THE OXFORD COMPANION TO

BRITISH RAILWAY
HISTORY

THE OXFORD COMPANION TO
BRITISH RAILWAY
HISTORY

FROM 1603 TO THE 1990s

EDITED BY

JACK SIMMONS

AND

GORDON BIDDLE

Oxford   New York

OXFORD UNIVERSITY PRESS

Oxford University Press, Great Clarendon Street, Oxford OX2 6DP

Oxford New York

Athens Auckland Bangkok Bogota Buenos Aires Calcutta
Cape Town Chennai Dar es Salaam Delhi Florence Hong Kong Istanbul
Karachi Kuala Lumpur Madrid Melbourne Mexico City Mumbai
Nairobi Paris São Paolo Singapore Taipei Tokyo Toronto Warsaw

and associated companies in
Berlin Ibadan

Oxford is a registered trade mark of Oxford University Press

British Library Cataloguing in Publication Data
Data available

Library of Congress Cataloging in Publication Data
Data available
ISBN 0–19–866238–6
ISBN 0–19–211697–5 (hbk)

Typeset by Interactive Sciences Ltd, Gloucester
Printed in Great Britain
on acid-free paper by
Butler & Tanner Ltd
Frome, Somerset

CONTENTS

Editorial Advisers · vi

Contributors · vii

Acknowledgements · viii

Introduction · ix

Important Note on the Maps · xii

Abbreviations · xiii

Notes for the Reader · xv

THE OXFORD COMPANION TO BRITISH RAILWAY HISTORY

Appendix 1: 1923 Grouping—Constituent and Subsidiary Companies · 577

Appendix 2: Imperial and Metric Measures · 578

Appendix 3: Historical Money Values · 579

Sectional Maps of the Railways of Great Britain, 1922 · 580

EDITORIAL ADVISERS

CONTRIBUTORS

CPA	Philip Atkins		JRH	John R. Hume
DHA	Professor Derek H. Aldcroft		MLH	Michael Harris
JA	Professor John Armstrong		TH	Dr Tom Hart
AB	Alan Blower		CRI	Christopher R. Irwin
DB	Dr David Brooke		MRLI	Reg Instone
DBi	Dorothy Biddle		AJ	Adrian Jarvis
GB-J	Gwyn Briwnant-Jones		AAJ	Alan A. Jackson
GAB	Grahame Boyes		DJ	David Joy
GJB	Gordon Biddle		NJ	Norman Jones
JMB	Dr J. M. Bourne		JK	John King
MB	Michael R. Bailey		MWK	Dr Maurice Kirby
MRB	Dr Michael R. Bonavia		PK	Peter Kay
PSB	Professor Philip Bagwell		RWK	R. W. Kidner
TB	Tim Bryan		MJTL	Dr Michael Lewis
TCB	Professor T. C. Barker		RVL	Robin Leleux
EC	Dr Edwin Course		GEM	Professor G. E. Mingay
FGC	Fred Clements		JEN	John Norris
GC	Dr Gerald Crompton		JAP	Professor Allan Patmore
GCh	Professor Geoffrey Channon		KUR	Keith Ratcliffe
GHC	Geoffrey H. Cope		MCR	Dr Malcolm Reed
GWC	George Carpenter		PJGR	P. J. G. Ransom
JC	James Carlisle		PWR	Peter W. Robinson
JAC	Dr John Coiley		RCR	R. C. Riley
MC	Mike Christensen		RMR	Michael Robbins
MMC	Michael Mark Chrimes		AJS	Andrew Scott
RC	Rex Christiansen		JEFS	Fleetwood Shawe
WPC	Paul Clegg		JS	Professor Jack Simmons
AD	Andrew Dow		PLS	Philip L. Scowcroft
AJD	Dr Alastair J. Durie		PWBS	P. W. B. Semmens
OD	Oliver Doyle		RAS-S	Robert Symes-Schutzmann
RJD	Richard Dean		RBS	Professor R. B. Schofield
ECE	Emma Eadie		RJMS	R. J. M. Sutherland
MGDF	Michael Farr		RTS	Dr R. T. Smith
JHF	Dr John Farrington		TRS	Tim R. Smith
RDF	Richard D. Foster		CPT	Chris Tennant
AG	Adrian Gray		DT	Dr David Turnock
DJG	Dorian Gerhold		MTT	Malcolm T. Tucker
MHG	Dr Michael Gould		RHGT	Ronald Thomas
OG	Oliver Green		RT	Robert Thorne
TRG	Dr Terry Gourvish		HW	Helena Wojtczak
CH	Charles Hadfield		LRW	Lawrence Roy Wilson
CSH	Chris Heaps		RW	Rodney Weaver
DJH	David Hodgkins			
DWH	Dieter Hopkin			
JH	Professor John Hibbs			
JHu	John Huntley			

CARTOGRAPHERS
Maps in text   Richard Dean
Sectional maps   Peter Fells

ACKNOWLEDGEMENTS

A BOOK of this kind cannot be produced without the support of numerous people, and the editors owe a considerable debt to all those who have given generous help in many ways.

Foremost are the members of our advisory panel listed on p.vi, whose assistance has been invaluable. We must additionally thank Michael Robbins for undertaking a substantial share of the arduous task of proofreading, and Terry Gourvish for preparing Appendix 3.

There are several contributors for whose ready assistance and advice in editorial and related matters, often given at short notice, we are especially indebted: Dr Michael Bonavia, Grahame Boyes, Rex Christiansen, Dr John Coiley, Andrew Dow, and Michael Harris.

Our thanks are also due to the following, some of whom are also contributors: George Carpenter, Michael Chorley, Alan Cooksey, Geoffrey H. Cope, Dr Edwin Course, Dr Alastair Durie, Colin Ford, John Gough, the late Charles Hadfield, David Jeffreys, Peter Johnson, Ted Labrum, Anthony Lambert, Shelagh Melling, Nigel Ogilvie, George Ottley, Professor Roland Paxton, Dr Malcolm Reed, Dr R. W. Rennison, James Sutherland, Malcolm Tucker, and Peter Waller.

Richard Dean has drawn the maps accompanying the text, and Peter Fells the sectional maps at the back of the book. To both we are grateful for the care and attention they have given.

Members of staff at a number of organizations have given valuable help: John Wilbur, former Group Public Relations Officer, British Railways Board; Michael Chrimes, Librarian of the Institution of Civil Engineers; Andrew Scott, Head of the National Railway Museum, and Philip Atkins, Christine Heap, and Dieter Hopkin from his staff; Jane Terry of Railtrack; Jean Rennie of the Timber Trades Association; S. R. Johnson of the Stephenson Locomotive Society. The North of England Institute of Mining & Mechanical Engineers, the Railway Correspondence & Travel Society, the Transport Salaried Staffs' Association, and the Railway Study Association also kindly provided information.

We also gratefully record the ready assistance from the staffs at the following libraries and archive repositories: the British Library; the Public Record Office, Kew; the Scottish Record Office, Edinburgh; the university libraries of Lancaster, Leicester, and John Rylands Manchester; public libraries at Croydon, Exeter, Kendal, Newcastle, and Nottingham; the Principal Registry (Family Division) at Somerset House, London.

We owe a particular debt to the staff of our publisher: Michael Cox, Pam Coote, Alysoun Owen, Alison Jones, and Wendy Tuckey, and their copy-editor Margaret Aherne; and to our typists Marian Armstrong of Levens, and Mrs J. E. Johnson and Robert Hulls of Leicester.

Finally, there must be an acknowledgement of deep gratitude for the patience, forbearance, and support of Dorothy Biddle, who for three years gave good advice, dealt with countless telephone calls, and lived with a mountain of paper.

INTRODUCTION

Several attempts have been made in Britain to produce an encyclopaedia of railways. Only two achieved publication: C. Hamilton Ellis's *Pictorial Encyclopaedia of Railways* (1968), which covered the whole world, largely in terms of 900 pictures; and the *Encyclopaedia of Railways* (1977), edited by O. S. Nock, and containing more detailed and comprehensive articles by a panel of authoritative writers, but again world-wide in scope.

There has long been a need for a work of reference covering the development of the British railway system in one substantial volume; the means by which it was promoted and financed; the technical devices and methods used in its building and operation; the lives of some of the people who planned, constructed, and ran it, their achievements and shortcomings; and the part it played in the history and development of the country in peace and war. It is important that such a work should stretch well beyond describing the railways in their physical terms, in addition to providing an account of the growth, consolidation, and eventual contraction of the system.

The published literature on the subject is very large, and the excellent bibliography compiled by George Ottley lists 13,000 entries. Their quality, however, varies considerably. There are important topics that have hardly been touched, and it must be remembered that the national archives relating to railways became available for study only in 1952. We hope that at some points the *Companion* offers a useful enlargement of knowledge, resulting from the exploration of these and other unpublished records. With great reluctance, we decided to confine the scope of the book to Great Britain—i.e. England, Wales, Scotland, the Isle of Man, and the Channel Islands. We should have liked to include Ireland, but the history of railways there has been in a number of important respects so widely different from elsewhere in the British Isles that a disproportionate part of our space would have been taken up in exemplifying and explaining its peculiarities. We do, however, offer accounts, under several headings, of the relationships between British and Irish railways, and the traffic between them.

Most accounts and studies of British railways have been approached from one of two viewpoints: from outside or inside. 'Outsiders' have looked at them mainly as a means of economic and social change, on a level with other contributors to the growth of the national economy such as the textile, coal, and power generation industries. 'Insiders' have studied them because they have a strong interest in railways as such.

Much favours both approaches. No one can fully appreciate railways, accurately and fairly, without a good understanding of how they work in all their many and varied aspects, what has governed their development, and the impact they have made. Those looking from the outside have seldom revealed a strong interest in these things, which sometimes has affected judgements on what the railways did for the community. Conversely, 'insiders', by concentrating mainly on railways as entities, especially in the mechanical field, have often shown little interest in the traffic that was carried, or its importance to the areas being served.

The *Companion* seeks to look at British railway history from both points of view: from external assessment and internal observation, examining what the railways have done, or not done, for the country, and the technologies they used in providing their services. In doing so it aims to set the railways in their context, displaying them and their multifarious activities as elements in the life, work, and thought of Britain in the past and in the modern world.

In planning this book our next decision concerned its time-span. Obviously it had to begin with the first recorded railway in 1603–4. In view of the widespread changes inaugurated by the Railways Act, 1993, the commencement of privatization of British Railways in April 1994 seemed an appropriate time at which to stop, although in a few instances we have gone beyond that date in order to give proper meaning within the context of the particular subject.

One of our hardest tasks was to decide how to allocate space within the predetermined total number of pages. In setting lengths of contributions we were particularly conscious that, over a total span of 400 years, it was in 1830–1914—the 'Railway Age'—that railways made their greatest contribution to the economic, political, and social life of Britain; a period, moreover, for which there is more copious and informative evidence than for the years before or since.

In the field of civil engineering and construction, special attention has been given to methods and structures. The treatment of mechanical engineering extends over all types of traction (excepting a very few freaks): from wind, horses, and men to gravity and cable haulage; steam, petrol, and diesel locomotives; pneumatic power; and electricity. Attention has also been paid to the services the railways provided and the vehicles they used. Emphasis is given to equipment that proved outstandingly successful, or was influential in development. All principal safety devices are discussed—notably signalling and brake systems—as well as a number of the accidents that occurred.

In other areas, treatment has had to be equally selective. It is a characteristic of British railways that whilst they tended to increase or create uniformity in life and business, their working was in some ways highly individual—more so than in most of Europe, where there was state control. The developments they helped to bring about showed much diversity too. For example, their effect on the communities they served varied greatly, yet clearly this must be discussed. But how widely? Which towns should have specific articles allocated to them? London and the largest cities obviously require surveys, as do the ports that the railways served most fully; seaside resorts, some of which they did much to create; 'railway towns' built by or for them. In the end we have included articles on 43 towns.

Again, turning to railway companies, by 1865 there were 366 authorized in Great Britain, though the lines of some of them were not yet built. The number then steadily declined, principally through the absorption of smaller companies by larger ones. When the big statutory amalgamation took place in 1923 it combined 120 into four, from 27 'constituent' and 93 'subsidiary' companies which are listed in Appendix I. But it still left nearly 50 small independent companies, possessing their own rolling stock. How many of these various entities deserved separate articles? Clearly all the chief pioneers that were subsequently absorbed into larger companies demanded attention, like the Kilmarnock & Troon, the Stockton & Darlington, the Liverpool & Manchester, and the London & Birmingham, together with later important lines, such as the Chester & Holyhead and the Blyth & Tyne. We therefore give separate accounts of each of the constituent companies of the four large groups, together with a number of the subsidiary companies, and others that merit inclusion. The selection of companies which had already been absorbed by amalgamation before 1923 is our own.

In due course there may be a second, updated edition of the *Companion* in which further developments in knowledge and opinion will be reflected. Constructive comments, suggestions, and any corrections will be welcomed by the editors. This printing includes minor corrections that were spotted following publication of the first impression.

JACK SIMMONS
GORDON BIDDLE

IMPORTANT NOTE ON THE MAPS

Sectional maps of the passenger railway system in 1922, at the end of the book, are to a common scale, except West Yorkshire which is enlarged separately. Limitations in the number and size of pages precluded showing every station. For the locations of those not included, readers are referred to the *British Railways Pre-grouping Atlas and Gazetteer* (1997 edn.).

Maps in the text. Complex areas enclosed in boxes on the sectional maps are enlarged on maps accompanying relevant entries, and are not to a common scale. On these text maps, the following symbols apply:

          □   main passenger station

          ○   other passenger station

                   main goods station at the end of a separate branch

                   point of change in ownership of line

Goods stations and depots adjacent to a passenger station are not shown separately.

The operative date for all maps is the end of 1922, except for the Central London Underground map on p.295 for which it is 1994.

Maps of the whole railway system in 1952 and 1985 are on pp.494 and 495.

ABBREVIATIONS

In text

*	words, or close derivatives, that are the subject of a separate article
ac	alternating current
BR	British Railways; British Rail
CME	chief mechanical engineer
dc	direct current
e.g.	for example
FRS	Fellow of the Royal Society
hp	horse power
Hz	hertz
ICE	Institution of Civil Engineers
i.e.	that is to say
IMech E	Institution of Mechanical Engineers
kV	kilovolts
kW	kilowatts
mph	miles per hour
NRM	National Railway Museum, York
T	tank engine (placed after wheel notation)
V	volts

Bibliographical references at end of articles

Following the title or abbreviation: volume number, year of publication, issue number (for periodicals), page number(s).

Note: small Roman numerals are used for book volume numbers; Arabic numerals for periodical volume numbers.

Acworth	W. M. Acworth, *The Railways of England* (1889 edn. unless otherwise cited)
Bagwell	P. S. Bagwell, *The Railway Clearing House* (1968)
BDE	J. Marshall, *Biographical Dictionary of Railway Engineers* (1978)
BL	British Library
Boase	F. Boase, *Modern English Biography* (1965 edn.)
BSRL	E. L. Ahrons, *The British Steam Railway Locomotive* (1927)
ch., chs	chapter(s)
CMCR	R. Christiansen and R. W. Miller, *The Cambrian Railways* (1967–8)
CMNSR	R. Christiansen and R. W. Miller, *The North Staffordshire Railway* (1971)
DBB	*Dictionary of Business Biography*
DNB	*Dictionary of National Biography*
Dow	G. Dow, *Great Central* (1959–65)
ed.	edited by
edn.	edition
ET	J. Simmons, *The Express Train and Other Railway Studies* (1994)
Findlay	G. Findlay, *The Working and Management of an English Railway* (1889 and subsequent editions)

Gourvish	T. R. Gourvish, *British Railways 1948–73* (1986)
GR	H. Parris, *Government and the Railways in Nineteenth-Century Britain* (1965)
Grinling	C. H. Grinling, *History of the Great Northern Railway* (1966 edn.)
GRSB	G. Biddle, *Great Railway Stations of Britain* (1986)
HLRO	House of Lords Record Office
HLT	T. C. Barker and M. Robbins, *History of London Transport* (1963–74)
Jackman	W. T. Jackman, *Transportation in Modern England* (1916)
JRCHS	*Journal of the Railway & Canal Historical Society*
JTH	*Journal of Transport History*
LLR	A. A. Jackson, *London's Local Railways* (1978)
LPA	Local & Personal Acts
LT	A. A. Jackson, *London Termini* (1985 edn.)
LTW	E. L. Ahrons, *Locomotive and Train Working in the Latter Part of the Nineteenth Century* (1951–4)
LYR	J. Marshall, *The Lancashire & Yorkshire Railway* (1969–72)
MacDermot	E. T. MacDermot, *The History of the Great Western Railway* (1964 edn.)
Mitchell & Deane	B. R. Mitchell and P. Deane, *Abstract of British Historical Statistics* (1962 edn.)
NRM	National Railway Museum, York
OED	*Oxford English Dictionary* (1991 edn.)
*Ottley	G. Ottley, *Bibliography of British Railway History* (1983 edn.) and *Supplement* (1988)
PGA	Public General Acts
PICE	*Proceedings of the Institution of Civil Engineers*
PP	Parliamentary Papers
PRO	Public Record Office, Kew, London
RCH	Railway Clearing House
Reg. Hist.	*Regional History of Railways* series (1960–95)
REW	J. Simmons, *The Railway in England and Wales, 1830–1914* (1978)
RM	*Railway Magazine*
RO	Record Office
Robertson	C. J. A. Robertson, *Origins of the Scottish Railway System* (1983)
RS	G. Biddle, *The Railway Surveyors* (1990)
RTC	J. Simmons, *The Railway in Town and Country 1830–1914* (1986)
RYB	*Railway Year Book*
SRO	Scottish Record Office, Edinburgh
Thomas	R. H. G. Thomas, *The Liverpool & Manchester Railway* (1980)
TNS	*Transactions of the Newcomen Society*
Tomlinson	W. W. Tomlinson, *The North Eastern Railway: Its Rise and Development* (1967 edn.)
VCH	*Victoria History of the Counties of England*
VR	J. Simmons, *The Victorian Railway* (1991)
VS	G. Biddle, *Victorian Stations* (1973)
Whishaw	F. Whishaw, *The Railways of Great Britain and Ireland* (1842 edn.)
Williams	R. A. Williams, *The London & South Western Railway* (1968–73)
WTT	working timetables

NOTES FOR THE READER

Termination date for the *Companion* generally is April 1994, which marked the change from nationalized to privatized railways in Britain.

Entries are self-indexing in alphabetical order, letter-by-letter up to the first punctuation mark, in accordance with current *Oxford Companion* practice.

Cross-references. Because many topics occur in several places, in different connections, cross-referencing is sufficiently frequent to knit a subject together as a whole. However, if it were done too copiously it would act as an irritant to continuity of reading, so in some cases the same subject-matter is referred to more than once in separate contexts.

Cross-references take three forms. An asterisk * in front of a word indicates that there is a separate article headed by that word, or a readily identifiable derivative. Other related articles are prefixed 'see' or 'see also'.

In only three instances are readers directed to two successive cross-references in order to find the definitive entry: the main London termini (grouped under **London Stations**); the individual lines that made up **London Underground railways**; and **gauge**. Although regrettable, these were unavoidable without cluttering the text with more repetitive cross-references than necessary.

Bibliographical notes at the end of each article are generally restricted to four printed books (published up to December 1996) as a guide to further reading, and to references for quotations or important statements.

Biographical entries exclude persons who were still alive on 31 December 1996, when the book was being prepared for press.

Place names are shown as the railways themselves spelt them. Consequently they include anglicized versions of Welsh and foreign names, for which, in the interests of historical accuracy, the editors hope they will be forgiven.

For the same reason, and also because there have been two changes in local government boundaries since 1974, towns and counties generally are referred to as they were before that year. The expression 'the City' refers to the City of London.

Railway company names. In each article, the names of railway companies are given in full the first time they appear. Thereafter, their initials are used.

Measures. Similarly, measures and money are given in imperial form. Appendix 2 contains tables of metric equivalents, and it is hoped that the table of historic money values in Appendix 3 will help to make more sense of quoted contemporary figures.

To
BRITISH RAILWAYMEN
AND WOMEN
PAST AND PRESENT

A

abandonment of railways. In early days a good many authorized railways were abandoned, either unbuilt or built only in part. A line might have proved more expensive than anticipated, or the paid-up capital too small to finish it. The shareholders had then to satisfy the company's creditors. If it had exercised its powers of purchasing land compulsorily, the vendors might now claim compensation. Some of the lines then abandoned were of considerable length: the *Northern & Eastern Railway's from Bishop's Stortford to Cambridge (25 miles), for example, in 1840; the *Eastern Counties' from Colchester to Norwich and Yarmouth (76 miles) three years later.

The very large number of railways authorized in 1844–7 (see MANIAS) included many that were hopeless. An abandonment procedure was established in the Abandonment of Railways Act, 1850, whereby application could be made to the Railway *Commissioners for powers to abandon the project, wholly or in part, making recompense for compulsorily purchased land, including any damage caused, with provision for arbitration. The Commissioners and the Board of *Trade (which soon succeeded to their powers) were then at liberty to authorize abandonment.

The first successful application was for the Lossiemouth branch of the Morayshire Railway in 1851. An apparently complete account of authorizations in 1868–82 is to be found in successive volumes of the Parliamentary Papers (see SOURCES OF RAILWAY HISTORY). Here are two examples.

In 1865 the *Great Northern Railway secured powers to construct a line between Hornsey and Hertford, through Enfield. It sought to abandon it in 1868, largely because completion of the *Midland Railway's London extension would remove that company's traffic from the GNR south of Hitchin, giving much-needed relief to the system. This was the first effort towards the construction of the 'Hertford Loop', not fully opened until 1924 (see SYSTEM, DEVELOPMENT OF THE). Compensation was ordered to be paid to an Enfield man who had established a brickworks, hoping to supply the railway.

Again in 1865, the Waterloo & Whitehall Railway proposed to tunnel beneath the Thames, with financial assistance from the *London & South Western Railway that was not furnished. By 1871, all the subscribed capital had been spent on preliminary works, so abandonment was authorized.

The Act, slightly amended in 1867 and 1869, is still in force, but applicable only to lines never opened. When the *Festiniog Railway asked the Ministry of Transport for power to abandon its line in 1950, it was refused because it had previously been open for traffic. As it happened, that refusal fortunately paved the way to the railway's preservation and revival.

See also RAILWAYS NEVER BUILT. JS

H. G. Lewin, *The Railway Mania and its Aftermath* (1968 edn.), 372–3, 480–3; PP 1851, xxx, 473 (Morayshire Railway); 1868–9, liv, 41 (GNR); 1871, xix, 49 (Waterloo & Whitehall Railway); J. I. C. Boyd, *Festiniog Railway* (1959), 341.

ABC Guide, see BRADSHAW'S GUIDE; TIMETABLES.

Aberdeen. Conscious of their relative geographical isolation, the merchants of Aberdeen were not slow to grasp the possibilities of the railway. Under the chairmanship of the Provost Thomas Blaikie, a prospectus for the Aberdeen Railway to link with the Northern Junction Railway at Forfar was issued in April 1844, and met with much enthusiasm. Work began in 1845, but there were problems in the construction: three arches in the viaduct on the southern approach to the terminus collapsed, and the bridge over the Dee was threatened by a spate in October 1847. There was no problem, however, with the acquisition of a site for a station close to the centre of Aberdeen from the Harbour Board, many of whose members were also shareholders. The financial crisis of 1848 hit Aberdeen hard, and it was not until April 1850 that the line from the south was opened for passenger traffic. One of the immediate effects was that Aberdeen lost 8 minutes and 22 seconds when the Post Office standardized on Greenwich Mean *Time.

Access to Aberdeen from the north was in the hands of the *Great North of Scotland Railway, whose shares were put on the market early in 1845. It approached the city from the north, and took over much of the route of the Aberdeenshire Canal, on occasion with such abruptness that boats were left stranded as the contractors drained the waters. Its terminus was at Waterloo Quay, 1½ miles from the Aberdeen Railway's terminus at Guild Street, and unfortunate passengers for the south faced a very uncertain trip between the two stations. Various schemes for the physical linking of the two railways were discussed, including a line via the western suburbs dubbed the 'Circumbendibus'; finally a line was driven through the Denburn Valley in 1867 and an iron-roofed *joint station constructed, to be replaced in 1915 by the present one in sandstone.

The railways benefited Aberdeen's economy greatly in allowing the movement of perishable commodities to the London market. Whereas the steamship had permitted a trade in live cattle to the south, the railway's greater speed allowed the movement of dead meat. Aberdeenshire farmers in the later 19th century concentrated on the breeding and fattening of cattle; Aberdeen butchers on their preparation for market. In the week before Christmas 1888, the *North British Railway carried over 1,000 cattle in six specials to London. Another industry to benefit was fishing: overnight fish trains to Billingsgate became an established feature, particularly after the building in 1889 of a municipal fish market with its own siding. Initially the fish were packed in ice in open wagons sheeted over, but later insulated vans were introduced.

Aberdeen also developed a surprisingly dense network of suburban stations. *Workmen's trains had been run to the paperworks at Stoneywood in the 1860s, but a much fuller service was introduced in 1887 from Aberdeen to Dyce, and seven years later on the Deeside line to Culter. The Aberdeen 'subbies' were well used, with over 2 million passengers in 1901. Stations were remarkably close: nine in the 8 miles to Culter, and eight in the 6 miles to Dyce. Bus competition in the inter-war years led to the withdrawal of the suburban services in 1937, a step long overdue, given the scale of the losses the railway had been suffering.

The 1960s saw further closures, including the Deeside line in 1966, and the loss of both passenger and freight business. The once substantial docks traffic ceased in the 1970s and the fish business transferred to road. The coming of oil did challenge the downward trend with, for example, large consignments of steel pipes being sent to the British Steel depot at Waterloo Quay. Some stations were reopened, including Dyce in 1984, to serve Aberdeen Airport and an expanding northern suburb. AJD

K. G. Jones, *The 'Subbies': The Story of Aberdeen's Suburban Trains, 1887–1987* (1987); H. A. Vallance, *The Great North of Scotland Railway* (1989); J. J. Waterman, *The Coming of the Railways to Aberdeen in the 1840s* (n.d., c.1978); *Reg. Hist.*, xv, ch. 5.

accidents. Railways were at all times dangerous contrivances. In April and July 1650 two boys were buried at Whickham (Co. Durham), each of them 'slain with a wagon' on a *wooden railway running from coalpits down to the Tyne. A broken rail, or the stumbling of a horse, might always cause death or injury. With the introduction of the steam locomotive, working at high pressure, dangers much increased. The first explosion of a locomotive's boiler seems to have been that on an experimental machine, under trial at Philadelphia (Co. Durham) in 1815. It killed 16 people, perhaps bystanders watching. On the *Stockton & Darlington Railway there were two such explosions in 1828. On the *Liverpool & Manchester there were numerous accidents of different sorts, beginning with the one that befell Huskisson at its inauguration; and as many as 12 on the Sutton incline in 1831–43.

Legal proceedings might arise from these accidents: claims for damages against railway companies, for example, in respect of property destroyed in them. If death occurred, a coroner's jury would inquire into it; and if it thought the accident due to negligence or irresponsibility it might bring in a verdict of manslaughter against the person or persons it held responsible. (See also DEODANDS.)

But neither coroners' juries nor any courts were well able to understand technical matters, and it soon became clear that railway management and machinery ought to be kept under more skilled observation. The companies had derived powers from the government to construct their lines; so it was reasonable that the government should also exercise a general surveillance over their operations, especially in matters concerning safety.

Accordingly, in 1840 the first *Regulation Act obliged railway companies to report all accidents causing injury to the Board of *Trade, which was to appoint *inspectors to 'enter upon and examine' the railways' works, buildings, and rolling stock. The Regulation Act of 1842 varied this requirement, applying it to 'serious accidents' only, 'whether attended with personal injury or not'. Neither Act authorized inspectors to investigate accidents. But the railways permitted them to do so nevertheless; the earliest of their reports on them date from 1840.

With one minor exception, all the inspectors were officers of the Royal Engineers. They had to learn about the railways' technology chiefly by observation. They made mistakes, having no previous knowledge of the power of steam, for instance, or the properties of metals as the railways used them; and they have been criticized—perhaps too severely—for their treatment of locomotive boiler explosions. But they were honest and careful, and they built up between them a large body of experience.

This became especially important where accidents were concerned. The inspectors had no power to compel railways to adopt safety appliances, however strongly they might feel they were desirable. They could only advise; but the reports were presented to Parliament and (from 1860 onwards) put on sale. So their advice, and the reasoning behind it, were public property.

Among the early accidents investigated was one that had important effects: that on the *Great Western Railway at Sonning in 1841, in which eight passengers were killed. They were travelling in open wagons, with a heavy load of goods behind them. That was obviously dangerous, and the inspector's clear and careful report led to much serious discussion of the conditions that the poor endured when being carried in trains, which came to be regulated by *Gladstone's Act of 1844.

Railway accidents were attributable to an infinitely wide variety of causes, chance playing a large part among them. A fundamental cause—for many years perhaps the most important one—lay in the growth of the *system itself, and of the traffic it carried. In the years 1852–61 the mileage of line open in Great Britain increased by 43 per cent, the mileage of the trains using it (passenger and goods together) by 71 per cent. This process continued almost without pause. In 1861–88 the mileage open grew by 81 per cent, the mileage of traffic carried by 180 per cent. This is the background against which the number of accidents occurring each year must be seen.

Certain problems in railway operation would come into particular prominence at any one time, to trouble both managers and inspectors. Then the appearance of a new precautionary device, or the improvement of an old one, offered the means of overcoming a danger—though sometimes at the cost of creating another one.

In the 1840s and 1850s numerous accidents arose from the practice of controlling the interval between a train and one following it on the same line by time alone (see SIGNALLING). If the first train was stopped for any reason, the second train could be prevented from colliding with it only if the guard of the first went back to meet the second. The failure to take this precaution caused a serious accident at Cowlairs, outside *Glasgow, in 1847 and another at Frodsham (Cheshire) in 1851.

But a remedy for that kind of accident was already appearing in the 1840s, with the electric *telegraph, leading to the development of the *block working system, which regulated the intervals between trains by distance, not time. It was adopted slowly, however. The equipment was expensive, and the companies shrank from the cost. Moreover, it was often alleged (though seldom with truth) that the block system made train-crews and signalmen less alert. Much the same happened when the interlocking (see SIGNALLING) of points and signals was developed, from 1860 onwards. Its adoption increased steadily—though meeting with similar objections—in the 1870s.

Accidents were now proliferating fast. Two very serious ones occurred within eight days of each other in August 1861, in Clayton Tunnel on the *London Brighton & South Coast Railway and on the Hampstead Junction line (worked by the *North London) at Kentish Town; 37 people died in them. Again, in 1865 two accidents took place only 50 hours apart, at Rednal (Shropshire) on the GWR and Staplehurst on the *South Eastern, the second of them celebrated because Dickens was among the passengers, and the effect of it on his mind contributed to shortening his life. Then in 1868 came the disaster at Abergele, west of Rhyl, when the Irish Mail collided with runaway wagons and caught *fire, killing all the 32 passengers in the front carriages.

The railway companies were widely blamed by public opinion for failing to adopt the safety precautions that were by now available. This was not always fair: only two of the five accidents just mentioned could have been prevented by their use. But in 1869 the Board of Trade asked each railway company for returns annually, showing the extent to which it had adopted the block system. This was received with explosive indignation by some of the leading companies. One, the *North Eastern, totally ignored the request. That folly received exemplary punishment in the autumn of 1870, when four serious accidents occurred on its lines, three of which could have been prevented had the block system and interlocking been available. The directors now grew alarmed, and the company's general manager, William O'Brien, was dismissed.

Two Regulation Acts, of 1871 and 1873, contained important provisions relating to accidents. Whereas the 1842 Act had required the companies to notify the Board of all accidents 'attended with serious personal injury to the public', that of 1871 extended the requirement to those involving loss of life or injury to 'any person whomsoever': i.e. it called for the notification of accidents occurring to the railways' own staff. It also empowered the Board to set up a special court of inquiry to investigate any major accident.

The Act of 1873 obliged each company to supply to the Board every year returns of the mileage of its lines controlled by the block system. These Acts produced some striking revelations. In the five years 1874–8 an annual average of 35 passengers were killed in train accidents, but 682 of the companies' servants—reduced to 487 in 1879–88.

The first of the new courts of inquiry was concerned with the accident to the principal *West Coast night express from London to Scotland, travelling through Wigan station at excessive speed in 1871. The *London & North Western company's officials said that the speed was forced upon it by its *East Coast rivals. Here one of the dangers arising from *competition was spelt out plainly. The hopeless demoralization of the staff of the *Somerset & Dorset Railway was exposed by thorough probing of the Radstock accident in another similar investigation in 1874.

The companies had resisted the passing of these two Acts as far as they dared, knowing that no British government would assume a direct responsibility for the safe working of the railways. But examination went further. In 1874 a Royal Commission was appointed to inquire into railway accidents. Lasting three years, it was among the most laborious investigations into the conduct of any kind of private business (except coal-mining) in Victorian Britain. It collected a great mass of evidence, but its work led to little result.

One other element in the cause of accidents, besides those concerned with signalling, had now become obvious: the inadequacy of brake power on trains. Progress was being made with the fitting of continuous *brakes to passenger trains, but various rival firms competed in their design and manufacture. Trials of these appliances were made before the Commission at Newark in 1876. No system showed any decisive superiority there, but the trials amply confirmed the inspectors' support of automatic continuous brakes, and in 1878 an Act required each company to make twice-yearly returns of the numbers of its passenger vehicles fitted with them. The debates between the braking systems gave the companies some justification for delaying commitment to one system rather than another. On the other hand, accidents cost them a great deal of money in *compensation to the sufferers and their families.

All this argument was suddenly muted after the fearful accident at Armagh in Ireland in 1889, befalling a runaway train fitted with no continuous brakes. The government decided immediately to legislate, and the Regulation Act of 1889 required every train carrying passengers to be fitted with them. It also compelled the companies to adopt the block system and the interlocking of points and signals.

The numbers of train accidents now fell strikingly. In 1901 and 1908, indeed, not a single passenger was killed in one through the railways' fault.

However, many accidents occurred that were not preventable by any of the devices discussed so far—provided, of course, that the devices were properly used; the most spectacular disaster in the history of British railways, the fall of the Tay Bridge (see NORTH BRITISH RAILWAY) in 1879, was among them. Three occurring to expresses travelling

accidents

too fast—at Salisbury, Grantham, and Shrewsbury in 1906–7—seem all to have arisen from unaccountable misconduct on the part of experienced train-crews. What was very much the worst British railway accident in terms of casualties (227 believed killed, 245 injured), a collision involving five trains at Quintinshill north of Carlisle in 1915, was due primarily to the flagrant carelessness of two *Caledonian railway signalmen.

But a further element in that disaster made it even worse than it would otherwise have been. One of the trains comprised old carriages lit by gas, which ignited. Anxiety had recently been expressed about the dangers from the use of gas in trains, arising especially from two accidents on the *Midland Railway at Hawes Junction (1910) and Ais Gill (1913). Electricity was now available to replace it, and very much safer (see CARRIAGE LIGHTING). But replacement was a large task, performed very slowly. At the inquiry into the accident at Charfield (Gloucestershire) on the *London Midland & Scottish Railway in 1928 it was revealed that half the company's passenger vehicles were still gas-lit (see also FIRE).

New safety precautions continued to be introduced: *track circuiting for instance, first installed in Britain in 1901; an electrically operated audible warning, in the engine-driver's cab, of distant signals at 'caution' (1906), developing into Automatic Train Control (ATC) (see AUTOMATIC WARNING SYSTEMS). But although the GWR progressively installed ATC on its main lines from 1929 onwards, none of the other *Big Four companies adopted it, applying mechanisms of their own choice over certain small sections of their lines.

Nature made her own contributions to accidents on railways. Heavy *snow was largely responsible for that at Abbot's Ripton on the *Great Northern Railway in 1876 and contributed to those at Elliott Junction (North British and Caledonian Railways' joint line) in 1906 and at Castlecary, east of Glasgow (*London & North Eastern Railway), in 1937.

A hurricane is fortunately rare in Britain, though one destroyed the Tay Bridge. Great cloudbursts did, however, occur sometimes, particularly in northern Scotland. In 1914 one of them swept away the Baddengorm Burn bridge on the *Highland Railway's new Inverness line. Here the bridge's construction was not blamed—nothing but the exceptional ferocity of the storm.

The danger of avalanches crossing the line, well known in Switzerland and Norway, arose at only three points in Britain. The *Chester & Holyhead Railway provided timber shelters at each end of Penmaenmawr Tunnel. At Friog Rocks, south of Barmouth on the *Cambrian Railways, special precautions were also taken against them, but they did not prevent two accidents, in 1883 and 1933, when locomotives were hurled down on to the seashore, killing their crews. After the second one the GWR built a reinforced concrete shelter across 200 ft of the track. In the Pass of Brander, on the *Callander & Oban line, a special warning system of possible danger from falling rocks, or from blockage by snow, was devised. No serious accident ever happened there.

One of the worst dangers affecting railway operation was *fog. *Findlay remarked in 1889 that this element 'entails more anxiety upon those engaged in the management of a railway than all others put together'. It continued to be a great menace until lessened from the 1960s onwards by the reduced employment of coal as a fuel. Three very serious accidents primarily or largely due to fog occurred in 1952–7, at Harrow, Lewisham, and Dagenham. The Harrow accident caused more deaths (112) than any other in British history except Quintinshill. That and the one at Lewisham involved main-line expresses and rush-hour suburban trains. In the Dagenham accident two suburban trains collided, which were carrying 1,000 passengers between them.

All these accidents took place in Greater London. It may seem surprising that only one occurring there has been mentioned earlier, considering that in 1939 more than one-sixth of the whole population lived within its boundaries, and that they were making far more daily rail journeys than *commuters anywhere else in Britain.

That is to be accounted for largely by the astonishing record of safety achieved by the *London underground railways. The *Metropolitan never killed one passenger in a train throughout all the years when it was worked by steam (1863–1906). The first serious accident on the whole underground system was a collision at Stratford in 1953, when 12 lives were lost through a signalling failure and what seems to have been a driver's error. Then in 1975 a very strange disaster occurred at Moorgate, when 42 passengers and the driver were killed. The train was running into a terminal platform. It overran a signal and crashed at a speed of 30 mph into the solid end-wall of the tunnel, with such force that its front cars were impacted into half their length. The causes of that accident remain mysterious, and are still debated. In his report the inspector was firm in placing the responsibility for it on the driver. But neither he nor anyone else has accounted for the driver's errors. Some medical opinion considers that his failure was due to physical causes, which were not revealed in the post-mortem.

This was followed in 1987 by a dreadful fire on an escalator at *King's Cross underground station, caused by the ignition of waste material lying underneath it, probably set off by the dropping of a lighted cigarette. Thirty-one people were killed in this disaster. It led *London Transport to forbid *smoking entirely within its trains and throughout its stations.

In the following year came another very serious accident at Clapham Junction, causing 35 deaths. This was due immediately to a low standard of work in connecting up a new signal, which reflected poor supervision by the BR signalling and telecommunications department. But that arose in part from numerous reductions in its staff and consequent reorganization, which were ultimately due to the steadily multiplying economies imposed on BR by the government.

And finally—this was the last serious accident that occurred in Greater London before *privatization began on

4

1 April 1994—there was a collision at Purley, again in the suburban system of the south-east, in 1989, in which five passengers were killed. A fast train ran into the rear of another one, which had been switched on to the same track; the driver of the fast train was held responsible for ignoring signals and travelling at too high a speed, and he was imprisoned for manslaughter and endangering life. The inspector recommended BR to proceed with installing an Automatic Train Protection system, which had been under consideration before the accident occurred.   JS

L. T. C. Rolt, *Red for Danger* (1982 edn.); C. H. Hewitson, *Locomotive Boiler Explosions* (1983); *ET*, 213–33; S. Hall, *Railway Detectives: 150 Years of the Railway Inspectorate* (1990).

accounting. Railways are highly complex commercial organizations, and their requirement for adequate accounting systems was recognized from an early stage. Three features particularly distinguished this requirement. The first was the railways' constitution as joint-stock companies, which made it necessary to account to shareholders both for the disbursement of *capital funds and for the allocation of profits. Secondly, the decentralized nature of railway operations demanded robust financial control which could function through dispersed units, often without specialized staff. Thirdly, the fact that the network was made up of separate but interconnected undertakings, which were statutorily obliged to provide facilities for through traffic, required arrangements for recording inter-company flows and allocating the costs and revenue arising from them. The *Railway Clearing House provided the mechanism for this, and its creation as early as 1842, when the network was still in its infancy, points to the sophisticated accountancy required to integrate even a relatively small number of railways into a cohesive system.

Though the forum provided by the RCH assisted in the harmonization of some procedures, the individual companies remained responsible for book-keeping and financial control systems. Passenger revenue, whether internal or inter-company, was relatively easily accounted for by the use of pre-printed numbered card *tickets. *Edmondson's invention of this form of ticket was an important early development in railway commercial practice, since it provided a ready means of balancing issues against revenue, leaving only infrequent journeys to be individually booked by completing blank card or paper tickets. Station abstracts of ticket sales gave a summary for audit purposes and inter-company settlements, while collected tickets provided a further check on revenue.

*Freight revenue was more demanding in accountancy terms: flows were diverse; charging classifications were multiplex; and extra services, such as cartage and craneage, might be required at either end of a journey. In addition, traffic might be sent pre-paid, on a consignor's account, or charged on delivery. The shipper's consignment note formed the contract for each transaction, and this was used to generate the railway's detailed invoice, which provided the basis for financial control, any inter-company adjustments, and customer billing. The originating station re-

tained a copy of the invoice, and another was sent to the destination: by summarizing outward and received invoices at the respective ends of the journey, consignments were accounted for twice. For example, goods sent from *Manchester to *Birmingham would appear on the Manchester abstract of invoices for consignments to Birmingham, and on the Birmingham abstract of consignments from Manchester. Though labour-intensive, this double-abstract system provided an automatic check on revenue, and enabled credits and debits to be balanced on the total flow between each pair of stations.

Traffic revenue provided a railway's main source of current income, and it was clearly essential to have secure systems to record takings and allow effective audit. However, virtually every aspect of a railway generated financial activity, and the need for adequate accounting arrangements extended throughout a company. This was reinforced by the departmental structure of all but the smallest railways, and by the statutory requirements to provide financial information about specific elements of expenditure, such as the maintenance and renewal of rolling stock and permanent way. Since engineering departments might undertake work on both capital and revenue accounts, it was also important to be able to allocate such expenditure accurately.

Most railways accordingly had well-developed financial control mechanisms, but several cases demonstrated the difficulty of preventing defalcations, especially during the infancy of the system. The most notorious of the individual scandals, Redpath's frauds (see CRIME) on the *Great Northern Railway between 1848 and 1856, related not to the company's revenue and expenditure but to the creation of fictitious stock. However, there were also instances of malpractice in the conduct of railway commercial affairs, and even so sound an undertaking as the *London & North Western Railway was not immune. Two senior officers were dismissed in 1856 for financial lapses, while later in the century the LNWR's then general manager openly acknowledged the need for precautions against 'ingenious' fraud by staff in goods depots.

Such problems were not, of course, unique to railways: any organization which has to place individuals in positions of financial trust is vulnerable, and many lines followed the common 19th-century practice of requiring personal sureties from appointees to some posts. But in the railway context most misappropriations by staff were small in relation to total turnover: even Redpath's £220,000 embezzlement, committed over several years, amounted to less than the GNR's half-yearly profits at the time when his deception was discovered. While such extreme instances affected confidence in the company involved, the aspect of railway accountancy that particularly exercised Parliament and financial commentators in the pre-*Grouping period was the accuracy of the total picture of a company's affairs which was presented in its published accounts. There were two main reasons for this concern: the examples, typified by George *Hudson's activities but by no means unique, of railways which buttressed dividends by drawing from capital to meet revenue charges; and the cases of companies which exceeded authorized financial powers, usually by borrowing beyond their statutory limits. Since such unauthorized borrowing was not legally secured, it amounted to a fraud upon lenders.

Despite early identification of such issues, statutory obligations were at first minimal: companies were required simply to keep 'proper' accounts and to submit these at six-monthly intervals to their proprietors. In practice, however, most railways published their accounts in some detail, and these were supplemented by financial returns required by the government. However, there was no uniformity of approach between undertakings, and there is also evidence that in practice some companies did not always maintain consistent accountancy principles, either because of professional incompetence or financial expediency.

The first detailed specification of accounting requirements was included in the *Regulation of Railways Act, 1868, which laid out a standard form of accounts, embodying 14 separate statements. The main reason for the codification seems to have been continuing concern about abuse of capital powers: half of the statements required by the Act related to capital, including a narration of the company's authorized powers and the sums raised thereunder. Because of its preoccupation with statutory capital, this Act formalized a particular characteristic of British railway accounts which survived until *nationalization. General commercial usage is to detail capital assets and liabilities in the balance sheet, but the form of railway balance sheet prescribed by the Act showed only the net difference between receipts and expenditure on capital account; the full figures were placed separately in a different statement. In this double account system, capital expenditure was shown at historic cost, and replacements were normally financed from the revenue account. Revenue therefore bore the adjustment if original assets were replaced at a different cost, though a contribution might also be made from capital if there was betterment, for example if iron rails were replaced by steel. Consequently, neither gross annual investment nor depreciation was explicitly shown in railway accounts, except when a company chose to state the latter separately.

While the 1868 Act was an advance, it did not address the problem of differences in the compilation of accounts, particularly in the way capital and revenue expenditure was defined. For example, in the decade from 1884 to 1894 the LNWR charged only £50,000 to capital account for new locomotives. During this period, however, *Crewe built around 800 engines, giving the company a more modern and more powerful fleet. Moreover, since serviceable locomotives were retained as 'duplicates' after displacement from the capital stock, the actual number of engines increased by 18 per cent. Though practice varied, several other leading companies similarly financed improvements in capital assets from revenue.

The next major development came in 1911, when the Railway Companies (Accounts and Returns) Act embodied most of the recommendations of a Board of *Trade committee which had previously examined the scope of the existing provisions. This owed its stimulus to criticism of the usefulness of existing railway accounts and statistics as management tools, and in particular the absence of data on passenger-miles and ton-miles. Though the government was not sufficiently convinced to add these to the requirements, the Act significantly increased the amount of detail in published railway accounts, and also gave the Board of Trade powers to alter or add to the requirements. One particular innovation in the Act was the separation of the accounts of ancillary businesses such as *hotels and *shipping services from those relating to railway operations.

Only the 1913 accounts appeared in the new format before the outbreak of World War I. Simplified accounts were published during the period of government control, and then conditions were further changed by the Railways Act of 1921, which led to the Grouping. The Railways Act added to the powers which the new Ministry of *Transport had taken over from the Board of Trade by enabling the minister to specify not only the form of railway accounts, but also the principles upon which they should be prepared. Though the general format introduced by the 1911 Act continued to be followed, from 1928 onwards each company's accounts were compiled on a standard basis.

Statutory accounting provisions were further altered by the Transport Act, 1947, which nationalized most railways along with other transport undertakings. The Act required the minister to direct the *British Transport Commission as to the form of its annual statement of accounts, and in terms of this direction the BTC produced consolidated revenue and net revenue accounts and a consolidated balance sheet, supported by detailed statements for subsidiary activities, including railways. The BTC also made an important change in the treatment of some railway capital assets: although infrastructure and other fixed assets continued to be valued at historic cost, a 'commercial' approach was taken to the valuation of rolling stock, ships, and plant, to align practice with that of *London Transport and the nationalized road transport undertakings. Inherited assets in such categories were brought in the balance sheet at a written-down value, and replacements were valued at their actual cost, with a corresponding depreciation charge against revenue spread over the life of the asset. The *British Railways Board maintained this distinction between fixed and depreciation-type assets when it succeeded the BTC in 1963, and, subject to the effects of the various financial reconstructions of the industry, this remained the basis of railway capital accounting until the implementation of the 1993 Railways Act.

See also FINANCING OF RAILWAYS; COSTING TECHNIQUES.

MCR

British Transport Commission, *Report and Accounts for 1948* (HC 235, 1949), 44–7, 196–7; C. H. Newton, *Railway Accounts* (1930); H. Pollins, 'Aspects of Railway Accounting before 1868', in M. C. Reed (ed.), *Railways in the Victorian Economy* (1969), 138–61; M. Robbins, 'The Redpath Frauds on the Great Northern Railway', *Points and Signals* (1967), 139–43.

Acts of Parliament, see PARLIAMENT AND LEGISLATION.

Acworth, Sir William Mitchell (1850–1925), writer; educated at Uppingham and Christ Church, Oxford, he was a master at Dulwich School 1875–85, and member of London County Council, 1889–92; he served on the Royal Commission on Accidents to Railway Servants (1901) and the Board of Trade Committee on Railway Accounts (1906). The greatly improved system of railway *accounting and *returns introduced in 1911–13 owed much to him.

His principal publications were *The Railways of England* (1889; 5th edn. 1900), *The Railways of Scotland* (1890), *The Railways and the Traders* (1891), and *The Elements of Railway Economics* (1905). They displayed his faculty of communicating directly and persuasively with readers; his mastery of telling example, which always lay to his hand from his reading and shrewd observation; and his power to make difficult matters intelligible to those who wanted to understand them.

During and after World War I he helped to conduct investigations into railway affairs in Canada, Rhodesia, India, Austria, and Germany. He was knighted in 1921. He gave his valuable collection of transport literature to the London School of Economics. JS
DNB.

Adams, William (1823–1904), engineer. Originally a marine and general engineer, Adams became locomotive superintendent of the *North London Railway in 1858 after helping to build its works at Bow. In 1863 he made his lasting contribution to locomotive technology by developing the Adams bogie, which could not only rotate about its pivot but also move sideways under spring control. This gave smoother and safer entry to curves, especially at high speed, and was widely used for steam locomotives with four leading wheels.

In 1873 Adams moved to the *Great Eastern Railway, then in 1878 to the *London & South Western, which he served until he resigned on health grounds in 1895. His LSWR locomotives were noted for their elegant and simple design, massively built and economical in both fuel and maintenance. Initially using outside-cylindered bogie locomotives (4-4-0s for express and mixed traffic duty, 4-4-2 tanks for suburban lines), he later adopted front-coupled locomotives as advocated by William *Stroudley and built 0-4-2 mixed traffic locomotives and 0-4-4 bogie tank engines. On the LSWR he introduced the 'Vortex' blastpipe, invented by his nephew Henry, with an annular nozzle intended to soften yet increase the effect of the blast. RW
C. H. Ellis, *Twenty Locomotive Men* (1958), 83–95.

Adams, William Bridges (1797–1872), inventor and writer. He was the son of a London coachbuilder, for whom he worked as a boy; he travelled in South America and then returned to his father's business. His book *English Pleasure Carriages* (1837) covered all forms of land transport, including railways, and discussed the vehicles with professional expertise. He took out 35 patents in 1835–72, including one for fish-joints for railway *track and another for a radial axle-box on locomotives, still called 'the Adams axle' on the

Continent 60 years later. He established Fairfield Works, Bow, London, for locomotive building c.1844, specializing in light machines with engine and carriage combined, precursors of *railcars. Unsuccessful in business, he died poor.

Adams maintained his interest in new transport developments to the end of his life, supporting mechanically operated *tramways and the use of armoured trains in *war in his book *Roads and Rails* (1862). He was a genuine originator. His writings are confused and his second book ill-organized, but he is one of the few Englishmen who have made the effort to study land transport as a whole. JS
C. H. Ellis, *Twenty Locomotive Men* (1958); M. Robbins, *Points and Signals* (1967); J. W. Lowe, *British Steam Locomotive Builders* (1975).

administration, see COMPANIES; MANAGEMENT.

Advanced Passenger Train. The concept was to exploit the potential of existing *British Rail main-line passenger routes rather than build new lines at prohibitive cost, as in Japan. This would be possible by the operation of Advanced Passenger Trains (APTs) whose technology, including tilt suspension, would make possible the combination of a high maximum speed—up to 155 mph—and, compared with conventional trains, an ability to maintain higher speeds on curves, typically 20–40 per cent above existing limits. Given that 50 per cent of BR's major routes comprise curvature the second factor was crucial.

The initiative for the APT project derived from BR research during the early 1960s into the dynamics of rail vehicles. This indicated that the critical speed of a vehicle was related to suspension and track parameters. By 1967, the experimental work had progressed to a proposal for a high-speed train whose tilting mechanism would allow much higher curving speeds. Further research led to the concept of the APT Experimental (APT-E) gas turbine-powered train (see TRACTION, TURBINE) whose construction was authorized in 1969.

Promising results from test running of the APT-E led to the building of three 25 kV ac electric APT-P (Prototype) trains, and these began trials in 1979. After an unhappy début in public service in 1981 there were further modifications and test running, but the project was abandoned in 1986. The unreliability of the APT-P trains' hydrokinetic braking, and failures of the tilt mechanisms and gearboxes were contributory factors. But by then InterCity had opted for the IC 225 trains (see SPEED), and a programme of route modernization to ease track curvature. MLH
J. Johnson and R. A. Long, *British Railways Engineering 1948–80* (1981); H. Williams, *APT—A Promise Unfulfilled* (1985).

advertising, see POSTERS; PUBLICITY.

aggregates, see STONE TRAFFIC.

agreements: leasing, working, pooling. Railway companies finding financial difficulty in completing their lines, or in working them after they were opened, sometimes leased themselves to individuals or stronger companies. The *Leeds & Selby Railway leased itself to the Hull & Selby in

1840, for 31 years. In 1844 the *Northern & Eastern Railway granted a 'perpetual' lease to the *Eastern Counties, which was to pay it 5 per cent on its paid-up capital. Some of these arrangements were very long-lived. The *South Eastern's lease of the *London & Greenwich lasted from 1844 to 1923.

An effort was made to regulate agreements of this kind in the Railways Clauses Act, 1845 (sections 112–13), which laid down leasing conditions to protect both lessees and lessors.

In addition, a large number of small companies simply persuaded other companies, or contractors (see CONTRACTORS' LINES), to work their railways, paying them at a fixed rate. By 1866, when the number of legally established railway companies in the UK reached its maximum, at 377, only 90 worked their own traffic.

In the later Victorian age many of these arrangements ended upon *amalgamation of smaller companies with larger. The *Great Western absorbed at least 35 minor companies in 1871–1910, 19 of them in 1892–8. The motive behind most of these transactions was to protect the larger company's territory against 'invasion' by a competitor—in this case, generally the *London & South Western.

But the force of *competition had for a long time been tempered by agreement between the larger companies themselves, usually based on a division of the total receipts from traffic over routes where competition was intense, in agreed proportions. The Americans called it 'pooling'. The Iowa Pool of 1870 was quickly followed by others.

But this device had already been employed in Britain 20 years earlier, under the vague name of 'agreements', arising mainly from the opening of the *Great Northern's new competing route between *London and *Edinburgh. These apportioned the passengers and goods receipts of the Great Northern, *London & North Western, and *Midland companies, together with some others involved with them on their routes between London, Scotland, and some industrial towns, all but one in Yorkshire. The first, the Octuple Agreement, regulating the receipts from Anglo-Scottish traffic (eight companies were involved in it), and the Six Towns Agreement, relating to traffic between London and *York, *Leeds, Wakefield, *Sheffield, *Doncaster, and Lincoln, were signed in 1850–1, to be succeeded by others modifying them in later years.

Pooling became a subject of violent political controversy in the USA, but although the legality of the British agreements was sometimes questioned, none of them was overturned in the courts. Early in the 20th century they were adopted to end insensate competition. In 1910–11 evidently reliable pooling arrangements were reached, regulating the competition between the GWR and the LSWR for the traffic between London and the west of England, and the wild rivalries in the *shipping services (most of them, directly or indirectly, controlled by three railways) on the Clyde.

See also FREIGHT TRAFFIC RATES.   JS

W. A. Robertson, *Combination among Railway Companies* (1912), 41–51; for the number of companies in 1866, preface to *Bradshaw's Shareholders' Manual*, 1869.

agricultural traffic. Initially the railways had a generally beneficial impact on British farmers, bringing in fertilizers to districts cut off from water transport and extending the range of outlets for farm products. However, the spread of railways and steamship services to other continents was later the primary cause of the long agricultural depression that began in 1879, by allowing competition from large-scale cheap imports, particularly of North American grain. The *Light Railways Act, 1896, which sought to promote railway construction in agricultural districts, was a belated response to this problem. Railways also led to the closure of many small town markets and concentration on bigger, regional markets.

Fertilizer traffic comprised a variety of natural manures and chemical fertilizers. The *Great Northern Railway carried stable manure from London, some of it as far as Lincolnshire, as a return load for wagons bringing produce into the *King's Cross potato market. In the opposite direction shoddy (woollen waste) was carried from the mills of *Bradford and Kidderminster to fertilize the Kent hop fields. The early chemical fertilizer industry, concentrated in East Anglia following the discovery of coprolite deposits there in 1842, eventually amalgamated under the name of Fisons Ltd. But the use of chemical fertilizers grew only slowly and the other big names did not enter the market until much later: ICI in 1926 from its Billingham, Teesside, complex and Shell in 1969 from a plant at Ince, Cheshire, adjoining its Stanlow oil refinery. More recently there have been large-scale imports of Norwegian fertilizer distributed by rail from Immingham docks.

The movement of *livestock and of farm and market garden produce for immediate consumption—*meat, *milk, *fruit and vegetables, and *flowers—is dealt with in other articles. It only remains to mention here the transport of bulk agricultural commodities to the next stage of production.

The main destination for wool was Bradford, where there were four railway warehouses (see GOODS SHEDS) for storing up to 126,000 bales until required by the mills. The traffic grew enormously during the 19th century, but by 1900 wool was mainly imported from Australia, New Zealand, and South Africa through the ports of London and the Humber.

Coastal and inland navigation (see SHIPPING, COASTAL; CANALS) were already well established in the grain trades and only ever partially displaced by rail transport. Nevertheless, the railways were significant transporters of barley and malt for the brewing and whisky industries—particularly the malt whisky industry, which was remote from water transport (see FOOD AND DRINK TRAFFIC); about 100 new rail-connected maltings were built, some in the barley-growing districts of East Anglia, others near large breweries.

Railways also seem to have competed successfully in the new market for animal feed compounds. J. Bibby & Sons, who became one of the biggest producers, were located adjacent to *Liverpool Waterloo goods station, the oldest part of their mill being leased from the *London & North Western Railway in 1886. The biggest in the field, British

Oil & Cake Mills Ltd (BOCM), formed by amalgamation in 1899 and later part of Unilever, had ten rail-connected mills around the country, the best-known being alongside the *East Coast main line at Selby.

In 1920 the railways carried some 2½ million tons of fertilizers and 12 million tons of bulk agricultural products. However, the agricultural sector of their freight business suffered particularly severely from *road transport competition between the wars; serving individual farms was not something the railways could do well. By 1939 agricultural traffics had generally fallen by over 50 per cent.   GAB

B. A. Holderness, 'Agriculture and Industrialization in the Victorian Economy', in G. E. Mingay (ed.), *The Victorian Countryside* (1981), 179–99; *RTC*, 51–2, 325–7.

agriculture. Before the introduction of railways, specialization in British farming had always been restricted by distance from *markets. Grain, cheese, hops, and potatoes could be moved long distances by sea, river, *canal, and road; and livestock, also, travelled by water as well as on their own legs. But perishable products, such as *milk, butter, eggs, *fruit and vegetables, and poultry were more difficult and costly to transport, although poultry travelled on foot as well as by cart. Generally, unless good means of water transport were at hand, dairying and market gardening were confined to a day's journey by road from the market. The railways made it possible for specialization in perishable products to spread much more widely. Fresh *fish could be taken from the ports to the cities, and fruit-growing came to be concentrated in the Vale of Evesham and central and east Kent.

The greatest effects on farming in general, however, were felt where there was easy access to railway stations. There, farming became more profitable and hence more intensive, and rents rose accordingly. Old local monopolies created by transport difficulties were broken down, and throughout the country prices of agricultural products became more uniform. Remote areas never reached by railways were relatively little affected, and remained dependent upon local markets until the coming of the motor lorry.

The most striking example of the breaking down of an old-established local monopoly was seen in dairying, and particularly in the production of milk for the *London market. It was only after 1865, when a rinderpest epidemic wiped out four-fifths of London's cows, that 'railway milk' secured a firm grip on this huge market, aided by innovations in methods of treating milk and providing for its efficient transport by rail. By 1878 London's demand was affecting farms up to 150 miles from the capital, with Derbyshire, for instance, becoming the northern limit for milk supplies. The revolution took a long time to complete, however, for even in the 1880s there were still some 700 licensed cow-houses in London, and 'town dairies' persisted similarly elsewhere. Further, from 1867 competition from canned condensed milk, a cheap and convenient alternative to the frequently adulterated fresh product, limited the growth of the dairy farmers' market.

British home-produced butter and cheese were also subject to competition, from both imports and alternatives such as 'butterine', a mixture of butter and margarine. The imported products set high standards of quality, freshness, and regularity of supply, owing to superior efficiency in production and distribution. In Britain, dairying off grass meant that little butter was made in the winter, and British farmers readily withdrew from the labour of making butter and cheese on the farm as factories appeared from the 1870s. After 1920 British dairying was hit by low prices, a problem which persisted until World War II. Subsequently, the influence of railways on dairying declined as road transport of milk in bulk tankers made the railway churn obsolete.

The marketing of *livestock was also revolutionized by railways. Not only were the expenses of droving and loss of flesh on the road eliminated, but more distant areas could rear cattle for the great centres of consumption. In Scotland new markets for livestock appeared at railheads such as Lairg, Lockerbie, Lanark, and Oban; and in England Ludlow and nearby Craven Arms dealt with large numbers of cattle coming from north and mid-Wales and from Ireland. Moreover, with the spread of the railway system the trade in dead meat developed, and it became possible for various parts of the carcass to be sold in different markets, wherever happened to be most profitable.

From the mid-19th century railways also influenced the use of fertilizers on farms. Supplies of cheap coal, carried by rail, enabled lime to be produced more widely and encouraged its greater use on the land. The first manufactured fertilizers, superphosphate of lime (1843), bone meal, and imported Peruvian guano were also affected, transported by rail from factory or docks. Other fertilizers which similarly became more readily available included nitrate of soda, muriate of potash, rape-dust, and sulphate of ammonia or basic slag. The use of expensive manures encouraged farmers to maximize their effects and avoid waste by draining wet soils and investing in machinery—also brought to them by rail—for reducing weeds and spreading the fertilizers more effectively. Thus, costly fertilizers encouraged both drainage and machinery, the most prominent advances in mid-19th-century farming, and all three contributed to the greater efficiency of leading farmers.

Railways played a significant role in the increased inflow of food imports, which depressed prices for British farmers in 1879–1914. A further spur was given to innovation, although in the worst-affected areas of East Anglia radical changes in farming came mostly from men new to the district, West Country farmers, and particularly Scots, who brought their Ayrshire cattle with them by rail, and in former arable areas practised economical forms of dairying and potato-growing for the London market.

Ease of rail travel was also one of the factors in the migration of labour from villages. By the end of the century the farm labour force was so reduced as to bring an upward pressure to bear on wage levels, and farmers bemoaned the shortage of skilled men. Farmers also attacked the railways for giving preferential rates to transporting imported foodstuffs while offering farmers a more expensive service for their home-grown produce.

Overall, the effects of railways on British agriculture were considerable, although it has to be remembered that large areas in remote parts of the country were never adequately reached by rail. Perhaps the most important effect was on the enterprise of the more advanced farmers. New access to markets, new availability of machinery and fertilizers, the wider spread of information through the farming press, and better facilities for attending local meetings and national shows, stimulated the willingness and ability to innovate, and helped farmers through the hard times of the late 19th century and inter-war years.   GEM

P. S. Bagwell, *The Transport Revolution from 1770* (1974), ch. 5; D. Taylor, 'The English Dairy Industry, 1860–1930', *Economic History Review*, 2nd ser., 29 (1976); C. S. Orwin and E. H. Whetham, *History of British Agriculture 1846–1914* (1964), ch. 5; E. H. Whetham, *The Agrarian History of England and Wales*, viii (1978), ch. 2; J. H. Clapham, *Economic History of Modern Britain*, ii (1932), ch. 8.

Ahrons, Ernest Leopold (1866–1926), writer; born at Bradford, of a Danish father, he became a pupil at the *Great Western Railway's Swindon works in 1885–8, after which he was a draughtsman in commercial engineering firms, with an interlude in Egypt. During World War I he worked for the Department of Overseas Trade. From 1919 he devoted himself wholly to writing.

The only books he himself published were very short. But he wrote two long series of articles of permanent value, later reissued in book form. The first was a set produced for the centenary of railways, published in 1927 as *The British Steam Railway Locomotive, 1825–1925*. It remains the best general account of its subject.

The other set first appeared in the *Railway Magazine* in 1915–26, on 'Locomotive and Train Working in the Latter Part of the Nineteenth Century', reprinted under that title in 1951–4. They record Ahrons' personal observation and experiences in travelling about the British Isles, with his accounts—lucid, shrewd, humorous, and sometimes caustic—of the practices he encountered. Much of what he tells us is based on notes made at the time, but recollection—not always accurate—also played its part in them. They are the best account we have of the daily running of British trains in 1870–1900, concentrating on the work that was actually done and on the equipment used by the men who did it.

JS

L. Pendred, introductory note to *The British Steam Railway Locomotive* (1927).

air-conditioning. *Carriages may be described as air-conditioned when fitted with an automatic system by which air entering the passenger accommodation has been filtered and brought to a pre-determined humidity and temperature, which is then maintained without variation at different positions within the vehicle. A comfortable atmosphere should be established, without objectionable draughts, and for effective working the windows are sealed.

Fully air-conditioned passenger stock was in service in the USA during 1930. However, a partial air-conditioning system, better described as pressure ventilation, was fitted

to *royal saloons built by the *East Coast companies in 1908. From the early 1930s the *London & North Eastern Railway made increasing use of pressure ventilation for prestige stock, principally first-class sleeping cars. Such carriages retained opening windows. At first, the heating and ventilation system was all-electric, but the LNER found that it was more practical to retain steam heating to ensure adequate warmth at the start of a journey. Comprising filters, fans, and thermostats, the equipment was usually mounted on the underframe and electrically powered from the carriage batteries. Air was distributed to the carriage interior through ducting, usually at floor level. A set of pressure-ventilated carriages entered service between Kings Cross and *Newcastle in 1934, and the Silver Jubilee and other prestige LNER train sets built in 1935–9 were so equipped.

A pair of *restaurant cars introduced in 1935 by the *Great Western Railway were the first fully air-conditioned carriages on British railways. Air-conditioned stock was not generally used by *British Rail until the Mark 2D carriages built from 1971.   MLH

M. Harris, *LNER Carriages* (1994).

Airey, J., see MAPS AND PLANS; JUNCTION DIAGRAMS.

air transport and railways. When the main-line railways obtained air powers from Parliament in 1929, only the *Southern Railway responded, albeit with an unsuccessful attempt to gain control of Imperial Airways. When a small number of internal airlines sprang up in different parts of the country in 1932, the railways did take note, the *Great Western Railway initiating a service between *Cardiff and *Plymouth in 1933, but only for the prestige of being the first in the air. In 1934 the *Big Four railways formed Railway Air Services Ltd with Imperial Airways as a nominal shareholder but also providing pilots and engineering.

The first service in 1934 was sponsored by the SR between Croydon and the Isle of Wight and was followed by a GWR one between Plymouth and *Liverpool, but it was the *London Midland & Scottish Railway that sponsored most services, its main ones being between *London, *Birmingham, *Manchester, Belfast, and *Glasgow. Competition was intense, however, especially in the Irish Sea area. The *London & North Eastern Railway alone did not sponsor services in 1934, nor subsequently. Each railway financed the necessary aircraft.

The objective of the railways was to control the new internal airlines if they persisted in staying the course. One of the weapons of the railways was the booking ban whereby there was a threat to withdraw the franchise of agents who sold tickets for airlines not on the *Railway Clearing House approved list. The ban on some airlines was lifted when they agreed to restrict their operations. In several cases, the railways actually withdrew their services in favour of a new airline owned jointly with the competitor.

The behaviour of the railways was to a large degree influenced by the LMS chairman Sir Josiah (Lord) *Stamp and the SR general manager Sir Herbert *Walker, who both never flew and wasted a lot of time worrying about the airlines. During World War II, when many services were suspended, the railways gradually bought out their partners in the jointly owned airlines. In 1944 the railways published a plan for the development of air transport to Europe. A change of government in 1945 altered the ownership plan and brought to an end the railway involvement in air transport. The Railways Act, 1993 extinguished the 1929 air powers which *British Rail had inherited in 1948.

See also ANCILLARY SERVICES.   JK

J. Stroud, *Railway Air Services* (1987).

alarm systems, see COMMUNICATION IN TRAINS.

Alexandra (Newport & South Wales) Docks & Railway. This originated as a dock company, incorporated in 1865 to build a large new dock—very much needed—at Newport. Hampered by financial difficulties, it was slow to complete even one part of the work, but as soon as the dock was opened in 1875 Newport interests began to argue that a railway connection with the Rhondda could divert some of the Rhondda coal away from Cardiff, which had now grown manifestly inadequate to handle it all.

Accordingly, in 1878 the Pontypridd Caerphilly & Newport Railway was incorporated, which, with the assistance of running powers over five other companies' lines, established a route from Pontypridd to Newport docks, opened in 1884. Two years earlier the Alexandra had turned itself into a 'Docks & Railway' company. In 1897 it purchased the Pontypridd Caerphilly & Newport. For a short time it ran a passenger service between Pontypridd and Newport, but that was taken over by the *Great Western Railway in 1899, and thereafter the Alexandra's passenger traffic was confined to one busy stretch of line between Pontypridd and Caerphilly, later extended to Machen.

The docks were gradually enlarged up to 1914, when they covered a continuous area of 124 acres. The company was paying 5 per cent when it was taken into the GWR in 1922. With its 9½-mile railway system it was the smallest of all the 28 constituent companies named in the Railways Act, 1921.   JS

Reg. Hist., xii, 103–9.

Allan, Alexander (1809–91), mechanical engineer, made one lasting contribution to locomotive design but has been incorrectly credited with developing the 'Crewe' type of locomotive.

Apprenticed under Gibb, the millwright of Montrose, he joined Robert *Stephenson & Co. at Newcastle in 1832 and two years later moved to George Forrester of Liverpool where he was involved in constructing outside-cylinder, double-framed locomotives for the *Liverpool & Manchester Railway. Two were ordered by the *Grand Junction Railway shortly before their locomotive department—then at Edge Hill—was reorganized under *Buddicom: Allan applied for the position but was instead appointed foreman of workshops. Buddicom resigned in 1841 and was replaced by Francis Trevithick who continued development of the 'Crewe' type designed by his predecessor: Allan may have

suggested the use of outside cylinders. When *Crewe works opened in 1843 Allan became foreman of locomotives and assistant to Trevithick, in effect works manager. In 1853 he disagreed with one of Trevithick's instructions, overstepped the mark in his reaction, and later resigned, subsequently becoming locomotive superintendent of the *Scottish Central Railway.

In 1854 he developed his well-known straight-link *valve gear, combining elements both of *Stephenson and *Gooch types. A compact gear giving excellent steam distribution, it was widely used by the *London & North Western, *Highland, and other railways over the next 50 years. The SCR was absorbed by the *Caledonian Railway in 1865 and Allan finished his career as manager of the Worcester Engine Company.   RW

D. H. Stuart and B. Reed, *Locomotives in Profile 15: The Crewe Type* (1971), 62–70.

Allen, Cecil J. (1886–1973), engineer and author, educated at the Grocers' Company's School and Finsbury Technical College of City & Guilds of London. Having joined the *Great Eastern Railway as a junior draughtsman in 1903 for the projected track widening between Temple Mills and Broxbourne, he was later transferred to the Permanent Way Department, becoming inspector of materials in 1908, which involved travelling by train well over 40,000 miles annually. He continued this work until retirement from the *London & North Eastern Railway in 1946.

His first article was written for the *Railway Magazine* in 1906. After the death of *Rous-Marten, Allen became one of the four authors who, in 1909, continued that magazine's 'British Locomotive Practice & Performance' articles, now the longest-running railway series in the world. In 1911 he became its sole author, contributing over 500 articles until handing over to O. S. *Nock in 1958. He then continued writing on the same subject in *Trains Illustrated*. During this period he took part in many notable high-speed runs. So well known was his series that in 1949 *Punch* published a parody, 'British Bus Practice & Performance'. The first of his 38 books (including eight 'for younger readers') was published in 1915. He also undertook many professional speaking engagements, as well as giving talks on radio and television.

He was a keen organist, playing in venues such as the Albert Hall for rallies of two Christian organizations with which he was associated. At various times he was president of the *Railway Club, the Railway Service Christian Union, and the Fleet Street Railway Circle.   PWBS

C. J. Allen, *Two Million Miles of Train Travel* (1965).

all-night services. The first British railway to offer round-the-clock services was the *Great Eastern, which began to run them every half-hour throughout the night between *Liverpool Street and Walthamstow in 1897. No other company followed this example until 1910, when the *South Eastern & Chatham Railway put on two trains in the small hours from Ludgate Hill to Beckenham and Bromley, partly to convey newspaper workers from Fleet Street. By 1922 the

*London & South Western Railway was running five such trains on the 'Kingston Roundabout', leaving *Waterloo between 1 and 3.35 a.m. These services were not then extended further in Britain. The arrival of the cheap motor-car presently reduced the demand, and in 1963 the news-papermen's trains ceased.

But similar services had just then reappeared, for a quite different purpose. In 1962 an hourly service was introduced between Victoria and Gatwick Airport, at first on Mondays only, then daily. They run still.   JS

C. J. Allen, *Great Eastern Railway* (1955), 63; *LT*, 202.

alloys have been defined as substances having metallic properties, consisting of two or more metallic elements, or of metallic and non-metallic elements, which are mixed with each other when molten and have not separated into distinct layers when solid. Steel is one of the oldest alloys, composed essentially of iron and carbon. Alloys are gen-erally divided into two main types—ferrous, or iron-based, and non-ferrous, defined by the most important metal pre-sent, brass thus being a copper-based alloy.

Mild carbon steel is most widely used for railway vehicle bodies and structures, but special steels have also been used in applications where increased resistance to wear is re-quired, also increased corrosion resistance. Thus the man-ganese content of rail steels increases working life, and in especially severe conditions, such as V-sections of pointwork (see TRACK) carrying heavy traffic, a higher manganese content can be used. Similarly, the provision of manganese liners to steam locomotive axle-boxes reduced the wear rate, and enabled mileages between overhauls to be greatly increased.

Alloys, especially aluminium, are also used to reduce the weight of railway vehicle bodies, the reduced weight for a given number of vehicles enabling train performance to be improved for a given applied power. Mild steel vehicle bod-ies can suffer from corrosion when running in heavily salt-laden air. Stainless chrome nickel steel *carriage bodies have been widely used in North America, France, and else-where. Nickel and vanadium steels have been used to re-duce the weight of driving and motion rods on steam locomotives, improving balance and reducing hammer-blow stresses on the track.   GWC

Allport, Sir James Joseph (1811–92), manager. The son of a Birmingham small-arms manufacturer, he joined the *Birmingham & Derby Junction Railway in 1839, becoming manager in 1843, then successively manager of the New-castle & Darlington Junction Railway (1844–50), Manches-ter Sheffield & Lincolnshire Railway (see GREAT CENTRAL) (1850–3), and *Midland Railway (1853–80, except 1857–60, when he was managing director of Palmer's shipbuilding company, at Jarrow).

Allport's policies for the MR were strongly ambitious. In 1853 its lines extended from *Derby to *Leeds, Lincoln, Rugby, and *Bristol. At his retirement they reached Lon-don, *Swansea, and *Carlisle; jointly owned lines took its traffic to *Lowestoft, *Liverpool, and *Bournemouth. All-port did not originate this expansion, but supplied a power-ful momentum.

In handling traffic his work was highly individual. The steady rise in third-class passenger journeys persuaded him to court this traffic instead of trying to force people to travel first or second, and from 1872 the company provided third-class accommodation on all its trains. Two years later it abolished second class (see CLASS DISTINCTIONS). At the same time it introduced *Pullman cars into Britain. The financial gains from these policies were strongly disputed, and have never been thoroughly examined.

Allport was not a progressive everywhere. He mistrusted interlocking (see SIGNALLING) over which he fought the gov-ernment *inspectors ferociously. But the inspectors pre-vailed.

In 1884, after retirement, he was knighted, the first rail-way manager so honoured. No other has ever enjoyed such widespread respect. 'Upon the population of the country at large', wrote *Acworth, 'he conferred a boon that entitles him to rank with Rowland Hill as a benefactor of his spe-cies.'   JS

DNB; *GR*, 189, 193, 196, 200; Acworth (5th edn., 1900), 206.

amalgamation. In Britain 'amalgamation' of railway com-panies might be of three types: (1) a combination of two companies whose lines converged; (2) the purchase of a smaller company by a larger one; (3) a merger of several, creating a coherent system. Any of these might also be achieved by leasing or working *agreements, or by two or more companies taking over lines in which they had com-mon interests, as *joint railways. Any fusion of capital re-quired an Act of Parliament.

The first such Act, sanctioning an arrangement of type 1, formed the *North Union Railway from the Preston & Wigan and Wigan Branch Railways in 1840. Type 2 ap-peared next year, when the *Grand Junction Railway was permitted to absorb the Warrington & Newton. Type 3 emerged in 1844, the *Midland Railway then being estab-lished by the amalgamation of three companies meeting at *Derby; this was followed in 1846 by the bigger amalgama-tion of the *London & Birmingham, Grand Junction, and Manchester & Birmingham Railways to form the *London & North Western.

Type 1 amalgamations usually sought to produce work-ing economies, and sometimes to end hostility. Type 2 became the commonest: the purchase of a small branch or connecting line by a larger company. Minor lines were often promoted locally, and a few might be bought up at par—e.g. the Selkirk & Galashiels by the *North British in 1859—or even at a profit to the smaller company, like the Vale of Llangollen Railway when it passed to the *Great Western in 1896. Usually, however, the sale was at a loss, made accept-able perhaps by the benefits the railway had conferred on local communities. With that in mind, the *Cornwall Rail-way shareholders agreed to accept only 40 per cent of the value of their shares on amalgamation with the GWR in 1889. A large company might also acquire a smaller line to protect its territory from invasion by a neighbour. The

*Great Northern, anxious about the Midland's London extension, bought the Edgware Highgate & London Railway in 1867 at a price well above what it was intrinsically worth.

Type 3, forming a new system by merger, was often a device for ending a ruinous competition. Such an amalgamation might lead to a *monopoly of railway services over a whole district, as in 1862 with the creation of the new *Great Eastern Railway. It must be remembered that stage *coaches had now virtually disappeared from the populous parts of Britain, which meant that the railways monopolized all overland travelling and, as much larger corporations, might exercise a dangerous new social power. Moreover, in the 1860s the issue of *season tickets began to attract wide attention, making *commuters into London and other big cities into a captive market.

It was in 1852 that *Punch* (a good reflector of middle-class opinion) began to attack railway amalgamation. In 1868 it published a strong cartoon by Tenniel exposing the proposed amalgamation of the *South Eastern and *London Brighton & South Coast Railways as an expedient for raising fares. It was chiefly on that ground that the House of Lords destroyed the plan.

In 1872 the LNW and *Lancashire & Yorkshire Railways asked Parliament to allow them to amalgamate. The proposal would have created an almost complete monopoly in most of industrial Lancashire, including such large towns as Bolton, Burnley, Blackburn, and *Preston; also between *Manchester and *Leeds. Every other similar district in Britain except Tyneside had strongly competing railways: the Black Country, South Wales, West Yorkshire, and the Forth–Clyde basin. The advantages of competitive services, in providing traders and passengers with a choice, seemed clear enough.

A joint committee of both Houses of Parliament now considered railway amalgamation in general, taking account of other similar plans (several already under discussion), leading towards the creation of some six great commercial bodies, dividing most of the British railway system between them; to be followed, as the committee thought likely, by the establishment of a single mammoth private or state corporation. Disliking this prospect, it recommended against the amalgamation of these two companies, and Parliament duly rejected it; twice indeed, for they tried again in 1873. This ended similar ideas there for some time.

Undeterred, Sir Edward *Watkin, as chairman of the Manchester Sheffield & Lincolnshire Railway (see GREAT CENTRAL), tried to secure amalgamations with its neighbours. In 1875 he sought one with the *North Staffordshire, which failed. In 1877 he turned to a much bigger fusion, with the Midland and the Great Northern, the MSLR shares to secure a guaranteed ordinary dividend of 4 per cent. However, when he demanded 4½ per cent, alleging that the security for the guarantees was insufficient, negotiations broke down. The shareholders would have been grateful for that 4 per cent: during the remaining 23 years of the company's life, their dividends averaged 1.8.

Some other amalgamations, of type 3, succeeded. The line from London to Penzance had been built by five companies. The *Bristol & Exeter amalgamated with the GWR in 1877; the *South Devon the following year; the Cornwall Railway in 1889. The *West Cornwall had lost its independence in 1866. These amalgamations set up no new monopolies, and Parliament accepted them readily.

It also sanctioned the 'working union' of the South Eastern and *London Chatham & Dover companies in 1899, something less than total amalgamation. Both companies remained as financial entities. It was management that was now to be unified. Their struggles all over Kent to damage each other (and those who used them) had long been notorious. Four other important amalgamation proposals made before 1914 met with varying fates. The GN, GE, and Great Central companies tried to form another 'working union' in 1908, but Parliament rejected it. Nor would it agree to an amalgamation of the *Taff Vale, *Rhymney, and *Cardiff Railways in 1909. On the other hand it allowed three of the eight *London underground railways to amalgamate in 1910, one more being added in 1912 and two more in 1920. Finally, in 1912 the Midland was permitted to absorb the *London Tilbury & Southend—on strict conditions, the most important of which the Midland dishonoured with impunity.

Amalgamation aroused many fears, but it offered substantial advantages too. It allowed some small and useful railways to be kept going, whereas if left alone they would have had to close down. It produced economies in working, not necessarily reducing charges but helping to prevent increases. And it could eliminate a tiresome multiplicity of stations, notably in Kent. One of the earliest termini to be closed was that of the *Canterbury & Whitstable Railway, after its amalgamation with the SER in 1846. Some of the last before *Grouping were at Ashford, Chatham, and Dover.

By 1914 the British railway system represented the consolidated aggregate of more than 1,000 separate companies. Under the Railways Act (1921) all the larger railways, 120 in number (excluding the London underground railways and the *Metropolitan), were amalgamated into four (see GROUPING). Nearly 40 other very small railways, each on average some nine miles long, remained independent. Only one more important amalgamation remained, forming the London Passenger Transport Board—including the Metropolitan—in 1933 (see LONDON UNDERGROUND RAILWAYS), until all but the very smallest railways in the UK were merged in 1948 into the single state-owned corporation, foreshadowed in *Gladstone's Act in 1844 and the deliberations of 1872.

JS

W. A. Robertson, *Combination among Railway Companies* (1912); E. Cleveland-Stevens, *British Railways* (1915); W. E. Simnett, *Railway Amalgamation in Britain* (1923); Tenniel cartoon, *Punch*, 54 (1868), 279; P. S. Bagwell, 'Rivalry and Working Union of the South Eastern and London Chatham & Dover Railways', *JTH*, 2 (1955–6), 65–79.

ambulance trains, see WAR.

ancillary services. In their authorizing Acts railway companies were seldom given any powers that might encroach on other people's privileges or rights, except what were judged essential. They were intended to be railways, and railways alone.

Presently some companies began to secure extensions to these powers, for activities related to railways and yet not part of them. For the most important see BUSES; CANALS; HOTELS; HOUSING; PORTS AND DOCKS; SHIPPING SERVICES. The railways' published accounts do not indicate the direct contributions made to their revenue by all ancillary services. These large ones brought in nearly £9 million in 1912: about 7 per cent of the railways' total receipts from traffic. Here some of the minor services are mentioned. Most of them contributed nothing directly; they were devices to save the companies money.

When the railways sought powers to extend their activities in this way, they were frequently opposed by interests which claimed they would suffer, and in 1847 the House of Commons laid down a special procedure to be followed in such cases. But in the 1860s this attitude changed materially (see PARLIAMENT), and most of the extensions applied for were allowed.

Some of the railways' smaller ancillary services were adopted simply in order to cheapen or speed up their work. The *London & North Western Railway, for example, had its own brickworks at *Crewe from 1862 onwards, for buildings throughout the system. The *Great Western likewise manufactured bricks at *Swindon from about 1880 up to 1908. At Crewe there was also a leather-works, and soap was made from the oil and grease removed from locomotives under repair.

But there were some industrial activities that even Crewe never touched. The LNWR did none of its own printing, contracting it to McCorquodale's, of *Liverpool and Wolverton. The *Great Eastern and *London Chatham & Dover companies, however, undertook their own. The GER printed all its *timetables and working notices at Stratford (London), employing over 100 people and claiming positive economy.

The railway companies became great capitalists, ready to spend money on anything that might profit them, directly or indirectly, including some things that also benefited places they served. A number established, or helped to establish, *markets, linked to their own systems. The *Great Northern company built a large potato market at King's Cross, the Midland a general vegetable market at St Pancras (see LONDON STATIONS). But the GER's Bishopsgate vegetable market, set up in 1882, had to be closed 18 months later because there were no statutory powers. The *Midland Railway and *Leicester Corporation collaborated in opening a new cattle market, rail-connected, in 1873, and the same happened later at *Nottingham and *York. This is all evidence of the range of the railways' interests and the extent to which they permeated the communities they served.

In the changed world of the nationalized railways ancillary services began to be reduced, and with the first privatizations of the 1980s they disappeared altogether.   JS

W. H. Chaloner, *Social and Economic Development of Crewe* (1950), 73; A. S. Peck, *Great Western at Swindon Works* (1983), 97; printing: Acworth, 440–1; markets: *RTC*, 49–50, 161, 186.

Andrews, George Townsend (1805–55), architect. A close associate of George *Hudson, Andrews was sheriff of York when Hudson was returned unopposed to Parliament. Although he is considered to have been heavily indebted to Hudson's patronage, Andrews' large output of railway work over a short period was of high quality, employing sensitive use of local materials. It comprised most of the stations on Hudson's lines in the north-east from Tadcaster to Gateshead, including *York's first station and the arch cut in the city walls by which the railway reached it. Andrews designed a light iron pitched roof on continuous side walls that became a characteristic of his trainsheds, such as Scarborough, Beverley, and Durham (Gilesgate). His façades were generally in a classical manner, Whitby and *Hull being among the best, while Pocklington displayed an arcade of considerable merit. His small wayside stations were plain 'house' types, although equally characteristic of him. But on lines where the scenery was more dramatic he favoured a Gothic style, most notably at Richmond where a heavily buttressed colonnade and steep-pitched roof afforded a remarkably medieval aspect. His other work included Richmond School, and a number of churches. Hudson's financial collapse left Andrews with heavy debts.   GJB

M. J. Minett, 'The Railway Stations of George Townsend Andrews', *JTH* (1965), 1st series, 7, 1; D. Ware, *A Short Dictionary of British Architects* (1967); *VS*, 56–60; K. Hoole, *Railway Stations of the North East* (1985).

angling. Railway companies, always keen to exploit special traffic, realized at an early date that many anglers wished to travel to riverbank and seaside in pursuit of their hobby. Tickets on the Manchester Sheffield & Lincolnshire (see GREAT CENTRAL) and *Cambrian Railways printed specifically for anglers date from the 1870s.

All major companies participated by 1902, when the *Railway Clearing House instructed that 'Third Class Return tickets may be issued to *bona fide* Fishermen at the agreed reduced fares for Anglers, minimum 1s. per Passenger'. Most companies insisted on membership of a recognized fishing club, and all required the rod and tackle to be produced when buying tickets and when they were examined *en route*.

Many smaller companies, including the *Isle of Man and Derwent Valley Railways, also offered reduced fares for anglers, and railway shipping services allowed them to fish from their piers. Daily or weekly fishing permits were available at ports such as Holyhead and Ryde.

See also SPORTS, FIELD.   MGDF
Railway Clearing House Coaching Books; *Rule Books* of various railways.

animals, see LIVESTOCK TRAFFIC.

Annett's key. The primary purpose of this mechanical lock-and-key device was to control *siding points situated between *block posts on double lines of railway, avoiding the need for a *signal box. It was devised by James Edward Annett and patented in 1875. The siding points were controlled by a ground frame with an additional lever which locked all the others. The lock was attached to it and had to be unlocked by the 'Annett's key'. If any of the levers were reversed, the key was held in the lock.

The key was kept in another lock in the signal box at one end of the block section. Removing it normally locked the levers against any conflicting movements. The key was taken to the siding by the shunter or train crew. On completion of the work the key had to be returned to the signal box to allow resumption of normal traffic.

Most railway companies and manufacturers made the locks and keys to their own designs and hence they varied considerably in appearance.

On *single lines the staff, tablet, or token normally released the siding points, but an Annett's lock could be used, with the key attached to the train staff.   RDF

L. P. Lewis, *Railway Signal Engineering* (1920).

announcing of trains. Until very recent times the transmission of information from the railways' staff to their passengers was haphazard, usually depending on nothing but question and answer. In 1861 at almost every station on the *Edinburgh & Glasgow Railway a parrot or starling was kept, which called out its name 'most distinctly' on the trains' arrival. Elsewhere *porters' voices were used for this purpose. They were untrained, and many of their announcements were inaudible or unintelligible. Since the station might have only one name-board on each platform, easily missed as the train drew in, a railway journey could be an anxious business to the traveller, particularly if he or she had to change trains *en route*. Edison invented the megaphone in 1879, but it was a long time before one was regularly used on any British railway station. Although the Tannoy company started in 1928, its products were not quickly adopted by railways in the UK. The *London & North Eastern Railway introduced loudspeakers at York in 1927, but growth in their use was slow until after World War II.

*British Rail installed electric public-address systems at its larger stations and made serious efforts to train the staff to use them well. Their use is now widespread, often transmitting pre-recorded messages. At some small stations the voice is that of a *signalman from a box some miles away. Yet at *Sheffield in the 1980s a member of staff had often to stand by the footbridge staircase to tell bewildered passengers where to find connecting trains, the announcer being either silent on the matter or incomprehensible.

Announcements could not be satisfactorily made within British trains while their vehicles were divided into *compartments. But when BR adopted the open coach as standard, announcements by 'intercom' throughout the train became possible. Their quality has been steadily improved, and they now usually work well.   JS

Edinburgh & Glasgow Railway: *Builder*, 19 (1861), 341.

archaeology, railways and. In the course of their construction railways were not infrequently carried into and through sites of ancient occupation. Most of these were then unknown and unrecorded; none was at first protected legally against destruction.

A very early case of this sort concerned one of the most famous antiquities in Britain: Hadrian's Wall, which the *Newcastle & Carlisle Railway cut through in two places in 1835–6. The work was managed carefully, without serious damage to the structure. The first important discovery due to railway building was of a Roman pavement near Bath, made while the *Great Western line was under construction in 1836–8. It was lifted and placed at Keynsham station, though subsequently destroyed. The building of the *Manchester & Leeds Railway produced discoveries of skeletons and weapons, described in a pamphlet in 1838.

Such published accounts contributed to knowledge, and won some applause for that. The *Chester & Holyhead Railway was said in an academic journal to have made 'even that most unpoetical and innovating of modern inventions—the railway—to serve the cause of Archaeology'. But there were other ways of considering this matter. The railways' ruthless passage through Lewes and Dorchester in the 1840s provoked public outcries, the second of them successful.

Some of the battles between railway projectors and preservationists are dealt with here in the article VANDALISM BY RAILWAYS. Particularly important arguments of this kind arose at *York and *Leicester, and during the construction of the deep-level *London underground railways after 1890. In 1900 the London County Council tried to persuade the companies to hand over to it all objects of archaeological interest found when such work was being carried through, to be placed in the Guildhall Museum, but the attempt failed.   JS

Chester & Holyhead Railway: *Archaeologia Cambrensis*, series 1, 4, 372; Great Western Railway: MacDermot, i. 54; Manchester & Leeds, *Ottley 7687; London (1900), PRO, RAIL410/2042.

archaeology of railways may be taken as the study of railway history from surviving traces and artefacts. Of the early era of *wooden-railed wagonways, the perishable nature of wood means that little remains. By far the most important is Causey Arch, near Stanley, Co. Durham, built of stone with a 105 ft span for the Tanfield Wagonway about 1726. Iron *tramroads have left many traces, notably the tramroad–canal interchanges at Froghall (Staffordshire) and Buxworth (Derbyshire), and the stone block sleepers to be found in numerous locations either on their original sites or built into walls nearby.

Iron tramroads have also left the prominent remains of the inclined planes upon which *cable haulage was used, like the Lancaster Canal tramroad at *Preston. Also prominent are remains of the *Stockton & Darlington Railway inclines at Brusselton, which overlapped into the steam railway era. At Chatsworth Street cutting, *Liverpool, traces of the *Liverpool & Manchester Railway's incline machinery installations were excavated in the late 1970s.

The LMR (1830) was above all the prototype steam main line. Early station buildings survive at Liverpool Road,

*Manchester, and at Edge Hill, Liverpool. Its nine-arched Sankey Viaduct was the prototype for many to follow: one of the first examples was the *Grand Junction Railway's Dutton Viaduct over the River Weaver. This continues in main-line use, like many other structures from the great age of railway expansion: *tunnels at Kilsby and Box; the great stations at *Paddington, *King's Cross, *St Pancras, *New-castle-upon-Tyne, and *Bristol; the great bridges—the Royal Albert Bridge over the Tamar, the Tay Bridge, and above all the *Forth Bridge (see also BRIDGES AND VIADUCTS). In many lesser structures, features characteristic of the old companies may still be found: the saw-tooth platform awnings and diagonal-railed platform fences of the *Midland Railway, for instance, and the distinctive styles which many companies used for their *signal boxes and indeed for the signals themselves.

These are still in use on the railway, though decreasingly so; but on some preserved railways they form the frame for the picture presented by contemporary steam locomotives and rolling stock. It was in their styling that some companies—notably the *Great Western—were at their most distinctive, and it is to railway *museums and railway *preservation groups that we owe the continuing opportunity to study them. So, too, can be studied the developing technical features of past locomotives and rolling stock: steam locomotives preserved range from *Hedley's primeval locomotives of 1814 down to the last to be built for *British Railways, *Evening Star* of 1960. As for traces of the large portion of the railway system which has been closed, it is impossible to move far in Britain without encountering abandoned trackbeds, redundant viaducts, and station buildings put to new uses.

See also CONSERVATION.   PJGR

G. Biddle, O. S. Nock, and others, *The Railway Heritage of Britain* (1983); P. J. G. Ransom, *The Archaeology of Railways* (1981); P. J. G. Ransom, *The Archaeology of the Transport Revolution 1750–1850* (1984).

arches, use of, see CONSERVATION.

architecture and architects. Railways, more than any other activity in Britain, have faithfully reflected architectural taste by creating a large class of widely disparate buildings which have epitomized the ideas and fashions of the times in which they were built. From the *Liverpool & Manchester Railway's Moorish Arch at Edge Hill in 1830 to the exposed structural elements of East Croydon station in 1992, they have expressed 160 years of change.

Railway architecture owed little to that of its predecessors, the *canals. Except for the great aqueducts and warehouses, canal architecture, although always seemly, was essentially domestic in character and, moreover, has undergone relatively little change. But railways, throughout their existence, have run through a profusion of styles and standards. Until about 1855 most construction was superbly inspired. Then it entered a century of increasing mediocrity which often descended to the banal, yet which at times was interspersed by surprisingly visionary work. After World War II there was a slow but significant awakening which,

from the 1960s, produced some contemporary buildings of high quality.

The early period coincided with the close of the Classical Revival, in which private and public power and wealth were expressed in great neo-Greek and Roman buildings. It was a natural idiom for those railways which sought to demonstrate their pride and confidence in the new economic power they were creating. The greatest was the Doric portico at *Euston (1838), which symbolized the *London & Birmingham Railway as London's gateway to the north. Philip *Hardwick, a well-known architect, was appointed to design it, together with an Ionic counterpart at *Birmingham.

Others followed: more modestly at *Leicester Campbell Street (1840) and *Glasgow Bridge Street (1841); on the grand scale at Monkwearmouth (1845); magnificently so at Huddersfield (1850), and—British railway architecture's crowning achievement—the 600 ft-long frontage at *Newcastle (1863), originally designed by John *Dobson but completed in modified form by Thomas Prosser. They, like the designers of the others and many more, were local men.

Classicism was applied to smaller places, too, like the first stations at Lytham and Lewes (both 1846), and Ashby-de-la-Zouch (1849), generally with restraint, although Newmarket (1848) was so amazingly opulent as to be compared with a baroque orangery. Surprisingly late for the style, Bath Green Park (1870) was given an Ionic façade that accorded with its Georgian surroundings.

This sure sense of 'place' was evidenced by the designers of many early stations, encouraged by the railways' recognition that, in small towns and villages, stations in a familiar style would help to persuade apprehensive inhabitants to travel by the new, often feared, railway. Consequently, many were made to resemble gate-lodges and cottages on country estates, with such homely, picturesque effects as half-timbering, steep gables, dormer windows, decorated bargeboards, and elaborate chimney stacks. Good-neighbourliness was achieved by using local materials: stone where it was available, brick from local clays, flint in East Anglia. Less affluent companies used timber, although even the *South Eastern Railway's wooden stations observed the Kentish clapboard tradition, continuing to be built in this way for many years.

Embellishments were also applied to some *civil engineering structures. The proportions of *bridges and viaducts spoke for themselves, although the architect David Mocatta was employed to decorate J. U. *Rastrick's Balcombe Viaduct with Classical balustrades and end-pavilions, and Francis *Thompson executed the detailing on Robert *Stephenson's *Britannia and Conway bridges. *Tunnel portals, though, were often considered to need special attention. Gothic arches, turrets, and battlements were seen as particularly appropriate preludes to the awesome gloom within, like those at Clayton Tunnel, Sussex, and Red Hill, Nottinghamshire. I. K. *Brunel preferred a Classical western entrance to Box Tunnel, Wiltshire, and Thompson chose Egyptian styling at Bangor.

When the first railways were built, Classicism and its

Renaissance derivatives were steadily being outmoded by Gothic as the fashionable style, a term stemming from the late 18th and early 19th century Romantic movement's interest in medieval architecture that came to embrace anything from Norman to Tudor. For some years Italianate and Gothic were equally popular, the former on railways to the extent that it was called the 'English Railway Style'. It had the advantage of cheapness. The brick and stucco of Mocatta's Palladian station at *Brighton (1841), for instance, and T. M. *Penson's charming Florentine stations at Gobowen and Ruabon (1846), cost much less than the dressed and carved stone required for Brunel's Tudor building at *Bristol Temple Meads (1840) or William *Tite's *Carlisle (1847).

Variations abounded in both styles: on the one hand, imitation Italian villas and *palazzi*, like Roberts and Smith's first *London Bridge station (1844), complete with campanile, and Thompson's enormously long Venetian frontage at Chester (1848); or, on the other hand, the cloister-like façade at Richmond, Yorkshire, by G. T. *Andrews (1846), and Henry Hunt's rich Jacobean at *Stoke-on-Trent (1850). Vernacular styles lasted longer in Scotland, where the variety of smaller stations was less marked. They were mostly stone and often plainer in the local tradition, with excellent masonry-work, and perhaps embellished with characteristic crow-stepped gables, although stations designed by Andrew Heiton, Jr of *Perth were more ambitious, particularly Dunkeld (1856). The *Highland Railway had some particularly rugged cottage stations in the far north, such as Rogart and Kinbrace.

Brunel was one of a number of early railway engineers who did their own architectural work, generally with skill. Others employed architects for specific tasks. Contractors occasionally took on architects, too, but in the main they were employed direct by the company, either on a contractual basis or, later, on a longer-term retainer, like Hadfield and Weightman of Sheffield for the Manchester Sheffield & Lincolnshire Railway (see GREAT CENTRAL). But Paley and Austin of Lancaster, who in 1865–82 carried out at least 13 major commissions for the small *Furness Railway, seem merely to have had a close relationship with the company, like some others.

As they moved from job to job, some architects developed distinctive features which they repeated on stations and lineside buildings along the railway on which they were working, giving it a visual entity of its own; William Tress's work in Kent, for example, and that of John *Livock and Sancton *Wood elsewhere. Such 'line-styles' were very prevalent in earlier work, none more so than Brunel's Tudor wayside stations on the *Great Western between London and Bristol, with their integral all-round awnings, and varying only in the choice of local building material. He developed an Italianate version that appeared on many of his later lines, which was continued by his successors. It seems probable that Brunel introduced the concept of the platform canopy or awning, and that most characteristic of British station features, the decorative wooden valance,

which spread overseas to nearly every country in the British sphere of influence.

Line-styles led the larger railways to adopt a recognizable company style, or sometimes several, which was the beginning of corporate architecture. The *Midland Railway's familiar single-storey station building, comprising a pair of gabled pavilions linked by a recessed centrepiece forming a waiting shelter, represented over 30 years of continuously evolving style: Beeston, Nottinghamshire (1847); Thornbury, Gloucestershire (1872). It was copied by the MSLR and several other railways, which introduced their own variations.

Mid- and late Victorian architecture was nothing if not eclectic, as Classical formality and true Gothic principles gave way to a mixing of styles and periods, often coarsely executed. Again, railways followed the fashion. In large cities, as stations grew or were rebuilt to keep pace with increasing traffic, great façades with towers and turrets—often a station *hotel—competed with new town halls, banks, and market halls for supremacy in the townscape.

Noted architects were engaged, such as E. M. Barry at *Cannon Street and *Charing Cross, Matthew Digby Wyatt for the Paddington hotel and the new frontage at Bristol, and Sir Gilbert Scott at *St Pancras.

Company styles naturally led to greater standardization in the design of small and medium-sized stations. Local building styles all but vanished, replaced by near-universal brick brought to the site by the railway itself, and mass-produced cast-iron and wooden components, leading to the appearance of complete standard stations regardless of locality. In a throw-back to earlier years, large numbers were all-wooden, particularly on the *London & North Western. At some stations, a number of them important ones, the Great Western continued to build the wooden, overall-roofed, barn-like structures developed by Brunel, curiously contrasting with the charm of his small stations.

Because the system was now virtually complete, the impact of the so-called Domestic Revival and the Arts and Crafts movement of the late 19th to early 20th century was not as great. But it did cause a small but welcome return to individuality in station design, employing decorative terracotta, tile-hanging, and pseudo-half-timbering for effect, particularly in southern and eastern England, although there was a notable Scottish example at Wemyss Bay (1903), while the Swiss chalet styling on the West Highland Railway (1894) reflected the influence of *tourism.

During the early 1900s some distinctive buildings enlivened London's streets at stations on the Underground Group of railways designed by Leslie W. *Green, notable for the use of dark maroon glazed tiling. A number of the succeeding surface lines had domestic-style stations that reflected the new suburbs they served, a theme intermittently followed for a time by the main-line companies after the 1923 *Grouping in the few new stations that they built. In the 1930s C. H. *Holden on the *London Underground and, to a lesser extent, J. R. Scott on the *Southern Railway, set an admirable new standard in functional station design: a revival of corporate railway architecture that was more complete in detail than anything before. Holden's LT headquarters at St James's Park was in a class apart among railway buildings, and with his stations attracted world-wide interest. Both architects laid visual emphasis on the entrance hall or concourse, to form—as at Cockfosters and Bishopstone—the focal point of the station, and in London there was much use of reinforced *concrete for columns and awnings. To a limited degree the *London Midland & Scottish also experimented with this medium, while the spacious new concourse at Leeds City was rightly acclaimed. Station reconstruction on the Great Western, however, was far more conservative, as, for example, its somewhat clumsy essays in Classicism at *Cardiff and neo-Georgian at Newton Abbot.

Towards the end of the 19th century some larger railways began to employ official architects and to establish architectural departments. Most companies allowed them to continue in private practice; only a few were full-time senior officials, like Charles *Trubshaw on the Midland and William *Bell on the *North Eastern, and generally they answered to the civil engineer. Some became chief officers in their own right, a trend that increased after the Grouping, although outside consultants might still be brought in for specially important work. After nationalization in 1947, *British Railways formed an architectural department in each of its regions, each having considerable autonomy, with a chief architect at headquarters in London.

As in other buildings of the time, new ideas and forms of construction were tried. There was extensive use of materials like pre-cast concrete panels, glass, and plastics, with varying degrees of durability. Banbury, Folkestone Central, Manchester Oxford Road, and *Coventry are examples. The last was particularly successful. Meanwhile, in 1965–70 the Southern Region went in for modular prefabricated buildings using the 'CLASP' system, although time, exacerbated by insufficient maintenance, was not always kind to them. Latterly, timber has been more widely used, and much more satisfyingly, as at Knockholt and Windermere. Tower blocks, too, have appeared at stations as everywhere else, including Euston, *Plymouth, *Manchester Piccadilly, and Milton Keynes Central, not all for railway use. As part of a large and lucrative programme of maximizing property values and revenue, large stations are increasingly becoming part of office and shop developments: disastrously in visual and user terms at Birmingham New Street (1967); triumphantly at Charing Cross (1991).

BR's Architects Department continued to produce very creditable work until, after being redesignated the Architecture and Design Group, it was disbanded under the *privatization programme in 1995. Although one or two railway businesses still employ a procurement architect, design has now reverted to private practices. The wheel has turned full circle.

The architecture of other railway buildings was strictly utilitarian and functional, in which sparingly applied features betrayed the owning company as surely as on the stations. Occasionally a *goods shed of distinction might match an adjacent station, usually earlier ones like Stroud, Hampton Court, and a series between Newcastle and Berwick by Benjamin *Green. *Signal boxes had particularly strong company characteristics, with decorative bargeboards and finials. Again, a very small number matched the station, like the Domestic Revival example at Nutfield, the brick lower storeys (but not the standard superstructures) at Kenilworth and Tenbury Wells, and those that accompanied the stations rebuilt in 1930–2 by the *London & North Eastern Railway on the *East Coast main line between York and Pilmoor.

See also TRAINSHEDS; STATIONS.   GJB

C. Barman, An Introduction to Railway Architecture (1950); VS; M. Binney and D. Pearce (eds.), Railway Architecture (1979); GRSB.

archives and records. The original records relating to the history of railways in Britain are of three main kinds: those of government (national and local); those of the railway companies and of commercial undertakings associated with railways—the builders of locomotives, for example, and the carriers of goods; and those descending from or held by institutions, societies, and private persons.

The phrase 'original records', where it is applied to railways, must be interpreted broadly. It should not be confined to documents written by hand. Many documents were printed, or reproduced by some other means, for circulation in government departments or among railway directors and officers, frequently stated to be confidential or understood to be such, copies of which now survive only in archive collections. They are part of the railways' records—unseen by the public and usually unknown to those who investigated their history until the companies' archives were thrown open to students and other interested people from 1951 onwards.

Moreover, there are records of some kinds that may be valuable and yet were never written at all: photographs especially, but pictures of other sorts too. These can sometimes provide authoritative historical evidence not to be found in any written documents known to us (see PHOTOGRAPHY and ART).

The most important records of the central government concerning the authorization of railways are to be found in the House of Lords Record Office at Westminster, to which the public has access. These records relate to both Houses of Parliament, but a great many of those of the Commons before 1835 were destroyed in the great fire that burnt down their House in that year. One may hope to trace in these records the whole process of legislation, from the promoters' submission of plans and books of reference (see PROMOTION PROCEDURE; LAND AND PROPERTY; LANDOWNERS) and introduction of their Bill into Parliament to the examination of it in committee, with verbatim transcripts of the evidence given to support or oppose it. Having heard all this evidence, the committee would decide on its report, and that would usually settle the fate of the Bill when it went back for the consideration of the Houses: to be enacted, if it came to be approved, in the same session (see PARLIAMENT AND LEGISLATION).

This office also contains much other material that may be of importance for the study of railways: petitions, for example, favouring or opposing projects under consideration by Parliament, and some records of judicial proceedings.

Not very much seems to be discoverable now about the keeping of records by the old railway companies. They were, as a rule, entrusted to the secretary (the chief legal officer) and dealt with by his clerks; almost nothing is heard of an archivist, or any other officer specially responsible for them. In 1859 the *North Eastern company had a 'keeper of muniments', Benjamin Dunn, who drew the attention of the secretary to the deplorable state of the documents he had found when he visited the Old Rectory House at Gateshead, where records of business at individual stations were then kept: 900 volumes of them lying about on the floor, in rooms with unglazed windows. In 1880 the company established a muniment room in the basement of the old station building at *York. The *Great Northern Railway kept the records of its day-to-day commercial business for seven years and then pulped them. In 1926 an effort was made on the *London Midland & Scottish Railway to destroy 'this junk', accumulated at Euston station. An order to this effect is said to have gone out, and to have been disobeyed. But is that statement wholly true? The quantity of records now extant from the LMS in the Public Record Office at Kew, London, relating to its business in England and Wales, is strangely meagre: with the result that the largest of the four companies created in 1921 is now represented there by what is proportionately the smallest number of records.

Some individual members of the staff of the old railway companies devoted themselves to assembling, sorting, and preserving record material of many kinds concerning them. D. M. Levien, for example, of the *Great Western Railway had a sharp and intelligent eye for them all, as well as for miscellaneous objects that he thought worth preservation. A selection from this material was exhibited in the 1930s in the long corridor that ran above no. 1 platform at Paddington station. The papers whose preservation we owe to him include important groups relating to *Brunel and Sir Daniel *Gooch, now at the PRO. The objects have passed to the Great Western Railway Museum at *Swindon.

The *British Transport Commission adopted a responsible attitude towards the preservation of the records it inherited from the companies in 1948, appointed an archivist (L. C. Johnson), and opened an office at Porchester Road in London to accommodate the documents, and readers who wished to consult them. Most of those that have survived from the English and Welsh companies are now held at the PRO, which also holds those of the Railway Department of the Board of *Trade. It issues a useful free guide to the main classes of its railway records, updated from time to time. Those of the Scottish companies are at the Scottish Record Office, Edinburgh. But most of the records of the companies that built railways specifically to serve London, notably those running underground, are divided between the Greater London Record Office (40 Northampton Road,

EC1) and the headquarters of London Transport (55 Broadway, SW1).

Many unofficial collections of records relating to railways, of widely different kinds, are to be found in the hands of other bodies. The British Library holds a large quantity of the *prospectuses issued by people who wished to launch railways, particularly in the 1840s, and its Department of Manuscripts contains letters and other documents relating to railways: e.g. in the *Gladstone papers (which are well indexed) and the diaries of the engineer C. B. *Vignoles. Other libraries containing large manuscript collections as well as printed books include the Bodleian at Oxford, the Cambridge University Library, the National Libraries of Wales and Scotland at Aberystwyth and Edinburgh, and the Bristol University Library, which holds the voluminous personal papers of I. K. Brunel—many more than those known to survive from any other British railway engineer. The surviving papers of Robert *Stephenson are at the Science Museum. Other important collections of such engineers' papers are those of J. U. *Rastrick in the Goldsmiths' Library of London University, and Henry *Robertson's at Aberystwyth and in the Clwyd Record Office at Ruthin.

Each of the Regional, County, and City Record Offices throughout Great Britain is usually the custodian of the records of the local council under which it was set up (together with those of its predecessors), and much communication might pass between it and the railway companies in its district, for example concerning the services provided and the rates or fares charged for them. These offices have now taken in large quantities of landowners' papers, which contain much material important for the student of railways: the Buller papers at Exeter, for example; those of the Earls of Radnor at Folkestone; and the Senhouse family's at Carlisle.

A good many records of industrial firms that had close connections with railways are now in such repositories too: those of Ruston & Hornsby, builders of cranes and railway engines, are at Lincoln; the Birmingham Carriage & Wagon Company's at Stafford; those of the Dowlais Ironworks (heavily engaged in the production of rails) in the Glamorgan Record Office at Cardiff. The surviving records of the North British Locomotive Company are with the University of Glasgow.

Collections of the papers of professional firms handling the railways' business have been deposited in local record offices: by solicitors, for instance those of Nicholson Hett & Freer of Brigg in the Lincolnshire office; by land surveyors and valuers like Rowley Son & Royce of Royston, now at Bedford.

These are a few examples from a list of this sort that is still growing. How can one discover who may hold what, and where? There is now a surprisingly simple answer to that question, and it is heartening. Anybody seeking to trace records of this kind—whether from an individual person, an institution, or a business firm—should visit the National Register of Archives, Quality Court, Chancery Lane, London WC2 (no previous appointment is necessary). The

Register is a constantly expanding master-index of the collections in all the record-holding bodies throughout England and Wales. The searcher who finds a group of documents recorded there that seems to be of interest can then inquire further about it from its present custodian by post or telephone. The Register assembles and puts into very good order a collection of references that might never even have been searched for without it, and would surely have had little chance of being discovered by a student of railways. JS

H. S. Cobb, 'Railway and Canal Records in the House of Lords Record Office', *JRCHS*, 27 (1986), 226–7; L. C. Johnson, 'Historical Records of the British Transport Commission', *JTH*, 1 (1953–4), 82–96; D. B. Wardle, 'Sources for the History of Railways at the Public Record Office', *JTH*, 2 (1955–6), 214–34; J. Simmons, 'The Scottish Records of the British Transport Commission', *JTH*, 3 (1957–8), 158–67. For Benjamin Dunn see PRO, RAIL 527/1255; for the GNR's practice, *RM*, 6 (1900), 318; for the LMS's, R. C. Willis, *My Fifty-one Years at Euston* (1939), 125–6.

armoured trains, see MILITARY RAILWAYS; WAR.

army, see MILITARY RAILWAYS; WAR.

Arrol, Sir William (1839–1913), *contractor. A cotton-spinner's son and a mechanical engineer's nephew, he was apprenticed to a blacksmith. He established himself in a contracting business in Glasgow (1868), his firm becoming reputed for the construction of iron railway bridges. In 1878 he secured a contract for the *Caledonian Railway's bridge over the Clyde into *Glasgow Central station, and next year one to cross the Forth, designed by Sir T. *Bouch, which was cancelled on the failure of the Tay bridge (see BRIDGES AND VIADUCTS). But a new firm, Tancred Arrol, gained the contract for another in 1882, built successfully; then the largest steel bridge in the world (see FORTH RAILWAY BRIDGE). Arrol was knighted on its opening in 1890. The firm was extensively employed on large bridge construction; e.g. the rail-and-road bridge at Sunderland; Tower Bridge, London; Hawkesbury River Bridge, Australia; Nile Bridge, Cairo.

Arrol was a director of the Union Castle steamship company, the Union Bank of Scotland, and Stewarts & Lloyds, steelmakers. One of the ablest, most honourable, and most consistently successful late-Victorian engineering contractors, he left £317,749. JS

R. Purvis, *Sir William Arrol* (1913); *Dictionary of Scottish Biography*, i (1986).

art. British railway art falls broadly into three divisions: a first period of enchantment (*c*.1825–*c*.1850), a period of realism (*c*.1850–*c*.1900), and a second period of enchantment (*c*.1900 to the present).

The first British artists to turn their attention to railway subjects were those who already specialized in topographical views. They coped well with landscape and civil engineering features, but few represented the rolling stock effectively, or reflected the euphoria which attended the early schemes.

One of the earliest locomotive drawings was by Thomas Rowlandson. He portrayed an experimental engine, *Catch-*

me-who-can, in Euston Square, London, in 1809, whilst a sketch by J. D. Harding at Hetton Colliery *c*.1825 exemplifies an early colliery engine.

Appraisal of authentic railway, as opposed to locomotive, images was not possible until the opening of the *Stockton & Darlington Railway in 1825. Here, John Dobbin presents a charming account of the event, though portrayal of the locomotive and train is undeniably primitive.

In 1830, the opening of the more advanced *Liverpool & Manchester Railway increased the demand for images of the new phenomenon, which was met initially by T. T. *Bury whose drawings were made on site and published in two series in 1831. They record well the railway's environs, structures, and civil engineering, but the new rolling stock was not fully understood by the early artists.

David Octavius *Hill in the same year produced informative and detailed images of the Garnkirk & Glasgow Railway. His keen observation of the general railway scene resulted in well-composed and competently drawn views. The same fastidious approach and dedication to accuracy is evident in his depiction of the impressive *Ballochmyle Viaduct* (see BRIDGES AND VIADUCTS), recorded in oils in 1849. The several paintings of this subject by Hill rank among the finest of railway images.

Other early railways to receive attention from topographic artists were the horse-operated *Whitby & Pickering Railway, well recorded by G. H. Dodgson in 1836, and the *Newcastle & Carlisle Railway, portrayed in 1836–8 by James Wilson Carmichael. They concentrated on scenic aspects and dealt adequately with these and civil engineering features but, again, Carmichael's drawing of locomotives was less effective. Both, however, were eclipsed by the exceptional talent of a 22-year-old Londoner.

John Cooke *Bourne was inspired by the sights and sounds of the *London & Birmingham line. He worked for three years on an extensive and invaluable set of drawings, of which 36 were lithographed by Bourne himself and marketed in association with Ackermann in 1838–9. Bourne could assess the main proportions of a composition, whilst simultaneously evaluating the relevance of a multitude of details. Problems of perspective, or the more mechanical aspects of the railway, held few terrors for him and his compositions always appear accurate and natural. Through his enthusiasm and industry, we are privileged to witness the revolutionary construction of a great railway, captured with a vigour and directness seldom equalled by others, or by the camera. Bourne's other major work was an ambitious *History and Description of the Great Western Railway* (1843–46).

The *Great Western also inspired the best known and most important painting to feature railways: *Rain, Steam and Speed—The Great Western Railway* (1844) by J. M. W. Turner (1775–1851). Turner, a master of both topographic and high art, was intrigued by the effect of light and the forces of nature, elements which featured increasingly in his later works. *Rain, Steam and Speed* not only demonstrates Turner's mastery of chiaroscuro but reflects an ambivalence between the sublime past and infernal future: it was decades ahead of its time and pointed clearly towards Impressionism and Abstract Expressionism. No other railway painting has been as influential.

David Cox (1783–1859) responded to *Rain, Steam and Speed* by producing *Wind, Rain and Sunshine* (1845). Cox, unusually for a Victorian artist, produced a further two paintings on railway themes: *The Birmingham Express* (1849) and *The Night Train* (c.1857). In the latter a horse is startled in the dark by the sound, light, and smoke of an advancing train, thereby reflecting the ambivalence demonstrated earlier by Turner in *Rain, Steam and Speed* when he portrayed a hare, previously one of the fleetest animals afoot, about to be destroyed by the rapidly advancing train.

T. H. Hair recorded aspects of railways in his *Sketches of the Coal Mines in Northumberland and Durham* (1844), but a more popular series featuring railways was produced by A. F. *Tait, who drew *Views on the Manchester & Leeds Railway* in 1845, which were subsequently lithographed. As with most of his contemporaries, Tait also revealed little empathy with the mechanical side of the subject but presented good views of the civil engineering, and the railway within the landscape (e.g. the Calder Valley).

William *Dawson first portrayed Brunel's *atmospheric railway in Devon. His album of water-colour drawings depicted views from both sides of the carriage along the route from Exeter to Newton Abbot and presents a unique attempt to marry the skills of surveying, cartography, and art. Undeterred by the failure of the atmospheric system, Dawson also undertook a series of more conventional coloured lithographs, published by William Spreat in 1848, depicting views along the *South Devon Railway's broad-gauge line which extended towards Plymouth.

The closest approach to Dawson's initial venture emerged in 1852 as a lithographed 'aerial' impression of the whole of the route of the Shrewsbury & Chester Railway, drawn on stone by A. Maclure.

The *Chester & Holyhead Railway provided engineers and artists with exciting new challenges. Robert *Stephenson was the engineer, and his design for the *Britannia Bridge attracted particular attention. Among those who recorded the construction were Samuel *Russell and George *Hawkins. Russell, a skilled and experienced observer of railways, had produced pictures of the *North Midland Railway whilst Hawkins, hitherto specializing in churches and landscape, adapted to the new subject with remarkable ease. Of all the topographic railway artists in Britain, Hawkins alone matched the skill of Bourne. His work arguably reveals a tighter technique, more akin to the style of an engineer, but between them, Bourne and Hawkins represent the prime exponents of the genre in Britain.

Very few of the established artists of the period of realism included any reference to the railway in their normal work. Even those that did generally ignored the more mechanical aspects of the subject.

Following Turner and Cox, John Martin (1789–1854)—a painter of some of the most spectacular and melodramatic canvases of the early nineteenth century—proved one of the few to incorporate the railway in his serious historical paintings. He reflected conventional Victorian values and general disapproval of the railways at this time. In his *Last Day of Judgement* (c.1853) the demon train plunges, with the damned, into the abyss. Moral disapproval of the railways also emerged in a popular though much later print extolling the virtues of the narrow and more difficult path to heaven (as opposed to the broader and 'easier' route). In *The Broad and Narrow Way*, Sunday trains were portrayed as evil.

Most artists of the period of realism were more concerned with social implications and travel by rail, rather than the subject itself. Only a handful found sufficient motivation for more than a single painting and none produced so many as Monet, later, in France.

Railway paintings of this era frequently highlight moments of departure, or circumstances during a journey. Robert Musgrave Joy's *Travelling in 1860*, and Abraham Solomon's paintings *Second Class—The Parting*, and *First Class—The Meeting*, are typical examples. *Return to the Front*, by James Collinson, depicting a soldier leaving for the Crimean War, also exploits the melancholy theme of parting.

Rail travel during the final decades of the 19th century was beset by a multitude of *accidents, which increased alarmingly in frequency and severity as the century progressed and featured prominently in the mind of the travelling public. Further criticism of late services, excessive charges, or goods damaged or lost in transit, ensured that the railways were no longer objects of wonder and marvel but were now taken for granted, censured accordingly, and effectively relegated among the more mundane aspects of Victorian life. Few of the paintings produced during this era resulted from any affection or respect by the artist for the railways themselves.

The popular press, particularly *Punch*, provided a ready forum for exhibiting a succession of criticisms, comments, and absurdities. Richard Doyle (*Raylway Statyon*, etc., 1849) provided light-hearted observations, whilst George and Richard Cruickshank were great questioners of the age of steam. An unsigned drawing of *The Patent Safety Railway Buffer*, depicting an affluent director strapped to his seat on the front of one of his own engines, epitomizes this aspect. Perhaps the most able and perceptive in this respect was John Tenniel, who lampooned the directors and constantly agitated for improvements.

If railways held little appeal for conventional, mainstream artists, the topic managed, none the less, to attract competent exponents. E. Duncan's fine 1854 portrait of *Kennard's spindly *Crumlin Viaduct* almost rivals Hill's Ballochmyle masterpieces, whilst Henry George Hine painted a charming picture of a locomotive negotiating a series of arches on the approach to Euston, in *Railway Line at Camden Town* (c.1857).

Gustave Doré (1832–83), a satirical but highly skilled illustrator, recorded scenes of deprivation and misery in his depiction of London (1869). His sombre subjects were keenly observed and powerfully drawn.

Commercially, one of the most successful of all railway pictures was *The Railway Station* (1862), by William Powell Frith. His accurate presentation of *Paddington station was prepared with the full co-operation of the authorities, who obligingly shunted carriages and locomotive into position for his benefit. The work took a year to complete. Each figure was posed and modelled individually; each group expressed a narrative so beloved by the Victorians. John O'Connor also featured the railway in the metropolis with his atmospheric *From Pentonville, Looking West—Evening* (1884) which captured the great stations at *St Pancras and *King's Cross, rising through a haze above the drab city scene.

Later artists attracted to different aspects of railway painting included Camille Pissarro who, whilst seeking refuge in London from the Franco-Prussian conflict, painted *Lordship Lane Station*. He returned to the genre when his period in exile ended. Lucien Pissarro painted *Wells Farm Railway Bridge, Acton* (1907). James Tissot was another Franco-Prussian refugee; he produced charming portraits against a railway background, exemplified by *Waiting for the Train*, set at Willesden Junction. Lionel Walden also painted railway scenes, notably *The Train at Night* and *Cardiff Docks* (1896).

The second 'period of enchantment' dawned as the railways sought to improve their image during the early decades of the 20th century. They were successful to a degree and the general dislike of railways gradually diminished, although the enthusiasm and high level of expectation of the early years were never fully recaptured.

The use of colour printing in advertising at this time led to the work of many established artists appearing on railway *posters, although railway scenes were not always depicted. Norman Wilkinson, an early advocate of the large-format pictorial poster for the *London & North Western Railway and later the *London Midland & Scottish, pioneered a new development in 1923–4 when he persuaded no fewer than 17 Royal Academicians to produce such posters for the LMS. Among them were Sir Arnesby Brown, Sir D. Y. Cameron, Sir William Orpen, and Stanhope Forbes. Forbes also produced some fine 'serious' paintings on railway themes, notably *Penzance Station* and *Through the Marshes*. The *London underground railways also undertook an important role in this context by commissioning work from, for example, Edward Bawden, Frank Brangwyn, Paul Nash, Eric Ravilious, and Graham Sutherland. Among posters of this period, some of the best were comic. Hassall's *Skegness is So Bracing*, for the *Great Northern Railway, became famous, whilst the work of W. Heath Robinson (*Railway Ribaldry*—for the Great Western's centenary in 1935), Fougasse (London Transport), and Rowland Emett (*Punch*) was also in a lighter vein.

Indeed, poster artists who portrayed the more glamorous trains of 1920–30 helped to establish a trend which flourished later with the implementation of the *Beeching Report in the 1960s. C. Hamilton *Ellis had confined himself to historic trains of the past, but Terence Cuneo's career effectively spanned the period of the 'real' railway and the current *preservation scene; his work ranged from 1940s posters to later commissions by the nationalized network, railway societies, and *museums. David Shepherd continues to portray the preservation of wildlife and railways with

equal success, whilst the late Peter Owen Jones, who displayed finer artistic skills and integrity than most, best represents a host of competent transport artists who specialize in the topic.

Nowadays, the movement relies heavily on nostalgia as the railway and its artefacts are almost invariably portrayed in pristine condition. Technical standards revealed by many contemporary exponents are impressively high: locomotives, particularly, are usually recalled with unerring accuracy—almost a Pre-Raphaelite fidelity—although features such as railway carriages, track, foliage, or human figures are not always represented as effectively.

During the pioneer years of the 19th century photography seldom challenged the dominance of the artist, but with 20th-century improvements in equipment and materials, the artist's role appeared to be confined to the poster.

But the demise of the steam engine in regular commercial use and the disappearance of vast tracts of the railway network during the 1960s generated renewed interest in railway art, demonstrated by the formation of the *Guild of Railway Artists in 1979. Many now acknowledge the advantage of the artist's imagination when recreation of the past is a prime objective.

It will be regrettable, however, if the current resurgence of interest reflects no other ambition than to emulate photographic standards. GB-J

S. F. Eisenman, *Nineteenth Century Art: A Critical History* (1994); F. D. Klingender, *Art and the Industrial Revolution* (1968); C. Hamilton Ellis, *Railway Art* (1977); J. Simmons, *Image of the Train—The Victorian Era* (1993); G. Rees, *Early Railway Prints* (1980); *VR*, ch. 5.

articulated carriages. Articulation describes two vehicles supported on, or connected with, their common supporting bogie through brackets or the like fitted to the vehicle ends, and adapted to engage with each other and serve as a coupling between the vehicles.

The first articulated *carriages resulted from complaints at the bad riding of six-wheeled carriages in *East Coast Joint Stock. In 1907, H. N. *Gresley was responsible for mounting two of these carriages on three new bogies, the centre one being the articulation bogie. The existing underframes were retained. The principle was patented in Gresley's name, and conversions of *Great Northern Railway non-bogie stock took place until 1914. New suburban four-coach articulated stock was built by the GNR from 1910, known as 'quad-arts', and from 1915 for main-line service, in units of up to five coaches.

Advantages claimed for articulated carriages were derived from the reduced number of bogies, and included a lower first cost, a saving in weight, improved riding, and greater resistance to collision.

Gresley made use of articulation for a variety of *London & North Eastern Railway carriages from 1923, for suburban and main-line use, the most notable being the train sets built in 1935–7 for the prestige Silver Jubilee and Coronation services. The *Great Western and *London Midland & Scottish Railways made a limited use of articulation for main-line and suburban trains. From 1938, articulated diesel trains were built for export by the English Electric Co.

The *Advanced Passenger Trains built by *British Rail in the 1970s were articulated, and the current application on BR comes in the Eurostar trains working to Paris and Brussels (see CHANNEL TUNNEL).   MLH

   M. Harris, *LNER Carriages* (1994); D. Jenkinson, *British Railway Carriages of the 20th Century*, ii (1990).

asbestos. This non-combustible material was used extensively in the past by railways, particularly for *locomotives and rolling stock. Steam locomotive boiler barrels were insulated with asbestos lagging which was covered with steel clothing plates. Asbestos was also used for lagging pipework, and in paints for heat-bearing surfaces.

Concern to reduce the fire hazard in *carriages led to its use in flooring, and to protect train heating radiators, and also to serve as heat and sound insulation between exterior body panelling and interior decorative trim. The asbestos was used in sheet form, or sprayed directly on to the inside of the panelling. The material was also used in various bearing surfaces.

Earlier passenger stock ordered under *British Railways' *Modernization Plan was largely free from blue asbestos, but this was used increasingly from the late 1950s, until the mid-1960s. When dust from this material was identified as a serious health hazard, BR was concerned to eliminate it from rolling stock and elsewhere, a process which had to be carried out under carefully monitored conditions, and which resulted in various expensive vehicle refurbishing programmes during the early 1980s. The alternative was to scrap the stock, its demolition being restricted to a few contractors. BR imposed a deadline for the withdrawal of asbestos-filled vehicles, or removal of the material, and, with a few exceptions, this programme was achieved in 1987.

Stringent government regulations were applied during the 1970s regarding the discovery, removal, and disposal of asbestos and these had implications for the railway *preservation movement. Many of the steam locomotives at Woodhams' Barry scrapyard retained asbestos boiler lagging, and some passenger rolling stock presented a hazard. The regulations prohibited the resale of vehicles containing asbestos, and its removal was mandatory before they could change hands.

During and after World War II asbestos sheeting and panelling was widely used in repairing buildings, particularly to replace glass in platform canopies, in which resin-bonded glass fibre sheets were used to admit light. Although cheap, durable, and easily worked, its poor weathering properties rapidly made it unsightly, while its brittleness made it dangerous in maintenance work.   MLH

   V. Pendred, *The Railway Locomotive* (1908); D. P. Madden, *Asbestos*—Association of Railway Preservation Societies Information Paper No 10 (1987).

Ashfield, Albert Henry Stanley, Lord (1874–1948), chairman of the Underground group and *London Transport, migrated as a small child with his family (Knattriess, who took the name of Stanley in 1897) from Derby to the USA, where his father found work in Detroit. Albert Knattriess joined the Detroit Street Railway at 14 as a messenger and odd-job man. He was given charge of scheduling on the first electrified route (1893). He rose to be general superintendent before he was 28, transferring to the Public Service Corporation of New Jersey in 1903 and to the general managership of the Underground Electric Railways of London in 1907.

The Americans who had financed and supplied the technical supervision for the electrification of the *Metropolitan District and tube lines were dissatisfied with earnings. Stanley's job was to make the group pay. By 1914 he reorganized the Underground (see LONDON UNDERGROUND RAILWAYS), deployed extensive publicity (see PICK, FRANK), and acquired the profitable London General Omnibus Company to form the 'Combine' in 1912. Naturalized as a British subject in 1913, he was knighted in 1914. In 1916–19 he was President of the Board of *Trade in *Lloyd George's government, for which he received his peerage (1920).

He returned to the Underground group as chairman and managing director in 1919, and from then until 1933 he ceaselessly worked towards co-ordination of all London's local passenger transport facilities under a single management. He was supple and pragmatic, indeed opportunistic, in his approaches. Finally, in 1929, Herbert *Morrison, Labour Minister of Transport, decided that Ashfield was a man he could do business with; and four years later (under a Conservative government) the London Passenger Transport Act was passed (see LONDON UNDERGROUND RAILWAYS—LONDON TRANSPORT). It fell short of what Ashfield wanted in one respect—the four main-line railways pooled their London area passenger receipts with the new LPTB, but without common management. Ashfield was the obvious choice to head the new board, and he remained chairman almost throughout its life. In the 1930s important investment in new railways and equipment was undertaken, coupled with renovation of the bus services and replacement of trams by trolleybuses, largely under guarantee of interest (not subsidy) by the Treasury. After *nationalization in 1948, when London Transport became a subsidiary of the *British Transport Commission, Ashfield was appointed a full-time member of the BTC.

Ashfield's special gift was an outstanding sense of the possible. He was an unrivalled manager of men and opinions, and he knew, from the bottom up, what the transport business was.   RMR

   DNB; DBB; T. C. Barker and M. Robbins, *History of London Transport,* ii (1974). Information from research by Alison Sharp; personal knowledge.

Ashford, see WORKS.

Aspinall, Sir John Audley Frederick (1851–1937), engineer. Trained at *Crewe under *Ramsbottom and F. W. *Webb, Aspinall became locomotive superintendent of the Great Southern & Western Railway of *Ireland in 1883 where he made significant contributions to the development of the automatic vacuum brake. In 1886 he moved to the *Lancashire & Yorkshire Railway, where his priority was to accelerate and build upon the improvements begun by his predecessor, Barton Wright. He completed the new works at Horwich, which produced its first new locomotive—the prototype of Aspinall's celebrated 2-4-2 tanks—in 1889. Aspinall's locomotives were simple and robust, like those of his tutors: notable among them were the 'High-flyers', large inside-cylinder 4-4-2s with 7 ft 3 in wheels which confounded the sceptics with their performance over Pennine gradients.

Aspinall's engineering and management qualities would have made him the ideal successor to Webb at Crewe had not his employers taken the unusual and imaginative step of appointing him general manager in 1899. His engineering background enabled him to make valuable contributions to the *electrification of the *Liverpool–Southport (1904) and *Manchester–Bury (1915) lines. He also found time to become Associate Professor of Railway Engineering at Liverpool University, another unusual step for a former locomotive superintendent. Much in demand as an engineering authority outside the LYR, he continued to make valuable contributions to railway technology for some years after his retirement in 1919, for example to the enquiry following the Sevenoaks disaster of 1927.   RW

H. A. V. Bulleid, *The Aspinall Era* (1967).

Associated Society of Locomotive Engineers and Firemen (ASLEF).

When the first railways were opened in Britain, skilled engine *drivers were in short supply. In 1840 they were paid between 5s. 6d. and 7s. weekly. This was more than double the rate of pay of other grades employed on the railways, and even in excess of what could be earned by turners in the engineering industry. This differential, though not in such an extreme form, has been maintained for more than 150 years.

However, competition between railway companies was often intense and the pressure to reduce working expenses compelling. The costs of running locomotives were reduced by employing footplatemen for excessive hours and by increasing the number of years they were required to serve as *firemen before being promoted as drivers. These practices resulted in impaired health and a greater incidence of accidents. Not surprisingly, therefore, when the first unions of footplate workers were formed their principal demands were for a shorter working day and safer railway working, rather than wage increases.

ASLEF was established in 1880 through the efforts of a small group of footplatemen employed on the *Great Western Railway. They had learnt caution and determination through the failure of earlier attempts to organize the locomotive staff on the *North Eastern Railway in the mid-1860s. The GWR men were led by Charles Perry who in 1879 handed to Sir Daniel *Gooch, the chairman, a petition against new and inferior promotion prospects, signed by 2,000 men; but Gooch's reply to the deputation is said to have been: 'Damn the signatures, have you got the men to back them up?' The blunt fact was they had not. But it was a challenge which was taken up by contacting staff in the leading locomotive depots in England and Wales. After

branches of the new Associated Society of Locomotive Engineers and Firemen were formed in the course of 1880, the first executive committee meeting was held on 8 March 1881 and the society registered under the Trade Union Acts with its headquarters in *Leeds. Membership grew slowly to reach the 1,000 mark only in March 1884.

Two decisions of the executive helped to generate a steady, if unspectacular, increase of membership in the late 1880s. On 5 August 1887 the footplatemen employed on the *Midland Railway struck in protest against the abolition of the guaranteed weekly wage and an insensitive and arbitrary system of discipline. Their action was impetuous and taken without authorization of the national executive. None the less, three days later the committee decided to back the Midland footplatemen. This strike was beaten and it drained the financial resources of the union. But a sense of solidarity was established.

The second decision of the committee was to give full legal assistance to Driver Taylor and Fireman Davies, who were prosecuted for manslaughter, following a fatal collision of two trains at Hexthorpe on the Manchester Sheffield & Lincolnshire Railway (see GREAT CENTRAL) in 1887. The two men were acquitted when the union's lawyers proved that the guilt lay with the company. This case demonstrated that ASLEF protected its members. It was (and is) a craft union looking after the fraternity of locomotivemen, rather than the interests of railway workers as a whole.

Albert Fox, who was general secretary in 1901–14, fully understood the need for political action to supplement the union's industrial strength. In 1903, when its membership exceeded 30,000 for the first time, it affiliated to the Labour Representation Committee, the forerunner of the Labour Party.

In 1907, under the threat of a strike of all unions in the railway industry, David *Lloyd George, President of the Board of Trade, established Railway Conciliation Boards with equal representation of unions and management, with the aim of settling disputes over wages and hours of work. However, the scheme failed to bring improvement in wages and working conditions. Starting in the Merseyside area, discontent culminated in the first national railway strike of 17–19 August 1911, sponsored by all railway unions except the Railway Clerks' Association (see TRANSPORT SALARIED STAFFS' ASSOCIATION). In the settlement which followed, the companies came closer to full union recognition.

In World War I a Railway Executive Committee, appointed by the government to manage the railways, negotiated a series of flat-rate war bonuses to offset the rise in the cost of living. This for a time severely eroded the differentials enjoyed by the footplate grades. But at the end of the war pressure from ASLEF and the *National Union of Railwaymen (which still had more footplate members than its rival) secured a promise of the eight-hour day from the managements. From 26 September to 4 October 1919 ASLEF backed the NUR in a successful strike against the Lloyd George coalition government's proposals for drastic economies at the expense of railway staff. But the two unions disagreed on the question of differentials, and in January 1924, when ASLEF members were called out on strike against worsened mileage allowances, a special general meeting of the NUR determined to advise its members to continue working.

In World War II another Railway Executive Committee managed the railways and flat-rate war bonuses were agreed. In the post-war years there was a leapfrogging of claims for their skilled members by ASLEF and the NUR. From 28 May to 14 June 1955 ASLEF members were on strike to restore the pre-war levels of differentials. They gained very little, though the solidarity they displayed was remarkable. A two-week strike in 1982 failed to stop *British Rail's plans for flexible rostering.

In September 1921 the headquarters of the union moved from Leeds to No. 9 Arkwright Road, Hampstead, London. This spacious, beautifully decorated house was bought from Sir Thomas Beecham, the famous musician, and his brother (of Beecham's Pills) for £10,000 and has remained the headquarters of ASLEF to the present day. But the membership of the union has fallen from its peak of nearly 72,000 in 1955 to 15,000 in 1994, and a move to smaller premises, less expensive to maintain, may well prove necessary. The future of the union's headquarters, as well as of the union itself, will depend upon whether the nation wills that more traffic should be carried on the railway system.

See also TRADE UNIONISM; EMPLOYMENT; STRIKES.   PSB

J. R. Raynes, *Engines and Men* (1921); N. McKillop, *The Lighted Flame* (1950); F. McKenna, *The Railway Workers, 1840–1970*, chs 5–7 (1980); B. Murphy, *ASLEF 1880–1980* (1980).

Association of Independent Railways. In the late 1930s the surviving small railways that had not been included in the 1923 *Grouping formed the Association of Minor Railways in order to present a combined viewpoint to the government, and act on matters of common interest. After *nationalization in 1947 membership declined, but in 1970 the organization was revived as the AIR in order to represent the growing number of new railway companies being formed as part of the railway *preservation movement. Although the primary purpose of independent railways shifted from being a provider of transport to becoming an important part of the tourist and leisure industry, the organization's objects remained unchanged. In 1996 it combined with the *Association of Railway Preservation Societies as the Association of Independent Railways and Preservation Societies.   GJB

Association of Railway Preservation Societies. Formed in 1959 to help and co-ordinate the activities of groups concerned with railway *preservation, ARPS grew to have over 100 member organizations, together with private members and overseas affiliates. The society provides advice and assistance by publishing information papers on all aspects of preserved railway operations, aimed at maintaining the highest standards of public presentation and safety. Regular meetings and seminars are held on administrative, technical, commercial, and legal subjects; competitions and award schemes are organized; and members

receive a quarterly journal. The association represents its members in relationships with government, the Railway Inspectorate, other transport bodies, and industry. In 1996 it combined with the *Association of Independent Railways to form the Association of Independent Railways and Preservation Societies.   GJB

atmospheric railways were an early but short-lived attempt to replace steam locomotives by stationary engines and, in Robert *Stephenson's words, a rope of air. The only system actually to be installed and operated commercially was that developed by Samuel Clegg and Joseph Samuda, in which trains were propelled by a piston running in a tube between the rails, connection to the train being by means of a cranked plate emerging through a greased leather flap that sealed a slot along the top of the pipe. Stationary pumping engines exhausted the tube ahead of the piston, creating a vacuum; air admitted through the leather valve behind the piston provided the motive power.

First tested at Wormwood Scrubbs in 1840, the Clegg and Samuda system was used on part of the Dublin & Kingstown Railway (1843–54), on the *London & Croydon Railway (1846–7), and on the *South Devon Railway between Exeter and Newton Abbot (1847–8). Right from the start it was a pawn in a game of railway politics, apart from having been installed for the wrong reasons. It would have been an excellent way of running a frequent service of light trains—on the *Metropolitan Railway, for example—but could not replace locomotives on a main line. Technically a brilliant near-miss, it was abandoned on both the English railways after little more than a year—but the popular story that rats ate the leather valve is a myth.

T. W. Rammell's system came later and used a larger tube in which ran a narrow-gauge carriage that formed its own piston. Needing only a comparatively low-pressure differential, it could be operated by large fans that blew or sucked according to the direction of travel. The nearest it came to commercial application was the Pneumatic Despatch Company's demonstration tube linking Euston station with several of the principal London postal sorting offices, through which experimental services operated spasmodically from 1863 until 1874, but the Post Office declined to adopt the system (see POST OFFICE RAILWAY).

Compressed air was proposed as an alternative to steam as early as 1797, and the principles of a successful compressed-air locomotive were patented by George Carpenter Bompas (Dickens' model for Serjeant Buzfuz) in 1827. Arthur Parsey demonstrated a successful passenger-hauling model in 1845 and in 1852 tested a 1½ ton home-built locomotive on the *Eastern Counties Railway near Cambridge. Following the passage of the 1870 *Tramways Act several engineers developed compressed-air trams and tram locomotives, by far the most advanced of which were those of Frederick Beaumont (1833–99), inventor of the first successful deep drilling equipment and an engineer on the abortive *Channel Tunnel project of 1878–83. Two prototypes tested on the *South Eastern and Metropolitan Railways demonstrated the feasibility of working the Channel

Tunnel with compressed-air locomotives, for which purpose Beaumont designed a remarkable 2-2-2-2 locomotive with 10 ft uncoupled driving wheels intended to traverse the tunnel in 70 minutes hauling a 70-ton load.

A handful of simple mine locomotives built by the Grange Iron Works, Durham, to the designs of Lishman and Young in 1876–80, principally for the Earl of Durham's collieries, were Britain's only successful compressed-air locomotives, but inspired thousands of such machines built in the USA, France, Germany, and Japan between 1880 and 1969.

See also TRACTION, UNUSUAL FORMS OF.   RW
C. Hadfield, *Atmospheric Railways* (1967).

automatic warning, and train protection and control systems. *Safety on the railway is primarily provided by *signalling but, to eliminate the risk of signals being passed at danger, secondary systems have been developed to give the driver an advance indication by means of audible or visual warnings in the driving cab.

The earliest schemes involved activation of an audible warning by mechanical contact between the locomotive and a lineside 'stop' or treadle co-acting with the signal. This principle was later refined by the introduction of electrical activation, as employed by the *Great Western Railway from 1906 in its Automatic Train Control (ATC). Physical contact was made between a shoe mounted under the locomotive and a ramp placed between the rails in advance of a distant signal. The ramp was energized or not depending on whether the signal was clear or at caution; if the latter, an electromagnet on the locomotive became de-energized and a siren sounded in the cab. From 1912, the GWR modified the system to include a brake application, and introduced ATC on its main lines.

A refinement of the GWR's ATC came with a system employing magnetic induction with a permanent magnet placed between the rails in place of the ramp, and a receiver on the locomotive. Named after its inventors, the Strowger–Hudd system was developed during the 1930s, and only installed on the *London Tilbury & Southend section of the *London Midland & Scottish Railway in 1948.

A third approach is the automatic train-stop system used by *London Underground. When a signal is at danger and an approaching train fails to stop, a trip mechanism on the track strikes a *tripcock on the train and applies the brakes.

*British Rail refined the magnetic induction ATC system during the 1950s, to include a visual warning in the cab as well as the audible indications. If the warning is not acknowledged and cancelled, the brakes are fully applied. This is known as the Automatic Warning System (AWS) which since 1956 has been applied to 70 per cent of the national network. A permanent magnet only is provided on the approach to speed restrictions.

A development of AWS has come with Automatic Train Protection (ATP) in response to situations in which drivers had acknowledged an AWS warning but failed to brake. ATP features an on-board computer, and the train receives messages from the track electronically. An indicator in the cab tells the driver if he needs to slow down or stop. If the warnings are ignored, ATP will apply the brakes. It also monitors train speed throughout the journey. Two versions are on trial, between *Paddington and *Bristol, and on the Chiltern lines from *Marylebone.

Automatic Train Operation (ATO) was introduced by London Underground on the *Victoria Line, and employs combined safety-signalling and driving-command systems. The former is based on coded *track circuits; the latter employs audio frequency signals. The combined effect is to provide automatic control of train speeds and of braking for station stops, and when a signal ahead is at danger.   MLH

J. Johnson and R. A. Long, *British Railways Engineering 1948–80* (1981); S. Hall, *BR Signalling Handbook* (1992); G. M. Kichenside and A. Williams, *British Railways Signalling* (1978).

B

Baker, Sir Benjamin (1840–1907), engineer. Son of an ironworks manager, following an apprenticeship at Neath Abbey Ironworks (1856–60), Baker worked for William Wilson, an associate of John *Fowler, on *Victoria station and Grosvenor Bridge. In 1862 he joined Fowler, then heavily engaged on the *Metropolitan and associated railway lines. Fowler, recognizing his abilities, persuaded Baker to remain in Britain rather than emigrate to the colonies. Together they became one of the great Victorian consulting partnerships.

In 1869 Fowler made Baker his chief assistant on the *Metropolitan District Railway between Westminster and Mansion House. Baker subsequently became a world authority on urban railways and tunnelling, acting as consultant on the City & South London, Central London, and Bakerloo lines (see LONDON UNDERGROUND RAILWAYS), and the Hudson River Tunnel in New York.

From the 1860s Baker produced a series of articles, in *Engineering*, and for the ICE, which established his international reputation. His ideas on long-span bridges (1867) were finally realized when he designed the *Forth Railway Bridge (1883–90), as Fowler's partner but principally responsible for it.

Overseas, Baker, with Fowler, was consultant to the New South Wales Railways and was engineer to the Crown Agents. He was consultant to the Cape Colony Public Works Department. In Egypt his most important work was the Aswan Dam. MMC

DNB; PICE, 170 (1907), 377–83.

Baker, William (1817–78), civil engineer. After being articled to G. W. *Buck, Baker worked on the *London & Birmingham, Manchester & Birmingham, and other railways until 1852, when he was appointed engineer of the Southern Division of the *London & North Western, becoming chief engineer of the whole railway in 1859.

He supervised the building of New Street station, *Birmingham, the first reconstruction of *Crewe, and the rebuilding or extension of *Liverpool Lime Street, *Manchester London Road, *Preston, and other large stations. He was responsible for building the company's new lines and for widening and other improvements during his term of office, including the Dundalk Newry & Greenore Railway in *Ireland, and LNWR lines in Dublin. His greatest achievement was the Runcorn Bridge across the Mersey (1869). Baker died in office, aged 61. GJB

Boase; *BDE*.

Bakerloo Line, see LONDON UNDERGROUND RAILWAYS.

Baker Street station, see LONDON STATIONS.

bankruptcy, see FINANCING OF RAILWAYS; SPECULATION.

banks, see FINANCING OF RAILWAYS.

Barlow, Peter William (1809–85), civil engineer. He was the son of Professor Peter Barlow and brother of William Henry *Barlow; pupil of H. R. Palmer on the Birmingham & Liverpool Junction Canal and London docks. In 1836 he became resident engineer under Sir William *Cubitt on the South Eastern Railway, later becoming engineer-in-chief.

Other railways on which Barlow worked included the Londonderry & Enniskillen and the Oswestry & Newtown, and the abortive scheme of the Londonderry & Coleraine to lay their line across Lough Foyle, reclaiming land. He was also interested in air resistance on train velocities. In 1858 he studied the use of light girders to stiffen suspension bridge decks, and in 1862 was engineer for the suspension bridge at Lambeth, then the largest using wire ropes.

He advocated *London underground railways, and was chairman of the Tower Subway Co., which in 1869 used for the first time a tunnelling shield forced forward against the cast iron lining. His son was its engineer, and J. H. *Greathead the contractor.

In 1854 he became FRS. MHG

PICE, 81 (1884–5).

Barlow, William Henry (1812–1902), engineer; he was the younger brother of Peter William *Barlow. After training as a dock engineer, he worked on ordnance for the Turkish government at Constantinople (Istanbul) in 1832–8. He entered British railway service with the Manchester & Birmingham and *Midland Counties companies, and then with the *Midland (1844). Though setting up in private practice in 1857, he remained a consulting engineer with the Midland until his death. He was involved with the building of its London extension, and particularly with *St Pancras station (1868). In 1879 he was one of the engineers who inquired into the Tay Bridge disaster, and he was primarily responsible for the second bridge (1887).

His name is attached to the 'saddleback' form of rail that he patented in 1849 (see TRACK), but the St Pancras *trainshed is his outstanding monument. His ICE paper describing it is a masterly exposition. It displays Barlow's great intellectual breadth, explaining the form and history of the roof as it evolved, stage by stage, with a proper tribute to the contribution made by R. M. Ordish (a specialist structural engineer), in language addressed to engineers, railway managers, and the general public alike.

He was elected FRS in 1850 and president of ICE in 1880. JS

DNB; *DBB*; *PICE*, 30 (1869–70), 78–105 (St Pancras); 151 (1902–3).

Barrie, Derek S. M. (1907–89), born in Newport, Gwent; he was a journalist until 1932, when he joined the Advertising and Publicity Department of the *London Midland & Scottish Railway. He had already contributed historical articles to the *Railway Magazine*, and embarked on a sequence of histories of South Wales railways: the *Taff Vale, *Rhymney, *Brecon & Merthyr, and *Barry Railways, concluding with the South Wales volume in the *Regional History of Railways* series. He also wrote several other histories and brochures, including the centenary history of the *London & Birmingham Railway.

After distinguished war service he returned to the LMS, and in 1948 became *public-relations officer first to the nationalized Railway Executive and then the *British Transport Commission. In 1955 he became assistant secretary-general of the BTC.

In 1962 Barrie went to York as assistant general manager of the North Eastern Region of BR, followed in 1967 by appointment as chairman of the combined Eastern Region Board and general manager of the Eastern Region. He remained at York until retirement in 1970, having received the OBE.

Derek Barrie, distinguished both as a manager and as a historian, had a lively wit that enriched his conversation, and he never lost his affection for his Welsh roots. MRB

Barrow-in-Furness: an isolated town at the south-west tip of Cumbria which was the headquarters of the *Furness Railway company. Transformed from a fishing village into an industrial complex in little over 30 years with one of the largest iron and steel works in the world, its population grew to almost 50,000 by 1881, since when its industries have increasingly concentrated on ship-building. Iron-smelting and steel-making finally ended in 1963, though local haematite iron-ore mining had ended in the 1940s.

The railway and its promoters dominated the town and its industries. An extensive dockland was developed by the railway company to serve them and to ship rails, for building railways in all parts of the world. A master plan for the town was prepared by the FR in 1856 and land sold for building. The railway company in effect governed the town and provided services until the incorporation of the borough in 1867. Railway domination continued even then, with ten of the initial 16 members and aldermen connected with the railway or the iron industry, and with council meetings held in the FR board room.

The first railway station to serve Barrow, from 1846, was at Rabbit Hill close by the Barrow Channel, which was enclosed to become the Devonshire and Buccleuch Docks, opened in 1867 and 1873 respectively. The second station, at the Strand, opened in 1863 (still standing at St George's Square, close by the one-time site of the company's offices and extensive engineering works), was replaced by the present station on a new loop line in 1886, rebuilt in the 1960s after severe war damage.

Barrow was also developed jointly by the *Midland and Furness Railways as an Irish Sea packet station. Boat trains connected with steamers at Ramsden Dock station from 1881 until the Midland completed diversion of its steamer services to Heysham in 1907. From then until 1915 it was used only by the FR's own steamers on summer services to and from Fleetwood (see SHIPPING SERVICES).

See also RAMSDEN, SIR J.; PORTS AND DOCKS. PWR

Reg. Hist., xiv (1983), 117–30; J. D. Marshall, *Furness and the Industrial Revolution* (1958).

Barry, E. M., see ARCHITECTURE AND ARCHITECTS; LONDON STATIONS (CANNON STREET, CHARING CROSS).

Barry Railway. Steam-coal exports from the Rhondda grew enormously from the 1850s onwards, shipment taxing the port of *Cardiff severely. The Bute Trustees enlarged their docks somewhat, but the coalowners began to consider *Swansea and other *ports.

A group of them, headed by David *Davies, sought powers to build a dock at Barry, south-west of Cardiff, with a railway in 1883. The *Taff Vale and *Rhymney Railways successfully opposed their Bill, but another succeeded in 1884, authorizing a 19-mile line from Trehafod (north of Pontypridd), where it would meet the TVR, and three short branches. Heavy works included two long tunnels. It was opened in February 1889; the port five months later, with a 73-acre dock, followed by another of 37 acres in 1898.

The company was essentially a dock-and-railway one, whereas all its rivals served docks they did not control. The railway scarcely entered the coalfield itself; traffic consigned to Barry was brought on to it by other railways: at Trehafod; at Peterston and Bridgend, where it connected with the *Great Western (1900); and through a link with the *Brecon & Merthyr Railway outside Caerphilly (1905).

The port immediately succeeded. In 1890–2 nearly one-third as much coal passed through it as through Cardiff. By 1914 it was handling more than Cardiff and Penarth put together. Barry grew from a tiny village into a substantial town (see TOWNS, RAILWAYS AND THE DEVELOPMENT OF).

Dividends were impressive: 9½–10 per cent in 1894–1920. But they were partly earned by under-maintenance, revealed in confidential reports by experts (1906, 1909) showing, for example, that up to one-third of the locomotives were out of service at a time, awaiting repairs. The locomotive engineer, H. F. Goulding, left in 1909. John *Conacher became managing director in 1910, securing some improvement before he died in 1911. The company became a constituent of the GWR in 1922. JS

D. S. Barrie, *Barry Railway* (1962); *Reg. Hist.*, xii, chs 6, 7; H. S. Jevons, *British Coal Trade* (1915), ch. 5; Conacher papers: SRO BR/SPC/9/3.

'battles' between railways. Physical confrontations, often involving 'armies' of *navvies, marked the intense rivalries following the *'mania' of 1845–7. They usually concerned disputes over interpretation of *agreements or statutory powers permitting one company to use the lines of another, and generally had to be resolved by the courts.

In 1849–51, for instance, several companies tried to prevent expansion of the *Great Northern Railway. The Manchester Sheffield & Lincolnshire Railway (see GREAT CENTRAL) blocked the line into Grimsby, and the *Midland Railway forcibly seized a GNR engine at *Nottingham, locked it in a shed, and lifted the rails to prevent its removal. It stayed there for seven months.

Twice in 1850–1 the *London & North Western Railway stopped traffic from the Shrewsbury & Birmingham Railway—allied to the rival *Great Western—reaching *Birmingham from Wolverhampton, first by preventing transhipment to *canal. Only the police, troops, and the reading of the Riot Act avoided violence. Then, when the railway was finished, the LNWR blocked the SBR's first train and, to the cheers of a large crowd, rival locomotives 'bunted' each other.

In 1849, when the *Lancashire & Yorkshire Railway blocked the line at Clifton Junction to stop *East Lancashire Railway trains reaching Manchester, engines tried to push against each other. A year later the ELR retaliated at Daisy Field Junction, Blackburn, blocking it with wagons.

*Carlisle was the scene of a unique incident in 1849 when, contrary to an agreement, the *Maryport & Carlisle Railway refused to surrender its Crown Street site for a new *joint station. The *Lancaster & Carlisle and *Caledonian companies obtained a court order for possession and, watched by the county under-sheriff, removed the MCR station and track.

In the south the *London Brighton & South Coast Railway was beset on either side by the *South Eastern and the *London & South Western. In a dispute with the SER in 1851 over access from Bopeep Junction into Hastings, the SER took up the track and prevented a horse-bus hired by the LBSCR from leaving the station. The affair was only ended by a legal injunction against the SER.

In 1858 the LBSCR had an injunction served on itself when it confronted an LSWR train trying to reach Portsmouth from Havant, removed the junction points, and stood an engine on the line. LSWR men promptly seized the engine and replaced the points, whereupon the LBSCR 'army' removed a rail and blocked the LSWR train with two engines, watched by a crowd of local inhabitants.   GJB

Nottingham: *Reg. Hist.*, ix, 124; Wolverhampton: MacDermot, i. 186, 193; Clifton Junction and Blackburn: G. Biddle, 'The Daisy Field Junction Dispute', RM, 101 (1955), 711; Carlisle: G. O. Holt, 'The Battle of Carlisle Crown Street', RM, 109 (1963), 575; Hastings: *Reg. Hist.*, ii (1982 edn.), 34; Havant: Williams, i, 145; G. Body, *Railway Battles* (1994).

bay or dock: a short platform, recessed into a larger one, sometimes one of a pair side by side. It was used for accommodating branch-line trains terminating at the *station, or short stopping trains connecting with others going forward over longer distances, although some large stations have bays capable of accommodating quite long trains, e.g. Edinburgh (Waverley). In Scotland a bay is sometimes called a 'dock', a term elsewhere applied to a similar platform usually reserved for milk, parcels, and light goods traffic.   JS

Beattie, J. H. (1804–71), engineer. Locomotive superintendent of the *London & South Western Railway from 1850 until his death, Beattie possessed an active and inventive brain and throughout his career patented many improvements in locomotives (see TRACTION) and other aspects of railway engineering. He is remembered for his distinctive engines and for his attempts to burn coal efficiently in their boilers. Advanced in some of his thinking—the LSWR was the first major railway to abandon engines with a single pair of driving wheels for main-line work—he was conservative in other directions, and the archetypal Beattie locomotive was a 2-4-0 with outside cylinders, a rather short wheelbase, low centre of gravity, and flexibly mounted leading wheels. In the interests of economy his locomotives used hot feed water, heat being recovered from the exhaust steam either by a jet condenser mounted in front of the chimney or, later, by a simpler concentric-tube heat exchanger alongside the boiler.

He devised several complicated coal-burning boilers with double fireboxes, combustion chambers, and other unusual features, but though very efficient they were heavy on maintenance and, being vulnerable to thermal stresses, required hot feed water to survive long in regular traffic.

RW

C. H. Ellis, *Twenty Locomotive Men* (1958), 12–20.

Beeching, Richard, Lord (1913–85): one of the most controversial figures in the history of British railways. After Imperial College and wartime armaments research, he became in 1957 technical director of ICI. In 1961 he was appointed as chairman of the *British Transport Commission and chairman-designate of the *British Railways Board set up in 1962.

He quickly obtained the facts needed to identify BR's losses. The result was two reports: the first, *The Re-Shaping of British Railways*, suggested closure of some 2,000 stations, and withdrawal of some 250 train services, on strictly economic grounds. It caused a furore, partly obscuring Beeching's second report, *The Development of the Major Trunk Routes*, which proposed substantial investment in a 'backbone' network.

Disagreement with a new Labour government in 1964, when 'Re-Shaping' had begun, brought his resignation in 1965. He was made a life peer. He returned for a few years to ICI, but his main later achievement was chairmanship of the Royal Commission which established the Crown Court system.

Those close to Beeching were impressed by his grasp of unfamiliar subjects, analytical approach, and lucid exposition. Unfortunately he was expected to produce quick solutions to problems that were deep-seated and not susceptible to purely intellectual analysis.   MRB

R. H. N. Hardy, *Beeching: Champion of the Railway?* (1989); Gourvish; M. R. Bonavia, *British Railways: The First 25 Years* (1981); D. Heenan, *The Great Railway Conspiracy* (1991).

beer

beer, see FOOD AND DRINK TRAFFIC.

Bell, Richard (1859–1930), born in Glamorgan, was the son of a quarryman. In 1876 he joined the *Great Western Railway as a *shunter and experienced the dangerous character of this employment. He joined the Amalgamated Society of Railway Servants (see NATIONAL UNION OF RAILWAYMEN) in 1881, was appointed an organizer in 1892, and was elected general secretary in 1898. He became MP for Derby in 1900. Though sponsored by his union as a Labour candidate, he sat with the Liberals in the Commons. He campaigned for accident prevention through enforcement of the Railways (Prevention of Accidents) Act of 1900. He advocated industrial conciliation and arbitration. Increasingly at odds with the socialists on his union executive, in 1909 he resigned both his post as general secretary and his parliamentary seat. In 1910 he joined the employment exchange branch of the Board of *Trade. After retirement in 1920 he was elected in 1922 to the Southgate (London) urban district council, which he chaired in 1925–6.

See also TRADE UNIONISM.   PSB

G. W. Alcock, *Fifty Years of Railway Trade Unionism* (1922); F. Bealey and H. Pelling, *Labour and Politics, 1900–1906* (1958); D. Martin, 'Richard Bell', *Dictionary of Labour Biography*, ii, eds. J. Bellamy and J. Saville (1974); C. Benn, *Keir Hardie* (1992).

Bell, William (1844–1919), architect. For 20 years Bell was an assistant architect on the *North Eastern Railway, beginning under Thomas Prosser in 1857, during whose time he supervised the building of *Leeds New Station, opened in 1869. After continuing under Prosser's successors, Benjamin Burleigh and William Peachey, he was appointed chief architect in 1877, when he became responsible for completing their new station and hotel at *York in 1877–8.

During the 37 years until he retired in 1914 at the age of 70, Bell designed large new stations at Sunderland, Darlington, and *Hull, giving them distinctive arched *trainsheds which he also used when he extended *Newcastle Central, and in a smaller version at Alnwick. He enlarged the Station Hotel at Newcastle. For the numerous smaller stations built or rebuilt during his term of office he produced a number of standard design features that appeared all over the NER system. In addition they were used in many warehouses, such as those at West Hartlepool, Tyne Dock, Hull, and Leeds which were built under his direction, and at the locomotive and carriage works at Gateshead, Darlington, and York. His designs were not notable for their delicacy, except for the art nouveau tea-room on the station at York, and the wooden pavilions on the concourse at Hull, which were quite charming. The fine booking hall and ticket office at Hull have been restored to their original condition. His Darlington clock tower became a prominent landmark in the town.   GJB

Building News, 59 (1 Aug. 1890), 146; *Builder*, 117 (17 Oct. 1919), 381.

Bennett, Alfred Rosling (1850–1928), writer. An electrical engineer, his main professional work was done in the development of the telephone, with the United and London Telephone Companies and as engineer to the municipal systems

of *Glasgow, Tunbridge Wells, *Portsmouth, *Brighton, and *Hull.

He was much interested in railways and wrote two books contributing to their history: *The First Railway in London* (1912), an account of the *London & Greenwich Railway, a pioneer work in its own field but now superseded; and *Chronicles of Boulton's Siding* (1927), recounting the curious, sometimes bizarre, history of the locomotive contracting firm of I. W. *Boulton at Ashton-under-Lyne. His *London and Londoners in the 1850s and 1860s* is still worth reading.   JS

BDE.

Betts, E. L., see CONTRACTORS AND CONTRACTING.

Beyer Peacock, see WORKS.

bicycles, carriage of. As cycling became popular during the 1870s, the organizations representing cyclists' interests lobbied the railways for cheaper carriage rates, but without success. Bicycles were usually carried on the same terms as passengers' *luggage, and loaded in the *brake vans of passenger trains. In some cases, bicycle tickets were issued, and bicycles were also accepted as luggage in advance. In left luggage offices, higher rates were charged for bicycles, as compared with other items.

This discriminatory attitude by the railways did nothing to discourage appreciable quantities of bicycles being carried by train by the end of the 19th century. The *Caledonian Railway was more accommodating. The *carriages built in 1905 for its Glasgow and Edinburgh to Aberdeen Grampian Corridor Express had bicycle racks fitted in the guard's brake compartments. Generally, cycles were carried in the caged, or enclosed section of the brake compartment, but some special vans were built for bicycles.

In the 1960s and 1970s cyclists' excursion trains were run from London to the Sussex coast, and affinities between railways and cycling within the public transport lobby resulted in BR's decision to carry bicycles free of charge on trains. On the other hand, the increased use of diesel and electric *multiple-unit trains with restricted storage space has imposed some restrictions on the carriage of bicycles. From 1988, the introduction of Express Sprinter cross-country services was accompanied by compulsory reservations for accompanied bicycles on these trains, while in the London area bicycles are barred from most trains entering or departing from the main termini at rush-hours.

For some years around the turn of the century the *London & North Western Railway carried bicycle traffic from the Coventry factories in specially adapted wagons.   MLH

VR, 305–6; *RM*, 7 (1900), 26–32; 17 (1905), 42–7.

Bidder, George Parker (1806–78), engineer. Famous when young as 'the Calculating Boy', his extraordinary mathematical powers lasted, to serve him well in adult life as a witness before parliamentary committees. He attended Edinburgh University in 1820–4, then learnt surveying and worked for H. R. Palmer, J. U. *Rastrick, and Robert *Stephenson, with whom he laid out the *London & Blackwall

Railway, which used the electric *telegraph. The same pair were also responsible for the Yarmouth & Norwich Railway (1844: see NORFOLK RAILWAY), the continuation of which to Brandon (1845) crossed the River Wensum outside Norwich, where Bidder provided the first balanced swing bridge (see BRIDGES AND VIADUCTS).

He now undertook many railway and dock works (particularly the great Victoria Docks in London) at home and abroad, constructing the first Norwegian railway (1851–4). A very active director of the Electric Telegraph Company, he helped to negotiate terms with the government in 1868. He was president of ICE 1860–1.

Bidder was a most able designer, and his works succeeded well in service. His pioneer swing bridge, for example, lasted for 60 years.   JS

E. F. Clark, *George Parker Bidder* (1983).

Big Four, The, nickname for the four large companies established under the Railways Act, 1921: the *London Midland & Scottish, *London & North Eastern, *Southern, and the enlarged *Great Western. See also GROUPING OF 1923.

JS

'birdcage', see DUCKET.

Birkenhead, see LIVERPOOL AND BIRKENHEAD.

Birmingham. History was reversed here, Birmingham having started to grow into 'the workshop of the world' and become the centre of the Midlands *canal network long before railways arrived, when it became a British 'grand junction' from which main lines radiated in several directions. The backbone of two north–south trunk routes was built by companies later owned by the *London & North Western Railway: the *Grand Junction which, with *Liverpool & Manchester connections, forged a link with north-

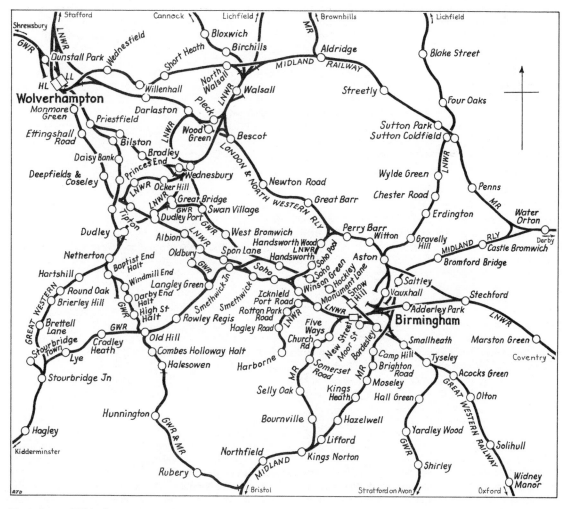

Birmingham and Wolverhampton area, 1922

west England on opening from Warrington in 1837; and the *London & Birmingham, completed in 1838, the year Birmingham was incorporated as a borough. The GJR ran to a temporary terminus at Vauxhall, before extending in 1839 to its own station adjoining the LBR's imposing terminal at Curzon Street (see ARCHITECTURE), which survives.

The rapid growth of long-distance passenger services to and through Birmingham caused congestion which was eased when it was bypassed as an Anglo-Scottish route by the Trent Valley Railway, opened between Rugby and Stafford in 1847.

Curzon Street station received extra traffic on completion of the *Birmingham & Gloucester Railway, the first of two main lines forming a north-east to south-west axis. Climbing the Lickey Incline, the BGR reached the city's outskirts in 1840 and joined the LBR in 1841, using Curzon Street for passenger trains and Camp Hill for goods. The other trunk line, the *Birmingham & Derby Junction, used its own station at Lawley Street from opening in 1842 until services were moved to Curzon Street in 1851 by the *Midland Railway, of which both now formed part.

In 1846 the MR acquired the Birmingham & Gloucester and *Bristol & Gloucester companies just as they were about to be taken over by the GWR. The LNWR was greatly relieved that the MR's action had blocked advance of the broad gauge to Birmingham from *Bristol, and gave it access to its spacious New Street station, which replaced Curzon Street in 1854. LNWR guide books noted New Street station as 'a fine structure close to the centre of the best street in Birmingham, roofed entirely with glass and iron, in this age of iron architecture' (see TRAINSHEDS).

The Midland consolidated its position at Birmingham by building lines to the east and west. It linked the city with *Leicester and eastern England by the Whitacre–Nuneaton line in 1864. Farmers in the richly agricultural Vale of Evesham got produce to Birmingham markets more quickly as local companies and the MR built the loop between Barnt Green and Ashchurch in 1859–68.

Thwarted at Gloucester, the GWR pursued its route to the Mersey (see LIVERPOOL) by acquiring two companies which completed Birmingham's main-line pattern. Both were planned to break the LNWR monopoly between London, the west Midlands, and Merseyside. Most strategic was the Birmingham & Oxford, opened in 1852. Two years later the route through the Black Country to Wolverhampton (where the broad gauge dream finally died) was completed by the Birmingham Wolverhampton & Dudley Railway. Birmingham and the Black Country were already served by two LNWR lines: the GJR and the Birmingham Wolverhampton & Stour Valley Railway, opened in 1854.

The broad-gauge companies shared Birmingham Snow Hill station (1852), as central as New Street, to which the southern approach was in tunnel to conserve valuable land.

To serve Birmingham industry, renowned as the home of 1,500 trades, the railways built large goods *stations, and many factories had private *sidings. A major industry, still busy on a reduced scale today, is private rolling stock manu-

facture. One of the earliest carriage works was established at Saltley in 1845 by Joseph Wright, owner of most London–Birmingham stage coaches (see WORKS, RAILWAY MANUFACTURE AND REPAIR).

Almost a decade separated construction of main lines and the building of branches penetrating growing residential areas. Sutton Coldfield grew into a town after an LNWR-worked branch opened in 1862, and the MR Walsall–Castle Bromwich line 17 years later. In the 1930s Birmingham Corporation classed Sutton Coldfield among 'charming residential areas for many who work in Birmingham'. In 1874 a short branch worked by the LNWR was opened to Harborne, an affluent village within sight of the city centre, and in 1879 the MR completed a line between Walsall and Castle Bromwich. Gradually, more desirable, leafy *suburbs covered surrounding hills, development accelerating after the MR virtually rebuilt the privately promoted Birmingham West Suburban Railway of 1876.

The MR's main purpose was to get a more direct and faster approach to New Street for the Bristol–Derby main line by extending the West Suburban line from its Granville Street terminus into New Street, through tunnels and deep cuttings with heavy engineering works beyond the promoters' financial resources. In 1885 the MR was given its own platforms at New Street and re-routed expresses from the Bristol–Derby direct line via Camp Hill to the West Suburban line. In 1897, New Street became an LNWR and MR *joint station.

GWR suburban services served industrial towns to the north and west of Birmingham including Wolverhampton, Dudley, and Kidderminster, and residential areas south to Leamington Spa, a natural frontier shared with Stratford-upon-Avon, reached via Bearley and the more direct Birmingham & North Warwickshire Railway. This line was far more important than suggested by the company's promotion of it as serving 'Birmingham and its Beautiful Borderlands'. It opened between Tyseley and Bearley in 1907–8 as part of a GWR Birmingham–Bristol main line competitive with the Midland. Construction also removed the threat of other companies invading the west Midlands from London and southern England. Local trains had their own small terminus at Moor Street (1909), again well-situated in the city centre, to relieve pressure on Snow Hill which itself was rebuilt as a fine, airy station in 1912. Together with the new London–Banbury direct route (1910), this line enabled the GWR to compete with the LNWR's, which was now slightly longer.

The competition finally ended in 1967 when *West Coast main line *electrification confirmed the Euston route as the faster. New Street station, completely rebuilt during electrification, has been classed as an 'underground' station since the King's Cross *fire of 1987 (see ACCIDENTS). Although millions of pounds were spent on safety and other improvements, for a modern station New Street is notoriously inconvenient to use.

Paddington–Snow Hill–Birkenhead expresses were withdrawn in 1967, but Snow Hill local trains lingered until 1972 when all services were concentrated on New Street and the station was demolished. In 1987 it was rebuilt as a terminus for suburban services, as part of an office and car-park development. At the same time Moor Street terminus was closed and a through station built alongside. Both are served from London Marylebone by Chiltern Line 'Turbo' diesel multiple units which reintroduced a second, semi-fast, Birmingham–London service in 1994.

The first 'Cross City' line, Lichfield–Redditch, was created in 1978 from the Sutton Coldfield branch (extended to Lichfield in 1864), the West Suburban and the single-line Barnt Green–Redditch section of the Ashchurch loop. It was electrified in 1993. Snow Hill has again become a through station since designation of a second Cross City line from Leamington Spa and Stratford-upon-Avon to Kidderminster and beyond in 1995, involving reopening the line between Snow Hill and Smethwick, with new stations.

Birmingham International, the largest wholly new station built by BR, completed in 1976, is beside the National Exhibition Centre and the city's airport, to which it was linked by elevated *Maglev train.

The west Midlands local network extends far beyond the conurbation on several routes. The West Midlands *Passenger Transport Authority, the largest outside London, with Centro as its brand image, has more than 300 miles of passenger routes linking 19 towns and cities, and 119 stations. Boundaries are Shrewsbury, Stafford, Rugby, Leamington Spa, Stratford-upon-Avon, and Great Malvern. People now get about the west Midlands with an ease and frequency which old company boundaries and rivalry made impossible. New Street, meanwhile, has become the country's main interchange station between north-west/south-east and north-east/south-west services (see CROSS-COUNTRY SERVICES). In the early 1990s an ill-conceived scheme for a new interchange at Aston, with a shuttle service to New Street for local passengers, was quickly abandoned.   RC

C. R. Clinker, *Railways of the West Midlands: A Chronology 1808–1954* (1954); P. Collins, *Britain's Rail Super Centres: Birmingham* (1992); J. R. Kellett, *The Impact of Railways on Victorian Cities* (1969); *Reg. Hist.*, vii (1991); *VCH—Warwickshire*.

Birmingham & Derby Junction Railway. This was originally conceived as a continuation of a line already planned to run from *Leeds to *Derby, which later became the *North Midland Railway. It was to run to Stechford, close to Birmingham, with a branch to Hampton-in-Arden joining the *London & Birmingham Railway there. Meanwhile, another proposal was being discussed, for a *Midland Counties Railway from Derby to meet the LBR much further south, at Rugby or Northampton, offering a route 10 miles shorter. These three railways were all authorized in 1836. The NMR was the largest and strongest; the other two were rivals for its traffic to London. The BDJR was opened in 1839, the other two in 1840.

George *Stephenson was the engineer responsible for the BDJR, as he was for the NMR. In 1837 his son Robert replaced him. The line traversed flat country; the largest work on it was the 20-arch viaduct at Tamworth. At Hampton all trains between Birmingham and Derby had to reverse. In 1840 the BDJR took powers for a line from

Whitacre into Birmingham, replacing the original Stechford line, which had not been built. This was opened in 1842.

The BDJR never prospered. In 1841–3 its dividend averaged only 1.8 per cent, half as much as that paid by the other two companies. The BDJR and MCR were both gravely weakened by their *competition, involving frequent reductions of fares and rates. Though proposals were made that they should amalgamate, none succeeded until in 1843 the NMR, now forcefully led by George *Hudson, suggested a merger of all three. Terms were then hammered out, and the three companies were authorized to combine as the *Midland Railway in 1844.   JS

C. R. Clinker, *Birmingham & Derby Junction Railway* (1982 edn.); P. S. Stevenson (ed.), *Midland Counties Railway* (1989).

Birmingham & Gloucester Railway. Plans for a railway between *Birmingham and *Bristol had first appeared in 1824, but none succeeded until 1836 when this line was authorized, covering about half that distance. To be built on the standard gauge, it was backed by the *London & Birmingham and *Grand Junction companies (whose lines were then under construction) as a device for preventing a broad-gauge railway from being thrust up to Birmingham from Bristol.

It had one big physical difficulty to face: the abrupt change of level occurring south-west of Birmingham, where a direct line would have to descend 300 ft from the Lickey Hills to reach Bromsgrove. This could be avoided only by a considerable detour. Both *Brunel and George *Stephenson, when consulted, favoured the diversion. However, the company's engineer, W. S. Moorsom, did not, neither did his directors; consequently the line had to negotiate the Lickey Incline for two miles, at 1 in 38. American engines were imported to work it, but did so with little success. But it remained a serious impediment to traffic until diesel traction supplanted steam. For the rest, Moorsom's engineering was competent (his fine iron bridge at Defford won a medal from the *Institution of Civil Engineers); but it was badly managed, as sharp-eyed critics noted. The line was opened throughout in 1840.

Meanwhile another railway had been authorized to come up from Bristol and join it at Gloucester, supposedly on the standard gauge. But in 1843 this company decided to adopt the broad gauge instead, which meant that the two gauges would meet head-on at Gloucester. For the troubles that ensued when this line was opened see BRISTOL & GLOUCESTER RAILWAY. In 1846 both Gloucester companies were merged into the *Midland Railway.   JS

C. E. Stretton, *History of the Midland Railway* (1901), ch. 12; P. J. Long and W. V. Awdry, *Birmingham & Gloucester Railway* (1987); F. R. Conder, *The Men who Built Railways*, ed. J. Simmons (1983), chs. 10–13.

Bishop's Castle Railway. Authorized in 1861 to go from the *Shrewsbury & Hereford Railway to Montgomery on the *Cambrian Railways' main line, it was opened in 1865 as a 10-mile branch with Bishop's Castle as its terminus. It was already bankrupt, and remained so throughout its life.

The services it afforded over the next 70 years were basic, sometimes hardly that, and it became a byword for decrepitude. In wet weather umbrellas were put up inside the carriages, and water rose through the floors. Motor-buses affected it slowly; there was too little traffic in that remote country to make them profitable. When the railway closed at last in 1935 it was mourned in the neighbourhood, and later honoured by an admirable history.   JS

   E. Griffith, *Bishop's Castle Railway* (1969 edn.).

Blackfriars, see LONDON STATIONS.

Blackpool was first served by a branch of the *Preston & Wyre Railway in 1846, when it was a small seaside resort receiving about 3,000 visitors a year. By 1900 the population was 50,000, when some 3 million people visited its seven miles of promenade, three piers, and the famous tower; since 1885 the town had been using the first electric trams in Britain (see TRAMWAYS, STREET). None of this would have been possible without the railway, which in 1861 was augmented by an independent coastal line from Lytham to a separate terminus, although it was 1874 before this was connected to the *Preston line to form a second route to Blackpool. Both lines were now owned jointly by the *Lancashire & Yorkshire and *London & North Western companies, the respective termini becoming Blackpool Talbot Road (later North) and Central. The former was rebuilt in 1898 with 15 platforms; Central in 1900 with 14. In 1903 the coast line was bypassed by a direct line from Kirkham, allowing faster running and shortening the distance from Preston by five miles.

These improvements stemmed from long-standing complaints about poor services. The town council had formed a Railways Committee which supported a proposed Blackpool Railway backed by the Manchester Sheffield & Lincolnshire Railway (see GREAT CENTRAL). A company was formed and land purchased, but nothing more.

It has been suggested that Blackpool's growth and popularity would have been even greater had it not been for the railways' earlier lethargy, which is possible, although the heaviest traffic was at summer weekends, much of it comprising day and half-day *excursions. After 1903 the main congestion was caused at Preston which, despite expensive improvements, was still a bottleneck at those times. The highly seasonal nature of the traffic made plans to eliminate congestion, at enormous cost, impossible to justify commercially.

After World War II cars and coaches made increasing inroads into rail traffic. Central station was closed and the coast line terminated at Blackpool South in 1964. The direct line closed in 1967, and main-line services were concentrated at Blackpool North, which was rebuilt in 1974. In 1992 through services from London were withdrawn, although they continue from *Manchester, *Leeds, and East Lancashire.   GJB

   J. K. Walton, *The Blackpool Landlady* (1978), 40–2; *LYR*; *RTC*, 248–51; *Reg. Hist.*, x (1986 edn.), ch. 9.

block working: the normal method of train *signalling in Britain, whereby an interval of space is maintained between following trains on the same track with the object of preventing collisions. In early days it was soon apparent that reliance on a time interval between trains was dangerous, and from 1841 the 'block system' began to be developed (see TELEGRAPH, ELECTRIC).

A line was divided into 'sections' of suitable length (usually station-to-station or junction, but on busier lines closer spacing was often necessary). A block telegraph circuit was set up for each section with fixed instruments. They provided permanent indications at both ends of the section for each direction, and were set at the advance (arrival) end of the section, where the signalman's action of accepting trains was commonly known as 'pegging up'. A series of coded rings on the single-stroke electric bell was used to ask permission for different classes of train to enter sections ('is line clear?') and record trains entering and leaving them ('train entering' and 'train out of section'). Companies originally used their own bell codes but after 1880 a comprehensive set of codes, largely common to all companies, was gradually evolved.

The original block instruments were of the 'needle' type, the needle pointing to written indications on the instrument face. They generally gave two indications, 'line clear' and 'train on line' (wording and practice varied from company to company). Some instruments showed three positions, the third (needle vertical and no line current) usually representing 'line closed'; these were of the 'three-wire' type (one wire for the *up needle, one for the down, and one for the bell) with earth return.

Instruments of the 'single-wire' type were also available. The indications were obtained by transient currents which had the disadvantage that they could be changed or even reversed by the effects of lightning or faults. Despite this they were popular with a number of companies because much less wire was needed, which reduced the capital cost. Edward Tyer, who formed Tyer & Co. of Dalston, London (initially Tyer and Norman), did much to promote and develop them.

Some people felt that *signalmen found it difficult to relate needle indications to the state of the line and the outside signals. W. H. Preece devised his 'semaphore block' in 1862, where the needle was replaced by an electrically worked miniature semaphore signal, operated by a switch in the form of a small lever. It was thought that the men would better relate to this by its similarity to the lever frame and outdoor signals, and others soon followed suit. Edward Tyer adapted his needle instrument to show indications by semaphore arms, but they were still operated by plungers, while C. V. Walker combined a single-stroke bell with a double semaphore housed within the glass window of the instrument. Semaphore block instruments of various kinds were very popular on many lines and were installed extensively over the next 30 years or so.

An alternative idea was developed by Charles Spagnoletti of the *Great Western Railway who, about 1862, replaced the needles by 'flags' labelled with the block indications ('train on line', etc.) and the appropriate flag appeared in a window in the instrument. 'Spagnoletti' instruments were standard on the GWR until *nationalization and were also used on the *Metropolitan Railway.

Preece developed a single-wire version of his semaphore block in 1866 (improved in 1872), in which the 'line clear' signal required the concurrent action of both signalmen, thus reducing the possibility of erroneous signals. Spagnoletti introduced his 'induced needle' in 1869; it proved very reliable and was adopted in most subsequent three-wire instruments. The reliability of single-wire instruments was further improved over the years.

In the 1880s it began to be realized that the two indications of most instruments were not sufficient, since mistakes arose because one of the indications meant two things. What was needed was three indications, normal or 'line blocked', 'line clear' to indicate a train had been 'accepted' to proceed into the section, and 'train on line' when a train was actually occupying the section. The three-wire system could easily be adapted to show three positions but the single-wire instruments could not. Some companies began changing their single-wire lines to three-wire but others shrank from the cost.

An alternative, obviating the need to install additional wires, became available in 1901 when Tyer devised single-wire instruments capable of showing three positions (necessitating needle indications). Two-position semaphore and needle instruments were then completely obsolete but despite this a few survived into the 1990s.

In its normal form the block system allowed only one train in a section at once and was known as the 'Absolute Block system'. On goods lines and in some station areas this was not flexible enough and a 'permissive block' was used whereby additional trains were allowed to enter an occupied section after receiving a caution signal. Similarly, in appropriate circumstances, a train, after being warned, could be allowed to enter a section that was clear but where the safety 'overlap' beyond was not clear ('warning arrangement').

The biggest weakness of the basic block system was that the only link between the block circuit, the lever frame, and the trains was the signalman, who could make mistakes. Special forms of 'interlocking block' were devised where track, signals, and the block system were linked by means of track circuits, treadles, and electric locks. The best known of these systems were 'Sykes Lock and Block', originally devised by W. R. Sykes in 1875, and the Midland Railway's 'rotary block'. In due course all forms of block had additional 'block controls' of various kinds added to improve security. In the more sophisticated forms a similar degree of security to the special systems is achieved.

Originally, the block system necessitated a *signal box at the end of every block section. Some signal boxes were provided with 'block switches' which permitted the sections each side to be combined at quiet times, allowing the box to be 'switched out' for periods to save manpower. The introduction of 'intermediate block signals' worked from one box allowed two or more trains to occupy the section between it and the next one, thereby increasing line capacity.

This principle was developed further into 'Track-Circuit Block'. Here the running lines are *track-circuited throughout allowing the locations of the trains to be continuously detected. This permits the block sections to be effectively reduced to the space between successive signals (with suitable safety 'overlaps' in front of, and behind, the train). It also allows the block instruments to be replaced by 'train describers' with the locations of the trains indicated on a control panel or television screen. Track-circuit block is the form of control in most power or multiple-aspect signalling schemes.

All the forms of block working so far described have utilized a succession of physical spaces between fixed points on the railway to keep the trains apart. While this achieved the safety object it inevitably meant that the minimum space between trains varied as they proceeded, owing to the characteristics of the line. A 1990s development is 'moving block', where the block section moves with the trains allowing them to run closer together, so increasing line capacity and reducing delays from adverse signals ('signal checks') as long as the trains keep the same distance apart.

See also SIGNALLING EQUIPMENT MANUFACTURE; SIGNALLING, AUTOMATIC. RDF

W. E. Langdon, *The Application of Electricity to Railway Working* (1877, 1897); M. G. Tweedie and T. S. Lascelles, *Modern Railway Signalling* (1925); J. Aitken, *Railway Block Telegraph Regulations* (1945); S. Hall, *BR Signalling Handbook* (1992).

Blyth & Tyne Railway. This company, established in 1852–3, brought together a group of small railways, open or under construction, extending from Morpeth to Blyth and Tynemouth.

The trade of Blyth harbour grew rapidly, in coal from the neighbouring pits and in fish. In 1862 the company concluded an agreement for the exchange of traffic at Morpeth with the *North British Railway, thrusting down from Scotland. Two years later the BTR opened a branch into *Newcastle.

Since 1854 the *North Eastern Railway had been battling to fuse the companies of Northumberland and Durham into a single *monopoly. By 1863 the BTR was the only important one that remained independent.

It was financially strong. In 1854–64 its annual dividends averaged about 9 per cent; from 1868 onwards they were 10 per cent, peaking at 12½ in 1872. Three-quarters of its revenue came from coal traffic, but its passenger business was well managed, and also prospered.

However, its assets were wasting. The port of Blyth (entirely outside the railway's control) needed deepening to take larger coastal steamships. The exchange traffic at Morpeth had proved disappointing. Anxious to round off its empire—and wealthy itself—the NER was willing to purchase the BTR on generous terms, and the two companies were merged in 1874.

The improvement of the port of Blyth began in 1880, with astonishing results. Its annual coal traffic had sunk to 235,000 tons: 30 years later it was 4,164,000, and it was half as large again in 1961. So Blyth's full potential had by then been handsomely realized.　　　　　　　　　　　JS

Tomlinson; *Reg. Hist.*, v. 206–12.

Board of Trade, see TRADE, BOARD OF.

boat trains. These were trains timed to connect with steamers running between Great Britain and *Ireland, the outlying islands, and the European mainland.

The first trains of this sort began to run from 1840 onwards on the Thames and the west coast of Scotland. The *London & Blackwall Railway ran to Blackwall pier, whence ships sailed to European ports. But none of its trains was specifically a boat train, for they ran every quarter of an hour throughout the day. Various efforts were made to establish boat-and-train connections at Greenock and Ardrossan, but none of them entirely succeeded, from discordances between the railway and shipping companies.

From 1843–4 cross-Channel steamships began to connect (inconveniently at first) with trains at Folkestone and Dover, running to Boulogne and Calais. But the depth of water at all these ports varied greatly with the tides, and so the railways' services had to be 'tidal', leaving London at times varying from one day to another. This nuisance was not finally eliminated until 1889.

The Irish services were not similarly affected, and the Irish Mail (see NAMING OF TRAINS) was the first British boat train, in the full sense of the word, carrying mails and passengers between London and Holyhead at fixed times, changing only a little over the years to suit the convenience of the *Post Office and the *London & North Western Railway.

Restrictions were placed by some companies on the use of these trains, confining them to the conveyance of steamship passengers. To the end of its life in 1922 the *Great Eastern Railway would admit no others to its night boat trains from London to Harwich, for Antwerp and the Hook of Holland.

Special sets of carriages were built for some of these trains (e.g. by the *South Eastern & Chatham Railway), offering a higher standard of comfort than that afforded in their ordinary vehicles. The quality of the catering on the two Great Eastern trains just mentioned was renowned, a tradition that was maintained long after both the company and its successor had gone. Dinner on the Hook Continental was still in the 1960s a special pleasure to be looked forward to as a start to a journey from London.

A number of these trains were given official names, appropriate to the destinations they served: The Manxman, for example, and The Ulster Express. The Danes courteously named their boat train from Copenhagen to Esbjerg Englaenderen, i.e. The Englishman.　　　　　　JS

Robertson, 262–5; R. Bucknall, *Boat Trains and Channel Packets* (1957).

bogies, see SUSPENSION SYSTEMS.

bombing, see WAR.

Bonsor, H. Cosmo (1848–1929). He was director of the Bank of England, 1885; MP for Surrey North East (Wimbledon), 1885–1900; one of the immediate successors to Sir Edward *Watkin as chairman of the *South Eastern Railway, March 1898; and was a major figure in the brewing industry. He was made baronet in 1925.

Bonsor was instrumental in the establishment of a working union between the South Eastern and *London Chatham & Dover Railways, and became chairman of the joint *South Eastern & Chatham Managing Committee set up on 1 January 1899. This dealt successfully with the wasteful competition which had existed between the two railways, and passenger services were rationalized and improved, accompanied by the building of Dover Marine station. As a consequence of some £1 million invested in the reconstruction of the way and works of the South Eastern, and its other main lines, the SECR was well equipped during World War I to handle military traffic to the Channel ports.

Bonsor was almost alone in his scepticism in 1918 regarding the coalition government's expressed intention to *nationalize the railways. He retired as Chairman of the SECR at the end of 1922, having faced strong opposition from LCDR shareholders towards the terms for the grouping of the undertaking in the *Southern Railway.　　MLH

DNB; C. F. Dendy Marshall, *History of the Southern Railway* (1963 edn.); *Railway Gazette*, 21 Feb. 1919.

booking office, see TICKET OFFICE.

bookstalls and shops, see STATION TRADING.

boosters used the trailing wheels of a steam locomotive, or the wheels of its *tender, to transmit additional power without increasing axle-loading. As early as the 1860s Archibald Sturrock equipped some 50 *Great Northern Railway 0-6-0s with 'steam tenders': their wheels were coupled and driven by an additional pair of cylinders. The complexity of steam tenders proved excessive, and his successor soon converted them to the ordinary type. In 1928 the 15-in gauge Ravenglass & Eskdale Railway provided its 2-8-2 *River Esk* with an eight-coupled steam tender: this too proved shortlived.

Meanwhile, in 1923 on the *London & North Eastern Railway H. N. *Gresley had fitted Ivatt 4-4-2 no. 4419 with a booster of American make. An auxiliary steam engine drove the trailing wheels through gears: it was engaged to provide additional power to start heavy trains or ascend steep gradients. Technically satisfactory, it was not repeated because construction of 4-6-2s in quantity enabled 4-4-2s to be reserved for light trains. Gresley also fitted his two P1 class 2-8-2 mineral locomotives with boosters when they were built in 1925, but these locomotives proved to be overpowered for available traffic and the boosters were removed. About 1931 he fitted three 0-8-4T shunting locomotives with boosters, and articulated two former *North Eastern Railway 4-4-2s to their tenders with fourwheeled bogies which incorporated boosters. But none of these applications seems to have had lasting influence.

Boosters were much more widely used in the USA than in Britain. PJGR

C. Fryer, *Experiments with Steam* (1990).

Booth, Henry (1788–1869), manager. A Liverpool corn merchant, he was secretary and treasurer of committees for building the *Liverpool & Manchester Railway from 1822 onwards and remained in those offices with the company until it was merged with the *Grand Junction Railway in 1845. He was a director of the *London & North Western Railway, which included both companies, in 1848–59.

Booth was more than a capable and conscientious administrator. He interested himself in railway technology, contributing to the evolution of the multi-tubular boiler and inventing a screw coupling. More still: he was a man of imagination, who foresaw some of the effects of railway building. In his admirable account of the LMR (see LITERATURE OF RAILWAYS), published shortly after its opening, he wrote: 'Speed—dispatch—distance—are still relative terms, but their meaning has been totally changed within a few months: what was quick is now slow, what was distant is now near, and the change in our ideas ... will pervade society at large.' Later he became the chief proponent of working all British railways to one standard *time. JS

DNB; R. Smiles, *Memoir of Henry Booth* (1869); Thomas.

Bouch, Sir Thomas (1822–80), engineer; remembered as the designer of the first Tay Bridge (see NORTH BRITISH RAILWAY), which was blown down in 1879, drowning over 70 people.

Bouch trained under *Locke and Errington, and became manager and engineer of the Edinburgh & Northern Railway, for which he designed the world's first train *ferries for crossing the Forth and the Tay. He built many lines in northern England and Scotland, and the Sevenoaks–Maidstone line in Kent, gaining a reputation for cheapness of construction which often needed expensive remedial work later. But his brick and masonry viaducts (see BRIDGES AND VIADUCTS) stood well, notably Hownes Gill, Co. Durham, and Smardale Gill in Cumbria. He built two spectacular iron trestle viaducts, Deepdale and Belah, now demolished, on the Barnard Castle–Tebay line, and one over Bilston Glen south of Edinburgh, later rebuilt. His Esk viaduct at Montrose, however, had to be partly rebuilt before opening.

He was knighted for his work on the Tay Bridge, but its collapse, for which he was blamed, led to his early death. The disaster has been attributed to inadequate design, bad workmanship, weak supervision, and poor maintenance, but the degree of responsibility due to each remains a matter of speculation even today. GJB

BDE; A. Earnshaw, 'Sir Thomas Bouch, C.E., Hero or Villain', *Backtrack*, iv, 5 (Sept./Oct. 1991), 231–40; Tay Bridge: J. Prebble, *The High Girders* (1975 edn.).

Boulton, Isaac Watt (1823–99), engineer. His father, John Boulton, seems to have been related to Matthew Boulton, James Watt's partner. He was born at Stockport, the son of a millwright, and was apprenticed to Richard Peacock, loco-

motive superintendent of the Manchester Sheffield & Lincolnshire Railway (see GREAT CENTRAL).

In 1856 he set up as an engineer in Ashton-under-Lyne, where he remained for the rest of his life. By 1859 he was into the business that made him famous: the purchase of old locomotives, which he hired out. An astonishing assortment of machines passed through his hands, which he adapted with great ingenuity to meet his customers' needs. The records of his undertaking, though imperfectly kept and preserved, furnish a unique account of his specialized form of contracting and some important links in the history of the locomotive. JS

A. R. Bennett, *Chronicles of Boulton's Siding* (1927); J. W. Lowe, *British Steam Locomotive Builders* (1975), 76–7, and *Supplement* (1984), 17; W. M. Bowman, *England in Ashton-under-Lyne* (1960), 366–7.

boundaries. *Fencing was not provided by railways simply to observe their statutory obligations. They indicated the boundaries of their property as well. Generally, railway boundaries follow the edges of cuttings or the foot of embankments, although there is at least one example of a boundary along the top of an embankment: near Eckington, Gloucestershire, where the *Birmingham & Gloucester Railway Act reserved to the vendor of the land all rights on the slopes.

As time passed boundaries tended to become obscured in some places, particularly where the railway, in staking out the original line, first marked it with a fence, dug a ditch inside it, and then planted a hedge inside that. The object was to protect the hedge while it grew, but in time the fence disintegrated and cattle encroached up to the ditch. Debris from years of ditch-cleaning was thrown into the hedge, eventually creating a mound which came to be regarded by the landowner as the boundary. To resolve resulting disputes the railway's only recourse was to the original deeds, which after successive amalgamations might not always be available. In 1870, for instance, the *Great Eastern Railway was still trying to trace some 130 deeds executed over 16 years previously.

The ideal solution was an iron fence, but that was too expensive except for protection of the public. A second hedge planted on the line of the original fence was hardly practicable because it could be eaten or damaged by animals whilst growing. At one time the *Great Western Railway marked some of its boundaries by posts made from old rail at 100 yd intervals, and on one of its lines the *South Eastern tried planting short iron rail stumps, but they were easily obscured by long grass, or became covered over.

A stout wooden or post-and-wire fence on the actual boundary was the only real answer, but where it was not possible a boundary marker was erected. Early lines used stones incised with their initials, but in later years cast-iron posts bearing the company's name or initials became general. The *London & North Western had a distinctive round-topped post of T-section; the Great Western's was topped by a horizontal circular disc bearing the words 'Great Western Railway Boundary' and the year. Occasionally a post was impracticable, as for instance on the street corner next to a bridge over the joint Longridge line in *Preston, where encroachment had been permitted to ease access. To mark the legal boundary the railways' initials—LNWR and LYR—were cut in the paving stones around the curve of the corner.

Boundaries between different railways at *junctions and other points where they met were occasionally marked on the ground, although usually it sufficed to keep detailed plans showing the juxtaposition of each company's property. They were important as the basis for agreeing tolls and charges for *running powers, and the maintenance of junctions.

On *nationalization in 1948, railway property was divided for administration purposes between the railway itself and its former *ancillary activities: docks and inland waterways, hotels and refreshment rooms, and some road transport functions. This entailed complicated boundary agreements, particularly at ports, and even more so at hotels which formed parts of stations. The artificial boundaries created for legal and financial purposes were often meaningless in practice. *Privatization has brought an even greater spate of expensive boundary-creation, this time more important because it can be part of contracts between the numerous units and, latterly, independent companies.   GJB

RS, 184–5, 200; *Trans. Surveyors' Institution*, xx (6 Feb. 1888).

Bourne, John Cooke (1814–96), a London lithographer who set himself in 1836 to depict the construction of the *London & Birmingham Railway in a series of delicate pencil drawings, 36 of which were published as *Drawings of the London & Birmingham Railway*, lithographed by himself, in 1838–9. He then did the same thing for the *Great Western Railway after it was completed. These drawings were lithographed in colour and published as a *History and Description of the Great Western Railway*. Some copies appeared in 1843, the main edition in 1846. No series of pictures of any other British railway work was produced on this scale or of such high quality (see ART). Bourne alone depicted the railway with this detail and accuracy: the men who made and worked it, its buildings, and the landscape through which it passed.

In 1848 he went with the engineer C. B. *Vignoles to Russia to record the building of the Dnieper road bridge at Kiev in drawings and photography, in which he had already come to take an interest. His later pictorial work was undistinguished, bringing him neither reward nor notice. He died at Teddington (Middlesex) in 1896, a bitterly disappointed man.   JS

*Ottley Supplement, 5930; F. D. Klingender, *Art and the Industrial Revolution* (2nd edn., 1968), 153–9; A. Elton, 'The Piranesi of the Age of Steam', *Country Life Annual*, 1963. The surviving finished drawings of the LBR are now at the NRM; other drawings (mostly sketches) relating to the GWR are at the Ironbridge Gorge Museum.

Bournemouth. Although Bournemouth owed a great debt to railways, the progress they made there was slow.

Cottages appeared at the mouth of the Bourne stream from 1810 onwards, but no coach came nearer than Poole, 6 miles west, where a railway arrived via Ringwood in 1847. The Ringwood Christchurch & Bournemouth Railway (authorized in 1859), leased to the *London & South Western, was not finished until 1870 owing to opposition in Bournemouth. Its station (East) was on the edge of the settlement. A second railway, the *Somerset & Dorset, arrived in 1875 from Bath, where it left the *Midland Railway, which leased it jointly with the LSWR in 1876. Despite a difficult route, cheap construction, and a separate station (West), this line became important to the town. The MR provided through carriages in 1876 from *Birmingham. By 1880 they were running from *Bradford, *Leeds, and *Sheffield; later from *Liverpool and *Manchester too.

The town was incorporated in 1890, with a population of 38,000: an indicator of success, albeit achieved only by defeating those who wished to keep Bournemouth select.

The LSWR, fearing that a shorter railway might be built to Bournemouth from the *Great Western, opened a line from Brockenhurst to Christchurch in 1888, reducing the London–Bournemouth journey by 8 miles, to 108. It also provided a new Central station and a connection to Bournemouth West, the conservatives insisting that it should be hidden largely in a cutting.

The developers' victory soon put Bournemouth in a position unique among English seaside resorts: easily reached from London (in two hours by 1914), and from the North and Midlands, with four through trains a day. But it was not only a holiday resort. Its mild winter climate attracted people to retire there, some of them well-to-do. More cross-country trains came from the GWR and the *Great Central line, exchanged with the LSWR at Basingstoke. Bournemouth eventually had through carriages from all the ten largest English provincial cities, except *Hull.

It became a large town, with a population sustained at around 150,000 since 1951. The railway has still some advantages here, even over the motorway. Hourly London trains (electric since 1967) take 112 minutes. Closure of the SDJR in 1966 caused the route from the north to be diverted via Basingstoke, on which there are eight trains each weekday now extending as far as *Edinburgh and *Glasgow.   JS

L. Popplewell, *Bournemouth's Railway History* (1973); Williams, ii, chs 5 & 6; R. Atthill, *Somerset & Dorset Railway* (1970 edn.).

Bow, see WORKS.

Bradford has traditionally been a rival of *Leeds, only 10 miles distant. That it has remained the smaller of the two cities is partly due to mid-19th-century railway politics, which denied the town a through railway route and thus impeded industrial and commercial growth.

Bradford's situation in a bowl with the only level exit facing north did not help. Early promoters were discouraged and it was not until 1846 that the Leeds & Bradford Railway, taking an indirect course along the Aire valley via Shipley, was opened to a terminus at Market Street.

At the time it seemed the LBR was on the point of merging with the *Manchester & Leeds Railway. A continuation through Bradford to serve Halifax and join the MLR was promoted, but then the merger proposals turned sour and the LBR fell into the clutches of George *Hudson. He would have no truck with the MLR, and as a result the link across Bradford was abandoned.

The line from Halifax was completed in 1850 by the *Lancashire & Yorkshire Railway, trains terminating at a station that became known as Bradford Exchange. It was only 300 yds from Market Street (later Forster Square), but the gap was never bridged.

The town briefly gained a third terminus in 1854 with the opening of the direct Leeds Bradford & Halifax Junction Railway into Adolphus Street. It was too distant from the town centre and in 1867 the successor *Great Northern company transferred services into Exchange. In 1878–84 the GNR opened mountainous lines to Halifax and Keighley via Queensbury, intended to be competitive but in reality hopelessly uneconomic. They closed in 1955.

In 1913 the *Midland booked 1,195,514 passengers at Bradford, compared with just over a million at Sheffield and 882,000 at St Pancras, which partly explains why it was so keen to put the town on a direct Anglo-Scottish link, avoiding Leeds, from Royston through Dewsbury and the Spen valley before plunging across Bradford from a tunnel over two miles long. Authorized in 1898 with a capital of over £2 million, it was a brave vision destined never to be fulfilled.   DJ

Reg. Hist., viii, ch. 3; S. R. Batty, Rail Centres: Leeds & Bradford (1989); passenger statistics: PRO, RAIL 491/676.

Bradshaw, George (1801–53), compiler of timetables. Born at Pendleton, Lancashire, and apprenticed to a Manchester engraver, he produced a map of British canals, rivers, and railways in 1830. He turned to printing and publishing railway timetables in 1838, and began to issue *Bradshaw's Monthly Railway Guide, in partnership with W. J. Adams, in London, in 1842. It was continued uninterruptedly until 1961. He also published a Continental Railway Guide monthly from 1847 until 1939 (except during World War I). His Railway Manual, Shareholders' Guide, and Official Directory, appearing annually 1847–1922, became a standard work of reference and is still of great value to students of railway history.

Bradshaw was an active member of the Society of Friends, engaged in supporting many of its causes, especially world peace. He died suddenly of cholera at Christiania (now Oslo) in 1853 and was buried there.   JS

G. R. Smith, The History of Bradshaw (1939); C. E. Lee, The Centenary of 'Bradshaw' (1940); ET, ch. 12.

Bradshaw's Guide. First issued as a monthly publication in 1842 by George *Bradshaw in Manchester and W. J. Adams in London, it quickly established itself as the sole guide to railway services throughout the British Isles. (See also TIMETABLES.)

The work was based wholly on information supplied by the railway companies. 'The proprietors do not hold themselves responsible in any way for inaccuracies'—those words came to appear at the beginning of each issue. What the companies normally did was to supply proof-sheets of their own public timetables, from which the Guide was printed. No important legal action ever arose out of a misstatement in the Guide that was attributable to Bradshaw's staff.

For this very reason the Guide became a book that was difficult to use; each company managed its business independently, and no full editorial control of the information given was ever established by the publishers. Complaints about the book's arrangement and the obscure instructions given in it were constantly made. Punch ran a series of jolly articles on the subject in 1865; the matter found its way into English *literature.

But with all its faults the Guide was never displaced by any rival showing the exact times at which trains were appointed to run over the whole system, and it is an indispensable tool for the railway historian for the period 1842–1961. It must be noted, however, that it deals with passenger services only.

It can be used to reveal much more than the times of trains. It displays the whole of the *Sunday services run throughout the British Isles—quite different from those afforded in the rest of Europe. It also shows the growth of new Saturday afternoon services; it is an important witness to the emergence of the 5½-day week and of the *weekend holiday, which became British social institutions. Anyone wishing to study the development of *commuting in Britain must use the Guide. It records for us some of the *class distinctions that the railways helped to raise, and to lower. The numerous advertisements it carried are a mine of miscellaneous information: about *hotels, for instance, their facilities, and often their charges. Taken in conjunction with the main text, they also furnish a broad view of the *shipping services linking Great Britain with *Ireland, the Scottish islands, and the European mainland.

After the railways were nationalized, they made use of the Guide as the timetable of all their services. That produced a change in the format and much new typographical awkwardness. The Guide was issued for the last time in May 1961. British Railways did not manage to produce a successor to it in one set of covers until 1974.   JS

Bibliography as in BRADSHAW, G.

brakes on railway vehicles usually operate brake blocks applied to the wheeltread, pads clasping the faces of the wheel, or similar pads clasping separate brake discs mounted on the axle. An alternative though rarely used form of braking for electric trains is to turn the motors into generators and dissipate the electrical energy either through air-cooled resistances (rheostatic braking) or by returning it to the supply (regenerative braking). The ill-starred *Advanced Passenger Train was to employ hydrokinetic brakes in which turbines would extract energy from the axles, to be dissipated by a cooling system.

Early locomotives often had no brakes at all, unless there was a handbrake on the *tender, rapid stops being effected by putting the engine into reverse. For many years brakes were not applied to driving wheels for fear of overheating

brakes

The automatic vacuum brake in the 'off' and 'on' positions

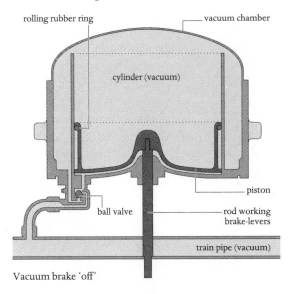

Vacuum brake 'off'

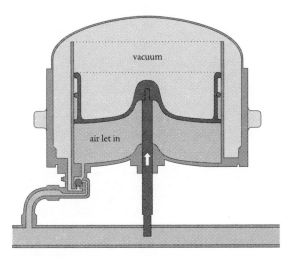

Vacuum brake 'on'

and loosening the iron tyres. There were a few attempts to employ sledge brakes instead but they were soon abandoned because of damage to points and increased risk of derailment. As better materials evolved, steam brakes came into use for locomotives; latterly these could be applied by the continuous brakes. Some companies' locomotives had automatic air or vacuum brakes instead of steam. Diesel and electric locomotives usually have straight air brakes.

For many years goods *wagons had handbrakes only, the earliest acting on just one wheel, applied by a lever at the side of the wagon, which was pushed down and secured by a pin or ratchet. They were usually operated from the trackside but occasionally by men riding on the wagon. Until the

modernization of *British Railways, this was the only form of brake fitted to most freight stock, and except when pinned down to help control trains descending steep inclines they played no part in controlling moving trains.

Until the end of the 19th century many wagons had only one brake lever, which caused frequent accidents as shunters (see SHUNTING) crossed from side to side of the train applying or releasing brakes. To reduce accidents, the *Railway Clearing House encouraged the development of brakes which could be applied and released from either side, requiring a complicated mechanism, and only the *Dean and *Churchward brake on the *Great Western Railway ever achieved widespread application. But either-side application allowed brakes to be applied from the same side of the train, which solved the problem, and the requirement for either-side release was later dropped. The most widely used of these simpler systems was the Morton four-wheel brake developed by the *Lancashire & Yorkshire Railway. Large, non-standard wagons, breakdown *cranes, etc. were usually fitted with screw-down handbrakes.

From the 1880s a limited number of wagons were equipped with continuous brakes, usually vacuum, for working fast freight services, but not until the 1950s was there any serious attempt to extend the use of continuously braked freight stock, simultaneously with the replacement

The Westinghouse brake in the 'off' and 'on' positions

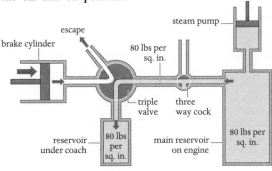

Westinghouse brake 'off'

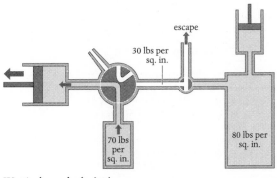

Westinghouse brake 'on'

of the four-wheeled loose-coupled wagon; freight trains are now braked to the same standards as passenger trains.

In hump *marshalling yards, free-running wagons were braked either by hand or by sledges placed under one wheel and knocked aside by a fixed ramp after the wagons had travelled a predetermined distance. More modern yards were equipped with rail-mounted retarders operated from a control tower; these gripped the sides of the tyres to slow wagons down.

Early passenger *carriages were either without brakes or provided with screw-down handbrakes, operated by two or more guards riding in the train. The driver had no control over the train brakes, but signalled to the guards by whistle. Later special brake compartments or vans were introduced. *Brake vans were also introduced for freight trains.

Increasing weights and speeds brought a need for more effective brakes and from the mid-1840s various schemes were produced for braking all the wheels of a train simultaneously (a 'continuous brake'), ideally from the footplate. The problem was to develop a simple system that could be broken and re-made whenever vehicles were attached or detached. Three were tried: mechanical, hydraulic, and pneumatic. The best-known and most widely used mechanical system was the Clark chain brake, in one version of which a friction clutch on one axle of the brake van operated a windlass to tighten a chain which operated the brakes on adjoining vehicles. As developed by F. W. *Webb of the *London & North Western Railway, the Clark & Webb brake was a 'sectional' rather than continuous brake with two or more brake vans and their adjacent carriages forming independent sections of the train. Being self-energizing, it was a crude form of anti-lock brake, superior to any but the best compressed air brakes of the period, but it did not act on all the axles of a train.

Hydraulic brakes were short-lived despite their remarkable power. There was considerable loss of fluid every time the hoses were coupled and uncoupled, which made the use of oil unpleasant, dangerous, and expensive, while water could not be used for fear of freezing.

It was eventually realized that air was the cheapest and most practical medium and two systems emerged: 'vacuum brakes' in which the pressure of the atmosphere acted against a partial vacuum, and 'air brakes' using compressed air.

From the mid-1860s there were repeated attempts to fit continuous brakes to all passenger trains, frustrated by a number of quite separate factors, and certain authors writing about the so-called 'battle of the brakes' have not recognized the real issues. There were different opinions as to whether the brake should be 'automatic' or 'simple' ('straight'). A simple brake is applied by being energized, so any breakage or leakage renders it unusable, whereas an automatic brake is energized to release it and therefore 'fails safe'. The Board of *Trade, backed by public opinion, wanted automatic brakes as being the safer kind but many railways resisted on the grounds of expense. Engineers such as Webb were not opposed to continuous brakes, but resisted their introduction until they had been proved reliable.

Webb maintained that a driver provided with a powerful brake acting throughout the train would not reserve it for emergencies but would use it for controlling his train, so it must work correctly every time. But for his chairman's opposition to anything specified by the Board of Trade, Webb would have developed his own automatic vacuum brake, but instead made extensive use of the Clark & Webb system, which was eventually made automatic in action by holding it off with a tensioned chain. In terms of failures per thousand applications it was the most reliable brake in use before 1880.

Three pneumatic systems competed to become the national standard. Simplest and cheapest was the 'simple' vacuum system developed in America by James Young Smith. An 'ejector' on the locomotive exhausted a pipe running the length of the train and connected to simple diaphragm cylinders beneath each carriage. Steam was turned on to the ejector—which is similar to an *injector but pumps air—to exhaust the train pipe and apply the brakes. It was quite powerful, although rather slow to act, and while very reliable in use was open to the objection that should a hose connection part or the train pipe be damaged the brake became useless.

The automatic vacuum brake perfected by James Gresham had much in common with Smith's brake. An ejector on the locomotive was turned on all the time the train was moving (unless there was a motion-driven vacuum pump to take over once the train started) which maintained a vacuum in the train pipe and in both sides of each cylinder, one of them by way of a non-return valve. To apply the brake the vacuum was destroyed in the train pipe, whereupon air flowed into one side of the cylinder but could not pass the non-return valve. This pressure difference applied the brake. Clearly an accidental breakage of the train pipe would automatically apply the brake, so it was fail-safe.

The erratic performance of early ejectors caused substantial fluctuations of vacuum while the brakes were off. This led to brake blocks rubbing on the wheels, not hard enough to stop the train but wasting fuel and, more seriously, overheating and loosening the tyres. Gresham solved this by developing a high-performance ejector fitted with a 'limit valve' to control the vacuum drawn in the train pipe.

Lastly there was the compressed air brake, notably that introduced by George *Westinghouse in the USA in 1869. It was only a simple brake, but following a demonstration on the *London Brighton & South Coast Railway in 1875 he was encouraged to develop an automatic version, which became the basis of practically all modern air brakes. In the Westinghouse system the locomotive carries an air pump, air pressure regulator, and air reservoir(s) from which air is admitted to the train pipe by the driver's valve. Under each vehicle are an air reservoir, brake cylinder, and 'triple valve'. When charging the train pipe, the triple valve vents the brake cylinder to atmosphere and charges the reservoir, continuing to do so until the pressures in train pipe and reservoir are almost equal. If the train pipe pressure is now reduced, the valve cuts it off from the reservoir and admits air from the latter to the brake cylinder in proportion to the depression in the train pipe. It is quick-acting and powerful, but had one characteristic that did not appeal to many British engineers: once applied it was not possible to ease the brake off without fully releasing and re-applying it. This lack of 'graduable release' led to a number of accidents in the early days of continuous brakes when drivers unwittingly released their brakes completely while trying to avoid stopping short.

In 1875 the Royal Commission on Railway Accidents arranged for a series of trials of different brakes to be held at Newark. The best were the Westinghouse and Steele–McInnes automatic air brakes, and some thought that this should have settled the issue, but for the reasons already mentioned they did not. Certain lines, notably the LBSCR, *Great Eastern, *Caledonian, and *North British Railways, chose the Westinghouse brake, while others tried two or more kinds before making up their minds. A key decision was that of the London & North Western Railway to adopt the vacuum brake, albeit the Smith simple version, allegedly after Westinghouse's representative unwisely offered a bribe to Webb. In the face of continued opposition to automatic brakes from his chairman, Richard *Moon, Webb subsequently encouraged a group of undecided companies to adopt a standard form of Smith's brake, though privately recommending the automatic vacuum brake as early as 1883.

Four years later a number of *accidents had exposed the limitations of Smith's brake (though they were not actually caused by that brake, as some writers have claimed), persuading most of the doubters to use the automatic vacuum, and by 1889 its installation was proceeding steadily on most railways, though the simple brake remained in use alongside it. In 1889 there was a major disaster at Armagh when part of an overloaded excursion train fitted with simple brakes ran back down an incline and collided with a following train. Under the pressure of public opinion, legislation was quickly passed to compel the fitting of continuous automatic brakes to all British passenger trains. Many thought that a single type should have been specified, too, but it was not; some companies used Westinghouse, but the majority adopted vacuum, leading to dual-fitted carriages for through workings. The government had seized the opportunity to enforce by law what years of persuasion had already set in motion.

The early vacuum brakes did not act as quickly as Westinghouse, because all the air required for application or release had to pass through the driver's valve and along the train pipe, instead of being supplied and exhausted locally by the triple valve under each vehicle. An accident at Slough in 1900 resulted in the introduction of the 'direct admission (DA) valve' which admitted air directly to the train pipe if the pressure began to rise rapidly, thus accelerating brake application in the manner of a triple valve.

Following the 1923 *Grouping the *'Big Four' companies standardized on vacuum brakes for locomotive-hauled stock. New suburban electric trains were, however, fitted with air brakes because compressed air had to be provided for electro-pneumatic controls. Subsequently electro-pneumatic brakes were introduced on this stock: these had electrically operated valves in parallel with the triple valve, by means of which normal braking was performed, drawing air directly from the train pipe, keeping the reservoirs fully charged, the action of the brake being even quicker than that of the normal triple valve. In emergency, however, the brake could still be applied conventionally by discharging the train pipe, using what is still known as the 'Westinghouse' position of the brake lever.

Though very reliable, the vacuum brake with its low working pressure requires very large brake cylinders compared with air brakes. For this reason British Railways decided to adopt compressed air brakes for future new construction and the vacuum system is now confined to a small number of carriages retained for use with preserved steam locomotives, and on many preserved railways.　　RW

A. Oliver, *The Vacuum Automatic Brake* (1930); J. T. Hodgson and J. Williams (rev. C. S. Lake), *Locomotive Management* (1939), 281–332.

brake vans. For 150 years the principle was followed by British railways that all trains should be under the control of a *guard who normally rode in a brake van equipped with a handbrake.

Passenger brake vans, often referred to as 'full brakes', were used on nearly all railways. They worked either on passenger trains which did not have a carriage with its own brake compartment, or as the brake van of parcels, mails, newspaper, and milk trains. The van space was used for the carriage of letter-post, railway parcels, livestock, and passengers' luggage.

Goods brake vans did not come into general use until about 1850. A *Great Western Railway rule of 1852 required a brake van at the end of every goods train. The goods guard had an altogether more onerous job and less salubrious working conditions than his passenger counterpart. Placed at the rear of a train that might be ¼ mile long, he rode in a small, usually four-wheeled, van, without internal lighting and equipped only with a coal-fired stove and handbrake. Vacuum-braked vans were in the minority until at least the 1920s. Design of vans varied between railways but in general the body was box-like, usually built with a verandah at one or both ends, windows to the ends of the main compartment, and side *duckets. The van was ballasted to increase its weight and braking power.

Brake vans changed little over the years. The *London & North Eastern Railway was responsible for the main innovations, in 1929 producing a 20-ton van with 16 ft wheelbase and a short body located between, but above, the two axles to ride better on fast, fully vacuum-braked freight trains. The general design was used by *British Railways for its standard goods brake built up to the early 1960s. Also in 1929 the LNER built one brake van with a heavy reinforced concrete body, aimed at eliminating ballasting. Bogie brake vans were built in small numbers from the early 1930s by the *Southern Railway; the four braked axles made them especially suitable for heavy engineers' trains, and some are still in use. With the virtual elimination of unbraked and partially fitted freight trains during the 1980s, the few brake vans retained by BR are principally for engineering works trains.   MLH

Brassey, Thomas (1805–70), the greatest railway contractor of his generation. His early career was as surveyor and land agent, involved in the development of Birkenhead.

With access to building materials, Brassey turned to contracting, first (1834) on the New Chester Road near Bromborough. In 1835 he successfully tendered for the Penkridge contract on the *Grand Junction Railway. The engineer, *Locke, persuaded Brassey to reduce his tender, and the foundation of a lifelong working relationship was laid. Further work with Locke followed on the *London & South Western Railway and elsewhere.

He became a leading contractor in 1841. In partnership with William *Mackenzie he successfully tendered for the majority of the contracts on the Paris–Le Havre Railway, where Locke was again engineer. Over the next decade the partners were to build railways in France, with interests in many other continental schemes.

From 1843 they took contracts in England. After some bargaining about the tenders they formed a partnership with John Stephenson to obtain the *Lancaster & Carlisle Railway contract. Further contracts included the *Caledonian Railway. Stephenson's death in 1848, and Mackenzie's serious illness in 1849–50, ended the partnership.

The *Great Northern Railway contract from London to Peterborough was mostly Brassey's own work. In the 1850s he continued to take contracts in his own name but was most famously associated with *Peto and Betts (see CONTRACTORS), on the Grand Trunk Railway in Canada and elsewhere. Together they financed Victoria Docks and the associated *London Tilbury & Southend Railway, which was operated by Brassey, as was the *Shrewsbury–Hereford line. At various times Brassey had other partners, including Ogilvie, *Falshaw, Field, Harrison, and *Wythes.

Brassey built over 6,500 miles of railway, including one-sixth of the British network. Unlike many leading contractors he survived the Overend Gurney Bank failure (see SPECULATION), and left a colossal fortune (£3.2 million).

MMC

ICE Archives, Mackenzie collection; Clwyd Record Office, Penbedw (Buddicom) papers; A. Helps, *Life and Labours of Mr. Brassey* (1872); C. Walker, *Thomas Brassey: Railway Builder* (1969).

breakdown train. As they developed, railways created a need for movable heavy lifting capability greater than anything previously known. Levers, block-and-tackle, and crude jacks had sufficed to build them but something better was needed for a working railway to speed up maintenance or, should the worst happen, to clear up after an accident. An early advance was George *England's traversing jack (1839) which greatly assisted the re-railing of locomotives and rolling stock: on some lines one or two traversing jacks were carried on each locomotive. The next development was the provision of permanent trains equipped with a sup-

ply of jacks, packing, and other tools, often including a crane, which could be sent wherever needed using the first available locomotive.

Simple rail-mounted hand cranes were used from an early date but their lifting capability was limited. To deal with locomotives and rolling stock of ever-increasing weight the first steam breakdown cranes—of 5 tons capacity—were introduced on the *Midland Railway in 1875. Lifting capacities soon increased and by 1910 35-ton cranes were in use. The traditional breakdown train remained more or less unaltered except in size, as did the range of tasks it performed, until the 1950s, by which time cranes up to 75-ton capacity were in use, but the advent of diesel and electric *traction with multiple bogies required more specialized lifting techniques, as did the spread of overhead electric wires which restricted crane usage.

The development of compact and reliable hydraulic equipment began to challenge traditional mechanical systems in the 1950s, an early instance being the replacement of heavy screw jacks by lighter aluminium-bodied hydraulic ones of similar capacity but quicker and easier to operate. The 1970s saw the last stronghold of steam, the breakdown crane, modernized by the introduction of hydrostatic transmission: a diesel engine driving one or more pumps to supply small hydraulic motors attached directly to the various working parts. Continuing development of hydraulic equipment saw the introduction of portable power packs able to drive remotely controlled jacks and other equipment.

Speed and flexibility of response to any emergency has been greatly increased by the use of road transport, and today's 'breakdown train' might be a four-wheel-drive all-terrain vehicle packed with sophisticated equipment, driven to the nearest point on the line concerned. Here it is driven athwart the track, lifted using its built-in jack-turntable, lined up with the rails, and lowered on to the track. A set of guidewheels is lowered just outboard of the road wheels, the steering locked, and it becomes a rail vehicle to complete its journey.   RW

J. S. Brownlie, *Railway Steam Cranes* (1973).

Brecon & Merthyr Railway. Of all the companies in south-eastern Wales this had the most complex history.

Its system was divided into two main sections, separated by 2½ miles of line belonging to the *Rhymney Railway, from Deri Junction to Bargoed South Junction, over which it exercised *running powers. The northern section (authorized in 1858, opened in 1867) ran between Brecon and Merthyr Tydfil. The southern section took the BMR to Bassaleg and thence over three miles of the *Great Western Railway into its station at Newport. This involved the purchase in 1861 of the 'Old Rumney' Railway, running down the left bank of the Rhymney valley (the Rhymney Railway taking the right), and its conversion into a workable modern line, completed in 1865. The upper part of the Old Rumney line acquired fresh importance in 1905, when it was linked to the *Barry Railway, enabling minerals (though not passengers or merchandise) to be brought down from Rhymney for shipment at Barry instead of Newport.

brickmaking

The making of this little system, 60 miles long, provoked ceaseless warfare with all its neighbours, eating into its revenue. Its lines were hard to operate, the northern section climbing up towards the Brecon Beacons and then plunging down the Seven Mile Bank; it was a dangerous line worked dangerously, and the scene of a shocking accident in 1878. The company never made a true profit. It passed to the GWR in 1922.   JS

D. S. Barrie, *Brecon & Merthyr Railway* (1957); *Reg. Hist.*, xii, 90–4, 99–100, 134–40.

brickmaking. Up to the middle of the 19th century the process of brickmaking had changed little and bricks for the early railways were handmade, often in temporary brickworks using clay from local deposits as close to the site as possible. Brickmakers therefore had to follow the work, but in spite of their skills the quality of the bricks produced was not always of the best, being dependent on the materials available. Sometimes clay excavated from a *tunnel was used on the spot to make bricks for the lining, as was the case at Grimston Tunnel (1874–7) in Leicestershire.

Bricks for Bletchingley Tunnel (1840–1), between Nutfield and Godstone in Surrey, were made by hand on the surface along the line of the tunnel, the brickyards being so arranged on each side of the shafts as to enable the bricks to be lowered down to the underground workings.

In 1827 the *Liverpool & Manchester Railway set up a brickworks on Newton Common to supply bricks for the Sankey and Newton viaducts, which were then clad with stone. Whalley viaduct (see BRIDGES AND VIADUCTS), Lancashire (1850), was constructed in bright red bricks made from clay deposits found in a field alongside, introducing a new material into an area hitherto dominated by stone. Deposits found along the *Settle & Carlisle line yielded bricks suitable for arch soffits, and as late as 1880 the *Great Eastern made many of the bricks for reconstructing Bishopsgate goods station at a works at Temple Mills, on land used later for a marshalling yard. Bricks for Harringworth viaduct (1876–8) were made by sub-contractors at nearby Seaton, using local clays.

The *London & North Western Railway began making its own bricks at Crewe works in 1862, and constructed in 1871–2 a 100-ft diameter Hoffman kiln and steam plant, with a consequent reduction in cost. Its coarse, pale red bricks could be seen all over the system.

See also BRICK TRAFFIC; BRICKS, USE OF.   KUR

R. V. Brunskill, *Brick Building in Britain* (1990); B. Reed, *Crewe Locomotive Works and its Men* (1982); R. V. Brunskill and A. Clifton-Taylor, *English Brickwork* (1977); F. W. Simms, 'Account of Brickmaking in Bletchingley Tunnel 1840–41', *PICE*, 25 Apr. 1843.

bricks, use of. Extensive use was made of bricks in the construction of railway structures of all kinds. The railways caused rapid expansion of the brick trade both by their own requirements and by the subsequent improved transport they provided (see BRICK TRAFFIC). In general bricks, when available, were cheaper and easier to use in construction and handling than stone, sometimes being used with the latter in composite work. Typically, many arched bridges and viaducts, apparently built in stone, have brick arch ribs and soffits.

Enormous quantities of bricks were used. For example, approximately 300,000 were needed for the average single-span road overbridge, and 14 million per mile in the average *tunnel lining. Harringworth viaduct (see BRIDGES AND VIADUCTS), the longest in Britain outside South London, is said to contain 20 million bricks. Local bricks were used at first, but as the railway system extended, the use of bricks spread to areas where they were not traditional. Numerous fine brick structures were built, including many miles of often-unnoticed retaining walls in cuttings. Bricks were also used extensively in drainage works.

The simultaneous and complementary growth of the brick trade and railways caused distinctive bricks to be used over a wide area. The familiar buff bricks used on the *Great Northern Railway came from the Bedfordshire and Peterborough brick fields; Accrington red bricks were supplied to the *Lancashire & Yorkshire Railway; Ruabon and Bristol 'reds' featured at many *Great Western Railway stations. The durability and high compressive strength of Staffordshire 'blue' engineering bricks made them particularly suitable for civil engineering work where there was high atmospheric pollution such as in tunnels, urban cuttings, and bridges. The Oxford Worcester & Wolverhampton (see WEST MIDLAND RAILWAY), and Birmingham Wolverhampton & Dudley Railways in particular used 'blues' for their stations—for example Worcester Shrub Hill, Wednesbury, and Wolverhampton Low Level, together with viaducts such as Hoo Brook near Kidderminster. The GWR later used blue bricks extensively, including for repair work, often quite unsympathetically on red brick structures, to the detriment of the local environment.

Sir Gilbert Scott, architect of the Midland Grand Hotel at *St Pancras, insisted on Gripper's bricks from Nottingham being used throughout, very finely pointed, as they later were at Somers Town goods station alongside. Glazed bricks, which were easy to clean, were used towards the end of the century; white in lavatories and in subways, where they reflected light. Other colours were used decoratively, for instance on platform building exteriors such as those at Bolton on the Lancashire & Yorkshire Railway, and coloured tiles at stations designed in the early 1900s by Leslie W. *Green for the *London Underground, which also used white for the platform tunnels.

The use of terracotta decoration was already popular, as in the partial rebuilding of Grantham station by the GNR in 1878; particularly on the *Midland Railway from the 1880s onwards where examples could be found at Kettering and other stations of the period; and at Pontypridd on the *Taff Vale Railway (1907).

See also: ARCHITECTURE; CONSERVATION; STONE; TIMBER; GLASS; IRON AND STEEL; ASBESTOS; PLASTICS; BRICKMAKING.

KUR

F. W. Sims, *Practical Tunnelling* (1877); B. Morgan, *Railways: Civil Engineering* (1971); Sir A. Pugsley (ed.), *The Works of Isambard*

Kingdom Brunel (1976), esp. ch. 9; F. Turton, *Railway Bridge Maintenance* (1972).

brick traffic. Until the mid-19th century brickmaking was a local, seasonal craft carried out close to where the bricks were needed. Water transport was used to extend the market of brickyards situated close to a canal or river, but only over short distances. The spread of railways broadly coincided with the beginnings of mechanization of brick manufacture. Larger brickworks grew up alongside railways, enabling them to compete in markets over a wider area and to serve those districts which had hitherto relied upon other building materials. Typical successful examples were the brickworks of Ruabon, which sold into areas of North Wales, Cheshire, and Shropshire that were previously poorly supplied with bricks, and the Accrington Brick & Tile Works, whose distinctive flame-red bricks were used for mills and houses over much of Lancashire.

The most notable use of railways for transport of bricks was from the brickfields in the Lower Oxford clay beds. In the 1880s it was discovered that this clay had a high carbon content, requiring much less coal for burning, and characteristics which particularly suited year-round, mass-production methods. These 'Fletton' bricks as they were called, having first been made at Fletton on the *Great Northern Railway main line south of *Peterborough, could therefore be produced at a price which, even after paying the rail transport costs, could compete over a wide area—notably in London. Other brickmaking centres were soon established south and east of Peterborough and then around Bedford and at Calvert, Buckinghamshire, all alongside railways. As the Fletton industry increasingly dominated the market between the wars there was further expansion south of Bletchley and along the Bletchley–Bedford line. At this period the railways were carrying 4–6 million tons of bricks per year.

Bricks were generally carried in standard 4-wheel open wagons, except on the GNR, which in 1921 built a fleet of bogie *wagons of 50 tons (20,000 bricks) capacity especially for the Fletton traffic to London (more were built in 1930). Until the 1950s bricks were laboriously stacked in wagons by hand and breakages were high. Not surprisingly, this was one of the first industries to adopt palletization and fork-lift trucks on a large scale. To reduce handling costs further, the London Brick Company (by then controlling the entire Fletton industry) turned to containers. In 1973–4 it launched the 'Fletliners': *Freightliner trains from the Stewartby brickworks to Trafford Park (*Manchester) and Garston (*Liverpool), and to *King's Cross, carrying bricks loaded in 20-ft-long open containers. They ran until the mid-1980s.

Specialized types of brick (e.g. engineering, refractory, and facing bricks) could also command prices that would pay for transport over relatively long distances, albeit on a smaller scale. The best-known engineering bricks were the Staffordshire 'blues', widely used by the railways themselves. In the 1980s some of the few remaining non-Fletton brickworks began to use the Speedlink wagonload freight service for distributing their facing bricks, but this last brick traffic came to an end when the service was withdrawn in 1991.

See also BRICKS, USE OF; BRICKMAKING.   GAB
R. Hillier, *Clay that Burns: A History of the Fletton Brick Industry* (1981); *VR*, 348–9; C. Fisher, 'Whittlesea Central Brickworks', *Industrial Railway Record*, 11 (1989–92), 181–96; 'Bricks by Fletliner', *Modern Railways*, 31 (1974), 312–14.

bridges and viaducts. Viaducts resemble long bridges (the terms are sometimes confusingly interchangeable) and are chiefly remarkable for the number of their moderate spans and the heights of their piers. They are built as economic, and often more stable, alternatives to high embankments across undulating country and wide valleys.

Masonry and brick

Arch construction in masonry and brick was a recognized technology long before the Romans used it, yet arch bridge design was still based mainly on rule of thumb during the 18th-century *canal era. Good examples of *tramroad structures of that period include the world's oldest, the Causey Arch (*c*.1726), and the Laigh Milton Viaduct (1812), Kilmarnock & Troon Railway.

Theoretical understanding developed slowly, in spite of the analyses published by Lahire (1695) and others in France, and in Britain by Emerson (1742) and Hutton (1772). These methods largely relied on the simplistic assumption that a cord suspended between two points took up different approximate curvilinear shapes, depending on the location and value of weights fixed to the cord, and that these could be considered similar to inverted arches. When inverted, 'line arches', as they are called, became lines of thrust from the loads, which transmitted forces to the abutments and foundations.

These principles worked satisfactorily in practice because numerous arch bridges and viaducts were built for the railways using such designs. Outstanding structures include: George *Stephenson and Jesse *Hartley's Sankey Viaduct (1830), 60 ft high with 8 arches of 50-ft span, and one 60 ft; James Jardine's Glenesk Viaduct (*c*.1830), a single-span bridge on the *Edinburgh & Dalkeith Railway; G. T. Landmann's *London & Greenwich Railway (1836), built entirely on a viaduct of 878 arches over 4 miles; G. W. *Buck's Stockport Viaduct (1842), 110 ft high with 27 arches and overall length of 600 yds; Robert *Stephenson's Royal Border Bridge (1850), crossing the Tweed at Berwick on 28 arches, each of 61 ft 6 in span, 126 ft above water level; J. S. *Crossley's Ribblehead Viaduct (1875), 104 ft high with 28 arches and a total length of 440 yds. These are but typical examples of the highest *civil engineering skills of that time.

Arches were commonly semi-circular or segmental, but a combination of circular curves, approximating to a semi-ellipse, was sometimes adopted. The type selected depended mainly on the levels of the adjacent earthworks.

I. K. *Brunel chose an unusually flat, semi-elliptical arch for the *Great Western Railway's crossing of the Thames at Maidenhead. There are two river spans, each 128 ft with a rise of 24 ft 3 in, and these combine with four semi-circular

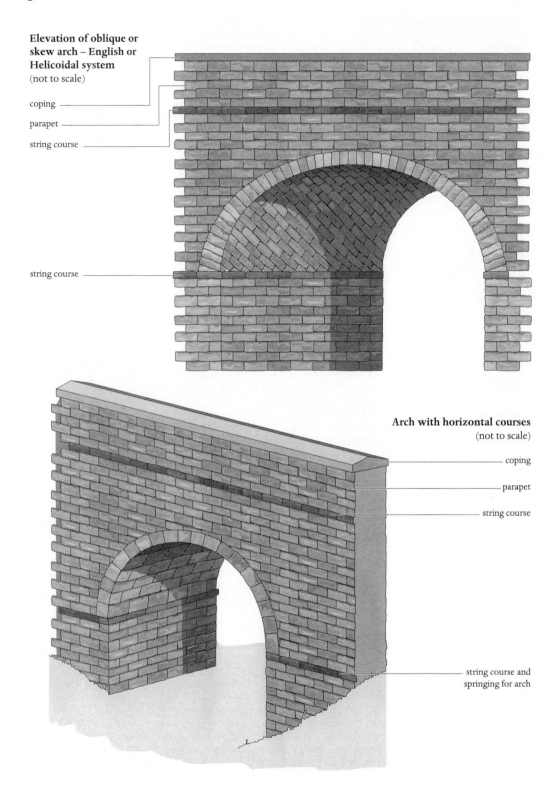

Elevation of oblique or skew arch – English or Helicoidal system
(not to scale)

coping

parapet

string course

string course

Arch with horizontal courses
(not to scale)

coping

parapet

string course

string course and springing for arch

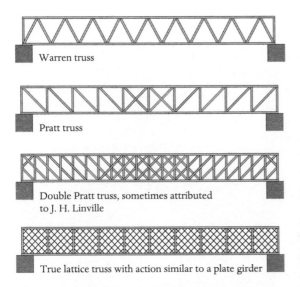

Warren truss

Pratt truss

Double Pratt truss, sometimes attributed
to J. H. Linville

True lattice truss with action similar to a plate girder

**Types of triangulated trusses developed in the 19th century
and used in railway bridges, often called lattice trusses**

flood arches, one of 21-ft and three of 28-ft span, at each
end. Brunel's critics declared that the bridge would fail, and
indeed the eastern arch distorted after the timber scaffold-
ing was removed. Brunel was unconcerned, confident that
damage was due to defective work, which he instructed the
contractor to remedy. When completed, the bridge's shape
was perfect and remains so today.

Many skew bridges were built to suit the alignment of
river or highway crossings, recognizable by their distinctive
parallel, spiral courses which terminate at an angle to each
abutment. Whilst building the Kildare branch of the Grand
Canal of Ireland in 1787, William Chapman first devised a
technique to maintain the alignment of certain highway
crossings, one of which was oblique to the canal by 39 degrees. He realized that the conventional practice of building
the voussoir bed-joints parallel to the abutments was likely
to result in failure so, instead, he set them out perpendicular to the face of the bridge at the crown of the arch, which
meant that they were also perpendicular to the thrust lines
across the bridge at that level. The masons then worked
outwards towards each abutment, laying courses parallel to
the first.

If the surface of the intrados (underside of the arch) is
spread out flat (called the 'development' of the surface), the
faces of the arch will become sinuous lines. The thrust acts
outwards from the crown to the abutments following paths
parallel to the latter and, for stability under load, all bed-
joints should be perpendicular to these sinuous lines. In
Chapman's method this occurs only at the crown, hence his
solution was not ideal, although it proved satisfactory in
practice.

A modified version, which came to be known as the
'English' or 'helicoidal' system, was widely adopted for rail-

way bridges. It involved minor changes to the setting-out,
the bed-joints being laid parallel to one another and perpendicular to the direction of the bridge, simplifying construction, although it was a no more exact solution to the
problem than Chapman's.

That variation may possibly be attributed to Peter
Nicholson, a Scottish mathematician and architect, who
explained the procedures in his *Treatise on Stone-cutting*
(1828). He also described unique designs of templates used
for cutting the complex, twisted voussoirs in the quarry, so
that they could be fitted into the spiral courses on site without need for further dressing. His *Guide to Railway Masonry*
(1846 edn.) includes a number of bridge designs, and several
testimonials, notably one from Henry Welch, the Northumberland bridge surveyor, who followed these procedures
when building the Croft Viaduct (1838–40), a four-span
structure of 50 degrees obliquity, for the *Great North of
England Railway. The earliest skew overbridge is that crossing the *Liverpool & Manchester Railway at Rainhill (1831),
probably designed by Jesse Hartley, although the technique
employed is unknown.

Buck published a book on *Oblique Bridges* (1839), in which
he described the techniques of setting out a skew arch. The
faces of the arch, which are straight in plan, were pencilled
over the lagging, i.e. the planks covering the arch centre,
and the positions of bed-joints were taken from a drawing
and marked off along these lines. A long, flexible straight-
edge of ½-in-thick timber, 12 in wide, was then rolled over
the lagging for pencilling in the spirals to provide for the
guidance of masons. Buck based his writings on his experiences as resident engineer on the *London & Birmingham
Railway. He knew of Nicholson's treatise although he
claimed that this did not 'sufficiently enter into detail'.

An exact solution for skew-bridge design was published
by the French engineer M. F. Lefort in 1839 (although its
precise origins are uncertain). In this 'French', or 'orthogonal', method, the bed-joints are everywhere perpendicular
to the direction of the thrust lines. This results in a series of
curving, tapered courses, the last of which meet the abutments at a tangent.

In Britain this method may have been discovered independently by Alexander J. Adie, resident engineer for J. U.
*Rastrick on the Bolton & Preston Railway, and also about
the same time by William Froude, resident engineer for
Brunel on the *Bristol & Exeter line. Froude had built two
brick bridges north of Exeter by about 1844, but a more
impressive structure in stone, completed by Adie in 1842, is
the semi-elliptical arch across the Leeds & Liverpool Canal
near Chorley. Not many were built for the railways; the
orthogonal system was complex and expensive, even
though Adie claimed that it saved stone and labour.

Mass concrete and blocks

A departure from traditional masonry and brick construction came with the use of mass and precast *concrete in
arch bridges, perhaps the first in Britain being an experimental structure built across the *Metropolitan District
Railway in London's Cromwell Road during the 1860s. Two

Britannia Tubular Bridge: perspective view from F. S. Williams, *Our Iron Roads* (1883 edn.).

viaducts were built entirely in concrete blockwork at Derriton and Woolstone Mill, near Holsworthy on the Bude branch of the *London & South Western Railway in 1898, but in Scotland concrete arches were constructed earlier at the Falls of Cruachan on the *Callander & Oban Railway (1880), followed in 1886 by Dochart Viaduct on the Killin branch: three skewed arches cast *in situ*. Most bridges on the West Highland Extension Railway (1901) were of mass concrete, notably the 416-yd-long Glenfinnan Viaduct, with 21 arches on a curve (see NORTH BRITISH RAILWAY).

The arch was an obsolete structural form by 1900, but recently there has been a re-awakening of interest in it. When maintenance costs over a structure's design life are compared with its initial capital cost, brick arches emerge favourably, compared with other materials.

Timber

This was also used in bridge construction, particularly in the early days when railways were anxious to open quickly and earn revenue. John and Benjamin *Green built two laminated timber-arched viaducts at Ouseburn and Willington Dene on Tyneside in 1839, later replaced by iron. But nobody was more knowledgeable of its properties than Brunel. The high cost of wrought iron, coupled with his mistrust of cast iron, led to experiments with both plain and laminated timbers for arches, continuous beams, struts, and piers. Brunel's successful 240-ft-long road bridge across Sonning cutting on the GWR encouraged him to use laminated timbers elsewhere, notably in the two 86-ft skew spans crossing the Avon at Bath. Each span incorporated six paral-

lel ribs at 5-ft centres, each rib being made from five 6-in laminations.

Moreover, Brunel's Devon and Cornwall lines required many crossings of deep, narrow valleys. For economy, 48 timber viaducts were built on the 111 miles of main line from Newton Abbot to Penzance, and a further 14 on branches, by 1863. They had horizontal, continuous, laminated beams, on struts fanning out from the tops of masonry or timber piers, cross-braced with timber and iron rods. All were graceful and light in appearance; several were spectacular, such as the 443-yd-long Truro Viaduct, and that at St Pinnock, 151 ft high. They were built when superb quality Memel pine was cheap and plentiful, but 16 of them, also the laminated sections of the Avon bridge, were replaced before the end of the century. The remainder became uneconomic to repair when the only available timber was Oregon pine, with a life-span of 8 years, compared with Memel pine of 30 to 60 years. The last, College Wood, was demolished in 1934, after 71 years' service. The masonry piers of a number of them still stand alongside their successors.

Three timber viaducts remain in use today: Barmouth (800 yds) and Traethmawr in North Wales, and Aultnaslanash near Inverness.

See also BRICKS; STONE, USE OF.   RBS

Iron, steel, and reinforced concrete

Ignoring a few earlier curiosities like Pont y Cafnau tramroad bridge and aqueduct at Merthyr Tydfil (1793)—probably the world's oldest iron railway bridge—and the short-span Gaunless Bridge (1823–4) on the *Stockton and Darlington Railway, the effective use of iron in railway bridges dates from the mid-1830s. Samuel Brown's railway suspension bridge of 1830 over the Tees proved a failure because of its deflection under heavy train loads, thus all but eliminating suspension bridges for railways. In contrast, cast iron proved very successful in the 1830s and 1840s, with single cast-iron beams up to about 45 ft, and segmental arches for longer spans.

To meet a growing need in the 1840s for longer spans with shallow decks and flat soffits, much thought went into means of extending the spans of cast-iron beams, leading to an unsound form of composite cast- and wrought-iron bridge beams being used quite widely, notably by Robert Stephenson for the *Chester & Holyhead Railway bridge over the Dee at Chester. Here one beam failed in 1847, dropping a train and killing five people. This shattered faith in wholly cast-iron bridge beams. A three-year Royal Commission investigation into the use of iron in railway structures followed (1849). Meanwhile, actual applications of iron were continuing, for instance Robert Stephenson's High Level Bridge at *Newcastle (1849), and, most important of all, the design and construction of his vast and wholly innovative *Britannia Bridge over the Menai Strait, all of wrought iron.

The first wholly wrought-iron railway bridges date from around 1840, but it was not until after 1850 that it virtually superseded cast iron except for arches, coinciding with a more scientific attitude. Truss forms were developing and their performance could now be calculated, as could that of riveted beams. Nevertheless, cast iron lingered on for compression members (e.g. *Cubitt's Newark Dyke Bridge, 1851), and until almost the end of the 19th century for supporting piers.

Many major iron railway bridges were built after 1850, all predominantly of wrought iron, including John *Fowler's Torksey Bridge of 1850, Brunel's tubular structures at Chepstow (1852, spanning 308 ft) and Saltash (1859, with main spans of 455 ft), *Hawkshaw's Charing Cross Bridge of 1863, and numerous others. Foundations varied widely from pad or piled footings to deep caissons of iron: sunk, excavated, and filled, and sometimes using compressed air as at Rochester Bridge (1851), Chepstow, Saltash, and many later ones.

Tall viaducts, with wrought-iron trusses between cluster-piers of slender cast-iron tubes braced together, became a feature of railway construction in the second half of the 19th century. Crumlin Viaduct (1857) was one of the earliest and most impressive, nearly 200 ft high. Others followed, such as Thomas *Bouch's successful Belah and Deepdale viaducts (1858–9), often seen as the prototypes for the ill-fated Tay Bridge of 1871–9.

Although carrying only a single track, the Tay Bridge was large: almost two miles long, with 84 pairs of wrought-iron trusses of sizes varying up to the 245-ft spans of the 'high girders', through which the trains ran within their depth. Originally all piers were planned in brickwork, but in practice only 14 were built prior to the decision to change to iron cluster-columns to reduce weight because of soil problems. On 28 December 1879, less than a year from the opening of the bridge, all 13 of the high girders and their intermediate supporting piers crashed into the water, together with a train, during a terrific gale. There were no survivors. What exactly caused the failure is still disputed, but it is clear that the wind resistance of the braced cast-iron piers was inadequate. A more substantial two-track replacement designed by W. H. *Barlow, using many of the girders from Bouch's bridge, was built between 1881 and 1887 (see also NORTH BRITISH RAILWAY).

Although most aspects of bridge design in wrought iron had become commonplace by the 1880s, wind took on a new significance, especially in relation to the *Forth Bridge, and the use of cast iron, even for piers, almost ceased. Steel gradually replaced wrought iron, following the Forth

Name or location	Between	and	Opened	Brief details
Bilston Glen† (Midlothian)	Loanhead	Roslin	1874 (rebuilt 1891–2)	Unusual steel lattice, 330-ft single span, 134 ft high across narrow gorge
Coventry (Mile Lane) (W. Midlands)	east of station		1838	Skewed masonry; possibly first flying arch on a railway
Shugborough (Staffs)	Colwich	Milford	1847	Ornamental masonry arch for Earl of Lichfield
Wicker Arch (Sheffield)	Sheffield Victoria	Neepsend	1848	72-ft span decorated masonry arch; 'Gateway to the Don Valley'
Windmill (Middlesex)	Southall	Brentford	1859	Three in one: road over canal over railway

A selection of some notable bridges and viaducts not referred to in the text

(1) Bridges

bridges and viaducts

Name	Between	and	Length (yds)	Height (ft)	Opened	Brief details
Ballochmyle (Ayrshire)	New Cumnock	Mauchline	179	163	1848	Masonry; 181-ft span central arch
Crimple (N. Yorks)	Spofforth	Harrogate	624	110	1848	Masonry, slender piers; dramatic landscape feature
Culloden Moor (Inverness-shire)	Daviot	Culloden Moor	550	180	1898	Masonry; longest in Scotland
Harringworth or Welland (Rutland)	Harringworth	Manton	1,275	60	1879	Brick; longest in UK (exc. South London lines)
King's Mill† (Notts)	Mansfield	Sutton	—	—	1817	Masonry; early tramroad
Leaderfoot† (Roxburgh)	St Boswells	Earlston	307	125	1865	Masonry; very slender and graceful
Meldon† (Devon)	Okehampton	Bridestow	180	144	1874–9	Curved twin interlaced iron trestles
Moorswater† old piers (Cornwall)	Liskeard	Doublebois	—	—	1859	Gothic-arched stone piers of original timber trestle, alongside 1881 replacement
Ouse Valley (Sussex)	Balcombe	Haywards Health	492	96	1841	Brick; classical decoration; pierced piers
Runcorn (Cheshire)	Runcorn	Ditton Junction	315	75	1869	Tracks inside iron lattice; 59-arch approach viaduct at N end on 1 in 114 gradient
Smardale (Cumbria)	Kirkby Stephen	Crosby Garrett	237	130	1875	Masonry; highest on Settle & Carlisle Ry
Speymouth† (Moray)	Garmouth	Spey Bay	317	20	1886	Steel lattice; bowed central 350-ft span
Victoria (Co. Durham)	Penshaw	Washington	270	120	1838	Masonry; 160-ft central span; 3 × 100–144-ft side spans; based on Roman Trajan's Bridge, Alcantara, Spain

† Closed.

Note: to identify locations, see British Railways Pre-Grouping Atlas (1963).

Bridge, but for many decades was still fabricated by riveting.

Opening bridges were built across some navigable waterways, allowing shipping to pass. They were usually swing types, like Trowse Bridge, Norwich (one of the earliest), Selby over the Yorkshire Ouse, Hawarden across the Dee near Chester, and one at each end of the Caledonian Canal.

Scherzer rolling-lift bascule bridges replaced earlier swing bridges at Carmarthen and across the Trent at Keadby, the latter with a 160-ft span.

From the early 1900s reinforced concrete was used for many road bridges over railways but virtually never for bridges carrying trains. One of the next technical changes was the introduction, after 1950, of pre-stressed concrete for both types of railway bridge, notably the Besses o' th' Barn Bridge over the M62, with its deep central beam, and the more elegant bowstring Frodsham Bridge. Welding replaced riveting at this time, while the development of new techniques for rapid or phased replacement became a more dominant requirement than new construction. For instance, the Grosvenor Bridge at *Victoria in London was replaced by Freeman Fox in the 1960s, keeping eight out of the ten rail tracks open at all times.

See also IRON AND STEEL, USE OF. RJMS

J. Binding, *Brunel's Cornish Viaducts* (1993); W. Humber, *Cast and Wrought Iron Bridges and Girders as applied to Railway Structures* (1857); P. S. A. Berridge, *The Girder Bridge after Brunel and Others* (1969); F. A. W. Mann, *Railway Bridge Construction: Some Recent Developments* (1972); Sir A. Pugsley (ed.), *The Works of Isambard Kingdom Brunel* (1976), esp. chs 5 & 6.

Brighton developed as a seaside resort in the 18th century, when sea-bathing was recommended by some doctors. The Prince Regent first visited it in 1783 and soon had his own residence there, the Pavilion. The town became both fashionable and popular, and by 1836 at least 16 principal coach services ran the 50 miles from London daily, taking an average of 5½ hours.

Six rival schemes were promoted for railways between London and Brighton in 1834–5. Parliament approved the most direct and the costliest in 1836, and the London & Brighton Railway opened in 1841. The town was then becoming less fashionable. Queen Victoria never visited the Pavilion after 1845. The railway company quickly started running *excursion trains, bringing crowds of visitors into the station at the north end of the town. Another new consequence, resulting from the reduced journey time of 1½–2½ hours, was a great increase in the number of people owning houses in Brighton and travelling up to London to work (see COMMUTING).

Another social change was also caused by the railway. In 1852 the *London Brighton & South Coast company moved its locomotive and rolling stock works from London to Brighton. They became the sole industrial enterprise of any important kind in the town. Six per cent of its population was dependent on railway work in 1903. The company's position as an employer and rate-payer bound it and Brighton together—something uncommon in a town served by only one railway (see MONOPOLY).

The *South Eastern and *London Chatham & Dover Railways attempted to reach Brighton in 1864 and 1876, but they failed. Another potential competitor offered a much superior express service between Brighton and London in 1901: an electric railway running without intermediate stations. This project collapsed, and the LBSCR retained its monopoly. But it electrified some of its London suburban lines in 1909, and might have extended the system to Brighton had it not been for World War I and amalgamation into the *Southern Railway in 1923. Brighton got electric trains in 1933, producing an altogether better passenger

service. By that time carriage and wagon building had been removed to Lancing, eight miles away. Locomotive building ceased at Brighton in 1958.

In 1841–71 the population of Brighton doubled, growing further by 37 per cent in 1871–1901, to reach 123,000. Hove, physically adjacent but a separate municipality, added another 37,000. In 1994 the two made up a total of 216,000. The railway continues to carry a great many commuters, and large numbers of holiday-makers bound for this 'London by the sea'. JS

E. W. Gilbert, *Brighton* (1964); *RTC*, 236–9. Coach services: A. A. Bates, *Directory of Coach Services, 1836* (1969), 7–10.

Bristol. The dashing, visionary spirit of the Merchant Venturers, who made Bristol into an important port for Atlantic trade and British coastal shipping by the 19th century, was lacking when it came to building railways. Wealthy Bristol businessmen were reluctant to invest in them until they were assured of good returns. Although the first docks opened in 1809, it was not until June 1841 that the broad *gauge *Great Western Railway, promoted in *London and Bristol and engineered by I. K. *Brunel, linked the two cities. As engineer of the *Bristol & Exeter Railway, Brunel continued the broad gauge west, promoted by Bristol businessmen. Authorized after the GWR, the first section to Bridgwater opened 16 days ahead of it.

The lines met at right angles at Temple Meads station, nearly a mile from Bristol city centre—a handicap never corrected. The GWR *trainshed was magnificent—befitting Brunel's vision of a London–New York route with steamships he largely designed—but the layout was chaotic. The London and Exeter lines were linked only by a curve on which through trains used an 'express platform'. The spur crossed the mouth of the BER's own small station. The arrival of the *Bristol & Gloucester Railway, also engineered by Brunel, in 1844 caused more congestion at Temple Meads.

With the BGR, Brunel took the broad gauge to Gloucester, but his aspirations to continue it to *Birmingham were defeated by the *Midland Railway's last-minute acquisition of the BGR and *Birmingham & Gloucester Railway in 1845 as the GWR was preparing to take them over. The MR introduced standard-gauge trains between Bristol and Birmingham in 1854—an early victory in the gauge war. From 1870 MR stopping trains from Gloucester and Bath via Mangotsfield ran to St Philip's, a single-platform station on the opposite bank of the Floating Harbour to Temple Meads.

Broad gauge extension battles made the GWR and Brunel unpopular in Bristol, where the civic authorities and merchants felt it partly isolated the city from the national railway network. Several strong, though unsuccessful, attempts were made to promote a second direct line to London. They began in 1861 with the Bristol & South Western Junction Railway running 40 miles to join the

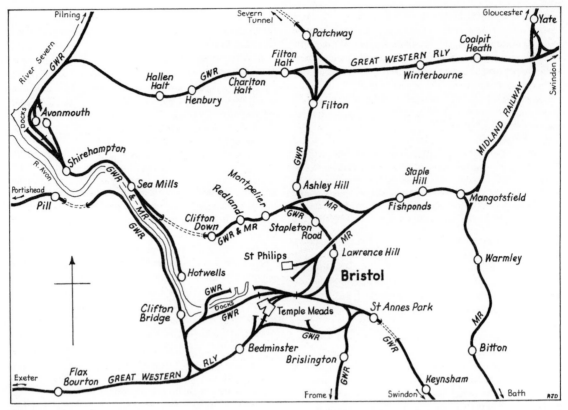

Bristol, 1922

*London & South Western Railway route to Waterloo. Other schemes followed in 1882 and 1902, all loosely associated with attempts to build a central station in Bristol.

The Midland's take-over of the Gloucester companies denied the GWR a direct route between the West Country and the Midlands, northern England, and Scotland. The setback was alleviated, and the GWR's standing at Bristol improved, by a north-to-west route via *Shrewsbury and the Welsh border, established after the *Severn Tunnel opened in 1886, and a Bristol (Temple Meads)–Birmingham (Snow Hill) express service via Stratford-upon-Avon in 1908 after the GWR was victorious in legal battles. Trains used the Midland main line between Yate (reached by a spur from the Badminton line) and Cheltenham.

Bristol and South Wales were linked from 1852 by trains running over the Bristol & Gloucester and *South Wales Railways. By sea and the River Severn, Bristol and Newport were only 25 miles apart; by rail, 82 miles. That distance was diminished in 1863 by the Bristol & South Wales Union Railway, with a broad-gauge line to New Passage, whence a steam *ferry ran to Portskewett, which was connected by a short branch to the South Wales Railway. When the *Severn Tunnel displaced the ferry, much of the BSWUR was adapted to serve as an approach line. Most South Wales–London services, including heavy coal traffic, were now worked through Bristol and Bath because the route

was shorter than via Gloucester, although a spur kept through freight trains and South Wales expresses clear of Temple Meads station.

In 1878 the GWR and MR rebuilt Temple Meads into a spacious *joint station, perpetuating the Gothic style of Brunel's original terminus. Equally attractive are the restored Jacobean-style offices of the Bristol & Exeter Railway (1852), which flank the station approach (see ARCHITECTURE).

Several developments around the turn of the century helped to relieve, though not eliminate, congestion at Temple Meads. The Bristol Avoiding Line, within sight of the platforms, was opened in 1892, and the 'Great Way Round' to the west via Bristol was abolished by the Castle Cary cut-off of 1906 which reduced Paddington–Taunton journeys by 20 miles (see SYSTEM, DEVELOPMENT OF THE). The well-aligned South Wales & Bristol Direct Railway of 1903 crossed the edge of the Cotswolds via Badminton, making the Paddington–South Wales route 25 miles shorter than via Gloucester and 10 miles shorter than through the Bath–Bristol bottleneck. Effectively, it quadrupled the main line between Swindon and Bristol, cut the distance by a mile, and made possible the GWR dream of two-hour London–Bristol expresses.

The Severn Tunnel also shortened distances between South Wales and the Solent, and a Cardiff–Bristol–

Southampton–Portsmouth Harbour passenger service introduced in 1896 still runs today. Another cross-country link, between Bristol and Weymouth, shares the route between Bristol and Westbury. Trains call at Frome, which had a direct local passenger service to Bristol via Radstock until 1959.

The GWR and Midland built lines to docks at Avonmouth, opened from 1877 when ocean-going ships became too large to enter Bristol. The railways' quick response contrasted with laggardly GWR attitudes at Bristol itself, where 30 years elapsed before three short dock branches were built. After the docks were virtually doubled in area by the Royal Edward Dock (1908), new lines connected Avonmouth to the South Wales main line at Patchway and the Badminton route at Stoke Gifford. Smaller docks at Portishead were linked to a broad-gauge branch opened from the Bristol & Exeter line in 1867. Railways were vital to a major port within 120 miles of London, and even closer to Birmingham and the Black Country.

The popularity of family holidays in the West Country in the 1930s resulted in the GWR and *London Midland & Scottish Railway being given borrowing powers to finance major extensions and improvements at Temple Meads and associated main-line quadrupling. In recent years the traffic has jammed Bristol's motorways rather than its railways. Road competition led to the withdrawal of passenger services in 1959–64 to Portishead, Frome, and Bath (Green Park); and from Avonmouth to Filton, and Pilning to Severn Beach. Today, the only local services are to Severn Beach, and stations on main lines to Cardiff, Gloucester, and Weston-super-Mare. High Speed Trains (see SPEED) introduced in 1976 revolutionized Paddington–Bristol and South Wales services. South Wales trains call at Bristol Parkway, opened in 1972 on the site of Stoke Gifford marshalling yards. Modest in concept, with only two platforms, but so successful in generating passenger traffic that it has been upgraded several times, it lies close to the M4 and Severn Bridge road network. From it HSTs reach Paddington, 112 miles, in 82 minutes.   RC

M. Harris (ed.), *Brunel, the GWR and Bristol* (1985); MacDermot; C. Maggs, *Rail Centres: Bristol* (1981); *Reg. Hist.*, i and xiii.

Bristol & Exeter Railway. Directly the *Great Western Railway was authorized in 1835, *Bristol merchants proposed an extension to Exeter, authorized in 1836. The engineer was *Brunel. The two companies were separate, with no common directors, but necessarily interdependent. The BER leased itself to the GWR in 1840. Bridgwater, 34 miles from Bristol, was reached in 1841, including a branch to Weston-super-Mare; *Exeter (42 miles more) in 1844. Apart from deep cuttings at Ashton and Uphill, and the Whiteball tunnel, no heavy engineering works were required. Branches were opened in 1847–53 to Clevedon, Tiverton, and Yeovil. The BER also worked the Exeter & Crediton Railway in 1851–62.

When the GWR's lease terminated in 1849 the BER took over operation itself. It remained a partner in the service between London and *Plymouth, bound to the GWR by

the broad *gauge—more plainly when the *London & South Western Railway completed its standard-gauge line from London to Exeter via Salisbury (1860), by which much of the BER's potential traffic to and from the Midlands and the north went, to avoid the break of gauge at Bristol or Gloucester.

The BER continued to build branches, alone or through associated companies: to Chard, Portishead, Wells, Barnstaple, and Minehead (1866–74). It leased the Somerset Central Railway from Burnham to Wells in 1854–61, but in 1862 that company united with the Dorset Central to form the *Somerset & Dorset Railway. The lease of that line jointly to the *Midland and LSW companies in 1875 angered the BER and GWR, and for their better defence they amalgamated in 1876.

The BER became modestly prosperous. In 1844–74 its annual dividend was 4½ per cent. It was managed with rigid economy, to the detriment of its track. Its *fares were high. However, it was the first substantial railway in England to operate the *block system, and it claimed never to have killed a passenger.

Among its officers were C. H. *Gregory, engineer, 1846–51; J. C. Wall, a vigorous commercial man, goods manager, goods agent, and then general manager, 1855–75; and James Pearson, remembered for his strange, unique express engines. In 1846–65 the chairman was J. W. Buller; his papers show a country gentleman devoting himself completely to the management of an important railway company.   JS

MacDermot, ii, ch. 5; Buller: Devon RO (Exeter), 2065 m. 551–22.

Bristol & Gloucester Railway. This grew out of the horse-worked Bristol & Gloucestershire Railway, opened in 1832–5, built chiefly to carry coal 9 miles from Coalpit Heath to *Bristol. In 1838 I. K. *Brunel surveyed a railway from it at Westerleigh to Gloucester, and the Bristol & Gloucester Railway was incorporated in 1839, absorbing the older company.

In 1843 connections were authorized with three other established railways. A ½-mile junction line was authorized to the *Great Western Railway at Bristol, and a junction with the broad-*gauge Cheltenham & Great Western Union Railway (Swindon–Gloucester) at Standish Junction, with *running powers thence for 7½ miles to Gloucester, where it was to meet the standard-gauge *Birmingham & Gloucester Railway coming from the north. The Bristol & Gloucester Railway, however, was influenced by the GWR (which had purchased the CGWUR) to adopt the broad gauge, and it was opened in that form in 1844. Gloucester therefore became a point of confrontation between the two gauges, where all passengers (with their luggage) and freight had to be transhipped. Daniel *Gooch designed special equipment for moving goods from one train to another, but it did not work well. A Royal Commission was appointed (1845) to investigate the whole problem arising from different gauges nationally, and when some of its members visited Gloucester they were confronted by horrible confusion, made worse by the deliberate contrivance of the Birmingham & Gloucester's goods manager.

The two warring companies now agreed to form a single Bristol & Birmingham Railway, but this plan was superseded by their acceptance of an offer from the *Midland Railway, into which they were merged in 1846, their proprietors exchanging their shares at par for Midland shares, then producing 6 per cent.

The confusion at Gloucester continued to be notorious. The MR took powers to lay down a third rail, permitting its standard-gauge trains to run into Bristol, although financial difficulties delayed completion until 1854, when the broad-gauge monopoly in the city was broken.   JS

C. G. Maggs, *Bristol & Gloucester Railway* (1969).

Britannia Tubular Bridge. The building of the Britannia Tubular Bridge (1845–50) must rank as one of the very greatest engineering advances of the 19th century. Faced with the need to carry the *Chester & Holyhead Railway across the Menai Strait with only one existing rock for intermediate support, Robert *Stephenson needed spans of over 450 ft. Additional piers, even if practicable, were ruled out as an obstruction to sailing ships, as were cast-iron arches, while normal suspension bridges had been shown to be too flexible for railway loads (see BRIDGES AND VIADUCTS). No existing type of beam, truss, or bowstring girder had been proved to more than about one quarter of this span.

Starting in 1845 with the concept of two very stiff wrought-iron tubes, each supported by chains and with the trains inside, Stephenson, assisted by William *Fairbairn and Eaton Hodgkinson, undertook a massive two-year programme of research and testing. As a result, the chains were eliminated and the original circular or elliptical tubes became rectangular with cellular tops and bottoms for greater stiffness. Further, they were made to act as continuous girders over five spans, a quite unprecedented application of beam action, even for their own weight alone.

The bridge was opened in 1850, preceded in 1848 by the single-span Conway Tubular Bridge, of the same form and on the same line. Regrettably Fairbairn and Stephenson quarrelled over the credit for the work, and Fairbairn resigned in May 1848.

In spite of this conflict, the joint achievement of the three main participants was enormous. Apart from developing and designing two major bridges of quite novel form in a remarkably short time, they advanced the understanding of materials, wrought iron in particular, to the extent that the design of bridges in Britain, and other structures, moved from a semi-empirical art to a science where performance could be calculated with reasonable accuracy.

Both bridges served the railways well until the accidental burning in 1970 of the highly combustible protective cover on top of the Britannia tubes. The heat resulted in a sagging at midspan, loss of structural continuity, and then splitting of the iron over the supports as the metal cooled. The Britannia Bridge was replaced by the present road and rail bridge designed by Husband & Co, and supported on arches, by now allowed because of the virtual extinction

of sailing traffic. The Conway Tubular Bridge remains, although strengthened (see also HAWKINS, G.).

See illustration, BRIDGES AND VIADUCTS.   RJMS

E. Clark, *The Britannia and Conway Tubular Bridges* (1850); R. J. M. Sutherland, 'The Introduction of Structural Wrought Iron', *TNS* (1964).

British Railways and British Rail (BR): the commonly used titles (the shorter one only since the 'corporate identity' campaign of the 1960s) of the railways nationalized on 1 January 1948.

The Transport Act, 1947, vested railways owning 19,639 route-miles, 20,023 steam locomotives (see TRACTION), 36,033 locomotive-hauled passenger vehicles, and 4,184 electric *multiple-unit vehicles. Diesel traction was negligible; the *wagon fleet numbered 1,223,634 (about half had been compulsorily acquired from *private owners).

Management was originally entrusted to the Railway Executive which, although a legal entity, was incorporated in the *British Transport Commission also set up under the Act. The BTC was empowered to issue 'Directions' to the RE; it was the financial arbiter and had statutory duty to integrate the forms of nationalized transport.

The relationship was not easy. The Executive Members, being ministerial appointees, felt that their judgement on railway matters should be final. Under the chairmanship of Sir Eustace *Missenden, former general manager of the *Southern Railway, RE policy was aimed primarily at restoring pre-war standards, and unifying the practices of the former railway companies. The whole system was divided into six regions largely based on former company boundaries. The Eastern Region comprised only the southern areas of the former *London & North Eastern Railway; the London Midland Region was virtually the former *London Midland & Scottish in England; the North Eastern Region was the North-Eastern Area of the LNER; the Scottish Region, however, was an amalgamation of the Scottish lines of the LMS and the LNER; the Southern Region was virtually the *Southern Railway, and the Western the *Great Western Railway.

A few initial changes were made; the *London Tilbury & Southend line was transferred to the ER and the former *joint lines were each assigned to a single region. Further boundary changes followed, sometimes controversially, until fully geographical regions were ultimately established.

Under 'functional' management, RE members issued instructions directly to departmental officers in the Regions, where Chief Regional Officers acted mainly as local representatives of the Executive and co-ordinators of the departments. Friction between the Regions and the Executive often surfaced; but after (Sir) John *Elliot was appointed to succeed Missenden in 1951 measures to reduce this were adopted.

Elliot's chairmanship was short, since a new Conservative government passed the Transport Act, 1953, abolishing the RE (considered over-centralized) and appointing Area Boards under the BTC. It appointed Sir Brian (Lord)

*Robertson as BTC chairman and thus also chief executive of the railways.

The RE headquarters had been in the former Hotel Great Central, renamed 222 Marylebone Road. The BTC, which had been housed in the London Transport head office at 55 Broadway, Westminster, moved into No. 222 and a complex new organization was set up covering all forms of nationalized transport.

Rising costs, road competition, and industrial action in 1955 soon began eroding rail finances, an operating surplus of £19m in 1948 having become a deficit of £17m by 1955. Concern at this, and a desire to appear more progressive than the RE (the BTC had been unhappy at the policy of building new classes of standard steam locomotives), led to the publication in 1955 of a *Modernization Plan providing for investment of £1,240m (soon revised to £1,500m) over a 15-year period. Its main features were abandonment of steam in favour of electric and diesel traction; replacement of loose-coupled hand-braked *freight wagons by larger wagons with power braking; replacement of many small *freight yards by fewer large mechanized yards; and modernization of many passenger and freight *stations.

*Electrification of the main lines from *London to *Birmingham, *Liverpool, and *Manchester, also to *Leeds and possibly *York, was proposed. The principal suburban lines from Liverpool Street and King's Cross would be electrified, along with the *Glasgow suburban lines. The Southern Region's main lines to the Kent Coast would be electrified 'as soon as circumstances permit'.

On non-electrified lines, diesel locomotives would replace steam for freight and important passenger trains, while multiple-unit sets or *railcars would serve branch lines and routes of light traffic.

Unfortunately, technical resources were found inadequate to execute the two major electrification schemes simultaneously, and priority was given to the London–Birmingham–Liverpool–Manchester project, which ran into planning difficulties. The work was also complicated by the decision to change from the hitherto preferred 1,500 V dc overhead system to the 25 kV ac system. On the diesel side, lack of experience led to too many types of locomotive being ordered, several proving unsatisfactory. The initial choice of the vacuum *brake for freight wagons had to be reversed in favour of the technically superior air brake. And the decline in freight traffic turned some of the new *marshalling yards into white elephants. But the principal objectives of the plan on the technical and operating sides were realized and the railway of 1970, at the end of the 15-year period, was utterly different from that of 1955.

Even so, the financial position continued to worsen and two government reports (one confidential to the Minister of Transport) concluded that the organization of the BTC was unwieldy and its outlook insufficiently commercial. The Transport Act, 1962, broke up the BTC into its main components, railways coming under a new British Railways Board from 1 January 1963. Its chairman was Richard *Beeching, former technical director of ICI, who had been made BTC chairman in the previous year. He gave the BRB

a much simpler organization and also recruited from industry a number of senior managers; most stayed only a few years.

To fulfil his remit from the government to reduce, if not eliminate, the deficit, Beeching demanded and was given data showing costs and receipts attributable to each section of line and each train service. He concluded that there was a case for substantial line closures and service withdrawals. In a published report, *The Re-Shaping of British Railways*, he quoted the inadequate receipts at many stations and low utilization of rolling stock, suggesting that on economic grounds some 2,000 stations and 250 train services were candidates for *closure.

The report produced a furore even though in effect it merely proposed accelerating drastically a closure process that had been long under way. The Beeching regime had a constructive side, with the origin of the *Freightliner concept (originally as 'Liner Trains') of timetabled fast container-carrying trains, with road collection and delivery at main centres; also the *'merry-go-round' coal trains to power stations with non-stopping discharge arrangements. A further report advocated investment in selected major trunk routes.

Beeching retired, with a peerage, in 1965 and was followed from within the railway by (Sir) Stanley Raymond, whose period in office was difficult; the deficit continued to rise and the Labour Minister of Transport, Barbara Castle, appointed a Joint Steering Group reporting to her and to the BRB chairman. Much internal debate took place over the proper headquarters organization. Disagreements with the government arose.

Raymond's enforced departure at the end of 1967 led to the appointment of an experienced railwayman, H. C. (Sir Henry) Johnson, as chairman. He had come from the London Midland Region, where he had carried through the troubled electrification project.

Johnson's period as chairman was eased by the Transport Act, 1968, by Mrs Castle. It wrote off much of the capital debt inherited from the BTC; instituted a system of specific grants for unremunerative but socially necessary services; transferred to a new National Freight Corporation the loss-making 'sundries' (small consignments) freight traffic, as well as—more controversially—the expanding Freightliner company. The Act created *Passenger Transport Authorities and Executives in the major provincial conurbations, with power to enter into agreements with BR for local train services, and make subsidy payments if necessary.

The 1960s represented the greatest decade of change for the railways. In 1967 the first main-line electrification of real significance (if one excludes the pre-war Southern Railway and the Manchester–Sheffield–Wath line, principally freight, of 1954), linking major centres and catering for both passengers and freight, was opened to Birmingham, Liverpool, and Manchester, with the completely reconstructed terminal at Euston opened in the following year. The Southern Region's two routes to the Kent Coast were electrified in 1959 and 1961, and were followed by electrification to

Bournemouth in 1967. The last standard-gauge steam train ran on BR in 1968.

An important feature of the period was the dramatic fall in staff numbers, arising from line closures, new methods of traction, and decline in wagonload freight. Great efforts were made to increase productivity by adopting 'work-study', and negotiating new working conditions. These included single-manning of diesel and electric locomotives to some extent, and the abolition of *guards on continuous-braked freight trains. The decade also saw the adoption of a corporate identity programme, including shortening the title, adoption of the double-arrow logo, and new standard *liveries for carriages.

Johnson retired towards the end of 1971 and was succeeded by Richard (Lord) Marsh, who had been Minister of Transport in a former Labour government. The system Marsh came to was very different from that of 1948, with 41 per cent less route miles and 67 per cent less passenger and freight stations. Some 20,000 steam locomotives had been replaced by 3,633 diesel and 317 electric locomotives, or by multiple-unit electric and diesel trains. Passenger carriages had fallen from 40,000 to just over 17,000. Wagon numbers were 22 per cent of 1948, and were to continue falling, partly offset by later growth in private owners' fleets.

The Railways Act, 1974 replaced the system of specific grants for socially necessary services with a lump sum known as the Public Service Obligation. It also provided for grants to industry for the construction of private siding facilities to encourage use of the railway.

The same year saw the culmination of planning for the *Channel Tunnel, in which BR had been engaged for some years jointly with the Department of the Environment, the French railways, and British project managers. This included the development of a high-speed rail link from the tunnel to London. Work was close to starting when the Labour government cancelled the project in January 1975, much to the disappointment of Marsh and the BRB.

Marsh was openly critical of the government's failure to support with ample research funding the experimental *Advanced Passenger Train, which was abandoned later. But the successful High Speed Train or IC 125—train sets with a high-power diesel unit at each end—entered service in 1974 and pioneered 125 mph running (see SPEED).

In September 1976 Marsh was succeeded by (Sir) Peter Parker who inherited an improving situation, with net surpluses on operating account, although, like his predecessor, he was dissatisfied with the investment ceilings imposed by the government and coined the phrase 'the crumbling edge of quality'. But he did secure authority for the St Pancras–Moorgate–Bedford electrification in 1976, a year in which the Great Northern line suburban electrification started to function as far as Welwyn Garden City and Hertford North.

The freight situation continued to be difficult, though Freightliners Ltd was returned to BR control under the Transport Act, 1978. A serious, though ultimately unsuccessful, attempt was made to retain the general wagonload traffic, so susceptible to road competition, by introducing a timetabled service of fast long-distance freight trains under the marketing title of 'Speedlink'. It had a hard struggle to survive until 1991. But bulk traffics held up well, with the fleet of private owners' wagons expanding.

Electrification continued, though on a piecemeal basis. Electric power was extended to reach Glasgow in 1974, and the Glasgow suburban network was expanded; the Great Northern suburban network reached Royston, short of Cambridge, in 1978. But the St Pancras and Moorgate–Bedford services were delayed until 1983, owing to an industrial dispute over single-manning.

The arrival of a Conservative government in 1979 raised the question of *privatization. Initially, BR was directed to dispose of its non-rail interests. *Sealink UK, formed out of the former BR Shipping & International Services Division, was sold in 1984, and the *hotels were disposed of piecemeal. The workshops had been reorganized as British Rail Engineering Ltd, and a separation made between the manufacturing and routine maintenance activities; the former group was sold in 1989.

To harmonize with government thinking, a move towards a more 'business-led' railway was made in 1982 with the establishment of 'Sectors' (originally InterCity, Freight, London & South-East, and Other Provincial Services), each under a director charged with preparing a business plan for execution by the Regional managements, and monitoring its execution. At the same time, Area managers in the Regions were given wider powers, foreshadowing a diminution in the importance of Regional headquarters, which had in any case been symbolized by the removal of all but the Southern from London. The Eastern had been amalgamated with the North Eastern in 1966, with headquarters at York. The London Midland was moved to Birmingham, and the Western to Cardiff. Less symbolic was the move of Board headquarters to Rail House, a modern block beside Euston station, followed by a second move into Euston House, originally built by the LMS.

Parker was followed by a career railwayman, (Sir) Robert *Reid, in 1983. As Chief Executive (Railways), Reid had been associated with the build-up of Sector management; he was, in the words of Modern Railways, a 'man of iron will, strong political awareness and strong management'. He coped with directives from Ministers imposing ever-tighter limitations upon funding and investment, and was assisted for some years by buoyant passenger traffic and the boom in property values, which enabled the British Rail Property Board to boost BR finances very substantially until the financial crash of 1988.

Reid was successful in obtaining authority for electrification of the East Coast Main Line in 1984; other electrification works—to Cambridge, Norwich, and Hastings—were under way, although this was a year in which a disastrous coal strike involved BR in a loss of £200m and helped to accelerate the run-down of the coalmining industry and the loss of BR's traditional basic traffic. The following year saw the closure of a London terminus—Broad Street—although Marylebone, threatened with closure and conversion into a coach station, was reprieved and later face-lifted in connection with the modernization of the Chiltern Line to Aylesbury, High Wycombe, and Banbury.

The process of sectorization continued with the transfer of functions to the sector directors and away from the regional managers, although (surprisingly to some) a new Anglia Region was carved out of the Eastern Region in 1988. The sectors engaged in numerous reorganizations, with sub-sectors emerging as operational units, clearly paving the way for privatization. The Freight Sector was originally divided into Railfreight Distribution and Trainload Freight; RfD was then amalgamated with the Freightliner Company. Parcels was for a time a sub-sector; and Network SouthEast replaced the London & South-East Sector. The 'Other Provincial Services' sector at last received the more prestigious title of 'Regional Railways'. The last remaining territorial unit from the regional system was 'ScotRail', which—probably because of political overtones—was a blend of sector and regional management, with a single director covering a dual role.

Attaching valid financial results to sectors was, in view of the extensive sharing of tracks and facilities, a matter of some accounting difficulty. Eventually all operations, and the engineering services required to support them, were transferred to the Sectors and the Regions disappeared in 1992.

The revival of the Channel Tunnel project by an Anglo-French government decision in 1986 involved BR in much work described elsewhere, including the formation of subsidiaries, Union Railways to plan a high-speed rail link to the tunnel and European Passenger Services to organize the rail services to and from the Continent.

Government pressure to reduce financial support was met by cost-saving, mainly in labour. Single-manning of locomotives and abolition of guards on some multiple-unit trains were accompanied by reductions in station staffs. Unstaffed stations presented problems of vandalism and provision of passenger information. Conductor-guards issuing tickets on minor lines, and on-train ticket controls accompanying an 'open station' policy, led to problems of fare evasion only partly checked by flying squads, designated 'revenue protection' staff, on-spot fines, and machines (where booking offices were closed) issuing 'permits to travel', showing journey origins.

These draconian measures led to BR, on statistical comparisons with almost all major European railways, showing the highest productivity and also the lowest level of funding by government. That did not affect public perception of shortcomings in service quality in some areas.

The collapse of the property market at the end of the 1980s seriously reduced the BR Property Board's ability to support BR finances, though major schemes were completed, especially in London, at Liverpool Street, Cannon Street, Charing Cross, and Victoria.

Completion of the *East Coast Main Line electrification, with its projection from *Edinburgh to Glasgow, as the InterCity flagship route, left two major investment problems. One was the updating and replacement needed for the *West Coast Main Line, after a quarter-century of intensive use of the tracks, motive power, and rolling stock; the other was the replacement of the older trains still running on Network SouthEast. Although the government claimed that investment levels had been substantial, much of the funding had perforce to be applied to the construction of the Waterloo International terminal and upgrading the former Southern Region London–Folkestone line in preparation for the Channel Tunnel trains. Domestic investment had been held back in consequence.

Sir Robert Reid retired in April 1990 and was followed by Sir Bob Reid, former chairman of Shell (UK). He inherited a situation in which, while some improvements were in the pipeline and had been initiated by his predecessor, the future was dominated by the issue of privatization, and major investment decisions were held in suspense.   MRB

Gourvish; G. Freeman Allen, *British Rail after Beeching* (1966); M. R. Bonavia, *The Organisation of British Railways* (1971); and *British Rail: The First 25 Years* (1981); J. Johnson and R. A. Long, *British Railways Engineering, 1948–80* (1981); Annual Reports of British Transport Commission to 1962, and of British Railways Board from 1963; files of *Modern Railways*.

British Transport Commission. The first conspicuous effect of the creation of the Commission (BTC) on 1 January 1948, under the Labour government's Transport Act, 1947, was railway *nationalization. But the BTC had a duty to 'integrate' all public inland transport and be financially in balance 'taking one year with another': it was not to be just a state railway.

The Commission's first chairman was Sir Cyril (later Lord) *Hurcomb, a distinguished former civil servant, aged 65, the other full-time members being Sir William *Wood (65), Lord *Ashfield (73), John Benstead from the *National Union of Railwaymen (50), and Lord Rusholme from the Co-Operative movement (57): not a young team for the vast task set them, though day-to-day management was delegated to Executive organizations. Even this was to create problems.

Under the Act, 'vesting' of the railways (along with *London Transport and the *canals) in the BTC automatically transferred ships, ports, hotels, and investments in *bus, coach, and haulage companies as a nucleus to which were soon added two bus combines (Tilling and Scottish Motor Traction) as well as road hauliers engaged predominantly in long-distance carriage.

For several years the Commission's staff laboured to obey the Act by planning Area Schemes designed to establish regional monopolies for road passenger transport, and for ports and harbours, involving further substantial takeovers. 'Integration' was also to be promoted through Charges Schemes where the true costs of different modes were to be reflected in charges designed to attract traffic to the most economic and efficient mode of transport.

Progress was disappointingly slow, partly because at management level the Executives dragged their feet and staff attitudes were hostile. Both within the Commission and in public there was criticism of the Railway Executive as over-centralized and slow to modernize.

Broad Street station

A new Conservative government passed the Transport Act, 1953, which abolished the Executives (except London Transport) and required the setting up of area authorities to decentralize the railways. The newly acquired road haulage firms were to be sold off, and 'integration' was no longer a duty. Abolition of the Executives meant that all activities were to be directly controlled by a greatly enlarged BTC subject to any powers granted to new area authorities.

Lord Hurcomb retired in September 1953 and was succeeded by Sir Brian *Robertson, who had to cope with a somewhat chaotic headquarters situation. His own reorganization, including Area Boards for the railways, duly received government approval, though it was cumbersome in practice. Disposal of the haulage fleet was pushed ahead energetically but sales stopped for lack of buyers with about one-third left in BTC hands.

Competition from *road traffic in all forms, together with rising costs, caused financial problems by 1955, relief from which was sought by the launch of the Railway *Modernization Plan. This long overdue measure was bedevilled by pressure to show speedy benefits, and by the complexity of the headquarters organization. Industrial relations had deteriorated, with a strike in 1955. Parliamentary and press criticism focused on allegations that the BTC was unwieldy in organization and insufficiently commercially minded, whilst the Modernization Plan had not been adequately tested on its financial justification.

After a report by the Select Committee on the Nationalized Industries and another by a Special Advisory Group, on 31 May 1961 Sir Brian Robertson retired and was replaced by Dr Richard *Beeching. Under the Transport Act, 1962 the BTC was abolished, Dr Beeching becoming chairman of the succeeding *British Railways Board, on 1 January 1963.

The BTC thus had two distinct phases during its 15-year lifespan. From 1948 it pursued the goal of integration, though latterly without conviction owing to the arrival of a Conservative government in 1951. The second phase opened in 1953, after which financial viability was the fast-disappearing objective. In each phase it must be said that the organization imposed by legislation militated against realization of its objectives.   MRB

Annual Reports of the British Transport Commission, 1948–62; Gourvish; M. R. Bonavia, *The Nationalisation of British Transport: The Early History of the British Transport Commission, 1948–53* (1987); and *The Organisation of British Railways* (1971).

Broad Street station, see LONDON STATIONS.

Brunel, Isambard Kingdom (1806–59), engineer. Born at Portsmouth, he was the son of the engineer Marc Isambard Brunel. He was educated in Paris, and then obtained practical skills in the workshops of the watchmaker Louis Breguet and Henry Maudslay. After working together in London on the construction of the Thames Tunnel, Isambard and his father produced the accepted design for the Clifton suspension bridge, *Bristol. This connection with that port paved the way for his appointment as chief engineer of the *Great Western Railway between London and

Bristol which, completed in 1841 with 7-ft broad *gauge track, remains his greatest single achievement. The broad gauge was laid on about 1,000 miles of line in those parts of the country whose companies had Brunel as their engineer. A man of many talents and great ingenuity, he worked on a wide variety of assignments, ranging from dock and harbour improvements to prefabricated hospitals during the Crimean War, and thus escaped the trend amongst his fellow engineers towards specialization. Much of the second half of his career was spent on the construction of the steamships *Great Britain* and *Great Eastern* to his advanced designs.

Brunel's bold and imaginative approach was inspiring, but his drive for originality could lead to serious financial loss—as occurred on the *South Devon Railway following the failure of the *atmospheric system of propulsion—or could be the source of a masterpiece such as the Royal Albert Bridge, Saltash. His assistant engineers and *contractors often found Brunel a peremptory and overbearing master and, on the evidence of the events at Mickleton Tunnel (see RIOTING) on the Oxford Worcester & Wolverhampton Railway (see WEST MIDLAND RAILWAY) in 1851, he was prepared to use physical violence against those who stood in his way. The 'great triumvirate' of engineers of the mid-19th century to which he belonged took the reputation of the profession to a uniquely high level in British public esteem although, unlike the other two, *Locke and Robert *Stephenson, he did little work abroad.

Brunel died in London leaving an estate of only £90,000; this was more a measure of his indifference to money than of 25 years of outstanding attainment.   DB

PICE, 19 (1859–60), 169–73; Sir Alfred Pugsley (ed.), *The Works of Isambard Kingdom Brunel, An Engineering Appreciation* (1976); L. T. C. Rolt, *Isambard Kingdom Brunel* (1957); A. Vaughan, *Isambard Kingdom Brunel, Engineering Knight-Errant* (1991).

Brunlees, Sir James (1816–92), engineer. Born at Kelso, he studied at Edinburgh University. He became an assistant engineer successively on the Bolton & Preston, *Caledonian, and *Lancashire & Yorkshire Railways; then engineer on the Ulverston & Lancaster Railway, a line crossing the broad Leven and Kent estuaries. Brunlees and the *contractors, Galloways of Manchester, devised a new method of penetrating down to the rock through sand 70 ft deep, and the work was completed in 1857. At the same time Brunlees was engaged on the São Paulo Railway in Brazil, climbing up through jungle by cable-worked inclines. In 1865–9, as engineer to the Solway Junction Railway, he built a high iron viaduct over the Solway Firth a mile long. It was severely damaged by ice-floes in 1880 and partially reconstructed.

His most important work followed in 1881–6: the *Mersey Railway, undertaken jointly with Charles *Fox, mainly in tunnel with an incline as steep as 1 in 27. This and the *Severn Tunnel, then also under construction, were the biggest underwater tunnels yet completed anywhere. Brunlees was also engineer with *Hawkshaw for the first *Channel Tunnel scheme (1872–86). He was president of the ICE (1882–3) and knighted in 1886.   JS

DNB; *PICE*, 111 (1892); *Reg. Hist.*, xiv, 107–8.

Buccleuch, Walter Francis Scott, 5th Duke of (1806–84), landowner. He succeeded his father in 1819. He was Lord Privy Seal and then Lord President of the Council in Peel's government, 1842–6. His estates (extending in 1883 to 460,000 acres) were both agricultural and industrial. More than half lay in Dumfries-shire, but in 1835–42 he spent £½ million on the development of the port of Granton serving *Edinburgh.

When in 1837 a *Carlisle–*Glasgow railway was proposed, running up Nithsdale close to his great house Drumlanrig Castle, he fought it energetically and it was defeated. But the plan succeeded in 1846, as the Glasgow Dumfries & Carlisle Railway (see GLASGOW & SOUTH WESTERN), though at the price of constructing a tunnel at Drumlanrig, partly in order to screen the railway from the house. His opposition also helped to delay until 1862 the building of a line from Carlisle to Edinburgh through Hawick. On the other hand the Duke supported the *Edinburgh & Dalkeith Railway, in the interest of his collieries there, and the building of a line to Granton. His attitude towards railways was almost wholly determined by the view he took of their effect on his estates.   JS

DNB; V. Gibbs and others (ed.), *Complete Peerage* (1987 edn.); Robertson; J. Bateman, *Great Landowners of Great Britain and Ireland* (1971 edn.), 63.

Buck, George Watson (1789–1854), engineer, Montgomeryshire Canal, 1818–32. He worked on the construction of the *London & Birmingham Railway under his friend Robert *Stephenson, and then became engineer of the Manchester & Birmingham Railway, again in association with Stephenson; with a brief interlude in Germany, he carried it through to completion in 1842. The chief structure on it, the massive and noble Stockport viaduct, is his masterpiece (see BRIDGES AND VIADUCTS). Bedevilled by ill-health, he retired to the Isle of Man, where he devoted himself largely to literary work. His most important book was *Practical and Theoretical Essay on Oblique Bridges* (1839). His son J. H. W. Buck became a senior engineer on the *London & North Western Railway.   JS

BDE.

Buddicom, William Barber (1816–87), engineer. After apprenticeship with Mather Dixon of *Liverpool, he was a resident engineer on the *Liverpool & Manchester Railway, and then on the Glasgow Paisley & Greenock under *Locke.

In 1840–1 he was locomotive superintendent of the *Grand Junction Railway. The Robert *Stephenson locomotives used on that line had all broken their crank axles, and it was one of Buddicom's chief tasks to devise straight axles, requiring inclined outside cylinders. The engines on this principle were usually known as the 'Crewe type', though the first of them were constructed not at *Crewe but by outside manufacturers. Their attribution to Alexander *Allan (the Crewe works foreman) is fallacious.

Locke was now constructing the Paris & Rouen Railway, and he persuaded Buddicom and William Allcard (another Crewe man) to superintend that company's locomotive works. From this they developed manufacturing works of their own at Sotteville, outside Rouen, which became a great commercial enterprise. Buddicom worked the PRR under contract until 1860. In 1870 he retired, living thereafter on his Penbedw estate in Flintshire. Important relics and records of his work are now in the Clwyd RO, Hawarden.   JS

PICE, 91 (1887–8), 412–21; D. H. Stuart and B. Reed, 'The Crewe Type', in *Locomotives in Profile*, ed. B. Reed (1971–4), ii, 49–72.

buffers perform essential functions for the marshalling of stock, in easing the movement of vehicles on curves, and in absorbing forces during collisions.

With the earliest railway vehicles, buffers were simply extensions of the wooden side-frames, to help protect the body ends from those adjacent. Then came wooden blocks or 'dumb buffers' for *wagons, while other vehicles had horsehair pads covered in leather. Dumb buffers remained in use on British railways until 1913. By the mid-1830s, *carriages were being built with sprung buffers mounted on the headstocks, supplementary buffing springs being placed within the underframe. From the 1850s some sets of carriages for suburban use were close-coupled, often with a central buffer between carriages, and coupling chains.

By the 1870s steel, sprung buffers were widely used. Within a forged or cast shank the buffer head was able to move, absorbing shunting forces by a steel or rubber buffing spring placed behind. Drop-forging of the buffer head produced a bearing face which was usually convex. These side buffers were accompanied by a spring mounted behind the drawgear at each end of the vehicle. Typically, the buffers extended 12–13 in from the headstock, and were mounted on the frames 3 ft 6 in above the rail. Colliery lines used wagons with the buffers mounted lower on the frames, with the result that some steam locomotives, e.g. on the *Maryport & Carlisle Railway, were fitted with two sets of buffers, one above the other.

Carriage buffers generally had a double action, offering relatively light resistance; some railways used oval buffers. Locomotive buffers were not greatly different.

From the 1890s railways began to use automatic *couplers, the shocks imparted to the central buffing and drawgear being absorbed by springs mounted transversely behind the headstocks. Side buffers were provided, but these were retracted when the carriage was coupled to another with an automatic coupler, and extended only when the carriage was coupled to a vehicle with a screw coupling, and side buffers. Automatic couplings were used by the East Coast companies from the 1890s (and later the *London & North Eastern Railway), by the *Pullman Car Company, and the *Southern Railway, and adopted by *British Rail as standard for gangwayed carriages.

The traditional sprung buffers absorb some kinetic energy when rakes of wagons are marshalled in yards, but severe shunting shocks are transmitted to the wagon structure, and the payload may suffer damage. With the effect of reducing impact shocks by some 75 per cent, the hydraulic buffer was developed in which oil, as an almost incompressible substance, fills a chamber within the buffer shank, and is surrounded by a chamber of compressible air. The energy of impact is converted into heat energy as the buffer closes, and during this movement the air in the reservoir is trapped as the oil raises the level in the reservoir. In some designs, a coil spring is mounted to the rear of the buffer head. Hydraulic buffers were introduced on BR in the early 1950s, and became standard for freight stock.

From the 1970s, most designs of electric and diesel unit trains have had automatic couplers, and lack side buffers.

Buffer-stops are provided at the ends of running lines, and in sidings. Traditionally, these were built up from rails, or rails and sleepers, with a horizontally-mounted baulk of wood to absorb the impact of the buffers. By the late 19th century hydraulic buffers were provided at terminal stations. Buffer-stop accidents account for some 40 per cent of all passenger injuries in train accidents. As a consequence of the exceptional *accident in 1975 on the *London Underground at Moorgate, buffer-stops are nowadays accompanied by preventive measures in the form of automatic speed-checking devices, and control is exercised through the *signalling and *automatic warning systems.   MLH

J. Johnson and R. A. Long, *British Railways Engineering, 1948–80* (1981); L. Lynes, *Railway Carriages and Wagons—Theories and Practices* (1959).

buffet car, a carriage provided for the service of light refreshments and drinks, with limited kitchen facilities not capable of serving main meals; not to be confused with a restaurant-buffet car (see RESTAURANT CAR). In some cases, the catering facilities were only part of a vehicle with normal seating accommodation. The prices charged were sometimes lower than in restaurant cars. The vehicles carry external lettering to denote their purpose.

In a buffet car, the facilities generally include a bar counter, with usually a hot water boiler/coffee machine and toaster, and a kitchen with a gas or electric ring, water tanks, and a refrigerator. Variations on the theme included tea or pantry cars which were no more than a compartment or two equipped with a hot water boiler and sink, and miniature buffet cars, popular with *British Railways from 1956, which dispensed drinks and snacks.

The first buffet cars were built in 1899 for the London extension of the Manchester Sheffield & Lincolnshire Railway (see GREAT CENTRAL). The general introduction of buffet cars did not come until the 1930s and they were often converted from carriages or dining cars. Others were purpose-built for services previously without train catering, e.g. the Cambridge Buffet Expresses, or for *excursion traffic.

MLH

building materials, see IRON AND STEEL; CONCRETE; BRICKS; GLASS; TIMBER; ASBESTOS; PLASTICS; STONE.

Bulleid, Oliver Vaughan Snell (1882–1970), mechanical engineer. He was apprenticed under Henry *Ivatt, *Great Northern Railway; in 1908–11 was assistant manager, Westinghouse brake and signal works, Paris; 1911–15, personal assistant to H. N. *Gresley, GNR; and assistant carriage and wagon engineer 1919–22. In 1923–37 Bulleid was assistant to Gresley after he became CME *London & North Eastern Railway in whose innovative locomotive and rolling stock developments he was closely involved.

After being appointed CME *Southern Railway in 1937, Bulleid pressed strongly for new and more powerful steam locomotives, investment in which had been restricted to assist in funding *electrification. From 1941 onwards he built 140 4-6-2 locomotives, embodying welded fireboxes and totally enclosed chain-driven *valve gear, representing a step-change in locomotive performance. He also introduced a prototype C-C type general purpose 'Leader' locomotive on two steam-driven power bogies, which was not developed further, together with new and more comfortable main-line and suburban electric stock. He was responsible for the mechanical design of prototype 1Co-Co1 1,750 hp diesel-electric locomotives, later the basis for 350 more powerful types built for *British Rail.

In 1949–58 Bulleid was CME Irish Railways (CIE), where he introduced diesel locomotives and *railcars; also modern passenger and freight stock of welded construction, and a prototype C-C type steam locomotive burning indigenous turf fuel.   GWC

DNB: Missing Persons (1993), 99–100; H. A. V. Bulleid, *Master Builders of Steam* (1963); H. A. V. Bulleid, *Bulleid of the Southern* (1977).

burrowing junctions, see JUNCTIONS.

Burton-on-Trent, see FOOD AND DRINK TRAFFIC; INDUSTRIAL RAILWAYS; LEVEL CROSSINGS.

Bury, Edward (1794–1858), engineer. Proprietor of the Clarence Foundry, Liverpool, Bury came to prominence in 1830 by designing *Liverpool*—the first locomotive to combine horizontal inside cylinders with a horizontal tubular boiler and a continuous metal chassis separate from the boiler. He introduced the bar frame and was the first to employ extensive standardization, not only between individual parts but between individual designs. Though overshadowed by *Stephenson practice at home, the Bury locomotive contributed much to the American school of design which eventually became universal outside western Europe.

As the first locomotive superintendent of the *London & Birmingham Railway, Bury effectively devised the position and duties of that office. His scientific approach to locomotive design and grasp of management principles applied to a large railway were widely admired, leading to his becoming in 1844 the first of only two locomotive superintendents elected to the Royal Society. At Wolverton he laid out the first railway *town, advised on *Swindon, and, later, when briefly general manager and engineer of the *Great Northern Railway, began similar development of *Doncaster.

Being the Stephensons' principal competitor, Bury attracted several vociferous critics and has been portrayed as a life-long believer in small four-wheeled locomotives. In fact he believed in building locomotives of the right size for the job, not hesitating to use six wheels where necessary, and by 1846 his latest LBR locomotives were larger than their Crewe-built contemporaries. He differed fundamentally from George Stephenson over frame design and subsequent experience has proved him correct.   RW

Bury, Thomas Talbot (1811–77). After training as an architect under A. W. N. Pugin, Bury became known chiefly as a pictorial artist. In 1831 two sets of prints of the *Liverpool & Manchester Railway from his drawings, 13 in all, 'made on the spot', were published by Rudolph Ackermann in London. These are perhaps the most widely known railway pictures ever produced. They treat the LMR's civil engineering and architecture admirably. Bury's understanding of its machinery was, however, imperfect: but then this was the first of all fully mechanized railways, and he was only 19 at the time. He seems never to have touched railways again.   JS

DNB; C. F. Dendy Marshall, *Centenary History of the Liverpool & Manchester Railway* (1930), 127–34.

buses have been an established part of passenger transport far longer than train services. Rural carriers who switched from horses to motors after 1919 had been carrying people as well as goods to the market towns from at least the 12th century, while the hackney carriage, which appeared about 1625, was one of the predecessors of the omnibus, the other being the stage-coach, whose services developed from around 1650 to provide a national network (see COACHES, ROAD). The first mail coach service began in 1784, between *London, Bath, and *Bristol, a route which was to be taken by the first true express motor-coach service in 1925.

But whereas the stage-coaches fell back before the advancing railways, having failed to compete successfully with the *Liverpool & Manchester, they retained their importance as 'short-stage' coaches in many places, often acting as feeders to railways, and eventually metamorphosing into horse-buses in towns and horse-drawn omnibuses or coaches in rural areas. Even so, the stage-coach between Wendover and London was withdrawn only in 1892, when the *Metropolitan Railway reached the town. Neighbouring towns where the rail journey was roundabout, such as Sudbury and Halstead on the Essex–Suffolk border, continued to be linked by 'long coaches', or omnibuses, until motors were available.

In serving and encouraging the growth of towns and cities in the 19th century, the horse-bus often played a more important part than the railway. Shillibeer's service between Paddington and the Bank in London started in 1829, copying developments in France, where the name 'omnibus' had been coined. In less than a year there were 39 omnibuses running in London, and within a decade the bus had become the accepted form of transport in *Birmingham, *Manchester, and most of the larger towns, a function it retained, since railway services within cities tended to provide chiefly for *commuters. After the Great Exhibition had

attracted many new firms to the London trade, over-supply led to combination, and from 1856 the London General Omnibus Company, financed in Paris, began to dominate the industry in the capital.

The law permitting motor-buses to be used was embodied in the Locomotives on Highways Act, 1896, and the first motor service commenced in *Edinburgh on 19 May 1898. The same year saw services started at Falkirk, Mansfield, Llandudno, Mablethorpe, Torquay, and Clacton, and, in December, the first rural service, between Newport Pagnell and Olney, Buckinghamshire. London had to wait for the motor-bus until 1899. It ran between Kennington Park and *Victoria station, and lasted just over a year.

Nevertheless, development in the early 20th century was rapid. In 1910 there were more motor than horse-buses in London, and by 1912 it was easier to identify those parts of the country where motor-buses were unknown than to list their local existence. In 1916 the foundations were laid for a system of territorial monopolies in England and Wales, itself reflecting the balance of power between two great holding companies, the British Electric Traction Co. (BET) and Thomas Tilling Ltd. Municipal bus operation started at Eastbourne, where the council in 1908 acted to avoid the construction of an electric *tramway, whose poles and wires were felt to be unsuitable for the town.

Some spontaneous road and rail co-ordination appeared early, when horse-cabs met trains and horse-buses served stations. The railways' own road operations were small; there were inter-station buses in London, and the Metropolitan Railway at various times operated 15 cross-London bus routes.

By 1919 the industry was poised for expansion, which proved so rapid that 10 years later there were motor-bus services everywhere, while express coach services by 1931 linked all the main towns of England and Wales. By 1929 technical development produced vehicles like the Leyland Titan double-decker, which could stand comparison with the tramcar, and diesel engines became widespread by 1939. Territorial expansion was matched by the growth of numerous small firms, and motor-buses were used to replace smaller tramway systems, and to complement most of the others.

The railway companies also diversified to some extent into motor-bus operation, notably the *Great Western, which, starting in 1903, owned just over 300 buses in 1928. Few of the GWR bus services were designed specifically to feed its trains, and over much of Wales and the south-west of England it was a territorial operator in its own right. Like most of the large companies, it faced competition from small firms using light, fast buses, often imported, or war-surplus vehicles sold off by the military after 1919. The *Great Eastern and some other railways also ran bus services. Ex-service gratuities and cheap hire-purchase contributed to growing investment in the bus industry, along with the policies of the so-called combines, and the municipalities.

Some railways had legal powers to run buses; others did not. The GWR's were extremely doubtful, and it was partly to rectify the situation that the *Big Four main-line companies promoted the Railway (Road Transport) Act of 1928, which authorized their operations. The *London & North Eastern then moved to acquire United Automobile Services, one of the largest remaining 'independents', with an east-coast territory stretching from the Scottish border to south Suffolk. The 'combines' (BET and Tilling) responded with a campaign to limit the threat of a railway-owned bus industry, and a settlement was reached whereby the main-line companies could acquire no more than 50 per cent of the shares in their subsidiaries. A similar settlement in Scotland made Scottish Motor Traction (SMT) the railways' partner there. As a result, the railways put over £9 million into the bus industry, much of it to be used to buy up smaller independents, while the expected co-ordination of services proved largely nugatory. The *London Midland & Scottish Railway also had interests in municipal undertakings at Huddersfield and Todmorden, and jointly with the LNER at Sheffield and Halifax. Railway directors or senior officers on bus company boards were instructed to pursue the profitability of the railway's investment, and not to try to protect the railway's operations. This policy continued to be followed after the railways, and many of the bus companies, had been acquired by the *British Transport Commission.

It was no coincidence that the settlements were accompanied by the passage of the Road Traffic Act, 1930. This legislation gave bus operators protection from competition on each of their routes, so that smaller firms could be acquired with no risk of new ones appearing next day. After 1930 there was thus a period of consolidation of ownership, equally marked in the express motor-coach business. Competition from long-distance coaches had threatened the railways more than that from buses. So, even when railways had invested in a coach operator, they would on occasion oppose the granting of licences for extra services by the Traffic Commissioners established by the Act, which also put an end to price competition, and rail cheap-day return *fares then tended to settle at the same level as the return fare by bus over the parallel route.

After the passage of the Transport Act, 1947, the Tilling and SMT group's companies were sold voluntarily to the British Transport Commission, as were those of the Red & White group, but no serious co-ordination followed. The BET companies were also acquired by the Transport Holding Company in 1968, to be transferred with the company's other bus holdings to the newly formed National Bus Company or Scottish Bus Group, while many municipal fleets passed to the *Passenger Transport Executives. The link between railway and bus management now became merely a duty to co-operate, itself removed by the Transport Act of 1985. When uneconomic rail services were withdrawn, bus companies, whether nationalized or independent, were often reluctant to adjust their routes and timetables to replicate a withdrawn rail service. This was an enduring problem; and after *privatization and deregulation of the bus industry, co-ordination could only appear to worsen.   JH

D. N. Chester, *Public Control of Road Passenger Transport* (1937); J. Cummings, *Railway Motor Buses and Bus Services in the British Isles* (1978–80); C. S. Dunbar, *Buses, Trolleys and Trams* (1967); J. Hibbs, *History of British Bus Services* (1968); C. F. Klapper, *Golden Age of Buses* (1978); Gourvish.

bye-laws, orders, rules, and regulations. Since a very early date railway companies were given power in their Acts of Parliament (see PARLIAMENT AND LEGISLATION) to lay down their own ordinances for the conduct of their business. These were, speaking broadly, of two different kinds: those applicable to the railways' customers, as conditions for the conveyance of themselves or their goods, and those designed to enforce discipline among the companies' own servants, necessary for the safe and efficient operation of the trains.

On the face of it, 'bye-laws' were intended to be a branch of the general laws governing railways. 'Orders, rules, and regulations' might be supposed to apply to railway staff alone, and to concern the complicated details of working. But that distinction quickly became eroded, and the whole group is treated here as one.

The earliest broad view of these ordinances is to be found in the first appendix to the report of the House of Commons committee on railways of 1839, which reproduces all those bye-laws that it had been able to collect, made under the authority of any Acts relating to railways and imposing penalties for their infringement upon persons other than the companies' own employees. Some companies had apparently made none: the *Grand Junction, *Newcastle & Carlisle, and *London & Greenwich, for instance. The *Stratford & Moreton and *North Union Railways' bye-laws prohibited the running of trains on *Sundays. Various *'rules of the road' were laid down. The awareness of them was necessary for the general public (e.g. at any stations where double lines might have to be crossed on the level) as well as for the companies' own staff. On the Monkland & Kirkintilloch and Ballochney Railways in Scotland anybody who made use of 'cursing, swearing, or other scurrilous language to the superintendent, collectors, or any other of the companies' servants, or to each other' might be fined 5s. by the company.

The first general *Regulation Act, of 1840 (sects. 7–10), refers to 'bye-laws, orders, rules and regulations' as a single group. Considering it necessary that the companies' exercise of their powers to impose them ought to come 'under proper control', it required that copies of them all should be sent to the Board of *Trade. None might take effect until it had been lodged there for two months; and the Board was given authority to disallow any of them, at that time or afterwards.

In the Railways Clauses Act, 1845 (sects. 109–11), it was ordained that the companies' bye-laws must not be 'repugnant to the laws of that part of the United Kingdom where the same are to have effect', and insisted that they must be displayed prominently at every station belonging to the company issuing them.

The same confounding of bye-laws with rules and regulations can be found in the companies' rule-books. The first produced by the Manchester Sheffield & Lincolnshire Railway (see GREAT CENTRAL) cut right across the distinction, for it bore the title *Bye-Laws for the Government of the Company's Servants*. But the *London & North Western tried to maintain the separation. It published a set of 10 bye-laws applicable to passengers shortly after its formation, in 1847, duly certified by the Board of Trade. They gave the company power to impose fines (of £2–5) for various offences—entering a train in motion, for instance; being intoxicated at a station or in a train; and damaging the fabrics of carriages. They also set down other offences that passengers might commit in respect of their *tickets. There will be more to say of that kind of conduct later. In 1849 the railway published a set of 'regulations' governing the work of its servants in various departments of its business. There were 291 of them, and every employee had to carry a copy of this rule-book when on duty, under pain of a 5s. fine for failure to do so.

As the railway system grew, with a number of each company's lines—sometimes a large number—meeting at junctions, it became clear that there would be a gain both in safety and in convenience if some of their operational practices could be made common to them all, by agreement. The Board of Trade thought in this way, and proposed that the companies should try to frame a uniform rule-book. Accordingly, a meeting of directors and officers from 19 companies was held at Birmingham in 1841, chaired by G. C. *Glyn. It did not achieve its object, but in the following year the establishment of the *Railway Clearing House, though it was intended primarily for the settlement of inter-railway accounts, also provided a forum for negotiations on matters affecting its members in common. Discussions of company rules went on there intermittently, and external critics were soon pointing out the undesirability of maintaining these diverse practices. Where signalling was concerned, the *Engineer* distinguished six different systems in force on British railways in 1856. The only serious defence of this conduct of their business was that it was unusual, even where *through carriages were provided from the line of one railway company to another, for the engines of the trains to which they were attached to run through; they were as a rule changed at the junctions, each being in the charge of a driver on his own line, and hence familiar with its signalling.

In 1867 the Clearing House, after five years' work by a committee, issued a set of *Rules for Working over Foreign Lines*, intended to form an appendix to each company's rule-book. This proved unsatisfactory and was superseded in 1876 by a much more comprehensive volume of *Regulations to be Observed by all Persons in the Service of the Railway Companies*, which was a great improvement on it, extending much more widely into the life and work of railwaymen and covering all devices and methods of operation, signalling systems prominent among them. Not all the companies adopted all its provisions, however. The bad consequences of that were demonstrated in an *accident at Canonbury in 1881, four trains being involved in successive collisions in a tunnel. It seems extraordinary that no more than five deaths resulted from it. The cause was a disparity of *telegraph

signals passing between one *signalman and another, which arose from the two different bell codes in force on the *Great Northern and *North London Railways. As the government would not legislate to impose uniformity of practice, that had to change gradually by agreement—sometimes facilitated by the retirement or death of stubborn officers who were not prepared to consider any changes whatever in the rules of their own companies. The lessons taught by the Canonbury accident led to the adoption of a standard set of rules governing bell codes in 1884. The 1876 *Regulations* were issued in five successively revised editions in 1883–1904.

Turning to the ordinances applicable to passengers and to their relationship with the railways conveying them, one general observation has to be made at the beginning. The companies' powers to make their own bye-laws were set down plainly enough in the Acts that established them; but the validity of any of these could be challenged in the courts, and many of them were declared void by the decisions reached there. The conditions imposed by the companies might be held to be unreasonable or (from 1845 onwards) to be in conflict with the established laws of the country, and invalid on that account. As H. W. Disney, a competent legal authority, put it, 'many of the bye-laws made by the railway companies of England were disapproved by the courts, and were practically worthless'. However, in 1905 the leading companies issued carefully revised collections of their bye-laws, evidently after consulting one another, in a wise attempt to explain themselves better and to obviate arguments in the future. These books continued to be standard throughout the remainder of the old companies' lives.

The most frequent disputes between the companies and their passengers arose over tickets. Their bye-laws gave prominent attention to them from the start. The earliest set promulgated by the *Great Western Railway in 1838 numbered 10, eight of which were concerned with tickets alone.

Both the companies and their passengers faced a difficulty here. The complexity of railway working absolutely demanded a control of passengers' behaviour at their stations and in their trains, far closer than what had been called for in the service of the horse-drawn *coaches. Those had been small units, seldom carrying more than 20 passengers each. Any arguments that might arise could be thrashed out at the coach office before the journey began; and if there was serious misbehaviour by passengers *en route* the coachman could stop his vehicle and refuse to go any further until the matter had been settled. But the contingencies arising in railway travel were more numerous, and some were difficult to resolve. The legislation governing it soon grew correspondingly complex, and so did the rules that the companies found it necessary to lay down in order to regulate the operation of their trains. An argument at a coach office could impede the departure of perhaps 20 people; at a railway station it might hold up a train containing 200, or many more, and the delay could easily affect the working of all other trains on the same line. The companies therefore took to printing on the front or the back of each of their tickets a phrase stating that its issue was subject to the 'regulations' or 'conditions' (whatever that vague word might mean) that governed the use of it; sometimes the 'bye-laws' were mentioned here too—a practice adopted at various times by the *North British and *Taff Vale companies, and occasionally in later days also by the *Southern.

It is true that the 'conditions' themselves, or some of them, were displayed at stations. But was it reasonable to expect that every passenger should familiarize himself with all these regulations, or—on the other side—that the companies' servants should point out the risk of any infringement of them to the passenger before it was committed? There was much to occupy the time of the courts here, and the companies could generally bear the cost of litigation better than those who travelled with them.

A few important matters that were at first dealt with under the companies' bye-laws came to be settled by Acts of Parliament: *smoking on trains, for instance, under the Regulation Act of 1868 (sect. 20). The Regulation Act of 1889 (sects. 5–6) did something to simplify the procedure concerning tickets. A passenger failing to produce one now must pay his fare from the station at which his journey began, or give one of the company's officials his name and address. If he refused, any of the company's officers was empowered under the Act to detain him until he could be brought in front of a magistrate.

A kind of case that sometimes came before the courts turned on a passenger's intention. If he had travelled beyond the station to which his ticket was valid, was he hoping to evade detection, or had he genuinely changed his mind about his destination in the course of his journey? The *London & South Western Railway's regulations included one worded thus: 'The company's servants have no authority to issue a cheap ticket to a passenger intending to travel to a station short of or beyond the station to which a cheap ticket may be obtained.' But how could his *intention* be known?

As far as passengers were concerned, these ordinances were a jungle, difficult for many of them to negotiate. But in 1906 they were offered valuable help, from G. B. Lissenden's *Railway Passenger's Handbook*: brief, crisply worded, and small enough to go into a capacious pocket.

There were many rules governing *freight traffic as well, but the situation here was, in one important respect, different. A trader dealing with a railway company over the carriage of his goods *was* a trader: almost bound to be familiar to some extent with the processes and practices of the law. He did not often have to be in any great hurry, as many passengers were at a booking office. If he was a careful man of business, he could negotiate with the goods agent at the station he was dealing with, and ask for explanations too. Legislation concerned itself with bye-laws much less in this department of railway business. Indeed, only one important Victorian Act dealt with it specifically, the Explosive Substances Act of 1875, which authorized the companies to make bye-laws regulating the loading, conveyance, and unloading of gunpowder and similar substances carried by train (see DANGEROUS GOODS). The courts had much to do with the handling of goods and the charges they made for it. After 1873 these cases were dealt with by the Railway Commission, and then the Railway and Canal Commission of 1888 (see FREIGHT TRAFFIC RATES).

Each of the *Big Four companies of 1923 consolidated its bye-laws from those of the companies it had absorbed, a relatively simple task since the general homologation of them in 1905. Their power to make bye-laws continued to rest almost wholly on the Clauses Act of 1845. After nationalization, under section 68 of the *British Transport Commission Act of 1949, it passed to the Railways Board and the *London Transport Executive.

See also LAW OF RAILWAYS. JS

The GWR bye-laws are in MacDermot, i, 368–9; the LNWR regulations and bye-laws are printed in full in Sir F. B. Head, *Stokers and Pokers* (1849), 159–208; H. W. Disney, *Law of Carriage by Railway* (1905 and later edns.); O. Kahn-Freund, *Law of Inland Transport* (1939 and later edns.); Bagwell; L. James, *Law of the Railway* (1980), 231–62; M. A. Vanns, *Signalling in the Age of Steam* (1995), prints the BR signalling regulations of 1960 (pp. 90–112).

C

cable haulage. Some early *tramroads had steep inclines, where horses were replaced by a stationary engine working a rope between the rails, or sometimes an endless chain, as on those of the Lancaster Canal *tramroad near Preston (1803). On railways this system was briefly seen as an alternative to locomotives, usually but not exclusively on inclines. Complete railways worked this way were the *London & Blackwall Railway (1840–9) and the *Glasgow Subway (1896–1935). Until 1844, when locomotives took over, trains were rope-hauled up Camden bank—the 1 in 70 climb out of *Euston—while on the climb out of Queen Street station, *Glasgow, trains complete with locomotives were assisted by rope until 1909. On much steeper inclines only two or three loaded wagons could be handled at a time, and many of these survived until line closure, notably on the Cromford & High Peak line in Derbyshire and on the Bowes Railway in Co. Durham.

With an endless rope, wagons might be attached using a pair of tapered chains which were wrapped around the rope in opposite directions before being tied off, producing a self-tightening temporary splice, but on the Glasgow Subway the rope ran continuously and the cars were provided with grippers to pick up or drop it. Where the rope was wound on and off a drum, a hook would be provided at its free end.

Another form of rope haulage was the Handyside system (1874), whereby a locomotive provided with its own winch doubled as a winding engine when clamped to the rails at the top of an incline. Despite well-publicized demonstrations there were no permanent British applications.   RW

B. G. Wilson and J. R. Day, *Unusual Railways* (1957), 53–64.

Caerphilly, see WORKS.

Caledonian Railway. The company's grand title was matched by its cavalier assumption of the Royal Arms of Scotland as its crest. Its position arose from its original conception as a northern extension of the *West Coast main line from *London to *Carlisle. The engineer was Joseph *Locke. When it received its Act in 1845, it was expected that it would be the only main line into Scotland from England, and it was therefore laid out on a Y plan, dividing at Carstairs, to serve both *Edinburgh and *Glasgow. The proposed grand terminals in these cities failed to materialize, as did an authorized cross-country line, and the company did not at first prosper, owing to serious management deficiencies.

The Caledonian made use of existing railways to gain access to Glasgow. The Garnkirk & Glasgow (later the Glasgow Garnkirk & Coatbridge), and the Wishaw & Coltness Railways, opened in 1831–44, took the railway east and north of the city centre to Buchanan Street station. The temporary wooden *trainsheds there lasted until the 1920s. This was the first city terminus for trains to Carlisle and the south. An alternative route using the Clydesdale Junction (a new line) and the upgraded Polloc & Govan Railway brought the Caledonian into a new South Side station (1849), somewhat inconveniently sited. This station was shared with the Glasgow Barrhead & Neilston Direct (1848). The Caledonian's third Glasgow terminus was jointly owned with the *Glasgow & South Western: this was Bridge Street, serving the Greenock line. The construction of the new Central and St Enoch stations in the late 1870s allowed South Side to be closed, and Caledonian services to the south to be moved to Central, but Bridge Street remained in service until the extension of Central station between 1899 and 1906; Buchanan Street continued to serve *Aberdeen, *Inverness, and Oban trains until the 1960s.

The West Coast route was extended to Aberdeen by the *Scottish Central, Scottish Midland Junction, and Aberdeen Railways, all opened by 1850. The last two amalgamated in 1856 as the Scottish North Eastern Railway, and in 1865–6 they all became part of the Caledonian. This consolidated group had the finest main lines in Scotland, and proved to be the most aggressively successful of all the Scottish companies. It penetrated the western Highlands by way of the *Callander & Oban Railway (1880), and in the 1880s and 1890s built a network of lines north and south of the Clyde to compete with the *North British and Glasgow & South Western Railways. The north-side lines provided lucrative suburban and tourist traffic (including steamers on Loch Lomond) with access to shipbuilding yards, docks, and other industrial establishments, providing outlets for Lanarkshire *coal, *iron, and steel. Those south of the river served steamers (see SHIPPING SERVICES) from Gourock and Ardrossan (the latter also a coal and iron port), and also the branch lines to Irvine, Kilwinning, and Kilbirnie which cut into GSWR territory. These lines were expensive to build, requiring extensive tunnelling. Their services were aggressively promoted, with fast trains, fine steamers, and elegant stations, of which Wemyss Bay was the apogee. The increased traffic to and from Glasgow and Edinburgh, and between them, led to the rebuilding of the company's terminals there. In Edinburgh the Lothian Road station, never satisfactory, was replaced by Princes Street, which had a *hotel added to it. In Glasgow a new terminus for coast trains at Bridge Street station was completed in 1890, but it had a short life, being superseded by the massive rebuilding and extension of Glasgow Central in 1899–1906. This now has 17 platforms on two levels, and is one of Britain's finest stations, still exciting admiration. The expansion of short-haul passenger services in the Glasgow area was halted by the electrification and extension of horse *tramway systems, and one line, the Paisley & District, was completed but never opened for passenger service.

North of the central belt expansion was more muted, but the company built new tourist lines from Connel to Balla-chulish and from Crieff to Lochearnhead. It took a leading part in remodelling joint stations at *Perth (1885–7) and Aberdeen (1914), and rebuilt its own station at Stirling in 1912.

From the 1880s onwards the passenger was aware of the Caledonian's gleaming trains and bright, well-designed, handsome stations. The glamour of the West Coast Joint Stock trains hauled by powerful blue locomotives was undeniable, as was that of the smart *boat trains and the company's steamers. The bread and butter of the railway was, however, its suburban services, which opened up new suburbs in Edinburgh and Glasgow, and above all its *freight traffic. The Lanarkshire coalfield, one of the richest in Scotland, was almost exclusively served by the Caledonian. Most of the Scottish steelworks were also in its territory, and it served virtually all the Clyde shipyards, together with many of the heavy engineering works. As older mineral fields were exhausted, lines were built to new ones, especially in Lanarkshire, and in 1880–1900 many private sidings were laid.

As befitted the nature of its traffic the Caledonian regarded access to docks as of the utmost significance (see PORTS AND DOCKS). Its main interests were on the Clyde, where it served all the Glasgow, Greenock, and Ardrossan docks. On the east coast the company also served Leith, *Dundee, and Aberdeen docks, and owned those at Grangemouth, the first of which it acquired when it took over the Forth & Clyde Canal in 1867 and proceeded to extend greatly in the early 20th century.

The Caledonian and North British Railways had intense rivalry for a variety of traffics. The *East Coast and West Coast routes in which they were partners were effectively in competition, especially for traffic from Edinburgh to London, and after the opening of the *Forth and Tay Bridges, to Aberdeen. There were also rival routes from Edinburgh to Carlisle and Perth. More locally there was competition within both Edinburgh and Glasgow, for the Forth ports and the North Clyde estuary, and for the West Highland trade. As extensions of their estuary competition both companies operated steamer services which were seriously competitive on the upper Firth of Clyde.

In taking great trouble to present an attractive face to the travelling public, the railway evolved a style unique in Scotland and rare anywhere else in Britain, with good design carried through all its activities, exemplified in particular by its hotels in Edinburgh and Glasgow, and finally and most grandly at Gleneagles, with its golf courses and splendid new station. The Caledonian's locomotives and rolling stock were among the best and most handsome in Britain. At the 1923 *Grouping it became part of the *London Mid-land & Scottish Railway, contributing a total mileage of 1,057.

JRH

O. S. Nock, *The Caledonian Railway* (1962); J. Butt and J. T. Ward, 'The Promotion of the Caledonian Railway Company', *Transport History*, 3 (1970), 164–92, 225–37.

Callander & Oban Railway. The line was the realization of a dream which began in the 'Railway *Mania' with the Glasgow & North Western Railway—an over-ambitious project, even in Mania terms, and which collapsed. In the 1860s, when confidence in railway investment had returned, the notion of linking Oban to the south was revived. By that time Oban was well established as a hub of west Highland steamer services and was becoming a select resort. The line was promoted by Oban men, and the cheapest route was sought for a line 71 miles long from Callander, terminus of a branch of the *Caledonian Railway from Dunblane. The engineers were Blyth & Westland of Edinburgh, and they introduced the then-new bowstring girder iron bridges on the first part of the line, up Strathyre. When it proved impossible to raise enough capital to complete the line, a temporary terminus was constructed at Tyndrum, from which horse-drawn coaches ran to Oban. It was not until the later 1870s that enough capital was raised to complete the railway, which reached Oban in 1880. The engineer for this section was John Strain. Steep gradients made the line difficult to operate, and the Caledonian Railway, which worked it, designed a succession of small-wheeled locomotives with low axle-weights. The most awkward section was in the Pass of Brander, a deep cleft, where stone-falls were a constant threat. A system of trip wires operated signals to warn drivers if a large stone fell on the line. The Callander & Oban remained an independent company until the 1923 *Grouping. Three branches were built: the shortest, to Killin, was opened in 1886; the longest, to Ballachulish, was opened in 1903; and the last, to Comrie and Crieff, completed in 1905. The Comrie line closed in 1964 and the other two in 1965. The section of the main line between Dunblane and Crianlarich was closed in 1966 and the remainder of the Callander & Oban is now reached by the former West Highland Railway (see NORTH BRITISH RAILWAY).

JRH

J. Thomas, *The Callander & Oban Railway* (1966); *Reg. Hist.*, xv, 38–40.

Cambrian Railways: the largest of the independent Welsh companies absorbed into the *Great Western Railway in 1922 (see GROUPING). Despite twice going bankrupt and being loosely, if not badly, run, in 1913 it carried some 3 million passengers and almost a million tons of freight. Cambrian enterprise helped isolated watering places to grow into small thriving resorts. It enabled Welsh industries to flourish and local people to stay, live, and work in their native land rather than having to emigrate.

Railways arrived late in mid-Wales, yet the core of the Cambrian's 295 miles was completed within a decade from the time when horse-teams delivered the locomotives for the isolated 12-mile-long Llanidloes & Newtown Railway, opened in 1859. It was constructed and leased by two pioneers of mid-Wales railways: David *Davies, a local man who later became an internationally known leader of the South Wales coal industry, and his partner, Thomas *Savin, a speculator who later constructed several other lines.

In 1864 the LNR was among four small companies which formed the Cambrian Railways to keep scheming English companies out of mid-Wales. The others were the Oswestry & Newtown, Newtown & Machynlleth, and Oswestry Ellesmere & Whitchurch. The system almost doubled in length when the Aberystwyth & Welsh Coast Railway was absorbed in 1865.

The last major addition was the Mid-Wales Railway, from Moat Lane to Talyllyn Junction (with *running powers to Brecon), opened by an independent company in 1864. It was Cambrian-worked from 1888. Wrexham, by far the largest town the Cambrian served, was reached by the Wrexham & Ellesmere Railway of 1895. The Cambrian was completed by its absorption or working of three standard and two narrow-gauge *light railways of highly individual character serving lead-mining districts. The standard-gauge lines were the 6½-mile Van Railway, built in 1871; the Mawddwy Railway of similar length through the Upper Dovey valley, opened in 1866 and, after closure, revived in 1911; and the 19½-mile Tanat Valley Light Railway of 1904. The 1 ft 11½ in gauge Vale of Rheidol Railway was opened in 1902, and the 2 ft 6 in gauge Welshpool & Llanfair in 1903.

Oswestry, an English market town, became a small railway *town as well when the Cambrian chose it for its headquarters, locomotive, carriage, and wagon *works, and main *engine shed. 'Whilst many small towns have been damaged by the introduction of railways, Oswestry has wholly benefitted; its trade has increased, its borders are enlarged, its shops have improved and there is a greater air of business about its inhabitants', noted the *Gossiping Guide to Wales* in 1871.

The Cambrian saw its strength in connections with the *London & North Western Railway, 'its closest ally', at Whitchurch, Welshpool, Builth Road, and Afonwen; with the GWR at Oswestry, Buttington, and Dolgelley; and with the *Midland Railway at Three Cocks Junction. Its biggest handicap was the length of its main line from Whitchurch over which most holiday traffic ran: 96 miles to Aberystwyth and 54 miles from Dovey Junction to Pwllheli. The LNWR helped to give the Cambrian an undeserved reputation for unpunctuality because of the late handover of main-line expresses at Whitchurch.

A classic head-on collision between an express and a stopping train at Abermule in January 1921 killed 17 people, arousing nationwide concern about single-line safety that was still being discussed when the GWR took over (see ACCIDENTS; SAFETY; SINGLE LINES, WORKING OF). To GWR chagrin, the Cambrian succeeded in becoming a constituent company, securing a seat on the board, while its 4,000 shareholders got a good guaranteed annual income. No major change took place in the era of the GWR. The coast line was refurbished to handle extra summer traffic and improve *punctuality. Halts were opened on a number of lines, including the Mid-Wales through the Wye Valley, and slowly,

GWR locomotives and rolling stock replaced the Cambrian's, but it was left to *British Rail to make economies which reduced it to 140 miles, with Shrewsbury the only access since 1965.

Years of closure threats to the coast line receded after extensive repairs to Barmouth *Bridge. When it was reopened in 1986, and modernized *signalling introduced, BR declared the Cambrian to be Britain's most up-to-date rural railway.   RC

CMCR; C. P. Gasquoine, *The Story of the Cambrian* (1922).

Campbell, Lord, see LORD CAMPBELL'S ACT.

canals and river navigations

The Canal Era

Railways were preceded and then accompanied by two other transport networks: roads and inland navigations. The first carried passengers, small freight loads, and animals; the second mainly bulk freight.

Where rivers ceased to be navigable, canals took over, giving access to mines, industries, and farms. Indian cotton and Australian wool reached Lancashire and Yorkshire mills; Birmingham manufacturers found a world-wide market; South Wales exported coal and iron, and London imported timber.

Inland waterways were the products and servants of the Industrial Revolution, and from c.1750 to c.1830 were essential to its growth, notably by carrying coal to ironworks, mills, or factories, as also other home products; and copper, tin, salt, and china clay. They also spread through the countryside, to carry wheat, barley, and cheese to the towns for food and beer, and to bring back coal and groceries.

Waterways that served mining areas threw out branches, sometimes as canals, sometimes as *tramroads, laid with L-shaped plates or edge-rails, their wagons horse-hauled or dragged up inclines by horse-gins or early steam engines.

Waterway lines also grew to link rivers served by seaports: *Liverpool to *London, *Hull to *Bristol, in a great cross. Three of its arms were then themselves linked: Mersey to Humber and Severn, Thames to Severn; but from Thames to Humber, trade continued to use the sea. In *Scotland, Forth was joined to Clyde, and a sea-to-sea canal was built across the Highlands.

Canals having made the Industrial Revolution at first practicable, then dramatically successful, men and their families moved from the countryside to find work in the new towns; they had to be fed, housed, and warmed with products largely brought by water. Seaports expanded to bring raw materials and food from abroad and carry Britain's manufactures away. By 1830 Britain had created some 4,000 miles of inland navigations, not counting their tramroad branches.

They were built within a world very different from that faced by all except the earliest railway engineers and managers. A national system of land mapping was not begun until the Ordnance Survey published its 2-in to the mile *map of Kent in 1801; only in 1844, after the canal age had ended, did OS maps reach northwards to the Hull–Preston line. Instead, local *surveyors had to work from scratch.

Roads were slowly being improved with the growth of *turnpike trusts. They became of increasing use to busy engineers, but little use for transport of materials for canal building. There was, however, an expensive postal service, although not until 1784 did Royal Mail coaches carrying passengers and *mail start running.

Early locomotive railways learned from canal and tramroad practice in many ways. Their engineers had gained experience in building embankments, cuttings, aqueducts (the model for viaducts), and *tunnels, like the great embankment that crosses Burnley; Tyrley cutting in Shropshire; Pontcysyllte aqueduct over the Dee, 1,007 ft long and 124 ft high; and Strood tunnel in Kent, 3,946 yds long, now used by trains.

The best canal engineers found themselves involved in soil mechanics, as well as the technical problems of their profession. Fortunately, they were soon helped by the development of steam engines for pumping and stationary haulage. They had learned to cross wetlands with heavy weights before ever George *Stephenson had seen Chat Moss, and build steam-powered inclined planes over hilly ground before Robert *Stephenson had essayed the Stanhope & Tyne Railway.

To build a major canal demanded skills which often had to be created. Land had to be bought in long strips, which divided farms and estates which then had to be rejoined. *Landowners seldom acquiesced willingly; some accepted an enhanced price, most needed to be faced with compulsory purchase. That meant a Private Act of Parliament.

Navigation building was also expensive, far beyond the capacity of mortgage finance. A few were built by public authorities—city, county, or state; a few privately. But most needed shareholders. A market was created in canal company shares. Joint-stock companies already existed, but they were few compared to those created by canals. The economic and financial success of early trunk canals like the Trent & Mersey or the Staffordshire & Worcestershire caused the businessmen, merchants, and landowners who had financed them to be joined by smaller men, and a crowd of speculators interested only in quick capital profit. This 'Canal Mania' extended from 1789 to 1796, peaking in 1793. In those years the country's leading civil engineer, William *Jessop, appeared before House of Lords Committees on 27 waterway Bills, followed by John *Rennie with 16. So the procedures of promoting Private Bills and getting them through Committees of Lords and Commons and then Parliament itself became known to a score of engineers and a hundred firms of lawyers before the first independent railway Act.

This burst of waterway activity created the *contractor as a firm. Formerly canals had been built by small men, each undertaking a mile or two, or perhaps a lock, under the eyes of resident engineers. Only in tunnelling had specialists begun to appear. The first group prepared to undertake canal and drainage contracts anywhere were the Pinkertons, headed by John and his brother James. They first appeared in 1768 in Yorkshire, then expanded in scope and reputation. Numbering at least seven of that name, they

worked in Lancashire, the Midlands, eastern and southern England, and South Wales, and were still active in 1825. The Pinkertons had a chequered career, as befits pioneers, but on the whole they succeeded, and showed the way to the great railway contracting firms. Beside the contractors grew up a corps of professional *navvies.

Thanks to roads and canals, London, Britain's greatest city and seaport, grew. Wharves, and later wet-docks, were built to receive goods carried in or out by sea. Food such as vegetables, grain, cattle, or sheep moved into London to feed its people, along with great quantities of fodder for the horses that provided its motive power, while manure and nightsoil moved out to the surrounding market gardens.　　　　　　　　　　　　　　　　　　　　　CH

The Railway Era

Canal companies bitterly opposed railway proposals until the 1845–7 *Mania, when attractive offers persuaded many to sell out. Usually railways' motives were simultaneously to overcome opposition, and control or destroy competition. Several canals were bought for conversion, wholly or in part, while some turned themselves into railway companies, like the Thames & Medway (see SOUTH EASTERN RAILWAY) and the Manchester Bolton & Bury (see LANCASHIRE & YORKSHIRE RAILWAY). Others leased themselves to railways. The Birmingham Canal came under *London & North Western Railway control for feeding traffic to exchange depots, in return for a guaranteed dividend. The *North Staffordshire Railway bought the Trent & Mersey to penetrate other railways' territory, and the LNWR leased the *Shropshire Union partly for the same purpose. The Leeds & Liverpool and the Rochdale Canals both leased part or all of their tolls to railway consortia for a period. One canal, the Lancaster, uniquely did the opposite and for six years leased a penurious railway—illegally (see LANCASTER & CARLISLE RAILWAY). Ultimately, around 30 per cent of waterways were railway-controlled, by no means all neglected; some, in fact, were improved and traded profitably into the 20th century.

Canals had four main disadvantages, compared with railways: a multiplicity of dimensions which dictated different sized craft, from 35-ton narrow boats to 300-ton barges or larger, severely restricting through traffic; vulnerability to extreme weather, e.g. freezing or drought; statutory reliance on independent carriers; and the levying of separate tolls by each canal, again discouraging through traffic.

Canals that stayed independent endeavoured to compete. Some failed and closed. The larger, better-run waterways had some success, at the expense of rate-cutting, or traffic *agreements with railways, and maintained respectable dividends: the Oxford was still paying 8½–6½ per cent in 1868–92, and the Leeds & Liverpool 17 per cent or more in 1875–90, after which they nose-dived, although both were still declaring small ones at *nationalization in 1948. Waterways with established bank-side industries did best. They could compete with railways for short hauls and, for a while, for larger ones, where speed did not matter. But eventually trade slowly, inexorably declined. From 1845 canals were enabled to act as carriers, but they continued to be hampered by the toll system. There was little attempt until the 1880s to negotiate through rates or emulate the *Railway Clearing House. From 1888, railway-owned canals were statutorily obliged to quote through tolls, but it was all too late.

Towards the end of the century there was talk of a revival, particularly after the success of the Manchester Ship Canal (see MANCHESTER), and a 1911 Royal Commission advocated selective nationalization and enlargement, but railway opposition and government inaction dashed hopes. Meanwhile, steam power was introduced, followed by diesel-engined craft, although horse-boats persisted until the early 1950s. After World War I decline accelerated, caused not by the railways but by a common enemy: the motor lorry.

Nationalization

In 1948 most canals were nationalized under the *British Transport Commission, but in 1963 they were transferred to the government-subsidized British Waterways Board, which divided them into commercial, cruising, and 'remainder' waterways, the last comprising those that were abandoned or wholly uneconomic. These categories were substantially recognized in the Transport Act, 1968. The 'Cruiseway' network enabled the public for the first time to think of a system instead of separate canals, while the increasingly popular pleasure-cruising business could rely on a stable and growing market. Meanwhile voluntary canal support and restoration organizations had sprung up, to both of which the change gave impetus, and they have had some remarkable successes. Commercial traffic, though, is virtually limited to broad waterways leading to the Humber, the seaward end of the Manchester Ship Canal, and the tidal Thames.   GJB

J. Boughey (ed.), Hadfield's *British Canals* (1994); E. Paget-Tomlinson, *Illustrated History of Canal and River Navigations* (1993); A. Burton, *The Canal Builders* (1981); C. Hadfield, *The Canal Age* (1993).

Cannon Street station, see LONDON STATIONS.

Canterbury & Whitstable Railway. This was the first railway in the world to convey both passengers and freight regularly by mechanical power.

Canterbury people had long been dissatisfied with their means of getting coal by road or by water from the coast. In 1825 some of them took powers to construct a 6-mile railway to the port of Whitstable. It was laid down by William *James, but he underestimated its cost, and George *Stephenson became the company's engineer. It required gradients as steep as 1 in 28 and a tunnel nearly half a mile long.

Opened on 4 May 1830, it was worked chiefly by stationary engines, but on a level stretch of one mile by the locomotive *Invicta*. That machine failed, however, and from 1839 traction was by stationary engines and horses. In 1844 it was leased to the *South Eastern Railway, which reached Canterbury in 1846 and then restored locomotives to the Whitstable line. The SER purchased the railway in 1853. It was closed to all traffic in 1952.   JS

R. B. Fellows, *A History of the Canterbury & Whitstable Railway* (1930); I. Maxted, *The Canterbury & Whitstable Railway* (1970).

capital. Before a railway can earn any revenue from carrying traffic, considerable sums have to be sunk in building and equipping its route. This requirement for a large fixed capital distinguished the first public railways from most contemporary industrial ventures, where investment in plant or working capital could usually be built up gradually from a small initial commitment, using profits to expand the capacity of the business. However, when railways began to emerge in Britain, the *canals already provided examples of highly capitalized transport undertakings, and the similarity of the funding requirements of the two modes was reinforced by the fact that railways made use of the same parliamentary authorization and incorporation processes (see PROMOTION PROCEDURE). These included the concept of a statutorily defined capital, which was readily applicable to railway companies: the total amount an undertaking was entitled to raise by virtue of its parliamentary powers determined its *authorized* capital. This definition also included additional means of authorization, such as Board of *Trade certificates.

Authorized capital encompassed two types of funds: shares and loans. Parliament almost invariably required a new railway's share capital to equal its estimated construction costs, and borrowing was initially envisaged as a means of enabling companies to deal with short-term delays in raising share capital or to provide for cost overruns. However, loan capital quickly became a permanent feature of British railway finance, and borrowing powers were soon standardized at one-third of authorized share capital. The same proportions were generally applied when companies sought additional financial powers, either because initial estimates had been inadequate or because extra funds were needed for extensions or improvements.

The difference between shares and loans was the most fundamental distinction in railway capital: shareholders were the owners of a company, and their shares represented individual portions of the capital embodied in the undertaking. Proprietors were entitled to a proportion of any profit remaining after all other expenses and charges had been met, and this was distributed as dividends. There was a legal distinction between shares and stock: shares were denominated in specific amounts and separately numbered, whereas stock could be represented in any amount. Stock was created when the requisite majority of proprietors agreed that an undertaking's shares should be consolidated; as this provision was applied in most large railway companies, their equity capital was formally classified as stock, and in many instances listed on the markets as 'consols'.

Unlike the owners of shares or stock, lenders had no proprietary rights: they simply made money available for a fixed or indefinite period, and in return were entitled to an agreed rate of interest. Because these payments were predictable and were more secure than dividends, companies usually found it easy to raise money in this way, so borrowing powers were generally exercised more fully than powers to issue shares: indeed, during the 1830s and early 1840s there were several significant instances of borrowing beyond authorized powers. Railway Acts also specified the manner in which loan capital should be raised; again, there were temptations to exceed powers, but legislation defined two main forms of borrowing: a mortgage, which was secured against the revenue and assets of the undertaking; and a bond or debenture, which in case of default entitled the lender to recover an additional penal sum. If a company failed to meet its obligations to its mortgagees, they were entitled to have receivers appointed to run the railway until its debts were discharged: however, default did not entitle lenders to seize a company's assets.

In the early stages of railway development, most borrowing was negotiated through separate transactions, but companies soon appreciated the disadvantages of having a multiplicity of loans outstanding for varying periods and on differing terms. While mortgages and debenture bonds were transferable, again their form required individual transactions, making it more difficult to maintain a ready market in such securities. Redeemable loan issues were therefore generally superseded by perpetual fixed-interest debenture stocks, which could circulate easily on the stock markets. By 1872 the capital funded in this way exceeded all other forms of railway borrowing, and by the end of the century debenture stock accounted for 96 per cent of loan capital.

Loans, whatever their form, always retained priority over shares in the distribution of earnings, but the convergence between the two forms of capital which was demonstrated in the emergence of debenture stocks was also found in the development of alternative share classifications. These were largely prompted by the restrictions on borrowing powers, which forced companies to adopt other devices to overcome difficulties in raising equity capital. Such issues carried special privileges in order to make them more attractive to investors, and though various terms and descriptions were employed the two most general classes of security were preference and guaranteed shares, both of which entitled holders to a fixed percentage dividend before any distribution was made to ordinary shareholders. Preferred dividends were usually contingent upon a railway's earning sufficient profits in each accounting period to meet its obligations on such shares; in some cases, however, the entitlement was cumulative, and any shortfall was carried forward to be set against future earnings. Guaranteed shares offered even greater security: their dividends ranked before those of preference shares, and remained a perpetual prior charge if for any reason they were not met in any accounting period. Guaranteed shares were therefore often issued when one railway took over another on the basis of a fixed future revenue.

The sum of the various classes of security which a company had issued by virtue of its parliamentary and any other powers established its *created* capital. This could not exceed its authorized capital, and was generally less, but in most instances there was also a difference between the nominal value of the created capital and the amount a company had actually received. The latter figure, its *issued* capital, reflected three adjustments: the balance of securities which, while created, had not yet been disposed of to the public; instalments on recent issues which had not yet been called up from holders or which were in arrears; and any difference between the cash value of an issue and the amount on which dividends or interest were calculated. Such nominal additions to or deductions from capital were frequently made to facilitate stock consolidation or conversion operations: for example, when the *Grand Junction Railway absorbed the Chester & Crewe Railway in 1840, the latter's £50 shares were replaced with an equal number of £25 GJR shares. This left the amalgamated company with a nominal capital some £120,000 less than had actually been received from shareholders, but, because the GJR dividend was higher, former CCR holdings maintained an equivalent earning capacity despite their lower nominal value.

Another source of nominal adjustments was the 'watering' of stock, which became increasingly common from the 1880s onwards. The *Regulation of Railways Act, 1868, had given companies permissive powers to divide their ordinary capital so that part received a preferred dividend; however, the Act required this to be done within existing totals, for example by replacing each £100 of equity with £50 preferred and £50 deferred stock. Several railways instead subsequently obtained authorization to increase the nominal value of their capital as part of this process, usually in a way which aligned the resultant total value more closely with the current Stock Exchange price. The most significant of these conversions was the *Midland's one-for-one issue in 1897, which inflated the company's nominal capital by more than £34 million and made it the most highly capitalized of all the pre-*Grouping undertakings.

The final stage in defining a railway's capital was to correct the total of its issued capital by the amount of any premiums or discounts at the time of issue. In principle such adjustments were similar to nominal additions or deductions, since they represented a difference between the amount actually received and the value on which dividends or interest were calculated; in practice, however, they were usually small in relation to total capital, reflecting minor fluctuations in the terms on which capital was retailed rather than the wholesale adjustments that were embodied in nominal additions or deductions. *Total receipts on capital account*, adjusted in this way, were then brought to account against total expenditure; though the two were expected broadly to correspond, and companies gauged their capital issues accordingly, it was virtually impossible to achieve an exact match. While a favourable balance might suggest financial prudence, significant surpluses implied either unnecessarily inflated loan charges or premature demands on shareholders. Since a deficit on capital account could generally be covered temporarily by favourable balances elsewhere in a company's books, such as undistributed revenue reserves, superannuation or savings funds, or accumulated depreciation provisions, such deficits became increasingly common among even the soundest companies. However, in some cases (for example, the Manchester & Milford or *Great Central Railways) a persistent excess of capital expenditure over receipts was a symptom of chronic financial weakness, representing expensive short-term indebtedness to bankers or suppliers.

See also FINANCING OF RAILWAYS; INVESTMENT IN RAILWAYS.

MCR

S. A. Broadbridge, *Studies in Railway Expansion and the Capital Market in England, 1825–1873* (1970), 64–76; R. J. Irving, *The North Eastern Railway Company 1870–1914* (1976), 144–57; C. H. Newton, *Railway Accounts* (1930), 30–41; W. W. Wall, *How to Invest in Railways* (1903), 28–44.

Cardiff. From 1766 the lords of the manor of this ancient town at the mouth of the River Taff were the Earls (later Marquesses) of Bute. The opening of the Glamorganshire Canal in 1794 brought iron, and presently coal, from Merthyr Tydfil and the Taff valley for shipment, and the river quays grew seriously congested. The 2nd Marquess built a dock, opened in 1839. The canal was by then also inade-

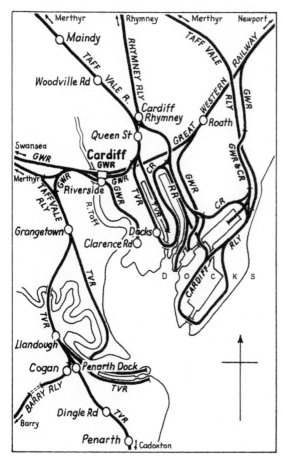

Cardiff, 1922

quate and the *Taff Vale Railway was opened from Merthyr in 1841, affording an alternative.

Merthyr, Newport, and *Swansea were then all larger than Cardiff. But its population trebled in 1851–71, and by 1881 it was the largest town in Wales. The quantity of coal shipped grew relentlessly after 1850. A second dock, the East Bute Dock, was completed in 1859, and the Bute Trustees were authorized to build a third, but they delayed its completion until 1887.

Railways had played a great part in this development. The TVR, with its rival the *Rhymney Railway (reaching Cardiff in 1858), served the port well until they too became choked with traffic. A harbour and dock at Penarth, two miles away, were opened in 1859–65, with a railway leased to the TVR. The broad-*gauge *South Wales Railway served Cardiff from 1850 onwards, but it handled little mineral traffic until the coal and iron masters secured its conversion to standard gauge in 1872.

In 1882 some coalowners, angered by the delays in shipment, secured powers to build the *Rhondda & Swansea Bay Railway, to take their traffic away from Cardiff altogether. Two years later others got authority to make a new port and dock at Barry, eight miles from Cardiff, served by a new *Barry Railway coming down from the Rhondda. Opened in 1889, it established itself very quickly. This enterprise necessarily damaged Cardiff. But the South Wales coal output was still increasing (doubling in 1889–1913). There was traffic enough to keep all these railways, harbours, and docks busy.

In the inter-war years the economy of Cardiff and the coalfield began to change. In 1922–38 the annual production of South Wales coal fell from 50 million tons to 35 million. Cardiff was hit with particular force because it had no important manufacturing industries—not even shipbuilding, unlike *Middlesbrough, Sunderland, or *Glasgow.

At the 1923 *Grouping Cardiff's local railways, with their docks, were incorporated into the *Great Western Railway, which was frequently alleged to neglect them thereafter, not always justly.

The decline of the coal industry inevitably affected the railways. The GWR closed some 25 miles of line to passenger traffic in the Cardiff valleys, and further reductions followed under *British Rail (see WALES). But the former Taff Vale and Rhymney main lines remained, carrying regular *interval services, subsidized by government grants amounting to nearly £2 million in 1974, including some reopenings. Improvements and new developments in Cardiff itself and the district to north and west are contemplated in a Cardiff Region Public Transport Study, issued in 1994.

JS

Reg. Hist., xii; M. J. Daunton, *Coal Metropolis: Cardiff 1870–1914* (1977).

Cardiff Railway. The Bute Docks Company (see CARDIFF) made repeated efforts, from 1888 if not earlier, to participate in railway operations by securing arrangements, of different kinds, with established companies like the *Taff Vale and the *Rhymney. When all these had failed, the Docks

Company gained Parliament's sanction in 1897 to changing its name to the Cardiff Railway, and to building new lines of its own from Cardiff northwards to link up with the Taff Vale at Treforest and near Pontypridd. The total system actually brought into use amounted to 11½ miles, though the company also owned 120 miles of railway line within the Bute Docks. It had its own locomotives and two steam rail-cars. Once constituted, it was in protracted dispute with neighbouring railways, involving profitless litigation.

The Cardiff was almost the only coal-carrying railway in South Wales that was a financial failure. Its Ordinary shareholders were paid a dividend of 1 per cent in 1921, when the Rhymney's were still getting 9 per cent. Although its dock interests were substantial, it seems strange that the Cardiff figured as a constituent company of the new *Great Western created by the Railways Act of 1921, when the much larger *Brecon & Merthyr became no more than a subsidiary one.   JS

Reg. Hist., xii, 128–30, 142–4.

Cardwell, Edward, Viscount (1813–86), politician. The son of a Liverpool merchant, he was educated at Winchester and Balliol College, Oxford; he was an MP 1842–74, and president, Board of *Trade 1852–5. He was chiefly responsible for the Railway and Canal Traffic Act, 1854 (often called 'Cardwell's Act'), obliging the companies to afford the public 'reasonable facilities' for the receipt, carriage, and delivery of traffic, and forbidding them to give any customer an *undue preference.

Though it did not afford complainants satisfactory legal remedies, the Act established the criteria by which the companies' conduct in these very important matters came to be tested, and it pointed the way to much subsequent legislation. In 1912 it was remarked that 'there is hardly a railway traffic case that comes into the courts in which it is not only referred to but is the keystone of the argument'.

Cardwell took no leading part in railway business again. He is chiefly remembered for the far-reaching army reforms he carried through while Secretary for War, 1868–74. He was created Viscount in 1874.   JS

DNB; W. A. Robertson, Combination among Railway Companies (1912), 17; E. Cleveland-Stevens, English Railways (1915), ch. 8.

Carlisle, a historic garrisoned town on the Scottish border, developed a new frontier role between the railways of England and Scotland. By the dawn of the *'Railway Age' it had already become an important textile manufacturing centre, linked to the outside world by the Carlisle Canal, opened in 1823. With the trains of seven companies operating into Carlisle Citadel station from 1876 to 1922, Carlisle became perhaps the most interesting and varied of Britain's railway centres.

Despite its important location on two of the Anglo-Scottish trunk route systems, Carlisle's first railways were of regional origin. The *Newcastle & Carlisle Railway opened into the city in 1836, and the *Maryport & Carlisle in 1843. The former was the successor to a proposal for a cross-country canal that dated back to the 1790s. All goods

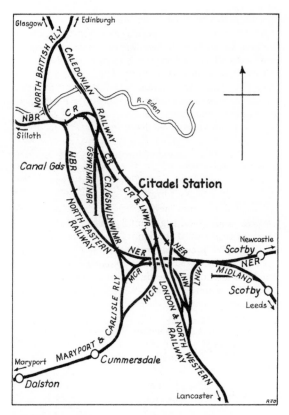

Carlisle, 1922

brought into Carlisle were liable to a toll levied by the Corporation which was commuted to a fixed annual payment by the railways.

The *Lancaster & Carlisle (1846) and the *Caledonian Railways (1848) completed the first Scottish trunk route, meeting at Citadel station. Trains of the *Glasgow & South Western Railway entered Carlisle from 1850, followed by the Port Carlisle Railway, after its conversion from the canal, in 1854. The latter was taken over by the *North British Railway when the Waverley route was extended from Hawick in 1862. *Competition between companies for the Scottish traffic was intense, with obstructive tactics from the *West Coast partners (*London & North Western Railway and CR) leading the other companies to propose new lines. The inadequate layout and facilities became acutely overloaded in the 1860s and 1870s; two railway level crossings added an element of danger, eventually resulting in a bad *accident in 1870.

The construction of the *Midland Railway's *Settle & Carlisle line (opened in 1876) finally necessitated the major reorganization of Carlisle's railways. New passenger approaches and goods avoiding lines were built, level crossings abolished, and Citadel station greatly enlarged (1880), with a new island platform and seven acres of overall roof. All this was largely paid for by the Midland as its price for entry to Carlisle, though the benefits were mainly to the West Coast partners. There remained, however, the multiplication of traffic and locomotive facilities which necessitated much wasteful, and delaying, interchange trip working and shunting. The many yards (11 in 1922), seven goods stations, coal yards, and private sidings probably required between 30 and 40 locomotives, and several times as many crews to work them round the clock. Only limited rationalization was attempted after the *Grouping. The problems remained until 1963 when Kingmoor *marshalling yard opened, but it was already obsolescent, and contraction began as early as 1972.

The railways fundamentally affected life in Carlisle. The 1901 census recorded 2,072 men working 'in Railways'. With related industries they accounted for over one in five working men as local engineering firms had become railway suppliers. Cowans Sheldon was the best known for its manufacture of cranes and turntables for railways the world over. The works closed in the mid-1980s but a design unit continues in Carlisle. Tweedy, later part of Tyers, made *signalling equipment for local railways.

The railways from early days occupied the Caldew valley below the walls of the old city, separating it from its industrial suburb of Dentonholme. Access was by a tunnel under Citadel station until 1877 when the City Corporation opened the Victoria viaduct over the north end of the station.

Although Anglo-Scottish expresses worked through Carlisle from the start, Citadel was a terminal station for all the pre-Grouping companies which worked into it. The frontier role remained until the end of steam with many trains changing engines. Carlisle's role as an operating centre has greatly declined since, although its power box controls over 70 miles of the West Coast main line. PWR

P. W. Robinson, *Rail Centres: Carlisle* (1986); *Reg. Hist.*, xiv (1983), ch. 4.

Carmarthenshire Railway. This was the earliest company promoted to work a railway and dock as parts of one undertaking. Incorporated in 1802 to bring limestone down from quarries at Castell-y-Garreg to a dock 16 miles away at Llanelly, it was opened in 1804 or 1805, using edge rails mounted on stone blocks (see EARLY IRON RAILWAYS), and worked by horses. Though it handled a considerable traffic, the company went into liquidation in 1844. In 1875 the new Llanelly & Mynydd Mawr Railway purchased what remained of its rights and laid a new line, suitable for locomotives, largely on the old track bed. JS

Reg. Hist., xii, 223–5; B. Baxter, *Stone Blocks and Iron Rails* (1966), 224.

carriage, composite, a *carriage which has segregated and identified accommodation for more than one *class of passenger. In the early days, the disparity in standards meant that the combination of first- and third-class would have been unthinkable, but by the 1870s composite carriages were well established.

The pre-*Grouping railways' fondness for *through carriages from main centres to a variety of destinations sometimes led to the complications of tri-composite vehicles, with accommodation for three classes, separate lavatories for each, and a brake van. Until 1928 and the introduction of third-class sleeping facilities, there were the so-called composite *sleeping cars, with first-class sleeping berths and seated accommodation for third-class. The last new locomotive-hauled composite carriages entered service on *British Rail during 1964. The decline in demand for first-class facilities, other than on InterCity and prime commuter routes, has seen a rapid fall in the number of composite carriages in recent years. MLH

carriage building. In the early days of passenger carriages, the resemblance of their bodies to stage-coaches was not merely imitative. Many were supplied by workshops that built road vehicles, a notable example being Joseph Wright, originally an operator of stage-coaches, whose Metropolitan Company (later the Metropolitan Railway Carriage & Wagon Co.) established a factory at Saltley, Birmingham, which by 1847 had 800 work-people. The Midlands became a centre of carriage building, another notable firm in the area being the Birmingham Railway Carriage & Wagon Co., founded in 1854. Such contractors prospered from exporting rolling stock, as well as supplying it to home railways. Railway companies soon began to construct their own carriages at centres that were often separate from the locomotive works, and managed by a carriage and wagon superintendent. Principal workshops in terms of output were: *Swindon (*Great Western Railway); Wolverton (*London & North Western Railway); *Derby (*Midland Railway); Newton Heath (*Lancashire & Yorkshire Railway); and Stratford (*Great Eastern Railway).

Carriage building followed the crafts and practices of the road vehicle industry. Workmen were skilled in woodworking and smithy work. Until at least the 1920s, individual carriages were constructed by a team who assembled all the woodwork and carried out all fitting. Drawing on the experience of the motor-car industry, production was thereafter arranged for sectionalized construction at workstations, with gangs of workmen engaged on different stages of assembly.

Iron and steel components such as *wheels, axles, and underframe fittings were often purchased from contractors, as were complete bogies. Some specialized carriages such as catering vehicles tended to be ordered from carriage and wagon manufacturers.

The typical Victorian carriage comprised an almost entirely wooden body, mounted on a wooden underframe with iron or steel running and drawgear. The body framework was usually of imported oak or teak, with teak or mahogany exterior body panelling and oak or deal roof boards, covered in canvas. The external finishes were ornate and time-consuming, several coats of protective varnish being applied. Rather than complete repainting, carriages were touched up and revarnished at intervals. By 1914, steel panelling was used for cladding the body, sometimes with steel roof panels. All-steel underframes had replaced wood,

Date	Type	Length & weight	Details	Cost per vehicle (£)
1905	GNR clerestory dining car (12 whl)	64' 2½" 40 tons	Gas-lit, incl. kitchen and pantry	2,980
1907	GNR/NER Jt Stock dining car (12 whl)	65' 6" 41 tons	Elec-lit, incl. kitchen and pantry	2,304
1924	LNER triplet articulated restaurant car set	various	Elec-lit, incl. kitchen, pantry, with elec. cooking equipment	11,506 for three cars
1931	LNER dining car	61' 6"	Elec.-lit, incl. kitchen, pantry, with elec. cooking equipment	5,223
1922	ECJS twin artic. sleeping car	113' 6" overall	Elec-lit, 20 first-class berths	12,628 for two cars
1923	LNER first-class sleeping car	61' 6"	Elec-lit, 10 first-class berths	5,917 each
1906	GNR first-class corridor brake	58' 6"	Elec-lit, 16 seats	1,580
1922	GNR first-class corridor brake	61' 6"	Elec-lit, 20 seats, compound bolster bogies	4,554
1927	LNER first-class corridor brake	61' 6"	Elec-lit, 30 seats, compound bolster bogies	3,440
1936	LNER first-class corridor brake	61' 6"	Elec-lit, 18 seats, compound bolster bogies	2,600
1906	ECJS third-class corridor	53' 6"	Elec-lit, 42 seats	1,547
1914	GNR third-class corridor	58' 6"	Elec-lit, 48 seats	1,565
1921	GNR third-class corridor	52' 6"	Elec-lit, 48 seats	3,487
1923	LNER third-class corridor	61' 6"	Elec-lit, 48 seats	3,571*

* As part of an order for 49 such vehicles built by company's workshops

| 1935 | LNER third-class corridor | 61' 6" | Elec-lit, 64 seats | 2,400* |

* As part of an order for 60 such vehicles built by contractors

| 1935–6 | LNER third-class corridor | 61' 6" | Elec-lit, 48 seats* | 2,707 (Met Cam) 2,797 (BRCW) 2,800 (Cravens) |

* Policy change to three-a-side seating

| 1947 | LNER third-class corridor | 63' 0" | Elec-lit, 42 seats | 5,732* |

* As part of an order for 263 such vehicles built by contractors

| 1911 | GNR twin artic. third-class suburban non-corridor | 88' 0" overall | Gas-lit, 192 seats | 1,680 for two cars |

Comparative costs of railway carriages from 1890: Great Northern, East Coast Joint Stock, and LNER carriages

Date	Type	Length & weight	Details	Cost per vehicle (£)
1925	LNER quint. artic. third-class suburban non-corridor	225' 0" overall	Elec-lit, 436 seats	7,800 for five cars
1935	LNER five-car suburban non-corridor (first, second, and third-class accommodation)	54' 1½" each	Elec-lit, 424 seats	7,500 for five cars

ECJS East Coast Joint Stock (GNR, NER, & North British Ry) LNER London & North Eastern Ry
GNR   Great Northern Ry   NER   North Eastern Ry

or wooden main members plated with iron or steel. During the 1920s external paintwork was simplified while the traditionally intricate varnished and polished wood of the interiors gave way to painted woodwork and, later, to leathercloth and plastic finishes.

The decline in exports of rolling stock to British-influenced railways, combined with the completion of the extensive rolling-stock orders of the *British Railways *Modernization Plan, caused contraction of the industry by the late 1960s. Manufacture had become concentrated on all-steel or alloy integral vehicles whose assembly required only semi-skilled workers.   MLH

carriage lighting. Early illumination was by *oil lamps in pots lowered when lit into the compartment roof, although the *Great Western Railway, for example, provided no lighting until 1842. Burning rape oil, the light generated by the pot lamps was feeble. Two lights were supposed to be placed in each compartment, according to a Board of *Trade regulation. Experiments began with gas lighting in 1857 but the first railway to use low-pressure coal gas lighting regularly was the *North London, as from 1862. The gas was stored in large containers in the brake vans.

Improvements in lighting were slow to come. The American-built *Pullman cars used from 1874 had effective kerosene lamps with Argand burners separate from the reservoirs. Meanwhile, carriage lighting using compressed oil gas stored in cylinders, usually beneath the vehicles, was invented by Julius Pintsch in the 1870s. It and similar systems were adopted by British railways later in that decade. Compartments had fishtail-jet burners in globes.

The use of electric lighting was pioneered in *Beatrice*, a Pullman car used between *Victoria and *Brighton on the *London Brighton & South Coast Railway. It appears to have been the first railway carriage in the world lit by electricity and, with three other similarly illuminated Pullmans, was demonstrated to the press on 14 October 1881. The current came from Fauré cells slung under the cars, and the Edison lamps had bamboo filaments. But the charging plant for the cells was expensive. Pullman adopted the Pintsch oil-gas lighting in 1885 for most of its cars, the exception being

the Brighton service where new cars in 1888 had electric current generated by an axle-driven dynamo located in a van which ran with the Pullmans.

Early electric train-lighting was not always satisfactory and shed a yellowish or orange light. An efficient battery lighting system was patented by J. Stone in 1894, later improved considerably by double batteries, charged by axle-driven dynamos. Gas lighting remained popular on some lines and was given a new lease of life by the invention of the incandescent mantle. Serious *fires in train accidents were caused by escaping gas and encouraged the retreat from gas lighting after 1914.

Manufacturers' electric lighting systems—and the railways' own versions—were universal for new carriage construction after 1918 and altered very little for over 40 years. Most interior lighting consisted of ceiling-mounted bulbs, increasingly augmented by reading lights. Fluorescent lighting was an obvious attraction for carriages although early equipment was heavy as a high-frequency current was required. It was used to a very limited extent before lighter, transistorized equipment became available in the late 1950s. Gas lighting remained until the early 1950s. *British Railways continued to build new carriages with tungsten filament lighting until the early 1970s.   MLH

carriages. Rail vehicles carrying fare-paying passengers date back to 1807 and the Oystermouth Railway, later the *Swansea & Mumbles. Its passengers were conveyed in horse-drawn coaches with flanged wheels.

A purpose-built rail carriage named *Experiment* ran on the *Stockton & Darlington Railway. It comprised a chassis, basically that of a *tramroad wagon, upon which was built a coach body with a door at each end, windows, and a table, seats and soft furnishings inside. Its use on the opening of the SDR in 1825 was short-lived but this was the first occasion on which passengers rode behind steam on a public railway.

With the opening of the *Liverpool & Manchester Railway in 1830 came regular passenger services using carriages owned by the operator. These pioneering carriages for first- and second-class passengers were light, small, and with

Weight and earning capacity of some British main-line carriages 1890–1990

	1890 Six wheeled corridor and non-corridor		1910 Bogie; corridor		1930 Bogie; corridor		1990 Bogie; open layout	
							First Class (Mark 4 stock)	Standard class (Mark 4 stock)
	First class	Third class	First class	Third class	First class	Third class		
Weight (empty) in tons	GER (6-whl, non-corridor) 13–14 ECJS (6-whl, corridor) 1893 18	GER 13 ECJS (1893) 17¼	LBSCR 23 GER 27½ GNR (1912) 34	GER 26½ GWR (1908) 27 GNR 28	LNER 32	LNER 31¼ GWR (1933) 32¼	39	39
Cost	GWR (1895 similar spec. to GER) £400–450 MR similar spec. £641 GER N/A	MR similar spec. £524 GER N/A	LBSCR £1,485 GNR £1,894 GER N/A	LBSCR £775 GWR £1,250 GNR £1,497	LNER £3,400	LNER £2,965 GWR (1933) £3,600	£275,000 approx. (1986 prices)	£275,000 approx. (1986 prices)
No. of seats provided	GER 24/30 ECJS (1893) 16	GER 60 ECJS (1893) 30	GER 36 LBSCR 26 GNR 28	GER 56 LBSCR 66 GWR 56 GNR 42	LNER 36	LNER 56 GWR 64	46	74
Deadweight hauled per passenger (cwt)	GER 9.1–10.8 ECJS 22.5	GER 4.4 ECJS 11.5	GER 15.1 LBSCR 17.6 GNR 24.2	LBSCR 7.0 GER 9.4 GWR 9.6 GNR 13.3	LNER 18	GWR 10.1 LNER 11.1	17.0	11.3
Cost per place	£13–16 based on GWR costs £21–27 based on MR costs	£8 GER based on MR costs £17 ECJS based on MR costs	LBSCR £57 GNR £68	LBSCR £20 GWR £22 GNR £36	LNER £94	LNER £53 GWR £56	£5,978	£3,716

Key: ECJS   East Coast Joint Stock   GNR   Great Northern Ry   LBSCR   London Brighton & South Coast Ry
         GER   Great Eastern Ry   GWR   Great Western Ry   MR   Midland Ry

compartments often no more than 5 ft in height. The bodies were the equivalent of three or so stage-coaches on a railway chassis. Third-class passengers were conveyed in little more than goods wagons, without glazing and sometimes lacking a roof or seats. In the worst cases, passengers stood and rainwater drained through holes in the floor. From the roofless road carriage came the nickname of Stanhopes for third-class—and the even more basic fourth-class—carriages.

Early developments brought improved suspension and patent screw couplings to link vehicles together more effectively and to reduce jerking from the chain couplings previously used. By the mid-1830s, dumb *buffers were replaced by those fixed to the underframe and properly sprung. Spoked iron *wheels initially employed for carriages were generally outmoded by 1850, in favour of the *Mansell pattern, in which the wheel comprised a cast-iron core and rim bolted to wooden segments. Earlier carriages tended to be four-wheelers but six-wheeled stock was preferred by the *Great Western Railway. At first, not all carriages had *brakes. Those so fitted were of a screw type, manually operated by a guard who occupied a box seat on the roof, to operate them and accompany the luggage. A separate brake carriage at the end of the train began to be provided from the 1850s.

Carriage bodies were chiefly of wood (see TIMBER, USE OF) although some had *papier mâché* exterior panels. Iron construction was pioneered by the GWR. First-class carriage interiors followed stage-coach practice, with cloth upholstery, armrests, and headrests. From the late 1830s, with the conveyance of mails by train, there came combined mail and bed carriages, a good example of these being Queen Adelaide's saloon of 1842 which is in the NRM. This was also the first genuine *royal saloon.

Oil lighting was provided in first and second class from the 1840s while separate *smoking carriages were generally introduced from about 1860. Saloon carriages were in favour from the 1850s for family and party travel and inspections by railway officials. By 1860, the typical carriage was 27 ft long, weighed eight tons, and ran on four wheels. The adoption of gas lighting (see CARRIAGE LIGHTING) and continuous, mechanically operated train braking were the major developments in this period.

Many of the significant features in carriage design date

from the 1870s. There was the liberating effect of allowing third-class passengers to travel on all trains. The abolition of second class by the *Midland Railway in 1875 had the effect of improving the specifications of third-class carriages. The limitations of a small, four-wheeled vehicle were overcome by the introduction of eight-wheeled bogie carriages from 1871, the pioneer in regular operation being the *Festiniog Railway. Bogie vehicles permitted higher seating capacity and were soon adopted by main-line railways, too. Before long, there were 12-wheeled carriages, particularly for *sleeping and dining cars. One important influence was the importation from 1874 of day and sleeping cars built by *Pullman in the USA. The first regular *restaurant car service on British railways began during 1879.

Apart from bogie vehicles, from the late 1860s some railway companies used six-wheelers with radial axles or those on swivelling frames—the Cleminson principle. Rigid eight-wheelers were favoured by the *Metropolitan, GWR, and *Great Northern Railway, some engineers resisting bogie stock until the 1890s.

The typical main-line carriage of the 1890s was bogied, featuring a clerestory roof, gas lighting, and lavatories. Electric lighting was still largely experimental. Meanwhile, effective continuous and automatic braking and passenger *communication systems had been standardized. Movement between vehicles in a train was made possible by the use of gangway connections from 1882. The first through-out corridor train was operated by the GWR between Paddington and Birkenhead in 1892. For secondary services, four-wheeled stock was constructed until at least 1900, the very last being some built for the *Caledonian Railway in 1922.

Footwarmers had been the sole form of *train heating until the 1890s. Thereafter, carriages were heated by steam supplied from the engine through pipes to radiators under seats. Although screw couplings continued to be used by some railways until *nationalization, from 1889 others adopted the Gould centre coupler and Pullman-type gangway. Their effect was to improve passenger safety in accidents as telescoping was resisted by the more rigid coupler and greater strength of the Pullman gangway.

Clerestory roofs were more expensive and not as strong as elliptical roofs, which made their appearance from the 1900s. Steel (see IRON AND STEEL, USE OF) underframes became the rule from the late 1900s, at first retaining wooden headstocks. Immediately before World War I the concern at the incidence of train fires led to use of fire-resistant materials. All-steel carriages were rare, but the risk of *fire was reduced by the adoption of electric lighting and patented fireproofed flooring.

Most of the pre-1914 improvements were consolidated after 1923 in the designs of the *'Big Four' companies, which otherwise were noticeably conservative. There was limited use of all-steel carriages by the *London & North Eastern and *London Midland & Scottish Railways in the late 1920s, but until 1951 carriages were normally of composite construction with wooden body framing and steel panelling. The main developments in the inter-war period

were the introduction of third-class sleeping cars from 1928, increased use of centre corridor 'open' vehicles, and *buffet cars. The late 1930s saw a number of innovations in passenger facilities and the placing in service of specialized carriages for prestige services. The all-steel passenger carriages built in quantity by *British Railways from 1951 had separate underframes and bodies and are referred to as Mark 1s. Integrally constructed vehicles, Mark 2s, did not enter full-scale production on BR until the mid-1960s, later versions having full air-conditioning. Stock of 23 m length used in High Speed Train diesel units, or as locomotive-hauled vehicles, is classified as Mark 3 and those marshalled in the IC 225 electric units as Mark 4 (see SPEED).

The effect of the improvements in 1880–1914 was greatly to change the earning capacity of main-line carriages, for the new facilities and requirements added to the tare weight and also reduced their payload. The trend towards higher speeds meant that within 20 years express passenger locomotives needed to be more powerful to haul heavier trains faster, thereby increasing operating costs.

Little changed in the years to nationalization, although some 1930s luxury stock had additional features such as pressure ventilation, thus adding to the deadweight per passenger figure. The design of the BR standard Mark 1 stock sacrificed cost and weight for the greatly improved safety of all-steel construction. The Mark 2 integrally constructed carriages improved the deadweight per passenger figure, which was comparable with that of the carriages of 1910, but the later batches featured *air-conditioning and were some 1½ tons heavier. The Mark 4 stock gains by having electrical power supplied from the locomotive, and the standard class has higher density seating than in the Mark 2s.

Little analysis has been done to relate weight and cost to earning capacity. The accompanying table covers the most significant period, 1890–1990.

See also CARRIAGE BUILDING; CARRIAGE, COMPOSITE; CLASS DISTINCTIONS; SLIP CARRIAGES; COMPARTMENT; DUCKET; OBSERVATION CAR.   MLH

C. Hamilton Ellis, *Railway Carriages in the British Isles 1830–1914* (1965); A. J. Hill, *Presidential Address* to the Institution of Locomotive Engineers, 12 Jan. 1912; D. Jenkinson, *British Railway Carriages of the 20th Century* (1988–90); J. Johnson and R. A. Long, *British Railways Engineering 1948–80* (1981).

Castle, Barbara, see BRITISH RAILWAYS.

catering, train, see RESTAURANT CAR; BUFFET CAR.

catering on stations, see REFRESHMENT ROOMS.

cattle, see LIVESTOCK TRAFFIC.

Cawdor, Lord, see GREAT WESTERN RAILWAY.

cement traffic. Railways had a close association with the cement industry. Few stations were without advertisements for Ketton cement or Earles', which would be sold from a merchant's store in the yard.

For centuries the industry had comprised small kilns near suitable mineral deposits. In 1877 T. R. *Crampton patented a rotary kiln, but it was not commercially successful until an American version was built in 1900 at Northfleet, Kent.

Thereafter a number of large works were established in the Medway basin, and in other chalk or lime-bearing areas.

They relied on rail for coal, and for despatching the bagged finished product in covered vans. After World War II special pressure-discharge tank *wagons were developed for carriage in bulk, and some large works adopted *merry-go-round coal deliveries. In 1982, for instance, Northfleet received over a million tons annually, and despatched over 1½ million tons of cement. Several lines which would otherwise have closed remained partly open, such as the Weardale branch to the Eastgate works (Durham), the Rugby–Marton Junction–Southam line for works at Bilton and Southam (Warwickshire), and the Watlington branch as far as Chinnor in the Chilterns. But despite block trains and new or improved sidings, in the 1980s *road transport started taking over, one of the last works being at Clitheroe (Lancashire) in 1994, where only a few years earlier access had been upgraded, leaving rail traffic flows only from Hope (Derbyshire), Dunbar (East Lothian), and Ketton (Rutland). GJB

Reg. Hist., ii, iv, viii, ix, x, xiii; K. Hudson, Building Materials (1972); B. D. Stoyel and R. W. Kidner, The Cement Railways of Kent (1990).

cemeteries. The huge growth of London and the large industrial towns in the early 19th century raised difficulties in arranging for the hygienic burial of the dead. Public alarm on this matter expressed itself strongly during and after the epidemic of cholera in 1848–9. There came to be strong support for the idea of laying out large new cemeteries well beyond the built-up urban areas, served by railways that could convey the dead bodies and the mourners. A London Necropolis & National Mortuary Company got an Act in 1852, authorizing it to acquire land for this purpose at Brookwood, west of Woking, beside the *London & South Western Railway's main line. The cemetery was opened on 7 November 1854; interments began there in the following week. The funeral trains started out from a station in London adjoining the LSWR's terminus at Waterloo, the mourners' carriages and the engines that hauled them being provided by that company, whilst the Necropolis company supplied its own hearse vans.

From 1854 to 1900 a train (for a time two) ran daily to the cemetery from London; thereafter the service was provided on weekdays only. A branch line ran into the cemetery, about ¾ mile long, with two stations: North, for the funerals of Protestant Nonconformists, Roman Catholics, Jews, and Parsees; South, for those of Anglicans. In London the station was rebuilt in 1902, on a new site. This second station was largely destroyed in an air-raid in 1941. The railway service then ceased. This enterprise made no large contribution to solving the original problem. In 1854–74 the interments in the cemetery averaged about 6 per cent of the total number of deaths in London.

A similar plan was brought forward by the Great Northern Cemetery Company, which acquired land for the same purpose at Brunswick Park, East Barnet, close to the railway about 7 miles out of London. Trains began to run into

its stations there from one that the Cemetery Company erected at Belle Isle, a little north of King's Cross, in 1861. The clientele here seems to have been less affluent than that at Woking. The effort did not succeed; the trains were discontinued only six years later.

Here was a social service that might have proved valuable if it had managed to generate more support, with the railways coming to do as much for this branch of public *health as they did for some hospitals and asylums. But since the arrangements demanded were made for small numbers of people, the organizations priced themselves out of all but a narrow market.

See also STATIONS, PRIVATE. JS

J. M. Clarke, The Brookwood Necropolis Railway (1983).

census, see POPULATION, CENSUSES OF.

Central Line, see LONDON UNDERGROUND RAILWAYS.

Central London Railway, see LONDON UNDERGROUND RAILWAYS.

chairmen of companies, see COMPANIES.

Channel Islands, see FRUIT AND FLOWER TRAFFIC; SHIPPING SERVICES; SYSTEM, DEVELOPMENT OF THE.

Channel Tunnel. The inauguration of the Channel Tunnel by Queen Elizabeth II and President Mitterrand on 6 May 1994 marked the end of nearly two centuries of planning such a link between England and France. Albert Mathieu-Favier, a French mining engineer, put forward the first idea at the beginning of the 19th century. Two tunnels were to meet on an artificial island constructed on the Varne Bank in mid-Channel, where the horses hauling the coaches would be changed. The proposal was far in advance of the technology of its day, but it caught people's interest, and the idea never subsequently receded from the public's attention for long.

In the 1830s Thomé de Gramond began more than 20 years of investigations into the strata under the Channel, and he is considered as the 'Father' of the Channel Tunnel. In 1875 a protocol between Britain and France was signed, under which private companies would have a concession to build the tunnel, with an international commission to oversee the construction and operations. A similar framework was followed in subsequent proposals.

After the French and two British tunnel companies had been formed in the late 1870s, trials started on both sides of the Channel. Compressed-air boring machines successfully tunnelled for about a mile through the chalk-marl stratum that lies some 150 feet below the Channel's floor. However, the British military saw the tunnel as a potential threat to the nation's security, and Parliament stopped the work. During the 20th century the idea of a tunnel was raised again unsuccessfully at intervals, with a Royal Commission considering it in 1929 following proposals for a broad-*gauge line from London to Paris. Not until 1955 was the Minister of Defence, then Harold Macmillan, prepared to state that a tunnel presented 'scarcely any' adverse military implications.

Following a 1973 White Paper, the boring of trial lengths began. There was also a need for a high-speed, Berne-gauge (see CLEARANCES), link between London and the tunnel entrance, to accommodate the first stage of the French 'Europolitan' project, now known as *Trains à Grande Vitesse* (TGV). Overcoming the opposition to these latter proposals increased the overall cost, and, after a government change, the project was abandoned in January 1975.

Planning was continued by interested parties, and in 1980 the UK government indicated that it had no objection to a privately funded tunnel, as suggested by the Channel Tunnel Study Group. In 1987 the Treaty of Canterbury was ratified, giving an Anglo-French company, Eurotunnel, a concession to develop, finance, construct, and operate the Channel Tunnel.

Eurotunnel raised some £10 billion, in the form of loans from banks and pan-European bodies, with approximately a quarter as equity. They signed a 'design and build' contract for the tunnel system with Transmanche-Link, a consortium of ten French and British contractors. During construction there were various disputes over delays and costs between Eurotunnel and these firms, which had earlier formed the Channel Tunnel Study Group.

Three 31-mile tunnels connect the terminal sites at Folkestone and Calais. There are two parallel rail tunnels, each 25 ft in diameter and carrying a single rail track. Between them is the smaller service tunnel, which forms a continuous safe haven if passengers have to be evacuated from a train. It also provides access and serves as part of the ventilation system, all three tunnels being linked at intervals by cross-passages. Piston-relief ducts connecting the rail tunnels reduce the aerodynamic drag of trains travelling at up to 100 mph. At two points below the Channel the rail tunnels come together in large chambers containing crossovers, permitting trains to operate by *single-line working during maintenance on part of one tunnel.

Half the tunnel's capacity is leased by the British and French railways for international passenger and freight trains. The smaller British loading gauge (see CLEARANCES) necessitates special wagons for intermodal and car-carrying services, and plans are being considered for increasing some UK clearances to accommodate road trailers on piggy-back trains.

Daytime passenger services are operated by the fleet of 31 Eurostar trains jointly owned by the British, French, and Belgian railways, and capable of operating on their three different electrified systems. These connect *Waterloo International with Brussels and Paris, and will later be joined by another seven, slightly different, British sets serving destinations as far away as *Glasgow. With 18 coaches between the two 8,000 hp power cars, Eurostars travel at 186 mph on the French TGV tracks, which gives journey times of 3 hours between London and Paris. When the Belgian high-speed line is completed in 1997, times to Brussels will be shorter than those to Paris, and there will be a further reduction of some 30 minutes when the high-speed railway from *St Pancras to Folkestone is completed. Overnight services connecting Glasgow, *Manchester, the West Midlands, *Plymouth, *Swansea, and London with destinations in France, the Netherlands, and Germany started in 1996.

Eurotunnel has its own services ('Le Shuttle') for accompanied road vehicles, operating on a 'Turn Up and Go' basis, with as many as four departures per hour. To avoid delays on arrival, vehicles pass through both countries' customs and immigration formalities on entering the terminal. They then use platforms to drive on to the largest railway vehicles in the world, 18.4 ft high and 13.5 ft wide. Each train is ½ mile long, powered by a 7,500 hp Bo-Bo-Bo locomotive at each end, with the driver in charge at the front. In an emergency the train captain in the rear locomotive can reverse the train out of the tunnel, after dividing if necessary. Private cars travel in double-deck wagons, while coaches and caravans, requiring more headroom, use the single-deck variety. All these are fully enclosed and air-conditioned, enabling passengers to remain with their vehicles for the 35-minute journey. Heavy lorries use semi-open wagons, their drivers travelling in a club car where they are provided with a meal during their statutory break. After emerging from the tunnel the shuttle trains traverse a semicircular loop to reach the platforms, so avoiding the need to reverse when running in normal service. PWBS

M. R. Bonavia, *The Channel Tunnel Story* (1987); W. Collard, *Proposed London and Paris Railway* (1928); C. Kirkland (ed.), *Engineering the Channel Tunnel* (1995); P. Semmens and I. Machefert-Tassin, *Channel Tunnel Trains* (1994).

Chaplin, William James (1787–1859), coach proprietor and railway chairman. In partnership with B. W. Horne he built up the largest coaching and carrying business in Britain. But he was quick to appreciate the future of railways and was one of the original promoters of the London & Southampton (later the *London & South Western) company. On the impending completion of the *London & Birmingham Railway, in 1837 the partners sold out of coaching altogether—in contrast to their chief rival Edward Sherman, who relied on lowering fares to meet the railways' competition, lost, and died in misery.

Chaplin became a director of the LSWR in 1837, deputy-chairman in 1840, and chairman in 1843–52 and 1854–9. It was a difficult position to occupy, the board and the proprietors being exceptionally quarrelsome. But he was astute, commanded his temper well, and held on. He constantly advocated a westward extension, to bring the LSWR, with its standard *gauge, to *Exeter, as a rival to the established broad-gauge *Great Western. It was opened, after many vacillations, in 1860, immediately after his death. He had become a considerable figure in the West of England and was MP for Salisbury in 1847–57. JS

Boase; Williams (i).

Charing Cross station, see LONDON STATIONS.

charities, railways and (see also RAILWAY BENEVOLENT INSTITUTION). Railway companies frequently contributed to the funds of charitable bodies, especially to hospitals that had treated their own or contractors' employees. The *Liverpool & Manchester Railway gave £100 to the Manchester

Infirmary on this account in 1831. The *Bristol & Gloucester subscribed £5 5s. a year to the Bristol Infirmary, adding £20 in 1843 to defray part of the cost of treating 13 'expensive' casualties during the previous year.

A number of railways set up their own institutions of social welfare. The *Great Western inaugurated a medical fund in 1847, which led to the establishment first of a dispensary, and later of a hospital at *Swindon. Some companies established orphanages of their own for the children of men killed in their service. The *Midland's at Derby opened in 1875 with 11 children, going on to occupy a much larger building 12 years later. The *London & South Western's, started in London in 1885, moved out to impressive purpose-built quarters at Woking in 1904.

Such activities lay within the companies' statutory powers since they provided solely for their own employees, and their families. But their contributions to the building of churches were occasionally questioned by shareholders (see RELIGION), and some proposals that they should build or subscribe towards the cost of educational institutions met with disfavour (see EDUCATION). The range of the railways' charitable gifts appeared to grow broader, nevertheless, and some of them were alleged to be merely devices for purchasing support. In 1908 Parliament required returns of their charitable subscriptions and donations during the previous year. The total proved to be small: less than £16,000, 54 per cent being devoted to medical purposes. The seven-mile Bideford Westward Ho! & Appledore Railway contributed 5s. towards Bideford regatta. After three years' returns, the matter was taken no further.

With few and unimportant exceptions the expenditure of the *Big Four companies created in 1923 was confined to maintaining the obligations to the charitable services of their predecessors. After 1947 most of them became a charge on the National Health Service. JS

PP 1909, lxxii; 1910, lxxx; 1911, lxx.

Charlewood, Rawdon Edward (1879–1950), railway officer and author. As a young man, Charlewood (the middle 'e' was pronounced) lived on Morecambe Bay, adjacent to the *London & North Western Railway's *Lancaster & Carlisle section, over which he had travelled for some 28,000 miles by 1904. After reading law at Oxford, he joined the family legal firm in *Manchester, but was afterwards offered a job in the *Midland Railway's Trains Office at *Derby, which had received numerous suggestions from him for improved services. From then until his early retirement in 1934 his knowledge, experience, and advice were invaluable to the Midland and the *London Midland & Scottish Railways. On one occasion he retimed the return working of a press special on the back of a dining-car menu after a locomotive failure.

He wrote his first article for the *Railway Magazine* in 1902, and briefly contributed to its 'British Locomotive Practice & Performance' series after the death of C. H. *Rous-Marten.

In 1935, travelling between Cologne and Mainz, he was arrested by the German police after sketching a station lay-out. After being held for some time in Berlin Moabit prison, he was released following the intervention of Sir Josiah *Stamp, the LMS president, and Dr Julius Dorpmüller, the German Minister of Transport. PWBS

Chartered Institute of Transport. The Ministry of Transport was created in 1919 and in the same year prominent figures in transport united to create an institute 'to promote and encourage knowledge of traffic science and of the art of transport'; to hold meetings, lectures, and examinations. The minister, Sir Eric *Geddes, was the first president and Lord *Ashfield the second. Corporate members were graded (M. Inst.T. or A.M. Inst.T.) and normal entry was to graduateship by examination before reaching corporate status. Later, grades became Fellows, Members, and Associate Members.

The railways generally supported the educational work of the institute, which received a Royal Charter in 1926. It set up a number of local sections in the UK and also overseas centres where examinations were held. Maximum membership, in 1985, was 21,380, but entry by examination has declined. The *Journal* of the institute originally published papers and lectures. Now it is a current review of events in the transport world. MRB

S. Woolley, *The First 70 Years: A History of the Chartered Institute of Transport* (1992).

Cheap Trains Act, see PARLIAMENTARY TRAINS.

Cheshire Lines Committee. Largest *joint railway after the *Midland & Great Northern (the biggest of Britain's joint railways), the CLC was judged far more important, having created a profitable network in north-west England despite competition from powerful, long-established companies. Its title was misleading because the most important of its 143 route miles were in Lancashire, where the bulk of its capital was spent and most revenue earned.

The largest of its 70 stations were also in Lancashire: *Liverpool Central and *Manchester Central (see TRAINSHEDS). Over its main line between these stations, the CLC ran 40-minute expresses renowned for their punctuality, outclassing those of the rival *London & North Western and *Lancashire & Yorkshire Railways.

The CLC developed from the 1860s when the Manchester Sheffield & Lincolnshire Railway (see GREAT CENTRAL), under Edward *Watkin, was trying to break the LNWR monopoly around Manchester with the *Great Northern and later the *Midland Railway as its allies. The three formed a joint committee in 1865–6 and controlled companies which slowly built lines in the Manchester and Stockport areas linked to the MSLR. The CLC's only main line in Cheshire was to Chester Northgate, where it joined GCR lines to North Wales and Bidston, from which it reached Birkenhead docks over the *Wirral Railway. A line around east Liverpool to Southport Chapel Street gave the CLC access to Liverpool docks. The *London Midland & Scottish Railway estimated in 1932 that the CLC captured nearly a fifth of Port of Liverpool goods and mineral traffic. Although it had its own rolling stock, it owned no locomotives: four steam Sentinel *railcars were its only motive power, locomotives being supplied by the owning companies, notably the *London & North Eastern Railway after *Grouping.   RC

P. Bolger, *An Illustrated History of the Cheshire Lines Committee* (1984); N. Dyckhoff, *The Cheshire Lines Committee Then and Now* (1984); R. P. Griffiths, *The Cheshire Lines Railway* (1958 edn.).

Chester & Holyhead Railway. One of several projects to speed up communication between London and Ireland, the Chester & Holyhead Railway, 84 miles long, was authorized in 1844. The *London & Birmingham Railway subscribed £1 million, and provided half of the directors. The engineer was Robert *Stephenson.

The line kept to the coast as far as Bangor, opened in 1848, and beyond Abergele had difficult sections along cliffs. The tubular bridge at Conway gave experience for building the much larger *Britannia Bridge over the Menai Strait, and in 1850 the line opened throughout to Holyhead. In 1849 the CHR purchased and opened the Mold Railway from Chester, and in 1852 it leased the Bangor & Carnarvon Railway which opened in that year. A branch to Llandudno was opened in 1858, and a year later the CHR was bought by the *London & North Western Railway.

The railway built the inner harbour at Holyhead and steadily developed it as a packet port, from which the LNWR operated extensive *shipping services to *Ireland. The population rose from 3,800 in 1841 to 12,600 in 1988.

Added to its strategic importance was the line's value in opening up North Wales coastal resorts (see HOLIDAY-MAKING), which the LNWR fully exploited. Between 1858 and 1912 branches were opened to Denbigh, Bettws-y-Coed and Blaenau Festiniog, Dyserth, Bethesda, and Holywell Town; and on Anglesey to Amlwch, and Red Wharf Bay. In 1852–67 the Carnarvon line was extended to meet the *Cambrian Railways at Afon Wen near Pwllheli, with a branch to Llanberis (1869). Primarily intended for slate and stone traffic, some of these lines also encouraged *tourism. The LNWR used them for combined rail-and-road excursions, which the *London Midland & Scottish Railway and *British Railways perpetuated, including the latter's 'North Wales Land Cruise' trains from Rhyl in the 1950s.

Most of the expresses ran through to Holyhead or Llandudno, and in the 1880s a daily Llandudno–Manchester businessmen's service began, which from 1908 included a *club carriage. In 1909 the LNWR's longest non-stop run was a summer express from *Euston to Rhyl, with through carriages to Llandudno and Pwllheli, which the LMS later named The Welshman. The best-known train was the twice-daily Irish Mail from Euston.

The original CHR stations were designed in a distinctive style by Francis *Thompson, and a number still exist. In 1860 the LNWR installed the first water troughs (see WATER SUPPLIES) at Mochdre, near Colwyn Bay. Today only the main line, and the Amlwch, Blaenau Festiniog, and Llandudno branches remain open, the first-named for freight, and the four tracks from Chester to Abergele that once carried enormous holiday traffic have been reduced to two.

Holyhead is still a busy port, mainly for roll on-roll off ferries, and the much-reduced through services from Euston are provided by IC 125 trains. For local and other services, 16 of 31 intermediate stations remain open.   GJB

Reg. Hist., xi; J. M. Dunn, *The Chester & Holyhead Railway* (1948); P. E. Baughan, *The Chester & Holyhead Railway*, i: *The Main Line up to 1880* (1972) (vol. ii has never been published).

Churchill, Lord, see GREAT WESTERN RAILWAY.

church interval, see RELIGION.

Churchward, George Jackson (1857–1933), mechanical engineer. The son of a Devon farmer, he was a pupil under John Wright, *South Devon Railway, and William *Dean at *Swindon, *Great Western Railway, 1873–7; assistant to Swindon carriage works manager, 1882–5, when he worked on an improved vacuum brake system, and improved axle bearings to minimize overhauls and delays. From 1885 he was carriage works manager, and in 1895 locomotive works manager. From 1897 he was also principal assistant to Dean, whom he succeeded as CME in 1902.

From 1903 to 1911 Churchward introduced nine standard locomotive types, with maximum component standardization, of which 1,100 were built up to 1921. They were of advanced design, based on latest American and European practice, embodying free-steaming tapered boilers and long-lap, long-travel *valve gear, providing economical use of steam. His four-cylinder express engines used divided drive and other features from three French locomotives imported by the GWR for tests against Churchward's. He was, with George *Hughes of the *Lancashire & Yorkshire Railway, the British pioneer in introducing superheating, which increased power and efficiency. He was the outstanding British locomotive engineer of his time; his design practice was continued by his successors until 1947 and largely adopted by the CMEs of the other railways grouped in 1923. He remodelled Swindon works, with a new 1½-acre boiler and erecting shop, and in 1904 built the first successful *locomotive testing plant in Europe. His 70-ft main-line carriages and other passenger stock gave a considerable advance in comfort.   GWC

H. Holcroft, *An Outline of Great Western Locomotive Practice 1837–1947* (1957); H. C. B. Rogers, *G. J. Churchward, A Locomotive Biography* (1975); *DNB: Missing Persons* (1993), 132–3.

cinema. Railways have been a popular subject for the cinema since the beginning. A French programme was first seen in London in 1896, accompanied by a man with a bottle of compressed air to make steam noises. The result was so realistic that people in the front rows are said to have leapt back lest they should be mown down by the engine coming towards them on the screen. From 1897 a series of 'Phantom Rides'—taken from the front of trains in various parts of the country—became popular; surviving films include a journey from Barnstaple Junction to Ilfracombe, a *View from an Engine Front down Exeter Incline*, and a recently discovered journey from Kyle of Lochalsh to Strome Ferry made in 1898, the year the line was opened.

The next step was to move towards a story film by cutting in a simple staged scene between two sections of a

'Phantom Ride', as in *Kiss in the Tunnel*, made in 1898. One version used a *View through Shillamill Tunnel* on the *London & South Western Railway, whilst the other started with a train entering Queensbury Tunnel on the *Great Northern Bradford–Halifax line but emerging into Monsal Dale in Derbyshire.

The first world-acclaimed fiction film was a railway subject: the American *Great Train Robbery* of 1903, after which films with railway backgrounds proliferated, with the British making use of the LSWR and *London & North Western, *South Eastern & Chatham, and *London Brighton & South Coast Railways in particular. They provide the finest collection of pre-*Grouping action scenes that still survives.

In addition to story films, documentaries now began to be popular; the best railway subjects include a tour of *Crewe works in 1911, and a visit to *Swindon to see a Star class locomotive being built in 1921. As early as 1907 the LNWR was collaborating with an American company to produce a film depicting the beauties of North Wales.

Feature films of the 1920s included *The Wrecker*, from Britain, in 1927. The coming of the talkies intensified the trend towards railway-based movies, now with the added bonus of the sound of steam locomotives. From Britain came *Rome Express* (1932), to be followed by Alfred Hitchcock's marvellous use of railways for added excitement and suspense in *The Thirty-Nine Steps* (1935), which featured the journey from *King's Cross to *Edinburgh, via Box Tunnel on the GWR; and *The Lady Vanishes* (1938), with French expresses, a *Southern Railway boat train, and some shots taken on the Longmoor Military Railway. *Seven Sinners* (1936) reworked the real crash staged on the Basingstoke & Alton Light Railway for *The Wrecker*, adding a cleverly staged train crash in a tunnel somewhere in France. During this period the classic *Post Office documentary *Night Mail* (1936) was made, featuring *London Midland & Scottish Railway *mail trains on the London–*Glasgow run. The *London & North Eastern Railway celebrated the *Stockton & Darlington centenary in 1925 with an official film of the parade of locomotives; the GWR celebrated its own in 1935 with *Romance of a Railway*, but never released the film; and the LMS, the first railway to have its own film unit, filmed the American tour of *Royal Scot* in 1933. Perhaps best remembered from that era was the Will Hay comedy *Oh! Mr Porter*, also shot on the Basingstoke & Alton Light Railway after it had closed, with track being lifted as the film crew strove to finish before it had all gone. The Kent & East Sussex Railway locomotive No. 2 *Northiam* was cast in the role of *Gladstone* for some of the film's best scenes.

The Ghost Train, turned into a film from Arnold Ridley's famous stage play in 1927 and 1931, was filmed once more in 1941 with Arthur Askey. An opening journey starts at Paddington with a King class locomotive, arriving at Teignmouth with a Castle, slowing up with bullet-nosed streamlined *King Henry VII*, and coming to a halt with a Saint class engine. For the rest, the railways were left to documentaries like *Women at War* (1945), shot entirely on the GWR, or *The Army Lays the Rails*, a 1941 tribute to the Longmoor Military Railway. But best remembered of the British films with a railway setting was the Noël Coward classic play *Brief Encounter* (1957), filmed on Carnforth station.

After the war and *nationalization, the British Transport Film Unit made numerous excellent documentaries, including travel films to popularize rail services and a number about the railway itself, for which it gained a number of awards. Meanwhile, the celebrated Ealing comedy *The Titfield Thunderbolt* (1952) acted as a precursor to steam railway preservation, using the historic *Liverpool & Manchester locomotive *Lion* on the Limpley Stoke–Camerton branch in Somerset. Since the demise of steam locomotives on *British Railways, preserved railways have been extensively used for filming period scenes, one of the first being the Keighley & Worth Valley Railway for making *The Railway Children* in 1970.

A recent film of the 1855 *Great Train Robbery* on the SER was made in Ireland, but the film with the same title based on the 1963 robbery was made in 1967 near Market Harborough.

See also PHOTOGRAPHY; RADIO AND TELEVISION.   JHu

J. Huntley, *Railways on the Screen* (1993); Catalogues of Transport & Travel Film Library (incl. British Transport films), 1952 onwards.

Circle Line, see LONDON UNDERGROUND RAILWAYS.

circus trains were first used in 1872 by Barnum & Bailey in the USA, closely followed by Ringling Bros. Although travelling circuses by road originated in Britain, European circuses kept to permanent buildings until the 1920s.

For Barnum's European tour of 1898–1902, four complete trains totalling 68 bogie vehicles, each 59 ft long, were built by W. R. Renshaw of Stoke-on-Trent. They were of American design, reduced in size for the British loading gauge (see CLEARANCES), with special small wheels to enable ground-level loading, and American buckeye couplers, except on the end-vehicles which had British *couplings. They included three special elephant cars, a double-deck pony car, and eight sleeping cars. The passenger vehicles had American-style end-verandahs. The trains toured Britain for two years before being shipped to the Continent.

Later, 50 of the vehicles were used for Buffalo Bill's Wild West Show, which toured Britain and Europe in 1903–6. Afterwards some of the coaches were used for carrying miners at Chatterley Whitfield colliery, near Stoke, and others went to the *Alexandra (Newport & South Wales) Docks & Railway. The Welsh Industrial and Maritime Museum at Cardiff has the body of a sleeping car.

Loading and unloading were meticulously organized so that a show could arrive, parade through the streets, give two performances, pack up, and move on to the next town, all in 24 hours. The only British tented circus to tour by rail was Bertram Mills', which started in four trains in 1929. The railways provided locomotives, but by the 1930s made little or no profit from the traffic.   GJB

New Encyclopaedia Britannica (1994 edn.), art. 'circuses'; C. B. Mills, *Bertram Mills Circus: Its Story* (1983 edn.); B. White, 'The

Circus Comes to Town', in Southampton University Industrial Archaeology Group *Journal*, 2 (Nov. 1993), 16–19; profitability: R. H. N. Hardy, *Beeching, Champion of the Railway?* (1989).

City & South London Railway, see LONDON UNDERGROUND RAILWAYS.

civil engineering was defined as 'the art of directing the great forces of nature for the use and convenience of man' when the founders of the *Institution of Civil Engineers petitioned for their Royal Charter in 1827. However, the term 'civil engineer' had already been in use for 70 years, having been coined by John Smeaton to distinguish between civilian and military engineering, after the manner of the French.

Civil engineering then encompassed everything from bridge, highway, harbour, and *canal construction to steam engine manufacture, but advances in the sciences during the 19th century brought new developments in mechanical, gas, and electrical engineering and other specializations. These led to the formation of other institutions, beginning with the *Institution of Mechanical Engineers in 1847, of which George *Stephenson was first president. Civil engineering then became associated only with works such as harbours, highways, railways, dams, water supply, and waste-water treatment, and, more recently, airports and offshore engineering.

The railway booms, which had dominated civil engineering, ended in the 1860s although substantial works still remained to be completed, including the notoriously difficult *Settle & Carlisle line (1869–76) and the *Great Western Railway's *Severn Tunnel, opened in 1886. Many lesser lines were still under construction by the 1890s, and the last main line, the *Great Central, was completed in 1899.

In those years, the emphasis and strengths of civil engineering practice lay in the practical aspects, in contractual procedures, and the management of manpower, these having evolved during the railway era. The fame and practice of British civil engineers spread overseas, and the Paris to Havre railway in France, designed by Joseph *Locke, was built by Thomas *Brassey and William *Mackenzie during 1841–3. By 1845 these two men had 13 railway contracts in Europe totalling £36 million, and in 1852 Brassey and others were building the Grand Trunk Railway in Canada, to be followed by works in India, Australia, and South America.

British civil engineers also turned to other tasks abroad such as the training of the Danube in 1861, the construction of the Aswan Dam in 1898–1902, and the Mulberry prefabricated harbours of World War II, to mention but a minute selection of achievements which continue to this day.

Meanwhile, in Britain during the 1850s, John Simpson developed his water purification systems for London at the same time that Joseph Bazalgette was directing construction of the immense sewerage system for the city, comprising 1,400 miles of trunk and branch sewers. In the 1880s Edward Leader Williams was engineering the Manchester Ship Canal, with its vast array of mechanical excavating equipment; and in 1890 the City & South London tube railway

opened (see LONDON UNDERGROUND RAILWAYS), using electric-powered locomotives.

The profession continued to contribute to British needs, to the motorways of the 1960s, to the building of *light rapid transit systems, and the *Channel Tunnel, and the redevelopment of the country's infrastructure of today.

At the beginning of the 19th century, British engineers placed no particular emphasis on the need for scientific education. This attitude was unlike that of the French, who had established, early in the 18th century, the élite 'Corps des Ingénieurs des Ponts et Chaussées', a body of highly educated men trained for the public works service. The corps was a national academy of engineering which offered opportunities for both study and research while carrying, at the same time, executive responsibility for the country's public works.

In Britain, courses for engineers were instituted only piecemeal, first by Professor Robison at Edinburgh University during the 1790s. This was followed in 1838 by the establishment of the first school of engineering at King's College, London, then the founding of chairs in civil engineering at Glasgow University and University College, London (of which C. B. *Vignoles was first professor), in 1840 and 1841 respectively. These modest beginnings were followed by other universities in response to the educational demands of a new generation of engineers, eager to take advantage of opportunities in the industrial developments of the age.

Subsequently, marked advances were made in all the branches of civil engineering through teaching and research, notably by Professor Rankine of Glasgow University who, from the 1840s, produced a stream of original contributions on theoretical and applied aspects of engineering, and a series of textbooks, containing much of what was then known of engineering theory. He, and other outstanding teachers and practising engineers since, displayed a practical outlook which is a traditional aspect of British civil engineering: the ability to combine common sense and experience with abstract theories, to the solution of problems.   RBS

C. M. Norrie, *Bridging the Years* (1956); J. P. M. Pannell, *Man the Builder* (1977); various authors, *Civil Engineering Heritage*, a continuing regional series from 1981.

Clapham, Sir John Harold (1873–1946), historian, born in Broughton, Salford, Lancashire, and educated at Leys School and King's College, Cambridge. He was a Fellow of King's College, 1898–1902, 1908–46; Professor of Economic History, Cambridge, 1928–38; and knighted in 1943.

His *Economic History of Modern Britain* (3 vols., 1926–38) displays the railways' contribution to that history, treating also the external influences that helped to shape the railways themselves. Its language is lucid, vigorous, and terse; the range of the whole study impressively wide. Clapham's brief account of the development of the electric *telegraph (i. 207–10), from 'a railway convenience' into a national necessity, is masterly. So is his survey (ii. 498–503) of the 'series of landscapes' of Britain; e.g. the disafforestation caused by the building of the *Highland Railway northward from Blair Atholl, the felled timber going partly into making railway sleepers.

Much more is known now about some of the matters that Clapham handled: about investment in railways, for example, and some aspects of their *management. But no subsequent writer has placed the railways so surely and firmly in the context of the Victorian economy. His book still affords the clearest introduction we have to that study.   JS

  DNB.

Clapham Junction, see JUNCTIONS.

Clarence Railway. This was the first railway to be authorized in Britain that was promoted for the express purpose of competing with another one already at work.

The *Stockton & Darlington Railway, opened in 1825, carried coal from the Auckland mines down to the Tees at Stockton for shipment. The facilities afforded there were unsatisfactory, however. A new port was needed on deep water, nearer the mouth of the river. The Stockton & Darlington extended its line on the south bank to *Middlesbrough. Thereupon a plan came forward for a second railway, branching out of the Stockton & Darlington at Simpasture to run to a new port on the north bank; it was named the Clarence Railway, in compliment to the Duke of Clarence (afterwards King William IV). Parliament sanctioned both these schemes in 1828.

They were clearly rivals. The Clarence Railway aimed at undercutting the Stockton & Darlington by accepting a much lower scale of maximum tolls for freight than the older company's. The coalfields they tapped were just beginning to be fully exploited, and their owners' sights were set on the coastal trade to London, by far the biggest market in the country.

The Middlesbrough line was opened in 1830, but the Clarence Railway not until 1833–4, with two shipping points: one at Haverton Hill, the other (named Port Clarence) closer to the sea.

The new company's traffic increased steadily, but it was beset by difficulties. The Clarence company had borrowed a large sum from the Exchequer Loan Commission (see SUBSIDIES). The Commission pressed for repayment, and when none was forthcoming in 1842 it virtually foreclosed, intending to put the line up for sale. When this threat had been averted, the company struggled on, leasing it in 1844. When the lessees merged with the *Hartlepool West Harbour & Dock Company in 1853 the new combine purchased the Clarence Railway outright, itself in turn passing to the *North Eastern in 1865. The Stockton & Darlington had fallen into the same hands two years earlier.   JS

  Tomlinson; N. Moorsom, *Stockton & Darlington Railway: The Foundation of Middlesbrough* (1975), 170–3; *Reg. Hist.*, iv (1986 edn.), 128–32.

Clarke, Seymour (1814–76), manager. Having been *Brunel's chief clerk, he toured railways in Belgium and northern England in 1837 and next year went to the *Great Western Railway as traffic superintendent of the London

division, under C. A. *Saunders. He testified on its behalf to the *Gauge Commission in 1845. Resenting a cut in salaries, he resigned in 1850, to become general manager of the *Great Northern Railway, at a salary of £900.

When he arrived, its main line from London to Doncaster was not quite complete. The 'towns line' through Newark and Retford was opened almost immediately afterwards, *King's Cross station not until 1852. Clarke's principal task was to organize the traffic from London to the north by this new route, in hot competition with the established one of the *London & North Western and *Midland Railways via Rugby, Derby, and Normanton. Here he was most successful, doing much towards the establishment of the GNR's lasting reputation for high speed. He was a first-class manager; but he was not an imaginative originator, nor an astute diplomat. The company appreciated his merits, raising his salary several times, until it stood at £4,000 in 1866. He over-drove himself, and his health suffered. A long illness obliged him to retire in 1870, aged 56.   JS

  BDE; MacDermot; Grinling; J. Wrottesley, *Great Northern Railway*, i (1979).

class distinctions. Before the arrival of the railways, four different charges had been levied on passengers travelling in public road vehicles. The highest fares were payable on *mail-coaches. Next, in the stage-coaches were those paid by passengers travelling inside the vehicles. Then came the fares levied on passengers carried in the open. The lowest fares were charged to passengers who went by slow goods wagons. The word 'class' was never applied to any of these categories of travel: they were simply designated 'mail', 'inside', 'outside', and 'wagon'. The early steamships never spoke of 'class' either. They used two self-explanatory terms: 'cabin' and 'deck'.

The *Liverpool & Manchester Railway adopted 'class' at first only to describe trains, the 'first-class' being the quickest. But this categorization was soon extended from the trains to passengers. Announcing its opening arrangements in 1837, the *Grand Junction Railway spoke of 'first-class passengers' and 'second-class passengers'. Hitherto 'first-class' and 'second-class' had been used in speaking of persons only in the English universities, where they denoted the examination performance of students.

The segregation of travellers by different classes in trains soon applied also at the stations. At *Manchester (Liverpool Road), for example, first- and second-class passengers had separate booking offices and *waiting rooms in 1830.

But a new class of passengers was now emerging. The *Stockton & Darlington Railway carried some to and from *Middlesbrough in open wagons in 1835. The *Leeds & Selby introduced a 'third class' in 1837, the *Manchester & Leeds two years later. In Scotland that class quickly became a mainstay of the railways' income. In 1843, on the lines from *Glasgow to Greenock and *Edinburgh, third-class travellers represented more than 60 per cent of the whole, furnishing 35 per cent of the companies' passenger revenue.

A *Great Western Railway train met with a serious

*accident at Sonning in 1841, in which eight third-class passengers were killed, all travelling in low-sided open wagons. This moved the Board of *Trade to make inquiries of each company concerning its arrangements for conveying third-class passengers. Great varieties of practice then appeared. In 1844 a Commons committee on railways attended earnestly to these matters, recommending that all companies should be obliged (under threat of a fiscal penalty) to provide at least one service every day, at maximum fares of a penny a mile and affording specified minimum standards of security and comfort. What were soon called *parliamentary trains were then introduced, complying with requirements the government laid down. But the old third class continued on many lines, free of the conditions that the Act imposed. This stringency encouraged the provision of a 'fourth class', at less than parliamentary rates. Extra-cheap trains had already been established by the Manchester & Leeds Railway. The *Edinburgh & Glasgow provided a 'fourth class' in 1845, besides a parliamentary one. So the number of classes on British railways was now rising to five.

A sixth was already beginning to appear. In 1844–5 *express trains started to run from London to *Brighton and *Exeter, soon becoming general. Third-class passengers were usually excluded from them. First- and second-class passengers were charged supplements, and that constituted in effect the creation of another class. Most of these supplements were moderate in amount, but they became very unpopular, and were abandoned on the northern main lines from London from 1859 onwards. South of the Thames express fares lasted much longer, though most of them had gone by 1890.

Meanwhile, yet another new class of railway passengers was emerging. The demolition of houses consequent on building railways through built-up urban areas presented a grave social problem from 1860 onwards (see TOWNS, RAILWAYS AND THE DEVELOPMENT OF). Some of the companies were now compelled to provide special early-morning services to carry 'persons of the labouring classes' into the centres of towns at exceptionally cheap rates. These *workmen's trains, first run in 1864, clearly provided a new class of travel. They carried passengers who had to fulfil stated conditions, for example relating to their employment. Moreover, the times of running were regulated, and subject to government approval.

By 1865 the number of classes of travel in Britain had therefore reached seven. Various new forms of luxury were introduced later, notably *Pullman and *sleeping cars, but they were merely additional facilities, and paid for as such. The subsequent history of classes on the British railways now became one of reduction.

Fourth class, having been extensively tried out, was gradually withdrawn, the last traces of it vanishing from Great Britain in the 1870s, and with the passing of the Cheap Trains Act of 1883 (see PARLIAMENT AND LEGISLATION) the designation 'parliamentary' began to disappear.

But the most important of these reductions related to the second class. This had been abolished as early as 1841 by the little Sheffield & Rotherham Railway. The first company that never offered second class was the *Great North of Scotland, which began work in 1854. The results of that policy were inquired into some 20 years later by E. S. Ellis, chairman of the *Midland Railway, and his company determined to dispense with second class from 1 January 1875. No other company did the same until 1885, when the *Great Northern withdrew second class from certain industrial districts it served. The Manchester Sheffield & Lincolnshire (see GREAT CENTRAL) and the *Cheshire Lines followed suit in 1891–2, and in 1893 (except in some suburban services) second class was abandoned by the *Great Eastern and *North Eastern Railways, and entirely in Scotland. After more withdrawals in 1912, second class survived in the main-line services of only two companies, the *London & South Western and the *South Eastern & Chatham, from which it disappeared in 1918 and 1923. Second-class accommodation continued to be provided on the *London & North Eastern Railway's London suburban services until 1938, and on the *Southern boat trains to the Channel ports until after *nationalization. When most of the European railways went over to a two-class system (1956) the British railways did the same, the classes now being everywhere designated 'first' and 'second'. 'Second' became 'standard' in their parlance in 1987.

The amount of accommodation provided by the companies was strongly influenced by their anticipations of revenue. The early (and at first surprising) growth in the sale of the lower-class tickets convinced some managers that they would provide more revenue than those sold to richer travellers. Moreover, third-class accommodation was much less expensive to provide than first- or second-class: each vehicle was cheaper to build (see CARRIAGE BUILDING) and carried many more passengers. In the 1860s up to 50 could be seated in a third-class carriage, 32 in a second, 24 in a first. The allocation of carriages of each class in a train now required very careful consideration. Some companies imposed restrictions on the use of trains, confining them to first-, or first- and second-class passengers alone. But when the Midland Railway decided in 1872 to admit third-class passengers to all its trains, its rivals felt obliged to do likewise wherever their services and the Midland's competed. By 1890 third-class passengers were being conveyed in all British trains running 100 miles and more. In consequence trains grew heavier, and either they had to run more frequently, so splitting the loads (as on the Midland Railway), or the locomotive power had to be increased. Both expedients added considerably to the cost of providing the services.

No other European country went so far in this direction before 1914, except Denmark. Even between Paris and Bordeaux, where the Orleans Railway treated third-class passengers more liberally than any other French privately owned company, they were still excluded from four of the principal trains. Between Berlin and Düsseldorf they were debarred from three. Moreover, continental third-class passengers travelled on wooden seats, vertically backed, and not upholstered, whereas in Britain they enjoyed comfort at least equal to the continental second.

A few British companies tried having one class only. The Newcastle & North Shields did so briefly in the early 1840s. From the 1870s onwards, *trams reduced the railways' traffic in many urban districts. Like the *buses, they levied fares at one rate only, without any division into classes. The first successful deep-level tube railway, the City & South London (1890), had only one class, and that became the usual practice on the *London underground railways except the *Metropolitan and *Metropolitan District. They offered three classes until they were electrified in 1905–6.

It has been contended that all these practices strengthened existing social distinctions between classes. In early days that may perhaps have been true. But it soon came to be argued that railways did more to break down class barriers than to reinforce them in 19th-century Britain.

The snobberies of coach travelling had often been derided, particularly the obsequious behaviour of inn landlords on the road, favouring their richer and grander guests. Satirists poked fun at the conduct of some railway officials towards different classes of passengers. But as early as 1849 the *London & North Western company was instructing *stationmasters to see that its staff behaved 'respectfully and civilly to persons of every class'. Two years later the journalist Samuel Sidney portrayed a dignified peer (who would formerly have travelled in his own carriage, with four post-horses) sharing a first-class compartment at *Euston with the travelling representative of a wine merchant and a newspaper reporter travelling to *Birmingham to attend a railway meeting. In the past no one of high dignity or of great wealth ever travelled in a public coach, in the company of strangers. Yet here was this Lord sitting enclosed with people he had never seen before, of a quite different social class from his own. He was making a huge economy by doing so, paying a first-class railway fare amounting to one-twelfth of what he would have been charged for post-horses. And the wine merchant and the journalist, in travelling like this, were buying time. Here, Sidney remarked, one saw 'the universal and levelling tendency of the railway system'. The novelist Surtees, himself a country gentleman, wrote that railways had 'annihilated the prejudice against public conveyance. They have opened the world out to everyone.'

But these were early days in the process of 'levelling'. Two other forces accelerated it. The first was sheer demand. Up to 1844, third-class railway facilities were provided extensively in industrial districts. But parliamentary trains now had to run on all railways alike. By 1850 half the passenger journeys in Great Britain were being made at the lowest fares. By 1875 that proportion had become 78 per cent.

Railway managements that disliked this tendency were nevertheless in the grip of another force: *competition. The Midland's decision to abolish second class in 1875 evoked loud protests from its rivals. But it was received with dismay also by many passengers who were not wealthy enough to travel first class but paid a little extra to avoid the rowdiness of the third. Some commentators supported them, maintaining that there were three classes in all societies, and advising the railways to go on respecting them. *The Times* said this in a leader (12 October 1874). Several railway managers, like *Findlay and *Scotter, went on voicing this opinion for years to come, and despite the resultant economies enjoyed by the Midland company, the demand for these classes weighed with them as a stronger consideration.

It was at its most powerful in suburban business, involving daily double journeys in crowded trains. Many passengers who might otherwise have travelled third went second, so three classes made good sense, without recourse to disputable social theories. Some of the leading railways, together with the *Taff Vale, continued providing second-class accommodation resolutely into the 20th century.

However, when on 1 July 1893 the LNW and *Caledonian companies put into service their newly built corridor trains between London and Glasgow they made them up of first- and third-class carriages only, with *restaurant cars accessible through corridors to both classes of passenger. They were a conspicuous landmark in the progress of the democratization of travel in Britain. Here, to an extent not even contemplated anywhere in France, Belgium, Germany, Austria, or Italy, the third-class passenger had attained equal rights with everybody else on the train. By 1913, 96 per cent of British passenger journeys were third-class.

The *Big Four companies of 1923–47 went somewhat further. Three introduced sleeping cars for third-class passengers in 1928. (The fourth, the Southern, did not provide any of its own.) There remained then on the British railways no important type of facility that was restricted to first-class passengers only.

Another change made by the two larger companies represented an important gain for third-class passengers. The *compartments in new third-class corridor carriages had seats for six passengers instead of eight—three on each side, not four—with armrests between them. And the compartments were enlarged by reducing the number in each carriage from eight to seven. These vehicles now accommodated a maximum of 42 seated passengers instead of 64, increasing the cost of hauling each of them by 50 per cent. The Great Western and Southern companies declined to make this change, on the ground that their traffic included a large proportion of holiday-makers in the summer, forcing them to cram as many people as possible into each compartment.

The London Underground railways withdrew first-class facilities on some lines in 1934–6, and on the rest in 1940–1, under the pressure of wartime traffic. In 1940 the government laid it down that all trains beginning and ending their journeys within the London area should carry passengers in one class only.

After 1947 the nationalized railways introduced no further important changes, except that from 1960 onwards its third-class vehicles reverted to seating four passengers a side. Rigid egalitarians demanded that the railways should abolish first-class altogether. Why should 1 per cent of passengers enjoy its greater comforts, merely by paying for them? The argument was not as simple as that, however. The additional revenue from first-class travel was not negligible, particularly from passengers whom the railways wished to attract from air and road. So there are still two classes of travel on British railways today, though no longer five—or seven.

One more innovation, curious and unforeseen, has to be recorded. First-class passengers had always enjoyed superior facilities. But in September 1992 they began to be deprived of one that remained available to standard-class passengers, albeit much restricted. On certain trains smoking was not permitted in *first-class* vehicles. So the first-class passenger, having paid his much higher fare, found himself penalized.   JS

C. E. Lee, *Passenger Class Distinctions* (1946); early Scottish fares: Robertson, 234–43; VR, 359–64.

clay traffic. The principal deposits of ball clay for the pottery industry are on the Isle of Purbeck in Dorset, and in north Devon. *Narrow-gauge railways were laid from Purbeck pits to quays on Poole Harbour in the early 1800s, but by the 1930s most of the clay was being transferred to the *Southern Railway's Swanage branch—some 30,000 tons annually. Rail traffic ceased in 1984. In Devon the main rail outlet was the Halwill Junction–Torrington line, opened in 1925 partly on the route of a narrow-gauge *tramway of 1880. Until 1970 the clay was exported from Fremington quay, near Barnstaple, and Fowey in Cornwall, or went to the Potteries, totalling some 300,000 tons a year. Traffic ceased in 1982.

China clay for the pottery and paper industries is produced in central and north Cornwall. An early tramroad ran from St Austell to Pentewan harbour in 1829–1918, and from 1847 a network of mineral lines grew in the 'China Clay District', based on St Blazey, which remains the centre of the traffic today, mainly for export from Fowey. *BR introduced a 'liner' train to the Potteries, replaced in 1982 by a Speedlink service (see FREIGHT TRAFFIC). Bogie hopper wagons have been used since 1986, when some 701,000 tons were carried. China clay forms Britain's longest freight haul, from Par to paper mills at Irvine and Aberdeen.   GJB

Reg. Hist., i; A. Bennett, *The Great Western Railway in Mid Cornwall* (1958); C. F. D. Whatmath and D. Stuckley, *The North Devon & Cornwall Junction Light Railway and the Marland Light Railway (Torrington to Halwill)* (1963); W. J. K. Davies, *Pike Bros., Fayle & Co. Ltd., Furzebrook* (Narrow Gauge Railway Society Handbook No. 1) (1958).

cleaners, engine and train. Locomotive cleaning was the responsibility of the locomotive department, while *carriage cleaning came under the traffic or carriage departments, and was usually controlled by the *stationmaster in charge of local carriage sidings or depots.

The engine cleaner was the entry grade in progression towards the positions of *fireman and *driver. Engine cleaners started as school-leavers, and were organized in gangs of six or seven boys and men, under a chargeman cleaner. There was a rigid system of advancement, and the usual pattern was for a man to progress to become a passed

cleaner, as a result of which he could act as a spare fireman, particularly at peak times. With the completion of the requisite number of turns of duty, the passed cleaner became a fireman.

Young cleaners were given the dirtiest tasks, such as cleaning *tender and engine wheels, including the insides, and then progressed to the tender-tank and framing-cleaning before promotion to the engine's frames, tender-sides, side-tanks, boilers, and brightwork; finally the side-rods and motion. Apart from cleaning, the intention was that cleaners should learn the function and design of the locomotive parts. Cleaning the engine was reckoned as a day's work, and the tender, half a day's work. The locomotive was usually allocated in 'quarters' as piecework to individual cleaners. Some enginemen recorded in personal notebooks the details of all the engines they had cleaned: an example can be found at the NRM.

Various cleaning agents were used, with bath-brick and emery-paper employed for scouring boiler mountings and buffer heads. In Victorian days the cleaned paintwork on boilers, tenders, and tank-sides was protected by a coating of tallow worked up by cleaners into a fishscale pattern, using pads of cloth. There was considerable rivalry between the cleaning gangs at a shed, and between sheds, to turn out the smartest locomotive.

After World War II there were considerable difficulties in recruiting engine cleaners, and the standard of cleanliness was often poor. At Camden depot in 1960, for instance, just two out of 32 positions for cleaners were filled.

Carriage cleaning was undertaken by men or *women working in sidings, at ground level, or from staging, and using buckets and long-handled brushes. Some main-line railways fitted water hydrants at ground level and, more rarely, electric points for vacuum cleaners used in cleaning the interiors.

Routine cleaning of carriages comprised no more than washing down the exteriors, sweeping out the floors, and dusting the woodwork. At monthly intervals, more thorough cleaning was carried out. The interior panelling and floors of carriages were cleaned with proprietary preparations dissolved in water. An acid and glycerine solution was applied by brush to the exterior panelling for the removal of grime and grease. This was rubbed in, and then washed off with water, and the handles and windows were polished. For prestige sets of carriages, wax polish was rubbed into wooden body panelling, and the exterior panelling polished; steel-panelled exteriors of *London & North Eastern Railway trains of the 1930s were cleaned with a solution of soap-flakes and warm water.

Although a pioneer mechanized carriage cleaning plant was recorded on the GWR as early as 1902, manual cleaning methods persisted and washing plants were not generally introduced until the 1930s. With the more recent examples of these, a unit train or set of carriages passes slowly through a shed to undergo five or so stages: pre-wetting by water jets; acid brushing with revolving brushes (or flails) which apply oxalic acid to the vehicles' sides, roofs, and ends; then brushes applying neutralizer; the water brush stage; and a final rinsing with spray jets. Modern rolling stock depots have sophisticated mechanical washing plants, activated by the approach of the train, and automatically closing down. Trains are usually put through the plant when coming to the depot for examination, or for routine maintenance. MLH

P. S. Bagwell, *The Railwaymen* (1982–3); J. Hodgson and J. Williams, *Locomotive Management from Cleaning to Driving* (1908); P. Ransome-Wallis, *Men of the Footplate* (1954); P. Townsend, *Top Shed* (1989).

clearances: strictly, the spaces between the load gauge and structure gauge, essential for safe passage of vehicles, but sometimes the actual distances between track and structure. The limitations imposed by the overline structures on the cross-sectional dimensions, lengths, and wheelbases of rolling stock proposed to be used on a route, and vice versa, taking account of *superelevation and curvature, are expressed as 'route restrictions' (see ROUTE AVAILABILITY). *British Railways inherited numerous load and structure gauges from its predecessors, and it was its policy progressively to modify both rolling stock and structures so as to standardize route restrictions as much as possible.

Load gauge
(not to be confused with 'loading gauge'): the maximum cross-section permitted for a railway vehicle placed centrally and at rest on straight, level track. The Berne gauge is the load gauge with which internationally operated European railway wagons must comply. It resulted from the need, perceived by the Swiss in the 1870s, to control the dimensions of international traffic through the trans-Alpine tunnels. It evolved at a series of conferences held in Berne by *Unité technique des chemins de fer* (UT), starting in 1882, and was finally implemented in 1914. The UT agreements were eventually incorporated in the *Rules for the Reciprocal Use of Wagons in International Traffic* (RIV). No routes on BR are currently able to accept vehicles to the Berne gauge.

Loading gauge:
apparatus for checking that a load does not exceed the load gauge. As common carriers, railways were until 1962 legally obliged to accept for transit any practicable consignment offered by customers, who often brought to local goods yards quite large objects for loading on to wagons. These were checked by a 'loading gauge' consisting of a lightweight metal outline of the upper part of the applicable load gauge, hanging from a bracket. The person preparing a train to leave the yard would arrange for any load appearing to be too large to be passed under the gauge, and if the load fouled it, or its width was obviously too great, the 'out-of-gauge load procedure' would be invoked. The wagon would be withheld from transit and the local 'out-of-gauge load inspector' would be sent for. He would measure the load and if necessary ascertain from the district engineer the route and conditions under which the wagon could be allowed to travel.

Although both common carrier liability and loading gauges are largely things of the past, the procedure remains, and an 'out-of-gauge load' can be accepted for transit only with special permission and over an approved route.

Structure gauge:
the desirable minimum size of any opening through which a track passes, usually expressed as horizontal and vertical co-ordinates related to the intersection of the running face of the nearest rail of the track concerned, and the plane of the rails, not allowing for curvature. Ideally all openings should be equal to or greater than the structure gauge, and must never be less than the kinematic envelope (the area swept by a moving vehicle allowing for swaying and pitching due to dynamic forces, and to wear and tear of track, wheels, and suspension), plus a safety margin or 'clearance', whose minimum size is specified by the Railway Inspectorate (see INSPECTORS, GOVERNMENT).

Records are kept of the actual sizes of all openings over the track throughout the railway. Updating used to be done by surveying, and revising drawings, but it is now possible to use automated on-track measuring equipment and a computer databank. GHC

G. H. Cope (ed.), *British Railway Track* (1993 edn.); 'Transit international et Unité technique', *La Vie du rail*, no. 1869 (1982); *Bulletin des transports internationaux par chemins de fer*, Berne (1982), no. 9/10; Office fédéral des transports (ed.), centenary booklet, *Unité technique des chemins de fer (UT)*, Berne, Administration gérante de l'Unité technique (1982).

Cleobury Mortimer & Ditton Priors Light Railway, see LIGHT RAILWAYS.

cliff railways. The typical cliff railway comprised two parallel tracks on a steep gradient, each with a *cable-operated car. Twenty-one lines were built at seaside resorts in Britain, with another four at inland locations. In 1994, 15 of the seaside and two of the inland lines were still open. They carried passengers only, although the Lynton & Lynmouth has carried freight. Finance was provided by independent companies or local authorities, the Lynton & Lynmouth relying on the support of Sir George Newnes the publisher, who lived nearby. The first line to be opened was at Scarborough in 1875; the peak period for construction was the 1890s when eight lines were built. Most lines closed in winter, and all the lines were closed during World War II. Only the Metropole Lift at Folkestone failed to reopen. The inland line at Bridgnorth was the only one to operate throughout the year. In 1994, Scarborough had four lines in operation, Bournemouth had three, and Hastings two.

Four of the seaside lines had only a single track. Most lines were straight, on a uniform gradient and at right angles to the cliff face. The steepest gradient, 1 in 1.28, was on the East Cliff at Hastings. The Sandgate line ran obliquely up the slope, with curves and changes of gradient, because of which the cars could not counterbalance each other, so each was attached to a weight in a vertical shaft. This system was also used on the other single-track lines, as at Hastings. The longest line was the Lynton & Lynmouth: 890 ft. *Track gauge varied from 3 ft for the Devil's Dyke line near *Brighton, to 6 ft on West Hill, Hastings. The rails were usually of a standard railway pattern, but to prevent downhill creepage, they were specially supported. Communication between the cars and the winding house was either mechanical or electrical.

Until 1903, with two exceptions, the lines were operated by the water balance system. Each car had fitted to it a water tank of up to 700 gallons capacity, which was filled at the top of the incline and emptied at the bottom, the extra weight of the descending car pulling up the car with the empty tank. In most cases, the discharged water was pumped back up by a steam or gas engine. In 1994 the water balance system was still in use at Saltburn, Lynton, and Folkestone's other line. Elsewhere the winding drum was worked electrically.

The cars had horizontal floors on a triangular chassis which accommodated the gradient, thus keeping the cabin level. The chassis housed the water tank. They were well appointed, with end-doors and longitudinal seating, like a *tram car. At Aberystwyth there were longer cars with stepped floors and side entrances reached from stepped platforms. Carrying capacity was up to 35 passengers.

There were no intermediate stations, and the principal station was usually at the lower end. There was no timetable, cars running on demand between about 9.00 a.m. and 6.00 p.m. A signal to start could be given from either station. Journey times varied from about 20 seconds at Saltburn (207 ft long) to two minutes at Lynton (890 ft long). Single or return tickets were issued, sometimes with different fares for ascending and descending.

Design, construction, and ownership were often local. For instance, the line at Devil's Dyke was designed by Charles Blaber who lived nearby, and built by Courtney & Birkett, engineers and yacht builders from Southwick, who had experience of patent slips for hauling yachts out of the water. The Lynton line was designed and constructed by Robert Jones, a local builder. The Torquay street tramway undertaking leased the Babbacombe Cliff Railway, although it was built by the National Electric Construction Co., an associate of Waygood Otis, makers of *lifts and escalators. However, in the 20th century, most of the lines have been owned by local authorities. For instance, the three Bournemouth lines (two opened in 1908 and one in 1935) were built and operated by the corporation—perhaps significantly by the Tourist and not the Transport Department.   EC

J. Woodhams, *Funicular Railways* (1989); E. Course, *Railways of Southern England*, iii (1976); M. E. Tighe, 'Cliff Lifts and Railways', *Sussex I. A. Society Newsletter* (Apr. 1992).

Clinker, Charles Ralph (1906–83), historian; he served with the *Great Western Railway 1923–46, during which time and afterwards he wrote numerous magazine articles on railway history, a subject on which he later conducted evening classes in the Midlands. He was not a writer of books, although he published several valuable company monographs, preferring to assemble chronologies of authorizations and openings. Despite being now largely superseded by R. V. J. Butt's *Directory of Railway Stations* (1995), Clinker's most valuable work was his *Register of Closed Passenger Stations and Goods Depots*, based on the work of M. D. Greville and J. G. Spence, which went through three editions. His most important, though least known, achievement was to set up Locomotive & General Railway Photographs (LGRP) in partnership with W. Vaughan Jenkins and V. Stewart Haram in 1948–9, a large, valuable, and painstakingly assembled collection which includes the work of early or well-known photographers such as T. F. Budden, E. Pouteau, H. Gordon Tidey, R. E. *Charlewood, H. L. Hopwood, and others (see PHOTOGRAPHY). A supply of contemporary subjects was ensured by providing film and free prints to established photographers, in exchange for copyright. Now, these also are a valuable historical record. The venture was a commercial failure, however, and after passing into Clinker's sole ownership it was sold and eventually acquired by the NRM.   GJB and JS

clock-face services, see ALL-NIGHT SERVICES; COMMUTING; INTERVAL SERVICES.

closure of railways. When proposals have been made for the closure of passenger railways they have in recent years often aroused opposition from public bodies and individuals. The history of closures falls into three distinct periods.

Before 1922–3, when the lines were owned by the old private companies, such closures were rare. The first was the withdrawal of passenger services from the Oystermouth Railway (see SWANSEA & MUMBLES RAILWAY), about 1827, after a new road had been built beside it that carried horse-buses; they were restored by the railway in 1860. The first line to be closed permanently to passenger traffic was the *Stockton & Darlington's branch to Yarm, ¾ mile long, on which services were discontinued in 1833. In the 1840s and 1850s a number of services were withdrawn, either because they were little used or because there were newer and better routes, but only two were longer than 10 miles: the Newmarket Railway from Great Chesterford to Six Mile Bottom (12 miles, closed in 1851), and the *Stratford & Moreton Railway (19 miles, closed in 1859; 9 miles reopened in 1889). The first line in Scotland closed permanently to passengers was the very short one from Milton Junction to Glasgow (St Rollox), replaced by a line into the new station at Buchanan Street.

The closure of a line already opened must be distinguished from the abandonment of one that was authorized but not built, the procedure for which was laid down in legislation of 1848–50 (see ABANDONMENT). Closure was never directly regulated by any Act of Parliament in the Victorian age, although the Railway and Canal Traffic Act (1854) bore upon it at one point in an important way. Section 2 required railway companies to 'afford all reasonable facilities for the receiving and forwarding and delivery of traffic'. If any of them did not, a complainant was entitled to take his case to court, which could result in a fine imposed on the company up to the then enormous sum of £200 a day until the facilities were restored.

Plainly, the withdrawal of passenger services without a satisfactory alternative amounted to a refusal of that sort.

But the procedure under this Act was cumbrous and costly, and though it was somewhat eased under further Acts of 1873 and 1888, it was not until 1890 that any complaint about a withdrawal of passenger services—in this instance the local board of Winsford, attacking the *Cheshire Lines Committee—won its case on these grounds. Four years later in a similar case concerning Darlaston (Staffordshire) the *London & North Western, ordered to reinstate a discontinued passenger service, took the case to the Court of Appeal and won it.

Some 400 miles of line were closed to passengers in Britain before 1922, 70 of them in Scotland. Nearly a third of these closures were World War I economy measures, but few were reinstated.

A new phase opened in 1922–3, when the main-line railways were *grouped into four companies. Because they were so much larger than the old ones they tended to look more critically on small units like country branch lines, and they now had to meet increasingly severe competition from mechanical *road transport.

Yet that was by no means new. Street *tramways, which began to be mechanized in the 1870s, had already gained a great deal of the traffic that had previously been carried by train in urban districts. Before 1914 motor-*buses, both urban and rural, had started to do the same thing. In the 1920s and 1930s this process was rapidly extended, until there was scarcely a rural line in the country that was unaffected by their competition.

The extent of this change must not be exaggerated. The railways were damaged in these years more severely by the loss of goods traffic to the roads, which occurred everywhere, on main lines as well as on branches. Between 1923 and 1939 the numbers of buses and coaches carrying passengers doubled. But the lorries on the roads multiplied eight times over.

Passenger services were withdrawn from more than four times as many miles of line in Britain in 1922–47 as during the whole of the previous century: a total of about 1,650 miles, 20 per cent of them in Scotland. Some were branches, succumbing to others that had been built to compete with them: at Marlborough, for instance, and Ramsey (Huntingdonshire). Others included more extensive lines that had never succeeded in generating any large passenger traffic. The two longest of these were both on the *London & North Eastern system: Alnwick–Coldstream (36 miles), closed in 1930; and most of the main line of the former *Hull & Barnsley Railway from South Howden to Cudworth (29 miles, 1932). The longest line then closed in Scotland was the branch to Fort Augustus off the West Highland Railway (24 miles long, 1933).

In 1928 the large railway companies secured powers to own and operate buses themselves. Though some had previously done that, their authority to do it had been doubtful. Now it was made certain. One of their chief reasons was to enable them to profit from replacement road services: not as a rule directly through running buses themselves, but by investment in bus undertakings, to an extent that within three years amounted to nearly £10 million.

So the four railways showed, in one way and another, that they took the threat of competition from mechanized road transport seriously. The *Southern Railway succeeded best in meeting it. But it could not truthfully be said that any of them came near to 'solving' the problems presented by lines that were unremunerative, whether in terms of passenger or goods transport, or both. Nowhere in Britain was any real effort made to achieve an integration between rail and road services, comparable with what was then being done in some parts of rural France. But there the task was eased by the much tighter control that the French state exercised over all transport services.

In 1948 the British government assumed that control for the first time (see NATIONALIZATION), working through its instrument the *British Transport Commission. Under this new management the railways began to accelerate the closure of lines. In 1948–53, some 1,253 miles were closed to all traffic, 1,167 miles to passenger services.

That process had now grown more complicated. Under the nationalization Act *Transport Users' Consultative Committees were established, which had power to consider plans to withdraw services. The public—local authorities, business firms, private persons—gained an opportunity to comment on what was proposed. Although the new committees were advisory bodies only, not executive, their opinions (which were published) could not be disregarded.

The railways' management had to take on a new task, which brought it widespread unpopularity. It was set on overhauling the whole railway system under a plan for its *modernization, requiring a massive investment of public money. In order to succeed, that plan (published in 1955) had to prove that it made all justifiable economies in the railways' working. One of these was to reduce expenditure on unprofitable lines, either by closing them totally or by withdrawing passenger services. The general argument convinced thinking people, but its application aroused intense opposition from those who were (or thought they would be) disadvantaged by the proposals, backed by a chorus of people who were saddened, or instinctively enraged, by them.

Richard *Beeching was appointed chairman of the BTC in 1961, and of the *British Railways Board when the BTC was abolished in 1962. Before the end of that year he had set up the means for collecting together in one place information about the commercial performance of all the individual lines and stations on the railway system. The committee charged with analysing it, chaired by Stanley Raymond, prepared a report, which appeared in 1963 under the title *The Re-shaping of British Railways*.

At its beginning the report stated, quite truly, that 'there had never been before any systematic assembly of a basis of information upon which planning could be founded'. It was a well-written and well-argued analysis, and the statistics required to support it were clearly presented. Having set down in detail some examples of the traffic handled by unremunerative lines, the report concluded by recommending the closure of about 280 lines to passenger traffic and of 1,850 stations, all of them individually listed.

As these lines and stations were scattered over the whole of Great Britain, from Caithness to Cornwall and from Anglesey to Kent, we cannot be surprised by the outcry that the report raised. But the protesters paid hardly any attention to the rest of the report—some of it concerned with the means of providing new or additional services. They made no effort whatever to face the compelling economic arguments that the report adduced.

There was, however, another element that received little immediate attention, though it had a future before it. The reshaping committee's remit was concerned with economic matters alone. But at two points (pp. 22, 55–6) it alluded to another way in which unprofitable lines and stations might still be retained if their closure would bring demonstrable hardship to the communities they served. That could perhaps be met, partly or wholly, by grants from public funds (national and local). Social 'cost–benefit studies' of this matter were already being made at the Ministry of *Transport, though not as yet with any positive results.

In 1964 a new Labour government was returned, later bringing as Minister of Transport Barbara Castle, who was prepared to take these proposals seriously (see SUBSIDIES). Before very long they began to be applied to the railways, where they became a policy so firmly accepted that it had to be continued by the Conservatives, back in power in 1970. Closure of lines and stations still proceeded apace, including some long lines like the Waverley Route from Edinburgh to Carlisle; also the last surviving fragment of the *Great Central main line from London to Sheffield. But the brake was now applied, gradually yet quite firmly. No line of much length or importance was closed during 1973–93, the last 20 years of BR's life.

Some lines severely threatened on economic grounds now received something much like an indefinite reprieve as grants became available to keep them going: the 'Heart of Wales Line' from Craven Arms to Llanelly, for example; the Cambrian Coast line from Machynlleth to Pwllheli; the Highland line from Inverness to Wick and Thurso; and, although the circumstances were somewhat different, the *Settle & Carlisle line. They were bound to remain commercially unprofitable, but the cost of new or improved roads to take the traffic from some of them was discouragingly high.   JS

M. D. Greville and J. Spence, *Closed Passenger Lines in Great Britain, 1827–1947* (1974 edn.); R. V. J. Butt, *Directory of Railway Stations* (1995); M. R. Bonavia, *British Rail: The First 25 Years* (1981); Gourvish.

club trains described trains which included 'club' carriages, and ran each morning and evening between residential towns and cities, mainly to and from *Manchester.

Club carriages were introduced by the *Lancashire & Yorkshire Railway in 1895, on *Blackpool–Manchester services, after an approach from first-class season ticket holders who asked that in return for a guarantee that a specified number of annual seasons were purchased, a carriage should be provided by the LYR for their exclusive use, and a supplementary fee charged to members of the club. Elec-

tion by the club committee was mandatory and there were rules for members, one being that all windows were to be kept closed while the train was travelling. Members had their own particular seats, usually in armchairs, while cups of tea were served from a galley. By 1902, the main Blackpool club train had two saloon club carriages, and a third-class club was also later established on this service.

The *London & North Western Railway introduced similar club trains before World War I on morning and evening residential trains between Llandudno and the other North Wales coast towns, and *Liverpool and Manchester. A club train was also operated from 1912 between Windermere and Manchester. Another operator was the *North Eastern Railway, with club cars working between Bridlington and *Hull into the mid-1930s.

Some of the club carriages were saloon vehicles converted for the purpose, but a new vehicle was built for the Blackpool service as late as 1935. The club carriages ceased to run during World War II, and were not reintroduced. Some were used for cruise trains operated in North Wales during the 1950s and 1960s.

A so-called club train composed of ordinary stock ran between Blackpool and Manchester for several years up to 1996.   MLH

C. J. Allen, *Titled Trains of Great Britain* (1967); G. O. Clayton, 'Club Trains of the LMS', *Locomotion* 7 (1936) 21, 33; E. Mason, *Lancashire & Yorkshire Railway in the Twentieth Century* (1954).

coaches, road. The first stage-coaches—horse-drawn vehicles open to the public, who paid fares reckoned by stages on the journey—began to run in the 1650s. By 1760 they had become established on all the principal English roads, which had themselves been much improved as a result of the *turnpike system, imposing tolls for its use.

The speed at which the coaches travelled was now gradually rising, from 50–60 miles a day *c.*1700 to 80 or even 100 by 1775. Further acceleration arose from some changes in the coaches' construction (they were beginning to be built with steel springs, for example, by 1755) and from new demands made upon them. The most important came from the *Post Office, which introduced mail-coaches of its own in 1784. Besides the mails, each of them took a small number of passengers: usually four or five to begin with, whereas the stage-coaches took 15–20.

There had long been competition between stage-coaches running on the same roads. They were usually owned by syndicates, the members of which included innkeepers at whose houses the coaches stopped in order to change horse, and allow passengers to dine. The mail-coaches now made competition strenuous. Their fares were at first somewhat higher, but the vehicles were better and they carried an armed guard, an important security when there were still highwaymen on the roads.

Competition also produced some increase in speed. After 1784 the best services ran at 7–8 mph. They did not approach 10 mph until after 1815, and only a few travelled faster in normal service. The speediest were generally those between London and *Brighton, *Plymouth, *Shrewsbury, and *Manchester. Some fares came down at the same time, although it is difficult to make exact statements about them. Coach proprietors were free to fix their own charges, and to alter them without notice. In 1784 most seem to have been, for inside passengers, 2½–4d. a mile. They rose in the 1790s, with the increased price of horse-fodder, but fell again after 1815.

The railways' competition with the coaches became formidable immediately. When the *Liverpool & Manchester line was opened in 1830, offering a service between the two cities twice as fast, at scarcely more than half the coaches' fares, nearly all of them disappeared. The railways' superior speed grew even more marked as the long-distance routes were completed. By coach the journey from London to *Birmingham took at least 12 hours. When the railway was completed in 1838 its trains took five, at comparable fares. Some desperate efforts were made to maintain coach services, but they failed (see CHAPLIN, W. J.). Horses had reached their limits, while the locomotive was still at the beginning of its development.

Extension of the trunk railways destroyed coach services running parallel with them, but they survived in districts into which railways had not yet penetrated (between Dover and Deal, for example, until 1881), and as feeders to the railways. A few were still running in 1900, like those to Hartland, St David's, and Nevin, to be displaced in the end by motor-*buses.   JS

Jackman, chs 4, 8, and appendices 5, 6; J. Copeland, *Roads and Their Traffic, 1750–1850* (1968); A. A. Bates, *Directory of Stage-Coach Services, 1836* (1969).

coal (as fuel). Before 1830 coal could only be sold in lump form by measure (volume), making broken coal or slack unsaleable waste, and all colliery steam plant, early locomotives included, burnt this waste with no thought of economy or smoke prevention. On public railways, however, locomotives were required by law to consume their own smoke and this led many companies to burn coke instead, erecting batteries of coke ovens which, being static, did not have to consume their own smoke. But coke is an expensive fuel, destructive of fireboxes and tubes, and several engineers attempted to burn coal without the emission of smoke. Some, like J. E. McConnell, J. H. *Beattie, and W. Cudworth, employed complicated and short-lived fireboxes, but the best and simplest method was that developed on the *Midland Railway by Matthew *Kirtley and Charles Markham using the admission of air above the fire with a deflector plate and firebrick arch to ensure proper mixing of the gas streams. Successfully represented as being designed to consume its own smoke in compliance with the law, this modification became standard for coal-burning locomotives after 1860. The importance attached to fuel economy by different designers depended upon the cost of buying and transporting coal for their respective locomotives. Apart from some experiments using *oil fuel, coal dust mixed with oil (colloidal fuel), and mechanical stokers, British steam locomotives were always fired by hand.   RW

BSRL, 23–56.

coal traffic. The importance of coal to the British economy in the last two centuries cannot be overstated, and the use of railways to carry it was crucial. Britain's plentiful supplies were found mainly in the north of England, the Midlands, South Wales, and across central *Scotland. The coalfields produced different grades of fuel, each having its own properties for specific purposes. For centuries coal was dug only where it outcropped, and was carried away mainly by cart or packhorse for local use. Coal from the north-east and Scotland was sent by sea to London and to the Continent. It was shipped from Ayrshire and Whitehaven to *Ireland, from South Wales to the West Country, and down the River Severn from Shropshire. The building of *canals reduced transport costs and allowed coal to be carried further afield. But it was railways that allowed full exploitation of deposits, the presence of which could influence the location of new pits.

Although people everywhere used coal for heating the home, over 75 per cent used in Britain went to industry, gasworks, ironworks, and, later, power stations. It was brought to most of its consumers partly or wholly by rail. Nearly every line had some coal traffic. Some carried prodigious quantities, amongst them the most profitable railways in the country.

The railways' long association with coal began with the wagonways of the 17th century (see WOODEN RAILWAYS; EARLY IRON RAILWAYS) and, though in decline, continues today. In the north-east, wagonways halved the cost of taking coal from local pits to the staiths on the Rivers Tyne and Wear, where it was loaded into keels for transfer to sailing colliers anchored in mid-stream. Later, at huge timber jetties, such as those at Dunston Staiths, coal was 'teemed' (emptied from bottom-opening wagons) down spouts or chutes directly into waiting colliers. Every effort was made to reduce breakage, since large lumps brought higher prices; dust was practically worthless.

The *Stockton & Darlington Railway (1825) was built to take coal from south-west Durham to the River Tees for shipping, allowing coalowners to break into the lucrative London market hitherto monopolized by the Tyneside and Wearside cartel (see GRAND ALLIES). A short branch line from Darlington to a coal depot at Croft, on the Great North Road, was opened in 1829. An extension westwards from Darlington to Tebay and Penrith enabled Durham coke to be supplied to the West Cumberland iron industry. In 1866 this line carried over 300,000 tons of coke.

By 1859 the *North Eastern Railway was carrying 1.6 million tons of coal and 117,000 tons of coke annually to depots and industries on its own lines in the north-east and Yorkshire. Ten years later those figures had risen to 4.7 million tons and 1.7 million tons respectively, only part of the increase being attributed to the SDR, which the NER had absorbed in 1863. Coal was the NER's dominant traffic, making it highly profitable, although unlike its passenger traffic it did not have a monopoly. In 1866 only about 30 per cent of coal shipped from Sunderland arrived there by NER, the rest being carried by the private railways of Lord Londonderry and other coalowners. On Tyneside the situation was similar.

Some railways were promoted specifically to carry coal, among them the *Clarence Railway in Co. Durham, the *Leicester & Swannington, and the *Edinburgh & Dalkeith. The *Hull & Barnsley Railway, opened in 1885, carried south Yorkshire coal for export. Some railway promoters were coalowners looking for cost reductions or new markets. Conversely, some railway builders became involved in coal-mining: George *Stephenson at Snibston, Leicestershire, and at Clay Cross, Derbyshire; David *Davies, the railway contractor, in the Rhondda.

In South Wales competing railways linked pits in the valleys with docks in *Cardiff, Newport, *Swansea, and a host of smaller ports. Coal traffic grew apace, checked only by the capacity of railways and docks to handle it. Small companies, such as the *Taff Vale and *Rhymney Railways, vied with each other and with the larger companies, the *Great Western, the *London & North Western, and the *Midland, but as markets grew there was more than enough for all. The constant, but slow, procession of coal trains down the valleys made the little companies very prosperous.

In the Rhondda, where there were vast quantities of high quality Welsh steam coal, coalowners became concerned at delays caused by congestion in the docks at Cardiff and limits being imposed on the markets by the transport system. They successfully set up the *Barry Dock & Railways Company to divert traffic from the TVR at Trehafod to a new dock at Barry, which eventually outranked Cardiff as the main coal exporting port in South Wales. Not all South Wales coal went for export; some was used locally and some was carried further afield by the GWR, LNWR, and MR.

Coal was moved throughout the Scottish lowlands by rail, to local towns and to ports on the Forth and Clyde. In 1867 the *Glasgow & South Western Railway carried some 900,000 tons to west coast ports, 340,000 tons to local stations, and nearly 500,000 tons to Scottish ironworks. In the same year the *North British Railway carried 2.7 million tons from 168 collieries, and the *Caledonian Railway carried a total of 3.2 million tons of which 2.2 million tons was delivered to CR stations. As elsewhere, competition was rife. The CR, for example, supported a line to Ardrossan in 1888 to capture coal traffic from the GSWR, and later took it over.

Away from the coalfields other ports received coal for distribution by rail. The *London Brighton & South Coast Railway carried coal to stations along its lines from Deadman's Dock, London, and Shoreham, on the south coast. The *South Eastern Railway distributed coal delivered by sea to Whitstable and Angerstein Wharf, London. The *Highland and *Great North of Scotland Railways distributed coal landed at ports on the Scottish east coast.

The railways enabled inland coal producers to compete in the London market hitherto dominated by sea-borne coal (see SHIPPING, COASTAL). In the five years to 1850, canal- and rail-borne coal accounted for only 1.6 per cent of the total sold in London. When the *Great Northern Railway

entered the trade in 1851, as both carrier and merchant, the amount brought to London increased dramatically. In the same year the Northumberland & Durham Coal Company began to run its own trains on the *North London Railway from Poplar Dock to its own depots. The following year the first iron-hulled, screw-driven steam collier, the *John Bowes*, entered Poplar Dock. The sea-borne coal faction had retaliated. Within a few years steam colliers had ousted the brigs. Unloading was mechanized with the introduction of hydraulic cranes. Other railways began to join the trade; the LNWR, MR, and *Great Eastern all brought substantial quantities of coal to London, the last via the Lancashire Derbyshire & East Coast Railway (see GREAT CENTRAL) and the GN & GE Joint line. In 1870 London's rail-borne coal traffic was handled by ten different railway companies. Of these, the GNR, MR, LNWR, and GER carried 3.24 million tons, 86 per cent of the total. The LNWR brought 835,000 tons from pits in 12 coalfields, including 29 pits in South Wales.

By 1867 rail-borne coal reaching London exceeded sea-borne coal. The building of Beckton gasworks, with coal jetties on the Thames, reversed rail's supremacy by 1897, and Thames-side electric power stations helped sea-borne coal to maintain its lead. Railway companies established wharves and docks along the Thames for transhipping coal to barges for delivery to riverside establishments and for bunkering steamships. Northern railway companies delivered coal traffic to southern companies and even established their own coal depots in south London.

The importance of the London traffic was reflected in special engineering works undertaken to ease gradients against loaded coal trains, increasing the loads that one engine could haul, thus reducing costs. The MR did this at Sharnbrook in 1884; the GWR on the new up line from the *Severn Tunnel between Pilning and Patchway.

In the north-east, the NER controlled the local market for coal through a network of depots. Rural depots were generally run by NER staff whilst those in towns were often leased out to merchants. Each depot comprised a number of 'cells' in which coal, coke, or lime could be stored. The dividing walls supported one or more railway lines so that wagons could be run over the cells to empty the contents through bottom-opening doors. Sometimes called 'drops' or 'bays', more sophisticated cells were found at depots in West Yorkshire and London, with intermediate hoppers from which merchants could bag coal as required.

Coal depots were noisy, dusty places, and caused much annoyance to their neighbours. More common was the straightforward yard with wide-spaced sidings. Merchants formed storage bunkers of old sleepers or simply sold from the wagon, a practice frowned on by wagon owners, whether they were railway or colliery company. Hence they charged *demurrage. Failure to return sufficient empty wagons to the pits could jeopardize coal production.

The maximum possible size of wagon depended on terminal facilities. At collieries, rotary tipplers inverted tubs to empty their contents past screens into wagons. At gasworks, wagons with end-doors were emptied by hydraulic tips. At ports, wagons were emptied at chutes, drops, tips, conveyors, and hydraulic hoists, which replaced balanced gravity tips from 1850. Changing any of these was expensive and was often not in railway control, so increases in wagon size were slow to materialize. Mechanization had its penalties.

From 1829 until the 1860s most locomotives burnt coke, some early railways having their own coke ovens. Others bought supplies from gasworks. Railways serving coalfields were at an advantage. The GWR benefited from its access to best quality Welsh steam coal. Railways in the south suffered from lack of local supplies. In periods of coal shortage oil-firing was tried (see OIL AS A FUEL). From 1893 the GER successfully oil-fired some 60 locomotives using waste oil from its plant producing gas for its Pintsch's *carriage lighting. Even the GWR converted some locomotives to oil-firing after World War I.

Distributing coal by wagon-load to a large number of widely scattered depots ended in the 1960s with the establishment of highly mechanized 'coal concentration' depots at strategic locations to which coal was more economically delivered by the train-load. Declining household coal traffic increasingly transferred to road haulage and the new depots were gradually closed down. In the 1960s *'merry-go-round' trains were introduced between particular collieries and the new, larger power stations.

Within the coalfields a pattern developed of short-distance coal trains to local communities and industries, and to nearby ports. Longer-distance trains took coal to other areas, particularly to London. From the inland coalfields there was also some long-distance traffic to coastal ports like *Hull and Grimsby. Some Erewash Valley coal from Derbyshire was even shipped from Morecambe. But with steam-powered and coal-using industry located mainly in the coalfields, much of the traffic travelled over short distances. The average haul before World War II was about 44 miles; during the war it rose to about 57 miles as traffic was transferred from the vulnerable east coast colliers to rail, a trend that continued afterwards. The peak year for coal and coke traffic was 1913, when the railways carried 225 million tons. By 1945 this had fallen to 143 million tons but it rose again after the war. In 1950 the railways were still responsible for carrying 70 per cent of Britain's coal traffic.

The passing of the Clean Air Acts in the 1950s, the wholesale abandonment of steam power by industry, and the switch to North Sea gas all contributed to the decline of traditional coal traffic. As electricity generating capacity was concentrated in large power stations railway coal traffic patterns changed to relatively short-distance haulage. Wholesale pit closures in the early 1990s reduced the railways' coal traffic still further in the preparations for *privatization of both industries.   TRS

A. R. Griffin, *The British Coalmining Industry* (1977); R. Smith, *Sea Coal for London* (1961).

coastal shipping, see SHIPPING, COASTAL.

Collett, Charles Benjamin (1871–1952), mechanical engineer. After a pupilage with marine engineers Maudslay Son

& Field, he joined the *Great Western Railway as a draughtsman at *Swindon in 1893, becoming assistant works manager in 1900, works manager in 1912, and in 1920 deputy to the CME, G. J. *Churchward. He was CME 1922–41. Collett's locomotive designs were derived from Churchward's, his 'Castle' class four-cylinder 4-6-0 express type, of which 171 were built or converted in 1923–50, being an enlargement of the 'Star' class, whilst the 410 'Hall' and 'Grange' class two-cylinder 4-6-0s were mixed-traffic derivatives from the 'Saint' express type. Collett's 'King' class express locomotives of 1927–30 were the heaviest and most powerful 4-6-0s in Britain, made possible by a relaxation in permissible axle loading. All were highly successful types.

Collett carried out a major programme of workshop re-equipment and greatly improved locomotive erection methods. Greater engineering precision gave appreciably increased mileages between overhauls. He extended the use of the GWR Automatic Train Control system (see AUTOMATIC WARNING SYSTEMS) to almost all important routes and was a member of the 1927 Pringle Committee studying the use of such systems in Britain. From 1936 he modernized the Swindon *locomotive testing plant to absorb the maximum power of larger locomotives. His later locomotive policy was rather conservative, but he was among the first to consider complete dieselization.   GWC

The Engineer, 194 (1952), 289–90; H. Holcroft, *An Outline of Great Western Locomotive Practice 1837–1947* (1957).

commissions and parliamentary committees. Any student of British railway history may be puzzled by references to bodies bearing these titles. This article tries to clear a path through the jungle.

Commissions

Those affecting railways were of four different kinds, as follows.

1. A *Royal Commission* was one issued by the sovereign at the government's request, appointing named members to report on named matters. It selected witnesses to appear before it and examined them, sometimes at great length. All the evidence given was published word by word, together with a number of other papers (often statistical), submitted in support of the evidence or called for by the Commissioners themselves. The evidence and appendices are often of great historical importance.

There were eight of these Commissions:

1845	*Gauges
1846	*London termini
1865	Railways (general, especially *nationalization; the 'Devon Commission')
1874	*Accidents
1900	Accidents to railway servants
1903	London traffic
1911	Wages Conciliation scheme
1914	Railways (general)

The last of these, overtaken by war, never reported. Valuable material relating to railways is also to be found in the papers of Royal Commissions dealing with other subjects, e.g. those on the Housing of the Working Classes (1883), on Canals (1906), and on Transport (1928).

2. *Standing Commissions*. In 1846 (during the *Mania) Parliament decided to remove the responsibility for the supervision of railways from the Board of *Trade, transferring it to a body of 'Railway Commissioners', chosen by itself. They comprised an MP (chairman), a peer, a retired judge, and a Royal Engineers officer who had been director of works at the Admiralty, with another RE officer as their secretary. Though individually able men, they did not cohere to make a satisfactory administrative body for the railways, and they were disbanded in 1851, their powers reverting to the Board of Trade. In 1896 the Board was statutorily authorized to appoint another Commission 'for the purpose of facilitating the construction and working of *light railways in Great Britain'.

3. *Legal tribunals*. Following a recommendation of a House of Commons Committee, a Railway Commission was set up in 1873, constituting a legal court to which complaints could be taken arising from the working of the Railway and Canal Traffic Act, 1854 (see CARDWELL, VISCOUNT), and especially from the 'reasonable facilities' that the Act required the companies to provide for the conveyance of passengers and freight. Though the principles of the Act had not been impugned, the cases in dispute had gone to the old-established courts, where the procedure was cumbersome and costly. The Commission of 1873 effected some improvements, but not enough, and a further Act was passed in 1893 replacing it by a Railway and Canal Commission, with a simplified procedure, which lasted until its powers were taken over by the Transport Tribunal in 1921.

4. *British Transport Commission*. This, the last of these commissions, stood on its own: established by Act of Parliament in 1948 to administer the railways and all other transport undertakings that were nationalized. It was disbanded in 1962.

Parliamentary Committees

Many committees were set up by Parliament to inquire into railway business, only a small sample of which can be mentioned here.

Parliament constantly referred matters requiring much discussion of detail to Select Committees of one House or the other, or to Joint Select Committees, comprising members of both. These were often instruments for devising principles on which Acts were subsequently based. Most of the chief *Regulation Acts emerged in this way: the Commons Committee of 1844 was especially important for its rehandling of some of *Gladstone's original proposals.

One other Committee of the 1840s may be referred to, from which no legislation emerged. The Commons Committee on Railway Labourers (1846) made a serious effort to investigate the conditions of their employment, and the evidence it took, from a wide range of witnesses, records a good deal about the *navvies that we should not otherwise know.

Another group of parliamentary committees worked particularly hard at this time: those charged with the examination of private Bills, which included all those promoted by railway companies (see PARLIAMENT AND LEGISLATION). They

numbered 116 in 1846–7, the committees' work occupying a total of 1,502 days.

Nobody could be satisfied then with the procedure for examining and pronouncing on railway Bills, and several committees were concerned with proposals for improving it, two in 1845–6, others in 1852 and 1858, but none produced an acceptable plan for improving the current arrangements.

The committee system appeared more effective when applied to the principles on which the *amalgamation of railway companies should rest, arising from the attempts of the *London & North Western and *Lancashire & Yorkshire Railways to amalgamate in 1872–3. The second of these two reported so firmly against these and other similar proposals as to settle the question. Apart from a GNR, GER and GCR scheme in 1909, no other plan for the same sort of amalgamation came up until 1921 (see GROUPING). Here a strong committee recommendation was decisive.   JS

E. Cleveland-Stevens lists the parliamentary committees dealing with railways in 1838–72 in his *English Railways: Their Development and Their Relation to the State* (1915), 62–4, 331.

communication in trains. From early days, as trains began increasingly to run over considerable distances without stopping, there was an evident need of communication between the *driver at the front and *guard at the rear; and equally, in emergency, between passengers and train crews. Fifty years of argument passed before wholly satisfactory appliances were evolved to meet these demands.

The first step was taken by the *Great Western Railway in 1847, when it began fitting a hooded seat to the back of each of its engines' tenders to contain a 'travelling porter', who could look along the train and communicate with the driver if he saw anything untoward. But this arrangement proved to be of very limited efficacy, and it was much resented by the porters themselves.

In 1853 the *London & South Western Railway adopted a mechanism by which the guard could warn the driver of any mischance by activating a distinctively toned whistle on the engine. Equally the driver could, at need, blow a very shrill whistle to tell the guard to apply his brake.

The Board of *Trade reviewed all such expedients and kept abreast of developments in France and Belgium. On some British lines cords were suspended along the train which, when pulled by passengers, were supposed to ring a bell on the tender, but that arrangement often proved ineffective. In 1853 and 1858 parliamentary committees urged the companies to find better solutions to the problem, but little progress was made. Then after 1860 the incidence of *crime committed on trains grew steadily more alarming. There was another parliamentary investigation in 1865, aided by a most efficient paper from the *inspector H. W. *Tyler, reviewing the whole range of appliances. The *Regulation Act of 1868 (section 22) required every passenger train travelling more than 20 miles without stopping to be provided with 'such efficient means' of communication as the Board might approve. Against the inspectors' advice it accepted a cord-and-bell system devised by

T. E. *Harrison, chief engineer of the *North Eastern Railway, which proved so unsatisfactory that the Board had to rescind its approval in 1872.

This grimly farcical situation continued unchanged for many years. Electrical systems had been adopted by the LSWR, *London Brighton & South Coast, and *South Eastern Railways by 1877 and approved by the Board, but they found no general acceptance. The breakthrough came at last as a consequence of the Regulation Act of 1889, requiring all passenger trains to be fitted with continuous *brakes. In 1891–2 the Manchester Sheffield & Lincolnshire Railway (see GREAT CENTRAL) and LBSCR adopted devices enabling passengers to apply the brakes themselves, in case of emergency, by means of chains or handles. They were quickly accepted by the Board and a reliable system emerged, in the passengers' hands. Its rapid adoption was impeded by some companies' refusal to find the money, but they all fell gradually into line.

Opposition to use by passengers arose from fear of trivial or malicious activation; penalties for those offences had already been laid down in 1868, which were now invoked, and enforced. No change in principle has occurred since. The Act of 1868 still stands, the maximum penalties imposed for improper use of the equipment being increased from £5 in 1868 to £50 in 1977. The mechanism itself is different, the chains used at first giving place entirely to handles, and tools being provided for the breaking of window-glass in emergency.

See also SAFETY.   JS

Tyler's paper is in PP 1865, i. 17–29.

commuting. The word 'commute', i.e. to change one form of obligation into another, was adapted in the USA in the 19th century for the specialized meaning of 'to travel regularly by public transport to and from work in a city or town centre', the 'commutation' being by payment for the journeys in advance. It and its derivative 'commuter' were still unfamiliar enough in 1944 to require explanation to British readers, but by 1960 they were in general use, extended somewhat imprecisely to cover everyone travelling some distance between residence and workplace, including travel by private car. On British railways the term normally used was 'season-ticket holders' (the word 'contract' was used in the north of England). *Season tickets offered regular travellers between two stations unlimited travel for a fixed period (usually a month, three months, or a year); they often included travel to and from intermediate stations also (see FARES; TICKETS; PASSES).

The first recorded season tickets were offered by the *Canterbury & Whitstable Railway in March 1834, for 'Family and Personal Tickets from Lady Day [25 March] to 1st November'. The name may have been adopted from the River Thames steamboats, where it was familiar enough to be used without comment by Charles Dickens in his sketch 'The River' (1835) included in *Sketches by Boz*. The *London & Greenwich Railway in 1836 offered 'Free Tickets' at £5, £4, or £3 per quarter, according to *class; these appeared also on the *Stockton & Darlington Railway in the 1830s. In

1835 there were 'subscriptions' on the Dublin & Kingstown Railway in Ireland. 'Composition' for tickets, rejected by the *Leeds & Selby Railway in 1834, appeared on the Hull & Selby Railway in 1841. On the *Liverpool & Manchester 'commutation' tickets were introduced in 1842, annual tickets to shareholders in 1843 and to the public in 1845. The *London & Brighton in 1843 offered first-class season tickets between terminals for £100 a year; this had been reduced to £43 by 1914. The *South Eastern sold annual tickets between *London Bridge and Gravesend for £26 5s. in 1849 and offered favourable rates in 1854 to outer-area stations to encourage house-building there. The *London & North Western and *Eastern Counties offered low-price seasons for new residents in outer suburban areas in the 1850s, but the results were disappointing. The *Great Western refused to issue any season tickets until 1851, when they were adopted between Paddington, Windsor, and Maidenhead. Until the 1890s growth in season-ticket traffic was slow. It is impossible to discover from available statistics how many season tickets there were at any date or how frequently they were used; most estimates of the journeys made on these tickets, including the railways' own, appear to be too high.

From the turn of the century railway policies changed from comparative neglect to active cultivation of the season-ticket market. From 1913 the statistics become more reliable, though still perhaps on the high side for journeys made on season tickets; in that year they were 39 million out of a total of 169 million passenger journeys.

Season tickets were normally issued only to first- and second-class passengers. They were by no means universally available, but conceded by managements in particular cases where it suited them. On the Whitehaven & Furness Junction Railway they could be had in 1850 only between Whitehaven and St Bees, the terms to be learned on application at those stations. Third-class seasons were rare in the 19th century (the SER issued some experimentally at Dartford in 1884); the *North London Railway issued them generally from 1902; the *Great Central sold 'weekly zone seasons' at Manchester and Sheffield in 1904, claimed to be the first in the country. Weekly seasons came into general use in some areas in the 1920s.

During World War I the popularity of season tickets grew fast, particularly when in 1917 other fares were increased, but not season rates (as again in 1940). It is surprising that it was only in 1917 that a railway bye-law required season tickets to be shown on demand; presumably until then their holders were few enough to be known by sight to local station staff. Between the wars season tickets, generally at bargain rates, became increasingly popular and went with electrified or otherwise improved train services, especially on the *Southern Railway, as an important feature of the railway's passenger commercial scene. Not only *London, but *Glasgow, *Liverpool, *Manchester, and *Newcastle felt the effects.

Railway managers found it difficult to decide whether they wanted to encourage season-ticket traffic or not. It was steady, and they got their money in advance; but the commuter 'peaks' imposed severe operational burdens, and they could never decide (or did not make public) whether the business was financially worthwhile. Some talked of 'the suburban incubus'; others had their hunch that it should be encouraged.

Season tickets themselves were originally produced for individual holders, either engraved on ivory or metal medallions, or specially shaped and coloured folding passes, leather- or linen-covered and usually stamped in gold. Later seasons, for all classes, were typically on card, more than twice the size of ordinary *Edmondson tickets.

The effect of increasing season-ticket traffic, or 'railway commuting', was slow to be felt. Apart from striking particular cases, like *Brighton and Southend from London, Harrogate from *Leeds and *Bradford, or *Blackpool and Lytham St Anne's from Liverpool and Manchester, every large city and many smaller towns like *Aberdeen and *Exeter enjoyed some form of local 'suburban' railway service; but the results were different in every case. Railway commuting could not exist without a railway in operation, but it depended equally on the development of residential property, which was patchy. Surbiton, *London & South Western Railway, was extensively developed from the opening of the London & Southampton line in 1838; but growth at Raynes Park, nearer London on the same line, was delayed for many years after that station was opened in 1871. While the train and the season ticket were necessary conditions of commuting until about 1950, they were not more than partners, if active ones, in a process that had wider and deeper roots in Britain's economic and social development.

RMR

J. P. Thomas, *Handling London's Underground Traffic* (1928), 12, 168–9; K. K. Liepmann, *The Journey to Work* (1944); J. R. Kellett, *The Impact of Railways on Victorian Cities* (1969); A. A. Jackson, *Semi-Detached London* (1973); *REW*, Appx. II, 277 n.

companies. With the exception of a few short lines that were ancillary to other undertakings or were built by individual owners (such as the Londonderry Railway or the Sandy & Potton), public railways in Britain before *nationalization were constructed and operated by companies formed for that purpose. This was almost invariably achieved through the promotion of a Private Bill, since parliamentary authority was necessary for the compulsory purchase powers that were generally required to enable a line to be built. In addition, an Act of Parliament provided the vehicle for incorporating the company and defining its objects, powers, and constitution.

The requirement to obtain parliamentary authority for the incorporation of a railway company stemmed from the restrictions that had been placed on joint-stock enterprises in England by the so-called Bubble Act of 1720, which made it necessary to obtain a royal charter or a special Act to establish an undertaking with corporate status. Without this, members were each individually liable for the firm's obligations. The importance of this protection was amply illustrated at an early stage in the development of the railway system by the unhappy experience of investors in the Stanhope & Tyne Railway, which was set up under partnership law rather than with parliamentary authorization, and adopted the practice of building private wagonways (see TRAMROADS) in the north-east of England by obtaining its right-of-way through wayleave agreements. The line was opened in 1834, but financial difficulties soon emerged and by 1840 debts amounted to £440,000. This left the undertaking's 49 proprietors, who included Robert *Stephenson, with a potentially disastrous personal liability, which was removed only by writing off their original capital and by the parliamentary incorporation of a new company to take over the STR's obligations.

While the restrictions of English partnership law had not been a hindrance to most 18th-century businesses, the long-term nature of the investment needed for infrastructure projects and the scale of their capital requirements made joint-stock status a virtual necessity. The Stanhope & Tyne Railway was therefore atypical, since the *canal companies already provided an obvious precedent for the railways. The development of the canal system was largely achieved through the parliamentary incorporation of joint-stock companies with powers of compulsory purchase, and in fact some of the earliest railways to receive parliamentary authorization were built as feeders to canals.

At first canal precedents extended even into the details of the *parliamentary processes adopted for railway Bills: these were initially subject to the same standing orders as canal Bills, and relevant sections in canal Acts provided a source for the drafting of railway Bills. However, during the 1830s Private Bill procedures were extensively overhauled in response to the growing demands of railway business on parliamentary time. As part of this process, specific requirements were introduced which affected the internal operation of a company and its relations with its shareholders. For example, besides being required to provide Parliament with a list of subscribers to the scheme, an obligation carried over from canal Bills, the promoters of a railway Bill were obliged to deposit part of the estimated cost of their line (see PROMOTION PROCEDURE). They were also obliged to include clauses to ensure adequate arrangements for audit, and to limit the company's borrowing powers to a third of its share capital. Another significant requirement introduced by the House of Lords in 1838 was the necessity for a general meeting of shareholders to consent to the terms of any Bill which sought to confer extra powers on their company.

By 1843 model Bills were available which, though unofficial, enjoyed considerable authority as an indication of the provisions that promoters should include within a Bill in order to satisfy parliamentary requirements. A further step was taken in 1845 with the passage of general Acts which brought together various standard clauses, making it unnecessary to rehearse them individually in each Bill to which they applied. Separate Acts were passed for England and Scotland: the Lands Clauses and Railways Clauses Consolidation Acts assembled the provisions relating respectively to compulsory purchase and to railway construction and operation, while the Companies Clauses Consolidation Acts effectively prescribed a standard format for railway and other companies incorporated by Act of Parliament. Later legislation—including the Railways Clauses Act, 1863, the Companies Clauses Acts of 1863 and 1869, and the Railway Companies Acts of 1867—amended the 1845 consolidation provisions and carried the process further.

The provisions of the 1845 Companies Clauses Acts were not novel: they simply embodied general principles and practices that had been built up as Private Bill legislation had evolved. They provided for the division of a company's share capital into prescribed amounts, and regulated the recording and transfer of share ownership. The Acts governed the calling-up of instalments on shares and the liability of shareholders who were in arrears, and also laid down the conditions upon which a company could borrow money. They required general meetings of shareholders to be held at half-yearly intervals, with written notice of any special business that was to be transacted. Quorums were prescribed, and voting procedures and provisions for the election of directors were specified. The legislation also laid out the powers and duties of the board of directors, subject to any more specific provisions contained in a company's special Acts. Directors were obliged to elect a chairman and keep records of their proceedings; they were empowered to manage and superintend the affairs of the company, to enter into contracts, and to fill casual vacancies in the directorate; they were also permitted to delegate any of their powers to a committee. Certain matters, however, could only be decided by a general meeting, including the regular election of directors and any variation in their numbers, the declaration of a dividend, the authorization of borrowing, the augmentation of capital, and the remuneration of directors, auditors, treasurer, and secretary. In addition, the legislation provided that a special general meeting called for that purpose could regulate the powers of the board of directors. The Acts also specified the directors' duty to ensure that proper accounts were kept, and to make these available for inspection for prescribed periods before and after each half-yearly general meeting. They also laid down procedures for matters such as arbitration, the making of bye-laws, and the recovery of penalties or damages.

This codification of the basis of parliamentary incorporation was preceded by two 1844 Acts which modified English company law. While principally intended to simplify the position of companies which did not enjoy the protection of either a royal charter or parliamentary incorporation, both Acts affected railway companies, particularly at the pre-incorporation stage. Though Scots law recognized the status of a company formed under a contract of copartnery, in English law a railway company remained a private partnership until its Act was obtained, leaving its individual subscribers with a potential liability for the full extent of its obligations. Because of the costs involved in promoting a railway, this could be a significant deterrent to some investors, and even when a Bill was introduced into Parliament there was of course no guarantee that it would pass.

The Joint Stock Companies Registration Act of 1844 established formal registration procedures for all new companies, whether or not they sought parliamentary incorporation. This went some way towards regularizing the position of a railway company and its subscribers at the pre-incorporation stage. The related Joint Stock Companies Remedies Act, 1844, which applied to any company in England and Wales whatever its status, provided further safeguards by making it necessary to exhaust proceedings against a company before any remaining debt could be recovered from individual members. While shareholders in an incorporated railway company enjoyed limited liability, this Act's provisions gave additional protection to subscribers if for any reason a project was wound up before it attained parliamentary authorization.

Company legislation was developed as the century progressed, and an increasing range of business undertakings adopted joint-stock, limited liability status by means of registration. Nevertheless, the particular characteristics of railway companies made it necessary for them to continue to adopt the parliamentary route to incorporation, with only one, relatively minor, exception, designed to cater for lines which fell into a special category. This was introduced by the *Light Railways Act of 1896, which, in order to encourage industrial and agricultural development, borrowed from Irish and tramway precedents by establishing a commission to deal with applications for the building of light railways. Besides having powers to approve the route of a proposed light railway and any necessary compulsory purchase rights, the Light Railway Commission was also able to agree to the incorporation of a company to carry it into effect.

With this exception, the framework within which railway companies in Britain conducted their business was provided by the requirements of their individual authorizing Acts (which specified the capital structure and particular powers of each undertaking), the Clauses Consolidation Acts (which laid down obligations and procedures of general application to railways and other similarly constituted companies), and the relevant provisions of the Companies Acts. Various other statutes modified or added to existing procedures: for example, the Railway Companies Securities Act, 1866, extended registration obligations and introduced additional requirements relating to borrowing, while the *Regulation of Railways Acts of 1868 and 1871 prescribed in considerable detail the form in which railway accounts and statistics should be presented to shareholders and returned to the Board of *Trade. A further enactment in 1911 increased the amount of financial and statistical information to be reported, but also removed the time-honoured obligation to hold general meetings and present audited accounts twice a year. From 1913 onwards, general meetings were required only annually, and directors were empowered to declare an interim dividend for the first half of each year.

Though this change was made in order to offset the administrative burdens imposed by the government's requirements for more detailed statistical and financial returns, it was also in practice an acknowledgement of the diminished role of company general meetings. While the theory of railway administration embodied in legislation and repeated in contemporary textbooks was that ultimate authority within a company rested with its shareholders, in practice control was rarely exercised at this level. One obvious reason was the sheer number of shareholders in the larger undertakings —as early as 1855, the *London & North Western Railway had 15,000 proprietors, and by 1902 the number of its ordinary shareholders stood at over 36,000. Direct participation on such a scale would clearly have been impracticable, while in any event the formalities of procedure meant that large general meetings were not an appropriate forum for debating complex policy issues. In reality, therefore, railway companies were no different from most large modern business undertakings, with effective control resting with the board of directors and its various committees. Within larger boards, this power was in turn often concentrated mainly in the hands of the chairman and a few colleagues, who determined policy, appointed chief officers, and in some cases exercised considerable influence over routine administration. While, especially in the unsettled times following the Railway *Mania, it was not unknown for directors' recommendations to be overturned at general meetings, or for individual directors or whole boards to be replaced because of the shareholders' dissatisfaction, this became increasingly rare as the system matured. The statutory provisions that directors should be elected in rotation rather than en bloc, and that boards themselves should appoint to casual vacancies, ensured that most directorates were in effect self-selected.

The Railways Act, 1921 (see GROUPING), which resulted in the formation of four large undertakings out of the 120 separate companies which by that stage accounted for the bulk of the British network, perpetuated the same basic concept of the joint-stock railway company, albeit on a larger scale. However, the *London underground railways, though included in the Ministry of *Transport's initial grouping proposals, were left out of the ultimate structure. They continued until 1933, when the London Passenger Transport Act vested them in the London Passenger Transport Board, together with the capital's bus and tramway undertakings. Unlike the four main-line railways, the LPTB was established as a public corporation, not a company: it had no shareholders, and its directors were appointed by trustees designated under the 1933 Act.

The LPTB was dissolved along with the main-line companies and their subsidiaries when the railways were *nationalized in 1948 under the terms of the Transport Act, 1947. Their assets were vested in the government-appointed *British Transport Commission, and the companies themselves were wound up once their residual affairs had been concluded. This did not, however, put an end to the existence of independent railway companies in Britain: as in 1921, a number of minor undertakings, such as the North Sunderland Railway, the Easingwold Railway, the *Liverpool Overhead Railway, and most Welsh narrow-gauge lines, were excluded from the Transport Act's provisions. Many were later abandoned, but despite nationalization a

niche continued to exist for independent railway companies because of the growth of the *preservation movement.

The Railways Act, 1993, fundamentally changed the position once more by reviving the role of the company in the provision of mainstream railway services in Britain (see PRIVATIZATION). However, the Act's provisions for the establishment of new railway companies differed in one important respect from those which applied to the traditional British railway company: the basis for the legal identity of such new undertakings was found in the Companies Acts rather than through parliamentary incorporation. Although the new companies were made subject to the railway licensing and regulation procedures introduced by the Railways Act, it embodied only one modification of general company legislation to reflect the particular circumstances of railway undertakings: special arrangements in cases of insolvency. With this exception, the Act left any new railway companies established as a consequence of its provisions within the same framework of company law as other business undertakings.

See also PARLIAMENT AND LEGISLATION.   MCR

The Jubilee of the Railway News (1914), 59–61, 78–86, 99–112; *Modern Railway Administration* (1925), i, 81–90, 122–7; E. V. Morgan and W. A. Thomas, *The Stock Exchange* (1962), 100–12, 125–39; L. T. C. Rolt, *George and Robert Stephenson* (1960), 262–9; Tomlinson, 441–4.

compartment. The earliest passenger *carriages built for the British railway companies owed their design to the road *coaches. The first-class vehicles on the *Liverpool & Manchester Railway essentially comprised three coach bodies, fixed together and mounted on an iron frame. Each of these bodies formed a compartment, though the use of the word in that sense is not recorded before 1862. This became the usual form of first- and second-class carriages, but the interiors of some of those used in *parliamentary trains were open (without partitions), with some seats round their walls and in the middle.

The same practices were generally followed on the European mainland, but not in the USA, where all passenger vehicles were open, with transverse seats in pairs, separated by central gangways. When that pattern was introduced into Britain in 1874, in the American-built *Pullman cars, it got a mixed reception, many passengers preferring the 'privacy' of the compartments to which they were accustomed.

One objection to the compartment plan was that it afforded new opportunities for *crime, horribly demonstrated in two murders, in France and England, in 1861 and 1864. They helped to prompt the German Heusinger Von Waldegg to devise a side-corridor vehicle in 1870, preserving the compartment but also giving access to it from the rest of the carriage. It gradually came to be adopted in Britain as the standard for *express trains, though hardly ever by the *London Brighton & South Coast or *South Eastern & Chatham companies. The open plan was also used for some purposes by all the *Big Four railways in the 1920s and 1930s, save the *Great Western. *British Rail adopted it increasingly, and wholly for second or standard class from 1965, and for first class from the 1970s.　　　　　JS

C. H. Ellis, *Railway Carriages in the British Isles* (1965); W. Schivelbusch, *The Railway Journey* (1980), ch. 5.

compensation. Railways' liability to provide compensation, other than in respect of the compulsory purchase of land (see LAND ACQUISITION), either absolute or on proof of negligence, fell into three broad categories: loss of or damage to goods; injury to, or death or delay of, passengers; death of or injury to employees. Liability was laid down both by statute and in case law (see LAW OF RAILWAYS). There were also other, less important areas of absolute liability, such as those prescribed in the Railway Fires Act (see FIRE).

Until 1962 railways were common carriers (see FREIGHT TRAFFIC RATES) and subject to the law relating to them, including absolute liability for the safety of whatever was carried, together with passengers' *luggage. The Carriers Act, 1830, excluded specified articles exceeding £10 in value (increased to £25 under the 1921 Railways Act) which can be loosely described as small in bulk but large in value. Otherwise carriers were liable at common law, without limit except when a special contract had been entered into, which was held to include a *ticket or printed conditions. But responsibility for passengers' luggage in a left-luggage office was subject to the liabilities of a warehouseman, and negligence had to be proved. Under the Railway & Canal Traffic Act, 1854, damages in respect of loss of or injury to animals in transit caused by negligence were limited to £10 per horse, £15 per head of cattle, and £2 for a pig or sheep, unless a higher value was declared at consignment, and a higher charge agreed. Liability for other damages was determined at common law.

With regard to passengers, the Fatal Accidents Acts, 1846 and 1976 (see LORD CAMPBELL'S ACT) extended the right to sue railways for damages in respect of pecuniary loss (but no other) arising from death in a railway *accident. Otherwise the railways had a common law liability to take due care to carry passengers safely, and were liable on proof of negligence. The 1846 Act resulted in a steady rise in compensation payments, and in 1867–71 the annual average was nearly £324,500, or 1.8 per cent of passenger revenue. Compensation might be awarded for pecuniary loss, for pain and suffering, and in reimbursement of expenses incurred. In *Phillips* v. *London & South Western Railway Company* (1879), a plaintiff was awarded £16,000, of which £1,000 was for bodily suffering. Under the 1868 *Regulation Act the Board of *Trade could be called upon to appoint an arbitrator to determine the amount of compensation.

Liability for compensation for pecuniary loss from delay rested on there being false representation by a company in its timetable. The expense of any reasonable action by the passenger to mitigate his loss or inconvenience could be recovered, including the cost of physical inconvenience such as the need to walk home if he were taken to a wrong station late at night, and was unable to procure conveyance.

In 1991, under pressure from the Conservative government, *British Rail introduced its Passenger's Charter (see also PUNCTUALITY) whereby for delays of more than an hour passengers could claim an *ex gratia* refund of 20 per cent of the fare, and a full refund in respect of a cancelled train. Discounts were offered to *season ticket holders where annual punctuality did not reach stated targets.

Railway employees had no statutory right to claim compensation from employers following an accident until they were included in the Employers Liability Act, 1880, which merely gave them the same right to sue as any other person in a case of negligence, with a limit of three years' wages. Hitherto railwaymen had to rely solely on the bounty of their directors, although many companies accepted an implicit duty to care for employees injured in their service, and for the dependants of men killed. Some gradually evolved a rough scale of *ex gratia* payments, according to circumstances, grade, and seniority, such as the payment of all or part of wages during a period of disablement, perhaps including medical expenses as well. Others simply paid a gratuity on evidence of distress, or paid the difference between wages and company sickness fund benefit.

Permanent disablement was usually compensated with payment of a lump sum, although the loss of a leg (not infrequent) might be compensated for by providing a free artificial limb. Alternatively, a disabled employee might be found other work. Payments to dependants of men killed were usually a small lump sum, varying according to the deceased's grade, the numbers of dependants, and the company's views on the degree to which the employee himself might have been responsible. Payment of funeral expenses was general, and occasionally a widow or orphans might be found jobs.

But it was not until the passage of the 1897 Workmen's Compensation Act that railwaymen, along with other workers, became entitled to statutory compensation.　　　GJB

E. E. G. Williams, *An Epitome of Railway Law* (1912); G. Gaunt, 'The Law Relating to Railways', in *Modern Railway Administration*, ii (1925); P. W. Kingsford, *Victorian Railwaymen* (1970), 165–7; L. James, *Law of the Railway* (1980); British Rail, *Passenger's Charter* (1991).

competition, inter-railway

Before 1844

Rival groups of coalowners had built railways in the 18th century that competed with one another—those running down to Derwenthaugh on the Tyne, for example; but they were solely aids to competition already existing within the coal trade itself.

Competing projects for railways running between important towns (*London–*Bristol, London–*York) were promoted during the *mania of 1825 (see SPECULATION), but none succeeded.

The first railway intended to compete with another, already open, was the short *Clarence, authorized in 1828. As the *Liverpool & Manchester Railway approached completion, the idea emerged that a second line might be built to link the two towns, running at some distance from it. After all, the rival stage-coaches between London and *Manchester took three different routes. Why should not railways do likewise? That represented a customer's view. Railway promoters and managers looked at the matter differently. A coach ran on an existing road, for the use of which it paid tolls, reflected in its fares, whereas a railway company had to make its own road. To build a second railway line, where one already existed, needed very careful consideration.

The establishment of railway companies in Britain called for two different types of men. The first comprised promoters who were often largely speculators, content to buy and sell their shares at a profit quickly; and they employed engineers and lawyers, who had their own profits to make too. The second were managers, who had to operate the line when completed, and to ensure that it was profitable. This division of responsibility was particularly significant in the early years of railway expansion. The speculators were not necessarily interested in a profitable working railway.

The promotion of competitive schemes first gained wide publicity in 1836, when six were laid before Parliament for a 50-mile railway from London to *Brighton. One was authorized, and built (see LONDON BRIGHTON & SOUTH COAST RAILWAY). This was decisive. Other attempts to build competing lines all failed.

1844–67

In 1844–5 many of the immensely numerous railway proposals were wholly or partly competitive. The long fight to build the direct line between London and York, which became the *Great Northern Railway, was the most celebrated. Others were proposed between London and Dover, *Exeter, *Birmingham, and Manchester, but these all failed except the last. Divergent attitudes towards competition now appeared. Samuel *Laing, then a powerful officer at the Board of *Trade, opined that competition between railways was 'out of the question'; wherever it appeared it would end in *amalgamation. The Railway *Commissioners, on the other hand, favoured the Oxford & Rugby Railway precisely because it would compete with the *London & Birmingham's established route.

By 1852 there were competing services from London to Birmingham, *Nottingham, *Leeds, and *Edinburgh; and from *Liverpool to Leeds and *Hull. By 1867 there were also competing routes between London and Dover, *Portsmouth, Exeter, Manchester, and *Sheffield. Laing's prediction had been disproved. Amalgamation had eliminated competition on only two trunk lines. The *Eastern Counties Railway controlled both routes between London and *Norwich through leasing and working *agreements, followed in 1862 by a full amalgamation as the *Great Eastern Railway. And the competitive routes from Leeds to the Wear and Tyne, via York and via Ripon, passed into the single ownership of the *North Eastern Railway in 1854. But those examples stood alone. By 1867 Britain had opted plainly for a railway system much more highly competitive than any other except that in the USA.

All these routes were competitive, however, only between their terminal points, each one serving a different district on its way. Between London and Dover, for example, one went by Tonbridge and the Weald, the other by Chatham and Canterbury, although the principal trains made few or no stops, which limited their value to intermediate places. Walter Bagehot's observation in 1864 that competing railways benefited only the customers at their extremities was over-simplified: every trunk railway naturally served large towns better than small ones. But he was right in emphasizing that competition benefited the large towns disproportionately more than country districts.

The multiplication of competing lines had another cause. After most of the English and Welsh trunk lines were completed, the remaining construction was largely of connecting lines and branches, resulting largely from inter-company politics.

By 1867 there were 12 companies with long-distance lines in England, one (the *Cambrian) in Wales, and five in Scotland. Each had what it regarded as its own territory. New branch lines were promoted to serve places lying off the main routes: either by one of the large companies (perhaps invading a neighbour's territory) or by a small new company, promoted locally, which might then try to sell itself to the company whose line it joined, or to a 'poaching' neighbour. Alternatively, a town might get two lines, reaching it from different directions, each owned or supported by one of the large railways. Chard, Midhurst, Brecon, and Peebles were all favoured in this way in 1855–67.

1867–1922

Some important new lines, principally competitive, were completed in these years.

The *South Eastern Railway, faced with the competition of the *London Chatham & Dover, built a direct line to Tonbridge in 1868, reducing its distance from London to Dover by 14 per cent. The *Caledonian began competing with the original *Edinburgh & Glasgow Railway (now in the hands of the *North British) when it opened its line via Shotts in 1869.

Most striking of all was the *Midland Railway's *Settle–Carlisle line, authorized in 1866. When it tried to abandon the scheme owing to financial difficulties, other supporting companies forced it to continue in order to serve their own interests. Opened in 1876, it was the longest British railway built at a single stretch for competitive purposes alone.

While it was still under construction, competitive railway building came under parliamentary scrutiny. In 1872–3 the *London & North Western and *Lancashire & Yorkshire Railways twice unsuccessfully sought to merge (see AMALGAMATION). In support of this and other similar plans it was frequently reiterated that competition would be superseded by amalgamation, or at least by inter-company agreements, based on the sharing of profits. Either of these expedients would certainly be cheaper than the construction of long new railways. On the other hand, both were strongly disliked by some of the railways' customers. Several important towns (*Southampton and Hull, for instance), even large districts like the whole of Suffolk, were in the hands of a single company, creating what many people there dreaded: a *monopoly.

Close on the opening of the Settle & Carlisle line, *London & South Western trains reached *Plymouth, side by side with the *Great Western's. In the next year the *Cheshire Lines Railway initiated energetic competition for the lucrative Liverpool–Manchester traffic, offering a much better service than the LNWR and LYR, over an improved line from a new Liverpool terminus.

Other competing lines were still to be opened: the *Hull & Barnsley, the *Barry, the *Great Central's London extension, the West Highland and its extension (see NORTH BRITISH RAILWAY), together with the GWR 'cut-offs' of 1906–10 creating new main lines that were highly competitive from London to Exeter and Birmingham. It seems strange that intelligent people were still contending that the competitive principle was now dead in Britain.

Only one important merger was achieved in those years, in 1899 between the SER and LCDR (see AMALGAMATION). But Parliament rejected a similar union between the Great Northern, Great Eastern, and Great Central companies in 1908.

On the opening of the GNR in 1852 the whole traffic between London, Leeds, York, Newcastle, and Edinburgh had become competitive with the established route of the LNWR and Midland. In 1857 the GNR and Manchester Sheffield & Lincolnshire (see GREAT CENTRAL) began to compete in speed with the LNWR between London and Manchester. By 1900 that journey could be made by two other routes also, at competitive timings. And yet in 1914 the fastest trains anywhere in Europe between two large cities were London–Bristol expresses of the GWR, which had no competitors.

There were other ways in which the companies fought out their battles. The Midland—the arch-competitor from the 1860s onwards—employed most of them. Though its new route to Scotland was longer, it tempted passengers (particularly third-class) by more comfortable vehicles than its rivals'; by 1881 it was using eight- and twelve-wheeled *carriages, riding much better than theirs. It also introduced *restaurant cars, providing a service that earned a very good name. All the companies had *hotels too: 11 at London terminal stations; three, competing lustily, at Liverpool and Glasgow; two each at Leeds, Bradford, and Edinburgh.

A number of railways were also competing to provide steamship services. From 1860 onwards one company after another succeeded in getting powers to do so; others let the business out to associated companies. Competition became hot on the Channel services and on those from Fleetwood, *Barrow, and Portpatrick (later Stranraer) to the north of Ireland. In the 1880s it became hottest of all on the Clyde, until that was tempered by pooling agreements 30 years later.

1923–47

One of the purposes behind the fusion of the railways into four large groups in 1923 (see GROUPING) was to reduce or, where possible, eliminate wasteful competition. This represented a clear reversal of British government policy for 70 years past. But the Act was a compromise. Although it removed competition wherever the companies merged within each group, it did not discourage competition between the groups themselves, let alone end it. It still afforded *Leicester, Nottingham, and Sheffield, for example, extravagantly lavish services, provided by the *London Midland & Scottish and *London & North Eastern Railways. In the summer of 1939 these were as shown in the following table. Competitive services to the much larger cities of Birmingham and Manchester numbered only 17 and 19 respectively. Bristol and Southampton, to which there was no competition, had 11 and 12.

	Shortest route (miles)	Number of express trains	LMS	LNER
London–Leicester	99	29	19	10
London–Nottingham	123	29	17	12
London–Sheffield	158	27	15	12

In other rail matters the railways acted together to regulate competition. The LMS and LNER joined with the Ellerman's Wilson Line to operate all the railway shipping services across the North Sea. They also acted together to gain a controlling interest in the two largest firms of road carriers, Pickford's and Carter Paterson. And they ventured jointly into the provision of *air services within Britain. Such actions, dampening down competition between themselves to help them to face potentially dangerous rivals, would have been unthinkable before 1923.

Competition was abandoned, of course, with *nationalization in 1947. A competitive spirit could still be detected here and there, however, notably on the former GWR and in the behaviour of the other British Railways Regions towards it. But that was no more than an attitude of mind, which gradually melted away as the years passed. To what extent the competitive spirit will revive, in any real or important terms, under *privatization remains to be seen.   JS

E. Cleveland-Stevens, *English Railways* (1915); A. Marshall, *Industry and Trade* (1919), 455–506; W. Bagehot, *Collected Works* (1965–86), x, 455.

competition with other forms of transport, see AIR TRANSPORT; BUSES; CANALS; COACHES, ROAD; SHIPPING, COASTAL; ROAD TRANSPORT; TRAMWAYS, STREET.

compounding on locomotives, see TRACTION, STEAM.

computers. As self-contained systems, with trains running within a finite network of running lines, railways are ideal for computer applications.

From 1949, *British Railways made use of computers for statistics and accounting. By 1963 computers were proving invaluable for calculating train performance and timings, producing locomotive diagrams, for wagon control, and in processing scientific data; attempts to use computers for timetable production were unsuccessful, however, and not achieved for another decade.

From the late 1960s BR and other operators steadily increased their use of computers, and some notable applications occurred during the next decade. The most comprehensive data-based system was the *TOPS freight information system, implemented by the mid-1970s; the control of automatic train describers in *signalling centres; the control—from 1975—of *track renewal programmes; *Junction Optimization Techniques for train control in complex areas, from the late 1970s; and, from the early 1980s, the computer-assisted design of overhead line electrification structures.

From the mid-1980s increased computer power has been able to process even the most complex set of variables, and applications include: the use of microprocessors in solid-state interlocking signalling, the pilot scheme for which dates from 1985; moves towards the computerization of train control by the co-ordination of Integrated Electronic Control Centres; Automatic Train Protection (see AUTO-MATIC WARNING SYSTEMS), making use of an on-board computer which receives signals from trackside beacons, and loops between rails, to provide visual indication to the driver and, if necessary, apply the brakes; the on-board computer-based Informatique control and communication network in Eurostar trains (see CHANNEL TUNNEL); and automatic *fare collection and revenue collection systems, progressing to 'Smartcard' *tickets. MLH

J. Johnson and R. A. Long, *British Railways Engineering 1948–80* (1981).

Conacher, John (1845–1911), manager. He entered the service of the *Scottish Central Railway at 16 and then worked in the audit office of the *Caledonian until he moved to the *Cambrian Railways as their accountant at 22. He was general manager of that company from 1885 to 1891, when he took up the same post on the *North British.

He inherited much difficulty there, with a divided board and a poorly disciplined staff. But he restored order with fair success, until he was sacked through a sordid directors' squabble in 1899, then becoming general manager of the London Metropolitan Electric Supply Company. In 1907 the government asked him to report on the South African railways, and appraise their recovery from the war of 1899–1902. He subsequently investigated the railway systems of Uganda and Nyasaland.

In 1909 he returned to railway service, becoming chairman of the Cambrian, and in 1910 managing director of the *Barry Railway as well. But he died before he could leave his mark on the policies of these two Welsh companies. JS

Engineering, 112 (1911), 429. Important papers of his, throwing light on the unsatisfactory state of the Barry Railway in 1910–11, are in SRO, BR/SPC/9/3.

concrete, use of. Concrete is a composite material consisting of cement, water, and aggregates of gravel or crushed rock.

Lime mortar was often used as cement in construction during the 19th century although pozzolana, a volcanic deposit, was frequently imported from Italy for the manufacture of cements suitable for underwater work. Similar cements were derived from natural deposits found on the Isle of Sheppey in 1796 and known as Parker's, or Roman, Cement. The variable composition of all these products gave uncertain results.

Modern developments began in 1824 when Joseph Aspdin, a builder, patented an artificial cement described as Portland Cement because of its likeness to the building stone. This was manufactured under factory conditions, commencing with the grinding of a mix of clay, chalk, and water, which was run into vats before drying. After calcining at high temperature, the residue was ground to powder. Frequent testing ensured a consistent quality. By 1852 four firms were manufacturing cements in the Medway valley where deposits of chalk and clay were plentiful.

Plain concrete, frequently known as 'beton' (a word borrowed from the French), was used throughout the railway era in building and bridge foundations, in retaining walls faced with brickwork or masonry, and in the manufacture of building blocks, but for very little else, apart from a few viaducts after 1860 (see BRIDGES AND VIADUCTS).

Concrete is strong in compression and weak in tension, but the inclusion of steel bars on the tension side produces the construction medium of reinforced concrete. A patent was obtained by the canal engineer Ralph Dodds in 1808, but his applications were unsuccessful owing to the unreliable nature of the cements available. The patent was neglected and the initiative, and credit for the invention, passed to continental engineers during the 1860s. British engineers then proved conservative and uncertain about the durability of reinforced concrete and were reluctant to use it. Even advanced engineering manuals of the 1890s make no mention of this valuable material.

There was only slow acceptance of 'ferro-concrete', as reinforced concrete was often described after 1900, following the introduction into Britain of the Hennebique (1897), Coignet (1904), and other systems. However, the material was successfully used by the *North Eastern Railway during 1903 for the construction of offices in Newcastle, and in 1906 the company also erected close by a massive warehouse 480 ft long by 180 ft wide, 4 storeys high (see GOODS SHEDS). The ground floor was designed to carry a working load equivalent to six goods trains, besides travelling cranes and other heavy equipment.

Some interest was also aroused at the time in the possibilities of bridge construction in reinforced concrete, and this induced engineers, notably William Marriott of the *Midland & Great Northern Joint Railway, to precast many items, such as signal posts, sleepers, and even gates and fences, in the material, particularly in World War I.

By the 1930s reinforced concrete was widely used in the construction of frames or complete buildings for *engine sheds and coaling plants (of which that at Carnforth, a listed building, is the sole survivor) and for many *stations, of which those at Apsley, Lea Hall, and the post-war canopies at *Derby are but a few examples.

Cement manufactured today is a compound of lime, silica, alumina, and iron oxide. Different cements are obtained by varying these constituents, ordinary and rapid-hardening Portland cements being the commonest types used. Modern concrete comprises coarse aggregates graded down from various nominal maximum sizes (generally 40 to 10 mm), a fine aggregate of sand, and a cement–water paste. The proportions of these components are determined by specified design strengths and, accordingly, reinforced concrete is now a material which can be confidently designed with precision for incorporation in a wide range of structures. A development, which proves more economical in certain situations, is the prestressing of concrete, which was first exploited successfully by the French engineer Freyssinet in 1928.

Recently, prestressed sleepers, with anticipated life-spans from 60 to 80 years (see TRACK), have proved successful on British railways and a further development of this experience is continuous, concrete slab-track construction for train speeds exceeding 100 mph. Moreover, numerous railway bridges have been partly rebuilt, or entirely replaced, in both reinforced or prestressed concrete as a result of electrification, or as part of highway or urban redevelopments.

Concrete is a useful, reliable, and economical building material when properly manufactured and quality-controlled.   RBS

Institution of Civil Engineers, *Report of the Committee on Reinforced Concrete* (1910); R. Hammond, *Modern Civil Engineering Practice* (1961).

conductors, see GUARDS.

conservation. Until recent years the railways' record has generally been poor (see VANDALISM BY RAILWAYS). Appropriate 19th-century extensions to historic stations, such as *Bristol, *Paddington, Lancaster, and *Carlisle, and the careful widening of some notable viaducts like Maidenhead and Stockport, were far outweighed by many other unfeeling alterations and additions and, particularly in the case of *bridges and viaducts, repairs with inappropriate materials. The Bath stone of Rennie's Dundas Aqueduct on the Kennet & Avon Canal, and *Brunel's railway viaduct through Bath itself, for instance, was patched by the *Great Western Railway in blue brick, while many Scottish viaducts have been disfigured by steel bracing made from old rails.

Much of this was done by the post-*Grouping companies and, in its first 30 years, *British Rail, until the demolition of the *Euston portico in 1961 marked a turning point. Deplorable loss though it was, the public outcry drew attention to the steady loss or disfigurement of important 19th-century railway (and other) buildings, and eventually BR took note. Under the chairmanship of Sir Peter Parker, a director-environment was appointed, responsible immediately to him. Policy now turned towards conservation wherever possible.

It was recognized that in many instances, with appropriate treatment, Victorian buildings had much useful life in them, and that it could be cheaper to restore and renovate than to demolish and rebuild. Furthermore, careful restoration of a period building could make surplus space attrac-

tive to prospective tenants, producing revenue to offset the cost. Impetus grew when government 'listing' of railway buildings began to gather pace. By 1994 there were 1,246 listed railway-owned structures and 62 scheduled as Ancient Monuments, while 895 Conservation Areas included railway property.

In the late 1960s BR also set about cleaning the external fabric of its large stations, usually with local authority support. Carlisle, *Sheffield, *Manchester Victoria, *Newcastle, and *Shrewsbury were early examples, revealing details long concealed by soot. Stations started to regain their place as visual assets in the townscape. Grimy urban viaducts, too, were cleaned; some, like Stockport and Accrington, were even floodlit.

Although a seemingly unending problem, new uses began to be found for large redundant buildings. In Manchester, for instance, the original Liverpool Road station of 1830 was restored for occupation as the Greater Manchester Museum of Science and Industry, while the long-disused Central station *trainshed was at last converted into a fine exhibition hall.

In the 1980s BR began a programme of refurbishing its 8,000 tenanted arches beneath urban viaducts, many a by-word for squalor, but earning some £14 million in rentals. Still in progress, the scheme has produced dramatic local environmental improvements in areas like south London and *Glasgow, as well as numerous smaller places. Viaducts on closed lines present a particular problem. The railway has a statutory liability to maintain them, from which it can escape only by demolition—difficult if the viaduct is listed —or by disposal to a new owner to whom liability can be confidently transferred, usually a local authority. Despite many efforts and some successes, the inherent difficulties in the disposal of nearly 50 redundant listed viaducts make it a slow process, although a number have been restored with financial help from outside sources. One method is to encourage the formation of a charitable trust to acquire a viaduct for a token sum, generally accompanied by a 'dowry' in the form of repairs—a cheaper long-term alternative to BR's retaining ownership.

Much of this work has been aided by the independent Railway Heritage Trust, set up by BR in 1985 to disburse funds allocated to historic structures and to act as a catalyst in attracting contributions from a variety of local and national sources, including English Heritage and Historic Scotland. The Trust has taken a leading part in restoring a number of viaducts, including the noble Leaderfoot Viaduct in the Borders, and the nationally acclaimed work at Ribblehead.

In the wider field, the Trust has played a highly successful role in many and varied projects, from small ones like restoring or replacing station clocks and ornamental railings, to larger tasks such as refacing the inappropriate modern entrance building at *Perth to achieve a more harmonious relationship with the station, extensive repairs to historic trainsheds, and retiling the roof at *Stoke-on-Trent to the original specification. Long-term schemes include continuing works at Paddington, Newcastle, and Bristol. The Trust has also been prominent in advocating 'non-aggressive' stone-cleaning techniques.

Railway building restorations have gained a number of awards. Under the auspices of the Association of Railway Preservation Societies, the Ian Allan National Railway Heritage Awards scheme has, since 1979, made annual presentations for meritorious work by BR, London Underground, preserved railways, and owners of former railway structures. In 1994 Wemyss Bay station had the distinction of winning both a Railway Heritage award and one in the biennial Brunel Award International Design Competition.

Good design of inescapable new features is equally important in conserving the old. Compare the care taken in installing overhead wires at *St Pancras and on the *East Coast main line viaducts north of Darlington, with the hideous impact of earlier electrification work at *King's Cross and on the *West Coast main line.

Following the widespread closures in the 1960s many small passenger stations were demolished. But the planning laws allowed the goods yards to be let, only too frequently for 'environmentally unfriendly' purposes such as builders', haulage contactors', and scrap dealers' yards, creating prominent eyesores in the town- or landscape. Thankfully, a more enlightened attitude in the 1980s began a slow but steady reduction as leases became due for renewal.

BR also established a very successful Community Unit, with its own funding, charged with bringing together local communities and BR in partnership ventures in the wider field of environmental care. They included improving station forecourts and passenger facilities, particularly for the *disabled; colourful repainting of bridges; upgrading lineside environments, taking account of natural habitats for flora and fauna; and projects offering training in skills for the long-term unemployed. The unit made a very substantial contribution to the overall appearance of the railway in town and country, but following *privatization of BR did not survive as such.

See also ARCHITECTURE AND ARCHITECTS; LAND AND PROPERTY OWNERSHIP; LAND, SURPLUS. GJB

Annual Reports of the Railway Heritage Trust, 1985–94; GRSB, 213–17; RS, ch. 9.

construction, process of. The system whereby capital works are conceived, designed, and constructed is known as the *'civil engineering procedure'. This has origins in the *canal era of the 18th century when promoters often embarked on engineering schemes with inaccurate cost estimates, and outline design proposals developed after work commenced. Eminent civil engineers, notably Thomas *Telford and John *Rennie, influenced their profession early in the 19th century by their efforts to improve cost-estimating and contract methods.

The procedure developed throughout the railway era, aided by the emergence of general *contractors able to accept binding commitments and offer guarantees for all constructional and financial aspects of a project. Other measures which helped stabilize industrial practices included the Companies Acts of 1856 and 1867, which dis-

couraged speculative proposals for attracting finance, and developments in local *government towards the end of the century, leading to more stringent control of public expenditure on capital works, which were also applied to railways.

Today the procedure requires a stable working relationship between the promoter who provides finance, the consulting engineer responsible for the conception, design, and technical direction of the project, and the contractor who successfully tenders for its execution. The system provides value for money and protects the interests of all.

There are three stages: first, the engineer investigates possible design solutions leading to a proposal and estimate for the promoter's approval; second, designs are refined, specifications and contract conditions are formulated, then tenders are invited; third, construction begins, concluding with final payments, and completion of the agreed maintenance period.

Contracts are agreements between promoter and contractor. The engineer is not party to the contract; his duty is to remain impartial and independent of both parties.

Types of contracts include fixed-price contracts (bill of quantities, schedule of rates, and lump-sum contracts); cost-reimbursement contracts (cost plus percentage fee, cost plus fixed fee, cost plus fluctuating fee, and target-price contracts); all-in contracts (design-and-build contracts, often called turnkey contracts) which can be executed as either fixed-price or cost-reimbursement contracts. The bill of quantities contract is the commonest, for which the contract documents comprise: conditions of contract, drawings, specifications, the priced bill of quantities, schedules of rates, the tender, and contract agreement.

The consulting engineer's representative on site is the resident engineer. He works with the partner, or project engineer, at head office responsible for the scheme, who issues working drawings and instructions. The resident engineer supervises the contractor and decides on minor design details. Experienced tradesmen known as clerks-of-works are employed to examine quality of workmanship and materials.

Much responsibility devolved on the resident engineer of the railway era because numerous details were undecided until work began. Although lines and levels were fixed, many major structures, culverts, walls, and drainage details were designed by resident engineers, with the approval of their principals. That would not happen today, but G. W. *Buck of the *London & Birmingham Railway, also William Froude of the *Bristol & Exeter, were typical of such engineers. Both were able theoreticians and designed some fine structures on their contract sections; indeed, Buck later published his designs.

Nowadays, the contractor's staff includes the agent, who is concerned with overall management and, particularly, the planning of works, engaging manpower and machinery resources, and directing progress through sub-agents, foremen, and the labour force. Site engineers are employed, whose principal tasks are the setting-out of works, ensuring accuracy of construction and checking the quality of materials. They may make regular tests of *concrete and other materials to ensure compliance with the specifications.

On site, the contractor is responsible for preparatory works including provision of temporary offices, workshops, stores, and services, and making arrangements with statutory undertakers for the diversion of highways and mains. He may employ sub-contractors for specialist tasks such as piling and earth-moving; meanwhile he decides on the construction methods, although the resident engineer ensures that the equipment and methods provide the specified quality finish. Both parties will be concerned with aspects of health and safety on site for which the contractor, in particular, will carry considerable legal obligations.

Payments for work are made monthly, subject to measurements of finished work. On completion of the contract, agreement is reached on any variations and on claims for works unforeseen. These are costed according to the schedule of rates, and final payments made. A maintenance period is invariably required and sums are retained until conclusion of this period.

The present contract system evolved from practices of the past and particularly those developed in the *railway age. Contractors then had far less responsibility to employers, employees, and the general public. Their agents would employ labour-only sub-contractors, many of them casual combinations of labourers organized for the job in hand. Failure to complete through inept estimating was common and resident engineers could find themselves completing abandoned sections by direct labour. Moreover, protracted litigation between companies and contractors, as a result of insufficient preparation of specifications and other contract documentation, was not unknown.

A measure of governmental control over railway construction and operation was desirable to counteract malpractices, and the Board of *Trade was empowered, through various enactments such as the Regulation of Railways Act 1840 and the Railways Clauses Act 1845 (see PARLIAMENT AND LEGISLATION), to superintend these ventures in public transport, and also to impose conditions on their operation.

The Board's authority included the examination and certification of changes in design notified by the engineer, and extended to such matters as negotiations with parties concerned to avoid disputes over highway bridge crossings and rights of way, and the approval of regulations for *level crossings. Moreover, on completion of works, railways could not be opened without acceptance by the Board's *inspectors, whose powers extended beyond the permanent way to railway stations and buildings, locomotives and carriages, and approval of *bye-laws. Such measures were rightly seen as essential for the safety of the general public. The railway inspectorate passed to the control of the Ministry of *Transport in 1919 and is now part of the Health & Safety Executive.

See also EARTHWORKS; BRIDGES AND VIADUCTS.   RBS

T. Brassey, *Work and Wages* (1872); F. McDermott, *Life of Joseph*

Firbank (1887); F. Harris and R. McCaffer, *Modern Construction Management* (1985).

construction costs. It has often been claimed that British railways were characterized by unduly high construction costs, and in particular that they were burdened by the expenses associated with the parliamentary authorization procedures and by excessive *land acquisition charges. In 1858 Joseph *Locke suggested that these were among the reasons why British railways were then around £5,000–£7,000 per mile more expensive than those in France, and similar comparisons continued to be made. For instance, in 1911 it was claimed that the average cost per mile of route in Britain was £55,712, whereas foreign examples ranged from £10,884 in Denmark to £37,088 in Belgium.

In assessing such figures it is necessary to distinguish between the total capitalization of British railways, their cumulative investment in 'way and works' (i.e. excluding rolling stock and ancillary undertakings such as docks or steamships), and the cost of constructing individual lines. The total capital expenditure of Britain's railways at the end of 1913 was equivalent to about £56,000 per mile of line then open; however, way and works accounted for only £40,000 of this. Moreover, the latter average masked considerable variations: for companies in England and Wales the figure was £43,000 per route mile, whereas for those in Scotland it was £27,100, reflecting the different conditions in those countries. The importance of traffic density in determining the ratio of investment to route mileage is confirmed by comparing the figure for a heavily used system such as the *Lancashire & Yorkshire—£79,000—with the *Cambrian Railways' £24,000. A busy network required not only more multiple track, with the extra land and engineering costs which this entailed, but also greater investment in *signalling, *sidings, and *stations.

These 1913 averages represented accumulations of investment which in some cases dated back to the 1820s. For all but the smallest companies, they also reflected the sum of the construction costs of numerous component undertakings. Some rural lines were built for less than £10,000 per mile: for example, the Bedale & Leyburn Railway, completed in 1855, cost £5,400 per mile, while the Wainfleet & Firsby Railway, which opened in 1871, was built for £5,600 per mile; its later extension to Skegness cost £7,200 per mile. Initial outlays of between £10,000 and £25,000 per mile were perhaps more typical of rural single-track routes: the *London & North Western's Northampton–Market Harborough branch had cost about £12,600 per mile when it opened in 1859, while the East Gloucestershire Railway, completed in 1873, required just over £20,000 per mile. Heavier expenditure was of course necessary for railways built to higher standards or where topography was more demanding: the LNWR's investment in its Leeds New line, which opened in 1899, was over £66,000 per mile. However, some quite substantial undertakings were comparatively inexpensive: the *Highland main line between *Perth and Forres, which included several viaducts, was built during the 1860s for £8,860 per mile, while the *Great North of

Scotland's total capital expenditure on way and works up to the end of 1913 was less than £14,200 per route mile. This included a significant proportion of double track. The equivalent ratio for the *Furness Railway, £19,700 per mile, and the Cambrian figure of £24,000 provide evidence that moderate system costs were not confined to Scotland.

While it is not difficult to find instances of British railways that were constructed relatively cheaply, expenditure varied considerably, and this became apparent as soon as the network began to be developed. Because the first trunk routes were built as separate undertakings, it is possible to isolate figures for individual lines, though in using them two qualifications should be noted. Firstly, there are problems in establishing final construction outlays in exact detail, since disputed *contractors' or property claims might still be outstanding several years after opening. Secondly, costs from railways completed in the 1830s and 1840s reflected the prevailing levels of provision: additional investment in track, signalling, or stations was generally needed subsequently.

The available evidence is, however, sufficient for comparative purposes, and shows that the construction costs of early trunk lines ranged from about £20,000 per mile to over £50,000 per mile. One of the cheapest was the *Grand Junction Railway, which unfortunately did not publish a detailed breakdown of its capital account; though figures as low as £14,000 per mile have been quoted, total expenditure by the early 1840s was around £21,000 per mile. However, this was about half the cost per mile of its southward continuation, the *London & Birmingham Railway, and an even lower proportion of that of its later tributary, the Manchester & Birmingham Railway: the latter's route from *Manchester to *Crewe cost over £51,000 per mile. Other expensive early lines were the *Great Western, on which around £50,000 per mile had been spent by 1842, and the Manchester & Leeds, which cost more than £49,000 per mile.

While some railway Bills were strenuously contested—the companies competing for the London and Brighton route spent £193,000 before an Act was obtained in 1837—in general it would be wrong to over-emphasize the contribution of parliamentary expenses to total construction costs. The *Liverpool & Manchester and London & Birmingham companies were both unsuccessful when they first applied to Parliament, and had to overcome further strong opposition before authorization. However, the LMR's parliamentary expenses, which were equivalent to around £1,000 per mile, were only 4 per cent of initial construction costs, while the LBR spent an even smaller proportion in this way, 1.2 per cent of total capital outlay, or less than £650 per mile. J. R. *Kellett's analysis of returns from 26 companies in 1849–50 shows that only 6 per cent of their total constructional expenditure of £76.6 million was attributable to parliamentary expenses.

Parliamentary costs may have been overstated partly because of subsequent failures to distinguish them from other preliminary expenses. While a detailed survey was necessary before a company could seek authorization, it was also an essential prerequisite to building a line. Some companies nevertheless included all their *surveying costs among parliamentary expenses, while others failed to separate the latter from other legal charges. However, the argument that the costs of railway construction were unduly inflated by Britain's adversarial authorization processes was attractive to apologists for the industry, and it is probably no coincidence that it was renewed in the 1920s and 1930s, when the *Big Four companies, struggling in the face of road competition, sought to demonstrate that they were financially disadvantaged by their inherited capital obligations.

To some extent, similar reservations can be applied to comments about the high costs of purchasing land for railway building in Britain. Land did, however, account for a higher proportion of the total capital expenditure of the companies included in the 1849–50 returns: about 20 per cent on average. It is also apparent that outlays for land contributed to some of the relative differences in construction costs already mentioned: the cost of land for the Highland's Perth–Forres main line averaged only £673 per mile, whereas the London & Birmingham spent £4,800 per mile and the Great Western over £6,200 per mile.

However, two further points need to be taken into account in assessing the influence of land acquisition costs on the overall level of railway constructional expenditure in Britain. The first is that engineering costs made up the bulk of the total capital outlay of the early railways cited above, and were also the main reason why their initial estimates were significantly exceeded. While the LBR's actual expenditure on land was more than twice the original estimate, it was only 12 per cent of outturn, exclusive of locomotives and the Euston extension. Engineering costs, 81 per cent of the final total, accounted for more than 70 per cent of the overrun: for example, major difficulties arose with Kilsby Tunnel. The Manchester & Leeds encountered similar problems: though land purchases exceeded the estimate, works such as Summit Tunnel were the main reason why this railway eventually cost more than the £1.3 million originally envisaged.

These examples are from the infancy of railway *civil engineering, when the task of planning and supervising construction projects on this scale clearly tested the professional competence of several of those involved. Even the *Stephensons and *Brunel did not acquit themselves well in the performance of their estimates, and it is surely significant that two of the cheapest of the early trunk routes, the Grand Junction and London & Southampton (see LONDON & SOUTH WESTERN RAILWAY), were completed by Locke, who avoided expensive alignments and structures wherever possible; he went on to apply his engineering techniques with considerable success in mainland Europe. There was also a conscious move towards more economical construction standards in Britain during the 1840s, as part of the reaction against the high costs of some lines built during the previous decade. This 'cheap principle' was typified by the adoption of single track on many branches, the acceptance of tighter curves and steeper *ruling gradients, and by greater use of *level crossings instead of bridges. While such reductions in initial outlay generally brought the subsequent penalty of higher operating costs, the comparison between Locke's *Lancaster & Carlisle Railway and Robert Stephenson's contemporary *Chester & Holyhead Railway demonstrates the capital savings that could be achieved when a lightly engineered route proved possible. The LCR, which followed river valleys whenever feasible, was built for less than £21,000 per mile, while the Holyhead line, which was obliged to cut across the grain of some extremely difficult terrain, cost over £45,000 per mile. Though the CHR's land expenditure was higher, this accounted for less than 6 per cent of the difference, whereas the *Britannia Bridge alone increased the company's average cost per mile by almost £8,000.

The second point about the relationship between land purchases and total construction costs is that the impact was naturally greater where land was expensive, in good agricultural areas, in towns, and above all in the great cities. This was evident from the outset of railway building in the capital. The *London & Blackwall Railway, completed to Fenchurch Street in 1841, cost over £308,000 per mile; of this, land purchase and compensation took almost half, £146,000 per mile. High urban land values became an even more significant factor when companies found it necessary to improve their terminals and widen or extend their routes in response to traffic growth and competitive pressures: as early as 1848 the *London & South Western Railway had invested £1.25 million in building its 1¼-mile four-track extension from Nine Elms to a new terminus at *Waterloo. In the 1860s the *Midland Railway spent around £5 million to provide itself with an independent station in London; while this outlay included the 49-mile extension from Bedford, the estimate for the whole project was initially £1.75 million, and the main reason for the increase was the cost of land for *St Pancras station and its approaches. The Manchester Sheffield & Lincolnshire Railway (see GREAT CENTRAL) encountered comparable difficulties when it in turn extended to London: the estimate for *Marylebone station and its associated works had been just under £3 million, but the final cost of the terminus and the last two miles of line was £6 million. In 1892, when the MSLR's London extension was authorized, its existing capital outlay per mile of operational route was £43,000; a decade later the equivalent figure for the then Great Central Railway stood at £64,000, and the company had ceased to pay an ordinary dividend.

To the extent that Britain's railways contributed to the urban development that created such land values, they were the victims of their own success. Outside the main conurbations, however, engineering costs were the principal determinant of total constructional outlays, and though expenditures on land and engineering were also influenced by traffic density and competitive pressures, these factors reflected the operating environment of the pre-*Grouping companies. While lower route construction and system costs might have been possible if authorization and regulatory procedures in Britain had been different, these processes themselves reflected the actualities of the political and economic context within which the nation's railway system had to evolve and develop.

See also CONSTRUCTION, PROCESS OF; FINANCING OF RAILWAYS; COSTING TECHNIQUES.   MCR

J. Locke, 'Address on Election as President', PICE, 17 (1858), 128–52; J. R. Kellett, The Impact of Railways on Victorian Cities (1969), 277–9, 427–31; A. W. Kirkaldy and A. E. Evans, The History and Economics of Transport (1924), 141–2; Whishaw.

containers. These were not a modern invention. Very large wooden boxes were specially designed to ride on railway flat *wagons, and were in common use, e.g. at *Swansea, *Liverpool, and Wigan in the 1850s. To counter road competition and the delays caused by transhipment, from the 1920s the railways increasingly adopted such containers for through consignments from door to door. They were used particularly for the house-removal business which the railways then cultivated to some extent. The containers were fitted with chains for lifting and were carried, usually on flat wagons, secured by chains. Railway cartage lorries completed the transits.

The development of freight container traffic continued after 1948, with the emergence of specialized varieties. By 1957 some 35,000 containers were owned by *British Railways. There were different types for general merchandise, insulated containers for meat, fish, and frozen food consignments, and some were designed to carry lime.

In 1959 a freight service named Condor was introduced between *London and *Glasgow and offered overnight door-to-door transits to traders. Existing types of container were carried on four-wheeled flat wagons, but the charges made were per container irrespective of contents. Later, bogie wagons were used and the maximum speed raised to 70 mph. New, metal 10-ton containers conveyed on four-wheeled flats were used for a similar service called Speedfreight which was inaugurated between London and *Manchester during 1963.

Concern that a more radical approach was needed to capture new freight business encouraged the development from 1962 of a nationwide container service: this was the Liner Train principle (see FREIGHTLINER). Metal containers of different types—boxes, flats, curtain-sided, and tanks—to International Standards Organization dimensions, are loaded on to rakes of flat, low-height bogie wagons.

MLH

1850s: MacDermot, ii, 7; LYR, iii, 101.

continental traffic, see EUROPEAN TRAFFIC.

contract, working of railways by. A number of the early railway companies, and some *tramroads that preceded them, let out the maintenance of their engineering works to contractors; a few entrusted them with the whole running of their lines.

Arrangements of this sort, if properly made, could relieve their directors and managers of much laborious work, and so offer substantial economies. But the plan succeeded only if the contractor was able, careful, and honest, and a good many of those who entered into these arrangements were inefficient or grasping. A company might guard itself against incompetence or fraud by requiring its engineer to make frequent inspections of its system, but that extra outdoor work had then to be paid for by increasing his staff, to carry on the normal office work when he was away.

The commonest form of contractor-working concerned only the track. The whole of the *London & Birmingham Railway's line was at the outset maintained by two contractors, respectively south and north of Rugby. Thomas *Brassey undertook the same task for the London & Southampton and *London & South Western Railways from 1840 to 1856. Here he was maintaining works for the construction of which he had himself been, to a large extent, responsible. On a small line, the contractor who had built it all might be entrusted with its maintenance immediately, as in the case of the Blackpool & Lytham Railway, under the terms of a contract of 1863 that survives.

Sometimes the contract was for the supply of locomotives or rolling stock, or both, and that might be especially tempting to a company that had raised all its authorized capital, in shares and loans, before any revenue came in from traffic. The *North Staffordshire Railway did this, for example, with the Birmingham carriage-builder James Wright, on the recommendation of the engineer primarily responsible for the construction of the line, G. P. *Bidder, who subsequently fully approved Wright's work.

In 1850 the *South Staffordshire company entered into an agreement with its own engineer, J. S. McClean, who had just completed the main line, handing its operation entirely over to him for a term of 21 years, the treaty being confirmed by Act of Parliament. He seems to have behaved with quite unnecessary arrogance towards everyone connected with the company, including the directors, until his health collapsed in 1858, when the *London & North Western Railway took over his work. In 1861 the LNWR and *Midland companies leased the South Staffordshire jointly, McClean being compensated with £110,000 for loss of anticipated profits. This striking case shows how far the power of the contractor might extend. In 1850-8 McClean autocratically controlled the whole operation of the company's system, leaving the directors little to do but to pay the small number of their own employees.

The contractor who undertook more of this work than any other was the greatest one of all, Brassey. His English contracts of this sort ranged from north Devon to the Welsh border, where he worked the *Shrewsbury & Hereford Railway in 1854-62. He evidently did well out of this contract; and the company too, for by 1860 it was paying a dividend at 6 per cent from the income received from him. The railway was run with the utmost economy, as a single line throughout; one of its stations, Moreton-on-Lugg, provided no more shelter than the hollow ruin of a tree.

The most important railway worked by Brassey was the *London Tilbury & Southend, which he leased in conjunction with two partners, *Peto and Betts (see CONTRACTORS) —engaged with him on the construction of the line—in 1854. It was to run for 21 years, the contractors working the railway and paying the shareholders 6 per cent on its share capital. Two other companies also worked over part of the line, the *London & Blackwall and the *Eastern Counties,

and their relations with the contractors were never amicable. Again economy was Brassey's watchword—and he spoke for all three contractors when his two partners became bankrupt in 1866. Partly through the efforts of these three men, a new town was arising at Southend (they were all engaged in building houses there), and the potential development of traffic was obvious. But as early as 1863 the lessees complained that they were losing money on their contract, and they ran the railway on a shoe-string, without the *telegraph or *block signalling. In the end (Brassey having died in 1870) everyone was dissatisfied with the lease, and the shareholders did not renew it in 1875.

By that time such leases had grown rare. When short branches were promoted by local people, they were now nearly always worked under *agreements with the established companies from whose lines they sprang—at Barnoldswick in Yorkshire, for instance, in 1871, and at Harborne on the edge of Birmingham in 1874. Almost three-quarters of the British railway system had been completed by 1875, and most British contractors were now more interested in securing work overseas, in the colonies, in South America, and Mexico.

These contracts proved their worth, however. Without them some lines would probably not have been built, or would have been completed more slowly. Their weakness was that the interests of the railway companies and the contractors seldom coincided for long. Both of course had their eyes on profits, but the ways of making them were often in conflict, and the fixed term of years for which contracts ran obliged companies and contractors to continue working together with mutual resentment, often with recrimination. Similar disputes could arise out of working agreements, but they were usually easier to settle; especially, if acceptable terms could be devised, by the *amalgamation of the small company with the larger. JS

For bibliography, see CONTRACTORS AND CONTRACTING.

contractors and contracting. The foundations of railway building in Britain were laid by the engineers and contractors who built the *canals and docks of the late 18th and early 19th centuries. Their achievements in tunnelling, excavation work, the management of large bodies of workers, etc., both served as an inspiration for the entire profession of *civil engineering and, on an individual level, gave experience in the development of transferable skills to men such as Thomas Townshend, Hugh McIntosh, and Joseph Nowell, who later became prominent railway contractors.

The framework of the legal and business relationship between contractors and companies for the accomplishment of a particular piece of work (see CONSTRUCTION, PROCESS OF) took the form of a contract which, amongst other matters, stated a date for the job's completion and an overall price in payment, and named the contractor's sureties. Some early lines, for example the *Stockton & Darlington and *Newcastle & Carlisle, were built in minor 'lots' by many small contractors, but by the mid-1830s, with the arrival of schemes for great trunk lines, contracts became arrangements for more substantial and expensive undertakings.

Thus the 30 original contracts for the *London & Birmingham Railway were let at an average price of £56,546, with six for work valued at over £100,000. The growing financial commitment required for railway building could tax the resources of even major contractors. Thomas Grissell and Samuel Morton *Peto, the leading London property builders, became financially overstretched on the *Great Western in their first attempt at railway construction. Similarly, but with a different solution, Thomas *Brassey's extensive involvement in railway building, both at home and abroad, in the 1840s led to the formation of a partnership with two other leading contractors, William *Mackenzie and John Stephenson, in order to share responsibilities and financial burdens. Some highly successful contractors, amongst whom were T. A. *Walker and Joseph *Firbank, worked alone but, if the example of Weetman Dickinson Pearson (Lord Cowdray) is a guide, this was only possible through accommodation from bankers.

The most serious recurring expense for contractors was that of remuneration for their men. In addition, investment in plant and materials often totalled many thousands of pounds within a few months of the commencement of work. In the category of fixed capital, the purchase of wagons, rails, sleepers, and horses entailed an onerous financial outlay. A number of locomotives could also be found at work as early as the 1830s, an example being William Mackenzie's purchase of the *Comet* in 1832 from the *Liverpool & Manchester Railway for use in the construction of Wapping Tunnel, *Liverpool. Full-scale mechanization of railway construction did not, however, take place before the final two decades of the century, when drills, stationary engines, steam cranes, locomotives, and steam excavators appeared on several major projects, including the contracts of the *Hull & Barnsley Railway and the London extension of the Manchester Sheffield & Lincolnshire Railway (see GREAT CENTRAL).

Following the collapse of the Railway *Mania and the completion of most of the trunk network, railway extension in the 1850s began to pay greater attention to rural areas. The lines of this period frequently belonged to recently established companies and, because many were little more than speculative adjuncts to the main system, they encountered problems in raising finance for construction work. Contractors were sometimes required to purchase a quantity of their shares. A stage beyond this in financial involvement was the so-called *'contractors' lines' for which a contractor agreed, usually in co-operation with the finance house which acted as his banker, to find all or the greater part of the capital required for construction in return for company shares and debentures. Negotiations between companies and contractors over a mutually satisfactory arrangement could be lengthy and years might elapse—in the case of the Swindon Marlborough & Andover Railway, it was six—between an Act and the start of construction. John Dickson, contractor of the Whitby Redcar & Middlesbrough Union Railway, who soon became a bankrupt for a third time, even sat on this company's board of directors and yet contrived to produce one of the century's most

shoddy pieces of work. One contractors' line, the *London Chatham & Dover, played a major role in bankrupting Peto and E. L. Betts in the financial crisis of 1866. The part of the country that benefited most permanently from the attention of contractors as railway promoters and financiers was undoubtedly mid-Wales where the absence of local resources was more than balanced by the enterprise of David *Davies, Thomas *Savin, and Henry *Robertson in rural rail construction.

The ultimate nexus between contractors and railways came in the form of lines that were not only financed and built by contractors but also operated by them. John Waddell and his family took on all these responsibilities for the Llanelly & Mynydd Mawr Railway and operated it with efficiency for at least 25 years in association with their coal-mining interests. Brassey, Peto, and Betts did the same (badly) with the *London Tilbury & Southend line in an attempt to develop property at Southend and Westcliff-on-Sea.

From the 1840s, when Brassey and Mackenzie built lines in France, British contractors and engineers took their skills in railway building abroad to many European countries and beyond into the colonies, Central and South America, and Africa. Weetman Pearson in the 1890s held contracts worth over £10 million in Mexico alone and had the distinction, rare for a non-American, of being awarded a large contract in New York City. Late in the century, as the pace of construction in Britain slackened and the drive for *light railways and urban *tramways proved only a palliative for the aspirations of the ambitious contractor, work outside the country became relatively more important. Nevertheless, amongst the last of their domestic assignments before 1914, the Great Western's South Wales and Bristol direct and the Ashendon–Aynho extension lines, confirmed their reputation for producing civil engineering work of the highest standard.

Some contractors accumulated a fortune—George *Wythes and T. A. Walker left £1,524,787 and £597,394, respectively—but Thomas Nicholson, builder of Standedge railway tunnel, died a poor man. But in public esteem and in wealth, no contractor of the 19th century equalled Thomas Brassey.   DB

In the decade after World War I considerable effort was expended by the railway companies in upgrading existing lines to carry the heavier loads imposed by new rolling stock. These loads had increased by up to 50 per cent since the mid-19th century. Typical examples were strengthening of the *Forth Bridge and underpinning and repairs to the High Level Bridge in *Newcastle-upon-Tyne, both by Sir William *Arrol.

Other more recent major railway works mainly involved the enlargement of *tunnels for electrification, or boring new ones needed for the expansion of the *London Underground. The latter has included the Victoria Line (1963–71) and the extension to the Jubilee Line. Such projects have employed shields with mechanical excavation and ground feezing using liquid nitrogen (Victoria Line), and the use of the new Austrian tunnelling method (Jubilee Line).

A major partner in the consortia constructing the Jubilee

Line and the *Channel Tunnel has been Balfour Beatty &
Co., who also constructed what was perhaps the most interesting tunnelling project arising from electrification: the
new Woodhead twin-track tunnel through the Pennines,
constructed in 1949–53 by enlarging a pilot tunnel from
intermediate chambers.

In view of the high risk involved, the Woodhead Tunnel
was let as a target-contract, with time and cost savings or
overruns being shared between client and contractor. However, to provide greater certainty when pricing or comparing tenders, plus an accepted basis for administering
contracts and sharing the risks involved, most contracts
were on a standard form such as that published by the
*Institution of Civil Engineers in 1945.

The other principal contractual development since the
1920s has been the standardization of the way in which
works are measured. In 1933 the Institution of Civil Engineers published a report laying down 'uniform principles
for drafting bills of quantities for civil engineering work'.
In the light of experience this was followed in 1953 by a
'Standard Method of Measurement of Civil Engineering
Quantities'.   JC
M. Chrimes, *Civil Engineering, 1839–1889* (1991); *DBB*; H. Pollins,
'Railway Contractors and the Finance of Railway Development
in Britain', in M. C. Reed (ed.), *Railways in the Victorian Economy*
(1969).

contractors' lines. These were lines promoted (at least in
part) and built by contractors who were willing to accept all
or some of their payment in shares, or bonds guaranteeing
payment in the future.

Most of the great trunk lines, likely on their merits to be
profitable investments, were open or nearing completion by
1850. But the *Mania of 1844–7 left behind it a trail of lines
unbuilt. It then grew more difficult for railway companies
to raise cash in the open market, and some turned elsewhere for the capital they needed. There were contractors
ready to supply it. In 1848 *Brassey accepted part of his
payment in shares or bonds for work on the *Great Northern and *North Staffordshire Railways when they were
nearing completion.

There were good reasons why some contractors were
interested in promoting and financing railways. They might
gain all the contracts, the company seeking no tenders.
Contractors had to build up their work-forces, and it could
be advantageous to move them *en bloc* from one task to
another. Waring Bros, for example, followed this practice in
Lincolnshire and Norfolk in 1858–63 (see MIDLAND & GREAT
NORTHERN JOINT RAILWAY), and later around Poole and
*Bournemouth (see SOMERSET & DORSET JOINT RAILWAY).
Soon one main line was being built with very considerable
financial support from a contractor, Charles Fox: the East
Kent (later part of the *London Chatham & Dover). By
1855 the *Railway Times* could dub it 'a contractors' line'. Fox
presently pulled out, to be succeeded by *Peto. However,
he went bankrupt in 1866, and the LCDR itself was in
receivership from 1866 to 1871.

Meanwhile another long line, the Aberystwyth & Welsh
Coast (see CAMBRIAN RAILWAYS), had been opened in 1863–7:

a contractors' line to an even greater extent. Thomas
*Savin, its chief promoter, undertook not only its building,
but also housing development designed to help the growth
of holiday resorts along it. He again, like Peto, crashed in
1866.

Contractors' lines in that full sense now disappeared. But
contractors might still give financial assistance to railway
companies whose lines they were building, sometimes
through specialist finance houses (see FINANCING OF RAIL-
WAYS). One of the first tube railways, the *Central London,
found contractors willing to accept shares in lieu of payment in 1895.   JS
H. Pollins, 'Railway Contractors and the Finance of Railway Development', in M. C. Reed (ed.), *Railways in the Victorian Economy*
(1969); *Railway Times*, 18 (1855), 1247; *CMCR*, i, ch. 4; *HLT*, ii
(1974), 141.

control, systems of train: systems whereby information
about the operation of traffic and trains is collected in a
central office and dispersed to other locations to aid
decision-making. Most effective systems of control also
require decisions to be made by the control officers, and the
issuing of instructions.

A prerequisite to an efficient control system is a rapid
form of communication, i.e. the *telephone. Early schemes
were intended to improve the working of goods and mineral traffic, the rewards being more efficient utilization of
locomotive power and the reduction of trainmen's excessive
hours. The means of achieving these ends included cancella-
tion, or termination of trains short of destination, and sending the traffic forward by other services where capacity was
available; re-routing of trains or traffic; holding trains at a
yard to connect with others; instructing signalmen to send
certain trains in front of others; rearranging trainmen's
relief; or indeed the requisitioning of additional locomotives
and train crews to meet heavy demand.

In theory, a distinction is made between train control and
traffic control: that is, authority given to instruct signalmen
regarding the movements of trains, or authority limited to
making arrangements for the traffic to be despatched economically. In practice it is virtually impossible to divorce the
two functions, and all real control offices combine elements
of both.

The first control office in Britain was opened at Masborough, Rotherham, *Midland Railway, in 1907, for the local
mineral traffic, followed by others on the same railway in
Yorkshire and Derbyshire in 1908–9. The system was next
taken up by the *Great Western for the Monmouthshire
valleys coal trains in 1909, but further development on that
railway was limited, until five offices were established during World War I.

The *North Eastern Railway introduced a goods and
mineral control office at *Middlesbrough in 1910, initially
only for recording information. Further installations followed at *Newcastle in 1917, *York (for the *East Coast
main line, including passenger trains) in 1922, and *Hull
(primarily a traffic control) in 1923. The *Lancashire &
Yorkshire introduced control at *Liverpool in 1912 and
*Manchester in 1913, concentrating them in a central office

in August 1915, which was extended to cover the entire railway by 1917. The *London & North Western opened its first control offices between 1911 and 1913 and rapidly established a comprehensive network under a central control at *Crewe. The *South Eastern & Chatham is also believed to have established a form of control about the same time.

After the *Grouping of 1923 the *London Midland & Scottish and *London & North Eastern Railways had comprehensive systems of control; but that of the GWR was less well-developed, and the *Southern Railway, on which freight traffic was less important, had no control offices until World War II.

The development of the control system is generally credited to the successive general superintendents of the MR, Cecil Paget and J. H. Follows, and Arthur Watson on the LYR, although the corresponding officers of the NER and LNWR undoubtedly did much the same.

As the experience and familiarity of the staff accumulated, additional functions were attached to the control offices, which might in any one case include: passenger and goods trains on main lines, including intense suburban services; *marshalling yards; regulation of shipment *coal traffic; scheduling of *excursion trains; carriage and wagon distribution; control of goods brake vans; and compiling records of train working for analysis. There were significant differences between the LMS and LNER systems, the former generally concentrating more functions and authority in their offices. Indeed, under the LMS Operating Manager's Department, the district controller was the chief operating officer for his district. On the contrary, a road cartage control existed at Somers Town goods station, London, which had nothing whatever to do with the working of trains (a 'pure' traffic control).

An important feature of most control offices was the train board, representing geographically the network of lines controlled, on which were placed cards with particulars of each train and the men working it. This visual appreciation of the state of traffic in the area was felt to be very important, especially as impending congestion could be foreseen much more rapidly than by using paper records. An alternative was a set of continuously updated train graphs.

During World War II, the importance attached to control offices resulted in the construction of 'protected' offices, usually in concrete blockhouses. On the LNER the protected offices were some miles from their peace-time locations, but on the LMS they were close by and work was only transferred on receipt of a 'red' air-raid warning. Some of these offices continued in use after the war, and many are still standing.

There was little change to control offices after *nationalization until reorganization as a system of Regions, Divisions, and Areas in the 1960s. A control office was instituted at each regional and divisional headquarters, some in new purpose-built offices, some of which were out of view of the railway. Further changes came in the 1980s when the divisional level was abolished and new Area Operations Centres

(AOCs) were created, in many cases on the operating floor of a large power signalbox. The new Integrated Electronic Control Centres (IECCs) (see SIGNALLING, AUTOMATIC) encompass the functions of the control office.

Also in the 1980s 'retail controls' were created, with the primary function of managing customer-care during periods of disruption.

The reorganizations of 1992 and 1994, in preparation for *privatization, again resulted in many relocations of control offices. Responsibility was divided between Railtrack and train operating units (TOUs). TOUs retain the 'retail controls' and control of locomotives, rolling stock, and train crews; they also monitor train running, produce performance statistics, and attribute blame for delays.   MRLI

P. Burtt, *Control on the Railways* (1926).

Cook, Thomas, & Son, *travel agents. Thomas Cook (1808–92) was born at Melbourne (Derbyshire) and became a wood-turner, giving much time to the Baptist community. He started a business of his own at Market Harborough (Leicestershire) in 1831 and grew much interested in the *temperance movement.

On 5 July 1841 he took a party from Leicester to Loughborough, for a temperance fête, in collaboration with the *Midland Counties Railway, he himself selling the tickets and travelling on the train. He soon moved into Leicester, as a printer, and began organizing *excursions every summer, reaching out in 1845–6 to North Wales and Scotland. But he over-stretched himself financially, going bankrupt in 1846. Recovering, in 1851 he became the *Midland Railway's agent for its excursion traffic to the Great Exhibition. Assisted by his son John Mason Cook (1834–99), he handled it successfully, claiming later to have brought 165,000 people to London for this purpose. He was soon working in conjunction with the *Eastern Counties and *London Brighton & South Coast Railways, organizing excursions to France, and he began offering coupons, sold to his excursionists in London, and accepted at hotels with which he made arrangements. He may be said to have introduced the 'package tour' to Britain and Europe. His success was not uninterrupted, however. In 1862–3 the Scottish railway companies withdrew their excursion business from him, to run it themselves.

In 1865 he opened a London office on Fleet Street, placing it under his son's charge, and this quickly became the firm's headquarters. They were both determined to extend the firm's business beyond Europe. Thomas visited the USA in 1865, sending a tour there in the following year. In 1868 the first of his tours went to Egypt and Palestine. In 1872–3 Thomas went round the world, paving the way for similar tours by the firm's clients, which came to be offered almost annually.

The two men were very different. Thomas always looked on the firm's work as a religious and social service. John Mason was intent on expanding it into a world-wide commercial undertaking. He was a first-class business manager (Thomas was not), and he considered that his father's philanthropical interests impeded the firm's progress. The two quarrelled constantly, until the younger man edged his father out of the business in 1879, to retire to Leicester, living there on an annuity into a very sad old age.

John Mason saw his ambitions fulfilled. The firm totally outdistanced its rivals in Europe, doing profitable business right across the world. In 1887–8 it opened offices in Melbourne, Adelaide, Sydney, and Auckland. It fulfilled large contracts with the British and French governments and made all the arrangements for the German Emperor William II to visit Palestine in 1898. But John Mason, who was escorting him, caught dysentery there and died in 1899. He left a fortune of £622,534 gross; his father's had been £2,731.

This was the peak of the firm's power. John Mason's two sons Frank and Ernest, though able men, lacked his dynamic force. And at the beginning of the new century a formidable rival appeared in Europe, reaching out across the Atlantic: American Express.

World War I suspended tourist business. When normal times returned, the conditions under which it worked changed rapidly. Hitherto based almost entirely on railways and steamships, it now had to take account of motor vehicles and aircraft. The firm made an impressive show in 1926 with a palatial new headquarters building in London, on Berkeley Street. But in 1928 Frank and Ernest Cook suddenly sold it to the Wagons-Lits company, the great providers of sleeping and restaurant cars for railways on the European mainland. The headquarters of that firm were in Brussels, and in 1940 it passed into the grip of the Germans. The *British Transport Commission acquired it in 1948. It has again been sold off three times more: to the Midland Bank in 1971, then briefly to German purchasers, and in 1996—most ironically—to American Express.   JS

W. F. Rae, *The Business of Travel* (1891); E. Swinglehurst, *Cook's Tours* (1982); P. Brendon, *Thomas Cook* (1991).

Cooke, C. J. Bowen (1859–1920) was chief mechanical engineer of the *London & North Western Railway from 1909 until his death. Trained at Crewe under F. W. *Webb, he became southern area running superintendent under Webb's successor George *Whale when the latter was appointed CME in 1903. Bowen Cooke's impressive performance during difficult negotiations with the unions in 1908 made him favourite to succeed Whale. He introduced superheating in the George the Fifth class of 1910 which, with the four-cylinder Claughton class of 1913, set new standards of performance and ensured his fame. Bowen Cooke wore himself out in the service of his country during World War I, and his death in October 1920 prevented him from tackling certain weaknesses in his locomotives which had been exposed under wartime conditions of reduced maintenance.   RW

R. Preston Hendry and R. Powell Hendry, *The LNWR at Work* (1990).

Cornwall Railway. This was incorporated in 1846 to build a 66-mile line, from the *South Devon Railway (already authorized) at Plymouth to Falmouth, linking up at Truro with the *West Cornwall, projected to run on to Penzance. The original engineer was W. S. Moorsom, but I. K. *Brunel improved his survey and completed the work. Just over one-fifth of the capital was subscribed by the *Great Western, *Bristol & Exeter, and *South Devon Railways (known as the 'Associated Companies').

Cornwall's one source of wealth came from mining tin and copper, but they went away by sea. Most mine-owners ignored the railway; however, some landowners and commercial men backed it. The line was opened to Truro in 1859 and to Falmouth in 1863. It had sharp curves and crossed numerous deep valleys on 44 *bridges and viaducts, all except Brunel's great Royal Albert Bridge at Saltash being of timber. It was managed jointly by the Cornwall Railway and the Associated Companies.

When it opened, Cornish mining was near to collapsing in face of overseas competition. Many of the mineworkers sought new employment abroad. The railway could offer little help but it tried to assist the development of the *china-clay industry, though it was slow to succeed.

However, the railway began immediately to aid Cornish agriculture, which took advantage of the warm climate to produce early vegetables. The railway conveyed them overnight to the markets in London and the big provincial cities, a service lucrative to growers and railway alike. It also served the fishing industry in the same way.

The railway enabled growing numbers of people to take holidays in Cornwall. New hotels were built at Penzance and Falmouth. St Ives, Newquay, and smaller places established themselves as resorts. All this helped to create new employment. The railways employed about 1,000 men in Cornwall in 1874, an annual figure that fluctuated very little.

The Cornwall company made no working profit until 1882. The line was still single, which, coupled with its curves and gradients, severely limited traffic. Nevertheless, the number of passenger journeys increased by 68 per cent in 1860–88, its total receipts by 144 per cent. The company was amalgamated with the GWR in 1889.   JS

MacDermot, ii, ch. 7; *ET*, ch. 4.

corridor train, see CARRIAGES.

corruption, see CRIME.

costing techniques

capital

A railway company's directors and shareholders naturally required financial information before endorsing any significant capital project. In addition, any railway construction work which required parliamentary powers involved the submission of estimates. Consequently, anticipated outlays for *land acquisition and on engineering and equipping a line had to be costed at the outset, and since parliamentary estimates were liable to detailed scrutiny during the committee stages of a Bill it was essential that they should be able to withstand such examination. It was therefore necessary for estimates of land acquisition costs to be based on justifiable assumptions about price and compensation, and for engineering estimates to reflect the expected quantities and costs of materials and labour.

costing techniques

In the early days of railway construction such estimates frequently proved inadequate. Six companies authorized in 1836 provide typical examples: the parliamentary estimates for the *Birmingham & Derby Junction, *Birmingham & Gloucester, *Manchester & Leeds, *Midland Counties, *North Midland, and *York & North Midland railways totalled £5.66 million, yet by 1843 these companies had spent £11.6 million on capital account, more than twice their original estimates. Much extra expenditure was attributable to the difficulty of costing substantial engineering works accurately: for instance, the original estimate for the Summit Tunnel on the Manchester & Leeds Railway had provided for 4,567 lineal yards of tunnelling at £38 per yard; as built, 5,432 yards of tunnel were required, at an average cost of £80 per yard. While such variations can be partly ascribed to relative inexperience of railway surveying and civil engineering, problems in estimating the costs of major construction projects were not unique to the initial phases of railway development.

revenue

Estimates of expected traffic income and operating costs were also a prerequisite for companies' investment decisions, and these could likewise be subject to detailed parliamentary scrutiny if opponents questioned the need for a proposed line (see PROMOTION PROCEDURE). Levels of service—and therefore operating costs—could of course be adjusted to meet actual traffic requirements, and while this did not eliminate the major financial problems facing companies which significantly exceeded their forecasts of land and engineering outlays, early estimates of net revenue generally proved to be more robust than those for capital expenditure. However, this was sometimes because errors tended to be self-cancelling: in particular, during the initial stages of the development of the system, parliamentary estimates of passenger revenue were exceeded on a number of lines, whereas freight traffic often fell short of expectations. As the system developed, such deficiencies were usually observed, and the growth in railway commercial and operating experience enabled estimates of traffic revenue and costs for new lines to be more firmly based.

Adequate costing information was of course also needed for the ongoing *management of a railway undertaking, and statutory reporting requirements involved the compilation of extensive financial data. This was categorized into the main components of income and expenditure, so by relating the various elements in the revenue account to traffic volume and to route and train mileage, basic costing data could be assembled, expressed as averages per unit of traffic or per route- and train-mile. In addition, however, many leading railways investigated aspects of their operating costs in considerably more detail: analysis of items such as average fuel consumption per engine-mile or the renewal costs of rails was common as companies sought to compare technological alternatives or establish appropriate accounting principles, and on some lines relatively sophisticated costing procedures were developed to assist management. On the *London & North Western, *Huish initiated statistical and financial analyses of several key operational and commercial policy issues: for example, decisions on contractual arrangements for goods collection and delivery were based on detailed assessments of the cost of the work involved. The company also appears to have maintained ton-mile statistics until 1875, when they were discontinued because of the clerical costs involved in their compilation. However, in 1902 the *North Eastern Railway took up the regular collection of ton-mile data as part of the modernization of its management systems, a process which drew heavily on the current practice of leading railroads in the USA.

The value of ton-miles in traffic costing was that they allowed fuller interpretation of the traditional management accountancy tools employed on British railways, which took train miles and traffic volumes as their basic units of measurement. By including ton-miles in the calculations additional information about *freight traffic could readily be obtained, such as average loading per train or average length of haul. Similar analysis of passenger services could be undertaken by using passenger-mile statistics. However, while ton-miles and passenger-miles, in common with the other indicators in more general use, could provide yardsticks for analysing the relative performance of different sections of the system or various types of traffic, they shed little additional light on the dynamic structure of railway costs.

This was because such financial statistics were simply averages, compiled on a basis which reflected a fundamental characteristic of railway traffic accounts: the difficulty of disentangling costs and relating them to individual revenue-earning activities. The problem was partly a consequence of the high proportion of railway costs which, once incurred, were either fixed or could be varied only over relatively long periods, and therefore had to be provided for regardless of prevailing traffic volumes. It also resulted from the extent to which expenditure was common to different types of traffic, including not only the more obvious examples of *track maintenance, *signalling, and locomotive facilities which benefited both passenger and freight movements, but also the various categories of revenue which might contribute to the earnings of a single train in the course of its journey.

Accordingly, while a railway company could easily determine its total expenditure, and the contribution of specific functions, the assumptions required to allocate costs against particular revenues inevitably caused ambiguity, leaving railways vulnerable to accusations that they were carrying some traffics at a loss to undermine competition from other lines or from *canals, and that where there was no competition they were exploiting their monopoly to make excess profits. The companies could reply that their maximum charges were statutorily defined, and that a further safeguard was provided by the principle, first enacted in 1845 and subsequently refined, that there should be no discrimination between customers: that any rate offered to one consignee should be available for all comparable consignments for the same journey. These arguments did not prevent continuing criticism, but though the issue remained politically controversial, the basis of railway charging withstood numerous official investigations and the scrutiny of the specialized courts that had jurisdiction over traffic disputes. In practice, therefore, companies retained considerable commercial freedom to set their rates within the permitted maxima.

British railway charges evolved on the principle of imposing what the traffic would bear, a principle which Parliament recognized in the different tonnage rates authorized for the various classes of traffic. Charges therefore bore no direct relationship to costs; indeed, railway managers freely conceded before successive Select *Committees and Royal Commissions that the nature of their industry made it virtually impossible to determine the real cost of carrying particular consignments. Instead, the main influences on individual point-to-point rates were the charges by competing railway routes or other means of transport, or, in some cases, the charge for bringing a commodity such as *coal to the same destination from an alternative source. Given the extent of fixed costs, these practices enabled separate undertakings to maximize their gross revenues, though they also implied the dilution of combined net revenue when two or more lines with different cost structures competed for the same traffic.

However, charging principles could not be wholly divorced from costs. The concept of charging what traffic could bear rested on the fundamental premise that, while each consignment should at least yield its direct costs, it was necessary for the combined revenue from all traffic to generate a sufficient margin to cover the undertaking's overall expenditure. In addition, rate structures, though price-led, embodied some cost factors: lower charges were offered to secure bulk consignments which could be cheaply conveyed in trainloads, while classifications distinguished between traffic consigned via private sidings and that which required the railway to provide additional services at each end (see TERMINAL CHARGES). Classifications also reflected the cost implications of the 'loadability' of traffic—its volume-to-weight ratio, and its ease of handling—and the carrier's potential exposure to claims for loss or damage. However, since systematic costing data was retrospective and largely based on averages, its immediate relevance as an input to rate determination was limited. In practice, outturns were heavily dependent on actual traffic volumes, and detailed cost control was an essentially pragmatic activity, which relied on the supervision of train loading and mileage to maximize financial and operational productivity.

Thus, though *Acworth's classic formulation of the principles of railway charging—'Get traffic. . . . Charge no rate so high as to stop the traffic from going. . . . Never make a rate so low as not to cover the additional cost incurred in dealing with the traffic to which the rate applies'—explicitly recognized the need to set the lower limit of any charge by reference to costs, data were simply not available in the detail necessary to ensure that this condition was fully met, and it would have been impracticable to generate it for the entire range of station-to-station rates that the complexity of the system demanded. Commentators sometimes questioned whether particular traffics were remunerative at the

charges that were available—for example, railway spokesmen frequently claimed that statutory *workmen's trains ran at a loss—but it remained difficult for companies to establish detailed costings even after the railway rates legislation of 1894 obliged them to justify any increased charge by proving that there had been an increase in the costs specific to the traffic to which that charge applied.

So long as Britain's railways remained in profit, the revenue implications of limited costing information were masked by cross-subsidy, but the growth in road competition after the 1923 *Grouping provided a new constraint, imposing a lower ceiling on many passenger and freight rates. The *Big Four companies responded by increasing their efforts to control overall costs, and, on the passenger side, by expanding their bus interests, but after *nationalization the *British Transport Commission established a traffic costing service to analyse with greater accuracy the costs of handling different categories of traffic. This reflected the fact that the BTC initially had responsibility for bus and road haulage operations as well as railways, and the view that the national economic interest would be best served if charges encouraged the redistribution of traffic to achieve more cost-effective use of the various modes of transport.

These efforts to refine costing techniques came up against the classic problems of railway financial analysis: the basis on which shared costs should be allocated, and how the incremental costs of specific traffics could be assessed. Although both the technical content of parts of the analysis undertaken by the traffic costing service and the application of some conclusions derived from its findings were therefore subsequently questioned, the underlying processes assumed wider significance after 1955, when the railway operating account moved into persistent deficit. Besides being commercially necessary to improve the BTC's rate-setting machinery, enhanced costing data became strategically important in determining the future of the industry. The more rigorous identification of the avoidable expenditure associated with particular revenue-earning activities accordingly laid the foundation for the *Beeching report and for subsequent policy developments.

This process was assisted during the 1960s by the development of a more scientific approach to the measurement of factors such as the track wear imposed by different categories of train, and by reappraisal of the infrastructure capacity required to handle existing and potential volumes of traffic with modern operating techniques. A joint British Railways and Department of Transport steering group was established in 1966 with the prime task of reviewing the basis of railway costs, including the establishment of detailed costings for individual loss-making services so that the government could determine whether they should be grant-aided for social and economic reasons.

The steering group accepted, with some reservations, its consultants' recommendation that joint and fixed costs should be allocated in proportion to traffic volumes. However, it also recognized that this 'Cooper Bros. formula' was inappropriate when services were retained for social and economic reasons, because of its failure to reflect the full costs of maintaining a passenger service when complete line closure was the alternative. Instead, what became known as 'Method 2' costing was proposed for grant-aided services: when a route was retained for a subsidized passenger service, its full infrastructure costs (including replacement depreciation) became eligible for grant. While any other services over the same line should of course meet their direct operating costs, they were charged only for infrastructure resources specifically attributable to them, such as sidings required solely for freight traffic.

After parliamentary scrutiny it was agreed in 1970 that freight should also be charged for the wear and tear it imposed on grant-aided infrastructure, and this principle was maintained with the change to system-wide passenger grant support in 1975, which left freight and parcels to bear only the avoidable costs of their operations. Under this 'prime user' charging, all the residual costs of a particular route—i.e. those costs which could not be allocated to a specific traffic—were assumed by the principal traffic using that route. The concept was refined in 1984 in a way which lessened the burden on the prime user: under the 'sole user' principle, the main operator over a route was charged with only those notional costs which would be unavoidable if there was no other traffic—the basic track, signalling, and station facilities needed for its services. Any additional costs were then charged to other users as appropriate. However, such developments did not detract from the fundamental change in railway costing principles established by the joint steering group, which replaced the traditional emphasis on seeking to recover aggregate system costs across the total revenue base, and instead drew on more transparent procedures, and an appreciation of the changing economics of railway operation, to achieve a closer identification of resources with traffics on a route-by-route basis.   MCR

W. M. Acworth, *The Elements of Railway Economics* (1924 edn.), 57–169; Cmnd 3439, *Railway Policy* (1967); C. D. Foster, 'Some Notes on Railway Costs and Costing', *Bulletin of the Oxford Institute of Statistics*, 22 (1962), 73–104; Gourvish, 108–12, 194–8, 394–6, 436–60; T. R. Gourvish, *Mark Huish and the London & North Western Railway* (1972), 130–55, 223–4, 234–51; S. Joy, *The Train that Ran Away* (1973).

costs, see FINANCING OF RAILWAYS; CONSTRUCTION COSTS; OPERATING COSTS; COSTING TECHNIQUES.

couplings are used to connect together the vehicles of a train. The earliest trains were coupled by chains or rigid bars, but the advent of locomotive haulage made necessary a more robust form of coupling that was easily connected or disconnected, a stout central chain being adopted. This hung from or was attached below a central hook, one or both chains from adjacent vehicles being used to couple them together. For coupling freight *wagons the chains were left slack ('loose-coupled') but for passenger *carriages a screw was incorporated so that the coupling could be slackened to get it over the hook and then tightened to take up the slack and bring the *buffers into contact to eliminate surging ('screw-coupled').

A chain cannot work in compression, so the buffers of a

vehicle were an essential part of the coupling system as they absorbed compressive (or buffing) loads during braking or when pushing the vehicle or train. The loose-coupled freight train, a feature of the British railway scene for over a century, had the advantage that the load could be taken up gradually on starting, but braking had to be equally gradual to prevent massive surging which could and did break couplings. A variation of the standard three-link coupling chain was introduced on the *Great Western Railway in which the central link was triangular and could be turned upright to reduce the slack (the 'Instanter' coupling).

A disadvantage of side-buffer couplings is that a long train cannot safely be propelled (pushed from the rear) at any appreciable speed because the thrust line on curved track is displaced inwards, creating instability. For this reason British railways were forbidden to propel more than two occupied passenger carriages, except in emergency. With central buffer-couplers this problem does not arise.

From the central buffers used on some narrow *gauge lines there was developed in about 1870 the 'Norwegian' coupler which employs a vertically pivoted hook working through a slot in the buffer head. On standard gauge the American knuckle or 'buckeye' coupler, which works horizontally and when engaged resembles a pair of hands firmly clasped, was introduced to Britain on the *Pullman cars imported by the *Midland Railway in 1873. Initial incompatibility with British couplings was overcome by attaching a hinged knuckle behind the hook of an existing drawbar, whereby either system could be employed. Buckeyes being more robust than chains, they are better able to prevent overturning and telescoping of carriages in an accident and slowly gained acceptance as an alternative to screw couplings except at the outer ends of the train.

Since the 1950s the use of centre buffer-couplers has greatly expanded, enabling for example the propelling of long trains at 110 mph or more, and the traditional buckeye has been challenged by newer and more complex designs. The couplings fitted to the latest diesel *multiple units do not merely couple the vehicles together but also complete all the electrical and pneumatic circuits, being operated from the adjacent driving cab.   RW

Coventry. The growth of this ancient city to contain 313,000 people in 1990 was mainly a 20th-century development, principally attributable to the motor and aviation industries. At first it had the most important intermediate station on the *London & Birmingham Railway (1838), which ran south of the city. Through peculiarities of land rights and ownerships eventual expansion was northward, while successive ribbon, clock- and watch-making, and cycle industries produced only small-volume railway traffic. Branches were opened to Warwick in 1844 and Nuneaton in 1850, but otherwise Coventry did not become a railway centre and was the only town of its size to largely escape 'railway blight'. Right until the 1950s its rail approaches other than from Nuneaton were surprisingly rural.

The virtual *monopoly of the *London & North Western Railway resulted generally in through trains only on London–*Birmingham–Wolverhampton, and Birmingham–Peterborough services. Changes were usual for all other destinations. The *Midland Railway had *running powers for goods trains from Nuneaton. A number of local schemes for links to other lines were abortive. In 1914 a goods *loop line was opened to serve new industries in the north of the city, linking the Rugby and Nuneaton lines, and avoiding the station which, despite enlargements, was cramped and still had only two platforms. Complete reconstruction with four platforms in 1962 for *electrification resulted in one of *BR's most successful new stations.

Leamington and Nuneaton passenger services ceased in 1965, but were resumed in 1977 and 1987 respectively as part of new *cross-country services which gave Coventry infinitely better rail communications than ever before, including trains over former *Great Western and Midland lines.   GJB

Reg. Hist., vii, 142–6; G. Biddle, 'Railway Monopoly at Coventry', *Railway World*, 23 (1962), 43–9; J. M. Prest, *The Industrial Revolution in Coventry* (1960); G. Hurst, *LNWR Branch Lines of West Leicestershire and East Warwickshire* (1993).

Cowlairs, see GLASGOW; WORKS.

Crampton, Thomas Russell (1816–88), mechanical and civil engineer. Crampton trained in mechanical engineering, first under John Hague, then Marc Brunel, and finally Daniel *Gooch of the *Great Western Railway, with involvement in the design of the successful Firefly class locomotives. In 1843 he took out his locomotive layout patent, with a single driving axle behind the firebox, and outside cylinders. It combined in standard-gauge engines a boiler of ample capacity, comparable with those of GWR 7-ft gauge locomotives, with a low centre of gravity for maximum stability at speed.

The first Crampton 4-2-0 was built in 1847 by Alexander *Allan at *Crewe for the Northern Division of the *London & North Western Railway. A total of about 25 Crampton engines were built in Britain, but about 300 in France and Germany where some ran until well into the 20th century, when heavier trains made multiple driving axles necessary. Their large and direct steam pipes and great stability enabled Crampton locomotives to attain the record of 90 mph with a 160-ton train in French locomotive trials in 1889. The most successful British Cramptons, to his second patent, ran on the 4-ft gauge Padarn Railway in North Wales. *Fire Queen* is preserved at Penrhyn Castle.

Crampton acted as civil engineer in railway construction on the *London Chatham & Dover Railway, in eastern Europe, and in the Middle East; for laying the first international submarine cable, between Britain and France; and the proposal for a chalk-cutting and slurry-removal machine for the first *Channel Tunnel project.   GWC

Proc. IMechE (1888), 437–9; BSRL; *Locomotive Railway Carriage & Wagon Review* (1940), 67–70.

cranes. Materials handling is a fundamental feature of railway freight operations, necessitating the use of suitable cranes in *goods depots, at loading and discharge points for *coal, *iron ore, and other *minerals, and at *ports, many of which were railway-owned. Cranes are also required at railway workshops for locomotives and rolling stock, at *engine sheds and maintenance depots, and at permanent way and bridging depots. Also, *breakdown cranes are used for re-railing in cases of serious derailment.

Goods depot operation normally involves the transhipment of freight between road and rail vehicles and vice versa, and in some cases transhipment between one wagon and another or to and from warehouses (see GOODS SHEDS). All these operations require suitable cranes.

Freight-handling at the smaller goods depots was normally carried out by fixed hand-operated cranes, to and from which wagons had to be moved. Whilst this method was acceptable at wayside depots handling only a few wagons daily, where traffic was heavier it was slow and extravagant in use of manpower, and from the 1930s onwards increasing numbers of petrol-electric and diesel-electric mobile cranes were introduced. This greatly improved the flexibility and economy of goods depot operation. From 1945 onwards large numbers of mobile cranes, built during the war for use at military stores depots, were acquired for railway use.

At larger freight depots electrically powered travelling overhead gantry cranes, capable of spanning several tracks and roads, have been widely used, both inside goods sheds and in open yards. These were supplemented by mobile cranes operating in other areas of the depot.

Grabbing cranes are widely used for the loading and discharge of coal, iron ore, and other minerals at mines, coal depots, steelworks, power stations, and docks.

In the days of steam traction, steam travelling cranes were used widely for the transhipment of coal from wagons to coal stages, or directly to locomotive tenders or bunkers at motive power depots; British steam locomotives burned some 15 million tons a year. In later years locomotive coaling plants were introduced at the larger depots, in which coal wagons were transported bodily to the top of a tower structure and manipulated to discharge into bunkers from which the locomotives were coaled. Steam travelling cranes were also widely used in permanent way storage yards, and for handling lengths of pre-assembled track at relaying locations. At storage depots where material was located at a considerable distance from the loading and unloading site, long-jibbed Scotch derrick-type cranes, with a tripod frame structure and limited slewing radius, were sometimes used. These were normally steam or electrically powered.

At railway-owned ports, where careful positioning of the load into the ships' holds was required, transfer to and from wagons was generally by rail-mounted portal-type cranes, whose superstructure was located above a four-leg travelling frame. Frequently these cranes had a level luffing member at the top of the jib, enabling the load to be maintained at a constant height whilst raising or lowering the jib, an important factor when manoeuvring the load within the confines of a ship's hold. These cranes were normally powered electrically.

In repair workshops for locomotives and rolling stock, electric overhead travelling cranes were provided for lifting, traversing, and travelling inside the shops, handling locomotives, bogies, boilers, diesel engines, transformers, and other components. Crane tank locomotives, with a crane jib mounted at the rear, were also used to some extent in workshop yards. At locomotive running depots sheerlegs were often used, where no wheeldrop was available, to lift one end of a locomotive to enable a bogie or wheelset to be run out, for example when overheated axle-boxes had to be remetalled. At railway construction and relocation sites, bucket-type crane excavators or dragline excavators were often used.

Breakdown cranes, with a lifting capacity of up to some 50 tons each, were required for re-railing overturned or damaged locomotives and rolling stock, in conjunction with re-railing ramps, jacks, winches, and wire rope. These incorporated retractable blocking-out sub-frames for use when the load required the crane jib to be luffed out to a considerable radius, to provide the necessary stability. Most British breakdown cranes were steam-powered, but a few were diesel-electric.

With the advent of *container trains, special depots have required overhead Goliath-type straddle cranes for transferring containers between rail and road vehicles.   GWC

Crewe. Despite contraction, Crewe retains its whole railway complex with six important junctions, a large marshalling yard partly fed by a complex of independent goods lines burrowing under the large station, electric and diesel traction depots which replaced once-famous steam *engine sheds, and the now-privatized locomotive *works. The town was born in 1837 when the Chester & Crewe and Manchester & Birmingham Railways (see LONDON & NORTH WESTERN RAILWAY) were authorized only four days ahead of the opening of the *Grand Junction Railway between Warrington and Birmingham. Crewe, a hamlet which had only a primitive wayside station beside a turnpike road, became the junction of the three lines. The Chester & Crewe was absorbed before completion in 1840 by the GJR, which enlarged the station and also worked the Manchester & Birmingham from its opening in 1842.

The GJR bought large areas of land at Crewe in 1840 and moved its locomotive and carriage works from Edge Hill, *Liverpool, partly because Crewe was more centrally situated on its main line. By 1843 it had built 200 *houses, and about 800 men, women, and children moved into them, 160 men being employed in the new works. Its successor, the LNWR, went on to build more houses, and also churches and schools, and to provide gas and water and the town's first policemen.

The works expanded quickly as it concentrated on locomotive building and repair. Subsequently, the wagon workshops moved north to Earlestown and *carriage-building and repair work was transferred south to Saltley, *Birmingham, for a short time before a permanent move to Wolverton. Although Crewe was now the hub of the LNWR, two other lines entered it: the *North Staffordshire Railway from Stoke in 1848; and the *Great Western from Market Drayton in 1863 and Wellington in 1867, completing a second route from the Midlands. The GWR used *running powers from Nantwich over the *Shrewsbury–Crewe line of 1858.

The LNWR replaced the original station in 1849 by one with ornate buildings and through lines in the middle. Then in 1867 the station was again rebuilt with widened platforms and bays to keep local and other stopping trains clear of the main line.

'Rejoicings' to mark the golden jubilee of Crewe in 1887 embraced the 50th anniversaries of Queen Victoria's reign and the opening of the GJR, the dedication of Queen's Park, a gift from the LNWR, and completion of the 3,000th engine made in the works, which continued to grow. In 1868 the Chester line had been moved a short distance south to allow further improvements. In 1871–1903 the works was dominated by the autocratic F. W. *Webb whose influence there, in the town, and throughout the company, was far wider than his title of locomotive superintendent would suggest. He was twice mayor, and a Cheshire magistrate and alderman, although his attempts to influence politics did not succeed. He formed a Railway Engineer Volunteer Corps of LNWR workers (see WAR) and nearly 300 men served in the South African War (1899–1902). He left a third of his large estate to found the Webb Orphanage at Crewe for the children of LNWR employees.

For years the Mechanics Institute, dating from the GJR days, was a focal point of railway and town life, a training centre for thousands of apprentices and workmen.

An LNWR Guidebook writer once noted wryly that 'most of the people have a railway look', and in late Victorian years the company employed 10,000 people at Crewe, almost a quarter of the population, mainly in the locomotive works, supporting its claim that the town was 'wholly dependent on the railway for its prosperity'. More than 8,000 locomotives—an average of one a week—were built between 1843 and 1990. Coronation Scot streamliners, introduced in 1938, were among the most notable.

The build-up of passenger, goods, and mineral traffic through Crewe was unrelenting. When congestion became acute in the 1870s, the LNWR presciently bought more land, this time south of the station. Twenty years later, when 1,000 trains a day were passing through, it built the 'Independent' goods lines and Basford Hall marshalling yard, with a 2,350-wagon capacity. It included a tranship shed, which the LNWR pioneered in 1901, to handle small traffic with 600 men clearing 1,100 wagons a day. As the Independent lines were being built, a third island platform almost doubled the size of the station. NSR trains from Derby and GWR services from Wellington used south bay platforms, where they were handled by a small staff from each company. The NSR also ran Potteries–Llandudno summer expresses through the station.

Crewe ceased to be purely a railway town in 1938 when Rolls-Royce built a 'shadow' factory to make engines for wartime aircraft. It employed 10,000 people in 1943, the total dropping after it changed to car production in 1946.

Diversification has continued, and now the railway works is about a quarter of its peak size.

Early *British Rail local passenger service economies included the closure of wayside stations on the main line to Stafford. Norton Bridge survives, though used only by Stoke-on-Trent services. The last of several remote village stations between Crewe and Chester closed to passengers in 1966.

BR concentrated the first stages of the 25 kV *West Coast main line *electrification on the Manchester, Liverpool, and Birmingham routes from Crewe. It embraced more than 70 miles of track within a 1-mile radius of the station and the Independent line tunnels were used for flashover tests. The Manchester scheme was completed in 1960 and that to Liverpool in 1962, but four more years elapsed before Birmingham services began. Since major resignalling, track alterations, and station modernization in 1985, expresses have run at high speed through the station while the approach speeds of those booked to stop have been raised.

See also TOWNS AND VILLAGES, RAILWAY-CREATED; HOUSING. RC

W. H. Chaloner, *The Social and Economic History of Crewe 1780–1923* (1950); R. Christiansen, *Rail Centres: Crewe* (1993); B. Reed, *Crewe Locomotive Works and its Men* (1982); *Reg. Hist.*, vii (1991), esp. ch. 10.

crime. From the magnitude of their operations, the speed at which their trains ran, the great diversity of the business they dealt with, and the huge sums of money that was poured into them or passed through their hands, railways were sometimes a great focus and agency of crime. They were seldom guilty of fomenting it for their own purposes, but they offered opportunities for violence, robbery, and fraud on a scale hardly imaginable before.

At first the crimes were petty. The *Liverpool & Manchester Railway often suffered from the placing of sleepers and other heavy objects across its lines, causing the death of a *contractor just before its opening; but except on that one occasion the results were never serious.

The earliest widely heard complaints of crime connected with railways arose from the lawless habits of some of the *navvies building them. In 1830 eight Acts were passed authorizing the appointment of special constables (paid for by the companies) to deal with such offenders. Some companies appointed constables of their own (see POLICE).

By the 1840s railways were taking a valuable part in the suppression of civil disorder (see RIOTING). In the same decade they began to assist the police in the arrest of criminals, aided by the electric *telegraph then being laid along their lines. This became celebrated in 1845 when John Tawell, having committed a murder at Slough, travelled by the *Great Western Railway to *Paddington station, where he was spotted by a policeman, who recognized him from a description that had been telegraphed from Slough, shadowed him to his lodgings, and arrested him next day. In due course Tawell was hanged.

Railways became associated with crimes of violence in another way too. The small compartments of the carriages used on most European railways almost invited them.

When a French judge was murdered in one in 1860 an English newspaper published in Paris remarked that 'a certain feeling of uneasiness has arisen at the idea of the extreme facility with which the crime appears to have been perpetrated'. Uneasiness became something much stronger in Britain when a similar murder occurred on the *North London Railway in 1864, for which a German, Franz Müller, was executed.

A small number of other murders are known to have been committed in British trains, but only three of them brought the criminal to conviction and death. P. M. Lefroy killed a wealthy corn merchant in a *London Brighton & South Coast Railway train in Merstham Tunnel (1881); G. H. Parker, who murdered a farmer between Surbiton and Vauxhall on the *London & South Western Railway 20 years later; and J. A. Dickman, who killed the cashier of a colliery company, on the *North Eastern Railway, near Morpeth, in 1910.

Railway carriage compartments were equally convenient for sexual assaults, and they were frequently brought before the courts. But another element was involved in some of them. The woman alleged to have been assaulted might levy blackmail on the man. The court had then to adjudge the probabilities of the tale largely by the impression that the two parties made on it. The most famous of all these cases was that of Col. Valentine Baker on the LSWR in 1875.

Financial gain was the root of many railway crimes. But that had been demonstrated, on the largest possible scale, by George *Hudson. Though by no means all of his financial dealings were illegal, and some of the results undoubtedly promoted the general interest of railways, much of what he did was indefensible. He escaped trial and imprisonment only by living abroad after 1850. There were numerous mini-Hudsons too, without his brains or vision, who played with the finances of the companies they were involved with: William Chadwick, for example, whose scandalous manipulation of the business of the North Wales Railway was closely scrutinized by a House of Lords committee in 1849.

Two very notable crimes on railways came to public notice in 1857. Leopold Redpath, a clerk in the share registration department of the *Great Northern Railway and its head since 1854, applied himself to creating bogus shares in the company and forging transfers in its books. By 1856 he had made well over £200,000 for himself in this way, but he was then detected and sentenced to transportation for life. He emerged at his trial in 1857 as a very curious man, living comfortably but without ostentation, a supporter of numerous charities (he was a governor of Christ's Hospital), pursuing fraudulence one might almost say as an art. The lax supervision of his work damaged the GNR's reputation, and it contributed to a long discussion of railway companies' *accounting, eventually expressed in legislation in 1866–8.

A more sensational trial (though involving a much smaller sum of money) took place later in the same year when four men were convicted of stealing gold bars, to the value of £15,000, from the *South Eastern Railway's night mail train between London and Dover. Two of them were the company's servants, a guard and a clerk. The job merely involved unlocking the safes in the guard's van that contained the gold, by means of duplicate keys, and replacing it with lead of the same weight. But the participants quarrelled, and one of them turned Queen's evidence.

Trains afforded convenient opportunities for a multitude of small crimes: card-sharping, for instance, and crooked gambling games of all sorts, loaded to trap the unwary—though since gaming was illegal in any 'public place', these tricksters had to operate in private, reserved compartments. Rowdyism was endemic in trains, and sometimes very alarming. It grew commoner for a time in the 20th century, when compartments were abandoned in favour of open carriages, with central gangways.

One more outstanding crime remains to be mentioned: the 'Great Train Robbery' of 1963. This involved 15 principal conspirators and was designed to remove a big consignment of bank-notes *en route* from the Glasgow–London night mail train. The complicated plan was ingeniously devised, but its execution was careless. The train was stopped at Cheddington (Buckinghamshire) by a signal that had been tampered with. The driver was coshed, and £2.6 million of notes were taken away to a house hired for the purpose. Only 13 per cent of that sum was ever recovered. The criminals all received heavy sentences of imprisonment. One escaped, and was still at large in Brazil 30 years later.

So railways may be said both to have enlarged the facilities for the commission of crime and to have made great improvements in the methods by which the criminals could be caught.

The crimes that have been considered here must be seen in their right proportion. It remains true that no major railway accident ever occurred in Britain that is certainly attributable to criminal planning. There might have been one of great magnitude in 1880 between Bushey and Watford, when a charge of dynamite was laid across the line to blow up the Irish Mail; but the perpetrators bungled their job, and the explosion never occurred.   JS

W. Schivelbusch, *The Railway Journey* (1980), 84–92; Tawell: MacDermot, i, 327; Redpath and the SER robbery: M. Robbins, *Points and Signals* (1967), 139–47; robbery of 1963: M. Fewtrell, *The Train Robbers* (1964), and P. P. Read, *The Train Robbers* (1978).

cross-country services. These were trains that ran through, with no change of carriage, across the grain of the trunk routes, particularly those radiating from London. They are different from *through carriages, which usually ran over branches after being detached at junctions from long-distance trains.

Stage and mail *coaches offered some cross-country services: between Gloucester and *Brighton, for example, and between *Manchester and *York. In 1836 the longest distance over which any cross-country stage coach ran seems to have been from *Birmingham to Yarmouth (199 miles).

England

The first long-distance cross-country services on railways ran between the Mersey and the Humber, from 1849 onwards. Four companies came to have stakes in three competing routes from *Liverpool and Manchester to *Hull and Goole. Soon afterwards the *Lancashire & Yorkshire and *London & North Western began to compete in the provision of through trains between Manchester and York, later extended to form through services between Liverpool and *Newcastle.

There were greater inducements to the running of such services in the north of England than in the south. In Lancashire and Yorkshire, stations serving industrial towns lay close together. Of the two routes between Manchester and York, one served Rochdale, Todmorden, and Wakefield on the way; the other Stalybridge, Huddersfield, and Dewsbury: so these trains could do good business at all those stations too.

The north of England had also another particular use for through services. Railway speed enabled well-to-do people to go to the warmer south of England for holidays, or to retire there, providing they could maintain their connections easily with friends and relatives in the north. Their journeys, however, meant crossing London and then going on by another train, which deterred people who otherwise liked the idea.

The pioneer in providing a through service of this sort was the *Midland Railway, in conjunction with the *Somerset & Dorset and the *London & South Western. In 1874 through trains began to run between Birmingham and *Bournemouth, coming off the Midland at Bath, a run of 165 miles. Six years later the service was extended northwards to Newcastle (370 miles), involving the collaboration of a fourth company, the *North Eastern.

This principle was adopted in 1880 by the LNWR and the *Great Eastern companies, which put on a through service between Birmingham and Harwich, for GER steamers to Antwerp, connecting at Rugby with others from *Scotland and *Ireland, which arrived at the same platform.

Other cross-country services had been run since 1850 for the benefit of a very different kind of passenger: through trains from Hull to Liverpool, conveying emigrants in transit from Russia, Germany, and Scandinavia to North America; 61,000 passengers were still being taken across England in this way in 1903.

The holiday business now called for the multiplication of through trains. In the 1880s there were such services in the summer to Llandudno from Manchester and Liverpool, Birmingham and *Leicester. But none ran west of Bristol, on account of the break of gauge there (see TRACK GAUGE). When the GWR line beyond Exeter was converted to the standard gauge in 1892 an early consequence was the provision of through carriages, and later whole trains, between Liverpool, Leeds, and Torquay. Trains also ran to *Plymouth from Liverpool and Manchester, through Shrewsbury and the *Severn Tunnel, which had been opened in 1886.

In 1900 a new and energetic protagonist of cross-country

services appeared: the *Great Central Railway, coming southwards from Manchester and *Sheffield and feeding traffic on to the GWR by its branch line to Banbury. It too served Bournemouth, from Manchester via Nottingham and Basingstoke, where the trains passed on to the LSWR.

Another new set of through services had now grown important: those from the north and the Midlands to the coasts of Sussex and Kent. These had two purposes: to ease communication with seaside resorts like Brighton, Eastbourne, and Ramsgate; and to assist travellers crossing the Channel by serving Folkestone and Dover. These services soon proliferated, taking a variety of routes: through Reading and Redhill; by Willesden and the *West London line. One of the most steadily popular of the trains ran from the LNWR to Brighton and Eastbourne from 1905 (later known as the Sunny South Express), conveying also through carriages from Liverpool to Dover. After World War I it acquired others for Margate and Ramsgate; eventually yet more, from Sheffield and the Midland line. It ran in this shape every summer and on Saturdays in the winter until 1939, but was never successfully restored thereafter.

Wales and Scotland
Cross-country services in *Wales and Scotland were very few.

In 1895 a through train between Manchester and Aberystwyth was put on by the *Cambrian and Manchester Sheffield & Lincolnshire (see GREAT CENTRAL) companies. By 1900 the Cambrian and LNW Railways were offering another. Southwards, a through train was introduced between Aberystwyth, Newport, and *Cardiff, the Cambrian's partners here being the *Brecon & Merthyr and *Taff Vale companies.

The north–south main roads in Wales were poor, but indirect railways did not provide any through communication even by the one circuitous route available, via *Crewe and Hereford. *British Rail at last established a service of this kind in 1987, but it did not last long.

In Scotland the main trunk lines connected all the most populous places, and the need for trains like these was therefore much less than in England. Still, in summer there were through trains on the *North British Railway from *Glasgow to the coast of Fife, terminating at St Andrews. Penetrating into England, there were through summer services from Glasgow to *Blackpool and Scarborough.

new competition
Most cross-country services were withdrawn during World War I. Many of them had been resumed by 1922, and some new ones had been introduced, including a train between *Portsmouth and Plymouth on the LSWR. Another appeared crossing South Wales between Aberystwyth and Treherbert in the Rhondda coalfield, which ran on Mondays and Saturdays, perhaps indicating the diffusion of the idea of the *weekend holiday. What became striking now was the multiplication of services on branch lines reaching seaside towns—Blackpool and Scarborough, also Skegness and the other resorts on the Lincolnshire coast.

The railways were now under pressure from a new competitor: the long-distance motor coach. It could be a formidable rival to the cross-country train. On journeys of moderate length the coach offered its own attractions, picking up and setting down passengers much more flexibly than the trains. Moreover, until 1930 the coach operators were free to provide services as and when they chose. For the railways that was more difficult. An engine and carriages must be found, with a crew of three or four men. For an extra train a *path would have to be laid down, often through a tangle of junctions—as at *Preston, on the approach to Blackpool. Yet there were still 30 through trains from stations beyond Crewe to Llandudno on Saturdays in the summer of 1939—more than twice as many as in 1922.

British Rail
World War II brought a considerable destruction of the railways' rolling stock, and no large-scale replacement began until four years after *nationalization. The demands of main-line and commuters' services were then paramount. Not only were there few vehicles to spare for holiday trains; the demand for them rapidly fell away with the beginning of cheap overseas holiday air travel from the mid-1950s onwards. Motor coaches and private cars now captured more and more of the business that remained.

The regular long-distance trains continued. But line closures necessitated changes of route for three important cross-country services. The first of these came in 1959, when all passenger services were withdrawn from the 84 miles from Saxby (Leicestershire) to Melton Constable (Norfolk). In the past, a substantial through traffic had gone this way in summer from the Midlands to Yarmouth and Lowestoft (see MIDLAND & GREAT NORTHERN JOINT RAILWAY). It was now mostly taken via Leicester, Peterborough, and Ely. The running-down of the Somerset & Dorset line required the diversion of the old-established through services from the north and the Midlands to Bournemouth: from September 1962 onwards they went by Oxford and Basingstoke. Then the Sheffield–London line of the old GCR was closed, removing another long-favoured cross-country route, via Banbury.

Another, different change was taking place simultaneously, affecting many important cross-country services: the total reconstruction of New Street station, Birmingham, in 1964-7. For passengers it now became the greatest meeting-place for long-distance services at one station anywhere in Great Britain, London included. All the cross-country through services from the north to southern and south-western England now ran through Birmingham. Through trains were available from New Street to each of the ten other largest provincial cities in the island, except Hull. The station claimed to be, in BR's words, 'the finest interchange centre in the country'. It was so indeed, on paper; but in practice it has never worked to passengers' satisfaction, owing to constant unpunctuality, causing missed connections. The Bournemouth services were notorious, from delays they met with at Basingstoke. Altogether by 1994 there were 26 long-distance cross-country trains running north and south every weekday via Birmingham, originating from points as far off as *Aberdeen, *Swansea, and Penzance.

One group of these services, however, did not pass through Birmingham: those between East Anglia and northern England. Some of them went, as they had long done, via March, Spalding, and Doncaster; others via Peterborough and the *East Coast main line, or (later) via Melton Mowbray and Loughborough. A number of them went as far as Blackpool.

All in all, cross-country services underwent a remarkable development in these years, doing a great deal of business on their way. The Aberdeen–Plymouth train stopped at 26 stations on its 645-mile journey.

services crossing London

Something akin to cross-country services has also been provided traversing London. In 1910 through trains were introduced to run from Ealing to Southend, by the underground *Metropolitan District and the *London Tilbury & Southend Railways jointly. They proved successful, and the service continued until 1939.

No other through trains like this one ever crossed London from west to east. But in 1988 an elaborate set of *Thameslink trains was introduced from north to south, providing through services over distances substantially greater than from Ealing to Southend: 104 miles from Bedford to Brighton, for instance; 69 from Luton to Guildford.

The Thameslink trains are essentially suburban trains (some of them stopping at all stations *en route*), extended into the outer suburban area or beyond. But they fulfil one of the chief purposes of many of the services reviewed here: they run through without obliging their passengers to change from one train or one station to another in central London. JS

Bradshaw's Guide and BR Timetables; emigrant traffic through Hull: *Reg. Hist.*, v, 224; Manchester–Aberystwyth services: *CMCR*, i, 129, 133; ii, 74–6; proliferation of services in 1905: *RM*, 17 (1905), 198–205.

Crossley, John Sydney (1812–79), civil engineer. An orphan from the age of two, he was articled to his guardian's son who was engineer of the Leicester Navigation, which included *tramroads. Crossley was appointed engineer in 1832, later becoming a director, which he remained until his death.

He began railway work on the *Leicester & Swannington Railway in 1833, going on to the *Midland Counties Railway. Apart from a period in 1851 when he worked for Leicester Waterworks, Crossley remained with the Midland Railway or its constituents for the rest of his life. Surviving a stroke in 1852, he became chief engineer in 1858, constructing some 225 miles of new line, including Clay Cross *Tunnel (1 m 26 yds) and Barnsley Viaduct.

His greatest work was the *Settle & Carlisle line (1876),

which he supervised throughout, although, not surprisingly, his estimates failed to take sufficient account of Pennine winters. The arduous responsibilities of such a difficult project made Crossley ill in 1874, and in 1875 the company accepted his resignation provided that he completed the line, after which he would be retained as consultant. His wife laid the last stone on the highest viaduct, Smardale, and the railway opened in 1876. Although the Settle & Carlisle undoubtedly contributed to his death three years later at the age of 66, Crossley will always be associated with it. GJB

BDE; P. E. Baughan, *The Midland Railway North of Leeds* (1987 edn.).

Cubitts, the. The son of a Norfolk miller, (Sir) **William Cubitt** (1785–1861) first worked as a millwright, then with the agricultural engineers Ransomes of Ipswich (becoming a partner), before practising as a civil engineer in 1826–58. He improved the Oxford Canal, was engineer of the Birmingham & Liverpool Junction Canal (1835), and built the *South Eastern Railway (1843), including the difficult coastal section near Folkestone. He was consulting engineer for the construction of the *Great Northern Railway (1844–55), and supervised erection of the Crystal Palace (1851), for which he was knighted.

His brother **Benjamin** (1795–1848) managed two engineering works before turning to railways, first as superintendent for the *London & Croydon, London & Brighton (see LONDON BRIGHTON & SOUTH COAST), and *South Eastern locomotive pooling committee, and then, in 1846, the GNR, where he died in office.

Sir William's son **Joseph** (1811–72) was apprenticed under Benjamin. He became chief engineer of the GNR under his father, succeeding him as consultant, and built the *London Chatham & Dover Railway (1861), and a number of other lines.

The brothers Thomas (1788–1855), William, and Lewis Cubitt (1799–1883) appear to have been not directly related to William. In 1824 they founded a large and successful speculative building business. Their railway contracts included part of the *London & Birmingham Railway, for which they erected the Doric portico at *Euston. Lewis was an architect who had trained under H. E. Kendall, and he designed many of the houses on the Cubitts' estates, notably in Bloomsbury, Belgravia, and Clapham Park in London, and Kemp Town, Brighton. The brothers also worked on Buckingham Palace and built Osborne House for the Queen and Prince Albert. Lewis designed *King's Cross station and *hotel on the GNR, and the SER's first London terminus at Bricklayers Arms. GJB

BDE; L. G. Booth, 'The Cubitts on the Great Northern Railway: One Family or Two?', *JRCHS*, 32, Pt 3, 163 (1996), 3–11.

culverts, see BRIDGES AND VIADUCTS.

Cuneo, T., see ART.

cut-off, applied to steam locomotives, is the percentage of the piston stroke during which steam is admitted to the cylinder behind the piston. For the rest of the stroke the steam is allowed to expand before being released from the cylinder at the end of the stroke. Increasing cut-off increases the amount of steam admitted during each stroke, the work performed during the stroke, and the tractive effort developed by the locomotive, but recovers a smaller proportion of the energy stored in that steam, so more steam is used per unit-power output, and of course more fuel and water are consumed to provide it. A long cut-off (e.g. 75 per cent) is used to start a train from rest because it requires much more tractive effort to accelerate a train than to haul it at a constant speed. As speed rises, however, the boiler would be unable to sustain the demand for steam were the cut-off not reduced progressively, and at full speed it may have been reduced to 15 per cent or less.

Because steam is used more efficiently at reduced cut-off, the tractive effort is not reduced in proportion to the cut-off: with the same steam chest pressure the locomotive will develop about half the tractive effort at 33 per cent cut-off that it does at 75 per cent. It is, however, capable of developing considerably more power (tractive effort multiplied by speed) for the same steam consumption.   RW

cut-off (route), see LOOP; SYSTEM, DEVELOPMENT OF THE.

cuttings, see EARTHWORKS.

D

Dalhousie, James, 10th Earl and 1st Marquess of (1812–60), politician; educated at Harrow and Christ Church, Oxford. He succeeded his father in the House of Lords, 1838. He was vice-president, Board of *Trade, under *Gladstone, 1843–5; president, 1845–6. He was heavily involved in government policy towards railways during the *Mania. In 1844 the Board was required to report on all railway schemes submitted to Parliament, for which task a committee was established comprising Dalhousie (chairman) and four of the Board's senior officers. They were rudely nicknamed the 'Five Kings'. Gladstone gave little help, partly because he was preoccupied with carrying the Bill that became known as *Gladstone's Act. The Prime Minister, *Peel, never appreciated Dalhousie's true worth.

The committee had a formidable assignment. It reported on 245 railway Bills deposited in 1844; Parliament accepted 87 per cent of its recommendations. Nevertheless, Peel dismissed it after one year's work. The far larger quantity of proposals submitted in 1845 was dealt with, much less satisfactorily, by parliamentary committees.

In 1847 Dalhousie was appointed governor-general of India, where he put his experience to good use, establishing a railway system for the whole sub-continent. He returned in 1856, his health broken, and retired from public life.

JS

GR; DNB.

dandy-cart, car. The *OED* traces 'dandy-cart' back to 1861, in the sense of 'a kind of spring-cart used by milkmen, etc.'. But the railways had used the term 30 years before that, when 'dandy-carts' were in service on the horse-worked inclines of the *Stockton & Darlington Railway. They were low, flat trucks on to which the horses were led after they had hauled the trains to the top of a hill, in order to ride back again by gravity, regulated by a brakesman on the train, a technique that was found to produce an economy of one third in the animals' energies. The horses liked it very much; the men reported that when getting on to the carts they 'laughed again'. The same practice was followed on other railways, including the *Festiniog, and it was still to be observed on a colliery line at Newburn, Northumberland, as late as 1907.

The dandy-car was a horse-hauled passenger carriage. The best-known, and the longest-lived of them, were those used on the Port Carlisle branch of the *North British Railway, which continued in service until 1914. One is still to be seen in the NRM.

JS

Tomlinson, 153–8, 527–30; A. Earnshaw, 'The Port Carlisle Branch', *Back Track*, 3 (1989), 132–7.

dangerous goods. Although railway companies were, for most legal purposes, common carriers, i.e. they were obliged to carry the goods of anybody who was willing to pay their charges, that obligation did not extend to the conveyance of dangerous goods. The Railways Clauses Act, 1845, laid down that no one might require a railway to carry 'any aquafortis, oil of vitriol, gunpowder, lucifer matches', or any other goods that it considered dangerous. When a company did agree to carry such goods, the consignor was bound to label them as dangerous before handing them over; if he did not, he was liable to a forfeit of £20 to the company. The Explosive Substances Act, 1875, greatly stiffened the penalties. Today the conveyance of dangerous goods is governed by Section 20 of the British Railways Board's Conditions of Carriage, ampler and more precise than the earlier regulations.

The railways usually carried such substances in their own specially designed vehicles. These were not very numerous —though the small *London Tilbury & Southend Railway had as many as 25, required chiefly for traffic to the Royal Artillery's works and testing-ground on its line at Shoeburyness. But the petroleum industry, which started in Britain in the late 19th century and became exceedingly important in the 20th, carried much of this highly flammable liquid in its own vehicles which were permitted to travel on the main railway lines, subject to close inspection. One dating from as early as 1883 is at the NRM.

See also WAGONS; OIL, CARRIAGE OF.

JS

L. James, *Law of the Railway* (1980), 330–2; R. J. Essery, *Illustrated History of Midland Wagons* (1980), ii, 14–21, 142.

Darlington, see WORKS.

Davies, David (1818–90), *contractor, helped his father, a farmer and surveyor from Llandinam, Montgomeryshire, before taking local bridge and road contracts. He tendered successfully for the first section of the Llanidloes & Newtown Railway, 1855 (see CAMBRIAN RAILWAYS). Further contracts followed, and Davies began to operate the line. This entrepreneurial spirit characterized his career, and over the next 10 years he built further lines in mid-Wales, often with his own capital. In 1857 he took as his partner Thomas *Savin on the Vale of Clwyd Railway, completed in 53 weeks. After completing the Newtown line in late 1858 they began to extend it to Aberystwyth, Davies building the section from Caersws to Machynlleth.

His other contracts were for the Pembroke & Tenby Railway, its Narberth extension, and the Manchester & Milford Railway.

While Savin financially over-reached himself, Davies

diversified. He obtained a mining concession in the Rhondda in 1864, and made a fortune out of the Ocean collieries. Although no longer a contractor, he played a key role in Welsh railway development: as the chief protagonist of the *Barry Dock and Railway (1884), and director of the Cambrian Railways (1868–79). He left £404,425, but probably passed more to his only child Edward, who left £1,206,311 (1898). MMC

DNB: *Missing Persons*; I. Thomas, *Top Sawyer* (1938, 1988 repr.); H. Williams, *Davies the Ocean* (1991).

Dawson, William (1789–1878), artist. Nothing seems to be known of his life, except that on the title-page of *Landslips in East Devon*, which he produced jointly with the distinguished geologist W. D. Conybeare in 1840, he appears as 'civil engineer and surveyor'. He went on to execute a complete set of water-colour drawings of the *South Devon Railway, from *Exeter to Newton Abbot, in a form that is surely unique: a map of the line, with engineering plans and sections, flanked by strips of drawings that depict the landscape on each side of the line, mile by mile, accompanied throughout by separate drawings of individual buildings. Some of them are informative about the equipment and operation of a railway worked on the *atmospheric system. In 1848 he published eight lithographs, lightly tinted, of civil engineering structures on the SDR, outstanding in the delicacy of their draughtsmanship. JS

The large and elaborate set of drawings is in the ICE library, unpublished—though some are reproduced in black and white in C. Hadfield, *Atmospheric Railways* (1967).

dead centre is the position of the crank of a reciprocating (piston) engine at which the piston rod, connecting rod, and crank are in a straight line at either end of the stroke. In this position piston thrust has no leverage on the crank and cannot cause the wheels to rotate, but increases frictional resistance to rotation of the axle. Should a steam locomotive stop with one cylinder on or near dead centre, therefore, it may be unable to start even though another cylinder is receiving steam with its crank at a favourable angle. This condition is known as 'stopping on centre' and is usually cured by backing the locomotive slightly to move the offending cylinder away from dead centre before trying again. RW

dead man's handle. The dead man's handle is a safety device on diesel or electric locomotives (see TRACTION) or *multiple-unit trains to guard against inattention or incapacity on the part of the driver. In its basic form, the driver must maintain a constant pressure on the spring-loaded handle of the controller at the driving position. Should he release his hold, the controller returns to the 'off' position, an electrical contact opening the motor contactors, to cut the supply of current to the equipment. Then, usually after a predetermined interval, the brakes are applied. Alternatively, a dead man's handle may comprise a foot-operated treadle.

The initiative for fitting dead man's handles came on *London's underground railways. At first, an assistant motorman was employed as a back-up to the motorman (driver), but by the mid-1900s the fitting of dead man's han-

dles, and introduction of automatic *signalling, allowed the companies to introduce single-manning. Early applications were on the experimental *Westinghouse-equipped train for the *Metropolitan District Railway's electrification in 1903, and on the stock built for the *Yerkes tube railways from 1906.

With the original dead man's devices, it was possible either for an incapacitated driver to fall forward on to the handle so that the train would proceed unchecked, or for the handle to be tied down improperly, as happened on the Tyneside electrification at Manors in 1926 when a collision resulted. Similarly, the dead man's device did not respond to the apparent incapacity of the driver in the Moorgate *accident of 1975.

A more sophisticated system was designed in the 1960s, usually referred to as a driver's safety device, or a vigilance unit. This requires the driver to confirm his alertness at intervals by pressing a button on the control desk, or by completing a monitoring cycle as a result of depressing a foot-operated control.

See also SAFETY. MLH

J. G. Bruce, *Tube Trains under London* (1968); J. Johnson and R. A. Long, *British Railways Engineering 1948–80* (1981); English Electric Co. Ltd, *Know the Locomotive You Drive* (1952).

Dean, William (1840–1905), locomotive engineer. Apprenticed under Joseph Armstrong, locomotive superintendent of the *Great Western Railway's northern division, at the age of 24 Dean took charge of Wolverhampton works. After succeeding Armstrong at *Swindon in 1877, Dean had to deal with the prolonged period of gauge conversion up to 1892 by modifying standard-gauge locomotives for broad gauge.

With a few exceptions, Dean built simple, robust, and effective locomotives, including 280 0-6-0 goods engines (1883–98)—many used for overseas service in both world wars—and his elegant 4-2-2 express locomotives, one of which averaged 72 mph from Bristol to London in 1904. His Duke class 4-4-0 of 1895, highly successful on heavily graded routes in Devon and Cornwall, was repeated 40 years later when their successors were improved and rebuilt for the *Cambrian line. Dean's larger carriages embodied his centreless, pendulum-suspended truck, lighter and less satisfactory than a true bogie, and included the prototype modern *sleeping car, with transverse berths. All broad-gauge carriages from 1877 were convertible to standard gauge. In 1880 he began development of the GWR improved vacuum *brake, working to a higher degree of vacuum than that used elsewhere. Dean also established the Swindon chemical and materials testing laboratory. GWC

Locomotive Railway Carriage & Wagon Review (1940), 180–5; H. Holcroft, *An Outline of Great Western Locomotive Practice 1837–1947* (1957).

Deltic. D. Napier & Son, one of the companies in the English Electric group, gave the name Deltic to a two-stroke, high-speed opposed-piston triangular diesel engine (see TRACTION, DIESEL) developed during the early 1950s for use in naval patrol boats.

In 1951 the English Electric Co. Ltd started building at its Preston works a prototype Co-Co diesel electric locomotive, powered by a pair of these engines and developing 3,300 hp. Known as the Deltic, it had a striking pale blue paint scheme. On entering trial service on *British Railways in late 1955, it was the most powerful single-unit diesel locomotive in the world.

A contract to supply 22 Deltics, including a then unique contract for maintenance of the engines, was placed with English Electric in 1958, their entry into service being planned for 1960–1.

The production Deltics differed from the prototype by virtue of reduced weight, altered engine and main generator drives and bogies, and a revised superstructure design. They entered service from early 1961 and in time allowed *East Coast express passenger services to be greatly accelerated. The Deltic fleet successfully ran at sustained speeds of up to 100 mph. With the introduction of InterCity 125 units (see SPEED) from 1979, the Deltics were gradually phased out, and all were withdrawn by early 1982.

The only other Deltic-engined locomotives were ten 1,100 hp single-engine units delivered to BR in 1959. These proved much less successful, and were withdrawn by 1971.
MLH

A. Baker and G. Morrison, *Deltics at Work* (1985); J. Johnson and R. A. Long, *British Railways Engineering 1948–80* (1981).

demurrage is, most commonly, the payment of compensation for undue detention of a *wagon, but it also applied to *carriages. It was introduced in 1842 as an inter-railway transaction administered by the *Railway Clearing House, which employed 'number takers' at exchange points to record the movement of rolling stock between companies. Payment became due to the wagon-owning company by the company holding the wagon after a specified number of 'free days' (the details varied over the years). From 1847 it applied also to wagon sheets and ropes. The railways later extended the scheme to traders.

The inter-company demurrage scheme was abandoned during World War I and, when resumed, was much simpler as the principal companies had agreed in 1917 to operate their non-special wagons as a common pool.

The number of free days allowed to traders was generous and the scheme was not an effective disincentive against using wagons for temporary storage. The scheme was tightened up at the beginning of World War II to encourage more disciplined wagon utilization. At the same time a simpler 'standage' scheme was devised for larger traders, based on daily wagon counts rather than the detention of individual wagons. But the railways were still burdened with a culture of measuring wagon turn-round in days rather than hours and the extra costs were very damaging once the railways were faced with road competition.
GAB

Bagwell; R. Bell, *History of the British Railways during the War, 1939–45* (1946), 105–8, 271–2.

Denison, Edmund Beckett (1816–1905) acted as parliamentary counsel for the *Great Northern Railway, 1845–81; QC 1854. He changed his name to Sir Edmund Beckett in 1874, in succession to his father who had held the baronetcy since 1813. He was created Lord Grimthorpe in 1886.

He was a member of the Denison dynasty (originally Beckett), associated with the GNR from its inception. His father was Edmund Denison, first chairman of the GNR, 1847–64, and his brothers were Christopher, director, 1864–80, and William, director, 1887–90.

His adversarial skills were tested when representing the GNR as leading counsel during examinations by House of Commons committees on Bills either promoted by the company, or inimical to its interests. Notable examples of the latter were during attempts to construct a new route for coal traffic from South Yorkshire into the eastern counties, such as the Coalowners' Associated (London) Railway Bill in 1871, and other 'railway-political' designs of the chairman of the Manchester Sheffield & Lincolnshire Railway (see GREAT CENTRAL), Sir Edward *Watkin.

Denison's advocacy for the GNR was demonstrated best when promoting—with Watkin—the jointly presented Bill for the Manchester–Liverpool line in 1865 (see CHESHIRE LINES COMMITTEE); the GNR's Derbyshire & Staffordshire Bill of 1872; and by undermining the *Great Eastern Railway's 1878 bid for a route into Yorkshire, and achieving instead joint ownership of lines with that company.
MLH

DNB; *Who Was Who*, i, 1897–1915; Grinling; J. Wrottesley, *The Great Northern Railway*, ii (1979).

deodands (Latin: things to be given to God). In medieval English law any personal chattel that had caused the death of a human being was forfeited to the Crown. It came to be accepted that either the chattel itself or its price could, on the verdict of a Coroner's jury, be applied to charitable purposes, the jury fixing the amount. Steam engines involved in fatal accidents were brought within the scope of these provisions. A deodand of £1,400 was placed on the locomotive *Raby Castle*, which was involved in an accident near Middlesbrough in 1839; but that was a freakishly high sum. The earliest official accident reports of 1840–2 record the amounts of deodands, wherever they were imposed, varying from £25 to a few shillings only. Deodands were abolished altogether in 1846.
JS

OED; Tomlinson, 426–7.

Derby was an important place long before the railway came: a county town and regional trading centre, with an old established silk-manufacturing trade, and by the 1820s a growing variety of other industries. Its location made the town a strategic point for railways, and in 1839–40 three companies' lines met there: the *Midland Counties from Rugby and *Leicester, and from *Nottingham; the *Birmingham & Derby Junction; and the *North Midland from *Leeds. The council's offer to sell them land if they agreed to a common station outside the town was accepted with reluctance, and they each built engine sheds and workshops nearby. When they merged to form the *Midland Railway in 1844 the nucleus of Derby's railway quarter was in place, next to but separate from the town, with land for expansion to the east and south; quite unlike *Crewe and *Swindon where the station, works, and company town were virtually one unit.

Although the company built no more important new lines into Derby itself, apart from a long southerly curve from the Nottingham direction, the Erewash Valley line of 1847–62 and a series of connecting lines and junctions some miles to the south and east permitted the heavy coal traffic from north Derbyshire and Nottinghamshire to flow southwards and west without passing through Derby. After the Midland's London extension was opened in 1868 these lines became invaluable. A large *marshalling yard for general freight was laid out at Chaddesden, ultimately capable of handling 2,500 wagons a day.

The station was impressive. Designed by Francis *Thompson and opened in 1840 before completion, it had a 1,050-ft long frontage and an elegant iron *trainshed covering a long single platform. It was designed expressly for passengers changing trains, and *Whishaw called it 'the most complete structure of the kind in the United Kingdom, or, perhaps, in the world'. Over the years more platforms were added, although the trainshed remained until World War II bombing destroyed part of it, and in 1952–4 it was replaced by concrete platform canopies. Meanwhile, the original frontage had been obscured by piecemeal additions. That, too, was rebuilt in 1984–5.

The works of the Midland's three constituents were quickly made into one, which during the next 30 years quadrupled in area. Locomotive building began in 1851, and by 1862 some 2,000 were employed, doubling by 1891. In 1873–7 the carriage and wagon works was moved to a large new site at Etches Park, allowing more locomotive work to be undertaken at the main works. Derby was in the forefront of diesel locomotive development on the *London Midland & Scottish Railway, of which it became part in 1923, and on *British Railways. The last steam locomotive was built in 1957, the 2,941st since 1851, and diesel locomotive construction finished in 1967, but multiple-unit and carriage-building continued.

The expansion of the works was accompanied by the growth of the company's headquarters. Unlike any other British railway, the Midland concentrated in one place the entire control of all its functions—commercial, engineering, and administrative—and large offices were built next to the station to accommodate the staff. When the London extension was under way there were thoughts about transferring the administration to St Pancras, but they were discarded and the Midland kept its centre of power at Derby.

The relationship between the company and the town was one of distant acceptance. By 1900 the railway employed over 12,000 out of a population of around 100,000, and other industries depended on it. Andrew Handyside's foundry, for instance, supplied most of the Midland's ironwork and castings, gaining a world-wide reputation; William Bemrose supplied and printed the company's stationery, thereby also securing a much wider market; and James Smith became a well-known supplier of uniforms, based on those he made for the railway. Yet there was never any significant railway representation on the town council, and not

until 1914 did a railwayman become mayor. This was due to the town having a long-standing, closely knit 'establishment' of local business interests which the railway was never able to enter. It may also have been because Midland employees had more opportunities for other employment than, say, the *Great Western's at Swindon and the *London & North Western's at Crewe. The North Midland built 80 houses opposite the station, but the Midland left it to others to provide homes for its work-force, mainly in the Litchurch area near the works. It built an institute and an orphanage, and contributed to schools and a church, but apart from employment was unable to command electoral influence by other means.

In the 1870s the Midland's monopoly was attracting local criticism, particularly over *freight rates. The council, largely composed of local industrialists, supported the *Great Northern's Bill for a line from Nottingham through Derby into north Staffordshire. Opened in 1878, the GNR did not provide the 'independent railway competition' its Derby supporters had naïvely anticipated, and created considerable hardship and disruption when it sliced through the town. Although its station was more central than the Midland's, it was inferior to what had been proposed. Moreover, the GNR's real interest lay in gaining some of the Midland's traffic in Derbyshire coal and Burton beer. Serving Derby was incidental, and it did no more than temporarily dent the Midland's position in the town, although James *Allport, the general manager, failed to become elected to the council in 1877.

Diversification began in earnest when Rolls-Royce moved to Derby in 1907, attracted by the skilled labour available at the railway works. By the end of World War II it had supplanted the railway as the town's largest employer.

After the 1923 *Grouping Derby was the headquarters of the LMS locomotive department until 1932, when Crewe took over. The LMS developed Derby's carriage-building capacity, a policy continued by *British Railways, and in 1938 the LMS opened its School of Transport, the first railway staff training college in Britain. Events turned full circle in 1964 when BR opened its Railway Technical Centre (see RESEARCH AND DEVELOPMENT), attracted in part by the aviation-based skills at Rolls-Royce.　　　　　GJB

Reg. Hist., ix (1976), ch. 9; J. B. Radford, Derby Works and Locomotives (1971), Rail Centres: Derby (1986); RTC, 178–80; M. Higginson, The Friargate Line: Derby and the Great Northern Railway (1989); P. Billson, Derby and the Midland Railway (1996).

Derwent Valley Light Railway, see LIGHT RAILWAYS; YORK.

development of the system, see SYSTEM, DEVELOPMENT OF THE.

Didcot, see STATIONS, PARKWAY; TOWNS AND VILLAGES, RAILWAY CREATED.

diesel locomotives, see TRACTION, DIESEL; MULTIPLE UNITS.

diesel multiple units, see MULTIPLE UNITS.

dining cars, see RESTAURANT CAR.

directors, railway, see COMPANIES.

disabled passengers. Special provision was made on British railways, at least from 1850 onwards, for invalids wishing to travel by train, yet too weak to endure journeys in the upright seats of ordinary *carriages. In that year the *London & North Western Railway had an 'invalid carriage' in service: a saloon with seats that could be laid together to form a bed, and a water-closet. The *South Eastern built something similar, slightly improved, in 1860. Another was offered by the *Great Northern company in 1872, with an open platform at one end, to ease the loading of a stretcher or wheeled chair. Substantial supplementary fares must have been charged for the use of these special vehicles. There is little trace of any provision for the assistance of less wealthy invalids or disabled people, until recent times.

The only railway ambulances were those constructed or converted for wounded servicemen in *war-time. *British Rail took to making special arrangements for the disabled generally, advertising them in its timetables and producing a booklet, *British Rail and the Disabled Passenger*, giving clearly worded advice on planning journeys, information on the services that could be expected at stations and on trains, and particulars of the fares concessions for holders of Disabled Persons' Railcards. Here was a notable social improvement. The care with which BR produced it will be one of the tests by which its successors are judged.   JS

C. H. Ellis, *Railway Carriages in the British Isles* (1965), 11–12, 32–3, F. A. S. Brown, *Great Northern Locomotive Engineers* (1966), 178.

disused railways. Very few 1/50,000 Ordnance Survey maps do not show a 'Track of old railway', mostly closed branch lines and secondary routes, although many are of considerable length. There are main lines, too, usually those which duplicated others, such as nearly all of the *Great Central from Beighton Junction, South Yorkshire, to Calvert, Buckinghamshire (97 miles); the *London & South Western from Okehampton to Plymouth (34 miles); and the former *Caledonian main line between Stanley, north of Perth, and Kinnaber Junction, south of Aberdeen (45 miles).

But disused railways have not resulted solely from the mass *closures of the 1960s. Parts of early *tramroads can still be seen: many in the north-east, for instance, including the Causey Arch (see BRIDGES AND VIADUCTS) of c.1726; the Penydarren Tramroad in South Wales (1802–c.1880); or the Plymouth & Dartmoor Railway (1823–69). Traces can also be found of short 19th-century connecting railways, long gone but once of great significance, like the east–west spur at Yarnton, north of Oxford, designed to provide a route from Euston to Worcester, which carried passengers only from 1854 to 1861. At Carstairs, Lanarkshire, the first curve used for through running from the south to Edinburgh in 1848–60 is still visible, bisected by another line of earthworks, the Carstairs–Dolphinton branch of 1867–1950.

Often there are gaps where the trackbed has reverted to agricultural use or been redeveloped, leaving no trace; elsewhere it is punctuated by *bridges, viaducts, and *tunnels.

Considerable numbers of viaducts are listed structures (see CONSERVATION). Tunnels are often bricked up for safety, although a few have found new uses. A high-voltage cable passes through one of the Woodhead tunnels, Devizes is a shooting gallery, and mushrooms have been grown in Scotland Street Tunnel, Edinburgh.

Many old railway routes now form footpaths. The first conversion, the Leek & Manifold Railway in the Peak District, happened as long ago as 1937, followed by the Welsh Highland Railway through the Aberglaslyn Pass in North Wales. Now there are over 400 miles of railway footpaths in England alone.

A registered charity, Sustrans, is very active in promoting the use of disused lines as footpaths and cycle-ways, the first of which was from Mangotsfield to Bath (10 miles). One long-term project is a cycling and walking route, partly on old railways, from Glasgow to Killin in Perthshire.

After closure in 1968, the straighter parts of the Abergavenny–Merthyr line formed the new Heads of the Valleys road, an early example of the increasingly common practice of using disused railway formations for road schemes, although generally they have been relatively short lengths for widenings or re-alignments. Railway formations on their own are not wide enough for a modern road. Relaying track on a closed line, once rare, is now increasing (see REOPENED RAILWAYS).

See also ABANDONMENT OF RAILWAYS; RAILWAYS NEVER BUILT, OR UNCOMPLETED.   GJB

M. D. Greville and J. G. Spence, *Closed Passenger Lines of Great Britain, 1827–1974* (1974 edn.); P. J. G. Ransom, *The Archaeology of Railways* (1981); RS, 213, 245–9, 253–4, 260; Carstairs: J. Gough, 'Two Caledonian Branches', *JRCHS*, 30, Pt 7, 150 (March 1992).

Dobson, John (1787–1865), architect. Born in humble circumstances, Dobson was apprenticed to David Stephenson, architect of *Newcastle. In 1813 he established his own practice, and also travelled extensively in Europe. He did an immense amount of work in northern England on country houses, schools, churches, docks, bridges, and other public works. He was also a proficient landscape gardener and town planner, and worked with Richard Grainger in replanning central Newcastle in 1830–45—during which he designed a number of public buildings—and for George *Hudson on developing Whitby.

His achievements in Newcastle included Central station (1846–50) which, although his original design was subsequently modified, ranks with Huddersfield and Monkwearmouth among Britain's great classical stations. His other stations were limited to the original Manors and Gateshead stations, and a design for an elaborate Gothic terminus for the *Newcastle & Carlisle Railway which was not executed. The drawing in the RIBA collection does not state for which city it was intended; probably it was *Carlisle. His apparent claim to have designed the roof at Newcastle Central has recently been questioned, and his relationship with Robert *Stephenson and T. E. *Harrison, the engineers, has still to be clarified. Dobson was the first president of the Northern Society of Architects.

See also ARCHITECTURE AND ARCHITECTS.   GJB
H. M. Colvin, *A Biographical Dictionary of British Architects, 1660–1840* (1978 edn.); L. Wilkes, *John Dobson, Architect and Landscape Gardener* (1980).

dock, see BAY.

Docklands Light Railway, built and equipped on *'Light Rapid Transit' principles as a hybrid of railway and developed street *tramway practices, was authorized in 1984–5 to run from Tower Gateway, Minories, at the eastern edge of the City of London, to Island Gardens (North Greenwich) and from Poplar to Stratford, 7½ miles, largely occupying existing railway locations. It was opened in 1987.

*London Transport acted at first as general consultant for the DLR, which, however, became wholly independent. The detailed design and construction was done, exceptionally, on a 'turnkey' or 'design, build, and equip' contract. Apart from the 4 ft 8½ in track gauge, the designs owed nothing to current *London Underground practice and make any future through working impossible: current supply at 750 V dc is by an outside third rail with underside contact; trains are automatically controlled with no lineside signals; curves are sharp, and trains limited to two two-car articulated units; platforms are 30 ft long, normally approached by stairs from ground level. In operation the system proved unreliable and its capacity unequal to peak demand, so that much modification and virtual rebuilding at some points had to be undertaken. The terminus at Tower Gateway, not physically connected with any Underground station, was recognized to be unsatisfactory even before services began, and a one-mile deviation and extension to the Bank, authorized in 1986, was opened in 1991; this was at the time perhaps the most expensive mile of railway in the world. Extension east from Poplar to Beckton was completed in 1994, making a total mileage of 14. Projection south of the Thames to Lewisham is under way.
                                                         RMR
S. Jolly and B. Bayman, *Docklands Light Railway* (1986); D. F. Croome and A. A. Jackson, *Rails through the Clay* (1993 edn.).

dock railways, see INDUSTRIAL RAILWAYS.

docks, see PORTS AND DOCKS.

Doncaster was one of the great railway towns of Britain, the main source of employment being 'the Plant', principal locomotive *works of the *Great Northern Railway and later the *London & North Eastern.

The Great Northern reached the coaching town from the south in 1849, making and end-on junction four miles north with the *Lancashire & Yorkshire Railway, over which it operated through services to *Leeds and *York via Knottingley until new routes were developed in 1869–71.

By this time 'the Plant' was well established, its opening in 1853 having added nearly 3,000 to the local population. With true Victorian spirit the Great Northern built two schools to cater for the influx of children, and the shareholders subscribed to the erection of a church. By the turn of the century the works had grown to such an extent that it covered 200 acres, employed 4,500 men, and had 60 miles of sidings. Doncaster was now also an important junction for a line to *Sheffield (1849) and a direct one to *Hull (1869).

Every September the locomotive and carriage shops were closed for a week in order to free as many sidings as possible for St Leger race traffic (see HORSE-RACING). The railway transformed this event from a small and élite gathering into a popular festival. By mid-Victorian times some 70 special trains were arriving in the town on St Leger Day, and in the Edwardian era over 100,000 passengers were being conveyed. In the evening, *excursion trains were dispatched at the rate of one a minute for over two hours.

The other huge traffic through Doncaster was in coal. Even in the early 1850s the Great Northern was working an almost hourly service of coal trains south from the town to London. 'Black diamonds' also figured prominently in the annals of the homespun South Yorkshire Railway, which connected the coalfield around Barnsley with Doncaster, Thorne, and later Scunthorpe steel works. The deeper coal measures around the town were not developed until the turn of the century, leading to a whole network of important mineral lines, the last of which was opened as late as 1916.   DJ
Reg. Hist., viii, ch. 8; S. R. Batty, *Rail Centres: Doncaster* (1991); P. S. Bagwell, *Doncaster: Town of Train Makers, 1853–1990* (1991).

double-deck carriages. The restricted loading gauge (see CLEARANCES) of British railways has made it almost impossible to accommodate a carriage with two self-contained decks, one above the other. These were not uncommon overseas during the 19th century. More recently, what may be described as staggered level or mezzanine floor double-deckers have been built overseas and ingenious design has made possible their use in Britain.

At first sight, overcrowding during the late 1940s on trains using the North Kent routes of *British Railways Southern Region, such as from Charing Cross to Dartford, could be alleviated only by an expensive programme of extending platform lengths and increasing power supplies for the longer trains that would be necessary. There was an alternative. The Regional CME, O. V. S. *Bulleid, produced a design for a four-car double-decker electric *multiple unit which was within gauge on the North Kent lines, although increased height precluded its use elsewhere. There was an ingenious arrangement of interlocking compartments at two levels. Ventilation was limited at the upper level and the compartments had restricted headroom. Even so, the total seating capacity of the eight-car train formed from the only two four-car trains to be built was 1,104, 30 per cent more than a normal SR eight-car suburban train of the time. The two units were used from 1949 until 1971. Two of the cars have been privately preserved.

The 'Le Shuttle' cross-Channel service makes use of 12 double-deck vehicles for cars and their passengers. Passengers remain in their cars or can walk around the bi-level carriages (see CHANNEL TUNNEL).   MLH

Dover, see PORTS AND DOCKS.

Dow, George (1907–87), railway officer and historian. Born in Watford, Herts, an estate accountant's son, he joined the *London & North Eastern Railway as a clerk in the chief general manager's office, 1927. Encouraged by Robert Bell (see LONDON & NORTH EASTERN RAILWAY), he designed route diagrams for use in LNER suburban *carriages, like those on some of the earlier *London Underground lines. Dow was appointed information agent (later, press relations officer) for the LNER in 1939. During the war, when many railway centenaries fell but could not be celebrated, he wrote several official histories for the LNER. He moved to the London Midland Region of *British Railways in 1949 for six creative years as public relations and publicity officer, when he commissioned award-winning posters, and carriage panels that became collectors' items. He retired as divisional manager, Stoke-on-Trent, in 1968.

He was founding president of the Model Engineering Trade Association, the *Historical Model Railway Society, and the Midland Railway Trust. He was a member of the BR Locomotive Naming Committee, 1948–58, lectured extensively, was a keen modeller, and wrote 21 books on a wide range of railway subjects, including definitive works on railway *heraldry and *Midland Railway carriages. His *magnum opus* was the classic trilogy *Great Central*.   AD

down, see 'UP' AND 'DOWN'.

drama, see THEATRE.

drivers, engine. Richard *Trevithick is believed to have walked beside his locomotive when driving it upon the Penydarren Tramroad in 1804, but the drivers of *Murray's *Middleton Railway locomotives of 1812 stood on a platform at the rear of the frames. The Wylam locomotives of *c*.1814 had the driver at one end and the *fireman at the other, positions perpetuated for decades by *Hackworth on his locomotives for the *Stockton & Darlington Railway. On *Locomotion*, the SDR's first locomotive (1825), and some other early *Stephenson engines the driver perched on a footboard beside the boiler; on later locomotives he gained what became the conventional position, on the footplate at the rear with the fireman.

Some of the early drivers' names survive. *Locomotion* was regularly driven by James Stephenson, George's elder brother. Driver of *Royal George* was William Gowland, who went on to drive *Sans Pareil* for Hackworth at the *Liverpool & Manchester Railway's *Rainhill Trials (1829). *Novelty* was driven at Rainhill by Charles *Fox, later a noted civil engineer; just who drove *Rocket* on that occasion does not seem to be recorded—probably George Stephenson himself. He was certainly not averse to driving on special occasions, as when inspired by the presence on the footplate of the beautiful young actress Fanny Kemble to achieve 35 mph with *Northumbrian*. For 1830, that was a phenomenal speed.

Rocket's regular driver was Robert M'Cree of Killingworth. Many of the LMR's earliest drivers came from northeast England; later on, newer lines in turn poached drivers from the LMR as the railway system spread. By 1840 the

*London & Birmingham Railway, for instance, was employing 35 drivers; in 1860 there were 3,756 engine drivers on nearly 8,000 miles of railway in Great Britain.

By the mid-1870s, and possibly earlier, the engine driver's task had crystallized into a form which would last as long as steam locomotives themselves, and in some respects longer. He had to come on duty an hour or so before his locomotive was due out, to read the notices of speed limits and so on affecting his day's work, and to examine minutely the working parts and lubrication. *En route* he had to drive safely and punctually, using regulator and reversing lever with care and skill, listening constantly for sounds which would indicate defects, and keeping a good lookout ahead for signals and obstructions. At the end of his turn of duty, he had to return his locomotive to its shed, and complete a report of work done, materials used, and defects needing attention.

Over the years technical developments both on and off the locomotive affected the driver's task. Reversing the earliest locomotives was a highly complex business, which involved disconnecting the valves and moving them by hand. The introduction of gab gears in the late 1820s made things simpler, and of link motions from 1842 very much more so (see VALVE GEAR). The locomotive could then be reversed, and the *cut-off adjusted, by moving a single lever. This was important not only for economical working but also because the normal means of stopping a train quickly was to reverse the engine: compression of steam in the cylinders braked the engine until the wheels actually started to revolve backwards. Otherwise the driver had the options of whistling for brakesmen on the train to act, and applying a screw brake on the tender or, if a tank engine, the locomotive itself.

Continuous *brakes under control of the driver were introduced gradually during the 1870s, and automatic continuous brakes under his control were made compulsory by law in 1889 on passenger trains. Other equipment under the driver's control included steam rail-sanding gear, introduced in the late 1880s, and steam heating for passenger trains at the turn of the century.

Under the time-interval system of operation (see SIGNALLING), which originated on the LMR and spread to most other railways, a good lookout ahead was absolutely vital. There were signals to be watched for, too: at first signals by hand or flag given by *'policemen'; later fixed signals in the form of discs, crossbars, and, from 1841, semaphores. Drivers were warned by these signals when danger was present. Then through the 1850s–1870s came the gradual change from the time-interval system to the *block system, in which the line was assumed to be blocked unless declared clear by *telegraph. Now the signals were used to show drivers when the line was clear. On *single lines, a driver had the security of the one-engine-in-steam and train-staff-and-ticket systems, and, from the 1880s, the electric train staff, tablet, or token. It was vital that he checked that the staff he held was the one for the section he was entering. Early 20th-century developments which eased the driver's task were Automatic Train Control (see AUTOMATIC WARNING

SYSTEMS), first installed by the *Great Western Railway in 1906, and colour-light signals with their bright illumination.

It is a minor mystery why, since even the driver of a stagecoach was allowed to sit, drivers of locomotives were expected to stand; but seats seem to have become general only in the 1930s. The driver's cab, too, showed for many years a marked reluctance to develop beyond a front weatherboard; drivers in the 1870s wore beards, and coats of pilot cloth. Soon afterwards, roofed cabs started to provide some protection from the weather. Early engravings of LMR locomotives show the driver sporting an outsize cap of dark cloth at a jaunty angle. Perhaps the traditional footplateman's cap developed from this.

For working long hours in bad conditions, and carrying great responsibility although within a limited compass, a driver around 1870 earned at most £2 10s. a week, at a period when an agricultural labourer earned 13s. Drivers were often at odds with management, with its wider responsibility for total operation of the railway. LMR enginemen went on *strike as early as 1836; the *Midland Railway had a serious drivers' strike in 1887. Yet drivers were noted as steady, sober, trustworthy men. Throughout the 19th century they were kept as much as possible to their own locomotives; in the latter days of steam, economics dictated that most locomotives were 'common-user', which may have pleased accountants but did nothing for drivers' morale. By the late 1880s it had become usual for drivers to be grouped into promotion grades or 'links' to cover particular routes and tasks.

The LMR considered that those seeking the position of fireman—with eventual advancement to 'engineman' —should first gain experience of maintenance in the repair shops, and such became the accepted practice over several decades. Towards the end of the century the bottom rung of the promotional ladder changed, to become the position of *cleaner in a running shed. Knowledge was gained largely from the experienced men among whom the cleaner—in due course, fireman—found himself working. The consequence was that eventually senior drivers, despite the efforts of mutual improvement classes and the like, tended to lack engineering knowledge, in marked contrast to their counterparts on the Continent. They also tended to be elderly, as promotion was often by seniority.

That did not discourage them from high speeds when needed. Between the wars record-breaking drivers became famous: J. H. Street who drove the Cheltenham Flyer, then the fastest scheduled train in the world, for the GWR in 1931; Tom Clark who achieved 114 mph for the *London Midland & Scottish Railway in 1937; and above all, Joseph Duddington of the *London & North Eastern Railway who achieved 126 mph with *Mallard* in 1938, faster than any man has driven a steam locomotive before or since. Not that Bill Hoole (*British Railways, Eastern Region) would have been averse to trying, had authority permitted: he reached 112 mph with A4 locomotive *Sir Nigel Gresley* as late as 1959.

With the change from steam to electric and diesel *traction, which started at the turn of the century but was at its most rapid in the 1950s and 1960s, there came for drivers the change from footplate to fully enclosed and glazed cab, with much improved view ahead, and from control by lever and steam valve to handle and push-button. The Automatic Warning System, to warn a driver to slow down or stop, became widespread; Automatic Train Protection, to ensure that he does so, is under test (see AUTOMATIC WARNING SYSTEMS). Since 1984, introduction of Radio Electronic Token Block on single-line routes in Scotland, Suffolk, and Mid-Wales has meant that drivers there no longer have to handle a physical token.

With modernization there came, too, though more gradually, single-manning. As early as the 1920s the *Southern Railway introduced single-manning on its electric *multiple-unit trains, and renamed the driver 'motorman'. Today it is only on train services which operate at more than 110 mph that there are two drivers in the cab. Driver Only Operation, with neither second man nor *guard, was introduced in 1982 between Bedford, St Pancras, and Moorgate, and is becoming widespread on freight trains, empty coach trains, and passenger trains with power-operated doors.

In 1948, British Railways employed 46,302 drivers, and in 1969, 21,486. In 1994 there were 14,200 drivers, employed by the operating units into which BR had been divided; they still, where appropriate, work in links. The reduction in numbers is evidence not merely of contraction of the system, but also of more efficient use of motive power.

Until 1976 most training to become a driver still took place on the job. In that year a specific training course was introduced for all new drivers, who needed at least two years' experience in the industry. In 1988 the course was lengthened and drivers were recruited from outside the industry also. In 1994 the basic driver-training course lasted 38 weeks, or more where routes were complex; simulators and inter-active videos are now used. A rail drivers' National Vocational Qualification has been introduced.

The most striking change, however, has been the increase in the speeds which are expected in everyday service. In the 1950s, trains which ran at more than 60 mph were considered fast; in the 1960s, maximum speeds on parts of the *East Coast route were increased to 100 mph and in 1976 speeds up to 125 mph were introduced between *Paddington, *Bristol, and South Wales. Subsequently the same speed limit was introduced on the East Coast main line, and the Midland and the *West Coast main lines speed limits were raised to 110 mph.

None the less, the railway *preservation movement has ensured that the skills of driving steam locomotives have not been lost. Drivers, both paid and unpaid, drive steam locomotives in passenger service on preserved railways and at steam centres throughout Britain, and British Rail's crews drive steam specials over the main line. Anyone now can find out what it is like to drive a steam locomotive by taking part in one of the driver-experience courses offered by many steam centres: such courses do not, of course, qualify participants to drive public trains, but are in themselves a fascinating experience.

See also ASSOCIATED SOCIETY OF LOCOMOTIVE ENGINEERS AND FIREMEN.   PJGR

L. T. C. Rolt, *George and Robert Stephenson* (1960), esp. chs 7 and 9; Anon., *Railways and Railwaymen* (1892), ch. 9; British Transport Commission, *Handbook for Railway Steam Locomotive Enginemen* (1957); 'The Diary of a London & North Western Engineman, 1855–62', in *ET*.

driving and firing techniques, see DRIVERS; FIREMEN.

Drummond, Dugald (1840–1912), locomotive engineer, son of a permanent way inspector on the Caledonian & Dumbartonshire Junction Railway.

Trained on his father's railway and with *Peto, *Brassey, and Betts, *contractors, in 1865 he became manager of the *Highland Railway's workshops at Inverness under William *Stroudley and in 1870 followed him to a similar post with the *London Brighton & South Coast Railway.

As locomotive superintendent on the *North British Railway (1875–82) he modernized Cowlairs workshops and introduced improved locomotives, including 4-4-0s whose leading bogies provided greater stability at speed on curves. He built similarly successful types for the *Caledonian Railway (1882–90), where he carried out extended locomotive efficiency trials. After five years in private industry he became CME on the *London & South Western (1895–1912). He replaced the inadequate works at Nine Elms with new, well-equipped workshops at Eastleigh, and developed excellent locomotives from his previous designs, although his later 4-6-0 types were less successful. Drummond introduced innovative features to improve locomotive efficiency, including firebox water-tubes, smokebox steam-driers, and feedwater heating. He was forceful and could be dour, but was fair to and respected by his men.   GWC

Locomotive Railway Carriage & Wagon Review (1938), 192–6; *RM*, 89 (1943), 213–15; *DNB: Missing Persons* (1993), 193.

ducket. A passenger train *guard was expected to keep a sharp lookout to ensure the safe operation and good order of his train. In the earliest days, guards rode on the roof of carriages, and applied a hand *brake in concert with the application of the brake on the locomotive or tender. Having transferred from roof to brake compartment, the guard was provided with what were variously called roof observatories, lookouts, projections, or duckets (etymology dubious). These facilitated his view alongside the train, and sometimes along the roof line.

Built out of the carriage body side, the ducket was usually a fairing or faceted projection, with small glazed lights for viewing in either direction of travel, and padded inside. A side lamp was often fitted above each ducket. The roof observatories favoured by the *South Eastern Railway and the *London Chatham & Dover Railway were raised portions of the roof with extensive glazing, at least to front and rear. In this form as used for *South Eastern & Chatham Railway carriages in the 1900s, they were popularly known as 'Birdcage' roofs. Of the *'Big Four' railways after 1923, the *Great Western Railway did not fit duckets. The *Southern's new electric stock from 1932 (steam stock from 1945) instead was fitted with roof-top periscopes facing in

each direction, as were the earlier *British Railways standard carriages.   MLH

dumb buffers, see BUFFERS.

Dundee. Some of the earliest railways in Scotland were constructed in and around Dundee in the 1830s. The line to Newtyle (1831) struck up north over the Sidlaw Hills by such a direct route that there were three inclines worked by stationary engines and ropes, the steepest of which was that at Law with a gradient of 1 in 10. These were eventually phased out in 1861 by a more circuitous route via Lochee. The Dundee & Newtyle Railway was standard *gauge, but the Dundee & Arbroath (1840), thanks to its engineer Thomas *Grainger, adopted the unusual gauge of 5 ft 6 in: both lines had to be relaid in 1847 as the network integrated and the Dundee & Perth Railway (later the *Caledonian) opened to Perth and the south, and a route led north to *Aberdeen in 1849. Ferry services were operated by the *North British Railway across the estuary between Tayport and Broughty Ferry. The Tay was bridged in 1878 only for the bridge to collapse in December 1879; it was replaced by the present one eight years later (see BRIDGES AND VIADUCTS). It enabled the North British to compete effectively for traffic to the north-east, and set off a further bout of competition with the Caledonian route via Forfar (see RACES TO SCOTLAND).

Though much of the city's textile trade was handled through the docks, greatly enlarged in the 19th century, and serviced by a rail network, quantities of jute were also brought in from further afield by rail: 23,000 tons in 1860. The development of suburbs such as Broughty Ferry, and Newport and Tayport across the river, owed much to rail services. The railways were also popular for excursions from Dundee but the charabanc and the car were to take away that traffic; the inland lines closed in the 1960s; the harbour branches saw less and less trade. The city had had the inconvenience of three stations, all close to each other; the 100-year old Dundee East station closed in 1959 and the West station, a handsome Caledonian Railway building from 1889, was demolished in the mid-1960s in order to make way for the approaches to the Tay Road Bridge, leaving the Tay Bridge station for all traffic. All suburban services had disappeared by the 1970s, apart from a few local trains to Carnoustie, but the closure of the Strathmore line did result in the diversion of Glasgow–Aberdeen services by way of Dundee, producing better frequency.   AJD

W. Duncan, *Newtyle: A Planned Manufacturing Village* (1979); A. C. O'Dell, *The Railways of Scotland* (1984); *Reg. Hist.*, xv, ch. 86.

dynamometer car. The principal purpose of a dynamometer car was to measure drawbar pull, i.e. the pull exerted by the locomotive (see TRACTION) on its load. The coupling attaching the car to the locomotive was usually designed such that, when in motion, the locomotive was pulling against a system of springs, its effort being continuously recorded inside the car on a moving graph. Effectively, the vehicle was a moving laboratory for what later developed as controlled road-testing of steam locomotives. It was fitted out internally much in the manner of the saloons used for railway officials, with some seating, a lavatory, and a galley. Other parts of the locomotive were also linked with instrumentation in the dynamometer car. Adhesion and braking characteristics (and much else) were studied in the last-built dynamometer car (1961) which had electrical load cells in place of a hydraulic dynamometer. In the case of diesel and electric motive power, the usual traction and resistance characteristics were obtained, as well as transient effects arising from their control and traction equipment. The need for a dynamometer car declined from the late 1960s with the reduced requirement for the road-testing of locomotives (see LOCOMOTIVE TESTING).

The first idea for a dynamometer car is attributed to I. K. *Brunel who in 1841 used a vehicle to measure the performance of a locomotive in motion. What was mundanely termed a 'measuring van', designed for resistance tests of locomotives, was built in 1856 by Daniel *Gooch, when locomotive superintendent of the *Great Western Railway. This was supplanted by the prototype of all modern dynamometer cars, built in 1901 to the specification of G. J. *Churchward. Other early dynamometer cars were built by the *London & North Western (1882 and 1908), *Lancashire & Yorkshire (1896 and 1913), and *North Eastern (1906).   MLH

T. D. A. Civil, *The Western Dynamometer Car* (1985).

Dyos, Harold James (1921–78), writer. Born in London, of Greek extraction, he served in the Royal Artillery for five years, gained his Ph.D. at the London School of Economics, and joined the staff of Leicester University in 1956.

His principal contributions to railway history were three. Two were pioneering papers. The first (published in 1953), on *workmen's trains in south London, 1860–1914, expounded the need that these services were designed to meet and analysed what they did, and did not, achieve. The second (1957) treated some of the social costs arising from the construction of railways into London.

Then, in 1969, came *British Transport: An Economic Survey from the Seventeenth Century to the Twentieth*, which he wrote jointly with D. H. Aldcroft (2nd edn., 1974). Railways are set very well here in the context of the transport system as a whole: 40 per cent of the book (a fair but not excessively high proportion) is devoted to them. It remains a standard work on the subject, much valued.

His *Victorian Suburb* (1961) studied Camberwell, with careful attention to the part played by railways in its development. *The Victorian City* (edited with M. Wolff, 2 vols., 1969) devoted a separate chapter to 'The Power of the Railway'.   JS

D. Reeder in *Urban History Yearbook*, 1979–80. The two articles mentioned appeared in *JTH*, 1 (1953–4), and 3 (1957–8).

Earlestown, see WORKS.

early iron railways occupied the intermediate period —about 1790 to 1830—between *wooden railways and the *Railway Age. They played the same basic role as before, serving *industry and especially the *coal industry, but developing and expanding in every sense. Where wooden railways totalled hundreds of miles, early iron ones ran to thousands. They spread outside the coalfields to almost all areas and to many more industries: ironworks, metal mines, quarries, clay pits, limekilns, *ports, land reclamation, and construction projects such as *canals, docks, and *bridges. As before, they often fed down to rivers, ports, and canals, and could now reach 25 miles in length (the Plymouth & Dartmoor, and several in South Wales) or even 36 miles (the Hay and Kington Railways together). They were also increasingly found as purely internal lines within industrial complexes.

While the majority were still private, public railways made considerable headway, at first built by canal companies (or at least under canal Acts), like the Loughborough & Nanpantan of 1794, the Little Eaton Gangroad in Derbyshire of 1795, and a plethora of canal feeders in the South Wales valleys from a similar date. Then followed public railways independent of canals and authorized by their own Acts of Parliament. The *Surrey Iron Railway (opened 1803), usually considered the first, had many successors like the Gloucester & Cheltenham (1811) and the trio of lines between Abergavenny and Hereford (1814–29). These might carry general, even agricultural, goods rather than a single dominant mineral, and traffic could be two-way

rather than, as hitherto, essentially one-way. By 1800 railways were becoming such a commonplace that visionaries were already dreaming of a national network.

The expansion in iron output and the growing cost of timber encouraged the development of the all-iron rail which, within 20 years, largely superseded wood. First the flat cast-iron bar spiked to a wooden rail, a Coalbrookdale invention, was deepened sufficiently to dispense with the wood altogether. This was the work of South Wales, where it was employed extensively from 1791; but soon a variety of better designs was developed elsewhere, notably the fishbelly. All these rails, being of cast iron, short (usually 3 to 4 ft), and mounted on stone blocks rather than wooden cross-sleepers, gave a bumpy ride and were distressingly prone to break (see TRACK). The way forward lay in wrought iron, stronger and rolled in much greater lengths, experiments from about 1805 culminating with John Birkinshaw's patent fish-belly rail of 1820; at George *Stephenson's insistence most of the *Stockton & Darlington Railway was laid with it. All these were edge rails for traditional flanged wheels; wheels with double flanges, despite suggestions to the contrary, were still almost or entirely a monopoly of North Wales.

At the same time, however, the rival plate rail, of L-shaped section for unflanged wheels, entered the fray and made astonishing headway. Imitating in cast iron the existing underground wooden tramway, and first made by John Curr at Sheffield in 1787, it rapidly came to the surface; and from 1795, under the influence of Benjamin *Outram of Butterley Ironworks, it spread far and wide, both on new lines and replacing earlier edge railways. Had its popularity continued, it might have driven the edge rail and flanged wheel to extinction, for of the major railway areas only Tyneside remained loyal to the old order. In theory, though very rarely in practice, plateway wagons could run on ordinary roads, and road vehicles (if the *gauge was right) on plateways. Plates, however, proved to be a greater technical aberration than the later broad gauge: weight for weight, they were weaker than the best edge-rails, and dirt lodging on their wide tread much increased the friction of the wheels. Wisdom finally prevailed, and by 1825 plateways were on the wane, although in redoubts like South Wales new lines were built for several decades more, and the odd example survived at work well into the 20th century.

Terminology was loose. On Tyneside, 'waggonway' remained the norm. Elsewhere, 'railway' was either a generic word or tended to mean an edge railway, while 'tramway' (*'tramroad' in South Wales) often denoted a plateway; but the distinction was far from universal. Finally, 'railway'

Sections of tramroad plate and edge rails

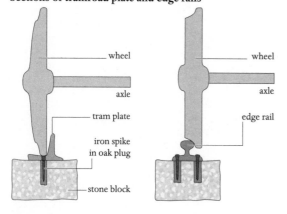

came to imply a more important line, 'tramway' a lesser one, again with no hard-and-fast definition.

Gauges varied widely according to terrain and traffic: often 2 ft or less in mountainous country or underground, 3 ft 6 in or 4 ft 2 in commonly on plateways, 4 ft or more on large edge railways. *Earthworks, bridges, and viaducts grew in scale, *tunnels reached 1½ miles in length (at Ebbw Vale), rope-worked inclines proliferated, and double track was found wherever traffic justified it. Since gradients were easier and iron rails generated less friction than wood, wagons were often linked together, thus inaugurating the concept of the train.

While horse traction remained almost universal, the combination of growing traffic, iron rails, the rising cost of horses, and the new high-pressure steam engine led to experiments with locomotives. These began with Richard *Trevithick's at Coalbrookdale (1803), Penydarren (1804), and elsewhere; reached a degree of efficiency with Matthew *Murray's rack locomotives at *Middleton near Leeds (1812); and culminated with George Stephenson's engines at Killingworth and elsewhere (from 1814); but cast-iron rails were too fragile for their weight, and only the wrought-iron rail of the 1820s allowed the locomotive to approach maturity.

Passengers were not infrequently carried on a quite informal basis, but some railways began to cater for them with proper carriages operated by contractors, notably on the Oystermouth (*Swansea & Mumbles) Railway from 1807, though such services were utterly subsidiary to freight carriage, which remained the almost exclusive function of every railway.

In short, the early iron railway saw the piecemeal adoption of most of the ingredients that finally came together to create the 'modern' railway. The Stockton & Darlington of 1825 was among the last to be built in this formative period of railway history; the *Liverpool & Manchester of 1830 was, for all practical purposes, the first representative of the Railway Age.   MJTL

N. Wood, *A Practical Treatise on Railroads* (1825); C. von Oeynhausen and H. von Dechen, *Ueber Schienenwege in England* (1829), trans. by E. A. Forward as *Railways in England, 1826 and 1827* (1971); C. F. Dendy Marshall, *A History of British Railways down to the Year 1830* (1938); C. E. Lee, *The Evolution of Railways* (2nd edn., 1943); B. Baxter, *Stone Blocks and Iron Rails* (1966).

early railways, see EARLY IRON RAILWAYS; WOODEN RAILWAYS; TRAMROADS.

earthworks. An important factor in the design of railway earthworks is the gradient line which is limited by the *'ruling gradient', although finished levels are also influenced by *bridges and *level crossings.

Early railways are renowned for their immense earthworks, a result of slack gradients necessitated by the limited power of the locomotives available. The *London & Birmingham Railway, with a ruling gradient of 1 in 330, has spectacular earthworks for that reason, notably Tring cutting which is 40 ft deep over 2½ miles. With improvements in locomotive design, railways such as the *Great Central

(1899), with a ruling gradient of 1 in 176, could be constructed to maximize speed, and natural obstacles were overcome without substantial earthworks (see also ROUTE SELECTION).

When determining the dimensions of earthworks, account was taken of the width of the formation, i.e. the finished level some 18 in below track level, which for a standard *gauge averaged 18 ft for single lines and 30 ft for double lines. Other factors included the width of land-take and the nature of the soils, because that decided slope angles. Experience shows that in cuttings, compacted soils and drained clays are normally stable at slopes of 1 (vertical) in 1½ (horizontal), although wet clays may require slopes of 1 in 3. Embankments of good materials are generally stable at slopes between 1 in 1½ and 1 in 2. Where space restricted the construction of slopes, retaining walls were built in masonry or brick, but nowadays reinforced concrete proves more economical.

Formerly, it was common practice to draw longitudinal sections, on which formation levels were sketched, to equalize approximately the volumes in cuttings and embankments. This crude method was aided by calculations, using tables published by G. P. *Bidder and others, which took into account differing slopes and volumetric changes of compacted soils.

Drainage systems for earthworks are essential, and designs have changed little. They often comprise: drains situated each side of the formation; catchwater ditches above cuttings and at the bases of banks; and rubble drains down the cutting slopes. All these run into ditches below embankments and connect to nearby watercourses, which may be culverted through the earthworks.

When construction began, topsoil was continuously stripped, ahead of sub-soil excavation, and stockpiled. Peat and other unsuitable materials exposed during excavations were removed to a tip. Embankments should not be built over such strata, although the construction of the four-mile embankment across Chat Moss in 1826–7 for the *Liverpool & Manchester Railway, under the supervision of George *Stephenson, proved that with much persistence and expense, such works are possible. Parallel drains were dug across the moss to drain a 48-ft wide causeway on which vast quantities of peat and fascines (bundles of brushwood and heather) were laid. These materials continually subsided into the morass until, eventually, a stable embankment formed. A platform of fascines was finally placed on this bank, covered with earth and gravel; then ash was spread and levelled to carry the sleepers and track.

The early railways were built entirely by manual labourers (*navvies) who combined in organized gangs, were often paid piecework rates, and needed no supervision except guidance on lines and levels. Outputs were high; one excavator working a face of, say, 6 ft width, assisted by pickmen and barrowmen, or 'wheelers', could shovel up to 20 cu yd per day of loose soil, or 16 cu yd of compacted clay.

A short trench, or 'gullet', wide enough to accommodate one or two railway tracks, was first driven into the centre of

Embankment and cutting, showing typical drainage systems
(not to scale)

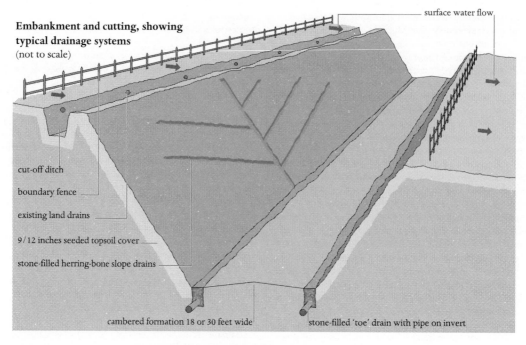

surface water flow

cut-off ditch

boundary fence

existing land drains

9/12 inches seeded topsoil cover

stone-filled herring-bone slope drains

cambered formation 18 or 30 feet wide

stone-filled 'toe' drain with pipe on invert

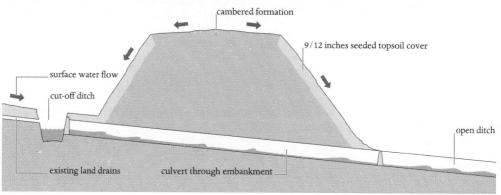

cambered formation

9/12 inches seeded topsoil cover

surface water flow

cut-off ditch

open ditch

existing land drains

culvert through embankment

Method of excavating a cutting by manual labour
(not to scale)

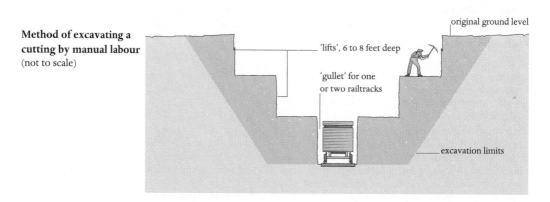

original ground level

'lifts', 6 to 8 feet deep

'gullet' for one or two railtracks

excavation limits

a cutting. Horse-drawn tipper-wagons removed spoil, but for a long 'lead', i.e. the distance to the embankment, locomotives provided motive power. Steps or 'lifts', 6 to 8 ft deep, were cut each side of the gullet to provide working faces. Work progressed, inwards and outwards, until the cutting was finished back to the slopes. Excavating, or 'getting', could be hastened by the dangerous practice of undermining, or 'falling', earth each side of the gullet and simultaneously loosening this from above by a line of stakes driven downwards, a short distance back from the face.

Wagons were end-tipped on to embankments, although those over 30 ft in height were generally built in 10-ft layers. Earthworks settled and might not stabilize for several months, hence settlement was often determined by experiments and bank heights adjusted accordingly. Embankments were seldom built by compacting thin, successive layers as is done today; this was considered too time-consuming, although that practice was used behind the abutments of underbridges. When slips occurred, slopes were rebuilt in sound materials or broken stone and often supported, until consolidated, by rows of stakes.

When leads were long, *contractors preferred to excavate from side-cuts on land adjacent to the embankments; similarly, surplus material was often dumped alongside the tops of cuttings. A wheeler would then run his loads up planks on the slopes, with a chain hooked on to his barrow, pulled by a horse at the top. This practice was said to be efficient and relatively safe. If the barrow toppled over because of a faltering horse, or a wheeler slipped on a treacherous, greasy plank, he would often adroitly leap to safety on the opposite side to his falling barrow.

After completion of earthworks, the slopes were protected by top-soiling and seeding, and the formation was shaped prior to the placing of an overlay of aggregate and the laying of track.

A steam navvy of American manufacture was first used for earth-moving in 1843 on the *Eastern Counties Railway and in spite of operational inexperience, outputs of 100 cu yd per day were achieved at costs of £2 10s. However, scepticism, capital costs, also plentiful cheap labour, stifled interest in mechanical excavators until the 1870s when Dunbar & Ruston machines were used on several lines, notably Castle Eden to Stockton in 1876, where a maximum output of 1,964 cu yd per week was achieved in tenacious clay, maximum daily output being 392 cu yd. Another machine on the West Lancashire Railway excavated 24,000 cu yd in 165 summer working days during 1877.

Outputs of 300 to 600 cu yd per day were achieved on several railway projects in those years, with savings between 3d. and 1s. per cu yd over manual excavation. The Ruston navvy cost about £1,200 and was operated by three men. One contractor equated its performance to that of 30 or 40 navvies; clearly, the era of the manual labourer was ending.

The development of diesel-engined tracked vehicles during two world wars further refined the techniques of construction; modern earth-moving plant speeds up the progress of works and now requires a very small labour

force. However, for efficiency and economy, capital and running costs of such equipment necessitate close control and co-ordination by engineers concerned with operational planning, setting-out, concrete technology, and soil mechanics.

Planning is aided by 'mass haul diagrams' which are based on earthwork computations, taking into account the bulking of soil during excavation and its shrinkage when compacted in embankments. These diagrams give the directions in which earth should be moved to achieve balances of cut and fill, and also simplify calculations of 'mean haul distances', which are the average distances from cut to fill. These and other techniques are invariably computerized and aid management decisions regarding type, capacity, and numbers of machines required; sequence of operations; and sites of tips and borrow pits.

See also CONSTRUCTION, PROCESS OF.   RBS

J. Day, *Construction and Formation of Railways* (1848); P. Lecount, *Practical Treatise on Railways* (1839).

Easingwold Railway, see LIGHT RAILWAYS.

East Coast main line (ECML). The east coast route from *King's Cross to Scotland comprises the main lines of the *Great Northern, *North Eastern, and *North British Railways. The northernmost 38 miles to *Aberdeen were over the rival *Caledonian Railway.

After climbing out of London there is only one steep gradient south of Darlington—between Peterborough and Grantham—on a line characterized by long straight stretches. More tortuous between *Doncaster and *Newcastle, the original route has been shortened several times. North of Newcastle the main climb is southbound over four miles at 1 in 96 to Grantshouse in Berwickshire. Reversals were necessary at *York until 1877, and Newcastle until 1906.

The route was only fully completed when the *Forth Bridge was opened in 1890, allowing the east coast companies to extend their competition with the *West Coast main line throughout to Aberdeen, on a route that was now shorter and more easily graded, although south of Doncaster this advantage was offset by only two tracks over the GNR. In the 1920s and 1930s the Hertford Loop and quadrupling between York and Darlington were completed, and in 1935 the *London & North Eastern Railway introduced Britain's first streamlined trains.

A 13-mile diversion was opened in 1983 to allow mining of valuable coal deposits near Selby without fear of subsidence, and in 1991 *electrification was completed from London to *Leeds and *Edinburgh. New InterCity 225 high speed trains were built, running at up to 140 mph (see SPEED).   GJB

Reg. Hist., iv, v, vi, viii, ix, xv; P. Semmens, *Electrifying the East Coast Route* (1991).

Eastern Counties Railway. This was authorized in 1836 to run from London to Yarmouth, via Colchester, Ipswich, Diss, and *Norwich; but it got no further than Colchester, reached in 1843, and the remainder had to be built by three other companies, which did not complete it until 1849. Although arrangements for through working were made between them, the companies were never on easy terms, and they squabbled continuously until they were fully merged in 1862.

The ECR had also to meet a threat from another line on its western flank, the *Northern & Eastern, making up with the *Norfolk Railway an alternative route from London to Norwich via Cambridge. But agreements were concluded between the ECR and these companies too, which kept their competition under some control.

The entire history of the ECR was dominated by its initial failure to secure a firm grip of its own territory. The efforts involved in making these arrangements, the compromises and losses they entailed, weakened what might have been a strong corporation securely founded on the rich agriculture and fisheries of East Anglia.

Its energies were soon drawn off in quite different directions, when in 1845 George *Hudson became its chairman, and for 3½ years it had to play a considerable part in thwarting the ambitions of the *Great Northern, Hudson's chief enemy, in matters that hardly concerned it at all. The financial mismanagement disclosed after his resignation impaired the company's already weak credit. It managed with difficulty to pay an average dividend of 2 per cent in 1849–62.

The services the ECR provided were slow and uncomfortable, a subject of complaint and ridicule in *Punch* and elsewhere (see HUMOUR). Its London terminus (Bishopsgate) was inconveniently located, and the early efforts it made to develop *shipping services to the Continent via Harwich failed, Parliament refusing it powers to own and work steamships itself. Until 1844 its *gauge was 5 ft.

But though the company's public image was bad, its true position was fundamentally sound. Together with its allied companies, it commanded the whole railway traffic of East Anglia. Its chief weakness lay in management. The direction of the smaller companies was imperfectly co-ordinated with the ECR's, and little effective control was applied to the whole group. The amalgamation of them all to form the *Great Eastern Railway in 1862 was a necessary step in this direction. It worked no wonders immediately: the financial history of the GER was worse in 1865–8 than the ECR's had ever been, and few signs of lasting improvement appeared until after 1875. But patient and careful management, firmly applied, brought the new company through in the end to creditable success, and that rested on the foundations the ECR had laid for it. JS

C. J. Allen, *Great Eastern Railway* (1955); *Reg. Hist.*, v.

East Kent Light Railway, see LIGHT RAILWAYS.

East Lancashire Railway. With a capital of £530,000, this railway was formed in 1845 from two smaller lines, to which more were soon added, forming a roughly T-shaped system. It ran from Clifton Junction, on the *Lancashire & Yorkshire Railway's *Manchester–Bolton line, northward through Bury to Accrington, where it divided: eastward to Burnley and Colne, and westward to Blackburn, *Preston, Ormskirk, and *Liverpool. With branches, the system's

length was 88 miles, and the company's headquarters and workshops were at Bury.

Early years were marked by squabbles with the LYR, which it met at eight places, including uneasy *joint ownership of Tithebarn Street station, Liverpool. The most crucial point was Clifton Junction, whence the ELR had *running powers to Manchester. By 1848 it had a through route to West Yorkshire via Colne and the *Midland Railway which, though roundabout, alarmed the LYR, provoking a quarrel and physical confrontation over tolls between Clifton Junction and Manchester (see 'BATTLES' BETWEEN RAILWAYS). The dispute was finally resolved only by placing the Clifton Junction–Salford line under joint ownership in 1854.

A year later the ELR tried tit-for-tat when it refused opening-day trains of the Blackburn Railway (Bolton–Blackburn–Chatburn), worked by the LYR, passage over ¼ mile of its line at Daisy Field Junction, Blackburn, unless exorbitant tolls were paid. Again the eventual result was joint purchase, the Blackburn Railway being taken over in 1858, by which time relations had improved to the extent that the ELR and LYR amalgamated in 1859.

The ELR's eastern lines were characterized by steep gradients and numerous viaducts (see BRIDGES AND VIADUCTS), some of which were originally of timber. The company was among the first to try out continuous *brakes, patented by its carriage and wagon superintendent, James Newall. It started fitting them to its carriages, but not quickly enough to prevent an LYR excursion train, composed of former ELR stock, parting on the 1 in 78 gradient up to Haslingden from Bury in 1860. Twelve runaway carriages crashed into a following train, killing ten people.

The lines to Accrington and Bacup were closed in 1966–80, except Radcliffe–Bury which was part of the LYR's 1916 *electrification, now used by Manchester's *Light Rapid Transit system. The Bury–Rawtenstall section, however, now forms the new, private, East Lancashire Railway on which steam locomotives operate (see PRESERVATION OF RAILWAYS). GJB

LYR, i, chs 6–7; iii, 55–6, 102–3; G. Biddle, 'The Daisy Field Junction Dispute', *RM*, 101 (1955), 711.

Eastleigh, see WORKS.

East London Railway, see LONDON UNDERGROUND RAILWAYS.

Edinburgh & Dalkeith Railway. Authorized in 1826, to bring coal from Midlothian collieries to *Edinburgh, it was opened in 1831, 8½ miles long. A 4-mile branch to Leith, under a nominally separate company, was opened in 1838. Haulage on both lines was by horses, except on a short inclined plane at Edinburgh, worked by stationary engine. The company did not carry its own freight.

Passengers were conveyed from the outset, in a leisurely way that aroused much amusement. The company's affectionate nickname was 'the Innocent Railway'. The manager said to a parliamentary committee in 1839: 'Many people could not tell, or did not make up their minds, where they were going, which causes great confusion in issuing tickets.'

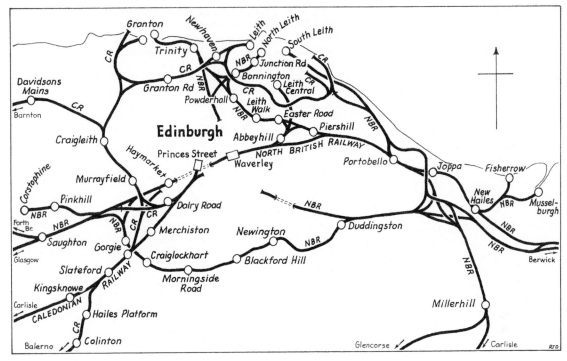

Edinburgh and Leith, 1922

So tickets were not used. Travelling was slow, but nevertheless over a million passenger journeys were made on the EDR in 1842–4, a substantially larger number than on any other Scottish railway then opened. The *North British Railway purchased it in 1845 and converted it to carry locomotives in 1846.   JS

Whishaw; Robertson, 63–5, 293.

Edinburgh & Glasgow Railway. The first project for a railway between *Edinburgh and *Glasgow followed the opening of the *Liverpool & Manchester line in 1830. It would have connected with the Garnkirk & Glasgow Railway (see GLASGOW), but would have been much less satisfactory than the line which received its Act in 1838 and was opened in 1842. Designed by *Grainger and *Miller, it was and remains a magnificent railway with easy curves and gradients, achieved at the expense of large viaducts (see BRIDGES AND VIADUCTS), deep cuttings, and three long *tunnels. The main problem in working was at Glasgow, where a *cable-worked incline was necessary to reach the central terminus at Queen Street. The *track gauge was not settled until quite late in construction: there was a real possibility that 5 ft 6 in would be adopted, as chosen by the Arbroath & Forfar and Dundee & Arbroath lines (see DUNDEE), but wisely the standard gauge was adopted. At first the Edinburgh & Glasgow competed with the parallel Union Canal, which it eventually bought out in 1847.

The pivotal role of the Edinburgh & Glasgow Railway in the geography and politics of central Scotland was reflected in the takeover battles that were waged over it from the

1840s until the *North British Railway secured it in 1865. Its influence expanded by the construction of a branch to Lennoxtown in 1858 and the working of the Glasgow Dumbarton & Helensburgh Railway from 1857. It also had a branch to Falkirk (Grahamston) and Larbert (authorized in 1846). At various points it had connections with the Monkland Railways, which it actually took over the day before its absorption by the North British Railway.

After a very hesitant start, with locomotives that were not up to sustained work, the Edinburgh & Glasgow built some very fine engines, which served the North British Railway for many years after 1865. The Cowlairs *Works of the EGR became the principal workshops of the North British.

The original main line is unquestionably the finest early railway in Scotland, and the quality of its engineering still commands respect. The Almond, Avon, and Castlecary viaducts are among the finest in the country. It is one of Scotland's busiest railways.   JRH

Robertson; Reg. Hist., vi.

Edinburgh and Leith. The railways here were of some complexity. The keys to their development were the restricted topography, with pronounced east–west ridges; the existence of an amenity-minded middle class; and the ambivalent relationship between Leith, the port and industrial centre, and Edinburgh, the capital city. The first railway into the conurbation was the *Edinburgh & Dalkeith, a horse-worked line built by the noted Scottish engineer Robert Stevenson and opened in 1831. This supplied both the burghers of Edinburgh and the harbour of Leith with coal, and was little more than a *tramroad of the kind which had operated in the Lothian coalfield since the 1720s. The next railway to reach the capital was the *Edinburgh & Glasgow, which at first terminated at a handsome station at Haymarket. After the opening of the *North British Railway in 1846 a connecting line was constructed to a new *joint station in the centre of Edinburgh, now Waverley. A third line north, the Edinburgh Leith & Granton, followed with platforms at right angles to the joint station, and a tunnel under the New Town to Scotland Street. The siting of what became Waverley station caused, and continues to cause, a degree of public opposition. The valley between the Old and New Towns of Edinburgh had become part of a designed landscape, and the construction of a railway through it seemed desecration. The initial proposals in 1843–4 aroused bitter opposition, but with the coming of the North British Railway in 1846 the logic of a link with the Edinburgh & Glasgow proved compelling. In 1848 the *Caledonian Railway reached the west end of the New Town, at Lothian Road, but was unable to build its planned grand station. Though the North British was at first solely a Scottish railway, after the opening of the Royal Border Bridge at Berwick in 1850 it became the northern link in the *East Coast main line from London. In 1850 the Hawick branch was opened, giving access to the main border towns, becoming a through route to *Carlisle after construction of the Border Union Railway in the 1860s, and giving the North British a second outlet to the south (the Waverley Route), via the *Midland Railway. The strategic network of railways to Edinburgh was completed in 1890 when the *Forth Bridge was completed, giving the capital direct links to Fife, and via the Tay Bridge to *Dundee, *Aberdeen, and further north.

Within this framework, a network of local lines developed. To the south and east the North British either built or acquired originally independent companies forming branch lines to Penicuik (1876), Polton, North Berwick (1850), and Gullane (1898), and a *light railway to Gifford (1901). A long branch to Peebles (1855) joined a cross-country line to Dolphinton (1864) and a link line to Galashiels.

The peculiar nature of Edinburgh's topography limited the possible impact of railways on the city's southern expansion. To the south-east the Waverley Route and its associated branches served neighbouring villages and small towns, and the Caledonian line from Princes Street had some suburban stations to the south-west. The gap between was not filled until 1884 when the Edinburgh & District Suburban Railway was opened by the North British. This formed a flat oval, passing through some of the select outer suburbs. Its importance was always restricted by the indirect service it offered, and it was badly affected by competition from *tramways.

All these fed passenger services into Waverley station, as did the Edinburgh & Glasgow, and Glasgow via Bathgate lines, creating enormous pressure on this restricted site. The station was rebuilt in the 1890s in its present form, but

still proved inadequate. To relieve the pressure, a major new station was built at Leith Central, opened in 1903, and though it did not generate much traffic it fulfilled a role as a safety valve. The improvement of tramways between Edinburgh and Leith prevented the station realizing its full potential.

Though Edinburgh's railways were largely operated by the North British and its predecessors, the Caledonian's presence was not negligible. In the earliest days the Caledonian offered services to the south and to Glasgow via Carstairs. In 1868 a more direct route to Glasgow via Shotts was opened. The Caledonian also built a branch to Leith docks (1876, upgraded for passenger trains 1880), with a passenger station at Leith (1879), and suburban lines to Barnton (1894) and Balerno (1874). The last-named had sharp curves, for which special 4-wheeled carriages were built.

The North British had two large locomotive sheds in Edinburgh: St Margarets and Haymarket. The former was also the locomotive *works of the North British from its inception until after amalgamation with the Edinburgh & Glasgow, when most repair and all building work was transferred to Cowlairs, *Glasgow. At an earlier stage the Edinburgh Leith & Granton had a small works at Warriston. The Caledonian's locomotive shed was at Dalry Road. For goods, the North British had a large depot at Waverley, and the Caledonian at Lothian Road. As in other cities, most passenger stations had associated coal yards and small goods sheds, but Edinburgh inherited from its first railway, the Edinburgh & Dalkeith, a specialist coal depot at St Leonards. There was also a fair number of private *sidings associated with, among others, breweries, distilleries, sawmills, and engineering works.

Edinburgh suffered more severely from closures from the 1950s onwards. Some of the outer branch lines went as early as the 1930s, and in the early 1950s the Barnton and Balerno lines closed, as well as Leith Central in 1952. The Bathgate line closed in 1955, and services to Leith North in 1962. The *Beeching cuts resulted in the complete closure of the Waverley Route and associated suburban services, Princes Street station, and the District Suburban line passenger services. Since then residual freight services, for example to Leith Docks, have also gone, but as a minor counter the Bathgate line was reopened in 1986, and some new stations have been opened on the surviving main lines.

The *West Coast main line *electrification did not at first take in the route from Carstairs to Edinburgh, which was not completed until 1993. Electrification of the East Coast main line reached Edinburgh in 1991. Apart from significant improvements in both the timing and the frequency of inter-city services, electrification also made it possible to run suburban services to east, and more recently to west, on a scale not seen since the 1960s.   JRH

D. L. G. Hunter, *Edinburgh's Transport* (1964); *Reg. Hist.*, vi.

Edinburgh Perth & Dundee Railway: this became part of the *North British Railway in 1862 in the wave of Scottish amalgamations. The line originated as the Edinburgh & Northern Railway, opened from Burntisland, Fife, to Tayport in 1847–50. The grandly titled line reached neither *Edinburgh nor the north of Scotland, but was a link between them, connecting the train *ferries across the Forth and the Tay and thereby providing the shortest (but not most popular) route from Edinburgh to *Dundee. It built a grand classical terminus at Burntisland, with a locomotive shed and workshops. The line then ran through Fife via Kirkcaldy, Ladybank, Cupar, and Leuchars to Tayport. Splendid stations were provided, at the expense of rather tight curves on some sections of line. The station buildings at Cupar and Ladybank are the most handsome early through stations in Scotland. Ladybank became the junction for a line to the *Scottish Central Railway at Hilton Junction, south of *Perth, in 1848. The company's name then changed to Edinburgh Perth & Dundee Railway in 1849, and it was absorbed by the *North British Railway in 1862, although the ferries remained until the bridges were built across the Tay (1878) and Forth (1890). With the opening of the latter the original Edinburgh & Northern became fully integrated with other east coast lines to give the North British an all-rail route to Dundee and *Aberdeen. It at last had the capability to compete fully with the *Caledonian, of which the NBR took full advantage. All of the original system remains open, though the Ladybank–Perth line is lightly used.

The Edinburgh & Northern's southern partner (which it acquired in 1847) was the Edinburgh Leith & Granton Railway. This took advantage of the construction of a harbour at Granton, to rival Leith, as a ferry terminal for services to Burntisland. The difficulty, as with any north–south route in the city, was to find a reasonably direct way into central Edinburgh. A tunnel was therefore constructed from the north side of the New Town to what is now Waverley station, where the ELGR had platforms at right angles to those of the *Edinburgh & Glasgow and North British Railways. This tunnel was on too steep a gradient (1 in 27) for locomotive working, and it was therefore *cable-worked. It was closed in 1868, though Scotland Street station remained in use for goods traffic until the 1960s. Until the opening of the *Forth Bridge, ferry traffic from Granton continued, but an alternative route via Piershill Junction was used after the closure of the tunnel.   JRH

W. S. Bruce, *The Railways of Fife* (1980); *Reg. Hist.*, xv.

Edmondson, Thomas (1792–1851), born at Lancaster, pioneered a *ticket system destined to be used by transport systems in the UK and abroad for more than 150 years.

Edmondson, a Quaker, trained as a cabinet-maker but joined the *Newcastle & Carlisle Railway in 1836 after his Carlisle furniture business failed. He was appointed *stationmaster of Milton station (now Brampton) where he became concerned about the lack of revenue control with the NCR fare-collection systems.

He prepared serially numbered card tickets ready to be sold to passengers, the first examples being handwritten. He used his woodworking skills to make a simple ticket-printing frame and to design a wooden press for dating them through an inked ribbon.

With John Blaylock, a Carlisle clockmaker and iron-founder, he produced an improved dating press in iron and an automatically fed ticket-printing machine. An example of his early model, operated manually, is in the Science Museum; later printing machines were run by belts from overhead shafts.

Edmondson moved to the Manchester & Leeds Railway in 1839 to introduce his fare-collection system, leaving that railway two years later to establish a ticket business in Manchester which traded under the name of his son, John B. Edmondson.

From the 1840s the Edmondson ticket system was adopted by most British railways, each company paying him a royalty of 10s. per mile. It continued in use until *British Rail finally replaced Edmondson tickets in February 1990, although they are still issued by many independent lines.

MGDF

J. B. Edmondson, *The Early History of the Railway Ticket* (1968), 3–6; M. Farr, *Thomas Edmondson and His Tickets* (1991); D. G. Geldard, *The First Fifty Years (The Early Development of the Railway Ticket)* (1984), 5–23.

education. When Dr Arnold, the great reforming headmaster of Rugby, saw one of the first trains on the new *London & Birmingham Railway, he remarked: 'I rejoice to see it, and to think that feudality is gone for ever.' He voiced the opinion of many liberal-minded men in seeing the railway as a great step forward in the march of civilization, but conversely contemporary schooling had contributed little to the early development of railways, or indeed the other industrial and commercial advances which Britain made in the century prior to the Great Exhibition (1851).

The apprenticeship system and other professional training were far more useful in developing a man's practical outlook, whether for managers like William *Hedley, who trained to be a colliery viewer (superintendent), or artisans like Timothy *Hackworth, who became his foreman blacksmith. George *Stephenson, the third of these locomotive pioneers from Wylam, had neither schooling nor apprenticeship.

The 'Railway Revolution' was accompanied by considerable demand for educated artisans to handle routine engineering, clerks for the ledger work, and better technical, scientific, and commercial education for the managers, not just for the railways but for the greatly expanded industry and commerce. The railways might look after their own in company towns like *Crewe, *Swindon, or Wolverton, or suburbs like New England (*Peterborough), or even occasionally in remote rural locations like Waskerley in Co. Durham, and to some extent the better day-schools, catering for aspirant managers, responded by introducing specialist and technical subjects; but the great public schools were much slower to react, preferring to educate Christian gentlemen. The state was even slower, reflecting middle-class concern that the working classes should not be educated above their station. Even the celebrated Education Act of 1870 was hard-fought, and it was not until the 20th century that state education really progressed beyond the primary stage.

The railways played a more direct part in the expansion of adult education. The mechanics' institutes, which emerged in the 1820s, were the skilled working men's answer to the earlier middle-class philosophical societies. The railways both brought visiting lecturers and provided *excursion trains for classes, the former becoming a highly developed system under the university extension movement from Cambridge in the 1870s. Mechanics' institutes were popular with railwaymen and, as mutual improvement classes, were set up at major, and many lesser, depots. The initiative often came from below; on the *Midland Railway at *Derby, for example, a group of employees began meeting in 1850 as a Reading Society; within weeks 423 of them successfully petitioned the directors for free accommodation, thus initiating the Derby Railway Literary Institution. In 1894 the chairman of the Midland opened the impressive Institute which still stands opposite the station. Any young *fitter, or aspiring shed-master, was expected to learn the realities of his trade that way. They continued well into the 20th century, as the state's provision for technical education remained woefully inadequate; at *Paddington the GWR Lecture & Debating Society (1904) was renowned for its long series of published papers.

Although the traditional universities were reluctant to abandon classical studies, engineering was soon regarded as sufficiently respectable for courses to be provided regularly at Durham (1838), then Glasgow, Edinburgh, and King's College, London, which set out to attract students of railway *surveying. Ultimately the railways also provided their own specialist training with the premium apprenticeship schemes of the *London Midland & Scottish and *London & North Eastern Railways and the latter's traffic apprenticeships for managers.

Just as the railways made possible the university extension movement, so, thanks to their unique ability to handle vast quantities of luggage and boys six times a year, they fostered the rapid growth of English public, and later, preparatory schools, at a time when their popularity was increasing with the reforms of Arnold and later headmasters, like Thring at Uppingham. Old-established schools were joined by a host of new ones like Cheltenham, Rossall, Epsom, and Haileybury. Success could not, however, be assumed; Oundle had to rely on the *London & North Western Railway but nearby Uppingham had two choices, being served by the more distant *Midland at Manton before the LNWR branch—noted in 1860 by Thring as under consideration—was belatedly opened in 1894. The school may have had a contract for school specials with the LNWR, but the boys continued to prefer Manton.   RVL

S. J. Curtis and M. E. A. Boultwood, *An Introductory History of English Education since 1800* (1966 edn.).

electricity, use of (other than traction). Railways have often been pioneering users of new electrical engineering developments, although subsequent widespread application might take many years. They were the first users of the electric *telegraph (1837), which gave rise over the next 40 years to a whole family of battery-powered *signalling devices for improving safety.

They were also early in adopting electric lighting. Arc lamps were first used at the Tay Bridge construction yard (1876–7) and then for station lighting at *London Bridge, *Liverpool Street, and some *underground stations, as well as at *Glasgow St Enoch (1878–9). Incandescent lamps were installed at Holborn Viaduct in 1882. These were mainly trial installations, but by 1886 electric lighting was sufficiently established as an alternative to *gas for the *Great Western Railway to install it between Paddington and Westbourne Park, including the goods station and yards. Electric lighting of carriages was introduced from 1881 (see CARRIAGE LIGHTING).

Electric motors soon began to supersede steam and *hydraulic power for *lifts, *cranes, *shunting capstans, and workshop machinery—and indeed for locomotion (see ELECTRIFICATION). The first electric and electro-pneumatic power signalling systems were completed in 1898–9.

Until the 1920s the railways often had to provide their own generating stations, because there were no local public supplies to draw upon. At nationalization there were still six, but only *London Underground still generates its own power at Lots Road and Greenwich power stations.

The railways began to install *telephone circuits from the mid-1880s, not long after the first public networks, and radio telegraphy was in use on railway ships by 1909. However, radio telephony was not regularly used until three decades after it had been developed, when in 1948 radios were first installed in *marshalling yard shunting engines and in railway *police cars. Only in the 1980s was radio equipment introduced in trains for signalman–driver communication (initially for radio electronic tokenless *block signalling) and for on-train public telephones.

Since the late 1950s developments have reflected the advances in solid-state electronics across a wide range of applications. Sometimes *British Railways has been in the vanguard (it was a pioneer user of electronic computers and it adopted solid-state telephone exchanges long before the *Post Office); sometimes it has been conservative, lagging behind the continental railways, notably in power systems for electric locomotives and trains.   GAB

electric lighting of trains, see CARRIAGE LIGHTING.

electric locomotives, see TRACTION, ELECTRIC.

electric trains, see MULTIPLE UNITS; TRACTION, ELECTRIC; ELECTRIFICATION.

electrification. The first experimental full-size battery-powered rail vehicle was built by Robert Davidson of Aberdeen in 1837. His locomotive *Galvani* was demonstrated at an exhibition at the Egyptian Hall in London in 1841 and subsequently on the *Edinburgh & Glasgow Railway. Following the public demonstration by Werner von Siemens of the first electric locomotive drawing its current from a third rail, at the Berlin Exhibition in 1879 and at London's Crystal Palace in 1881–2, three electric railways were built in the

British Isles in 1883–5: Volk's Railway at *Brighton, and the Giant's Causeway Portrush & Bushmills and Bessbrook & Newry Railways in Northern Ireland, the last two being powered by hydro-electric generators.

Most of the applications of electric traction in Britain up to the end of the 19th century can be divided into two groups: new minor railways, often associated with tourism (including *pier railways and several in the *Isle of Man), mostly *narrow-gauge, running individual single-deck cars; and street *tramways, generally with double-deck cars. Typically the direct current (dc) was supplied at 500 V either from a third rail between the running rails or from an overhead conductor wire, with return through the running rails.

During 1890–1900 the first four standard-gauge electric urban railways, using trains of carriages, also opened: the underground *City & South London, *Waterloo & City, and *Central London Railways, and the *Liverpool Overhead Railway, all initially central third-rail systems at 500–550 V dc. Whereas earlier schemes had generated direct current at the voltage required, the CLR was the first to generate and distribute a high-voltage alternating current (ac) by cables to substations, where it was reduced and converted to dc for feeding to the third rail—more economical over long distances from the power station.

By the end of 1900 the electrified route mileage in the British Isles was: 55 miles of minor railway, 348 of street tramway, and 19 of urban railway. Although British engineers had played a significant pioneering role, the adoption of electric traction was slow compared with Germany and especially the USA. Nevertheless, by 1902 the electric tramway competition compelled main-line railway companies to consider electrification of their suburban lines.

The first steam railway to be electrified was the *Mersey Railway (1903), followed in 1904 by the first sections of the *Lancashire & Yorkshire Railway's Liverpool–Southport and the *North Eastern Railway's North Tyneside systems. The NER scheme included the first electrically hauled freight trains on a main-line railway. After a trial service between Earl's Court and High Street Kensington in 1900, the *Metropolitan District Railway began to electrify its lines in 1903, followed by the *Metropolitan Railway in 1905. It was now the normal practice to place the positive conductor rail outside the running rails. A central insulated negative rail was also provided on the underground railways to avoid the return current leaking from the running rails and causing electrolytic corrosion of tunnel linings, underground pipes, etc. The voltage for all these lines was now 600–650 V dc, the District's 630 V four-rail system setting the standard for all future *London underground railways; the earlier tube lines were also later converted.

The next development was the adoption of higher voltages, which offered advantages for the long-distance main-line electrification that some companies were beginning to contemplate. Three rival technologies were by then available: dc, single-phase ac, and 3-phase ac. The last was never used in Britain, although the Metropolitan came close to doing so, but the single-phase ac overhead system, at a frequency of 25 cycles per second (or hertz—hz), was adopted by the next two main-line railway companies to enter the field. The 6,600 V ac electrification of the *Midland Railway's Lancaster–Morecambe–Heysham line in 1908 was intended as a trial for future electrification of the Derby–Manchester line. From 1909 the *London Brighton & South Coast Railway, with the vision of electrifying its main line to Brighton, progressively electrified much of its South London suburban network at 6,700 V ac but World War I prevented completion until 1925.

The first high-voltage dc systems were commissioned during 1913–16. The NER adopted 1,500 V dc with overhead wiring for working 1,400-ton mineral trains from Shildon to Newport, on Teesside, and for its planned electrification of the *York–*Newcastle section of the *East Coast main line. Following trials with a 3,500 V dc overhead system, the LYR decided upon 1,200 V dc third-rail for its Manchester–Bury line, the first of a planned series of electrifications in the *Manchester area; for safety reasons the collector shoes made side-contact with the conductor rail, so that it could be almost entirely protected by timber boarding. Meanwhile, the *London & North Western Railway began electrification of its Euston–Watford and Broad Street–Richmond services, using the London Underground standard 4-rail system to allow through running from the *Bakerloo Line; and the *London & South Western Railway electrified the first sections of its London suburban network at the slightly higher voltage of 660 V, but with an outside third rail only. By the 1923 *Grouping, there were 363 miles of electrified standard-gauge railway.

After World War I the multiplicity of systems threatened to grow even further when the *South Eastern & Chatham Railway proposed suburban electrification using a 3,000 V dc four-rail system. However, the *Grouping delayed it and the *Southern Railway quickly decided to adopt the LSWR's 660 V third-rail system for a major electrification programme that continued without a break until 1939 (including the conversion of the LBSCR network). By now the need for standardization, to facilitate inter-running, had become apparent. Following recommendations by the Kennedy Committee (1921) and Pringle Committee (1928), the Railways (Standardization of Electrification) Order, 1932, established two standard systems: 750 V dc third-rail (or four-rail for tube lines) and 1,500 V dc overhead. The future possibility of 3,000 V dc was also allowed for.

Until now most electrification schemes had to provide their own generating stations. The Committee on Main Line Railway Electrification (the Weir Committee) was set up by the Ministry of *Transport to review the prospects for electrification following the creation of the new Central Electricity Board's national grid, then under construction. Its report (1931) considered the case for suburban electrification, combining reduced running and maintenance costs and generation of additional traffic through more frequent and faster services, as already proven. Although it believed that main-line electrification would also generate more revenue, it felt unable to quantify it and its calculated 7 per cent return was less impressive than it might have been.

Even if the Weir Committee had been bolder, the course of history may have been no different. Except for the Southern, the *Big Four companies were generally lukewarm towards main-line electrification, not just because of their financial position, but also because of the influence of those who argued that the potential of steam traction had not yet been fully exploited. Before World War I the *Great Northern Railway had built a fleet of powerful 0-8-2 tank engines and the *Great Eastern Railway a prototype 0-10-0 tank (the 'Decapod') in an attempt to demonstrate that the acceleration of electric traction could be matched by steam, but they were too heavy for the track of that time. The GER's intensive 'Jazz' service was, likewise, specifically introduced to avoid investment in suburban electrification. The chief response to the Weir Committee's report was the accelerated steam express train schedules of the later 1930s.

Nevertheless, in 1931 the *London Midland & Scottish and *London & North Eastern Railways electrified their jointly owned *Manchester South Junction & Altrincham line at 1,500 V overhead; and in 1938 the LMSR's *Wirral lines and LNER's South Tyneside line were electrified using the third-rail system for compatibility with the contiguous Mersey and North Tyneside lines. In the mid-1930s the LNER, aided by cheap government loans for relief of unemployment, began work on the Liverpool Street–Shenfield (later extended to Chelmsford and Southend) and Manchester–Sheffield–Wath 1,500 V dc electrification schemes, but World War II deferred completion until after *nationalization. All these were passenger schemes, except the last which was primarily justified by the heavy coal traffic. Although the *Great Western Railway twice commissioned consultants to carry out studies, it was the only one of the Big Four not to undertake any electrification, except on lines jointly owned with *London Transport. In 1948 the *British Transport Commission took over 1,052 electrified route miles. The *Glasgow Subway (6½ miles, electrified in 1935) and Liverpool Overhead Railway (6¾ miles) were not nationalized.

Technical innovations during the inter-war period included: the first unmanned substation, remotely controlled from an adjoining manned substation, on the Morden extension of the *Northern Line (1926); mercury-arc rectifiers, superseding rotary converters in substations; and the first electrical control room, controlling substations over a large area, at Three Bridges on the Brighton line (1932).

An early act of the *British Transport Commission was to set up another Committee on Railway Electrification. Reporting in 1951, it broadly endorsed the Pringle Committee's recommendations: 1,500 V dc overhead was to be the standard, except on the Southern Region and London Transport. The 1955 *Modernization Plan included a massive programme of electrification: the *London Tilbury & Southend, the GNR suburban, and the remainder of the GER suburban lines (200 route miles); the *Glasgow suburban network (190 route miles); further lines in the Southern Region's Eastern Section (250 route miles); and 820

miles of trunk routes from London to Ipswich, to *Leeds (and possibly York), and to *Birmingham, *Liverpool, and Manchester, and some branches therefrom.

Meanwhile, electric rolling stock technology was shifting the balance in favour of ac electrification at 50 hz, the frequency of the national grid. Following an extended trial on the specially re-equipped Lancaster–Morecambe–Heysham line, and the highly publicized success of the French Railways' first essay with 25 kV ac, the BTC announced in 1956 that it was adopting a dual-voltage, 25/6.25 kV ac system as the future standard in place of 1,500 V dc (6.25 kV was to be used for the conversion of the GER 1,500 V lines and in areas where it was difficult to achieve the necessary clearances).

The Modernization Plan's electrification schemes were substantially completed by 1967, except for the GNR Suburban and East Coast main line schemes which had been dropped. By now electrification had to be justified in comparison with diesel traction; the cost benefits were much less than they had been in comparison with steam, but the 'sparks effect' of a faster electrified service on revenue was now recognized. The overhead catenary has thus been progressively extended to Bedford, Norwich, King's Lynn, and over both the West and East Coast routes to Glasgow and Edinburgh; the third rail now covers most of the former Southern Region, the principal exception being the Basingstoke–*Exeter line. The *Paddington–Heathrow Airport scheme will bring electric traction to the former GWR at last. The electrified route mileage at 31 March 1994 was: British Railways 3,087 (30 per cent of its total route mileage); London Underground 245; other metro and light rail systems 78; Isle of Man 22.

Technical developments during this period concentrated on reducing the capital cost and developing performance for higher speeds. On some lines third-rail dc trains achieve 100 mph and ac trains 125 mph (the ECML's overhead line equipment is designed for future speeds of 140 mph). At the other end of the scale, Light Rail technology (see LIGHT RAPID TRANSIT SYSTEMS) has reduced the cost of urban electrification as a successor to electric tramways in cities. Experience with 25 kV, particularly after the withdrawal of steam, showed that electrical clearances could safely be reduced, allowing conversion of the 6.25 kV sections to this voltage. Semi-conductors (initially germanium and then silicon) have made a notable contribution, at first replacing mercury-arc rectifiers in both dc substations and on ac locomotives and *multiple units. Their derivative, the thyristor, has been used to improve control systems on both dc and ac rolling stock, and more recently made possible the use of cheaper and more reliable ac traction motors in place of the traditional dc machines. They have also greatly simplified the design of dual-voltage ac/dc traction, employed with great advantage on the *Thameslink trains linking the ac and dc networks north and south of the Thames, and on the Eurostar trains and class 92 locomotives operating passenger and freight services from the UK through the *Channel Tunnel to the Continent. GAB

J. C. Gillham, *The Age of the Electric Train: Electric Trains in Britain since 1883* (1988); J. G. Bruce, *One Hundred Years of Development of Electric Traction* (1986); A. A. Jackson, *Volk's Railway, Brighton: An Illustrated History* (1993); C. F. Klapper, *Sir Herbert Walker's Southern Railway* (1973).

elevated railways, see OVERHEAD RAILWAYS.

Elliot, Sir John (1898–1988), son of R. D. Blumenfeld, editor of the *Daily Express*. After World War I he became assistant editor of the *Evening Standard* and adopted the maternal surname of Elliot.

In 1925 he joined the *Southern Railway, and became public relations assistant to the general manager, Sir Herbert *Walker. In 1930 he became assistant traffic manager and in 1938 assistant general manager. When Sir Eustace *Missenden, then GM, was appointed to the Railway Executive (see BRITISH TRANSPORT COMMISSION) Elliot became acting general manager; and after nationalization, chief regional officer of, first, the Southern Region of *British Railways, then in 1950 the London Midland Region. In 1951 he succeeded Missenden as chairman of the Railway Executive. Later that year a hostile Conservative government made Elliot's position difficult.

When the Executive was abolished under the Transport Act, 1953, Elliot became chairman of the *London Transport Executive until 1959. He was knighted in 1954. Thereafter he was non-executive chairman of Thomas *Cook & Son and of the *Pullman Car Company, and was consultant to the Commonwealth Development Corporation and the World Bank.

Elliot was a fluent and skilful manager. Although coming to the railway later in life than most, he developed an intense loyalty which he retained to the end.   MRB

Sir J. Elliot, *On and off the Rails* (1982); C. F. Klapper, *Sir Herbert Walker's Southern Railway* (1973); M. R. Bonavia, *British Rail: The First 25 Years* (1981).

Ellis, Cuthbert Hamilton (1909–87), writer and artist. Educated at Westminster School and briefly at Oxford, he became one of the most prolific of all British writers on railways; *Ottley lists 36 of his books, the first of them published when he was 21. He was interested above all in steam locomotives, which he observed affectionately in Britain, Holland, Germany, and Sweden. And yet perhaps his most notable book was *Railway Carriages in the British Isles, 1830–1914* (1965).

He became highly knowledgeable, and much of his knowledge was interesting and lay out of the way; but unfortunately he scarcely ever gave any references to support his stories, so nobody can judge how far they are reliable. His writing is always lively, and picturesque in the literal sense of that word, because he was a painter too. His largest work, *British Railway History* (2 vols., 1954–9), despite some errors, was a brave attempt to provide something badly needed (and still wanted): a general account of the whole subject. But he worked uneasily on a large scale, and the book does not make a satisfactory, continuously informative whole.   JS

RM, 133 (1987), 559.

Ellis, John (1789–1862), chairman. A Quaker farmer and corn merchant in Leicestershire, he supported a proposal

for a railway from the collieries in the north of the county to *Leicester itself. He secured George *Stephenson's interest, and the *Leicester & Swannington Railway was opened in 1832–3. He became a director of the *Midland Counties Railway, and deputy-chairman of the *Midland company on its formation in 1844. The chairman was George *Hudson, whose abilities he respected, while avoiding involvement in his malpractices. Ellis was chiefly instrumental in the Midland's acquisition of the *Bristol & Gloucester in 1846. On Hudson's resignation in 1849 he became the Midland's chairman.

Only a very tough and courageous man would have accepted the post. The company's finances were in great disorder. In 1844–8 its dividends had been above 6 per cent; in 1848–52 they were under 3. But Ellis inspired great confidence, and his integrity was unquestioned. He was MP for Leicester in 1848–52. Under his guidance the Midland company carried through its southward extension to Hitchin in 1857, giving it access to London. He resigned the chair in 1858. His son Edward Shipley Ellis was also a good chairman of the company in 1873–9.   JS

DNB; C. R. Clinker, *Leicester & Swannington Railway* (1977 edn.); C. E. Stretton, *History of the Midland Railway* (1901).

embankments, see EARTHWORKS.

Emett, Rowland, see ART.

employment. The number of persons in full-time railway employment (excluding those engaged in construction) is difficult to determine accurately because of different statistical approaches. Figures based on statements of occupation in the census returns understated the total by at least one third (see POPULATION, CENSUSES OF). In broad outline (to the nearest thousand) there appear to have been 47,000 in 1847, more than doubling to 98,000 in 1855, nearly trebling again to 275,000 in 1873, and rising to 368,000 in 1884 (all UK). At its peak in World War I the number (Great Britain) rose to nearly 650,000 (including 56,000 *women); in 1932 it was 598,000, in 1945 622,000. *British Railways began in 1948 with 629,000, dropping to 251,000 in 1970 and 116,000 in 1994. By contrast, *London Transport railway staff, 17,000 in 1948, were 18,000 in 1994.

The principal sources of recruitment in the early years were: *drivers and mechanics, from the existing mining and manufacturing districts, especially in the north-east; *guards and *signalmen, largely from the navy and army; *porters from agriculture; clerks by nomination by board members, with testimonials of character; managers from the armed forces. The companies had little difficulty in picking the men they wanted. In time, sons of railwaymen came forward into the service, and the 'railway family' was an important stabilizing element. Some women were employed before 1914; then and after World War I in increasing numbers.

Physical and educational standards were set for eyesight, height, and *literacy (the last not always applied to enginemen at first). Uniforms were provided. Discipline was rigorous, with a military tinge to the rules: 'Every person is to come on duty daily, clean in his person and clothes, shaved, and his shoes blacked' (*Taff Vale Railway, 1856). Penalties were fining and ultimately dismissal, with no chance of re-engagement. There was some dissatisfaction with wages and long hours of work (see STRIKES; TRADE UNIONISM); but the disputes were rarely disruptive, and in general the security and respectability of working for the railway prevailed over immediate grievances.

Railway communities were formed at hitherto country places—*Swindon, *Crewe, Wolverton, Melton Constable, Horwich, Inverurie—where the companies took a paternalistic interest in supplying *housing, schools, churches, and dispensaries. Beginning in 1838 on the *Great Western, friendly societies (medical, accident, and pension funds) were established on all the principal railways. They also encouraged mutual improvement classes for technical instruction. Apart from works outings (Swindon went *en masse* by train to Weymouth for a week), *passes and privilege tickets (that included families) became a perquisite of the railwayman's job; so were the *stationmaster's house and the crossing-keeper's cottage at low rent, and in some areas cheap coal.

As the 19th century went on, the railways could find all the employees they wanted; but apart from engineers who needed professional qualifications, they did little to extend the range of their recruitment or to look for more than what an intelligent man might learn from experience on the job. At the turn of the century there was a marked change: in 1895 the London School of Economics set up railway courses, with some support from the companies; and on the *North Eastern Sir George *Gibb in 1896 started recruiting men with university degrees. Textbooks began to be written. The North Eastern's traffic apprentice system worked well, and through it the *London & North Eastern Railway built up a highly qualified *management team. The other three post-1923 groups copied it. Clerical grades were encouraged to improve their knowledge; so were workshop and maintenance staffs.

Most junior employees stayed at one place throughout their railway lives; but the middle management were liable to be transferred from one end of their company's territory to the other. The railwayman's way of life in some ways set him apart from the community he dwelt in; but his loyalty to his employer was unusually strong. As it used to be said, 'Once a railwayman, always a railwayman'.   RMR

P. S. Bagwell, *The Railwaymen* (1963, 1982); P. W. Kingsford, *Victorian Railwaymen* (1970); H. A. Simmons, *Ernest Struggles* (1879), reprd. as *Memoirs of a Station Master*, ed. J. Simmons (1974); F. McKenna, *The Railway Workers* (1980); R. S. Joby, *The Railwaymen* (1984).

engineers; engineering, see CIVIL ENGINEERING; MECHANICAL ENGINEERING.

engine sheds, sometimes called running sheds or, latterly, motive power depots, were familiar features on steam railways. Many were 'straight' sheds containing parallel tracks with inspection pits between the rails. The *Great Western Railway's *Swindon shed in 1841, for instance, was 500 ft long with space for 48 engines.

A significant number, however, contained a central turntable with radiating tracks, which saved ground space but slowed entry and exit as only one engine could use the turntable at a time. The first were built in 1839–40 by the *North Midland Railway at *Derby, and the *Manchester & Leeds Railway at Miles Platting, *Manchester. The Derby shed had 16 sides with a slated roof on iron columns, and held 30 engines. In 1847 the *London & North Western Railway built the celebrated Camden circular 'roundhouse', from which all future sheds of this type took their name, whatever their shape. A year later the Manchester Sheffield & Lincolnshire Railway (see GREAT CENTRAL) opened a unique roundhouse at Gorton, Manchester, with an iron-and-glass roof supported on a single central column around which the turntable revolved. In an attempt to reduce conflicting engine movements the table had two pairs of parallel tracks.

Large roundhouses had more than one turntable. The rectangular example at Gateshead had five, serving 60 tracks, while the largest on the GWR, at Old Oak Common in west London, had four. It was built in 1906, with two entrances to reduce congestion, and interconnected turntables enabling engines to be moved about inside the shed. But straight sheds had the advantage that they could be extended easily.

Sheds varied in size according to need and location. The *South Eastern Railway kept one third of its stock of 413 engines at one place—Bricklayers Arms, London—and dispersed the rest among 24 other sheds. Large railway centres might have several sheds. *Crewe, for example, had two very large ones belonging to the LNWR—North and South—and one very small one for the GWR. At the opposite end of the scale a small branch-line terminus might have a shed only big enough for the branch engine, with minimal facilities.

Density of traffic also influenced locations. In the 29 miles between *Preston and Colne the *Lancashire & Yorkshire Railway had four large sheds: Lostock Hall (Preston), Lower Darwen (Blackburn), Accrington, and Rose Grove (Burnley), and a medium-sized one for 16 engines at Colne, where the *Midland Railway also had a small shed.

Sheds were usually built of brick or stone, with a slated and glazed roof in pitched longitudinal bays containing smoke vents; or, particularly on the LNWR, northlight roofs. The vents might be single louvres or more elaborate inverted wooden troughs, usually one over each engine pit but sometimes continuous, exhausted by a row of chimneys. Some sheds were wooden, despite the *fire risk. The first at *Paddington was a polygonal wooden roundhouse. The large railways eventually adopted standard designs.

From the 1930s a considerable amount of modernization and rebuilding took place, particularly on the *London Midland & Scottish Railway, with widespread use of structural steel and reinforced concrete. A new brick and concrete roundhouse replaced three sheds at *Leicester in 1945, for instance.

As well as office and staff accommodation, the larger sheds had workshops for locomotive repairs. At the main ones quite large repairs and overhauls could be undertaken, including re-profiling of driving wheels where wheel-lathes and drops were provided.

Depots needed yards for ancillary equipment. All but the very smallest straight sheds had an outside turntable. Coaling was at first done from a wagon on an elevated stage, where coal could be shovelled into an engine tender alongside, a method which continued at the smallest sheds, perhaps with the aid of a small crane and an iron skip. In time, larger stages were covered over and handling devices provided, such as tubs on rails which were pushed to chutes above the tender. Mechanical handling slowly started to appear, increasingly in the 1930s when numbers of large coaling towers were built, in which tubs carried coal up to overhead hoppers, or coal wagons were hoisted and tipped bodily. Ash disposal, usually done with a shovel into a pit, also began to be mechanized. Numerous water columns were required about the yard (see WATER SUPPLIES), fed from an elevated tank which in some places formed the coaling stage roof. Small sand stores and drying stoves were also necessary for replenishing engine sand-boxes.

Straight shed yards were laid out as far as possible for a common sequence of operations, whereby arriving locomotives were turned, coaled, watered, emptied of ashes, and finally taken on to (never 'into') the shed.

Very few sheds now remain. Those that do are used for other purposes. The roundhouses at Camden, Derby, and Leeds are listed for preservation. But the only complete depot is at 'Steamtown', Carnforth, in Lancashire, where the 1940s reinforced concrete shed, coaling tower, and ash plant are listed. Although the concrete is deteriorating and the coal and ash plants unfortunately are unusable, they are the only examples left in Europe. GJB

C. Hawkins and G. Reeve, 'Engine Sheds', in M. Binney and D. Pearce (eds.), *Railway Architecture* (1979); C. Hawkins and G. Reeve: a series of detailed historical surveys and descriptions of engine sheds, on a company basis (1979 onwards); *VR*, 46–7.

England, George (c.1811–95), proprietor of the last private locomotive works in London, invented the traversing screw jack in 1839 and shortly afterwards set up the Hatcham Iron Works in New Cross, where he began building locomotives in 1850. England was a poor businessman, a bad employer, but a competent engineer: his products were well made, attracting orders from main-line railways, including the *Great Western. In 1862 he collaborated with Charles Holland to design the first locomotives for the *Festiniog Railway and in 1869 built for them the *Fairlie locomotive *Little Wonder*, Robert Fairlie being his son-in-law. England then retired and Fairlie took over the works to develop his own ideas, but following the death of England's son the following year this venture collapsed. A typical England locomotive, once owned by the *Wantage Tramway, is preserved at Didcot Railway Centre. RW

enthusiasts. Many professional railwaymen and women are enthusiasts, with an interest extending far beyond their job. One of the first was Edward T. Lane, a *Great Western Railway apprentice who in 1847–9 made meticulous scale drawings of locomotives from his own observations. But in the amateur sense the first enthusiasts were 19th-century authoritative writers on railways, like J. *Francis and F. S. *Williams. The hobby of timing trains also dates back. When giving evidence at the Wigan *accident enquiry in 1873, an Eton schoolmaster stated that it was his practice to time trains during journeys (see also AHRONS, E. L.). Later, specialist magazines were published (see PRESS) for an expanding body of interested people. Despite discouragement from railway companies the amateur interest grew, societies were formed, and books increasingly appeared covering many aspects, particularly steam locomotives from which many readers' fascination sprang (see LITERATURE OF RAILWAYS). Boys collecting engine numbers would gain an appreciation of how they worked, and progress to a wider knowledge of railways. After World War II, published lists of engines gave impetus to 'train spotting', a term first used in 1959. Now there are societies devoted to every feature of railways, including the *preservation of steam and diesel traction. Although, as in most popular movements, irresponsible behaviour by a small lunatic fringe has earned them a bad name, leading many serious devotees to eschew the term 'railway enthusiast', there is also a growing academic interest. GJB

Train timing: *REW*, 269; E. T. Lane: *VR*, 125.

environment, see LANDSCAPE, RAILWAYS IN THE; CONSERVATION.

European Passenger Services, see CHANNEL TUNNEL.

European relationships. As the centre of railway activity during the 1830s and 1840s, British practice soon spread to Europe. The British *track gauge was largely adopted in continental Europe, but not the restricted loading gauge (see CLEARANCES) that came to characterize British railways, and restricted the interchange of vehicles.

During the 1840s rails were rolled at Dowlais, Glamorgan for Germany and elsewhere, and John Hughes went from Dowlais to Russia's Don Basin in 1869 to set up a rolling mill for rails. Robert *Stephenson and Co. and the Vulcan Foundry supplied engines to France, Germany, Austria, and Russia in 1835–9. *Signalling equipment was also exported, notably by Saxby & Farmer which from the 1860s sold signal frames to continental railways, and in 1878 set up a factory at Creil, France. The company also signalled some Italian railways, and a modified British lower-quadrant semaphore signal was adopted by the Italian State Railways.

The Western Railway of France from Paris to Rouen and Le Havre was built with British capital. *Brassey and *Mackenzie were the contractors, with *Locke as the engineer. Brassey also supplied rolling stock, and Locke engaged *Buddicom to build and run the locomotives. Buddicom and Brassey contracted to work other French railways. Brassey also built railways in Italy, Belgium, Spain, and elsewhere.

Links between the managements of British and continental railways were otherwise limited, other than with *shipping interests, but most British railways maintained commercial offices in European cities. Edward *Watkin was unusual in being a director of the Nord Railway, France.

British and French railways jointly promoted through travel between London and the Continent, and notably just before World War I they combined to speed up London–Paris services. Some pre-*Grouping railways participated in *agreements and conferences, and in 1875 the *Great Eastern Railway joined the predecessor of the European Timetable Conference which arranged train connections throughout Europe.

British locomotives were exhibited on the Continent, notably the *London Brighton & South Coast Railway's 0-6-0T *Brighton* at the Paris Exhibition of 1878, its 0-4-2 *Edward Blount* sent there in 1889, and the GER's *Claud Hamilton* exhibited at Paris in 1900. *Edward Blount* and the *South Eastern Railway's 4-4-0 *Onward*, also at Paris in 1889, took part in comparative trials on the Paris Lyons & Mediterranean Railway.

Although early links between British manufacturers and most continental railways were soon lost, Beyer Peacock and Sharp Stewart were long associated with the supply of locomotives to the Dutch State Railways (see WORKS). Other instances included the *Highland Railway 4-6-0 design ordered in 1911 by the French State Railways, and the 4-4-0s and 0-6-0s built for the Belgian State Railways by a Scottish builder from 1898 to 1913, based on *Caledonian Railway drawings.

In 1902, G. J. *Churchward of the *Great Western Railway ordered from Société Alsacienne the first of three compound 4-4-2s designed by du Bousquet and de Glehn, similar to those on the Nord (see TRACTION, STEAM). Named *La France*, it was to provide comparison with Churchward's simple 4-6-0s. Continental-built engines on British railways were rare, but in 1914 the German builders Borsig supplied ten 4-4-0s to the *South Eastern & Chatham. French and Hungarian manufacturers built electric stock for the *Yerkes tube railways in 1906 because of lengthy delivery times quoted by British companies.

Commercial links between British and European railway operations included Lord Dalziel's dual involvement in the *Pullman Car and Wagons-Lits companies, which in the 1920s led to the supply of British-built Pullman, dining, and sleeping cars for continental services.

Consultation between H. N. *Gresley and A. Chapelon of the Nord led to the incorporation of a Kylchap double blastpipe, chimney, and smoothed steam passages in the *London & North Eastern Railway's 2-8-2 *Cock o' the North* of 1934. The engine was tested at the French national testing plant at Vitry.

Regulations relating to rolling stock used for international traffic were established from the 1870s, and following World War I they were incorporated in the International Wagon Union (known as RIV) and International Carriage and Brake Van Union (RIC). At first, there was little British participation in technical and rolling stock committees organized by the Paris-based Union Internationale des Chemins de Fer (UIC) until the advent of the train *ferries; it increased from the 1960s. *British Rail has been concerned with Interfrigo, which promotes the development of refrigerated rail traffic, and Intercontainer, a jointly owned subsidiary of the European railways, in promoting large freight containers. Legal conventions for international rail traffic were instituted by European railways in the 1870s, but Britain's isolation from mainland Europe meant that they were not ratified until the 1950s.

Interworking with European railways has changed with the opening of the *Channel Tunnel. The Eurostar tunnel services are jointly managed by Eurostar (UK), and French and Belgian Railways, while *sleeping car services between Britain and France, Germany, and the Netherlands are run by European Night Services, jointly owned by Eurostar, and French, Dutch, and German Railways. There is similar collaboration in running international freight trains through the tunnel.

The major railway manufacturer GEC Alsthom is a joint British and French company which has supplied the Eurostar and French TGV trains, and rolling stock for the *London Underground. MLH

M. Robbins, *The Railway Age* (1962); *BDE*; H. C. B. Rogers, *G. J. Churchward* (1975); J. Johnson and R. A. Long, *British Railways Engineering 1948–80* (1981).

European traffic was already growing, stimulated by the introduction of regular steamboat services in the early 1820s on the Dover–Calais and Newhaven–Dieppe routes, but it was the opening and extension of railway links on each side of the Channel that provided the chief impetus for expansion. It became possible to travel by train and steamer from London to Brussels and Cologne via Dover–Ostend in 1844, to Paris via *Southampton–Havre in 1847, and via Folkestone–Boulogne or Newhaven–Dieppe in 1848, to Basle in 1852, Marseilles in 1855, and Brindisi in 1865. Regular services across the North Sea took longer to become established: from the Humber in 1851, Harwich in 1863, and *Newcastle in 1884. (See SHIPPING SERVICES.)

One of the first traffics to benefit from the faster links was the overseas *mail to and from India, as well as to the Continent. By crossing to Calais and then taking a train to pick up the P & O ship in the Mediterranean, passengers as well as urgent mail could save three days compared with the sea journey from Southampton.

In the 1860s Thomas *Cook and other continental tour organizers began to have a major influence on the growth of tourist traffic. The great international exhibitions held periodically in London and Paris also generated considerable traffic, up to 180,000 extra passengers being recorded in exhibition years. Until 1914 another substantial, but one-way, business was emigrants from Scandinavia, Germany, the Baltic states, and Russia *en route* to America; the *Great Central Railway was one of the North Sea shipping companies that provided cheap accommodation on their ships specifically for bringing emigrants across to *Hull or Grimsby, whence they were carried, usually by special train, to *Liverpool or Southampton for embarkation on the transatlantic steamships.

But most international travel was undertaken by those

who could afford the comforts of a superior class; as late as 1928 only 15 per cent of passengers on the short sea routes booked third class, with 46 per cent going first class and 39 per cent second. Three-quarters of all passengers were British. Even though the two railway companies in most direct competition, the *South Eastern (*Charing Cross–Folkestone–Boulogne) and the *London Chatham & Dover (*Victoria–Dover–Calais), had reached a revenue pooling *agreement soon after the latter route opened, there was keen competition between the several routes for this lucrative traffic. Journey times between London and Paris were progressively reduced from 11 hours in 1851 to 6½ hours by 1913. On all routes successive generations of boats and *boat trains offered ever greater comfort. The growing demand for luxurious rail travel beyond the Channel was met by the formation of the Compagnie Internationale des Wagons-Lits et des Grands Express Européens in 1876. Although standards were never the same after 1914, the tradition of providing a superior service for international passengers continued until the demise of the London–Paris through sleeper train, the Night Ferry, in 1980.

The number of passengers using the Channel and North Sea routes grew from 150,000 in 1850 to half a million by 1880, one million by 1900, and nearly 2 million in 1913. Further growth between the wars was interrupted by five lean years following the 1931 sterling crisis, when traffic fell below 1½ million per year in response to the government's 'Holidays in Britain' campaign. The inter-war peak was 2.4 million, the vast majority being railway passengers; although provision had been made for carrying cars on some shipping routes before World War I, the numbers were still low. Likewise the *air services to France, begun in 1922, were not yet seriously competitive. But the competition grew rapidly after World War II, with roll-on roll-off car ferries and air package holidays both being introduced in the early 1950s. Nevertheless, the market expanded so enormously (30 million passengers crossed by sea to or from the Continent in 1992) that the railways also experienced further growth of their business to over 4 million passengers per year, not including the passengers carried by rail to airports *en route* to and from Europe.

The railways transported, to and from the *ports, a large proportion of Britain's trade with the Continent, which grew more than eightfold between 1853 and 1913. However, they were more particularly associated with traffics carried by their own shipping services. These were generally of a *perishable or high-value nature, such as imports of *fruit and vegetables, wines and spirits, and other *food and drink traffic, and exports of *fish and wool; by 1913 they totalled 3.0 million tons per year, one third in *Lancashire & Yorkshire Railway vessels. As early as 1864 the amount of continental fruit and vegetables carried by the SER justified a special 'Grande Vitesse' depot, first at *London Bridge and then at nearby Southwark.

The inter-war period saw the introduction of superior services that eliminated the problems of damage and loss during transhipment at the ports: train ferries carrying specially built wagons that conformed to both continental tech-

nical requirements and the British loading gauge (see CLEARANCES); and door-to-door transits in railway-owned *containers. But trade was depressed and there was no further significant growth in traffic until the 1960s.

A Harwich–Zeebrugge container ship service was introduced in 1967 to link the *Freightliner network to an equivalent network on the Continent operated by Intercontainer, a company established in the same year and jointly owned by the principal railways of Europe including *British Railways. By the early 1980s one million tonnes of freight were being exchanged annually by this route, complementing the 1.2 million tonnes carried by the train ferries; at this time the UK's total 'unitized' trade with the European Community (i.e. that carried in lorries, wagons, and containers) was about 30 million tonnes. The train ferries still carried large amounts of fruit, vegetables, and other perishables. A new depot was built for this traffic at Hither Green in 1960. Wagons regularly seen there included vans with interchangeable axles for bringing produce from the 5 ft 6 in gauge Spanish railways, and refrigerated vans operated by Interfrigo, another joint company in which BR had a share, formed in 1949. But increasingly the train ferries were being used to transport heavy freight, such as *timber and steel (see IRON AND STEEL INDUSTRY).

A much larger share of both passenger and freight traffic is expected to use railway services through the *Channel Tunnel.

International traffic in Europe is governed and facilitated by a large corpus of procedures, regulations, and standards agreed under the auspices of a number of international bodies (see EUROPEAN RELATIONSHIPS).   GAB

A. R. Williams, 'The Southern's Continental Freight Depot at Hither Green', *Modern Railways*, 16 (1962), 332–4; Sir R. L. Wedgwood, *International Rail Transport* (1946).

Eurostar, see CHANNEL TUNNEL.

Euston, see LONDON STATIONS.

Euston Square Confederacy, see LONDON & NORTH WESTERN RAILWAY.

exchanges, locomotive, see LOCOMOTIVE TESTING.

Exchequer Loan Commission, see SUBSIDIES; FINANCING OF RAILWAYS; GOVERNMENT, RAILWAYS AND NATIONAL.

excursion train. In 1800 an 'excursion' might mean a journey of pleasure, whether in a carriage or on horseback or on foot. The idea of providing it for a large body of people first began on the water.

*Canals were conveying substantial numbers of passengers, many purely for pleasure purposes. Some boats could carry several dozen people at a time, far more than road vehicles. When steamboats entered regular service on the Clyde, the Thames, and other estuaries from 1815 onwards, their capacity was larger still. This change of scale was important, opening the way to commercially organized trips available to anyone paying the fare.

The railways could undertake this business much better. An ordinary train was able to accommodate at least 100 people; with more than one engine that total might extend to 1,000, far more than any horse-drawn vehicle could manage, or a shallow-draught steamboat.

The *Liverpool & Manchester Railway went into the excursion business in its first year of operation, taking a *Manchester Sunday-school party of 150 to *Liverpool and running special trains to *horse races. These may be seen as the first excursion trains, run (usually at reduced fares) either by a railway company or in concert with a private organizer. In 1840 two railways carried between them 24,000 passengers from *Glasgow to Paisley and back during the two days of a race meeting.

Pleasure was soon mingled with instruction, when mechanics' institutes (see EDUCATION) began to offer trips to their members. In 1840 the *Leeds Institute arranged an excursion to *Hull, in a 40-carriage train carrying 1,250 passengers. This was perhaps the first of what came to be called 'monster trains'. Another Leeds–Hull excursion, far bigger, ran in 1844, said to have conveyed 6,600 passengers in 240 carriages hauled by nine engines: probably not in a single train but in a series run in succession.

A less bold development was occurring in the south of England, one which gained wide public attention in 1844. The London & Brighton Railway (see LONDON BRIGHTON & SOUTH COAST RAILWAY) stood out here, and it was the first of the London companies to treat the revenue from excursion business as a regular part of its income, watching out for any signs that the provision of these trains was diminishing the proceeds from ordinary traffic; but few such appeared. The business developed in both directions. The *Eastern Counties company noticed that at the Easter holiday, nearly half as many people again booked to come into London by these trains as to leave it. There were even excursions to France, the *South Eastern Railway taking 300 passengers to Boulogne in May and following up this success by running six more such trips in the late summer.

The monster train was not unknown in London, the Brighton company carrying 1,710 passengers in 46 carriages on an August Sunday (and, even so, leaving 300 behind); but that was something far less monstrous than the great efforts in the north.

The *Railway Chronicle* observed on 1 June 1844 that railway excursions were now 'becoming our chief national amusement'. Still there was much debate about this general expediency. Were they desirable socially, or were they no more than an incentive to the poor to waste their money? The discussion of these matters was complicated. Not all the passengers in these trains were poor; the mechanics' institutes included many members who were not mechanics; some of the trains comprised first- and second-class carriages as well as third and open wagons. How could anyone generalize about their social effects?

Other commentators questioned the profitability of these trains. Taking everything into account, was it less than the companies' chairmen claimed? That was a matter to be calculated carefully by managers, and it was squabbled about by shareholders at their meetings.

On a different question, however, there was more certainty. Railway safety appliances were still primitive in 1844, above all *brakes. The use of the electric *telegraph was then confined to two very short railways. The difficulty in clearly communicating between several engines on a train caused danger.

The Board of *Trade became anxious about the running of excursions between regular service trains, and it circularized the companies that October, offering guidance, but little attention was paid to its warnings. With the growth of traffic, these dangers only increased—and the total number of passenger journeys in Great Britain more than doubled in 1844–8.

Meanwhile a new force had appeared: the *travel agent. The first railway excursion organized by an individual, who travelled with it himself, was from Leicester to Loughborough in 1841, taking 570 people to and from a temperance fête. The man was Thomas *Cook, who soon made a wide reputation. Operating from Leicester, he extended his business soon as far as North Wales and Scotland. Another temperance group, led by Richard Stanley and Joseph Dearden of *Preston, organized trips (at very low fares, especially for the poor) to Fleetwood, for bathing, and to Liverpool, from 1846 onwards.

The demand for excursions to London was much increased in 1851 during the 24 weeks of the Great Exhibition. At its close in October just over 6 million admission tickets had been sold. How many of those had been bought by railway excursionists? Precise figures are few and inconsistent. The *London & North Western company's agent said that it had conveyed 90,000 people in excursion trains into *Euston while the Exhibition was open; but Thomas Cook later claimed that he and his son had brought 165,000—nearly all of them to Euston too.

Though the figures are unhelpful, some other more generalized statements are valid. Obviously, with the population of London and the Home Counties nearly 4 million, most of the people entering the Exhibition arrived in horse-drawn vehicles or on foot. Taking all the indications together, it is plain that the number who travelled by excursion trains was much lower than has usually been imagined. But that does not mean that their part in the Exhibition's success was unimportant. It is accepted that they made a powerful impression. A modern French historian sees the railways as chiefly responsible for turning the Great Exhibition into 'a huge popular festival', and the example it set was followed by others in many countries.

These trains still had their sharp and persistent critics. The LNWR showed little liking for them. Technically, it did not run any, usually preferring to call them *'special trains', although it had to provide them (see HOLIDAY-MAKING). The LNWR's reluctance may have been strengthened by the practices of the *Lancashire & Yorkshire company (its neighbour and, for many purposes, its partner), which could scarcely have been worse. In 1859, the LYR responded to a Board of Trade objection to the carriage of excursionists in open wagons by fitting temporary roofs to about 200 cattle trucks, half of them without *buffers. Their use continued until 1872, when the company at length felt able to improve matters, having paid an average annual dividend of 7.1 per cent from 1866.

They continued to be trains of pleasure, though the pleasure was sometimes grim. In 1849 railway excursionists considerably augmented mobs attending two public executions, at *Norwich and Liverpool. One of the Norwich excursions had come 120 miles from London. Moreover, crowds of excursionists could contribute substantially to public disorder (see PRIZE-FIGHTING).

The running of these trains on *Sundays aroused fierce opposition and much debate within some of the companies: particularly in *Scotland, and on the *Newcastle & Carlisle Railway in 1847–62. At first treated entirely in religious terms, from the 1860s onwards it influenced other questions too: the working hours of railwaymen (see EMPLOYMENT) and the revenue that excursion traffic earned.

Because the excursion train makes no separate appearance in the railway *returns, analysis is difficult. It never figured in an Act of Parliament; it was entirely unnoticed, as such, by the government. Among the chief investigations only the Royal Commission on Railways of 1865–7 called for evidence about it. Our knowledge has therefore to rest largely on occasional remarks at shareholders' meetings or miscellaneous documents in the companies' records, on newspaper accounts, and government *inspectors' reports on accidents. Of all the main branches of the Victorian railways' passenger business this one is much the most obscure.

The Royal Commission discovered that the LNWR, LYR, and *Midland Railway had carried 1,140,000 excursion passengers in 1865. On this basis, the profits for all companies seem to be about 3 per cent of the total for passenger traffic. But they were subject to large variations. In February 1870 Samuel *Laing, chairman of the LBSCR and an advocate of excursions, told the shareholders that the company had paid out £100,000 in compensation for death and injury to excursionists involved in two accidents, and he doubted whether its excursion traffic really paid for itself.

The first serious *accident to an excursion train occurred at Burnley in 1852, the second at Round Oak, Staffordshire in 1859; over the next 30 years there were eight more in Great Britain. There was a decline in the number of all excursion-train accidents investigated by the inspectors, serious or slight; in 1855–69 they averaged eight a year, in 1870–89 only five. The Regulation Act of 1889 (see PARLIAMENT AND LEGISLATION), by requiring that all passenger trains must be worked on the *block system with interlocking of points and signals (see SAFETY) and be fitted with continuous brakes, effected a substantial reduction in accidents. The impulse that led to its passage had been a disaster befalling excursion trains at Armagh in Northern Ireland.

Excursions increased rapidly after the establishment of the August Bank Holiday in 1871. Some railway companies entrusted the arrangements partly to agents. The LBSCR had a long, satisfactory relationship with John Restall, particularly after he began half-day trips, well suited to the short runs on the company's system, in 1894. In 1901–9 the takings and the company's annual revenue rose every year

without interruption, coming to average £243,000—well over 10 per cent of its entire passenger receipts.

Not all the agencies involved were commercial. The National Sunday League, founded in 1855 to secure the opening of public parks and museums on Sundays, turned its attention in the 1870s to organizing excursions, as another means of providing activity for many to whom the day was bleak and dreary. In 1889 it offered 22 such trips; by 1914 the number was 540, some of them running on weekdays as well.

The 'monster trains' of earlier days had now disappeared. But what might be called 'monster excursions' were still organized, the travellers going in numerous trains instead of one. Bass & Co., brewers from Burton-on-Trent, began in 1865 to offer their employees and families a day trip to the seaside. From 1889 this became an annual event, when as many as 15 trains might set out from Burton, carrying 10,000 people. Some railway companies did similar things for their own employees: particularly the *Great Western, with the annual 'Swindon Trip', a compendious name for a whole group of excursions, which in July 1914 took 26,000 people away from the town—more than half its population.

Britain went much further into the excursion business than continental countries. In 1909–10 its government found, on inquiry, that there were very few trains like British cheap excursions, for which there seems to have been very little demand in Europe. Wages in Britain were generally somewhat higher, and working hours less, which may have been one explanation. One thing stood out: the excursion train was a peculiarly British institution.

The *Big Four companies maintained their predecessors' practices after 1922. But first the motor coach and then the private car developed as rivals, allowing holiday-makers to take their families away where and when they chose (see ROAD TRANSPORT). Excursions ran as before to special events, notably horse races and football matches. Occasionally they carried visitors to railway works, and some ran great distances, involving overnight stops: from London to the Highlands of Scotland, for example.

The nationalized railways continued excursions after 1947, though with less enthusiasm. They were anxious to reduce the number of spare locomotives and vehicles kept for holiday periods. Occasionally an interest in them flickered up again, as when in 1971 *British Rail introduced 'Merrymakers'—the old excursions renamed. Thereafter 'excursions' disappeared from the railways' official language.

Yet they continued, and were extended in another form. In 1938 the *London & North Eastern Railway ran excursion trains from London to Cambridge and back, commemorating the 50th anniversary of the first *Races to Scotland, using an engine and carriages of the types used in that contest. Other excursions were also provided for societies of *enthusiasts. This practice continued and grew commoner after 1947. It diminished from the 1970s onwards as suitable spare rolling stock grew scarce.   JS

VR, ch. 12; Paisley races: Robertson, 245; Stanley and Dearden: Lancashire Record Office, DD Pr 35; LYR, i, 258; continental enquiries: PP 1909, lxvii; 1910, lvii.

Exeter. On the opening of the *Bristol & Exeter Railway in 1844, Exeter was a prosperous cathedral city of some 31,000 people. When the original St David's station was rebuilt in 1864 it was also an important junction. Lines dominated by the *Great Western Railway continued westward to *Plymouth (see SOUTH DEVON RAILWAY) and around Torbay to Kingswear (for Dartmouth), while the rival *London & South Western had arrived from Salisbury and was pushing north into Devon. In 1876 it completed its own, competitive route from London to Plymouth. Both railways brought new trade, particularly the LSWR whose stations on the Exmouth branch helped to develop dormitories for the city, which quietly continued to expand.

St David's station was on the natural riverside route outside the town. The LSWR's Queen Street station was central, but at the expense of a tunnel and a steep, difficult curve down to St David's, through which its trains had to pass—with a compulsory stop—to reach its north Devon line, creating the curious situation of GWR and LSWR trains to and from Plymouth passing through the station in opposite directions, a feature repeated at Plymouth North Road.

In 1862–92 St David's was a transhipment point for standard- and broad-gauge traffic, and although it never witnessed the chaos of Gloucester in the 1840s (see TRACK GAUGE), the inconvenience was real enough.

St David's was again rebuilt in 1911–14, and Queen Street in 1933 when it was renamed Central. In 1905 the GWR thwarted an LSWR attempt to build a line bypassing St David's, but a revived plan in 1935 gained parliamentary approval, only for preliminary work to cease when World War II intervened.   GJB

Reg. Hist., i (1988 edn.), ch. 4; GRSB; Transhipment: 'Notable Railway Stations, 40—Exeter St David's', RM, 21 (Oct. 1907), 286–7.

exhibitions. Public exhibitions grew familiar in some towns early in the Victorian age, and railways quickly became involved in them. In 1840 the *Liverpool & Manchester Railway agreed to convey objects to be shown in one organized by the Manchester Mechanics' Institute (see EDUCATION) without charge, provided that admission was free. Later in that decade discussions began about holding a big international 'exhibition of manufactures' in London. It was held in Hyde Park in 1851, in a building constructed mainly of glass and iron, which became known as the Crystal Palace. The facilities that railways could offer were an essential element: for bringing in exhibits (some of them enormous, including two of the largest locomotives yet built), together with the multitude of visitors expected.

How large that multitude actually was cannot be known. The exhibition was open from 1 May to 15 October, and just over 6 million tickets were sold. But that does not mean that 6 million individuals came, for many people made several visits. The proportion of them carried to London by railway is also undiscoverable. A large majority lived in London and arrived on foot (there was no railway station on the site), on horseback, or in carriages. Still, when the exhibition closed it was generally agreed that its evident success could not have been achieved without the help of railways.

The next large exhibition held in Great Britain was at *Manchester in 1857. A temporary station was built at Old Trafford specially to serve it. In material terms it was not a success, but among those who helped to redeem it from failure was Thomas *Cook, who brought visitors in substantial numbers, some of them travelling long distances overnight. A second international exhibition was held in London in 1862, but the results were disappointing compared with the first, always spoken of as the 'Great Exhibition'.

Such huge shows (we would call most of them trade fairs) now became common in large cities across Europe and the USA, the railways and some manufacturers sending exhibits to them. Three were held in Scotland, at Edinburgh (1866) and Glasgow (1888, 1901). The southern railways profited from the additional traffic arising from visitors to the exhibitions at Paris in 1878, 1889, and 1900. An extension to the *Central London underground line was opened in 1908, partly to serve the White City exhibition building from a new Wood Lane station.

After World War I a British Empire Exhibition was held in an impressive building at Wembley. The *Great Central Railway initiated special provision for it, with a new station served by a loop line, completed by its successor the *London & North Eastern in time for the exhibition's opening in 1924.

It is perhaps significant that the last of these shows, the Festival of Britain in 1951, had only inconvenient rail access from Waterloo station, and that although *British Railways had a presence there, that was hardly more than a ghost.

                                              JS

Great Exhibition: C. R. Fay, Palace of Industry (1951); for numbers of visitors: VR, 275–6.

explosives, see DANGEROUS GOODS.

express train. Before the coming of railways the word 'express' had long been applied to a special messenger travelling on horseback on urgent business. It first came to denote a train in 1840, meaning then a *special train, chartered by someone for his own use. Express trains open to the public were introduced by the London & Brighton Railway (see LONDON BRIGHTON & SOUTH COAST) in 1844 on its 51-mile run. Their full potential was revealed by those of the *Great Western running from London to Exeter (194 miles) from May 1845, at the quite unprecedented speed of 43 mph.

Express trains raised two objections: they were expensive, and they were dangerous. They cost more to run than ordinary trains, so supplementary fares were usually charged; but even so, they were held not to pay. The risks in running expresses on the same tracks as slower trains were evident, with the primitive *signalling equipment then in use. True, the Exeter expresses met with no serious accident in the 1840s or 1850s attributable to speed, but those provided by the *Great Northern from 1852 were much less fortunate.

For a time all these trains were slowed down, and their number reduced, until competition caused a resumption of higher speeds. The payment of supplements began to be rescinded. The *Midland Railway abolished them in 1859, and all other companies north of the Thames did the same by 1870. This contrasted sharply with the practice of the continental railways, which continued to levy them (at rates up to 40 per cent) into the 20th century.

By the 1880s it was usual to define a British express train as one that ran at 40 mph, including stops. Foxwell and Farrer, in 1888, considered that a sensible definition of one in northern Europe was that it should attain not 40 mph, but 29. If a 40-mph standard were imposed there, the British Great Northern Railway alone would show more express mileage than the whole of Europe. By 1900, however, a number were appearing, particularly in France, that made 50 mph and more, and some people were concluding that Britain's supremacy had passed. Still, in 1914 the best GWR London–Bristol expresses ran faster than any between two large continental cities. And in some other respects the British trains were, in many passengers' eyes, superior. No supplements were charged on any covering a distance of more than 80 miles, and every one of those carried third-class passengers, who were excluded from most of the best trains in Europe except those in Switzerland and Scandinavia.

It should be added that there were 'express goods' trains too, running at a lower speed than the passenger trains (few of them were fitted with continuous *brakes before 1923)

but still considerably faster than other goods trains. A sample of eight of these in the 1880s shows them running at 23–30 mph, including stops.

In the inter-war years the British express-train service remained good. The GWR's Cheltenham Spa Express ran from Swindon to London in 1929 at 66.2 mph, then the fastest schedule in the world, and the streamlined trains on the *East and *West Coast main lines, introduced in 1935–9, were excellent. But in this field the achievement of the German railways—still more of the American—was greater still.

The nationalized British railways' efforts were designed largely to keep their traffic in competition with *air services and cars on the motorways. But the diesel and electric trains (see TRACTION) provided from 1967 onwards a fast, frequent, and (at least until the later 1980s) a generally dependable service. Cramped by increasingly tight financial restrictions, the British railways could by then hardly have done more.

The word 'express' is now falling into disuse. Only seven trains on BR carry it as part of a title—the oldest of them perhaps the Pines Express from the north and Midlands to *Bournemouth (see also NAMING OF TRAINS). With modern methods of operation the trains on every line fall into groups, each having a more-or-less standard schedule, under which no train runs at a speed significantly higher than the rest.   JS

ET, ch. 2; E. Foxwell and T. C. Farrer, *Express Trains English and Foreign* (1889), 30–1 (goods trains), 93 (definition of speed); P. W. B. Semmens, *History of the Great Western Railway, 1923–47* (1985), ii, 44–6.

F

fabrics and upholstery. The materials used in the earliest compartment *carriages followed closely the practice of stage-coaches. Each first-class compartment was distinguished by full-height partitions, and seats formed by a padded backrest and cushioned seat. There was cloth upholstery pulled tight over a base, usually stuffed with horsehair, but sometimes hay, and secured with buttons to give a quilted effect.

By the 1850s upholstery was usually provided in the second class. The seating was more perfunctory than first class, comprising a stuffed strip to support the back, and a cushion to form the seat. In the first class, one distinction becoming commonplace was the provision of curtains, sometimes of tapestry, to be drawn across to exclude sunlight or darkness.

*Royal saloons such as the pair built for Queen Victoria by the *London & North Western Railway in 1869 featured ceilings and upholstery lined with quilted silk.

With the passing of the Railway Regulation Act, 1868, all main-line railways were required to provide *smoking accommodation. Morocco leather was the preferred material for upholstery in compartments designated for smoking.

A velvet moquette began to be introduced in the 1870s. Following the abolition of second class by the *Midland Railway in 1875, the disparity between first- and third-class furnishings began to narrow but, for the next 80 years or so, the types of material used in the classes varied. In the first class, plain blue broadcloth was used by many of the principal railways, usually secured by leather buttons and trimmed with braiding. In the third class, there was woollen rep upholstery, stuffed with curled horsehair.

In the 1890s railways began to adopt moquette, a durable woollen material with a hemp or linen base, in uncut-tapestry or cut-plush versions. One exception was the *Lancashire & Yorkshire Railway, which covered its third-class seating in a horsehair material, in order to resist the grease on millworkers' clothes.

Utility and hygiene were important considerations as carriages were seldom reupholstered in under seven years, and the condition of some passengers meant that the disinfestation of carriages was often required. Patented woven wire seating was introduced in the mid-1890s, and this was covered by an upholstered cushion, with a stuffed squab as the backrest.

Restaurant cars tended to be upholstered in buffalo hide up to the 1920s. Indeed, there were few innovations in the use of furnishing materials in the 1920–70 period, other than a liking of the *London & North Eastern Railway in the 1930s for Rexine, a coated and textured artificial cloth,

used for lining compartment walls and for trim and window blinds. That era, with its fondness for art deco patterns, had the effect of brightening up carriage interiors, although some of the jazz upholstery patterns were garish.

From the 1970s, *British Rail has moved to easily removable seat covers, in preference to the upholstered bench-type seating of the previous 100 years.

See also CLASS DISTINCTIONS. MLH

C. H. Ellis, *Nineteenth Century Railway Carriages* (1949).

Fairbairn, Sir William (1789–1874), engineer and contractor, born in Kelso. After apprenticeship to a millwright and varied engineering employment, Fairbairn formed a manufacturing partnership (1817) with James Lillie (dissolved in 1832). He became a member of the ICE in 1830. He built the iron-hulled canal boat *Lord Dundas* in 1831, and was engaged on wrought-iron shipbuilding (1830s and 1840s) in Manchester and London, patenting a riveting machine in 1839. He was also concerned with 'fireproof' mills and testing cast-iron beams (partly with Eaton Hodgkinson). In 1845 Robert *Stephenson consulted him on the *Britannia and Conway tubular bridges and he carried out extensive structural experiments. He withdrew before completion, following a dispute over credits.

Fairbairn took out a wrought-iron beam patent in 1846, built many iron structures, and wrote extensively on mill construction, iron shipbuilding, properties of iron, and other engineering subjects. He became president of the IMechE in 1854; FRS 1850 (Gold Medal 1860); and baronet 1869. Forceful and undoubtedly influential, the true depth of his engineering understanding is hard to assess. RJMS

W. Pole, *The Life of Sir William Fairbairn, Bart, Partly Written by Himself* (1877); DNB; Fairbairn's publications.

Fairburn, Charles Edward (1887–1945), son of Robert Fairburn, who was chief engineer, Traction Department, English Electric Co. Fairburn was a pupil of Henry *Fowler at Derby locomotive *works, 1910–12, then joining Siemens Dynamo Co. where he was responsible for the overhead line system and putting locomotives into service on the *North Eastern Railway's Newport–Shildon freight line *electrification. In 1919 he set up the English Electric Co.'s electric traction department, and became general manager of its Preston and Stafford works.

Joining the *London Midland & Scottish Railway in 1934 as chief electrical engineer, he became deputy to *Stanier in 1937, and CME 1944–5. He was responsible for large-scale introduction of diesel-electric shunting locomotives, and initiated proposals for 1,500-hp main-line diesel-electrics. He introduced a modified 2-6-4 steam tank locomotive in 1945.

An engineer of great perception and powers of analysis, his premature death was a great loss to railway engineering.   GWC

Proc. I. Mech. E, 154 (1946); E. S. Cox, Locomotive Panorama, i (1965); DNB: Missing Persons (1993), 219–20.

Fairlie, Robert Francis (1831–85), engineer; he trained on the *London & North Western Railway, later became locomotive superintendent on the Londonderry & Coleraine Railway, then worked in India. Fairlie considered that enlarging conventional locomotives to haul heavier trains incurred unnecessarily high operating costs because they required higher axle loads and longer wheelbases than the wagons they hauled. Reasoning that the ideal locomotive would be as flexible and as kind to the track as the train behind it, he patented in 1864 a double-ended, all-adhesion locomotive mounted on two powered bogies. Successful trials of the 2-ft gauge Fairlie *Little Wonder* on the *Festiniog Railway in 1869 gave world-wide publicity to the type. This was the first successful application of articulated steam locomotives and was copied elsewhere; the Festiniog still uses Fairlie locomotives.

After 1869 Fairlie began to advocate 3-ft gauge railways worked by articulated locomotives as a means of opening up undeveloped parts of the world, but while promoting his ideas in Venezuela he caught a fever which left him an invalid for the remainder of his life. His unusual double-ended steam locomotive became, for the very reasons he gave, the ancestor of today's main-line diesel or electric locomotives.   RW

R. F. Fairlie, *Locomotives, How They Are and How They Ought to Be* (1865).

Falshaw, Sir James (1810–89), *contractor and railway chairman, born in Leeds. He worked with *Brassey on construction of the *Caledonian and *Scottish Central Railways (1845–8) and again in 1853–63 on the Inverness & Nairn and *Inverness & Perth Junction Railways (later parts of the *Highland company). He was then based at Perth, but moved to Edinburgh, where he became Lord Provost in 1876 and was created baronet. He was chairman of the *North British Railway, 1882–7: the only contractor who ever presided over a great British railway company, unless we except *Peto, who was chairman of the much smaller *Chester & Holyhead Railway, 1851–9.   JS

J. Hobson, *Life of Sir James Falshaw* (1903).

fares. The aim of any transport fares system is to set prices at a level that will bring the maximum income without being so high as to encourage passengers to seek an alternative carrier.

The earliest reference to a fare being charged to travel by public transport appears in the Bible (Jonah 1: 3) on Jonah's travels by boat from Joppa to Tarshish. In Britain, travellers by stage-*coaches paid fares at the inns between which the services operated, and were charged appropriately for seats inside or outside.

When the *Stockton & Darlington Railway opened in 1825 the single fare for the whole distance (approximately 12 miles) was 1s.; the following year a cheaper fare of 9d.

was introduced for travelling outside the coach. The SDR appears to have offered the earliest incentive fares, cheaper rates on market days having been advertised by 1835.

From 1832 revenue duties were raised on rail travel at the rate of ½d. per mile for every four passengers carried. Railway travel was then aimed at the wealthier classes and the duty brought little hardship, but a mileage tax was seen as a deterrent to cheap or excursion fares and in 1842 the duty was revised to the rate of 5 per cent of gross passenger receipts.

A major feature of *Gladstone's 1844 *Regulation of Railways Act was its requirement that companies should operate at least one train daily on which passengers could travel in covered coaches at 1d. per mile. On these trains the duty was abolished (it remained on other fares until 1929), and half-fare for children aged between 3 and 12 years was introduced, accompanied children under 3 being carried free. The *Liverpool & Manchester Railway (1830) had carried children under 3 free from the outset; half fares for those up to (probably) 10 had been introduced by 1840.

A list published in 1865 showed that the price per mile varied widely from one railway company to another. Second-class travel on the *North London Railway cost 0.4d. per mile, whereas the *Great Eastern and some minor lines charged 2d. for the same distance. The average fare was 1½d., as charged by the *Great Western, its first-class rate being 2d. and third 0.9d., with premium fares for travel by *express train of 2.4d. first class and 1.7d. second. The *Midland Railway introduced 1d. per mile fares on many fast trains to London in 1868 and throughout the system in 1875, when it also abolished second class.

Urban development from the mid-18th century resulted in workers being rehoused further away from city centres, although their work remained there. To enable those displaced to reach their employment, workmen's fares were introduced under the 1883 Cheap Trains Act, although several railways were already required to provide *workmen's trains. The Great Eastern had to offer prescribed workmen's fares in part-compensation for demolishing property on its Liverpool Street extension, under its Act of 1864.

Early *tickets seldom indicated the fare, but the 1889 Regulation of Railways Act required that every ticket sold at normal prices 'shall bear upon its face, printed or written in legible characters, the fare chargeable for the journey for which such ticket is issued'. Exemptions applied to excursion, party, and other reduced-fare tickets.

By 1914 ordinary passenger fares averaged slightly less than 1d. per mile third class, and in an effort to discourage the general public from using the railways during World War I all ordinary fares were increased by 50 per cent in 1917. Following the *Grouping in 1923 mileage tables were recalculated and a new fare basis of 1½d. per mile was introduced nationally in 1928.

Ordinary return tickets had generally been sold at double the single fare, exceptions being where companies operated competing routes or where tram services ran parallel with railways in urban areas. After the abolition of Railway Passenger Duty in 1929, a cheap monthly return ticket was introduced to offer the incentive of travel at 1*d*. per mile overall.

Special fare-scales were offered for particular classes of traffic, including *anglers, ramblers, picnic parties, commercial travellers, and the police. Military personnel travelled extensively by rail, with separate fare-scales for duty travel and for journeys on leave.

In World War II fares were again raised, to 40 per cent over the 1928 base-rate, and the range of scales was simplified with the aim of discouraging pleasure travel. Full single and monthly return fares were offered, a pattern which continued until after *nationalization in 1948 when cheap day return fares were reintroduced for many local journeys.

Third-class fares, calculated purely on a mileage basis, were reduced from 2.44*d*. to 1.75*d*. per mile in 1952. The term *workman* had become unacceptable, and *British Railways now renamed this range of fares as early morning returns until withdrawal in 1961.

New marketing strategies were introduced in the late 1960s using selective pricing. Fares (or prices, as they became known) were led by market forces and not calculated purely on a mileage basis—BR was the only European railway to do so. The aim was to compete with road or air travel and to achieve even loading of trains throughout the day, with off-peak fares considerably lower than those charged during the morning and evening peak travel hours.

To reduce the effect of fare increases on off-peak leisure travel, railcards were introduced for specific classes of passenger. By investing in a railcard, valid for one year, fare reductions could be obtained by families, young people, senior citizens, and disabled people.

The *London Underground railways had introduced 'scheme' fares on the Bakerloo line in 1911, with one fare covering a number of stations. This was extended throughout the Underground network and was developed further in 1983. London was divided into concentric rings of zones, and travelcards were offered giving unlimited travel on almost all public transport within them for a flat daily, weekly, monthly, or annual fare. Similar fare-zoning has been introduced in several other British cities.

In preparation for *privatization of the BR system, a network of permitted routes for journeys on lines of more than one operating company was agreed, so that the revenue collected can be distributed fairly. Competitive pricing was offered where more than one operator provided services between the same points, such as between London and Gatwick Airport.

See also PASSES AND PRIVILEGE TICKETS; SEASON TICKETS.

MGDF

C. E. Lee, *Passenger Class Distinctions* (1946); D. N. Smith, *The Railway and its Passengers* (1988), 32–7; D. G. Geldard, 'Tickets and Fares on the Stockton & Darlington Railway', *Journal of the Transport Ticket Society*, 144 (1975), 425–45; J. P. Thomas, *Handling London's Underground Traffic* (1928), 152–4; R. H. G. Thomas, *The Liverpool & Manchester Railway* (1980).

Farrer, T. H., SEE TRADE, BOARD OF.

Fay, Sir Sam (1856–1953), manager; he was christened Samuel, but always known as Sam. Of Huguenot origin, he joined the *London & South Western Railway in 1872, becoming assistant store-keeper in 1891. With two colleagues he started the *South Western Gazette* (see PRESS, RAILWAY), and he wrote a short history of the company, *A Royal Road* (1881).

In 1892 he became manager of the bankrupt *Midland & South Western Junction Railway. Alert, hard-working, and skilful, he brought it to solvency in 1897. He returned to the LSWR as superintendent of the line in 1899. In 1902 he became general manager of the *Great Central Railway, then financially very weak.

Fay exploited its central position, making it an important *cross-country route and developing high-class London suburban traffic in conjunction with the *Metropolitan and *Great Western Railways. He energetically pursued the GCR's project for a new port at Immingham (see PORTS AND DOCKS). He was knighted in 1912. In national life, he devised 'conciliation boards' in 1906, to prevent *strikes, and served at the War Office in 1917–19. After the 1923 *Grouping Fay became chairman of Beyer Peacock (see WORKS), the *Manchester firm of *locomotive builders, remaining there until 1933.

JS

DNB; *DBB*; Dow, iii.

Felixstowe, SEE PORTS AND DOCKS.

Fell system, SEE MOUNTAIN RAILWAYS.

Fenchurch Street station, SEE LONDON STATIONS.

fencing. As soon as railways were empowered to purchase land and were no longer merely devices in the hands of private owners whose land they were intersecting, they had to be enclosed with fences and, where they ran across public highways, with gates. The *Surrey Iron Railway was obliged to do this in 1801; any person found guilty of leaving a gate open could be fined £2–5. General statutes governing the railways spelt out the companies' obligations here: the *Regulation Act, 1842 (sect. 10) and the Railways Clauses Act, 1845 (sect. 68).

The main purpose was to protect the owners of land compulsorily purchased, by fencing off lines to prevent their cattle from straying on to them, but the interest of the general public quickly asserted itself. As soon as railways began to use steam locomotives, loud complaints were heard about the frightening of horses passing along nearby roads, sometimes causing serious accidents. In 1832 an important case was brought against the *Stockton & Darlington company for 'allowing and committing a nuisance'. But the judges held that the legislature had specifically permitted the company unrestricted use of locomotives, and that the public benefits fully justified that practice.

There were means by which the 'nuisance' might be lessened. In 1834 the Basingstoke Canal Company claimed that if the London & Southampton Railway (see LONDON & SOUTH WESTERN) was built, running close by it past Woking for 12 miles, the engines would frighten the horses on the tow-path, and the railway company had to build banks or brick walls as screens. The Railways Clauses Act permitted any road authority to apply to the Board of *Trade for an order requiring the erection of screens, and many were set up.

Methods varied according to the materials available. *Whishaw tells us that south of *Liverpool and *Hull fences were nearly all wooden posts-and-rails. On the Bodmin & Wadebridge Railway they were of turf. Upright stone flags were used in some parts of Lancashire, and slate in North Wales. Over a large part of the *Northern & Eastern Railway's line between Stratford and Broxbourne (1840) an interesting experiment was made with iron posts supporting horizontal wires. But this practice was costly, and did not begin to come into widespread use until the end of the Victorian age. It grew common in the 20th century, using concrete posts.

The attitudes of the courts and of the public towards fencing requirements have changed over the years. The protection of horses is today barely a consideration, and the rights of landowners are no longer sacrosanct. Accidents to human beings on railways that were inadequately fenced, or which occurred because the fencing was in bad repair, came to be seen as a responsibility of the companies, made greater with the spread of electrification, particularly on the *Southern Railway from 1925 onwards, with live rails only a little above ground level. Here the sufferers were often children, trespassing on the line. In the past the responsibility had usually been held to rest with the children's parents. Now, however, the state of the fence (which was undoubtedly the railway's responsibility) became the subject of much closer scrutiny, until the decision of the House of Lords in *Herrington's Case* (1972) was seen 'to impose a Common Law duty to fence in favour of potential child trespassers almost as onerous as the statutory duty to fence in favour of owners and occupiers of the adjoining land'.

See also BOUNDARIES. JS

Whishaw; W. H. Mills, *Railway Construction* (1898), 73–4; E. S. Fay, 'Fencing the Railway: Then and Now', *British Transport Review*, 4 (1956–7), 235–42; L. James, *The Law of the Railway* (1980), esp. 158–64, 185.

Fenton, Sir Myles (1830–1918), manager. Son of a Kendal postmaster, and a clerk on the Kendal & Windermere Railway at 15, Fenton moved to four other lines before becoming secretary of the *East Lancashire Railway in 1854. In 1862 this wide experience helped him in becoming at 32 the operating superintendent of the *Metropolitan Railway, and general manager in 1863.

In 1866 he pioneered feeder bus services in London, long a feature of the Metropolitan. Emerging unsullied by *Watkin's investigation into discreditable practices of John Parson, the previous chairman, Fenton became responsible for implementing Watkin's policies, including the grand plan to use an extended Metropolitan as a link between his other lines, the Manchester Sheffield & Lincolnshire (see GREAT CENTRAL) and the *South Eastern, to form a through route from Manchester to Dover. In 1880 he became general man-

ager of the SER where he applied the skills gained in handling Watkin's squabbles with the *Metropolitan District Railway to a similar relationship with the *London Chatham & Dover. He markedly improved the SER's notoriously poor reputation, and its finances, and interceded with the Belgian king when the Dover–Ostend steamer service was in danger of moving to the *Great Eastern's port of Harwich. A Lieutenant-Colonel in the Engineer & Railway Volunteer Staff Corps (see WAR), he was influential in planning the use of railways for wartime troop movements. Fenton was the first railway officer to be knighted while still serving, in 1889. He retired in 1896. GJB

Who Was Who; 'Men of the Day, No. 455, Sir Myles Fenton, KB', *Vanity Fair* (1890); A. A. Jackson, *London's Metropolitan Railway* (1986); A. Gray, *The South Eastern Railway* (1990).

ferries. This article deals with the most important of the railway-owned ferries that crossed river estuaries: Tay, Forth, Humber, Dart, Severn, and Mersey. (For sea-crossings, now commonly called ferries too, see SHIPPING SERVICES.)

An early proposal for a railway ferry appears to be a failed scheme of 1825 for a *tramroad from *Birmingham to Rock Ferry on the Mersey, including vessels to carry the wagons to *Liverpool.

In 1840–5 railway companies acquired existing ferries over the Mersey at Birkenhead and the Humber at *Hull: both irregular transactions. The Birkenhead ferry was transferred to independent commissioners. Some directors of the Great Grimsby & Sheffield Junction Railway, who bought the Humber ferries and then sold them to the railway at a profit to themselves of more than 100 per cent, were threatened with legal action and eventually disgorged their gains.

Railway companies got parliamentary powers in 1846–7 to establish ferries over the Tay, Forth, and Severn. The second became historically important because the Edinburgh & Northern Railway (see EDINBURGH PERTH & DUNDEE RAILWAY) began to work it in 1850 with the world's first train-ferry, designed by the company's engineer Thomas *Bouch, to take wagons from Granton (outside *Edinburgh) to Burntisland: a British invention that was little used, however, in Britain itself. The Severn ferry, by the New Passage at Portskewett, offered, in conjunction with a railway, a much shorter route between Bristol and Cardiff than the detour via Gloucester; but this plan was not realized until 1864. The ferry was discontinued immediately the *Severn Tunnel was opened in 1886.

Some important railway-owned ferries were replaced by bridges (see BRIDGES AND VIADUCTS), most notably those over the Tay and Forth. After the first Tay Bridge blew down in 1879 the ferry was reopened, and maintained until the completion of the second bridge in 1887. The Forth Bridge, opened in 1890, naturally diminished the use of the old Queensferry service running beneath it, but this continued until 1964.

Only three railway-owned ferries then remained in Britain: from Hull across the Humber to New Holland, carrying a substantial traffic until the completion of the Humber Bridge in 1981, when it closed; from Kingswear to Dartmouth, opened in 1864; and the Tilbury–Gravesend ferry on the Thames. When the *London Tilbury & Southend Railway was established in 1852 it had powers to run a ferry, and after lapsing for a time they were resurrected in 1875. The LTSR had a maximum of six paddle-steamers in service. This ferry and the Dartmouth one are still running.   JS

> Rock Ferry: W. H. Chaloner, *Social and Economic Development of Crewe* (1950), 15; *Reg. Hist.*, x, 45–6 (Birkenhead), xv, 69–70 (Forth and Tay); P. Sulley, *History of Ancient Birkenhead* (1907), 114–25; Dow, i, 89–90, 143 (Humber); MacDermot, ii, 2–3 (Portskewett), ii, 124–5 (Kingswear); H. D. Welch, *London Tilbury & Southend Railway* (1951), 32–3.

Festiniog Railway. Authorized in 1832 to provide a rail outlet from slate quarries around Blaenau Ffestiniog to the newly created harbour of Portmadoc, it opened in 1836. Of 2-ft *gauge, it was laid for much of the distance on a continuous gradient of approximately 1 in 80 to facilitate gravity working. In 1863 it introduced steam locomotives and in 1865 became a public railway, partly to increase capacity, partly to counter a rival standard-gauge line. It adopted *Fairlie articulated locomotives in 1869, trials of which attracted world-wide attention, and in 1871 the first bogie coaches with integral iron framing, the ancestors of all modern railway *carriages. By demonstrating what could be achieved on a very narrow track with a restricted loading gauge (see CLEARANCES), it influenced railway development in many parts of the world.

Both the *slate industry and the railway declined after 1900. In 1934 it leased the ailing Welsh Highland Railway, which ran from Dinas through Beddgelert to Portmadoc where it connected with the Festiniog. This move contributed to the company's undoing, and three years later the WHR was closed. Passenger services (summer only after 1932) ended at the outbreak of World War II and the last slate train ran in 1946. The railway lay derelict until 1954 when a group of enthusiasts gained control and began restoration using volunteer labour. A short length reopened in 1955 and restoration proceeded steadily, including 2½ miles of new railway to bypass a reservoir, until services to Blaenau Ffestiniog were restored in 1982. The railway has its own works capable of building locomotives and rolling stock and is now one of the principal tourist attractions in North Wales.

See also NARROW-GAUGE RAILWAYS; SPOONER FAMILY.   RW

> J. I. C. Boyd, *The Festiniog Railway* (1975).

financing of railways. So rapid was the development of Britain's railways that by 1843, less than two decades after the opening of the *Stockton & Darlington line, their total capitalization, £60 million, was greater than that of any other category of joint-stock company. With the boom in promotion in the mid-1840s and the successive waves of further investment, railway *capital continued to grow spectacularly for most of the rest of the 19th century: by 1850 railway share and loan capital stood at £227 million; by 1881, at £709 million, it equalled the funded national debt,

and before the turn of the century it had exceeded £1,000 million. Growth slackened during the early years of the 20th century, and World War I and subsequent events then complicated the picture, but at *nationalization in 1948 the capital of the vested railway undertakings was approximately £1,250 million.

In contrast with much of Europe and many British overseas territories, where government funding or guarantees played a significant part, railway investment in Britain prior to nationalization relied almost entirely on private capital. Though railways were also able to raise money by borrowing, legislative restrictions meant that share capital was their primary means of finance, and indeed a new company was obliged to have the bulk of its shares subscribed before it could obtain parliamentary authorization. For the promoters of the first public steam railways in Britain, those authorized in the 1820s, the magnitude of this task was increased by two additional considerations: the transport technology they were seeking to finance was still in its infancy and was little known outside the coalfields of northeast England; and they had to raise relatively large sums of venture capital at a time when the organized market in financial securities was mainly limited to government stocks and was concentrated in London, remote from the areas where railways were being developed.

Surviving evidence from the earliest railways suggests that none was able to place all its shares with subscribers in its own area, and that various methods were employed in order to dispose of the balance needed for a successful flotation. The pioneering Stockton & Darlington Railway raised only half of its initial capital in Durham and North Yorkshire; most of the rest was obtained through the personal links of the Quaker businessmen who played a leading role in the line's development, with the result that significant blocks of SDR shares were held in East Anglia, the West Midlands, and the south and west of England. Such connections provided one means of tapping additional sources of funds for new railway undertakings; another was to resort to direct canvassing. In 1835 the secretary of the *Great Western Railway described the 'sad harassing work' of 'calling upon and pressing perfect strangers to contribute'.

However, these direct methods of seeking capital had obvious limitations, and most railways were obliged to take additional steps. Newspaper advertisements provided one means of inviting subscriptions on a more general basis, and from an early stage companies found themselves looking particularly to the principal commercial centres to supplement their other sources of finance. At first, the main focus of transactions in company securities was in London, where the Stock Exchange and its fringe markets were quick to respond to additional trading opportunities. The mid-1820s saw considerable City interest in new flotations, including many railway companies, and while most of these ventures were unsuccessful, the two largest undertakings to be authorized during the 1820s, the *Liverpool & Manchester and *Newcastle & Carlisle, each drew a significant proportion of their initial subscriptions from London. Though it would be wrong to associate this interest solely with the

Stock Exchange's contemporary enthusiasm for new issues, there is sufficient evidence to suggest that much of the metropolitan participation in early railway schemes differed in character from that from a line's locality. Those shareholding records that have survived from the 1820s and early 1830s indicate that original subscribers based in London tended to dispose of their holdings sooner than others, and the financial press provides secondary evidence of the speculative nature of much Stock Exchange activity in railway shares at this time.

However, following the opening of the LMR, significant changes took place in the railway share market, leaving London with a less distinctive role. *Liverpool and *Manchester investors, with first-hand experience of the effectiveness of the new mode of transport, played a key part in this process: their enthusiasm for new railway projects during the 1830s was channelled not only into the rapid expansion of the Lancashire network, but also into substantial stakes in more distant schemes, such as the London & Southampton (see LONDON & SOUTH WESTERN) and Glasgow Paisley & Greenock Railways. Liverpool also provided the largest block of subscriptions to the *London & Birmingham Railway; although this line offered advantages to Lancashire, since it completed the trunk route to London, its promotion was initiated and led from the cities named in its title. Despite this, the combined financial input from these sources was less than that from Liverpool, and within three years of the company's authorization in 1833 Manchester funding also exceeded the aggregate from both *Birmingham and London.

Lancashire interest in railway investment was reflected in the establishment there in 1836 of the first provincial stock exchanges, in Liverpool and Manchester. While City involvement in railway projects did not cease (and found particular expression in some London-funded schemes such as the *North Midland or *Preston & Wyre), the emergence of the two Lancashire exchanges demonstrated the way in which the institutional apparatus of the capital market was expanding along with the railways. These developments during the mid-1830s were repeated on a larger scale during the great Railway *Mania of the 1840s, which saw the creation of stock exchanges in most of the larger urban centres. In addition, stockbroking expanded as a profession even in towns which did not have a dealing floor, and financial information about railways was circulated widely through the daily press and new specialist periodicals. In parallel with the growth of the railways, therefore, a nationwide financial network emerged which was specifically geared to transactions in their shares. Besides extending the opportunities for investors to direct their savings into railway schemes, and increasing the liquidity of such investments, these developments gave new companies easy access to the capital market, and the use of stockbrokers as agents for raising funds in distant areas was already becoming apparent before the end of the 1830s.

Railway shares accordingly became a widespread outlet for savings: there were over 700,000 separate holdings in British railway companies in 1902, and though many investors would have held shares in more than one undertaking, individual stakes were typically quite small—average holdings in most companies were under £1,500. While some local loyalty usually remained evident, surviving records show that proprietors were widely dispersed. In 1860 more than 40 per cent of the *South Eastern Railway's shareholders lived in Lancashire and Cheshire, compared with around a quarter in London, Kent, and Sussex. About a third of GWR shareholders in 1900 lived outside the areas served by the line (including London); this was a lower proportion than in 1870, when more than 40 per cent were non-local. The *North Eastern Railway provides another example: despite this company's strong regional identity, less than half of a sample of shareholders in 1921 lived in the counties which it served.

The emergence of this widely dispersed and essentially impersonal market in railway shares meant that stock-exchange fluctuations quickly became an important influence on railway companies' ability to raise funds. Investors were naturally deterred from entering into extra commitments when the prices of existing railway shares were depressed, as can be seen from the dearth of successful promotions in the early 1840s and during the aftermath of the Railway Mania. However, market sentiment also affected established lines when they needed extra capital to fund extensions or improvements, since they had to compete for funds with other available investment opportunities. These included colonial and foreign securities (among them many high-yielding overseas railways), utilities, and an increasing range of commercial and industrial firms. The functional efficiency of the capital market which the railways had helped to create was such that 'Home Rails' were frequently at a disadvantage compared with other issues, and the consequent difficulties in raising equity capital made it necessary for British railway companies to tap additional forms of finance.

The most obvious means available was borrowing. Lending to a railway was relatively risk-free, since the loan was secured and a predetermined rate of interest was guaranteed, even while a line was under construction and unable to pay an ordinary dividend. Accordingly, borrowed capital played an important part in railway finance from the outset, and though at first loan instruments were generally negotiated as separate transactions, from the 1860s onwards there was increasing reliance on debenture stocks, which were certificated like shares and could be traded in a similar way. The distinction between share and loan capital was also elided by the development of preference and guaranteed shares, which offered a fixed return rather than the fluctuating dividends of ordinary stock. In these ways, railways were able to draw funds from investors who were either unwilling to bear the risks attached to ordinary shares or whose investment options were legally restricted, as was the case with trustees. Loan capital in particular offered a useful outlet for the funds of institutional investors such as banks and insurance societies; lenders in these categories can be traced during the earliest stages of railway development, and in 1842 the Bank of England itself began to include railway debentures in its portfolio. In 1900 borrowed funds accounted for 26 per cent of the total nominal capital of Britain's railways, and a further 36 per cent was made up of preference or guaranteed shares, demonstrating the importance of prior charge issues in overcoming bottlenecks in the supply of ordinary share capital.

Publicly issued share and loan capital made up the overwhelming bulk of British railway finance, and both forms of funding had clear statutory recognition, though on occasion legal powers were exceeded. However, three other financial devices were sometimes employed, which, although small in relation to the total, could be particularly significant for the companies involved. The first was simply to allow the capital account to go into deficit: this was sometimes a sign that a railway was in serious difficulties, but became increasingly common as a matter of financial convenience if credit balances were available in other accounts.

Another device was to arrange for a *contractor to finance all or part of a line's construction, a common practice during the mid-Victorian years, when new undertakings found it extremely difficult to raise capital. Instead of cash, contractors took securities in payment for work done, and either used them as collateral for their own borrowings or sold them, thus effectively acting as underwriters. Since contractors took a discount or commission for employing their own credit in place of the company's, this inflated eventual *construction costs; in addition, considerable use was made of promissory notes in such transactions. Such securities tended to find their way into the short-term money market through the refinancing operations which contractors had to undertake to maintain their own liquidity, and the Overend Gurney collapse of 1866 (see SPECULATION) demonstrated the vulnerability of the credit pyramids that could develop when railways were financed in this way.

A third financial variant was the acquisition of rolling stock through a hire or finance company. This reduced a railway's immediate capital outlay, but at the cost of later recurrent charges. In principle, this was similar to the practice followed by the many small undertakings which obtained rolling stock through a working *agreement with a larger railway, and apart from the costs involved there was no inherent drawback. However, as with reliance on contractors, it was often a symptom that a company was in straitened circumstances, and unable to raise the necessary finance on its own account.

See also ACCOUNTING; INVESTMENT IN RAILWAYS.   MCR
S. A. Broadbridge, *Studies in Railway Expansion and the Capital Market in England, 1825–1873* (1970); R. J. Irving, *The North Eastern Railway Company 1870–1914* (1976), 139–57; M. W. Kirby, *The Origins of Railway Enterprise: The Stockton and Darlington Railway, 1821–1863* (1993); MacDermot, i, 8–11; M. C. Reed, *Investment in Railways in Britain, 1820–1844* (1975).

Findlay, Sir George (1829–93), manager. Son of a Scottish superintendent of masonry on the *Liverpool & Manchester Railway, he began life as an engineer, overseeing the construction of part of the *Shrewsbury & Hereford Railway, 1850–2. He became its manager under the contractor *Brassey, 1852–62; goods manager, *London & North Western Railway, 1864–74, then its chief traffic manager, 1874–80; general manager 1880–93. He refused chairmanship of the company in 1891. He was knighted in 1892.

Findlay was largely responsible for welding the LNWR's far-flung system into a coherently managed and, in normal times, smooth-working organization which he described and explained in his book *The Working and Management of an English Railway* (1889 and six subsequent editions). Lucid and easily comprehensible, this is the most satisfying account of the administration of a British railway company ever produced by one of its own officers. What he has to say of the handling of its *freight traffic (chs 9–12) is perhaps of special value and interest.   JS
The Times, 27 Mar. 1893; Sir G. Findlay, *The Working and Management of an English Railway* (1976 edn.).

Firbank, Joseph (1819–86), railway *contractor, was the son of a miner in the Auckland coalfield, Durham. After entering railway building in 1840 as a *navvy, he obtained a series of sub-contracts before being awarded a maintenance contract on the Rugby–Stamford line of the *London & North Western Railway in 1850. His career, having been launched from a most unpromising position, benefited from the recommendations of the engineer Charles *Liddell. Firbank's railway building, which took place principally in the east Midlands, south-eastern England, and South Wales, included contracts on the *Midland Railway's Bedford–St Pancras and *Settle & Carlisle lines; he developed mutually advantageous relationships especially with that company, and with the *London Brighton & South Coast Railway.

Having failed to find a satisfactory partner, he depended on the assistance of his nephew, Ralph Firbank, and eldest son, Joseph Thomas. Firbank's activities were confined to England and Wales and he was one of the last major contractors to spend his entire life in railway building. Competence, integrity, and reliability were his hallmarks. He died at Newport, Monmouthshire, leaving £348,528.   DB
F. McDermott, *The Life and Work of Joseph Firbank, J.P., D.L., Railway Contractor* (1887).

fire. Sparks from locomotives caused a considerable hazard in steam days. In the late 1860s, for instance, 24 houses were destroyed by fire from a flying cinder at Stoke Canon on the *Bristol & Exeter Railway. Fire claims were expensive to deal with, and in 1864 the Central Wales Railway paid £50 to replace thatched roofs with slate near Dolau, in return for a binding disclaimer. Fraudulent claims were frequent, and under the Railways Fires Act, 1905, liability for damage to agricultural land was limited to £100, and the companies were empowered to enter property to extinguish fires, and to reduce the risk by clearing undergrowth. Lineside fires could disrupt services; today even more so when electric *signalling cables laid on the ground are damaged.

*Station fires were relatively uncommon, considering the large number that were built of wood. In 1885 the wooden buildings at Didcot were burned down; in 1912 Bramford station on the *Great Eastern Railway; and, shortly after closure in 1953, Gosport, leaving only the shell. Part of the *trainshed at Chester was destroyed in 1972 when petrol tank wagons ignited.

Steam locomotives were generally banned from entering goods depots. Large, multi-storey warehouses (see GOODS SHEDS), with wooden floors and gas lighting, presented high risks. The huge Bishopsgate goods station in London, opened in 1881, burned down in 1964. As less hazardous forms of construction evolved they were adopted by the railways for new buildings, such as the *Great Northern's 'fireproof' Deansgate goods station at Manchester (1885–98). *Hotels, too, were vulnerable, as the Great Northern realized when it used fireproof construction for the corridors in the hotel at *King's Cross (1854). But in 1906 its *Leeds hotel was badly fire-damaged, and the *Great North of Scotland's Palace Hotel, *Aberdeen, was destroyed in 1941.

Precautions were in line with the standards of their day. Stations and *signal boxes had fire buckets and portable extinguishers; larger stations, *engine sheds, and goods depots had hydrant systems, with staff trained to use them. But there was reluctance to incur the expense of automatic detection and sprinkler systems. Large *works had their own fire brigades and often a fire-fighting train with an engine kept in steam, which could also be despatched to incidents elsewhere.

Train fires present one of the greatest risks to life. In early days engine sparks were liable to ignite baggage carried on the roofs of carriages, but little worse. Fire in wooden coaches following a collision was the great hazard, as when the Irish Mail collided with runaway wagons carrying paraffin at Abergele in 1868, killing 32 passengers. Gas lighting materially increased the danger: nine died in the Hawes Junction fire on the *Settle & Carlisle line in 1910, 14 only two miles away near Ais Gill in 1913, and 15 at Ditton Junction, near Widnes, in 1912. The same combination at Britain's worst train disaster, at Quintinshill, near *Carlisle, in 1915, caused 227 deaths, and in 1928, 15 died at Charfield, Gloucestershire. Thereafter, steel coaches and electric lighting steadily reduced the risk, although defective design and poor maintenance caused a series of fuel tank fires in diesel *multiple units in the 1960s.

The hazards of flammable interior finishes were realized after a sleeping car train fire at Taunton in 1978 killed 12 passengers, mostly by asphyxiation from fumes. It brought about the complete redesign of passenger vehicles to include non-flammable materials, automatic alarms, and suppression systems.

A train fire in a tunnel is the most feared, although fortunately they have been few. One in Welwyn North Tunnel in 1866 burned for 36 hours, while the most spectacular occurred in 1984 in Summit Tunnel through the Pennines, when a derailed petrol train caught fire, melting the brickwork and closing the tunnel for eight months—fortunately with no casualties. A different kind of tunnel, the tube forming the *Britannia Bridge over the Menai Strait, was so weakened when the combustible lining caught fire in 1970 that it had to be replaced by steel arches. Fires on the *London Underground have also been rare. Usually the cause has been arcing of electrical equipment, as happened near Holland Park in 1958. But the most tragic incident in recent years occurred at King's Cross Underground station in 1987, when 31 people died. Following a public enquiry, stringent policies were adopted, including provision of automatic alarm and extinguishment systems in plant rooms and under escalators, improved means of escape, and prohibition of smoking. They also covered other stations below ground level; Birmingham New Street, for example, is classed as 'underground' for these purposes.

In November 1996 a serious fire occurred in a lorry shuttle train in the *Channel Tunnel. Fortunately there were no fatalities, and despite serious damage from intense heat, limited train services were resumed in two weeks.

See also ACCIDENTS; SMOKING. GJB

L. T. C. Rolt, *Red for Danger* (1982 edn.); 'Fire Safety', *Modern Railways*, 52 (Aug. 1995), 563.

firemen, locomotive. 'Fireman' was latterly a rather inappropriate title for the second crew member on a steam locomotive, for his duties included far more than simply tending the fire and the water level in the boiler. In the days of mechanical signalling—and before that of little or no signalling at all—he was, when not firing, the *driver's second pair of eyes and in an emergency was capable of undertaking any of the driver's duties.

Fireman was a step on the promotional ladder to driver. One began as a *cleaner whose job was literally to clean locomotives inside and out—firebox and smokebox included—when they were being prepared for service. It was a hard and dirty job but, as so often in railway service, had a dual purpose, for the cleaner became familiar with the workings of a locomotive, learnt how to carry out certain routine servicing tasks, and would eventually inspect the locomotive as he cleaned it. Having at the outset learnt how to dispose of a dead fire, he would then learn how to lay a fresh one and to tend it while the locomotive raised steam. He would then progress to simple firing duties on shunting engines and, after taking an initial test of his knowledge of locomotives and of the rule book, would become a 'passed cleaner' permitted to fire locomotives on the main line as a means of gaining the necessary experience to become a fireman. Firemen started on local freight trains and worked up to main-line passenger turns, not only improving their firing technique but also learning more of the driver's responsibilities and—most importantly—learning the intimate details of the routes on which they worked. Eventually becoming a 'passed fireman', he would be allowed to drive trains over those routes for which he had sufficient route knowledge, then progressing to driver.

The fireman's job developed over a lengthy period of time. In the early days he was simply a stoker, who lit the fire, built it up, and then maintained it at a suitable thickness to produce enough steam when the locomotive was at work. Anything else he did was at the behest of his driver, who was in sole charge of the locomotive and alone responsible for maintaining the water level in the boiler. This was particularly so on lines where coke was used, for it was difficult to maintain constant steam output with a coke fire. Most of the time the fireman waited until steam pressure began to fall, showing that the fire was burning thin, then filled the firebox up and became a spectator as the fire recovered, pressure rose, steadied, and finally began to fall again over a cycle of about 10 minutes' duration.

From the 1850s, the introduction of efficient fireboxes designed to burn coal made it possible to fire more consistently and to maintain pressure within closer limits than had hitherto been normal. There was, however, some resistance to the new fuel because the fireman now had to tend his fire more frequently. He could now judge the condition of his fire from the density of the smoke at the chimney top. Firing became more skilled, and following the introduction of injectors in place of pumps to feed the boiler the fireman was at last permitted partial control over water level.

The driver's job became more complicated, too, as track layouts and signalling installations became more complex, and trains became heavier and faster. Certain duties therefore began to be shared between both crew members. This raised the status of the fireman somewhat; indeed, senior drivers and firemen were well paid and enjoyed better than average job security. On the other hand, those lower down the ladder, particularly those working goods and mineral traffic, often had to work very long hours. As often happens when two people have to work together a lot, the relationship between a driver and his regular fireman was often very close: they worked as a team and might also share their off-duty pursuits. But human nature is fickle and there were instances of a driver and fireman who simply did not get on, even to the extent of seldom talking to one another, yet still managed to do a good job of work. Sometimes the most senior jobs were in effect, if not in reality, let out to a driver on contract, in which case his fireman and perhaps a regular cleaner were paid by their driver rather than by the railway company (e.g. on the *London Brighton & South Coast Railway under William *Stroudley).

The introduction of larger locomotives in the early years of the 20th century made life harder for those who fired them, particularly on long runs in the years immediately prior to the introduction of superheated locomotives (see TRACTION, STEAM) having significantly lower fuel consumption. On many lines extra payments were negotiated for firemen rostered to locomotives above a certain size, for example 1,500 sq ft of heating surface in the case of the *London & North Western Railway.

Railway *safety has long embodied a principle that two separate mistakes must occur to create a hazardous situation, and for this reason there were times when a fireman was permitted to give orders to his driver: were a train running without a *guard the latter's overall responsibility for the safety of the train passed to the fireman so that decision-making was still split. In practice, of course, driver and fireman usually double-checked each other and were sometimes required so to do—for example, the man collecting a *single-line token read out the section to which it referred so that both could verify that they had the right one.

The advent of diesel traction removed the need for a fireman as such, but until modernization and rationalization of track layouts and signalling were carried out the rest of the fireman's traditional tasks remained and he became the 'second man' or 'driver's assistant'. In recent years it has been necessary to train a new generation of firemen in order to work preserved steam locomotives.

See also ASSOCIATED SOCIETY OF LOCOMOTIVE ENGINEERS AND FIREMEN.   RW

Fishguard, see PORTS AND DOCKS.

fish traffic. Among perishable foodstuffs fish and *milk were the first to benefit from the great increase of speed in transit offered by the steam railways.

Fish had long been conveyed inland from the sea by horse-drawn road vehicles. By 1765 there was a regular service from the south coast to Billingsgate market in *London. In 1777 the market at *Leicester (almost as far from the sea as any English town) was 'remarkably well stocked with fish'. Most of what was so transported must have been salted or dried, and the selling price of it was high.

By the mid-1840s, with the opening of railway communication inland from *Hartlepool and *Hull, the supply of rail-borne fish to *Manchester began to be commented on, and especially the consequent reduction in its market price, by two-thirds or more. Captain Laws, of the *Lancashire & Yorkshire Railway, was credited with special energy in fostering this traffic.

In the 1850s a very old *port was rejuvenated as a fishing port by railways. The Manchester Sheffield & Lincolnshire Railway (see GREAT CENTRAL) took over the Grimsby Dock Company and presently opened a new fish dock there (1856). The *Great Northern Railway also served it by a line through Louth. Grimsby moved ahead steadily to the forefront of this trade. In the 1880s and 1890s it was handling a quarter of all the rail-borne fish distributed over England and Wales.

Other leading fishing-ports were Whitby, Scarborough, Yarmouth, Lowestoft, and Harwich on the east coast of England; on the south coast *Plymouth, and several smaller ports in Cornwall; Milford Haven and Fleetwood, facing the Irish Sea. In Scotland the fisheries were particularly important in the north-east, handled at ports all along the coast from *Aberdeen to Wick. The Wick & Lybster *Light Railway, opened in 1903, was built largely to convey this traffic, its construction persuading the Duke of Portland to assist very substantially in the improvement of Lybster harbour. Some fishing ports that lacked railway communication made efforts to secure it: in Cornwall, for example, Mevagissey, where that attempt failed in 1884; successfully at Padstow in 1899.

The development of steam-worked railways had been accompanied by that of steam trawlers. Together, they produced great changes in British diet. Alexander's comment on this process is quite unhesitating: 'extended consumption [of fish] was a function of a radical change in transport technique'. The consumption of salted and pickled herrings (a staple food in many London working-class families) now declined. As fresh fish became more widely and cheaply available there was an early sign of a gradual diversification of eating habits. It should be added that when, in the 1880s, fish merchants complained loudly that the rates charged by the railways were a factor in keeping prices higher than they would otherwise have been, *Acworth demonstrated conclusively that this allegation was not true.

The railways' transport of fish was managed in various ways. The *Great Western company carried all fish in open *wagons until 1909, when its first purpose-built van for the trade was turned out. The Lancashire & Yorkshire adopted this practice whole-heartedly. In 1923 it had a fleet of 450 fish vans, larger than any other British company, built since 1906. They were based at Fleetwood, which the company had developed as a fishing port with great determination, building a fish market, and dispatching fish trains (or through vans) as far afield as London, Birmingham, and Scotland.

This traffic presented one special problem in railway operation. The droppings from fish-carrying vehicles made the rails greasy, which could impede the effect of braking. That was observed as early as 1866, when the *North Eastern Railway was attaching 'fish-trucks' to the East Coast night express at Berwick. It was an element in what might have been a very serious *accident at *St Pancras station in 1894.

With the arrival of the long-distance road motor vehicle, and some improvement in the roads themselves, much of the fish traffic eventually passed to them after World War I. This mode might be superior, from the fish merchants' point of view, offering greater flexibility in the choice of routes and reducing the need for transhipment. But the shift from rail to road took place gradually, over a long period of time, and it was managed so as to reduce possible antagonism and avoid dispute. By the mid-1970s the traffic had dwindled to a few containers a week on the Eastern Region of *British Rail, which had handled the largest proportion. So it simply decided to discontinue them. JS

D. Alexander, *Retailing in England during the Industrial Revolution* (1970), 12–18; RTC, 47–8, 129, 175–7, 218–22; Dow, iii, 264–5; LYR, i, 93, 111, 122, 154.

fitters, as their name suggests, were originally employed to assemble pieces of machinery. Their job was to ensure that parts fitted snugly together, rigidly so where rigidity was necessary, or with the right clearances to work properly if required to move. By thus selectively assembling machinery it was possible to achieve superior fits and clearances to those that were possible with fairly basic machine tools. The fitter took over where the machinist left off and, using a variety of hand tools such as files and scrapers, removed minimal amounts of metal—or added them by means of shims—so that nominally identical shapes became precise, matching, and generally usable only in the machine for which they were intended. Fitting as just described has largely been eliminated, obsolete by modern manufacturing techniques but still necessary for the maintenance of older equipment—preserved locomotives and rolling stock, for instance.

Almost everything on a railway has to be assembled to a greater or lesser extent, and several different classes of fitter were eventually to be found on the payroll, often employed as much in maintenance as in original assembly. The heavy work of assembling a steam locomotive (see TRACTION, STEAM) involved much fitting but was normally performed by erectors; once the locomotive left the erecting shop, however, all necessary adjustments and minor repairs would be performed by locomotive fitters.

The *carriage and *wagon department likewise had its own fitters who, again, became responsible for routine servicing and maintenance once a vehicle had left the works. C & W fitters were responsible not only for the basic vehicle but also for its associated fittings such as *brakes and lighting (see CARRIAGE LIGHTING). As with locomotive fitters, they would be expected to attend to minor problems without taking the affected vehicle out of traffic; thus the *driver or *guard of a train might request the attendance of a fitter at the next stop.

Well into the 20th century, the greatest user of basic mechanical systems was the *signalling department. Each signal or pair of points was a mechanism in its own right; it was operated mechanically by rodding or wire from the *signal box in which the levers were interlocked mechanically by locking frames of varying and occasionally awesome size and complexity. There was plenty for the signal fitter to do, and despite the gradual introduction of electrical and pneumatic systems it has remained an important job.

Times and technologies move on: it was said of the early diesel locomotives that it took a day to find out what had gone wrong and five minutes to fix it, unlike a steam locomotive where you knew what had happened straight away and needed a day to put it right. This may have been an exaggeration, but as equipment has become more complex, more compact, and, through the use of modern technology, more reliable, the emphasis on problem-solving has indeed shifted from hands-on dexterity to prompt and accurate diagnosis. Today's fitter attending a defective High Speed Train (see SPEED), for example, will know what symptoms the driver has reported and have a good idea of what has gone wrong before the train stops at the platform. He may simply unplug one PCB (printed circuit board), insert a replacement, carry out a functional check, and report the job complete. Knowing what to change has become more important than knowing how to repair it, either because it cannot realistically be repaired or because it is essential to minimize the time a piece of capital equipment is idle.

RW

'Five Kings', see DALHOUSIE, JAMES.

Fleetwood, see PORTS AND DOCKS.

Fletcher, Edward (1807–89), mechanical engineer. Apprenticed at Robert *Stephenson's works, *Newcastle, he was involved in the building and trials of *Rocket*. In 1830 he joined the *Canterbury & Whitstable Railway as engineer, driving its first locomotive *Invicta* at the opening. From 1837 he worked under T. Cabry on the construction of the *York & North Midland, becoming in 1845 locomotive superintendent of the Newcastle & Darlington Junction Railway, and from 1854 to 1882 of the *North Eastern Railway.

His 4-4-0s of 1864 for the sinuous *Whitby & Pickering section of the NER were amongst the first in Britain to be fitted with leading bogies. Fletcher's 2-4-0 passenger, 0-6-0 freight, and 0-4-4 tank types were simple and reliable machines which gave good service for many years. In the interregnum following the premature resignation of his successor, William McDonnell in 1885, the NER management built an enlarged, modernized version of his successful 2-4-0 type for express service. Known as the Tennants, they gave excellent results.

Fletcher ran his department paternalistically and on a light rein, taking a great interest in his men who greatly respected him and his engines. GWC

BSRL; *Locomotive Railway Carriage & Wagon Review* (1938), 274–8.

flooding. So far as they affect railways, floods come in two principal types: total inundations by swollen rivers or exceptional tides, and flash floods which damage bridges and other structures.

Over the night of 31 January and 1 February 1953, a spring tide combined with an onshore gale to break through sea defences and in East Anglia 145 miles of railway were either flooded or cut off. Floods up to 10 ft deep stranded trains, inundated tracks, washed away embankments, and flooded stations, marshalling yards, motive power depots, and rail-connected industries. For their gallantry that night, four railwaymen were awarded the BEM. Locations particularly badly affected included King's Lynn, Yarmouth, Felixstowe, Harwich, and the *London Tilbury & Southend line in three places. Locomotives and rolling stock were isolated by floods, and train services had to be diverted or truncated. Clearing up and repairs took several weeks.

It was not the first time that certain sections of that line had been flooded: the Brightlingsea branch, for instance, had been flooded by a high tide in 1897, and again in 1903 and 1928. The LTSR was flooded again in September 1958, but on that occasion Southern Region lines bore the brunt of violent thunderstorms accompanied by torrential rain. The resulting earthslips blocked one or both tracks at 39 places in the London Central and Eastern Districts; Clock House station, Beckenham, was under 2 ft of water.

The Dawlish–Teignmouth coastal section of the *Great Western is particularly vulnerable; in 1986 it was closed for five days. As recently as December 1994 *Glasgow Central Low Level station was inundated: the water reached to tops of the windows of a train, and closed the line for nine months.

Probably the earliest serious accident caused by a washout occurred in 1846, when the River Medway carried away a timber bridge; the locomotive and leading wagons of a *South Eastern Railway freight train plunged into the gap. A particularly unlucky accident of this type occurred at Carrbridge, *Highland Railway, in 1914, when the Baddengorm Burn rose in spate following a cloudburst. A road bridge collapsed, forming a dam which eventually gave way to send a wall of floodwater down on the railway bridge. This subsided sufficiently to derail a Glasgow–Inverness train, and then collapsed completely beneath it.

In 1948 torrential rain in the Lammermuir Hills sent floods sweeping down on the *East Coast main line. Between Dunbar and Berwick seven bridges were washed away, three large landslips affected the track, and there was much minor damage. By a feat of engineering, the line was reopened in less than three months, but meanwhile secondary lines such as the Border Counties and the Kelso branch found themselves carrying diverted main-line trains.

Fortunately no trains had been directly involved in the disaster. A Shrewsbury–Swansea train in 1987 was less lucky: Glanrhyd bridge over the River Tywi had been damaged by a raging flood and collapsed under the train, leading, sadly, to four deaths.

In 1989 part of the railway bridge over the River Ness at Inverness was swept away during a flood, isolating the lines to Kyle of Lochalsh and Wick. It was eventually replaced, but on at least two occasions flood damage has prompted complete closure of lines. The *narrow-gauge Corris Railway was closed in 1948 after the flooded River Dovey had eroded an embankment up to the track. Closure of the Ruabon–Dolgellau line had been announced for January 1965, but flood damage including a breach rendered the Llangollen–Bala Junction section unusable in December previously, and it was not reopened.

See also ACCIDENTS. PJGR

L. T. C. Rolt, *Red for Danger* (1955), ch. 4; East Coast floods: H. E. P. Grieve, *The Great Tide* (1959), and G. F. Fiennes, 'BR and the East Coast Floods of 1953', in M. Harris (ed.), *Railway World Annual 1982* (1981); Dunbar and Berwick: O. S. Nock, *Scottish Railways* (1950), 98–101; RM, 104 (1958), 738, 746–50.

flower traffic. This was a particularly welcome branch of the railways' business: a luxury trade, commanding high prices, the goods themselves light and arriving from the growers already packed, their conveyance calling for no specially constructed vehicles. The traffic came chiefly from the Channel Islands and Cornwall.

There was a profitable trade in Guernsey lilies and in carnations carried to England throughout the summer by the normal *shipping services and the *Great Western and *London & South Western Railways. It maintained itself steadily, though interrupted during the wars, until the 1970s, when the greater part of it went by air.

The Cornish flower traffic began to become important in the 1880s. The narcissus and other spring flowers were grown chiefly in the Scilly Islands and shipped across to Penzance, going on to Covent Garden market in London by the night mail train. As many as 100 tons were dispatched in 1887. In 1901–5 the tonnage each year was over 700. The traffic also included lilies, gladioli, irises, and wallflowers. No other method of transport then available could have handled it satisfactorily.   JS

F. F. Dalley, *The Channel Islands: A Guide* (1860), 241–4; Acworth, 287–8; *VCH Cornwall*, i (1906), 579–80; J. H. Lucking, *The Great Western at Weymouth* (1971).

flying junction, see JUNCTIONS.

fog (and falling *snow, as for most purposes the impact and implications were the same) was, until recent years, the single greatest impediment to the safe and expeditious working of the railway. Most obviously, fog prevented drivers seeing the arms of semaphore signals, while the oil lamps in the signals were no match for it either, and in the worst fogs the lights might be visible for only a few yards. While city 'smogs' (the combined effect of fog and the smoke from a myriad chimneys) were the worst, natural fogs, mists, and low cloud could (and still do) also reduce visibility to a few yards. Fog obliterated landmarks and the surroundings, and deadened sound. Most railwaymen could ascertain their location at night by the sounds of the trains on the track: a useful aid in observing the signals and regulating the speed of their trains. In fog and snow these aids disappeared. Things felt quite different and it was easy to become lost. Some fogs were so thick that even when a train was standing at a signal the arm could not be seen and the crew might have to climb the post to see its indication.

In these circumstances the need to ensure that trains were kept apart, and that the drivers were aware of the location and aspect of the distant signals (see SIGNALLING), took on even greater importance. Fog signalmen, or 'fogmen', were therefore employed at distant signals to supplement them. They also attended at certain stop signals and other locations to suit circumstances. The fog signalmen had flags and lamps for giving hand signals to passing trains, as well as detonators. These were invented by E. A. Cowper in 1841 and consisted of flat disc-shaped metal boxes containing a small explosive charge. They were fixed to the rail by soft metal straps a short distance before the signal. The detonator was left on the rail while the signal was at danger and removed when it showed clear. A train, as it passed over the detonator, exploded it, alerting the driver to his location and the fact that the signal was at danger. Placing the detonator before the signal gave the driver an opportunity to try to see it, and any handsignal from the fogman.

Without fog signalmen it was easy for drivers to miss the signals. As a precaution, if there was no fogman, the signalman could not accept a train until both his section and the section ahead (or a similar arrangement) were clear. This effectively gave a double space ('double block') between trains. Well-defined rules were made for calling out fogmen and providing equipment and relief. At a fog post there was usually a small hut and brazier for the men. Fogmen were normally platelayers, and some were allocated cottages specially built near to their designated fog post. At difficult or busy locations fogmen were also employed as ground-men

to pass messages to signalmen and confirm positions of trains.

Fog working was clearly very expensive, and if it persisted (city fogs could last for days or even weeks) would play havoc with the timetable. Almost every activity was affected; many operations had to be done differently and took much longer. Even with all the fogmen in place, trains had to proceed cautiously and late running was endemic. Line capacity also dropped, leading to congestion and further delay. On many lines, particularly in busy commuter areas, special fog timetables were available. Ordinary freight trains would be cancelled and the number of passenger trains reduced to a level that fitted the circumstances. Prolonged fog created a massive backlog of freight traffic, as well as maintenance work.

A number of mechanical devices such as Clayton's, Pinder's, and Woodhead fog machines were invented to assist the fogmen in placing detonators on the rail. They also allowed the detonators to be placed from some distance away, reducing the danger to fogmen in crossing tracks. They gave a quicker response and enabled one man to cover several signals. In some cases miniature repeaters of the signal arms were provided adjacent to the fog post.

The introduction of the day colour-light signal, with a beam that penetrated fog, allowed exemption from the requirement to have a fogman in attendance. This, together with the clearer light, encouraged companies to provide colour-light distant signals on main lines. The introduction of Automatic Train Control and the *Automatic Warning System also helped.

The Clean Air Act ensured that there were no more great city fogs after the late 1960s. Together with progress in colour-light signalling, this has much reduced the impact of fog on railway operations. The rules and regulations have consequently been much simplified in recent years.

See also ACCIDENTS.   RDF

M. Taylor, *Railway Signalling* (1949).

Folkestone, see PORTS AND DOCKS.

food and drink traffic. A vital function of the railways was to keep the growing urban populations supplied with fresh *perishable foods, particularly *fish, *fruit and vegetables, *meat, and *milk, thereby contributing to the improved diet and health of the nation. By the late 19th century this included large-scale distribution of imported food from the ports. Until World War I the main supplies of eggs came from Russia and Germany, at first through *Hartlepool docks and later through *Hull and *London. Irish butter was brought in through Holyhead by *London & North Western Railway ships from at least the 1880s. In 1905 the *Lancashire & Yorkshire Railway introduced a Copenhagen–Goole service with refrigerated vessels for importing Danish dairy produce and bacon; it continued, except for the war years, as a railway-operated service until 1965. Both companies had sizeable fleets of butter vans for onward distribution of these traffics.

The growth of the railway network led to more uniformity in the availability and price of food. Food manufacturers could now supply the nation, not just a local or regional market. Old-established firms which moved into larger factories with their own private *sidings included J. & J. Colman at *Norwich (1854), Huntley & Palmer at Reading (1873), Cadbury Brothers at Bournville (1884), and Rowntree & Co. at *York (1895). New enterprises established on rail-connected sites included the sugar refineries of Henry Tate & Sons and Abram Lyle & Sons at Silvertown, east London (1878 and 1883), and the preserves factories of Chivers & Sons at Histon, Cambridgeshire (1875), James Keiller & Sons at Silvertown (c.1880), and Wilkin & Sons at Tiptree, Essex (1885). Notable 20th-century examples were J. Lyons & Co. at Greenford (1923), H. J. Heinz & Co. at Willesden (1925)—both in west London—and the Kellogg Company on the Barton Dock Estate, *Manchester (1938).

The railways were similarly instrumental in the establishment of the large centralized manufacturing units of the English and Scottish Co-operative Wholesale Societies. These included a lard refinery and egg warehouse at West Hartlepool, a preserves, pickles, and vinegar factory at Middleton Junction, a margarine works at Irlam—both near Manchester—and a preserves factory at Reading, each with its own sidings.

The impact of the railways on the long-established brewing industry was mixed. Nowhere was there a more dramatic demonstration of how the railways could expand markets than at Burton-on-Trent, where production of ale increased 50-fold between 1840 and 1900. The industry grew to take over most of the town centre, which was crisscrossed by a complex network of branch lines and private railways serving the many breweries and maltings. Two of Burton's brewers, Bass & Co. and Allsopp & Sons, together with Arthur Guinness & Son of Dublin, distributed their products nationally. There were a further 30 or so brewers that used the railways to expand into firms of regional significance. One of the first was Ind Coope & Co., which had a siding laid into its Romford brewery in 1853, primarily to serve the London market. In 1881 Eldridge Pope & Co. moved its Dorchester brewery to a site by the *London & South Western Railway's station and began a policy of buying public houses that could easily be served by train. But most breweries remained as local businesses; even the majority of the 150 with private sidings probably only used them for receiving coal and raw materials (see AGRICULTURAL TRAFFIC; HOP-PICKERS' TRAINS).

The growth of malt whisky production in the Highlands into a modern industry followed the opening of the *Great North of Scotland Railway, on which most distilleries were dependent for their coal and barley and for transporting casks of whisky to the blending houses in the Scottish Lowlands.

The limited available statistics suggest that the total traffic in manufactured foodstuffs carried by the railways in 1920 exceeded 6 million tons. Beer, wines, and spirits added another 2¼ million tons. Losses to road competition appear to have been relatively light until the 1950s; indeed, new traffics such as ice-cream and frozen foods in highly insu-

lated *containers were still being won. But by the late 1960s most forwarders had gone over entirely to road, although some traffic was transferred to *Freightliner and Speedlink services, whose regular customers included Rowntrees, Campbells Soups, Guinness, and Spillers Petfoods.   GAB

VR, 351–4; R. Scola, Feeding the Victorian City: The Food Supply of Manchester 1770–1870 (1992); T. R. Gourvish and R. G. Wilson, The British Brewing Industry 1830–1980 (1993); I. P. Peaty, Brewery Railways (1985).

footwarmers, see TRAIN HEATING.

Forbes, James Staats (1823–1904), manager and chairman. Forbes trained as an engineering draughtsman. He joined the *Great Western Railway in 1840, becoming goods superintendent at Paddington. Next he became manager of the Dutch Rhenish Railway, and it was claimed that his continental experience gave him an insight 'into methods of railway management less purely traditional than in this country'. In 1861 he was appointed general manager of the *London Chatham & Dover Railway. When the company became bankrupt in 1866, he became joint manager and receiver. He joined the board in 1871 and in 1874 became chairman. For nearly 25 years he was involved in bitter competition with the *South Eastern Railway, led by Sir Edward *Watkin. In 1870 he became part-time managing director of the *Metropolitan District Railway, and was chairman from 1872 until 1901. He was also chairman of two smaller railways and held positions in electricity, finance, and telephone companies. By 1884 he was reported to be earning £15,000 a year. A man of taste and discernment, he sometimes lacked conviction; this he made up for with a charm and eloquence which made him a shrewd negotiator. He left £135,367.   EC

Obituaries: The Times and Railway Times (Apr. 1904); A. Gray, London Chatham & Dover Railway (1984).

Forth Railway Bridge. The first railway crossing of the Firth of Forth near its mouth was Thomas *Bouch's successful train-*ferry (1850) between Granton and Burntisland. This was followed in the 1860s and 1870s by several proposals for fixed bridges, culminating in Bouch's stiffened suspension bridge on which William *Arrol started work in 1878. Construction was halted when Bouch's Tay Bridge collapsed in 1879 (see BRIDGES AND VIADUCTS) but it was not until January 1881, some time after the publication of the enquiry report, that his Forth Bridge scheme was finally abandoned. Visually, few are likely to mourn its loss.

Fresh proposals were invited and in September 1881 Sir John *Fowler and Benjamin *Baker were instructed to complete their proposed design based on three double cantilevers with suspended spans between. This was developed into the present widely recognized bridge with main spans of 1,700 ft—greater at the time than any other bridge in the world. It appears to have been almost wholly Baker's idea and it was he who took the lead on the design of the project until its completion, although Fowler was responsible for the complex system of approach railways.

The shift from a stiffened suspension bridge to rigid framing was an understandable reaction to the Tay Bridge collapse, although the wind force of 56 lb per sq ft stipulated by the Board of *Trade may now seem excessive. Above all, the bridge needed to be stiff and to feel stiff. It is often said that the design of the Forth Bridge was over-cautious. However, there were many novel features apart from its vast scale. The form alone was unusual, even if not totally without precedent. It was the first major, if not the first, British bridge to be built in steel, rather than in wrought iron, a change made possible by the comparatively recent perfecting of the open-hearth process which produced much more reliable steel than the Bessemer one. The design stresses for steel, 7.5 tons per sq in, rather than the Board of Trade's 6.5 tons per sq in, were justified by quality control. The vast tubular struts—actually quite slender—needed novel thinking, as did the allowance for thermal movement without loss of rigidity. Testing, of both materials and wind pressure, was paramount.

On the construction side, great credit is due to William Arrol, the *contractor, not only as an organizer but as an extremely creative designer of special plant for rapid but controlled construction. Once the foundations (caissons made on the site and sunk, using compressed air) were finished in 1886, erection of the steelwork started and in a little over three years the bridge—fully tested—was opened by the Prince of Wales on 4 March 1890.

The bridge was owned by a consortium of the *North British, *Great Northern, *North Eastern, and *Midland Railways, called the Forth Bridge Company, which maintained the structure. The NBR worked and maintained the railway.

Looked at broadly, the Forth Railway Bridge, like the *Britannia Bridge, was a landmark in the development of scientific thinking and control on bridges. Never again could wind and lateral stability be left to intuitive judgement, nor could workmanship be left solely to the skill and integrity of contractors.   RJMS
    W. Westhofen, *The Forth Bridge* (1989), reproduced from *Engineering* (1890); R. Paxton (ed.), *100 Years of the Forth Bridge* (1990).

Fowler, Sir Henry (1870–1938), mechanical engineer. Son of an Evesham cabinet-maker, Fowler was CME of the *Midland Railway in 1909–22, and the *London Midland & Scottish Railway in 1925–30. He was knighted for wartime services.

Fowler made a major contribution to improved production methods in railway and government workshops, and to metallurgical improvements in locomotives and rolling stock. Apprenticed under *Aspinall at the *Lancashire & Yorkshire Railway's Horwich works, he joined the MR in 1900, becoming assistant works manager, *Derby, in 1905, and works manager in 1907.

On the formation of the LMS he was deputy CME to George *Hughes. The integration of six companies' design, building, and repair practices was extremely difficult, at which he was not really successful. He oversaw early, partially successful attempts at line-production in locomotive repairs aimed at reducing overhaul time, and a standardization policy that eliminated small locomotive classes and

those which were costly to maintain. Fowler developed Hughes' proposals for more powerful 4-6-2 and 2-8-2 passenger and freight engines as four-cylinder compounds (see TRACTION, STEAM), using his MR experience, but the designs were rejected by the operating department partly because larger turntables would be needed. His Royal Scot class 4-6-0s built in 1927–30 were adequate, but were rebuilt by his successor *Stanier.

In 1931–3 he was adviser to the vice-president (research) of the LMS and authorized the purchase of prototype diesel shunting locomotives (see TRACTION, DIESEL), later introduced on a large scale.   GWC
    Jnl Inst. Loco. Engineers, 28 (1938), 606–8; H. A. V. Bulleid, *Master Builders of Steam* (1963); E. S. Cox, *Locomotive Panorama*, i (1965).

Fowler, Sir John (1817–98), engineer. Son of a Sheffield land surveyor, he worked with the engineers J. T. Leather and J. U. *Rastrick before becoming engineer of the Stockton & Hartlepool Railway in 1841, and later general manager. He and T. E. *Harrison of the *North Eastern Railway were the only leading Victorian engineers with practical experience of running railways.

His early work was on railways in Yorkshire and Lincolnshire, including lines which became part of the Manchester Sheffield & Lincolnshire Railway (see GREAT CENTRAL) and the *Great Northern. He moved to London in 1844, and in 1852 became engineer of the Oxford Worcester & Wolverhampton Railway (see WEST MIDLAND RAILWAY). He became engineer for the *Metropolitan and *Metropolitan District Railways, beginning in 1853 and overcoming great difficulties. Fowler continued as engineer or consultant for almost all the *London underground railways built before his death. He was responsible for very many railway schemes at home and abroad, was consultant to the *Great Western after the death of *Brunel (whom he greatly admired), and to the GNR, *Cheshire Lines, and *Highland Railway. He was consulted about major termini like *Liverpool Central and *Glasgow St Enoch, and was engineer for Grosvenor Bridge and *Victoria station in London, including the graceful arched *trainshed on the 'Chatham' side.

As a bridge engineer, his most notable works were Torksey Bridge (1849–50); the first *concrete railway bridge, on the Metropolitan District (1867–8); and above all the *Forth Railway Bridge, the last with Sir Benjamin *Baker. It was the culmination of 30 years' work on long-span bridge design. A cultivated man with a collection of pictures, he was considered grasping in money matters. He bought two estates in Ross-shire, and left £179,000. He was president, ICE, 1866–7, and was knighted in 1885.   MMC and JS
    DBB; *DNB*; T. MacKay, *Life of Sir John Fowler, Engineer* (1890); M. M. Chrimes, 'Sir John Fowler', *PICE*, 135 (1899), 328–37; *PICE*, 97 (1993), 135–43.

Fox, Sir Charles (1810–74); **Sir Charles Douglas** (1840–1921); **Sir Francis** (1844–1927), engineers. Charles Fox abandoned a family medical tradition to become a pupil of John Ericsson at the age of 19, working on the *Novelty* engine for the *Rainhill trials. He then joined Robert *Stephenson's staff.

In 1838 Fox became a partner in Joseph Bramah's Smethwick ironworks, from 1841 known as Fox Henderson & Co. The firm became leading structural ironwork contractors, also supplying railway equipment and Fox's patent switches. In addition to the Crystal Palace, their works included station roofs at *Birmingham New Street and *Paddington, and major iron bridges such as Rochester, and Newark Dyke. The firm were also railway *contractors, building lines in France, Germany, and Denmark. Their most important in Britain was the East Kent (1852) (see LONDON CHATHAM & DOVER RAILWAY).

In 1856 the company went bankrupt. Fox set up as a consultant, taking his sons into the practice, Douglas in 1860 and Francis in 1861. Major works included the Battersea railway approach to London, *Mersey Railway tunnel (with Sir James *Brunlees), *Liverpool Overhead Railway, and the southern extension of the *Great Central Railway. They were engineers for the Charing Cross–Hampstead, and the *Great Northern & City underground railways in London.

Overseas, Sir Charles was a successful advocate of economical methods of construction in the colonies. The practice designed lines in Queensland, Canada, South America, and, particularly, in southern and central Africa.   MMC

DNB; Charles: *PICE*, 39 (1875), 264–6; Douglas: *PICE*, 213 (1921), 416–21; F. Fox, *River, Road and Rail* (1904); F. Fox, *Sixty-Three Years of Engineering* (1924).

fox hunting. England's hunting men did not view the arrival of the railways with any enthusiasm: how could one chase a fox with iron tracks criss-crossing the fields at every turn? But the warnings of sporting journalists *Nimrod* and *Druid* were not borne out. Far from it: the rail revolution greatly extended the appeal of the chase, both socially and geographically, significantly altering both the composition and the organization of the local hunts and influencing the way in which the sport was conducted. By using the train a man could now take his own horse to hunt much further afield.

Inevitably the appearance of the rail horsebox, allowing a man to breakfast in London and hunt the same day in Leicestershire, had a huge impact on the sport. A stay in a country house lasted now not for a month but for a long weekend, with hunting on Saturday and Monday if one was lucky. And as more country houses came within the traveller's orbit, so did more hunts. This appealed not only to those, such as Lord George Bentinck, who already hunted and now found it easier to mix work with pleasure, but also to those among the middle class, now granted their first chance to hunt.

This middle-class influx was not always welcome in the shires. As well as the ambitious young barristers depicted by Anthony Trollope, the railways brought R. S. Surtees' horse-dealing crook, Mr Sponge, and countless vulgarians intent on climbing the social ladder through their hunting exploits. The honest, if rough and ready, Jorrocks was

eclipsed by the crass Mr Jawleyford. Within a few years of the arrival of the railways some hunts, such as the Quorn, took to emphasizing their social exclusiveness.

This change in the composition of a hunt inevitably influenced its organization. The railways did indeed presage the end of the private, proprietorial hunt, such as that in the feudal grip of Surtees' Duke of Tergiversation, but they did not do so alone. Hunting was an expensive business—a proprietor would expect to pay £4,000–6,000 a year to maintain a top-flight hunt, and so few could afford proprietorship. In addition, 'London' huntsmen, like Trollope, preferred the relative independence of the 'subscription' hunt where hunters paid for their sport as they enjoyed it, and were thus under no obligations.

Popularity brought to hunting other problems, the most pressing of which was the scarcity of foxes, hence the seriousness with which vulpicide was treated. The nature of the sport changed too. Hunting visits were, although more frequent and varied, shorter. Runs thus became briefer and much faster, a development which refinements in the breed of both horse and hound assisted.

Trains, therefore, stimulated a great interest in hunting. However, the sport could not, or would not, always enjoy its new-found popularity, and the almost defiantly upper-class image of some hunts was partly a reaction to the democratizing effects of steam. But a startling new interest in the sport had been created. Far from destroying the nation's hunts, the railways gave them a whole new lease of life.

ECE

R. Carr, *English Foxhunting* (1976); K. and F. Lawley, *The Racing Life of Lord George Bentinck* (1892); R. S. Surtees, *Mr Sponge's Sporting Tour* (1852), *Mr Facey Romford's Hounds* (1865).

Francis, John (?–?), writer. Little is known of his life. He was evidently not the same man as John C. Francis, publisher of the *Athenaeum*. He worked for the Bank of England, 1835–76, becoming chief accountant, and producing a *History* in 1847, followed by *Chronicles and Characters of the Stock Exchange* (1849) and in 1851 by a *History of the English Railway; Its Social Relations and Revelations, 1820–45*, its preface indicating an intention of continuing it down to 1851, which remained unfulfilled.

The *History of the English Railway* is a spirited piece of writing, easily enjoyed. It is dedicated to G. C. *Glyn, chairman of the *London & North Western company, and the promoters and directors of railways make a large figure in it. The treatment of *Hudson, written after his fall, is perceptive and, on the whole, just. The book remains a good reflector of the excitement aroused by the railways' early expansion.   JS

M. Robbins, *Points and Signals* (1967), 52–5.

fraud, see CRIME.

freight depots, see STATIONS, GOODS.

Freightliner was the brand-name adopted for the *container 'liner train' concept, first expounded in the *Beeching Report, that sought to bring the economies of trainload operation to wagonload-size consignments. The 75-mph container train had been developed, first in the London–Glasgow 'Condor' service (1959) and then in the London–Manchester 'Speedfreight' service (1963), as a means of competing for the traffic of customers without private *sidings; but, by eliminating the delays and costs of *shunting individual wagons and double-handling of their loads, Beeching saw it also as a way of turning much of the unprofitable wagonload traffic into a viable business.

The first Freightliner service began in 1965. Four years later the network had grown to 140 trains per day serving 33 terminals, with *Sealink container ship services extending it to Belfast, Dublin, and Zeebrugge. In 1969 the enterprise was vested in Freightliners Ltd, initially a subsidiary of the new National Freight Corporation but returned to *British Rail ownership in 1978.

With great foresight Freightliner had been designed around the newly recommended international standard container dimensions. Thus, when container ships began to replace conventional deep-sea cargo vessels from 1968, it was destined to be a major carrier of containers to and from the deep-sea *ports: principally *Southampton, Tilbury, Felixstowe, and *Liverpool. In fact this soon proved to be its premier business. As *road transport prices fell, Freightliner became less competitive for domestic traffic involving two sets of road–rail transfer costs. The company reached its zenith in 1983 when it carried the equivalent of 968,000 20-ft containers; since then there has been some decline in the size of both network and traffic.   GAB

British Railways Board, *The Re-Shaping of British Railways* (the Beeching Report) (1963), 42–4, 142–8; Gourvish, 491–3, 544–7; M. J. Collins, *Freightliner* (1991).

freight traffic. The early trunk railways took on the commercial practices of road and *canal transport, including use of the term 'goods', whereas American railroads adopted the shipping term 'freight'. The American usage arrived in Britain in the early 1900s and since 1948 it has predominated.

At first some of the new railway companies relied partly or wholly on established road carriers such as Pickford & Co. to organize their goods business and provide handling, collection, delivery, and documentation services. By the mid-1850s the railways were generally managing the business themselves, although the carriers might be retained as cartage agents.

Goods traffic developed only slowly until the *Railway Clearing House was established to facilitate through carriage over more than one railway. Goods revenue did not overtake passenger revenue until 1852, but from the 1860s until 1965 it was 30–50 per cent higher. Annual carryings grew to 367 million tons in 1913 and probably 400 million in World War I. Since then, except for a respite during World War II, there has been a generally downward trend under the effects of competition from *road transport and the decline of the basic industries that were the railways' largest customers; 300 million tons were last carried in 1943 and 200 million in 1970. In 1993–4 carryings were almost down to 100 million tonnes (metric tonnes had been

adopted in 1975), less than by pipeline, reflecting the change from coal to oil and gas for electricity generation. By then freight revenue was only one quarter of passenger revenue. The railway's freight 'workload', as measured in ton-miles, has fallen rather less dramatically; indeed it was higher in the years 1946–57 than in any of the inter-war years, reaching a peak of 22.9 billion ton-miles in 1951, but has since fallen below 9 billion.

Goods traffic was divided into 'full loads' (consignments occupying complete *wagons) and 'smalls' or 'sundries'; the latter were quite distinct from *parcels, which were charged at a higher rate and carried by passenger train. Where possible sundries were consolidated into 'mixed loads', all consigned to the same station but for several consignees. Alternatively they were sent to an intermediate depot, where they were sorted and transhipped into consolidated loads for the destination stations. Several small stations on the same line might share a 'road van' or 'road box' ('road' here meaning a railway line or route, not a highway); each station unloaded and loaded its traffic as the van passed through on the daily local goods train. In 1901 the *London & North Western Railway opened a central transhipment shed at *Crewe, which received and despatched a through van or road van daily from and to every other goods station on its system. This is an early example of a 'hub-and-spoke' distribution system, now widely used by air-cargo carriers.

At each end of the journey goods might be consigned direct from or to a private *siding in the customer's premises; or from or to a station or public siding with the customer arranging handling and cartage; or they might be collected and/or delivered by railway, or railway agent's, cartage (see FREIGHT TRAFFIC RATES). At many stations the railways also offered warehousing (see GOODS SHEDS).

Carriage of goods was regulated by an elaborate system of documentation and checking, designed to prevent loss of goods, charging errors, and dishonest dealing by customers and railway employees, to facilitate collection of charges and inter-railway financial settlements, and to provide statistical data. The consignment note, on which the sender declared the nature and weight of the goods, was the basis of the contract of carriage and was retained by the forwarding station. The information was transcribed to the waybill, on which were added the charges and whether paid by the sender or to be paid by the consignee. Originally this accompanied the goods, but was later called the invoice and sent ahead by passenger train. The route and destination were displayed on the wagon for the information of *shunters and *guards. These primary documents were supplemented by sundry other documents and account books at both forwarding and receiving stations, and by abstracts, summaries, and returns submitted to the company's audit office and the *Railway Clearing House.

In the days of horse-drawn road transport the railways needed to provide a cartage service at most goods stations. Where there was sufficient regular work, railway companies would either employ a large carrier as sub-contractor or establish their own cartage service. Elsewhere a local carrier was hired as required. Some of the contract carriers were eventually bought out: the LNWR took over *Chaplin & Horne in 1878; Pickford & Co., the large Scottish carrier Wordie & Co., and several others were purchased in the 1930s.

The *Lancashire & Yorkshire Railway used a steam lorry for cartage of goods as early as 1900 and several railways experimented with steam, petrol, and electric vehicles before 1914. In 1922 the railways already owned 1,947 motor vehicles for cartage work, more than half with the LNWR, alongside 18,000 horses. By then they were beginning to be reliable enough to be employed on 'zonal' collection and delivery over a much wider radius, allowing concentration of sundries services on fewer stations. Motor lorries also enabled the introduction from 1926 of door-to-door *container services. The Karrier Cob three-wheel tractor and the similar Scammell Mechanical Horse, introduced in 1930–3, were specifically designed for mechanization of railway cartage work in towns, their manœuvrability being ideal for narrow streets and awkward premises. In 1948 *British Railways inherited nearly 6,000 of them, and subsequently bought 7,500 of the post-war Scammell Scarab design.

Unless there were enough to make up a full trainload, the loaded wagons were collected and delivered by a pick-up goods train or local 'trip' working, which started and terminated at the nearest *marshalling yard, visiting all the stations and sidings along its route to shunt, detach, and attach wagons as required. At the marshalling yard the wagons were formed into a trunk train to take them forward to the yard nearest their destination, or perhaps in stages via one or more intermediate yards along the appropriate route. If they had to pass from one railway to another, they were generally handed over at an exchange yard near the inter-company boundary. Transfer trips operated frequently between the various companies' yards encircling London and other major cities. Unless the sender specified a route, the sending railway generally selected the one that kept the traffic on its own lines for the longest distance, giving it the maximum share of the total charge.

Long-distance express trains for *perishable goods, running at passenger train speeds, evolved from the early practice of attaching vans to passenger trains; by the 1880s they had continuous *brakes. Fitting of automatic brakes to other wagons did not begin until the early 1900s, when it became necessary to run fewer, but heavier and faster, goods trains to overcome track capacity constraints on the main lines. A 'fitted head' of braked wagons, marshalled behind the engine, provided the extra braking power to match the higher tractive power of the new goods engines then being built. The first train and traffic *control offices were also established at this period to improve freight train working in congested districts.

Protection of the general merchandise business against road competition was the main impetus for service improvements between the wars. The number of fully- and partially-braked, long-distance, fast freight trains, running at average speeds of 35–50 mph, steadily increased, the aim being to provide overnight transits wherever practicable. By

the 1930s 72 per cent of wagonload goods and 64 per cent of 'smalls' were recorded as arriving on the next day, with only 1 per cent taking more than 3 days. There were also commercial initiatives such as the 'Green Arrow' registered transit service, instituted in 1928, which monitored the progress of registered consignments to ensure delivery by the quoted time. A comprehensive distribution service was offered to manufacturers of consumer products, including warehousing, documentation, and delivery to retailers in road vehicles painted in the customer's livery.

In World War II, even more than in the first, the railways were required to undertake a greatly increased workload: ton-mileage in 1943 and 1944 was one third higher than in the best of the preceding years. At the end, the railways emerged in a very run-down condition, physically and financially (see PROFITABILITY). Recovery was slow, and it was not until 1951 that fast freight train services were reinstated to their pre-war level; horse-drawn cartage did not disappear until 1959.

The newly *nationalized BR generally pursued its predecessors' freight development policies that had been left unfinished in 1939. However, they faced two new problems: shortages and increasing costs of labour; and the post-war trend of locating industrial estates distant from the railway. So there was a new emphasis on mechanical handling and road–rail transfer techniques: pallets (adopted surprisingly slowly by customers), fork-lift trucks, and pallet vans; specialized containers, e.g. for liquids; covered hopper wagons for bulk traffics such as grain; pressure-discharge containers and wagons for bulk powders such as cement; conveyors, electric tugs, and mobile cranes for sundries and parcels depots; and the Roadrailer (see ROAD-RAIL VEHICLES). The new equipment was introduced at new or modernized 'concentration' depots, each of which replaced many small terminals.

The 1957 Merchandise Charges Scheme, which was the first step towards giving BR freedom to negotiate contract terms and rates with customers, gave a boost to commercial innovation. An Export Express Service, with guaranteed delivery deadlines at *ports, was inaugurated in the same year, followed by assured overnight services for domestic traffic. *Named express freight trains were introduced in 1959–60, resurrecting a *Great Western Railway practice of the 1930s. New traffics attracted to rail included motor cars and frozen foods. By 1959–60 the progress that had been achieved in terms of modernization of equipment, service improvements, and commercial successes was beginning to look impressive; it seemed that at last the railways were winning back. Behind the scenes, however, results from traffic-costing studies were revealing that wagonload general merchandise traffic, other than between private sidings, and sundries were seriously loss-making.

The 1963 *Beeching Report announced a significant change of direction. The strategy was now to concentrate on 'doing what the railways can do best': by using BR's new commercial freedom to induce customers to consign their traffic in trainloads rather than wagonloads; by concentrating station and public siding traffics on many fewer concentration depots; by developing traffic through private sidings; and by creating what became known as *Freightliner services to bring the benefits of trainload operation to wagonload and 'groupage' (consolidated sundries) traffics.

Conversion of wagonload movements into trainloads proceeded rapidly, the first 'company train' contracts being announced in 1963. By 1972 two-thirds of freight tonnage was moved in trainloads. Except for cars and inter-factory supplies of automotive components, the commodities that moved in sufficient volumes to fill a train were largely bulk goods: petroleum products and chemicals (see DANGEROUS GOODS), fertilizer (see AGRICULTURAL TRAFFIC), *stone, china *clay, iron ore and other industrial *minerals, *cement, inter-factory movements of steel ingots and billets (see IRON AND STEEL INDUSTRY), and, of course, *coal (see also MERRY-GO-ROUND). Even these might only justify a once- or twice-weekly train.

The new trainload contracts were often associated with the introduction of the new generation of high-capacity wagons that began to appear in 1963 in response to major changes in BR's technical standards. In 1962 the wagon axle-load limit was raised from 17½ to 22½ tons (increased in 1966 to 25 tons on specific routes). In 1956 BR had decided to start moving towards a fully vacuum brake-fitted regime, but then in 1963 announced that the more effective air brake was to be adopted for the new trainload services, allowing higher speeds for heavy trains: 60 mph became the normal maximum, increased to 75 mph when the axle-load did not exceed 20 tons as on Freightliner and car-carrying trains. In 1948 only tank wagons had been excluded from the nationalization of *privately owned wagons, but it now became the practice for all customers requiring specialized wagons (except the nationalized coal, electricity, and steel industries) to buy or lease their own.

All these innovations combined to transform the efficiency and economics of bulk freight transport, which, with a few isolated exceptions, had hitherto changed little from 19th-century methods. Considerable new business was generated. The new style of trainload operation was competitive with road even over short distances. It became economical to transport waste fly-ash from power stations and domestic waste from major conurbations for land reclamation. In the 1980s more powerful diesel locomotives allowed further cost reduction by increasing trailing loads from, typically, 1,000 tonnes to 2,000 or, in some instances, 4,000–5,000 tonnes.

Opening of concentration depots for sundries, coal, and steel, and closure of traditional goods *stations also proceeded apace. In 1962 there were 5,200 BR freight terminals (down from 6,400 in 1948), 950 of them handling sundries traffic. By 1968 there were fewer than 1,000; by 1975 fewer than 500. Much traffic was shed in the process, either by withdrawal of facilities or by increasing rates to a viable but uncompetitive level. There was a parallel decline in the number of private sidings from 5,900 to 2,000. A separately managed Sundries Division was created in 1966, which was

renamed National Carriers Ltd and vested in the new National Freight Corporation on 1 January 1969. BR's entire cartage fleet of 9,600 motor vehicles and 23,100 trailers was taken over by NCL, those required for the parcels and full-load goods businesses being leased back to BR.

Progress was made towards answering the question left open in the Beeching Report: what to do with the residual wagonload flows between private sidings too small for conversion to trainloads. Although there had been some rationalization, many of the pre-1923 traffic routings were still used in 1965. The National Freight Train Plan, implemented in 1966–7, introduced a radical new routing pattern designed to minimize train operating costs and allow closure of many marshalling yards. Yard working was improved by the introduction of an Advance Traffic Information (ATI) system, a precursor of *TOPS, that used teleprinters to transmit train consist information ahead to the next yard.

A strategy gradually emerged for an orderly withdrawal from the old-style wagonload network; and in parallel the development of a limited range of reliable 60 mph overnight services for traffics that could justify investment in modern wagons. The first of the new trains was launched in 1972 and the system, named 'Speedlink' in 1977, grew steadily until 1984 when the last of the old-style services was withdrawn. By then it was carrying 8 million tonnes a year, including *food and drink traffic, *bricks, *timber, paper, and finished steel, as well as the smaller flows of trainload commodities. It also provided services for *European traffic connecting with the Harwich and Dover train ferries (see SHIPPING SERVICES). But profitability proved to be elusive.

BR's overall freight business was unprofitable for the first 30 years, but in 1977 the government announced that no further financial support would be provided for Railfreight, as it was now known, beyond that year; and so it has been, although this was made easier by treating the railway infrastructure as a passenger system and charging Railfreight only as a marginal user. Except for major strikes, trainload profits were sufficient to cover wagonload losses. However, the worsening trend led to the decision to close Speedlink in 1991, although services for European traffic were maintained until superseded by the new *Channel Tunnel freight services.

See also FRUIT AND VEGETABLES TRAFFIC; LIVESTOCK TRAFFIC; MEAT TRAFFIC; SLATE TRAFFIC. GAB

G. L. Turnbull, *Traffic and Transport: An Economic History of Pickfords* (1979); E. Paget-Tomlinson, *The Railway Carriers: The History of Wordie & Co.* (1990); R. T. Munns, *Milk Churns to Merry-Go-Round: A Century of Train Operation* (1986); A. Vaughan, *The Great Western at Work 1921–1939* (1993); British Transport Commission and British Railways Board, *Annual Reports* (1948 onwards).

freight traffic rates. The first concept of a public railway incorporated by Act of Parliament was of merely a special type of highway (not unlike a canal or turnpike road) available to all carriers of goods on payment of a toll. Simple lists of goods, in Acts of Incorporation, specified tolls per ton per mile based on their value and presumed consequent ability to pay. But soon the adoption of locomotive traction involved haulage charges, maximum scales for which, including the toll element, began to be prescribed for each new railway.

The need to quote through rates for traffic between connecting railways, and the huge increase in the variety of goods offered for carriage, obliged the railways to expand the primitive class rates very considerably, and also to introduce another factor: *terminal charges for services such as loading or cartage, expected from a public carrier. These might be performed by the railway company or very often by an established carrying firm such as Pickfords. Rates thus grew into three categories, not necessarily mutually exclusive: private *siding (PS) traffic was from or to a trader's own siding where the railway provided no terminal services; station-to-station (S to S) traffic was from and to a railway goods *station, where the railway might or might not perform all the terminal services; and lastly, collection and delivery (C & D) rates which included cartage from and to a trader's premises.

Rates were subject to variation according to whether the traffic passed in the railway's wagons or those of a private user; there was also a cheaper 'owner's risk' (OR) rate widely available, where the railway was exempt from the liabilities of a public carrier.

In addition to developing their own systems of class rates, usually on similar principles, the need to provide for through traffic led most of the railways as early as 1842 to join in forming the *Railway Clearing House, made a statutory body in 1850. The Clearing House, after much patient work, produced a General Railway Classification which assigned charging classes (originally two for minerals and five for general merchandise) for everything likely to require transport. By 1886 there were 2,753 items listed. The RCH also produced ready reckoners for calculating charges, and mileage tables for ascertaining 'chargeable distance'; also a handbook of all stations with freight facilities, which eventually numbered about 7,000.

The 'class rates' were based upon a combination of value, which assumed ability to pay, and cost elements such as bulk in relation to weight ('loadability'), liability to damage, ease of handling, and so on. Each goods station had not merely the Clearing House publications, but also its own rates book, recording charges peculiar to the owning company. Where there were alternative and competing routes to any destination, the charge for the shorter distance also applied to the longer route. And although charges were always expressed as per ton per mile, an element of 'taper' usually applied over long distances.

Apart from the classification system, and below the maximum class rates, a network of 'exceptional rates' grew up covering important flows of traffic to such an extent that eventually it was calculated that over three-quarters of the total traffic was charged under them. Quotation of these rates played an important part in bargaining with traders and competing with rival railways.

Although it imposed rather rudimentary maximum charging scales in private railway Acts, Parliament passed no general legislation on railway rates for some time. An Act of 1854 required the railways to afford 'reasonable facilities' for forwarding traffic, and to refrain from showing *'undue preference' in quoting rates. It also set up a Railway and Canal *Commission with power to deal with specific grievances of rail users.

By the mid-19th century, however, there was much criticism of the level of railway rates, and in 1888 a new Act required the railways to prepare a classification for government approval. This was done, but the railways, pleading insufficient time to reassess the millions of rates in the rate books, started to impose everywhere the new maximum charges, in Classes A, B, and C for minerals, etc., and 1 to 5 for merchandise traffic. This led to a public outcry and the passing in 1894 of a further Act which in effect froze charges at their previous level except where the railways could prove before the Railway & Canal Commission that increases were justified.

After World War I, with the creation of a Ministry of *Transport, a new policy towards railway rates was adopted in the Railways Act, 1921. For the first time, the level of charges was to be related to profits. The railways, *grouped in four major companies, were allocated a 'standard revenue' (roughly, their 1913 net receipts) and any excess over the 'standard' was to be followed by reductions in charges calculated to absorb 80 per cent of the excess. To earn the 'standard revenue', new 'standard rates' in a fresh set of 21 classes were introduced from 1928; they were mistakenly expected to replace the so-called 'jungle' of exceptional rates. A Railway Rates Tribunal was set up in lieu of the Railway & Canal Commission to administer the new charging policy by authorizing changes in rate levels overall, and also new individual exceptional rates which were more than 40 per cent below the standard.

Due largely to intense road competition (both 'for hire or reward' and 'own account') the 'standard revenue' was never earned and the railways had to continue quoting 'exceptional rates'. In 1933 they obtained parliamentary powers to quote 'agreed charges' under which traders were charged a fixed sum per ton despatched, irrespective of destination. Such schemes, of course, required approval by the Tribunal.

The loss of merchandise traffic to the roads continued, and in 1938 the main-line railways launched a 'Square Deal' campaign for release from all statutory controls over charging. After concessions had been made to meet objections from road haulage interests and traders' organizations such as the *Mansion House Association, the government conceded in principle but World War II intervened in 1939 before anything was done.

Soon after the war ended the railways were *nationalized along with other forms of public transport under a policy of transport integration, to be achieved by guiding traffic to use the most cost-effective mode through charging policy. This required the devising of charges schemes, meant to be based upon scientific traffic costing. Meanwhile the pre-war charges remained in force. But before a Freight Charges Scheme that included road and rail services could be completed, a change of government started both the de-nationalization of road haulage and the step-by-step de-regulation of rail charges.

The Transport Act, 1953, began the process by allowing charges schemes to be, in effect, based on ordinary commercial principles and the objective of integration was dropped. Then, ushering in the *Beeching era on the railways, the Transport Act, 1962, abolished charges schemes completely, allowing the railways to make charges 'as they think fit'. From this time onwards, railway commercial policy, whilst still bearing in mind the need to attract or retain traffic by not quoting rates in excess of 'what the traffic will bear', subordinated this principle to insistence upon covering costs. That meant discarding operations where a profitable rate could not be charged, usually because of the effectiveness of road competition.

Although statutory fixing of rates had lapsed, the advent of government policies for prices and incomes in 1964 led to interference in the shape of ministerial instructions to nationalized industry, such as the railways, not to implement proposed general increases in charges, even where justified by increasing costs. After the abandonment of the prices and incomes policies, market forces were unchallenged.

However, the character of the rail freight business was changing drastically (see FREIGHT TRAFFIC; FREIGHTLINER). Overwhelmingly, from the 1970s onward, freight traffic receipts came from bulk traffic in trainloads—*coal, aggregates, liquids, chemicals—where contract rates (unlike former 'exceptional rates') were unpublished. A return to the position before the 1947 Act, which nationalized the large stock of *private-owner wagons, was that many major customers invested in their own fleets of modern wagons, thereby merely being charged for haulage. *British Rail could find this advantageous in view of severe government restrictions upon their investment in rolling stock, but the loss of receipts from wagon provision in some ways was putting the clock back.   MRB

W. M. Acworth, *The Elements of Railway Economics* (1924 edn.); T. C. Barker and C. I. Savage, *An Economic History of Transport in Britain* (1974 edn.); S. Joy, *The Train that Ran Away* (1973); Gourvish; A. M. Milne, *The Economics of Inland Transport* (1955); British Transport Commission (1948–61), and British Railways Board (1962 onwards), *Annual Reports*.

Freshwater Yarmouth & Newport Railway, see ISLE OF WIGHT RAILWAYS.

fruit and vegetables traffic. The biggest commodity in this group was potatoes—2.2 million tons in 1920. Both the *Great Northern and *Midland Railways established wholesale market premises for potatoes brought from Lincolnshire and the Midlands into their London goods *stations at King's Cross and St Pancras. Similar facilities were also provided in other cities. Even after the main potato traffic had all been lost to road, *British Rail continued to carry seed potatoes from east Scotland to the potato-growing districts of England until the mid-1980s.

Sugar beet traffic was also substantial, but not until the development of the beet sugar industry in the 1920s following wartime shortages of cane sugar. By 1928 18 sugar-beet factories had been opened, mainly in eastern England; rail carryings reached a peak of 1.6 million tons (concentrated into the 4-month season) in 1935. This traffic ceased around 1980.

In 1879 the *Great Eastern Railway built Stratford Market, a rail-connected wholesale fruit and vegetable market for East London, at a period of rapid development of market gardens. Their produce demanded considerable flexibility from the railways: the seasons of the individual commodities were short, with pronounced peaks, and the size of the harvests depended on the weather; the quantity and pattern of trade changed from week to week as early crops from the south-west (including those landed at *Plymouth and Weymouth) were displaced by later crops grown further east and north; the traffics were not only highly *perishable, but also easily damaged, and individual consignments were small; both the handling and the clerical work were, therefore, labour-intensive, requiring the posting of temporary additional staff to the forwarding stations.

Market-garden traffic extended almost throughout the year: home-grown spring green vegetables from March onwards, preceded from early January by supplies from western France, Jersey, Guernsey, and the Scilly Isles; peas and soft fruit from May to August; plums, damsons, and tomatoes from July to September; and finally apples and pears through the autumn. The railways' national distribution capability encouraged districts to specialize and become famous for particular commodities: the Channel Islands for broccoli and tomatoes; Penzance for broccoli; the Vale of Evesham for asparagus and plums; the Tamar Valley, Swanwick (Hampshire), and Wisbech (Cambridgeshire) districts for strawberries; West Yorkshire for rhubarb. Other important districts included the Home Counties, the Fens, and the Fylde.

In 1901–2 Elders & Fyffes established a distribution network of rail-served ripening warehouses for bananas imported through Avonmouth and *Manchester docks. Manchester was replaced by Garston dock, *Liverpool, in 1912 and *Southampton was used increasingly from the 1930s. Geest Industries began a rival business in 1952–3 using *Barry and *Preston docks. Banana vans were the only freight wagons fitted for steam heating, to prevent frost damage to the fruit. Following a period of using *Freightliner services in the 1970s, the traffic was finally lost to road in 1979. Since 1907 the railways have also been involved in the distribution of South African citrus fruit, which more recently has arrived in *containers. Italian and Spanish produce continue to be important traffics (see EUROPEAN TRAFFIC).

Fruit traffic totalled 1.0 million tons and market-garden vegetable traffic 0.7 million tons in the early 1920s.

See also AGRICULTURAL TRAFFIC.   GAB

W. F. Downing, 'The Fruit Traffic of Evesham', *RM*, 15 (1904), 404–8; 'Fruit Traffic on the Great Eastern Section of the London and North Eastern Railway', *RM*, 53 (1923), 209–13; R. Webber, *Market Gardening: The History of Commercial Flower, Fruit and Vegetable Growing* (1972); P. N. Davies, *Fyffes and the Banana: Musa Sapientium: A Centenary History 1888–1988* (1990).

funicular, see CABLE HAULAGE; CLIFF RAILWAYS.

Furness Railway; originally built as an isolated local line to convey iron ore and slate from the mines and quarries of the Furness peninsula to *Barrow-in-Furness for shipment. By a process of takeovers it eventually comprised a main line from Carnforth to Whitehaven, with branches into the Lake District and connecting steamer services on Windermere and Coniston Water. The company had a monopoly of the enormous *iron and steel traffic of the Furness area and an important share in that of West Cumberland.

The first sections opened from Kirkby-in-Furness to Roa Island and Dalton to Barrow in 1846. Over the next few years extensions were completed to Ulverston and Broughton-in-Furness, where a connection was made in 1850 with the Whitehaven & Furness Junction Railway, which was absorbed into the FR in 1866. The link eastwards to Carnforth and the south was not completed until 1857, and then by the independent Ulverston & Lancaster Railway, which was taken over by the FR in 1862.

The company prospered greatly during the 1870s and 1880s when Furness and West Cumberland played a vital role in the development of the British steel industry. The ending of the monopoly of haematite-based steels started a long process of decline, which would have been far more severe for the railway but for its imaginative promotion of *tourist traffic, benefiting from, and further encouraging, the popularization of the Lake District. The FR became part of the *London Midland & Scottish Railway in 1923.   PWR

Reg. Hist., xiv (1983), ch. 5; R. W. Rush, *The Furness Railway* (1973).

G

Galbraith, William Robert (1829–1914), engineer, born at Stirling. He was articled to John Errington in 1846, working under him on the Aberdeen and *Scottish Central Railways; and was resident engineer, Yeovil–Exeter line of the *London & South Western Railway, 1856–60. In 1862 he became the LSWR's engineer for new works and was chiefly responsible for the lines from Yeoford Junction to Bude, Padstow, and Plymouth (1865–99), and the awkward Barnstaple–Ilfracombe line (1874).

With R. F. Church, he became a consultant in Edinburgh; they worked on the northern approaches to the *Forth Bridge (1890) and the reconstruction of Waverley station, *Edinburgh (1900).

Galbraith also participated in making the *London underground railways: first the Waterloo & City line in association with J. H. *Greathead, then with Church and Benjamin *Baker on the Bakerloo and Northern lines.

Galbraith kept well abreast of developments. His two *concrete viaducts on the Bude line (1898) were among the first on an English railway (see BRIDGES AND VIADUCTS). He established an unusual position for himself in railway engineering, flexible and independent. He never became the 'chief engineer' of a company. JS

PICE, 197 (1914), 328–9.

Galt, William (?1809–?94), reformer, was a solicitor; the first systematic advocate of the *nationalization of British railways, explaining his case and his plans for managing the business in his *Railway Reform* (four editions, 1843–4). The book may have influenced the proposals for dealing with the matter in *Gladstone's Act. It was republished, much enlarged, in 1864–5. Galt gave evidence before the Royal *Commission of 1865.

He was no political doctrinaire. He set out his plans cogently in terms of what he considered the interests of the country at large. Though his views were not accepted, the 1865 edition of his book remains the most useful broad survey of the political economy of the British railways at that time. JS

*Ottley, 4309, 4377; P. Rayleigh, *The Cogers of Fleet Street* (2nd edn., 1908), 54.

gardens. The long tradition of station gardens appears to have begun on the *North Eastern Railway, followed by the *Great Western. Gardens were seen by management as a means of encouraging staff to take pride in their workplaces, and making them attractive to passengers. Competitions were held for various classes of station, judged by a group of directors and senior officials.

Most of the other railways did the same, providing materials and tools, and cash prizes for winners. Some *stations gained high reputations for their flower beds and hanging baskets, from *York to the tiny Tan-y-Bwlch on the narrow-gauge *Festiniog Railway. Stirling has long had its own nursery and greenhouse for its famous summer floral decorations.

Station staff showed great ingenuity in designing displays which have included topiary work, palm trees, and fishponds, and often incorporating the station name. In the 1950s, for example, Verney Junction, Buckinghamshire, had an extraordinary display that included a pool, dovecote, mermaid, stork, three gnomes, a rabbit, and a windmill.

In 1930 the *London & North Eastern Railway fitted a seat to the front of a locomotive which was used for judging all the stations in its Southern Area, but although it saved time, the experiment was not repeated.

Outsiders, too, have helped. In 1963 the Great Western Society gave plants for Hanwell and Taplow stations, and in more recent years *British Rail's Community Unit successfully encouraged voluntary organizations to help in maintaining gardens at small or unstaffed stations. At others, displays have been provided commercially by local garden centres. GJB

G. A. Wade, 'The Prettiest Railway Stations', *RM*, 6 (1900), 46; 'Railway Gardens', *RM*, 18 (1906), 308; LNER inspection locomotive: *RM*, 94 (1948), 374, 410; R. E. G. Read and G. Biddle, 'Station Gardens', *Railway World*, 26 (1965), 149.

gas lighting of premises. Gas light predated the steam railway and was quickly taken up as a means of lighting city streets, being seen as an important deterrent to crime. In the larger towns and cities, gas was therefore available for lighting stations and other railway premises from the start, for example in *Liverpool where the *Liverpool & Manchester's tunnel from the original Crown Street terminus to Edge Hill was lit throughout by gas when the railway opened in 1830. As the manufacture of gas spread so did its use on the railways.

Until the end of the 19th century, gas lighting used the open, luminous yellow flame of a fishtail burner. Though more effective than candles, it was dirty and little better than one of the better forms of oil lamp. The Welsbach incandescent mantle was invented in 1886 but made little headway in Britain until the development of the inverted mantle about 10 years later. It was much more efficient than an open flame, burning a smaller volume of gas in a hotter and cleaner flame to produce a greater output of almost pure white light; not only did it quickly supplant the old fishtail burners but for a few years outclassed the pale, yellowish gleam of the new electric light with its carbon filament bulbs. It was still being installed in the 1930s and survived on many smaller stations until they were closed or modernized in the 1960s—as did oil lamps.   RW

gas lighting of trains, see CARRIAGE LIGHTING.

gas turbine locomotives, see TRACTION, TURBINE.

Gateshead, see NEWCASTLE AND GATESHEAD.

gauge, see TRACK GAUGE; CLEARANCES; ROUTE AVAILABILITY.

Geddes, Sir Eric Campbell (1875–1937), businessman and politician, born in Agra, India, son of a Scottish civil engineer. He joined the *North Eastern Railway in 1904, and made his mark in management techniques and statistical analysis, rising to general manager in 1914. Co-opted into the service of the state during World War I, he dealt successively with munitions output, transport organization in France, and naval supply, becoming Minister of Transport in the Lloyd George coalition government where he conceived grandiose schemes for reorganizing and streamlining the whole of Britain's transport system and electricity supply. He was responsible for the passage of the Railways Act, 1921 (see GROUPING), but returned to private enterprise in 1922 and joined the board of Dunlop Rubber Co., becoming its chairman in the same year. Two years later he became part-time chairman of Imperial Airways, and devoted most of his time to these two interests until his death.

His main claims to popular fame arise from his attitude to the treatment of Germany after World War I (squeezing Germany 'until the pips squeak'), his association with national expenditure cuts in 1922 (the 'Geddes axe'), and his organization of essential supplies during the General Strike of 1926.   DHA

DNB; K. Grieves, *Sir Eric Geddes: Business and Government in War and Peace* (1989).

Gibb, Sir George Stegmann (1850–1925), general manager. Son of Alexander Gibb, civil engineer of the *Great North of Scotland Railway, he was born and educated at Aberdeen. Qualified as a solicitor, he was with the *Great Western Railway before being appointed solicitor to the *North Eastern Railway in 1882 (see LAWYERS AND RAILWAYS). In 1891 he became general manager and proceeded to reform and vitalize the whole administration, at first somewhat hampered by a vague power given to his predecessor Henry *Tennant to provide counsel on 'important matters of policy'. Of the wide-ranging changes introduced by Gibb, the most significant were the development of operating statistics including ton-mileage figures, and the recruitment of university graduates as traffic apprentices (the first being R. L. *Wedgwood, later chief general manager, *London & North Eastern Railway). Gibb, unlike most of his contemporary railway managers, was broad-minded and accessible; he adopted many ideas from the best United States railroad practice after a visit in 1901. He kept in touch with the press

and with the transport economists William *Acworth and George Paish. He was knighted in 1904.

But Gibb was given less than the full support he felt entitled to by his board, and he left the NER in 1906 to be deputy chairman and managing director of the *Underground Railways of London—a position for which membership of the Royal Commission on London Traffic (1903–5) had prepared him—but he remained a director of the NER from 1906 to 1910. The Underground was in difficulties: expenditure was growing much faster than income. Gibb set up the first moves to co-operation among the London electric railways, and earnings slowly improved. But the American financial backers were impatient, and in 1907 they brought over Albert Stanley (see ASHFIELD, LORD) from the USA who succeeded him as managing director in 1910. Gibb then became chairman of the new Road Board, 1910–19. He worked for the War Office in World War I but was not actively engaged in railway management again.   RMR

Tomlinson; R. Bell, *Twenty-Five Years of the North Eastern Railway (1898–1922)* (1951); C. H. Ellis, 'Lewin Papers concerning Sir George Gibb', *JTH*, 5 (1961–2), 226; *HLT*, ii; R. J. Irving, *The North Eastern Railway Company 1870–1914* (1976).

Giles, Francis (1787–1847), worked as a waterway surveyor under the *Rennies. When it came to railways he discredited himself by giving evidence against George *Stephenson on the *Liverpool & Manchester project. Nevertheless he became engineer to the *Newcastle & Carlisle Railway in 1829 and was responsible for three magnificent works there, the deep Cowran cutting (see EARTHWORKS) and the Gelt and Eden bridges east of Carlisle. Having taken on too many engagements, he was edged out of office in 1833, before the line was completed. He was also engineer to the London & Southampton Railway (see LONDON & SOUTH WESTERN RAILWAY) 1831–7, but resigned when the directors criticized him for the same fault. He became notorious for it, and never found important railway work again.

JS

DNB; Williams, i, 14, ch. 2.

Gladstone, William Ewart (1809–98), politician: the only British prime minister to have had an extensive personal concern with railways.

His father, Sir John Gladstone, a Liverpool merchant, was a forceful promoter of Scottish lines. By 1843 he held £170,000 of railway stock. The young man entered Parliament in 1832, becoming president of the Board of *Trade under *Peel. Early in 1844 he chaired a Commons committee on railways. From its extensive and careful deliberations a Bill emerged, which Gladstone carried through the House (see GLADSTONE'S ACT).

He and other members of his family continued to be much concerned with railways as investments, and he was careful to avoid the charge that his policies were designed to further those private interests. Shortly after his railway measure became law he resigned office, partly because he wished to cease being responsible for railway policy, owing to this conflict.

He adhered to that decision for the rest of his long life. Although in 1852–3 he was a member of *Cardwell's Commons committee on railways, he attended only two of its sessions. When the Royal Commission on Railways was appointed in 1865 he seems to have evaded service on it.

He kept a constant watch on the railways, however. From 1867 onwards he was associated with (Sir) Edward *Watkin. In 1888–90 the two men became linked by support for the project of a *Channel Tunnel.

Gladstone was the only British political leader who used the railways for electioneering. He addressed crowds at stations and from carriage windows after the fashion of the 'whistle-stops' made by politicians in America. The first of these were at Dunfermline, Perth, and Aberfeldy on 1 December 1879.   JS
GR; F. E. Hyde, *Gladstone at the Board of Trade* (1934); R. Jenkins, *Gladstone* (1995).

Gladstone's Act, the title frequently given to the third Railway Regulation Act (see GOVERNMENT, RAILWAYS AND NATIONAL), based on a report of a Commons committee chaired by W. E. *Gladstone, steered through Parliament by him, and passed in 1844; remembered particularly for its provisions relating to *nationalization and to cheap travel facilities.

It laid down conditions under which the British government might purchase railway companies in the future. They applied only to those established after 1 January 1845 and could not be exercised before 1 January 1866. The price was to be 25 years' purchase of each company's annual profits, averaged out over the three preceding years.

These powers were much weaker than Gladstone had intended. The leading railway companies' chairmen brought strong pressure to bear on the Prime Minister, *Peel, over the provisions for state purchase, which survived in the Act in a form that could scarcely have been enforced. They were duly reviewed in 1865–7, and ignored thereafter.

The provisions relating to cheap travel were, however, implemented, providing for what came to be called *parliamentary trains, carrying passengers paying exceptionally low fares, and conforming to requirements of speed and comfort that the Act specified.

The Act also obliged the railways to permit the electric *telegraph to be carried alongside their lines, for use by the government and the public: an important aid towards securing the expansion of the great benefits this very new device offered.

To Gladstone himself the Act represented a defeat. But the power of the British railway companies was by 1844 too strong to be remoulded as he devised, and although the provisions relating to state purchase were a failure, the Act brought far-reaching benefits to the whole community.   JS
E. Cleveland-Stevens, *English Railways* (1915), ch. 5.

Glasgow. The place of Glasgow in the British economy in the 19th century needs no false emphasis. The city well deserved its supplementary title of 'The Workshop of the British Empire' with its many shipyards, engineering works, cotton mills, breweries, and other industries, including locomotive building (see WORKS) for which the city became world-famous. Accompanying this phenomenal growth of industry and commerce was the development of improved transport, and in particular the railways. By 1900 virtually every works of any consequence had its rail link and some, such as Singer's, chose their new factory site at Kilbowie in Clydebank because they could rely on cheap *workmen's fares to bring their work-force from central and eastern Glasgow. The links between industry and transport were underlined in 1904 when Glasgow, with a population just over twice that of *Edinburgh, had five times as many public goods *stations and private *sidings.

There had been some *tramroads for moving coal in the Glasgow area in the later 18th century, but the first proper railway was the Garnkirk & Glasgow, opened in 1831. Extended to a 'temporary' wooden station at Buchanan Street, this terminus became the *Caledonian Railway's station for Aberdeen, and also after 1849 for London (Euston) via Coatbridge. The next three lines for the city were promoted with passengers in mind; but there remained the problem of the Clyde. To the south of the river, the *Glasgow Paisley Kilmarnock & Ayr shared from 1840 a terminus at Bridge Street with the Glasgow Paisley & Greenock. English services after June 1849 used South Side Station at Gushetfaulds. North of the river was the *Edinburgh & Glasgow's Queen Street station, entered via a steep and inconvenient *cable-worked incline from Cowlairs. The Admiralty having effectively vetoed an attempt in the mid-1840s by the Clydesdale Junction Railway to establish a station at Dunlop Street by insisting on the construction of a swing bridge, it was 1876 before the Clyde was crossed from the south by the *Glasgow & South Western to its new St Enoch station, and three years later the Central station of the Caledonian was opened. As part of the City Union Railway, St Enoch also offered links to the north and east, but passenger services in those directions were limited and later withdrawn. There were problems of securing routes and sites; awkward landowners such as the Campbells of Blythswood were able to beat back various schemes, and the *North British Railway was fortunate to find the University of Glasgow willing in the 1860s to move from a run-down central area it wanted for a goods station to a more westerly site at Gilmorehill. The city authorities were supportive, as they were in the case of the St Enoch and City Union proposals which allowed for the demolition of some equally unsalubrious property.

Competition between the various railway companies for routes and sites in Glasgow was fierce, and so many projects were brought forward that Glasgow was the only 19th-century British city, other than London, to have had a Royal Commission set up, in 1846, to investigate the competing schemes for railway termini. It made little mark, however. The Union and the Caledonian seem to have had a particularly antagonistic relationship; if one wished to promote a scheme, the other was invariably in opposition. The big three companies—the CR, NBR, and GSWR (the latter

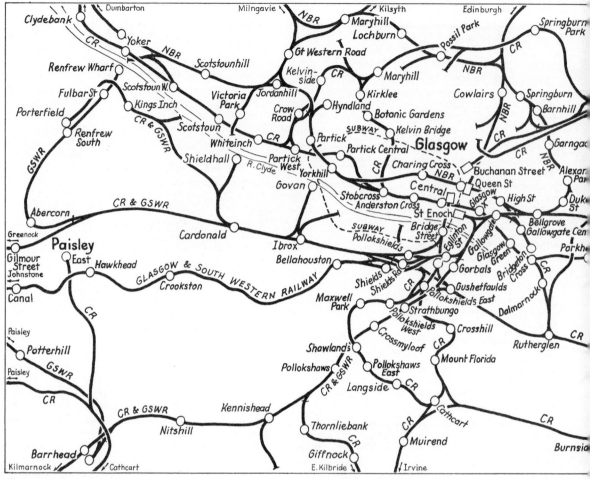

Glasgow area, 1922

two tending to be in loose alliance against the first)—gradually absorbed the smaller fry, and a network of suburban lines was built. The years 1885–1910 saw rival lines completed by the competing companies to allow them access to the river's new docks, and a 'Caledonian-free' GSWR route to Ayrshire via Paisley Canal was also completed.

There were also competing east–west routes through the city, the first being the Glasgow City & District in 1886, with three miles of tunnel below the city, and a low-level station at Queen Street. The Caledonian followed suit with its east–west route under Argyle Street and Central station, a costly line with no fewer than seven miles of steam-operated tunnel workings. The circular cable-hauled *Glasgow Subway was completed in 1896. As a purely passenger system entirely below ground and unconnected to the major rail companies, this has some claim to be considered the world's third true underground system after London and Budapest (see UNDERGROUND RAILWAYS). Other suburban services proliferated on the south side of the city and made use of the greatly expanded platform capacity available in

the first years of the 20th century at Central station and St Enoch. The best-known of these was the Cathcart Circle, actually a heart-shaped service operating from Glasgow Central. The volume of passengers and freight alike grew by leaps and bounds. While freight dominated the CR's income, passenger traffic through its Glasgow stations rose fourfold between 1848 and 1862, reaching 5.5 million by 1873; Central station alone had 4.75 million passengers in 1880, and 15.75 million in 1897.

The coming of the railways meant the demolition of some mostly slum or small business property. Local communities were divided and disrupted by the lines, viaducts, and depots, and the noise and smoke detracted from the urban environment. But their works also meant the addition of some striking Victorian *architecture, notably the GSWR's five-storey St Enoch *Hotel, at the time the largest in Scotland. The railways also had a social impact, not always foreseen: the expansion of Central station between 1901 and 1905 (see STATIONS) created a covered way over part of Argyle Street, and this became a favoured meeting place

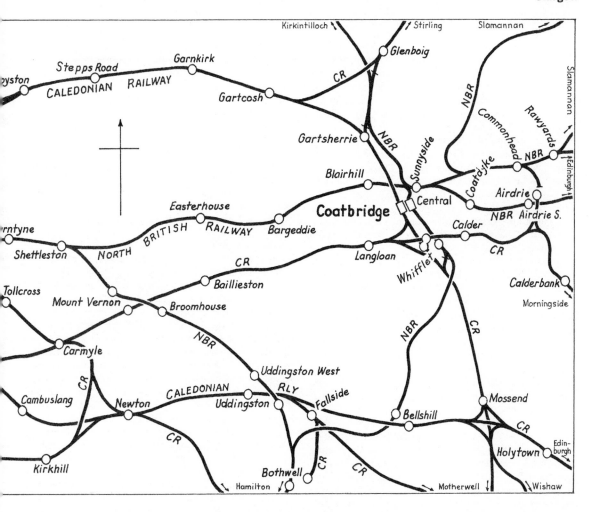

for exiled Highlanders, particularly on Sunday nights: 'the Hielanman's Umbrella' as it was called in Glasgow patois.

Yet this rail boom of the early 1900s was more fragile than it appeared. Successive alternative forms of transport in the shape first of the electric tram, then the motor-bus, the lorry, and the private car made their appearance and cut into the demand for rail services. The city's economy, too, lost the momentum it had during the 19th century; relative decline and prolonged unemployment were much more characteristic. Two World Wars brought short periods of flat-out production and intensified rail traffic but there was little opportunity otherwise for rail growth between 1910 and 1960. Although extensive closures were avoided, falling revenues made it difficult to justify new investment. Indeed, traffic at the newly enlarged Central station was declining by 1905, hard-hit by more frequent tram services extending ever further out into the suburbs. Buses and cars added still more competition, but the fall in passenger-use was at least slowed by issue of discounted *season tickets and bargain offers for trips to the coast or city centre. New stations on

existing lines such as those at Hillington, Cardonald, and Kings Park, were opened to take advantage of either new industry or housing development. The most positive step forward in the inter-war years was the municipalization and electrification of the Subway or Circle Underground, a popular step as 30 million passenger journeys a year proved. However, post-war plans for Glasgow's transport, which included proposals for the four terminal stations to be replaced by two new ones—one south of the river and the other a redeveloped Buchanan Street—came to nothing, as did a proposal for an enlarged Underground.

After 1960 freight traffic withered. The staple steel and coal traffic had all but gone by the early 1990s as had most of the rail-based dock traffic. A *Freightliner terminal was opened at Gushetfaulds but closed in 1993, with all such traffic being handled outside the city at Coatbridge, or at the Eurocentral terminal at Mossend and the Deanside transit depot. Large areas of ground previously used as goods yards, train maintenance depots, and locomotive works became available for redevelopment, including such famous sites as Cowlairs, Springburn, and St Rollox. Very few of the freight lines and sidings so important in 1904 remained in use.

By contrast, passenger traffic stopped falling in 1960 and has subsequently seen an increase. Glasgow still has the largest passenger rail network in Britain outside London, and many stations and a number of lines have reopened in recent years. Increased government funding for railways under *British Railways' 1955 *Modernization Plan allowed *electrification at last to begin while other lines gained from more frequent diesel services. The first electric trains, known locally as 'Blue Trains', started in 1960 on the Queen Street Low Level Line; services from Central soon followed. But this was also the time of the *Beeching Report and the reshaping of the rail network. Instead of being electrified, the Central Low Level service ceased in 1964, and all services from Buchanan Street and St Enoch stations had been diverted to Queen Street and Central by 1966. Apart from those closures and that of the Paisley Canal line in the early 1980s, the Glasgow suburban network survived and began to be more appreciated as a valuable alternative to increasing road traffic and congestion.

The formation of the Greater Glasgow *Passenger Transport Authority and its Executive, renamed in 1980 Strathclyde PTE, brought in a new era of rail regeneration. Since the late 1970s productivity improvements such as unmanned stations have helped Strathclyde to justify substantial support for local rail services and continuous expansion. The changes have included the complete modernization of the Underground, the reopening and electrification of the Glasgow Central Low Level line, the reopening of the Paisley Canal line, a new direct curve at Cowlairs for Cumbernauld–Queen Street trains, and new services on existing lines from Central to Whifflet and from Queen Street to Maryhill. Other schemes are under active consideration, such as the reopening to passengers of the City Union Railway under the name 'Glasgow Crossrail' to provide a north–south direct route, a rail link to Glasgow Airport, and the introduction of a Strathclyde *Light Rapid Transit route from Maryhill to Easterhouse through the city centre, which would use sections of disused railway as well as street running. The implications of Crossrail for the future roles of the existing termini at Queen Street and Central are interesting: the PTE has proposed a new city centre station at Bridgegate, at the east end of the former St Enoch station site, and a new interchange with the Underground at West Street. The situation is almost as fluid as it was 150 years ago, but it seems clear that the passenger railways of Glasgow are set for a fresh phase of development.

AJD and TH

W. M. Acworth, *The Railways of Scotland* (1890); C. Johnston and J. R. Hume, *Glasgow Stations* (1979); J. R. Kellett, *The Impact of Railways on Victorian Cities* (1969); *Reg. Hist.*, vi, ch. 8.

Glasgow & South Western Railway. The GSWR occupied the middle position of Scotland's five main railway companies prior to the 1923 *Grouping. The origins of the company lay in the need for improved links between the two main Ayrshire towns and both *Glasgow and the south. The *Glasgow Paisley Kilmarnock & Ayr Railway gained construction powers in 1837 and, by 1850, had absorbed the Glasgow Dumfries & Carlisle Railway to take the name GSWR. The Glasgow–Ayr line was completed in 1840, followed by the branch from Dalry to *Kilmarnock in 1843, which itself became the GSWR main line to *Carlisle via the Nith valley and Dumfries by 1850. This line had a summit level some 300 ft lower than the steeply graded *Caledonian Railway route via Beattock, but was 18 miles longer.

The GSWR absorbed other lines, notably 'Scotland's first railway'—the coal-carrying *Kilmarnock & Troon of 1811—and included many other branches in south-west Scotland by the early 20th century. One served the new railway golf *hotel at Turnberry from 1906, opening 18 years before the GSWR's great rival, the Caledonian, finished its own prestigious golf hotel at Gleneagles. The core business of the GSWR lay in Ayrshire with its twin attractions of coalfields and expanding coastal resorts. There was also rivalry with the Caledonian for Anglo-Scottish and Anglo-Irish traffic, which was a powerful influence on the railway politics of Glasgow and south-west Scotland.

Because of the importance of Anglo-Irish traffic, the GSWR never achieved total control of the direct route from Carlisle through Dumfries and Castle Douglas to Stranraer, which quickly supplanted Portpatrick as the main railserved port for northern Ireland. The major part of this route became a joint line shared with the Caledonian, and the *London & North Western and *Midland Railways of England. The secondary route, from Stranraer north to join the Ayr line, had tremendous problems of financing and operation. Direct shipping from Ireland to Ayrshire and the Clyde (see SHIPPING, COASTAL) was a very powerful competitor, delaying completion of the Glasgow–Stranraer route until 1877 and full incorporation in the GSWR until 1892.

From early in its history there were always prospects of the GSWR being absorbed by larger companies. Throughrunning to the *North British Railway became possible on completion of the City Union railway in 1870 and Glasgow St Enoch terminal station in 1876 while, to the south, through-running to the Midland increased on completion of the latter's *Settle & Carlisle Railway. Parliament rejected mergers with the Midland in 1867 and again in 1872, but a close working relationship developed with express trains from London *St Pancras to St Enoch.

On the other hand, local business soon resented the GSWR monopoly of Ayrshire traffic and welcomed the efforts of the Caledonian to construct competing lines. The company was forced to accept joint operation of the new direct Glasgow–Kilmarnock line (1873), and separate Caledonian routes had been built to Ardrossan, Kilbirnie (with a new steelworks), and Irvine by 1890. To maintain this competition and possibly extend it to Troon and Ayr, Parliament rejected a Caledonian attempt to absorb the GSWR in 1890. The company's later years brought further increases in industrial traffic, tourism, day-tripping, Clyde steamer connections, and longer-distance commuting. This encouraged plans for quadruple track, or equivalent loop lines, between Glasgow and Ayr—work which was substantially completed over the 30 miles from Glasgow to Kilwinning by 1914. The company's main *works were at Kilmarnock from 1856 but additional workshops were provided at Barassie, a suburb of Troon, in 1901. Barassie station also had a golf club close at hand, as had the coastal stations at Gailes, Irvine Bogside, Troon, and Prestwick.

In the 1923 Grouping the GSWR became part of the *London Midland & Scottish Railway, bringing a rapid elimination of a motley collection of GSWR locomotives and imposition of Caledonian traditions. However, the GSWR routes survived subsequent rationalization of competing lines in Ayrshire. Among the lines which closed in the 1960s, the direct route from Stranraer to Dumfries was the most prominent casualty. The Glasgow–Dumfries–Carlisle route survives, together with the short link from Kilmarnock to Troon and the Glasgow–Ayr–Stranraer route.

The last is one of Scotland's neglected scenic routes, combining steep grades and impressive views south of Girvan. Several GSWR buildings also survive, including passenger stations at Ayr, Kilmarnock, and Dumfries and, of course, the imposing hotel at Turnberry.   TH

D. Smith, *Tales of the Glasgow and South Western Railway* (1961); *Glasgow and South Western Railway, 1850–1923*, Stephenson Locomotive Society (1950); C. Highet, *Glasgow & South Western Railway* (1965); *Reg. Hist.*, vi, ch. 5.

Glasgow Paisley Kilmarnock & Ayr Railway. This was promoted in 1836 concurrently with the Glasgow Paisley & Greenock Railway, the two companies consenting that the seven miles of line between *Glasgow and Paisley should be owned and worked jointly (see JOINT RAILWAYS). *Grainger and *Miller were the engineers, Miller the active partner here. The section between Glasgow and Ayr was opened in 1839–40, the eight-mile branch from Dalry to *Kilmarnock in 1843.

Meanwhile the GPKAR had become involved in a struggle between two projected routes from Glasgow to *Carlisle: the Annandale line, which became the *Caledonian Railway, and the Nithsdale line promoted by the Glasgow Dumfries & Carlisle company. This was intended to run from Carlisle to Cumnock, where it would join an extension of the GPKAR (authorized in 1845 and opened in 1848). The GDCR was authorized in 1846; on its completion in 1850 the GPKAR merged with it to form the *Glasgow & South Western Railway.

The extension of the GPKAR southward from Kilmarnock included some of Miller's finest works, particularly the Ballochmyle viaduct (see BRIDGES AND VIADUCTS).

William Johnstone, Miller's resident engineer on the GPKAR, became manager of it and then of the GSWR in 1841–74: an unusual example of an engineer passing successfully into railway management.   JS

Robertson; C. Highet, *Glasgow & South Western Railway* (1965); Johnstone's unpublished letter-book, dating from his work under Miller, deserves attention: see SRO BR/GPK/4/7.

Glasgow Subway: one of a number of *underground railways projected in *Glasgow in the period 1880–90. The immediate stimulus was road congestion caused by population growth, made worse by rising living standards, which encouraged suburban living. The first underground line, the Glasgow City & District (opened in 1886), was a steam-worked adjunct of the *North British Railway, rivalled and paralleled by the Glasgow Central and the Lanarkshire & Dumbartonshire Railways, worked by the *Caledonian and opened in 1896. Neither served the rich and populous West End very effectively: the GCD's Hyndland station was on the edge of the district. There were, therefore, several proposals for an underground line to meet the need, and the Glasgow District Subway was successful, receiving parliamentary approval in 1889. It was a 4-ft-gauge line in twin tunnels, roughly circular, serving districts on both banks of the Clyde. As electric underground traction was in its infancy, the promoters chose continuous *cable haulage, operated by stationary steam engines at a power station in Scotland Street.

*Tramway electrification hit the company fairly hard, followed in the 1920s by economic depression. After 1919 it lost money and in 1922 was purchased by Glasgow Corporation, whose transport department was renowned for its efficiency. Under its auspices the line was electrified economically but effectively in 1932–5, and renamed 'Glasgow Underground', although it is still known as 'the Subway' today. By the 1970s the original train equipment was becoming increasingly difficult to maintain, and the Greater Glasgow *Passenger Transport Executive resolved to modernize the system, while recognizing that a subsidy would be required. The revitalized system was reopened in 1978, and has proved very successful. It is the only wholly underground passenger railway outside London and the only *narrow-gauge mass-transit line in Britain. Two of the original cars are in Glasgow Transport Museum.   JRH

D. L. Thomson and D. E. Sinclair, *The Glasgow Subway* (1964).

glass. Technical changes in the methods of flat-glass manufacture, making possible the greater availability of larger panes at lower cost, coincided with increased railway demand for glass for windows, skylights, and station roofs (see TRAINSHEDS) from the later 1840s. Before that, the way in which Britain's glass excise duty was exacted—by weight rather than by area—gave an overwhelming advantage to crown glass, from which only quite small panes could be cut. When small-scale production of sheet glass started in England in 1832 at one factory, at Smethwick, much of it was exported. It extended to other concerns after 1840. Growing competition and lower prices applied not only to sheet, but also to the far costlier cast plate glass from which thicker and larger panes were produced, for mirrors, shop windows, and more prestigious premises.

The earliest city railway terminals of the 1830s had few windows, and *stations along the line were at first little more than open-air halts. Similarly, first-class passenger coaches had small windows, like stage-coaches; but those paying lower—especially excursion—fares often travelled in the open. The benefits of glass came later for them, certainly by the time of *parliamentary trains after the mid-1840s. In so far as railways built *houses for their employees, they presumably paid the very onerous window tax when over seven windows were constructed. For offices, places of manufacture, or warehouses, however, the railways, like other businesses, were exempt. Booking offices had their windows; and illustrations of railway stations, including the very early photograph of Linlithgow of 1845 (see HILL, D. O.), do not suggest any lack of glazing. Windows were, of course, of greatest importance with the advent of *signal boxes.

The new and more impressive city centre termini called for window glass in greater quantity and size. These developments occurred after an even cheaper form of glass, known as rolled plate, was introduced in 1847. Translucent but not transparent, and fabricated in long, narrow panes, it was ideal for arched station roofs and for skylights.

The longer, heavier, and more numerous passenger carriages of the later 19th century required much more glass. So did the city and provincial railway stations in which great quantities were used when they were built or extended to handle the growing traffic. Waiting and refreshment rooms required windows. Railway *hotels increased the demand. More recently, as stations have been closed or simplified, and rolling stock fleets reduced, double glazing has had an offsetting effect on the reduced requirements.

Glassworks, benefiting from cuts in waterway costs arising from new railway competition, continued to send their heavy panes by canal or navigable river. Pilkington glass was still sent by canal to Widnes, for instance, after 1833 when the St Helens & Runcorn Gap Railway, of which the chairman Peter Greenall was also partner in the glassworks, linked those two places. With the creation of a railway network, however, sidings were stipulated in some railway Acts, as for Chance Brothers, Smethwick. Pilkingtons at St Helens had an extensive internal system.

Sheet and plate glass was normally packed in crates, although several railways built special wagons to carry large sheets of glass: the *Great Western began to do so in 1884, while the *Midland Railway built two in 1891–9 and two more in 1912. There was also an extensive traffic in glass bottles. The *London & North Western's Falcon Lane depot at Battersea, for instance, was used exclusively for bottles from the United Glass Bottle Co. at St Helens.

No account of the growth of rail-borne window glass traffic is available; nor has the total amount of such glass used by railways been calculated. It is impossible to guess how much of two completely different sorts of glass—bottles and drinking glasses—were bought, or broken in railway refreshment rooms, dining cars, and hotels.   TCB

T. C. Barker, *The Glassmakers* (1977); C. Ross, 'James Hartley', *DBB*, iii (1985); *RTC*.

Glyn, George Carr, 1st Lord Wolverton (1797–1873), banker and railway chairman, educated at Westminster School. He was a partner, bank of Glyn Mills & Co., 1830, and senior partner, 1864–73.

An original director of the *London & Birmingham Railway, he was chairman of it and its successor the *London & North Western in 1837–52. In that office he was tirelessly active, though never attempting to be an autocrat. He took great pains to secure a sound apportionment of responsibilities between the board and its chief officers. But he always watched their performance closely. By 1856 (when no longer chairman, though still a director) he had become convinced that the general manager, Mark *Huish, whose talents he appreciated highly, was a bad collaborator with his colleagues and with other companies, and that he must go.

In the 1830s and 1840s he was constantly anxious to secure co-operation between the companies for common purposes. He was a principal founder of the *Railway Clearing House (on a banking model) in 1842, and remained its chairman until his death. He was Liberal MP for Kendal (1847–68) and created Lord Wolverton in 1869. His personal estate was sworn at nearly £1m.   JS

Boase; T. R. Gourvish, *Mark Huish and the London & North Western Railway* (1972); Bagwell.

Glyn Valley Tramway, SEE LIGHT RAILWAYS .

Golden Valley Railway. Traversing 19 miles of remote Herefordshire from Pontrilas to Hay-on-Wye (opened 1881–9), it never came near to paying its way. It was kept going largely by the financial support of a few local landowners. Closed entirely in 1898, it was then sold to the *Great Western Railway, only the debenture holders receiving any of their money back. The line was reopened by the GWR in 1901. Its regular passenger service lasted just 40 years more.

Yet even this weak, unprofitable line cannot be written off as a social failure. In the 1890s, before the advent of mechanized road transport, it was carrying an average of more than 125 passengers on each working day. Its history was particularly well told by C. L. Mowat in his book *The Golden Valley Railway* (1964), perhaps the most satisfactory account we have of any small rural line in Britain. His judgement on it is this: 'We too easily forget how much of the railway system of England . . . [was] built at the cost of private persons and the unpaid or little-paid services of local directors, gentry and tradespeople; money and service for which there was no financial return, often serious loss. And even the Golden Valley performed a real service to the people of the valley when Shanks's mare or the horse were the only alternative means of travel.'   JS

Gooch, Sir Daniel (1816–89), engineer and chairman. After short spells of employment in ironworks and mechanical engineering he became the first locomotive superintendent of the *Great Western Railway in 1837, working under *Brunel, who had before his arrival commissioned experimental locomotives, which proved ineffective in service, except the strong and reliable 'Star' class from Robert *Stephenson's firm. Gooch developed from them his own first machines, built in 1840–2.

*Swindon works, established in 1841, began the con-

struction of new engines to his designs in 1846: notably *Great Western*, which at once performed brilliantly between London and *Exeter. The 'Iron Duke' class, a development of it (and later a little modified), handled all the fastest trains on the GWR until 1892. Gooch gained another success with his heavy 4-4-0 saddle-tank engines, employed on the steeply graded lines in Devon and Cornwall.

The direction of the company grew disunited in 1854–65, and in 1864 Gooch resigned, undertaking the chief responsibility for the laying of the Atlantic cable, for which he was made a baronet.

In 1865 he returned to the GWR as chairman of the board, facing grave confusion in its finances. He guided it with a firm hand until his death. Under him financial difficulties were overcome chiefly by most rigid economy. That undoubtedly lasted too long, to the detriment of the company's reputation; yet he was an unswerving supporter of the construction of the *Severn Tunnel in 1873–86, at a cost of nearly £2 million. He was Conservative MP for Cricklade in 1865–85.

Gooch had other business interests besides the GWR. He involved himself in the working of smaller railways by *contract, in the West Country and elsewhere, and also in coal-owning. He left £670,000. JS

MacDermot; *Sir Daniel Gooch, Memoirs and Diary*, ed. R. B. Wilson (1972); A. Platt, *Life and Times of Daniel Gooch* (1987).

Gooch, Thomas Longridge (1808–82), engineer, the eldest son of John Gooch, cashier at Bedlington ironworks, Northumberland; two younger brothers were John Viret Gooch (1812–1900), locomotive superintendent of the *London & South Western and *Eastern Counties Railways, and Daniel *Gooch of the *Great Western. He was apprenticed in 1823 to George *Stephenson at Newcastle. He made his way forward as a draughtsman and surveyor, first with Joseph *Locke on a preliminary survey for the *Newcastle & Carlisle Railway, then from 1826 as Stephenson's secretary and amanuensis on the *Liverpool & Manchester. In 1830 he succeeded Locke as resident engineer for the Liverpool end of the LMR and was responsible for the traffic arrangements for the opening of the line.

Six weeks later he was transferred to the projected *Manchester & Leeds Railway, on which his reputation chiefly rests. After a spell on the *London & Birmingham Railway he resurveyed the MLR, gave parliamentary evidence for it, and from 1837 to 1844 supervised its construction, under Stephenson, at a salary of £1,500 a year. The principal engineering works were the Summit Tunnel at Littleborough and the skilfully managed approach through Todmorden on the Yorkshire side.

Gooch resigned from the MLR in 1844. He undertook the Trent Valley Railway from Rugby to Stafford, opened in 1847, under Robert *Stephenson. By this time his health had been severely worn down by overwork, and he retired from professional activity in 1851. He remained a friend of all the engineers of the day outside the *Brunel camp, being particularly close to Robert Stephenson.

Gooch was a more than competent engineer; he stood only just behind the front rank. He left 'A Few Memoranda' of his professional life. RMR

DNB: Missing Persons; *PICE*, 72 (1883), 300; Library ICE, MSS 92, Gooch (including 'Few Memoranda'); M. Robbins, 'Thomas Longridge Gooch, 1808–1882', *TNS*, 56 (1984–5), 59.

goods sheds and warehouses. Traditional *stations handling *freight had various facilities, and all but the smallest included a goods shed. Its central feature was one or more loading banks or platforms, level with the floors of railway vehicles. Road vehicles backed up to other faces of the bank and goods were transferred between the two on barrows and trolleys. Platform-mounted swivelling cranes of up to 2 tons capacity could lift heavy articles. A bank was usually surfaced with heavy timber and was wide enough for consignments to be sorted and stacked while awaiting onward transport. Lift shafts might communicate with warehousing above or below the shed. In some goods stations on viaducts, there were additional platforms at street level, with rail access by wagon hoist or incline, but poor lighting made these spaces better suited to storage. In dockside transit sheds, where assembling and discharging ships' cargoes required much space, the bank was level with the quay, which it shared with wagons loading directly to the ships. Inland, a dock for canal boats was an occasional feature, alongside or beneath the loading banks, as in the *King's Cross goods shed shown in great detail in a painting at the *NRM.

Small goods sheds typically had a single siding, either beneath an external cantilevered canopy with doorways into the shed along the platform edge, or else running inside the building through a door in the end. Road access might mirror these arrangements, or vehicles might enter through side doors. At larger stations, trains needed to be broken down and formed up. In mid-19th-century practice, wagons were fed individually from *marshalling sidings to various positions along a bank or into short docks within it, by means of transverse tracks with turntables, set in embayments in the edge of the bank. There could be separate banks for arrivals and departures or, later, separate sheds. As destinations multiplied, the transverse system was superseded by multiple platforms between longitudinal tracks, facilitating capstan *shunting. Locomotives were never allowed inside buildings. Constructional considerations usually dictated a rectilinear layout, but an exception was the Outwards Goods Station of 1903 at Willow Walk, South London, where docks at an oblique angle were fed from an external spine track to permit locomotive shunting, at cost of very heavy, long-span girders carrying the superstructure across the severe skew.

Some sheds were lightly framed and clad in timber or corrugated sheeting, but sturdy brick or stone construction predominated in the 19th century, roofed with timber and slate. The larger sheds had partly glazed, multiple-span roofs on widely spaced columns. In the 20th century, metal-clad steel frames replaced solid walls, and long-span roof trusses gave more uninterrupted space. Some long-span concrete roofs appeared in the 1950s, as at *Liverpool Edge Hill.

goods traffic

Railway warehouses mainly served the storage needs of customers, and some were designed for particular commodities such as grain, cotton, wool, or maturing alcoholic beverages. Undercrofts of elevated stations were particularly suitable for the latter. Tenants sometimes cleaned, packaged, or bottled their goods within warehouses. Specially secure bonded stores were reserved for wines, spirits, and tobacco on which customs and excise duties had not been paid. Dockside warehouses provided for storage while awaiting ships, and during the slow process of cargo stowage.

The traditional warehouse developed at seaports and canal terminals, multi-storeyed for compactness and robustly built to carry heavy loads and for protection from theft and fire. Floors were supported on columns, between outer walls of brick or stone. Parapets extending above roof level gave greater fire protection, enclosed stone staircases slowed the spread of fire and assisted fire-fighting, and dividing walls, if provided, reduced the volumes at risk. Water tanks and fire mains might be installed, and naked lights were banned. With such precautions, heavy and expensive 'fireproof' construction was regarded as unnecessary. However, under incentive from insurance tariffs, non-combustible floors of brick or concrete jack-arches were used in a few large late 19th-century warehouses, mainly for textiles (e.g. Deansgate, Manchester, 1898), and more widely to isolate warehousing sections from general goods handling.

The earliest railway warehouses, at *Manchester Liverpool Road (1830), are internally wholly of timber. Cast-iron columns soon became standard for their greater strength, followed by rivetted wrought iron and then steel. Metal beams allowed wider spaces for flexibility of operation, but 3-in thick timber floors, which charred rather than burned, went on being installed after 1900. By that time, fire sprinklers gave additional protection. In the 20th century, construction was transformed by the light, non-combustible floor slabs, monolithic frames, and versatile foundations of reinforced concrete, first adopted by the *Great Western Railway in 1899.

Goods were often hoisted up the outside of warehouses by pulleys and taken in through loading doors or 'loopholes' at each floor. Overhanging timber enclosures ('lucams') sometimes provided shelter, especially on granaries. Sacks of grain returned downwards on chutes. Alternatively, wagons might pass beneath or into the warehouse, for goods to be unloaded on to banks or hoisted through trap doors. Lift cages were adopted later and, occasionally, wagon hoists, as at Huddersfield (1883), where wagons were later carried to docks on the second floor on an electric *traverser.

Hoisting was originally by hand winch. Steam power was applied, but inefficiently. From 1852 *hydraulic power was widely adopted, using wall-mounted rams with multiplying sheaves called 'jiggers'. Electric motors followed about 1900. Goods were distributed on each floor by barrows and trolleys, manhandling being assisted by levers, ramps, and lifting tackle. In the 20th century overhead runways, barrel conveyors, electric platform-trucks, and small fork-lift trucks were introduced where possible. Single-storey sheds, often open-sided, were used for high-stacking or heavy goods, such as hay and straw, timber or steel. After the 1950s, mechanical stacking, bulk transport, and *containerization made most multi-storey warehousing obsolete.

Elaborate *architecture was rarely afforded, although a few goods sheds at small stations received matching embellishment. Limited decoration persisted, such as lozenge-pattern window frames on the *Midland Railway and Gothic doorheads on Brunel's lines. Broad canopies and iron brackets could provide scope for expression, as at Helpston (MR). Simple cornices to parapets and Doric capitals to columns were common. The Granary at King's Cross (1851) is particularly fine, as was the massing effect of large warehouses in some northern cities. In the later 19th century, walls modelled in panels or in contrasting colours of brickwork were usual, but 20th-century warehouses in reinforced concrete failed to develop a satisfactory style.   MTT

goods traffic, see FREIGHT TRAFFIC.

Gorton, see WORKS; MANCHESTER AND SALFORD.

government, railways and local. In 1830 'local government', in the sense in which that term is used today, bore a very restricted meaning. The towns incorporated by royal charter had councils of their own; but their powers were not extensive, and a number of what had then become the largest English towns were never incorporated until the passing of the Municipal Corporations Act of 1835—*Manchester, *Sheffield, and *Birmingham, for example. The control of local matters rested chiefly with the magistrates, who were appointed by the crown. Many of these men were *turnpike trustees and shareholders in *canal companies, and they were understandably hostile to railways at the beginning (see OPPOSITION TO RAILWAYS).

The *Liverpool council, however, acted benevolently towards the *Liverpool & Manchester Railway, yet not with careless acquiescence. When the company sought powers in 1833–5 to build an extension to a new terminus on Lime Street, the council insisted that it must be used only for passengers, in order to limit extra street traffic in the centre of the city. But at the same time it agreed to contribute towards the cost of the station building, to give it a handsome frontage.

The governing bodies of some towns opposed, or were said to have opposed, the admission of railways: among them Maidstone, Abingdon, and Worcester. But that attitude was scarcely maintained after 1850, when it was plain that every town must have a railway if it could get one. The attention of townspeople now came to be concentrated on the facilities the railways offered after their opening. Where they were considered inadequate, some councils (those of *Southampton, *Plymouth, and *Bristol for instance) supported proposals for bringing in other, competitive lines. From the 1860s onwards the Liverpool council constantly hammered the *London & North Western Railway, trying to force it into improving services.

'Rates' for the conveyance of goods lay at the heart of

many of these wrangles. Liverpool council established a special committee on railway rates, which sat in 1880–6, and took a leading part in persuading other municipal bodies to fight the railway companies on this matter in Parliament, with a substantial measure of success (see FREIGHT TRAFFIC RATES).

In another sense 'rates' meant the local property taxes that the parishes were authorized to levy, which were applied to the relief of the poor and to some other general public purposes (see TAXATION, LOCAL). They were a frequent cause of dispute throughout the railways' history. The principles on which these taxes were assessed went back to 1601, and no attempt had ever been made to adapt them to the canals. So the railway companies had to fight new battles on such questions as 'What is a signal?', 'What is a siding?', with increasing difficulty as their operations became more complicated. The railways often contested the assessments and appealed against them, as other commercial organizations did. But at the turn of the century, when rating levies began to rise sharply, their protests grew louder, entering into the speeches of chairmen at shareholders' meetings, as they were called upon to explain the companies' declining *profitability and lower dividends.

In a good many towns that were centres of railway employment, some of the companies' servants were elected as councillors, though they seldom played a conspicuous role. That happened at *Derby, for instance, where the *Midland Railway became the largest employer in the town until 1914. Derby was an important place in its own right, a county town, having other manufactures besides its railway works. In the smaller railway *towns, established by the companies themselves, it might be different. At *Crewe, *Swindon, and Gateshead (see NEWCASTLE AND GATESHEAD) railwaymen formed a large part of the electorate. F. W. *Webb, locomotive superintendent of the LNWR, kept a close political control of Crewe in the Conservative interest, until his domination collapsed in 1889–90.

Outside the towns, as constituted in 1835, important changes arose when county councils were established in 1888. The administrative powers of the magistrates now passed to them. The most conspicuous of these bodies was the *London County Council. It soon started investigating the railways' provision of *workmen's trains, which varied very much from one company to another. This had some immediate results: the number of these trains provided in south London increased in 1890–4 by over 150 per cent, and this pressure continued thereafter, though no similar municipal action was taken with strong effect in any provincial city.

One other factor in the evolution of workmen's trains must also be remembered. From 1891 onwards the larger municipalities began to provide their own transport, particularly for the poorer classes, by means of electric *tramways. Local authorities were now proclaiming themselves openly as the railways' rivals.

The relationship was a haphazard one, never planned and seldom touched by any special legislation. In that it reflects the character of railway development in Britain (see GOV-ERNMENT, RAILWAYS AND NATIONAL) and that of British local government itself.　　　　　　　　　　　　　　JS

W. H. Chaloner, *Social and Economic Development of Crewe* (1950), 153–65.

government, railways and national. This article should be read with PARLIAMENT AND LEGISLATION.

The earliest railways were built by private individuals for carrying their own freight, requiring no permission from the government. But when in 1758 Charles Brandling and some associates wished to bring coal from their pits into *Leeds by a railway, interfering with other persons' established interests, they secured a private Act to validate their plans for the *Middleton Railway. In 1801 the *Surrey Iron Railway Act permitted the public to use the line for its own traffic, on payment of fixed tolls. This was the basis on which the *Stockton & Darlington Railway's first Act was passed in 1821, supplemented by another in 1823, authorizing the use of mechanical traction and the conveyance of passengers. The government did nothing to interfere until 1838, when it obliged the railways to carry mails, at a 'reasonable remuneration', for the *Post Office. Then in 1840 it passed an Act for regulating railways in general, followed by two more in 1842 and 1844 (see REGULATION ACTS). These established the Board of *Trade as the department responsible for railway matters, authorizing it to appoint *inspectors to examine lines before they were opened and to report on accidents; providing also for the compulsory running of cheap trains, on defined conditions, and for requiring railways to permit *telegraphs. But these Acts touched only on matters of broad political interest. The 1844 Act laid down terms on which, in or after 1866, the government might purchase the railways if it chose (see GLADSTONE'S ACT; NATIONALIZATION).

The government exercised almost no powers over the planning of a national railway *system, beyond setting up commissions to investigate rival routes from England to *Scotland and *Ireland and schemes for admitting railway lines into central *London. Some people thought that the politicians had shirked their responsibilities, and when the railways' development was thrown into confusion by the wild speculation of 1844–6 (see MANIAS), their voices grew louder; more so when its sorry results came to be examined.

All other European governments acted differently. They determined the lines of their railway systems; Belgium and some of the German states paid for construction themselves. In Britain the whole work was done by commercial companies, subject only to the few legislative restrictions mentioned. The power of British commercial interests was very much stronger than any on the Continent, and able to speak to the government on equal terms. Looking back in 1846, Macaulay comprehensively condemned the weakness of British governments, of both parties, in the handling of the railways. Questions affecting the convenience, prosperity, and security of the public had been treated as private matters. 'That the whole country was interested in having a good system of internal communication seemed to be forgotten', he said. The interests of speculators and land-owners had received careful attention, 'but nobody appeared to be heard on behalf of the community'.

There were demands that the government should create a strong Railway Board, more powerful than the civil servants at the Board of Trade could be, authorized to plan and supervise development; but they were successfully opposed by the railway companies. The British government was willing to prevent or rectify abuses, but it shrank from acting to promote improvement (see DALHOUSIE).

However, the Board of Trade quietly grew stronger and its authority, built up on the experience of the years, became increasingly recognized and respected. When the government chose to ignore its advice, it usually had in the end to give way (see COMMUNICATION IN TRAINS). Some railway chairmen and managers strongly disliked the Board, particularly its inspectors: *Watkin, *Moon, *Allport, T. E. *Harrison. But they did not prevail. They spoke only on behalf of the companies and their shareholders, the Board 'on behalf of the community'. In 1889 the Board emerged in triumph, when Parliament obliged railways to adopt safety precautions that had been urged on them by the inspectors for 30 years and more. Here the government was at last to be seen governing the railways.

During this time the British government had asserted the right to use railways for its own purposes. The Regulation Act of 1844 allowed it to require them to convey troops and police, and these powers were exercised at times of internal disturbances (see RIOTING). They gave the government new kinds of strength. Military witnesses before parliamentary committees spelt this out in detail. Cobden summarized it tersely in 1850: 'Since the introduction of railways the same number of troops gives a vast increase of power.' With the aid of the telegraph as well, the government could respond to events and, if need be, exercise control in a much shorter space of time than ever before.

Moreover, the railways offered the government effective help in time of *war. The Regulation of the Forces Act (1871) authorized it, in national emergency, to assume control of any railways it chose, as it did in 1914.

Meanwhile, railways had steadily assisted the government in developing its provision for defence, military and naval. The army's organization was greatly changed when bases were established at Aldershot and on Salisbury Plain; in the second of these developments the *London & South Western Railway played a valuable part from 1905 onwards. The same company had conducted the embarkation of troops at Southampton for the Boer War smoothly in 1899–1902. Great new naval bases were also being developed in Scotland, at Rosyth, Invergordon, and Scapa Flow, which were wholly dependent on railway access (see also HIGHLAND RAILWAY).

The great and essential support that the government received from the railways in World War I helped to convince some politicians that it ought to act more positively towards them than in the past. The idea of nationalization (which had been much discussed in 1907–14) was rejected, the government deciding instead to amalgamate 120 railways into four groups (see GROUPING), under the Railways Act, 1921, with a new Ministry of *Transport, inheriting the railway powers of the Board of Trade.

That ministry soon became responsible for the balancing of the railways' interests against those of mechanical *road transport. It controlled, for example, the licensing of road vehicles, and the administration of the new Road Fund for the improvement and extension of the road system. The railways complained of injustices done to their own interests, which the Transport Act, 1929, did something to rectify, permitting them wider participation in road transport than hitherto.

The establishment of the London Passenger Transport Board (see LONDON TRANSPORT) in 1933 was the first serious effort by any British government to integrate rail and road transport. The effort was incomplete, for it applied only to the *underground railways, disregarding the main-line companies' routes in London. But it worked satisfactorily, on the whole, and fortified the movement that wanted state ownership of railways, led by a Labour party fully committed to nationalization.

World War II again placed the railways under the government: much more absolutely than in 1914–18. The whole system was now vulnerable to air raids and the government became responsible for railway operations over which it had not previously exercised control: the movement of civilians, for instance, and supplies of fuel and food. When the Labour party achieved power in 1945 it promptly set about nationalization, effected in 1947.

The government now had complete control. The railways depended on *subsidies to supplement their insufficient revenue (see BRITISH RAILWAYS), which varied according to the attitude of the party in power, thereby inhibiting long-term planning. Finally, in 1993 the Conservative government took powers to return the whole system to private ownership (see PRIVATIZATION). JS

E. Cleveland-Stevens, *English Railways* (1915); *GR*; T. B. Macaulay, *Speeches* (1854), 438; R. Cobden, *Speeches*, ed. J. Bright and J. E. T. Rogers (1880).

gradient posts, SEE MILE AND GRADIENT POSTS.

Graham, George (1822–99), engineer, born of farming stock in Annandale, and apprenticed to Robert Napier, marine engineer, for whom he worked on the engines of the first Cunard steamship, the *Britannia*. His health gave way, and he was employed by Joseph *Locke to assist in the survey of the *Caledonian Railway, becoming involved throughout construction. He started the first public passenger train on the line. Appointed engineer-in-chief to the Caledonian in 1853, he retained the post until his death. Until 1880 Graham had general supervision of permanent way and works, thereafter being responsible for new lines including the extension of the Greenock line to Gourock, the Glasgow Central Railway, and lines in *Edinburgh. He wrote the first history of the CR, published privately in 1888. A conservative engineer, during his career the mileage of the Caledonian increased from 195 to 1,116. JRH

PICE, 137 (1899–1900), 424.

Grainger, Thomas (1794–1852), civil engineer. He worked in an Edinburgh surveyor's office 1809–16, then practised on his own. He surveyed and constructed the Monkland & Kirkintilloch Railway, 1824–6, and the Garnkirk & Glasgow Railway, 1826–31 (see CALEDONIAN RAILWAY).

He took John *Miller into his office in 1823, and into partnership in 1825. The firm was unusual in that many Scottish railways ascribed to 'Grainger & Miller' as engineers were dealt with independently by one or other of them. All the largest Scottish railways they undertook were handled by Miller. The firm was responsible for over 60 per cent of lines opened in Scotland before 1845.

Grainger was often criticized, not always justly, for extravagance and faulty estimating. The English engineers *Locke and Errington satisfied their Scottish clients better. His partnership with Miller ended in 1845, by which time Grainger was working in England on the Leeds Dewsbury & Manchester and *Leeds Northern Railways, each requiring a long tunnel and long bridges. He died in an accident on the LNR in 1852.   JS

PICE, 12 (1852–3), 159–61; Robertson, 191–5. No papers from the partnership seem to survive.

Grand Allies. Two sets of landowners joined forces in 1726, to protect their common interests in the North Durham coalfield. They soon became known as 'the Grand Allies'. The original partners were Sidney and Edward Wortley, George and Sir Henry Liddell, George Bowes, and William Cotesworth, who died only a month after the alliance was formed.

Among the matters agreed on were that the partners should pool their rights to grant 'wayleaves' and also pool their own wagonways (see TRAMROADS) for their common use. Among these was the Tanfield line, with its Causey Arch (see BRIDGES AND VIADUCTS).

This treaty became a very tight-fisted arrangement: the partners, for instance, would sometimes agree to pay rent to another landowner provided that he refused to grant a wayleave to one of their competitors: a subject of complaint before Parliament in 1727. But the treaty stood, and should be remembered as the ancestor of all the pooling *agreements between British railway companies in the 19th and 20th centuries.

The treaty of 1726 was long-lived. The consortium became important again in the history of railways nearly 100 years later. Still known as the Grand Allies, it leased the Killingworth collieries, north of Newcastle, in which the partners showed an active and far-seeing interest. They financed the building of George *Stephenson's first locomotive there in 1813. 'Yes!' he recognized gratefully in old age, 'Lord Ravensworth [Liddell] and partners were the first to entrust me with money to make a locomotive engine.'   JS

M. J. T. Lewis, *Early Wooden Railways* (1970), 122–3, 138; S. Smiles, *Life of George Stephenson* (1857 edn.), 82.

Grand Junction Railway. The Grand Junction gained its Act on the same day in 1833 as its southern neighbour, the *London & Birmingham Railway, but because of a comparative lack of heavy engineering works, it attracted far less attention, even though it was opened first, in 1837, thus becoming Europe's first trunk line. Its share capital was £1,040,000.

Running from a station alongside the LBR's at Curzon Street, *Birmingham, to the *Liverpool & Manchester Railway at Newton (later called Earlestown), Lancashire, it passed close to Wolverhampton and through Stafford and Warrington. The last 4¾ miles were built by the Warrington & Newton Railway, opened in 1831, which the GJR had absorbed in 1834. With the LBR and LMR, it formed a continuous railway from *London to *Liverpool and *Manchester.

The Grand Junction was also notable for being built on time and within its financial estimate. Initially the engineer was George *Stephenson, with Joseph *Locke as his deputy, although the latter did most of the work, thereby gaining the greater confidence of the directors who, tiring of Stephenson's apparent loss of interest, placed the entire work in his hands in 1834. Locke's efficient attention to detail made his reputation. The 78 miles to Warrington contained some modest viaducts and two major ones, both over the River Weaver in Cheshire: Vale Royal and Dutton, the latter at that time the largest then attempted.

Liverpool finance and a number of common directors ensured a close relationship with the LMR from the outset, including the running of through trains from Liverpool and Manchester to Birmingham, and the location of the GJR's works alongside the LMR at Edge Hill, Liverpool, before they were moved to *Crewe in 1840. In that year the GJR absorbed the Chester & Crewe Railway, shortly before it opened.

Seeing itself as part of a grand design for a railway from London to Scotland, the GJR supported the *North Union Railway, which took the line on to Preston, and invested in the *Lancaster & Carlisle and *Caledonian Railways. In 1845 it amalgamated with the LMR and absorbed two small lines to Bolton, consolidating its position in Lancashire by acquiring the NUR jointly with the *Manchester & Leeds company in 1846.

Despite complementary geographical locations, inherent jealousy between Liverpool and London financial interests on the respective boards created mutual acrimony with the LBR, particularly concerning the Manchester & Birmingham Railway which sought a shorter route to the LBR through the Potteries. After the Grand Junction reneged on an agreement by which it had persuaded the MBR to take its line to Crewe instead, the MBR found a ready supporter in the LBR.

In 1844 the antagonists made a 'non-poaching' territorial agreement, only to resume warfare a year later over the MBR's renewed efforts, which included a direct line from Stafford to Rugby: the Trent Valley Railway. The scheme failed, but not before the GJR uncovered a provisional agreement by the LBR to acquire the MBR.

The GJR retaliated with a brief flirtation with the *Great Western, ambitious to take the broad *gauge north-west, which sufficiently alarmed the LBR into agreeing to absorb a second, independent and successful Trent Valley Railway jointly with the GJR and MBR in 1846, followed immediately by the amalgamation of all three to form the *London & North Western Railway.

The GJR was very profitable. Since opening, its dividends were at least 10 per cent, and its final capital value reached £5,788,560. Its general manager, Mark *Huish, took the same position in the new company.   GJB

Whishaw, 124–37; N. W. Webster, *Britain's First Trunk Line* (1972); H. G. Lewin, *The Railway Mania and its Aftermath* (1968 edn.), chs 3, 4; M. C. Reed, *Investment in Railways in Britain, 1820–1844* (1975), esp. 126–33.

Granet, Sir William Guy (1867–1943), manager and chairman. A barrister, he became secretary to the *Railway Companies Association in 1900, where he expanded its activities and influence, and equipped himself to take a senior railway management position, albeit not via the conventional route from the operating department. In 1905 he joined the *Midland Railway as assistant general manager, becoming general manager in 1906 at the youthful age of 39. He was knighted in 1911.

He, *Fay, and *Thornton were the only railway general managers who served with the War Office, Granet doing so as deputy director-general of military railways in 1916, and of movements and railways, 1917.

Appointed to the board of the MR in 1918, he became its last chairman in 1922. At the *Grouping he became a deputy chairman of the *London Midland & Scottish Railway, and chairman the following year. He was largely responsible for the introduction of an American style of management to the LMS before retiring in 1927.   AD

RM, 19 (1906), 237; and 44 (1919), 97; Sir S. Fay, *The War Office at War* (1937).

gravity working took advantage of long, favourable gradients to propel loaded trains without attaching motive power. At first the horse merely walked or trotted behind but in 1826 George *Stephenson suggested attaching an open horsebox or *dandy to each train whereby the train could travel downhill as fast as was prudent while the horse relaxed in the dandy, thereby speeding up traffic and increasing the amount of work that each horse could perform in a day. Except in emergency, gravity working was seldom employed on locomotive-worked lines: a notable exception was the *Festiniog Railway on which loaded slate trains ran by gravity until 1939.

A more specialized use of gravitational motive power was hump *shunting in which trains were propelled slowly over an artificial hump where previously uncoupled groups of wagons ('cuts') accelerated away on the downhill side, creating space between successive cuts for points to be changed, directing them into the required sidings. Gravity was also harnessed by self-acting *cable inclines on which a heavier descending load hauled a lighter one uphill.

See also TRACTION, UNUSUAL FORMS OF.   RW

L. T. C. Rolt, *George and Robert Stephenson* (1960), 138.

Gray, John (1810–54), engineer, son of an engineer associated with George *Stephenson. Gray trained at the Ste-

phensons' Newcastle works and then, with his father, joined the *Liverpool & Manchester Railway where they were responsible for locomotive power until 1839. He designed a hydraulic press for forcing wheels on to and off axles and, with John Chanter, special smoke-consuming fireboxes for burning coal instead of coke. Gray's patent *valve gear, allowing expansive use of steam on the LMR *Cyclops*, reduced fuel consumption appreciably. He was appointed locomotive superintendent, Hull & Selby Railway (see LEEDS & SELBY) 1840–5, and *London Brighton & South Coast Railway, 1845–7. His 2-2-2 passenger engines for these railways were equipped similarly, whilst 0-6-0s for the HSR also had balance-weights on the driving wheels. Other innovations included a device for transferring weight to driving wheels at starting, tapered chimneys to improve draught, and shaped valve ports to reduce fire-throwing when engines were working hard.   GWC

BSRL; *Jnl. Inst. Loco. Engineers*, 33 (1943), 377–9; R. T. Smith, 'John Gray and His Expansion Valve Gear', *TNS*, 50 (1978–9).

Gray, Thomas (1787–1848), promoter. The son of a Leeds engineer, he was interested by the *Middleton Railway when he saw it at work. He was at Brussels in 1816, when a projected canal from Charleroi to Holland was under discussion, and urged that a railway should be built instead. In 1820 he published an anonymous pamphlet, *Observations on a General Iron Railway*, putting forward a plan for a British railway system; it was reissued in four more editions (1821–5), swelling from 22 pages to 233. Only the last edition bore his name.

His plan comprised two trunk lines, from London to Edinburgh and Falmouth, from which others branched. All were to be built, equipped, and maintained by the government and to remain under its control.

In his later years he lived at *Nottingham and *Exeter; well known as a monomaniac, talking of nothing but railways. He died in poverty, having seen railways projected into every part of the country by private undertakings, under no government plan at all.   JS

DNB; *Ottley, 256, 364, 372; Jackman, 507–9.

Great Central Railway. Its origins lay in the need for better communication across the Pennines between *Manchester and *Sheffield, achieved in 1845 by the Sheffield Ashton-under-Lyne & Manchester Railway, a company promoted by local interests. Its construction was bold, piercing the Pennines with the three-mile Woodhead *tunnel, then the longest in the country. Rapid expansion was planned both for profit and against competition. In 1847 the SAMR expanded by amalgamation with three other railways and the Grimsby Docks Company to form the Manchester Sheffield & Lincolnshire Railway: Grimsby flourished and foundations were laid for penetration of the south Yorkshire coalfield, achieved in 1863 by the absorption of the South Yorkshire Railway, to the disquiet of the rival *Great Northern Railway.

Westward expansion was secured that year by joint funding, with the GNR and later the *Midland, of the amalgamation of four railways then managed under the name of

*Cheshire Lines Committee. This eventually gave the MSLR access to Warrington, *Liverpool, and Chester, whence it gained access to coal and iron ore deposits in North Wales.

Most of the income of the MSLR came from coal and the products of the industry served. It supplemented its passenger services with *running powers over other railways, particularly in the West Riding. However, it was constantly on the defensive against competition from, and absorption by, stronger rivals such as the *London & North Western, GNR, and Midland, and later with new railways such as the Lancashire Derbyshire & East Coast, promoted in direct competition with the MSLR in 1891. In defence of its competitive position with the GNR in 1850 the MSLR had been drawn into an alliance with the LNWR, *Lancashire & Yorkshire, *East Lancashire, and Midland Railways known as the Euston Square Confederacy (see COMPETITION, INTER-RAILWAY); when this alliance was dissolved in 1857 the MSLR instead forged a 50-year alliance with the GNR.

In these times the company had as chairman (Sir) Edward *Watkin, who held numerous railway directorates and, soon after taking the chair in 1864, also assumed chairmanship of the *South Eastern, East London (see LONDON UNDERGROUND RAILWAYS), and *Metropolitan Railways. Watkin was a visionary and an adventurer, unceasingly pursuing his dream of a *Channel Tunnel while giving the MSLR a reputation for acting close to the limits of acceptable corporate behaviour. His battles with Mark *Huish of the LNWR, James *Allport of the MR, and, to a lesser extent, E. B. *Denison of the GNR, dominated railway development in late Victorian years.

Under Watkin, the MSLR flourished but was never rich. His determination to expand the railway, even beyond its means, resulted in low dividends. Chief among expansions was the extension to London, built in the 1890s and criticized as unnecessary and wasteful. It involved building a new railway from Annesley, Notts, to Quainton, Bucks, whence a *joint line developed with the Metropolitan Railway took the MSLR to a short new railway and a terminus at *Marylebone.

This undertaking transformed it from a provincial cross-country railway to a trunk route, and justified the then unusual step of giving the company a new name: Great Central. Thus it declared its rivalry to others and its confidence in its route to London, which opened in 1899. It ran through *Nottingham, *Leicester, and Rugby, all of which already had direct access to London, and could only be made to pay by taking traffic from other railways. Significantly, no ordinary dividends were paid after 1889.

The headquarters was moved from Manchester to Marylebone in 1905, by which time it had a new senior team equal to the tasks ahead: the chairman from 1899 was Alexander Henderson (later Lord Faringdon), a financier; the general manager from 1902 was (Sir) Sam *Fay, from the *London & South Western Railway; and the solicitor from 1900 was Dixon Davies, who had much experience of railways through his work for the LDECR, which the GCR had purchased in 1906. These three were ably supported by John

G. *Robinson, *Swindon-trained, who came as CME from an Irish railway in 1902; and Arthur Bound, promoted to signalling engineer in 1906.

Robinson equipped the GCR with powerful and singularly handsome locomotives, built mostly at the company's Gorton *works. His coaching stock, also built at Gorton prior to the opening of a new carriage and wagon works at Dukinfield in 1910, was well received by the travelling public who responded to the GCR's advertising slogan 'Rapid Travel in Luxury'. Notable freight stock included bogie vehicles both for fish traffic from Grimsby and for locomotive coal.

Among new developments was the construction of a new *port at Immingham, complementing busy Grimsby, for both goods and passengers, including significant emigrant traffic from northern Europe bound for the USA via the GCR and CLC to Liverpool. The full cost of Immingham, which covered 1,000 acres and incorporated 150 miles of sidings, was £2.6 million. It allowed expansion of the GCR's *shipping services to the Continent and competed strongly with the *North Eastern Railway at *Hull. During the opening ceremony by King George V in 1912, Fay was publicly knighted. It was a fitting reward for a distinguished railwayman at the height of his achievements.

One of Fay's early and characteristic initiatives had been to buy Dean & Dawson, an old-established *travel agency well placed to attract passenger business. Then there were new through workings to North Wales, the south, and south-west. With the *Great Western Railway the GCR ran a through service between *York and *Cardiff, including through coaches for *Newcastle-upon-Tyne and later for Hull and Barry.

The coal business also grew: in 1907 a hump *marshalling yard at Wath, in the heart of the south Yorkshire coalfield and capable of sorting 5,000 wagons in 24 hours, was commissioned. Here and elsewhere the GCR installed power *signalling, with pneumatically operated signals.

These and other innovations characterized the company, but railways were coming under increasing competition from *tramways and the motor car. Experiments in low-cost equipment such as steam and petrol-electric *railcars complemented the increasing efficiency of Robinson's locomotives. The last major route built by the GCR was a second approach to London via Princes Risborough and High Wycombe, constructed jointly with the GWR and opened to passengers in 1906.

The company was primarily a carrier of freight. In 1914, 67 per cent of its gross receipts came from freight, but only 22 per cent from passengers, far lower than that of any other large railway. It was marginally the largest carrier of freight among all the railways that served London.

World War I brought an end to further ambition, and diverted men and machines alike. Three of the GCR's ships were seized in Germany and the remainder were requisitioned by the Royal Navy. Workshops manufactured munitions, and traffic increased vastly to support the movement of men and weapons. Robinson's classic 2-8-0 heavy freight locomotive was chosen by the Ministry of Munitions as the standard locomotive for use overseas, and 521 were built to its orders. Fay became director of movements at the War Office for the last two years of the war.

The Government assumed control of the railways in August 1914 and did not relinquish it until after the groundwork had been laid for the *Grouping. The opportunities for further innovation were thus strictly constrained and there was a need to catch up arrears of maintenance from the war years.

The GCR contributed much to the country and to its successor, the *London & North Eastern Railway, not least its capable staff, modern equipment, the widespread network of passenger services which had been reinstated soon after the war, a notable flair for innovation, and a keen sense of publicity. It is seen in retrospect as a bold, innovative railway, and remembered for its beautiful locomotives. In recent years most of the line to London and its route across the Pennines have gone. Immingham remains its greatest living memorial, and Marylebone station a quiet reminder of a once great company.   AD

Dow; freight and passenger receipts: *Railway Year Book* (1914).

Great Eastern Railway. An amalgamation, authorized in 1862, of the *Eastern Counties Railway with the *Norfolk, the Eastern Union, East Anglian, and East Suffolk (all of which it already worked), giving the amalgamated company a railway *monopoly east of Cambridge.

The finances of these five squabbling companies took four years to sort out, and during the crisis of 1866 (see SPECULATION) the GER went briefly into receivership. But it slowly recovered, making good progress under the chairmanship of Lord Cranbourne (later Marquess of Salisbury) in 1868–71.

Among its chief defects was its inconvenient London terminus, Bishopsgate (see LONDON STATIONS—LIVERPOOL STREET; WOOD, SANCTON). In 1864–6 it had taken powers to buy land for a new one within the City. That station was opened on Liverpool Street in 1874–5. The company had just then completed a number of lines in the north-eastern suburbs, forming a dense network.

Henceforth its activities fell into six main divisions. (1) It was heavily committed to the development of London working-class suburban traffic. (2) It handled a large *agricultural business, though this was badly hit by the decline of English arable farming in the 1870s and 1880s. (3) It served five *ports: Harwich, Felixstowe, Lowestoft, Yarmouth, and King's Lynn. From the third and fourth of these it conveyed large quantities of *fish to London and the Midlands. (4) Lowestoft and Yarmouth were also large *holiday resorts, as were Clacton and Southend, served by GER branches opened in 1882 and 1889. (5) From Harwich the company operated steamship services to the Low Countries, unskilfully developed at first but growing successful from 1883 onwards. (6) After a long struggle, it secured part of the valuable coal traffic from Yorkshire into East Anglia by means of a *joint line undertaken with the *Great Northern, from a point near Doncaster through Lincoln, Spalding, and March, opened in 1882.

The GER enjoyed little luxury business except race traffic at Newmarket. There its services were so much appreciated that the wealthy Col. McCalmont handsomely paid for the building of a large new station in 1902.

Rather, the GER became primarily a carrier of passengers paying the lowest fares. In 1872 it copied the *Midland Railway immediately by providing third-class accommodation in all its trains. It was the first British company to admit third-class passengers to a *restaurant car (in 1891). Its suburban trains were seriously overloaded in the rush hours, but the numbers of passengers were more than could possibly have been conveyed in any degree of comfort. The service it gave them was brisk and, most notably, *punctual; in the circumstances, a great achievement.

Electric *tramways first ran in east London in 1901, depriving the GER of much of this traffic. It considered electrifying its own lines, but was deterred by the cost and believed it could develop its services further with steam traction. In 1914 an exceedingly able general manager, the American Henry *Thornton, reshaped the company's main-line services. He went on to produce in 1920 an ingeniously planned reorganization of its suburban system, which made it the finest of its kind, worked entirely by steam, anywhere in the world. First- and second-class carriages bore distinctive yellow and blue stripes, earning the nickname 'jazz trains'.

No conspicuous changes like these occurred in the company's rural districts. There it came to lose part of its monopoly. Some small lines appeared, feeding traffic into it but remaining independent: the Colne Valley & Halstead (completed in 1865), for instance, and the *Southwold Railway (1879). Other short lines had been built west of King's Lynn, supported by the Great Northern and Midland companies. These were gradually extended across Norfolk to reach Cromer, *Norwich, and Yarmouth, and were amalgamated by these two companies in 1893 to form the *Midland & Great Northern Joint Railway. It competed with the GER for the holiday traffic of the Norfolk Broads and the coast, and the conveyance of fish to the Midlands. Nevertheless the GER retained almost all the business between these places and London.

When the port of Harwich became inadequate to handle its growing continental traffic, the railway built a large extension, opened in 1883 and named Parkeston Quay after its chairman C. H. Parkes. The traffic grew further after the new port at the Hook of Holland opened ten years later. Harwich became the most important naval base on the east coast south of Rosyth. The GER made a large contribution to this work, much of its Parkeston Quay being turned over to the navy during World War I.

The company was well served. Two of its chairmen have already been mentioned here; for the last of them see HAMILTON, LORD CLAUD. Its locomotive engineers formed a distinguished group. Although three of these were with it for only a short time—S. W. *Johnson, William *Adams, and T. W. *Worsdell—they each did good work there. Robert *Sinclair and James *Holden served longer, Holden being remembered particularly for his successful experiments with *oil as a locomotive fuel. After 1878 most of the company's engines were built in its own works at Stratford. In signalling, it should be remembered as the first in Britain to introduce electro-pneumatic power operation, at its Spitalfields goods yard in London, in 1899.

Financially, the company made remarkable progress from its miserable start. Its dividend never attained 2 per cent until 1882, but by 1901 it was 6 per cent. Then the difficulties facing most British railways in the following years, aggravated by the sharp decline in its London passenger traffic, set the dividend back to 2 per cent by 1913.   JS

C. J. Allen, *Great Eastern Railway* (1956 and later edns.); *Reg. Hist.*, v; Acworth, ch. 14; T. C. Barker, 'Lord Salisbury, Chairman of the Great Eastern Railway, 1867–72', in *Business and Business Men*, ed. S. Marriner (1978), 81–103.

Greathead, James Henry (1844–96), civil engineer, born in South Africa. He was a pupil of P. W. *Barlow, 1864, and assistant on the *Midland Railway, Bedford–London line, 1867. He later assisted with unsuccessful projects such as the Regent's Canal Railway, 1880; the outer circle, 1881; and an Eastbourne line, 1883. He was joint engineer with Sir Douglas *Fox on the *Liverpool Overhead Railway, 1888–93.

Greathead is best remembered for his development of the modern tunnelling shield (see TUNNELS). In 1869 he built the Tower Subway for Barlow, some 900 ft long and with only 25 ft of cover. In 1868 he advocated compressed air in wet soils, and in 1874 patented a method of water excavation, extended in 1884. He held patents on grout injection and spoil removal. In 1884 he was engineer on the *City & South London Railway, opened in 1890, built using compressed air. At his death, he was working with W. R. *Galbraith on the *Waterloo & City Railway, opened in 1898.

MHG

PICE, 127, 1896–7.

Great Northern & City Railway, see LONDON UNDERGROUND RAILWAYS.

Great Northern Railway. Although the GNR's main line from *London to *Doncaster was not opened throughout until 1852, a London to *York scheme had been proposed as early as 1827.

Not until 1844 was an effective trunk route plan revived, by the London & York Railway, supported by Edmund *Denison, MP for the West Riding of Yorkshire, and with William *Cubitt as engineer. The scheme comprised a main line from London via Hitchin, *Peterborough, and Grantham; a loop line from Peterborough to Bawtry south of Doncaster via Boston and Lincoln; and branches to *Sheffield and Wakefield.

Essentially, this became the core of the future Great Northern Railway. The London & York Bill received Royal Assent in 1846, after protracted opposition involving heavy expenditure, and the first meeting of what was now the Great Northern Railway followed almost immediately. Edmund Denison became chairman in 1847.

The first section of line to be opened was leased: Louth to Grimsby (1848); and by 1849 services were offered between Peterborough and Doncaster via Lincoln. By 1850, the line was opened to Peterborough from a temporary station at Maiden Lane, London, and Doncaster to York via Askern. The London terminus at *King's Cross was completed in late 1852 and the railway's main *works was established in 1853 at Doncaster.

By 1853, the direct Peterborough–Grantham–Retford line was open, and by acquiring other railways, or *running powers, the GNR gained access to *Bradford, Cambridge, Halifax, *Leeds, and *Nottingham. By means of a working arrangement with the Manchester Sheffield & Lincolnshire Railway (see GREAT CENTRAL), by 1857 the GNR was able to run London–Sheffield–*Manchester express services. The *Midland Railway used the GNR's line into London from Hitchin from 1858. The result of both these developments was to undermine the 'Euston Square Confederacy' established by the *London & North Western Railway (see COMPETITION, INTER-RAILWAY).

By the late 1850s the GNR had access to all the important West Yorkshire towns. The revenue received from the coal traffic from this area to London and the south-east encouraged the *Great Eastern and *Lancashire & Yorkshire Railways to promote a Bill for a trunk line through Lincolnshire from Doncaster. Thrown out by Parliament in 1865, it was equally unsuccessful in 1871. The GNR improved its access to West Yorkshire in 1866 by the *joint purchase with the MSLR of the West Riding & Grimsby line (Doncaster–Wakefield). In due course, the ambitions of the GER were constrained by the establishment in 1879 of the Great Northern & Great Eastern Joint lines, from Huntingdon through March into Lincolnshire and to Doncaster, which were joined together by new construction.

For its part the GNR pursued territorial interests outside its original areas of interest by joint promotion with the MSLR of a Manchester–Liverpool route in 1865. It was soon committed to further extensions into Cheshire and Lancashire through its involvement in the *Cheshire Lines Committee, in concert with the MSLR and MR.

Initially, management of the railway was dominated by Edmund Denison, and the general manager, Seymour *Clarke. The former retired in 1864, the latter in 1870, to be succeeded by Henry *Oakley. Under F. P. Cockshott as superintendent of the line, the GNR established a reputation for well-run main-line services. By the early 1870s it was operating a more intensive service of express trains than either the LNWR or MR. Hauled by Patrick *Stirling's single driving-wheel locomotives (see TRACTION), they were some of the fastest in the world.

The railway expanded rapidly during the 1860s, and the GNR was at its most profitable in 1873. With a steady growth in traffic during the early 1870s, it had to invest heavily in the extension of the *block *signalling system, and interlocking, and in improvements to *stations and goods sidings. In 1875–80 the increase in revenue was outpaced by investment, and the railway risked over-extending itself by marginally profitable extensions to the CLC network, and by the construction of lines in Nottinghamshire and Leicestershire under joint control with the LNWR. To the east, the GNR gained access to the Norfolk coast by joint acquisition with the MR of the Eastern & Midlands Railway from 1889, the system becoming the *Midland & Great Northern Joint Railway.

An unsatisfactory arbitration, the Karslake Award of 1870, in the matter of *freight rates charged for coal traffic from south Yorkshire and the Derbyshire coalfield, led to a rates war with the MR. One consequence was the GNR's extensions into Nottinghamshire and Derbyshire, as far west—initially—as Burton-on-Trent.

The GNR's role in the establishment of an Anglo-Scottish *East Coast route was confirmed by the formation of the East Coast Joint Stock in 1860, by which a common pool of passenger vehicles was operated by the GNR, *North Eastern, and *North British Railways. Anglo-Scottish expresses had run over the GNR from 1852. The principal express trains became the 10 a.m. departures from King's Cross and from *Edinburgh Waverley; these began running in June 1862, and by the 1870s were known as the Flying Scotsman.

The GNR's expresses were steadily improved and expanded from the late 1870s, notably with the operation of the first regular *restaurant car service in 1879, and the fitting of continuous vacuum *braking by 1881.

During the mid-1890s the main line had to be relaid with heavier rail to accommodate larger and faster trains, and more powerful engines designed by H. A. *Ivatt which entered service from the mid-1890s. These worked fine sets of clerestoried *carriages built for the East Coast expresses and West Riding dining car trains. Elliptical roofed stock was designed by H. N. *Gresley for the GNR and East Coast Joint Stock from 1905; some of this was *articulated.

Long-distance excursion traffic was developed to Skegness, to the Norfolk coast, and to the St Leger race meetings at Doncaster.

Suburban development in north London brought a rapid increase in *season-ticket travel. City traffic was catered for by trains run to *Broad Street, following reciprocal arrangements set up in 1875 with the *North London Railway. Widening of much of the London end of the main line was completed in the 1890s.

The GNR's principal revenue was derived from freight, predominantly coal, for which major *marshalling yards were provided at Doncaster, Colwick (Nottingham), New England (Peterborough), and Ferme Park (London). For merchandise traffic, the GNR was a pioneer of fully braked goods trains. Under the 1923 *Grouping, it became part of the *London & North Eastern Railway.   MLH

Grinling; J. Wrottesley, *The Great Northern Railway* (1979–81).

Great North of England Railway. Originally planned to connect *York and *Leeds with *Newcastle, in continuation of lines from the south, this was in fact built only between York and Darlington. Its 43 miles, almost straight across the Plain of York, were nowhere steeper than 1 in 342 (for a very short distance), making construction easy. The two biggest bridges, Nether Poppleton and Croft viaducts, designed by experienced engineers, John and Benjamin

*Green, and Henry Welch, county surveyor of Northumberland, respectively, are strong masonry structures that have stood well. Trouble with a number of the smaller bridges, however, necessitated rebuilding, leading to the replacement of the company's engineer, Thomas Storey, by Robert *Stephenson. The York terminus was shared with the *York & North Midland Railway.

Part of the GNER's powers to continue to Newcastle was transferred to a new company, the Newcastle & Darlington Junction, authorized in 1842, controlled by George *Hudson and forming a section of the through route he envisaged from London to Edinburgh, via Rugby, *Derby, and Berwick-on-Tweed. To prevent the GNER uniting with the proposed direct line from London to York (see GREAT NORTHERN RAILWAY), Hudson leased it in 1845. In the following year it was purchased by the NDJR, which changed its name to, first, the York & Newcastle, and then *York Newcastle & Berwick in 1847.   JS

Whishaw; Tomlinson, 278–82, 285–6, 290–1, 348–52; *Reg. Hist.*, iv, ch. 5.

Great North of Scotland Railway: one of the constituent companies of the *London & North Eastern Railway in the 1923 *Grouping. It was promoted when the progress of the Aberdeen Railway created interest in extension north of the city and a prospectus was issued in 1844, though capital was not forthcoming until the railway from the south was finished in 1850. The GNSR was opened in stages from *Aberdeen to Keith in 1853–6 to meet the Inverness & Aberdeen Junction (*Highland Railway from 1865) which arrived in 1858. A plan for the lines to join at the Spey foundered through disagreement over the payment for the bridge and GNSR concern about running through unrewarding country. The Aberdeenshire Canal provided the alignment for the railway as far as Inverurie.

There were troubled relations with the HR over *running powers to *Inverness, but GNSR proposals for independent access failed to gain approval. From the 1880s there was a more conciliatory approach with pooling arrangements and through running of locomotives; even an amalgamation proposal in 1905. Meanwhile, there was no real interest in amalgamation with the Aberdeen Railway (*Caledonian Railway from 1866). The GNSR used a separate station and had a bad reputation for its treatment of long-distance passengers by failing to maintain connections when trains from the south were delayed. Initially, it declined to join the *Railway Clearing House. A new era dawned when a *joint station opened in Aberdeen in 1867. The reform of management later in the century produced a more accommodating attitude to passengers, summed up by the phrase 'little and good'.

The main line was doubled between 1861 and 1900 and the network was extended by routes to Elgin via Dufftown and via the coast, completed in 1863 and 1884 respectively. Both arose out of local railway projects: the Morayshire Railway connected Lossiemouth with Elgin and advanced south to Rothes; while the coast route originated in the Banff Portsoy & Strathisla Railway which ran from Grange, east of Keith Junction. There were major branch lines to Peterhead in 1862, Fraserburgh in 1865, Ballater in 1866, and Macduff in 1872, as well as many shorter branches. The general policy was to minimize the construction of new railway, so branches usually left the network at the nearest point to the destination, although this resulted in somewhat indirect journeys from Aberdeen. Further branch lines were considered in Buchan and Glenlivet, and some minor additions to the system were achieved: Boddam in 1897, and St Combs in 1903.

Technical innovations included *single-line tablet exchange and equipment for exchanging mails at speed; also the early use of electric light at stations. Locomotive building was transferred from Kittybrewster (Aberdeen) to Inverurie in 1902, where good housing was provided in a new quarter of the town.

Passenger journeys were predominantly local, with few *through carriages apart from Aberdeen–Inverness workings. Tourism was stimulated by a *hotel at Cruden Bay in 1899, served by an electric tramway from the local railway station. The Moray Firth was promoted as the Scottish Riviera. The Aberdeen suburban service to Dyce (1887) was extended to Culter on the Deeside line in 1894 and additional stations were built. The Deeside line was also regularly used by royal trains to Ballater, the station for Balmoral (see ROYAL TRAVELLING). The GNSR stimulated the fishing industry with its special trains, and concessionary fares for fish-sellers travelling inland from the coastal ports. There was also a growth of the fat cattle trade as country stations generated local markets, like Maud where a new village was created, and the Speyside distilleries prospered.   DT

Reg. Hist., xv, 5; M. Barclay-Harvey, *A History of the Great North of Scotland Railway* (1940); H. A. Vallance, *Great North of Scotland Railway* (1965).

Great Western Railway. Several proposals for a railway between London and *Bristol were produced from 1824 onwards, the first effective one in 1832. The Bristol promoters appointed I. K. *Brunel as their engineer and, with a committee in London, launched their 'Great Western Railway'. A parliamentary Bill failed in 1834, but in 1835 the company gained authorization to construct the line, with a capital of £2.5 million in shares and £0.83 million in loans.

Brunel proposed a *gauge of 7 ft, as against the 'standard' one of 4 ft 8½ in, considering that broad-gauge trains could be safely run at higher speeds. His ideas were accepted by the board. To the objection that it would prevent through running between the GWR and standard-gauge lines, Brunel answered that at such points of junction a 'mixed gauge' could be established, with a third rail laid outside each pair of standard-gauge lines: an arrangement that did not work well in practice.

Construction and Development to 1863
The first section of the line was opened between London and a station near Maidenhead in 1838. Its capable secretary C. A. *Saunders undertook the general management. The locomotives Brunel ordered were largely experimental,

intended for high speed but unsuited to the initial ordinary traffic. The difficult task of making them work rested on a very young locomotive superintendent, Daniel *Gooch.

By the end of 1840, 80 miles of line were completed from London and 11 miles from Bristol to Bath. At Box, east of Bath, a two-mile tunnel had to be built. The whole line, 116 miles long, was opened in 1841, by which time its cost had risen from £3.3 million to over £6 million. The blame for its slow completion and high price was widely attributed to Brunel's special requirements. Many shareholders considered that it had been a mistake to accept his broad gauge, but efforts to get rid of him in 1839 failed.

The system was soon enlarged by branches to Windsor, Basingstoke, Hungerford, Oxford, and Gloucester, all opened by 1849. Other companies had by then extended the line from Bristol to *Plymouth.

When in 1845 the GWR reached Gloucester the broad gauge met the standard gauge of the *Birmingham & Gloucester Railway, head on. Great confusion ensued. The *Midland Railway now leased the *Bristol & Gloucester intending to connect it with the standard gauge, a task that was finished in 1854, bringing standard-gauge trains into Bristol over Brunel's unsatisfactory 'mixed' track.

In another field of railway working, however, his ideas achieved great success. In 1845 the GWR introduced *express trains between London and *Exeter (194 miles) at 43 mph, including three stops, much faster than trains anywhere else. Brunel shared his triumph with Gooch, who had designed locomotives that showed complete mastery of their task.

In 1852 the GWR broke out of southern and western England by opening a mixed-gauge line from Oxford to Birmingham, enabling it to compete for London–Birmingham traffic with the *London & North Western Railway. When in 1854 the Shrewsbury & Birmingham and Shrewsbury & Chester companies amalgamated with the GWR, giving access, by *running powers, to Birkenhead, the GWR had a trunk route from London to the Mersey. It was extending its power in other directions too. The *Cornwall Railway, opened in 1859, depended on the GWR and its allies for the exchange of long-distance traffic at Plymouth. By 1867 *through carriages were being run between London and Penzance.

Finally, in these years the GWR began to establish strong interests in South Wales and in the traffic to southern Ireland. In 1845 the *South Wales Railway was authorized to build a broad-gauge line from the GWR near Gloucester across to the west coast. It reached Milford Haven in 1856, whence steamers sailed to Waterford. In 1863 the GWR amalgamated with the SWR and with the *West Midland Railway, whose system extended from Oxford to Wolverhampton, Hereford, and down to the Monmouthshire coalfields.

In 1862 the GWR had a total mileage of 595. These new additions increased it to 1,105.

Great Western Railway

Years of Difficulty

This expansion might look impressive, but the real state of the company was unsatisfactory. Bagehot remarked in 1863 that it had a 'board of directors and a sort of board at any rate of anti-directors'. After the highly respected Charles Russell resigned from his 16 years' chairmanship in 1855, five other chairmen came and went during the next ten years until Gooch, the former locomotive superintendent, was appointed in 1865. He confronted great difficulties, exacerbated by the financial crisis of 1866 (see SPECULATION). The company remained solvent only by the most rigid economy. Though Great Western stock nearly always commanded a good price, in 1841–79 its annual dividend was only 3.8 per cent.

In 1856–61 the mixed gauge was extended from Oxford to London. But in South Wales, industrialists' increasing dissatisfaction with the broad gauge persuaded the company to convert the SWR to standard gauge. This task, extending to just over 300 miles of line, was most efficiently performed over one weekend in 1872. By 1876 nearly all broad-gauge trains had disappeared from GWR main lines except the principal one, from London to Penzance.

The company made no further important extensions of its own until 1900. Three-quarters of its expansion from 1,331 miles in 1873 to 2,526 in 1900 were due to the absorption of other companies, by which time its system was the longest in Britain. Improvements requiring considerable expenditure were made only with great reluctance. No new main-line broad-gauge carriages were built after 1882, the old ones growing steadily shabbier. Express trains were hauled by renewals and enlargements of Gooch's 'Iron Duke' locomotives of 1847.

Yet the company had important merits—was even, here and there, an innovator. It led the way in introducing refrigerated vans for the new frozen-meat trade in the 1870s. Among the four largest British companies the GWR had fewest major fatal accidents: only one between 1874 and 1936. Moreover, in 1873–86 the company built the *Severn Tunnel, then the longest underwater tunnel in the world.

Rejuvenation

In 1889 Gooch died while still in office. Although his services to the GWR had been very great, his economies were excessive. He was succeeded by another former officer, F. G. Saunders, and he in turn in 1895 by Lord Emlyn (Earl Cawdor, 1898), a large landowner in Wales who served admirably for ten years. In 1888 N. J. Burlinson had become superintendent of the line, and he and his successor T. I. Allen reshaped the passenger services. J. C. *Inglis, chief civil engineer from 1892, became manager in 1903. These men, accompanied by a good locomotive engineer, William *Dean, and after his retirement in 1902 by a great one, G. J. *Churchward, completely transformed the company.

The broad gauge was entirely abolished in 1892: 385 miles, branches included, between London and Penzance. This allowed new services to be offered. Through standard-gauge carriages were at once provided, for example, from *Liverpool, *Manchester, and *Leeds to Torquay. In 1895 the company at last freed itself, at considerable expense, from the compulsory refreshment stop at *Swindon, allowing accelerations of chief expresses by ¼ hr. *Restaurant cars were at last introduced in 1896.

These improvements were accompanied by a steady increase in line capacity. By 1890 there were four tracks from London to Didcot (53 miles), except for a bottleneck at Reading, removed in 1899; and the single line through Cornwall was being progressively doubled.

Still one major defect remained: the company's circuitous principal routes from London, which earned it the nickname 'Great Way Round'. Consequently on two of them traffic passed largely to competitors. Even in Gooch's days powers had been secured to shorten the main line from London to Exeter by linking up existing lines, through Westbury to Taunton. Work now proceeded energetically. The GWR was also determined to develop its South Wales and Irish traffic by shortening its route between London and Cardiff. Simultaneously it had an opportunity to secure a direct line to Birmingham, in place of the one via Oxford, by collaborating with the new *Great Central Railway. The magnitude of the GWR's work in these years, compared with other companies', is revealed in the accompanying table.

Much faster trains were now run over these routes, composed of new carriages very different from the ageing broad-gauge vehicles and hauled by Churchward's fine new locomotives. Under Inglis the company showed that it understood the value of effective *publicity, to proclaim its new services. The handling of long-distance *freight traffic was improved, and safety precautions too: the GWR was the pioneer, among large British railways, in the adoption of

Route	Powers first taken for any part	Completed	Old distance (miles)	New distance (miles)	Distance by rival line (miles)	New construction (miles)
London–Cardiff	1896	1903	170 via Gloucester 155 via Bath	145	none	30
London–Exeter	1883	1906	194	174	172 (LSWR)	33
London–Birmingham	1897	1910	129	111	113 (LNWR)	58

GWR 'cut off' routes completed 1903–10

Key
LNWR   London & North Western Ry
LSWR   London & South Western Ry

*automatic warning systems from 1906 onwards (see SIG-NALLING).

To improve Irish services, the company built a large new harbour at Fishguard in 1906 and provided three turbine ships. It also competed for transatlantic traffic in 1909–14, when some of the Cunard liners—including *Mauretania* and *Lusitania*, then the two biggest ships in the world—called at Fishguard, whence the GWR conveyed passengers and mails to London (261 miles) in about 4½ hours.

In World War I the GWR suffered little damage, and less disruption of traffic from military demands than its neighbour the *London & South Western Railway. But it could not avoid political upheaval afterwards. The government was determined to amalgamate the railways into a small number of large units (see GROUPING). Although the GWR had a more tightly coherent system than the two other biggest companies, the LNWR and the MR, it had at its central point in South Wales 13 short independent railways which operated some 450 miles. And there was the system of the *Cambrian Railways in mid-Wales, with another 280. They all touched the GWR at numerous locations, and in 1922–3 they came under its control. The GWR failed in an attempt to have them regarded as subsidiary companies, without seats on its new board, and therefore had to find room for six representatives among its 25 members. It was unfortunate for future relationships that the author of this unsuccessful ruse was the new general manager, Felix *Pole.

The New Company

A great problem lay ahead. The South Wales coal industry, on which all these companies except the Cambrian depended, reached its peak in 1923, and then declined almost without interruption. The *ports and railways serving it suffered correspondingly, burdening the GWR with a shrinking business, which before 1923 had been highly profitable. Here it had a worse inheritance than any of the other new companies, though the *London & North Eastern was similarly damaged in north-eastern England and in Scotland.

However, it also enjoyed one great advantage in not having to establish new administrative structures in 1923, sparing it the internal power struggles that beset the other companies, the *London Midland & Scottish worst of all. The management continued smooth, stable, and self-confident. For many years the chief offices had been filled almost wholly by internal promotion, the only important exception being Louis Trench's appointment as chief engineer, from the LNWR, in 1891: an unhappy business, for he stayed little more than 18 months. This practice tended to produce a certain complacency, and perhaps to discourage innovation.

In 1938 the company employed consultants to estimate the costs and savings in electrifying its line from Taunton to Penzance (see ELECTRIFICATION). A major purpose here may have been to warn the South Wales coalowners that their charges for locomotive fuel were too high, and that another form of motive power was being actively considered. No result followed and the GWR remained alone among the large British railways in not employing electric traction. For the rest, the company strove to maintain its standards with well-publicized high-speed express trains. None, however, were completely streamlined, like those of the LMS and LNER.

It was affected much more severely by World War II than by World War I, both by intensified demands and by physical damage (see WAR). In 1940 the Severn Tunnel became one of the worst bottlenecks on the whole British railway system. The approach lines from Newport were quadrupled late in 1941; but it would have been impracticably expensive to build an additional tunnel.

The company emerged from the war to face the certainty that it would be purchased by the state (see NATIONALIZATION). Among the strongest critics of that measure was the GWR's general manager, Sir James *Milne. Nevertheless, the company's long history terminated in 1947.

Among the British railway companies the GWR bore a character all its own. Foxwell caught it admirably in 1888 when he remarked that it did 'some great things and many small, but all alike with the immovability of Jove'. That immovability remained to the end: symbolised, for the observing passenger, by the courtesy of its staff and their ritual at stations during the quite exceptionally long stops its express trains made, above all perhaps at Reading. JS

MacDermot; P. W. B. Semmens, *History of the Great Western Railway, 1923–47* (1985); Bagehot's comment: *Collected Works* (1965–86), x, 443; Pole's proposal: *Felix Pole His Book* (1968 edn.), 50; Severn Tunnel: C. I. Savage, *History of the Second World War, Inland Transport* (1957), 225, 233, 259, 425–6; Foxwell's remark: E. Foxwell and T. C. Farrer, *Express Trains English and Foreign* (1889), 27.

Green, John (1787–1852) and **Benjamin** (1811–1858), *architects. The Greens, father and son, had an extensive practice in *Newcastle. Their work is not very easy to separate. John built Scotswood and Bellingham bridges over the Tyne, the Newcastle Literary and Philosophical Institute, churches, and two laminated timber viaducts and bridges on the Newcastle & North Shields Railway, a novel form of construction he also used elsewhere, and with his son for the triple-arched *trainshed at North Shields station, which was widely followed by other engineers.

Benjamin worked with *Dobson in redeveloping central Newcastle, where he designed the Theatre Royal and the Grey Monument. When aged 25 he designed the simple but attractive stations on the *Newcastle & Carlisle Railway (1835–8), giving them a common stamp which also characterized some stations on the *Great North of England Railway (1841), and Alston station (1852), suggesting that he may have had a part in their design as well.

Ten years later on the Newcastle & Berwick Railway he produced powerful designs for the stations, no two of which were alike. Although the smaller ones had no clearly definable style they were carefully proportioned, while the larger stations—Warkworth, Longhirst, Christon Bank, Belford, Beal, Morpeth—were strongly neo-Tudor, delicately executed in finely dressed stone, and notable for their matching goods sheds. The most elaborate station, Tweedmouth, was Jacobean. GJB

L. G. Booth, 'Laminated Timber Arch Railway Bridges in England and Scotland', *TNS*, 44 (1971–2); *VS*, 69–71; H. M. Colvin, *Biographical Dictionary of British Architects, 1600–1840* (1978); N. Pevsner and I. A. Richmond, *The Buildings of England: Northumberland* (1992 edn.).

Green, Leslie William (1875–1908), the *architect (with Harry Wharton Ford as staff architect) for the *Underground Electric Railways of London from 1903. He was responsible for the design of stations above ground and their interior decorative work on the Bakerloo, Piccadilly, and Hampstead tubes (see LONDON UNDERGROUND RAILWAYS). The street-level elevations, each individually designed to carry later additions of upper storeys, were faced with glazed tiling of a noticeable ox-blood red colour, which made them distinctive and familiar to passengers before the later standard house-signs of the Underground were introduced. The same colour was used in most (not all) of the station interiors in the passage-way and platform tiling. Green is credited with over 40 tube station exteriors, probably more than any other single architect working for a railway, before his death, aged only 33. RMR

A. Gray, *Edwardian Architecture* (1988 edn.), 76–7, 198; L. Menear, *London's Underground Stations* (1983).

Greene, Sydney, see NATIONAL UNION OF RAILWAYMEN.

Greenock, see PORTS AND DOCKS.

Gregory, Sir Charles Hutton (1817–98), engineer. Apprenticed to a millwright, he worked as an assistant to Robert *Stephenson on the Manchester & Birmingham Railway and then, under James Walker, in dock-building at Woolwich. In 1840 he became resident engineer, under William *Cubitt, for the *London & Croydon Railway. For its junction with the *London & Greenwich line at Corbett's Lane he designed and installed semaphore signals (originally proposed by *Rastrick; the first used on any railway—see SIGNALLING) and the ancestor of *signal boxes. He accepted the plan for working his railway on the *atmospheric system, but he quarrelled with Jacob Samuda, one of its chief protagonists, and resigned in 1845 to become chief engineer of the *Bristol & Exeter Railway, then already in full operation, and of the two components of the *Somerset & Dorset Railway. In later life he did much work on colonial and foreign railways. He was president, ICE in 1867–8, and became KCMG 1883. JS

PICE, 132 (1897–8), 377.

Gresley, Herbert (Sir) Nigel (1876–1941), engineer; apprenticed at *Crewe, later with the *Lancashire & Yorkshire Railway. He was appointed carriage and wagon superintendent of the *Great Northern Railway, 1905, and succeeded H. A. *Ivatt as CME, 1911, then was appointed CME of the *London & North Eastern Railway, 1923. He was knighted in 1936, and was president *IMech E, 1936.

Responsible for the introduction of elliptical-roofed carriages on the GNR, and for East Coast Joint Stock in 1905–6, Gresley pioneered *articulation. He developed the com-

pound-bolster bogie from 1911. As CME, he introduced a modern 2-6-0 design to the GNR in 1912, then two- and three-cylinder 2-8-0s, the latter with derived motion for the inner cylinder (see HOLCROFT, HAROLD W.). Gresley's first A1 class Pacific was No. 1470 *Great Northern*, of 1922. Rolling-stock designs included the first five-car articulated dining car set in 1921, an articulated twin sleeping car in 1922, and four- and five-car suburban trains in 1923–30. He pioneered the use of electric cooking equipment for restaurant cars in 1921.

The Gresley Pacifics were progressively improved from 1926, with long-lap valves and higher pressure boilers, culminating in the A4 class streamlined engines, built from 1935 and used on the high-speed trains such as the Silver Jubilee and Coronation. *Mallard* of this type ran at 126 mph in July 1938, to set up an unbeaten world record speed for steam (see also SPEED).

The basic design of the teak-panelled carriages introduced for the GNR was perpetuated for the LNER, with features such as pressure ventilation and *air-conditioning in prestige stock, from 1930; welded underframes, from 1934. Other innovations included the use of aluminium, and plywood for body panelling.

Locomotive innovations included experiments with booster engines, from 1923; poppet valves, from 1925, fitted to the 2-8-2 *Cock o' the North*, built in 1934; the experimental 4-6-4, No. 10000, built in 1929 with a water-tube boiler. The versatile 'V2' 2-6-2 mixed traffic engines were built in quantity from 1936.

Despite the excellent design of his engines, the conjugated valve gear deteriorated in performance with the poor maintenance during World War II, overheated big-ends proving a cause of failure. (See THOMPSON, EDWARD.) MLH

F. A. S. Brown, *Nigel Gresley* (1961); F. A. S. Brown, *From Stirling to Gresley 1882–1922* (1974); M. Harris, *LNER Carriages* (1994); M. Harris, *Great Northern Railway and East Coast Joint Stock Carriages from 1905* (1995).

Grierson, James (1827–87), manager. He became secretary of the joint committee for managing the Shrewsbury & Birmingham and Shrewsbury & Chester Railways in 1851, and in 1857 chief goods manager of the *Great Western. He took a leading part in the difficult amalgamation of the *West Midland Railway with the GWR in 1863, the year he was appointed the GWR's general manager.

He became its chief diplomat, and a highly skilful witness before parliamentary committees. Though he had to work during the reign of economy under Daniel *Gooch, he steadily effected improvements in the company's services. He died in 1887 before they had been fully realized. Gooch then noted privately: 'His loss to me and the railway interest cannot be replaced.'

A year before his death he published *Railway Rates English and Foreign*: the most comprehensive discussion, from the railways' point of view, of their freight services and the rates charged for them, then being angrily criticized (see FREIGHT TRAFFIC RATES). Quiet in tone and very well informed, its comparative analysis of the subject in Britain and elsewhere was especially valuable. JS

guards

MacDermot; Boase; Sir D. Gooch, *Memoirs and Diary*, ed. R. B. Wilson (1972), 351.

Grinling, Charles H., writer. He was the son of William Grinling, accountant of the *Great Northern Railway in 1868–96, and he served in his father's department. In 1895 he published a *History of the Great Northern Railway* (2nd edn., 1903; 3rd, with additional chapters by others, 1966), much the best then published of any British railway company. From his position at headquarters he had access to many of the company's records, and he made good use of that. Enlivened by a flash of dry humour here and there, this is still among the best books of its kind.

He also wrote a popular book, *The Ways of Our Railways* (1905, new edn. 1910), and a guidebook to the Lancashire Derbyshire & East Coast Railway (see GREAT CENTRAL) in 1905. He contributed three articles to the first volume of the *Railway Magazine* (1897), but none thereafter.   JS

Grouping of 1923. When the railways were released from wartime control in 1921 they were not allowed to return to their pre-war competitive position. There was fairly general agreement that the benefits of unified operation should be retained in peacetime, and hence the Railways Act of 1921 amalgamated 120 undertakings into four large groups (see Appendix 1): the *London & North Eastern (LNER), the *London Midland & Scottish (LMS), the *Southern (SR), and the *Great Western (GWR), the first two of which controlled the bulk of the route mileage. These four groups remained in being until the railways were *nationalized after World War II.

The grouping was achieved rapidly, and when the Act came into force on 1 January 1923 the reorganization had been largely completed. Effectively it brought to a logical conclusion the trend towards company concentration evident since the mid-19th century. The chief objective behind the amalgamation was to diminish inter-company rivalry, reducing costs and inefficiency resulting from the duplication of facilities. It was also envisaged that substantial economies would accrue from more unified operation.

The second most important part of the Act related to charging policy. Here the aims were to codify and rationalize the system of charging and to provide a more flexible rate-making structure. A permanent control body, the Railway Rates Tribunal, was established, whose first duty was to approve a new schedule of standard charges submitted by the new companies. The Act did not guarantee the companies a fixed level of profit, but it did require that charges set should be at such a level as to yield an annual net revenue equivalent to that earned in 1913, amounting to £51.4 million (see FREIGHT TRAFFIC RATES).

Though the railways were to achieve considerable improvements in operating performance and economies from more unified control, their subsequent history was far from happy. Traffic stagnated throughout the inter-war years and the companies, either individually or collectively, failed to meet their standard net revenues of 1913 in almost every year. The decline in the staple heavy industries resulted in the loss of heavy goods traffic, especially coal, while the

rapid growth of *road transport seriously affected the railways' passenger and merchandise traffic on short- and medium-distance routes. The railways could not offer the same flexible delivery as road transport. The fortunes of the railways were also impeded by the restrictive charging powers of the 1921 Act, the continued use of antiquated costing and pricing systems, and the common carrier and social obligations inherited from the 19th century. Finally, despite the concentration of ownership, very little attempt was made to eliminate excess capacity. In fact the route mileage abandoned during the period was small.   DHA

D. H. Aldcroft, *British Railways in Transition* (1968), ch. 2; G. W. Crompton, 'Efficient and Economical Working? The Performance of the Railway Companies, 1923–33', *Business History*, 27 (1985).

guards. The term 'guard', for the railwayman in charge of a train, is derived directly from the armed guards in charge of *Post Office mail-coaches on the roads from 1784 onwards. The responsibilities of the 'mail guard' included not only security of the mails but also recording the timekeeping of the coaches. Operators of stage-coaches similarly placed their vehicles in the charge of guards, and so in due course did the *Liverpool & Manchester Railway (1830) and subsequent railways with their trains of coaches.

From November 1830, when mails were first carried by rail (on the LMR), there were two sorts of guard to be seen on trains: the companies' own guards, in charge of the trains, and the Post Office guards, transferred from road routes, who continued to take charge of the mails. At first they travelled on elevated outside seats, comparable to their previous position on road coaches, to keep watch upon the mails carried in boxes on carriage roofs. From 1838, however, they were also located within Travelling Post Office (see MAIL SERVICES) vehicles, where their duties included not only taking charge of the mails but also operating the bag-exchange apparatus. By 1841 the Post Office was employing mail guards on 19 railway routes. Because travelling outside was much more dangerous than on road coaches, on trains where there was no TPO mail guards increasingly travelled in ordinary compartments with the bags. In 1848 the Post Office made arrangements with the railway companies for conveyance of mail-bags in the charge of the companies' own guards, and the numbers of Post Office guards declined, although they continued to be a feature of trains until 1860 when the Post Office reorganized its TPO staff as 'sorters' and 'clerks'.

Like the mail guards, the railways' own guards at first travelled on elevated seats on the ends of passenger coaches. They applied the *brakes in response to whistles from the engine. If their train stopped other than at a signal they had to go back down the line to protect it from those following, either by hand signals, or by use of detonators after their invention in 1841. On goods trains, brakesmen who undertook the same task travelled on top of the wagons. *Brake vans first appeared in the late 1840s and early 1850s. Those for both goods and passenger trains were at first similar—the guard was still in the open, but at floor level, with most of the van enclosed to form luggage space.

197

guard's van

In 1860 there were 4,264 guards and brakesmen on the railways of Britain. The introduction of continuous brakes on passenger trains, and of the *block system (both made compulsory by the *Regulation of Railways Act, 1889), relieved the passenger guard of some of his immediate responsibilities, although he was still able to apply the brake in emergency, and had to protect his train in event of an out-of-course stop or accident. He continued, however, like his mail-coach predecessor, to record details of his train and its progress for the benefit of those in authority. This record, the 'guard's journal', included the number of the locomotive and name of the *driver, details of the vehicles and the load, and alterations as vehicles were attached or detached *en route*; it also included arrival and departure times at stations, with, particularly, causes of delay. F. S. Williams in *Our Iron Roads* (1883) records receipt of 1,600 guards' journals every day at the *Midland Railway superintendent's office.

The passenger guard was very much in the public eye; a popular figure. As well as passengers he had in his care mails, *luggage, *parcels, horses, and dogs. Children travelling unaccompanied were placed in his charge with instructions to make sure they got out at the right stop. Before the general introduction of dining cars (from around 1890) he arranged for passengers' orders for refreshment baskets to be telegraphed ahead. At stations he patrolled the length of his train, and it was his responsibility, after ascertaining that all was well, to give the driver the 'right away' by whistle and green flag or, after dark, handlamp.

Such important personages cut suitably imposing figures. Guards on the *Manchester & Leeds Railway wore coats of flaming red, those of the *London & Greenwich dark green with brass buttons, those of the *London & South Western, from 1847, coats of blue with scarlet collars (see also UNIFORMS). On the *London & North Western Railway passenger guards wore frock coats; prominent from right shoulder to left hip was the ornamental leather strap of the 'baldric', derived from the workaday strap and pouch in which the guards of mail-coaches had carried their vital timepieces. The baldric continued to be part of an LNWR guard's uniform until the turn of the century. Later guards sported the chains of fob watches, and carnations in their buttonholes.

The passenger guard was usually promoted from goods guard, who had in turn been promoted from *porter or shunter. Throughout most of the railway era, operation of loose-coupled *freight trains without continuous brakes meant that goods guards had a harder time than their passenger train colleagues. The goods guard travelled at the rear of the train in his van, equipped with lockers, brake handle, and stove but no illumination apart from his handlamp. Controlling his brake required much skill; the sudden impact of an unchecked brake van against the last wagon of a bunched-up train could send the guard flying from one end of the van to the other.

In 1948 there were 19,255 goods guards and 8,274 passenger guards on the railways of Britain, performing largely their traditional tasks. Subsequently, modernization has brought many changes. As freight trains fitted with continuous brakes spread, so brake vans were eliminated and the goods guard moved to the rear cab of a diesel locomotive, or was dispensed with altogether. Passenger guards have become accustomed to remote operation of doors, and to communicating with drivers by buzzer and intercom rather than whistle and flag, although the latter are still used at busy stations and in emergencies.

Introduction of 'pay trains' in the late 1960s made their guards responsible for taking fares, and they were retitled 'conductor guards'. The term 'conductor' for a senior passenger guard was used by the *Grand Junction Railway as early as 1837, and has appeared at intervals since. Since the mid-1980s, guards with responsibilities for checking tickets, taking fares, and operating a public address system have been called 'conductors', or 'senior conductors' on InterCity trains (see BRITISH RAILWAYS). A nation-wide paging network has been introduced to enable senior conductors to be contacted by *control offices, and some guards and conductors carry their own radio-telephones for outward communication. On some routes, starting with the Bedford–*St Pancras and Moorgate line in 1982, the functions of the guard have been combined with those of the driver under 'Driver Only Operation'. PJGR

Anon., *Railways and Railway Men* (1892), ch. 7; H. Chappell, *Life on the Iron Road* (1924); F. McKenna, *The Railway Workers 1840–1870* (1980); Post Office mail guards: P. J. G. Ransom, *The Victorian Railway and How It Evolved* (1990), ch. 5.

guard's van, see BRAKE VANS.

guidebooks. The conveyance of passengers by steam-worked railway created a public for guidebooks, pointing out features of interest in their working and describing what might be seen from trains as they went along.

Although J. S. Walker's *Accurate Description of the *Liverpool & Manchester Railway* (1830) combined both those elements, it was principally a general account of the work, not specifically addressed to travellers. The earliest true guidebook to this line—one to be held in the passenger's hand, objects of interest being identifiable from little drawings in the text—was the admirable *Railway Companion. By a Tourist* (1833), followed by E. Parsons' *Tourist's Companion* (1835), describing the rail and steamboat journey from Leeds to Hull.

The opening of trunk railways from 1837 onwards offered a bigger market for such books, for passengers making long journeys, and by 1840 there were guidebooks (sometimes more than one) to all the chief lines out of London, as well as to some in the provinces. Presently they came to be produced in series, each volume dealing with a separate line: the *Railway Chronicle Travelling Charts* in 1846, for example (folding route-maps, with places described and depicted on both sides of the line); and the fuller guides of George Measom, nine of them (1852–64), together with two to Irish railways (1866).

The railway companies themselves entered the business with their *Tourist Guides*, concerned more with landscape and history than with details of working, when those had ceased to be a novelty. Perhaps the best were produced by the *Caledonian and *Highland Railways in Scotland. In England and Wales the lead was taken by the *Great Western company, advertising its guides from 1904 onwards as 'the Holiday Books of the Holiday Line'. Two large ones were commissioned from distinguished authorities: one from M. R. James on the medieval abbeys in places served by the company (1925), the other on castles from Sir Charles Oman (1926).

Guidebooks have interesting things to say to students of railway history. Some record the conditions imposed by the companies on their passengers. Others illustrate details of construction and working. Thomas Roscoe's *London & Birmingham Railway (1839) deals with 'the home and country scenes on each side of the line' but also includes a useful discussion of its engineering by Peter Lecount. Tebbutt's Guide . . . to the *Midland Counties Railway (1840) supplies gradient profiles of its lines and illustrates its codes of signalling. Measom's guides were a thoroughly commercial enterprise, much commendation of individual factories and shops being introduced into the text, and each having a large section of interesting advertisements appended to it.

There was another type of Victorian guidebook, which must not be ignored in studying railways. *Murray's Handbooks for Travellers* and the successive editions of Karl Baedeker's *Great Britain* and *London* have much to say about the prices and types of accommodation that travellers might find on their way.   JS

Particulars of all the railway guidebooks mentioned are to be found in *Ottley. See also R. B. Wilson, *Go Great Western* (1987 edn.).

Guild of Railway Artists. Rationalization of *British Railways' network inadvertently stimulated additional interest in the system. Whilst the camera effectively recorded changes such as branch-line closures or last runs by individual locomotives, artists rapidly established their superiority at recreating historic scenes of the past.

The Guild of Railway Artists was established in 1979 after Frank Hodges and Steve Johnson recognized a need to coordinate the endeavours of many artists then new to the subject. The Guild helps to safeguard standards and provides a forum for the exchange of artistic, commercial, and practical ideas.

Submission of photographs of work by prospective members can lead to associate membership; full membership is offered to those whose original work is approved by a selection panel. The Guild also arranges regular exhibitions throughout Britain, with occasional publications; arguably the most successful were associated with the 1985 'Great Western 150' celebrations.   GB-J

H

Hackworth, Timothy (1786–1850), was one of that group of enterprising colliery owners and engineers in the northeast who saw the steam locomotive through its formative years. He was born in Wylam and in 1807 was appointed foreman blacksmith at Wylam Colliery where he assisted William *Hedley in building his *Puffing Billy* and two other locomotives, 1813–15.

In 1824 George *Stephenson asked Hackworth to supervise his newly established locomotive works in Newcastle and was so impressed that he first offered him a partnership, which Hackworth refused, and then appointed him resident engineer to the *Stockton & Darlington Railway where he remained until 1840. Its first locomotives were constantly too short of steam for the long hauls now demanded so, faced with proposals to abandon locomotives entirely, Hackworth determined to produce a better one. By developing the blast-pipe, which improved the fire, and using a return-flue boiler, which considerably increased the heating surface on *Royal George* (1827), he successfully combined power and reliability with economical operation. Hackworth entered his *Sans Pareil* in the 1829 *Rainhill trials, but although it put up a creditable performance it was no match for Stephenson's *Rocket*, not least because its vertical cylinders severely curtailed potential speed. Hackworth sold it to the Bolton & Leigh Railway where it covered 120 miles daily for some years.

Hackworth developed the SDR's Shildon Works from 1833 and simultaneously established his own Soho Works nearby. Although he began to use multi-tube boilers from 1830, and later inclined cylinders driving directly on to coupled wheels, as on his *Derwent* (1845), he remained essentially a builder of slow, heavy freight locomotives and was left behind by more progressive designers.   RVL

P. R. B. Brooks, *Where Railways Were Born* (1979); J. T. van Riemsdijk, 'The Early Locomotive', in B. Horsfield (ed.), *Steam Horse, Iron Road* (1972); R. Young, *Timothy Hackworth and the Locomotive* (1923).

Hadfield, Ellis Charles Raymond (1909–96), writer. Charles Hadfield's outstanding achievement was to conceive and edit the scholarly 15-volume history *Canals of the British Isles* (1950–71), of which he wrote seven himself and three jointly with others. In doing so he established himself as the leading historian of waterways.

After working in publishing, Hadfield became a senior civil servant, and was awarded the CMG in 1959. A strong advocate of water transport, he wrote 25 books and numerous articles on canals world-wide. He helped to found the Inland Waterways Association in 1946, and the *Railway & Canal Historical Society in 1954. In 1960 he established David & Charles Publishers with D. St J. Thomas, and was a member of the newly formed British Waterways Board in 1962–6.

*Tramroads and railways featured prominently in Hadfield's canal histories, and his extensive writing on other subjects also included an important railway book, *Atmospheric Railways: A Victorian Venture in Silent Speed* (1967). With A. W. Skempton he wrote a valuable biography, *William Jessop, Engineer* (1979), on which subject, and canals, he contributed to this *Companion*.   GJB

M. Baldwin and A. Burton (eds.), *Canals: A New Look* (1984).

halts, see STATIONS, PASSENGER.

Hamilton, Lord Claud (1843–1925), chairman; younger son of the 2nd Marquess (1st Duke) of Abercorn, educated at Harrow. Having served in the Grenadier Guards and Royal Inniskilling Fusiliers, he was a Conservative MP for 31 years (discontinuously), 1864–1918. He was a director, *Great Eastern Railway, 1872; vice-chairman, 1874–93; and chairman, 1893–1922.

By 1872 the GER was already overcoming past follies and blunders, its fortunes turning upward with the profitable development of suburban, agricultural, and continental traffic. Hamilton devoted the main energies of his life to the company, not only at headquarters but also through constant travelling over the system, observing its conduct and operation.

His concept of management was authoritarian, and entirely paternal, which occasioned frequent conflict with *trade unions, especially the *Associated Society of Locomotive Engineers & Firemen. He favoured fighting out confrontations to the end, above all in the *strikes of 1911 and 1919.

His services to his company were real, and great. The trust he inspired helped to improve its financial position strikingly in difficult times: its shares rose from 76 in 1874 to par by 1896, while a mere diehard could not possibly have supported the appointment of a young American, Henry *Thornton, as general manager in 1914. Hamilton stoutly defended what proved to be a brilliant choice, against those who thought a British candidate should have been selected.   JS

DBB; C. J. Allen, *Great Eastern Railway* (1955).

Hammersmith & City Line, see LONDON UNDERGROUND RAILWAYS.

Hampstead tube, see LONDON UNDERGROUND RAILWAYS.

Hardwick, Philip (1792–1870) and **Philip Charles** (1822–92), *architects. Hardwick senior was one of the third generation of an architectural family, and at 24 was appointed architect to the Bridewell and Bethlehem Hospitals, London. He later acted for St Katherine's Dock Company, was architect to the Duke of Wellington, and surveyor to the Portman estate. His best-known surviving work is the Goldsmiths' Hall in the City, but his finest was the noble Grecian Doric portico and its attendant lodges and gates at *Euston station, completed for the *London & Birmingham Railway in 1838, and wantonly demolished in 1963. He designed the two flanking *hotels (1839), and the complimentary Ionic terminal building at *Birmingham Curzon Street (1838), which still stands.

After being commissioned to design the Great Hall, Shareholders' Room, and Board Room at Euston, Hardwick's health broke down in 1847 and his son took the greater share of the work. Until his retirement in 1861, therefore, it is difficult to distinguish their individual work, although at Euston P. C. Hardwick would undoubtedly have charge. Completed in 1846–9, the hall was Italian Renaissance in style and distinguished by what was claimed to be the largest unsupported ceiling in the world, 62 ft high and deeply panelled. John Thomas provided rich sculpture, and a curved double staircase led up to the equally magnificent Shareholders' and Board Rooms.

P. C. Hardwick's other railway work was the Great Western Royal Hotel at Paddington (1850–2), which survives, although considerably altered in 1936–8 when much of Hardwick's and Thomas' decorative treatment was removed. When built it was the largest hotel in Britain.   GJB

Sir J. Summerson, *The Architectural History of Euston Station* (1959); H. M. Colvin, *Biographical Dictionary of British Architects, 1600–1840* (1978); *GRSB*, 48–50, 90–3, 135–6.

Harrison, Sir Frederick (1844–1914), manager. After joining the *London & North Western Railway as a clerk at Shrewsbury, Harrison became foremost in the group of 'high-flyers' under *Findlay, becoming assistant superintendent of the line in 1875 at the age of 31. Appointed assistant goods manager in 1884, and chief goods manager a year later, he succeeded Findlay as general manager when the latter died in office in 1893.

It fell to Harrison to follow Findlay's policy of thoroughgoing modernization, which he did with zest, giving particular emphasis to the concept of service to the public. His continuing improvements, particularly in train services and rolling stock, and including the complete reconstruction of the station and junctions at *Crewe, ensured that the LNWR entered the 20th century as a strong, up-to-date undertaking. After retirement in 1909 Harrison briefly served as deputy chairman of the *South Eastern & Chatham Managing Committee, sitting on the board until his death. He was knighted in 1902.   GJB

Who Was Who; G. P. Neele, *Railway Reminiscences* (1974 edn.); M. C. Reed, *London & North Western Railway* (1996), 78, 88, 96; C. F. Dendy Marshall, *History of the Southern Railway*, ii (1963 edn.), 367, 369.

Harrison, Thomas Elliott (1808–88), engineer. After a grammar-school education he was apprenticed to William Chapman, civil engineer, and worked on dock construction. He helped Robert *Stephenson with plans for the *London & Birmingham Railway. He then became engineer of the Stanhope & Tyne Railway (worked largely by inclined planes) and the seven-mile Durham Junction Railway (1834–8), including the remarkable Victoria Bridge over the Wear. He worked, again under Stephenson, on the Newcastle–Berwick line (1845–9), becoming chief engineer of the *York Newcastle & Berwick Railway. He played a large part in forming the *North Eastern Railway in 1854 and was its chief engineer for the rest of his life. He designed important swing bridges for it at Goole and Naburn and (in collaboration with the company's architects) the great station at *York.

Harrison was an all-round engineer, interested in railways as a whole. When young he was consulted by *Brunel, who had two locomotives built for the *Great Western Railway, *Thunderer* and *Hurricane*, incorporating Harrison's patents. Neither succeeded, but both were intended to remedy important defects in current design. Brunel also consulted him on matters concerning the *Taff Vale Railway in 1841. In the 1860s Harrison's mechanism for providing *communication in trains between passengers and crews was officially adopted by the Board of *Trade, although later abandoned, largely because it was applied with insufficient care. He was president ICE in 1874.   JS

DNB; *PICE* 94 (1888), 301–13; *BDE*; Tomlinson; MacDermot, i, 391–5; Brunel papers, Bristol University Library. Some of Harrison's sketchbooks are in PRO RAIL 1021/87.

Hartlepools, the. In the 1820s Hartlepool was only a shrunken fishing port. But the Durham coalfield was then needing new maritime outlets, and the Hartlepool Dock & Railway Company built a line from Haswell to Hartlepool, 12 miles long, opened in 1835. The dock was completed in 1841, by which time the company's dividend was 8 per cent. When a second dock was needed, the Hartlepool West Harbour & Dock Company was formed to build it, a mile away from the old town; it opened in 1852. The company then merged with the Stockton & Hartlepool Railway to form the West Hartlepool Railway & Dock Company. Its chairman, Ralph Ward Jackson, was its driving force, and also of a new town of West Hartlepool.

The railway companies found allies in different camps. The Hartlepool company passed to the *York & North Midland in 1848; the West Hartlepool looked to the *Leeds Northern. When both of these larger companies became part of the new *North Eastern Railway in 1854, the West Hartlepool remained independent, allied only with the remote *London & North Western. It made some efforts to expand, beyond its legal powers. These being revealed, Jackson resigned in 1865 and the company fell into the NER's hands.

Under its management, the two ports grew securely. The favour the NER showed them aroused intense jealousy in *Hull, an element in the enduring hostility displayed there towards that company.

The two towns remained separate, developing their trade in coal, timber, and fishing, West Hartlepool acquiring ironworks and shipyards. By 1900 their population reached about 90,000. Through a curiosity of English local government, they were united into one municipality only in 1967. JS

Tomlinson; *Reg. Hist.*, iv (1986 edn.), 146–51; *RTC*, 199–201.

Hartley, Jesse (1780–1860): remembered primarily as an outstanding dock engineer at Liverpool, where he was surveyor of docks, 1824–60. But he also had an important hand in the *Liverpool & Manchester Railway. Asked to advise on its original line in 1823–4, he became one of its consulting engineers in 1826, giving valuable help to George *Stephenson on civil engineering matters. He seems to have been chiefly responsible for the design of the principal bridges, including the Sankey viaduct and (probably) the Rainhill skew bridge. He was also engineer for the conversion of the Manchester Bolton & Bury Canal into a railway (1832–8). JS

Thomas, 17, 34–5, 37, 45, 54–5; *LYR*, i, 26–30.

Harwich, see PORTS AND DOCKS.

Hassall, John, see ART.

Hawkins, George (1809–52), artist. The son of a landscape painter, he became an architectural draughtsman (exhibiting at the Royal Academy) and worked as a lithographer for Day & Son (later Day & Hague). His most widely known published lithographs were those he made for *Monastic Ruins of Yorkshire*, with a text by Edward Churton (1844–56).

But he also produced a most impressive series of lithographed drawings of the construction of the *Britannia Bridge over the Menai Strait on the *Chester & Holyhead Railway, showing close observation of engineering processes and of the men involved in successive stages of the work. Together with the drawings of Samuel *Russell and Edwin Clark these give an unforgettable impression of the magnitude of the task, and the meticulous care required. He died very soon after this work was completed. JS

VR, 125–6; *Menai Bridge* (Welsh Arts Council, 1980).

Hawkshaw, Sir John (1811–91), engineer. After a pupillage under Charles Fowler, a Yorkshire road surveyor, around 1829 Hawkshaw joined Alexander Nimmo and surveyed a railway from *Liverpool via *Leeds to the Humber. In 1832–4 he worked for a mining company in Venezuela, then on Liverpool Docks under Jesse *Hartley.

In 1836 Hawkshaw became engineer to the Manchester Bolton & Bury Canal & Railway (see LANCASHIRE & YORKSHIRE RAILWAY). In 1838 he reported on the *Great Western Railway for Lancashire interests. He was critical of the permanent way, and the use of broad *gauge. Further appointments in the Lancashire area followed. He became engineer of the *Manchester & Leeds Railway (1845), and then the Lancashire & Yorkshire (1847).

In 1850 Hawkshaw moved to London. Among his more important works were the *Cannon Street, *Charing Cross and *Waterloo lines incorporated in the *South Eastern

Railway for which he was consultant in 1861–81. In the 1860s he began investigating a Channel crossing and in 1872–86 was engineer, with James *Brunlees, to the *Channel Tunnel Company. In the London area he was engineer for the East London Railway, and the Inner Circle completion from Aldgate to Mansion House (see LONDON UNDERGROUND RAILWAYS). His greatest tunnelling achievement was the *Severn Tunnel (1886).

Overseas, Hawkshaw was consultant to Indian railways, where he designed the Nerbudda viaduct on the Bombay Baroda & Central India Railway. He designed the Riga–Dünaburg–Vitebsk and reported on the Moscow–Kursk railways in Russia. He was president ICE in 1862–3, and knighted in 1873.

Hawkshaw embraced all branches of civil engineering at home and overseas, particularly in South America. MMC

PICE, 106 (1891), 321–35; *LYR*, i, 227–32, 266–7; *BDE*.

headcodes. Trains have always carried headlamps to give warning of their approach. By the 1880s, growth in traffic had created a need to distinguish between different classes of train: goods and passenger, fast and slow. The larger railways then used codes of headlamps—by position and colour—to identify each approaching train.

The use of coloured lights was largely abandoned about 1905, when agreement was reached at the *Railway Clearing House on the use of a standard code, albeit with some variations to suit local circumstances. Further local and company variations were introduced subsequently, and it was not until 1950 that a single national headlamp code was introduced. Railways south of the Thames had rather different requirements, based on route rather than class, and they developed their own codes, using white or patterned discs or diamonds. The *Southern Railway perpetuated white discs, and introduced large route numbers on the front of its electric *multiple units.

The *London Midland & Scottish and *Great Western Railways had also developed numbering systems for identifying individual trains, the numbers being exhibited on the front of the engines when required, and particularly relied upon for special trains, as well as workings on summer Saturdays. The growing areas controlled from signal box control panels later brought a need for every train to be identified by a number, leading to the introduction of four-character train descriptions ('headcodes') on *British Railways in 1960–1. Trains were classified 1 to 9 or 0, succeeding the previous classes A–K. The four-character code comprised a digit for the class, a destination letter, and two digits identifying the train. From about 1958 some locomotives were equipped to exhibit the codes. This practice was rendered redundant by the rationalization of traffic and *marshalling yards and the development of *signalling systems. It was discontinued in 1976. The train descriptions ('reporting numbers') are still in use internally.

See also CONTROL. MRLI

health. Railways did a good deal to improve health, both personal and public, and damaged it in some ways too.

The speed at which trains ran enabled new and salutary

changes of diet. They could bring *milk, *fruit and vegetables, *meat, and *fish rapidly, in good condition, into the fast-growing towns. Before railways' arrival, fish was eaten in London only by the well-to-do and on fast-days by the Catholic poor. When the railways were able to bring it in quickly and cheaply it soon became accepted as a standard food by poor people of all sorts, even in towns far from the sea. The railways' long-distance transport of milk—later in vans that were cooled in hot weather—also helped to enrich and diversify townspeople's diet. Moreover, speed of transit reduced the temptation to adulterate food with preservatives that were frequently poisonous.

The railways' services to public health were varied. They assisted some hospitals. The Three Counties Asylum at Arlesey (Bedfordshire), for example, opened in 1857, had a private siding on the *Great Northern Railway's main line, with a passenger station (see STATIONS, PRIVATE). This institution became huge, and would have been unworkable without rail transport: by 1880 it had 1,000 beds. A number of hospitals had private railways. Patients, staff, and visitors were conveyed in electric *trams from the main-line railways at Cheddleton (Staffordshire) and Hellingly (Sussex). The Bangour Railway, steam-worked and opened in 1905, was a two-mile private branch from the *North British company's Edinburgh–Bathgate line taken into the Bangour Village Hospital.

One more social service of a similar kind was also developed in association with railway companies, though it achieved only limited success: the laying-out of large new *cemeteries, away from town centres.

The railways could also convey medicinal supplies when they were needed, quickly and cheaply. Brine, for example, wanted for hydropathic purposes at Harrogate, came in that way from Teesside. Safe and pure water reached Lincoln by rail during a typhoid epidemic there in 1905.

The railways' speed benefited many invalids. Even the cheapest, *Parliamentary trains (which could take them to hospital), travelled more than twice as fast as horse-drawn *coaches. Specialists' fees were reduced as their travelling time to distant patients came down.

From an early date railway *stations had public lavatories (see SANITATION), which influenced their wider adoption by local authorities.

Most railway companies provided medical aid to their employees, especially those injured at work. The *Grand Junction and *Great Western set good examples at *Crewe and *Swindon in 1844–7, medical funds being established, to which the men contributed. Surgeons were appointed and remunerated by the companies; small hospitals followed in both towns, again partly supported by the companies. All this was done quietly, to avoid shareholders' criticism of the expenditure, and generous contributions were made by directors and officers. Half the capital cost of establishing the GWR fund came as a gift from Daniel *Gooch.

Other employers, in mining and manufacturing, acted similarly; some went further. Railways made important contributions, however, to the acceptance of a broader idea of employers' responsibilities, nowhere more clearly than in their provision of reliable and affordable medical aid (see also COMPENSATION).

It must be recognized, however, that the railways also damaged the lives of some people. Those who lived near them suffered much from atmospheric *pollution by smoke, and—almost as bad—from the din of nightly shunting in goods yards. Travelling by them could be dangerous, especially in 1860–80, when *accidents were most frequent. It was sometimes argued that the daily travelling of *commuters shortened their lives, and (inconclusively) that diseases of the heart and spine arose from sitting in railway carriages.

The journey itself might have its own private terrors, when passengers were enclosed in compartments with lunatics or ruffians, with no means of summoning help when needed (see COMMUNICATION IN TRAINS). Such episodes read horribly when reported in newspapers. Yet the news of hideous car crashes does nothing to reduce traffic on the roads today, and it was the same with the railways up to 1914.

The drawbacks that the railways brought to health and welfare were real, but they should not be over-emphasized. The new flexibilities they afforded, in work and leisure (see HOLIDAY-MAKING), did much to invigorate body and spirit, and that represented, in the largest sense, a true strengthening of health.   JS

J. C. Drummond and A. Wilbraham, *The Englishman's Food* (1957 edn.); G. Croughton, R. W. Kidner, and A. Young, *Private and Untimetabled Railway Stations* (1982); VR, 351–5, 373–5.

heating, see TRAIN HEATING.

Hedley, William (1779–1843), born in Newburn, Northumberland, trained as a colliery viewer (manager). Overshadowed among the locomotive pioneers because his interest lay primarily in efficient colliery operation, Hedley linked *Trevithick's and George *Stephenson's work by demonstrating that a smooth-wheeled locomotive could pull an economic load on smooth rails.

Christopher Blackett appointed Hedley as viewer at Wylam Colliery in 1805, having just ordered a second Penydarren locomotive from Trevithick. The state of the wooden track precluded its use, and Trevithick declined to build another after this was relaid with iron plate-rails, so, knowing of the successful Blenkinsop and *Murray locomotives, Blackett approached Hedley.

After some experimenting, Hedley built three successful locomotives (1813–15) with *Hackworth's assistance, using return-flue boilers and wheels coupled through gears. Modified as 8-wheelers (1815–17) to spread their weight over the brittle plate-rails, they pulled 50-ton loads until 1828–9, when they were replaced by two 4-wheelers of the same design (*Puffing Billy* and *Wylam Dilly*) now running on edge rails; these operated until the 1860s.

Hedley demonstrated his ingenuity again in 1822 when he converted one of his locomotives into a steam tug to circumvent the keelmen's strike on the Tyne which threatened to block his colliery's output.   RVL

P. R. B. Brooks, *William Hedley, Locomotive Pioneer* (1980); J. B. Snell, *Railways: Mechanical Engineering* (1971).

Heiton, Andrew, see ARCHITECTURE AND ARCHITECTS.

heraldry. Heraldic devices have long been used by railways to establish their identity and as a symbol of solidity and respectability. Usually based upon the seal of incorporation of the company, the coat of arms was highly decorative and widely used to add to the *liveries of equipment.

Commonly, the coat of arms took the form of a garter, complete with buckle, bearing the name of the company, which encircled one or more decorated shields, a monogram, or other symbol. Shields usually carried the arms of the principal towns served. The most extravagant example was the first device of the *Great Northern Railway, incorporating the arms of 12 cities or towns and those of England and Scotland.

Coats of arms also came in simpler form. Garters with no decoration, or shields without garters were widely used. The least informative were those of the *Maryport & Carlisle and *Central London Railways, neither of which bore any name or motto to indicate the identity of the company.

It was rare for a company to seek a grant of armorial bearings from the College of Arms. Those which did were the Manchester Sheffield & Lincolnshire and its successors the *Great Central and *London & North Eastern Railways, the *Southern Railway, and the *British Transport Commission. The College of Arms was also involved when the GNR incorporated the arms of the City of London in its coat of arms without the City's consent, as a result of which the GNR changed promptly to a simpler design. No objection appears to have been made about the *Caledonian Railway using the Scottish coat of arms, or to the *London & North Western Railway using the seated figure of Britannia both in its coat of arms and as a logo on uniform buttons.

Logos sprang from the crests of coats of arms. The *Midland Railway's wyvern (once the badge of the ancient kingdom of Mercia), the Staffordshire knot incorporated in the arms of the *North Staffordshire Railway, and the lion-and-wheel crest from the arms of the British Transport Commission used by *British Railways are the best known, and simplicity in reproduction was the major reason for the adoption of the logo in preference to the fully coloured and decorated coat of arms. However, one of the first companies in railway privatization, Waterman Railways, adopted a traditional coat of arms for its locomotives and rolling stock.   AD

G. Dow, *Railway Heraldry* (1973).

Herapath, John (1790–1868). The origins of his *Journal* reach back to the *Railway Magazine* of 1835, which he partly owned. He re-established the magazine as the weekly *Railway and Commercial Journal*, often called simply *Herapath*. Sometimes he figured in the paper as an outsider, writing about experiments he had himself made or observed; supporting the use of 4-wheeled against 6-wheeled locomotives, for example, and staunchly opposing *atmospheric

traction. He invested freely in railways himself, and his private financial interests often determined the favour shown by the *Journal* to one company against another. Those interests also influenced its attitude to questions of national policy: he was strongly opposed to *Dalhousie and the Board of *Trade in their efforts to regulate the expansion of railways during the *Mania.

Herapath revelled in controversy, not only in the *Journal* but at shareholders' meetings of the *London Brighton & South Coast Railway. On every railway issue he took a stand immediately, and seldom changed it. He supported the broad *gauge against the standard and commended *Sunday trains. On the other hand he always attacked *excursion and *express trains.

The tone of the paper's opinions grew quieter after his death, when it became less of a commentator and more of a chronicle. As such it remains particularly valuable to the student of Victorian railways.

The *Journal* became merged into the *Railway Gazette* in 1914.   JS

Heysham, see PORTS AND DOCKS.

Heywood, Sir Arthur Percival, see NARROW-GAUGE RAILWAYS.

Highbridge, see WORKS.

Highland Railway: a constituent company of the *London Midland & Scottish Railway in the 1923 *Grouping. It was created in 1865 by an amalgamation of the Inverness & Aberdeen Junction Railway and the Aberdeen & Perth Junction Railway. The inherited main lines from *Inverness to Keith (1858) and Dunkeld (1863) were supplemented by two northern lines: to Strome Ferry (1870) and Kyle of Lochalsh (1897), and to Wick and Thurso (1874). Here there was a possibility of a direct route across the Moray and Cromarty firths, but Sir Alexander Matheson, with estates at Ardross near Alness, was able to press for the roundabout Beauly–Dingwall route. The Duke of *Sutherland's Railway (Dunrobin–Helmsdale) had a separate existence until 1884. The *ruling gradient is as steep as 1 in 70 between Bonar and Golspie, and notable *bridges include the swing bridge over the Caledonian Canal at Clachnaharry, and the viaduct over the Kyle of Sutherland between Culrain and Invershin.

In later years many branch lines were proposed, but the growth of *road transport prevented them being built. Moreover, the company was threatened by proposals for new lines to Inverness. The 1883 project for a *Glasgow–Inverness railway (running through the Great Glen) proved abortive and the HR improved its defences by opening the direct line from Aviemore to Inverness in 1898. However, completion of the West Highland Railway (see NORTH BRITISH RAILWAY) (1894) and the Invergarry & Fort Augustus Railway from Spean Bridge to Fort Augustus (1903) generated further proposals for an extension to Inverness. *Running powers over the IFAR were denied when the HR Bill was approved but the plan was entirely defensive and the extension was never built.

There were only 47 miles of double track on the HR in

1914, comprising passing loops and a widened section between Clachnaharry and Clunes. *Single-line working practices were improved in the 1890s when train staff and tablet instruments were introduced, replacing the system of orders telegraphed to trains along the line. Automatic token-exchange apparatus was used later. Crossing loops were realigned to give a straighter road for the direction in which the faster running was expected.

*Mixed trains were common, with coaches separated from the locomotive by loose-coupled wagons without any continuous braking system. There were *accidents and the practice was threatened by the Railway Regulation Act 1889, which insisted on continuous *brakes. However, the company was allowed several years to make the necessary alterations and it was not until 1897 that there was full compliance.

The company faced hazards of *snow in winter and *fire in summer. Snow fences were erected at vulnerable points with palisades of old sleepers in rows two or three deep. A special blower was installed at Fairy Hillocks close to the Caithness–Sutherland county boundary. William *Stroudley, the first Highland Railway locomotive superintendent, designed a range of snow ploughs when he arrived in Inverness in 1865. His successor, David *Jones, produced efficient locomotives, including the first 4-6-0 to run in Britain: a heavy freight locomotive for the *Perth–Inverness line.

The fishing industry was transformed when *Liverpool and *Manchester could be reached in 14 hours from Buckie. Herring caught in Caithness could also be marketed fresh without concentrating on the best quality fish for curing. The railway also revolutionized the cattle trade, as it was no longer necessary to use the drove roads. Animals now arrived at southern destinations in a good condition. There was further investment in farm improvements to produce fat animals instead of store cattle. There was a growth of whisky distilling with new distilleries sited along the railway.

The HR tried hard to stimulate tourism. It provided a branch to the spa of Strathpeffer in 1885 and built its own *hotel there in 1911. The result was heavy seasonal traffic, especially when wealthy families transferred their households for the *shooting season. There was unprecedentedly heavy traffic during World War I with 'Jellicoe specials' (see WAR) taking coal and personnel to Thurso for the fleet at Scapa Flow. Kyle became nationally important as the port of entry for mines and American naval personnel required for the Northern Barrage—a defence line of mines across the North Sea with a base at Dalmore near Invergordon.

DT

Reg. Hist., xv, 6; J. Thomas and J. H. Farrington, The Skye Line (1990); H. A. Vallance, History of the Highland Railway (1985 edn.).

High Speed Train (HST), see SPEED; TRACTION, DIESEL; TRACTION, ELECTRIC.

Hill, David Octavius (1802–70), artist. The son of a Perth bookseller, he was secretary of the Edinburgh Society of Arts (later the Scottish Royal Academy), 1830–70. He became interested in railways as a young man and produced a set of engraved views of the Garnkirk & Glasgow Railway in 1831, the first pictures of a railway in which mechanical devices were rendered with meticulous precision. Ackermann's celebrated aquatints of the *Liverpool & Manchester Railway (1830), from drawings by T. T. *Bury, had displayed its civil engineering nobly, but they made almost no effort to depict its mechanical appliances.

In 1843 Hill went into partnership with Robert Adamson for the development of *photography. Pictures taken by them at Linlithgow in 1845 are the earliest known photographs of any railway scene. Hill was also a close friend of the engineer John *Miller, and he made at least three oil paintings of Miller's magnificent Ballochmyle viaduct (completed in 1848: see BRIDGES AND VIADUCTS) on the Glasgow Dumfries & Carlisle Railway, aided by photographs that he took himself.

Hill's partnership ended with Adamson's death in 1847, and after Miller's retirement in 1850 he seems to have concerned himself with railways no more. JS

DNB; Boase; S. Stevenson, David Octavius Hill and Robert Adamson (1981); J. Simmons, Image of the Train: The Victorian Era (1993).

Historical Model Railway Society. Founded in 1950 by historians and modellers to collect and exchange records, drawings, and photographs in the interests of historical accuracy in *modelling, the HMRS is the senior such society in Britain. The interests of individual members are cared for by stewards, each of whom specializes in a railway company or subject, and who acts as a clearing house for information between members. Its quarterly journal, archives, lectures at venues across the country, together with occasional publication of high-quality reference books written by members, has established the society as an authority in the modelling fraternity. AD

historic structures, protection of, see CONSERVATION.

Hodgson, Richard (1812–68) of Carham, Coldstream, chairman. He became chairman of the *North British Railway in 1855, when the company's fortunes were at a low ebb. The railway then consisted of the main line from Edinburgh to Berwick, a long branch to Hawick, and various shorter branches. At first Hodgson contemplated amalgamation with the *North Eastern Railway, but when terms could not be agreed he embarked instead on a remarkable programme of expansion, beginning with an extension of the Hawick branch to Carlisle by the Border Union Railway (1862), and purchased a line from Carlisle to Silloth which provided an Irish Sea connection. He consolidated the North British position in the borders by acquiring the Border Counties, Wansbeck, and Northumberland Central Railways, decisions perhaps influenced by his position as MP for Northumberland. He also took the North British to Fife and *Glasgow by acquiring the *Edinburgh Perth & Dundee and *Edinburgh & Glasgow Railways in 1862 and 1864. These moves made the North British a great company, but they were not soundly financed, and in 1866, having over-reached himself, Hodgson was forced to resign in disgrace. JRH

J. Thomas, The North British Railway, i (1969).

Holborn Viaduct station, see LONDON STATIONS (BLACK-FRIARS).

Holcroft, Harold W. (1882–1973), engineer, apprenticed at the *Great Western Railway works, Wolverhampton, later at *Swindon. He was appointed locomotive draughtsman for the *South Eastern & Chatham Railway, Ashford works, 1914, and served on the personal staff of the *Southern Railway CME, 1924–45.

Holcroft was in the drawing office at Swindon at the height of G. J. *Churchward's restocking of the GWR with standard engines, and contributed various features, such as streamlining the exhaust passage layout of the 'Star' class, and in 1911 was responsible for the overall design of the 4300 class 2-6-0, the first general utility engine on British railways. While at Swindon, he produced a concept for a three-cylinder engine with conjugated *valve gear, simpler than that at first adopted by H. N. *Gresley. This was incorporated by Gresley in his large-boilered 2-6-0s of 1920, and at first referred to as the Gresley–Holcroft valve gear. It was used for Southern Railway three-cylinder 2-6-0s. At Ashford, Holcroft's most significant work was in connection with *Maunsell's rebuilding of H. *Wainwright's 4-4-0 classes with long-travel valves. MLH

H. W. Holcroft, *Locomotive Adventure*, i, ii (1962, 1965); H. W. Holcroft, *An Outline of Great Western Locomotive Practice 1837–1947* (1957).

Holden, Charles (1875–1960), *architect. It was an inspired choice to appoint Holden as architect for, first, the *Underground Group and, after 1933, the London Passenger Transport Board (see LONDON TRANSPORT). Working with Frank *Pick, he designed many new stations in the interwar years, evolving an entirely new form of transport architecture that led the world in displaying a complete corporate identity, from equipment, signs, lettering, and advertising to every kind of printed material.

Holden was known as a visionary architect, town planner, and individual designer, with a reputation that had already won him the job of architectural adviser to the War Graves Commission. After designing the tube stations on the Morden extension (1926), and rebuilding a number of others, he completed his longest and what some consider his finest work, the Underground (later London Transport) headquarters at 55 Broadway (1929). His stations were so outstanding that it is almost invidious to choose Piccadilly Circus, Rayners Lane, Arnos Grove, and Osterley as examples.

Holden's large architectural output covered a long period, from King Edward VII Sanatorium, Midhurst, in 1906 to the English Electric Company's offices in the Strand in 1955. Among his many distinguished posts he was a member of the Fine Art Commission, and with Lord Holford produced the City of London development report in 1947. GJB

D. Ware, *A Short Dictionary of British Architects* (1967); C. Barman, *The Man who Built London Transport: A Biography of Frank Pick* (1979); L. Menear, *London Underground Stations* (1983).

Holden, James (1837–1925), engineer, apprenticed to E. *Fletcher at the Gateshead works of the *York Newcastle & Berwick Railway, then on the *Great Western Railway, where he later became chief assistant to William *Dean. He was appointed locomotive, carriage, and wagon superintendent of the *Great Eastern Railway in 1885, and resigned from this position in 1907.

Holden was not only responsible for some reliable and long-lived locomotive designs, but his reorganization of Stratford works, and standardization of the engine classes, placed the GER in the forefront of British locomotive practice. Holden's masterpiece was the 'Claud Hamilton' class of 4-4-0s, introduced in 1900.

When the GER was threatened by Bills for new electric railways in the London suburban area, Holden produced an 0-10-0T (the 'Decapod') that matched the acceleration of electric stock, and although it was too heavy for the track it helped the company to fight off the schemes. Also notable was his development of oil-firing for a number of steam locomotives, using a by-product from the manufacture of oil-gas for carriage lighting. MLH

C. J. Allen, *The Great Eastern Railway* (1955); Railway Correspondence and Travel Society, *Locomotives of the LNER* (1963–77).

holiday-making. This article deals primarily with holidays taken within Great Britain, not with those taken abroad (see TOURISM).

Before 1815 only a few well-to-do people went away on holidays involving any considerable amount of travel, except to visit relatives or where the effort promised some medical benefit at a spa or by the sea. But steamships began then to offer a new facility for this purpose: along the Thames estuary, for instance, from London to Margate and Ramsgate. Each of these ships could carry far more passengers than any horse-drawn vehicle, and it was they, not the railways, that introduced the conception of the mass movement of human beings. A glimpse of what that kind of travel was like can be got from Dickens' paper 'On the River' in *Sketches by Boz* (1836).

Railway trains soon began to offer accommodation for still larger numbers of passengers, and they ran throughout the year, whereas most steamers sailed only in the summer. The English railways at first displayed their capacity in this way only for single events, such as *horse-races or fairs (see MARKETS AND FAIRS); but in Scotland the *Kilmarnock & Troon Railway was credited in 1829 with making Troon 'a fashionable sea-bathing town'. By 1837 the railways' promotion of holiday-making along the Clyde was evident. Three years later a large traffic to and from the coast in summer was spoken of at Greenock and Dundee.

By that time two suburban railways were playing a part in this business: the *London & Greenwich and the Newcastle & North Shields (see NEWCASTLE AND GATESHEAD). It did not interest the earliest long-distance railways. But the lines running from London to *Southampton and *Brighton (completed in 1840–1) both concerned themselves with it. The Brighton company (see LONDON BRIGHTON

& SOUTH COAST RAILWAY) soon had some trains making the 51-mile journey in 2½ hours, which enabled it to carry many passengers on day and weekend trips, and from 1844 their number increased through the provision of cheap *excursion trains.

Railways were soon aiding the development of seaside resorts on other coasts too. In 1840 the *Preston & Wyre Railway was opened, running to a new *port, Fleetwood, which was intended to offer summer bathing. Next year Weston-super-Mare became the first established resort to which a branch was built off a main line. Another railway, from *York to Scarborough, followed in 1845. In 1846–9 branches were built to serve 14 more seaside resorts, including *Blackpool, Southport, Eastbourne, and Torquay.

We cannot judge the scale of the traffic these railways carried. The census reveals very little that is useful, since from 1841 to 1911 it was nearly always taken about 1 April, therefore showing only the resorts' resident population, seldom any substantial number of visitors. The railways hardly ever themselves took censuses of passengers as they arrived. The extant figures of tickets booked at individual stations relate only to people departing: yet these do of course include tickets issued for the short journeys that visitors might make to neighbouring places during their stay. Very few registers of English hotels survive, revealing their guests' home addresses.

Railway companies contributed directly to the establishment of some seaside resorts. At Silloth and *Barry they were developed in association with the building of new ports. Silloth failed to reach expectations, but Barry flourished. At Saltburn and Hunstanton, however, the railways did more.

In 1858 the *Stockton & Darlington company was authorized to extend its line eastwards from Redcar for the benefit of ironstone working, and for the creation of a coastal resort at Saltburn. When it was opened in 1861 plans were already in hand for a new town there, under the railway's control and with the co-operation of a large landowner, Lord Zetland. A substantial *hotel was opened in 1863, then assembly rooms, a pier, and pleasure ground. The place prospered modestly as a holiday resort and as a residence for businessmen working in and around *Middlesbrough. The revenue from this branch line rose by 40 per cent in 1864–8. The business of all these places fluctuated in accordance with the summer weather and the state of the national economy. But at Saltburn passenger bookings doubled in value in 1885–1913.

A railway company and a landowner, Henry L'Estrange, also collaborated in developing a seaside resort at Hunstanton, north of King's Lynn. L'Estrange joined in the promotion of the Lynn & Hunstanton Railway, opened in 1862 and worked by the *Great Eastern. It built its own hotel and paid an average annual dividend of 7.5 per cent in 1866–74, and then became part of the larger Hunstanton & West Norfolk company which immediately erected a second hotel at Hunstanton. When, in its turn, this company was absorbed into the GER in 1890, their stocks were exchanged more or less at par. Hunstanton proved a good place for quiet middle-class holidays. No large industrial town lay within 100 miles of it. Here was a successful resort, well supported by a railway, remaining that and little else, and prospering as such.

Railways were also at this time fostering the development of a series of small resorts in Wales and Scotland, lying close together on Cardigan Bay, in North Wales, and in Fife, each group linked by lateral lines.

The fun and high spirits of these early Victorian resorts were delightfully caught by Surtees in his novel *Plain or Ringlets?* (1860). He opened it thus: 'Railways have brought wealth and salubrity to everyone's door. It is no longer the class distinction that used to exist, this place for that set, that for another, but a sort of grand quadrille of gaiety, in which people always change places continually.'

By 1914 there were nearly 200 towns and villages on the coast of Great Britain served by railway, and recognizably resorts. Brighton remained by far the largest in population, with 180,000 in 1911 (including Hove): 2½ times the size of *Bournemouth (79,000), about three times that of Southend (63,000) and Blackpool (58,000).

Not all holiday-makers went to the seaside, however. Inland resorts, particularly the spa towns, offered relief from illness, hand in hand with amusement. Some lay close to large towns, and were soon linked with them by rail: Buxton with Manchester, for example, Leamington and Droitwich with Birmingham, Tunbridge Wells with London. By 1860 most English spas could be reached from any part of the country without the need to stay even one night on the journey.

The poor had always taken occasional holidays, and the railways assisted them too in that way. Many industrial towns had tracts of open country accessible on foot or by some kind of vehicle: the dales and moors outside *Bradford and *Sheffield, for instance; Mousehold Heath at *Norwich. London was surrounded by them: Hampstead Heath; Barnet Common; Epping Forest; Blackheath; Wandsworth, Streatham, and Wimbledon Commons. Partly in consequence of railway extension, facilitating large-scale suburban building (see SUBURBS AND RAILWAYS), these stretches of London common land were being eroded, and from 1866 onwards efforts were made to protect them from further encroachment, safeguarding them for different forms of popular recreation. Rough horse-races continued to be held on Streatham Common, and in Enfield Chase until 1880. A pack of hounds was kept at Enfield itself in 1885–99.

In 1863 the number of London East-Enders going out to Epping Forest on Sundays and Mondays (no railway yet helping them much) was put at 50,000, but on Easter Monday at 200,000 or more. Ten years later a branch of the GER reached Chingford, on the edge of the Forest. On Easter Monday 1888 the railway took more than 160,000 passengers to one part of the Forest and another, and there were many others who still travelled in the old ways.

In 1900–9 the LBSCR issued nearly 19 million excursion tickets, the revenue from them constituting about one-eighth of the whole of what it drew from passengers. It contracted out part of its excursion business to *travel agents, including a charitable body, the National Sunday League, which had been organizing excursions from the 1870s onwards.

Some cheap railway tickets aided more private kinds of holiday-making: among them *angling (the most private of all), cycling, and walking.

Cycling grew popular in the 1870s. But dwellers in the large towns, anxious to get into the country on their cycles, had first to negotiate long stretches of badly maintained roads. Railways could help them here by conveying them and their machines; and they did so at quite reasonable rates. In the summer of 1898 more than 60,000 cycles were handled at *Liverpool Street station. However, the machines not infrequently suffered damage on railway premises or in transit, and the companies were urged to provide specially devised accommodation for them in their trains. The *Caledonian Railway included cycle-racks in the vans of its newly built Grampian Corridor Express trains, introduced in 1905.

Country walking—often called 'rambling'—was now becoming more popular in Britain. That was not, of course, dependent on railways, but here they could get the ramblers comfortably over the first stage of their outing, to begin their walking sooner. In 1905–14 the *Great Western ran a special Sunday train from Paddington to five stations east of *Swindon, helping ramblers to explore the Vale of the White Horse. After 1923 the *Big Four companies developed this plan extensively, passengers with cheap tickets being allowed to travel out to one station and return from another. In 1930 the *Southern Railway produced a neat little book, Southern Rambles, detailing their facilities and offering guidance on routes.

The companies went further in the same direction, to rent out 'camping coaches': railway carriages converted into living accommodation, parked in sidings or on lengths of track in rural station yards. A camping coach at a station, say, on the line to Kyle of Lochalsh offered an attractive base for a family holiday.

Such were some of the varieties of holiday-making that the railways offered. What effect did they have on the seaside resorts, to which they gave the greatest attention? How far did they assist or disappoint them?

None of the larger ones had been deliberately established by a railway, though several of them owed their existence to railways built for other purposes—Whitley Bay, Westgate-on-Sea, and Penarth, for example. Saltburn (population 3,322 in 1911) remained the only one of any importance that a railway had itself founded. But railways did much to develop resorts that were already in existence when they were built: very obviously at Cleethorpes, where the line terminated at the sea-shore. Opened in 1863, it had to be doubled within ten years. Presently the Manchester Sheffield & Lincolnshire Railway (see GREAT CENTRAL) bought the pier and built a promenade with gardens, baths, and refreshment rooms.

Some of the stations at which the holiday-makers arrived

were enlarged specially to cater for them. At Llandudno the whole station was rebuilt, and two of its four platform faces were reserved for excursion trains. Both the big stations at Blackpool, extended in 1900–2, had ranges of excursion platforms. At Scarborough and Weston-super-Mare separate stations were provided, used almost wholly by excursion trains. At Brighton, where the station site precluded the building of additional platforms, the existing ones were ingeniously lengthened.

Railway companies did not meet all the demands made for the encouragement of holiday traffic, sometimes yielding more readily to other pressures. At a good many resorts there was a clear division of interests between those rate-payers who liked this kind of traffic and those who deplored it, considering that it lowered the social tone of the place. That appeared conspicuously at Bournemouth; and it was one of the elements that entered into the curious development of Folkestone.

More often there was complaint about the railway facilities themselves. That was expressed—with good reason—at Margate and Ramsgate, at Southsea, and very noisily at Blackpool where the issue was complicated. The two companies concerned could easily have increased the number of tracks on the two routes from *Preston with relatively little expense. But any corresponding expansion there, where they diverged from the *West Coast main line, was bound to be very costly. How far were the railways justified or, still more, morally obliged, to incur this expenditure in order to bring more and more people into Blackpool only in the holiday season? Much work was carried out, but not to the extent that some of the townspeople demanded.

After World War I this traffic changed greatly. With the development of popular motoring, at relatively low cost, much of it ceased to depend on public transport, and motor-coaches ate into what remained, with fares that were usually lower than the railways'. But the railway companies lowered their fares too, and exploited the great advantage they still enjoyed in speed. Very few of the trunk roads were extensively improved before the outbreak of World War II. This can be demonstrated from the summer of 1939 issues of *Bradshaw's Guide. The numbers of additional trains provided at weekends, many of them for out-and-back trips on Saturdays—to Blackpool and the resorts in North Wales, for example—were still substantial: on some routes indeed larger than in 1922.

After World War II the nationalized railways never recovered this traffic. They lost it to still cheaper motor cars and better motor-coaches, running on roads that were being much more rapidly improved. They still offered excursion trains (marketed for a time as 'merry-makers'), but most of them ran to sporting events rather than enabling their passengers to enjoy seaside holidays. And from the mid-1950s onwards more and more holiday travel was in aircraft flying cheaply and efficiently to the Mediterranean.   JS

J. A. R. Pimlott, The Englishmen's Holiday (1947); J. K. Walton, The Blackpool Landlady (1978), and The English Seaside Resort, 1750–1914 (1983); VR, chs 12 and 13.

Holyhead, see PORTS AND DOCKS; CHESTER & HOLYHEAD RAILWAY.

honours accorded to British railwaymen in recognition of their services have been of three types: (1) public honours bestowed by the Crown; (2) the presidency and membership of distinguished bodies; (3) awards for outstanding courage, in war or peace.

(1) No peerage has been conferred in recognition of railway work alone. G. C. *Glyn, for example, who became Lord Wolverton in 1869, had been chairman of the *London & Birmingham and *London & North Western Railways in 1837–52; but he was also a leading banker and had been MP for Kendal in 1847–68. Sir Josiah (Lord) *Stamp, president of the *London Midland & Scottish Railway, had also rendered many other public services when he was ennobled in 1938.

The first man much involved in railways to be made a baronet was the contractor S. M. *Peto (1854), followed by Daniel *Gooch in 1866, not as chairman of the *Great Western Railway, but for directing the laying of the Atlantic cable. Edward *Watkin (1880) was a politician besides a railway chairman. Richard *Moon, chairman of the LNWR, became a baronet in 1887; the engineer John *Fowler in 1890.

Few railwaymen were knighted under Queen Victoria. The first seems to have been Thomas *Bouch (alas!) in 1879. Then came *Gregory, *Allport, *Fenton, and the contractor *Arrol. In the 20th century the practice increased, from *Inglis and *Fay to Robert *Reid.

Many men well known for their work in Britain were decorated for services in other countries. Though he accepted no honours at home, *Brassey agreed to receive foreign decorations when they were offered. 'Mrs Brassey will be glad to possess all these crosses', he remarked.

(2) Though most leading railway engineers were elected presidents of their professional institutions, only a very few became Fellows of the Royal Society, in recognition of their scientific attainments. The first was *Rastrick (1837), followed by *Locke (1838), Robert *Stephenson (1849), and *Vignoles and *Hawkshaw (1855). Benjamin *Baker was elected in 1890, but no other railwayman until Sir William *Stanier (1944).

(3) Five railwaymen serving in World War I were awarded the Victoria Cross. In World War II the George Cross, instituted by George VI in 1940 as a similar award for valour by civilians, was bestowed on three railwaymen: Norman Tunna in the Merseyside blitz of 1940; Benjamin Gimbert and J. W. Nightall at Soham, Cambridgeshire, in 1944. The older Albert and Edward Medals were subsequently assimilated in the George Cross, and eight more railwaymen won them.   JS

DNB; A. Stanistreet, *Brave Railwaymen* (1989), which includes the citations.

hop-pickers' trains. The growth of the 19th-century brewing industry led to a great expansion in hop-growing, principally in the Weald of Kent where the large, short-term labour-force required for harvesting was provided by women and children who every September migrated *en masse* from the east end of London to spend several weeks in the hop fields. It was their only form of holiday and, with their necessary belongings, they lived in the fields. At weekends they were joined by husbands and friends.

The *South Eastern Railway first ran hop-pickers' trains in 1856 from Bricklayers Arms station, and then from *London Bridge. The fare was 2s. 6d. to stations in the Maidstone–Tonbridge area. Paddock Wood was the main centre; after it opened in 1892–3 the Hawkhurst branch received hop specials, and later even the Kent & East Sussex *Light Railway gained a share of the traffic.

The trains began leaving London Bridge in the early hours of the morning, and were notorious for violence and drunkenness among passengers; in 1863, for instance, the mayoress of Maidstone was assaulted on the platform. That year the SER conveyed over 11,000 pickers. The first trains were stated to comprise cattle trucks; certainly the company always reserved its oldest carriages for them, attaching vans for passengers' household effects.

During the 1930s over 33,000 hop-pickers were transported annually, and in September 1937 the *Southern Railway ran 30 outward and 33 return specials, together with 98 more during the intervening weekends for friends and relations. But by 1952 mechanical picking and increasing use of road transport reduced the numbers to 4,400 pickers and 23,000 friends in 56 special trains to Paddock Wood. The last train ran from London Bridge in 1960.

Smaller hop-growing districts near East Grinstead in Sussex and Alton in Hampshire attracted pickers from *Portsmouth and *Southampton, but the other main area was in Worcestershire and Herefordshire. Large numbers of pickers were carried from Black Country stations: upwards of 5,000 women and children in 1893. *Great Western Railway instructions in 1936 ordered that 'only third class carriages of the oldest type must be used', in no circumstances containing lavatories or first class compartments.   GJB

GWR Working Timetable General Appendix, 1936; B. Reed and C. E. Lee, 'London Bridge Station, Part II', *RM* (Feb. 1937), 102; *LT*, 166; A. Gray, *South Eastern Railway* (1990), 173; *Reg. Hist.*, ii, 32.

horse-buses, see BUSES.

horse-drawn carriages, conveyance of. When railways began to carry passengers, they necessarily were prepared to take wealthy people wishing to travel in their private carriages too. Although the earliest lines ran over short distances, they provided links between the main roads, and as trains were generally much faster than horse-drawn coaches it might be worth while to travel by the new conveyance, even for only part of a journey. Moreover, many of the wealthier passengers who were accustomed to using their own carriages did not like travelling in railway carriages in the company of strangers, losing a privacy they had always enjoyed.

Each carriage was placed on a four-wheeled flat truck, usually at the back of the train. Instead of hiring post-horses, one or more vehicles called 'horseboxes' were attached.

This practice was not free from danger. Most gentlemen's carriages were far more lightly built than the railways', sometimes causing unpleasant vibration; they were also apt to be badly shaken when other vehicles were carelessly shunted on to them.

As travelling by train became an ordinary feature of life, and railway carriages—first-class at least—improved in comfort, fewer people insisted on taking their own carriages with them. The Duke of Wellington always continued to do so, although he did occasionally travel in an ordinary carriage of the train; but his unique celebrity and his most distinctive appearance made the practice seem, in his case, natural. By the time he died in 1852 the conveyance of private carriages by passenger train was already declining, but it was still quite common in the 1860s. It survived where passengers were travelling into large districts not served by railways, most conspicuously during the *shooting season in Scotland when the convenience of the wealthy man's own carriage and horses, for the use of his family, was most obvious, although most travellers now rode in the trains. A 'Special Horse and Carriage Train' from Euston to the Highlands was still provided in the summer until the 1890s, on Mondays–Fridays, but it ran only until the night of 10–11 August; grouse-shooting began on the 12th.

In the 20th century the same provision was made for private motor cars (see MOTOR CARS, CARRIAGE OF).   JS
Thomas, 183, 191–3; *Wellington and His Friends*, ed. 7th Duke of Wellington (1965), 266–8; in the 1860s: W. Vincent, *Seen from a Railway Platform* (1919), 21.

horse-drawn coaches, see COACHES, ROAD.

horse-racing. The development, in the mid-19th century, of a rail network covering the greater part of England had important, if unexpected, consequences for British horse-racing. The arrival of the railways had an enormous impact. The easy movement of both man and beast across the country transformed it from the idle pursuit of a few gentlemen into a nationally organized sport complete with prize money and spectators watching carefully bred animals race across clearly defined courses. In turn the sport had an impact on the railway companies, requiring special train services, boosting profits, and occasionally determining the situation of new lines and stations.

Moving racehorses around the country before the 1830s was a time-consuming business. It took a fortnight to move the northern champion, Filha da Puta, from Middleham in North Yorkshire to Newmarket in 1819 and a fortnight to take it back again.

But, by 1848, when racing's headquarters, Newmarket, acquired a branch line, the situation was changing. Railways reached at least part of the way to Epsom, Ascot, and *Doncaster by 1838, Chester was well provided for by 1840, and in 1843 even the notoriously remote Goodwood could boast a rail link, albeit only as far as nearby Chichester. By leading the horse into a specially adapted railway vehicle or placing its usual travelling box on the train, horses could be moved from their training stables to a major course 200 miles away in a day.

Although the first horseboxes travelling on roads appeared in the mid-1830s, they were expensive and inconvenient, slow and unsafe. Only the rich, and possibly obsessive, like Lord George Bentinck, could afford to build them; even then, to little effect. It took four days to move his St Leger favourite, Elis, from Goodwood to Doncaster in a horsebox in 1839, and one of those was a rest day. Thus the railway companies predominated in this business until after World War I (see LIVESTOCK TRAFFIC). Their safety record appears to have been surprisingly good: it was not unknown for road horseboxes to topple over, but there were no such accidents on the railway. Racehorses were generally carried in special trains between Berkshire training grounds and Newmarket meetings, but otherwise horseboxes were attached to passenger trains. The traffic ceased around 1970.

Such developments were restricted to the wealthier owners. Transporting horses about the country was still not cheap: in 1853 John Bowes spent £300 moving his Derby winner West Australian from course to course. With prize money so meagre—in 1859 the seven most prestigious courses in England could manage prizes of only £15,000 between them—racing on a national scale was still the prerogative of the rich. Nevertheless, the attitude of racing men was changing. There was no longer talk of a northern and a southern champion. From the mid-1840s an Epsom Derby winner had to prove his worth in the north. A fixed annual calendar had developed by about 1835, mirroring to a certain extent the peregrinations of the upper classes and covering the whole of the country. The best horses were expected to follow their owners to the best meetings: a top-rate 3-year-old would run at Newmarket in April, Epsom in June, Goodwood in July, and Doncaster in September.

These changes had further repercussions, particularly for the nature of the sport. Just as people could reach a course more easily, so too could they leave it. A meeting had to be attractive throughout the event. A desire to see the St Leger no longer meant that spectators had to watch three days of sub-standard sport before the big race, as had been the case earlier, if the journey was to be worth while.

Emphasis on shorter races brought young horses, speedier than their older colleagues, to the fore. This could not have happened without the railway revolution. They no longer had to walk to a course. Improved means of transport allowed young horses to race widely as juveniles, as James Merry's Thormanby demonstrated. Racing as a 2-year-old at Northampton, York, Epsom, Chester, Ascot, Goodwood, and Newmarket, it was still strong enough at 3 to win the Derby in 1860.

Some felt that the railway companies did not sufficiently show appreciation for their profits. From the late 1840s many journalists were pointing out the discrepancies between the revenue gained by the companies from racing, and the paucity of rewards on offer to the competitors. There was talk of railway companies sponsoring races, contributing to the winner's purse, but only the *London & South Western Railway, briefly at Ascot, responded, provid-

ing £50 for a plate for a few years in the mid-1860s. The
*Great Western Railway subscribed to the prize stakes in
1850.

There were other reservations about the influence of the
railways. Some felt that they led to an unhealthy 'democratization' of the sport. Goodwood had lost much of its charm
now that it was no longer accessible only to the closest
friends of the course's owner, the Duke of Richmond. The
new popularity of racing prompted Lord George Bentinck
to invent the enclosure, to keep the masses at arm's length.
The Jockey Club long tried to hold up with horror the prospect of hordes of people trampling the hallowed turf, contending that the railway had, after all, been meant to move
horses, not people.

In general, however, courses were only too aware of the
benefits railways might bring. Course proprietors were frequently among those petitioning for local lines. They had
seen a dramatic rise in their fortunes, thanks to the train.
*York emerged from relative obscurity to become host of
one of the year's most prestigious meetings. Chester saw
record amounts wagered during its spring meeting,
although it was not unknown for horses to rear, frightened
by a train rattling past the course. When deciding on a site
for a new course, transport became one of the first considerations. In the 1860s Sandown Park was attractive to
investors partly because of its proximity to Esher station;
Kempton Park enjoyed the same attraction ten years later.
Epsom had two branch lines to it. And when the racing
establishment began building Newbury racecourse in 1905
it persuaded the GWR to build a special station next to the
course. Others included Cheltenham, Stratford-upon-Avon,
Wetherby, Westenhanger, and York, while Aintree had special platforms for race trains. Racecourses poorly served by
the railway network often had little chance of success; the
failure of Monmouth, Weymouth, and Stockbridge can, in
part, be attributed to their relative isolation.

In the 20th century, too, the railways continued to play a
major part. Although, since the inter-war period, trainers
have come increasingly to rely on roads to move horses,
spectators have still had recourse to rail. Until the outbreak
of World War II special race-day excursions were common,
for which the companies kept carriages in reserve. Vast
numbers of racegoers were carried, particularly to major
meetings like the Grand National and the St Leger, and the
trains were notorious for card-sharps and confidence tricksters. Even though members of the House of Lords were no
longer seen climbing into cattle wagons to get to the Derby,
as had been the case in 1840, *Waterloo station was
crowded on Ascot and Epsom race days, when entrance fees
were reduced for rail travellers. Despite the inroads made
by the private car, race specials are still run and London
stations like *King's Cross, *Paddington, and Waterloo can
still be extra busy on race days.

At some courses, such as Newbury, with a railway station
at the front gate and where access by road can be awkward,
the link has remained strong. On race days, InterCity services from London and *Bristol make special stops. Some
courses, keen to attract participants in what has become an
expensive day out, have sought once more to offer rail
travellers reduced-price entry. This has worked well for the
organizers of the Cheltenham National Hunt Festival, as
have their 'luxury' rail packages, an imaginative piece of
marketing for a course at least three miles from the town's
main-line station.

Horse-racing in England was, therefore, hugely affected
by the rail revolution. Even the nature of the sport changed;
it certainly became more organized, commercialized, and
professional, helping the railways to what became one
of their earliest sources of reliable profit, a source which
remains to this day.   ECE

See also EXCURSION TRAINS.

J. F. Fairfax-Blakeborough, *Chester Races* (1951), and *Doncaster St
Leger: The Oldest Classic Turf Race* (1958); R. Mortimer, *The Jockey
Club* (1957); W. Vamplew, *The Turf: A Social and Economic History
of Horseracing* (1976); A. and S. Jordan, *Away for the Day: The
Railway Excursion in Britain, 1830 to the Present Day* (1991),
79–93.

horses, use of. The earliest sources of motive power on
railways were human beings, horses, and the force of *gravity. The tunnels in early coal mines were too small for
horses to pull the trucks, but as soon as the coal had been
brought to the surface they took over.

Horses also worked the earliest passenger services on
railways. When the *Stockton & Darlington Railway was
opened in 1825, though all its freight traffic was handled by
steam locomotives, passenger trains were for some time
hauled by horses; but in 1833 locomotives were put in
charge of these too. The *Liverpool & Manchester Railway
used locomotives for almost the whole of its traffic from the
start. The railways appeared to be entirely replacing the
horse by the machine. But the horse continued to be used
in three different types of railway service well into the 20th
century.

A considerable number of short lines, mainly in rural districts, were, at times, worked by horse power. Some were
designed for it, like George *Stephenson's *Whitby & Pickering Railway, opened throughout in 1836. Some, laid out
for steam traction, proved commercially disappointing and
horses were substituted: the line from Huntingdon to St
Ives, for example, and the North Berwick branch in Scotland. Among the towns served by horse-worked branch
lines were Weston-super-Mare, Tewkesbury, and Ilkeston.
Two services lived very long: to Port Carlisle until 1914,
when locomotives took over; and to Inchture (Perthshire)
until 1917, the line then being closed altogether.

Horses continued to be used for shunting in goods yards;
not in the great *marshalling yards, where vehicles were all
moved mechanically, or by gravity, but in station *sidings,
which handled much miscellaneous traffic. Some of that involved the movement of only one or two wagons at a time,
where the flexibility of the horse could be an advantage
over a locomotive. Since it lived close by it could be called
up for service immediately, needing only one man to attend
it, whereas a locomotive needed two.

Many horses were also used for delivering goods by road
from the railway to the consignee's premises. These services

were turned over to motor vehicles from 1901 onwards; but it was not until after 1918 that this new form of traction proved itself to be thoroughly reliable.

In 1914 the 11 largest English railway companies were still using nearly 26,000 horses of their own; the *Big Four handed on 9,193 to the *British Transport Commission in 1947. Horses were then still being extensively used in shunting. Two of the last, at Newmarket, were withdrawn only in 1967.

See also DANDY-CARTS.   JS

ET, 17–20; B. Holden, *The Long Haul: The Life and Times of the Railway Horse* (1985).

Horwich, see WORKS.

hotels were beginning to be built before the *railway age. What the railways did was to rapidly develop them, creating the Victorian grand hotel, and pioneering the modern hotel industry. At various times they operated over 110 establishments, large and small. Hotels were built outright, purchased, or leased, and in 1913 net receipts exceeded £½ million.

The first hotel for rail travellers was built alongside *Crewe station by Lord Crewe, opened in 1837, leased by the *London & North Western Railway in 1864, and bought outright in 1877. The first to be built by a railway were the twin hotels at *Euston, opened in 1839 by the *London & Birmingham Railway.

They began a long period of building or acquisition of hotels by or for railways that lasted into the 20th century. In 1840, the *North Midland Railway opened a hotel for passengers needing to change trains at Normanton, designed by Francis *Thompson who built Cuff's Station Hotel at *Derby in 1841. It was bought by the railway in 1862 and renamed the Midland. In 1844 the first hotel adjoining a station was opened at Gateshead, followed in 1851 by the handsome Royal Station Hotel built across the head of the platforms at *Hull, in what became a customary position. A year later the opening of the *Great Western Royal Hotel at *Paddington, with 103 bedrooms the largest in the country, immediately set a new standard in comfort and marked the beginning of large palace-type hotels.

The Great Northern at *King's Cross was opened in 1854, and until company law legislation in 1856 and 1862 relaxed restrictions on share ownership and introduced limited liability, the railways were the only organizations with the capital resources to build hotels. Strictly, parliamentary powers were required. Few had them, and a number of companies obtained them only retrospectively, or made recourse to subsidiary companies, or financed others. The *London Brighton & South Coast Railway assisted a private company to build the Grosvenor Hotel at *Victoria in 1861, bought it in 1893 and quickly leased it out. Eventually all the London termini had a hotel, except *Fenchurch Street, *Blackfriars, and *Waterloo.

Nor were the provinces neglected, where railway rivalry often produced hotels. The LNWR opened the Queens Hotel at *Birmingham New Street in 1854; the GWR at Snow Hill in 1863. In *Leeds, the *Midland's Queens

opened in 1863, followed by the Great Northern Hotel in 1869. The same happened in *Glasgow where there were three, in *Edinburgh, and in *Bradford. At *Liverpool the LNWR's North Western Hotel had no rival from 1871 until the *Lancashire & Yorkshire opened its Exchange Station Hotel in 1888. Then the Midland bought the ageing Adelphi in 1892, and rebuilt it in neo-Classical style in 1912–14. Curiously, *Manchester lacked a comparable hotel until the Midland, through its energetic hotels manager William *Towle, built the massive Midland Hotel outside Central station in 1903.

Railways also owned hotels at *ports, like the London & Paris at Newhaven in 1847, and the Lord Warden at Dover in 1853. The Great Eastern Hotel at Harwich (1865) was largely superseded by one of the same name at Parkeston Quay in 1883. The *Chester & Holyhead Railway bought a hotel at Holyhead in 1850, replaced by the New Station Hotel in 1880.

Seaside resorts received rather less attention. The *Stockton & Darlington Railway built the Zetland at Saltburn (1863), as part of a railway-inspired development, and there were others like the Sandringham at Hunstanton and the Station Hotel at Ayr. The Great Western bought Tregenna Castle, a mansion near St Ives, for a country house hotel in 1878, possibly the first of its kind. The idea was not pursued until it bought North Bovey Manor, Moretonhampstead, in 1929, opening it as the Manor House Hotel, and the *London Midland & Scottish opened the Welcombe Hotel near Stratford-on-Avon in 1931. There were a number of smaller hotels which railways owned or held an interest in: for instance at Keswick, Windermere, and Rudyard Lake in North Staffordshire; but in general they ignored the popular inland resorts.

Golf received considerable attention, particularly in *Scotland, notably at Dornoch, Strathpeffer, Turnberry, and, above all, Gleneagles. The last two had championship-standard courses. But the *Great North of Scotland Railway's hotel and course at Cruden Bay, near Fraserburgh, was too remote to be successful.

*Architecture followed current fashion, becoming more flamboyant as the 19th century progressed. Well-known architects were employed: E. M. Barry at *Cannon Street and *Charing Cross, C. E. Barry at *Liverpool Street, Alfred Waterhouse at Liverpool's North Western, and George Gilbert Scott at *St Pancras, where the Midland Grand, opened in 1873, reached the apogee of High Victorian Gothic architecture and was the last word in hotels in its day. Interiors were no less lavish, with vast, impressive dining rooms and lounges. Some catered for special interests, such as City functions at Cannon Street, and exemplified by the two Masonic temples in the Great Eastern at Liverpool Street. The ultimate innovations were made at the Midland, Manchester, which included in its attractions a winter garden and an 800-seat theatre; and the Hotel Great Central (1899) at *Marylebone—built by a separate company—which boasted a palm court, and a cycling-track on the roof.

After the 1923 *Grouping some of the older hotels that could not be economically modernized were sold or converted to offices: the North Western at Liverpool in 1933; the Midland Grand in 1935. A degree of modernization took place elsewhere, and the LMS replaced two hotels: the 1848 Midland at Morecambe was rebuilt in *art deco* style by Oliver Hill in 1930; the Queens at Leeds in 1937, by W. Curtis Green and W. H. Hamlyn, setting a new high standard. Generally, only the *Southern Railway continued to use contractors to run hotels.

On *nationalization in 1948, hotels were divorced from railways under a separate Hotels Executive, only to return to them in 1962 as British Transport Hotels. The total of 61 in 1901 was now 37, mostly run-down after World War II. Uneconomic ones began to be sold, although one new hotel was built, the Old Course Hotel at St Andrews in 1968. A policy of refurbishment, aimed at the growing tourist market, was succeeding when the 1979 Conservative government ordered *privatization of ancillary railway activities.

The 29 hotels remaining in 1981 were sold, some to return to a new glory, albeit with new and unnecessary names like the Midland Holiday Inn at Manchester, the Copthorne (formerly North British) at Glasgow, and the Royal York (formerly Royal Station). After 41 years as offices the Hotel Great Central at Marylebone was re-converted to the luxury Regent Hotel, while the greatest of them all, the Midland Grand, has been splendidly restored externally. Painstaking sample restoration of the interior shows what treasures remain to be uncovered, but they await finance, which means finding a use for the building. That, sadly, still has to be achieved.

See also REFRESHMENT ROOMS. GJB

D. Taylor, *Fortune, Fame and Family: British Hotels and Catering from 1878 to 1978* (1978); C. Monkhouse, 'Railway Hotels', in M. Binney and D. Pearce, *Railway Architecture* (1979); N. Wooler, *Dinner in the Diner: A History of Railway Catering* (1987); O. Carter, *British Railway Hotels, 1838–1983* (1990); *ET*, 37–55.

housing. Early railways were aware of a need to provide houses for employees at remote locations, for example for men working *cable-operated inclines and for toll-collectors. *Level crossings required gate-keepers' cottages. The first main-line railways provided houses for country *stationmasters, often forming part of the station.

*Towns and villages sprang up at major railway locations, often where there was nothing before, *Crewe being the best-known example. There were also lesser-known settlements, some quite isolated like Waskerley on the *Stockton & Darlington, high on the moors of western Durham, and Riccarton Junction, on the *North British Railway in the Border hills, which had 30 houses, a school, and a recreation hall, all provided by the company and accessible only by rail. Some groups of houses formed enclaves on the edge of towns, such as the *Great Northern's colony of 220 houses at New England, *Peterborough, and the *London & North Western's at Mold Junction, outside Chester, both of which included a school.

Eventually the railways collectively became one of the country's largest private house landlords, owning some 27,000 employees' dwellings (not including those on stations) found clustered near stations, junctions, works, marshalling yards, carriage sidings, and engine sheds, or simply along the lineside. Provision depended on the availability of local accommodation. The stations at Rugby and Coventry, for instance, were outside the town. Needing houses nearby, the *London & Birmingham Railway built its own. Other railways bought up property to let to employees.

Motives were mixed. Some railways regarded housing provision as a means of promoting loyalty and discipline by keeping a work-force together. In 1857 Richard *Moon, later the chairman of the LNWR, stressed the importance of a house-building programme to prevent men having to seek poor lodgings where they became demoralized and mixed in bad company. Lineside cottages were needed for *signalmen at remote boxes, and for *platelayers, enabling them to be easily summoned for *fog duty. By 1921 that railway owned over 4,300 staff dwellings; the *North Eastern nearly 4,600. The companies with the best ratio of houses to employees, however, were the *Highland and the *Great North of Scotland, reflecting the sparsely populated areas they served; one of the worst was the *Great Western, despite the largest route mileage. A company not given to providing houses, it virtually stopped building in 1853, until it was forced to resume at Goodwick in 1907 for its new port of Fishguard. In general, therefore, companies provided housing only where it was essential to the running of the railway, and the number of jobs that included a house was relatively small.

Railway houses were usually, but not always, superior to contemporary agricultural and industrial artisans' dwellings, although the NER's house survey in 1862 revealed some appalling conditions, mainly inherited from smaller companies. A three-roomed cottage at Sprouston housed a platelayer, his wife, four daughters, and two drivers and firemen as lodgers. Tenants were encouraged to take lodgers, provided they were railwaymen.

Aided by the public health Acts, conditions steadily improved. Companies more consistently built standard patterns of houses with *sanitation and wholesome water supplies. Some, like the London & Birmingham, did so from the outset; its smallest terraced houses at Wolverton in 1844 had a parlour, kitchen, a hot water boiler, and two or three bedrooms. The *Grand Junction Railway's houses at Crewe, built from 1843, were considered models of their day. The LNWR continued the tradition, its characteristic red-brick houses appearing all over the system, singly, in pairs, or in long terraces. Other large companies' houses were equally distinctive, and although some tended to use local building materials, the design remained the same, and where they were built at an existing village they still stand out aggressively next to the vernacular, as at Woodford Halse, Tebay, Hellifield, and Rowsley. The *Great Eastern built some curious wooden station and crossing-keepers' houses having a distinctly colonial flavour.

Accommodation for engine crews working away from home was provided in hostels or 'barracks'. Never popular, some, like the LNWR's at Camden and Crewe, were better than others such as the GER's windowless establishment in the middle of Stratford locomotive yard, and the old carriages the GWR tended to press into use. Conditions barely improved until World War II, when some new hostels were built.

Tenements were built in *London for railway families: Culross Buildings at King's Cross, for instance; Polygon Buildings at St Pancras, Coronation Buildings at Vauxhall, and the euphemistically nicknamed 'Seaside Buildings' at Bermondsey, named after resorts served by the *London Brighton & South Coast Railway. *Glasgow, city of tenements, had 'The Blocks' at Cowlairs, intended by the *Edinburgh & Glasgow Railway to be part of a model 'village' that was never finished. The *Glasgow & South Western's at its Corkerhill engine sheds did reach completion. The small *Furness Railway built large, ornate sandstone blocks of tenements containing 564 'houses' at *Barrow that could have come straight from Glasgow.

At first, houses were often rent-free. The GWR deducted rent from wages from the outset, and in the 1840s other lines started doing the same. Companies hoped to get a 4–6 per cent return on the capital cost, but few did so. In 1914 the *London & South Western's return had dropped to 2–3½ per cent. Apart from a few fluctuations rents remained relatively stable throughout the 19th century.

After the 1923 *Grouping only the *Southern Railway continued to build houses in any quantity. Despite a shortage, staff attitudes were changing. Because of its long opposition to wide-scale housing the position was most acute in the GWR, which it solved by successfully forming co-operative housing associations, building 11 estates up to the late 1940s. The *London & North Eastern did the same on a smaller scale, but the *London Midland & Scottish, which had by far the largest housing stock, preferred to make cheap loans for house purchase. The scheme was transferred to a building society in 1934, subject to a guaranteed maximum interest rate.

*British Rail's policy was to sell its houses, and now there are only a few essential ones such as crossing-houses, which are dwindling rapidly. But despite alterations by their new owners, most former railway houses are still clearly recognizable.   GJB

Housing figures: Board of Trade Railway Returns; RS, ch. 6.

Hudson, George (1800–71), chairman. A farmer's son from the East Yorkshire village of Howsham, Hudson was educated locally before moving to *York. In 1827 he inherited a fortune of some £30,000 from a distant relative under dubious circumstances, enabling him to invest in early railway schemes. He also became active in local politics and by 1836 was leader of the Tories on York City Council, which paved the way for his election as chairman of the *York & North Midland Railway.

Although Hudson from the outset used questionable accounting practices, the YNMR appeared to be extraordinarily prosperous. He was seen as a supreme strategist and financial genius, and was easily able to assume control of other lines. In 1844 he master-minded the formation of the *Midland Railway with a capital of £5 million. By now Hud-

son was in charge of over 1,000 miles of line, including the trunk route from London to the North from Rugby through York to *Newcastle. He was nicknamed the 'Railway King' and became a favoured house guest of the influential and wealthy.

In 1845 Hudson was elected Tory MP for Sunderland. In a desperate bid to defeat the Bill for the direct London & York Railway (later the *Great Northern), he also assumed chairmanship of the struggling *Eastern Counties Railway. It was a tactical error, his resignation in 1849 precipitating a Committee of Inquiry which found that in three years over £200,000 in dividends had been paid out of capital. Similar malpractices quickly came to light on Hudson's other lines and by the end of the year he had been forced to resign all his railway chairmanships.

Hudson went to live abroad, in obscurity. Much of his later life was spent in fighting claims for misappropriated funds, especially from his relentless enemy the *North Eastern Railway. In a penetrating obituary, *The Times* commented: 'There was a time when not to know him was to argue one's self unknown; now he is only a tradition.'   DJ

A. J. Peacock, *George Hudson: The Railway King* (2 vols., 1988–9); R. S. Lambert, *The Railway King 1800–1871* (1934).

Hughes, George (1865–1945), mechanical engineer. Apprenticed at *Crewe, *London & North Western Railway, under F. W. *Webb, 1882–7, he then joined the *Lancashire & Yorkshire Railway in 1895, becoming principal assistant for carriages and wagons. In 1899 he was works manager, Horwich, and CME 1904–21.

He was, with *Churchward of the *Great Western, a British pioneer in the use of firetube superheaters, first applied to 0-6-0s in 1906 and two years later to 4-4-0s where, combined with long-lap, long-travel piston valves, performance was transformed. His large four-cylinder 4-6-0s of 1908 were extravagant with fuel, but after rebuilding with superheated boilers and improved valve-setting showed a 25 per cent economy, and more were built. He built substantial numbers of 0-8-0 freight engines with large superheated boilers, as well as 0-6-0s and 2-4-2 tanks. In 1913 designs for a very large four-cylinder 2-10-0 freight engine were opposed by the operating department. He became CME of the combined LNWR and LYR in 1922, and of the *London Midland & Scottish in 1923–5, where, realizing the need for more powerful locomotives, he had designs prepared for 4-6-2 passenger and 2-8-2 freight types, but construction was aborted. However, 245 of his excellent mixed traffic 2-6-0s were built after his retirement.   GWC

BSRL; E. Mason, *The Lancashire & Yorkshire Railway in the Twentieth Century* (1954); E. Mason ('Rivington'), *My Life with Locomotives* (1962); E. S. Cox, *Locomotive Panorama*, i (1965).

Huish, Mark (1808–67), general manager; born in Nottingham, son of a prominent hosier. After serving in the East India Company army, 1823–37, he became secretary to the Glasgow Paisley & Greenock Railway, 1837, and secretary and general manager of the *Grand Junction Railway, 1841–6 (salary £1,250 when the company merged with the *Liverpool & Manchester Railway, 1845). He engineered the merger with *London & Birmingham Railway to create the *London & North Western Railway, 1846, of which he was general manager, 1846–58 (salary £2,000 p.a.).

Huish contributed significantly to debates about rail safety, cost accounting and financial management, freight traffic management, permanent way costing, and telegraphic communication. He was, above all, a highly skilled traffic manager who established the early railway cartels, dominated by the LNWR, which divided traffic in agreed proportions among the major companies. A master strategist of 'railway diplomacy', he found it difficult to delegate and became the scapegoat for the collapse of his agreements in 1857. He was forced to resign in the following year after a directorial coup led by Richard *Moon, Edward Tootal, and George Carr *Glyn. He then retired to the *Isle of Wight, where he was persuaded to become a director of the Isle of Wight Railway. He also acted as chairman of two non-railway concerns, the Clifton Suspension Bridge Co. and the Electric & International Telegraph Co. A somewhat disgraced figure in the 1860s, he nevertheless acted as arbitrator in a number of inter-railway disputes, and gave evidence to the Royal Commission on Railways in April 1866.   TG

T. R. Gourvish, *Mark Huish and the London & North Western Railway* (1972); T. R. Gourvish, 'Captain Mark Huish: A Pioneer in the Development of Railway Management', *Business History*, 12 (1970), 46–58.

Hull, for long England's third *port, owes its importance to the channelling of traffic from the west along the corridor of the Humber. That estuary was difficult to navigate, but a suitable inlet for an early port came where the River Hull entered on the north bank. It was, however, inadequate for the late 18th-century surge of traffic, and a ring of docks was built around the original town—Queens in 1778, Humber in 1809, and Princes in 1829.

The first railway, the Hull & Selby of 1840 (see LEEDS & SELBY), was strongly influenced by the form and setting of the town. Its Manor House terminus abutted Humber Dock, and it then followed the bank of the Humber, with no gradient steeper than 1 in 572, and with 18 miles dead straight.

Within 25 years, most of Hull's eventual railway network evolved. In 1846 came the line to Bridlington, built by the *York & North Midland Railway, which leased the Hull & Selby in 1845 and became part of the *North Eastern Railway. With the rapid growth of traffic, better terminal facilities were needed. In 1848 Paragon station was opened closer to the town centre, in the grand style, with hotel and offices by G. T. *Andrews, though the present overall roof dates from 1905. Manor House remained for freight.

The early docks were becoming too small. Victoria Dock was opened in 1850, east of the River Hull, reached by rail in 1858 around what were then the outskirts of the town.

The next lines opened up the relatively unpromising terrain of Holderness to the east. The Hull & Holderness Railway (1854) ran to Withernsea. Its first terminus was at Victoria Dock, but after acquisition by the NER in 1860, its trains ran through to Paragon from 1864. The Hull &

Hornsea Railway of 1864 became part of the NER in 1866.

Surprisingly, Hull also had access from the south. From 1849, the Manchester Sheffield & Lincolnshire Railway (see GREAT CENTRAL) operated a ferry across the Humber from New Holland to Hull, and the facilities at Hull's Victoria Pier remained until the opening of the Humber Bridge in 1981.

Hull's logical railway pattern reflected the monopoly of a single company, the NER, which became intensely unpopular in the city. It was challenged by the promotion of and opening in 1885 of the *Hull & Barnsley Railway and the commissioning of its Alexandra Dock. This line approached Hull from the west across the Yorkshire Wolds, necessitating gradients up to 1 in 100. In Hull, a new line was built at high level around the outskirts of the town to reach the dock and the HBR's Cannon Street terminus, north of the town centre. Competition, however, was short. The HBR and NER opened the King George V Dock jointly in 1914, and were amalgamated in 1922.

The dock system at Hull spread both east and west of the River Hull, and the railways expanded accordingly, having at their zenith some 300 miles of sidings. In 1907 a new passenger station, Riverside Quay, was opened to serve liner traffic.

In the changed conditions since 1950, the decline of Hull's railway network has been as logical as its expansion. For passenger traffic, the first line to go was the duplicate HBR route in 1955 (closed completely in 1964). In 1964 the sparsely used branches to Withernsea and Hornsea succumbed. In 1968 the Victoria Dock branch closed, and future access to the eastern docks was by the high-level HBR route, reducing the number of Hull's notorious level crossings.

The decline of freight traffic has been even more dramatic. In 1952 there were 52 booked freight departures each day, including 11 fully fitted *fish trains to destinations as diverse as *King's Cross, Banbury (2), and *Manchester. Today, the fish traffic has long gone and only two freight flows remain. The port is now almost entirely road-served, with acres of derelict or redeveloped railway land emphasizing the change. Passenger services remain, with through trains to Scarborough, *York, Manchester, *Sheffield, and (once daily) *London.   JAP

Reg. Hist., iv, ch. 3; M. Nicholson and W. B. Yeadon, *An Illustrated History of Hull's Railways* (1993).

Hull & Barnsley Railway. The last substantial new, independent railway company, the HBR was a classic case of a line born in competition: a duplicate of existing facilities. Its purpose was better described by its full title, the Hull Barnsley & West Riding Junction Railway & Dock Company, which it retained to 1905.

It was conceived as an attempt, strongly encouraged by *Hull Corporation, to break the monopoly of the *North Eastern Railway and the Hull Dock Company on the trade of Hull. The line was authorized in 1880, and the railway and the integral Alexandra Dock were opened in 1885 after considerable financial and engineering difficulties. The main line ran 53 miles from the *Midland Railway at Cudworth, two miles short of Barnsley, to the relatively isolated passenger terminus of Cannon Street in Hull. The prime physical problem was the crossing of the hard chalk of the Yorkshire Wolds. The line climbed to 250 ft, with Drewton tunnel at the summit ¾ mile long, and a 1 in 150 gradient eastbound and 1 in 100 westbound; much more severe, particularly for eastbound mineral traffic, than those of the NER along the Humber. In Hull itself, a high embankment was built to avoid numerous level crossings, but at the additional expense of 34 bridges.

Having opened up the market, the prime purpose of the HBR was over. By the 1890s competition on *freight rates had ceased, though the splendid facilities of the Alexandra Dock gave a significant advantage, for it was the largest and deepest on the east coast. Closer working with the NER ensued, leading to the joint building of the King George V Dock, completed in 1914. The two companies were amalgamated in 1922, as a preliminary to the 1923 *Grouping.

In the 1930s the line continued to handle the coal export traffic for which it had been built, but after 1945 decline was swift. The remnants of passenger services ceased in 1955, no through freight was carried after 1958, and the last local freight, to Little Weighton, was withdrawn in 1964.

Only three legacies of consequence remain. Power station traffic is carried on a spur from Hensall Junction to Drax, Alexandra Dock still serves some traffic, and the HBR's high-level route remains the freight line in Hull to the eastern docks and Saltend.   JAP

K. Hoole (ed.), *The Hull & Barnsley Railway*, i (1972); B. Hinchcliffe (ed.), *The Hull & Barnsley Railway*, ii (1980).

Hull & Selby Railway, see LEEDS & SELBY RAILWAY.

humour. The railways' plans and practices were sometimes comic, especially in early days, or could be made to appear so by satirists in words or in pictures. Both of these are considered here; but see also ART.

They were an easy target for the pamphlets produced by their critics and enemies (see OPPOSITION TO RAILWAYS), bearing titles that indicate their purposes: e.g. *Railroad Impositions Detected*; *The Ghost of John Bull*; or *The Devil's Railroad; Pooh! Pooh! a Poem*, all published in 1834–9.

Very soon after *Punch* was established in 1841 it joined the critics, moved first by horror arising from *accidents. Sometimes it concentrated on the mismanagement of individual railways, over a long span of time: in the 1840s and 1850s the *West London Railway and the *Eastern Counties; in the 1860s the *London & South Western.

The *Mania of 1844–7 afforded ample scope for ridiculing railway schemes and their promoters. The stout person and spectacular career of George *Hudson invited caricature. They got it at its best in 1849 from A. H. Forrester ('Alfred Crowquill') in *How He Reigned and how He Mizzled*. At the same time *Punch* included a richly comic yet not unkindly view of a disappointed railway shareholders' meeting by Richard Doyle.

The misconduct of the ECR was not satirized in *Punch* alone. In 1856 G. E. Ancell, a solicitor, amused himself, and many other people, by issuing a series of broadsheets to announce that a costermonger had challenged that company to run his cart, hauled by a donkey, to race with its express train, showing the donkey's victory in the jolliest terms. In another the donkey is attached to the locomotive, hauling it as well as the train, with its passengers cheering.

Railway *refreshment rooms were the constant butt of satirists, headed by Dickens. Trollope remarked in 1869 that 'the real disgrace of England is the railway sandwich'.

The mood of the railways' critics now changed from ridicule to straightforward attack, its humour dying down. Their most prominent appearances in *Punch* were in the cartoons of John Tenniel, with their biting commentary on accidents. But, here and there, some quaint branch line might be lovingly depicted: as the Bodmin & Wadebridge Railway (see LONDON & SOUTH WESTERN RAILWAY) was by Quiller-Couch ('Q') in his 'Cuckoo Valley Railway', and the *Southwold Railway in the delightful postcards of Reg Carter.

Presently some first-rate comic draughtsmen paid attention to railways, headed by W. Heath Robinson, who 'made droll fun of the machine in an age which was enslaved by it'. The *Great Western Railway, by some inspiration, commissioned him to produce a set of 96 drawings, which it published as *Railway Ribaldry* to commemorate its centenary in 1935. Other cartoonists also enjoyed railways, their temper now not fierce but affectionate: notably Rowland Emett, a direct and worthy successor to Heath Robinson, and Fougasse, who produced war posters commissioned by the Ministry of Information, persuasive by comedy and beautifully clear drawing. Paul Jennings sketched the railways' oddities deftly. No one has recorded the obstacles encountered in making telephone inquiries about services better than he did in his 'Euston Sleepers', which gently leads him off into improbable fantasy.

But the grimmer kind of humour was not dead. In *Notes from Overground: A Commuter's Notebook* (1983) Roger Green ('Tiresias') set down some of the miseries of their journeys, as recorded by many authors, with an extended and witty running commentary.   JS

Pamphlets of 1834–9: *Ottley, 5218, 7686, 7689; Doyle on shareholders' meeting: *Punch*, 17 (1850) 32; Trollope on the sandwich: *He Knew He was Right* (Old World's Classics edn., i. 351); comment on Heath Robinson: *DNB*; 'Euston Sleepers': P. Jennings, *The Jenguin Pennings* (1963), 77–9.

Hunt, Sir Henry Arthur, see ARCHITECTURE AND ARCHITECTS.

Hurcomb, Cyril William, 1st Baron Hurcomb of Campden Hill (1883–1975), civil servant; chairman of the *British Transport Commission, 1947–53. Educated at Oxford, Hurcomb was a highly effective civil servant in several departments, including the *Post Office and the Ministry of Shipping (1915–18, 1939–41). As Permanent Secretary at the Ministry of *Transport, 1927–37, he did much to establish that comparatively new department's standing, and he enjoyed a close working relationship with Herbert *Morrison.

Hurcomb was at his most influential when Director-General of the Ministry of War Transport, 1941–7. He was one of the principal architects of the post-war *nationalization of much of Britain's inland transport, including the assets of the private railway companies. Indeed, his opposition to the idea of nationalizing the whole of inland transport was a key factor in the compromise represented by the Transport Act, 1947, which created the British Transport Commission. As first chairman of the Commission, he adopted an ambitious stance and, indeed, dominated policy-making. A first-rate administrator, he had a quick, analytical mind, and a great capacity for hard work. On the other hand, his shy, austere manner did not endear him to career railwaymen. He was at the centre of the battle with the Railway Executive (see BRITISH TRANSPORT COMMISSION), and in particular its chairman, Sir Eustace *Missenden, which did much to discredit the reputation of the railways in the early years of nationalization. A series of morale-sapping conflicts arose over operating issues, public relations, research, and motive power investment. Hurcomb made strenuous efforts to impose centralized control and at the same time improve the quality of regional railway management, but had limited success. He also tended to be too deferential to his political masters when dealing with pricing and labour relations (see TRADE UNIONISM). In 1953 a new Transport Act encouraged a new railway organization by abolishing the Railway Executive. Hurcomb, now 70, retired as chairman of the Commission and was succeeded by General Sir Brian *Robertson.   TG

Who Was Who; obituaries from The Times (1971–5); Gourvish; M. R. Bonavia, The Nationalisation of British Transport: The Early History of the British Transport Commission, 1948–53 (1987).

hydraulic power was much used by railway companies. As early as 1842 the double lift at the *Great Western Railway's *Bristol goods station was worked hydraulically. Later, central pumping stations distributed water, at a pressure of 600 lb per sq in, or more, through networks of pipes to dispersed hydraulic machines. Pressure was regulated by weight-loaded accumulators, placed in towers at the engine houses. Developed by William Armstrong (Baron Armstrong of Cragside), the system was first used commercially in 1850 by the Manchester Sheffield & Lincolnshire Railway (see GREAT CENTRAL) at New Holland, Lincolnshire.

The system was soon in widespread use. It turned large swing bridges, like those across the Yorkshire Ouse. Important *goods depots, particularly those in *London and *Liverpool, relied heavily on hydraulic *cranes, shunting capstans, wagon hoists, goods *lifts, and even chaff-cutters. Railway-owned *ports used hydraulic cranes, capstans, sluice gear, and lock gate mechanisms. Hydraulic *coal hoists and tips were found at ports handling coal traffic. Railway workshops had powerful hydraulic forging presses and materials-testing machines. Each site had its own steam-driven pumps, some, as at *Paddington, supplying over 100 machines. Some appliances used low-pressure, town's water mains.

With his crane of 1846, Armstrong introduced the hydraulic jigger, which formed the basis of many machines. Others, such as hoists, utilized the press, patented by Joseph Bramah in 1795. Circular motion, for capstans and lock gate winches, was produced by the hydraulic engine, or later, by the more compact Brotherhood motor and similar devices.

Availability of gas engines in the 1880s made smaller installations viable, like that of 1882 at Tynemouth. Public hydraulic mains were installed in London and some other cities, including *Manchester where they were used at the *Great Northern Railway's Deansgate goods depot of 1898. With increasing competition from electricity in the 20th century, some pumping stations were electrified, others closed, sometimes in favour of the local public supply.

TRS

I. McNeil, Hydraulic Power (1972).

I

IC 125; IC 225, see SPEED; BRITISH RAILWAYS.

industrial railways. The early history of industrial railways is that of railways themselves. For almost 200 years after the first *wooden railways were built in the early 17th century, they and the *tramroads which followed were private, carrying only the traffic of the owners of the industries they were built to serve.

When steam-operated public railways began to spread across the country, industrial railways also continued to expand and increase, connecting factories, mines, and quarries to main-line railways by a private siding or branch line, and carrying materials and products within or between industrial sites, or both.

Users of industrial railways became legion. Collieries remained probably the most important, both above and below the surface, and to ironworks were in due course added steelworks. Industrial railways were providing transport for *slate quarries from at least 1801 and were later used widely by them, and by quarries for *stone, chalk, sand, gravel, and iron ore (see IRON AND STEEL INDUSTRY). Such lines became known generically as mineral railways. Shipyards, *brickworks, gasworks, waterworks, and sewage works all had industrial railways. So did breweries, notably at Burton-on-Trent, and distilleries, particularly on Speyside (see FOOD AND DRINK TRAFFIC). Industrial railways were used in *agriculture for carriage of sugar beet from the 1860s and potatoes from the 1920s, and in forestry for extraction of timber, particularly during World War I. The 20th century saw extension of their use to electricity generating stations, oil refineries, and industrial estates. All three armed services, though not strictly 'industries', have used similar railways to serve storage depots and dockyards (see MILITARY RAILWAYS).

Some industrial railways, particularly the colliery lines, were immensely long-lived: the *Middleton Railway, Leeds, had been operating, in one form or another, for over two centuries before preservation in 1960. Some were comparatively short-lived, such as the system which carried materials for construction of Welwyn Garden City in c.1920–36. Some were wholly temporary; contractors' lines built to aid particular construction projects. Temporary railways were used in construction of the Caledonian Canal as early as c.1804, and they were subsequently much used to carry materials and remove spoil during construction of railways, reservoirs, tunnels, and (particularly during the 1920s) roads. Occasionally such lines were left in position, like the Lochaber Narrow Gauge Railway, built to assist construction of aluminium works at Fort William in 1924–9, and maintained to serve them until 1976.

Private sidings and other industrial railways connected to the national railway system had of necessity to be built to standard gauge. Elsewhere *narrow gauges were often used. The narrowest seems to have been 1 ft 6 in—within the *London & North Western Railway's *Crewe Works, and at Woolwich Arsenal, for instance. Gauges of 2 ft or thereabouts were often used for temporary lines; prefabricated removeable lengths of track were in use by the 1870s. Many other *gauges up to standard were employed, and broad gauges too on occasion. Contractors building Holyhead harbour breakwater in the 1850s used the 7 ft gauge, and after conversion to standard gauge about 1913 the line continued in use for repair work until 1979–80.

Before the locomotive era, traction on industrial railways was manpower, *horses, *gravity, or stationary steam engines with cables. Despite the introduction of locomotives, all four means of traction have survived into recent times. The last standard-gauge *cable-worked incline in commercial use, at Whitehaven, ceased operation in 1986, while one is still operated on the preserved Bowes Railway in Co. Durham.

The earliest steam locomotives—*Trevithick's, Blenkinsop's, *Stephenson's—were all built for industrial railways. Subsequently, they seem to have employed locomotives second-hand from public railways, or of similar types. By 1860–70, however, builders such as Manning Wardle and Hunslet Engine Co. were beginning to specialize in small locomotives suitable for industrial use and many other builders followed suit. Industrial railways such as that of the Harton Coal Co. in Co. Durham were using electric locomotives, both with overhead current collection and with batteries, by 1900. Industrial railways were pioneers of internal combustion locomotives also: use of these on gauges of about 2 ft was greatly boosted by the release of many Simplex locomotives as surplus after World War I. Nevertheless, steam locomotives continued in use on industrial railways into the 1980s, long after the end of steam on *British Rail.

The 18th-century wagonways of north-east England carried coal in chaldron *wagons, and some very closely derived from them were still in use there in the 1960s. The North Wales slate wagon seems first to have appeared on the Penrhyn Railway in 1801, and examples are probably still in use. Many lines carrying bulk materials used side- or end-tipping wagons; all-metal side-tipping wagons or skips for 2 ft gauge were in use by the 1870s and became ubiquitous. Specialized wagons have been used by industrial railways in immense variety—such as those to carry molten slag in steelworks, or *transporter wagons like those on the Padarn Railway, an industrial line which also had passenger carriages; one of several that provided passenger trains for employees. The South Shields Marsden & Whitburn Colliery Railway was owned by a colliery company but also ran a public passenger service. Several colliery companies in north-east England operated trains over not only their own tracks but also those of BR, as did the Wemyss Private Railway in Scotland.

Latterly industrial railways have fought a losing battle against lorries, dumper trucks, fork-lift trucks, and conveyor belts for movement of materials, and against the decline of the heavy industries, such as coal and steel, which were their main users. But there remain instances where they continue to prove their worth. In 1980–94, an extensive system of 900 mm gauge railways was used in construction of the *Channel Tunnel, to remove spoil and take in tunnel segments. The British section alone at its peak used 144 locomotives.   PJGR

Pocket Books and Handbooks of the Industrial Railway Society; F. L. Pugh, 'Industrial Railways', in O. S. Nock (ed.), Encyclopaedia of Railways (1977); Industrial Railway Record.

industrial relations, see TRADE UNIONISM.

industry, railways and. Through the 19th century and into the 20th they grew together, influencing and feeding each other's development. The relationship between railways and industry, especially heavy industry, has therefore always been complex.

Development

The mainstream of railway development played a major role in concentrating much of Great Britain's industrial activity in distinct manufacturing regions. Many had been established during the canal age or earlier, and the railways facilitated their growth. They also led to the creation of new industrial centres, and of new industries, but they were rather less significant in the overall patterns of industrial activity than in the general process of concentration.

The quality which gave railways such great utility for industry was their ability to move large quantities of raw materials—particularly *coal, *timber, iron ore, cotton, and wool—and products such as *iron and steel, machinery, textiles, and foodstuffs, more quickly, cheaply, and reliably over longer distances than competing modes of transport in most circumstances. Even when their *freight rates were comparable with other modes, they could often provide a service that was cheaper overall, when reliability and the costs of capital tied up in goods-in-transit, warehousing (see GOODS SHEDS AND WAREHOUSES), and handling were taken into account. However, *road, *canal, and coastal *shipping did continue as vital parts of the industrial process, particularly the last, either complementing or competing with rail.

The railways were arteries for the industrial growth of the 19th century, assembling materials for factory-based production, transporting its output, and feeding the rapidly growing urban populations which served the industries.

Coal dominated *freight traffic. It formed over half the total tonnage from 1850 onwards, and one of the railways' great contributions to industrial and urban growth was to make coal available at a lower price. The market expanded in size and in distance and railways allowed it to be met by facilitating the development of existing coalfields and opening up new, deeper deposits. As railways were built to tap the coalfields of central *Scotland, South *Wales, north-east England, Lancashire, Yorkshire, Nottinghamshire, Derbyshire, and the Midlands, dense networks led to new collieries being sunk, and production increased rapidly. Coal exports were also greatly helped by the construction of docks (see PORTS), such as *Barry Docks in South Wales.

The railways assembled coal, iron ore, and limestone for iron and steel-making, emphasizing and developing the earlier concentrations of the industry in the coalfields. Railway construction itself also stimulated the demand for iron production in South Wales, the Midlands, north-east England, and central Scotland in 1830–40, and steel production after the 1850s. It has been estimated that railways consumed about 20 per cent of total engineering output in the form of rolling stock between 1840 and 1851.

Mutual relationships

Coal and iron are two examples of close industrial relationships. Bargaining strengths could be extremely complex. To take an example, the United Steel Companies' works near *Sheffield and Rotherham were served by two formerly competing railway companies, which should have been a source of bargaining strength on freight rates; but the railways were also major customers of United Steel for rails, plates, sheets, castings, wheels and axles, billets and so on. There had to be some reciprocity of interest.

The closest relationship was traditionally with the coal industry, which required instant transport from the pithead to avoid the cost of storage. If the railway failed, the pit had to stop. Collieries therefore built extensive sidings for storage of empty wagons, and loaded wagons awaiting collection. Continuous contact between colliery managers and railway operators was thus essential, and many collieries provided their own wagons (see PRIVATE-OWNER WAGONS), which also justified their demanding a cheaper rate for carriage.

Conversely, the railways were important customers. They purchased large quantities of locomotive coal, though quality requirements somewhat restricted the number of sources, and locomotive designers had to accept variations in grades. The *Great Western Railway enjoyed access to high-quality steam coal from South Wales; the *Great Northern accepted a more bituminous quality from south Yorkshire. Haulage costs were important for the railways of southern England, not connected to major coalfields.

Similar relationships existed between railways and other industries.

Railway stimulus

Although care should always be taken in attributing a decisive role to any transport system in the establishment of new industrial areas, the rapid emergence of *Barrow-in-Furness as a major centre of iron mining and smelting after

1840 was largely due to the opening of the *Furness Railway in 1846. The *North Eastern Railway is also recognized as an essential element in the growth of *Middlesbrough as an iron-producing centre, using Cleveland ore. Certainly the railways were the direct cause of the introduction of engineering into areas which would not otherwise have experienced it, and of expanding populations of relatively small country towns and villages, by locating their engineering *works in centres such as *Swindon, Ashford, Inverurie, *Inverness, Melton Constable, *Crewe, and Horwich (see also TOWNS AND VILLAGES, RAILWAY-CREATED). New growth points in existing urban areas were also established as centres of railway engineering, such as Stratford in east London, Gorton in *Manchester, St Rollox in *Glasgow, *Doncaster, and *Derby. Railway engineering itself was a genuinely new industry created by the railway companies and their suppliers. Despite the decline, and often the disappearance, of railway engineering in these centres in the 20th century, traditions established in the 19th have survived in other, more recent forms of engineering, as at Swindon, Crewe, and Derby.

Railways in Britain were at first the sole buyers from these firms, until they began to undertake new construction in their own works originally established for repair purposes. In 1843 the *London & North Western Railway started to build its own engines, as did others at Swindon, Derby, and elsewhere. The private builders suffered from fluctuations in home demand; only when the railways' own works were overloaded did orders come their way, except in the case of small railways which bought all their locomotives from outside. But the private builders quickly established an export trade which became very important; starting in Europe it was soon concentrated upon British colonies and possessions, and other countries where British capital built the railways, notably in South America.

Relations between the railways and the private builders varied from the prickly (as when the *London Chatham & Dover Railway found it difficult to pay for engines) to the long-standing cordial, of which an outstanding example was those between Beyer Peacock & Co. of Gorton, Manchester (see WORKS) and the Manchester Sheffield & Lincolnshire Railway (see GREAT CENTRAL) next door.

Railway rolling stock builders similarly competed with the railways' own shops, and here too the export trade was important, especially for *carriages. There also rose firms providing ancillary equipment such as *signalling (e.g. Saxby & Farmer, McKenzie & Holland), *braking systems, and components such as locomotive boiler *injectors (Gresham & Craven).

The railways generally disliked paying royalties for the use of *patented components, such as superheaters, and would redesign them to evade liability. The Midland Railway contrived to quarrel with the *Pullman Car Company which had provided its first sleeping and *restaurant cars and with *Westinghouse which supplied its first proper brake system. Other companies maintained a long and mutually satisfactory relationship.

Purchasing

Railway policy regarding internal provision or outside purchase varied a great deal. Generally the largest companies, such as the *London & North Western Railway, sought to be self-sufficient. The Great Western was reputed to be able to provide from Swindon almost any wood or metal articles that it might require, down to ash-trays for hotels.

But despite the leaning towards self-sufficiency, the railways were still large customers of a wide range of suppliers, and their purchasing agents, usually the stores superintendents, wielded considerable bargaining power as bulk buyers, assisted by substantial investment in storage and warehousing facilities. For instance, the Midland had large centralized stores near Derby for tarpaulins and ropes for sheeting open wagons. The Great Northern had a similar warehouse at Peterborough, and the Great Western maintained a large provender store at Didcot for feeding its horses. It may be noted that despite the opportunities presented for financial irregularities, such as secret commissions, historians have recorded few, if any.

Distribution

As well as helping in the concentration and growth of basic industries the railways brought many changes in rural crafts and industries. They distributed factory-made products throughout the land, at lower prices than many locally produced goods. The economic activities of rural areas became less diversified as the enormous productive power of the industrial centres was spread through the rail network, and craftsmen became sellers of others' production. Textiles and clothing, foods and tools, beer and *bricks, and a host of other manufactured goods flooded outwards, and mass-consumption of standardized products became the new pattern of economic life. Foreign imports, too, were more readily available, so regional and national markets alike became part of a larger-scale system of economic interaction.

In short, without railways to assemble and distribute goods on a massive scale, factory-based and concentrated industrial production, with its economies of size and burgeoning urban populations, would scarcely have been feasible. Rail transport was increasingly substituted for geographical proximity to markets and raw materials.

However, business methods were changing by the end of the 19th century. Retailers (including the new chain stores) and local agents were reducing their capital by cutting their stocks. This was made possible by rapid and reliable rail transport, though in fact it began to create a traffic environment less suited to the railways, whose strength had traditionally been in heavy freight movements of bulk goods. Now they had helped to create a demand for the rapid, reliable movement of small consignments. This trend, together with fundamental structural and geographic changes in British industry, was to make the railways' relationship with it less pervasive.

Modern Industry

Railways and industry began to move apart, functionally and geographically, after World War I, due to changes in industrial structure, production methods, and location, and to the new competition from developing motorized *road transport. The dominance of the basic industries which had been at the heart of economic growth began to recede as new industries grew, including electrical engineering, motor vehicle production, and a wide range of consumer-oriented industries catering for the population's increasing purchasing power. They were less directly bound by the locational imperatives which had focused iron and steel, heavy engineering, shipbuilding, and textiles on or near the coalfields. Instead they could locate themselves close to the large and more affluent consumer markets and capital sources in London and the south-east. Assembly-line production methods required more factory floor space, and sites outside existing urban areas were ideal, notably in the south-east, but also for the new industries setting up around existing industrial areas in South Wales, the Midlands, northern England, and central Scotland.

Road transport allowed these changes to take place. Just as the railways had the advantage over canals in their ability to reach more industrial locations, so road transport's flexibility freed a growing section of industry from the need to locate on or near railways. The fiercely competitive road haulage industry captured a large proportion of the new industrial traffic, and ate into existing railway traffic. Also adding to the railways' problems in this period was the decline in their core traffics as basic industries failed to make the investment and changes in production techniques required to meet increasing foreign competition. The railways, with their small capacity *wagons, slow loose-coupled goods trains, and trip working between the numerous goods yards dating from the pre-*Grouping era, also found it difficult to meet the new competition, and were left with the least profitable traffic.

Although the railway system shouldered the bulk of the domestic burden during World War II, the industrial trends and patterns of the 1920s and 1930s became more pronounced after 1945. Heavy industry continued to decline. Coal was increasingly replaced, though not completely, by oil and other fuels; light industries located themselves away from rail facilities; and the freight market increasingly moved to horizontal integration in which component manufacture is linked with assembly plants by road haulage, operating on the 'just in time' principle, with precise delivery schedules, and low-cost, tightly controlled distribution systems. The integration of manufacturing has also become more international, particularly in Europe, and here again rail has found it difficult to accommodate the needs of industry. Rail freight has become increasingly focused on a diminishing core of economic traffics, squeezed by industrial change, road competition, and government investment policy. Regular trainload hauls are the main traffic, but as the coal and steel industries continue to decline, the railways have had to work hard to stay in the freight business on an appreciable scale.

Efforts have been made to meet industry's needs for rapid, reliable delivery. Automated *marshalling yards and Condor (London–Glasgow) container trains in the 1950s,

and the *Freightliner road–rail container system after the 1960s, tried but failed to stem the road-borne tide.

The carrier–customer relationship has often disappeared, and what may be called 'cosy contacts' with particular firms have now gone. The change from steam to diesel and electric traction—world-wide as well as in Britain—was fatal to many old-established locomotive builders, though a few adapted to the new technologies, aided by amalgamation. For their part, the railways accepted that they could not design and build diesel and electric motors, or control equipment, and that their workshops would at best become more assembly than processing plants. Some compromises were sought under the *Modernization Plan of 1955 by which, while industry was invited to supply complete prototype locomotives, railway workshops would be responsible in other cases for mechanical items, body shells, and underframes, with the traction elements being bought in. They were grouped as British Rail Engineering Ltd, and later were sold to the private sector (see PRIVATIZATION).

A loosening of railway links with industry can be traced back to the first years of *nationalization, when the *British Transport Commission queried such long-established practices as the tradition that the *Southern Railway's passenger ships should all be built by Denny Bros of Dumbarton. More evidence of competitive tendering was demanded. This challenging of relationships with industry was accentuated during the *Beeching era; privatization is carrying the process even further.

Personalities
Industrial personalities linked industry and some of the early railways. In South Wales the great ironmaster Sir John Guest was chairman of the *Taff Vale Railway, and the coal-owner David *Davies headed the Barry Railway. But in the north, Quaker commercial interests—particularly the *Pease family in the north-east—were pre-eminent. By the mid-19th century, with heavy industry marching towards its peak, industrialists were members of the boards of the great freight-carrying railways, continuing past the Grouping of 1923. The *London & North Eastern Railway was glad to have the chairmen of Dorman Long and Consett Iron as directors; its last chairman was Sir Ronald Matthews, a Sheffield steel magnate. The Great Western maintained a convention that South Wales must be properly represented on its board, and even the passenger-dominated Southern Railway had probably its most able and useful director in F. Dudley Docker, a Midlands industrialist. The *London Midland & Scottish gave industry several places, including one for a Wedgwood from the Potteries. It was, however, shaken by the appointment as chairman in 1926 of Josiah *Stamp from Nobel Industries, although he was by no means a typical industrialist.

Nationalization considerably weakened business links. The Railway Executive of 1948 had just one part-time member from industry, a ship-builder. The creation of part-time area boards after 1953 was meant to renew business contacts with the railways, but the effect was limited. From

1962 Beeching recruited some full-time board members from industry, most controversially P. H. Shirley from Unilever, and L. Williams from Shell, as well as some younger businessmen into regional management. Since then the *British Railways Board has been dominated by professional railwaymen as full-time executives, with some enlargement from outside business, and at the top, ministerial appointments have varied sharply; since 1965 there have been, very roughly alternating by origin, four railwaymen and three businessmen as chairmen.

The Future

Three recent developments suggest that railways in Britain may yet be able to align their freight operations more closely to the needs of industry at the end of the 20th century. Concern about the environmental consequences of a road-dominated transport system is already reducing road spending and perhaps also may increase the costs of road transport. The *Channel Tunnel presents real opportunities for the railway to take freight traffic from road transport through its network of terminals and rapid services to near- and mid-continental destinations. Privatization is creating new incentives for freight companies to go out and win traffic. If they can offer imaginative pricing, and guarantee reliability with speed of delivery, they could offer real competition to road haulage.

See also MINERALS TRAFFIC; articles on other individual traffics.　　　　　　　　　　　　　　　　MRB and JHF

G. Alderman, *The Railway Interest* (1973); P. S. Bagwell, *The Transport Revolution from 1770* (1974); M. R. Bonavia, *Railway Policy Between the Wars* (1981); H. J. Dyos and D. H. Aldcroft, *British Transport: An Economic Survey from the Seventeenth Century to the Twentieth* (1971); Gourvish; C. I. Savage, *An Economic History of Transport* (1966 edn.).

Inglis, Sir James Charles (1851–1911), engineer and manager. Born and educated at *Aberdeen, he became a pupil of James Abernethy and worked under him on the *Alexandra Docks, Newport. In 1875 he became assistant engineer of the *South Devon and *Cornwall Railways, transferring in 1878 to employment part-time on the *Great Western (which had absorbed them), and undertaking dock work for it at *Plymouth. He was resident engineer for the building of the difficult Princetown Railway in 1881–3. In 1892 he became full-time assistant engineer of the GWR, and almost immediately afterwards chief engineer.

He planned a series of improvements to the company's lines from London to South Wales and the West Country, and from *Birmingham to *Bristol. His greatest achievement was the construction of Fishguard harbour (with the approach railways), for Irish and transatlantic services.

In 1903 he became general manager of the company. There he was determined to maintain his full authority, attempting to centralize its entire management. His plan was accepted by the board in 1910 but then dropped, chiefly owing to the tenacious opposition of its locomotive engineer, G. J. *Churchward.

He was no narrow-minded technician. He grasped the importance of public relations and promoted the GWR's *advertising imaginatively. He played a part in public life, as a member of the important Engineering Standards Committee and of the Royal Commission on Canals and Waterways (1907–11). He was president of the ICE (unusually for two succeeding terms) in 1908–9 and knighted in 1911.　　JS

Engineer, 112 (1911), 635; *PICE* (1911); MacDermot, ii; O. S. Nock, *Great Western Railway in the 20th Century* (1971 edn.), 43–9.

injector, locomotive: since *c.*1870 the most widely used method of pumping water into a locomotive boiler against the internal pressure, superseding the motion-driven reciprocating pumps originally employed. The first injector was devised in 1858 by the French physicist Henri Giffard as a lightweight and reliable boiler feed pump for his steam-powered dirigible balloon; having obtained a British patent he sent samples of his invention to several locomotive builders, including Sharp Stewart & Co., where its importance was recognized by James Gresham who quickly developed an improved version suitable for locomotive use. First applied in 1861 it was adopted rapidly even by the most conservative designers because it eliminated the heavy maintenance necessary with mechanical pumps, and unlike pumps could be used when the locomotive was stationary. After 1870, pumps were used only to handle hot feed water, e.g. on condensing locomotives.

The apparent paradox of using the pressure in a boiler to pump water against itself is an early example of the application of thermodynamics: a pound of steam contains many times as much recoverable energy as a pound of water at the same temperature and pressure. The simplest injector consists of three cones. Steam expanded through the steam cone produces a jet travelling at more than 2,000 ft per second, which mixes with several times its own weight of cold water in the combining cone where it is condensed and transfers much of its momentum to the water. The resulting jet of hot water is still travelling faster than would a jet

Diagram of a simple injector

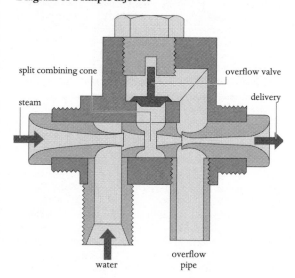

split combining cone

steam

water

overflow valve

delivery

overflow pipe

of water issuing directly from the boiler, and by means of the divergent delivery cone, sufficient of its momentum is destroyed to develop a pressure in excess of that in the boiler. This allows it to open the clack, or non-return valve, in the delivery line, and flow into the boiler.

Live steam injectors take steam directly from the boiler; later there were developed exhaust steam injectors which derived part of their energy from exhaust pressure, thereby recycling a proportion of the steam used in the cylinders and improving thermal economy.   RW

'The Inspector' (pseud.), *Locomotive Injectors* (1905); British Railways Board, *Handbook for Steam Railway Locomotive Enginemen* (1955).

Inner Circle, see LONDON UNDERGROUND RAILWAYS (METRO-POLITAN RAILWAY and METROPOLITAN DISTRICT RAILWAY).

inspectors. The term 'inspector' has held many connotations in a railway context. The earliest were probably the inspectors who, on behalf of the engineers employed by railway companies, inspected the masonry, *earthworks, *tunnels, and permanent way of railways under construction by *contractors.

The term soon came to be used for a supervisory position in the hierarchy of railway operation, and by 1860 there were almost 1,000 inspectors on the railways of Great Britain. Probably those most familiar to the travelling public, throughout the railway era, have been station inspectors. Subordinate to the *stationmaster at large stations, they took charge of trains standing at the platform and supervised passengers boarding, loading and unloading of luggage and parcels, attaching and detaching of vehicles, and getting the train away on time. While stationary the train was under the inspector's control rather than that of the *guard. The night inspector took over when there were night mails and similar important trains to attend to, subsequently reporting to the stationmaster on any incidents during his turn of duty.

On the *Midland Railway administration was highly centralized by the 1890s, and a large staff of inspectors represented headquarters departments, enquiring into irregularities, obtaining information for their superiors, and ensuring that orders were carried out, in an effort to reduce chronic delays to trains. They would descend upon country stations to take charge when a large but temporary increase in traffic was expected such as, for instance, the arrival of prize livestock for an agricultural show. On most railways, which were less centralized, two or three travelling inspectors carried out these tasks in each district. Such men were railwaymen of long service and great experience.

Locomotive inspectors, at both district and headquarters level, were drawn from the ranks of experienced engine *drivers. One of their main tasks was to ascertain whether *firemen were fit to be promoted to drivers, and *cleaners to firemen, by examining them on both theoretical and practical knowledge. Locomotive inspectors attached to large stations were responsible for arranging fresh engines and relief crews when needed, and for giving drivers special instructions. And for general supervision: J. W. Street recorded an encounter with a locomotive inspector. As a recently promoted driver, about 1902, he ran into Paddington very smartly with an empty train, but stopped several yards from the *buffers. Observing this, the inspector, from *Swindon, commented that he believed the men handling such trains knew how much brake power they had, but if one struck the end of the platform Mr *Churchward would take him off the footplate. Other matters with which locomotive inspectors were concerned included the siting of *signals for visibility, and investigating enginemen's complaints about particular locomotives.

Rolling stock inspectors were responsible for supply of rolling stock to meet fluctuating traffic needs; lamp and signal inspectors were responsible for investigating defects in signals and their oil lamps—matters of vital importance for safety—and the supervision and examination of *signalmen. In the early years, railways' inspectors of *police were responsible not only for investigating criminal activities, but also for supervising the 'policemen' who controlled railway traffic when signalling was still simple. Boiler inspectors, on the staffs of locomotive superintendents, were responsible for periodic examinations of steam locomotive boilers to ensure their safety. Permanent way inspectors supervised the activities of track gangs on behalf of district engineers. Many such grades no longer retain these titles: permanent way inspectors, for instance, became permanent way section supervisors in 1979 and then permanent way supervisory managers in 1990, with responsibility, typically, for 45 miles of track and a work-force of about 40.

When *British Railways created divisional operating managers in its early days, they controlled divisional and district operating inspectors for designated functions, such as signalling (the highest grade), passenger traffic, *freight, freight rolling stock, and, later, *electrification.

See also INSPECTORS, GOVERNMENT.   PJGR

Enginemen's examinations: F. S. Williams, *Our Iron Roads* (1883, reissued in facsimile 1981), ii, 353; G. F. Allen, *The Concise Encyclopaedia of World Railway Locomotives* (1959), 441; Anon., *Railways and Railwaymen* (1892), ch. 7; J. Macaulay and C. Hall (eds.), *Modern Railway Working* (1912), ii, 39, 55, 62; locomotive inspector: J. W. Street, *I Drove the Cheltenham Flyer* (1951).

inspectors, government. (See also ACCIDENTS; TRADE, BOARD OF.) In 1833 an Act was passed imposing conditions for the employment of labour in factories, and providing for the appointment of inspectors to see that its provisions were obeyed. The railways were subjected to a similar arrangement under the first *Regulation Act (1840), which empowered the Board of *Trade to authorize 'any proper person or persons to inspect any railway'. A second Act (1842) provided that no new passenger-carrying railway might be opened without an inspector's prior approval. It also obliged the companies to report to the Board any accident 'attended with serious personal injury to the public' using the line. The Board could then send its inspector to investigate.

With one exception, all the railway inspectors were officers of the Royal Engineers until 1982. The first, Sir Frederic Smith, appointed in 1840, held the post for only one year, but his last report, on the accident at Sonning on the *Great Western Railway, had most salutary consequences (see PARLIAMENTARY TRAINS). His successor, C. W. *Pasley (1841–6), kept a private diary that enables us to watch him at work.

If a company opened a line that the inspectors had not approved, it was liable to a fine of £20 for every day during which it was worked in that state. Any postponement, in order to meet the inspector's objections, of course deferred the earning of revenue. That appeared prominently in 1848, with the extension of the *London & South Western Railway from Nine Elms to *Waterloo. The inspector had refused to sanction its opening on 1 July because he considered its largest bridge unsafe. But despite the company's heavy pressure on the Board, in defence of 'the proprietors' rights', the Board remained adamant, and they were kept out of their dividend for ten days.

The inspectors were not always so well supported, however. The Manchester Sheffield & Lincolnshire Railway (see GREAT CENTRAL) was allowed to open Torksey Bridge over the Trent in 1850 against the inspector's advice, which a group of engineers rightly considered was unduly overcautious. Occasionally the Board refrained from enforcing penalties that the companies had undoubtedly incurred. For example, an accident happened at Leeds in 1880 on an important, though very short, linking line, which the *Midland Railway had opened in 1872, but not submitted for inspection. The Board pointed out that this dereliction had exposed it to an accumulated fine amounting to £60,000. Only when the MR had agreed to undertake the necessary work, secured the inspector's approval of it, and acknowledged its fault, was the fine dispensed with.

Some chairmen never disguised their hostility towards the inspectors—*Moon and *Watkin, for example; some managers too, such as T. E. *Harrison and *Allport. Time after time we see the inspectors defending the public against railway boards stubbornly determined to pursue economy at the expense of safety. One of them, *Yolland, became firmly convinced that the government must legislate, to make the companies adopt precautions that had proved their efficacy. As those precautions grew more useful and reliable (and as the toll of accidents mounted in the 1860s), these matters came to be debated in Parliament and in the country at large.

Public concern now extended to the companies' treatment of their own staff. Back in the 1840s, investigating accidents, the inspectors had sometimes pointed out as a cause the extremely long hours that railwaymen might be required to work. One of them, Henry *Tyler, repeatedly showed his anxiety to see that they had justice done to them: in the accidents at Carter House (*London & North Western Railway, 1872), for instance, and at McAndrews Siding (*Caledonian Railway, 1873). Here the inspectors were acting as mediators between the men and their employers.

These inspectors did not always work alone. When they had a boiler explosion to examine, the Board of Trade usually brought an expert from its Marine Department to join in the investigation.

One class of accidents raised issues of special delicacy: those involving the design or construction of great bridges, in which it was really the engineer who was in the dock. Yolland sat with another Board of Trade man (not a railway inspector) and the engineer W. H. *Barlow to inquire into the destruction of the Tay Bridge in 1879, and their investigation showed clearly that, of several possible causes, the overriding element in the disaster was the faulty design of its braced cast-iron piers, quite inadequate to withstand the exceptionally fierce winds along that estuary. For this the engineer, Sir Thomas *Bouch, was responsible, and they made that plain in their report. (See BRIDGES AND VIADUCTS.)

The battle over new safety equipment was long, and grim. The inspectors repeatedly pointed to accidents that would not have occurred if appliances, already proved efficient, had been in use: above all the *block system, the interlocking of points and signals (see SIGNALLING), and the provision of automatic continuous *brakes. The Regulation Acts of 1871 and 1873 required annual returns showing the extent to which these improvements had been introduced by each company. But the government would go no further towards compulsion until its hand was forced by the Armagh accident of 1889, when it assumed full powers, requiring every passenger line to be worked on the block system and with interlocking, and every passenger train to be fitted with the new form of brakes.

The expansion of the *system being greatly slowed down from 1900 onwards, not many new lines needed inspection before opening. The number of inspectors was reduced from four to three in 1913, their work being concentrated now almost wholly on accidents and their prevention.

A new branch of the inspectorate had emerged as a result of the Railway Employment (Prevention of Accidents) Act, 1900, requiring the companies to use appliances that had proved their efficacy in preventing accidents to their employees while at work, and to discard those that were dangerous. Under section 13 the powers of the Board of Trade to inspect railways were specifically extended to include inspection for these purposes, and that led to the establishment of Railway Employment Inspectors, a group separate from the old inspectorate.

*Nationalization did not require any formal change in the inspectorate or in its relationship with the railways. It continued to be responsible for the investigation of accidents and for advising on safety appliances. Many of these cost substantial sums of money. But whereas in the past the inspectors were seeking to persuade the privately owned railway companies to spend these sums, now their admonitions were addressed to another department of the government. They encountered just as much unwillingness to accept such charges in *British Railways as they had in their dealings with the companies. In spite of the inspectors' clear and repeated recommendations of the need for large-scale extension of *automatic warning equipment, reducing the danger of errors on the part of both *signalmen and *drivers, that extension did not really get under way until 1969. Even then, however, the system adopted by BR did not meet all the demands legitimately made on it.

Other new problems were continually figuring in the inspectors' reports. For example, the welding of substantial lengths of *track together, greatly reducing the number of rail joints, could produce breaks in the weld, causing derailments. But perhaps the most serious among these new problems was that springing from the introduction of automatic lifting barriers at *level crossings. The bad accident on one of them at Hixon (Staffordshire) in 1968 led to a large public outcry against barriers of this kind, which had always been much disliked by motorists. The inquiry into this accident was entrusted not to one of the inspectors, but to a QC, and the same procedure was followed with the investigation of the big Clapham Junction accident of 1988. In both these cases it could perhaps be argued that the accidents had occurred partly as a consequence of implementing proposals made by the inspectors themselves.

The Health and Safety at Work Act, 1974, codified and extended the government's powers in this field. Though it did not specifically mention railways, they fell fully within its scope. The new Health and Safety Commission concluded an agency agreement with the Department of *Transport, under which the railway inspectorate became its agent in dealing with railways.

One recent change must also be recorded. In the 1980s the practice of appointing only officers of the Royal Engineers to be railway inspectors came to be abandoned. In 1988, for the first time, a civilian, R. J. Seymour, became Chief Inspecting Officer. JS

Railway Inspection (Railway Gazette, 1946); L. T. C. Rolt, *Red for Danger* (1982 edn.); S. Hall, *Railway Detectives: 150 Years of the Railway Inspectorate* (1990); ET, ch. 14.

Institute of Railway Studies, see NATIONAL RAILWAY MUSEUM.

Institution of Civil Engineers was formed in 1818 by eight young engineers, led by Henry Palmer. The Smeatonian Society of Civil Engineers had been established in 1771 but membership was restricted to senior engineers and, although they helped to ensure that *civil engineering became recognized as a profession, they did little to organize instruction and training in scientific principles and practical applications for young entrants. The new institution proposed to rectify these omissions; the modest, initial purpose of its members was to meet weekly to consider engineering practice and the merits of scientific inventions, and to read papers on discoveries or select information.

In 1820 Thomas Telford became president and, through his influence, the membership and activities grew. A Royal Charter was granted in 1828 which guaranteed the place of the institution as guardian of all matters relating to civil engineering, a privilege retained to the present. Today its corporate members, known as chartered civil engineers. are internationally recognized and its published proceedings are authoritative sources of information. The institution, housed in fine premises in Westminster, is still concerned

with education and training, besides all aspects of professional practice, publishing, and the promotion of civil engineering in government and business. Its *Proceedings* are a valuable source of historical information. RBS

G. Watson, *The Institution of Civil Engineers* (1988).

Institution of Electrical Engineers: originated in the Society of Telegraph Engineers in 1871. With the rapid development in the 1880s of electric power, W. H. Preece, a member of the STE, proposed the formation of the IEE. It began in 1889 and now has over 100,000 members, and includes electronics and production engineering.

Electric traction was an important subject, especially with the rapid expansion of suburban railway *electrification in the early 1900s. Overhead single-phase ac electrification was strongly advocated by Sir Philip Dawson, but not adopted by BR for 50 years, while H. E. O'Brien proposed electrification of part of the *West Coast main line, only achieved 40 years later. GWC

W. J. Reader, *A History of the Institution of Electrical Engineers, 1871–1971* (1987).

Institution of Locomotive Engineers. Founded in 1911 by G. F. Burtt, a locomotive draughtsman, and his colleagues on the *London Brighton & South Coast Railway, the institution's object was the reading and discussion of papers, and dissemination of locomotive engineering and allied sciences. Its membership had increased from 75 at the end of 1911 to some 2,500 in 1969 when it merged with the *Institution of Mechanical Engineers, combining with that body's Railway Engineering Group to form a new Railway Division.

Papers given covered virtually all aspects of locomotive and rolling stock design, construction, and maintenance, and discussions were often forthright and searching analyses of the subject by engineers with wide practical experience. A substantial proportion of its members—25 per cent in 1956—worked on overseas railways, and their contribution to discussions was extremely valuable. The institution was a friendly and close-knit body, many of whose members shared common workshop training and early careers, which facilitated free exchange of professional knowledge and experience. Its presidents included the CMEs of three of the *Grouped railways, and invitation-lecturers included the general managers of the French, Netherlands, and Swedish railways. GWC

Journal Inst. of Loco. Engrs: J. F. B. Vidal, 'The History of the Institution', 46 (1956), no. 251; H. Holcroft, 'The History of the Institution—the First 40 Years', 50 (1961), no. 278; E. S. Cox, 'The History of the Institution—the Ten Years to the Golden Jubilee', 50 (1961), no 278.

Institution of Mechanical Engineers. Railway engineers played a major part in founding the institution in 1847 to cater for their needs and those of the new engineering industry. The *Institution of Civil Engineers had existed since 1818, but had been founded when engineers oversaw complete but relatively uncomplicated projects like *canals and roads. The requirement to prove both engineering and managerial ability excluded many highly skilled but more specialist engineers now needed by the railways. These men therefore set up a body catering for their needs. The IMech E's headquarters was appropriately in *Birmingham until 1877. George *Stephenson was the first president, followed by his son Robert—two of the 14 railway engineers to hold this office.

The institution's activities have also covered the iron, steel, and mining industries, power generation, ship propulsion, the internal combustion engine, gas turbines, agricultural machinery, and many others. Membership more than doubled to 67,000 between 1947 and 1966, and 13 specialized groups were established in 1960, including railway engineering. In 1965 the institution joined with 13 others to form the Council of Engineering Institutions, controlling the granting of chartered engineer status.

See also INSTITUTION OF LOCOMOTIVE ENGINEERS.   GWC
L. T. C. Rolt, *The Mechanicals* (1967).

Institution of Railway Signal Engineers. Technology in railway *signalling advanced rapidly after 1900 and it became obvious that a forum was required for developing the science and disseminating knowledge. The Institution of Signal Engineers was established in 1910 but reincorporated in 1912 as the Institution of Railway Signal Engineers to overcome a constitutional error. It advances the science of railway signalling, through technical meetings, conferences, and visits, and publishing proceedings, technical papers, booklets, and textbooks. The Institution holds examinations in signalling and telecommunications and operates a licensing scheme by which individuals can obtain certification of their competence to practise within the profession. Over half the members work outside Britain.   RDF
O. S. Nock, *Fifty Years of Railway Signalling* (1962).

insurance and railways come together in three ways: the insurance of passengers against accidents; railways' insurance of their own property and liabilities; and insurance companies as a source of investment.

When the Accident Compensation Act, 1846, allowed a deceased person's dependants to sue for damages against negligence, it prompted suggestions about insurance against railway accidents, and in 1849 the Railway Passengers Assurance Co. was incorporated with a capital of £1 million. Policies took the form of tickets, the same size as railway tickets, sold on commission at booking offices and covering a single journey regardless of length. They stated the amount insured, the premium, and the issuing station. Fixed premiums and benefits were 3*d*. for £1,000, 1st class; 2*d*. for £500, 2nd class; and 1*d*. for £200, 3rd class. Period tickets were also available and within a year 32 railways, including all the major ones, were operating the scheme through the *Railway Clearing House, during which time 110,074 single and 2,808 period tickets were sold, and 37 claims met, totalling £210. Railway employees were also accepted, other than train crews and porters, although they were admitted in 1850.

In 1852, £1,000 annual, 5-year, and 10-year single premium policies were introduced, and the company started transacting general personal accident business and, later,

public and employers' liability. Other insurers followed, although only the Railway Passengers sold insurance at stations. The whole range of modern accident and legal liability insurance stems from that company. *Class distinctions were abolished in 1896, when combined 'boat-and-rail' tickets became available but, curiously, baggage insurance was not sold at stations until 1912. The company was absorbed by the North British & Mercantile in 1910—but continued under its own name—and later became part of the Commercial Union Group.

In 1851 the *Lancashire & Yorkshire Railway insured its employees with the Railway Passengers, although poor claims experience quickly caused an increased premium, but generally railways limited themselves to insuring against fire. In 1871 only three other large companies provided employees with accident benefits: the *London & North Western, *London Brighton & South Coast, and *North British. Membership of schemes was compulsory, and the LNW Insurance Society was administered by a committee of 12 employees and three nominees of the company, which paid five-sixths of the premiums. Compulsory sickness, retirement, and pension funds followed, administered by the same committee.

Smaller companies tended to insure more comprehensively than larger ones which steadily became more selective, often forming their own contingency funds. In 1865 the *Edinburgh & Glasgow Railway insured certain property such as houses, offices, a hotel, and its works, but in 1903 the *Furness Railway still insured nearly all of its extensive property in *Barrow. The *Stratford-upon-Avon & Midland Junction Railway was typical of a small company in insuring all its buildings against fire, its legal liability for accidents injuring employees or passengers, forged transfers, and defalcations by staff handling money or materials. It also had to insure other companies' signal boxes at junctions where the two lines met, a common practice in such circumstances.

In 1853 the *Midland Railway established an insurance fund to which it transferred annual amounts, selectively moving risks away from commercial insurers as the fund grew. In 1872 the fund amounted to £350,000 and in 1878 was earning 4 per cent. In 1903 it started paying for the *Derby works fire brigade, by which time only leasehold and contractual liabilities were insured externally. Self-funding was continued by the *Big Four after the 1923 *Grouping, but in the 1970s *British Railways decided to insure commercially on a 'catastrophe' basis, whereby insurers took over liabilities above an agreed figure of several millions. *London Transport had earlier made a similar arrangement.

Insurance companies at first looked unfavourably on railways for investment, but were prepared to make loans secured by bonds. In 1838 the Royal Exchange Assurance invested £30,000 in *London & Birmingham Railway 5 per cent bonds, a practice that grew in the early 1840s. Later, debenture shares were the more usual form of investment in railways, and often the prospect of acquiring a railway's fire insurance acted as an inducement, although it was not always attractive. The Royal Exchange refused the Norfolk Railway's in 1847, while in 1849 a Leeds locomotive manufacturer was described as a 'repugnant' fire risk. When yields started to fall later in the century, insurers' investment in railways declined.

See also COMPENSATION; PENSIONS AND GRATUITIES; SALARIES AND WAGES; TRADE UNIONISM. GJB

F. H. Cox, *The Oldest Accident Office in the World: The Railway Passengers Assurance Co.* (1949); B. Supple, *Royal Exchange Assurance: A History of British Insurance, 1720–1970* (1970); LNWR: Sir G. Findlay, *Working and Management of an English Railway* (1899); EGR: SRO BR/EGR/1/2; Furness: PRO RAIL 214/87; SMJR: author's collection; MR: PRO RAIL 491/330–382.

InterCity, see BRITISH RAILWAYS.

interest, the railway, see POLITICS.

interlocking, see SIGNALLING.

interval services. Passenger trains running at regular intervals throughout the day, or a large part of it, first appeared in Britain on the *London & Blackwall Railway, which provided them every ¼ hour from its opening in 1840. The *North London did the same, uninterruptedly from 1850 to 1916.

The pattern was well suited to short-distance services and was an obvious convenience to frequent travellers. Over longer distances it was not applied until the 1870s, when it became a feature of services between *Manchester and *Liverpool. The *Cheshire Lines Committee led the way in 1877, with trains running at half-past each hour from both terminal stations from 8.30 a.m. to 9.30 p.m.; one element in the CLC's determined policy of competing with the older-established services of the *London & North Western and *Lancashire & Yorkshire Railways. The LNWR came to run trains every hour on the hour. The LYR ran a good many leaving each city at 40 minutes past the hour, but not with unbroken regularity.

An important step towards the introduction of interval services over much longer routes was taken by the *Great Western Railway in 1924, when it standardized the departure times of nearly all its principal expresses from London, at 10 minutes past the hour for *Birmingham, 15 for *Bristol, 30 for Devon and Cornwall, 45 for Worcester, and 55 for South Wales. But the trains did not run every hour. The *London Midland & Scottish company went one stage further with its trains from London (*St Pancras) to Manchester settling down by 1939 to run every two hours at 30 minutes past the hour. The *Southern Railway adopted the practice with its West of England trains from London (*Waterloo), and on electrification in 1933–7 its services from London (*Victoria) to *Brighton, Eastbourne, and *Portsmouth were timed at hourly intervals. All the company's electric suburban trains ran at standard timings throughout the day, varied a little during peak hours.

It was *British Railways that brought interval services fully into their own, worked by diesel and electric *multiple units with a new precision and reliability from the 1960s onwards. It now became possible to turn every main-line service into a shuttle, the trains running backwards and for-

wards without change of engines at termini. The service from London to *Edinburgh now bore much the same character as those introduced 100 years earlier between Manchester and Liverpool, but over a distance ten times longer. Services at regular half-hourly intervals were introduced from London to Birmingham (113 miles) on electrification in 1967. With High Speed Trains the same was done for *Leicester (99 miles) in 1992. JS

Bradshaw's Guide; BR *Timetables*.

Inverness is the Highland capital, and the *Highland Railway played an important role in the town's development. There was a steady growth of population during the 19th century: 8,732 in 1801 rising to 18,162 in 1861; 24,614 in 1921 and 45,498 in 1981. The Inverness & Nairn Railway of 1855 was extended by the Inverness & Aberdeen Junction Railway to Forres in 1857 and Keith in 1858, giving access to *Aberdeen. This important achievement by Inverness interests ensured that Aberdonians would not control the entire Aberdeen–Inverness route. The line also provided scope for *excursions to the seaside as well as a starting-point for an independent route to the south from Forres, opened in 1863 (see INVERNESS & PERTH JUNCTION RAILWAY). Extensions west and northwards to Kyle of Lochalsh, and Wick and Thurso, made Inverness an important junction. The direct line south through Aviemore was opened in 1898.

The railway presence was projected most visibly by the company headquarters, terminal station, and *hotel complex. Northbound and southbound platforms were built as a 'vee', but there was a bypass line that could be used (with reversal) to bring connecting trains into adjacent platforms. This was particularly necessary at the height of the tourist season. A plan to rationalize the entire station layout (1895) was never put into effect. The railway made a major contribution to industrial development after opening its Lochgorm workshops in 1855. The extensive part-roundhouse *engine shed with a distinctive water tower and arch (1863) was a significant architectural feature. A full roundhouse was intended but never completed. DT

O. S. Nock, 'Inverness: A Unique Railway Centre', *RM*, 72 (1933), 25–8; L. Maclean of Dochgarroch (ed.), *The Hub of the Highlands: The Book of Inverness and District* (1975); W. Vamplew, 'Railway Investment in the Scottish Highlands', *Transport History*, 3 (1970), 141–53.

Inverness & Perth Junction Railway: one of two principal companies that merged in 1865 to form the *Highland Railway. It was opened in 1863 between Forres and Dunkeld, closely following a path surveyed by Joseph *Mitchell in the 1840s for the proposed Perth & Inverness Railway which was rejected by Parliament in 1846. At the time, a railway through Drumochter Pass was considered an impossibility. But the prospect was not so daunting in the 1860s, given improved locomotive performance and the priority attaching to direct railways.

The junction with the Inverness & Aberdeen Junction Railway at Forres made the line convenient for Moray as well as for *Inverness. The railway required eight viaducts, 126 bridges over streams and 119 over roads. Some were built originally in wood to accelerate construction. Extensive drainage was provided, including deep drains on the summits. There was a link with land improvement in the Beauly and Cromarty Firths where it was thought new and valuable land might be created. Agriculture became more intensive, but large-scale land improvements did not take place.

The line was always difficult to work with major summits at Druimuachdar (1,484 ft) and Dava (1,052 ft). When the HR opened the direct line between Aviemore and Inverness in 1898 there was a third summit at Slochd (1,315 ft). At Druimuachdar (the highest point on a British main line) the greatest difficulty met northbound trains, with a 17-mile climb from Blair Atholl including more than eight at 1 in 70 and another four at 1 in 85. Summit sections were particularly vulnerable to *snow, although the hazards at Druimuachdar were eased by widening. Telegraph poles were placed in sheltered positions and signal wires were carried on high posts.   DT

Reg. Hist., xv, 6; H. A. Vallance, 'One Hundred Years at Druimuachdar Summit', RM, 110 (1964), 2–9; H. A. Vallance, The History of the Highland Railway (1985).

Inverurie, see WORKS.

investment in railways. It is generally agreed that railways had the greatest impact of any single innovation in 19th-century Britain. In assessing this impact economic historians have paid particular attention to the relation between the pattern of investment in the railway system and changes in the wider economy, not simply because of the sheer magnitude of the investment requirements of the railways themselves, but also because of wider theoretical interest in the linkages between capital formation and economic growth. Several studies have assembled statistics of investment by railway undertakings in Britain or the UK. While there are detailed differences in their compilation, the series all agree in showing a rapid initial acceleration in expenditure, from approximately £500,000 in 1831 to about £9 million at the end of that decade. After falling to an annual rate of under £4 million during the early 1840s, investment peaked at over £30 million in 1847 before declining again to around £8.5 million during the early 1850s. The next peak, of about £24 million, came in 1866, and expenditure continued to vary significantly throughout the next half-century, with annual levels ranging from less than £12 million to more than £20 million.

For most of the period before World War I, the course of these variations in railway investment conforms broadly with the generally accepted outline of the trade cycle, the economy's repeated swings between boom and depression. At times the relationship was weak: the economic recovery in 1853 was barely reflected in railway investment, which was still influenced by the reaction to the Railway *Mania, while the trough of 1894 was a faintly discernible interruption in a long upswing that peaked in 1900. In contrast, during some stages of the initial development of the network, changes in the level of railway investment activity were strong enough to affect the general economic cycle. In

the mid-1830s, and even more in the 1840s, enthusiasm for railway promotion contributed significantly to economic optimism in the upswing, and the amount of investment generated by these promotional booms meant that railway capital spending continued at a high level during the succeeding depression.

In real terms, the level of investment attained during the 1840s was unique in British railway history: it reflected the opportunities offered by a new transport technology that had proved its potential with the pioneer trunk lines, and now had the scope to develop into a national network. While the optimism which led up to the Railway Mania quickly turned into excess, and was followed by a collapse of confidence in the autumn of 1845, the inherent lags in the authorization and construction processes meant that capital expenditure did not reach its maximum until 1847. The £30 million invested in constructing and equipping railways during that year was £11 million more than in 1846, and about four times the level achieved in 1845. Though the decline in investment after 1847 was as steep as the preceding increase, expenditure during the next two years nevertheless totalled more than £29 million.

Contemporaries recognized the wider significance of such levels of investment, and it has subsequently been reassessed in more detail by historians. The consensus is that, at its height in 1847, UK railway investment accounted for almost 7 per cent of national income, and about 45 per cent of total gross domestic capital formation. Two schools of thought emerged about the immediate economic impact of this extraordinary investment activity. One, to some extent coloured by the speculative excesses of the Railway Mania and the scale of the following reaction, linked the depression of the late 1840s, and particularly the financial crisis of 1847, with the distortions of shareholders' expenditure patterns, investment in other industries, and monetary circulation, which all resulted from railway capital requirements. The other interpretation emphasized instead the beneficial effects of railway demand on an otherwise depressed economy: it has been estimated that railway construction alone employed around 4 per cent of the working male population in 1847, and that railway demand for iron from 1844 to 1851 was equivalent to almost 18 per cent of the UK's total pig-iron output. As Hawke has pointed out, however, these opposing views can be partially reconciled by taking account of the lags between the *raising* of capital and its *expenditure*, and by noting the phased impact of railway investment on different sectors of the economy. On this basis, it is possible to accept not only that railway funding demands contributed to the financial crisis of 1847, but also that the construction made possible by these funds was ultimately beneficial because of the economic stimulus it gave during the depression.

So much of the railway map was filled in between 1845 and 1852 that the future possibility of a comparable concentration of investment on such a scale was virtually eliminated. In addition, the disappointing short-term return on many schemes initiated during the Railway Mania left investors reluctant to commit themselves to new railway pro-

Railway Investment 1830–1973

Representative published series

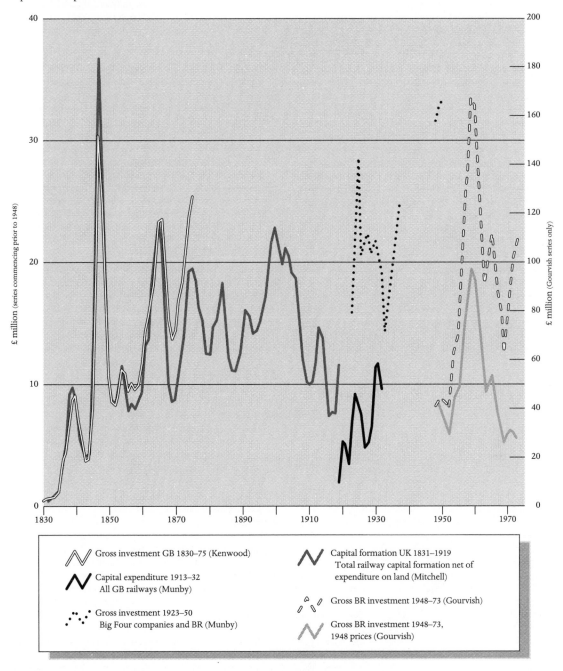

Sources:

Kenwood, A. G., 'Railway investment in Britain, 1825–1875', *Economica*, N.S. 32 (1965), 322

Mitchell, B. R., 'The Coming of the Railway and United Kingdom Economic Growth', repr. in M. C. Reed (ed.), *Railways in the Victorian Economy* (1969), 30–2

Munby, D. L. and Watson, A. H., *Inland Transport Statistics: Great Britain 1900–1970*, 1 (1978), Tables A5 and A6.

Gourvish, T. R., *British Railways 1948–1973* (1980), 595

posals in Britain for most of the 1850s. However, as traffic built up and revenues improved, a substantial new wave of railway investment was stimulated in the early 1860s, much of it in areas where sparse population and difficult topography had discouraged earlier development, or in *London, where high property acquisition costs had previously been a deterrent. The expenditure generated during these years peaked in 1865 and 1866 at a level comparable with 1848; however, the general growth of the economy since then meant that railway investment during the 1860s boom was proportionately less significant, amounting at its peak to under 3 per cent of UK national income and less than a third of total domestic fixed capital formation. And while the financial crisis of 1866 was followed by a sharp decline in railway capital expenditure, the recovery was not delayed, as it had been during the 1850s: there was a significant new upswing after 1869, and though fluctuations in levels of investment remained evident thereafter, they were generally less extreme.

Part of the reason for this was the stability and relative prosperity of the leading companies as the century progressed: much of their investment was prompted by the need to cater for growing traffic, by means such as widening existing routes or extending facilities in the main towns. Even when funds were required to extend the network, established railways were generally better able to obtain finance than a new company, since all that they required was a relatively small increase in their existing capital. In addition, as the system developed, the renewal of existing assets accounted for a greater proportion of total investment. Decisions on new capital expenditure were influenced by the ease with which additional funds could be raised: this explains much of the general conformity between fluctuations in the wider economy and variations in the overall level of railway investment. However, the timing of renewals depended primarily on the condition of the assets involved; while railway accountancy practice was not always precise in its treatment of such expenditure, most renewals were charged against revenue, and therefore funded internally. By the 1870s renewals comprised more than 40 per cent of the gross investment attributable to Britain's railway companies, and the nature of this expenditure provided a relatively steady underpinning which dampened the effects of cyclical fluctuations in new investment on capital account.

The last major wave of new investment in Britain's railways took place between 1894 and 1906. Besides the completion of the *Great Central main line, the building of major cut-offs such as the *Great Western's improved routes to Fishguard and *Birmingham or the *Highland Railway's direct link between Aviemore and *Inverness, and the opening of long rural outliers such as the West Highland Extension or the North Cornwall line, these years also saw the inauguration of several urban and suburban *electrification schemes. This activity was reflected in an increase in the amount of extra capital raised and in the proportion of total investment attributable to new works: capital expenditure by the *North Eastern Railway in 1904 reached £1.4 million, the highest level since 1876. After a trough

around 1910 investment had again resumed an upward trend when this was cut short by the wartime diversion of resources. The decline in the railways' financial position during the 1920s also had a depressing effect on levels of expenditure; while the injection of government-guaranteed funds provided some fresh opportunities for capital works in the 1930s, the outbreak of war in 1939 again resulted in the virtual cessation of new investment and the deferment of all but essential renewals. Post-war austerity delayed recovery from this backlog, and it was only during the brief years of *British Railways' *Modernization Plan that the *nationalized railways experienced anything approaching an investment boom. This too was short-lived, and by 1967 gross annual investment in BR was lower in real terms than it had been at the start of public ownership.

See also FINANCING OF RAILWAYS; CAPITAL.   MCR

M. R. Bonavia, *Railway Policy Between the Wars* (1981), 76–92; Gourvish, 68–90, 256–304, 507–29, 595–611; G. R. Hawke, *Railways and Economic Growth in England and Wales, 1840–1870* (1970), 197–212, 363–79; B. R. Mitchell, 'The Coming of the Railway and United Kingdom Economic Growth', in M. C. Reed (ed.), *Railways in the Victorian Economy* (1969), 13–32.

Ireland, relationships with. By the Act of Union, 1800, Ireland was placed under direct rule from Westminster. The *parliamentary procedure for creating Irish railways was therefore the same as for Great Britain, and until partition in 1921 they were regarded as part of the British railway system, although under the 1846 Gauge Act the Irish standard *gauge was fixed at 5 ft 3 in. An Irish *Railway Clearing House was set up on the British model. The railways of the Republic of Ireland and Northern Ireland are now two nationalized undertakings, the latter still directly controlled by the British Department of *Transport, as yet with no proposals for *privatization.

Inevitably, Ireland's first line, the Dublin & Kingstown (1830), was influenced by technical events in Britain. At first a canal was proposed, but as the *Liverpool & Manchester Railway approached successful completion, it was decided to build a railway of 4 ft 8½ in gauge, later widened to 5 ft 3 in, and the locomotives were ordered from England. Before they were delivered they ran trials on the LMR. After the railway opened in 1834 it provided a vital link in the chain between London and Dublin. Two English companies, the *London & Birmingham and the *Great Western, were concerned in abortive political manœuvrings over a possible extension southward towards Rosslare. The LBR also supported the Great Southern & Western Railway, and a year after it became part of the *London & North Western it invested in the GSWR in order to promote through traffic via Holyhead.

Although Westminster rejected the 1837–8 Royal Commission on Irish Railways' recommendation of state funding, over the years there was significant direct or indirect government support, by grants, loans, or guarantees, enabling lines to be completed. Under the so-called 'baronial guarantees', interest on capital and indemnification against losses on a number of lines were guaranteed through local authorities. In 1889 the Royal Commission on Irish Public

Works: Railways, under the chairmanship of Sir James *Allport, former general manager of the *Midland Railway (the 'Allport Commission'), recommended state aid, and under the *Light Railways (Ireland) Act, 1889, over 300 miles of line, mainly in the west, received grants. Called 'Balfour lines', after the then Secretary for Ireland, despite the Act's title they were mostly built to main-line standards. Many lines that received government aid would not otherwise have been built, and indeed few opened after 1885 were constructed solely with private capital.

British railways were always keen on promoting through traffic with Irish companies. Mails were an important source of income for the DKR. Close collaboration between the GSWR and the LNWR resulted in their operating a service for Atlantic mails in 1859–1914 between Queenstown (now Cobh), where they were transferred to and from the liners, and London via Kingstown (now Dun Laoghaire) and Holyhead. But despite the LNWR's attempts to secure the contract, Irish political interests ensured that the sea passage remained with the City of Dublin Steam Packet Co. from 1848 to 1920. In 1902 the LNWR lent £100,000 to the Dublin Wicklow & Wexford Railway to build a line from New Ross to Waterford, thereby securing a seat on the DWWR board. The arrangement continued under both companies' successors until 1933.

There was a considerable traffic in seasonal harvest-time labour to England, and sharply increased emigration after the Great Famine of 1846–7 brought a high volume of through traffic to the railways which was significant until the 1980s, when reduced air fares attracted many to air services. In 1877 the volume of Irish Sea traffic using LNWR services was so great that the company transferred its own maritime operations from Kingstown to North Wall, Dublin, as Kingstown was then unconnected to the rest of the railway system at Dublin. The LNWR built its own station, and a *hotel, although the station could never be used by its owner's trains. The three principal railways serving Dublin, the GSWR, Midland Great Western, and Great Northern Railway (Ireland), all operated regular boat trains to North Wall, whence large numbers of cattle were carried to Holyhead. In 1923 passenger traffic reverted to Dun Laoghaire, freight remaining at North Wall until it was superseded by road vehicle ferries.

Other British railways operated steamers to Ireland, including services to Belfast from Morecambe (later from Heysham), Fleetwood, and Stranraer (later to Larne), and to other Irish ports (see SHIPPING SERVICES). Vessels still operate the Holyhead–Dublin, Heysham–Belfast, and Stranraer–Larne services under private ownership, with connecting trains.

The last major Anglo-Irish scheme was the Fishguard–Rosslare route, a combined venture of the Great Western Railway and the GSWR, opened in 1906. Both companies promoted the joint Fishguard & Rosslare Railways & Harbours Company. In *Wales a railway was built from Goodwick to a new harbour at Fishguard; and in Ireland the small port at Rosslare was enlarged and a new railway built to Waterford. In connection with the new sea route, the British government contributed £25,000 and the GWR £15,000 towards a cross-city railway in Cork, to speed up *fish and vegetable (see FRUIT AND VEGETABLE) traffic for England. The works at Rosslare were carried out by British contractors: Sir Robert *McAlpine, Charles Brand of Glasgow, and William *Arrol.

The company still exists, jointly owned by Stena *Sealink and Coras Iompair Eireann as successors to the original promoters. It was very successful in attracting traffic to the south of Ireland and within a short time day excursions were advertised from *Paddington to Killarney, travelling out by the overnight service before being taken on by special train for sightseeing tours, and returning overnight to London. In 1964 *British Railways successfully introduced roll-on roll-off car services on the route, but the number of passengers travelling by rail is now small, owing to air and motor car competition. Other British railways with Irish connections promoted tourism in Ireland on an increasing scale in the latter part of the 19th century, using their steamer services; their successors in the maritime business still do so, but again mainly aimed at car owners.

Among personalities, Joseph Tatlow was a noted railway manager. He joined the GSWR from the Midland Railway in 1875, was general manager of the Belfast & County Down Railway in 1885–90, and of the MGWR in 1890–1912, after which he became a director. He was the only manager of Irish railways to serve on parliamentary and (British) Railway Clearing House committees.

In 1934 Sir Felix *Pole, general manager of the GWR, headed an enquiry into railway-operated road services in Northern Ireland, and in 1948 his successor, Sir James *Milne, reported on railways in the republic for the Eire government.

Many Irish railway mechanical engineers either came from British railway companies or left to join them. In 1845 John Dewrance left the LMR to join the GSWR. When he moved to the MGWR in 1847 he was replaced by John Wakefield, who worked for the *Stephensons. His successor, Alexander McDonnell, was impressed by the quality of Beyer Peacock (see WORKS) locomotives when working in eastern Europe. When he took charge at the railway's Inchicore works, Dublin, he soon had 12 locomotives built by that company, which continued to build locomotives for Ireland until 1951, when it supplied two tank engines to the Sligo Leitrim & Northern Counties Railway.

When McDonnell left Inchicore in 1882 to join the *North Eastern Railway he was succeeded by J. A. F. *Aspinall, who had previously worked for the LNWR at *Crewe, and in 1886 was succeeded by H. A. *Ivatt who had also trained at Crewe. After ten years Ivatt became locomotive engineer of the *Great Northern Railway at *Doncaster. After World War II, O. V. S. Bulleid of the *Southern Railway was called upon to advise on replacing the ailing Irish steam locomotive fleet. His experimental turf (peat)-burning steam locomotive, similar to his 'Leader' class for the Southern Railway, had only limited success, and with the locomotive position critical, in 1953 CIE purchased 60 AEC diesel *multiple units from Britain with bodies by Park

iron and steel, use of

Royal Vehicles, followed in 1954 by the largest single Irish order ever placed in Britain for railway locomotives, when 94 were ordered from Metropolitan-Vickers of Manchester. A further 12 were delivered in 1956 from the Birmingham Railway Carriage & Wagon Co. with Sulzer engines—the last locomotives bought in Britain by CIE, ending a 120-year-old tradition, although British Railways continued to supply passenger carriages.

Most of the narrow-gauge locomotives and *railcars were either purchased complete from British manufacturers or had significant components supplied by them. Irish railways were also dependent on Britain for coal.

Irish signalling followed British practice, and it was the tragic *accident at Armagh in 1889 that led directly to legislation requiring all railways in the British Isles to fit automatic continuous *brakes to passenger trains.

Two English railways controlled Irish lines. The LNWR took a controlling interest in the 26½-mile-long Dundalk Newry & Greenore Railway in 1873, aiming to secure a share of the Belfast traffic via Holyhead and Greenore. Local trains were operated with locomotives and carriages built at Crewe, and retained LNWR livery until closure in 1951. Through trains to Belfast were run by the GNR(I), which after partition took over the management, but not ownership. Curiously, the line passed to the *British Transport Commission when British railways were *nationalized in 1948.

The Belfast & Northern Counties Railway, some 200 miles long, amalgamated with the Midland Railway to form its Northern Counties Committee in 1903, the object being to provide the MR with its own route throughout to Belfast via the Stranraer and Larne steamer service in which it had a share. After the 1923 *Grouping the NCC formed an outpost of the *London Midland & Scottish Railway.

In 1906 the NCC and the GNR(I) purchased the 3-ft gauge Donegal Railway to form the County Donegal Railways Joint Committee, at 125 miles the longest narrow-gauge system in the UK. It was closed in 1952–60.

Between 1868 and 1964 several schemes were proposed for a tunnel from Scotland under the North Channel, but they all foundered through lack of government interest.

OD and GJB

Reg. Hist., xvi (1995); J. Tatlow, *Fifty Years of Railway Life* (1948 edn.); E. M. Patterson, *The Great Northern Railway of Ireland* (1962); K. A. Murray and D. B. McNeill, *The Great Southern & Western Railway* (1976); K. A. Murray, *Ireland's First Railway* (1981); M. H. Gould, 'The Effect of Government Policy on Railway Building in Ireland', *TNS*, 62 (1990–1); Irish Railway Record Society, *Journals*, i to date.

iron and steel, use of. The railway system developed from *tramroads built by the 18th-century coal and iron industries, many of which used cast-iron track. Even then the limitations of cast iron were seen as rails broke beneath the weight of overloaded wagons or experimental steam locomotives, but there was little the early railway builders could do about it: individual ironmasters were left to nibble away at the problem by hit-and-miss variations on the known methods of making iron. Some lessons were learnt the hard way, such as the unsuitability of cast-iron boilers, but before 1830 railways were not a big enough market to have much influence on the ironmasters.

A notable early advance was made by George *Stephenson, who, despite being co-patentee of an improved form of cast-iron rail, recognized the superiority of wrought-iron rails introduced by James Birkinshaw in 1818, and thereafter recommended this material. Rolled rails could be much longer, thus reducing the number of rail joints, and formed into true curves to produce a smoother track suitable for the safe achievement of 20 mph or more. The *Stockton & Darlington Railway objected to the higher cost of wrought iron and insisted on part of its line being laid in cast iron, but the cost of replacing broken rails soon proved Stephenson right. By similar empirical methods the early engineers began to identify the best materials for various applications (see also TRACK).

Besides seeking better materials, however, it was necessary to learn how best to employ existing ones. A foremost investigator who laid the foundations of materials technology as we know it today was William *Fairbairn, who, assisted by the mathematician Eaton Hodgkinson, identified and quantified such phenomena as 'fatigue' and 'creep'. His investigations led him to condemn as fundamentally unsound the 'compound' girder that became popular for long bridge spans in the 1840s, but his warnings were ignored until Robert *Stephenson's bridge over the Dee at Chester collapsed under a train in 1847 (see BRIDGES AND VIADUCTS; BRITANNIA TUBULAR BRIDGE). From that time engineers began to accept that knowledge of material properties and material selection were important aspects of mechanical design. The most notorious example of incorrect material selection was Thomas *Bouch's Tay Bridge (see NORTH BRITISH RAILWAY). Generally, though, engineers proceeded cautiously when changing from iron to steel: steel rails had proved successful straight away, but early steel boilers proved less satisfactory. Gradually they realized the need to develop confidence in a new material before using it in earnest.

An early development in this direction was the practice of serialization, whereby individual components vital to safety (for example wheels, axles, tyres, and springs) were marked to indicate the heat of metal from which they were made, samples of the latter being *tested to confirm that it was satisfactory. Were a part subsequently to fail, bringing into question the integrity of the original metal, all similar components could then be traced, examined, and—if deemed necessary—withdrawn from service. Serialization began before 1850 and promoted the principle not only of establishing confidence in a product, but also of being able to demonstrate it. That is the basis of modern safety procedures.

This is illustrated by F. W. *Webb's controversial three-cylinder compound locomotives. He once managed a steel-works and knew about an unsuccessful attempt to use steel coupling rods over 9 ft long. The large fireboxes of his new engines necessitated driving axles 10 ft apart, so they were built with uncoupled driving axles. Ten years later better steels were available and Webb's next design of compound was a four-cylinder four-coupled locomotive.

Compared with the USA, Britain was an early user of iron carriage chassis, but all-steel *wagons and *carriages were slow to develop and it was not until after World War II that wood was entirely supplanted. Besides locomotives, rolling stock, and bridges, however, the railways used iron and steel widely in lesser structures of all kinds. At an early date iron supplanted wood in *station roofs (see TRAIN-SHEDS) and platform awnings, in which wrought-iron trusses or cast-iron brackets were supported by hollow cast-iron columns which often acted as downpipes to carry away rainwater. Late in the 19th century steel girders and stanchions were introduced, notably by the *Great Western and *Midland Railways, riveted into the required sections and configurations. Iron tanks and water columns were familiar features of locomotive depots and stations, while many footbridges were of wrought-iron lattice construction with ornate cast-iron stairs, columns, and railings. The *North Eastern Railway had a very distinctive cast-iron footbridge built from sections.

A profusion of smaller articles was made of iron, from lamp-posts to platform seats, waiting room fire-grates, and office umbrella stands, often in intricate designs. Apart from wooden posts and arms, *signalling installations were assembled from a multitude of iron or steel components including thousands of miles of point-rodding and signal-wire. Around the turn of the century latticed steel posts and pressed-steel arms, previously used by a few companies, became more widely used, followed in the 1930s by simple tubular steel posts.

The companies developed close relationships with manufacturers. They kept a close eye on quality control, particularly of boiler plates, rails, axles, and tyres, having their own inspectors who paid regular visits to steel works and rolling mills. Products bought finished almost invariably bore the name of the manufacturer cast or rolled alongside the name or initials of their customer: rails by the Workington Iron & Steel Co.; roof columns by Mabon & Sons of Ardwick Ironworks, Manchester; footbridges by George Smith of the Sun Foundry, Glasgow; and all manner of ironwork for the Midland Railway by Handyside & Co. of Derby, to name but a few. Smaller local firms were used as well: Smith & Sons of Whitchurch, for instance, cast the iron trefoil awning brackets for that station and nearby Nantwich.

After 1900 railways gradually yielded their place at the forefront of materials technology, initially to the motor car industry, so although new *alloys and ways of using them continue to appear they now do so by adaptation from another technology. In the same way, iron and steel are no longer the almost universal constructional metals that they were during the railway era.

See also IRON AND STEEL INDUSTRY.   RW and GJB

iron and steel industry. Though iron has been produced in Britain for at least 2,000 years, the modern era began about 1709 when 'Dud' Dudley succeeded in smelting iron with coked coal instead of charcoal. Freed from its dependence upon wood, which was in great demand for shipbuilding, the industry was now ready to meet the growing demands of the infant industrial society. Iron became cheaper and more plentiful, enabling it to replace timber for bridges (Abraham Darby, Ironbridge, 1787), boats (John Wilkinson, also 1787), and for the rails of *tramroads used in and around coal or ironstone mines. For almost 200 years the destinies of the iron industry and of the railway were to become interdependent.

Initially iron was cast straight from the blast furnace (cast iron); impure, brittle, but hard-wearing and very strong under compression. Its conversion to steel, a superior alloy long used for weapons, edged tools, clock springs, etc., was a costly, small-scale operation even as improved by Huntsman's crucible process in 1721.

Henry Cort's puddling process (1789) removed much of the carbon, sulphur, and phosphorus from cast iron to produce 'wrought' or malleable iron. Being stronger in tension —though weaker in compression—and more predictable than cast iron, it became a very useful engineering material. Cast and wrought iron were the principal structural metals available at the beginning of the 19th century and made possible many engineering triumphs of the next 60 years, including the railways. The resultant demand created famous ironmaking centres such as Merthyr Tydfil, Coalbrookdale, *Sheffield, Furness, and Lanarkshire. Common to all was the ready availability of one or more of the essential raw materials (iron ore, coal, limestone) which led to the establishment of several ironworks in the same area; good transport links and availability of water power also helped to concentrate industry in this way. But the iron industry was by no means confined to these areas and many of the ironworks themselves were relatively small.

In 1856 Henry Bessemer announced his revolutionary method of making steel by blowing air through molten iron in a converter. Quick and relatively cheap, it made steel available in greater quantities than previously. In the next ten years the crucial though much under-valued work of David Mushet and development of the Siemens-Marten open-hearth furnace revolutionized the industry and established steel as the successor to wrought iron. The basic technology of the new iron and steel industry remained essentially unaltered until the introduction of the electric arc furnace in the 20th century.

In these developments the growing network of railways became involved at more than one level. Starting with the raw materials, railways were laid down to serve the expanding *coal and iron ore mining districts. Often these were built by the proprietors of those mines, either serving the ironworks directly or exchanging traffic with a main-line company over whose lines the proprietors' own wagons were often used. In the 19th century and well into the 20th iron-ore railways were laid down from mines and quarries in West Somerset, Oxfordshire, Northamptonshire, Leicestershire, Cleveland, and Cumbria, some of them quite extensive and requiring substantial engineering works.

Equally the main-line railways freed the industry from local supplies of fuel and ore. The South Durham & Lancashire Union Railway from Barnard Castle to Tebay (1861) was built to take rich Furness ore to Cleveland ironworks, and coke from Durham to the Furness and West Cumberland furnaces; the Solway Viaduct (1869) took West Cumberland ore to Scotland; while at their peak after World War II, Northamptonshire mines were sending ore to Cleveland, Derbyshire, and South Wales.

The output of the works might be in the form of ingots, standard rolled sections, unmachined or part-machined forgings, castings, etc., depending upon the type of steel produced, the capability of the works, and customer's requirements; until the middle of the 20th century most of this traffic would have been carried by rail. So too would the products of most of the intermediate processors who had received their basic raw materials from the steelworks by rail.

Increasing rail traffic created its own demand for increased *track and *siding capacity, which in addition to track replacement made the railways themselves a major customer of the steel industry: a mile of average track required at least 135 tons of rail and 75 tons of chairs besides fishplates, bolts, and screws. In a wider context, the expanding national economy generated not only additional business for the steelmakers but also thereby increased traffic for the railways. The development of both industries was therefore to a great extent complementary: for a considerable time railways and their related technologies led the way in demanding better and more specialized grades of steel which then found uses in other applications (see also INDUSTRY, RAILWAYS AND).

Some of the established iron-making centres developed to meet the demand for steel: in South Wales, for example, the ironworks around Merthyr Tydfil developed major steelworks at Dowlais and nearby Ebbw Vale. Furness, Cleveland, and Sheffield developed likewise, but despite railways' vast appetite for the material only one company, the *London & North Western, became self-sufficient in steel, with its own steelworks as part of its engineering complex at *Crewe.

All industries evolve. What was once a large number of quite small ironworks close to the source of at least one of their raw materials gradually became a smaller number of large units whose locations were dictated by different considerations, though still highly dependent upon rail transport. The industry began to switch from native ores to imported ones, prompted by dwindling British reserves. Spanish imports began about 1860, and this change gained momentum when British ores required different furnace linings from imported, usually Scandinavian, ores. Particularly after World War II, railways increasingly began to haul ore from *port to steelworks instead of mine to steelworks, and new, even larger, works were located to reduce the distance involved. This led to the establishment of specialized ore-importing terminals such as Tyne Dock, Immingham, Port Talbot, and Hunterston, each generation being larger and more directly associated with its sole customer than

was its predecessor. Tyne Dock was an existing installation adapted to importation in the early 1950s, and sent much of its ore uphill to Consett in trains of nine purpose-built high-capacity wagons hauled by two locomotives, a spectacular but clearly uneconomic showcase operation in the latter days of steam traction, which ended in 1980. Immingham, a general port, supplied the Scunthorpe works. Port Talbot was a new terminal built in 1970 at existing docks, and sent heavy trains over a shorter and almost level route to the giant steelworks at nearby Margam, while Hunterston was a purpose-built port on the Clyde with an equally easy route into Ravenscraig in 1979–92.

Not only iron ore but also coal was latterly imported. Just as the huge deposits of ore in Scandinavia made it cheaper to import it than to extract it from the comparatively small British fields, so did coal from the vast coalfields in, for example, the USA and Australia, delivered to the UK, become cheaper than native deep-mined coal. While much of this imported coal was moved by rail, it caused yet another change in traffic patterns over a contracting railway system.

Since the 1970s there have been dramatic changes in the British steel industry. Over-capacity and importation of cheaper foreign steel led to closure of many older and smaller plants, leaving a leaner and more competitive industry based on a handful of giant complexes. Rail transport is still used for bulk movement of raw and finished materials, but smaller consignments now go by road: no longer are the destinies of rail and steel so closely linked as they were in the past.

See also IRON AND STEEL, USE OF.　　　　RW and RVL
W. K. V. Gale, The British Iron and Steel Industry (1967); E. S. Tonks, The Ironstone Railways and Tramways of the Midlands (1961 edn.), and The Edge Hill Light Railway (1948); R. Sellick, The West Somerset Mineral Railway and the Story of the Brendon Hill Iron Mines (1962); R. H. Hayes and J. G. Rutter, Rosedale Mines and Railway (1974 edn.); W. Vamplew, 'The Railways and the Iron Industry: A Study of Their Relationship in Scotland', in M. C. Reed (ed.), Railways in the Victorian Economy (1969); Reg. Hist., i, iv, ix, xiv.

iron ore traffic, see IRON AND STEEL INDUSTRY.

iron railways, see EARLY IRON RAILWAYS.

Isle of Man railways and tramways. The Isle of Man is unique in having five differing rail systems dating from the 19th century still serving its tourist industry. Currently the 15½-mile-long 3-ft gauge steam railway between Douglas and Port Erin operates from Easter to October, whilst the Snaefell Mountain Railway and Douglas horse-trams run from May to September inclusive. The Manx Electric Railway operates throughout the year, with a reduced winter service. The 2-ft gauge Groudle Glen Railway runs on Sundays, Bank Holidays, and during the holiday season.

Following the formation of the Mona's Isle (Steamship) Company in 1829, increasing numbers of visitors crossed to the island annually, but as the roads were atrocious they mostly stayed in Douglas.

As tourism flourished the island needed a railway network to complement its steamships. Several schemes were proposed from 1847 onwards but it was not until 1873 that the Douglas–St John's–Peel line of the Isle of Man Railway was opened, followed in 1874 by one from Douglas to Port Erin via Castletown.

Beyer Peacock & Co. (see WORKS) built for the IOMR, in 1873, the first of a class of outside-cylinder 2-4-0T locomotives with a tractive effort (te) of 4,930 lb. Improved versions followed, the last being No. 16 *Mannin* of 1926 with 8,810 lb te. Locomotives used recently include No. 4 *Loch*, No. 10 *G. H. Wood*, No. 11 *Maitland*, and No. 12 *Hutchinson*, but the former County Donegal railcars Nos. 19 and 20, bought in 1961, are rarely used. Diesel locomotive No. 17 *Viking* is a recent purchase. The Metropolitan Railway Carriage & Wagon Co. supplied the original four-wheeled carriages. Later the bodies were removed and fitted in pairs on to new bogie underframes; the present purple-lake and white liveried coaching stock includes these and other vintage vehicles, comfortably upholstered and modernized.

The Manx Northern Railway opened a line from St John's to Ramsey in 1879, and operated the Foxdale Railway from St John's to Foxdale, opened in 1886. Both were absorbed by the IOMR in 1904.

Tourism and the railways boomed, with 615,000 summer arrivals in 1913, but in World War I holiday-makers were replaced by military personnel, internees, and prisoners-of-war, an internment camp at Knockaloe being served by a short branch from the Peel line, financed by the British government, but worked by the IOMR from September 1915, and lifted in 1923–4.

After the war the number of visitors failed to reach previous totals, although 534,000 holiday-makers arrived in May–September 1925 and rail passengers that year numbered 1,344,620. Furthermore, the IOMR now faced competition from motor-*bus proprietors, whom it bought out by 1930, combining the undertakings in its Isle of Man Road Services group, with joint timetables and advertising material. In 1937 the IOMR carried 775,000 passengers and 56,000 tons of freight over its 46¼ route miles.

Internees and aliens again replaced tourists in many Douglas sea-front hotels during World War II, and the horse-*tramway tracks and promenade were obstructed by barbed-wire enclosures. A decline in railway receipts of £16,417 in 1940 led to a successful request for government funding calculated on figures for 1935–7.

Turning to other lines, in 1892 Frederick Saunderson, a civil engineer and nominee of Alexander Bruce, the manager of Dumbell's Bank, Douglas, obtained an Act to develop the Howstrake estate north of Douglas and build roads and tramways; their Douglas & Laxey Coast Electric Tramway opened a 3-ft gauge line to Groudle in 1893, where R. M. Broadbent built a *hotel and 2-ft gauge railway, now restored.

The single-line tramway, relaid, doubled, and extended to Laxey by July 1894, had been absorbed into Bruce's new Isle of Man Tramways & Electric Power Co., which in May had acquired the horse-tramway inaugurated on the Douglas promenade in 1876 by Thomas Lightfoot, a Sheffield busi-

nessman who had retired to the island. In exchange for an extended lease on the horse-tramway, Bruce built a cable car system (opened 1896, closed 1929) for Douglas Corporation.

Another Bruce undertaking was the Snaefell Mountain Railway, opened in 1895, a 3 ft 6 in gauge electrified line, equipped with the 'Fell' safety system having a horizontal centre-rail engaged by guide wheels (see MOUNTAIN RAILWAYS).

A Laxey–Ramsey extension of the electric railway was authorized in 1897 and by July 1899 a half-hourly service of cars ran between Douglas and Ramsey. The Bruce conglomerate now embraced such undertakings as proposed electric lighting for Douglas promenade, quarries at Dhoon and Ballajora, hotels, refreshment rooms, and a brewery syndicate.

Dumbell's Bank failed in 1900, ruining many depositors. Bruce, disgraced magistrate and former town treasurer, died of heart failure six months later. The receivers were called in. Douglas Corporation got the horse-tramway and cable cars for £50,000, a 'Manchester Syndicate' paid £252,000 for the Douglas–Ramsey and Snaefell electric lines, and a new Manx Electric Railway company took them over in August 1902.

In the 1950s the electric lines were rescued from financial collapse by the Manx government, but the availability of cheap Mediterranean holidays started a permanent decline in the island's tourist industry.

The steam railway also had problems. By the end of 1964 the only winter working was between Douglas and Port Erin. The railway opened again throughout in June 1965, but all services ended in November, and in January 1966 it was announced that it would not reopen that year. In April 1967 it was reported that the Marquess of Ailsa had leased it, but this renaissance ended after the 1968 season.

The Peel and Ramsey lines were lifted (Foxdale had closed by 1942), and the spasmodic openings of the Port Erin line became a political issue, until in January 1978 it was bought by the Manx government and passed to the Manx Electric Railway Board, renamed the Isle of Man Passenger Transport Board in 1983 and subsequently the Department of Tourism, Leisure, and Transport.

Nowadays tourism ranks only third, after finance and manufacturing, in contributing to the Manx gross national product; but if the authorities avoid narrow-interest promotions and concentrate on the island's unique features, e.g. the vintage transport system, T. T. races, and motor sport, tourism can still play an important role. Significantly during the 1993 'Year of Railways' numbers of general arrivals increased by 25 per cent.

See also NARROW-GAUGE RAILWAYS. NJ

P. H. Abell, *British Tramway Guide* (1993); J. I. C. Boyd, *The Isle of Man Railway* (1995 edn.); A. M. Goodwyn, *Manx Electric* (1993); F. K. Pearson, *The Douglas Bay Tramway* (1956).

Isle of Wight railways. Before 1923 the Isle of Wight, 24 miles long by 14 broad, with a resident population of 85,000 (and a large summer tourist influx), had 56 miles of railway, all standard gauge, operated by three independent companies, while the most important section was owned jointly by two other companies which ran no trains of their own on it.

The Isle of Wight Railway, opened from Ryde to Shanklin in 1864 and on to Ventnor (11¼ miles) in 1866, was the soundest company, occupying the territory in the east of the island with best traffic prospects. It worked the 2¾-mile branch from Brading to Bembridge Harbour, opened in 1882, in connection with a wagon-ferry from Langston, Hayling Island, on the *London Brighton & South Coast Railway, abandoned in 1888. It took the branch over in 1898. The IWR enjoyed consistent, if modest, prosperity.

The Isle of Wight Central Railway did not. Its first constituent, the Cowes & Newport Railway, opened in 1862; this was isolated until the opening of the Ryde & Newport Railway in 1875. Amalgamation in 1887 produced the IWCR, 27¼ miles in all, with the inclusion of the impecunious Isle of Wight (Newport Junction) Railway from Newport to Sandown, and later of the Merstone–Ventnor branch of 1897–1900. It had a fair freight traffic loaded at Medina Wharf. It paid no ordinary dividend until 1913.

The *London & South Western and LBSCR, serving *Portsmouth, the main port for the island steamer services, frustrated by the inadequate tramway connection between Ryde Pier Head and the IWR station, opened their own *joint line in 1880 for operation by IWR and IWCR trains.

West Wight was unpromising ground for railway promoters, but finally the Freshwater Yarmouth & Newport Railway, 12 miles long, was opened in 1888–9, worked by the IWCR until 1913 when the FYNR began on its own. Schemes to link it with the mainland by a tunnel under the Solent came to nothing.

In 1923 the island railways became part of the *Southern Railway, which made many detailed improvements but no substantial changes in the system or its operation. In 1952 the Merstone–Ventnor branch was closed; from then until 1966 other lines followed so that only 8½ miles from Ryde Pier Head to Shanklin remain. This stretch was electrified on the third-rail system, and ex-*London Transport stock was adapted to work it.

The locomotives of the pre-1923 railways were an assorted collection of tank engines, many of them second-hand. The Southern scrapped most of them fairly soon and brought over seven LBSCR *Stroudley 0-6-0 tanks and 23 0-4-4 tanks of William *Adams' LSWR 02 class, built in 1888–96. With few exceptions the passenger rolling stock had been built for and worked in mainland service. There were 543 goods wagons in 1921. Train services were not speedy: in 1914 the Ryde–Ventnor journey (12½ miles) took 37–45 minutes, with 15 trains on weekdays. Fares were high; third class on all trains came only in 1914. Under the Southern there were generally more, but not faster, trains. All lines were single-track except for the first 2 miles from Ryde Pier Head. In 1921, 1,760,000 passengers were carried; in 1951, with train mileage more than doubled, some 3 million.

After closure of most of the island lines, a preserved railway was formed (see PRESERVATION OF RAILWAYS), and trains of ex-island stock have been operated based on Haven Street station.   RMR

P. C. Allen, *The Railways of the Isle of Wight* (1925); C. F. Dendy Marshall, *History of the Southern Railway* (1963 edn.), ch. 14; M. Robbins, *The Isle of Wight Railways* (1973 edn.).

Ivatt, Henry Alfred (1851–1923), engineer; apprenticed at *Crewe, he then joined the Great Southern & Western Railway, Ireland, where he became locomotive engineer, 1886. He succeeded Patrick *Stirling as locomotive engineer of the *Great Northern Railway, 1896. Ivatt retired in 1911; his successor was H. N. *Gresley.

In Ireland, Ivatt designed a variety of tank engines in the 1890s, some lasting into the 1950s.

On the GNR, Stirling's engines were no longer powerful enough for the heavier express trains with bogie stock, and so at first Ivatt produced 4-4-0s, then 4-4-2s from 1898, no. 990 being the first of its type in Britain. The larger versions appeared from 1902 and, once superheated, became outstanding performers, remaining on express duties until the mid-1930s. Ivatt experimented with compounding (see TRACTION, STEAM), but this showed no demonstrable advantage over his simple 4-4-2s. He designed a number of capable goods engines: 0-6-0s, and an 0-8-0 class—the 'Long Toms'; also 4-4-2 and 0-6-2 tank engines for suburban trains. Some were superheated at the outset, others were greatly improved by superheating. He patented a water-scoop and a built-up crank-axle.

Under his control, the GNR produced some notable 12-wheeled carriages—featuring the automatic coupler—for its own and East Coast Joint stock, in marked contrast to the non-bogie stock characteristic of the Stirling era.   MLH

H. A. V. Bulleid, *Master Builders of Steam* (1963); F. A. S. Brown, *From Stirling to Gresley 1882–1922* (1974).

Jackman, William T. (1871–1951), writer, educated at Toronto University and others. He taught at Vermont University, USA, 1901–15; was assistant professor of political economy, Toronto, 1915–23, and professor of transportation there, 1923–41. Jackman published *Transportation in Modern England*, 1916; *Economics of Transportation*, 1926; and *Critical Analysis of the Canadian Railway Problem*, 1939.

His *Transportation in Modern England* (the title is misleading, for its treatment extends only up to 1850) is the most successful attempt yet made to survey the history of English inland transport by road, water, and railway, and the interrelation of each mode with the others. It is a meticulous work of scholarship, including a massive guide to the sources consulted, in print and in manuscript.   JS

Who Was Who, 1951–60; W. H. Chaloner's introduction to the reprint of *Transportation in Modern England* (1962) usefully supplements Jackman's bibliography.

James, William (1771–1837), surveyor and engineer. After acting as land agent to the Earl of Warwick, James built up a surveying practice that by 1824 was said to be the largest in the country. He bought collieries and estates, and was reckoned to be a very rich man. Greatly interested in canals, he took over completion of the impoverished Stratford-on-Avon Canal, and then purchased the Upper Avon Navigation connecting with it.

James foresaw the future for railways and in 1800–20 he surveyed and tried to promote many lines at his own expense. None was adopted. He was a friend of George *Stephenson, and in 1821 he made the first survey for the *Liverpool & Manchester Railway, with Robert *Stephenson as one of his assistants. But James had overstretched himself and in 1823 was declared bankrupt. George Stephenson was appointed engineer in his place, although James maintained that Stephenson's route was based on his own and always regarded the LMR as his own creation. He retired to Cornwall where he died a poor man.

His family tried to establish him, not Stephenson, as 'Father of Railways', but all he had actually caused to be built was the *Stratford & Moreton Railway, and the Stephenson influence was too strong. James' visionary, single-minded drive led him to attempt too much too quickly. He was a man before his time.   GJB

E. M. S. P[aine], *The Two James's and the Two Stephensons* (1961 edn.); C. Hadfield and J. E. Norris, *Waterways to Stratford* (1962); J. E. Norris, *The Stratford & Moreton Tramway* (1987); Thomas, 12–19.

jazz trains, see GREAT EASTERN RAILWAY.

Jellicoe specials, see WAR; HIGHLAND RAILWAY; NAMING OF TRAINS.

Jessop, William (1745–1814), engineer, was born at Devonport, the son of Smeaton's foreman when building the Eddystone lighthouse. Later his apprentice, Jessop became a great canal, dock, and drainage engineer. In 1792 he joined *Outram as a founding partner of the Butterley Company, quickly to become a leading British ironworks.

So Jessop became involved in early railways. Best-known is his *Surrey Iron Railway, authorized in 1801, opened in 1803, running for eight miles from Wandsworth on the Thames to Croydon, with a Hackbridge branch. In a report of 1799 he wrote: 'Railways . . . have been brought to the degree of perfection which now recommends them as substitute for Canals . . .'

He went on to the Croydon Merstham & Godstone, authorized in 1803, and the *Kilmarnock & Troon, whose Act of 1808 was the first for a public railway in Scotland.

Of Jessop's sons, Josias (1781–1826) engineered the Cromford & High Peak Railway, and was consulted by the Bridgewater waterway interest upon whether to support the second Bill for the proposed *Liverpool & Manchester Railway. It was accordingly supported. William (1784–1852) managed Butterley ironworks after 1805. By 1830 it had supplied nearly 100 customers with railway products.   CH

C. Hadfield and A. W. Skempton, *William Jessop, Engineer* (1979).

Johnson, Sir Henry, see BRITISH RAILWAYS.

Johnson, Samuel Waite (1831–1912), engineer. The son of an engineer at *Leeds, he was trained in E. B. Wilson's locomotive-building works there. Having served the Manchester Sheffield & Lincolnshire (see GREAT CENTRAL) and *Great Northern companies, he was locomotive superintendent on the *Edinburgh & Glasgow (1864–6), *Great Eastern (1866–73), and *Midland at *Derby (1873–1903).

There he abandoned some of the practices of his predecessor Matthew *Kirtley, e.g. consistently preferring inside to outside frames on his locomotives. Nearly all his passenger engines were of the 2-4-0 and 4-4-0 types, all his large freight engines 0-6-0. His designs show a strong aesthetic sense, every part of the machine being rightly proportioned with the rest. He attended carefully to all aspects of the locomotives' work: the high-level coal stages he built greatly quickened their fuelling. His 4-2-2 express engines, built from 1887 onwards (the single driving wheels becoming acceptable through new rail-sanding mechanism prepared at Derby), were swift and powerful. In 1900 he began to use much larger boilers, which were fitted to his 4-4-0 compound engines. With some development they proved themselves well in service on the MR and its successor the *London Midland & Scottish Railway. JS

J. B. Radford, *Derby Works and Midland Locomotives* (1971); B. Reed (ed.), *Locomotives in Profile* (1971–4), i, 121–2.

Johnstone, John James Hope (1796–1876), chairman; proprietor of the Annandale estates. When in 1836 a route was surveyed for a *Carlisle–*Glasgow railway up Nithsdale, Johnstone and his factor, Charles Stewart of Hillside, formed an Annandale Committee to promote an alternative route up that valley. *Locke resurveyed in 1837, showing that, though much more difficult than the Nithsdale line, it was feasible. When the Royal *Commission on railways between England and Scotland reported in its favour in 1841, the *Caledonian Railway was promoted in 1844, with substantial English finance and Johnstone on the provisional committee. After its incorporation in 1845, he became chairman in the following year and vigorously pursued construction so that the line was opened throughout to Glasgow and *Edinburgh in 1848. But the company then encountered serious financial difficulties, and the board was dismissed by a committee of shareholders in 1850. Thereafter Johnstone played no further part in the Caledonian's affairs, although there is no doubt that his fiery advocacy and strong leadership played a major part in the rapid completion of what was at the time a very daring railway. JRH

J. Butt and J. T. Ward, 'The Promotion of the Caledonian Railway Company', *Transport History*, 3 (1970), 164–92, 225–57.

joint railways, i.e. lines owned by more than one company, were almost entirely a British phenomenon. What might have appeared to be a sensible solution to directly competing aims was, in fact, a particularly wasteful compromise. Not only was there the cost of legislation or a legal agreement needed to establish working arrangements, but most joint lines required a committee of directors or senior officials, while the larger ones had all the apparatus of a main-line company, with separate headquarters, officers, managers, staff, works, uniforms, and tickets. Further, the work in making returns for the apportionment of revenue and expenditure between the joint owners was considerable, even on smaller lines where management was undertaken by one of the owners, while the practice of taking it in turns, with consequent periodic administrative upheavals, in financial terms was quite indefensible. Joint ownership was undoubtedly a significant factor in the high cost of running railways in Britain, compared with other countries, the superfluities of which could have been avoided if, at the outset, the government had insisted on one company taking sole responsibility and charging others simple tolls for running rights; in other words, an extension of the principle of *running powers.

Joint railways came about in three ways: new construction by two or more companies as a consortium; joint acquisition or lease of an existing line; or the admission by one company to the joint ownership of its line by another. In 1922 there were 77 officially designated joint lines or committees (see table), excluding lines in the immediate vicinity of *joint stations but including the *Forth Bridge. The longest, the *Midland & Great Northern, had 183 route miles and, like the 105-mile-long *Somerset & Dorset (*Midland and *London & South Western), possessed its own locomotives and rolling stock. Two more had their own *carriages but used engines provided by the *Great Central: the *Cheshire Lines Committee (GCR, MR, and *Great Northern), and the *Manchester South Junction & Altrincham (GCR and *London & North Western). The others were either worked under agreement by one of the owners, or by both (or all) concurrently. Some were quite small, such as the ¼-mile joint curve of the *Caledonian and *North British at Clydebank. Despite being only three miles long, the Nantybwch & Rhymney joint line even had two sets of *mile posts, one on each side of the line, measuring the LNWR's distances from Abergavenny and the *Rhymney Railway's from Cardiff.

A smaller number formed links in important main lines of one or both of their owners. The *North Union joint line, for instance, simultaneously comprised 7¼ miles of the LNWR's *West Coast main line and the *Lancashire & Yorkshire's Manchester–Preston line, while 17 miles of the West Riding & Grimsby (GNR and GCR), between Doncaster and Wakefield, made up part of the former's main line from London to Leeds.

The southern end of the GCR's route to London divided into two legs, both joint. The first, the Metropolitan & Great Central (35 miles), was an existing *Metropolitan line which was made joint after the GCR reached it from the north, but the second, the Great Western & Great Central, was a combination of an existing *Great Western line and new joint construction. In 1910 it became even more important to the GWR as part of its direct line from *Paddington to *Birmingham.

The earliest joint line was the Glasgow & Paisley of 1840, a collaborative venture by two companies building lines to Greenock and to Kilmarnock and Ayr, which diverged at Paisley. It became Caledonian and *Glasgow & South Western joint, which in 1863 also built the Glasgow Barrhead & Kilmarnock Joint Railway. The first line to be jointly leased was the *West London, to the LNWR and GWR in 1846, which in 1863 continued it as the West London Extension Railway in partnership with the LSWR and the *London Brighton & South Coast Railway. As a north–south link around London, it was valuable to all their interests. For the same reason the North & South Western Junction Railway (in the same area) was worked jointly by the LNWR and LSWR from 1852 to 1866, when the *North London company became a third partner, followed in 1871 by withdrawal of the LSWR which preferred running powers. The Midland took its place.

Leasing was also adopted by the LNWR and the Manchester Sheffield & Lincolnshire (see GREAT CENTRAL) in 1862 when they gained control of the Oldham Ashton & Guide Bridge Junction Railway, a local venture opened a year earlier and aiming to break the LYR's monopoly of services to Manchester. It continued to have its own manager until the joint companies assumed direct control in 1879, although the MSLR ran most of the passenger trains.

Joint ownership was sometimes adopted as a compromise to end cut-throat *competition. In 1858 a devious and complex series of manœuvres by the LBSCR and LSWR over London–Portsmouth traffic culminated in the *'Battle of Havant'. As a sequel the disputed line from Cosham to Portsmouth was vested in both companies jointly, and extended to Portsmouth Harbour in 1876. Curiously, the nominally independent branch to Southsea, opened in 1885, was worked only by the LSWR until it was leased jointly in 1886. The companies also ran joint steamer services to the *Isle of Wight, where they owned 1½ miles of line from Ryde Pier Head to St John's Road station, although the trains were provided by two other railways, the Isle of Wight and Isle of Wight Central.

The short line on Portland Bill had extraordinarily complicated joint arrangements. The first 5 miles from the GWR at Weymouth formed the Weymouth & Portland: leased to the GWR and LSWR in 1862, opened in 1865, and originally of mixed *gauge. When, in 1900, the separate Easton & Church Hope Railway extended the line another 3½ miles, the GWR and LSWR only worked it. Each company ran the passenger trains on both lines alternately on a five-year cycle, but operated independent goods trains.

Intense competition for Norfolk coast traffic eventually led the *Great Eastern and MGNJR in 1898 to establish the Norfolk & Suffolk Joint Committee to control two new lines well over 20 miles apart: the MGNJR's from North Walsham to Cromer, and the GER's from Yarmouth to Lowestoft. The committee comprised four directors from each railway. These lines were unique in that one of the participants was itself a joint company.

The GCR and MR had a similar organization, the Sheffield & Midland Joint Committee, which was responsible for three widely separated lines, starting with a group in the *Manchester–Stockport area in 1872, to which was added the Widnes Railway—a loop off the Cheshire Lines—in 1875, and in 1904–7 a colliery line in two sections near Doncaster.

Competition of a different kind induced the Midland in 1872 to support the MSLR's proposal to obtain a more independent route to London by building a long new line from Doncaster to the MR at Market Harborough, Leicestershire. In return, the Midland would gain more direct access from London to York. The scheme failed, so instead the MR joined forces with the *North Eastern and built the Swinton & Knottingley Joint Railway, opened in 1879, which shortened its route to York from Sheffield. The NER, in fact, took little advantage of the new line until 1898. The same companies collaborated to reach Wharfedale from Leeds in 1865, when they opened the Otley & Ilkley joint line.

In addition to the West Riding & Grimsby and the Swinton & Knottingley, the railway map of the south Yorkshire coalfield around Doncaster was a maze of other joint lines owned by various combinations of the GCR, GNR, LYR, MR, NER—in one instance by all five—and the *Hull & Barnsley Railway. Most of them were colliery lines, but two had passenger services, neither of them very successful.

Occasionally joint ownership was undertaken as a means of securing the future of an important line, notably the ailing Castle Douglas & Dumfries Railway, worked by the Glasgow & South Western, and its westward continuation, the *Portpatrick Railway, worked by the Caledonian. Together they formed a route to *Ireland via Stranraer, and were rescued in 1885 when the two large companies joined with the LNWR and MR to form the quadripartite *Portpatrick & Wigtownshire Joint Committee. The Caledonian and GSWR provided locomotives for all four companies' trains.

Complementary objectives were behind the formation of the Great Northern & Great Eastern Joint Committee in 1879, which took over certain existing lines and built new ones to make up 123 miles of joint line from Huntingdon to Doncaster via Spalding and Lincoln. It allowed the GNR to penetrate further into Lincolnshire and Cambridgeshire, and gave the GER access to the South Yorkshire coalfield, but was curious in that there were three short gaps over one or other of the owning companies' metals, and one of 14 chains over the MSLR at Gainsborough. Until World War I the GER promoted it as the 'Cathedrals Route' to York from Liverpool Street, although it could not compete with the much shorter GNR main line and remained primarily a freight route that became important during both World Wars.

At times Parliament compelled the creation of a joint line, as happened when the Caledonian sought to control the route to *Aberdeen by absorbing the Scottish North Eastern Railway in 1866. As a *quid pro quo*, the enabling Act decreed that the rival North British company should be admitted to joint ownership of the CR's *Dundee–Arbroath line if, in the future, the NBR chose to build an extension to Montrose. As part of its own thrust to Aberdeen the NBR did so, and in 1880 the Dundee & Arbroath duly became joint and part of the NBR's main line to the north from *Edinburgh.

In an independently promoted Act, Parliament forced the Metropolitan and *Metropolitan District Railways to sink their differences and in 1884 complete London's 'Inner Circle', which for 13 years had suffered from a gap of little over a mile between Mansion House and Aldgate stations, by constructing a joint line, and also jointly building a link to the *East London Railway at Whitechapel. In the same year the two companies joined with the LBSCR, *South Eastern, and *London Chatham & Dover companies to lease the ELR. A year later the GER joined the consortium, making the ELR a six-party joint line.

Joint ownership was rarely apparent in a line's physical characteristics. After 1860, when the Birkenhead Railway succeeded in being taken over by the LNWR and GWR in order to rid itself of the responsibility of managing its 56½ miles of line, subsequent additions to stations and buildings were clearly of LNWR design, as was the signalling. Conversely, the same two companies' joint lines from Shrewsbury to Hereford and to Welshpool had a strong GWR

joint railways

Joint Railways at 1922 (excluding joint stations and short lengths of line in connection therewith)

Name	Location (where not in name)	Mileage	Owners or lessees	Name	Location (where not in name)	Mileage	Owners or lessees
Ashby & Nuneaton		29¼	LNWR, MR	Halesowen	Halesowen–Northfield	6	GWR, MR
Axholme	Haxey–Goole–Fockerby	28	NER, LYR	Halifax & Ovenden and Halifax High Level		5½	GNR, LYR
Birkenhead	Chester–Warrington–Birkenhead–West Kirby	56½	GWR, LNWR	*Hammersmith & City	Hammersmith–Westbourne Park	3	GWR, Metropolitan
Brecon & Merthyr and LNWR	Merthyr–Morlais Jcn	6	BMR, LNWR	HBR & GCR	Aire Jcn–Braithwell Jcn (Doncaster)	25½	HBR, GCR
Brynmawr & Western Valleys	Brynmawr–Nantyglo	1	LNWR, GWR	Kilsyth & Bonnybridge		8½	CR, NBR
Carlisle Goods Traffic Committee	Carlisle Goods Avoiding Line	1½	CR, GSWR, LNWR, MR	Lancashire Union	Cherry Tree–Chorley; and Adlington–Boars Head	12¾	LYR, LNWR
*Cheshire Lines Committee	S. Lancs & N. Cheshire	142	GNR, GCR, MR	*Manchester South Junction & Altrincham		9¼	LNWR, GCR
Clee Hill	Ludlow	6	GWR, LNWR	Methley	Lofthouse–Methley	6	GNR, LYR, NER
Clifton Extension	Bristol	9	GWR, MR	Metropolitan and District	Mansion House–Aldgate–Whitechapel	2	Metropolitan, Met. District
Cosham, Portcreek Jcn & Portsmouth		8½	LSWR, LBSCR	Metropolitan & GCR	Harrow–Quainton Road and branches	51½	Metropolitan, GCR
Croydon & Oxted		12½	LBSCR, SECR	Middlewood Curve		0½	LNWR, NSR
Dentonholme Joint Committee	Dentonholme Goods Lines, Carlisle	0¾	GSWR, MR, NBR	*Midland & Great Northern	Norfolk; Lincs.	183¼	MR, GNR
Dumbarton & Balloch		7	CR, NBR	Nantybwch & Rhymney		3	LNWR, Rhymney Ry
Dundee & Arbroath		23	CR, NBR	Newark Junction Line		0½	GNR, MR
*East London	Shoreditch–New Cross and Queens Road	7	GER, LBSCR, Metropolitan, Met. District, SECR	Norfolk & Suffolk	North Walsham–Cromer; and Yarmouth–Lowestoft	22¼	GER, MGNJR
Easton & Church Hope	Portland Bill	3½	GWR, LSWR	North & South Western Junction	Willesden–Kew	5¼	LNWR, MR, NLR
Enderby Branch	off Nuneaton–Leicester line, LNWR	2¾	LNWR, MR	*North Union	Euxton Junction–Preston	6	LNWR, LYR
Epsom & Leatherhead		3¾	LBSCR, LSWR	Oldham Ashton & Guide Bridge		6¼	GCR, LNWR
*Forth Bridge		4¼	GNR, MR, NBR, NER	Otley & Ilkley		6¼	MR, NER
Furness & Midland	Carnforth–Wennington	9¾	FR, MR	*Portpatrick & Wigtownshire	Castle Douglas–Stranraer–Portpatrick–Whithorn	82	CR, GSWR, LNWR, MR
Glasgow Barrhead & Kilmarnock		29¾	CR, GSWR	Prince's Dock	Glasgow	1¼	CR, NBR, GSWR
Glasgow & Paisley (incorporating Glasgow & Renfrew District)		12¾	CR, GSWR	Preston & Longridge		8¼	LNWR, LYR
GCR, HBR, & MR	Doncaster	4	GCR, HBR, MR	*Preston & Wyre	Preston–Blackpool–Fleetwood	45	LNWR, LYR
GCR & MR (formerly Sheffield & Midland)	Widnes; Manchester–Stockport; and Doncaster	40	GCR, MR	Quaker's Yard & Merthyr		6	GWR, Rhymney Ry
GCR & NSR	Macclesfield–Marple	11	GCR, NSR	Rothesay Dock	Clydebank	0¼	CR, NBR
GNR & GER	Lincolnshire and Cambridgeshire	123	GNR, GER	Ryde Pier & Railway	Ryde Pier–St John's	1½	LSWR, LBSCR
GNR & LNWR	Hallaton–Bottesford–Bingham	45	GNR, LNWR	Severn & Wye	Berkeley Road–Coleford, Lydbrook Jcn and Cinderford (incl. Severn Bridge)	39	GWR, MR
GWR & GCR	Harrow–Quainton Road; Northolt–Princes Risborough–Ashendon Jcn; and branches	41	GWR, GCR				

Name	Location (where not in name)	Mileage	Owners or lessees
*Shrewsbury & Hereford			
Shrewsbury & Wellington	}	82¾	GWR, LNWR
Shrewsbury & Welshpool			
*Somerset & Dorset	Bath–Broadstone Jcn (for Bournemouth) and branches	105	LSWR, MR
Southsea		1¼	LSWR, LBSCR
South Yorkshire	Doncaster	22¼	GCR, GNR, LYR, MR, NER
Stobcross & Kelvinhaugh	Glasgow	0½	CR, NBR
Swinton & Knottingley		19½	MR, NER
Taff Bargoed	Llancaiach–Dowlais (Cae Harris)	11	GWR, Rhymney Ry
Tenbury	Woofferton–Tenbury Wells	5	GWR, LNWR
Tooting Merton & Wimbledon		5¾	LBSCR, LSWR
Tottenham & Hampstead		4¾	MR, GER
Vale of Towy	Llandilo–Llandovery	11	GWR, LNWR
Wath Curve	Wath (Yorks)	0¾	GCR, MR, NER
*West London	North Pole Jcn–Addison Road (Kensington)	2¼	GWR, LNWR
West London Extension	Addison Road–Clapham Jcn	5	GWR, LBSCR, LNWR, LSWR
West Riding & Grimsby	Doncaster–Wakefield	31½	GNR, GCR
Weymouth & Portland		5½	GWR, LSWR
Whitechapel & Bow		2	Met. District, MR
Whitehaven Cleator & Egremont		36	FR, LNWR
Woodside & South Croydon		2½	LBSCR, SECR
Wrexham & Minera		3	GWR, LNWR

* See separate article.

BMR	Brecon & Merthyr Ry	LSWR	London & South Western Ry
CR	Caledonian Ry	LYR	Lancashire & Yorkshire Ry
FR	Furness Ry	MGNJR	Midland & Great Northern Joint Ry
GCR	Great Central Ry	MR	Midland Ry
GER	Great Eastern Ry	NBR	North British Ry
GNR	Great Northern Ry	NER	North Eastern Ry
GSWR	Glasgow & South Western Ry	NLR	North London Ry
GWR	Great Western Ry	NSR	North Staffordshire Ry
HBR	Hull & Barnsley Ry	SECR	South Eastern & Chatham Ry
LBSCR	London Brighton & South Coast Ry	SER	South Eastern Ry
LNWR	London & North Western Ry		

appearance, while the Shrewsbury & Wellington bore LNWR characteristics, bespeaking the division of responsibility. Most stations on the MGNJR and the Somerset & Dorset related to the originally owning companies—there had been several on both systems—but much of the signalling on the former was typically GNR, and on the SDJR was of LSWR design. Yet on the GCR & *North Staffordshire joint line from Macclesfield to Marple, stations and signalling were both of NSR pattern. Only the Cheshire Lines had its own distinctive signals and boxes, which from 1886 were manufactured in its own works at Warrington. The 45-mile-long GNR & LNWR joint line through Leicestershire and Nottinghamshire was unusual in having a clear territorial division at Melton Mowbray. Southwards, it had LNWR stations and signals; from Melton northwards they were Great Northern, showing the divided construction responsibility.

After the 1923 *Grouping had reduced the number of joint lines to 16, the *'Big Four' companies effected some management rationalization. The *London Midland & Scottish and *London & North Eastern Railways, which inherited more than the other two, put theirs into three groups for centralized administration purposes, including those joint stations which previously had their own committees. The GWR assumed responsibility for lines it formerly owned jointly with the GCR and LNWR, while the *Southern Railway took over the infrastructure of the Somerset & Dorset. After its foundation in 1933 the London Passenger Transport Board became responsible for the Metropolitan & Great Central joint line, and in all cases the apportionment of receipts and expenses reflected the consequent economies. The Cheshire Lines, however, kept its separate management at Liverpool.

Apart from these changes, no other effort was made to simplify the labyrinth of legal and financial agreements. It took *nationalization in 1948 to bring joint lines to an end. GJB

H. C. Casserley, *Britain's Joint Lines* (1968); *RYB*; Railway Clearing House junction diagrams and maps; *Reg. Hist.* (all vols.).

joint stations were owned and managed by more than one railway. Many were part of a *joint railway line or system; here we consider a selection of those that were joint in their own right, by either Act or agreement, but not those many more numerous stations that were entered by trains of more than one company though the ownership was entirely with one, such as York and Cambridge.

The first was the *Derby 'Tri-junct' station of the *North Midland, *Midland Counties, and *Birmingham & Derby Junction companies (1840). When they amalgamated as the *Midland Railway in 1844, the station ceased to be joint.

*Carlisle Citadel station (1847) was paid for by the *Lancaster & Carlisle Railway (later *London & North Western) and the *Caledonian equally. The *Maryport & Carlisle and *Newcastle & Carlisle companies declined to contribute, but entered later as tenants, as did the *Glasgow & South Western and *North British. On opening its *Settle & Carlisle line, the Midland contributed substantially to enlargement, yet secured acceptable terms only when it threatened to promote a parliamentary Bill. It still failed to get on the jealously guarded Citadel Station Joint Committee. The two owners maintained the station in turn on a five-year cycle, but in 1916 the Caledonian assumed responsibility for the immediate station area; the LNWR the associated joint lines and junctions immediately to the south.

Joint management could be established by formal *agreement, or by Act of Parliament. Sometimes an agreement was codified by a subsequent Act, as for Carlisle in 1861. An 1847 Act empowered the *Scottish Central Railway to build and manage *Perth General station 'without preference' on behalf of four railways, which were to share the cost. Later, another was granted access. A joint committee was set up in 1863, given statutory authority in an Act of 1865, and amalgamations shortly reduced representation to three: the Caledonian, North British, and *Highland.

Huddersfield joint station (1847) was the solution to a quarrel between the Huddersfield & Manchester and *Manchester & Leeds Railways, which respectively became part of the LNWR and *Lancashire & Yorkshire. Squabbling between owners marked the early years of the General station at Chester, opened by four companies in 1848. Three were allies, dominated by the powerful LNWR, while the fourth, the small Shrewsbury & Chester Railway, represented a prospective route from Birmingham to the north-west for the rival *Great Western. LNWR intimidation of the Shrewsbury & Chester, which included throwing its booking clerk out of his office, tearing down timetables, and forcing passengers to travel south by the LNWR's longer route through *Crewe, was ended only by the Shrewsbury & Chester gaining a court injunction. When the GWR acquired the Shrewsbury company, the LNWR was forced to accept it as joint owner.

Similar tactics were employed at *Manchester London Road (now Piccadilly), where the Manchester Sheffield & Lincolnshire Railway (see GREAT CENTRAL) enjoyed statutory tenancy in perpetuity. Each company had its own offices and staff, but as an economy in 1854 they agreed that the LNWR should act for both. In 1857 the MSLR allowed a LNWR competitor, the *Great Northern, to use its part of the station. The LNWR retaliated by refusing tickets for the GNR line, intimidating its passengers, and ejecting MSLR clerks when they tried to repossess their booking office. The MSLR and GNR alliance was finally ratified by Parliament.

Two of the three *Leeds stations were joint. Central was opened in 1849 by the GNR, LNWR, Leeds & Thirsk (later *North Eastern), and LYR, although continuous disagreements prevented completion until 1857. Only the GNR and LYR used it consistently, the NER and LNWR preferring the Midland's Wellington station until they opened their own joint Leeds New station in 1869. At *Aberdeen, the *Great North of Scotland and Aberdeen Railways, unable to agree on a joint station, built their own, necessitating a connecting horse-bus service for passengers hoping, often fruitlessly, to catch a supposedly connecting train. It was 1867 before Aberdeen Joint station was opened by the Caledonian and the GNSR.

Yeovil Town was owned jointly by the *London & South Western and GWR from the outset, and in 1877 the same companies built an enlarged station at *Plymouth North Road. The last of the big purpose-built joint stations was *Nottingham Victoria, opened in 1900 by the *Great Central and the GNR on the former's London extension.

Smaller joint stations were sometimes built where two lines met end-on, as at Colne (MR–LYR), Hawes (MR–NER), Ashbourne (LNWR–*North Staffordshire), Cockermouth (LNWR–Cockermouth Keswick & Penrith Railway), and Abersychan & Talywain (GWR–LNWR).

Two joint stations in particular became the hub of a system of joint lines. *Shrewsbury, built by the Shrewsbury & Chester and Shrewsbury & Birmingham companies, was also used by the *Shropshire Union and *Shrewsbury & Hereford. The first two passed to the GWR, the third to the LNWR, and the SHR to them both, jointly, along with lines to Wellington and Welshpool. They also had other lines of their own to Shrewsbury. In 1844 each of the four main railways entering *Preston had its own station. By 1866 they were all owned by the LYR or by the LNWR and LYR together, using a single joint station.

Some stations became joint when other lines arrived. Normanton was among the first, opened by the North Midland in 1840 and handed over to a joint committee of the NMR, *York & North Midland, and Manchester & Leeds in 1843. The Lancaster & Carlisle's stations at Carnforth, Tebay, and Penrith became joint after other lines made junctions: respectively the *Furness Railway, the NER, and, at Penrith, the NER and Cockermouth Keswick & Penrith Railway. In each case extra platforms were provided. From 1855 the Whitehaven Junction Railway's station at Whitehaven Bransty was shared with the Whitehaven & Furness Junction Railway (later LNWR and FR), although the latter had to wait 20 years for additional platforms.

Wakefield's two stations became joint: Kirkgate between the LYR and GNR; Westgate between the GNR, GCR, and Midland, to which the LYR also ran under *running powers. The Midland and GNR lines into Leeds crossed at Holbeck, where the low- and high-level platforms were connected by stairs, mainly for interchange purposes. Although the station became joint, in effect it continued to be operated as two separate stations. Similarly, at Egginton Junction the GNR and NSR had their own distinctive platforms. Joint ownership at Aylesbury was more complex, where the GWR station admitted first the *Metropolitan, and then the GCR, which formed joint lines with the other two companies respectively. After some squabbling the station was made the joint property of the two joint committees.

Two large stations became joint after originally being established by one company. The *Bristol and Exeter and the Midland quickly gained entrance to the GWR's terminus at *Bristol Temple Meads. The BER subsequently built its own terminus adjacent, but through working became so chaotic that the companies formed a committee under the Bristol Joint Station Act, 1865, to build a through station, completed in 1878 and incorporating the original GWR buildings. By then the GWR had absorbed the BER, leaving the Midland as the other joint owner.

At *Birmingham New Street the Midland exercised its statutory right to use the LNWR's station from the outset, effectively as tenant. In 1885 additional platforms were opened, virtually for the MR's exclusive use, but it was 1897 before a joint committee was formed. The companies took turns to appoint a joint superintendent, but the LNWR retained the freehold, and responsibility for maintenance and signalling, which was charged to a joint account.

Joint station committees comprised senior officers from the participating companies, with a joint superintendent or *stationmaster usually appointed in turn, and a joint staff, except in booking and parcel offices, of which there was invariably one for each company. In a peculiar exception at Manchester London Road, the station was divided into two parts, with separate stationmasters and staff. While the LNWR platforms were numbered conventionally, the MSLR's were lettered A–C, and there were separate signalling systems. Curiously, although it was only a tenant, the MSLR had its headquarters there until they moved to London in 1905, after it became the Great Central.

As a rule, joint stations displayed the characteristics of only one owner, whether in signals or uniforms. Bristol, for example, appeared outwardly to be wholly Great Western but for the initials 'BJS' on uniform caps and lapels; likewise Plymouth North Road where, indeed, the three tracks running through the centre of the station remained solely GWR property. The LSWR gained joint ownership of the station by contributing to buying the land needed on each side for a new station, and the cost of building it. Birmingham New Street and Chester General had all the appurtenances of the LNWR, and Perth those of the Caledonian. Shrewsbury, however, became hybrid, carrying many LNWR characteristics until the GWR carried out alterations in the 1920s. Although the signal boxes were unmistakably LNWR, the signals themselves were of both companies' patterns; latterly, even, GWR arms appeared on some LNWR posts, reflecting periodic changes of responsibility.

The unusual arrangements at Preston dated back to early disputes over boundaries and charges. The main platforms were jointly owned by the LNWR and LYR under a joint stationmaster, but those on the east side, known as the East Lancashire platforms, were the property of the LYR which had its own entrance, stationmaster, staff, and signalling. Preston and Perth each had a jointly owned *hotel.

Goods stations were less frequently joint, except on joint lines. There was one at Colne, and the LNWR and LYR had one at Leeds Central. The reverse applied at Stobcross, Glasgow, where the goods station was CR and NBR joint, but the passenger station was solely Caledonian.

The 1923 *Grouping ended many joint agreements. Bristol, Perth, Leeds Central and New, Manchester London Road, Plymouth North Road, Shrewsbury, Chester, and Aberdeen remained the principal joint stations of this kind.   GJB

Railway Clearing House junction diagrams (not always clear or impeccably accurate); 'Notable Railway Stations' series, in *RM* (1900–9).

Jones, David (1834–1906), locomotive, carriage, and wagon superintendent, *Highland Railway, 1870–96, son of an engineer.

Jones was responsible for the design of several excellent locomotive types, simple and robust, including the first 4-6-0s in Britain. He was apprenticed on the *London & North Western Railway under John *Ramsbottom. In 1858–65 he was principal assistant to William Barclay, locomotive superintendent of the HR, then locomotive running superintendent under William *Stroudley whom he succeeded.

The Highland's routes were severely graded and curved, and in 1874 Jones introduced outside-cylinder 4-4-0s following the *'Crewe-type' with double frames. His later types —the 4-6-0 heavy goods and 'Loch' class 4-4-0 passenger engines, which did excellent work for over 40 years—had outside cylinders with inside frames. His last design, an enlarged 4-6-0 for passenger service, was built by his successor Peter Drummond. In retirement he designed locomotives for overseas railways. His passenger coaching stock included the first bogie *sleeping cars designed in Britain.   GWC

The Locomotive (1937), 253–6.

Joy, David (1825–1903), engineer, best remembered for his development of Joy radial locomotive *valve gear, patented in 1879. It was widely adopted by both the *London & North Western and *Lancashire & Yorkshire Railways from the 1880s through to 1923.

Born in Leeds, he was apprenticed first to Fenton *Murray & Jackson and then transferred to Shepherd & Todd at the Railway Foundry. He was appointed acting chief draughtsman in 1845, playing a leading part in designing the famous 'Jenny Lind' 2-2-2s. Following a dispute, he left to become manager of the Nottingham & Grantham Railway and then superintendent of the Oxford Worcester & Wolverhampton (see WEST MIDLAND RAILWAY).

From the mid-1850s Joy largely devoted his energies to experimental work, his many inventions including an organ blower, a steam hammer, a revolving gun, and an improved earth closet.

Joy kept copious diaries, with detailed diagrams, providing a valuable insight into his achievements. Extracts were published in the *Railway Magazine*, May–December 1908, and the originals are at the Science Museum, London.   DJ BDE.

Jubilee Line, see LONDON UNDERGROUND RAILWAYS.

Junction Diagrams. As a specific term this relates to the series first issued by John Airey in 1867, based on the internal documents then in use within the *Railway Clearing House where he worked. Originally a book of 84 oblong lithographed sheets, these were revised and extended in many later editions to keep pace with the expanding railway system. Careful hand-colouring distinguished the ownership of the various lines and stations, with exact distances quoted in miles and chains to satisfy the principal purpose of the publication: the calculation of rates and division of receipts for through traffic between companies. A short text in the later volumes listed *running powers and working arrangements. Proof copies were sent out to the individual railways for checking, which ensured an unusually high standard of accuracy.

In 1869 Airey issued the first of his regional *maps of the railway system to which the Junction Diagrams were in many ways complementary, and both series were further developed after the RCH took over his business in 1895. Colour-printing replaced the old hand-colouring, and by 1915 the book had grown to 158 sheets, all drawn by J. P. and W. R. Emslie and lithographed by McCorquodale & Co. Ltd. Some sheets were made up of several smaller diagrams, and the depiction ranged from simple end-on junctions such as Sprouston or Dolgelley to the multi-company complexities of *Carlisle or Clapham. North Wales District has its own sheet, which conveniently fills one of the gaps in the coverage of the regional maps. Each sheet is dated, and supplements updated the set between editions.

The 1928 edition incorporated all the changes in ownership brought about by the 1923 *Grouping, and adopted a convenient loose-leaf format which assisted the difficult job of inserting amended or additional pages into what had hitherto been a fully bound volume.

Comprehensive collections of Airey and RCH Junction Diagrams are hard to find, but the David Garnett collection in Brunel University and the *British Transport Commission archive in the Public Record Office are good starting points. The series in its 1915 state was the subject of an excellent reprint by David & Charles in 1969.   RJD

junctions. In railway parlance, 'junction' has several meanings. It can be the place at which two routes diverge, the end-on meeting-point between two companies' lines, or a junction station. On a few railways, notably the *Midland, it also meant points and crossings on a section of line where there was no divergence of route.

The first junctions were formed by branches off early *tramroads, and then on the *Stockton & Darlington Railway (1825), which initially had three short branches. On a single line the junction is formed by a single set of points, or turnout, but a double-line junction requires two and a diamond crossing (see TRACK), known as a flat junction. In recent years, the simplification of layouts has produced single-lead junctions, where the turnout to a secondary route from a double line is on one track only, preceded by a cross-over, thereby eliminating the comparatively high maintenance cost of a diamond crossing. The diverging route either continues as a single line or becomes double again just beyond the junction. This type of layout means, however, that on the main (double) line, the track between the cross-over and the turnout is used by trains in both directions, sometimes for up to half a mile, requiring bi-directional *signalling. The arrangement has led to several collisions, notably at Newton, near Glasgow, in 1991, provoking criticism which was met by applying more strin-

gent working instructions and modification of some layouts.

On busy routes, flat junctions create a potential for delays, which has been overcome by building flying or burrowing junctions where one of the conflicting tracks is carried over or under the other, avoiding a diamond crossing. The earliest flyover was at Norwood, where in 1845 the *London & Croydon Railway's *atmospheric track was carried on a wooden viaduct over the London & Brighton's (see LONDON BRIGHTON & SOUTH COAST) diverging conventional line. The latter company constructed a flying junction at Sydenham in 1854, and when the *London & North Western shortened its route to Liverpool in 1869 it built a flyover at Weaver Junction, north of *Crewe, carefully graded and curved to allow high-speed running. Thereafter, flyovers and flyunders became more common, particularly in the congested areas of south London. Over the 14 miles between *Waterloo and Hampton Court Junction, for example, there are ten, three of them at Clapham Junction, while Hampton Court Junction itself has one of each, for the Hampton Court and Guildford lines respectively. The main line comprises four tracks, and the layout where the Hampton Court branch diverges enables five trains to pass through simultaneously.

Station names incorporating the word 'junction' took them either from the location, of which Clapham Junction is the best known, even though it is actually in Battersea; or from the place which the junction was *for*, as in Seaton Junction where passengers changed for Seaton. This could lead to long-standing confusion between stations, originating on the *Liverpool & Manchester Railway in 1831. That company appears to have been the first to use 'junction' in a station name, at Kenyon Junction where passengers changed for Bolton, ten miles away, and at Newton Junction, for the line to Warrington. But for some years Kenyon Junction was also referred to as Bolton Junction, and Newton Junction as Warrington Junction. In 1861 the latter became Earlestown Junction, after the town that had grown around it, and later simply Earlestown. St Helens Junction, on the same line, appears to have opened in 1832 when a branch was built to St Helens. Parkside station for a time enjoyed the alternative name of *North Union Junction, after the company which acquired the branch from the LMR to Wigan.

The use of 'junction' in this fashion commonly derived from the time when there was no nearby settlement from which to take a name. Chard Junction and Killin Junction were examples and, provided that passengers for the branch always had to change, the practice was reasonably sensible. But when there were also through trains which stopped at both stations, like those from Waterloo to Yeovil Town via Yeovil Junction, 1¾ miles away; or instances like Barmouth Junction and Barmouth (1½ miles apart), at both of which all trains stopped, passengers could be forgiven some anger if they mistakenly alighted at the junction instead of the town station.

Railways were far from consistent in these matters. Preston Junction, two miles from *Preston, was particularly ill-named, not only for the confusion it caused with the main station, but because passengers changed there into trains *from* Preston. It was renamed Todd Lane Junction in 1952, after a century of misunderstanding, although the signal box still retained the old name. Some junction stations of this kind retained their full names long after their branches closed and the junctions ceased to exist: Brampton Junction, Cumbria, for 38 years before it was renamed Brampton; Tiverton Junction, Devon, for 22 years until it was replaced by Tiverton Parkway. Others, like Buckley, Hyde, and Walton Junctions, never were junctions in the sense of being stations for changing trains. A few gave their names to subsequent settlements, at some of which the station may now have been long closed, such as Horbury Junction in West Yorkshire, or where the railway has entirely disappeared, like Halwill Junction in north Devon.

The Midland Railway used the same confusing terminology for its signal boxes at Shipley station, West Yorkshire, where at the apexes of the triangular junction they were respectively named Leeds, Bradford, and Bingley Junctions,

with a fourth, Guiseley Junction, nearby. They referred, of course, to the places to which the lines led, some miles distant. Yet at Ambergate, Derbyshire, where there was a similar layout, the junctions were conventionally named North, South, and East.

The same company frequently used the term 'junction' where there was no proper junction at all, but merely crossovers on a four-track line, like Aylestone Junction at Leicester; or Brentingby Junction, a box which only controlled the entry and exit to goods loops south of Melton Mowbray. *British Rail has continued the practice at some places where new pointwork has been installed on what hitherto was plain track, such as Springs Junction on the Leeds–Ilkley line where double track becomes single.

Even motorways have perpetuated the terminological uncertainty, verging on tautology, as in 'the interchange at Junction 21'.

See also STATIONS. GJB

For details of flying junctions, see Quail Map Co., *Railway Track Diagrams*, 5 vols. (1987–94).

K

Kellett, John Reginald (1925–91), writer, educated at Bradford Grammar School, Oxford, and Cambridge. He taught at the University of Glasgow, 1954–84.

Kellett investigated *Glasgow solicitors' records concerning sales of land to railways, surveying his discoveries in an article (1964), and extended his inquiry to *London, *Birmingham, *Manchester, and *Liverpool, resulting in his *Impact of Railways on Victorian Cities* (1969). Though based on the land transactions, its scope broadened to cover the social consequences of railway building. A model that everyone working in this field needs to study, it is well written and richly documented, and stands high in the literature of British transport history.

It was Kellett's only large book. He wrote many valuable articles. Among them, one (1969) attacked the way in which the history of British railway companies had so far been written. JS

Independent, 24 June 1991. Articles referred to here: *JTH*, 6 (1963–4); 'Writing on Victorian Railways', *Victorian Studies* (Sept. 1969), 90–6.

Kennard, Thomas William (1825–93), civil engineer, son of Robert William Kennard MP (1800–70), railway financier. In the early 1850s he took out several patents, including a wrought-iron variant of the Warren truss (see BRIDGES AND VIADUCTS) and columnar iron piles. These were immediately applied at Crumlin Viaduct. The contract had been awarded to his father's ironworks at Blaenavon, but Kennard decided to build a new works near the bridge site—the Viaduct Works. This became a major bridge works, using Kennard's patents.

The viaduct was completed in 1857. In 1859 he became engineer to the Atlantic & Great Western Railway, with which his father's bank was involved. He remained engineer until 1867 when the company passed into receivership.

Kennard retired early. Best known for his bridges, his design methods were described by Humber. MMC

Engineer, 76, 269; *Engineering*, 56, 330; W. A. Humber, *Practical Treatise on Cast and Wrought Iron Bridges and Girders* (1857); H. N. Maynard, *The Viaduct Works' Handbook* (1868).

Kent & East Sussex Light Railway, see LIGHT RAILWAYS.

Kilmarnock was, for a town of its size, one of the most remarkable railway centres in Britain; not for the traffic it handled, but for its extensive involvement with locomotive construction. Its first railway was the *Kilmarnock & Troon, opened in 1811, a horse-worked *tramroad. The town was first reached by conventional railway in 1843, by a branch from the Glasgow–Ayr line at Dalry, extended to Cumnock in 1850 as part of the *Glasgow & South Western's main line to *Carlisle. The GSWR moved its principal *works to Kilmarnock in 1855. By that time the Caledonia Works of Andrew Barclay was already building industrial locomotives, and others followed, including Grant Ritchie & Co., and Dick Kerr & Co. Andrew Barclay survived many vicissitudes to become Scotland's last locomotive builders, now part of the Hunslet Barclay group.

Kilmarnock grew as a railway centre with the building of the Irvine Valley line to Newmilns and Darvel (opened in 1850), and more significantly by the GSWR and *Caledonian Railway's joint direct line to meet the CR's existing line from Glasgow to Neilston, opened in 1873, which gave the GSWR a significantly faster main line to Carlisle and the south. The present station dates from that time. The original locomotive depot was beside it, but a much larger one was opened at Hurlford in the 1880s and lasted until the end of steam traction in 1967.

After the *Grouping, the *London Midland & Scottish Railway concentrated locomotive and *carriage repairs in Scotland at Glasgow and at *Inverness. It stopped building locomotives and carriages in Scotland. Kilmarnock works was therefore run down. The last buildings were demolished in the 1960s. That decade also saw the closure of local services; the Darvel branch closed in 1964, and passenger services on the Kilmarnock & Troon in 1969, while local trains on the main line also ceased, though reopened in a limited way in the 1980s and 1990s. A recent development has been the introduction of through services from Ayrshire to *Newcastle via Carlisle, which takes the 'Strathclyde Red' trains of the *Passenger Transport Executive into Newcastle Central. JRH

Reg. Hist., vi; R. Wear, *The Locomotive Builders of Kilmarnock* (1977).

Kilmarnock & Troon Railway: the first railway in Scotland to be established by Act of Parliament, the first to carry passengers there, and the first on which a locomotive was used.

In 1807 the Marquess of Titchfield, who succeeded his father as 4th Duke of Portland in the following year, commissioned William *Jessop to survey a railway from coal-pits at Kilmarnock down to the harbour he was developing at Troon in Ayrshire. It was authorized in 1808 and opened in 1811, a double line of 4-ft gauge. In 1817 the duke, having heard of the work of George *Stephenson at Killingworth, invited him to make a visit with one of his locomotives. Although it proved equal to its work, it was too heavy for the rails, and horse traction was therefore maintained. From the railway's early days passengers were conveyed in two carriages, *Caledonia* and *The Boat*. The line was leased to the *Glasgow Paisley Kilmarnock & Ayr Railway in 1846, and converted to standard gauge, with track strong enough for locomotives. The *Glasgow & South Western Railway purchased the company outright in 1899.

This little railway was outstandingly profitable. Of the 80 shares in it, 77 were in the hands of the Portland family, and an average dividend of more than 8 per cent was paid every year from 1817 onwards until the company was dissolved in 1902, except in 1858–9 when special charges had to be met for litigation with the GSWR. In the 1840s the dividend attained 18 per cent, and it still averaged 14 per cent over the whole of that decade. No other statutory British railway company rewarded its shareholders so handsomely and for so long as 85 years.   JS
  SRO, BR/KTR/1/1–2; A. S. Turberville, *Welbeck Abbey and its Owners*, ii (1939), i; G. Kilpatrick, in *Back Track*, 6 (1992), 41–8.

King's Cross station, see LONDON STATIONS.

Kirtley, Matthew (1813–73), engineer, son of a colliery owner. After training under *Hackworth on the *Stockton & Darlington Railway, Kirtley was an engineman on the *Liverpool & Manchester, Hull & Selby (see LEEDS & SELBY), and *London & Birmingham Railways, driving the first train into London on the LBR. He joined the *Birmingham & Derby Junction Railway in 1839 and became locomotive superintendent in 1841. On the formation of the *Midland Railway he was appointed locomotive and carriage superintendent, 1844–73. He expanded and re-equipped Derby works, from which the first new engines, 0-6-0s and 2-2-2s, emerged in 1851.

He was the first to fit a locomotive firebox with a brick arch and deflector plate in order to burn coal instead of coke, which became applied almost universally.

Kirtley's 0-6-0 freight and 2-4-0 passenger engines were simple, effective, and elegant, built in substantial numbers and the basis of his successor Samuel *Johnson's designs.   GWC
  J. B. Radford, *Derby Works and its Locomotives* (1971); BSRL.

Kyanizing, a process for preserving timber by saturating it in a solution of bi-chloride of mercury, contained in wooden tanks, patented by J. H. Kyan in 1832; much used in treating the sleepers in *track, and timberwork in bridges during the 1830s and 1840s. It proved too expensive, however, and creosote was in the end preferred.   JS
  MacDermot, i, 27; L. G. Booth in Sir A. Pugsley (ed.), *The Works of Isambard Kingdom Brunel* (1982), 110.

labour, see EMPLOYMENT; STRIKES; TRADE UNIONISM.

Laing, Samuel (1812–97), civil servant and chairman. Educated at Cambridge and called to the Bar, in 1840 he became law clerk (law secretary, 1844) in the Railway Department of the Board of *Trade. He was much involved in the preparation of *Gladstone's Act, and a member of *Dalhousie's Railway Board in 1844–5. When it was dissolved he resigned from the Civil Service. He was chairman of the *London Brighton & South Coast Railway in 1848–55 and 1867–94, and was MP (discontinuously) in 1852–85. In 1860–5 he was Finance Member of the government of India. Among all the mid-Victorian railway chairmen Laing's experience of public life was unique.

Each of his chairmanships began when the LBSCR was in a state of grave financial weakness (almost bankrupt in 1867), exacerbated by board-room squabbles. He successfully sorted out tangles, calmed tempers, and restored confidence, helped by able managers. Ever since his time at the Board of Trade he had been interested in providing cheap travel for the poor, and he steadily supported the LBSCR's *excursion business, which became exceptionally lucrative.   JS

   DNB; *GR* (correcting some of the *DNB*'s dates).

Lancashire & Yorkshire Railway. Although its 600 route miles qualified for only 11th place among British railways, this *Manchester-based company came fourth in number of locomotives, exemplifying its dense, thickly populated, intensively worked network.

In 1847 the *Manchester & Leeds Railway changed its name to Lancashire & Yorkshire Railway, simultaneously absorbing the Wakefield Pontefract & Goole, subsequently opened in 1848. The company came to own the *North Union and *Preston & Wyre Railways jointly with the *London & North Western, giving it access to *Preston and Fleetwood—where the docks were also jointly owned—and to *Blackpool and Lytham.

Successive acquisitions added lines in Yorkshire to Barnsley, *Bradford, and Huddersfield; and in west Lancashire from *Liverpool to Southport; while in 1859 a quarrelsome relationship with the *East Lancashire Railway ended in amalgamation, providing routes to north-east Lancashire, and from Liverpool to Colne. The main system was completed in 1880 when the line from Blackburn to Hellifield was finished. The West Lancashire Railway (Preston–Southport, 1882) was acquired in 1897.

The lines straddling the Pennines were characterized by lofty viaducts, tunnels, and steep gradients, many built by the noted engineer Sir John *Hawkshaw. Lines across the west Lancashire plain and the Fylde were relatively straight and level. From MLR days the company adopted a cavalier attitude towards its passengers; trains were slow, dirty, and unpunctual. Significantly, the dividend was highest when services were worst: 8⅜ per cent in 1872.

In 1883 Thomas Barnes, chairman for 31 years, retired, and John Pearson took his place. Although Pearson died in 1887, he began long-needed improvements which his successor, George Armytage, continued during 31 years in office. There was pressing need not only for new locomotives but for a new works to replace the old, cramped premises at Miles Platting and Bury. A site was chosen at Horwich (see WORKS) where the chief locomotive superintendent, W. Barton Wright, laid out large, up-to-date workshops which became a model of their kind. Miles Platting closed in 1887, the year after Wright was succeeded by J. A. F. *Aspinall.

Although Wright built some strong, simple, reliable engines, increasing traffic meant that many old ones had to be kept, and once Horwich works was complete Aspinall successfully set about their replacement, most notably by powerful 2-4-2 *tank engines which virtually took over all passenger services except main-line expresses; on occasions, they performed well on those, too. Between 1889 and 1911, 332 were built. In 1899 Aspinall became general manager, revolutionizing the company's operating and commercial practices.

Much of the LYR's earlier complacency may be attributed to its *monopoly. The only direct competitor was the LNWR, from Manchester to Liverpool and Leeds over considerably shorter routes, so the company preferred to make traffic *agreements. The LYR's Leeds route was so much longer that it concentrated instead on Bradford, from which no other line ran westwards.

When in 1888–9 new cut-off lines were opened to avoid Bolton and Wigan, however, considerable accelerations to Liverpool took place, culminating in highly creditable 40-minute expresses that equalled those of the LNWR and the *Cheshire Lines Committee, but over a more difficult route. By the early 1900s Manchester–Blackpool expresses took 65 minutes, and through trains were being run in conjunction with other companies, such as Colne–Euston; Liverpool and Manchester to Scotland; Bradford to North Wales, Sheffield, Southampton, and Bournemouth. After 1888 the Scottish services were provided by the *Midland Railway, which exercised *running powers from Liverpool and Manchester to Hellifield, for the *Settle & Carlisle line.

Simultaneously, passenger and goods *stations were

improved or rebuilt, and particularly busy parts of the east–west main line were quadrupled in the Calder Valley of Yorkshire, around Manchester, and on the approaches to Liverpool. Together with new *marshalling yards, these improvements enabled the company to expeditiously handle its enormous *freight traffic: cotton and wool from Liverpool, for which large warehouses (see GOODS SHEDS) were built at many towns; finished goods for export; *coal; and heavy engineering goods. Fleetwood docks were enlarged for *timber, grain, and *fish traffic, and *shipping services were operated to Belfast jointly with the LNWR, with fast connecting trains from London and Manchester. In 1902 the LYR began its own Irish service from Liverpool to Drogheda.

In Yorkshire the company dominated the port of Goole, from which it ran frequent passenger and cargo ships to France, Belgium, Holland, Germany, and Denmark. The LYR's 30 ships formed the largest number owned by a British railway. Such a transformation could only be executed with very large capital expenditure, resulting in dividends settling at around 3–4 per cent from 1900.

To handle better the heavy *suburban traffic between Liverpool, Southport, and Crossens, and meet electric *tramway competition, Aspinall advocated *electrification, using third-rail *multiple-unit trains at 600 V dc. The system was inaugurated in March 1904. In 1906 the Liverpool–Aintree line was also electrified. An experimental overhead system was installed on the Bury–Holcombe Brook branch in 1913, and in 1916 a third rail was installed on the Manchester–Whitefield–Bury line at 1,200 V dc. The Holcombe Brook system was similarly converted a year later.

The LYR introduced the country's first electro-pneumatic *signalling, first at Bolton in 1903, then on part of the Manchester–Rochdale line, and at Southport Chapel Street. The company's signalling school at Manchester Victoria had a unique model layout, used for training for over 70 years.

The close relationship with the LNWR led to amalgamation in 1922, as a prelude to the 1923 *Grouping. Although the LYR lost its separate identity, three of its chief officers took leading positions on the LNWR and, for a few years, the *London Midland and Scottish Railway: (Sir) Arthur Watson as general manager, H. Marriott as assistant, and George *Hughes as CME. A fourth, Ashton Davies, eventually became vice-president of the LMS.

The LYR was an example of a railway directly influencing rapid growth of an industrial area. After the 1880s it served it well, providing frequent trains for business and pleasure. Its Blackpool and Southport *'Club Trains' enabled Manchester businessmen to live by the sea and, not least, it conveyed vast crowds of holiday-makers to the Lancashire coast—in 1919, about 1 million to Blackpool from the Manchester area alone.   GJB

LYR; *Reg. Hist.*, x (1986 edn.); *LTW*, ii, 38–70.

Lancashire Derbyshire & East Coast Railway, see GREAT CENTRAL RAILWAY.

Lancaster & Carlisle Railway. In 1839 government commissioners, appointed to choose between *east and *west

coast routes to Scotland, advocated both. Between Lancaster and *Carlisle the most easterly of three alternatives was selected, subsequently amended to pass near Kendal and avoid a summit tunnel. The four existing west coast companies made substantial contributions to the Lancaster & Carlisle Railway's capital of £900,000.

Engineered by *Locke, with *Brassey as *contractor, the 69-mile line formed the largest single railway contract then placed, and was completed through remote, mountainous terrain in the remarkably short time of 2½ years. Six months after commencement, work was in progress at 75 places, and at the peak nearly 10,000 *navvies were employed. In 1846 the military had to quell *riots between English and Irish factions at Penrith.

At Lancaster the LCR joined the Lancaster & Preston Junction Railway, which in 1842 had been leased to the Lancaster Canal. Believing the lease to be defective, the LCR tried to acquire the LPJR, whose directors resigned, leaving the company with no authority and illegally in the hands of the canal. The LCR began running expresses over it to Preston in 1846, independently of the LPJR which continued to run its own local trains; 2½ years later there was an inevitable collision, whereupon the Board of *Trade instructed the parties to behave responsibly, forcing the canal to withdraw. In 1849 the LCR took over the line's management and in 1850 agreed to share Preston–Kendal freight traffic with the canal company.

At the outset the LCR was worked by the *London & North Western, which by amalgamation now owned the line from London, but in 1857 the company asserted its independence and bought its own rolling stock. Two years later, however, it agreed to lease itself to the LNWR, giving that company control of the entire Euston–Carlisle line. In 1879 the LNWR acquired it outright. The LCR was very prosperous, its dividends during independence rising to nearly 9½ per cent and, at one point during the LNWR lease, exceeding 12 per cent.

The LCR subscribed to the South Durham & Lancashire Union Railway (later part of the *North Eastern), opened to the LCR at Tebay in 1861 to carry Durham coke to smelt the rich iron ore of Furness.

The line was always difficult to work, particularly the long northward climbs to Grayrigg and up the notorious four miles at 1 in 75 to Shap, requiring contingents of banking engines at Oxenholme and Tebay until *electrification in 1974.   GJB

B. Reed, *Crewe to Carlisle* (1969); H. D. Bowtell, *Over Shap to Carlisle* (1983); *Reg. Hist.*, x, ch. 10 (1986 edn.); xiv, ch. 2 (1983); M. C. Reed, *London & North Western Railway* (1996), 28–30, 47–9, 73.

Lancing, see WORKS.

land, surplus. Under the Lands Clauses Consolidation Act, 1845, a railway was required to sell, within ten years of its completion date, any surplus land acquired under its Act (other than in towns, and building land), giving first option to the original owners or their heirs, or failing them, adjoining owners. Parliament reasoned that it was inequitable to allow railways to profit by developing land bought under statutory compulsory purchase powers, although there came to be a statutory limit of 15 acres that they might purchase beyond their immediate requirements, in case of unforeseen need. The companies responded that, compared with other lineside owners, it was unfair that they should be barred from realizing enhanced development opportunities that the railway itself had created.

The railways have always been accused of hoarding land, until recent years with some, but not entire, justification. In the days of rapid expansion they were prudently cautious about selling land they might need for widening lines or enlarging stations. Conversely, there were not always ready buyers. Often surplus land was of poor quality, or affected by severance, which companies had been obliged to purchase from an owner who was glad to get rid of it, as part of a bargain for land they really needed.

Periodically the companies took stock of what they might sell, usually when economies were ordered, although conclusions were invariably conservative. In 1867 the *Great Western, for instance, appointed a committee of investigation which in its two years' existence achieved very little. Sometimes shortcomings were uncovered: the *Great Eastern in 1870 found that land purchased in early years was no longer in its possession, yet it had no record of sales; the *Caledonian in 1902–5 discovered that for some years £60 feu duty had been paid for land of which it had never taken formal possession; while the *Cheshire Lines estate committee in 1924 found that it owned a large acreage of empty land at *Liverpool intended for docks that had never been built. Despite such instances, however, it was usual for committees to conclude that ample land should be retained for possible future requirements.

Only two pre-*Grouping companies successfully developed surplus land. The *Metropolitan had managed to secure clauses in successive Acts which overrode the Lands Clauses Act, enabling it to retain considerable amounts of land, with powers to lease. Acts of 1885 and 1887 empowered it to form a separate development company, through which it laid out a succession of housing estates between 1880 and 1933 (see METRO-LAND), including some on land bought expressly for the purpose. The *Great Central obtained an Act increasing the statutory ten years disposal period to 30, for surplus land at St John's Wood, in order to overcome difficulties with pre-emption clauses in its London Extension Act, thereby enabling it to arrange economic leases for development.

After the widespread rationalization that followed *Beeching's Re-Shaping Plan of 1963, *British Railways embarked on a massive programme of land disposal resulting from the closure of lines, *stations, and *goods depots. Wherever practicable, BR retained a stake in urban development schemes through its Property Board, which gained it valuable revenue. When the property market collapsed in 1990, income from this source was much reduced, although by then all that was left was mostly land difficult to dispose of, such as narrow strips remaining from closed lines containing bridges or viaducts.

However, disposals continue where opportunities occur,

and there has been close collaboration with local authorities in creating long-distance footpaths, and with organizations like Sustrans in converting *disused lines into cycle-ways.

See also LAND ACQUISITION; LAND AND PROPERTY, OWNERSHIP AND DEVELOPMENT OF.   GJB

Monopolies & Mergers Commission, British Railways Board: Property Activities (1985); RS, 107–8, 185–6, 199, 200, 203; Metropolitan Surplus Lands Committee: A. A. Jackson, London's Metropolitan Railway (1986), 238–42, 289–93; land development and disposals, 1974–90: Property Board News (1974–90).

land acquisition. *Tramroads built by *canal companies were sometimes on land acquired by the same means of statutory compulsory purchase as for the canals themselves, but on the early coal wagonways (see WOODEN RAILWAYS; EARLY IRON RAILWAYS) in the north-east, and some elsewhere, landowners granted the builders wayleaves for a fixed term of years at an annual rent. When some of the wagonways were later converted to railways, the wayleave system was often perpetuated. The Brandling Junction Railway ran over wayleaved land for 26 miles, and part of the *East Coast main line was originally the subject of a wayleave.

Excessive rents could give wagonway owners severe financial burdens. The £280–300 a mile paid to the bishop or the dean and chapter of Durham for 17 miles of line made a major contribution to the closure and sale of the Stanhope & Tyne Railway in 1841. The *North Eastern Railway inherited by far the largest number of wayleaves, and for seventy years fought against what it considered to be an archaic system that enabled grasping landlords to profit from railways.

Some early Scottish railways were granted wayleaves, although there the alternative to purchase was usually the payment of an annual feu duty: a type of perpetual lease. In 1875, for instance, the *Caledonian Railway had a large number of feus, including 12 on its main line north of Stirling. A feu could also contain stipulations, such as the provision of stations, the safeguarding of tenants' rights, replacement of interrupted water supplies, and, in the case of the Earl of Moray's feu to the Dunblane Doune & Callander Railway in 1856, acceptance by the railway of the local *turnpike's £3,000 debt.

The leasing of land for a railway was not common, other than on private and *industrial railways. In the Forest of Dean, however, tramroad and, later, railway land was leased from the Crown under licence, usually for 31 years. Licences were also required authorizing construction. The *West Cornwall Railway leased some of the land it needed, in order to avoid the capital cost of purchase, but that was unusual. Only in north-east England was leasing at all common, becoming even more widespread than wayleaves, and even today a number of long leases remain in force.

In general, it was regarded as essential that a railway should own the freehold of the land over which it ran, in order to safeguard its operations and its subscribers' capital, and this could only be done by obtaining a private Act of Parliament. One of the prime purposes of a railway's Act of incorporation, therefore, was to give the company the statutory right—albeit somewhat indirectly before 1845—to purchase land, within the limits shown on the *parliamentary plans and subject to whatever requirements and restrictions Parliament might impose. But the Act did not set out the price to be paid. That was a matter for negotiation between the parties. All it did was to lay down the procedure to be followed in settling disputes, which dated back to the days of *canal construction and required the summoning of a jury of 12 'sufficient and indifferent men', to sit in judgement. These words were included in the Lands Clauses Consolidation Act, 1845, which codified the procedure, so that it no longer had to be repeated in every individual Act. It legislated for disputes to be settled by an arbitrator or, if the parties could not agree to a single appointment, two arbitrators presided over by an umpire. Even so, in the last resort there remained the option of a jury.

Hitherto the market price of land had been generally considered as a fair basis of settlement, including reasonable compensation for loss of amenity, but the Lands Clauses Act established a new principle of separate awards for each. There is little doubt that it thereby opened the way for exorbitant claims, the most celebrated of which was Lord Petre's demand from the *Eastern Counties Railway of £20,000 for land on eight miles of line, and £100,000 compensation for loss of amenity on his estate as the price of his support in Parliament. The ECR's provisional committee accepted, only to repudiate the agreement once its Act had been passed. Lord Petre fought back and won (see LANDOWNERS). It was by far the largest sum paid by a railway to a single *landowner, and the legal wrangling delayed the opening of the railway by at least two years.

Companies sometimes negotiated prices before obtaining an Act. Wherever possible they tried to avoid taking a line through property where they knew it would be difficult to negotiate a reasonable price or, indeed, any price at all, resulting in deviations from the easiest or most direct route. Even so, total avoidance was impossible, and many cases were recorded of the subterfuges adopted by *surveyors when crossing land which they knew would be disputed, including sending out decoys to lure the landowner's men away from the intended route, and surveying at night by the uncertain light of shielded lanterns.

Sometimes special *civil engineering works were necessary to overcome a landowner's *opposition in Parliament, to prevent or reduce an excessive claim for land, or both. All sorts of bargains were driven to secure a route: perhaps the provision of a *tunnel to hide the line from the landowner's view; a viaduct instead of an embankment, in order to partly preserve a view; the provision of a private *station; a right to stop trains at the landowner's personal convenience; and all manner of lesser privileges.

The *London & Birmingham Railway, for instance, bought off the opposition of the Earls of Clarendon and Essex at Watford at a cost of nearly £73,000, a deviation, and a mile-long tunnel to avoid their parks. At Stapleford Park, near Melton Mowbray, the notorious 'Lord Harborough's Curve' caused a severe speed restriction on the *Midland Railway for 44 years until eventually it was re-aligned. Again, the Oswestry & Newtown Railway was compelled by one of its own shareholders to adopt a route that bypassed her land, needing a bridge over the Severn and a steep two-mile gradient that otherwise could have been avoided.

The Crown was no less demanding, asking a high price from the two railways desiring to build lines to Windsor, playing off one against the other; and insisting on the winding route the railway takes through the New Forest. The Admiralty secured £10,000 for its consent to a bridge at Rye, Sussex, and successfully insisted on severe restrictions on lines serving Dover and Portsmouth, on the grounds of national security.

But by no means were all landowners uncooperative, particularly those who had business interests that would be served, such as those who helped to promote the Dundee & Newtyle Railway in 1825, and the coalowners of Lothian who invested in the *Edinburgh & Dalkeith Railway in 1826. Although some of the great Scottish landowners like the Dukes of *Buccleuch and Atholl, whose vast estates no railway could avoid, were particularly difficult, others recognized the benefits railways could bring and lent their support. Land was given free to the Wishaw & Coltness and Slamannan Railways. Later, Highland landowners in particular supported railways, and offered land cheaply or free of charge in the expectation that they would open up the country and improve the economy. In England the Duke of Devonshire gave land for the Cromford & High Peak Railway in Derbyshire; other landowners bought railway shares, provided cheap land, and, frequently, became leading members of railway boards.

To reduce costs, railways at first tended to pass outside towns, where land was cheaper, although some municipalities like Cambridge actively discouraged them from entering. Others, though, quickly saw the advantages of having a railway. *Carlisle, for example, sold land to railways within the city, including the site of the station. *Derby did the same, although the town stipulated that the three railways concerned must share a common station on a carefully selected site.

On the whole, a new railway tended to increase the value of neighbouring land, particularly agricultural and land near stations, depending on proximity to the line. Increases in Scotland, outside the large cities, generally were lower than in England and Wales. It has proved difficult to generalize on the effect of railways on urban land although, again, in city business districts close to stations values rose rapidly. Later, when railways began to create 'land blight' close to city centres, land near by fell in value, particularly alongside viaducts, in the neighbourhood of busy junctions, and near goods depots and locomotive sheds. For a number of years railways considered it essential to own the strip of land over tunnels, but as time passed this was found to be unnecessary except around shafts, to which access was gained by easements granted by the landowner. However, railways were obliged to purchase buildings on the line of a tunnel, for which reason *underground railways were built beneath streets. The *Victoria Line in London was the first to be built by obtaining statutory tunnelling rights not following streets, opened in 1969, and all new tunnels are now built in this way wherever possible.

See also LAND AND PROPERTY, OWNERSHIP AND DEVELOPMENT OF; LAND, SURPLUS. GJB

RS, ch. 4; wayleaves: M. J. T. Lewis, *Early Wooden Railways* (1970); Scotland: Robertson; land in cities: J. R. Kellett, *The Impact of Railways on Victorian Cities* (1969).

land and property, ownership and development of.

The management of railway property built or acquired for operational purposes, such as locomotive and freight depots, workshops, *stations, *signal boxes, and *hotels, was usually the responsibility of the department concerned. Other property, such as offices, employees' *houses, and all 'non-operational' land and buildings, was managed by the estate department, which also purchased and disposed of land, fixed and collected rents, negotiated access agreements, controlled poster advertising hoardings and *station trading, was responsible for the upkeep of deeds and plans, and acted on behalf of the operating departments in property matters of all kinds. Among unusual examples, several companies owned quarries for *track ballast (see STONE, USE OF), while for different periods in 1854–1912 the *Great Western Railway owned or leased three South Wales collieries as a source of locomotive fuel. During World War I the *Great Eastern had a poultry farm on an estate it purchased in Suffolk, to encourage wartime poultry-raising and to provide its hotels with eggs. The estate was farmed until it was sold in 1928. All these activities were managed by the estate departments.

When they were *nationalized in 1948, the railways collectively were probably the country's largest single landowner, other than the Crown, including large and valuable areas in city centres. For instance, in 1900 railways owned 9 per cent of land in the historic centre of *Liverpool; more than in *London or any other large city. By 1985 *British Rail was still among the 12 largest landowners in Britain, although the railway estate was such that as little as 10 per cent could be compared with normal commercial property holdings.

In the past, when railways were contemplating expansion, they tended to quietly buy property as it came on the market, often through intermediaries in order to allay possible competition from rival companies or to prevent inflated prices. There might be no immediate plans, much less parliamentary powers. In 1919, for instance, the *North Eastern Railway started buying land on Tyneside for a series of lines intended to avoid the busy station and junctions in *Newcastle. The *London & North Eastern continued the same policy, although parliamentary powers were still not sought, but then abandoned it in the depression that followed World War I. The land was sold in 1931–51.

In the same period the GWR bought land on which to relocate its coast line in south Devon, but World War II caused the scheme's abandonment, together with one to replace the tortuous Looe branch in Cornwall with a more direct line (see RAILWAYS NEVER BUILT, OR UNCOMPLETED). The aim there was to create a new resort, where land was also bought for a hotel, houses, and a golf course, although only the last was completed. Part of the land was still unsold in 1990, like some near Shap where, long before, purchases had been made for a deviation line to avoid the 1 in 75 gradient. Powers first obtained by the *London & North Western Railway in 1898 were kept alive by the *London Midland & Scottish, but finally lapsed in 1930.

Resulting from fruitless statutory or non-statutory purchases like these, the railways became owners of a wide variety of properties to add to those which they had acquired in earlier times when they often found it expedient to buy property they did not want in order to secure more easily, or at a better price, the land necessary for their lines, but which later on they had been unable to resell (see LAND ACQUISITION; LAND, SURPLUS). They ranged from houses, shops, and pubs to farms, agricultural land, woodland, and marsh, and included such oddities as foreshore rights, pew rents, and bridge tolls. Ownership of *canals and river navigations brought additional varied responsibilities.

The main task of the estate departments was to manage the railways' property effectively, in order to maximize revenue, although the Lands Clauses Consolidation Act, 1845, precluded the development of lineside land for other than railway purposes. The *Metropolitan Railway very successfully overcame this restriction in 1885–7 by setting up a separate property development company (see METRO-LAND). Others were less venturesome. The *Great Central developed land away from the railway at Wembley, and the GWR at Park Royal and Brentford, but it was not until 1933 that the LMS and the LNER gained specific statutory authority to invest in land development in the vicinity of their lines. Both companies set up subsidiaries, but much positive activity was inhibited by the imminence of World War II. The *Southern Railway, preoccupied with *electrification, made no moves in this direction, but the GWR used similar powers obtained in 1936 to greater effect, forming a subsidiary in partnership with an insurance company in order to buy substantial acreages of development land in Berkshire and for the Looe scheme.

The Metropolitan also led in developing station sites, its commercial rents from these sources in 1914 amounting to over £171,000. In 1930 it completed Chiltern Court, a large block comprising flats, shops, a restaurant, and a function hall over and alongside *Baker Street station. Other mainline companies followed slowly. It was not until the 1970s that the newly formed BR Property Board embarked on an ambitious programme of urban site development in partnership with private sector companies, partly on land released by the closure of freight yards and passenger stations after the rationalization of the 1960s, and partly by exploiting the 'air space' over large stations. The first development of this kind took place several years earlier, at *Birmingham New Street, followed by a number of *London stations such as Cannon Street, Victoria, and Charing Cross. During the 1980s property boom this policy was crucial in offsetting BR's operating losses. Under the *privatization dismemberment of BR, property management has been split between Railtrack Property, dealing with operational assets, and a new British Rail Property Board, responsible for residual property, mainly non-operational.   GJB

F. C. Hockridge, 'The Work of the Surveyor's & Estate Department', *GWR (London) Lecture & Debating Society*, 282 (8.3.1934); Monopolies & Mergers Commission, *British Railways Board: Property Activities* (1985); *RS*, chs 7–10.

landowners. Their attitudes to railways were not always as hostile as has been asserted. Many raised bitter opposition and cost the railways far more money than their land was worth. Earlier opposition to *canals on the grounds of lost amenity lessened as they became assimilated into the landscape, but railways were different: they ran in straight lines, were more obtrusive, and were smoky and noisy.

The Atherton and Byrom estates in *Manchester and Salford opposed the intrusion of the *Liverpool & Manchester Railway on their new residential property, and in *London the Duke of Bedford's determination to preserve Bloomsbury was largely responsible for railways from the north not penetrating beyond Euston Road. Opposition was partly a reaction against a changing order, but more a fear of railways' new political and economic power.

There were sound practical reasons, too. Northamptonshire landowners in 1830 summarized their objections thus: unity of farms was destroyed; odd-shaped remnants of severed land were difficult to manage; cuttings could alter water tables and supplies; embankments could affect drainage; the width of land required often made provisions to reduce the impact of severance difficult and inconvenient.

Completion of the *London & Birmingham and *Grand Junction Railways in 1838 marked a turning point, particularly the former, which had paid large sums for land and compensation, with expensive deviations. Yet, despite them and formidable engineering difficulties, the 113 miles of line was built in under 5½ years, clearly demonstrating that although railways might be diverted, delayed, and subjected to extortion, they could not be stopped. Many landowners, therefore, drove the hardest bargains they could.

Unnecessary engineering works like *tunnels were demanded to hide the line from their residences, and stations were refused on their land. The Duke of Wellington objected to one within five miles of Stratfield Saye, although he relented later when the advantages were realized. But whatever the merits or otherwise of bargains made in the two most celebrated cases, those of Lords Harborough and Petre (see LAND ACQUISITION), these men were simply demanding the execution, in the first case, of an Act of Parliament, and in the second of a legally binding agreement. Both were in respect of properties on which large sums had been spent on improvements, and both peers won. A third case, Thomas Grissell's, more closely approached extortion. Having made his money from housing development and railway contracting, he knew every trick and turn of the trade, and made full use of them.

From the outset some landowners saw railways as a means of enhancing their interests. The largest investor in the LMR was the Marquess of Stafford, heir to the Bridgewater estates and industries, whose grandson, the 3rd Duke

of *Sutherland, did much to extend railways in the far north of Scotland at his own expense. In 1840 Sir Peter Hesketh Fleetwood founded Fleetwood and largely promoted the *Preston & Wyre Railway, much of it over his own land, beggaring himself in the process. Far more successfully, the Marquess of Londonderry built Seaham Harbour at the same time, with a railway from his pits that expanded into a self-contained little system. The 7th Duke of Devonshire led the building of the *Furness Railway and *Barrow; the Earls of Yarborough the revival of Grimsby, with a railway leading to it. Huddersfield received a well-planned, handsome town centre from the Ramsden family trustees, who owned most of it, mainly by selling land to the railway at four times the offered figure. It included one of Britain's finest classical stations. The railway in turn strengthened the Ramsdens' position by increasing the value of their land.

When it was clear that railways were becoming established, diehard attitudes started to change. Stations were demanded instead of being rejected, and members of the aristocracy subscribed to railways and joined their boards. Earls of Harrowby graced the *North Staffordshire's; Earl Vane was a director of the *Cambrian; the Marquess of Chandos chaired the *London & North Western in 1853–61, as did the first Lord *Stalbridge, brother of Britain's wealthiest landowner the Duke of Westminster, from 1893 to 1912. In the Highlands, even the implacable Duke of Atholl was won round by the persuasive engineer, Joseph *Mitchell.

Heavily mortgaged landowners were often glad to sell, while others were prepared to wait for their money in return for interest, or accepted shares partly in lieu. Where future advantage was foreseen—but not always realized—land might be sold at low prices, or given for a station. As late as 1912 the new station at Newmarket was built out of a landowner's personal pocket.

See also LAND AND PROPERTY, OWNERSHIP AND DEVELOPMENT OF; LAND, SURPLUS.   GJB

J. T. Ward, 'West Riding Landowners & Railways', *JTH*, 4 (Nov. 1960), 4; D. Whomsley, 'A landed Estate and the Railway: Huddersfield, 1844–54', *JTH* (NS) 2 (Sep. 1974), 4; *RTC*; *RS*, ch. 4.

landscape, railways in the. Although the railways' impact on the landscape depends on the terrain, it is less than that of a modern trunk road and much less than a motorway. Narrower, its grey or brown ballast, steep-sided embankments and cuttings, and brick or stone bridges blend far more easily into the landscape than concrete bridges and tarmac.

Because they hug the slopes in hilly country, railways there are often less obtrusive than on the plain, while local materials used for *bridges and viaducts have assured rapid assimilation into the local scene. Indeed, some viaducts are now considered to enhance it. Monsal Dale in Derbyshire, for instance, and Leaderfoot, near Melrose in the Scottish borders, although disused, have been restored. In the fens of eastern England, however, railways were more intrusive as they cut straight through the pattern of fields, roads, and

language

dykes, rising up to bridge navigable waterways. Aerial photographs show this strikingly. The Axholme *Joint Railway in north Lincolnshire (1904) cut clean across the most important surviving example of the medieval strip system of cultivation.

Coastal lines could change beaches, estuaries, and shorelines, but sometimes made opportunities to reclaim tidal marshes. Although intended near Fleetwood, reclamation was only partly begun when the railway was moved inland, but it happened near Abergele on the North Wales coast where the *Chester & Holyhead Railway built a sea wall behind which to construct its line; at Brading on the Isle of Wight; and along the shores of Morecambe Bay, where the Ulverston & Lancaster (later *Furness) Railway caused over 1,100 acres to be reclaimed in 1857–75. Conversely, its viaduct at Arnside restricted estuarial flow, creating 700 acres of new marsh upstream. The Norwich & Yarmouth Railway (1844) assisted in improving land drainage in Norfolk.

Railways were far more obtrusive in urban areas. Viaducts like those at Stockport, Mansfield, and Durham dominated town centres. South London was criss-crossed by many miles of viaduct, creating huge areas of urban degradation that have been tackled only recently, while Bordesley viaduct, *Birmingham, four tracks wide and nearly a mile long in grim blue brick, straddles streets that still echo Dickensian scenes and portrayals by Doré. A bridge, too, can spoil a fair prospect. Until 1991 one blocked the view of St Paul's up Ludgate Hill; one still does in Bath Street, Leamington Spa, in Friargate at Derby, and Foregate Street, Worcester, although in the last two some amelioration was attempted by erecting decorated arches. The view of Glasgow's Tolbooth Steeple (1626) from Saltmarket is ruined by a latticed railway bridge.

The square that fronted a handsome station, so common in Europe and North America, was unusual in Britain (see TOWNS, RAILWAYS AND DEVELOPMENT OF). Many stations required an approach road, but a fine new street to a station was equally uncommon. The commendably broad Manvers Street, Bath, was built by the *Great Western Railway under the compulsion of its Act, and important new streets were laid out by the town at *Norwich, *Brighton, and *Coventry. A few railway *hotels became prominent landmarks—the North British in *Edinburgh, and the North Western in *Liverpool, for instance—but by and large the physical presence of the railway in the town, unlike the country, either acted as a despoiler or, where it had merit, went unregarded.

See also VANDALISM BY RAILWAYS.   GJB

W. G. Hoskins, *The Making of the English Landscape* (1955), 254–69; D. Turnock, *Railways in Britain: Landscape, Land Use and Society* (1982); *RTC*; D. Lloyd, *The Making of English Towns* (1992 edn.), chs 16 and 17.

language, railways in the English. Railways contributed new words and phrases to the language.

'Stations', meaning fixed stopping-places, appeared on the *Canterbury & Whitstable and *Liverpool & Manchester Railways at their opening in 1830. 'Trains', as a single word on its own ('trains of waggons' had been known before), came into use at the same time. The railways' new machine was being called the 'locomotive', instead of the cumbrous 'locomotive engine', by 1828. It, its *'tender', and the 'signal' that controlled its progress were three words taken from English into every Western European language, virtually unchanged.

Phrases derived from railways also entered the speech of ordinary people. 'Getting up steam', 'running out of steam', 'going off the rails', were all in use by 1850. In Disraeli's *Coningsby* (1844) we find 'trains of thought', and a Manchester businessman can speak of his train as leaving 'at 9.45', an expression found strange by a visitor from the vaguer south. Dickens describes a new pump in his house as 'quite a railway terminus, it is so iron and so big'. In 1876 one of George Eliot's heroines feels herself to be 'treated like a passenger with a third-class ticket'.

We hear railway phrases less often today, and when we meet a new one it is sometimes degrading. 'Passenger'—recognized by everybody—was translated into 'customer' by British Rail in 1988: a plain misuse of language, for a 'customer' also means someone sending a consignment. Significantly, the airlines have not followed suit, and BR itself recognized its folly by continuing to publish a 'passenger timetable'.

The railways also generated a language—or at least a jargon—themselves, used in their building and operation. The origins of some of their words and phrases can be traced back to activities preceding their own. Many of the *navvies who built them had already worked on the *canals, and some of their terms came on to the railways. The 'ganger' or 'gaffer', for example, who superintended the platelayers maintaining the track, had also been heard of in canal-building. Similarly, some railway titles came from road coaches, like the *'guard' and the 'conductor'. The navy made its contribution here too: the 'capstan' used in goods yards; the 'semaphore' (see SIGNALLING); the 'tender', which attended on the locomotive as it had on a man-of-war.

It was the technical operation of running the railway that did most to produce a new branch of the language. Some of the words used there were entirely novel: the *'buffer', for instance; the 'fish-plate' (see TRACK). Signals might be 'on', requiring a train to stop, or 'off', allowing it to pass. Some old words were now put to fresh use. The locomotive had a 'boiler' and a 'firebox'. The track demanded a substantial number of such words: the 'chairs' on which it rested, 'points' (which included a rail tapering to a point), 'safety' or 'catch' points for diverting runaway vehicles off the rails.

A number of words in ordinary use came to be adopted by railwaymen instead of the official ones: for them see NICKNAMES.

See also PUBLICITY AND PUBLIC RELATIONS.   JS

OED; *VR*, chs 6 and 7; B. Disraeli, *Coningsby*, Bk IV, ch. 2; J. Forster, *Life of Charles Dickens* (Everyman edn.), ii, 210. The first glossaries of English railway terms were in F. Whishaw, *Analysis of Railways* (1837), and S. C. Brees, *Appendix to Railway Practice*

(1839). See also ch. 8, 'Language on the Railway', in F. McKenna, *The Railway Workers* (1980).

Lardner, Dionysius (1793–1859), writer. The son of a Dublin solicitor, he studied there at Trinity College. In 1827–32 he was professor of natural philosophy and astronomy in the new University of London, editing his *Cabinet Cyclopaedia* (133 vols., 1829–46) and making a name as a popular lecturer. He eventually settled in Paris, and died at Naples.

Lardner incurred criticism by some rash prophecies in scientific matters; his judgement was always erratic. But he revealed his mind at its best in his *Railway Economy* (1850).

Two things gave it particular value. Lardner treated the subject comparatively: British practices against Belgian, French, German, and American. Moreover, he was helped by an outstanding British railway manager, Mark *Huish, who perceived the value of publicizing some of his own policies through this intelligent and well-known writer.

Lardner supported his arguments by frequent use of *statistics, complaining however of a British insufficiency, here compared with those available for the Belgian railways. Sometimes his over-confidence in his own ideas led him astray. Chapter 14, on accidents, with its 'Plain Rules for Railway Travellers', afforded much merriment from its *naïveté* and hasty conclusions.

The book was respectfully received. But later Lardner's name was ridiculed in connection with railways because of some of his false prophecies, a view that was gradually modified in the 20th century. Alfred Marshall, Sir John *Clapham, Michael Robbins, T. R. Gourvish, and G. R. Hawke were right to take *Railway Economy* seriously.   JS

   G. R. Hawke, *Railways and Economic Growth in England and Wales, 1840–70* (1970), 93–9 (references to all discussions of Lardner).

law of railways. From the Act of Incorporation of the *Liverpool & Manchester Railway in 1826 until the present day, railways—like any other body or individual—have been subject to the statute law of the land, as well as to the common law of contract and tort so far as it has not been amended by statute, either generally or by special Acts relating to railway companies in particular.

Railway law is an amalgam of private and public statute law, and the common law. Much of the statute law relates to the particular rights, powers, duties, and responsibilities of individual railway companies, including the protection of the public; but railways are also liable under the common law of tort where they have breached a general duty of care, or where negligence can be demonstrated, and in cases of breaches of contract. Much contract case law—law evolved by decisions of judges creating precedents for the future —related to the inclusion in contracts of terms set out in other documents. They might determine the exact time when a contract between two parties was actually completed. This was developed particularly in cases relating to railway *tickets. For instance, should a passenger be bound by conditions of carriage not shown on the ticket but to which his attention would have been drawn by the words

'For conditions see back', had such words not been totally obliterated by the date stamp? Relations between railway companies and their employees are also covered by the law of contract, as well as by relevant public statutes relating to employment.

Many recent public Acts of Parliament concerned with transport have been complicated, detailed, long, and political, although originally each individual railway company was granted its statutory rights by a private Act of Incorporation. The current law is to be found in the Railways Act, 1993, which runs to no fewer than 244 pages. The Transport Act, 1947, had vested the *Big Four and a number of smaller companies in a national transport system run by the *British Transport Commission (see NATIONALIZATION). The 1993 Act, and the British Coal and British Rail (Transfer Proposals) Act, 1993, together provide a mechanism whereby the railway system is split up into a large number of individual companies suitable for private ownership (see PRIVATIZATION).

Governments of the day took a keen interest in the operation of the early railways, their *fares policies, and *safety, although the influence of railway company directors in both Houses of Parliament throughout the 19th century meant that attempts to impose regulations were often successfully opposed or watered down. However, *public opinion and the frequency of railway *accidents led to insistent pressure for change (see PARLIAMENT AND LEGISLATION).

The first major statutory incursions were the Railway *Regulation Acts of 1840, 1842, and 1844. These empowered the Board of *Trade to approve the completion of new railway works; to postpone the opening of new lines if the inspectors were not satisfied that they could be operated without danger to the public; and required railway companies to report all serious accidents. Later, under the Regulation of Railways Act 1871, provision was made for the holding of official enquiries into accidents. The Regulation Act of 1868 provided for the compulsory installation of means of *communication between passengers and staff on trains travelling more than 20 miles without stopping, and the Regulation Act of 1889 authorized the Board of Trade to require block *signalling on all passenger lines, the fitting of continuous *brakes, and the interlocking of signals and points.

Parliament was concerned not only for the safety of railway passengers but also for that of other members of the public, as it demonstrated in early Acts of Incorporation by requiring that lines should be securely *fenced. This obligation, intended to protect livestock as much as the public, may have been influenced by the large numbers of *landowners in Parliament, and is not generally imposed elsewhere in Europe. It was extended to all later lines by the Regulation Act of 1842. The standardization of statutory requirements was achieved by the Railways Clauses Acts, 1845 and 1863. Most of the provisions of these two Acts still remain in force. The 1845 Act and its Scottish equivalent provided that their terms should be incorporated in any subsequent Act of Incorporation unless expressly varied or excluded, but the provisions of the 1863 Act have to be expressly included. For example, exceptions from the 1845 Act and some of the provisions of the 1863 Act are specifically referred to in Schedule 2 to the *Channel Tunnel Act, 1987.

The 1845 Railways Clauses Consolidation Act empowered railway companies, among other things, to carry out construction works, alter the course of rivers, build railways on the shore with the consent of the Admiralty, impose penalties on persons not closing gates, use locomotives, convey all passengers and goods that are offered, erect *mile posts at quarter-mile intervals, and impose penalties on passengers knowingly travelling without having paid the fare. The 1863 Act empowered the Board of Trade to require a bridge in place of a level crossing; made provision for the signalling of junctions; and preserved public access to tidal waters and tidal lands.

These provisions relate generally to the powers and duties of railway companies, which themselves needed authority over passengers travelling on the railway system. This was achieved by way of *bye-laws. Statutory powers to make bye-laws were conferred by sections 108 and 109 of the 1845 Clauses Act, and are now set out in section 67 of the Transport Act, 1967, and its later amendments. It states 'The Railways Board and London Regional Transport may make bye-laws regulating the use and working of, and travel on, their railways, the maintenance of order on the railways, and railway premises, including stations and the approaches to stations, and the conduct of all persons, including their officers and servants, while on the premises.' In particular they relate to tickets and the evasion of fares; to interference with or obstruction of the working of the railways; to *smoking; and to the carriage of goods and bicycles. The bye-laws may also lay down fines, and under the 1993 Act these powers are extended to independent railway operators. For a bye-law to be enforceable, it must not be repugnant to general law and it must be certain, *intra vires*, and reasonable. Express powers to enable penalties to be imposed on passengers travelling without a ticket, but not necessarily with intent to avoid payment, have been granted by the *British Rail (Penalty Fares) Act 1989, and the London Regional Transport (Penalty Fares) Act 1992.

In several respects railway companies have also been legally bound by the huge body of case law precedents (common law) evolved over many centuries, although in one or two areas—occupiers' liability, for instance—case law principles have been embodied in statute. This is particularly so, for example, in liability for damage or injury to passengers and others, and in the law relating to carriage of goods or passengers.

Until the Transport Act, 1962, railway companies, like the stage-coaches and stage-wagons before them, were regarded as 'common carriers' and thus under a duty to carry for anyone who paid the carrier's (reasonable) charges. A common carrier's liability was 'absolute' in that it did not depend on negligence; although certain defences—like 'Act of God' or some fault of the consignor or owner of the goods—could be pleaded if the carrier was not himself neg-ligent (see also COMPENSATION). By contrast, private carriers (as the railways have been since 1962) could be selective in the business they accepted; their liability if goods were lost or damaged depended on their negligence. In practice, railway charges were for over a century largely regulated by statute, and nowadays rail freight contracts are mostly standard in form. Terms and conditions are complex, covering matters like risk, negligence, theft 'in transit', wrong delivery, packing, and labelling. Valuable goods, breakables, *dangerous goods, and animals are provided for separately (see FREIGHT TRAFFIC RATES).

The railways as passenger carriers are governed by different rules. A person's right to be carried in a railway train is again contractual. Like most contracts, this is made by 'offer' and 'acceptance', the offer basically being the railway company's timetable, and the acceptance the passenger's purchase of a ticket. There must be valuable 'consideration' on both sides, this being, generally speaking, the payment of the fare by the passenger, and on the railway's part, a promise to convey the passenger to his destination safely, subject to certain conditions embodied in the railway's regulations and bye-laws.

A ticket's purpose is twofold. It acts as a receipt; and, more importantly, is a means by which the railway transmits to the passenger the conditions, under which he will be carried. Two cases from the 1870s—*Parker v. South Eastern Railway* (1877) and *Harris v. Great Western Railway* (1876)—established that this could be done by words like 'for conditions see back' or 'for conditions see the company's timetable'. It made no difference if the passenger was illiterate, as held in *Thompson v. London Midland & Scottish Railway* (1930). If a ticket is, as so often nowadays, issued by a machine, the conditions should be printed by the machine. If the ticket is issued on the train, the passenger's prior acceptance of the conditions may be inferred, as established in *Wilkie v. London Passenger Transport Board* (1947).

Not all lawful passengers need have paid for a ticket. Some may travel gratuitously by licence of the railway. Even children for whom their parents fraudulently omitted to obtain a ticket may be lawful passengers, as in *Austin v. GWR* (1867). So may third (now standard) class passengers travelling 'first', as in *Vosper v. GWR* (1928). However, once the fraud is discovered the railway company can regard the culprit as a trespasser and eject him from the train, using reasonable force.

As common carriers, railways were bound to convey free of charge passengers' luggage reasonably necessary for a passenger's comfort and the purpose of the journey (but not, surprisingly, tools of trade), so long as it was in the form of a box, bag, or parcel (not, say, bicycles or animals). The railway company's liability was absolute, as for freight, and thus was higher than its liability for the passengers themselves, though the courts attempted to restrict the duration of a company's liability to the journey itself and a short time before and after (very short in the latter case). Now that railways are no longer common carriers, such rules do not apply; the position latterly has been governed by British Rail's Conditions of Carriage of Passengers and their Luggage. Liability depends generally on negligence.

Liability for injury and damage caused by railway operations, or in an accident, can arise in one of two ways: either, in the case of fare-paying passengers, by breach of the contract of carriage by failing to carry a passenger safely; or for all lawful passengers, in tort, by the railway company or its servants (but not third parties) being negligent. The standard of care expected of a railway company is the objective one that trains, rolling stock, and railway operations are as safe as they reasonably can be, and free from all detectable faults. It is stricter than the normal, more subjective occupiers' liability (now codified in the Occupiers Liability Act, 1957) which applies to other railway premises. The normal test of negligence is whether the incident was reasonably foreseeable. A railway's duty of care is owed not only to lawful passengers, but at common law to railway servants actually at work, even though the duty of care to employees prescribed by the Health and Safety at Work Act, 1974, is the lesser one of ensuring so far as reasonably practicable the health, safety, and welfare at work of all employees.

The duty of care in a railway context extends to railway platforms, which should not be too high or too low for the carriages, too slippery with oil or ice, or overcrowded; to other railway premises; and to matters like alighting from trains and shutting carriage doors before a train starts. Besides passengers and staff, this duty is owed to others such as neighbouring owners and occupiers affected by things like sparks or smoke from a locomotive. These can constitute a private nuisance, but liability basically still depends on negligence.

Subject to proof to the contrary, negligence can be assumed either by circumstances suggesting negligence on the part of somebody apparently within the railway's control (*res ipsa loquitur*) or by the railway's breach of a duty laid on it by statute (e.g. the Health and Safety at Work Act; provision of continuous brakes; or the requirement to fence the permanent way). Passengers, too, must exercise care, otherwise they may be defendants themselves—for instance if they open a train door and injure someone on a platform—or, if they are plaintiffs in an action, they may have their damages reduced by their own contributory negligence.

If a plaintiff proves his case, the remedy is usually monetary damages for personal loss (injury, pain and suffering, loss of enjoyment of life, etc.), or pecuniary loss (loss of earnings, medical and convalescence expenses, etc.), or both. Rarely, if ever, does an injunction lie against a railway.

Railway case law, whose surface has been barely scratched here, and then only in relation to England and Wales (Scottish law is often different), made a large contribution to the body of common law following the great expansion and popularity of railways in the century after 1830. Specific railway law is primarily statute law. Cases based on railway occurrences have, however, expanded and enriched pre-existing branches of the common law like con-

tract, particularly the law of carriage which derived from the stage-coach era, tort, criminal law (notably that concerning manslaughter), and, in the present age, the burgeoning field of employment law. The advent of railways brought about the Fatal Accidents Act, 1846 (now 1976)—see LORD CAMPBELL'S ACT—enabling relatives for the first time to sue for death caused by a tortious act. It remains to be seen how rail privatization will affect long-established legal principles. Contracts of carriage, passenger or freight, will presumably be made between, and be enforceable by, passengers or consignors and a franchise company; but Railtrack, as the inheritor of fixed railway assets, will surely be involved as a party in tort actions where it is claimed that injury has been caused by or to premises or track.

See also LAWYERS AND RAILWAYS.   CSH and PLS

W. Hodges, *Treatise on the Law of Railways* (1889 edn.); E. E. G. Williams, *An Epitome of Railway Law* (1912); L. James, *The Law of the Railway* (1980) and later supplements; *Halsbury's Laws of England*, esp. vols. 5(1) and 38, and supplements.

lawyers and railways. Railways are creatures of statute law, and lawyers have been associated with railways from their earliest days up to the present time, when numerous firms of solicitors are earning large fees dealing with the complexities of the Railways Act 1994 and the (literally) thousands of agreements that are required for the new contractual links between Railtrack, the train operating companies, and the hundreds of other independent companies that previously made up *British Rail (see PRIVATIZATION).

Although the steam engine and the concept of railways were the work of engineers, surveyors, and businessmen, the British railway system could not have developed without the assistance of lawyers. They have never been popular, and railway lawyers were no exception. Throughout the 19th century, railway promoters and directors objected to the legal costs incurred in the preparation of parliamentary Bills and their subsequent (but not always successful) passage through Parliament, and George *Bradshaw, the editor of a leading railway newspaper—*Bradshaw's Railway Gazette*, published in 1845–72—regularly railed against the legal profession. In 1848 the editor claimed that 'too great dominance of the lawyer breed' was the main source of the troubles faced by railways, and even claimed that the 'conduct of lawyers in reference to railway matters had created a heap of reckless fraud, injustice, misery, ruin and dishonour'.

In 1848, Bradshaw was referring to the losses suffered by many investors after the *Mania period. Although it is true that lawyers were active in the floating of many of the abortive schemes in which money had been invested and lost, it is unfair to blame lawyers alone for the greed and stupidity of investors in lines which never had any chance of success.

Railways were incorporated by private Acts of Parliament (see PARLIAMENT AND LEGISLATION) and constituted as joint-stock companies to which the public were invited to subscribe, and which were themselves created by lawyers. Contrary to the prejudice of Bradshaw, many solicitors and barristers properly provided legal and commercial advice to promoters. Their services were invaluable because the procedures for procuring Private Acts were (and still are) lengthy, expensive, and complicated (see PROMOTION PROCEDURE). Solicitors prepared the company documents, prospectuses, and letters of allotment, and subsequently dealt with the legal requirements in the purchase of the land for the lines, whilst barristers used their advocacy skills to persuade parliamentary committees to approve Bills.

Success in the parliamentary system could not be guaranteed, especially in the face of opposing petitions from competitors and influential *landowners—many of whom were peers or MPs—and even the *Great Western Railway failed in its first attempt to obtain an Act in 1834. The importance of advocacy before House of Commons committees is demonstrated by the fact that the 1834 Bill was considered for no fewer than 57 days; all was not wasted as the committee which considered a new Bill the following year accepted the previous report on the need for the railway and it gained Royal Assent.

A parliamentary bar made up of barristers expert in railway promotions grew up in 1840–70. The adoption of court-room tactics in the committee rooms created a lucrative monopoly for which railway companies had to pay high fees, and generally they were slow to conclude that they could run their systems without the help of independent legal advisers. Francis *Mewburn is considered to be the first railway solicitor (in private practice) and, eventually, rising legal costs led the *London & North Western Railway in 1862 to appoint the industry's first salaried solicitor, James Blenkinsop. The GWR soon followed the LNWR's example, and in 1864 appointed John Young. He remained in the post for 11 years.

The GWR was more successful than the LNWR in opposing claims for personal injury (real or imaginary) by passengers. Lawyers were active in developing the concept of personal injury litigation against railway companies perceived to have unlimited wealth, and received support from judges who realized that the coming of railways had brought the possibility of industrial injuries to the upper and middle classes for the first time. Early cases in 1838 and 1841 (*Bridge v. Grand Junction Rly.* and *Carpue v. London & Brighton Rly.*) resulted in damages being awarded to injured passengers against railway companies on the basis of the presumed negligence of their employees. Opportunities for claims increased after *Lord Campbell's Act of 1846 which enabled immediate relatives of a deceased to claim damages, and after then awards of large sums of damages were regularly awarded against railway companies as litigation increased to the 'most gigantic dimensions' (*Herapath's Railway Journal*, January 1849). In practice, these claims did not exceed 2 per cent of revenue (see also COMPENSATION).

Railway law continued to develop throughout the 19th century through the joint agencies of Parliament and the judiciary, and most (if not all) of the major companies followed the example of the LNWR and the GWR and set up their own legal departments. After nationalization 'The Solicitor' to the Board headed BR's legal department but, with the creation of Railtrack, much of the legal work (and certainly most of the legal property work) has now transferred to this new body. Railtrack also employs solicitors in private practice, as do the train-operating and other new companies formerly part of BR. The legal wheel has turned full circle.

See also LAW OF RAILWAYS. CSH

R. W. Kostal, *Law and English Railway Capitalism 1825–1875* (1994); [F. Mewburn], *The Larchfield Diaries: Extracts from the Diary of the late Mr. Mewburn, the First Railway Solicitor* (1876); MacDermot.

Lee, Charles Edward (1901–83), writer. After a grounding in accountancy, Lee was on the staff of the Tothill Press, publishers of *Railway Gazette, Shipbuilding & Shipping Record, Railway Magazine,* and *Railway Year Book,* from 1925 to 1966. He contributed, mainly anonymously, to all these publications. His articles and books set a new standard of careful analysis and terse and accurate statement for transport, especially railway, history. The most important were: *The Evolution of Railways* (1937; rev. edn., 1943); *The Centenary of '*Bradshaw'* (1940); *Early Railways in Surrey* (1944); *Passenger Class Distinctions* (1946); *The *Swansea & Mumbles Railway* (2nd edn., 1954); *The *Metropolitan District Railway* (1956); and booklets for *London Transport on its rail lines (1957–76). He made valuable contributions in the Newcomen Society's *Transactions* and elsewhere on the origins of railways on Tyneside, and he wrote also about other Welsh railways, horse- and motor-buses, and London tramways.

Always formal in his dress and manners, he was invariably helpful in supplying information from his copious files to other researchers. Apart from transport, he was devoted to St Pancras church, of which he was churchwarden and treasurer; his *St Pancras Church and Parish* was published in 1955. RMR

RM, 130 (1984), 78; *JRCHS*, 28 (1984), 52; personal knowledge.

Leeds, situated where the River Aire leaves the Pennines and starts to enter the Vale of York, has been an important centre of inland communications since the early 18th century. With its abundant supplies of *coal and a thriving textile industry, it became a focal point firstly of inland waterways and then early main-line railways.

Long before the arrival of the first passenger trains it had already established a place in railway history. On 9 June 1758 local colliery-owner Charles Brandling obtained the first Act of Parliament (see PARLIAMENT AND LEGISLATION) authorizing a railway, a 4 ft 1 in gauge double-track *wooden wagonway extending from pits at Middleton to Casson Close near Leeds Bridge. It was opened in the same year, giving Brandling a monopoly of the supply of coal to Leeds and helping to foster the town's rapid industrialization. The *Middleton Railway achieved further fame in 1812 when horse-haulage gave way to the first steam locomotives in the world to be used commercially on rails.

The earliest conventional line into the city was the *Leeds & Selby Railway, opened in 1834 to give a direct

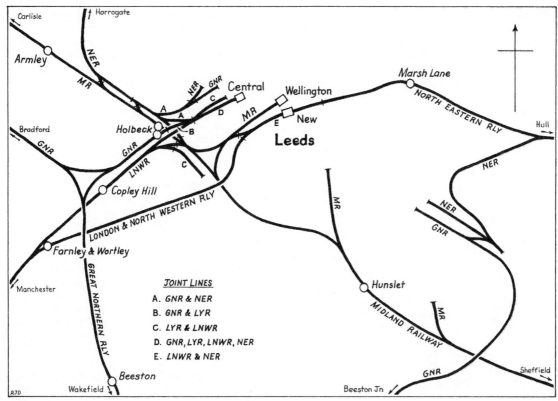

Leeds, 1922

connection with fast packet boats along the rivers Ouse and Humber to Hull. Its Leeds terminus was on the north side of the Aire at Marsh Lane. Just outside the station was the 700-yd Richmond Hill Tunnel (now a cutting), the first in the world through which passengers were drawn by a locomotive. In an attempt to calm terror-stricken travellers, the interior was whitewashed and copper plates installed at the foot of the air shafts to reflect light.

The wave of railway promotion in the mid-1830s brought two key trunk routes into Leeds. In a way remarkably similar to today's M1 motorway, George *Stephenson's magnificent *North Midland Railway swept north from Derby and then ended abruptly at Hunslet Lane almost a mile from the town centre. Opened in 1840, its tracks north of Normanton were from the following year shared with the *Manchester & Leeds Railway, providing a vital east–west link through the Pennines.

A town-centre terminus had to wait until 1846 and the opening of George *Hudson's Leeds & Bradford Railway, following a circuitous but easily graded course from Wellington station along the Aire valley. With the Railway *Mania at its height, plans were drawn up for a 'grand central' terminus costing some £500,000 and catering for the multitude of companies now seeking to serve the town. Protracted disagreements caused the concept to be stillborn, and a much smaller and unprepossessing Central sta-

tion came to be used by the *Great Northern and *Lancashire & Yorkshire Railways. (see also JOINT STATIONS).

There was equal congestion at what was now the *Midland Railway's Wellington terminus, which was also handling *London & North Western and *North Eastern trains. Eventually, these two companies decided to build the adjacent Leeds New station, on an impressive array of 'Dark Arches' straddling both river and canal. Designed by Thomas Prosser (SEE ARCHITECTURE), it covered over seven acres but had no frontage and, in the words of one contemporary historian, 'added nothing to the architectural embellishments of Leeds'.

At the same time the North Eastern constructed a connection to Marsh Lane, thus at last creating a direct route across Leeds to *York and *Hull. Opened in 1869, it cut straight through the graveyard of St Peter's church, the company being compelled to treat bodies reverently, replace gravestones on the embankment slope, and to lay rails on 'India Rubber' and use semaphore signals instead of whistling so as to minimize sacrilegious noise.

Leeds now had a network of radiating railways, which played a vital role in transporting the new and cheap cloths of mungo and shoddy from the neighbouring textile districts. The town was thus able to become a dominant centre of the clothing trade.

It was also famous for building locomotives. After its pioneering triumphs on the Middleton Railway in 1812, *Murray's Round Foundry had gone from strength to strength, reaching its greatest heights in 1840–2 when it turned out 20 7-ft single 'Firefly' class express engines for the broad-gauge *Great Western Railway. Soon it had been joined in Hunslet by such famous firms as E. B. Wilson, John Fowler, Kitsons, Hudswell Clarke, Manning Wardle, and the Hunslet Engine Co. Over 10,000 steam locomotives were produced in these 30 acres of Leeds, the various *works providing employment in the earlier stages of their career for such well-known engineers as J. C. Craven, S. W. *Johnson, Richard Peacock, and David *Joy.

From the 1870s there were few major changes to the railways of Leeds, although the need for a single central station continued to be raised every few years. It was not until 1938 that the first steps were taken when Wellington and New were interconnected to form Leeds City, the project including the rebuilding of the former MR Queens *Hotel in a style described as 'cosmopolitan classic with a decided transatlantic bias'.

A scheme to concentrate all passenger services at an improved City station was finally begun in 1959 but not completed until 1967. Leeds Central was then closed, with few tears being shed, and at the same time two men and a computer took over the work of 17 manual *signal boxes. Leeds City could not be more centrally placed, a fact that has led to a huge growth of suburban services in recent years as road travel has become ever slower. As a result, the station is suffering severe congestion at peak hours. The line from Doncaster and London was electrified in 1990 (see EAST COAST MAIN LINE), and continued to Ilkley, Skipton, and Bradford Forster Square in 1995. DJ

Reg. Hist., viii, ch. 1; S. R. Batty, Rail Centres: Leeds & Bradford (1989); for the various locomotive works, see J. W. Lowe, British Locomotive Builders (1975).

Leeds & Selby, Hull & Selby Railways. In the late 18th century the fast-growing *Leeds textile industry used *Hull as its main port for bringing in wool from the Continent and sending out finished cloth. Although the waterways were improved from 1775 onwards they became inadequate, and the Leeds & Selby Railway was authorized in 1830, connecting with steamboats down the Ouse to Hull.

James *Walker was the engineer. The 17-mile line was opened in 1834, emerging from Leeds through a 700-yd tunnel. The company purchased land wide enough for four tracks from its eastern mouth all the way to Selby, the first railway to do so. Some of Walker's over-bridges remain, though the outer arches were never used, two tracks sufficing for the traffic.

In 1836 the Hull & Selby Railway was authorized, joining it at Selby, with Walker as engineer again. It was 31 miles long (opened in 1840), crossing the Ouse with one of the earliest iron bascule bridges. Although the two lines were worked separately, goods and passengers could now be brought without transhipment from Leeds to the Humber Dock at Hull.

In 1840 the Leeds & Selby was leased to the *York & North Midland Railway, which purchased it in 1844. The other company was also leased to the YNMR in 1845, but otherwise remained independent until the *North Eastern Railway bought it in 1872.

*Whishaw's detailed account of the two railways is valuable, especially his 12 pages on the Leeds & Selby, which list the numbers and wages of staff in each grade, and itemize the whole cost of building and operation. JS

Whishaw, 162–7, 173–84; Tomlinson; Reg. Hist., v, chs 2, 3.

Leeds Northern Railway: originally the Leeds & Thirsk Railway, authorized in 1845, which was conceived both to serve Harrogate and to break George *Hudson's stranglehold on traffic between *Leeds and the north-east, over a roundabout route via *York.

Its route, cutting across east–west valleys, involved some major undertakings for the engineer, Thomas *Grainger. A 23-arch viaduct over the River Aire in Leeds preceded the 2 miles 241 yds Bramhope tunnel, which was almost immediately followed by a curving 21-arch viaduct across the Wharfe. Harrogate was served by a station at Starbeck, whence the line ran by way of Ripon and Melmerby to Thirsk.

The line was opened in 1849. A branch from Starbeck to Knaresborough should have been ready at the same time, but was delayed by collapse of the viaduct over the Nidd. A replacement structure, crenellated in an attempt to blend with the town but described by Nikolaus Pevsner as 'one of the most notable railway crimes of England' (see VANDALISM BY RAILWAYS), was completed in 1851.

By this time the company had achieved steady progress under the guidance of its manager Henry *Tennant and secretary Samuel *Smiles. It now set its sights firmly on the north-east, having obtained sanction for a line from Northallerton to Stockton in 1846 and for a cut-off from Melmerby to Northallerton two years later. These routes began to carry traffic in 1852, the major feature of the extension being a great viaduct over both the River Tees and the old town of Yarm. With 42 arches and a length of 760 yds, it cost £44,500. Grainger again was the engineer.

The previous year the company had declared its greater territorial ambitions in a change of title to the Leeds Northern. With a connection with the *London & North Western Railway at Leeds, and direct access to *Hartlepool's docks at the other end of its system, it now posed a major threat to the established *York & North Midland and *York Newcastle & Berwick Railways.

The result was an outbreak of cut-throat competition which became so ruinous that the companies instead began to talk about amalgamation. After initially rejecting the proposals of the two wealthier concerns, the Leeds Northern directors finally capitulated and the companies amalgamated as the *North Eastern Railway in 1854. DJ

Reg. Hist., iv, ch. 5; Tomlinson.

legislation, see PARLIAMENT AND LEGISLATION.

Leicester. A town of 40,000 people, with a long-established hosiery manufacture, linked by water to the Mersey, the Humber, and London, Leicester got its first railway in 1832: the *Leicester & Swannington, successfully enlarging and cheapening the supply of coal. In 1840 the *Midland Counties Railway arrived, putting the town on to a trunk line from London to Leeds. This became part of the *Midland Railway, which constructed a long branch from Leicester to *Peterborough (1848). The Midland's direct line to London via Bedford was completed in 1868. Direct routes from Leicester to *Birmingham and to *Manchester were opened in 1862 and 1867. The town had become the hub of a very good railway system.

Leicester had an important footwear manufacture. In 1875 George Oliver moved there from Wolverhampton, concentrating entirely on distribution; he had 100 branches by 1899. Rival chains soon appeared, such as Freeman Hardy & Willis. Leicester became a national distribution centre in some other trades too. Both Curry's and Halford's started there, dealing in cycles, in 1884 and 1901.

Although the Midland Railway had the largest share of the town's traffic, the *London & North Western's line to Nuneaton (over which Midland trains ran) took some on to its main line. The *Great Northern arrived in 1882, providing some additional services to and from west Yorkshire; and the *Great Central Railway, supported (not quite whole-heartedly) by the town council, took its Sheffield–London line through in 1899. But the Midland retained its hold. It issued 500,000 tickets at its main Leicester station in 1874 and half as many again in 1913. The railways all carried large numbers of the townspeople for seaside holidays.

Services on the chief line to London were accelerated slightly under the *London Midland & Scottish Railway. In 1937 the LMS speeded up four of its London trains to 60 mph start-to-stop. Services by the ex-GCR line were withdrawn in 1966. In 1994 the fastest took 69 minutes for the 99 miles; the average time was 84.   JS

J. Simmons, *Leicester Past and Present* (1974), i, 155–9; ii, 3, 44, 77. MR passenger bookings: PRO RAIL 491/673, 675.

Leicester & Swannington Railway. This was the first steam-worked public railway, conveying both passengers and freight, in the Midlands: 16 miles long, authorized in 1830, and opened in 1832–3. Its promoters were primarily coalowners in north-west Leicestershire, anxious to get their *coal into Leicester and thence southwards by water to London. They consulted George *Stephenson; his son, Robert *Stephenson, became their engineer and constructed the line. The first six of the railway's eight locomotives were built at the works of Robert Stephenson & Co. in *Newcastle. The 1 in 17 Swannington incline, at the north end of the railway, was worked by a stationary steam engine, built by the Horsley Company of Tipton, near Birmingham. Part of it is at the *NRM.

The railway successfully achieved its main aim as a carrier chiefly of coal, lime, and *stone; coal alone averaged 136,000 tons a year in 1833–45. It provided a regular service for passengers, conveying 77 a day during that time. These figures look modest, but they enabled the company to pay an average dividend of 5 per cent. When the *Midland Railway decided to buy it up in 1845 it could only do so by exchanging each £50 Leicester & Swannington share for a £100 one of its own, on which it was then paying 8 per cent.

Such was the reward of good sense. The company wasted no money on fruitless expansion or expensive alliances with weaker neighbours. It remained what its promoters had always intended, a railway between Leicester and Swannington.   JS

C. R. Clinker, 'The Leicester & Swannington Railway', in *Trans. Leicestershire Archaeological Society*, 30 (1954); reprinted separately, 1977.

leisure, see HOLIDAY-MAKING; TOURISM; SPORTS, SPECTATOR; CINEMA; WEEKEND; EXCURSION TRAIN; THEATRE; RADIO AND TELEVISION.

level crossings occurred on early *tramroads where they crossed roads. Horses and carts had to bump their way over the L-section rails; in time, tramroad Acts like those for the lines between Hereford and Abergavenny (1811–26) stipulated that the rails at crossings must not protrude more than one inch above the road surface. A course of stone blocks along the lower edge created a groove for the wagon wheels. Later a square U-section rail was used.

From the beginning gates were erected to prevent animals being driven over a crossing from straying on to the line. The Whickham (1645) and Tanfield Moor (1772) *wooden wagonways on Tyneside had gated crossings, the latter with gatehouses for attendants. Gates were kept closed across the line, but in 1834 the *Liverpool & Manchester Railway began keeping them closed across the road during the daytime, and bells were provided for road-users to summon the gateman.

The Highways Act, 1839, required railway level crossings on *turnpikes and highways to have gates attended by 'good and proper persons', and the earlier railway Acts usually required them to be kept closed across the road. But the 1842 *Regulation and 1845 Railways' Clauses Acts, recognizing that there could be circumstances where the opposite might be more appropriate, empowered the Board of *Trade to authorize exceptions when it considered them more conducive to public safety, and it eventually became usual for gates to be kept closed across the railway. Turnpike trustees could request screens where there was a risk of horses being frightened by trains. The 1863 Railways' Clauses Act went further in empowering the Board to demand a bridge where considered necessary on grounds of public safety. Compliance was rarely speedy, however, and in 1898, for instance, Warwickshire County Council obtained an injunction against the *London & North Western Railway, imposing a speed limit of 4 mph on trains where its main line crossed the busy Watling Street in Atherstone. Even then a bridge was not erected until 1903.

level crossings

Level crossings are of three main types: foot crossings, accommodation or occupation crossings, and those on public highways. Under the 1845 Act, bridleway crossings required gates, but on footpaths stiles were permitted as an alternative. Since the introduction of higher-speed trains the railway has tried to eliminate foot crossings wherever possible, by diverting footpaths or building footbridges or under-passes. Foot crossings at stations increasingly have miniature lights warning of an approaching train.

Private accommodation or occupation crossings were provided where land was severed by the railway. Under the 1845 Act gates were placed across the road, opening outwards, and the responsibility for closing them was placed on the user, under penalty of 40 shillings; hence the once-familiar notices. Again, high-speed trains and the increasing use of large, heavy machinery has increased the dangers, particularly at crossings with steep approaches which can cause grounding of road vehicles. The Transport & Works Act, 1992, authorizes 100 per cent grants for replacement by a footbridge or underpass, but elimination is not easy, especially where crossings were specified in an authorizing Act. A single owner, for instance, was given the right to 17 crossings in the eight miles of the Hoylake Railway on the flat land of the Wirral. In 1983 the position was eased by the Level Crossings Act which empowered the Department of Transport to authorize changes. In addition to re-alignment where necessary, strict requirements regarding visibility and safety are being applied to the many remaining accommodation crossings. They can include prominent notices, telephones, and, sometimes, miniature warning devices. At a few locations gates have been dispensed with in favour of audible warnings and flashing lights on both road and railway, operated automatically by approaching trains, but only when subject to a severe speed restriction.

Crossings on public highways required supervised gates. Most were operated from an adjacent *signal box, either manually, or by rodding and gearing connected to a large hand-wheel in the box itself, the gates being interlocked with the signals. Busier crossings were often provided with wicket gates as well, which pedestrians could use after the road gates had been closed. Shortly before a train arrived the signalman locked them by pulling a lever. Instead of wickets the *North Staffordshire Railway had curious iron turnstiles at some of its crossings. Less important crossings could be supervised by a crossing-keeper from an adjacent hut or a crossing-house, which was provided with bells and indicators connected to the next signal box in each direction. Interlocked signals might be provided as well.

In the 1950s the traditional heavy wooden gates began to be replaced by continental-style lifting barriers, and in 1961 the first automatic half-barriers were installed, operated by approaching trains. A fatal collision at such a crossing at Hixon, Staffordshire, in 1968, slowed down the programme while safety procedures were reassessed. Remotely controlled barriers are accompanied by closed-circuit television cameras which transmit a display to the signalman, who may be in a box or control centre many miles away. Barriers of both types have large warning notices, flashing lights, an audible warning, and a telephone.

The traditional level crossing was surfaced with wooden sleepers or, in towns, sometimes stone setts. Tarmac has been tried, but makes access to the track more difficult, and tends to break up where it abuts the rails. More recently, modern technological advances have produced heavy sections of thick rubber compound that are smooth, resilient, and removable. Occupation and foot crossings are nearly always still made of sleepers. The 1974 Railways Act authorized 50 per cent grants for the maintenance of public level crossings (following European Commission regulations), in order to compensate the railway for wear-and-tear by road users.

Certain places were notorious for the abundance of level crossings, particularly *Hull, Burton-on-Trent, and Lincoln. Railway closures, rationalization, and new bridges have brought much-needed relief.

An entirely different kind of level crossing is one where two rail routes cross on the level, as at Newark on the *East Coast main line. Others, like Llanelly, Bedford, and Wigston (near Leicester), have disappeared following closures; Retford crossing has been replaced by a bridge. Before 1877 St Nicholas crossing, Carlisle, was notorious for *accidents. After a fatal collision a coroner's jury found the LNWR directors guilty of manslaughter.   GJB

M. J. T. Lewis, *Early Wooden Railways* (1970), 160, 223, 248–50; R. A. Cook and C. R. Clinker, *Early Railways between Abergavenny and Hereford* (1984), 43–4; Thomas, 219; A. Lambert, 'Improving Crossing Safety', in [British Rail] *Property Board News* (Winter 1993), 11.

Lewin, Henry Grote, historian. A Cambridge graduate, one of the first to be recruited to the railway service, a course particularly favoured by Sir George *Gibb of the *North Eastern Railway, Lewin joined that company in 1898, rising to become mineral train superintendent in 1909. Disappointed in his hopes of further promotion, he left the company in 1912, returning to work briefly for the *London & North Eastern Railway in 1923.

His mind was now concentrated chiefly on the historical study of railways. He published two substantial books of great merit: *Early British Railways, 1801–44* (1925) and *The Railway Mania and its Aftermath, 1845–52* (1936). He was the first writer to make a detailed study of the British railway system from parliamentary papers and other contemporary government publications. He wrote lucidly, and his study was well organized. These two volumes still form an indispensable source of knowledge today. A revised edition of the second one, useful chiefly for its correction of some errors of dating, appeared in 1968.   JS

Sir R. Wedgwood's brief foreword to the 1936 edition of *The Railway Mania*; see also C. H. Ellis, 'Lewin Papers concerning Sir George Gibb', *JTH* 5 (1961–2), 226–32.

Liddell, Charles H. (*c*.1812–94), civil engineer. After working on the *North Midland Railway under George *Stephenson, Liddell was one of the *surveyors involved in the affray at Saxby on the *Midland Railway's Syston–Peterborough line in 1846 (see RIOTING). At this period he also worked with Robert *Stephenson on schemes in the south Midlands before becoming chief engineer on the MR's Leicester–Hitchin line of 1857, and the Bedford–Radlett section of its London Extension of 1868.

Liddell spread his activities widely. In 1851 he was engineer for the Newport Abergavenny & Hereford Railway and its Taff Vale extension—on which he selected T. W. *Kennard's design for the Crumlin Viaduct (see BRIDGES AND VIADUCTS); in 1853 for the Worcester & Hereford Railway, and other lines.

In 1873–93 he worked as consulting engineer for the Manchester Sheffield & Lincolnshire (see GREAT CENTRAL) and *Metropolitan Railways under the chairman, Edward *Watkin. He built lines for the MSLR in Nottinghamshire, and surveyed routes for its London Extension and for the Metropolitan's proposed line to meet it. He relinquished his position over dissatisfaction with Watkin's terms for the post of engineer for the MSLR scheme.

Jointly with Lewis Gordon and R. S. Newall, Liddell patented wire ropes, being concerned with manufacture and laying of over 4,500 miles of marine cable. In the 1860s he developed a system of lighthouse and marine telegraph stations, and was also director of a railway in northern Italy.

GJB

T. Constable, *Memoir of Lewis D. B. Gordon* (1877); *The Engineer*, (24 Aug. 1894); MacDermot; Dow; J. Gough, *The Northampton and Harborough Line* (1984); A. A. Jackson, *London's Metropolitan Railway* (1986).

lifts and escalators. Lifts were first used by railway companies for luggage and goods (typically between platforms and a footbridge or subway in most large stations) and for transferring wagons into city goods *stations built into a confined space below an elevated railway. The steam-powered wagon lift at *Glasgow Bridge Street (1840) was an early example, but *hydraulic power was soon preferred.

The earliest railway applications of passenger hydraulic lifts were in station *hotels, the Grosvenor Hotel at *Victoria station (1861) having one of the first in London. The first *underground station lifts—for London's Tower Subway (1870)—were unsuccessful, but the *Mersey Railway (1886) proved their suitability for London's proposed tube railways, which could not have been built without them. By 1900 electric lifts were normally selected, except for very large lifts or where there was already a hydraulic supply. The Otis Elevator Company supplied no fewer than 140 electric lifts to the *Underground Electric Railways Company for its three tube lines opened in 1906–7. 'Landing control' of lifts, whereby one attendant at the top and bottom landings could control several lifts, was introduced in 1914, but the first fully automatic lifts, at Earl's Court, did not come into use until 1932, following a 1928 experiment at Warren Street.

The first railway escalator, at Seaforth Sands, *Liverpool Overhead Railway (1900–6), and the unused spiral variant at Holloway Road (*Piccadilly Line, 1906), were both of the Reno inclined conveyor type. Stepped escalators were installed at Earl's Court in 1911 and were immediately successful; two escalators had the capacity of five lifts and they did not require an attendant. All tube stations built after 1912 had escalators only. The early type had flat treads which disappeared under a diagonal balustrade or 'shunt'; passengers stepped off sideways. The 'comb' type with slatted treads, from which passengers could step straight off, was first installed at Clapham Common in 1924.

Escalators have been increasingly incorporated in modernized and rebuilt *British Railways stations since the 1960s. The stepless 'travolators' at the *Waterloo & City line's Bank station (297 ft long, inclined at 1 in 7) were installed in 1960. Hydraulic lifts are again in vogue and have been installed at the new *Waterloo International station (1994).

GAB

I. McNeil, *Hydraulic Power* (1972), 111–16; O. Carter, *An Illustrated History of British Railway Hotels 1838–1983* (1990), 62–74; C. E. Box, *Liverpool Overhead Railway, 1893–1956* (1959), 42–4; D. F. Croome and A. A. Jackson, *Rails Through the Clay: A History of London's Tube Railways* (1993 edn.).

light railways. The object of a light railway was to open up a rural or undeveloped area at minimal cost. Although successful overseas, on both standard and narrow *gauge, few of them flourished in Britain.

Strangely, there was no official definition of a light railway, but it can be described as a railway built to a lower standard than a main line, with lighter engineering and *track, and free of the usual obligations regarding *signalling, *fencing, *level crossings, *station platforms, etc., but with restrictions imposed on speed and on the weight of locomotives and rolling stock, the object being to provide benefit to a poor district economically and cheaply.

The reason for their comparative failure in Britain was twofold. Firstly, agricultural decline gathered pace in the 1880s, by which time much of the country was well-served by a network of railways and branches built to main-line standards, so that the demand for better rural transport came from relatively few areas. Secondly, railway companies and the Board of *Trade by then had entrenched ideas about how railways should be built and equipped. Reduced standards were considered to be retrograde. Had light railways developed earlier their history might have been very different.

The first legislation that permitted some relaxation of standards was the Railway Construction Facilities Act, 1864. It allowed authorization by a Board of Trade certificate instead of a specific Act, thereby considerably reducing preliminary expenses (see PROMOTION PROCEDURE), but still subject to parliamentary approval and to the agreement of all interested parties such as *landowners. It was largely ineffective. The 1868 *Regulation Act was the first to refer specifically to a 'light railway': one authorized by the Board of Trade, with axle loads restricted to 8 tons, and a maximum speed of 25 mph. Because of the difficulty in gaining general consent, or opposition from existing railways, its effect was no more positive. A few lines were built, like the Easingwold and *Southwold Railways, while others such as the Glyn Valley Tramway were constructed under the 1870

*Tramways Act whereby they all bore the full cost of enabling Acts and buying land. The Wisbech & Upwell Tramway, built by the *Great Eastern Railway, was one that was steadily profitable.

In 1894 a Board of Trade conference on the matter received reports on light railway development overseas. Public bodies joined in the debate, and a generally favourable opinion led to the Light Railways Act, 1896, which was intended to facilitate construction to a much greater extent (see also PARLIAMENT AND LEGISLATION). Its main provisions were as follows.

1. It established a Light Railway Commission of three members to receive applications and determine their worth.
2. A simplified procedure was laid down to replace an authorizing Act, whereby the Commissioners could grant a Light Railway Order (LRO) subject to the Board of Trade's approval of the technical aspects.
3. Local authorities were authorized to participate in promotion, and to make loans or subscribe capital. Where money was advanced, a Treasury loan of 25 per cent was also available.
4. The Treasury itself could make grants or loans of up to 50 per cent of the capital cost if the Board of Agriculture certified that a light railway was necessary to develop a district, provided that co-operation of all interested parties was assured. £1 million was allocated for these purposes.
5. The Commissioners and the Board of Trade were granted powers which, in effect, allowed them to relax the provisions of general railway legislation.
6. Compulsory purchase of land was authorized (see LAND ACQUISITION). Landowners' compensation was to take account of benefits the railway would bring.
7. Existing railways could be converted to light railways by applying for an Order.

In 1898–1918 there were 687 applications, covering a total of 5,015 miles. Many were impracticable. From the 2,100 miles authorized only 900 were built, 350 miles of which were *street tramways because local authorities had been quick to use the Act to gain powers to build or extend their systems, a purpose for which it was never intended. Out of the remaining 550 miles, three-fifths were accounted for by lines built or converted by main-line companies, of which 80 miles received grants and 22 miles received loans. Only 23 miles of purely independent railway were built with loans, and only £203,000 was spent out of the Treasury's £1 million.

In practice, the Board of Trade was reluctant to abandon traditional attitudes, particularly regarding safety, despite the low speeds, so that many lines were obliged to provide level-crossing gates, signals, and full-height platforms. The Dornoch Light Railway in Scotland, for example, had many onerous conditions in its LRO of 1902, incurring heavy expenditure. It was worked by the *Highland Railway. Yet the *Great North of Scotland Railway's branch from Fraserburgh to St Combs, authorized in 1899, was allowed to be unfenced provided that the locomotives had cowcatchers fitted. The Wick & Lybster line, also worked by the Highland, was authorized in 1903 with a capital of £72,000, of which £25,000 was a Treasury grant. The bulk of the

remainder came from the HR, Caithness County Council, and the Duke of Portland.

Main-line railways not only promoted light railways but agreed to work some of the independents, and if they encountered financial problems—as most of them did—might take them over. The Kelvedon Tiptree & Tollesbury Pier Light Railway, for example, was worked by the Great Eastern company from the outset. The *Cambrian Railways worked or acquired several light railways, such as the Mawddwy which was built as a conventional line but was taken over and run under a LRO in 1910; and the Van Railway which closed in 1893 but was reopened for working by the Cambrian in 1896. It remained nominally independent until the 1923 *Grouping, with others like the Cleobury Mortimer & Ditton Priors Light which was fully independent until it was placed under the *Great Western. The Mid-Suffolk was left out of the Grouping, but was quickly taken over by the *London & North Eastern Railway.

Because independent light railways on the whole were poorly planned and equipped, usually relying on second-hand materials and rolling stock, progress in building them was slow. In their final report before their duties were taken over by the new Ministry of Transport in 1921, the Commissioners significantly commented that *road transport was becoming very competitive. In the event, only five more LROs were granted.

Most of the independent lines were penurious in the extreme, weighed down by over-capitalization resulting from unnecessarily elaborate construction and working methods, high interest charges, and unreliable second-hand equipment. After World War I road competition made matters worse, and when things wore out more were bought second-hand or a line simply closed down. Consequently light railways gained a reputation for ancient rolling stock and a certain decrepit, rustic charm. Those belonging to main-line companies were better-kept and lasted longer, their losses hidden in the overall financial picture.

By World War II only 16 independents were still operating. Three survived to be nationalized in 1948: the East Kent, Kent & East Sussex, and Shropshire & Montgomeryshire. Four of the remaining five independents soon closed. The other, the Derwent Valley Light Railway in Yorkshire, lasted until 1988. One of the most successful, it probably most closely represented the original light railway concept. One standard-gauge line, the Kent & East Sussex, has been reopened by a *preservation society.

Two names stand out in association with light railways. An ardent believer in them, Col. H. F. Stephens brought together a group of 13 under the name of Associated Railways which he ran from an office in Tonbridge. He also became engineer and locomotive superintendent of the narrow-gauge Welsh Highland and *Festiniog Railways in 1923, the year in which the former was completed and the latter granted a LRO. He exercised strict economy, and bravely experimented with an extraordinary collection of petrol *railcars for passenger traffic on several of his lines, although when they wore out he reverted to steam.

Sebastian Meyer promoted, built, and in some cases operated eight light railways in Yorkshire, Lincolnshire, and Northumberland. A ninth, the Dearne Valley Railway, was a conventional double-track line which included an impressive viaduct at Conisbrough. Apart from the North Sunderland Light they were all absorbed into other railways at the Grouping.

The term 'light railway' is perpetuated in the *Docklands Light Railway in London, and *Light Rapid Transit systems in some cities. Although their purpose is different, the principle of lightweight track, structures, and vehicles is the same. LROs, too, still have a purpose: they are used by preservation societies to gain authorization to operate restored railways.

See also NARROW-GAUGE RAILWAYS.   GJB

W. J. K. Davies, *Light Railways* (1964), chs 1 and 3; J. S. Morgan, *The Colonel Stephens Railways* (1978); Meyer: A. L. Barnett, *The Light Railway King of the North* (1992); P. Bosley, *Light Railways in England and Wales* (1990); numerous books on individual light railways.

Light Rapid Transit systems. Apart from *Blackpool, electric trams disappeared from British streets in 1962. However, they continued to be developed in urban areas in Europe and elsewhere as Light Rapid Transit systems (LRT), employing single-deck *light-rail vehicles for fast, frequent services, with unmanned stations, automatic ticket machines, and zoned fares. There are now over 300 systems throughout the world, and most major continental cities have one, variously combining street, underground, and open reserved tracks.

Britain's first was the Tyne & Wear Metro, opened in stages by the *Passenger Transport Authority (PTA) from 1980 onwards, running on former *British Rail tracks north and south of the Tyne, connected by a new bridge and tunnels beneath central *Newcastle. At Central station a circular route serving Whitley Bay, Tynemouth, and North Shields now meets lines to St James, Gateshead, Jarrow, and South Shields. Stations are under surveillance from a control centre by closed-circuit television, the first in Britain. Tyne & Wear was followed in 1987 by the *Docklands Light Railway in London, unique in having driverless trains controlled by computer.

The opening of *Manchester Metrolink in 1992 marked the first return to street *tramways in Britain. It uses former BR tracks from Bury to Victoria station, whence there is street running to Piccadilly station and to St Peter's Square, where the former BR Altrincham line is joined (see MANCHESTER SOUTH JUNCTION & ALTRINCHAM RAILWAY). Use of BR meant conversion of two different electrical systems to 750 V dc overhead for Metrolink. The two-car articulated sets were built in Italy and can be operated in multiple, with automatic coupling and uncoupling from the driver's cab. Low platforms are provided at street stops, and several streets have been declared 'tram-' or 'tram-and-bus-only'. The system was built for Greater Manchester PTA on the 'design, build, operate, and maintain' (DBOM) principle with some government funding under Section 56 of the 1963 Transport Act (see SUBSIDIES), and an operating com-

pany represents the PTA, DBOM consortium, and Greater Manchester Buses (included for their expertise). The system has been a great success, and extensions are planned.

*Sheffield followed in 1994–5 with its equally successful Supertram system, where street running is much more extensive: about half of the 18 route miles, all of which have been built new, some alongside BR, and including two major viaducts. Inevitably in a hilly city there are steep gradients, up to 1 in 10. Lines run from the city to Meadowhall shopping centre, where there is a BR interchange, to Hillsborough, and Halfway near Masborough. The system is operated by South Yorkshire Supertram Ltd, a wholly owned subsidiary of the PTA. The three-car articulated vehicles, built in Germany, are among the largest of the kind in Europe.

A number of other British cities have similar plans, some well advanced, particularly *Nottingham and *Bristol. At *Birmingham the first section of the Midland Metro is nearing completion. An ambitious 18-mile scheme named 'Tramlink' is approaching construction, centred on Croydon with lines to Wimbledon, Beckenham, and New Addington. It combines the conversion of existing rail routes, street running, use of disused BR lines, and entirely new routes. LRTs are also proposed elsewhere in the London area.   GJB

Light Railway Transport League, *Light Rapid Transit: The City System* (c.1979); P. Waller (ed.), *Light Rail Transit* (1991); Manchester: E. Ogden and J. Senior, *Metrolink Official Handbook* (1992); Sheffield: M. Harris, 'Sheffield Supertram', *Modern Railways*, 51 (May 1994), 548; Croydon: M. Harris, 'London to Widen Transport Systems', *Modern Railways*, 52 (June 1995), 561.

literacy. It is thought that in the 1840s some 30 per cent of British people could not read. By 1900 total illiteracy had become very uncommon. What part did railways play in bringing about this change? This question begs two more. How far did railways insist upon literacy as a qualification for entering their service? And what assistance did they afford to any of their employees who wished to acquire or improve a capacity to read and write?

Literacy was demanded of some railwaymen from the beginning: all those, for instance, who handled money and had to account for it, such as booking-clerks and goods-clerks. But it was unnecessary for *platelayers, providing that they worked under a literate supervisor who, on some railways, was told to read the instructions applicable to each piece of work aloud to the men engaged in it: on the Edinburgh & Northern Railway (see EDINBURGH PERTH & DUNDEE) in 1847, on the *Bristol & Exeter as late as 1864.

Between these two groups of railwaymen lay others, where the need for literacy appeared uncertain and was debated by experts. While C. H. *Gregory took it as a matter of course in 1840 that engine drivers on the *London & Croydon Railway should be able to read and write, *Brunel—for rather curious reasons—positively preferred those who could not. Before 1860, however, accident reports show that books of rules and regulations (see BYE-LAWS) were commonly being issued to them, to which obedience was demanded. As for station staff, a random sample of 87 men, taken on the *London Brighton & South Coast Railway in 1856, shows that all were literate.

At the companies' *works the men themselves took a hand by making educational provision, inside or close by, based on examples set by the Mechanics' Institutes (see EDUCATION). These emerged at *Crewe, *Swindon, and *Derby from 1843 onwards and some elsewhere, developing, with the libraries they all included, into valuable centres of adult education.

The Education Acts of 1870 and 1876, making primary education compulsory, began to have discernible effects in British society from the mid-1880s onwards, and railway employees who could not read must then have dwindled to a very small number. However, each boy appointed to Swindon works had still to declare that he would obey the rules and regulations there, which he had read 'or have had read to me'. That last proviso disappeared only in 1904.

Though the railway companies are not known to have made any special efforts to teach reading as one of the 'three Rs', except through the primary schools they opened at their important centres (at least 14 of them were established in 1840–59), they came to do a good deal towards improving the quality of literacy and extending its scope through their furtherance of technical education, in which they collaborated with some local authorities after the reform of local government in 1889.

Perhaps this subject, for which we have little precise evidence, can be best summarized in this way. The railways had secure employment to offer, at adequate wages. The multiplicity of the tasks that their servants had to perform brought a need for them to read and write, much more imperatively than mill-hands or miners. The companies were in a position to dictate here, and they did so. Thereby they quietly helped to raise the value set upon literacy in Victorian Britain.

See also EMPLOYMENT.   JS

VR, 186–90; K. Hudson, *Working to Rule* (1970), 35, 113; P. W. Kingsford, *Victorian Railwaymen* (1970), 73.

literature, children's railway. The Victorians often used railways as analogies in 'improving literature' for children. One of the first books with no deliberate moralizing was R. M. Ballantyne's *The Iron Horse*, which went through no fewer than 11 editions in 1871–9. In a chapter in Lewis Carroll's *Through the Looking Glass* (1871), Alice meets an extraordinary group of fellow-passengers in a railway carriage. E. Nesbit's *The Railway Children* (1906) went into a second edition in 1944, although it was its revival on film and television in the 1970s that made it probably the best-known of all children's railway stories.

From about 1900 instructive non-fiction works became popular. J. R. Harden's *Boys' Book of Locomotives* (1907) and *Boys' Book of Railways* (1909) each contained over 100 illustrations, and H. Golding's *Wonder Book of Railways for Boys and Girls* (1911) reached an amazing 21st edition in 1950. G. Gibbard Jackson was a popular and prolific writer in the 1920s.

Several well-known technical authors essayed children's books, including C. J. *Allen—'Uncle Allen' in *The Children's Railway Book* (1930)—O. S. *Nock, and Brian Reed who wrote two volumes on railways in the *Boys' Power and Speed Library* series in 1949–50. Allen also wrote *Famous Trains*, published by Meccano Ltd in 1928, whose *Meccano Magazine* from 1916 to 1989 carried authoritative articles on railway topics. At least one noted railway writer produced fiction for teenagers or adults. In 1939 C. Hamilton *Ellis wrote *The Grey Men*, an adventure story set on the West Highland Railway (see NORTH BRITISH RAILWAY). He followed it with *Dandy Hart* (1947), a historical novel based on the *London Brighton & South Coast Railway and others in 1830–60.

The train-spotting hobby can be said to have begun with Ian Allan's celebrated *ABC* booklets listing locomotive numbers and types, starting with the *Southern Railway in 1942. They were valuable for reference, too, and recently have been reprinted.

In the 1930s railway fiction for older children tended to diminish. There were a few like S. T. James' *Railway Stories* (c.1930), but generally railways featured more in books for young children. Rupert Bear frequently travelled by train, unlike Christopher Robin and Winnie the Pooh, and since World War II the market has been dominated by the phenomenal success of the Revd W. Awdry's *Thomas the Tank Engine* series. Beginning in 1945, it has accumulated 26 titles, appeared on television and in videos, and been translated into eight languages, including Gaelic, Welsh, and Japanese.

Numerous other popular children's titles have included D. Ross's *Little Red Engine* series (1956–69), the award-winning author Barbara Willard's *Stop the Train*, William Mayne's *Tiger's Railway* (1991), and Penelope Farmer's *The Runaway Train* (1980) which accurately portrayed a day excursion from London to Shoeburyness in 1947. The well-known children's writer Elizabeth Beresford foreshadowed the reopening of lines in *The Secret Railway* (1973).

See also LITERATURE, RAILWAYS IN ENGLISH; LITERATURE OF RAILWAYS.   DBi

literature, railways in English. The word 'railways' first appears in any literary work of importance in 1816, at the opening of T. L. Peacock's novel *Headlong Hall*, where they figure with *canals and *tunnels in an optimist's view of current 'remarkable improvements'. The first great writer who concerned himself with them was Sir Walter Scott, who joined in the promotion of several lines in Midlothian, Selkirk, and Roxburgh in 1820–5, investing £1,500 in one, which he lost.

The chief pioneers of the mechanically worked railway, the *Stockton & Darlington and *Liverpool & Manchester, were a long way from London, the centre of English literary life, where railways made little direct impression before 1836, when its first line was opened, the *London & Greenwich.

The young Dickens begins to refer to railways in 1836–7. A chapter in *Pickwick Papers* bears a title that includes the phrase 'the Course of True Love is not a Railway', and a 'locomotive engine' is mentioned in chapter 32. At the same time, in a satire on the British Association for the Advancement of Science, he throws out the idea of a railway running underground. He often introduced railways into his novels (particularly *Dombey and Son*, 1848), but never liked them. He disapproved of the *speculation they encouraged, and he always considered them dangerous. (He was in a bad *accident himself in 1865.) However, he could not have lived the life he did without them, especially when he was giving his public readings all over Britain and in America from 1858 onwards. He evoked railway scenes splendidly in some short pieces: 'A Flight', for instance, 'The Lazy Tour of Two Idle Apprentices', and 'Mugby Junction'.

Thackeray had something to say about speculation; he speculated himself, unsuccessfully. Trollope used railways and their stations as settings for several scenes in his novels: *Orley Farm* (1862), *The Belton Estate* (1866), and especially in his closely observed account of Willesden ('the Tenway Junction') in *The Prime Minister* (1876). They figure importantly in his ferocious satire *The Way We Live Now* (1875), though here it is a huge foreign railway hatched by his villain-hero Melmotte (modelled on Baron Albert Grant), into which gullible British investors get drawn. Like Dickens, Trollope was a constant railway traveller. Many of his novels were written in trains.

The construction of railways interested some Victorian writers. A young engineer employed in it figures in Mrs Gaskell's *Cousin Phillis* (1864). George Eliot recollected the survey for the *London & Birmingham Railway through Warwickshire in the 1830s, and the bewilderment it produced is recalled vividly in *Middlemarch* (1872). In an essay of 1856 she had traced the impact that railways were making on English people's thought and language: what she called 'the picture-writing of the mind'. That appeared several times in her last novel *Daniel Deronda* (1876). But Peacock, having noticed railways so early, came to detest them, attacking them towards the close of his last novel *Gryll Grange* (1860), above all for the horrible accidents they occasioned, arising from 'the insane passion of the public for speed'.

Ruskin shared that disapproval, and expressed it repeatedly. But his loathing of railways was above all aesthetic; he saw them as ravagers of the landscape, and he denounced their crimes passionately in brilliantly forceful language wherever he saw them, in Derbyshire or Furness or Switzerland. Even he, however, was compelled to salute one 'entirely divine' railway journey from Aix-les-Bains to Annecy in 1882.

Among the great Victorian writers the railways never found one staunch admirer or sympathetic defender; none seemed grateful for the resultant benefits, which simply came to be accepted, without remark, as part of the machinery of 'progress'. The means by which they were produced were merely technical, uninteresting to the literary public, which thought about quite different matters.

Some change, however, may be discerned from the 1870s onwards, coming from writers who had grown up with railways and saw them as part of the ordinary equipment of life. They were realists, and railways entered readily enough into the 'picture-writing' of their minds.

Railways were frequently in the mind of Thomas Hardy. An architect when he was young, he brought an informed eye to their construction, showing it memorably in his novel *A Laodicean* (1881), where his hero stands in a recess inside a tunnel while a train runs past, rejecting the doctrine that 'science, steam, and travel must always be unromantic and hideous'. But Hardy had an eye for something else about railways too: brief episodes figuring in them or on them, which he records in poems again and again. He called them 'Moments of Vision': 'Midnight on the Great Western', for example; 'The Waiting-Room'; 'At the Railway Station, Upway'; 'A Parting Scene'.

Robert Louis Stevenson stood close to railways by inheritance, for he came of a family of engineers, one of whom had published a book of essays on them in 1824. He never wrote anything about railways as machinery. But journeys made on them interested him very much, as he showed in two poems, in his essay 'Ordered South', published in *Across the Plains* (1892), and in his queer, entrancing novel *The Wrong Box* (1889), written in collaboration with his stepson Lloyd Osbourne. Who but he would have dared to publish a realistic account of a railway accident that was tinged with comedy? It was set on the *London & South Western Railway, known to him from residence in *Bournemouth. Again in 1889, Jerome K. Jerome guyed the ludicrous muddle of that company's *Waterloo station in *Three Men in a Boat*. And presently Kipling wrote his tale 'My Sunday At Home', a wry account of a crawling journey made on that day, again on the LSWR.

By that time one novelist had seized on railways as part of the structure of his realistic fiction. Arnold Bennett, when young, looked closely at the *North Staffordshire Railway, as he did at most things in his native Potteries. In *The Old Wives' Tale* (1908) he recorded traditions of the building of the Loop Line through Hanley and Burslem, some 40 years earlier. He repeatedly depicted *Stoke-on-Trent station as the setting for arrivals and departures, giving attention to the way in which it was operated (as in his stories 'Beginning the New Year' and 'The Death of Simon Fuge'), treating railways as an essential part of the community he portrayed.

One or two minor poets of the late 19th century wrote a little about railways, particularly John Davidson, who depicted the castaways hanging about the London stations, as well as desperately anxious suburban travellers 'a-scheming how to count ten bob a pound'. But he gracefully acknowledged the chance the *Great Eastern Railway gave him to spend an October day in Epping Forest, and he wrote a good comic poem about the tangle of stations at *London Bridge. Then, around the turn of the century, some younger writers produced delightful sketches of railways—'Q' and Max Beerbohm, for example—and several wrote good poems, at least two of which are affectionately remembered still: Siegfried Sassoon's 'Morning Express' and Edward Thomas's 'Adlestrop'.

Railways played a considerable part in detective fiction. To Sherlock Holmes they were an essential part of his work, Conan Doyle's observation of them (not always exactly correct) appearing, for example, in 'Silver Blaze' and 'The Bruce-Partington Plans'. Victor L. Whitechurch made a name with his mystery stories set on railway lines, devised with close and accurate observation. A better writer, Freeman Wills Crofts, was a former railwayman himself, displaying expert knowledge in 'Crime on the Footplate' and 'The Mystery of the Sleeping-Car Express', and later in his novel *Sir John Magill's Last Journey.*

In the 1920s and 1930s railways started to become romantic, an element in a vanishing past. Sassoon touched on it delicately in his poem 'A Local Train of Thought', with its closing line: 'That train's quite like an old familiar friend, one feels'. Edward Thomas's *Adlestrop* evoked a Cotswold station in summer. Presently some writers were reflecting on what railways had meant to them in their lives, notably John Betjeman, who had always enjoyed railways, and wrote an occasional poem about them. They figured in his autobiographical poem *Summoned by Bells* (1960), and from then onwards they became more prominent in his work; he even wrote a book about the London stations. He had a strong liking for the *Metropolitan Railway, shown in his 'Metropolitan Railway; Baker Street Station Buffet' and in his still-celebrated BBC television programme on *Metro-land.

No other English poet of the time wrote so much about railways. But a good many other writers devoted poems or sketches to aspects of their operation: T. S. Eliot, for example, W. H. Auden, A. L. Rowse, Patricia Beer, Philip Larkin. They figure frequently in the novels of P. G. Wodehouse —as in the opening of chapter 8 of *Uncle Fred in the Springtime*, set at *Paddington station. So also in a very different mood, grim and tense, is John Wain's novel *The Smaller Sky* (1967).

The best means of investigating this literature—scattered, diverse, and often rewarding—is a good anthology. There have been several. One that is particularly rich in extracts from the literature of the later 20th century is *The Train*, by Roger Green (1982).

The railways also played a direct and important part in literary life by transforming book production in Great Britain. Before 1840 almost all of it was undertaken in London, Oxford, Cambridge, and Edinburgh. But the growth of the railway system soon allowed publishers to send work to printers at a distance overnight; cheaply too, by the penny post (see POST OFFICE). By the 1850s some London publishers were regularly using printers 25 miles away at Hertford, even 100 miles away at Frome. Presently London printers, working then in very cramped premises, began to open branches or even to move their works out of London altogether, for example to Aylesbury, Beccles, and Fakenham.

The speed of book production that the railways made possible seems incredible today. George Eliot finished her novel *Felix Holt* on 31 May 1866. She was living in London, and the book was printed and published in Edinburgh. The final proofs had to travel 800 miles for her correction (Edinburgh–London–Edinburgh). But the book was in the shops within 12 days of its completion.

Like so many of the railways' services to the community, this one excited no remark. But they alone made possible the enormous increase in the dissemination of English literature during the Victorian age.

See also LITERATURE OF RAILWAYS; LITERATURE, CHILDREN'S RAILWAY.   JS

T. L. Peacock, *Headlong Hall and Gryll Grange*, ed. M. Baron and M. Slater (1987). On Scott see M. Robbins, *Points and Signals* (1967), 40–6; for George Eliot's 'picture-writing' see her *Essays*, ed. T. Pinney (1963), 267; for Ruskin's 'entirely divine' railway journey, his *Works*, ed. E. T. Cook and A. Wedderburn (1903–12), vol. xxxiii, p. xliii; for the publication of *Felix Holt*, G. S. Haight, *George Eliot* (1968), 387–8. Detective stories are well treated by P. L. Scowcroft in *JRCHS*, 33 (1977), 87–93. Individual poems cited here can usually be found in collected editions of the writers' works.

literature of railways. The railways called forth a literature of their own. Hardly any of it contributed to what is conventionally called English literature (see the preceding article). But it set some good standards in the interpretation of the railways' affairs to their customers and to the general public, and in recording their history.

One of the earliest general accounts of railways was in German by two Prussian mining engineers, C. von Oeynhausen and H. von Dechen, who compiled a detailed illustrated report following visits to Britain: *Railways in England, 1826 and 1827*. Apparently unknown here until 1921, it was subsequently translated, but was not published in full until the *Newcomen Society did so in 1971 under the editorship of C. E. *Lee and K. R. Gilbert.

In 1830 Henry *Booth published an excellent *Account of the *Liverpool & Manchester Railway* (he was its secretary), summarizing its history and explaining some of its practices. There had been good engineers' accounts of railways before, such as Tredgold's and Nicholas *Wood's. But Booth's little book is the first classic in the railways' own literature and easily readable still. In 1839 Peter Lecount did something similar for the *London & Birmingham Railway. A few of the writers of early railway *guidebooks attempted the same task more briefly, and succeeded, notably James Wyld.

The rapid building of railways called for engineers' textbooks and manuals. The largest and best was S. C. Brees's *Railway Practice* (four series, 1837–47; French translations published in Liège, Brussels, and Paris). At the same time Francis *Whishaw produced his *Railways of Great Britain* (2nd edn., 1842), describing all those then at work, company by company.

*Lardner's *Railway Economy* (1850) is different: an analysis of operation and management, attempting to lay down principles (not always successfully) and making useful comparisons between British and foreign railways, often to the disadvantage of the British.

The first attempt at any historical treatment was made in 1851 by John *Francis in his *History of the English Railway . . . 1820–45*, giving a spirited account of the emergence of the early railways, as joint-stock companies. Next year another good book was published: F. S. *Williams's *Our Iron Roads* (7th edn., 1888). Later he produced the first substantial history of a British railway company in his *Midland Railway* (1876; reprinted 5th edn., 1968).

Another new author soon appeared, from inside the railway service: Samuel *Smiles, whose books about George and Robert *Stephenson (1857–62, many reissues) laid the foundations of industrial biography in Britain.

The popularity of these works was well deserved. But it did not lead to any extended analytical treatment of British railways as a social and political institution. Several studies of great merit appeared in France and Germany in the 1870s, especially those by Charles de Franqueville and Gustav Cohn. But they were not translated into English, and nothing similar emerged in Britain itself until 1889, when W. M. *Acworth brought out his *Railways of England*: well informed about the past and the present, and most skilfully written (5th edn., carefully revised, 1900).

Except Smiles, none of these authors was employed by a railway company. But several railwaymen now produced good books about aspects of their own work. James *Grierson published *Railway Rates, English and Foreign*, a cogent defence of the companies' *freight traffic rates (1886); George *Findlay's *Working and Management of an English Railway* (1889) set out the *London & North Western Railway's practices very clearly; and C. H. *Grinling, an accountant on the *Great Northern Railway, produced a good history of his company in 1898.

A growing popular interest in railways was now cultivated by the establishment of two monthly periodicals, *Moore's Monthly Magazine* (later the *Locomotive*) in 1896 and the *Railway Magazine* (1897) (see PRESS, RAILWAY).

The history of British railways at last began to find comprehensive treatment in two books published in 1915–16: E. Cleveland-Stevens, *English Railways: Their Origins, Development and Relation to the State*; and W. T. *Jackman, *Transportation in Modern England*. World War I was chronicled well in E. A. *Pratt's *British Railways and the Great War* (1921).

The centenary of the *Stockton & Darlington Railway evoked an important book, *Early British Railways, 1801–44*, from H. G. *Lewin (1925), followed by his *Railway Mania and its Aftermath, 1845–52* (1936). Together, they constituted the first scholarly attempt to construct a general history of British railways. At the same time extensive historical study of the British locomotive began with J. G. H. Warren's account of the firm of Robert Stephenson & Co., *A Century of Locomotive Building* (1923), E. L. *Ahrons's *British Steam Railway Locomotive 1825–1925* (1927), and the essays of C. F. Dendy *Marshall, starting to appear in book form in 1928.

Grinling's history of the Great Northern Railway was followed up in 1915 by W. W. *Tomlinson's *North Eastern Railway*, much larger and based on a wider range of sources, though unhappily foreshortened towards its end. The first railway company to commission a history was the *Great

Western, which secured a very fine book from E. T. *MacDermot (1927–31).

Shorter histories, of much smaller companies, came out from the 1930s onwards. Some were very good—those on the South Wales companies by D. S. *Barrie, for example. The great majority, however, were scrappy and inadequate. A popular history of a railway company was easily put together, and it could be tricked out by its publisher with photographs, often bad, uninformative, and poorly reproduced (see PHOTOGRAPHY).

Most of the pictures were of locomotives and trains, to which a parallel output of books was also devoted. The pictures were as a rule accompanied by captions that were quite perfunctory. As this torrent poured out (*Ottley characterized it well as the 'Railway Book Mania') Brian Reed quietly set himself to demonstrate how much more there was to be learnt about steam locomotives, given expert knowledge, careful and well-documented research, and incisive, critical reasoning. He and a group of fellow-authors did much to redeem this study by their *Locomotives in Profile* (1963–74).

Much of the popular work, aimed at the nostalgia market, repeated itself again and again. One new phenomenon was the emergence of heavily illustrated books containing minute details of sections of line or branches, often with little appreciation of their significance in the railways' wider activities. Much more important, the attention given to locomotives broadened out into valuable studies of carriages and wagons, and of railway stations. The detailed history of signalling and safety was now investigated profitably. *The Signal Box*, by the Signalling Study Group (1986), is an outstanding example.

M. J. T. Lewis's *Early Wooden Railways* (1970), a work of impressive scholarship on the pre-locomotive railway, examined in more detail some of the ground covered by C. E. Lee in his admirable *Evolution of Railways* (2nd edn., 1943).

Some excellent large general works appeared in the years after World War II. George *Dow's *Great Central* (1959–65) was a strong company history, paying attention to some aspects of its life not usually noticed; so was *London's *Metropolitan Railway* by A. A. Jackson (1986). M. R. Bonavia did much to illuminate the history of the *Big Four companies, as well as the process of *nationalization. *British Rail commissioned T. R. Gourvish to write a history of its first 25 years, and got a distinguished one in 1986, *British Railways, 1948–73*. The 16 volumes of the *Regional History of the Railways of Great Britain* (ed. D. St. J. Thomas and others, 1960–89) made a valuable effort to fit the business of railway companies, and of BR, into the framework of the communities they served. London did best of all in this respect, with the *History of *London Transport* (1963–74), commissioned by LT itself, from T. C. Barker and M. Robbins.

The more general history of railways in Great Britain as a whole made slow progress. Hamilton *Ellis courageously attempted one in his *British Railway History* (1954–9). It was readable (no small merit) but did not advance the study very far. Although an excellent contribution was made by

C. J. A. *Robertson in his *Origins of the Scottish Railway System* (1983), that terminated in 1844. No work of this sort, comparable in depth and breadth of research, has yet been produced for England or Wales.   JS
   *Ottley.

liveries. The livery, or colour scheme, of physical assets is always an opportunity for companies to identify themselves in the public mind. This extends to equipment, buildings, uniforms, and printed material. Early railways had few precedents to follow, and they pioneered the development of corporate identity in all its essentials: house colours, distinctive standard designs, logos, typefaces, and signs.

The earliest locomotives were too small for distinctive liveries, but passenger carriages, following the colourful example of stage-coaches, were painted brightly, with different colours for each class of accommodation.

Standard liveries evolved following the establishment of company workshops, incorporating paint shops, from the mid-1840s, with locomotive engineers responsible for colour schemes. Specifications for paint and methods were particular to each company, and paint was mixed in the shops.

It was idiosyncratic of most railways before the *Grouping to use different colours for locomotives and passenger vehicles. The *Midland Railway, which used crimson lake for both from 1883, was a notable exception. The most popular colour for locomotives was green, although dozens of shades were to be found; varieties of reds, blues, yellows, and browns complemented the utilitarian black also widely used. The cheapness of skilled labour found expression in elaborate lining-out, often consisting of three or four colours in lines of different thicknesses with rounded corners (convex or concave), accompanied by brightly polished copper- and brass-work.

*Carriages were often painted a darker colour at the ends and below the waist, and a lighter colour above, the company's choice of colours becoming its hallmark. Teak finish was also popular. Frames and running gear were invariably black, and roofs were grey, black, or white. Lining-out in two or three colours, with rounded corners around the panelling, was common until the 1930s.

Freight *wagons were usually grey, complementing the almost universal use of black for freight locomotives. There were exceptions among companies, and on special-purpose vehicles.

Company identification on locomotives and passenger vehicles varied from full names to initials (perhaps in an elaborate monogram) and whatever legend appeared on the garter or coat of arms. Locomotives were usually numbered, often with a name in hand-painted shaded characters or on a name-plate, usually of cast brass. The invention of the transfer by Tearnes in 1856 was a notable device for saving time in the application of numerals, lettering, and coats of arms, and encouraged more elaborate designs. The ownership of freight vehicles needed displaying, because they travelled on other companies' lines. It was controlled by the *Railway Clearing House, and was restricted to standard abbreviations of company initials in large characters. *Privately owned wagons gave prominence to the name of the owner.

The Grouping reduced the variety but led to special new liveries when tourist stock was built by the *London & North Eastern Railway in 1933, followed by streamlined trains (of which some were not painted but covered in Rexine) introduced by the LNER and the *London Midland & Scottish Railway. Plainer liveries were used for suburban carriages. World War II brought further simplification, and use of plain black even for express locomotives.

*British Railways experimented with liveries, using three major schemes, with very little lining, for locomotives, and corridor and non-corridor carriages in its first 25 years. The division of BR into business sectors, and again into units for *privatization, has resulted in a proliferation of liveries for all vehicles.

The advancing technology of paint and its application has influenced liveries only in recent years. The art of painting and lining survived surprisingly long, and was always a great expression of pride and self-confidence for companies and employees alike.   AD
   G. Dow, *Midland Style* (1975); W. J. Gordon, *Our Home Railways* (1910).

Liverpool and Birkenhead. The *Liverpool & Manchester Railway (1830) was an instant success, yet it was 18 years before another arrived. In that time Liverpool's population had almost doubled to more than 350,000. Ocean trade was expanding and prosperity increased with the introduction of steam-propelled ships as well as locomotives. The first steam transatlantic crossing was made in 1833 and when the Cunard Steamship Company started a regular mail service to North America in 1840, the LMR had replaced its original Crown Street station by a central terminus in Lime Street. It opened in 1836 and by 1838 Liverpool was linked to *Birmingham and *London.

Lime Street was an impressive terminal for a fast-growing town and port, being enhanced by the council which contributed £2,000 to the façade. Platforms were approached through a long, steep *cable-worked incline from Edge Hill. The LMR and its successor, the *London & North Western, reached busy docks through long tunnels to Wapping in 1829 and Waterloo in 1849, also cable-worked.

The LNWR's Liverpool monopoly was broken by the *Lancashire & Yorkshire Railway which by 1859 approached from the north and east, from Wigan, *Manchester, *Preston, and Southport ('a bathing village'), coinciding with construction of nine large north docks as the port steadily became one of the world's busiest; all close to the LYR. Like the LMR, the LYR quickly replaced its original terminal, Great Howard Street, by Exchange nearby, completed in 1850.

Three more major companies reached Liverpool, again after some 20 years, but they never broke the dominance of the LNWR and LYR. The *Great Northern, Manchester Sheffield & Lincolnshire (see GREAT CENTRAL), and *Midland

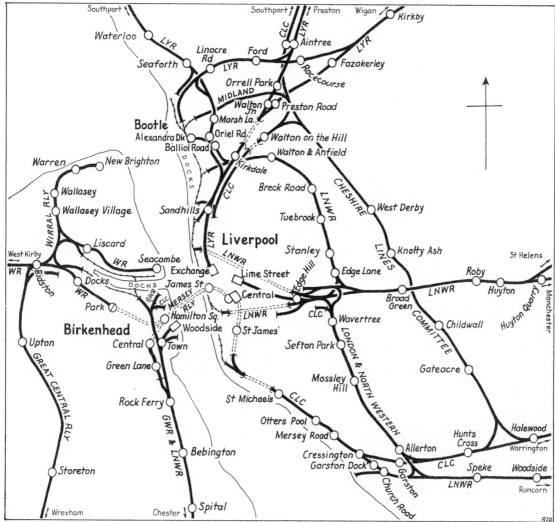

Liverpool and Birkenhead, 1922

Railways formed the *Cheshire Lines Committee in 1865. It built a third Liverpool–Manchester main line from Liverpool Central station in 1874. Later all three routes gained fame as the race tracks of 40-minute expresses.

The LNWR radically shortened its approach from *Crewe and the south by building the Runcorn bridge (see BRIDGES AND VIADUCTS) and a direct line in 1869. The company was now able to sharpen competition with the *Great Western Railway for west Midlands traffic which the GWR handled after reaching Birkenhead in 1854.

Its approach from Chester was over the Birkenhead Lancashire & Cheshire Junction Railway which, as the Birkenhead Railway, was vested *jointly in the GWR and LNWR in 1860. Dock building began at Birkenhead in 1847, nearly 150 years after the first had opened across the river. From the start, Birkenhead docks were well served with rails laid

to quays, but passenger facilities were poor until Woodside terminal, beside the Liverpool ferry, opened in 1878.

*Brunel's dream of broad gauge to the Mersey was never realized and GWR standard-gauge rails did not reach Liverpool itself, the company never being able to do more than ferry traffic between Birkenhead and its four city and dock depots in Liverpool. Even so, the GWR played an influential part in the development of the Port of Liverpool, being one of three parties which in 1857 promoted a Bill to set up the Mersey Docks & Harbour Board to take entire control and end disputes between rival interests at Liverpool and Birkenhead.

Merseyside's Victorian prosperity owed much to railways. As Liverpool's population approached 500,000 in the 1870s and its docks handled exports worth £55 million —twice that of London—the LNWR saw the city's rapid expansion as 'one of the most remarkable instances of prosperity the world has seen'. It was matched by a big rise in passenger traffic between Liverpool, the west Midlands, London, and the south, by far the busiest of Liverpool's long-distance express routes. Lime Street station, first rebuilt in 1849, was expanded again in 1867–74. A 208-bedroom *hotel built in French Renaissance style was added in 1871, much used by transatlantic liner passengers. Liverpool became the main port for North America, including emigrants from Britain and the Continent, but its position was soon challenged by *Southampton, far closer to London, and competition was intensified after 1892. The MDHB responded in 1895 by building Riverside station alongside the landing stage, where liners berthed and from which the LNWR ran luxury non-stop 4-hour Euston *boat trains. Like the station, they did not appear in public timetables. But the attractions of Southampton were only stemmed, not halted. Riverside closed in 1971 after the liner traffic had been destroyed by competition from airliners crossing the Atlantic in hours rather than days.

Once Birkenhead Woodside terminal was opened in 1878, the GWR competed for Birmingham and London traffic. GWR timetables showed ferry connections to Liverpool Landing Stage which it regarded as the terminus of the Birkenhead Joint line, and kept its interests afloat—literally —with a booking and parcels office, jointly with the LNWR. GWR main-line timetables also showed connections from Rock Ferry, Birkenhead, to Liverpool Central (Low Level) via the under-river *Mersey Railway. At Birkenhead, the MSLR challenged the LNWR and GWR for dock traffic after reaching Bidston in the 1890s over a roundabout route from South Yorkshire via Stockport and Chester, but its share of goods traffic remained small.

In the 1930s, the *London Midland & Scottish Railway, which now included the LYR, estimated that it carried 69 per cent of traffic in and out of Liverpool and Birkenhead docks. Of the remainder, the Cheshire Lines Committee dealt with 18 per cent, the GWR 10 per cent, and the *London & North Eastern Railway 3 per cent.

Thirty-eight miles of quays were once served by MDHB lines. The last closed when shipping was concentrated on the Gladstone and Royal Seaforth docks, to which *British Rail returned in 1980 as the port continued to expand. The decline which it suffered over some 40 years was in the number of vessels handled rather than cargo tonnage. The port still deals with millions of tons of freight, most carried in large container ships and bulk carriers. They use new and specialized complexes which incorporate Liverpool *Freightliner terminal, reached over the Bootle branch by trains which reverse at Edge Hill, where the LNWR built its innovative gridiron *marshalling yard in 1873–82. Ensnared between its approach lines and the Crewe line were Edge Hill *engine sheds, mostly for passenger engines; goods used Speke Junction shed. Liverpool's other Freightliner terminal opened at Garston in 1966. Nearby is Ford's Halewood vehicle factory, another generator of regular rail traffic. It has its own *industrial railway.

After *nationalization the pattern of Merseyside's long-distance and local passenger services changed, Lime Street becoming the terminal for the whole of the region. All main-line services were transferred after rationalization of services brought closure of Birkenhead Woodside in 1967, Liverpool Central (High Level) in 1972, and Exchange in 1977. InterCity services, except those to Scotland, travel via Crewe, a route *electrified in 1962. Four years later, Lime Street–Manchester express services were transferred to the CLC route via Warrington (Central), using a spur from the Crewe line at Allerton.

Under the Merseyside *Passenger Transport Authority, local lines were branded Merseyrail in 1971. They included the Southport, Ormskirk, and Wirral electrified lines. The LYR had electrified to Southport and Ormskirk in 1904–6 to serve growing residential areas, especially those near the Irish Sea. Both routes were linked to the *Liverpool Overhead Railway, but through running lasted only a few years, except to Aintree on annual Grand National days (see HORSE-RACING).

Residential growth along the north Wirral coast led to the electrification by the LMS in 1938 of the *Wirral Railway's West Kirby and New Brighton lines, and the integration of services with the Mersey Railway underground line at Birkenhead Park station.

In 1977–8 the old systems were united in central Liverpool by two underground lines with interchange stations at Moorfields, Central, and Lime Street. The Link Line was extended 5 miles from Central to Garston in 1978, and to the Manchester main-line interchange at Hunts Cross in 1983, by reopening the Liverpool end of the CLC closed in 1972. In 1985 electrification was extended over the former Birkenhead Joint line from Rock Ferry to Hooton; in 1993 to Chester, junction for the North Wales coast; and to Ellesmere Port in 1994. This was two decades after they became easily accessible via the M53 Mid-Wirral motorway and the second Mersey road tunnel.

Suddenly, after years of changing between terminals, cross-city rail journeys of over 20 miles were possible: direct from Hunts Cross to Southport; and from Chester to Southport and West Kirby with only a single change.

The steam locomotive, which arrived with the Liverpool & Manchester, departed in 1968 when the last BR standard-gauge steam-hauled train ran from Liverpool on a ceremonial round journey via *Carlisle.

See also PORTS AND DOCKS. RC

Reg. Hist., x (1986 edn.), esp. chs 1–3; A. Jarvis, *Docks of the Mersey* (1988); J. Joyce, *Roads, Rails and Ferries of Liverpool 1900–1950* (1983); Mersey PTE and BR, *The Story of Merseyrail* (1979); Thomas.

Liverpool & Manchester Railway. By 1821 the *Liverpool merchants and *Manchester mill-owners had long been seeking an alternative to the costly and inadequate services of the canals and roads linking their two cities at a time of booming trade. It was then that the wealthy Quaker Joseph Sandars met William *James, who proposed a railway which he undertook to build in 18 months at a cost of

£100,000. Though his offer was accepted, long delays then occurred and by 1824 he was succeeded by George *Stephenson as the company's engineer. The next year a parliamentary Bill was introduced, but it failed principally owing to Stephenson's inability to answer questions on his survey by opposing counsel. He was accordingly dismissed by the board, who appointed the professional civil engineers Sir John and George *Rennie; they, with their assistant C. B. *Vignoles, ensured the passage of the Bill in May 1826. The Act contained over 200 sections and was the pattern for railway Acts of Incorporation for many years (see PARLIAMENT AND LEGISLATION). At this time the capital of the LMR was £510,000, with power to raise £127,500 more in loans.

Stephenson was now reappointed engineer and with his assistants *Locke, Allcard, and Dixon, proceeded with the heavy engineering works at Olive Mount, Chat Moss, and the 1¼-mile tunnel under Liverpool to the docks. In 1828 the Exchequer Loan Commissioners (see SUBSIDIES), who had lent the company £100,000, sent *Telford to examine the works; he was extremely critical of Stephenson's methods, and of the board for allowing its engineer to act also as contractor.

Enormous crowds attended the opening of the LMR by the Duke of Wellington on 15 September 1830, but the celebrations were marred by the tragic death of William Huskisson, the Liverpool MP and steadfast supporter of the railway (see ACCIDENTS).

The *Rainhill trials of October 1829 had established the steam locomotive as most suitable for the LMR and a further 17 were supplied by Robert *Stephenson & Co. by 1831; thereafter several firms built engines for the company but from 1841 it built them in its own *works.

As other lines opened they offered the experienced engine *drivers higher wages to join their companies. Following a strike in 1836 the LMR guaranteed a minimum wage for drivers and *firemen. Among the LMR employees later to achieve high office elsewhere were Joseph Armstrong, engine driver in 1836, age 20, and Matthew *Kirtley, fireman.

A few weeks after opening, the LMR had run its first *excursion trains, carried the first *mails, and was conveying *road-rail *containers for Pickfords; by the summer of 1831 the railway was carrying tens of thousands by special trains to Newton Races.

Many minor accidents occurred in the early years but few resulted in the death of passengers, other than by their own negligence. Rules and regulations (see BYE-LAWS) gradually evolved from experience and in 1839 a revised set of 50 was published.

By the early 1840s several great railways were completed and working. In 1845 the LMR amalgamated with its principal partner, the *Grand Junction Railway, and in 1846 became part of the *London & North Western.   RHGT

Thomas; R. E. Carlson, *The Liverpool & Manchester Railway Project, 1821–1831* (1969); T. J. Donaghy, *Liverpool & Manchester Railway Operations, 1831–1845* (1972).

Liverpool Overhead Railway. Known for 60 years as the 'Dockers' Umbrella', the line provided dock workers' transport and a bird's-eye view of the docks for the public.

Built 16 ft above street level in 1893–6 to keep trains clear of the road entrances to miles of docks and reduce fire risk to warehouses alongside, the LOR was the first urban elevated electric railway in the world (see ELECTRIFICATION). It ran 6½ miles from Dingle to Seaforth and in 1905 was extended to meet newly electrified *Lancashire & Yorkshire lines to Southport and Ormskirk. It installed Britain's first automatic semaphore signals (see SIGNALLING) and replaced them in 1921 by colour-lights, again a 'first'.

Despite wider acceptance of railway closures after World War II, the end of the LOR, carrying millions of passengers every year, in 1956 came as a shock. But it was life-expired and, as a purely passenger line, losing money heavily against road competition. Neither the *British Transport Commission, the Mersey Docks & Harbour Board, nor Liverpool Corporation was prepared to find about £2 million to replace the steel decking, and a similiar sum to keep the railway running.

See also OVERHEAD RAILWAYS.   RC

P. Bolger, *The Dockers' Umbrella* (1992); C. E. Box, *Liverpool Overhead Railway 1893–1956* (1959).

Liverpool Street station, see LONDON STATIONS.

livestock traffic. Before the railways, animals were normally moved by driving them 'on the hoof', with consequent loss of weight and value. The railway's superiority for this trade was demonstrated as early as 1831, when the *Liverpool & Manchester Railway began to carry Irish livestock landed at *Liverpool. As the railway network expanded, it captured almost all except the short-distance flows. It opened up more distant markets for farmers and dealers and allowed them to select a time when prices were favourable to send their animals to market. The cattle dock and pens became as much a feature of the village and small town station as its goods shed and coal siding. The only significant competition was from coastal *shipping services operating southward from *Aberdeen.

The railways were involved in, and greatly influenced the development of, four distinct patterns of movement of livestock for consumption:

1. The traditional spring and autumn flows of lean cattle and sheep from the hill farms in the north and west, where they were reared, to the lowland farms in the south and east for fattening. The principal markets for this trade developed at locations convenient for rail transport: in the north and west at *Perth, Lanark, Hawick, Castle Douglas, Annan, *Carlisle, *York, *Doncaster, *Shrewsbury, Craven Arms, Knighton, *Bristol, and *Exeter; and in the east and south at Lincoln, Grantham, *Leicester, *Peterborough, *Norwich, Ipswich, Rugby, Banbury, Dorchester, Chichester, and Ashford.

2. Fatstock for slaughter. The chief markets supplying this trade were at Aberdeen, *Edinburgh, *Glasgow, *Leeds, Northampton, *Derby, Leicester, Norwich, and Lincoln. There dealers bought and despatched animals to markets in

the places where they were to be consumed, particularly to *London. In 1855 London's ancient livestock market at Smithfield was replaced by the new Metropolitan Cattle Market in Islington, served by cattle sidings at Maiden Lane (*North London Railway) and Holloway (*Great Northern Railway). However, this traffic to London was already in decline by the 1870s, as it became more usual to slaughter at the supplying market and forward the carcasses to London as *meat traffic, and the market closed in 1939.

3. A large trade in cattle and pigs shipped from Ireland and landed chiefly at Bristol, Fishguard, Holyhead, Liverpool, Heysham, and Glasgow, whence they were forwarded for fattening or slaughter.

4. Animals for slaughter imported from northern Europe. These were mainly shipped direct to London, but in 1851 the *Eastern Counties Railway was instrumental in setting up the Northern Steam Packet Co. which brought in Danish cattle through Lowestoft for forwarding to London; however, the venture failed in 1857. From 1863 the *Great Eastern Railway gained a share of the traffic with its own steamer services from Rotterdam and Antwerp to Harwich. Other ports handling continental livestock were *Hull, which also sent them on to London as well as the West Yorkshire towns, and *Newcastle. However, there were increasing restrictions from 1869 on the import of foreign livestock, for reasons of disease control, and the traffic had largely ceased by 1893.

Livestock traffic grew rapidly until the mid-1870s, when it was worth about £1m per annum in revenue. Thereafter it grew more slowly, reaching a peak in 1910–28. In 1913 4.4 million cattle, 12.9 million sheep, and 2.1 million pigs were carried, bringing in £1.3m in revenue; nearly half the business was in the hands of the *London & North Western, *Great Western, *North British, and *North Eastern Railways.

The movement of livestock between farm and market was one of the earliest losses to *road transport competition; by 1939 carryings had halved. This resumed after World War II and in 1962 *British Railways decided to concentrate on the regular flows, immediately reducing the number of stations with livestock facilities from 2,493 to 232. By 1968 only the Irish cattle trade through Holyhead was being served and this ceased in 1975.

The early cattle *wagons were merely pens on wheels, but covered wagons were built from 1848. At first the top one-third of the sides and ends was left open for ventilation, but the ends were later enclosed for better weather protection. A standard specification for cattle wagons, in three sizes, was agreed through the *Railway Clearing House in 1873. Thereafter there was little visual change in the design right up to 1954, when the last ones were built. The LMR also had double-deck wagons for sheep and pigs, but the only other railway to adopt this idea was the *Highland Railway, although the *London Midland & Scottish experimented with it again in 1929–30.

The practice of attaching horseboxes to passenger trains goes back to the early days when first-class passengers might be accompanied by their *horse-drawn carriages.

Horseboxes subsequently became associated mainly with the carriage of racehorses (see HORSE-RACING). The standard layout of three longitudinal stalls, divided by padded partitions, was established by the 1860s; a groom's compartment at one end, and then a tack and hay locker at the other, came later. In the 1880s similar vehicles, much superior to the common cattle wagon, were introduced for transporting prize cattle by passenger train to shows and sales; they were called variously Prize, Pedigree, Valuable, Special, or Passenger Train Cattle Vans. The last vehicles of both these types were withdrawn in 1972.

Various species of small livestock were (and still are) carried as parcels traffic. Homing pigeons deserve particular mention, as their rectangular wicker baskets were such a familiar feature of the rural railway scene from the early 1900s until the 1970s. For training flights they were carried in the guard's van of passenger trains to a station at the required distance from home and there liberated by the station staff. But many special trains were required every Friday night during the summer for the weekly races organized by the pigeon-fanciers' clubs. Each week they ran to ever-more distant stations until, at the end of the season, some were running to the Channel ports where the birds were transferred to the ferry services for release from the Continent or Channel Islands.   GAB

G. R. Hawke, 'Railways and Agriculture: Livestock Flows and Meat Supplies', in *Railways and Economic Growth in England and Wales 1840–1870* (1970), 131–56; G. Channon, 'The Aberdeenshire Beef Trade with London: A Study in Steamship and Railway Competition 1850–69', *Transport History*, 2 (1969), 1–24; R. J. Essery, D. P. Rowland, and W. O. Steel, 'Livestock Vehicles', in *British Goods Wagons from 1887 to the Present Day* (1970), 86–91; W. Smith, 'Pigeon Train to Frome', *Railway World*, 25 (1964), 127–9.

Livock, John (1814–?), architect. A little-known figure who practised in London, Livock is chiefly remembered for his charming Tudor and Jacobean stations on the Northampton–Peterborough line (1845) of the *London & Birmingham Railway, and the Trent Valley Railway (1847) of the *London & North Western, on both of which he was resident engineer under Robert *Stephenson. His stations and houses were outstanding examples of the picturesque movement applied to railways. The most handsome was Tamworth which, like all the others except Atherstone, Oundle, and Wansford, and a former crossing-house at Mancetter, has been demolished. He has been credited with the ornamental portals of Shugborough Tunnel and the bridge in Shugborough Park.

Livock also designed stations for the LNWR on the Buckinghamshire Railway (1850–1), and the frontage block and *hotel at *Birmingham New Street, a sober, mildly Palladian building that contrasted strongly with his earlier exuberance.

His only other works identified so far are the Clarendon Hotel next to Watford Junction station (1860) and the village schools at Bloxham, Oxfordshire (1864–70). On several occasions he exhibited at the Royal Academy. In 1837 he showed a design for a station, in 1848 some Trent Valley designs, and in 1853 designs for domestic buildings and schools. There is a folio of his sketches at the RIBA (none of them for railways), and he last appeared as an architect in London directories in 1877.

See also ARCHITECTURE AND ARCHITECTS.   GJB

G. Biddle, 'The Railway Stations of John Livock and T. M. Penson', *JRCHS*, 31 (2), 154 (1993), 61–71; 32 (2), 164 (1996), 141.

Lloyd George, David, Earl (1863–1945), politician. He

enters railway history at two points. As a solicitor at Criccieth he battled with the *London & North Western Railway in 1890–5 for its alleged discrimination against Welsh-speakers on its staff. He was MP for the Caernarvon Boroughs continuously from 1890 to 1945. As President of the Board of *Trade he undertook much negotiation with the railway companies and the *trade unions over a threatened *strike in 1906, in which he proved resourceful and untiringly patient, gradually gaining the confidence of employers and men. He was politically responsible for securing the acceptance of 'conciliation boards', a form of arbitration devised by Sam *Fay of the *Great Central Railway. This averted the immediately threatened strike and helped towards achieving an accepted procedure for the settlement of future disputes, though it did not prevent a national strike in 1911.   JS

LNWR dispute: PRO, RAIL 410/2053; P. S. Bagwell, *The Railwaymen* (1963), ch. 10.

Lloyd's bonds: a financial device enabling railway com-

panies to raise money to pay for completing their lines even when their statutory limits on borrowing were exhausted. They were devised in the early 1860s by John Horatio Lloyd (1798–1884), an able barrister much involved in railway promotion, and called after him. In such a bond the railway company acknowledged that a debt of a certain sum was still owing to a *contractor in order to complete the line, and he agreed to postpone the settlement of it until a date in the future, written into the bond, when it would be discharged with interest payable at a stated rate. On the security of this bond the contractor could expect to raise a loan himself, from a bank or some other financial house, sufficient to allow him to finish the work. The bonds did enable some lines to be completed that might otherwise have had to be abandoned—the long one between Carmarthen and Aberystwyth, for example. But in the frenzy of promotions in the early 1860s they were grossly abused, helping to encourage the building of some lines that should never have been made. Their issue contributed to the financial crisis of 1866 (see SPECULATION). They continued to be used, however, by railway companies: for example by the *Golden Valley Railway towards getting its work completed in 1879–81.

See also FINANCING OF RAILWAYS; CONTRACTORS' LINES.   JS

Lloyd explained the bonds with admirable clarity before a critical committee of the House of Lords in 1864: PP 1864 xi, 67, containing a specimen text, p. 81.

load(ing) gauge, see CLEARANCES.

local government, see GOVERNMENT, RAILWAYS AND

LOCAL.

Locke, Joseph (1805–60), civil engineer, son of a Yorkshire

colliery manager. With *Brunel and Robert *Stephenson, all born in 1803–6, Locke formed a triumvirate of great early railway engineers. Articled to George *Stephenson in 1823, he later worked for him on the *Liverpool & Manchester Railway, but his discovery of alignment errors in, first, Wapping Tunnel in 1827, and then Lime Street Tunnel in 1832 eventually led to estrangement, culminating in Locke replacing Stephenson as engineer on the *Grand Junction Railway in 1835, where hitherto he had been responsible for only the northern portion. In 1843 he laid out the GJR's *works and town at *Crewe.

Twice more Locke took over and completed the failing work of others: he replaced Francis *Giles on the London & Southampton (see LONDON & SOUTH WESTERN RAILWAY) in 1837, and C. B. *Vignoles on the Sheffield Ashton & Manchester (see GREAT CENTRAL RAILWAY) in 1839.

Locke's particular skill was as an organizer. He closely controlled *contractors and expenditure and, unlike many contemporaries, completed his lines on time and within estimates, on many of which he worked closely with the contractors *Brassey and *Mackenzie. Their work included railways in France, Spain, and Holland.

They built many lines in Britain, including most of those that eventually made the route between *Birmingham and *Aberdeen, where Locke's vision of what became the *West Coast main line to Scotland was one of the driving forces. His avoidance of tunnelling, wherever possible, reduced construction costs at the price of steeper gradients than had hitherto been attempted, such as Shap and Beattock, with consequent increases in long-term operating expenses. He was assisted on many of his works by John E. Errington, whom he later took into partnership.

Locke was MP for Honiton, 1847–60, and president of the *Institution of Civil Engineers, 1858–9. Like Brunel and Robert Stephenson, he died comparatively young from overwork. He is commemorated by a statue and Locke Park in Barnsley, where he spent his formative years.   GJB

BDE; N. W. Webster, *Joseph Locke, Railway Revolutionary* (1970).

locomotive building costs. The principal elements in the

total cost of a steam locomotive were materials (typically 50–70 per cent), wages (20–30 per cent), and works charges (which were often somewhat arbitrarily assessed).

Fluctuation in the price of materials accounted for the wide variation in the cost of a given locomotive type in the period before 1914, when monetary inflation was negligible. Prices increased during periods of economic prosperity and declined during spells of industrial depression, being related to the prevailing cost of *coal. This was admirably illustrated by the cost of S. W. *Johnson's 865 *Midland Railway 0-6-0 goods engines, built to substantially the same design from 1875 to 1902. Typically, these cost £2,250 each (£45 per ton empty weight) but fell to £1,965 in 1886, yet climbed to just over £3,000 in 1901, giving a range of approximately £40 to £60 per ton.

Rising prices in World War I and its immediate aftermath increased costs from 1915 to 1921, when two new 4-4-2s for

Locomotive Manufacturers' Association

Year	Railway and type	Railway works' costs	Contractors' costs	Average percentage increase, contractor/ railway works
1899–1900	CR 0-6-0	£2,189–£2,274	£2,985–£3,100	36
1903	GCR 4-4-2T	£1,866	£2,770	48
1906	GCR 0-6-0	£2,406	£3,300	37
1908	NER 0-6-0	£2,986	£3,500–£3,550	18
1925	LMS 4-4-0	£5,604–£6,456	£6,547–£6,651	9
1936	LMS 2-6-4T	£5,011	£5,672	13
1948	LNER 2-6-4T	£9,733	£14,349	47
c.1954	BR 2-10-0	£24,691	£30,058–£31,268*	24

Comparative costs of building steam locomotives simultaneously in railway workshops and by contractors, 1899–c.1954

* Quotations only (10 per cent profit assumed).

Key
BR	British Rys	LMS	London Midland & Scottish Ry
CR	Caledonian Ry	LNER	London & North Eastern Ry
GCR	Great Central Ry	NER	North Eastern Ry

the *North British Railway cost £15,450 each against an estimated 1913 price of £4,320. Prices had fallen sharply by 1923, when ten 4-6-2s built by the *London & North Eastern Railway at *Doncaster cost only £7,614 each. Levels thereafter remained virtually unchanged up to 1938 when both the *London Midland & Scottish Railway and the LNER could build a streamlined 4-6-2 for nearly £10,000.

From 1939 locomotive costs climbed unremittingly; after 1949 at a rate which exceeded the cost of living index. In 1950 *British Railways calculated that before World War II a typical LNER locomotive built in railway workshops cost £60 per ton, compared with £73 per ton by a contractor, whereas post-war figures were reckoned to have risen to £114 and £136 respectively. The private locomotive-building industry resented the extent to which British railway companies built their own, only resorting to the industry when they had insufficient capacity or required locomotives quickly. Almost invariably, where costs are available for locomotives of a given design being built simultaneously in railway works and by contractors, the former appear to be cheaper, not least because there was no profit margin. It is probable that railway works' and contractors' construction costs were not always strictly comparable. Railway works often used existing patterns and press blocks, etc., whereas these would have to be fabricated anew by a contractor, thereby adding to development costs. Furthermore, contract builders were almost entirely concerned with new construction, but railway works were predominantly devoted to locomotive repairs. Whereas contractors would therefore be obliged to ascribe high overheads, in a railway works these could be absorbed to a greater degree in general works charges spread over its entire operations. Even at *Crewe Works less than 10 per cent of the work-force was engaged in new construction.

During the brief overlap of steam and main-line diesel locomotive construction in 1958, a new BR Class 9F 2-10-0

weighing 101 tons empty cost £30,000, compared with £107,000 for a prototype English Electric 2,000 hp 1Co-Co1 diesel-electric locomotive of 124 tons. In real terms this was still considerably less than the reputed £2–3 million cost of a high-tech BR Class 60 diesel, or Class 91 or 92 electric locomotive of the early 1990s.

See also CARRIAGE BUILDING.   CPA

B. Reed, *150 Years of British Steam Locomotives* (1975); C. P. Atkins in R. J. Essery and D. Jenkinson (eds.), *An Illustrated Review of Midland Locomotives*, iii (1988), Appendix; various unpublished official sources.

Locomotive Manufacturers' Association, see RAILWAY INDUSTRY ASSOCIATION.

locomotives, see TRACTION.

locomotives, names of types, see WHEEL NOTATION.

locomotive testing. From the early days of steam railway traction, engineers have measured the performance and efficiency of locomotives. The interdependency between components which generate steam and those which turn it into movement necessitates testing the whole machine as a single entity. Testing confirms its ability to achieve designed performance and indicates the modifications required if it fails to do so.

In 1818 George *Stephenson and Nicholas *Wood developed a device for measuring the pull exerted by locomotives. In 1839 Charles Babbage's instruments for measuring tractive effort, distance, and speed were installed in a *Great Western Railway vehicle. In 1856 Daniel *Gooch developed this further in a measuring van (see DYNAMOMETER CAR).

Comparative tests between different locomotives were made at *Rainhill in 1829, to decide the most suitable type for the *Liverpool & Manchester Railway, and on many subsequent occasions. In 1948 *British Railways made extensive dynamometer car tests on service trains between locomotives of the four nationalized railways before starting design studies for its standard steam types.

The running of special test trains in constant-controlled conditions was pioneered by Borodin and Loewy in Russia and fully developed there from 1898 by Lomonossoff, whose test trains were run at constant power and speed over uniformly graded lines. Constant speed-testing over variable gradients was developed by Czeczott in Poland from 1921 using a second regulating locomotive, which assisted the test locomotive when climbing gradients or acted as a brake when descending to maintain constant speed. Then, in 1925, Nordmann and Gunther introduced road-testing in which up to three counter-pressure brake locomotives absorbed the power of the test locomotive in simulating a train of given weight. In 1947 H. I. Andrews' mobile testing units on the *London Midland & Scottish Railway replaced brake locomotives by motor braking vehicles, whose traction motors acted as generators providing a dynamic braking load under electronic control.

To overcome the difficulty of providing *paths for constant-speed test trains on busy main lines, S. O. Ell of the GWR introduced his controlled road-testing system in 1947. A steam-flow meter enabled the test locomotive's driver to work it at constant firing and steam production rates, train speed fluctuating with gradients as in normal service trains.

Whilst road-testing produced much valuable data, boiler and cylinder performance could only be fully analysed over lengthy periods on static test plants: virtual locomotive laboratories. Here the locomotive wheels ran on rollers, with power absorbed by hydraulic or friction brakes. The first test plant was built by Goss at Purdue University, Indiana, USA, in 1891, and Churchward's GWR Swindon plant dated from 1904.

From 1927 H. N. *Gresley of the *London & North Eastern Railway strongly advocated a British national testing station. The modern Rugby test plant, based on that at Vitry in France, was finally opened in 1948, and 37 steam types, some in both original and modified form, were tested under D. R. Carling until 1959. The enlarged Swindon plant also played an important part in BR locomotive testing. Modifications made after plant tests to improve the defective draughting of a 2-6-0 locomotive enabled its maximum power to be increased by 55 per cent.

Static plant tests cannot exactly simulate road conditions in the absence of air resistance to motion, and they were frequently followed by road tests. Locomotive performance curves derived from test data now enabled train performance and timings to be calculated scientifically—a great advance on previous empirical methods.

See also TESTING OF EQUIPMENT; TESTING OF MATERIALS; RESEARCH AND DEVELOPMENT.   GWC

D. R. Carling, 'Locomotive Testing on British Railways', *Jnl. Inst. Loco. Engineers*, 40 (1950), 406; D. R. Carling, 'Locomotive Testing Stations', *TNS*, 45 (1972–3), 105–82; S. O. Ell, 'Developments in Locomotive Testing', *Jnl. Inst. Loco. Engineers*, 43 (1953), 561; S. O. Ell, 'The Testing of Locomotives', in *Concise Encyclopaedia of World Locomotives* (1959), 386–410.

London. The site of London was originally fixed by the Romans at the lowest regularly used crossing-point on the River Thames, where a bridge was soon built at the upper limit of navigation for sea-going vessels. Roads converged upon it from the south-east coast and fanned out into the interior of the country to the east, north, and west. The approach from the south was over level, sometimes marshy, ground; on the north side there were minor elevations close to the river, with a supply of drinkable water, and a range of heights some 3–5 miles farther back. On the east the Lea valley was an obstacle, but there was no natural break to the west. By the early 19th century a large urban mass had been developed round the two poles of the City and Westminster and their immediate suburbs, with a much smaller conglomeration south of the Thames. In the census Greater London area (somewhat larger than the county established in 1965), population rose from 1,110,000 in 1801 (when London was far the biggest city in Western Europe) to 2,250,000 in 1841, 6,581,000 in 1901, and 8,187,000 in 1964; it then began to fall slowly as greater freedom of movement reduced the density of settlement in urban areas. England's capital was not only the focus of the national road system but also encompassed the government of the country and its expanding empire, a huge trading port, financial centre, and a host of manufactures.

When steam railways began to be built in London at the end of the 1830s they were confronted with these facts of geography and historical development: the fairly broad Thames, with heavy shipping traffic and docks to the east of the City; low ground with marshes, some parts only recently reclaimed and built on, to the south; heights to the north which discouraged direct approach except through tunnels; and a man-made obstacle, the Regent's Canal (1820), curving round the north side well within the continuously built-up area, which had to be crossed with clearance above or below. Acquisition of *land was likely to be particularly contentious because great estates—Bedford, Grosvenor, Portland, Portman—maintained their rights as ground landlords to control development in accordance with their intentions, which were mostly for high-class housing.

The first railway in the London area, the *Surrey Iron Railway (1803), was a horse-drawn *tramroad for conveyance of freight to and from the Thames at Wandsworth, of no significance for the future. The first two passenger railways, the *London & Greenwich and *London & Blackwall, short-distance lines with at the outset strictly local objectives, were able to build, largely on viaducts, up to the very edge of the central area. The housing they demolished was mostly in slum areas, where clearances caused distress to the occupants but involved no serious conflict with important property owners. The *London & Birmingham and *Great Western, however, approached from north-west and west, where better-class estates held most of the land; the prospect of dispute and high land costs forced them to terminate outside the edge of the existing town, at *Euston Square and *Paddington. The London & Southampton (see LONDON & SOUTH WESTERN RAILWAY) got no further in than

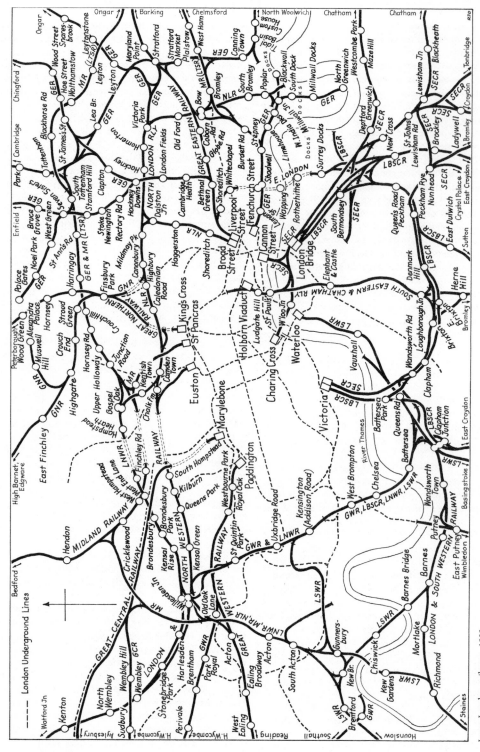

Inner London railways, 1922
Note: The North London Railway became part of the LNWR on 1 Jan. 1922

Nine Elms (Vauxhall); London & Brighton (see LONDON BRIGHTON & SOUTH COAST RAILWAY) and *South Eastern trains used the LGR line to *London Bridge; the *Eastern Counties got to Shoreditch, misleadingly renamed Bishopsgate. Authority was given in 1845 for the LSWR to extend from Vauxhall to the south end of *Waterloo Bridge, and the *Great Northern Act of 1846 authorized entry into *King's Cross, opened in 1852.

In 1846 Parliament, nearly overwhelmed by the quantity of railway legislation descending upon it, decided that a Royal *Commission should investigate the question of future railway facilities within an area of central London bounded by Park Lane to the west, up to the line of Marylebone and Euston Roads on the north, and down to Lambeth Road on the south. After examination of 19 projects, the Commission recommended against any extension of railway lines on the north side and any idea of a general central station, and against any new Thames railway bridge. They were prepared, however, to sanction a Waterloo–London Bridge link on the south (which came to nothing at that time); and they recommended a north–south communication between the railways approaching London, crossing the Thames somewhere west of Vauxhall bridge, and a connection with the docks, clear of the limits of their inquiry to the north. Their recommendations were published but not formally adopted; they were a guideline, not a ruling. Their recommended link with the docks became the *North London Railway. The 'box' north of the Thames remained free of surface railways until it was breached in a new railway promotion boom in the late 1850s. In 1858 Parliament sanctioned a river bridge at Battersea leading to a terminus at *Victoria, right on the edge of the box. SER extensions over river bridges were authorized, to *Charing Cross (1859, opened 1864) and *Cannon Street (1861, opened 1866). In 1860 the *London Chatham & Dover Railway got an Act to smash right through the western part of the City over a bridge at Blackfriars to Ludgate Hill (opened 1864), with a tunnel link to the *Metropolitan at Farringdon Street (opened 1866).

These developments were concerned with long-distance passenger and freight traffic and to some extent, especially on the south, with short-distance *commuter journeys; but they did nothing to resolve the problem of movement within the central areas where congestion was serious and much complained of. Sir Joseph Paxton testified that it took him as long to get from London Bridge terminus to a destination in the West End as the train journey time from Brighton. Cabs, omnibuses, private carriages, wagons, and cattle on their way to market combined to throng and jostle in the narrow streets in a way that was clearly wasteful and sometimes dangerous. There was not even room for the crowds of pedestrians: Charlotte and Anne Brontë, on their first visit to London in 1848, 'became so dismayed by the crowded streets, and the impeded crossings, that they stood still repeatedly' and were nearly an hour in covering the half-mile distance they had to go to Cornhill. The crowding and the pushing struck every foreign visitor (Gustave Doré did a ferocious cartoon in 1872) and one influential Lon-

doner in particular: Charles *Pearson, a man of progressive opinions who was in 1839–62 the City Solicitor. Largely through his advocacy, a project for an underground railway for both passengers and goods was surveyed, and an Act (North Metropolitan Railway, 1853, renamed Metropolitan Railway, 1854) was obtained for a sub-surface (mostly cut-and-cover) line linking the GWR and GNR terminals with Farringdon Street on the edge of the City, and serving Euston Square (for the *London & North Western Railway) on the way. This was opened in 1863 and was the beginning of the steam-hauled underground network which, with the Inner Circle (worked with the *Metropolitan District Railway) and numerous branches, served the central parts of London north of the river and became the nucleus of the later Underground and London Transport (see LONDON UNDERGROUND RAILWAYS).

In the 1860s also, the *Midland Railway opened its own London terminus at *St Pancras (1868), and the North London at *Broad Street (1865) on the eastern edge of the City; the *Great Eastern advanced to *Liverpool Street in 1874. All these stations were just on the rim of the Commission's 'box'; and that of the last main line to arrive, the *Great Central's *Marylebone (1899), also just north of the boundary, completed the ring of main-line terminals. There were attempts to make north–south links: the Metropolitan with its 'widened lines' afforded a connection between the GNR and Midland and the LCDR and later the SER to the south, which was used by freight and local passengers but not by long-distance passenger trains. The LNWR supported proposals for a Central London Railway in 1871 to link Euston with Charing Cross, but nothing came of them.

The difficulty and expense of carting goods between the different companies' depots were vexatious, and various working arrangements and connecting lines were made to enable freight wagons to reach points away from their parent lines but closer to their recipients. Completion of the *West London Extension Railway (1863) with a new river bridge at Chelsea, the South London line from Battersea to Deptford, and the *East London did not quite complete the 'girdle' that planners, looking at Paris, thought desirable; but they made it possible for the northern companies to establish their own goods and coal depots on lines near the City and the docks, and at several points in the south London suburbs well beyond the parents' territory.

There were from time to time grand conceptions of a central station serving all the lines terminating in London, from proposals put before the 1846 Commission by Charles Pearson and Thomas Page, through Paxton's 'Great Victorian Way' of 1855 to A. W. Gattie's 'goods clearing house' of 1910, but none came into being: the expense would have been enormous, the companies maintained their ingrained competitive outlook and disliked shared accommodation and joint arrangements, and the difficulties would probably have proved insuperable, not only on the railway operating side but in relation to the street traffic problem that a single location would have thrown up; and the administration would have been at least as cumbersome as the fragmented practices that the railways worked out by bargaining between themselves.

There were attempts from time to time to provide *through carriages or trains from the northern and western lines across London (see CROSS-COUNTRY SERVICES), using the West London line after 1863, including a Birkenhead to Dover *slip-carriage service in 1905–6, and a train from *Manchester to *Brighton and Dover before and after World War I (the *London Midland & Scottish's 'Sunny South Express'). *British Railways tried and gave up in the 1980s. The Midland used its Cricklewood–Acton link for a *Bradford–*Portsmouth train in 1905–8. But nearly all passengers wanted to go to London, not through it.

By 1874 the main pattern of surface railways serving inner London was complete, apart from the Great Central. The first two lines were concerned with local traffic; the others were at first principally concerned with traffic from middle and longer distances, only a few stations and depots being opened in the suburban area. The southern lines soon began to develop short-distance carryings; the GNR and GER did so from the 1870s, the LNWR, GWR, and MR only from later—very little before the end of the 19th century. But throughout the period a network of lines and a great number of stations proliferated in the suburban area. The Richmond & West End Railway, amalgamated with the LSWR shortly after its opening in 1846; the SER's Blackheath, Woolwich, and Gravesend line in 1849; and the ECR Enfield branch of 1849 initiated a continuous expansion of branches and opening of stations on existing lines that went on until 1939. Seen on the map, the results are bewildering, and everyone but the regular user was likely to be confused. *Dickens's Dictionary of London* remarked in 1879: 'Though it would be decidedly a triumph of ingenuity so to construct an equal number of lines of railway as to give less practical accommodation than is given at present, the London railway system is so vast that it serves every portion of the metropolis. To attempt any mere verbal explanation would be futile.' The somewhat inaccurate accompanying list showed 334 stations.

The destruction of house property, especially near the centre, finally caused Parliament to insist on the provision of cheap *workmen's fares to compensate in some measure those displaced from their homes. From the 1870s workmen's fares, into Broad Street and Liverpool Street in particular, stimulated the building of working-class housing in the north-eastern and eastern sectors of outer London, on both sides of the Lea valley, and to some extent south of the Thames as well.

London traffic and communications were periodically reviewed by Royal Commissions or parliamentary committees, again in 1872, 1884, 1895, and most notably by the Royal Commission on London Traffic of 1903–5, of which a senior railway officer, Sir George *Gibb, general manager of the *North Eastern Railway, was a member. Its report was based on the most searching inquiry ever conducted into the subject; but its principal recommendation, that a London Traffic Board with certain executive powers should be set up, was not pursued, and the various interests—the rail-

way companies, the omnibuses and trams, London County Council, and other municipal bodies—went on, either by continuous competition or by agreement or amalgamation, to do what seemed best to each of them.

The period from 1900 to 1914 was crucial for London railway and traffic development. *Electrification of the Metropolitan and the District, its beginning on the LBSCR South London line, and the building of new tubes, together with a growing interest in London suburban possibilities shown by the LNWR and the GWR, with new construction especially in Middlesex and Buckinghamshire to serve areas previously untouched by railways, led to a surge of local traffic that the railways both encouraged and found hard to cope with. Electrification of LNWR, NLR, and LSWR suburban services was in hand before 1914.

After the strains imposed by World War I and a decade of argument in the 1920s, the London Passenger Transport Act, 1933, placed all the purely local railways under the ownership of the new London Passenger Transport Board (see LONDON UNDERGROUND RAILWAYS), including the Metropolitan, which resisted to the end, claiming that it should be treated as a main-line railway; but not the Waterloo & City (see LONDON & SOUTH WESTERN) which remained with the Southern. A general pool of London area passenger receipts including the main lines was set up, though management remained separate. A standing joint committee of the four *Grouped railways and the board succeeded in getting approval, with a Treasury guarantee of interest, for an ambitious 'New Works Programme 1935–40', in which portions of LNER and GWR lines were included (see *CENTRAL LINE, *NORTHERN LINE).

The 1930s and around 1950 marked the peak of the railways' contribution to movement within London, of both passengers and freight. Suburbs of continuous building flowed over every usable piece of land; new railway facilities and intensified train services struggled to keep up with the demand. After World War II there was little land left for housing development in the immediate London area; 'New Towns' were created outside the 'Green Belt', which was used to check the apparently inexorable spread of the city; and further growth was diverted to areas that could not be considered London at all. The railways played first a substantial, then a declining part in moving this new relatively long-distance traffic.

But the need for improved communication within the central area was increased rather than diminished by these post-war shifts. London Transport built its *Victoria (1969) and *Jubilee (1979) lines; the long under-used and almost abandoned low-level connection between King's Cross and Blackfriars was brought back into service by BR as *'Thameslink' (1988). Elsewhere, the Jubilee line extension is following a devious course south of the river from Westminster before turning north to Stratford; the East London line is to be extended north to Hackney; and a main-line link is being constructed to Heathrow airport.

It is tempting to attribute the whole of the physical expansion of London during the period of railway dominance to the railway alone; but this is too simple an explanation.

London was already changing its social and residential pattern before 1845, when D. Morier Evans wrote in *The City; or the Physiology of London Business*: 'The City is not now much chosen for a residence . . . Regent's Park, and rows of villas that stud the neighbourhoods of Kensington, Brompton, Hammersmith . . . are thickly inhabited by City men.' In 1854 the number of the City's working population 'who now oscillate between the country and the City' was estimated as 54,000 (both ways) daily at London Bridge and *Fenchurch Street stations, 8,440 at Paddington, Euston, and King's Cross—this out of a total of 640,000 entering and leaving daily, not a high proportion. Workmen's fares certainly did very much, with the significant and often competitive contribution of street *tramways, to make possible the occupation of the artisan and working-class housing that flooded the areas on both sides of the Lea valley and parts of south-east London from the 1870s; but elsewhere development was patchy. The presence of a railway service did not automatically spur it.

Suburban development and commuting were heavily dependent on the railways down to the 1950s; but the decisions of landowners and local bodies and the facility of borrowing on mortgage were at least equally important for the speed and pattern of development. The railway was a necessary condition of suburban growth; but the railway alone did not ensure that it occurred at any particular time or place. Only in the 20th century did railways—the Metropolitan in particular through its associated Country Estates company—begin to promote suburban business so successfully that it nearly overpowered some of them (see METRO-LAND). The Southern Railway had to build new connecting loops at Lewisham (1929–35) to provide more capacity from the south-east, and the Metropolitan's bottleneck between Baker Street and Finchley Road had to be relieved by new *Bakerloo tube tunnels (1939).

It is impossible to tabulate the numbers of rail passengers travelling into central London because of inconsistency in the statistical methods. In 1854 there may have been about 6,000 daily commuters on the railways (against 200,000 arriving in the City on foot and 15,000 by steamboat). In 1904 passenger arrivals at London main-line terminals before 10.30 a.m. were 318,000; in 1949 374,000. A British Railways count in 1994 gave 630,699 passengers arriving at central London stations on a working day (396,295 between 7 and 10 a.m.).

London was also a manufacturing centre for railway equipment. John Braithwaite of New Road, with John Ericsson, built the locomotive *Novelty*, the popular favourite and runner-up at the *Rainhill trials in 1829, and was in business as Braithwaite & Milner until 1844; Maudslay Sons & Field of Lambeth and G. J. *Rennie of Blackfriars built engines between 1838 and 1843; William Bridges *Adams produced light locomotives and railcars from Fairfield works, Bow, in 1847–9; George *England, Hatcham Ironworks, Old Kent Road, turned out over 150 locomotives in 1849–72, including 19 for the *Somerset & Dorset and seven for the narrow-gauge *Festiniog Railway. Railway-owned locomotive, carriage, and wagon works were at Stratford, ECR and

GER, which built locomotives from 1851, and nearly all GER engines from 1882 to 1921, including an 0-6-0 erected as a 'stunt' in 9 hrs 47 min in 1891. Nine Elms, LSWR, opened in 1843, built all new engines from 1887 until the works moved to Eastleigh, Hampshire, for carriages and wagons in 1891, locomotives in 1909. Longhedge, Battersea, LCDR and *South Eastern & Chatham, built 50 locomotives in 1869–1904; Bow, NLR, made all that company's engines after 1863; Neasden works, Metropolitan Railway, built 3 engines in 1896–8. Several *signalling equipment manufacturers had London factories: Saxby & Farmer, Kilburn Lane, 1863–1903; W. R. Sykes Interlocking Signal Co., Clapham; Stevens & Sons, Southwark.

The original electrically operated railways (except the LBSCR) built their own generating stations for current supply: Stockwell (*City & South London); Waterloo (Waterloo & City); Shepherd's Bush (Central London); Poole Street, Islington (Great Northern & City); Neasden (Metropolitan); Lots Road, Chelsea (Underground group); Stonebridge Park (LNWR); Durnsford Road, Wimbledon (LSWR); Park Royal (GWR). From the 1960s onwards these were given up and power normally drawn from the national grid.

London did not contain railway towns like *Crewe, *Swindon, and Wolverton, owned and developed by the companies (see TOWNS AND VILLAGES, RAILWAY-CREATED), with minor exceptions: at Stratford, where 300 *houses were built by the ECR and GER (the nickname 'Hudson's Town' soon disappeared, but 'Waddington', ECR chairman in 1851–6, remains as a street name); Neasden, Metropolitan Railway, 1882, and GCR, 1899; and small 'garden villages' at West Acton and Hayes (GWR, 1923).

See also LONDON STATIONS; LONDON UNDERGROUND RAILWAYS. RMR

Royal Commission on London Traffic, *Report* Cd. 2597 (1905); F. A. A. Menzler, 'London and its Passenger Transport System', *Jnl. Royal Statistical Socy.*, series A, 113 (1950), 198; HLT; J. R. Kellett, *The Impact of Railways on Victorian Cities* (1969); LT; A. A. Jackson, *Semi-Detached London* (1973); D. J. Olsen, *The Growth of Victorian London* (1976); M. Robbins, 'Railway Electrification in London and its Social Effects', in *Perspectives in Railway History and Interpretation*, ed. N. Cossons and others (1992).

London & Birmingham Railway. Robert *Stephenson's first major undertaking as engineer-in-chief, the building of the London & Birmingham, captured public imagination like that of few other early trunk lines. After several abortive schemes, the 112-mile line was authorized in 1833 with a share capital of £2,500,000, but only after agreement to buy out some rapacious *landowners.

Originally intended to start at Camden, the London terminus was changed to *Euston. The line was opened progressively in 1837–8, including six months when road coaches covered the gap between Denbigh Hall, near Bletchley, and Rugby while Kilsby *Tunnel was being completed. Of the eight tunnels, Kilsby, south of Rugby and 1 mile 666 yds long, was the most formidable, causing constant difficulty from running sand. Deep cuttings had to be made at Tring and Roade, but the result was that beyond

London & Blackwall Railway

Camden the LBR was the best-graded 111 miles of railway in Britain. At Curzon Street Station, *Birmingham, the LBR joined the *Grand Junction Railway, forming a through route from *London to *Liverpool and *Manchester.

Until 1844 the 1¼-mile-long incline from Euston to Camden, rising as steeply as 1 in 70, was operated by stationary winding engines and endless *cable, locomotives being attached to or detached from trains at the top. In 1838 the great Doric portico was completed at Euston and a complementary entrance was erected at Birmingham (see ARCHITECTURE AND ARCHITECTS).

Five branches were made by quasi-independent companies backed by the LBR and taken over before or shortly after opening: Cheddington–Aylesbury (opened in 1839), *Coventry–Warwick (1844), Bletchley–Bedford (1846), Leighton Buzzard–Dunstable (1848), and Rugby–Leamington (1851). The company itself built a long cross-country branch from Blisworth through Northampton to Peterborough (1845).

In 1838 locomotive and carriage *works were established at the village of Wolverton, Buckinghamshire, and a town was built for employees. By 1844 there were 200 *houses.

In 1839 the *Birmingham & Derby Junction Railway brought traffic on to the LBR at Hampton, between Coventry and Birmingham, followed in 1840 by the *Midland Counties Railway from *Derby to Rugby via *Leicester. After 1844, when they became part of the *Midland Railway, Rugby was the sole traffic-exchange point, and from 1840 until the opening of the *Great Northern Railway in 1850 the LBR carried the entire traffic between London and central and north-east England, as well as the north-west.

An acrimonious relationship with what should have been the LBR's natural ally, the Grand Junction, reached its height over the proposed extension of the Manchester & Birmingham Railway and allied lines southward to join the LBR. To the west, the *Great Western threatened by furthering broad-gauge lines from Oxford to Rugby and to Wolverhampton via Worcester. LBR support for the MBR scheme led the GJR to ally itself with the GWR, while LBR investment in the Trent Valley Railway (Rugby–Stafford) provoked the GJR to reluctantly follow suit.

Ultimately the two companies' shareholders, many with cross-investments, sensibly prevailed on their boards to negotiate an amalgamation that included the Manchester & Birmingham. It was preceded by absorption of the Trent Valley Railway by all three parties, which were then incorporated as the *London & North Western Railway in 1846. Honours were even, the LBR chairman, G. C. *Glyn, becoming the new chairman and Mark *Huish of the GJR the general manager. GJB

L. T. C. Rolt, *George and Robert Stephenson* (1960), ch. 11; H. G. Lewin, *The Railway Mania and its Aftermath* (1968 edn.), chs 3 and 4; Whishaw, 218–55; M. C. Reed, *Investment in Railways in Britain, 1820–44* (1975), esp. 133–8, and *London & North Western Railway* (1996).

London & Blackwall Railway. Authorized in 1836 as the Commercial Railway, this 3½-mile line ran from the Minories to Blackwall via Stepney, the first section of 2½ miles to West India Docks on an 18-ft viaduct; the estimated cost was £600,000. In 1839 an extension to *Fenchurch Street was authorized, and the company changed its name to London & Blackwall, opening for traffic in 1840.

To eliminate the risk of fire to shipping in the docks, *cable-haulage was used and stationary engines were installed at the Minories and Blackwall to drive the 23-ft-diameter cable drums. Each track was furnished with seven miles of hempen rope, 3½ miles of which was wound round one of the drums, and a brakesman rode on each carriage to attach or slip his vehicle from the rope.

In practice, at each terminus a train of seven carriages would be waiting and at the intermediate stations a single coach stood on each track. At a signal by electric *telegraph both engines would start winding; the carriages from the local stations then travelled singly to their respective termini, followed by the main train which would deposit five of its coaches at stations along the way. On arrival at the terminus the remainder of the train would join the waiting five carriages from the intermediate stations to form a complete train, and the cycle would be repeated. However, travel between any two local stations was not possible.

In 1849 the system of rope haulage was abandoned and the *gauge was changed to standard from the original 5 ft. At this time the Blackwall Extension Railway was opened from Stepney Junction to Bow, *Eastern Counties Railway, and in 1856 the *London Tilbury & Southend Railway joined it at Gas Factory Junction, giving access to Fenchurch Street.

In 1866 the recently formed *Great Eastern Railway took over the LBR on a 999-year lease. RHGT

J. E. Connor, *Stepney's Own Railway* (1984).

London & Croydon Railway. Authorized in 1835 and opened in 1839, the 8¾-mile line ran from Corbetts Lane Junction on the *London & Greenwich Railway to Croydon (now West Croydon). The original intention to lay the tracks along the bed of the old Croydon Canal was abandoned as impracticable. The total cost of the line was £615,160, or £70,240 per mile. The railway reached *London Bridge over the LGR but had its own station alongside the LGR terminus.

By 1842 the trains of the London & Brighton (see LONDON BRIGHTON & SOUTH COAST) and *South Eastern Railways were using the LCR, greatly increasing congestion on that line; this led the company to adopt the Samuda Brothers' *atmospheric system for its own local traffic. The first railway flying *junction was installed south of Norwood to enable the atmospheric line with its large central pipe to cross the running lines of the other two toll-paying companies.

Public traffic started in 1846 but there were many breakdowns and delays; in the meantime all the atmospheric equipment was purchased for the extension to Epsom, authorized in 1844. In 1846 the Croydon and Brighton Railways amalgamated to form the *London Brighton & South Coast Railway and in 1847 the new company abandoned the whole atmospheric system. RHGT

J. T. Howard Turner, *London Brighton & South Coast Railway*, i

(1977); H. Clayton, *The Atmospheric Railways* (1966); C. Hadfield, *Atmospheric Railways* (1967).

London & Greenwich Railway. Plans for this 3¾-mile line were produced in 1831 by a Royal Engineer, Colonel G. T. Landmann. To avoid the numerous streets in the vicinity of the *London Bridge terminus, and to take the railway above the low-lying marshy ground in Bermondsey periodically flooded by the Thames, the line was to run on a brick viaduct 22 ft high.

Authorized in 1833, the original capital of £400,000 was raised with some difficulty by George Walter, the company's secretary and general manager until 1837. The viaduct was built by the contractor Hugh McIntosh, using materials purchased by the company: 60 million bricks, 12,000 yds of rails, and vast quantities of cement; when finished it contained 878 arches of 18 ft span and 28 ft wide. This, the first railway in *London, provided the pattern for other lines in built-up areas; by the end of the century there were approximately 25 miles of brick railway viaduct in the metropolis.

The railway opened in stages, Spa Road–Deptford in February 1836, London Bridge–Spa Road in December 1836, and Deptford–Greenwich in December 1838.

The board, apprehensive of trains falling off the viaduct, despite its 4 ft 6 in parapet walls, employed low centre of gravity carriages, the frames of which were only 4 in above the rail. They also had the viaduct illuminated by gas lamps at night as a safety measure.

When completed in 1843 the LGR had cost £993,000 in shares and loans, or £267,000 per mile. Among its costly mistakes was the employment of granite sleepers set in concrete on the brickwork of the viaduct.

The *London & Croydon, London & Brighton (see LONDON BRIGHTON & SOUTH COAST), and *South Eastern Railways all used the tracks of the LGR between London Bridge and Corbetts Lane, about 1¾ miles, upon payment of a toll of 3d. per passenger, increased to 4½d. when the viaduct was widened to accommodate them in 1842. This increase led to bitter disputes between the companies involved, and ultimately to the leasing in perpetuity of the LGR by the SER in 1845.   RHGT

R. H. G. Thomas, *London's First Railway: The London & Greenwich* (1986).

London & North Eastern Railway: the second largest of the groups created by the Railways Act, 1921. It linked the partners in the *East Coast route to Scotland—the *Great Northern, *North Eastern, and *North British Railways, as well as the small, isolated *Great North of Scotland Railway. Radiating from *London it also joined the 'Three Greats' (Great Northern, *Great Eastern, *Great Central Railways) that had once sought and been refused amalgamation. The small *Hull & Barnsley Railway had already been absorbed into the NER in 1922.

The LNER was more dependent upon *freight than any other main line and should have prospered; but it relied upon heavy industry in the north-east, Scotland, and Yorkshire, where there was long-term depression, and it had the weakest financial position of the *'Big Four'. So caution dominated the board, where the chairman, William Whitelaw, had come from the thrifty NBR, and the deputy chairman, Lord Faringdon, from the chronically hard-up GCR. Economy and productivity were sought with some success, staff falling from 207,500 in 1924 to 175,800 in 1937, though more train-miles were being operated. But investment had to be financed from internal sources, mainly renewal funds built up from revenue, instead of by borrowing.

Managerial salaries were lower than on the other main lines in general, but even so the LNER had probably the best resources of able young managers owing to the Traffic Apprenticeship Scheme which the chief general manager, Sir Ralph *Wedgwood, brought with him from the NER, attracting graduates and backed up by career planning personally supervised by the assistant general manager Robert Bell, also ex-NER.

On organization, Wedgwood originally favoured a straight departmental pattern, but the board adopted a strongly decentralized system of three Areas with headquarters in, respectively, *London, *York, and *Edinburgh (with a temporary sub-Area in *Aberdeen). Each Area was placed under a divisional general manager in charge of the principal departments, except for certain 'All-Line' officers, notably the chief mechanical engineer. There were also three Area Boards dealing with purely local questions. The effect was to leave the chief general manager free to concentrate upon board matters, major policy, and—if necessary—ruling in cases of disagreement between DGMs. Wedgwood was masterly in handling external relations.

Within the financial constraints, the LNER can be considered well managed. Strenuous efforts were made to retain the freight traffic, especially against road competition; fast overnight services between major centres were operated and modern mechanized *marshalling yards were built at Whitemoor, Cambridgeshire, and Hull in Yorkshire.

On the passenger side, there was a sharp difference between the principal express services and the London suburban network. The CME, H. N. (Sir Nigel) *Gresley, had come from the GNR, a line with a tradition of high speed. He built a range of handsome and effective express passenger locomotives, and new carriages for the Anglo-Scottish and other prestige services that caught the public eye, and which the LNER's very efficient *publicity department was able to exploit. Imaginative developments included the non-stop London–Edinburgh run of the Flying Scotsman, the introduction of all-Pullman trains such as the Queen of Scots, and the novel concept of train-cruising as a luxury holiday, with the Northern Belle.

Strongly supported by the management, Gresley took the LNER into the era of high speed trains with steam (instead of diesel traction then being tried out in Germany and the USA). His streamlined Silver Jubilee set of 1935 was followed in 1937 by the Coronation and then the West Riding Limited. A world speed record of 126 mph momentarily attained on a test run enhanced Gresley's prestige.

At the other end of the spectrum, the steam suburban services in north and east London were overcrowded, slow, and often dirty. They were heavily criticized, though ingenuity was shown in working an intensive service over crowded routes, particularly on the Great Eastern section; and the maximum number of seats for any given train-length was achieved by the principle of *'articulation' introduced by Gresley, whereby adjacent carriages were brought close together by sharing one bogie.

Like all the grouped companies, the LNER was a conglomerate. Its continental *shipping services based on Harwich (Parkeston Quay)—see PORTS AND DOCKS—were served by fine modern vessels; its *hotels, mostly less grandiose than those on the *London Midland & Scottish, were well patronized; and its investments after 1928 in *bus companies were significant, with the LNER in several cases sharing in joint boards with local authorities. But, alone among the grouped companies, the LNER was not interested in the development of *air services.

When in 1933 government loans at low interest were offered for approved railway schemes, the LNER embarked at last upon *electrifying the heavily used freight main line from *Manchester to *Sheffield and Wath yard, and lines in the London suburban area. The latter involved the transfer of several routes to *London Transport. Work on these schemes had to be suspended after the outbreak of war and most were not completed until after *nationalization.

Owing to its geographical position, the LNER suffered heavily from enemy action in 1939–45. It had also seen new men at the top. Whitelaw was followed by Sir Ronald Matthews in 1938 and Wedgwood by C. H. (Sir Charles) Newton in 1939. Although Whitelaw had once upset his fellow chairmen by suggesting that nationalization might not be disastrous, the board now only went so far as to suggest a 'landlord and tenant' scheme as a half-way house to nationalization. The government quickly rejected this, and on 1 January 1948 the LNER was divided up between the Eastern, North Eastern, and Scottish Regions of the new Railway Executive. The relatively high proportion of senior positions in *British Railways subsequently occupied by ex-LNER men was an eloquent tribute to the policies of management development pursued by Wedgwood and Robert Bell.   MRB

C. J. Allen, *The London & North Eastern Railway* (1966); G. Hughes, *LNER* (1986); M. R. Bonavia, *A History of the LNER* (1982–3).

London & North Western Railway. The company was formed in 1846 by an amalgamation of the *London & Birmingham, *Grand Junction, and Manchester & Birmingham Railways, putting under single operation 247 miles of trunk route from *London to *Birmingham, Warrington —where it connected with the *Liverpool & Manchester line—and *Preston. There it joined other lines leading to *Carlisle. The MBR ran from *Crewe to *Manchester, and there was a line to Chester and several others. The combined capital was nearly £17.25 million.

With a system more linear than regional, beset by strong competitors, the railway in its earlier years, under its first chairman George Carr *Glyn (later Lord Wolverton) and general manager Mark *Huish, had little option but to pursue an aggressively acquisitive policy, one that at times was quite unscrupulous.

Huish proceeded vigorously to form alliances with other railways, endeavouring to keep on LNWR metals as much as possible of the growing traffic between London, the Midlands, north-west and north-east England, and Scotland. The first, known as the Euston Square Confederacy (1850) (see AGREEMENTS), was directed against the *Great Northern Railway. When it began to collapse, Huish tried another tack with the Octuple Agreement, which pooled receipts between London and places north of York, virtually abolishing competition for ten years; this in turn was followed by the English & Scotch Traffic Agreement (1859–69) which in effect gave London–*Glasgow traffic to the west coast companies and *Edinburgh to the east coast. All were dominated by the LNWR.

Expansion continued. By 1859 the LNWR extended to Oxford, Cambridge, Peterborough, *Leeds, and, by leasing the *Lancaster & Carlisle Railway (later purchased), to Carlisle where a long-lasting alliance was formed with the *Caledonian Railway which extended the *West Coast main line to Glasgow, Edinburgh, and *Aberdeen. The LNWR also bought the *Chester & Holyhead Railway. By 1866 the company was established in west Cumberland and by 1868 was running trains from *Shrewsbury through central Wales to *Swansea and Carmarthen over a route 80 per cent wholly or jointly owned. It had also acquired an isolated group of lines between Abergavenny, Ebbw Vale, and Merthyr, reached by *running powers from Hereford and giving valuable access to Newport and *Cardiff. The company reached the City of London and the docks over its subsidiary, the *North London Railway, and the *Great Western and railways south of the Thames over *joint lines in west London.

But in 1851 and 1852 bold proposals to amalgamate with, first, the *Midland Railway and then the smaller *North Staffordshire were abortive. The LNWR also failed to prevent the antagonistic GWR from reaching Birmingham, Shrewsbury, and Birkenhead (for *Liverpool) via Oxford —although it retained joint ownership of the line from Chester onwards—resulting in competition between the two routes. The company suffered a further setback in 1858 when the MR secured an alternative route to London over the GNR from Hitchin, and after the pooling agreements ended in 1869 there was open competition for Manchester traffic with the MR and with a combination of the GNR and Manchester Sheffield & Lincolnshire Railway (see GREAT CENTRAL). The completion of the MR's *Settle & Carlisle line in 1875 also brought new competition for Anglo-Scottish traffic. In all cases the LNWR had shorter and easier routes, although in 1910 a new GWR line gave a slightly shorter route to Birmingham, Wolverhampton, and Shrewsbury, provoking intensified competition.

Three important cut-off lines (see LOOP; SYSTEM, DEVELOPMENT OF THE) were built in the first 23 years: the 51-mile Trent Valley Railway between Rugby and Stafford (1847), by-passing Birmingham; a short link north of Warrington avoiding tortuous junctions at Winwick and Golborne

(1864); and a direct line to Liverpool north of Crewe, via Runcorn (1869).

From early on the company enjoyed friendly relations with the *Lancashire & Yorkshire Railway. Apart from their competitive Manchester–Liverpool lines, their dense networks in south Lancashire and west Yorkshire were considerably complementary, and in 1863 they entered a series of traffic pooling agreements. Proposals for outright amalgamation in 1872 were rejected by Parliament. In 1908 the MR was admitted to an agreement under which the three railways undertook to consign exchange traffic by the shortest route.

The LNWR was fortunate in a succession of highly competent general managers. Huish, for all his aggressiveness, steered the company successfully through its formative years, while (Sir) Richard *Moon, chairman from 1861 to 1891, was a far-sighted, clear-thinking administrator, a rigid disciplinarian, a strong advocate of economy—for him 45 mph was fast enough—and able to pick out talented subordinates. Under them the former near-autonomous Southern and Northern Divisions were welded into a single, powerful organization which became one of the three largest railways in the kingdom and styled itself 'the largest joint-stock company in the world', with 'the finest permanent way in the world'. Its track was, indeed, superlative, extending at the 1923 *Grouping to 2,066 route miles. During Moon's 30 years' chairmanship the dividend rose from 4.25 per cent to 7.75 per cent by 1880, and thereafter seldom fell below 6 per cent. But it was at the price of a policy bordering on parsimony which, initially justifiable, went on too long.

Huish was succeeded by William Cawkwell, but in 1871 Moon elevated him to the board in order to make (Sir) George *Findlay chief traffic manager, later general manager from 1880 to 1893, who developed a highly efficient, sophisticated, and centralized management structure overseeing 15,000 employees around the country: an organization continued by able successors—Frederick *Harrison, Frank Ree, Robert Turnbull, and Guy Calthrop, all of whom were knighted.

In 1861 locomotive building was concentrated at Crewe and the former Southern Division works at Wolverton given over to carriage building. Wagons were built at Earlestown, near Warrington (see WORKS). The new CME, John *Ramsbottom, made a good job of the reorganization, while his successor, F. W. *Webb (1871–1903), proceeded to make the LNWR remarkably self-sufficient. In time Crewe works included a steel works producing nearly all the company's iron and steel components, with a rolling mill for 60-ft rails—longer than any other British railway's; a brickworks; workshops producing *signalling equipment; even a soap works and a ticket-printing shop, so that everything possible was made there, although no other railway emulated it to the same degree.

The company created the town, which for long was an LNWR hegemony where it provided all services, dominated politics, and, to a large extent, religion, firmly controlled by Webb. He inherited a stock of 2-2-2 and 2-4-0

passenger engines, small, hardworking, and reliable. He built more 2-4-0s, and then went on to pioneer compounding on main-line locomotives (see TRACTION, STEAM) as a means of gaining maximum power from engines limited to a 15½-ton axle load. Although he has been criticized, they largely handled the demands made until the end of the century. His eight-coupled freight engines were the first on a major British railway; large numbers were also built in modified form by his successors (see also BRAKES).

The company first introduced bogie coaches in the late 1880s, followed in 1893 by all-corridor trains for the Anglo-Scottish services operated jointly with the Caledonian. Designed by the LNWR carriage and wagon superintendent, C. A. Park, they set a new standard in luxury passenger travel.

The LNWR's huge freight traffic was derived particularly from the industrial west Midlands, the north-west, and west Yorkshire, providing a large traffic in *coal (also in South Wales), *minerals, engineering products, and raw and finished textiles, to mention a few. Much capital was expended on efficient handling facilities. To deal with the volume from its six Liverpool goods *stations, for instance, the company in 1882 completed extensive and novel *gravity-operated *marshalling yards at Edge Hill, known as 'the gridiron', which at the time were the largest of their kind, eliminating shunting. In 1864 Garston dock, near Liverpool, was acquired, and enlarged in 1876, principally for shipping coal to *Ireland.

To segregate fast and slow trains, by 1914 quadruple track or double-track alternative routes existed on 89 per cent of the 209 miles of the West Coast main line between Euston and Preston, the entire 38 miles between Stalybridge and Leeds—including Standedge *Tunnel, and nearly all of the 33 miles of the Chester & Holyhead as far as Abergele. Elsewhere, numerous goods loops and closely spaced *signal boxes were installed to speed up traffic. The flying *junction at Weaver Junction, north of Crewe, in 1869 was the first of a number built by the LNWR for the same purpose.

Despite carrying the Irish *mail from London to its *port at Holyhead from 1848, the company never succeeded in gaining the sea-going contract until 1920. Until then, for political reasons it remained in the hands of the City of Dublin Steam Packet Company, despite prodigious efforts by the LNWR to secure it, including a new harbour, completed in 1880; quays at North Wall, Dublin—more convenient than Kingstown (Dun Laoghaire); and a succession of improved and faster ships. However, the railway gained the lion's share of Irish goods and extensive cattle traffic, and in 1873 made a bid for the Belfast traffic with a service to Greenore, in connection with the Dundalk Newry & Greenore Railway in which it had a controlling interest and worked with LNWR-built engines and rolling stock. It also participated in a joint service with the LYR from Fleetwood to Belfast, and from Stranraer to Larne with the Midland, Caledonian, and *Glasgow & South Western companies. Great importance was given to the North American traffic through Liverpool. Splendid 12-wheel coaches were built for the 'American Specials'. But the attractions of South-ampton eventually overtook Liverpool's.

In 1914–22 London suburban services were *electrified on the fourth rail system from Broad Street and Euston to Watford and Croxley Green, and in 1927 to Rickmans-worth.

The company was in the forefront of railways' improved *publicity in the early 1900s, producing nearly 12 million postcards depicting engines, trains, stations, and lineside scenes, which are now collectors' items.

After World War I the company found itself bereft of its three most senior men. The chairman, Sir Gilbert Claugh-ton, retired in 1921 and the general manager, Sir Thomas Williams, at the end of 1920, in which year the CME, C. J. Bowen *Cooke, died. Partly due to this, the increasingly close relationship with the LYR culminated in the appoint-ment of the LYR's general manager, (Sir) Arthur Watson, to both companies, followed in January 1922 by amalgamation under the LNWR name, the first 'preliminary scheme' under the 1921 Transport Act. After the full Grouping a year later, the combined company became part of the *Lon-don Midland & Scottish Railway. It seems likely that the LNWR–LYR amalgamation also sought to counteract the Midland's influence in the new group. If so, it was hardly successful. GJB

W. L. Steel, *History of the London & North Western Railway* (1914); Findlay; G. P. Neele, *Railway Reminiscences*, new edn. (1974); M. C. Reed, *London & North Western Railway* (1996); W. A. Tuplin, *North Western Steam* (1963); *Reg. Hist.*, vii, xii, xiv.

London & South Western Railway. From its origin in the London & Southampton Railway, 77 miles long, author-ized in 1834 and opened throughout in 1840, the LSWR developed a London suburban and main-line network. Hav-ing changed its name in 1839, it extended to *Portsmouth (1848; direct line 1859), Dorchester (1847), Salisbury (1848), and *Exeter (1860). West of Exeter, it finally achieved through services to *Plymouth (1876) and Padstow (1899); it had purchased the isolated Bodmin & Wadebridge Rail-way in Cornwall in 1847. In 1922 the LSWR owned 862 miles with a further 157 miles of *joint line.

The South Western operated in three areas of markedly different character: London and its outer suburbs; the main-line territory, an elongated triangle between Woking, Ports-mouth, and Exeter; and a straggling tentacle beyond Exeter, where it was later a rival to the *Great Western.

In London the original 1838 terminus at Nine Elms (Bat-tersea) was soon found too remote; a 1¾-mile extension to *Waterloo was opened in 1848. This was still inconven-iently sited, and the South Western tried many expedients to get its trains into the City. Not until the *Waterloo & City electric tube was built in 1898 (absorbed in 1907), fol-lowed by two Underground Group tubes (*Bakerloo, 1906; *Hampstead line, 1926), was it satisfactorily linked with the north bank of the Thames. The first suburban branch was to Richmond (1846), extended to Windsor and Reading (1849–56); from this and the main line an extensive network was developed down to the 'new' Guildford line via Cob-ham (1885). To minimize conflicting train movements,

seven flying or burrowing *junctions were constructed along 42 miles west of Raynes Park, the greatest concentra-tion on any British main line.

After sharp disputes with the *London Brighton & South Coast Railway, joint arrangements were made for lines and stations at Portsmouth, a shared interest in the Isle of Wight steamers, and ownership of 2 miles of line at Ryde (see ISLE OF WIGHT RAILWAYS). *Southampton, where the docks were acquired by the railway in 1892, provided much of its most important business (see PORTS AND DOCKS). With Aldershot and Salisbury Plain in its area, military traffic grew to be of great importance; in the South African War and World War I movement and embarkation of men and supplies at South-ampton were handled wholly by this railway (see WAR).

The LSWR ran steamers from Southampton to the Channel Islands, Le Havre, and St Malo, and between Lym-ington and Yarmouth (see SHIPPING SERVICES). *Bourne-mouth, not on the original line to Poole, had a direct line from 1888, and holiday traffic grew.

Relations with the Great Western, its northern neigh-bour, were hostile or at best suspicious throughout. The GWR bitterly fought every LSWR attempt to enter its terri-tory, and accused it of bad faith when, with the *Midland, it secured joint control of the *Somerset & Dorset line in 1875. Competition was fierce, punctuated by occasional truces. Between Plymouth and London ocean passengers were carried by the LSWR at high speeds until the Salisbury *accident to one of these trains in 1906 put a stop to such timings. Of 43 passengers on the special train, 24 were killed. This was the railway's worst accident.

The LSWR was a steady dividend-earner, normally pay-ing 5½ per cent or more after 1871. It was primarily a pas-senger line, but its freight, steamship, and docks earnings amounted to nearly 40 per cent of the total revenue in 1908. The principal freight terminals (see STATIONS, GOODS) were at Nine Elms and Southampton; a large *marshalling yard, with hump shunting and electrically controlled points, was completed at Feltham, near Hounslow, in 1922, the year the 2ft. gauge Lynton & Barnstaple Railway was purchased.

After 1878 the locomotives under William *Adams, Dugald *Drummond, and R. W. Urie were a serviceable stock, with a fair amount of standardization and several mixed traffic designs. The train services were 'deliberate rather than lethargic' (Hamilton *Ellis). The earliest British automatic signals controlled by *track circuits were installed between Woking and Basingstoke in 1902–7.

Though widening and improvements (and at Waterloo they were very extensive) were continuous, the manage-ment proved slow to respond to rising demands, especially in the London area, until Herbert *Walker from the *Lon-don & North Western Railway was appointed general man-ager in 1912. He initiated *electrification of the suburban lines, inaugurated in 1915, and went on to be the master mind of the *Southern Railway, on which the LSWR firmly set its own stamp. RMR

S. Fay, *A Royal Road* (1883); G. A. Sekon, *The London & South-Western Railway* (1896); C. F. Dendy Marshall, *History of the Southern Railway*, i (1963 edn.); C. Hamilton Ellis, *South Western*

Railway (1956); Williams; J. N. Faulkner and R. A. Williams, *London & South Western Railway in the 20th Century* (1988).

London Bridge station, see LONDON STATIONS.

London Brighton & South Coast Railway.

The 'Brighton', as it was known, was formed by amalgamation of the London & Brighton and *London & Croydon Railways in 1846. It then operated from *London Bridge to *Brighton (opened 1841), Brighton to Shoreham (1840), and extended west to Chichester (1846) and east to St Leonards (1846). *Portsmouth and Newhaven were reached in 1847, Horsham in 1848, and Eastbourne in 1849. Within this triangle, with infilling lines built up to 1888, the Brighton established a virtual *monopoly, with the *London & South Western on the west and *South Eastern on the east. It built up a network of London suburban lines served from London Bridge and *Victoria (1860). Its total mileage, including *joint lines, was 457 in 1922. It operated *shipping services to France, jointly with the Ouest Railway, from Newhaven after 1867 and from Littlehampton in 1867–82. *Freight produced a quarter of the traffic receipts in 1913; the most important depots were at Willow Walk, Bermondsey, London, and Lovers Walk, Brighton. A *grande vitesse* goods train served Newhaven.

Overstretched finances, including 6 per cent dividends in 1856–62, led to near-insolvency in 1867, when Samuel *Laing returned to the chair and prudent retrenchment followed. After 1874 the dividend was near 5 per cent or higher. The Brighton was not aggressive towards its neighbours, but involvement with the SER at London Bridge and Redhill led to continual difficulty; the latter was largely removed when the Brighton opened its avoiding line from Coulsdon to Earlswood (the 'Quarry line') in 1900.

The London–Brighton passenger traffic was always a prime concern. The best times for the 50¾ miles were 90 min (1844), 75 min (1865), and 60 min (1898). The first *slip carriage service in Britain began at Haywards Heath in 1858; *Pullman cars ran from 1875, with electric lighting from 1881. But these were exceptional; the Brighton was much criticized in the 1880s and 1890s for poor provision for third-class passengers. For *carriage lighting, *braking, and *signalling, the Brighton scored high (Sykes' lock-and-block was installed in London and down the main line from 1880). The first 'fish tail' distant signal arm was at Norwood Junction, 1872. After William *Stroudley moved to Brighton to take charge in 1870, the mechanical department (which included steamships) was efficiently managed.

In the 20th century the Brighton was forced to modernize itself, by growth of traffic, competition from electric *tramways in London, and the threat of a competing line, the London & Brighton Electric scheme of 1901–2. The main line was quadrupled to Balcombe Tunnel (32 miles from Victoria) and general powers to *electrify were obtained in 1903. A 6,700 V ac overhead system was introduced on the South London line (Victoria–London Bridge) in 1909 and extended to Crystal Palace and Selhurst in 1912.

The impact of the railway on its territory was great, most of all at Brighton itself: first, by *excursion trains; then by making it possible to live in Brighton or Hove and work daily in London (see COMMUTING); and from 1852 by the *works, with its large labour force. It encouraged growth of coastal towns from Hastings to Bognor. Its services enabled the Crystal Palace to be re-erected at Sydenham (1854); it was essential to the development of the south London suburbs from Dulwich to Purley; and it brought all of Sussex within easy reach of London.　　　　　　　　　　RMR

[The Company] *The London Brighton & South Coast Railway Co. 1846–1922* (1922); E. W. Gilbert, *Brighton* (1954); C. F. Dendy Marshall, *History of the Southern Railway*, i (1963 edn.); J. T. Howard Turner, *The London Brighton & South Coast Railway* (1977–9).

London Chatham & Dover Railway.

This small company took an important part in shaping the transport network in south-east England because of its frenetic competition with the *South Eastern Railway, which ended only with the formation of the *South Eastern & Chatham Railways Managing Committee on 1 January 1899.

The origin of the LCDR can be traced to the decision by the South Eastern to adopt a Weald of Kent route for its Dover main line. This was compounded by a failure to extend the North Kent line east of the Medway. Thus it was Faversham interests that dominated the formation of the East Kent Railway in 1853; the first section of line, between Strood and Faversham, opened during 1858.

The EKR showed a tendency to become a *contractor's line from an early stage, with contractors like Sir Charles *Fox being instrumental in the promotion of early extensions such as the expensive line from Canterbury to Dover, following the opening of which the company was able to develop a steamer service to Calais from 1862. However, the SER mistakenly tried to starve the EKR into submission, with the result that the contractor Sir Morton *Peto encouraged the East Kent directors to extend successively to Bromley (1860), *Victoria (1862), and Farringdon (1866). As part of this process, the company changed its name to London Chatham & Dover Railway in 1859.

Rapid expansion and a lack of genuine capital soon brought financial disaster. The LCDR relied heavily on the contractors Peto and Betts, whose sharp decline following the Overend, Gurney & Co. bank failure (see SPECULATION) led to the bankruptcy of the LCDR itself in 1866—lasting until 1871.

The 1866 collapse strengthened the position of James Staats *Forbes, who had become general manager of the LCDR in 1861. He became chairman in 1874, from which time he dominated the business almost totally, waging an often bitter campaign against the South Eastern—led with equal stubbornness by Sir Edward *Watkin. This rivalry tempted the LCDR into promoting several lines which squandered capital and reduced operating profits, notably the Greenwich branch (opened in 1871, extended in 1886), the Gravesend West branch (1886), and—to a lesser extent —the Maidstone to Ashford extension (1884).

However, the errors of the SER were possibly even worse, so that the relative strength of the LCDR improved in the 1890s. Talks on a working union between the companies foundered in 1890 when the SER rejected LCDR requests for a 37 per cent share in traffic receipts, but the eventual arrangement of 1899 awarded the LCDR 41 per cent to the SER's 59 per cent. The 'Chatham' had much healthier receipts per mile: £142.6 per week in January 1898, against only £87.9 on the SER. The SER reached agreement 40 years too late.

The LCDR deserves some credit. It had no major accidents between 1878 and 1898, served the Kent coast efficiently, and built a line through the heart of London whose value has been confirmed comparatively recently for *Thameslink services. Even the duplicate route to Ashford is proving useful for *Channel Tunnel traffic. AG

D. L. Bradley, *The Locomotives of the LCDR* (1979); E. Course, *The Railways of Southern England: The Main Lines* (1973); A. Gray, *The London Chatham & Dover Railway* (1984).

London Electric Railway, see LONDON UNDERGROUND RAILWAYS.

London Midland & Scottish Railway. The largest of the four railways formed at the 1923 *Grouping, the LMS was a sprawling, unwieldy amalgamation of the *London & North Western (including the *Lancashire & Yorkshire with which it had already made a preliminary amalgamation) and *Midland Railways in England; the *Caledonian, *Glasgow & South Western, and *Highland in Scotland; a number of smaller lines; and two in *Ireland. Difficult to knit together, fusion was impeded by internal strife between LNWR and MR factions—with the latter prevailing—while in Scotland the Caledonian was dominant. Until 1927, therefore, the public saw little change.

The early application of Midland centralized train *control to the whole system was sensible. It was further developed by creating three (later four) operating divisions, and eventually became a feature of considerable pride on the LMS. At first it did little to speed up passenger services, which in 1929 were the slowest of the *Big Four compared with 1914, largely owing to perpetuation of the Midland's small-engine policy for new locomotives.

In 1926 Sir Josiah (Lord) *Stamp came from Nobel Industries as president of a four (later seven)-man executive, replacing the traditional general manager and an officers' committee; a revolutionary American concept. In 1927 Stamp also became chairman. This small but powerful team set about the difficult task of achieving a unity that was accompanied by a detailed analysis of costs, leading to radical combining of functions, together with the vigorous —some thought ruthless—standardization of operating methods and equipment. Set against trade depressions and increasing road competition, not surprisingly it took some years for a corporate identity to emerge.

To eliminate double-heading of expresses the CME, Sir Henry *Fowler from the Midland, was instructed to produce more powerful locomotives, but his 4-6-0 Royal Scots were only just adequate. After he retired, Stamp brought in (Sir) William *Stanier from the *Great Western in 1932. Quickly ending the factional quarrelling between *Derby

and *Crewe, Stanier began a locomotive building and standardization programme that by 1938 reduced the number of types from 404 to 132. Rationalization and modernization of locomotive and carriage workshops drastically reduced costs, repair time, and the number of locomotives required to work the system—the last by 26 per cent—producing an annual saving of some £2 million.

Stanier provided the motive power that the LMS needed, immediately improving train services. Simultaneously, he embarked on mass-production of new corridor *carriages that for space and comfort were regarded as the best in the country. In 1937 the streamlined Coronation Scot train was introduced, followed by others, while improved non-corridor stock was built for local services. He built numerous and highly successful Class 5 4-6-0 mixed traffic locomotives, which later formed the basis for a standard *British Railways design.

Stanier also speeded up *freight trains with his standard 2-8-0 locomotives, of which numbers were built for wartime service overseas as well. Following a work-study programme in 1933—another innovation—wide-scale rationalization of handling methods helped to make LMS freight business generally profitable in 1939. In 1938 there were seven scheduled daily freight trains running over 150 miles non-stop, and 57 over 90 miles, although the company was curiously slow to mechanize collection and delivery services and, unlike the GWR, refused to invest in large, 20-ton mineral *wagons.

The emphasis on modern technology and business methods extended to training and *research. At Derby a testing and research laboratory was established, followed in 1938 by the School of Transport, the first of its kind in the world. The LMS also paid great attention to *publicity by building up a highly successful organization that included the production of attractive *posters by well-known artists, and the pioneering use of films, many of which are now historic documentaries. As part of its drive for transatlantic business the company sent the Royal Scot train on a North American tour, and later the Coronation Scot.

The LMS claimed to be the world's largest transport organization, and the biggest commercial undertaking in Europe (but without stating criteria), including the largest chain of *hotels. In 1938 it was responsible for operating 6,870 route miles of railway, excluding its Northern Ireland lines. Yet, like the others in the Big Four, it failed to achieve significant *profitability. During World War II, when the dividends on its ordinary shares were based on the average net revenues for 1935–7, they amounted to only 2.7 per cent.

The LMS was a railway of contrasts, particularly in its secondary and branch-line trains which, compared with main-line services, were often slow and dirty. And despite the forward-looking policies elsewhere, the company had little interest in *electrification. The former *Wirral and *Mersey Railways were electrified, together with the *Manchester South Junction & Altrincham line jointly with the *London & North Eastern Railway, but that was all. Although in this respect better than the GWR, which did nothing, it was worse than the LNER which by World War II had several ambitious schemes in hand, and it bore no comparison with the *Southern.

Strict economy spread to stations, which were infrequently cleaned, seldom painted, and bore a generally shabby appearance. Unlike the other companies there was no general reconstruction or modernization programme, and the only large station to be partly rebuilt was *Leeds City, where economies were also made by combining two older stations, one jointly owned with the LNER. After Stamp's death Sir William *Wood became president in 1941–7, when war-time measures followed by impending *nationalization inhibited any long-term development. The system took a large share of the damage and neglect that the war caused to the railways. Afterwards it considered pooling receipts with the LNER, and with other companies an exchange of penetrating lines and the abolition of *joint lines. Nationalization, however, intervened, but not before the first British prototype main-line diesel-electric locomotive (see TRACTION, DIESEL) appeared bearing the initials LMS.   GJB

H. J. Dyos and D. H. Aldcroft, *British Transport* (1969), 293–6, 308–9, 347; M. R. Bonavia, *The Four Great Railways* (1980); P. Whitehouse and D. St J. Thomas, *LMS 150* (1987).

London stations

Baker Street

This was the headquarters of the *Metropolitan Railway, beginning as a sub-surface station on what is now *London Underground's Circle Line in 1863. In 1868 the St John's Wood line was opened from adjacent platforms known as Baker Street East. In 1892–3, after that line had been extended, the East station was enlarged, followed in 1910–25 by progressive rebuilding to incorporate the Circle Line platforms and the company's offices. In 1930 Chiltern Court, a prestigious block of luxury flats, was built facing Marylebone Road, including shops, a restaurant, and a large function hall. The *Bakerloo tube station was incorporated into the complex in 1940, and *Jubilee tube platforms were opened in 1979. The Circle Line platforms were restored in 1984 to represent their original appearance.   GJB

L. Menear, *London's Underground Stations* (1983); A. A. Jackson, *London's Metropolitan Railway* (1986); D. Leboff, *London's Underground Stations* (1994).

Blackfriars and Holborn Viaduct

The first Blackfriars station (1864–85) was on the south bank of the Thames on the *London Chatham & Dover Railway's cross-City line to Farringdon. In 1886 a combined through station and terminus opened on the north bank, called St Paul's, but renamed Blackfriars in 1937. *BR rebuilt it in 1971–9, preserving on the concourse a curious set of 54 British and continental destinations taken from the stonework of the old station, all supposedly accessible from it —mostly indirectly.

In 1874–7 the LCDR opened a six-platform terminus and hotel at Holborn Viaduct close by, to relieve congestion at its through Ludgate Hill station (1865–1929). Adjacent sub-surface platforms on the through lines were called Snow Hill,

renamed Holborn Viaduct Low Level in 1912, and closed in 1916. The severely bomb-damaged frontage of the terminus was rebuilt as part of an office development in 1963. It closed in 1990 on the opening of City *Thameslink station, virtually on the site of the old Ludgate Hill.   GJB

LT, 191–209, 359–61.

Broad Street

The station was the *North London Railway's City terminus, opened in 1865. Designed by the engineer William *Baker, probably assisted by the architect J. B. Stansby, its mixed French-Italian frontage was marred by a screen wall in 1913, when two ugly footbridges were built across the forecourt to improve access to the nine elevated platforms. Part of the *London & North Western Railway's goods *station lay underneath.

By 1969 the 50,000 daily passengers of 1900 had fallen to some 9,000, the two-bay *trainshed had been severely cut back, and the platforms reduced to five, mostly unroofed. Outside peak hours Broad Street had an air of quiet neglect. It was closed in 1986 to make way for redevelopment associated with the modernization of *Liverpool Street.   GJB

The Builder, 28 Oct. 1865, 769; *Illustrated London News*, 3 Feb. 1866; J. Betjeman and J. Gay, *London's Historic Railway Stations* (1972), 50–3; *LT*, 95–106, 350–1; *GRSB*.

Cannon Street

This station was built by the *South Eastern Railway in 1866 to gain access to the City. The 190-ft-span arched *trainshed, by *Hawkshaw, abutted on to his bridge across the Thames, flanked by two Baroque towers containing water tanks for hydraulic *lifts. The eight platforms—later nine—were built on arches. At the front, the City Terminus *Hotel was designed in French and Italian style by E. M. Barry. It was converted into railway offices in 1931.

After remodelling and *electrification by the *Southern Railway in 1926 the station reverted to eight platforms. World War II bombing severely damaged the trainshed and hotel. The former was dismantled, leaving only the arcaded walls and the towers, City landmarks which were restored later. A 15-storey office block replaced the hotel in 1965, and a new entrance and concourse were opened in 1974. In 1991 another office block was built over the platforms.   GJB

LT, 172–88, 306–9; *GRSB*.

Charing Cross

Close to Trafalgar Square, it is London's most central terminus. Opened in 1864 to give the *South Eastern Railway access to the West End, its small size, with only six platforms, belies a heavy commuter traffic and main-line services to Hastings, Folkestone, and Dover via Tonbridge, which in 1984 made it London's fourth busiest terminus.

The lofty single-arch *trainshed designed by Sir John *Hawkshaw suffered a spectacular collapse in 1905, killing six men. It was replaced by a low ridge-and-furrow roof, which in turn was demolished when the 'air space' over the station was redeveloped to form Embankment Place, a large office complex designed by Terry Farrell, completed in 1990. Viewed from the Thames, its great arched profile, derived from the Victorian trainshed idiom, has been highly acclaimed as one of London's most spectacular modern buildings.

Meanwhile the concourse, and the seven-storey hotel and forecourt facing the Strand, designed by E. M. Barry in 1865, were carefully restored as closely as possible to their original appearance, although it was impracticable to alter the unsympathetic top floor which replaced the war-damaged original. Sir John Betjeman considered the hotel dining room to be the most finely appointed in London.   GJB

J. Betjeman and J. Gay, *London's Historic Railway Stations* (1972), 86–95; *LT*, 243–66, 363–4; M. Binney, 'A Man with Ideas above His Station', *The Times Saturday Review*, 19 Jan. 1991.

Euston

Before 1962 it was both splendid and seedy. Philip *Hardwick's noble Doric portico truly proclaimed the *London & Birmingham Railway's station as the 'gateway to the north'. Opened in 1838, it immediately became a public spectacle, enhanced in 1849 by the resplendent Great Hall and Shareholders' Room. But beyond lay anticlimax: low light iron sheds covered two platforms. Designed by Robert *Stephenson and Francis Fox, they were cheap and easy to erect, and were forerunners of successive designs on the *London & North Western Railway and elsewhere during the rest of the century (see TRAINSHEDS).

The original concept soon eroded. From 1839 the portico was steadily hemmed in by *hotels and office blocks, becoming completely hidden by 1881, while the platforms haphazardly increased to 15. Euston became a labyrinth.

The *London Midland & Scottish Railway's plans to rebuild were stopped by World War II, and *British Railways made a fresh start when they *electrified the *West Coast main line. A public outcry and representations to the prime minister failed to prevent demolition of the portico and the Great Hall, to be replaced in 1968 by a low, bland frontage facing a piazza (see VANDALISM BY RAILWAYS). Despite complaints about the long walk to the 20 platforms, the new station was incomparably better, particularly the spacious concourse. All that remained of the old Euston were the 1870 entrance lodges, the war memorial, and the statue of Robert Stephenson that had graced the Great Hall.   GJB

[G. Royde-Smith] *Old Euston* (1938); Sir J. Summerson, *The Architectural History of Euston Station* (1959); *LT*, 31–58, 344–6; *GRSB*.

Fenchurch Street

Tucked away in a City side street, this is the quietest London terminus. Built on the end of the *London & Blackwall Railway's viaduct in 1841, it was rebuilt in 1854 by the company's engineer, George Berkeley, with a crescent-shaped overall roof that was reflected in the curved pediment above a restrained Italianate façade. The *Great Eastern Railway succeeded the Blackwall company and added a fifth platform. The layout was completely remodelled by the *London & North Eastern Railway in 1932–5 by which time, curiously, most of the trains were those of the *London Midland & Scottish Railway's *London Tilbury & Southend services. In 1967 the Tilbury line was electrified, and in 1987 the station was reconstructed beneath a pyramidal office block, leaving only the original façade.   GJB

J. F. Gairns, 'Notable Railway Stations and Their Traffic: Fen-

church Street', *RM*, 44 (1919), 359; J. Betjeman and J. Gay, *London's Historic Railway Stations* (1972), 44–9; *LT*, 128–43, 353–4.

King's Cross

It has always had an ambivalent reputation: admired as architecture but disliked by railwaymen as extremely difficult to operate. It was built in 1850–2 by the *Great Northern Railway primarily for main-line services, and like other stations of its time it was planned with distinct departure and arrival sides. Designed by Lewis *Cubitt, this duality was expressed in the two large glazed arches of the main elevation, presenting a dramatically functional façade. The 105-ft-span arches of the two *trainsheds were unusual in being of laminated timber: their rapid deterioration led to their replacement by wrought-iron ribs of the same profile.

A *hotel formed part of the original proposals, but was constructed as a separate building, also designed by Lewis Cubitt, completed in 1854.

The station is on a cramped site with tunnels close to the platform ends. These impeded train working, especially once suburban services began to increase. In 1863 connections to the *Metropolitan Railway were opened with their own platforms, and in 1875–95 a separate suburban station was progressively added. By the 1880s, suburban trains accounted for over half the traffic at King's Cross.

In 1987 ambitious plans were introduced to construct an international station beneath the existing building, and join the station to *St Pancras, but after six years' intensive design and promotion these were dropped in favour of proposals to bring *Channel Tunnel trains to St Pancras only.

For many years the frontage was notorious for a clutter of unsightly miscellaneous buildings, but is now much improved.   RT

G. Biddle, 'King's Cross and St Pancras: The Making of the Passenger Termini', in M. Hunter and R. Thorne (eds.), *Change at King's Cross* (1990); *LT*, 77–94, 348–50; *ET*, 99–106.

Liverpool Street

No other London terminus has had quite such a complex and contradictory history as Liverpool Street. Built in two stages, and with a frontage *hotel also of two parts, it remained a notoriously confusing station until its redevelopment in the 1980s property boom.

The station lies on the northern side of the City, and exists primarily to provide suburban services for City workers, together with trains to East Anglia. Its first part was built in 1871–5 by the *Great Eastern Railway to the designs of the engineer Edward Wilson. It was a ten-platform station, L-shaped in plan, set below street level. Gothic Revival station offices fronted a four-bay *trainshed with an unusual cantilever truss roof. In 1892–4 eight more platforms were added beneath a roof of simpler design. The longer main-line platforms of the original part created a major barrier between the two sides of the station, to the annoyance of generations of travellers.

The Great Eastern Hotel was built by the GER in 1880–4 and was added to in 1899–1901, filling the rest of the site left over by the extension of the station.

Despite the intensity of its suburban traffic, it was not

until 1949 that the first lines into Liverpool Street were *electrified. In 1975 plans were announced to rebuild the station totally as part of an office complex. The more conservation-minded scheme that was eventually carried out in 1985–91 rationalized the layout of the station, when the 1894 roof was replaced by an overhead office block whilst retaining the original trainshed which was extended in matching form: work which has been highly praised.   RT

[R. Thorne], *Liverpool Street Station* (1978); N. Derbyshire, *Liverpool Street, A Station for the Twenty-First Century* (1991); *LT*, 107–27, 351–3.

London Bridge

This station was hardly less confusing than the old *Waterloo. It was London's first terminus, opened by the *London & Greenwich Railway in 1836. In 1839 the *London & Croydon Railway opened from a terminus on the north side, running parallel before crossing over to the south at Bermondsey. The London & Brighton Railway began using the LCR's tracks in 1841, followed in 1842 by the *South Eastern. The Croydon, Brighton, and South Eastern companies replaced the original LGR station with a new *joint terminus in 1844, when the Greenwich company moved into the old Croydon station, thereby avoiding the conflicting crossing at Bermondsey.

The new station did not last long. In 1845–6 the SER leased the Greenwich line and the LCR and LBR amalgamated to form the *London Brighton & South Coast Railway. Unable to agree on enlargement, they divided the site by a wall and in 1863 opened two new adjacent stations. The SER's, designed by Samuel Beazley, was superior architecturally, but the Brighton's arched *trainshed was acclaimed for its style and cheapness. The Terminus *Hotel, opened alongside, was unsuccessful and the LBSCR bought it for offices in 1893.

The lines into London Bridge were on a viaduct which was steadily widened, eventually carrying 11 tracks. In 1864 the SER built five high-level through platforms on the north side when it extended to *Charing Cross, and later to *Cannon Street. It undertook further rebuilding in 1893–4, retaining Beazley's frontage, and after more extensions in 1902 there was a combined total of 21 terminal and six through platforms.

It was left to the *Southern Railway to unite the two stations in 1928, although confusion remained, made worse by makeshift repairs after World War II bombing destroyed most of the frontage buildings and the former hotel. In 1979 *British Rail built a new station, with a striking open-trussed covered forecourt having pyramidal lantern-lights in the roof, and a light, uncluttered concourse. New awnings covered the former SER platforms, but the arched Brighton roof was retained. With 16 platforms, the design was one of the best modern station reconstructions in Britain.   GJB

LT, 144–71, 354–6; *GRSB*.

Marylebone

It has always been a quiet terminus. Opened by the *Great Central Railway in 1899 for its London Extension, it had four platforms. Land taken for another six was never needed. The station has a three-span ridged roof, a broad concourse, and an undistinguished red brick frontage that is enlivened by a recently restored, elaborate iron-and-glass *porte cochère* that formed a covered way to the *Hotel Great Central opposite. The hotel was opened by a separate company in 1899, and in 1946 was purchased for railway offices. In 1948–91 it formed *BR's headquarters, but was restored for reversion to a hotel in 1993. Earmarked for closure after the demise of the Great Central route in 1966, Marylebone has latterly been restored and refurbished for trains to Birmingham via Bicester, and revitalized suburban services.   GJB

J. F. Gairns, 'Notable Railway Stations and Their Traffic: Marylebone', *RM*, 29 (Oct. 1911), 269–80; *LT*, 331–44, 370–1; *GRSB*.

Paddington

The *Great Western Railway of 1835 was intended to join the *London & Birmingham, its trains running into *Euston station. But that arrangement broke down, and in 1837 the company was authorized to make its terminus at what was then the suburban village of Paddington. The first station, opened in 1838, was a temporary one, abutting the west side of Bishop's Road and sketchily built of timber. Nevertheless, it lasted 16 years.

Expanding traffic needed something larger, and in 1851–3 the shareholders approved the construction of a new station and a hotel east of Bishop's Road. *Brunel designed the station with a three-span arched iron-and-glass *trainshed roof having two 'transepts', which gave it an unusually dramatic effect. Matthew Digby Wyatt was his 'consultant for the architectural details'. Its hotel, sited across a space behind the buffers, was the work of the architect P. C. *Hardwick. Because the station lay in a cutting, it had no effective façade of its own; but Hardwick's building provided that, towering above Praed Street. Adapted in accordance with later technological developments, these structures have all lasted until today, with three important additions.

In 1863 a separate station was added on the north side for the underground *Metropolitan Railway, enlarged in 1876, and subsequently incorporated into the main station. The arrival side, also on the north, was enlarged, under a fourth, matching, roof-span, in 1916. The company's chief offices and board-room on the first floor of the main block on the south side were very severely damaged in an air-raid in 1941, and never wholly reconstructed.   JS

MacDermot; *GRSB*; *LT*, 303–30, 369–70.

St Pancras

The *Midland Railway took powers in 1863 to extend its line from Bedford to London, allowing it to compete effectively with the *London & North Western and *Great Northern companies for traffic from Yorkshire. It was to terminate on the Euston Road. W. H. *Barlow, the engineer, conceived a vast, single-span arched *trainshed in iron and glass 110 ft high and 243 ft wide, exceeded in size by only three others subsequently built in the USA. The ribs are tied by the platform deck, so making the internal span entirely unobstructed and flexible, to allow for future changes of use. Below the platforms an undercroft with rail access accommodated Burton-on-Trent beer traffic.

The station was accompanied by a *hotel, forming a vast façade to the trainshed and proclaiming the arrival of the new railway in London. A competition was held in 1865, won by the well-known architect George Gilbert Scott, whose building was far larger than the rules of the contest permitted. The station was opened in 1868, the hotel finished in 1876. Their total cost is unknown, but it certainly neared £1 million. There was also a goods station, built west of the main one in 1883–7.

The trainshed was never enlarged, though its original six platforms were increased to seven by removing a carriage siding. The only serious fault in the station's design was that trains entered it on a falling gradient, causing four *accidents in 1891–1906. The platform lengths were just sufficient for MR trains (always short), but inadequate for those of its successor the *London Midland & Scottish. The LMS was also dissatisfied with the hotel which was no longer profitable, and it was closed in 1935.

*BR also considered the station a liability and proposed to demolish it in 1966, taking its traffic into *King's Cross. After a large public outcry the project was cancelled. Instead, the line was *electrified as far as Bedford, profitably. The goods station was abandoned, its site now accommodating the British Library. The exterior of the hotel was cleaned, to superb effect, the work being completed in 1995.

An ambitious £1.4 billion scheme to join the station to King's Cross as an international terminal was abandoned in 1993, in favour of a cheaper one to bring much of the traffic from the *Channel Tunnel into St Pancras alone.　　JS

J. Simmons, *St Pancras Station* (1968); GRSB, 112–15, 142–6.

Victoria

Until 1924 Victoria comprised two stations side by side. First was the *London Brighton & South Coast Railway's in 1860, followed by that of the *London Chatham & Dover and *Great Western (the latter used it very little) in 1862. The Brighton station had a transverse ridge-and-furrow roof over eight platforms, partly fronted by an independently owned *hotel in florid, French style by J. T. Knowles. The LCDR side also had eight platforms, and a two-span crescent-shaped roof by Sir John *Fowler; but the Victoria Street frontage shared with the LBSCR merely comprised wooden huts and hoardings, the modestly Italianate entrance building being at one side in Hudson Place.

In 1906–9 the Brighton company rebuilt its station, with a new entrance beneath a hotel extension, and, because there was no space for expansion sideways, lengthened platforms which two trains could use simultaneously by means of scissors cross-overs (see TRACK). A new longitudinal ridge-and-furrow roof covered the whole station. Not to be outdone, the *South Eastern & Chatham, as it then was, built itself a frontage block alongside the Brighton's, in ostentatious 'Second Empire' style by A. W. Blomfield.

After the *Grouping the *Southern Railway combined the stations by making an arch in the dividing wall. The platforms were renumbered consecutively, and European services mainly concentrated on the Eastern (SECR) side

under the name 'The Gateway to the Continent'. By contrast with its relative spaciousness, the Central (Brighton) side became increasingly cluttered, inside and out.

In the 1980s two large office and shop complexes replaced the roof over the Central station platforms, producing a tunnel-like effect. Because the Eastern side roof was listed, a third block could only be built beyond it, spoiling the vista.

By 1992 the Central side had at last been tidied up and enlarged, and the two concourses were finally given greater visual unity by a block of matching shops extending through the arches in the former dividing wall.　　GJB

J. F. Gairns, 'Notable Railway Stations and Their Traffic: Victoria', RM, 60 (April 1927), 253–69; LT, 267–302, 364–9; GRSB.

Waterloo

In 1848 the *London & South Western Railway replaced its original Nine Elms terminus with a new station near Waterloo Bridge. It was undistinguished, built on arches with four platforms beneath a wooden roof. During the rest of the century it was extended piecemeal, resulting in a station that was a byword for confusion. By 1885 its 16 platforms were divided between 'Central', 'South', 'Windsor', and 'North' Stations, while two sets of platforms were both numbered 1 and 2, and there were four areas that passed as concourses. Furthermore, a line crossed the central concourse on the level, passing out through the front wall on to a bridge over Waterloo Road to a junction with the *South Eastern Railway's *Charing Cross line at a station called Waterloo Junction (now Waterloo East). In 1898 the LSWR opened its *Waterloo & City tube line from a separate station in the basement to the Bank. A fourth Waterloo station was built adjacent by the London Necropolis Company for its funeral trains to Brookwood *cemetery.

Except for the relatively new 'North Station', Waterloo was entirely rebuilt in 1900–21 with 21 platforms, a vast ridge-and-furrow roof, and a spacious concourse, transforming it from one of Britain's worst termini to the largest and finest. The curved frontage by J. R. Scott housed the company's offices and incorporated the Victory Arch, an impressive entrance in Portland stone forming the company's war *memorial. The public rooms possessed considerable elegance, a little of which still remains.

Waterloo remained largely unchanged until the four platforms of the 'North Station' were demolished to make way for the International Terminus for *Channel Tunnel trains, completed in 1993. Designed by Nicholas Grimshaw & Partners, the curving platforms and novel, yet traditionally arched stainless steel and glass roof created a perspective that has received wide praise.　　GJB

J. F. Gairns, 'The Largest Railway Terminus in Great Britain', RM, 50 (1922), 299–313; LT, 210–42; GRSB; J. Macneil, 'Arch Arrival', *Building* (8 May 1992).

See also STATIONS, PASSENGER.

London Tilbury & Southend Railway originated in 1852 with an Act for a *joint line, owned by the *Eastern Counties and *London & Blackwall Railways, from Forest

Gate Junction on the ECR to Southend via Tilbury. This promotion followed years of unsuccessful rival attempts by the two companies to claim the territory. In political reality, however, both the LTSR and the previous schemes arose primarily from efforts by the engineer G. P. *Bidder and the *contractor Samuel Morton *Peto. Bidder became the LTSR engineer, and Peto (with fellow contractors Thomas *Brassey and E. L. Betts) built the line and then worked it on a lease from opening in 1854–6 until 1875.

Trains (run by the ECR under contract to the lessees) initially ran in two portions, from Bishopsgate and *Fenchurch Street stations, joining at Stratford. The primary objective was the *excursion traffic to Gravesend, for which the Tilbury–Gravesend *ferry was leased. Southend excursion traffic, soon much more important, was at first only a subsidiary target. In 1855 a branch was opened to Thames Haven, built by the independent Thames Haven Dock & Railway Company but taken over on completion. Congestion at Stratford demanded a cut-off line (see LOOP) through Plaistow, opened in 1858, this becoming the LTSR main line with trains now running from Fenchurch Street only.

In 1862 the LTSR became an independent company, but most of the directors were still appointed by the LBR and the *Great Eastern (as the ECR now was). When the lease expired in 1875 the company assumed the running of the line and appointed Arthur Stride as manager, later managing director, and then chairman. In 1876–80 the line was modernized and acquired its own 4-4-2T locomotives and rolling stock, the working of the trains by the GER ceasing in 1880.

In 1882 the appointed directors were dropped, and the LTSR henceforth was an entirely independent company. In 1885–8 a new shorter main line from Barking to Pitsea via Upminster was opened. The Shoeburyness extension (1884) and Romford–Grays line (1892–3) completed the system. Passenger receipts grew considerably with the development of the east London suburbs, and then of a vast Southend *season-ticket traffic. Tilbury docks (1886) boosted the small goods traffic and required *boat trains for ocean liners.

The Tottenham & Forest Gate Railway (1894), jointly owned with the *Midland Railway, and the Whitechapel & Bow Railway (1902), jointly owned with the *Metropolitan District, provided better links with other companies. The WBR was soon carrying frequent electric trains to Barking. By the 1900s the LTSR was one of the country's busiest, and most profitable, railways. To the surprise of those who had foreseen an eventual takeover by the GER, it was bought by the Midland in 1912.   PK

H. D. Welch, *The London Tilbury & Southend Railway* (1951); *RTC*, 74–5, 80–1.

London Transport, see LONDON UNDERGROUND RAILWAYS.

London Underground railways. The accompanying diagram shows in broad outline the development of the London Underground system. Asterisks indicate alphabetical sub-headings here, or other articles relating to the companies which make up its present-day lines. A section on London Transport itself will also be found in the article, positioned alphabetically.

Baker Street & Waterloo Railway (Bakerloo)
The 'Bakerloo', as it was invariably called after the portmanteau word was invented in 1906, was the first London tube to cross the centre north–south. Authorized in 1893, the project languished until it was taken up in 1897 by the London & Globe Finance Corporation of Whitaker Wright. Work began on the tunnel under the Thames in 1898, but it stopped after the London & Globe's failure in 1901. The powers were taken over by C. T. *Yerkes' *Underground Electric Railways group in 1902, and the line was opened from Baker Street to Elephant & Castle (3.6 miles) in 1906. There was at first a flat fare of 2*d*. In 1913 the line reached Paddington; in 1915 it was linked at Queen's Park with the *London & North Western Railway, over which its trains were projected to Watford in 1917. To relieve the inner section of the *Metropolitan line a tube link from Baker Street to Finchley Road was opened in 1939, over which Bakerloo trains were projected to Stanmore, making a total of 32 route miles operated. The in-town section soon became so much overloaded that the Stanmore branch was detached to form part of the *Jubilee line in 1979. At the southern end, extension to Camberwell was authorized in 1931 and briefly revived in 1949, but never proceeded with.

The Bakerloo shared the technical features of the other UER tubes; the original cars were of American build. The first 'passimeter' for issue and examination of *tickets was introduced at Kilburn Park in 1921.

C. E. Lee, *Sixty Years of the Bakerloo* (1966); *HLT*; D. F. Croome and A. A. Jackson, *Rails through the Clay* (1993 edn.).

Central London Railway and Central Line
The Central London Railway, authorized in 1892 and opened in 1900, linked Shepherd's Bush with the Bank (5¾ miles), traversing London's busy quarters on the west–east axis along the line of Oxford Street. Once it had replaced its original electric locomotives with *multiple-unit trains in 1903, it was recognizably the prototype of the modern tube. It had ample capacity, with 7-car trains and adequate platforms and access. *Signalling was by manual lock-and-block. The positive current rail was laid between the running rails, which conducted the return current. Originally there was a flat fare of 2*d.*, giving rise to the nickname 'The Twopenny Tube'; this lasted until 1907. The line was extended by a loop to Wood Lane, close to the White City exhibition site, in 1908, and to Liverpool Street in 1912. Motor-bus competition cut into CL traffics, and in 1913 the *Underground group took control. Extension to the west was begun over *Great Western tracks to Ealing Broadway in 1920.

The Central Line (as *London Transport named it from 1937) was radically changed under the 1935–40 New Works Programme, in the course of which the third-rail current collection was replaced by the standard Underground fourth-rail system. The line was extended beyond Liverpool Street to Leyton and thence over *London & North Eastern

London Underground railways

An outline of the evolution of London Underground

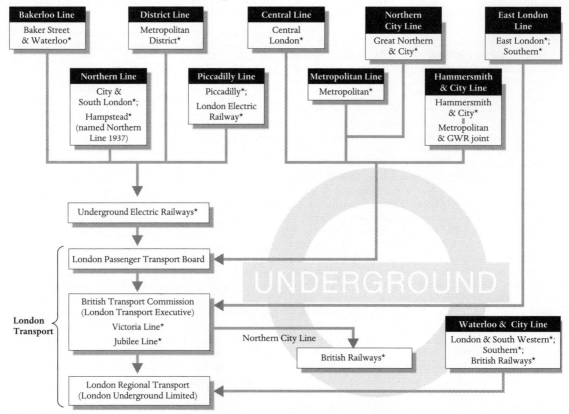

* Have subheadings within the entry **London Underground railways**, or are the subject of separate entries.

Railway tracks (with 4 miles of new tunnel) to Hainault and Epping in 1947–9, with its rural prolongation to Ongar electrified in 1957 but closed in 1994. At the western end new tracks beside the GWR line took Central trains to West Ruislip in 1948. West Ruislip to Epping trains had a run of over 34 miles; with the lines to Ealing, Hainault, and Ongar, the total route mileage was 51¼.

> B. G. Wilson and V. S. Haram, *The Central London Railway* (1950); C. E. Lee, *Seventy Years of the Central* (1970); *HLT*; D. F. Croome and A. A. Jackson, *Rails through the Clay* (1993 edn.).

City & South London Railway

This was the world's first deep-level electric railway. It successfully employed the technique of boring through soft soil by means of a 'shield', perfected by its engineer J. H. *Greathead. The original intention of haulage by *cable was discarded in favour of electric traction by locomotives, using third and fourth rails for current. Two *lifts at each station were hydraulically operated; *signalling was mechanical lock-and-block.

The original section, opened in 1890, ran from King William Street, in the City, under the Thames for 1¼ miles to Stockwell. From the outset it carried 15,000 passengers a day; but deficiencies were soon revealed. Almost everything

was too small. Capacity was inadequate at the City terminus; current supply was unreliable; the locomotives were underpowered; the two-car trains were insufficient; the 10 ft 2 in tunnel diameter was too restrictive. Despite these difficulties the CSLR showed that the thing could be done, with safety and a modest financial return. Other tubes learned from the pioneer's experience (see CENTRAL LONDON RAILWAY).

The CSLR was extended to Moorgate and Clapham Common in 1900, Angel in 1901, and Euston in 1907. The company, never financially robust, was taken over by the *Underground Electric Railways in 1913, and the railway was absorbed into the Underground system by links to the *Hampstead line, total reconstruction of the tunnels to the standard tube diameter in 1922–4, and re-equipment to Underground standards where possible, though some single island platforms survived. A 5-mile extension from Clapham Common to Morden, where the London County Council was to build a housing estate, followed in 1926. From then on the CSLR was operationally a part of the *Northern Line.

> T. S. Lascelles, *The City & South London Railway* (1955); C. E. Lee, *Sixty Years of the Northern* (1967); *HLT*; D. F. Croome and A. A. Jackson, *Rails through the Clay* (1993 edn.).

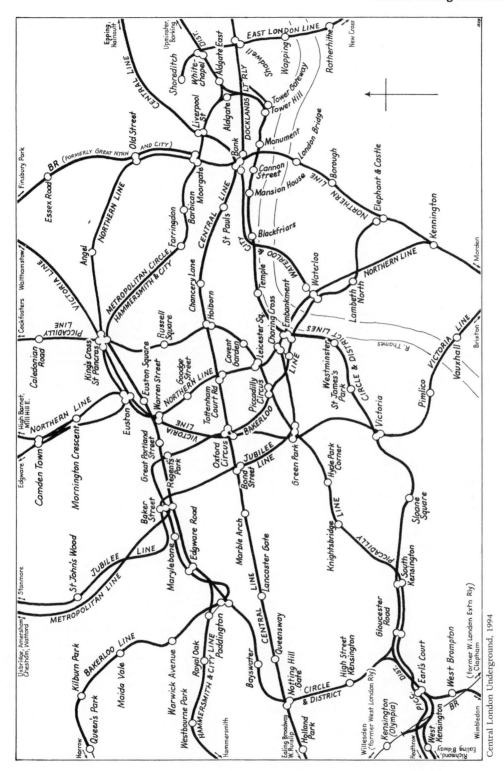

Central London Underground, 1994

London Underground railways

East London Railway

This line was authorized in 1865 as a link to connect all the railways entering London north and south of the Thames. Its under-river section was the Thames Tunnel built by Sir Marc Brunel in 1825–43, the first tunnel for public traffic driven beneath a river. In the event it was well linked at its southern end, above New Cross, but it never had an adequate connection to the north and so failed to provide a through route for more than a restricted amount of traffic.

The line was opened from New Cross to Shoreditch, 5¼ miles, in 1876, with access to *Liverpool Street. The ELR owned no rolling stock; its train services were operated by other companies, in a succession of complex variations. In 1882 a five-railway *joint committee (*London Brighton & South Coast, *South Eastern, *London Chatham & Dover, *Metropolitan, and *Metropolitan District) leased it; the *Great Eastern joined in 1885. From 1913, after *electrification on the fourth-rail system, the Metropolitan worked ELR passenger services; ownership was vested in the *Southern Railway in 1925. The whole was transferred to *London Transport in 1948. The connection to Liverpool Street was removed in 1966; the wagon-hoist at Spitalfields, which most of the through freight traffic had to use, had gone in 1955; and the ELR became a local passenger line of modest usefulness, without any through services from other lines. Extensions north to Dalston (2½ miles) and south to East Dulwich (4½ miles) are proposed.

HLT; C. E. Lee, *The East London Line and the Thames Tunnel* (1976); A. A. Jackson, *London's Metropolitan Railway* (1986).

Great Northern & City Railway

The GNCR, 3½ miles from Finsbury Park to Moorgate, was the 'odd man' among the London tubes. The tunnel bore was 16 ft, capable of accepting main-line rolling stock; it had no physical connection with the rest of the system; its signals, designed by C. E. Spagnoletti (see SIGNALLING), were then novel in having lights but no moving parts in them; and its current rails were laid outside the running rails.

The *Great Northern Railway originally encouraged the project in 1892 to provide relief on its congested approach to *King's Cross; but it soon shifted its support to the new *Piccadilly Line, and financing and construction were carried through, in the face of GNR indifference, by the *contractors S. Pearson & Sons. It was opened in 1904, with an awkward vertical interchange at Finsbury Park. Traffic rose to 16 million passengers in 1907 and then dropped to 12.8 million in 1912. In 1913 the *Metropolitan Railway, rather surprisingly, purchased it, with ideas of extending it southwards and establishing a direct connection with the GNR. But the Metropolitan could do little with it, apart from closing its generating station at Poole Street, Islington (later used as Gainsborough's film studio) and introducing the only first-class accommodation on a tube railway.

Under *London Transport the original rolling stock was replaced by small-sized tube cars and the current supply converted in 1939. It was then planned to run a through service from Moorgate over *London & North Eastern Railway lines to High Barnet, Edgware, and Alexandra Palace. This scheme was abandoned in 1953. The *Victoria line took over parts of the Northern City Line (as it was now called) for its alignment in 1968. Eventually its original purpose was achieved by transferring it to *British Railways for through running to the Great Northern section. On 28 February 1975, a few months before the planned handover, the Underground's worst train *accident occurred when a train ran at speed through Moorgate station and crashed into the tunnel headwall. LT trains last worked on 4 October 1975; BR services began in 1976.

HLT; J. G. Bruce, *The Big Tube* (1975); A. A. Jackson, *London's Metropolitan Railway* (1986), 218–22.

Hammersmith & City Line

The Hammersmith & City Railway was opened in 1864 from Green Lane Junction (later Westbourne Park) via Shepherd's Bush to Hammersmith, with a connection from Latimer Road to the *West London Railway, 3 miles in all. Built mostly on viaduct, it traversed some land that had been bought by Charles Blake and John Parson, directors of the company, who made a handsome profit reselling it to the railway. The line was mixed-*gauge until 1868–9. It became joint property of the *Great Western and *Metropolitan Railways in 1867. Both owners provided services with their own trains until *electrification in 1906–7 using jointly owned rolling stock. Trains were projected in stages over the Inner Circle and finally over the *East London Line to New Cross, *South Eastern Railway (1884). Through electric working between Hammersmith and New Cross began in 1914; it was discontinued in 1941.

The original HCR was transferred to *London Transport in 1948, and tracks from Westbourne Park to Paddington in 1970. London Transport's 'Hammersmith & City Line' now denotes a composite of the original HCR, part of the Circle, and an eastern terminus at Whitechapel, with a peak-hour extension to Barking, District Line.

MacDermot, ii; F. Sheppard (ed.), *Survey of London*, 37, 'Northern Kensington' (1973), 303–6; HLT; C. E. Lee, *The Metropolitan Line* (1972), and *The East London Line and the Thames Tunnel* (1976); A. A. Jackson, *London's Metropolitan Railway* (1986).

Hampstead Line (or Hampstead and Highgate)

Its full title was the Charing Cross Euston & Hampstead Railway. It was opened in 1907, and was the third of the *Underground Electric Railways' tubes. It was described at the time as 'The Last Link'. The original line, authorized in 1893, was varied by later Acts to run from the Strand at *Charing Cross station via Euston to Hampstead, with a branch to Kentish Town on the *Midland Railway; but nothing was done until C. T. *Yerkes and the UER syndicate took up the project (Yerkes may have been interested in its possibility since 1896). Work began in 1903, including extensions to Golders Green and Highgate. The line climbed steeply under Hampstead Heath to reach the surface at Golders Green. This was the first tube terminus situated in 'green fields' in the hope of stimulating housing development. At Hampstead the platforms, 192 ft below ground level, are the deepest on the London Underground; its lift shaft, 181 ft, is the longest. A short extension to the *Metropolitan District's Charing Cross station (1914) was in the form of a loop, avoiding reversal of trains.

The Hampstead line was extended and its character much changed under Acts of 1912 and 1913 by extension from Golders Green to Edgware, opened in 1923–4, through more 'green fields' and serving a London County Council housing estate to be built at Burnt Oak; and by new links to the *City & South London Railway at Euston and Kennington, together with rebuilding and absorption of the latter, completed with the Morden extension in 1926. Thereafter called the Edgware Highgate & Morden Line, it was renamed *Northern Line in 1937.

C. E. Lee, *Fifty Years of the Hampstead Tube* (1957), and *Sixty Years of the Northern* (1967); *HLT*; D. F. Croome and A. A. Jackson, *Rails through the Clay* (1993 edn.).

Jubilee Line

The Jubilee Line (so unaptly named by the Greater London Council in 1977) had its origin as the Fleet Line, authorized in 1969 to run from Charing Cross to Baker Street, 2½ miles, to relieve the over-pressed *Bakerloo line in the West End and to take over its Stanmore service. It was opened in 1979. Extension along the line of Fleet Street (hence the original name) through the City of London and south-east to Lewisham was authorized in 1971–2; but instead a route south of the Thames via Waterloo, continuing east to Docklands and then north to Stratford, was preferred, and construction began in 1993.

D. F. Croome, and A. A. Jackson, *Rails through the Clay* (1993 edn.).

London Electric Railway

This line was the former Great Northern Piccadilly & Brompton Railway (see PICCADILLY LINE), renamed in 1910 and enlarged to take in the *Bakerloo and *Hampstead lines. The tubes acquired in 1913 by the *Underground group (*Central London and *City & South London) retained their company structures, but chief officers were appointed for the whole group, and they were assimilated as far as possible to the technical and commercial standards of the LER. All were merged in *London Transport, 1933.

HLT, chs 7–9.

London Transport

The title was adopted by the London Passenger Transport Board, soon after its establishment in 1933, as the working name for its road and rail operations, and this has continued to be used under successive changes in higher organization. The LPTB was set up by its Act of 1933 to provide or secure the provision of an adequate and properly co-ordinated system of passenger transport by road and rail, in partnership with the main-line railways, within a widely drawn London area of nearly 2,000 square miles. The Board was appointed by five ex-officio trustees. In 1948, under the Transport Act, 1947, its system was taken over by the London Transport Executive, a subsidiary of the *British Transport Commission, LTE members being appointed by the Minister of *Transport. In 1963 it was followed by the London Transport Board, appointed by and directly responsible to the minister. From 1970 control was transferred to the Greater London Council, which appointed members of the (second) London Transport Executive. In 1984 the government removed LT from the GLC and appointed London Regional Transport to oversee separate companies operating the *bus and *Underground activities.

In spite of these organizational changes, development of the Underground railway system was carried forward consistently within varying financial constraints. Notable additions were made to the mileage (see CENTRAL, JUBILEE, NORTHERN, and VICTORIA LINES), and technical progress was maintained. In the 1980s there was a marked jerk towards the satisfaction of political rather than transport needs, with the decisions to build the *Docklands Light Railway and to divert the planned Jubilee Line extension away from Fleet Street to loop through south and east London in 1993.

HLT; D. F. Croome and A. A. Jackson, *Rails through the Clay* (1993 edn.).

Metropolitan District Railway

Usually known as 'the District', the MDR was the second underground passenger railway in the world when its first section was opened on Christmas Eve 1868, the *Metropolitan having been the first. The confusing similarity of names arose because the MDR was separately promoted for financial reasons as a move towards the completion of a circular railway for London, proposed by a House of Lords committee; the two companies were to be merged on completion. But that did not happen; their interests diverged; and the Inner Circle, completed in 1884, was the scene of incessant conflicts between the two partners.

Most of this line was difficult and expensive to build, especially within the City of London. The Thames Embankment, then under construction, was used for part of it. The railway was always hard up, having to issue loans and preference stocks with a heavy burden of fixed interest and arrears. The original section, South Kensington to Westminster Bridge (1868), was at first worked by the Metropolitan, which withdrew in 1871. By 1874 the District's line extended from Mansion House to West Brompton; then it reached out into western and south-western suburbs, working mostly over lines built by nominally independent companies. By 1889 its trains ran to Ealing Broadway, Richmond, Hounslow, and Wimbledon; to Whitechapel in the east; and to New Cross on the *South Eastern Railway over the *East London Railway. In association with the *London Tilbury & Southend Railway it reached Barking in 1908 and Upminster, on the *London Midland & Scottish Railway, in 1932.

*Electrification was seen as the solution to the District's poor state by the mid-1890s; but the Metropolitan disagreed with the traction method to be used. The District's system was adopted after arbitration, and electric services began on the new South Harrow line in 1903; all trains were electrically worked by the end of 1905.

There were no further extensions of the District; rearrangements involving the *Piccadilly line later removed District trains from the South Harrow and Hounslow branches.

London Underground railways

The District carried heavy traffic—51 million passengers in 1904—but unremuneratively; its earning record was poor. It did its best to stimulate exhibition traffic, first at South Kensington, then at Earl's Court, built on District property. Its steam locomotives, 4-4-0 tanks, were similar to the Metropolitan's; its four-wheeled carriages were serviceable if dingy. It had a good safety record.

There was a complete change after the American group headed by C. T. *Yerkes (see UNDERGROUND ELECTRIC RAILWAYS) built its generating station at Lots Road, Chelsea, and equipped the District and three tube lines for electric working. The District became the key line, virtually the backbone, of the London Underground system. By 1933 it worked over 58¾ miles of railway, of which it owned 25 miles. In 1994 three stations on the 3½ mile section between Putney Bridge and Wimbledon were transferred to it from *British Railways.

C. E. Lee, *The Metropolitan District Railway* (1956), and *100 Years of the District* (1968); *HLT*; A. Edmonds, *History of the Metropolitan District Railway to June 1908* (1973).

Metropolitan Railway
The world's first passenger-carrying underground railway was opened from Paddington (Bishop's Road) to Farringdon Street, City of London, on 10 January 1863, constructed by cut-and-cover mainly beneath existing streets. It was at first sponsored by the *Great Western Railway and was laid to the broad *gauge (7 ft); but the working partnership, never easy, was severed in 1867 and broad-gauge working was given up. The line was extended by 1884 so as to form, with the *Metropolitan District Railway, a continuous circle linking the principal main-line termini north of the Thames and providing by its 'widened lines' access for *Great Northern, *Midland, and *London Chatham & Dover trains to the City. Extensions, involving complex joint arrangements, were opened to Hammersmith in 1864, Harrow-on-the-Hill in 1868–80, and New Cross over the *East London Railway in 1884. The Harrow extension became the main line, reaching Aylesbury in 1892, with connections beyond to Verney Junction and Brill, Buckinghamshire. The Aylesbury line gave the *Great Central Railway its original access to London in 1899; north of Harrow it was jointly managed after 1906.

The Metropolitan tried to be a main-line railway which happened to lie under ground in the centre; it provided three passenger classes (two from 1905, one from 1941) and refreshment rooms, and it handled freight and parcels traffic. Electric working began in 1905, with change to steam at Harrow (later Rickmansworth) for through trains. With efficient traction and good signalling, the Metropolitan was reliable and safe for passengers, and it was commercially successful, with a substantial income from properties and its country estates subsidiary, from 1919 (see METRO-LAND). Competition from tube railways after 1900 and motor buses after 1910 forced it to concentrate on developing outer suburban services; even two *Pullman cars were provided. Uxbridge was reached in 1904, Watford in 1925, Stanmore in 1932. The *Great Northern & City tube was acquired in 1913, but there was no physical connection. The company's

claim to be treated as a main-line trunk railway when resisting incorporation in the London Passenger Transport Board in 1933 was unsuccessful.

The Metropolitan had a distinctive personality, with locomotives painted 'chocolate-lake' (from 1885), teak-finished carriages, and in later years cream glazed tiled station exteriors. Its technical innovations included roller bearings for axles in 1929 and centralized *signalling control on the Stanmore branch in 1932. Its publicity for *'Metro-Land', begun in 1915, gave a title to one of Evelyn Waugh's characters (*Decline and Fall*, 1928) and a word to the English language.

C. Baker, *The Metropolitan Railway* (1951); *HLT*; C. E. Lee, *The Metropolitan Line* (1972); A. A. Jackson, *London's Metropolitan Railway* (1986).

Northern Line
This name was given to the former Edgware Highgate & Morden (or Morden–Edgware) line of the London *Underground in 1937 (see CITY & SOUTH LONDON RAILWAY; HAMPSTEAD LINE). It was then under serious strain as suburban settlement in the outer areas it served grew faster than its carrying capacity, and a series of relief works, as well as higher-capacity rolling stock, was undertaken to deal with the pressure. These included extension from Edgware to Bushey Heath; a new tube link north from Highgate to join *London & North Eastern Railway branches to High Barnet and Edgware; and integration with the Northern City line (see GREAT NORTHERN & CITY RAILWAY) with projection of its service over LNER lines to East Finchley and Alexandra Palace. The new and converted lines north of Highgate were brought into use in 1939–41; the Bushey Heath and Northern City parts of the scheme were dropped in 1950 and 1953.

The total Northern line mileage is 40, including 17 miles 528 yds that from 1939 to 1988 formed the longest continuous railway tunnel in the world, from East Finchley via Bank to Morden. The Northern City section, not physically linked with the Northern line, was transferred to *British Railways in 1975.

C. E. Lee, *Sixty Years of the Northern* (1967); *HLT*; D. F. Croome and A. A. Jackson, *Rails through the Clay* (1993 edn.).

Piccadilly Line
The Piccadilly—formally the Great Northern Piccadilly & Brompton Railway—was the longest of the London tubes when it was opened in 1906 from Finsbury Park to Hammersmith, 8½ miles (7¾ miles under ground). It was a fusion of three separate projects: a deep-level scheme of the *Metropolitan District, the Brompton & Piccadilly Circus, and the Great Northern & Strand Railways, merged in 1902. The resulting line ran roughly east from Hammersmith through Kensington and the West End to Holborn, where it turned north to King's Cross and Finsbury Park on the *Great Northern Railway, with a short branch from Holborn to Aldwych, closed in 1994. The GNPB company was renamed the *London Electric Railway in 1910, when it absorbed the *Bakerloo and *Hampstead railways.

The line was constructed and equipped to the same standards as the other *Underground tubes. Nearly all its rolling stock was built in France and Hungary (probably the only Hungarian-built stock on a British railway). An experimental escalator on a double spiral system was installed at Holloway Road in 1906, but never put into service; the first railway escalator in London was brought into use between the District and Piccadilly platforms at Earl's Court in 1911. The escalators at Leicester Square, with a rise of 81 ft, are the longest on *London Transport (see LIFTS AND ESCALATORS).

The line was extended beyond both terminals in 1932–3: to the west over former District tracks to Hounslow and South Harrow and over the *Metropolitan branch to Uxbridge; to the north in new tube, with surface sections, to Southgate and Cockfosters, 7¾ miles. The end-to-end Piccadilly run from Uxbridge to Cockfosters, 32 miles, was then the longest on LT electric tracks. New station buildings, by or inspired by Charles *Holden, were a striking feature.

The Hounslow branch was projected to Heathrow airport in 1977, giving London the first underground railway connection to its international airport of any capital city in the world; a further loop to serve Terminal 4 was added in 1986.

C. E. Lee, *Sixty Years of the Piccadilly* (1966); *HLT*; [London Transport] *Underground to Heathrow* (1977); D. F. Croome and A. A. Jackson, *Rails through the Clay* (1993 edn.).

'Underground', and Underground Electric Railways Ltd
The word 'Underground' in relation to London railways has had several different shades of meaning. First it meant the financial group Underground Electric Railways of London Ltd headed by C. T. *Yerkes which, absorbing the Metropolitan District Electric Traction Co. (1901) in 1902, built the generating station at Lots Road, Chelsea, to supply power to the *Metropolitan District Railway and three tubes, the *Bakerloo, *Piccadilly, and *Hampstead lines. It converted the District to electric traction and completed the construction and equipment of the other three. Control of statutory undertakings by a non-statutory limited company was a novelty in Britain; there was suspicion that it was an American financiers' device to secure profits without responsibility. The original UER capital of £5 million was largely subscribed in New York, Boston, Amsterdam, Frankfurt, and Paris. The subsequent issue of anonymous bearer bonds made it difficult to know where the ultimate power lay.

The UER quickly brought in a team of Americans who proceeded to introduce standards and equipment which gave the London electric system its particular hallmark: current supply at 550–600 V dc by third and fourth rail; electric automatic *signalling; *multiple-unit trains; Otis *lifts and, after 1911, escalators; a common architectural style for tube stations (see GREEN, LESLIE); shared commercial management and publicity (see PICK, FRANK).

This last led to the second use of 'Underground'; its application was extended in 1908 when the *Metropolitan, as well as the *Central London, *City & South London, and *Great Northern & City, agreed to adopt the word for their exterior station signs and maps.

Thirdly, 'the Underground' was commonly used between about 1920 and 1933 to mean the whole group controlled by the UER, including its bus, tram, and trolleybus interests. Alternatively, it was called 'the Combine', especially by pirate bus operators; it was not a term of affection. After the formation of the London Passenger Transport Board in 1933 the term was applied colloquially to all the board's railways, below and above ground.

HLT.

Victoria Line
The Victoria line, so named in 1955, was the first new London tube across the central area since 1907. It was badly needed to distribute the growing traffic from and to the main-line terminals at *King's Cross, *St Pancras, *Euston, and *Victoria, with interchange to all existing *Underground lines. At its north-eastern end it served Finsbury Park, Tottenham, and Walthamstow; southwards it provided a new under-river crossing at Vauxhall and was projected to Brixton. The main section was authorized in 1955 and opened in 1968–9; with the Brixton extension of 1971, this made a mileage of 14. Improved methods of tunnel excavation and lining were used, including concrete segments, where suitable, in place of cast iron. The trains were from the start under full automatic control.

[London Transport] *The Victoria Line* (1969); *The Brixton Extension of the Victoria Line* (1971); *HLT*; D. F. Croome and A. A. Jackson, *Rails through the Clay* (1993 edn.).

Waterloo & City Railway
This tube line was opened in 1898 to afford direct access to the City from *Waterloo station, beneath which it had its own platforms. Although independent, it was worked by the *London & South Western Railway with purpose-built four-car electric trains, and the LSWR absorbed it in 1907. The 1½-mile-long line ran without intermediate stations to a terminus at the Bank. Vehicles were transferred by an electric hoist at Waterloo. After passing through *Southern Railway and *BR ownership, the line was transferred to London Underground in 1994. It still remains physically unconnected to other lines at both ends, and stock transfers are now made at Waterloo by crane.

J. N. Faulkner & R. A. Williams, *The London & South Western Railway in the Twentieth Century* (1988), ch. 2; *HLT*, ii, 50–1.

Whitechapel & Bow Joint Railway, see separate entry.

RMR

Longhedge, see WORKS.

loop. This word is used by railways in more than one sense. It can mean a line built to provide a new route, parallel with an established one but at some distance from it: the Loop Line in the Potteries for example, on the *North Staffordshire Railway; or the Hindley Loop, allowing the fastest *Lancashire & Yorkshire expresses between *Manchester and *Liverpool to bypass Wigan. Or it could mean a short curve between two converging lines, to form a triangle and so avoid the need for reversing, as at Newport, where the short Maindee East Loop allowed Western Valleys coal trains to run direct to Bristol and London. The most common uses of 'loop' are to describe a short section of double track on a single line, where trains can pass, called a 'crossing loop'; and a lay-by siding connected to the running line at both ends, enabling a slow train to be overtaken by a faster one.

See also TRACK. JS

Lord Campbell's Act. This Act (9 & 10 Vict., cap. 93), passed in 1846 on the initiative of Lord Campbell and usually referred to by his name (its official title was 'Fatal Accidents Act'), established the right of the dependants of anyone killed in an accident of any sort to claim *compensation from those responsible for it. Compensation had hitherto been payable only to the sufferers of injuries, so if he or she died no recompense was paid. The Act laid down that the family of the person concerned should be entitled to compensation—'family' being narrowly defined to include only the deceased's wife, husband, parents, or children. The amount of the compensation was to be settled by a jury, which could apportion the money between two or more of the claimants.

The Act was, of course, invoked in the majority of fatal railway *accidents. It remained in force for 130 years, being finally superseded by the Fatal Accidents Act, 1976, which did not alter its principles but widened the range of people who might claim under it.

See also LAW OF RAILWAYS. JS
H. W. Disney, *Law of Carriage by Railway* (1923 edn.), 178–80; L. James, *Law of the Railway* (1980), 393–7.

lubrication is generally necessary wherever one hard surface slides over another, a thin film of lubricant between the surfaces keeping them apart, reducing to a minimum the friction resulting from movement, and helping to dissipate heat generated by friction. Natural oils—chiefly of vegetable or animal origin—were used in the early days of railways, mineral oils—derived from crude oil—coming into increasing use after 1870. By refining and blending oils of different origin a wide range suitable for different purposes was developed: thin oils for light duty, more viscous oils for use under heavy loads and at high temperatures, and greases (oils thickened to a paste) where retention of lubricant was a problem. All these relied simply for their efficacy upon retaining a certain viscosity under operating conditions; thus a thicker oil would be used in the cylinders of a superheated engine than in those of a saturated steam engine because of the higher operating temperature.

At first railway lubrication was of the 'total loss' variety, so oils did not have to be particularly durable, but with the appearance of internal combustion engines, gearboxes, and similar recirculatory systems, oils were required to withstand long periods of use without breaking down and causing either loss of lubrication or corrosion of the system. One development was the use of film-building additives which enable a thin oil to behave like a thick one at elevated temperature (a multi-grade oil), together with anti-oxidants and stabilizers to delay breakdown, and detergents to prevent the build-up of contaminants in small passageways.

For still more demanding service conditions, synthetic oils have recently been introduced, likewise silicone-based

hydraulic fluids, while at the lighter end of the spectrum the use of self-lubricating materials such as polytetrafluorethylene has eliminated the need for oil in certain applications.

At first oil and grease were applied by hand as required, but simple automatic methods were soon developed. Axle-boxes and similar bearings were provided with reservoirs from which oil was fed to the bearing itself by woollen 'trimmings' which acted like lamp wicks, or were fitted with felt pads kept wet with oil and held in contact with the journal. For steam locomotive cylinders there was developed the displacement or hydrostatic lubricator in which a column of water (produced by condensing steam) displaces oil from a reservoir into the steam chests. With the advent of superheating most engineers changed over to mechanical lubricators in which small metering pumps are used to deliver the oil. Thanks to the advances in oil seal design over recent years, the modern roller-bearing axle-box has become a self-contained oil system which is merely topped up at specified intervals.

Flange lubricators are used to reduce the rolling resistance of trains on sharp curves. Actuated by the wheel flanges, they apply a minute, calculated amount of grease to the inner faces of the rails so that it is spread along the *track but does not creep on to the upper, running surfaces. RW

luggage. The stage-*coaches conveyed small quantities of their passengers' personal luggage with them, but they were not equipped to do more. Large quantities, and heavy baggage of all kinds, had to be transported separately, and more slowly, by carriers' wagons.

Railway trains were able to offer much better service. Luggage vans came very early to be attached to them, usually occupied by *guards (see BRAKE VANS), and at first luggage was also carried on the roofs of vehicles, strapped under tarpaulins. At the opening of the *Liverpool & Manchester Railway in 1830 passengers were permitted to take with them 60 lb of personal luggage each, free of charge; but the *London & Birmingham Railway at its outset in 1837 carried no luggage free. As the railway system grew, the rates of free carriage settled down to a standard, accepted by most companies, of 150 lb first-class, 120 lb second, and 100 lb third. This was a much more liberal arrangement than the railways made in many other countries. In Belgium, for example, nothing more than small hand-luggage was taken free of charge.

The conveyance of luggage on carriage roofs proved dangerous. It might drop off when fastened insecurely, and cinders from the engines were apt to set it on *fire. The practice was therefore gradually discontinued, all luggage being taken in vans; but it lingered on in some country districts at least until about 1870.

Victorian travellers habitually took with them quantities of luggage that would today seem enormous, and the process of stowing it away on the trains and getting it out again could be time-consuming and troublesome.

So were the arguments in the courts about what constituted the 'personal luggage' that was to be carried free. In 1869 it was held that a child's rocking-horse did not qualify; in 1873 that a sewing-machine did. After much dispute, it was decided in 1899 that passengers' bicycles were not part of their 'personal luggage', and must be paid for. Some companies weighed with extreme precision each article for which a passenger was liable to be charged: the *London Brighton & South Coast Railway, according to *Ahrons, with a care that 'would have done credit to the troy methods of a dispensing chemist in the poison business'.

Cloak rooms were established on railway stations for the temporary deposit of luggage as early as the 1840s.

The principles on which passengers' luggage was carried in the Victorian age continued, enlarged and refined as necessary, after *nationalization.   JS

H. W. Disney, *Law of Carriage by Railway* (1923 edn.); L. James, *Law of the Railway* (1980); *LTW*, v, 67.

Lundie, Cornelius (1815–1908), manager. Born at Kelso, he worked on the Broomielaw bridge, Glasgow, in 1835, and later as an engineer in Australia. Unable to support himself, he lived for a time in the bush. Having returned to Britain, he was employed on construction of the *Caledonian Railway, then as engineer and manager of the *Blyth & Tyne Railway, 1855–61; and finally general manager of the *Rhymney Railway. He occupied most of the company's other chief positions as well, for which he was criticized. But when he retired in 1903 (at 88) the directors asked him to join them.

The *Railway Magazine* then ignorantly dismissed him as 'a Welsh railway autocrat'. But his record speaks for him. He defended his company stoutly and effectively against its bellicose rivals. When he arrived, it was on the verge of leasing itself to one of them. Twenty years later it was paying dividends of 11 per cent.   JS

D. S. Barrie, *Rhymney Railway* (1952); *Engineer*, 105 (1908), 197; *LTW*, iv, 105.

Lynton & Barnstaple Railway, see LONDON AND SOUTH WESTERN RAILWAY; NORTH AMERICAN RELATIONSHIPS.

M

McAlpine, Sir Robert (1847–1934), *contractor. Born at Newarthill, Scotland, he entered the Lanarkshire collieries aged seven. In 1863 he began bricklaying and in 1868 started small-scale contract work.

By 1874 he owned two brickyards, but was ruined three years later by the failure of the City of Glasgow Bank. From the wreckage arose McAlpine & Co., and in 1885 he won the contract for the Lanarkshire & Ayrshire Railway, taking his five sons to work with him. In 1892 he began the Lanarkshire & Dumbartonshire Railway, and in 1896 completed an early British tube railway, the *Glasgow District Subway. In 1896 the firm undertook the Yoker to Dalmuir extension of the *North British Railway.

McAlpine undertook work at low cost partly by planning uses for the spoil—in 1893 he made that from the Cessnock Dock Railway into bricks—and partly by the widespread use of *concrete for railway works after 1892. Called 'Concrete Bob' (or the 'Concrete King'), he began building concrete houses in 1876, experimenting with various mixtures and reinforcement. By building up the concrete in layers he was able to advance railway bridge spans from 60 ft to 127 ft (see BRIDGES AND VIADUCTS).

In 1897 McAlpine commenced the Mallaig extension of the West Highland Railway, with difficult rock and many tunnels and bridges, mostly in concrete. The best-known is the curved 21-arch 100-ft high Glenfinnan Viaduct. Concrete was also extensively used in Methil docks (see PORTS AND DOCKS) for the NBR in 1913.

The company gained a reputation for fast construction, for example replacing a washed-out bridge on the Inverness main line in three weeks in 1914. Robert McAlpine & Sons developed as a large general contractor after 1900, and in 1918 Robert was made a baronet.   MHG

J. Saxon Childers, *Sir Robert McAlpine* (1925).

MacDermot, Edward Terence (1873–1950), writer. Educated at Downside and Magdalen College, Oxford, he became a barrister (non-practising). He wrote a large and much-admired *History of the Forest of Exmoor* (1911).

He took a long-continuing interest in the history of the *Great Western Railway, considered broadly as an element in that of the West Country. Felix *Pole, general manager of the company, persuaded its board to commission an official history of it from him.

Three members of the GWR staff had already made collections for its history, on which he drew: A. R. Burnell, G. T. Milford, and D. M. Levien. He had no specialized knowledge of railway equipment or working. The development of the company's locomotives, carriages, and wagons

was recorded in the book by E. L. *Ahrons and A. C. W. Lowe.

But the *History* is no work of scissors and paste. It is a highly finished achievement, bearing the strong marks of a single mind, and expressed very clearly in pure, precise English. MacDermot's was the first history of a large British railway company to be written by a well-qualified and practised historian.   JS

E. T. MacDermot, *History of the Great Western Railway* (1927–31), revised edition 1961 by C. R. Clinker.

McIntosh, David (1799–1856), civil engineering *contractor, was born at Cheddleton, Staffordshire, the son of the eminent contractor Hugh McIntosh. After attending Glasgow University, he assisted his father with the huge number of harbour, dock, bridge, and canal contracts undertaken by the McIntoshes in the 1820s. New burdens of responsibility came as a result of his father's blindness and the extension of their business into railway construction. Without entirely abandoning canal and bridge work, the McIntoshes in the 1830s held contracts valued at more than £1,175,150 on nine railways; David is especially associated with the building of Dutton Viaduct on the *Grand Junction Railway.

He abruptly retired after the death of his father in 1840 and devoted the rest of his life to a Chancery suit against the *Great Western Railway in which an award of £148,271 came nine years after his death.

He died in London, leaving £140,000.   DB

PICE, 16 (1856–7), 162; D. Brooke, 'The Equity Suit of McIntosh v. the Great Western Railway: the "Jarndyce" of Railway Litigation', *JTH*, 17, 2 (Sept. 1996), 133–49.

McIntosh, John Farquharson (1846–1918), mechanical engineer. The outstanding early 20th-century image of the *Caledonian Railway was largely due to the sky-blue 4-4-0 and 4-6-0 locomotives of J. F. McIntosh. He joined the Scottish North Eastern Railway in 1862, rising to become chief running superintendent of the CR in 1891, despite the early loss of his right hand in an accident.

With a background firmly based in locomotive operation rather than design, when appointed locomotive superintendent in 1895 McIntosh took as a basis the classic 4-4-0 and 0-6-0 designs of Dugald *Drummond, who had held charge at St Rollox Works in 1882–90. The 'Dunalastair' 4-4-0s of 1896, with 4-ft 9-in diameter boiler, were outstanding. In 1903 he produced a large 4-6-0 passenger engine, the forerunner of the legendary '903' or 'Cardean' class of 1906, having earlier built a small class of 0-8-0 heavy goods engines. Unusually, large numbers of locomotives of McIntosh design were built for the Belgian State Railways between

1898 and about 1910. McIntosh placed greater priority on reliability than fuel economy, and demonstrated a progressive attitude towards rolling stock design, producing 12-wheeled *carriages, and high-capacity bogie coal *wagons.

He became MVO in 1913, shortly before he retired in 1914.   CPA

A. B. MacLeod, *The McIntosh Locomotives of the Caledonian Railway* (1944); O. S. Nock, *The Caledonian Dunalastairs* (1968); H. J. Campbell Cornwell, *Forty Years of Caledonian Locomotives 1882–1922* (1974).

Mackenzie, William (1794–1851), civil engineering *contractor, was born near Nelson, Lancashire, the son of a small contractor. After an apprenticeship with a carpenter, he began a busy career of bridge and canal building which included working for Thomas *Telford and the great contractor Hugh McIntosh. In 1832 he took the contract for Lime Street Tunnel on the *Liverpool & Manchester Railway and thus shifted his considerable experience and skills into railway building. Mackenzie worked alone for the remainder of that decade and it was not until 1840 that a partnership with Thomas *Brassey and the maturing of an association with Joseph *Locke laid the foundations for an immense expansion of his business. Between 1840 and 1851 Mackenzie and Brassey constructed over 500 miles of line in France. In Britain, assisted by another partner, John Stephenson, they were responsible for about 620 miles.

Mackenzie's contracting was characterized by heavy financial investment in the companies for which he worked, and pioneering use of steam-powered equipment. He died at Liverpool, leaving £341,848.   DB

M. M. Chrimes *et al.*, *Mackenzie—Giant of the Railways* (1994); *PICE*, 11 (1851–2), 102–5.

Maglev defines surface transport systems suspended by electro-magnetic levitation, propelled by linear motor, silently, smoothly, and pollution-free on a levitation air gap. There is no mechanical contact, and no parts wear out, therefore maintenance is minimal. The vehicle is captive on a dedicated guide-way and cannot be derailed.

Britain held the lead in Maglev technology in the 1960s. Dr E. R. Laithwaite, then professor of heavy electrical engineering at Imperial College, London, was engaged in research as member of a group supported by industry and including *British Railways, the *British Transport Commission, Manchester University, and the University of Sussex Applied Science Laboratory. It undertook (with sponsorship by the Wolfson Foundation) the Wolfson Magnetic Suspension project. The 1-ton 4-passenger vehicle created and successfully tested can be seen at the Science Museum, Wroughton.

Exhaustive research was continued by British Railways at the BR Magnetic-Levitational Experimental Centre, Derby. The success of these tests made it necessary to find a suitable location where industry could build a commercial Maglev system. Coincidentally, plans were announced for a new passenger terminal at Birmingham International Airport, requiring passenger shuttle facilities to link the airport

with the BR station and National Exhibition Centre complex. An elevated Maglev people-mover had the characteristics required, plus the backing of industry and government funding for a project which had an element of development. The system was opened by the Queen in 1984, but was closed in 1995 because of the high cost of spare parts.

Research and development of high-speed Maglev has continued in Germany, Japan, Korea, and the USA with target speeds of 400 km per hour.

The development of high-powered super-conductive magnets has created an electro-dynamic suspension system, with repulsive force sufficient to provide a levitation air space of 10 cm, most important for very high speed operation, compared with 1.5 cm levitation gap for people-mover type systems as operated at Birmingham International Airport.

See also MONORAILS; OVERHEAD RAILWAYS; TRACKED HOVERCRAFT.   LRW

V. Nenadovic and E. E. Riches, 'Maglev at Birmingham Airport from System Concept to Successful Operation', *G.E.C. Review*, i (1985); E. R. Laithwaite, *Propulsion Without Wheels* (1970).

mail services. In 1830 the Superintendent of Mail Coaches of the *Post Office (PO) attended the board of the *Liverpool & Manchester Railway to discuss terms for conveying the mail twice a day in each direction between *Liverpool and *Manchester. It was agreed that the company would do so at a charge of 1*d*. per mile, or 2*s*. 6*d*. per trip, and the agreement was quickly put into effect, so inaugurating an important element of railway traffic.

There was no major development in Great Britain until the opening of the *Grand Junction Railway in 1837. The PO made immediate use of this facility by establishing on the previous night a new mail service, by road from *London to *Birmingham, then forward by a morning train to reach Liverpool in 16½ hours.

The limited requirements of the PO had so far been met by negotiation with railway companies individually. Now it sought special powers to ensure that full advantage was taken of their potential to speed the mail. The outcome was the Railways (Conveyance of Mails) Act, 1838, empowering the Postmaster-General (PMG) to require all railways, whether already made or to be made in the future, to carry the mails, by ordinary or special trains and at such hours of the day or night as the PMG might direct. If required, a railway company was to provide carriages exclusively for the conveyance of mails or for sorting letters while in transit. Only the remuneration of the companies was left for negotiation.

As an alternative to the use of railway *carriages, the PMG could require the conveyance of mail-coaches and mail carts on trucks or frames supplied by the companies for the purpose. The *Great Western Railway began carrying stage-coaches in this way two weeks after the opening of the first section of its line in 1838. From the end of 1839 the coach for the Cheltenham day mail was similarly conveyed, and likewise those for the Bath, *Bristol, Gloucester, and Stroud night mails early in 1840. On the London &

mail services

Southampton Railway (see LONDON & SOUTH WESTERN RAIL-WAY) mail-coaches were conveyed, probably from December 1838 between Nine Elms and the temporary terminus at Winchfield.

In 1842 mail was being carried over some 1,400 route miles of railway, involving 40 companies, 27 of which were acting under notices given under the 1838 Act, and the remainder under other arrangements. On most railways accommodation took the form of a compartment in a van or carriage, or a locked container on the roof known as an Imperial. The mail was generally accompanied by a *guard.

On the *London & Birmingham Railway, the GJR, and the *North Union Railway, provision for the mail had grown beyond a single compartment, and the Travelling Post Office (TPO) was well established. This was the carriage for sorting letters, envisaged in the 1838 Act. Such a vehicle had been introduced on the GJR in January 1838, working between Birmingham and Liverpool, using a converted horsebox.

It is unlikely that a TPO was used on any part of the LBR before its line was completed throughout in 1838, although mail trains were run as each section was opened. On 1 October a TPO started running between *Euston and Liverpool, and after the opening of the NUR, the TPO was diverted to run to *Preston instead. North from Preston the mails were rail-borne into *Carlisle for the first time in 1847, and the service was soon reaching the principal cities and towns of Scotland.

The postal network grew rapidly, and there were few main lines on which at least one TPO did not operate in each direction daily. Mails were also carried in the vans of passenger trains, while many small post offices received their bags of mail sent by early morning goods train from their main post town. Day mails were established, particularly working from London with bags which had arrived in the capital on the various night mails for onward despatch.

The first trains exclusively for mail ran between *Paddington and Bristol, inaugurated in 1855. This year probably also marks the beginning of TPO working on the GWR main line, the mail having been previously conveyed in a second-class carriage. A TPO was established between Bristol and *Exeter in 1847, and this is regarded as the forerunner of the Great Western TPO between Paddington and Penzance of later years. In 1869 the PO agreed to allow one first-class carriage to be attached to the mail train between Paddington and Bristol, and in 1884 the service started running without restriction on the number of passengers. It resumed as a purely mail train in 1902.

In 1855, following complaints as to the unreliability of the Anglo-Scottish service, due, it was claimed, to overloading, the PMG suggested that the postal portions should run solely for mail. This was finally implemented in 1885, although for some time afterwards passengers were conveyed northwards from Holytown, near Glasgow. The departure of the postal train at 8.30 p.m. from Euston to *Glasgow and *Aberdeen was to feature for more than 80 years.

Between 1916 and 1921, to cater for army leave traffic, passengers were conveyed on Saturday nights from Euston to *Perth and beyond, while for many years on Sunday nights carriages were attached at Euston for passengers to Dumfries, Stranraer, and beyond. On weekdays the southbound train carried passengers between Aberdeen and Stirling.

In 1882 posting-boxes were fitted to all mail trains in which sorters travelled, and letters bearing an additional ½d. postage as a late fee could be posted in them every day of the week at any station at which the trains stopped. Late-fee boxes, cleared direct into the same trains, were provided at some stations. The late fee was abolished in anticipation of the two-tier postal service, but the posting facility continued for letters bearing first-class postage. Registered letters could be handed to travelling postal staff, provided they bore stamps equal to the special fee charged.

In coaching days it was not unusual for the mail guard to exchange bags at wayside offices without stopping the coach, bags for his collection being handed to him on a pole as the coach passed. Those for delivery were thrown to the ground. Such practices continued on the early railways but were fraught with difficulty, mainly because of the higher speed. By 1842 the TPO was being fitted with apparatus by which mail-bags could be exchanged without reducing speed.

Credit for the concept of exchange apparatus is due mainly to Nathaniel Worsdell, carriage superintendent of the LMR. His device seems to have taken the form of a series of prongs on the side of the TPO, and on pillars at the lineside. With the prongs pointing in the direction of travel, a bag would be hung on the pillar by a large ring in which the prongs of the TPO would engage, the passage of the train causing the bag to be transferred. Worsdell tried to sell the device to the PO but it was finally rejected in 1838.

By this time the PO had become interested in equipment devised by one of its employees, John Ramsey. It took the form of an iron frame on the side of the TPO, across which was secured a net; the frame opened outwards, and the net caught the bag which was hanging from a standard at the lineside, held in place by a spring catch. A bag to be set down was hung from the TPO at a level below the net, and a device at the lineside caused it to drop to the ground, guard boards being fixed on the vehicle and along the track to prevent it from falling under the wheels. Trials took place at Boxmoor on the LBR in 1838, and were considered a success. The equipment was then installed on a permanent basis at Boxmoor, Berkhamsted, and Leighton Buzzard, to be followed by six more locations northward towards Preston in 1839.

Failures to make the exchange were far from rare, blame being put on such problems as the sinking of the rails, oscillation of the carriages, high winds, and loose tarpaulins which knocked bags from standards. Improved apparatus was tried on the *South Eastern Railway, and it went into use on that line in 1848 at New Cross, Croydon, and Edenbridge. The improvements included the use of leather pouches to contain the mail-bags, so preventing them from slipping through the wide mesh of the net. A lineside net to receive bags from the train was also introduced; this was close to the ground, the bags being hung from the TPO below floor level.

The use of the facility grew rapidly. In 1860 there were 101 locations at which exchanges took place, and by 1911 they had increased to 245. Increased use of motor vehicles to serve smaller communities led to a gradual reduction in use, and by early 1967 it was used at only 34 places in Great Britain. In 1971 working took place for the last time when a TPO delivered mail at Penrith.

The design and fitting-out of postal vehicles varied greatly, sometimes reflecting requirements of a particular route. Very typically, one side of a sorting carriage was given over almost entirely to sorting tables and racks of pigeon-holes identified to places served, while the other side had rows of pegs from which hung mail-bags ready to receive bundles of letters from the pigeon-holes opposite. If the carriage were fitted for lineside exchange working, the equipment was on the same side, together with the main doors for loading and unloading at station platforms. Doors were also provided on the same side as the sorting tables, but to allow space for sorting they often gave limited access, so that they were used as little as possible. This consideration, and the need to have exchange apparatus on the correct side, sometimes required postal vehicles to be turned after each journey, using a convenient triangular junction or even a locomotive *turntable.

As traffic grew, two or more postal vehicles were needed on one service, requiring openings in their ends so that the mail guard could move bags between them. Such a requirement goes back at least to 1858, anticipating the bellows-style corridor connection on passenger trains by more than 30 years. Some form of protection was given to the guard in crossing between vehicles, and a witness of the disaster at Abergele in 1868 (see ACCIDENTS) spoke of wide leather bands which passed from the TPO to the van next to it.

It was the practice to place end-gangway connections to one side of the vehicles, rather than centrally. On sorting carriages the side was the one away from the sorters, who would thus not be interrupted in their work by the shifting of bags to and from adjoining vehicles. It followed that communication was not possible between postal vehicles and rolling stock with centre-gangways. To remedy this a number of other vehicles were fitted with a side-gangway at one end, while retaining a centre-gangway at the other. In 1959 three new trains were built for the service between Paddington and the West of England; these had centre-gangways throughout, and all postal vehicles built since have been similarly equipped.

In anticipation of the introduction of the parcel post in 1883, the PO entered into an agreement with no fewer than 81 railway undertakings for its conveyance, and the whole was confirmed by the Post Office (Parcels) Act, 1882. Railway remuneration was to be 55 per cent of the gross receipts of the PO for those parcels carried by rail. To assist in apportionment of the receipts, the PO was to undertake a census for one week in each half-year, recording the number of parcels conveyed by railway and forwarded from the different post towns. In 1922 the railway companies agreed to a reduction in their remuneration to 40 per cent, and the PO agreed to send no more than 10 per cent of parcels by road. Some sorting of parcels was undertaken on trains.

As early as 1913 the PO was despatching some mail by road from London as far as *Bournemouth, *Derby, and Liverpool, a development which grew rapidly from the 1960s onwards. By the early 1990s parcel post had been transferred to road. The Scottish TPOs to and from Euston were withdrawn in May 1993, and first-class mail between London and Scotland, and between other principal cities, went over to air, with connections between air and rail through airports such as East Midlands and Bristol. Partly to counter it, BR set up its separate 'Rail express systems' subsidiary, which included carriage of mail under a penalty contract with the PO.

In December 1993 the PO launched Railnet, a far-reaching development for handling mail under a 10-year contract with Res. A new London postal terminal or 'hub' at Willesden, opened in 1995, handles 68 trains a day; 16 four-car electric *multiple-unit trains are in service, owned by the PO but driven and maintained by Res, and taking power from overhead wires or third rail. Railnet has retained the 1994 network of 24 TPOs, those serving London being diverted to Willesden, and regional 'mini-hubs' have been established at Glasgow, *Newcastle, Warrington, *Doncaster, Bristol, and Tonbridge. The key to the project is the substitution of *containers for the traditional mail-bags, the former being more easily handled and capable of use in all modes of transport. JEN

M. J. Daunton, *Royal Mail: The Post Office since 1840* (1985); H. S. Wilson *T.P.O.: A History of Travelling Post Offices in Great Britain* (1971–5); P. Johnson, *Mail by Rail* (1996); Annual Reports of the Postmaster-General; 'Railnet', in *Modern Railways*, 53, 571 (April 1996), 234–9.

malicious damage. Railways were much exposed to physical damage, almost by their very nature. Each occupied a large extent of land, with its track, sidings, stations, and minor buildings, and although this was *fenced in intruders could enter it with ease, for whatever purpose, for it could not all be kept under continuous observation; nor could the interiors of the railways' vehicles or buildings be constantly watched.

Each company was left to take the best measures it could to safeguard its property, with no special help from the law, until 1861, when a Malicious Damage Act laid down specific penalties—extending at their maximum to penal servitude for life—for setting *fire to the railways' stations and other buildings, or injuring bridges and track (including the unauthorized movement of points). Damaging wires, cables, and posts was now made a criminal offence, with appropriate penalties attached to it. Section 36 of this Act has been used to convict people guilty of altering railway signals.

Another measure was coupled with this one, passed on the same day: the Offences against the Person Act, including penalties for the throwing of stones at locomotives or vehicles, laying down that anyone endangering 'the safety of any person being conveyed or being in or upon' a railway should be liable to a maximum of two years' imprisonment, with or without hard labour. With minor amendments, these two Acts remain in force today.

There were many offences, not endangering life, that were committed against railways but were untouched by this legislation. Some of them were provided against by *bye-laws, rules, and regulations, but these could do little more than threaten, with small hope of success. Many occurred constantly on all railways. Two examples from the *London & South Western in the 1850s are typical. This instruction was appended to its working timetable in 1857: 'The disgraceful practice of making drawings and writings on the walls of water closets and other places must be prevented.' Each stationmaster was to visit all of them on his own station and 'cause to be removed or obliterated immediately anything of the kind'. In 1859 seat cushions in carriages were being slashed. A carriage that had been treated in that way was exhibited to the public, who were informed that if the practice continued the cushions would be removed altogether. The immediate result of this threat is unknown, but the LSWR was shortly obliged, under the pressure of competition from other companies, to continue the cushioning of its higher-class carriages.

No remedy against malicious damage of these kinds has ever been found effective, though the design of modern passenger vehicles has made the practice somewhat more difficult.   JS

L. James, *Law of the Railway* (1980), 371–3; Williams, i, 235.

management. Railway companies were among the very largest commercial enterprises in Britain during the 19th and much of the 20th century. Their size, number of employees, geographical dispersion, and complexity of operation required a previously unknown scale and depth of organization. For these reasons they came to exhibit a degree of separation of ownership and management long before this was detectable elsewhere. Even the smaller railways made demands on the *capital market which attracted investors in unprecedentedly large numbers, on an impersonal basis, and nationally rather than locally. The railways consequently helped to move business activity away from organizations run by owners, partners, and their relatives to corporations dependent on hierarchies of professional employees, and on bureaucratic procedures. The pioneering companies needed executives with a variety of skills, both traditional and new, and gradually developed line and staff distinctions, detailed planning systems, and increasing use of accounting techniques and statistical analysis to ensure effective administration. It has been claimed that American railroads faced more radical challenges in these respects, and were in a more decisive sense the founders of modern corporate management, with a more positive influence on the organization of other industries. But it cannot be doubted that British railway management also had a significant innovatory impact, and in some ways, such as the exceptionally dense network of routes and services,

or the unusual diversity of activities (manufacturing, *hotels, etc.), had at least as demanding a task.

Pressures on management varied according to the scale of operations, and at all times before 1923 there were marked differences between the largest and smallest companies. In the earlier decades of the *Stockton & Darlington Railway, management was immature, and heavy reliance was placed on the supervision of sub-contractors. In contrast, the much grander *London & North Western had a relatively comprehensive management structure by the mid-1850s. This consisted of a pyramid headed by the general manager, and containing two secretaries, three passenger and three locomotive superintendents, and four goods managers. Considerable powers were delegated to lower-level functionaries such as goods agents and *station-masters. Co-ordination depended not just on the role of the general manager, but also on committees, of which the most important (from 1855) was the executive committee of 13 directors.

Many companies initially lacked a clearly defined post of chief executive. Until at least the mid-19th century the most senior official below board level might be a traffic manager, engineer, or solicitor who would not be given overall responsibility. But well before 1914 the railway general manager had achieved strong definition as one of the most prestigious and highly paid professional employees in any sector of the British economy. A substantial proportion rose even higher and ultimately became directors.

The general manager headed an increasingly centralized organization, divided into departments which provided specialist services—*civil engineering, *mechanical engineering, operating, marketing, and so on. Although the work of many junior officials was usually co-ordinated at area or district level, the senior members of the central departments exercised great authority, subject only to the superior decision-making powers of the general manager and the board. Despite the existence of other career paths, the traffic or operating department normally offered its members the best prospects of advancement.

In their first few decades railways had to recruit managers with no previous experience of the industry. These included engineers, *lawyers, officers from the armed forces, and those from other forms of transport, such as *canals. But before long companies were able to fill managerial jobs through internal promotion. The more junior posts were taken by those who had performed well in the clerical grades, which were frequently staffed by young men recruited straight from school. The great majority of them came from business, professional, or other middle-class families, and had enjoyed above-average education. Increasingly the railways trained and developed their own managers. As early as the 1850s the Manchester Sheffield & Lincolnshire (see GREAT CENTRAL) had established a special apprenticeship scheme for particularly promising recruits. Ultimately, the best-known and most highly regarded of all management development programmes was the *North Eastern Railway's (later the *London and North Eastern's) traffic apprenticeship scheme. This consisted of a three-year training in all branches of railway management except engineering, followed by a series of junior managerial postings. It was filled by a combination of university graduates and promising junior staff. The products of this scheme were prominent not just in the LNER itself, but also in the senior ranks of *British Railways after 1948. Some were 'poached' by other businesses with less proficient management training. Other forms of management development included the courses on railway economics run by the London School of Economics, and various company training schemes, often (by the 1920s–30s) in their own residential schools.

The most common criticism of railway management was its alleged tendency to in-breeding and conservatism. Long-term employment and the absorption of a pervasive railway culture produced a type of loyalty and commitment, to both company and industry, which could be a weakness as well as a strength. It has been suggested that the railways became too dependent on single-company men whose careers had often in large measure been spent in one specialized department. Departments could become excessively isolated, and disagreements might be difficult to resolve except at high level. Lack of integration between revenue-producing and cost-producing functions was one implication. Arguably a gap existed which might have been filled by a layer of general management at headquarters, equipped with appropriate statistical information, and instructed to consider broader strategic issues. The most serious possible consequence of these shortcomings was a tendency to technical and organizational stagnation.

The economic record of the railways from the late 19th century onwards might be taken as confirmation, at least in part, of the validity of these criticisms. Clearly management did find difficulty in adjusting to major changes in their business, though they were of course far from unique in that respect. The early decades of continual expansion and frequent mergers required much rapid learning and acquisition of such skills as inter-company diplomacy over pooling and traffic *agreements. Later, conditions of more stable oligopoly emerged, but accompanied by rising costs and tightening government regulation. The scarcity of capital and relative labour abundance in 1920–39 were replaced after 1940 by conditions in which it became urgent to improve labour productivity. It is, however, not clear that financial results were closely determined by managerial efficiency. Returns were higher in the first few decades of railways than in the late 19th and early 20th centuries, although management was unquestionably better organized and more systematic from the 1850s onwards. In the inter-war period the most financially successful of the *Big Four was the most managerially conservative—the *Great Western. This paradox is attributable to the relative prosperity of the territory it served, and to the lesser disruption it underwent after the *Grouping of 1923. It seems likely that the generally low earnings and stagnation of traffic in the 1920s and 1930s were more the result of powerful external factors like the growth of *road competition and restrictive legislation, than of weak or ossified management. Slowness in *electrification, for example, was a penalty of financial weakness rather than a product of unthinking devotion to steam traditions.

Some charges of managerial conservatism have, in all periods, relied for their effect on some exaggeration: the accusation of in-breeding, for example. Even during the relative maturity of the railway system, between 1870 and 1922, more than a third of general managers had previously spent some time in a variety of non-railway occupations. There was also considerable mobility between railways in the 19th century, with companies such as the *Great Northern and the *London & South Western normally appointing their chief executives from outside. There is, however, only one recorded case between 1850 and *nationalization of the appointment of a chief executive with no previous experience of the industry: Josiah *Stamp joined the *London Midland & Scottish Railway as President of the Executive. His arrival was associated with a major restructuring of the company, which certainly demonstrated that railways had by no means lost their capacity for managerial innovation.

Stamp became president of a small executive committee (and soon afterwards also chairman of the company) which included four vice-presidents, each with responsibility for a defined area of company activity—finance, traffic, engineering, and research. They were supported by a relatively small headquarters staff of around 120. Under Stamp's leadership the LMS became the most effectively centralized of the four groups, and made the most rapid progress towards standardization and rationalization. This new structure may have owed something to American models. It could certainly be considered a significant early example of a version of multi-divisional corporate organization in Britain. Other groups responded quite differently to similar market and regulatory conditions. The GWR retained the closest equivalent of the traditional structure. The LNER remained the least centralized, with four (later three) divisions corresponding to former constituent companies, each headed by an influential divisional general manager.

The railways may, in principle, have stimulated business in other sectors of the economy by providing examples of advanced managerial practice, although, in fact, few other British firms before World War II were sufficiently large to have much incentive to emulate their methods. Railways did, however, make a contribution through the supply of managerial talent to other businesses. Firms in electricity supply, engineering, and insurance were prominent among those who found railway executives attractive recruits. Notable instances were Sam *Fay, who went from the *Great Central to Beyer Peacock (see WORKS), and Felix *Pole, who left the GWR for Associated Electrical Industries.

Since nationalization, management structures have, if anything, been subject to more continual and rapid change than previously. Despite unification of the system, there has been much instability in policy and organization, and a high level of somewhat inconsistent government intervention. In 1947–68 there were four major Transport Acts. The cumbersome *British Transport Commission gave way in 1962 to the *British Railways Board. An objective of greater centralization was pursued in the late 1940s and early 1950s, then decentralization from 1953, and then a measure of recentralization during the *'Beeching revolution' of the early 1960s. During the latter an attempt was made to ensure that the board was able to focus on corporate planning issues. Until the 1980s it ran a four-tier structure of headquarters, region, division, and area, the crucial layer being the multi-functional region, followed by a more streamlined 'field' organization, with five major 'business sectors' below board level, for freight, parcels, InterCity, provincial, and London & South East.   GC

T. R. Gourvish, *Mark Huish and the London and North Western Railway* (1972), *British Railways 1948–1973* (1986), and 'The Railways and the Development of Managerial Enterprise in Britain', in K. Kobayaski and H. Morikawa (eds.), *Development of Managerial Enterprise* (1986).

Manchester & Birmingham Railway, see LONDON & NORTH WESTERN RAILWAY.

Manchester & Leeds Railway. Under its Act of 1837 the Manchester & Leeds Railway was authorized to build a cross-Pennine line 51 m long from *Manchester through Rochdale to a summit at Littleborough, and thence down the narrow valley of the Yorkshire Calder through Todmorden and Sowerby Bridge to pass near Wakefield and join the proposed *North Midland Railway at Normanton, over which it would have *running powers to *Leeds. George *Stephenson was chief engineer. There were numerous tunnels and viaducts, and the most difficult work was Summit Tunnel, 1 m 1,125 yds long. The line was opened from its Manchester terminus in Oldham Road in 1839–40.

Branches were built to Heywood (1841), Oldham (1842), Halifax (1844), and Stalybridge (1846). In 1848 a connecting line was built across Manchester to the *London & North Western Railway, giving access to the south, and at the eastern end there were connections to *York and *Hull. The only gap in east–west communications lay between the MLR and *Liverpool & Manchester Railway termini in Manchester, which was filled in 1844 when a new, more central station was opened at Victoria, whereupon Oldham Road became a goods station.

In 1846 the Manchester Bolton & Bury Railway, opened in 1838, and the incomplete Liverpool & Bury Railway amalgamated with the MLR. In the same year the company leased the *North Union Railway jointly with the *Grand Junction company, and in 1847 it changed its name to *Lancashire & Yorkshire Railway.   GJB

LYR, i.

Manchester and Salford in the first half of the 19th century formed Britain's second city, although the twin towns have always maintained separate identities. They were likened by Leon Faucher in 1844 to the centre of a 30-mile spider's web of cotton-manufacturing towns. By 1804 Manchester had become a *canal centre linked to many of its satellite towns, to Yorkshire, the Midlands, and to *Liverpool, on which it depended for importing cotton and despatching finished goods.

Although the city gave only lukewarm support, the *Liverpool & Manchester Railway (1830) by 1838 provided rail communication from Liverpool Road station to London, considerably shortened in 1842 by the Manchester & Birmingham Railway (see LONDON & NORTH WESTERN) from London Road station to *Crewe. By 1845 the Manchester Bolton & Bury Railway was open to Bolton; the *Manchester & Leeds from Oldham Road throughout to Normanton, joining lines to *Leeds, *York, *Hull, and the east Midlands; and the Sheffield Ashton-under-Lyne & Manchester Railway, which shared London Road station with the MBR.

Thus Manchester had four termini—including Salford—serving five lines, only two being connected. In 1844 the Liverpool and Bolton lines were linked to the MLR and its new Victoria station, and Oldham Road and Liverpool Road became goods stations. But it was 1849 before the Crewe and *Sheffield lines were connected to the Liverpool line by part of the *Manchester South Junction & Altrincham Railway, a suburban railway running from London Road through a junction at Castlefield to Bowden. Some of its trains ran from the intermediate Oxford Road station, nearer the business quarter.

By 1847, amalgamations had put the LMR and MBR into the London & North Western Railway and the MLR and MBBR into the *Lancashire & Yorkshire, while the SAMR had become the Manchester Sheffield & Lincolnshire (see GREAT CENTRAL). A year later the LYR opened a line for goods trains from Miles Platting to the LNWR and MSLR at Ardwick.

Manchester was now almost enclosed by a horseshoe of viaducts (see LANDSCAPE) with two peripheral stations rendering through north–south travel impossible. London Road, where the LNWR and MSLR were at best uneasy partners, served the south, east, and, jointly, Altrincham; from Victoria the LYR covered almost the whole of Lancashire and parts of West Yorkshire, while the LNWR also used it for trains to Liverpool and North Wales, and Leeds via Huddersfield, reached by *running powers over the LYR as far as Stalybridge.

The growing network enormously speeded up manufacture in the surrounding cotton towns. As early as 1839 yarn despatched 30 miles by rail to *Preston at 3 a.m. was woven, finished, and back in Manchester by 7 p.m., ready for sale next morning. By providing the flexibility the characteristically fluctuating cotton trade demanded, the railways were now essential to its expansion. Moreover, the railways were paramount in the growing chemicals industry and heavy engineering, which included locomotive building, notably Sharp, Roberts (1833), and Beyer Peacock (1854) next to the MSLR's works at Gorton (1848) (see WORKS).

Such dependency attracted other railways wanting a share of the traffic. The *Great Northern came in over the lines of its ally the MSLR in 1857, provoking a physical dispute with the LNWR over the use of London Road; the *Midland Railway, by the same means in 1867. Even the *Great Western gained running powers over the LNWR

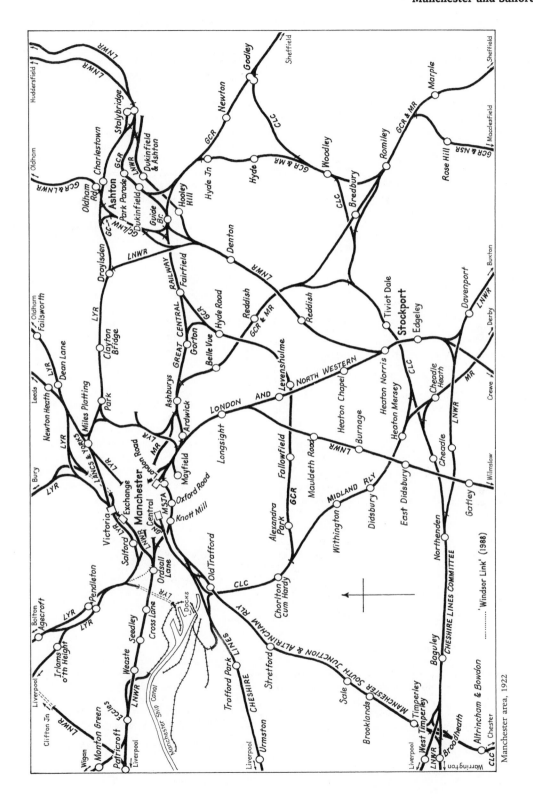

Manchester area, 1922

from Warrington in 1858 and had a warehouse at Liverpool Road.

In 1880 the *Cheshire Lines Committee, comprising lines owned jointly by the MSLR, GNR, and MR south and west of Manchester, completed Central station, to which the GNR and MR promptly transferred. At Victoria, the LYR's refusal to accept the LNWR as joint owner led to the latter opening Exchange station, adjacent, in 1884. After they became part of the *London Midland & Scottish Railway in 1923 the two stations were joined by a through platform 731 yds long: the longest in Britain. Manchester's last terminus was Mayfield, a small adjunct to London Road built by the LNWR in 1910 for residential trains, but in the event used more for mail and parcels. But none of these developments provided the cross-city through route that Manchester needed.

The suburban Manchester South District line of 1880 gave the MR access to Central, made more direct in 1902 by a new line through the 2½-mile Disley Tunnel, enabling it to compete seriously with the LNWR for London traffic and to a degree with the Great Central, as the MSLR became in 1897. At Chorlton Junction the South District was joined in 1891–2 by an MSLR line from Fairfield, giving that company direct access to Central too. Both carried considerable suburban traffic, like the MSLR's lines into London Road, including an Oldham service competing with the LYR's two routes from Victoria. That company had the most intensive local services, some from east Lancashire continuing to terminate at Salford. But at the end of the century a growing electric *tramway network started eating into this traffic, and in 1916 the LYR electrified its Bury line with a 1,200 V dc third-rail system (see ELECTRIFICATION); the MSJAR was electrified from Oxford Road at 1,500 V dc overhead in 1931.

Two major companies were based in Manchester: the LYR at Hunts Bank (Victoria), and the MSLR at London Road until it moved to London *Marylebone in 1905 after becoming the GCR.

The centre of Manchester was remarkable for its large goods *stations that in other cities would have been located further out. The LNWR's at Liverpool Road, and at London Road alongside the MSLR's in Ducie Street, and the CLC's at Central next to the GNR's massive Deansgate goods station, were typified by large multi-storey warehouses (see GOODS SHEDS). The LYR's yard sprawled along the opposite bank of the Irwell in Salford; that company had a second at the former Oldham Road terminus, and the MR's was at Ancoats; all close to the central mercantile district.

The Manchester Ship Canal (1894) was more than a response to Liverpool's monopolistic dock dues, but also to railway charges. Large docks were constructed in Manchester and Salford, to which the LYR and CLC built connecting lines, and to the Ship Canal Company's own extensive railway.

In 1954 *British Railways electrified the Sheffield line from London Road at 1,500 V dc, and in 1960 the line to Crewe at 25 kV ac as part of its *West Coast main line

electrification from Euston. The short stretch to Oxford Road was included; later the whole of the MSJAR was converted to the same voltage. In 1981 Stockport–Hazel Grove, on the Buxton line, was electrified, and in 1984 Glossop and Hadfield services were converted to 25 kV ac following closure of the Sheffield line as a through route in 1981 in favour of the former MR route via Chinley.

To this end London Road, including the MSJAR platforms, had been remodelled and renamed Piccadilly, enabling Mayfield to be closed in 1960. Further rationalization, withdrawal of local trains, closure of the former MR route to Derby, and reversion of the ex-LNWR services to Victoria meant that Central and Exchange could be closed in 1969. Manchester now had only two main passenger stations. Exchange was demolished and Central, with its notable arched roof, mouldered as a car park until its exemplary conversion to the G-Mex exhibition hall in 1986. Only two central goods warehouses remain: Ducie Street and Deansgate, both listed but not in railway use; goods traffic is concentrated at Trafford Park *Freightliner depot, where a large regional *Channel Tunnel freight depot is located.

In conjunction with the Greater Manchester *Passenger Transport Authority rail services since the early 1980s have been slowly but steadily revived. The Hazel Grove chord, opened in 1986, speeded up Manchester–Sheffield trains. The Windsor Link, opened in 1988 between former LYR and LNWR lines, at long last provided direct running from Preston and north-east Lancashire to Piccadilly, the south, and east, via the MSJAR and Oxford Road. An entirely new pattern of services was made possible, helped by a new interchange station at Salford Crescent. Salford station itself was rebuilt for vastly improved services. The opening of Manchester Airport station enabled many services to start and end there, although the electrified system unfortunately remains incomplete until the Manchester–Preston line is tackled.

In parallel, the PTA has very successfully pioneered a British tram revival in Metrolink, a *Light Rapid Transit system using converted BR tracks from Bury to Victoria and Altrincham to Castlefield, connected by street tracks through the city centre, with a spur to Piccadilly station. Further extensions are planned. Victoria station is undergoing redevelopment as a large hotel, offices, shops, and sports complex, with new platforms but retaining most of the historic portions—the largest of its kind on railway land outside London. Meanwhile, the world's oldest surviving station, Liverpool Road, is enjoying a new career as the Greater Manchester Museum of Science & Industry, where railways play a prominent part.   GJB

L. Faucher, *Manchester in 1844: the Present Condition and Future Prospects* (1844); G. S. Messinger, *Manchester in the Victorian Age* (1985); J. R. Kellett, *The Impact of Railways on Victorian Cities* (1969), ch. 6; *Reg. Hist.*, x (1986 edn.), esp. ch. 5.

Manchester Sheffield & Lincolnshire Railway, see GREAT CENTRAL RAILWAY.

Manchester Ship Canal Railway, see MANCHESTER.

Manchester South Junction & Altrincham Railway.

Formed in 1845 by the *Liverpool & Manchester and Sheffield Ashton & Manchester (see GREAT CENTRAL) Railways to provide a 1½-mile link between them on a viaduct across the south side of *Manchester, the line was opened from Ordsall Lane to London Road station in 1849. Almost as an afterthought, an eight-mile 'branch' from Castlefield to Altrincham was included, which quickly became the busier line, forming one of the earliest suburban railways and materially influencing the growth of the district. The *joint owners, by now the *London & North Western and Manchester Sheffield & Lincolnshire companies, ran frequent services to Altrincham from Manchester Oxford Road, although regular trains to London Road did not begin until 1879. The Ordsall Lane line fully answered its purpose as an important link, but it never had a significant local train service. Junctions at Altrincham allowed use of that line for other destinations, including Chester by *Cheshire Lines Committee trains.

Disagreements between the two owners became so frequent that an Act of 1858 provided that an arbitrator should attend all meetings. The company owned its own rolling stock, but locomotives were mainly provided by the MSLR. In 1931 the line was *electrified on the 1,500 V dc overhead system, which in 1971 was converted to the 25 kV ac system of the Manchester–*Crewe line, enabling an integrated suburban service to be run from Crewe to Altrincham via Oxford Road. The Windsor Link of 1988 gave even greater importance to the Ordsall Lane section. In 1993 the Castlefield–Altrincham line was again converted, as part of the Metrolink *Light Rapid Transit system, although the route still carries Chester trains.   GJB

Reg. Hist., x, 113–17; F. Dixon, *The Manchester South Junction & Altrincham Railway* (1973).

manias, railway.

Histories of railway development in the United Kingdom have placed considerable emphasis on the great 'railway mania' of the mid-1840s, when parliamentary powers were obtained for the building of over 9,000 route miles and the raising of more than £500 million by British and Irish railway companies. However, while this was the most extreme manifestation of promotional fever, it was not unique, nor was the phenomenon confined to railways. Besides the precedent of the South Sea Bubble of 1719–20, the 19th-century railway booms were foreshadowed by the *'canal mania' of 1791–4, when 42 new inland navigations were authorized.

The first promotional boom involving railways occurred in 1824–5, when changes in company legislation and the easy availability of money encouraged a large number of new flotations. While much attention was devoted to foreign loans and mining and utility undertakings, railways also featured significantly among the proposed ventures, despite their infancy. *Prospectuses were published for at least 70 lines, of which around 40 reached the parliamentary stage. Though the *Liverpool & Manchester—which in fact originated before the boom—was the only substantial railway to emerge successfully, other proposals current in 1825 included ambitious schemes for trunk routes linking *London with *Birmingham, Lancashire, *Bristol, South Wales, and Falmouth.

The poor harvest of 1825 and a series of banking failures ended the boom, but even before the general collapse of commercial confidence the prospects of many railway projects had been undermined by the defeat of the first Liverpool & Manchester Bill in June 1825. However, the LMR's opening in 1830 revived interest in railway promotion: though an incipient boom in 1831 was checked by the Reform crisis, several major schemes were authorized between 1833 and 1835. This was the prelude to the first tangible railway mania, which began in the autumn of 1835 and resulted in a peak of parliamentary activity in 1836–7. Over 1,500 route miles and £34.6 million capital were authorized in these two years.

In most respects except scale, the railway mania which began in 1844 followed a pattern similar to that of the mid-1830s. Economic recovery was accompanied by an upsurge in railway promotion, initially based mainly on sound projects. However, as commercial confidence grew, railway securities were soon in wider demand as an apparently easy way for individuals to share in the growth in prosperity, primarily through the realization of capital gains on a rising market. As the booms moved into the mania phase, expectations became increasingly unrealistic, and more speculative, sometimes fraudulent, schemes were able to attract eager subscribers.

Inevitably, such over-optimism could not be sustained, and the lack of real substance behind some schemes increased the markets' reaction against railway shares when confidence wavered and credit tightened. Nevertheless, the lengthy processes in preparing a Private Bill meant that much legislative activity continued after the speculative peaks had passed, in May 1836 and August 1845 respectively. Accordingly, new lines continued to be authorized despite the worsening financial climate, but as recession deepened even firmly based companies found it difficult to raise funds for construction. Over a third of the mileage authorized between 1844 and 1847 was not built.

Even if investors had been prepared to ignore the lessons of the 1840s, the increasing dominance of the established railway undertakings afterwards meant that new companies' shares could no longer play so important a part in the stock market. Consequently, though there were lesser booms in 1852–3 and the early 1860s, the excesses of the great railway mania were never repeated on a comparable scale.

See also SPECULATION; ABANDONMENT.   MCR

T. R. Gourvish, *Railways and the British Economy 1830–1914* (1980), 12–19; J. R. T. Hughes, *Fluctuations in Trade, Industry and Finance* (1960), 184–206; H. G. Lewin, *The Railway Mania and its Aftermath* (1968 edn.); R. C. Michie, *Money, Mania and Markets* (1981), 78–100; H. Pollins, *Britain's Railways: An Industrial History* (1971), 35–54.

Mansell, Richard C.,

carriage superintendent, *South Eastern Railway, c.1848–1882. He is chiefly known for the patented design of wheel bearing his name. Around an iron, later steel, centre boss, a disc was built up from 16 teak segments. The disc was forced on to a bevelled inner face of the tyre by hydraulic pressure. Two grooves were formed in the tyre and two securing rings were fixed in the grooves —one on each side—and all were bolted together by screw bolts and nuts. The first patent was taken out in 1848. By 1874 there were over 20,000 sets of Mansell wheels in use, but no incidence of failure had yet been reported to the Board of *Trade. Mansell wheels ceased to be manufactured for new stock just before World War I.

Mansell was responsible for an ornate royal saloon built by the SER in 1851, and for some of the earliest standard-gauge bogie *carriages, built from 1878.

In 1876, as a result of a dispute with the SER's chairman, Sir Edward *Watkin, the locomotive superintendent, James Cudworth, resigned. Watkin's son was his immediate but temporary replacement, after which Mansell took charge of locomotive matters, three new classes of engine appearing before James Stirling was appointed locomotive superintendent in 1878. MLH

C. F. Dendy Marshall, (ed.), *History of the Southern Railway* (1963); D. Gould, *Carriage Stock of the SE&CR* (1976).

Mansell wheel, see MANSELL, R.; CARRIAGES.

Mansion House Association on Railway and Canal Traffic. Widespread dissatisfaction with railway *freight rates led in 1889 to the formation of the Mansion House Committee at the instigation of the Lord Mayor of London, Sir James Whitehead. It represented trade and agricultural organizations, chambers of commerce, local authorities, the Railway & Canal Traders' Association, and the Lancashire & Cheshire Conference on Railway & Canal Rates. After 1891 it was the principal body negotiating with railways and the government on rates and charges. In 1892 the Traders' Association formally merged with the committee to form the Mansion House Association, followed in 1897 by the Lancashire & Cheshire Conference. GJB

P. M. Williams, 'Public Opinion and the Railway Rates Question in 1886', *English Historical Review*, 68 (1952), 45; G. Alderman, *The Railway Interest* (1973), 127, 303–4.

Manx Electric Railway, see ISLE OF MAN RAILWAYS.

Manx Northern Railway, see ISLE OF MAN RAILWAYS.

maps and plans. Railway maps in Great Britain reflect its position as the best-mapped country in the world; others have fared less well. British railway cartography is as old as railways themselves—Staffordshire Record Office holds a manuscript of *c.*1680 with a rough plan of the 'footrails' built by Andrew Yarranton to take coal down to the short-lived River Stour navigation, and the complex arrangement of wayleaves (see LAND ACQUISITION) for early *wooden railways in the north-east generated contemporary surveys for legal and estate purposes. During the 18th century they began to appear as topographical features on the larger-scale engraved county maps, but Gibson's fine *Plan of Collieries on the Rivers Tyne and Wear . . .* of 1788 must be one of the earliest printed maps with a major railway content.

As the science of engineering improved during the In-

dustrial Revolution, so expertise developed in surveying and planning transport routes by road, water, and rail, with the resulting maps becoming more sophisticated. The parliamentary process enhanced this trend, with accurate detailed plans being required for public deposit (see PARLIAMENTARY PLANS). Initially the skills needed were drawn both from the ranks of *canal and road builders and from land *surveyors, with the engineer undertaking the surveying work or a surveyor some engineering. This interdependence survived later trends towards specialization; surveying and plan production formed an integral, and expensive, part of railway development.

Any attempt at classification of the huge variety of railway maps can be neither definitive nor comprehensive, but a number of types or families with similar characteristics have evolved over the years. There is no clear dividing line between plan and map—the former are usually large in scale and show detail exactly as it appears on the ground, whilst the latter necessarily involve generalization, distortion, and symbols; in the extreme they become line diagrams.

Contract or centreline plans are the engineering surveys on which construction is based. The route of a railway would be staked out on the ground using the parliamentary plan, and the surveyor would then plot this alignment and add all the topographic detail to construct an accurate plan of the area up to 400 ft either side, firstly as a dimensionally accurate but roughly finished draft, which would then be inked-up or fair-copied and perhaps enhanced with water colour. This finished plan might remain in manuscript, with further copies being laboriously traced by hand, or it could be printed. With the assistance of levels it would then be used to calculate the exact size of the *earthworks, and to position *bridges, *tunnels, *fences, *stations, and permanent way. Copies could then enable *contractors to cost out and tender for the job, and it was also used to compute areas and negotiate *land purchase. The scale was variable, with two or three chains to the inch normally sufficient in rural areas, but often larger in towns. Where these plans have survived they are invaluable in showing features which were swept away by the railway, together with the minor adjustments which had to be made to the route itself to improve the alignment or to satisfy *landowners. Some remain in railway ownership; a few have migrated to record offices; many are now lost.

Line or land-plans were produced by many of the larger railways to record and administer their property, and they are the railway equivalent of the landowner's estate map. Often on the scale of two chains to the inch, they may be based on the contract plan and show all the property which had been purchased together with details of the vendors, leases, and other estate management information. Some, such as those prepared by the *Lancashire & Yorkshire Railway, show little else, but the value of most is that they were based on a proper dated survey and record the *track, bridges, *signals, stations, and other infrastructure exactly as it then existed, sometimes with later notes of any changes. Lithography enabled copies, often delicately hand-coloured and bound in books or rolls, to be issued to various departments as required, where they served for a variety of engineering and record purposes. The *London & North Western Railway, for example, systematically covered most of its lines with new or revised surveys in the late 1860s and early 1870s. Still produced, retained, and used by Railtrack (see PRIVATIZATION), many earlier ones have found their way to local record offices.

The clear and accurate depiction of topography has made Ordnance Survey maps and plans indispensable, not least to the railway industry, but OS have published only one or two specific railway maps—the quarter-inch scale coverage in 1839 for the Irish Railway Commission was probably the first. The Old Series of one-inch sheets produced between 1805 and 1874 was not comprehensively revised or kept up to date, but a policy of adding new railways to the plates as required has made them, and the comparable Scottish and Irish series, into useful *de facto* railway maps. Later editions were better at showing stations. From the 1840s coverage spread at larger scales of 6 in, 25 in or more to the mile, recording on thousands of plans a huge amount of railway information that was perhaps not exploited as well as it should have been by contemporaries, but is now being recognized as a major historical source. For England and Wales the largest collection is that of the British Library, but good coverage can often be found in local depositories, and the expanding series of Godfrey reprints includes many urban sheets of great railway interest.

Railway *guidebooks and *publicity often made use of a range of maps. Despite their titles these were frequently not really railway maps, but some suitable local survey with the line emphasized. They can be useful, for example in locating the position of closed stations, but need to be approached with a degree of caution—lines could be badly misplaced, and it was a common practice, shared with many general map publishers, to show a railway without checking whether or not it had actually been built. Such errors were often perpetuated for many years and faithfully transcribed from one publication to another, although the situation gradually improved as the use of Ordnance Survey maps developed.

Timetable or system-maps were published by nearly every railway and whilst the standards varied, the usual format was to ignore geography and portray the home line as a bold direct route or routes, with competitors either omitted or distorted to aimless loops. Stations were prominently shown and named, and the margins and reverse were often adorned with advertisements or illustrations. Some are really diagrams rather than maps, such as the well-known depiction of the *London Underground. An even-handed but somewhat sketchy treatment is given by *Bradshaw in the map which accompanied his annual guide: it should not be confused with his large map of the railways of Great Britain first published in 1839 which is a much more attractive production that was soon emulated by others, often less satisfactorily.

*Prospectus maps were usually issued as part of a document aimed at potential shareholders, and both document

and map used considerable licence to enhance the attractiveness of the investment. Cartographic accuracy is missing (as are many competitors' lines) since the map strives to present even the most minor proposal as central to the railway network and of the utmost importance. Treated cautiously, with information cross-checked against more reliable sources, they remain as a testimony to an era when millions of pounds were speculated in railway investments (see MANIAS, RAILWAY). Some libraries hold good collections of these documents.

In contrast, *Railway Clearing House maps were sober working documents with a deserved reputation for accuracy. Zachary Macaulay, one of the RCH clerks, had published in 1851 a map recording comparatively accurately the railway system of Great Britain which had emerged from the boom years of the 1840s, and he was well placed to receive information about new lines and stations which justified several later editions. Macaulay died in 1860, but the work was later taken up by his colleague John Airey, who published a book of *Junction Diagrams on a semi-official basis in 1867, followed in 1869 by a map of the Manchester area. Other regional maps followed, and by 1893 the series had grown to 15, with a general railway map of England and Wales which was a big improvement on Macaulay's. Airey's maps are clear and detailed, naming every passenger station and most sidings and goods facilities. Early experiments with colour-printing were not pursued at the time and the series settled down to carefully applied colour wash on each sheet as a means of distinguishing line ownership, with the distances between stations given in miles and chains to assist in the calculation of rates. The maps rapidly became essential tools in many railway offices, with new editions being produced at frequent intervals, and the system of sending proofs to the railway companies for checking avoided most errors. Copies could be purchased mounted on rollers for wall display or dissected and folded on cloth in leather covers for the shelf. In 1895 the business was purchased by the RCH, with subsequent sheets being redrawn and issued as colour-printed official publications. The output slowed following the 1923 *Grouping, and the last map to be published was the 1960 edition of Scotland. The David Garnett Collection in Brunel University Library is an excellent source for these maps, as is the BTC archive in the Public Record Office. One sheet is the subject of a modern reprint, and two railway atlases are largely based on RCH map data.

Engraving was traditionally the printing process for maps, with the outline and lettering of the work being skilfully cut in reverse on a smooth copper plate with a steel point. A thick ink was then wiped over the surface and polished off, and the plate put in a press with a dampened sheet of soft paper: under pressure the fibres of the paper were squeezed into the minute incisions in the copper where they picked up the residual ink. Although engraving continued to be used for the best work until the middle of the 19th century, it was rapidly replaced during the railway period by lithography, a process which involved drawing or transferring the image to a smooth porous slab of stone using a greasy ink. When the stone was dampened it would then reject further applications of ink which would cling only to the previously treated areas from where it could be picked up on a sheet of paper in a press. This was both quicker and cheaper than engraving; in either case the resulting maps could be finished by hand colouring, soon to be rendered obsolete by the development of colour printing. Single monochrome copies could also be made from tracings by various photographic processes, of which the 'blueprint' is the best known, and dyeline the most used.

Whilst paper was always the commonest medium for railway maps, others have included cloth, silk, pottery, glass, metal, and plastic. The large map of the LYR which still adorns Manchester Victoria station is prepared on glazed tiles.   RJD

RS; P. Hindle, *Maps for Local History* (1988); A. Jowett, *Jowett's Railway Atlas* (1989); R. Oliver, *Ordnance Survey Maps—A Concise Guide for Historians* (1993); D. Smith, *Maps and Plans for the Historian and Collector* (1988).

market garden traffic, see FRUIT AND VEGETABLES TRAFFIC; AGRICULTURAL TRAFFIC.

markets and fairs. These played a large part in the *agricultural economy of Victorian Britain. The majority were governed by ancient rights granted by the crown or large landowners.

Every market town was served by road carriers converging on it from the surrounding country. Though the markets dealt primarily in vegetables, *fruit, dairy produce, cattle (see LIVESTOCK TRAFFIC) and *meat, and *fish, they also competed with the towns' shops in selling other miscellaneous goods.

The expansion of railways soon alarmed towns lying off their proposed routes, especially those with prosperous markets, such as Devizes, Marlborough, Maidstone, and Stamford. The railways often destroyed the business of small markets, concentrating it in larger towns, particularly those that were junctions. In Somerset, Wiveliscombe and Wellington both saw theirs drawn away to Taunton. The railways encouraged people to travel to markets by issuing market tickets, at reduced rates.

Here and there the railways facilitated the provision of new markets, adjoining stations. The Earl of Portsmouth established one at Eggesford in north Devon about 1860. In Cumbria in the 1870s the *Midland Railway itself created a market at Lazonby (snuffing out an ancient one at Kirkoswald, 1½ miles away), and an 'auction mart' for cattle on its land at Appleby.

Every small market was under threat. The number in England was approximately halved in 1792–1888, and reduced by one-third in Wales; a decline attributable, however, not entirely to reduced business but also to 'rationalization'. Grain, for instance, was concentrated into new 'corn exchanges'. The one at Halstead (Essex) was built in 1865 adjoining the railway station.

Cattle trading near town centres caused disruption of traffic and much fouling of streets. At *Leicester and *York separate cattle markets were built in 1871–9, served by

branch railways. Something much bigger was attempted in London at Smithfield, though with incomplete success.

At Salisbury a handsome general market house was erected in 1859 adjoining the old open market, with a branch railway running into it. But nothing so comprehensive appeared anywhere else.

In the late Victorian age most markets encountered new competition from chain-stores—Lipton's and the Home & Colonial, for instance. Their bulk-buying—an easy matter by railway—lowered their prices. The old open markets were now increasingly transferred into market halls, none of them physically connected with railways.

The history of fairs in Great Britain is different. Unlike markets, they were not held throughout the year, but for as much as a week at certain fixed times. They dealt principally in livestock. Among the most celebrated in England were those at Cambridge (Stourbridge Fair), Barnet (Hertfordshire), and Weyhill (Hampshire). Most of the sheep and cattle were brought in on the hoof; some of the drove-roads are still traceable. Railways were usually late in penetrating many cattle-raising districts, and meanwhile the drovers' work continued. The greatest centre on which they converged in Scotland, Falkirk Tryst, died out at the end of the 19th century (see LIVESTOCK TRAFFIC).

But there were also other fairs: 'pleasure fairs' selling numerous cheap goods, and 'fun fairs', which often accompanied them. These attracted day-trippers, a high proportion of them arriving by train before 1914. Several of the best known developed from traditional fairs: the Birmingham Onion Fair, for example. That lapsed in 1939, but some survive, like St Giles's Fair at Oxford in September and the *Nottingham Goose Fair in October, which used to bring large crowds from considerable distances. The heavy *excursion traffic to this last caused a serious accident in 1869 at Long Eaton.   JS

Royal Commission on Market Rights and Tolls: PP 1888, lii, liii, 1890–1, xxxvii; *RTC*, 161, 186, 287; A. R. B. Haldane, *Drove Roads of Scotland* (1961 edn.), 219–21.

Marples, Lord, see TRANSPORT, MINISTRY OF.

Marsh, Lord, see BRITISH RAILWAYS.

Marshall, Chapman Frederick Dendy (1872–1945), writer; he graduated from Cambridge and was called to the Bar, but never practised. He took up the study of engineering and evolved a *valve gear applied to a *London & North Western Railway locomotive in 1915. In World War I he worked in the Ministry of Munitions. He was a founder of the *Newcomen Society in 1920 and its president in 1934–6. He published a paper on the motion of vehicles on a curved railway line and another on the resistance of *express trains.

He produced several collections of papers on early British locomotives, and three books besides. One is most valuable: *A History of British Railways down to the Year 1830* (1938, handsomely reissued in 1971). His *Centenary History of the *Liverpool & Manchester Railway* (1930) was an unsatisfactory account of its subject. Dendy Marshall was a collector of railway rarities—pictures, maps, medals, pottery, textiles—

and the book is devoted largely to illustrating and discussing them. As a history of the company it was entirely superseded by R. H. G. Thomas's excellent work of 1980.

He also wrote a commissioned *History of the *Southern Railway* (1937), a large work of uneven value, some of its errors being corrected in a second edition of 1963.   JS

marshalling yards. A marshalling yard received *freight traffic over a wide area, so as to save extensive sorting at the initial concentration point. Short-distance transits were sorted out for local distribution, and full trains of longer-distance transits were made up and despatched to a marshalling yard nearer to the destination of the *wagon's payload. In the days of *private-owner wagons, empty coal wagons were concentrated at marshalling yards to form trains for return to the collieries.

Some yards were located at a convenient collecting point for originating traffic, on the outskirts of a city, or in the proximity of a coalfield. Along the main lines of the pre-*Grouping railways heavily involved with coal traffic, there were marshalling yards at strategic centres, usually 60 miles apart. The distance was significant in that this provided suitable staging points for servicing steam locomotives, for the relief of train crews, and to meet the requirement for wagon examination, vital in the days of grease-*lubricated axle-boxes.

The earlier marshalling yards were usually built on level ground, consisting of a series of parallel *sidings leading from an entry line. Facilities were provided for controlling points (see TRACK) and *signals from a *signal box or lever-frame, and for the shunters who had to pin down and release the wagon hand-brakes, and couple and uncouple wagons. Yard *shunting was carried out by horses, or a shunting locomotive usually termed the 'yard pilot'.

The task of shunting in and out of sidings to make up rakes of wagons was time-consuming. A solution was provided by gravitational yards, by which wagons were shunted over a hump, from which they gravitated into the appropriate siding, and were then marshalled to form a train. The earliest example was probably on the *North Eastern Railway at Tyne Dock, where gravity shunting began in 1859. Then came the NER's conversion in 1869 of Shildon yard which served the West Durham coalfield, achieved by laying-in new tracks and providing a hump.

In 1873–82 the *London & North Western Railway pioneered the 'gridiron' marshalling and sorting sidings at Edge Hill, *Liverpool. The name was derived from the grid-iron pattern of the grouped sidings, an inclined plane being constructed at the yard to allow marshalling by gravity. The procedure used there was followed at nearly all other gravitational yards. An incoming local 'pick-up' goods train entered one of the reception sidings where its engine was detached, and each wagon was chalked with the number of the sorting siding for which it was intended. The wagons were then uncoupled singly or in groups. As each wagon had its brake released, it began moving down the inclined plane and, in accordance with hand-signals, shunters operated points at the entry to the sorting sidings, thereby

routeing the wagon appropriately. From the sorting sidings, the wagons gravitated into the gridiron marshalling sidings when required to make up a train. The wagon brakes were held down by 'wagon-chasers' to reduce speed, and there was a cable-operated restraint to deal with runaways. Wrongly shunted wagons were retrieved using horses.

Major yards of the late Victorian period included Toton, near *Nottingham, *Midland Railway, where shunting was almost entirely carried out using horses until the down yard was converted to hump working in 1901; Temple Mills, East London, *Great Eastern Railway (1880); and Colwick *up yard, also near Nottingham, *Great Northern Railway (1878).

During the early 1900s, pressure to reduce operating costs led to the construction of several major yards. The *Great Central Railway's Wath concentration yard was opened in 1907, and served 45 collieries in the South Yorkshire coalfield. It was the first power-operated gravitational yard in the country, extended a distance of 1½ miles, and comprised 36 miles of sidings, laid out for gravitational working in up and down yards. Each hump had a cabin which controlled all compressed-air operated facing points at its end of the yard.

In hump yards such as Wath, wagons of an incoming train were first uncoupled, singly or in groups, to form 'cuts', and then propelled over the hump by a powerful yard engine. The wagons accelerated, and descended gradients as steep as 1 in 40, to enter the sorting sidings. Major hump marshalling yards built at this time by the NER included Gascoigne Wood, near Selby (1907), and Erimus, on Teesside (1908).

Exchange of freight traffic between the northern lines and those south of the Thames was never easy. To improve its exchanges with the northern companies, in 1922 the *London & South Western Railway completed construction of an entirely new hump yard at Feltham, Middlesex. The yard points were electrically worked, and extensive use was made of *track-circuiting. As many as 3,390 wagons were dealt with in 24 hours, and an incoming train of 70 wagons could be sorted in 12 minutes.

March, in Cambridgeshire, was the meeting-point of routes linking the eastern counties, and the east side of London, with the coalfields of the east Midlands and Yorkshire. By the late 1920s the existing yards had become overloaded, and in 1928 the *London & North Eastern Railway completed the new up Whitemoor yard, immediately north of March. The new down yard was opened in 1933. Whitemoor was partly modelled on the yards at Hamm, Germany; German and American practice was ahead of Britain by the early 1920s.

The combined Whitemoor yards contained 68 miles of track, and handled 7,000 wagons daily. The up yard dealt with loaded traffic and was Britain's first mechanized yard: i.e., the points controlling access into the sorting sidings were remote-controlled, and sets of power-operated retarders decelerated wagons descending from the hump. At Whitemoor, the operator in the up yard control tower preset the points according to the destinations of the 'cuts' of wagons, and manually controlled the action of the Frölich hydraulically operated retarders.

During the early 1930s the *Great Western Railway used finance available under the Loans & Guarantees Act, 1929, to construct a gravitational yard at Banbury, and to enlarge its existing yards at Severn Tunnel Junction, and Rogerstone, near Newport (Mon).

In 1935 the LNER commissioned the fully mechanized New Inward Yard at Hessle, near Hull; this also featured hydraulic retarders. The last major pre-war marshalling yard scheme was that at the *London Midland & Scottish Railway's Toton down yard which was mechanized in 1939. As at Hessle, colour-light signals were used to indicate to the driver of the (diesel) hump shunting engine the speed required for humping a particular 'cut' of wagons, the control tower operator at Toton having received information by teleprinter from the shunters making the 'cuts'.

Some 10 per cent of investment in *BR's *Modernization Plan was devoted to building large, mechanized marshalling yards in place of numerous small ones of pre-Grouping origin. The list included Thornton, Fife (1956); Ripple Lane, Barking (1959); Temple Mills (1959—rebuilding of existing yard); Margam, near Port Talbot (1960); Perth (1962); Millerhill, Edinburgh (1963); Kingmoor, Carlisle (1963); Healey Mills, near Wakefield (1963); Tees-Newport, Teesside (1963); Tyne-Lamesley (1963); and Tinsley, near Sheffield (1965). Abandoned at the planning stage were completely new yards at Gloucester, Stourton (Leeds), and Shrewsbury.

BR had overestimated the need for investment in new yards as, by the early 1960s, the trend was towards trainload movements, and away from single wagonloads. Too many new yards resulted, often of excessive size and some proving disappointingly inefficient.

The Plan yards were fully or semi-automatic, the latter indicating that the control tower operator had some discretion in the operation of the secondary retarders; in fully mechanized yards, radar scanning and a weigh-rail combined to assess the 'rollability' and distance to travel of a 'cut', and activated the retarders automatically. Automatic operation caused damage to the wagons' contents, but a solution was found in automatic wagon control, by which a series of hydraulic retarders or booster-retarders laid inside each running rail accelerated or decelerated wagons during their progress from hump to sorting sidings. This equipment was provided at Tinsley and the rebuilt Bescot yard, near Wolverhampton (1966), and also in the last major marshalling yard scheme, Scunthorpe (1972).

Lord *Beeching believed that only a radical restructuring of the system of wagonload traffic would reduce losses, and produced the National Freight Train Plan of 1967 which involved the re-routeing of trains, and their concentration on the main yards. Longer transit times lost traffic, with the result that there was a spiral of cut-backs and reduced freight movements, accentuated by a rapid decline in demand for household coal. By 1982 there were only 59 marshalling yards in use, and the super-yards of the 1960s were working at well below capacity. Under BR's 1983–8 Corporate Plan, it was decided to phase out the non-airbraked wagonload traffic completely. Effected by May 1984, this spelt the end for all marshalling yards, and of hump shunting.

See also STATIONS, GOODS; GOODS SHEDS AND WAREHOUSES; CONTAINERS; FREIGHTLINER.   MLH

R. T. Munns, *Milk Churns to Merry-Go-Round* (1986); J. Johnson and R. A. Long, *British Railways Engineering 1948–80* (1981); M. Rhodes, *The Illustrated History of British Marshalling Yards* (1988); Dow, iii; C. F. Klapper, *Sir Herbert Walker's Southern Railway* (1973).

Marylebone station, see LONDON STATIONS.

Maryport & Carlisle Railway: formed in 1837 to continue the *Newcastle & Carlisle Railway westwards and to develop the northern part of the west Cumberland coalfield. Laid down by George *Stephenson, it was 28 miles long and opened in 1840–5. Having passed briefly under George *Hudson's control in 1848, after complicated disputes its tangled finances were sorted out by 1850, and it then settled down to a well-maintained prosperity. The average ordinary dividend it paid each year in 1850–1922 was 6.6 per cent; at its height, in 1870–82, it was 11.1 per cent.

The company kept its territory to itself. The Solway Junction Railway, coming from Annan, threatened to convey much of the Cumberland iron ore to Scotland, but the creation of new works to smelt the ore for steel-making on the spot soon destroyed its main business. The *North British Railway's port of Silloth, nearby, handled chiefly passengers and grain.

The MCR built two branches. The 'Bolton Loop' through Mealsgate (1866–77) proved disappointing, but the 'Derwent branch' to Brigham (1867) afforded useful access to Cockermouth. The company's system now extended to 43 miles.

It was carefully run. No serious accident ever occurred on it. As early as 1859 ten of its locomotives were burning *coal instead of coke. Possibly the first of all-steel locomotive boilers was made for one of its engines in 1862.

The MCR became a subsidiary of the *London Midland & Scottish Railway in 1923.   JS

J. Simmons, *Maryport & Carlisle Railway* (1947); *Reg. Hist.*, xiv, ch. 6; N. Mason, *Unprofitable Railways* (1986).

Maunsell, Richard Edward Lloyd (1868–1944), mechanical engineer. Following pupilage at the Great Southern & Western Railway of Ireland's Inchicore works under H. A. *Ivatt, in 1891 Maunsell joined the *Lancashire & Yorkshire Railway, gaining experience in workshops, drawing office, and running sheds. In 1894 he became assistant locomotive superintendent, East Indian Railway, returning to Inchicore as works manager in 1896. He was appointed CME, *South Eastern & Chatham Railway, 1913, where he built up an outstanding design team with Pearson and *Holcroft from *Swindon, and Clayton from *Derby, who developed modern 2-6-0 and 2-6-4 tank locomotives and radically improved existing 4-4-0 passenger engines. The team, with Lionel Lynes for carriage design, continued during Maunsell's tenure as CME, *Southern Railway, 1923–37. The ex-*London

& South Western Urie 4-6-0s were greatly improved to form standard types, the 'Schools' class three-cylinder 4-4-0s were outstandingly successful, and heavy four-cylinder 4-6-0 and some 0-6-0 freight engines were built. Modern and comfortable main-line steam and electric *multiple-unit stock was built. The capital demands of *electrification restricted steam locomotive modernization, and the civil engineer rejected Maunsell's proposed four-cylinder 4-6-2 and three-cylinder 2-6-2 types. Ashford and Eastleigh works were remodelled and line production methods introduced.

GWC

C. S. Cocks, 'History of Southern Railway Locomotives to 1938', *Jnl. Inst. Locomotive Engineers*, 38, No. 206; H. Holcroft, *Locomotive Adventure*, i and ii (1962–5).

Mawddwy Railway, see CAMBRIAN RAILWAYS; LIGHT RAILWAYS.

meat traffic. An early benefit of the railways was to open up new sources of fresh meat for the growing cities. By 1850, when the railway reached *Aberdeen, supplies came to *London from as far away as north-east Scotland. However, the trade tended to be concentrated in the cooler months—one reason why a parallel trade in *livestock for slaughter existed for many years.

When the new London Central Market for meat and poultry was opened at Smithfield in 1868, a goods *station was provided in its basement by the *Great Western Railway alongside the *Metropolitan Railway's 'Widened Lines' and linked to market floor level by *hydraulic *lifts. However, the other companies continued to deliver by road from their own goods terminals direct to the butchers' stands.

There was little import of dead meat until the development of mechanical refrigeration in the 1870s allowed chilled and frozen meat to be shipped from Canada, the USA, Argentina, Australia, and New Zealand. By the late 1880s it was a major trade, entering mainly through the Mersey and London (Victoria, Royal Albert, West India, and Tilbury docks) although *Cardiff, *Manchester, *Glasgow, Avonmouth, *Southampton, *Hull, and *Newcastle were also used. Much of it was then forwarded by train to provincial centres, where cold stores were established. The first cold store in Britain was opened in 1877 in the undercroft of *Cannon Street station; however, in this case the meat came in by river barge and went out by road van.

At the same time, a substantial trade developed in live cattle from Argentina, the USA, and Canada. The disease control regulations required animals from the first two to be slaughtered at the port of entry after 1878, and similarly for Canadian cattle from 1893. Most of this traffic came in through specially built lairage and abattoir facilities at Birkenhead docks (see LIVERPOOL), served by the Great Western and *London & North Western Railways, and at the Foreign Cattle Market, Deptford, opened in 1871 when similar restrictions were first imposed on livestock from continental countries, and later connected to the *London Brighton & South Coast Railway. However, this trade steadily declined in favour of the frozen meat trade and finished entirely by 1914.

Together, these colonial and American meat trades generated considerable volumes of rail traffic. In 1903–4, for example, the annual tonnage of Scotch beef taken from Aberdeen to London was 6,750 tons, but the GWR and LNWR carried ten times this weight of imported meat from Birkenhead and Liverpool to London.

At first fresh meat was packed into hampers, which could be hired from the railway companies; later, carcasses were sewn into canvas. Although both types of packaging were being loaded into open wagons and covered by a tarpaulin sheet as late as the 1880s, refrigerator vans had been introduced for the imported chilled and frozen meat traffic from 1879; these were heavily insulated and cooled by end-tanks containing ice, or ice and salt. Ventilated vans (see PERISHABLE TRAFFIC) were introduced for fresh meat from 1881; later designs were also insulated and had rails of hooks in the roof from which the carcasses were hung. For the relatively short distance from Southampton docks, the *London & South Western Railway ran trains of flat trucks, each carrying two horse-drawn road vans, to its Nine Elms goods depot for direct delivery of imported frozen meat to the London market traders.

In 1920 the railways' meat carryings amounted to some 600,000 tons, but they were soon being eroded by lorry competition; by 1930, 40 per cent had been lost to *road. Meat *containers, in both ventilated and insulated variants, were introduced from 1928 to match the road hauliers' 'door-to-door' capability; by this time the method of refrigeration was packs of 'dry ice' (solid carbon dioxide), dispersed among the carcasses. Thereafter containers progressively replaced vans in this traffic and in 1966 the Scottish meat business was transferred to the new Aberdeen–*King's Cross *Freightliner service. However, rail could not match the temperature-control standards offered by road transport and the traffic was finally lost in the 1970s.

On a much smaller scale were the seasonal flows of game from Scotland and, from about 1900, rabbit carcasses from Devon and Cornwall. The latter were suspended from horizontal poles in open wicker hampers and despatched by passenger train. During the food rationing of World War II, this traffic grew to such proportions—up to 15,000 per night from the Barnstaple branch alone—that it required a special evening train to Taunton, for overnight connections to London, *Birmingham, and beyond.

GAB

J. T. Critchell and J. Raymond, *A History of the Frozen Meat Trade* (1912); R. Perren, *The Meat Trade in Britain 1840–1914* (1978); E. A. Pratt, 'The Carriage of Dead Meat', in *Railways and Their Rates* (1905), 134–53; G. R. Hawke, *Railways and Economic Growth in England and Wales 1840–1870* (1970), 131–56; R. J. Essery, D. P. Rowland, and W. O. Steel, 'Vans for Perishable Traffic', in *British Goods Wagons from 1887 to the Present Day* (1970), 86–91.

mechanical engineering developed as a distinct branch of the profession during the emergence of railways largely, though not exclusively, to meet the needs of this new technology. 'Engineer' originally meant a military engineer, who had received a fairly broad formal training, as opposed to the millwright, smith, clockmaker, etc., with his practical training as an apprentice. The Industrial Revolution created a civil market for the engineer's skills and the new profession of *'civil engineer' who, like his military counterpart, would usually take total charge of a large project such as a *canal or railway. *Surveying and building a railway was not greatly different from surveying and building a canal, but whereas a canal could be operated and maintained using existing skills a railway required ongoing maintenance and the development of new and, to many, rather complex pieces of mechanism such as locomotives (see TRACTION) and rolling stock.

To meet this need a new breed of engineer appeared who dealt principally in mechanisms, in ways of making things and in small but complex structures, which were outside the province of the traditional civil engineer. At first known rather deprecatingly as 'mechanics' they soon became indispensable to the railways, indeed to industry in general, and became known as 'mechanical engineers'. For a long time mechanical engineers designed, built, and maintained locomotives, machine tools, the mechanical parts of *carriages and *wagons, points (see TRACK), and *signals. On some lines they also became involved in steamships and, later on, in motor vehicles. The growing status of the profession was mirrored in successive titles given to the chief of the locomotive department: locomotive foreman, locomotive superintendent, and finally chief mechanical engineer.

Several established crafts came under the umbrella of mechanical engineering, such as iron-founding, pattern-making, even carpentry, but remained separate professions: the mechanical engineer had to understand what they could and could not do in order effectively to design the machines they would help to make.

What might be termed a mechanical engineering apprenticeship, though rarely so described on the railways, involved moving round the various departments of a railway *works learning how to make, build, or repair things. According to aptitude, apprentices often ended their training in a department where they might expect permanent employment, though in theory—and usually in practice—no apprentice was ever guaranteed a job at the end of his training. For those lucky enough to have made the right impression a vacancy would always occur at the right moment, but even if it did not a railway apprenticeship was valued in many other industries and many eminent engineers totally unconnected with railways started out that way.

As the scope of engineering grew ever wider, further categories were defined to cater for those who worked in newer technologies such as electrical engineering, and thus the field of mechanical engineering has become more and more specialized, though it has never lost its early association with mechanisms.

The pace of change has accelerated since the 1960s, particularly with the advent of *computers. It would now be possible for an engineer to design a locomotive, manufacture it, test and maintain it using 'virtual reality', then pass instructions—electronically—to the machines and men who are to build the real thing in the knowledge that his design works correctly. At no time need he see or handle any actual metal. Not everyone is enthusiastic about such developments, seeing in them the seeds of stagnating innovation.

See also INSTITUTION OF MECHANICAL ENGINEERS. RW
L. T. C. Rolt, *The Mechanicals, Portrait of a Profession* (1967).

medical services, see HEALTH.

Melton Constable, see WORKS; MIDLAND & GREAT NORTHERN JOINT RAILWAY.

memorials. The term is here taken to mean objects (not institutions) designed to commemorate persons or events in railway history.

Personal memorials in the form of stones or tablets in churches or graveyards range from the simple one for George *Stephenson, 'G. S. 1848', on the floor of Holy Trinity, Chesterfield, to the brass by G. G. Scott to Robert *Stephenson in Westminster Abbey, 1859. There are statues of George Stephenson at the *National Railway Museum, York (from *Euston); *Liverpool, and *Newcastle; I. K. *Brunel at Embankment Gardens, London, and *Paddington; medallion plaques to H. A. *Walker at *Waterloo; and to Albert Stanley, Lord *Ashfield, at *London Transport headquarters, 55 Broadway, Westminster. There is a tablet at Soham, Cambridgeshire, to two *London & North Eastern Railway enginemen killed by the explosion of an ammunition wagon in 1943, who stayed on their engine to draw the train away from the town. C. J. Bowen *Cooke is recorded on his grave at St-Just-in-Roseland, Cornwall, as CME, *London & North Western Railway; but Mark *Huish, general manager of the same railway, is buried at Bonchurch, Isle of Wight, under an inscription stating only: 'Former Captain, 74th Bengal Native Infantry'.

Memorials to individual promoters of railways can be found at Rannoch, West Highland Railway (see NORTH BRITISH RAILWAY), to J. H. Renton, in relief carved on rock; and at Rosebush, Dyfed, to E. Cropper, Maenclochog Railway.

Personal memorials arising from railway *accidents are found in many churches and at outdoor sites. A lineside memorial to William Huskisson, MP, killed at the opening of the *Liverpool & Manchester Railway on 15 September 1830, was erected by the company at Parkside, Lancashire. Railway accidents are mentioned as the cause of death at many places: examples are Harrow, Middlesex (Thomas Port, LNWR, 1838); Bromsgrove, Worcestershire, commemorating a locomotive boiler explosion in 1840, but depicting an engine of another type; Ely Cathedral cloister, with verses 'The Spiritual Railway', 1845; Chacewater, Cornwall, to the Revd H. W. Phillips, killed at Shrivenham, *Great Western Railway, in 1848; and St Ninian's cathedral, Perth, to A. I. and A. M. Campbell Kinloch, killed at Cudworth, *Midland Railway, 1905.

Collective memorials commemorate the victims of accidents during construction or operation. The most singular monument to loss of life during construction is in the churchyard at Otley, West Yorkshire—a scaled-down replica of the north portal of Bramhope tunnel, Leeds & Thirsk

Railway (see LEEDS NORTHERN RAILWAY), to the 23 men lost in building it in 1849. Others are: a tablet and headstone at Chapel-le-Dale church, North Yorkshire, to those who lost their lives in building the *Settle and Carlisle line in 1869–76; a lineside slab inscribed '+ August 20th, 1868', at Llandulas, North Wales, at the site of the accident to the LNWR Irish Mail, and a monument in Abergele churchyard; and a monument in Salisbury cathedral to those killed in the Salisbury accident, *London & South Western Railway, in 1906. Few major accidents have been commemorated in this way, not even Quintinshill, on the *Caledonian Railway, in 1915, the worst of all. There is a mean metal plaque at *King's Cross underground station to the victims of the fire there in 1987; a memorial garden plot beside the cutting at Spencer Park, near Clapham Junction, is a memorial to those killed there in 1988.

War memorials were erected to railway staff. The MR placed a tablet at *Derby and the LNWR one in Queen's Park, *Crewe, for staff lost in the war in South Africa, 1899–1902. The large losses of railwaymen in World War I led to memorials being erected by practically every company, mostly at their headquarters and main workshops. The most prominent outdoor ones are at Euston Square, LNWR, and Waterloo, LSWR (the Victory Arch of the new station, 1921). The GWR memorial at Paddington has a fine statue by C. S. Jagger. Memorials to local staff were put up at Attenborough, MR, and Mexborough, *Great Central Railway. At several of these the dead of World War II have been economically recorded on additional panels. Three locomotives were designated as 1914–18 war memorials: LNWR 'Claughton' class 4-6-0 *Patriot*; GCR 4-6-0 *Valour*; *London Brighton & South Coast Railway 4-6-4T *Remembrance*.   RMR

merry-go-round (MGR) is the name that was coined for the method of train operation developed in the early 1960s for supplying *coal to the new generation of large electric power stations then being planned. The aim was to maximize the benefits of rail operation by treating the train, rather than the *wagon, as the transport unit. The concept comprised: a permanently coupled train of fully air-braked hopper wagons; rapid loading while passing at ½ mph under a large storage hopper at the colliery, each wagon being automatically weighed before and after; and automatic discharge and weighing while passing over the power station's receiving hopper, located on a circular loop to avoid uncoupling the locomotive. The new wagons had a capacity of 32 tons, 30 per cent more than their predecessors. The result was a massive reduction in the requirement for locomotives, wagons, train crews, ground staff, and land for sidings, making rail transport competitive even over short distances.

Following the first MGR scheme, serving West Burton power station, Nottinghamshire, in 1965, operation of MGR coal trains was extended to several *cement and steel works as well as to power stations. The principle was also applied to other mineral traffics, including imported *iron ore.
                                                          GAB

G. F. Allen, 'Coal by Merry-go-Round', in *British Railfreight Today and Tomorrow* (1984), 29–37; R. T. Munns, 'Merry-go-Round', in *Milk Churns to Merry-Go-Round: A Century of Train Operation* (1986), 148–71.

Mersey Docks & Harbour Board, see LIVERPOOL AND BIRKENHEAD.

Mersey Railway: notable as the first British railway fully converted from steam to electric operation; for steep gradients (1 in 27 under the river); for Chicago-style clerestory coaches with stable-like half doors; and for diverse architecture. Hydraulic lift towers 120 ft high at James Street and Hamilton Square stations contrasted with a modest, two-storey head office.

The Mersey Pneumatic Railway of 1866 became the Mersey Railway two years later, suggesting a change in motive power plans: steam when the first 2¼ miles, dropping to nearly 130 ft below Ordnance Datum, opened between James Street, close to the docks and *Liverpool's commercial heart, and Green Lane, Birkenhead, in 1886.

Extension from Hamilton Square to a surface station at Birkenhead Park, *joint with the *Wirral Railway, followed in 1888; Green Lane–Rock Ferry, junction with the Birkenhead Joint Railway, in 1891; finally, James Street–Liverpool Central (Low Level), in 1892; total mileage 4½.

Steam operation using powerful condensing tank locomotives was disastrous, filling coaches, stations, and tunnels with smoke and soot. The company was bankrupt from 1887 to 1900, but rescued by third-rail *electrification at 650 V dc in 1903, immediately successful against competition from Birkenhead Corporation ferries which claimed to sail 'the health route'. By the 1930s passengers were some 17 million a year.

It survived *Grouping but in 1938 was integrated with the newly electrified Wirral section of the *London Midland & Scottish Railway, later *nationalized and today forming the heart of Merseyrail.   RC

J. W. Gahan, *The Line Beneath the Liners* (1983); G. W. Parkin, *The Mersey Railway* (1965).

Metro-land. Alone among the railways, the *Metropolitan overcame statutory sanctions on developing *land. Over a period in the 19th century, it secured parliamentary powers to purchase and hold land for non-railway purposes, initiating residential development at Willesden Green in 1880. More followed at Pinner (1900) and Wembley Park (1906). This policy was accelerated by the formation in 1919 of a subsidiary, Metropolitan Railway Country Estates Ltd, over which the parent had virtually total control. In 1915 the railway produced its well-known *Metro-land* slogan, which it used successfully in promoting some ten Estate Company estates alongside the line in 1920–33. Controlling the nature of these developments, which also set a standard for others to emulate, the Metropolitan was able to generate much remunerative suburban traffic; by the mid-1920s, it was earning more than twice per third-class seat than were the three largest main line companies, whilst the Estate Company's dividends reached 8 per cent in 1930 and 1931.

See also SUBURBS.   AAJ

[Metropolitan Railway] *Metro-land* (annual editions 1915–32); A. A. Jackson, *Semi-Detached London: Suburban Development, Life and Transport 1900–39* (2nd edn., 1991), 174–82; and *London's Metropolitan Railway* (1986), 134–43, 203–5, 238–44, 249–50.

Metropolitan District Railway, see LONDON UNDERGROUND RAILWAYS.

Metropolitan Railway, see LONDON UNDERGROUND RAILWAYS.

Mewburn, Francis (*c*.1786–1867), solicitor. Involved in the *Stockton & Darlington Railway project from 1818 onwards as one of the company's solicitors, he played an important part in securing its first Act (1821). He wrote on the law of real property in 1830 and became chief bailiff of Darlington in 1846.

The main energies of his life were devoted to his railway company. Highly critical of the *North Eastern Railway after its formation in 1854, he worked against proposals to amalgamate the Stockton & Darlington with it. The merger took place, nevertheless, in 1863.

Extracts from his diary were published as *The Larchfield Diary* by his son in 1876, but they were unskilfully made and inaccurate. Much of the original manuscript survives, divided between the Durham County Record Office and the Chesterfield Public Library. It deserves printing in full, in a better version.   JS

Boase; Tomlinson, 57–69.

Middlesbrough. This town owed its foundation to the *Stockton & Darlington Railway, opened in 1825, the purpose of which was to convey coal from Auckland to the River Tees at Stockton. But the depth of water proved insufficient for large vessels, and some of the SDR proprietors searched for a site for a better port lower down the river. They selected Middlesbrough, and the railway opened a line to it in 1830. Staiths allowed six ships to be loaded simultaneously, lying in deep water.

The land had been purchased by the group that had chosen it, who became known as the Middlesbrough Owners. A small town was laid out on a grid street-plan approved by them, centred on a market-place. In 1831 the population of Middlesbrough parish was 383; ten years later 5,709.

The place was then starting to grow into an industrial centre. In 1840 John Vaughan bought land from the Owners to erect an ironworks, in partnership with the German F. W. Bolckow; its development was much assisted by Vaughan's discovery of workable ironstone in the nearby Eston Hills in 1851. Presently steel-making came to be established at Middlesbrough too. In 1879 the first successful use of the Bessemer basic process was made there by Bolckow Vaughan.

A second town grew up, adjoining the first but far larger, accommodating the people engaged in this business. Middlesbrough was incorporated as a borough in 1853. Its population grew from 8,000 in 1861 to 56,000 in 1881 and 109,000 in 1911; in 1994 it was 146,000.

Railways continued to play an active part in this extraordinary development. The SDR supported the construction of the South Durham & Lancashire Union Railway (opened in 1856), which brought high grade ironstone from Furness across the Pennines, to enrich the local product. The SDR had purchased the dock from the Owners in 1849; its successor, the *North Eastern, undertook a big enlargement, completed in 1874. And in 1877 a new station arose, flamboyantly Gothic: 'an architectural tribute to the greatness of Middlesbrough'.   JS

W. Lillie, *History of Middlesbrough* (1972); N. Moorsom, *The Stockton & Darlington Railway: The Foundation of Middlesbrough* (1975); Tomlinson (the final quotation here is from p. 682); *RTC*, 145–7.

Middleton Railway. The first railway Act of Parliament was obtained by Charles Brandling in 1758 for a 4 ft 1 in *gauge horse *tramroad from his collieries at Middleton into *Leeds. It did not actually authorize construction, but ratified agreements he had made with landowners. In 1812 two rack-and-pinion locomotives, designed by John Blenkinsop and built by Matthew *Murray, started work: the first railway engines in the world to be operated commercially. In 1835 worn-out locomotives and a sharp reduction in fodder prices caused a reversion to horse-traction until 1862, when steam working was resumed by new owners, using conventional adhesion. In 1881 the line was converted to standard gauge.

By 1890 the pits had closed and the line, now connected to the *Midland Railway, was used by adjacent factories. In 1958 all but a short section had closed. In 1960 the volunteer Middleton Railway Trust was formed to restore and operate the historic line, and the first section was reopened to carry commercial traffic from local firms. It was the first standard-gauge *preservation society to begin operation, and in 1969 the line again reached Middleton.   GJB

Middleton Railway Trust, *A History of the Middleton Railway*, Leeds (1994 edn.); *Reg. Hist.*, viii.

Midland & Great Northern Joint Railway. This system, at 183 miles the longest of the *joint railways, comprised three units. The first consisted of four little *contractors' lines crossing the district between *Peterborough, Bourne, Spalding, and King's Lynn, opened in 1858–66 and promoted by Waring Bros. They were worked by the *Great Northern and *Midland companies, both wanting to extend into north Norfolk—then little provided with railways. The second was an independent line from Yarmouth to North Walsham, opened in 1879–81. With this a third railway, the Lynn & Fakenham, was merged in 1882 to form the Eastern & Midlands company. Its completion (1883) created the spine of a new trunk route across Norfolk, with a branch to *Norwich.

The *Great Eastern Railway now had lines reaching the coast at Wells and Cromer. Though the EMR opened a branch to Cromer also (1887), it passed into receivership (1890). The MR and GNR agreed to purchase it, and all the three units were now combined as the Midland & Great Northern Joint Railway (1893). Next year this company opened a line westwards from Bourne, meeting one at Saxby built by the MR and affording through communication with *Leicester, *Birmingham, and *Nottingham.

Though some doubling was undertaken after 1893, 77 per cent of the system remained a single line. An efficient new tablet-exchange apparatus (see SINGLE LINES, WORKING OF), introduced in 1906, much improved their working.

The MGNJR carried three specially remunerative kinds of traffic: cattle (see LIVESTOCK TRAFFIC); *fish from Yarmouth and Lowestoft, requiring five trains daily in the summer; and *holiday-makers to Cromer and Yarmouth, with through trains from the north and Midlands. The GNR ran through services between London and Cromer, though this route was 174 miles long, against the GER's 139.

The popularity of north-eastern Norfolk for holidays grew steadily, and the MGNJR and GER fought for it. In 1896, however, they wisely agreed to promote the Norfolk & Suffolk Joint Railway. Only two parts of it were built, from Cromer to North Walsham (opened in 1898) and from Yarmouth to Lowestoft (1903), giving the MGNJR its own access to Lowestoft, which it had long desired.

In 1923 the MGNJR passed to the *London Midland & Scottish and *London & North Eastern Railways, though in 1936 the LNER undertook the entire local administration. The railway's holiday traffic was gradually reduced by motor competition, and the fish moved away in large numbers from Yarmouth and Lowestoft. By 1958 the line was hopelessly unremunerative, and the *nationalized railways closed the whole of it in 1959.

The company's locomotive *works were at Melton Constable, the central junction on the system, under the energetic William Marriott, engineer and locomotive superintendent 1884–1924 (see also CONCRETE).   JS
A. J. Wrottesley, *Midland & Great Northern Joint Railway* (1970); *LTW*, i, 135–43.

Midland & South Western Junction Railway: a line linking Cheltenham with *Southampton, to carry traffic brought by the *Midland Railway from *Manchester and *Birmingham, narrowly missing incorporation in 1845. In 1873 the Swindon Marlborough & Andover Railway was authorized, offering a route between *Swindon and Southampton, aided by *running powers over two existing lines. Opened in 1881, it was extended northwards by the Swindon & Cheltenham Extension Railway to Andoversford in 1891, reaching Cheltenham over the *Great Western Railway. The two lines were merged as the Midland & South Western Junction Railway in 1884.

Its 62 miles of line were costly to build and work. In 1879–84 the SMAR was financially assisted by contractors (see CONTRACTORS' LINES); but in 1884–97 the MSWJR was in receivership.

In 1892, however, it secured Sam *Fay from the *London & South Western Railway as receiver and general manager. He believed in its prospects and set about upgrading the system piecemeal. A new line was undertaken enabling the MSWJR to bypass the eternally hostile GWR near Savernake. By 1897 the company was solvent. When in 1899 Fay

returned to the LSWR he was said to have 'made an empty sack stand upright'.

The line had two short branches. One joined the GWR at Swindon. The other, to Tidworth, was constructed by the War Office to serve a military base and was leased to the company in 1903. Tidworth earned more passenger revenue than any other MSWJR station.

Long-distance traffic was developed, with *through carriages from *Sheffield and Birmingham to Southampton in 1893; later from *Bradford, *Leeds, and *Liverpool; from Manchester in 1911; and even from Whitehaven to Southampton, taking emigrants from the depressed west Cumberland ironfield.

At the *Grouping the MSWJR was absorbed by the GWR. The last regular services ran in 1961.   JS
T. B. Sands, *Midland & South Western Junction Railway* (1959); C. G. Maggs, *Midland & South Western Junction Railway* (1967), quotation on p. 66.

Midland Counties Railway. This originated as a scheme, launched in 1832, to build a line from Pinxton to *Leicester, backed by Derbyshire and Nottinghamshire coalowners. Presently they decided to carry it on to join the *London & Birmingham, calling it the Midland Counties Railway. It was incorporated in 1836 to run from *Derby and Leicester to Rugby, fed by a branch from *Nottingham.

Its engineer was C. B. *Vignoles. The only big works on the line were a bridge over the Trent and one over the Warwickshire Avon at Rugby. It was opened in 1839–40. At the same time the *North Midland Railway was opened from Derby to *Leeds, so that the Midland Counties became the central section of a great trunk line (owned by three companies) from London to Yorkshire.

Another 'central section' was, however, available: the *Birmingham & Derby Junction, running from the London & Birmingham line to Derby through Tamworth. Though this route was 11 miles longer from London than the MCR's, the two companies fought for through traffic with a ferocity that soon threatened to ruin them both, until they agreed to join together with the NMR to form the amalgamated *Midland Railway in 1844.

Throughout its independent life T. E. Dicey was the company's chairman, a Leicestershire banker and landowner. He acted rather like the chairman of a *turnpike trust: without technological knowledge (though he knew a good deal about money), yet interesting himself carefully in the railway's performance. When he had to defend the board's policies at shareholders' meetings he did so manfully, but he could not match George *Hudson and his associates, who opposed him, either in guile or in force. Though he did not go on to the board of the Midland Railway, he was a useful director of the *North Staffordshire in 1846–58.   JS
P. S. Stevenson (ed.), *Midland Counties Railway* (1989); K. H. Vignoles, *Charles Blacker Vignoles* (1982), ch. 6. Vignoles's day-to-day work for the MCR is recorded in his Diary from September 1835 onwards: BL, Add. MS 34528, from fo. 154.

Midland Railway, a combination, authorized in 1844, of the *North Midland, *Midland Counties, and *Birmingham

& Derby Junction Railways, whose lines converged on *Derby. This was the earliest large-scale *amalgamation sanctioned by Parliament.

The Midland differed from most later amalgamations, however, in that from its birth it served the competitive principle. The Birmingham & Derby and the Midland Counties had been fierce and futile competitors with each other, which amalgamation was designed to end. But the MR's first chairman, George *Hudson, shared those instincts in his own rather different way.

The MR formed the central component of a trunk line from *London to *York, with traffic fed to it from the *London & Birmingham Railway at Rugby and taken on from Normanton by Hudson's *York & North Midland. Despite this alliance's claim that it could handle adequately all traffic from London to north-east England, long-standing schemes for a more direct railway from London to York had surfaced again by the time of the MR amalgamation. A battle was fought for two years. The MR lost when the new railway, the *Great Northern, was authorized in 1846 and opened in 1850–2.

The MR thrust expansionist tentacles into territory that the GNR was to cross: long branches to Lincoln (1846) and *Peterborough (1848), and in other directions also. In 1846 it leased the Leeds & Bradford Railway, already empowered to extend to Skipton, whence the 'Little' North Western Railway (so nicknamed to distinguish it from the *London & North Western) was to continue it to Lancaster and Morecambe; and it lunged south-westwards by purchasing the *Birmingham & Gloucester and *Bristol & Gloucester companies, which took it into the preserve of the *Great Western at *Bristol.

There, for the present, expansion stopped. The decline of Hudson's power was then beginning. In the general collapse of the stock market in 1847–8 his policies were questioned, and soon his integrity (see also SPECULATION). In 1849 he resigned the chairmanship of the company.

He was succeeded quietly by his vice-chairman, John *Ellis, who had not been a party to Hudson's deals for his own enrichment. Ellis had the qualities needed in this extremely difficult position, commanding general respect, and the company owed much to him for his calm and resolute leadership over the next nine years. Even at the worst (1849–51), it never passed a dividend. In 1852–9 it paid an average of 4 per cent annually; in the 1860s (including two years of special difficulty, 1866–7), well over 6 per cent.

Earlier plans for expansion to London and *Manchester were carried out in 1857–68. First came an extension from *Leicester to Bedford and Hitchin, whence the GNR afforded *running powers into London (*King's Cross). This arrangement proving unsatisfactory, the MR built its own line from Bedford to London, with a new and spectacular terminus at *St Pancras, opened in 1868. The company had then reached Manchester by a line through the Peak District, arriving in 1867 by running powers over the Manchester Sheffield & Lincolnshire Railway (see GREAT CENTRAL) from New Mills.

Simultaneously another long extension was in progress.

The MR wished to increase its traffic between England and Scotland. Since 1861 much of that had been taken over the 'Little' North Western Railway on to the *Lancaster & Carlisle, but this worked badly, and the MR secured powers in 1866 to build a line of its own from Settle to Carlisle.

The project received Royal Assent two months after the collapse of the stock market. The company tried to abandon the enterprise, but the *Lancashire & Yorkshire and *North British Railways, which had backed it to serve their own purposes, stopped it from doing so. The line took ten years to complete. The London extension (including the St Pancras *hotel) and the *Settle & Carlisle line, taken together, cost the MR well over £6 million.

The company was also acquiring control over numerous other railways. Two were notable. The *Somerset & Dorset passed under lease to the Midland and *London & South Western companies jointly in 1875, enabling the MR to run profitable through trains from the North and Midlands to *Bournemouth. And in 1876 the MR acquired a set of lines from Hereford (reached by running powers) to *Swansea, so admitting it into the South Wales coalfield.

Nevertheless it still remained true to its name. It was the only large English company that was managed from one centre. The head offices were to have moved from Derby to the London hotel building; but in the end they remained at Derby with the locomotive, rolling stock, and signalling works.

From 1853 to 1880, with one short intermission, the company's general manager was James *Allport. He backed competitive policies strongly. In 1872 the MR suddenly announced that it would carry third-class passengers in all its trains. Three years later it discontinued second class, reducing first-class fares and raising the comfort of third-class accommodation to the former second-class standard. This angered the MR's competitors, which had, however, to take account of it in their own services—though second class did not disappear from the LNWR until 1912 (see CLASS DISTINCTIONS). The abolition of second class arose from the uninterrupted growth of third-class travel. It also simplified operating practices, by requiring only two classes of accommodation, each with *smoking and non-smoking sections, in each train.

Further, in 1874, after a visit to America, Allport persuaded his board to inaugurate in Britain the running of *Pullman cars, at a supplementary fare.

Although these policies' commercial results have never been fully analysed, they contributed beyond doubt towards increasing the MR's popularity, its passengers riding in newly built vehicles (designed under T. G. Clayton) that were more comfortable for both classes than those on other railways (see CARRIAGES).

Among Allport's successors as general manager was Guy *Granet (1905–18), who initiated or helped to secure important reforms (some of them very much needed) in the company's internal administration.

On the *civil engineering side, the MR was well served by a succession of outstandingly able officers. W. H. *Barlow had been resident engineer on the Midland Counties

Railway and was the Midland's engineer from 1844 to 1857, when he set up in private practice in London. But he remained its consultant thereafter, and himself designed the roof of St Pancras station. He was succeeded as the company's chief engineer by J. S. *Crossley, who stayed in office until 1875, when his largest and most testing work, the Settle & Carlisle line, was almost completed.

The first two of the MR's locomotive superintendents served it between them for almost 60 years: Matthew *Kirtley (1844–73) and S. W. *Johnson (1873–1903). The engines produced under them were straightforward in design, and very long-lived. By no means all were built in the company's own works at Derby; it turned freely to commercial manufacturers when that seemed advantageous.

The MR was a major *freight carrier; even more after its extension to London, which gave it a full share in the railborne coal trade of the metropolis and much-improved access to the docks. The company embarked in 1874 on the purchase of *private owners' wagons running on its system, not with complete success but pointing towards a change that many managers desired.

The MR's interests extended throughout the British Isles. In England it made two more additions to its system. In 1893 it entered into a partnership for the purchase of lines from Peterborough and Bourne (Lincolnshire) to Norwich and Yarmouth, to form the *Midland & Great Northern Joint Railway; and in 1912 it bought the prosperous *London Tilbury & Southend Railway, promising to undertake (but not carrying out) *electrification.

In Scotland the MR was linked closely to the NBR and *Glasgow & South Western Railways, which took its trains on to *Edinburgh and *Glasgow. It provided 30 per cent of the capital for building the *Forth Bridge, opened in 1890. It also held a quarter of the capital in the *Portpatrick & Wigtownshire Joint Railway, from Castle Douglas to Stranraer, connecting there with *shipping services to Larne in *Ireland, an interest strengthened by its outright purchase of the Belfast & Northern Counties Railway in 1903. By then it was building a new port at Heysham, for services to Belfast, opened in 1904; but this venture never fulfilled its ambitions.

So the MR continued competitive to the end. From 1899 it had itself a new competitor to face, the *Great Central, pushing its way from *Sheffield southwards; no real threat to passenger business, but a serious one to the MR's freight traffic.

The MR's operating policies differed from those of its old rivals the LNWR and GNR. Most of its routes were somewhat longer than theirs, steeper and more sharply curved; so its practice was to run a more frequent service, of lighter trains, hauled by smaller engines. The MR's very heavy freight traffic had to be kept clear of the faster passenger trains, requiring *multiplication of tracks: between London and Leeds, a much higher proportion of quadrupled line than the GNR ever provided on its route. Even this very expensive work did not achieve all that was expected. Though some MR passenger services appeared in the time-

tables to be a trifle faster than their rivals', they were notoriously unpunctual (see PUNCTUALITY). Competition had led the company to promise what it could not perform. From 1910 onwards punctuality was somewhat improved, however, by the introduction of a central *control office at Derby, with powers throughout the system.

On the other hand, Midland trains offered their own pleasures to the traveller. The scenic landscapes they traversed—from Derby to Manchester, for example, and from Leeds to Carlisle—were a positive inducement to travel by those routes. The trains continued notably comfortable, and the *restaurant cars bore a good reputation for food— as some other railways' did not. As for freight, no more impressive demonstration of the scale of the British coal trade could be had than in the continuous procession of long trains carrying it over the MR line between Wellingborough and London. JS

F. S. Williams, *Midland Railway* (1876 and later edns.); C. E. Stretton, *History of the Midland Railway* (1901); J. B. Radford, *Derby Works and Midland Locomotives* (1971); R. E. Lacy and G. Dow, *Midland Railway Carriages* (1984–6); J. Gough, *The Midland Railway: A Chronology* (1989).

Mid-Suffolk Light Railway, see LIGHT RAILWAYS.

mileage, route and track. Route mileage represents the total geographical distance covered by a railway or line. Published figures, however, must be treated with caution, as it is not always clear what they mean. Leased lines are usually included, but *jointly owned lines, and those over which a company has *running powers, may or may not be.

Track miles comprise the total mileage of individual track making up a given route or *system, including *sidings, lines in yards and depots, and all other locations where a company's rails are laid. GJB

mile and gradient posts. Lineside mile, half-mile, and quarter-mile posts indicate distances along the railway that correspond to the engineers' line plans. They derive from ancient road practice and were required on the *Surrey Iron Railway under its Act of 1801 to enable rates of carriage to be calculated. The Railways Clauses Act, 1845, compelled all railways to erect them, and today they are principally used to identify locations. Because distances were measured by the original owning company, they are now not necessarily continuous along a particular route. Northward from Parkside Junction, for instance, the *West Coast main line is measured only to *Preston, and then to Lancaster; at both places the distance starts again at 0. Some main lines have, however, been re-measured throughout.

Posts took many forms, from the *Stockton & Darlington Railway's incised stone blocks to cast iron in many distinctive designs and, more recently, reinforced concrete. The *Great Western's showed each quarter by a vertical line beneath the mileage figure, a method copied by *BR, which used a large dot.

Maintenance of gradient posts or boards is no longer kept up. They indicated changes in gradient on an arm each side of the post, varying in precision from company to company. Some meticulously recorded even the slightest change. At least one post between Dewsbury and Bradford on the *Great Northern Railway showed the gradient to three decimal places.   GJB

'Mileposts and Their Peculiarities', RM, 92 (1946), 217.

Miles Platting, see WORKS; LANCASHIRE & YORKSHIRE RAILWAY.

military railways: installations not open to public traffic within dockyards, bases, or depots of the armed forces, and lines solely used for military traffic.

At Woolwich Arsenal a *tramroad of 2 ft 6 in to 3-ft *gauge was in use from 1824; in 1873–80 some 25 miles of 18-in gauge line with 11 steam locomotives and 11 passenger carriages were installed. The Royal Engineers took over responsibility in 1891. There was a *siding from the *South Eastern Railway in 1870, and the Arsenal railway then constructed its own standard-gauge network, 120 miles long by 1918.

At Chatham dockyard a narrow-gauge tramway was built in the late 1860s for communication between workshops and fitting-out basins; in 1877 a 2-mile *London Chatham & Dover Railway siding was opened from Gillingham (New Brompton), and in the 1930s the narrow gauge disappeared. The Admiralty and the Royal Engineers built a standard-gauge line west of the Medway—the Chattenden Naval Tramway—and the 2 ft 6 in Chattenden & Upnor Railway. At Lydd, Kent, a standard-gauge military railway was opened in 1881 and extended in 1893 with second-hand materials from the Suakin-Berber railway in the Sudan. Before 1914 there were dockyard lines at *Portsmouth, Keyham (Devonport), Chatham, and Rosyth, and in naval ammunition depots.

The ordnance depot at Weedon, Northamptonshire, served by a branch (1806) from the Grand Junction Canal, had a siding from the *London & North Western Railway main line (1888), and an internal 2-ft gauge system was built.

Extensive internal rail systems were developed at numerous military installations such as Chilwell, Nottinghamshire; in the Gretna area, Dumfries-shire; Bicester, Oxfordshire (one of the longest—48 miles); and Catterick Camp, North Yorkshire. The Royal Air Force had a short line linking its depot at Cranwell, Lincolnshire, with the *London & North Eastern Railway at Sleaford; a branch into Manston airfield, Kent; and a narrow-gauge line at Calshot, Hampshire. At Spurn Point, Yorkshire, a 3½-mile standard-gauge line carried naval and lighthouse traffic, c.1915–51.

Fireless steam locomotives were developed from 1912, principally by Andrew Barclay of Kilmarnock, for use within service depots and munitions areas, with particular attention to low axle loads and restricted clearances. There were 114 built for this work and for electricity generating stations by 1962, when diesel locomotives took over the remaining duties.

The first railway built and operated in the field in direct support of operations by the British (or any other) army was at Balaclava in the Crimea, 1855–6; but the home railway companies contributed nothing to it—men and materials were provided by the *contractors *Peto, *Brassey, and Betts. For the Egyptian and Sudan campaigns, units of the Royal Engineers were specifically allocated to railway work: the 8th (Railway) Company, Royal Engineers, in 1882, and 10th (Railway) Company in 1885. They were given hasty training on the LCDR, *London & South Western, and SER. Training was done for a time at Woolwich Arsenal, and from 1905 on the Woolmer Instructional Military Railway, renamed in 1935 the Longmoor Military Railway, Hampshire.

Longmoor became No. 1 Railway Training Centre when No. 2 was opened at Derby in 1939, using the *London Midland & Scottish Railway Staff College and the Melbourne Military Railway—the former *Midland Railway branch from Weston-on-Trent to Ashby-de-la-Zouch, Leicestershire. Part of the Shropshire & Montgomeryshire Railway (see LIGHT RAILWAYS) was also used for training. Royal Engineers operated extensive systems built to serve the ports at Faslane on Gareloch, and Cairnryan, in Scotland. Longmoor was shut down in 1969; some of its memorabilia are preserved at the Museum of Army Transport, Beverley, Humberside.

Volunteer corps raised in 1859 in the face of a French invasion threat included railwaymen. The first specifically railway unit was the Cheshire Railway Volunteers, based on the LNWR at *Crewe. The first Manual of Military Railways was produced in 1889. Reductions after the South African campaign meant that there were just three Royal Engineers Railway Companies by 1913. World War I saw the development of specialist units, including Railway Construction Troops, the Military Camp Railways, and the Railway Operating Division RE (formation of which began in April 1915 to provide for the working of overseas railways). Post-war retrenchment saw the strength of the Railway Companies reduced to some 200, but from 1924 new Supplementary Reserve (Railway Units) were formed, based on the *Big Four companies. Again, World War II saw substantial increase in the numbers of personnel in the Railway Companies. Military railways in Britain came under the control of Staff Branch TN3, and then No. 1 Railway Operating & Maintenance Group RE. Renamed 1 Railway Group in 1945, it remained in the Royal Engineers until becoming part of the Royal Corps of Transport in 1965. Trade training was based on the Longmoor Military Railway until it closed in 1969; then on 79 Squadron in Germany. The organization passed to Railway Wing, Army Freight Organisation, in 1971; Army Department Railway Staff in 1977; Army Railway Organisation in 1985; and Railway Staff Office in 1993, under which many of the military railways are effectively part of the units in which they operate. The RCT itself has been absorbed into the Royal Logistical Corps.

See also WAR.   RMR and MC

W. Porter, *History of the Corps of Royal Engineers* (2 vols., 1889);

E. A. Pratt, *The Rise of Rail-Power in War and Conquest 1833–1914* (1916); H. M. Sinclair, 'History of the Railways & Road Training Centre, RE, Longmoor', *Royal Engineers Journal* (July 1919); D. W. Ronald and R. J. Carter, *The Longmoor Military Railway* (1974); A. Baker and A. Civil, *Fireless Locomotives* (1976); M. Christensen, 'Military Camp Railways', *Archive*, 6 (1995).

milk traffic was regularly carried to *Liverpool by the *Liverpool & Manchester Railway from 1832, to *Manchester by the Manchester & Birmingham Railway from 1844, and to *London by the *Eastern Counties Railway from 1845. However, most milk still came from cows kept in cities; only gradually was it supplemented by milk brought in on passenger trains from up to 25 miles away.

London's supplies of 'railway' milk were initially poorly organized: the farmers supplied their own cans and paid the transport costs to the London terminal; trading between the many small wholesalers and retailers took place on the station platform, where the milk was transferred into the retailers' cans. There was more scope for accidental contamination and deliberate adulteration than with 'town' milk, quite apart from deterioration during the rail journey. It therefore gained a reputation as a poor man's drink.

It was the emergence of new, large wholesale companies, set up specifically to develop more efficient and wholesome supplies of railway milk, that changed this. The Express Country Milk Supply Company, formed in 1864 by (Sir) Charles Barham and renamed the Express Dairy Company in 1882, was the best-known and most successful; it adopted a 2-2-2 locomotive *Express* as its trademark to emphasize its railway associations. By controlling distribution from farmers to retailers, and to an increasing extent retailing too, wholesalers were able to impose higher standards of hygiene and negotiate better facilities and terms with the railway companies. This development received considerable impetus when thousands of town cows had to be slaughtered during the cattle plague of 1865–7, and replacement milk supplies for London quickly arranged from Berkshire, Wiltshire, Leicestershire, Derbyshire, and even further afield. A period of rapid development ensued.

The problem of deterioration during transit was overcome by initial cooling of the milk, both at the farm and, increasingly, at a railhead depot, the first of which was opened at Semley, Wilts., in 1871. Northallerton milk depot was built by the *North Eastern Railway in 1905 for lease to the Wensleydale Pure Milk Society, a farmers' co-operative. Many depots were also creameries, balancing milk supplies with the cities' demands by turning the surpluses into butter or cheese.

The dairy companies, who now provided the cans (popularly called 'churns'), introduced more substantial and hygienic designs, standardizing on a conical shape of 17 gallons capacity. When full they weighed nearly 2 cwt, requiring two men to lift them. Much later they were superseded by less cumbersome cylindrical cans holding 8–12 gallons.

For their part, the railway companies introduced special rates to encourage longer-distance traffic; they adjusted the passenger services on which it was carried (generally twice daily) to suit the trade, and from the 1890s began to introduce special milk trains; from 1873 they introduced ventilated vans to keep the milk cool in transit; and they provided special reception accommodation at Ordsall Lane goods depot, Manchester (1869) and later at *Paddington, *St Pancras Goods, *King's Cross, and Finsbury Park in London.

The quantity of milk carried annually to London by the railways grew during the period of the cattle plague from 2 million to 7 million gallons. By 1875 they were supplying 14 million, more than half the city's consumption; by 1897, 50 million, and in 1914, 93 million gallons, 96 per cent of consumption. Comparable figures applied to large provincial cities. This portrays not just a substitution of supply sources, but a major economic shift within the agricultural industry and an improved diet for the urban poor, both made possible by the railways. As imports reduced the price of wheat, meat, and cheese (see AGRICULTURAL TRAFFIC and MEAT TRAFFIC), farmers found it more profitable to produce liquid milk, and consumption per head increased sixfold.

The inter-war period saw further considerable changes in milk distribution. London's milk was now coming from as far as Devon and Cornwall, Carmarthenshire and Pembrokeshire, Shropshire and Staffordshire, North Yorkshire and Westmorland. It was increasingly consigned to new bottling plants being established alongside the railway around central London, such as Vauxhall, Wood Lane, South Acton, and Cricklewood, as bottled pasteurized milk grew in popularity. Although by now suffering from *road competition, particularly after the 1919 rail strike, the railways still carried 280 million gallons in 1927. The introduction of milk tank *wagons in that year secured their position as carriers of long-distance bulk supplies. A standard design carrying 3,000 gallons in a glass-lined or stainless steel barrel on a six-wheel chassis was adopted in 1933. Road tank trailers carried on flat wagons were also introduced to collect from creameries without sidings. In 1932 the *London Midland & Scottish Railway was carrying 72 million gallons—more than any other railway—to London, the north of England, and Scotland.

The rationalization undertaken by the Milk Marketing Board, which took control of all milk distribution in 1942, steadily reduced the need for long-distance movements. By the late 1960s the only regular milk trains were from the West Country and west Wales to London. These ceased in 1980, although the MMB retained an emergency reserve fleet of tank wagons until 1989.   GAB

B. Morgan, *Express Journey 1864–1964: A Centenary History of the Express Dairy Company Limited* (1964); P. J. Atkins, 'The Growth of London's Railway Milk Trade, c.1845–1914', *JTH*, N.S. 4 (1977–8), 208–26; J. Hosegood, 'Milk Traffic on Rail', *Railway World*, 43 (1982), 286–9, 542–3; R. Scola, *Feeding the Victorian City: The Food Supply of Manchester, 1770–1870* (1992), 71–9.

Miller, John (1805–83), civil engineer. He worked for an Ayr solicitor 1818–23, and then went into Thomas *Grainger's office, becoming a partner in 1825. He built roads in

Scotland and Ireland 1829–31; his first railway was the Dundee & Arbroath, 1836–7. He then became engineer for all the principal lines in central Scotland except the *Caledonian.

His *Edinburgh & Glasgow Railway was a splendid achievement: the most nearly level of all British trunk lines —except where it plunges steeply into Glasgow—achieved at the expense of heavy engineering works. The masonry is superb, as in the Winchburgh cutting and in the Almond and Avon viaducts (see BRIDGES AND VIADUCTS). The same is true on his *Glasgow Paisley Kilmarnock & Ayr Railway. Its Ballochmyle viaduct is among the finest masonry bridges in Britain.

His *North British Railway proved less satisfactory. Shortly after opening in 1846, it was closed when torrential rain destroyed bridges and embankments. Skimped contractors' work had been inadequately inspected. Though Miller was not directly blamed, the ultimate responsibility was his. On completion of the Glasgow Dumfries & Carlisle Railway in 1850 (see GLASGOW & SOUTH WESTERN RAILWAY), Miller gave up railway work. He purchased two estates in the counties of Peebles and Kincardine and was MP for Edinburgh in 1868–74.   JS

PICE, 74 (1883), 268–9; Robertson, esp. 119, 138, 190, 195–6, 202.

Miller, John (1872–1942), civil engineer. An Ulsterman by origin, he went from London to the USA to work on the Pennsylvania Railroad in 1909. Henry *Thornton recruited him to the *Great Eastern Railway's civil engineer's department. He became chief civil engineer in 1919 and, after the GER had passed into the *London & North Eastern Railway, chief civil engineer of its North Eastern Area. He retired in 1937.

Miller is remembered for the extreme care he took with every aspect of the physical maintenance of the track and the land it crossed. He insisted on the most precise ballasting and on the trim upkeep of every grass verge, neatly and firmly boarded. Frank *Pick greatly admired his work. 'When the train slows down to approach the Selby swing bridge', he remarked, 'I put away my papers. I always look forward to a sight of the Miller country.'   JS

BDE; C. J. Allen, London & North Eastern Railway (1971 edn.), 218; Pick: in C. Barman, The Man who Built London Transport (1979), 234.

Milne, Sir James (1883–1958), manager. Having graduated in engineering at *Manchester, he entered the locomotive department of the *Great Western Railway in 1904. He then moved into the company's head offices, becoming much concerned with *statistics, and gaining some practical experience of operations also. In 1919 he became director of statistics at the new Ministry of *Transport. But he returned to the GWR in 1922 as assistant general manager, becoming general manager in 1929.

The company was then heavily burdened by the South Wales railways it had inherited (see GROUPING), with their declining industrial traffic; suffering heavily too, like its fellows, from increasing *road competition, and very soon

from the general effects of the economic depression. Milne had to give priority to reducing expenditure; but his policies were meticulously planned, and forward-looking. They included considerably increased involvement in road transport, and he led the companies into the development of internal *air services. Plans for main-line *electrification had to be rejected on account of their cost. He was knighted in 1932.

In World War II Milne was deputy-chairman (in effect, chairman) of the Railway Executive Committee, which controlled the railways for the government. Though outspokenly opposed to *nationalization, he was offered the chairmanship of the Railway Executive (see BRITISH TRANSPORT COMMISSION), but refused it.   JS

DBB; Gourvish, 35, 37.

minerals traffic comprised chiefly: *coal, coke, and patent fuel; *iron and other ores; *clay, including china clay; sand and gravel; *stone blocks, roadstone, and limestone for steel-making; *salt; and lime, marl, and other mineral fertilizers (see AGRICULTURAL TRAFFIC).

From 1856 the railway companies were required to separate minerals from merchandise traffic in their annual statistical *returns to the Board of *Trade, but the distinction was not clearly defined until 1903, when the minerals category became synonymous with classes A and B of the General Railway Classification of Goods (classes 1–6 from 1928—see FREIGHT TRAFFIC RATES). Thus the minerals *statistics came to include other low-value bulk traffics that loaded at least 4, if not 6, tons to a wagon, such as: organic fertilizers (stable manure, compressed peat); industrial by-products (tar, basic slag); *bricks, tiles, *slates, and concrete blocks; pig-iron, steel ingots, and iron and steel scrap; and even sugar beet.   GAB

miniature railways, see NARROW-GAUGE RAILWAYS.

Missenden, Sir Eustace J. (1886–1973): son of a Kent stationmaster, he became a junior clerk, *South Eastern & Chatham Railway, in 1899, progressing to be a district traffic superintendent; a divisional operating superintendent, *Southern Railway, 1923; assistant superintendent of operations, 1930; docks and marine manager, Southampton, 1933; and traffic manager, 1936.

After the outbreak of war in 1939, the War Office requested the services of G. S. *Szlumper, SR general manager. Missenden took his place and when Szlumper was free to return Missenden was chosen to continue.

With *nationalization, Missenden was appointed chairman of the Railway Executive (after Sir James *Milne of the GWR had declined the post), but he disliked the organization and the relationship with the *British Transport Commission; he retired in 1951, having ensured that his successor would be a former Southern man, John *Elliot.

Missenden was a competent railwayman, with few outside interests. He disliked public appearances and was suspicious of politicians and civil servants. He was intensely loyal to his former railway, and he took care to reward those who had given him good support.   MRB

M. R. Bonavia, The History of the Southern Railway (1987); and

The Nationalisation of British Transport (1987); Sir J. Elliot, On and Off the Rails (1982); Gourvish.

Mitchell, Joseph (1803–83), engineer: born in Forres, son of a mason on the Caledonian Canal. Apprenticed to his father at the Fort Augustus locks, he was then recruited as an assistant by Thomas *Telford and carried out the first survey of St Katharine's Dock, London. He was the first recorder of the proceedings of the *Institution of Civil Engineers. In 1824–63 he was Inspector of Highland Roads and Bridges in succession to his father, during which he was responsible for the construction of 30 churches. In the mid-1840s he became concerned with railways, surveying what became the *Scottish Central Railway from Coatbridge to *Perth, and a scheme for a line from Perth to *Inverness. He was engineer for the Inverness & Nairn (1855), Inverness & Aberdeen Junction (1858), *Inverness & Perth Junction (1863), and Inverness & Ross-shire (1868) Railways, which all became part of the *Highland Railway. In 1862 he took Murdoch and William *Paterson into partnership, and surveyed the Dingwall & Skye and Caithness Railways. He gave up business in 1867, owing to ill health.

He was noted for his boldness of concept, and for the grandeur of his major works. The summit of the Inverness and Perth Junction at Drumochter is still the highest on a main line in Britain. He was a pioneer of the use of iron truss bridges in Scotland, examples surviving at Dalguise, Forres, and Logierait, but his masonry structures as at Nairn and Killiecrankie are also particularly noteworthy. A dominant figure in Scottish railway engineering, with *Grainger and *Miller he stands at the head of his profession.   JRH

PICE, 74 (1883–4); J. Mitchell, Reminiscences of My Life in the Highlands, ii (1884).

mixed train. The mixed train—one including both passenger and freight vehicles—did not quickly become a regularly used device on the railways. It was unknown on the *Stockton & Darlington, where at the outset passengers were hauled by horses and freight by locomotives; the *Liverpool & Manchester seems never to have run any train of this description in normal service. By 1840, however, the *Great Western company was providing vehicles in which it arranged to carry passengers, and they were attached to freight trains (see ACCIDENTS). In Scotland the mixed train became established quite early. The Glasgow Paisley & Greenock Railway introduced fourth-class fares in 1844, payable by passengers travelling in wagons attached to coal trains. The resultant economy in locomotive power and in operations was obvious; but it found favour mainly on small branch lines where trains were few, small, and slow.

In the 1860s the government *inspectors showed some uneasiness about the safety of these trains, expressed for instance in the report on an accident at Drem on the *North British Railway in 1867. Since mixed trains usually made frequent stops to shunt wagons in station sidings, it was clearly convenient to place these wagons at the front of the train, next to the engine. But this impaired the passengers' safety. When continuous *brakes were introduced

on passenger carriages (but not for a long time on freight vehicles) there could be no continuity between the engine and carriages if they were at the back. The inspectors repeatedly advised that in mixed trains all passenger vehicles should be at the front; but some companies resisted this practice.

The *Regulation Act of 1889 laid down conditions that, strictly speaking, forbade the running of mixed trains altogether; but some latitude was allowed to the Board of *Trade in enforcing this requirement. It had acrimonious disputes with the *Highland Railway, which in 1892 ran 113 mixed trains, in most of which the freight vehicles were at the front. The company did not give in until 1897.

Mixed trains, marshalled as the Board required, continued to run in small and decreasing numbers on branch lines. All trains to Thaxted (Essex) were mixed until the *British Transport Commission closed the line in 1952.   JS

Robertson, 239; Drem accident: PP 1867, lxxii, 80; H. A. Vallance, Highland Railway (1985 edn.), 110–11; J. Thomas, Skye Railway (1977), ch. 5; P. Paye, Thaxted Branch (1984), 97.

modelling developed simultaneously with full-size prototypes, when manufacturers had scale working models of their locomotives made for demonstration purposes. Some still exist in *museums, often the only remaining record of a particular type, built by craftsmen having skills akin to watch- and clock-making.

From about 1850, complete railway layouts began to be constructed by individuals for their own pleasure, ranging from about 3½-in to 8-in *gauge, with steam locomotives. Interest also began to grow in scale models of contemporary locomotives made by craftsmen or professional engineers, sometimes for sale; thus the term 'model engineer' came into being.

The popular hobby of model railways began in the 1890s when the toymakers of Nuremberg, Germany, produced 'carpet trains' of tinplate, wood, or cast iron for children. Local clock-makers developed driving mechanisms, and clockwork engines became popular. By the end of the century complete systems with many accessories, all in lithographed tinplate, were readily available.

In 1900 W. J. Bassett-Lowke realized the potential market among adults. He ordered tinplate replicas of British locomotives and rolling stock from Bing of Germany, designed by Henry Greenly, a railway engineer and builder of small-scale steam engines. They were more authentic than anything previously on sale, and included steam-driven models as well as clockwork. Carriages and wagons were of lithographed tinplate, but some of the locomotives were hand-painted in Britain, correctly portraying contemporary liveries, and those that survive form a valuable record of their prototypes. Relatively expensive, they were not considered merely as 'toys'. Specialist 'one-man' manufacturers of accessories such as turntables, signals, and station buildings also appeared. Several railway companies built sophisticated layouts for staff-training purposes.

After World War I the hobby began to gain wide popularity. Smaller scales were made possible by small electric motors as an alternative to clockwork, using a central third rail to carry the current, while semi-mass production methods brought prices within a wider range of pockets. Names like Mills Bros, Bonds, Leeds Model Co., Jubb, and Hull joined the growing industry. In 1920 Frank Hornby, of Meccano fame, brought out his range of tinplate clockwork and electric Hornby Trains, catering for the toy market. At this time gauge '0' (1¼ in) predominated, although already there were signs of a further reduction in popular sizes. Bing produced their 'table top' railway in '00' gauge (⅝ in) as early as 1922, followed by Hornby Dublo in the 1930s, a period when many firms made models in 4 mm or 3.5 mm scales, thereby laying the foundations of the present-day business.

Small scales became the popular standard after World War II, three-rail giving way to the more realistic two-rail systems in which current was taken through the wheels of the locomotive. Keen competition between British and European manufacturers soon extended to the Far East. Injection-moulded plastics brought accurately detailed models at an affordable price, complete with accessories; the unskilled could now assemble layouts which compared favourably with the hand-made, while plastic or die-cast models in kit form enjoyed growing popularity.

Concurrently, mass-produced simple 1¼-in and 1¾-in gauge steam locomotives were manufactured, creating an enthusiasm for outdoor small-scale railways which is still growing, together with the more expensive German-made electric systems, mostly based on *narrow-gauge prototypes. Many garden railways are quite elaborate, calling for small-scale civil engineering as well as mechanical skills. Hand-built 'super detail' model railways, complete with rural and urban three-dimensional scenery of considerable complexity, can be seen at exhibitions, museums, and commercial displays; no longer the domain of the spare-time modeller but now often produced by a small craft industry specializing in such work, as well as in individual models.

There is also a thriving model railway press publishing magazines and books, the best of which can also be invaluable to the railway historian, while nearly every town of consequence has its model engineering society or model railway club.

See also HISTORICAL MODEL RAILWAY SOCIETY.   JEFS
H. Greenly, *Model Steam Locomotives* (1922); E. Beale, *Scale Railway Modelling Today* (1939); P. Whitehouse and J. Adams, *The World of Model Trains* (1970); R. Fuller, *The Bassett-Lowke Story* (1984).

Modernization Plan. The *British Railways Modernization Plan was detailed in the *British Transport Commission's document *Modernisation and Re-equipment of British Railways* published in 1955.

The first comprehensive investment plan for the railways, it proposed the spending of £1,240 million over 15 years. By making rail services more attractive, the object was to recover traffic lost to road and so improve BR's financial results. Cost reduction was also an important aspect.

Principal areas for investment were: *electrification of

principal routes; large-scale introduction of diesel and electric *traction, and new coaching stock; resignalling, and track renewal. Soon after publication, the BTC was asked to review its deteriorating financial state and prospects, as a result of which a reappraisal of the plan and its finances was underwritten by the government in a White Paper of 1956. This promised that modernization would help eliminate BR's financial deficit by 1962.

Although the theme of modernization improving the prospect of reduced losses was pursued in the 1950s, BR's finances worsened and a second reappraisal of the plan came in 1959. This promised to speed up modernization, particularly the introduction of diesel traction and resignalling, accompanied by rationalization of route *mileage and stations, but also indicated deferment of the *East Coast electrification. The Modernization Plan was superseded by the provisions of *Beeching's *Re-Shaping of British Railways* report of 1963.   MLH
British Transport Commission, *Modernisation and Re-equipment of British Railways* (1955); HMSO, *British Transport Commission: Proposals for the Railways*, White Paper (1956); HMSO, *BR: Re-appraisal of the Plan for the Modernisation and Re-equipment of BR*, White Paper (1959); Gourvish, 256–304.

monopoly. Parliament never set out deliberately to give a railway company a territorial monopoly until 1921. Ten monopolies of this kind did emerge in different parts of Great Britain during the 19th century, but none was created for that purpose. Most became larger and more powerful units by successive *amalgamations, generally from the desire to end unprofitable *competition.

The word 'monopoly' had long and unpleasant associations in the minds of English people. The granting of monopolies to individuals had been one of the complaints that led to the Civil War. In more recent times there had been fierce attacks on the East India Company's monopoly in the importation of valuable goods from the east, abolished altogether in 1853. There were now fears that communications within Great Britain would become monopolies.

'We often hear of the "monopoly" of the railroads', the *Edinburgh Review* remarked in 1841, continuing that 'this "monopoly" is given by nothing but superiority; railroads have no legal privilege'. When in that year the *Great Western Railway was opened throughout between London and Bristol, its trains made the journey in about 4½ hours. The coaches did it in 12–15 and were more expensive than the railway. They had ceased to run by 1843, leaving the railway with a 'monopoly'. The railways acquired and kept a monopoly of this kind of passenger traffic, over most of Great Britain, for more than 80 years thereafter, owing it to 'nothing but superiority'.

Parliament supposed at first that it had provided against monopoly by allowing the companies no more than the right of taking tolls for the use of their lines, anticipating that carriers would use their own vehicles, as they did on *turnpike roads. But the introduction of locomotives made this impossible, for few of the carriers would own such machines. Instead, railway companies provided the motive power and some of the vehicles, though much freight went in the customers' *private wagons.

Another device intended to guard against monopoly appeared in 1828, when the *Clarence Railway was authorized, deliberately competing with the *Stockton & Darlington, already at work. A line that would compete with the *Liverpool & Manchester for the traffic across south Lancashire was being surveyed only a week after the first railway was opened in 1830.

Some railways were authorized in those years that did unintentionally turn out to be monopolistic, such as the successful scheme from the six proposals in 1836 for a line from *London to *Brighton (see COMPETITION). The *London Brighton & South Coast Railway owed this chiefly to the remarkable directness of its line; again to 'nothing but superiority'.

When the great extension of the railway system that was authorized in the 1840s had come into full use, few similar monopolies had been set up. By 1853 there were competitive services between London and *Birmingham, between England and *Scotland by the western and eastern routes, and between *Liverpool, *Leeds, and *Hull. Yet the contrary policy was adopted in 1854, when Parliament sanctioned the amalgamation of four companies to make the *North Eastern Railway, which would have a heavily preponderant power in north Yorkshire, Durham, and Northumberland. Again, in 1862 the *Great Eastern Railway was established, creating a monopoly over much of East Anglia.

Walter Bagehot analysed this confused situation lucidly in 1863, contrasting the big regional monopolies in France with what he called 'competing monopolies' in Britain: the companies being monopolists in the territories traversed by their main lines but fighting for the districts that lay between them, by building branches or absorbing small companies. This he thought very dangerous; their directors, he said, '*must* quarrel, fight, and spend'.

There came to be ten substantial districts where one of the pre-1923 railway companies established a virtual monopoly:

1. The far north of Scotland (*Highland Railway).
2. Scotland north and north-west of *Aberdeen (*Great North of Scotland).
3. Scotland between Tay and Forth (*North British).
4. North-east England from Beverley and Selby to the Scottish border; westwards to Harrogate and Hawes (North Eastern).
5. The Potteries, and outwards to Macclesfield and Burton-on-Trent (*North Staffordshire).
6. Mid-Wales (except some short lines), from Shropshire to Aberystwyth and Pwllheli (*Cambrian Railways).
7. Norfolk south of Norwich, and Suffolk (Great Eastern).
8. South Hampshire and east Dorset (*London & South Western—except the *Somerset & Dorset Railway, owned jointly with the Midland).
9. Eastbourne–Redhill–Chichester triangle (London Brighton & South Coast).
10. Kent (*South Eastern & Chatham, after 1899).

All these areas except 4 and 5 were predominantly rural.

Among the 12 largest British cities only *Newcastle-upon-Tyne was served virtually by one railway alone.

A number of smaller towns were aggrieved because they had only one railway: e.g. *Southampton, where the corporation tried repeatedly to get a second line to compete with the LSWR. *Plymouth was more successful, where with much local support the LSWR broke the monopoly of the GWR and its allies in 1876.

Arguments on this matter came to a head in 1872–3, over the abortive merger proposals by the *London & North Western and *Lancashire & Yorkshire companies (see AMALGAMATION).

Complaints about *freight traffic rates and services continued, although lessened by considerable improvements that some monopolist companies made. Hull and Southampton benefited from the railways' heavy investment in their docks.

Some towns recognized the benefits a railway monopoly brought. In 1880 Ipswich council recorded its thanks to the GER for the improvement of its services, 'which now leave hardly anything to be desired'. The waste arising from competition was now attacked, as helping to keep fares high. The NER was widely commended for providing, as its chairman claimed, 'the best possible service at the lowest cost'.

Parliament's attitude varied. In 1899 it sanctioned the 'working union' of the rival companies in Kent, but in 1908–9 it refused to do the same in eastern England and South Wales.

After World War I, when the railways were managed under government control, advocates of *nationalization urged that this practice should be continued. Instead, the *'Big Four' were created under the Railways Act, 1921 (see GROUPING). Each had monopolies over large areas: the *London & North Eastern Railway, for example, over almost the whole of eastern England north of the Thames.

But generally the debate was subsiding. *Road competition reduced the fear of rail monopoly, whilst the *Southern Railway's *electrification programme showed that the railways still had great potential for development. Parliament set up the London Passenger Transport Board (see LONDON UNDERGROUND RAILWAYS) in 1933, to run the Underground with most of the tram and bus services in Greater London —though not the main-line railways. It quickly demonstrated the advantages of a well-directed common management, as a monopolist, in a huge conurbation.

In World War II the railways (and the LPTB) were again unified under government control. On 1 January 1948 a Labour government put them, with trifling exceptions, under one state monopoly.   JS

Edinburgh Review, 72 (1840–1), 481; Jackman, 572–83; E. Cleveland-Stevens, *English Railways* (1915), chs 8–10; GR, 219.

monorails. A patent of 22 November 1821, registered by H. R. Palmer (engineer to the London Dock Co.), provides the first documentary evidence of a monorail, built in 1824 to convey merchandise from the Thames to warehouses at Deptford. Palmer's second monorail, built in 1815, carried building materials across the Cheshunt marshes to the River Lea. Both systems were propelled by horse power, with loads balanced pannier-fashion from the extended axles of wheels running on a single elevated load-bearing rail. In 1830 the first passenger-carrying monorail, the 'William the Fourth Royal Car', ran around the Royal Panarmonion Gardens in London. The carriage was suspended asymmetrically from 2-wheeled bogies in tandem and propelled by man-power through pedals.

Trials of an original towing system took place in August 1839 on the banks of the Forth & Clyde Canal. The unusual 6-wheel locomotive employed two wheels on the single load-bearing rail and four driving wheels to provide traction upon the level roadway. In 1872 Sharp Stewart, *Manchester, received an order from Lisbon Tramways, Portugal, for 15 locomotives operating on the same principle.

A monorail patent was lodged by John Barraclough Fell in 1868. His locomotives were initially designed with twin boilers mounted on either side of the elevated load-bearing rail. Horizontal stabilizing wheels were incorporated in the design. In 1887 Hunslet Engine Co., Leeds, built three twin-boiler locomotives for Lartigue's Listowel & Ballybunion monorail, Ireland, which operated in 1887–1924.

Behr's 'Lightning Express' monorail was designed in 1900 to link *Liverpool and Manchester with a regular 110 mph service. The Gloucester Carriage & Wagon Co. built a demonstration car in 19th-century *Pullman style. The track was similar to that erected by Lartigue for his Tothill Street, Westminster demonstration in 1886.

In December 1903 Louis Brennan applied for a master patent relating to his remarkable Gyroscopic Monorail. A full-scale vehicle was constructed and successfully demonstrated in 1909. A new monorail concept was successfully demonstrated in model form by E. W. Chalmers Kearney in 1908. The cars ran on a single support rail and were stabilized by an overhead guide rail. A full-scale car was constructed by the Brush Engineering Co. at Loughborough. The 'George Bennie Railplane' full-scale monorail demonstration track was constructed between Milngavie and Hillfoot, near Glasgow, in 1929. The car was suspended by 2-wheel bogies from a single rail and stabilized by a single rail beneath the car. It was self-propelled by four-bladed propellers fore and aft.

The novel 'Air Rail' monorail was one of the schemes proposed for the London–Heathrow Airport link in the 1950s, incorporating dual-purpose coaches designed to operate as road vehicles at the terminals and to straddle a concrete beam for the fast overhead run to and from the Airport (see also MAGLEV). LRW

D. G. Tucker, 'F. B. Behr's Development of the Monorail', *TNS*, 55 (1983–4), 131–52; *Jnl Inst. Loco. Engineers*, Paper No. 631/1962; B. and R. Wilson, 'Monorail to Maglev', Friends of the National Railway Museum *Newsletter*, 65 (Nov. 1993)–83 (Summer 1998).

Moon, Sir Richard (1814–99), elder son of a Liverpool merchant, director of the *London & North Western Railway 1851–91 (deputy chairman 1861, chairman 1861–91), created baronet in 1887.

Moon was one of the longest-serving British railway chairmen, and the pre-eminence of the LNWR gave him a status which was reinforced by his business acumen and his commitment to the company's interests. The LNWR was formed by amalgamation in 1846, and by 1851, when he became a director, the company was experiencing a marked deterioration in its financial position because of the rapid expansion of the network. Moon identified himself with the reformist element on the board, and in 1855 chaired an investigation which led to the establishment of an executive committee of directors to supervise the company's management more directly. He became chairman of the general stores and locomotive expenditure committee in 1858, and used this position to give practical effect to his view that expenditure required more rigorous control, championing the rationalization of the separate *works inherited from the LNWR's constituents, and advocating functional rather than divisional management.

Moon's appointment as chairman in 1861 came at the nadir of the LNWR's fortunes, but with further management reform and through careful financial management and progressive restructuring he restored and enhanced its standing. Though some subsequent commentators have criticized the conservatism of his approach, the effectiveness of Moon's long stewardship of the LNWR, at that time Britain's largest business undertaking, was incontrovertibly demonstrated in the company's strength when he retired. MCR

DBB; T. R. Gourvish, *Mark Huish and the London and North Western Railway* (1972), 170–8; B. Reed, *Crewe Locomotive Works and its Men* (1982), 46–51, 251; D. Stevenson, *Fifty Years on the London & North Western Railway* (1891), 31–5; M. C. Reed, *London & North Western Railway* (1996).

Morrison, Herbert Stanley (1888–1965), son of Henry Morrison, a London policeman. He was a voracious reader and throughout his life often got the best of an argument through being well-briefed. In 1906 he joined the Independent Labour Party and in 1915 he became secretary of the London Labour Party. As a councillor in Hackney in 1919–25 he became its mayor in 1920. He served on the London County Council as representative for Wandsworth from 1922. He was elected Labour MP for South Hackney in 1923, was defeated in 1924, but re-elected in 1929. In the first Labour government of 1924 Morrison served as Secretary of State for the Colonies.

Until the late 1920s Labour Party thinking was that future publicly owned industries should be run as departments of state, like the *Post Office. Morrison considered that they should be run by independent corporations, as in the case of the BBC from 1926. As Minister of Transport in the Labour government of 1929–31 he put these ideas into practice in the National Government's London Passenger Transport Act of 1933. Harold Clay, for the transport workers, argued at Labour Party conferences in 1931, 1932, and after 1945 that employees in the industry should be given a major part to play on the corporate boards that were planned, so that they should feel a real involvement in 'their' industry; but Morrison preferred management by a predominance of 'outside' business experts.

Morrison was Home Office Minister and Minister of Home Security in the coalition government in World War II, and Lord President of the Council in 1945–51, when he had influential oversight of *nationalization. It enabled him to carry through this policy for the Railway Executive (1948–62) which ran the nationalized industry under the *British Transport Commission, and continued after 1962 under the *British Railways Board. Morrison's plans for integrated transport in which there would be an appropriate balance between road and rail were undermined by the Transport Act of 1953, which privatized the Commission's Road Haulage Executive.

Morrison was created Baron Morrison of Lambeth in 1959.   PSB

H. Morrison, *Socialisation and Transport* (1933); and *Autobiography* (1960); B. Donoughue and G. W. Jones, *Herbert Morrison: Portrait of a Politician* (1973); Ross M. Martin, *TUC: The Growth of a Pressure Group, 1868–1971* (1980).

motive power depots, see ENGINE SHEDS.

Motorail, see MOTOR CARS, CARRIAGE OF.

motor cars, carriage of. From the earliest days, trains conveyed private *horse-drawn carriages, usually on open *wagons known as carriage trucks, but later in covered carriage trucks, attached to passenger trains or run in special 'horse and carriage' trains. As better-off families took up motoring, their cars were conveyed in the same fashion—on the *Midland Railway from 1904. The usual rates charged by the railways comprised the cost of hire of the carriage truck, and a supplement for mileage.

By 1934, the *London & North Eastern Railway was conveying 505 cars annually in this manner from *King's Cross, 70 per cent of these during the high summer, to Scotland. Their passengers mostly used the *sleeping-car trains, and sometimes there were enough motor cars to justify running a separate train. The *Great Western Railway operated a service through the Severn Tunnel from 1909, to save motorists the lengthy detour then necessary via Gloucester. This lasted until the Severn road bridge was built in 1963, and was advertised in the public timetables.

The first long-distance car-carrying train as such was introduced in 1955 as a twice-weekly overnight service between King's Cross and *Perth and return, the passenger accommodation including sleeping cars. The service was soon expanded, and a daytime car-carrier came in 1960, between Holloway (London) and *Edinburgh, and return. Ordinary end-loading vans were supplemented by double-deck covered vehicles in 1962.

Services were also operated between *Marylebone and Scotland in the 1960s, but in 1966 better loading and reception facilities were provided at Kensington Olympia, and in time this became the London base, with trains to Stirling, *Inverness, and Perth, now routed via the *West Coast main line. There were also services from the provinces to Scotland from the mid-1950s, such as those from *York to Inverness, and Sutton Coldfield (*Birmingham), or

Newton-le-Willows (Lancashire), to Stirling. They were re-named 'Motorail' in 1966.

London to the West Country and west Wales trains started in the 1960s, the best-known being the Kensington to St Austell Motorail introduced in 1966, and London–Fishguard in 1965. There were numerous changes to the routes and stations served by Motorail, and with the end of steam traction, bogie open wagons were normally used to convey cars. The construction of motorways, combined with increased charges, caused the peak carryings of 100,000 cars annually in the early 1970s to decline rapidly during the next decade to 50,000, and services were greatly reduced for the 1982 season. In time, Motorail reverted to the provision of a limited number of vans on overnight sleeping-car trains, but even these were discontinued in 1995.

The only car-carrying rail service currently offered in Britain for motorists and their vehicles is Le Shuttle, operated through the *Channel Tunnel.

From the late 1950s, *BR became heavily involved in the carriage of new cars from their point of manufacture, or place of import, to distribution depots. This traffic reached its peak in the 1980s, by which time the car distribution companies had built up fleets of double-deck, articulated car-carrying wagons.   MLH

J. Norris and others, *Edwardian Enterprise GWR* (1987).

motors, steam rail, see PUSH-AND-PULL TRAINS; RAILCARS.

mountain railways. Britain has two mountain railways in the generally accepted sense, i.e. employing a supplement to adhesion, excluding *cable-operated railways and funiculars.

The first, opened in 1895, was the Snaefell Mountain Railway on the *Isle of Man, using single-deck electric tram-cars taking current from overhead wires. Operated by the Manx Electric Railway, they ascend 1,823 ft in 4½ miles from the MER's Laxey station to a summit terminus, mainly at 1 in 12. The 3 ft 6 in *gauge, 6 in wider than the MER, was selected to enable use of Manx Northern Railway steam locomotives during construction, thus precluding a physical junction. In 1995 steam engines were again used during centenary celebrations.

The cars were equipped with the Fell *braking system, which comprises pairs of horizontal wheels which grip a centre-rail laid on the hill section. Devised in 1863 by J. B. Fell to assist propulsion as well, two locomotives were successfully tried on experimental track alongside a 1 in 7 cable incline on the Cromford & High Peak Railway, Derbyshire, before being adopted overseas. As the Snaefell cars have been fitted with electric regenerative braking, the Fell system now acts as an additional safeguard.

The other line, the Snowdon Mountain Railway, operates on the Swiss Abt system. It was opened by the Snowdon Mountain Tramroad & Hotels Company in 1896. The 2 ft 7½ in gauge line climbs 3,140 ft in 4½ miles from Llanberis, on a *ruling gradient of 1 in 5½. Swiss-built 0-4-2 tank locomotives, which have a forward-tilted boiler and firebox to maintain a horizontal water-level, haul themselves up the mountain by a pair of co-axial pinions which engage in staggered teeth on a central double rack-rail. They also provide braking downhill, assisted by counter-pressure steam brakes. A single uncoupled coach is pushed up the mountain, and descends behind the locomotive. In recent years a diesel locomotive has also been obtained.

Other mountain railways have been proposed, particularly in the Scottish Highlands. In 1893–1913 several ideas were advanced for a line up Ben Nevis, while more recently a scheme for a *winter sports centre on Ben Wyvis included a railway.   GJB

F. K. Pearson, *The Snaefell Mountain Railway, 1895–1970* (1970); K. Turner, *The Snowdon Mountain Railway* (1973); Ben Nevis: J. Thomas, *The West Highland Railway* (1960), 82; Ben Wyvis: *Reg. Hist.*, xv, 263.

'Müller's lights', see NORTH LONDON RAILWAY.

multiple tracks. Railways designed as trunk routes nearly always had double track, although on some secondary routes built to take a double line only one was laid in order to reduce initial costs. Generally they were soon doubled, like the *London & Birmingham Railway's Northampton–Peterborough line (1845), but some later ones such as the Meon Valley line in Hampshire (1903) never justified it.

As traffic grew, lines were widened to increase capacity by segregating passenger trains from slow-moving freight. On the *London & North Western Railway, for instance, freight traffic increased in 1865–1900 from 9 million to 35 million tons a year, much of it on the main line. By 1859 the company had laid a third track from north of *Euston to Bletchley, and in 1890 there were four tracks from London to Roade, whence alternative routes provided the equivalent to Stafford, followed by four tracks to *Crewe. The *Midland Railway's prodigious coal traffic required similar measures, and in 1873–1910 it widened lines or built alternative routes that in effect provided four tracks for over 200 miles from London to Shipley, beyond *Leeds. The volume of coal traffic forced even the small *Taff Vale Railway to quadruple over 12 miles of its line into *Cardiff, and by 1914 the *Glasgow & South Western Railway had quadruple tracks or *loop lines for most of the 30 miles from *Glasgow to Kilwinning. The *Leeds & Selby Railway (1834) was probably the first to build part of its line wide enough for four tracks from the outset, although only two were laid.

The high cost meant that such work was done over a long period. *Tunnels and viaducts (see BRIDGES AND VIADUCTS) were the most expensive obstacles. Watford Tunnel on the LNWR, and Belsize on the MR, had two sets of interlaced tracks until second tunnels could be made. Two tunnels totalling ¾ mile had to be duplicated to widen the 1¼ miles between Haymarket and Waverley stations in *Edinburgh, while Wharncliffe and Maidenhead viaducts slowed up the *Great Western Railway's widening (the latter by nine years) between London and Didcot (53 miles) in 1875–99.

Most of the large *London stations are approached by multiple tracks. The final 1½ miles into London Bridge

from the east have 12 and then 11; Waterloo has eight. Where passenger traffic alone was heavy, segregation was between fast and slow, as over the 50 miles from Waterloo to Worting Junction which was progressively quadrupled in 1862–1909 by the *London & South Western Railway, a company which earned only one third of its revenue from freight. The *London Brighton & South Coast Railway experienced the same pressure: by 1864 it had four tracks from London Bridge to South Croydon (11 miles), and eventually used four from Victoria to Balcombe Tunnel (32 miles).

Rapidly growing suburban traffic was the main reason. It created severe problems on the *Great Northern Railway, which spasmodically widened its notoriously congested line from King's Cross, hampered by a cramped terminus and seven tunnels in the first 12 miles. Starting in 1871, the 59 miles to Huntingdon had been quadrupled by 1901, but were still interrupted by bottlenecks at three tunnels, Welwyn Viaduct, and two unreconstructed stations. Although the chairman declared in 1882 that the tunnels must be duplicated, it did not happen until 1953–5, and the viaduct has never been widened. It has been suggested that the company itself was partly to blame by deliberately encouraging suburban traffic on a line which could scarcely accommodate passenger and coal trains, without having properly weighed the added revenue against the cost of widening. Desultory construction of the Hertford Loop as a relief line, and initial refusal to support *Underground schemes in north London, made matters worse (see SYSTEM, DEVELOPMENT OF THE).

Similar uninformed judgement may have been applied elsewhere. The LNWR quadrupled most of its North Wales coast line from Chester to Abergele in the early 1900s, mainly for heavy seasonal holiday traffic lasting three months of the year, which the company had done much to promote. It has been argued that the opposite happened at *Blackpool (see also HOLIDAY-MAKING).

Where full-scale widening was not justified, line capacity could be increased by providing *loops where slow freight trains could be overtaken. For instance, over the 88 miles between *Preston and *Carlisle there were 12, some long enough for two trains. A number of stations had extra tracks enabling expresses and freight trains to overtake other trains standing at the platforms: at large stations like Darlington, and small ones like Gerrards Cross.

Single lines which became trunk routes, but had a combination of highly seasonal traffic and formidable engineering works, took a long time to widen, like most of the GWR through Cornwall where doubling begun in the early 1870s was not finished until 1929, leaving only Saltash bridge single. The *Highland Railway constructed extra passing loops and doubled 29 miles of its long and remote main line in 1896–1914, principally for summer tourist traffic but undoubtedly easing the difficult working of military traffic in both world wars.

Although only a few double lines had been singled before the 1960s—usually lightly used branches—reduced freight traffic and lighter, faster passenger trains enabled *British Rail to revert to sections of single track on these routes, on the LSWR west of Salisbury, and elsewhere. Paradoxically, an upturn in traffic required 23 miles of the Highland to be doubled for a second time 12 years later. Significant increases in line capacity provided by modern *signalling have also enabled some four-track lines to be reduced to three or two. GJB

Reg. Hist. (all volumes); GWR: MacDermot; GNR: J. N. Young, Great Northern Suburban; J. Simmons, 'Suburban Traffic at King's Cross, 1852–1914', JTH (3rd series), 6, 1 (1985), 71–8; LSWR: J. N. Faulkner and R. A. Williams, The LSWR in the Twentieth Century (1988), 64–6.

multiple units. Diesel- or electric-powered vehicles are said to be able to operate as multiple units when they can be coupled to others for operation from one driving position as a single train. The driver then has control of power and braking throughout, so permitting the other driving positions to be left unmanned. The term has become generic to diesel and electric unit trains although some may not be able to work in multiple because of incompatible control circuits, or the need to avoid overloading the lineside power supply.

Multiple-unit vehicles are connected by 'jumper cables' which carry control wiring from the driving cab. Recent developments combine control connections with automatic mechanical couplers, typically of the Scharfenburg type. A multiple-unit control system was invented in Chicago in 1898 by Frank J. Sprague. The first British trials were on the *Central London Railway while the first European operator to place an order for electric multiple-unit trains was the *Great Northern & City Railway in 1901, although the Central London's were the first to enter service, in 1903. The control equipment was supplied by British Thomson-Houston. One master controller utilized a number of low-current electrical circuits for operating control switches on the separate motor cars: these made and broke the main power circuits. This was the basis of all subsequent control systems on dc electric units. Generally, there has been a limit of 12 cars operating in multiple, usually in units of two or four cars.

On the *Southern Railway, after 1936 all electric rolling stock equipment was supplied by the English Electric Co. Ltd so that different classes of unit could run in multiple with each other. In post-war years the system was extended so that electric, electro-diesel, and diesel locomotives, and electric passenger and parcels units, could all run in multiple. Multiple-unit control was adopted for 25 kV ac electric stock, and the suburban units put into service by *BR from 1959 onwards all had a standard control system.

A variety of multiple-unit control systems was available for diesel *railcars from the mid-1930s, usually pneumatic, electro-pneumatic, or electric. These variously enabled remote control of fuel pumps, gearboxes, and braking. From 1950, the Great Northern Railway (Ireland) built up a fleet of diesel mechanical railcars able to work in multiple. Of the 3,600 diesel multiple-unit vehicles put into service by BR from the mid-1950s, there were five main coupling types, each mutually exclusive. Most of the current generation of diesel railcars, both the Class 14X 'Pacer' two-car, four-wheeled types and the 15X 'Sprinter' two- or three-car types, are able to work in multiple with each other. Several current classes of dc and ac electric units are only able to work in multiple with other units of their class.

See also TRACTION, DIESEL; TRACTION, ELECTRIC. MLH

J. Johnson and R. A. Long, British Railways Engineering 1948–80 (1981); J. Graeme Bruce, Tube Trains under London (1972).

Murray, Matthew (1765–1826), engineer; he produced the first commercially successful steam locomotives by developing the ideas of James Watt and Richard *Trevithick. Born near Newcastle upon Tyne, and apprenticed as a millwright, he settled in Leeds where he quickly established his reputation as an engineer, and designed lighter, more compact, and self-contained stationary steam engines for Fenton Murray & Wood which effectively challenged Boulton & Watt's monopoly. His slide valve was a major step forward, followed by improved cylinder-boring and other precision machines.

To counter the soaring cost of horse fodder, in 1810 John Blenkinsop sought Murray's assistance in providing steam power on his *Middleton Colliery wagonway nearby. Murray's locomotives used two vertical double-acting cylinders with a single-flue boiler, giving a smoother action. Blenkinsop's patent toothed drive was incorporated into locomotives and track to ensure that heavy loads could be drawn by a locomotive which was still light enough not to break the iron plate-rails, although others' use of edge rails demonstrated that this was being unduly cautious.

Demonstrated in June 1812 before thousands of spectators, the four locomotives performed well, hauling up to 100 tons on level track at 3½ mph, and replacing 50 horses and 200 men. The last engine was retired in 1835. Although they declined to build locomotives for the *Stockton & Darlington Railway in 1825–6 'until they became a regular article of commerce', Fenton Murray & Wood supplied the *Great Western in the 1830s. RVL

L. T. C. Rolt, Great Engineers (1962); J. B. Snell, Railways: Mechanical Engineering (1971).

museums, railway. This is a term commonly used to describe a wide variety of organizations involved in the *preservation of Britain's railway inheritance, ranging from the *National Railway Museum, which is trustee of the nation's collection, through local railway museums, general museums which contain railway collections, and preserved working railways, to sites which hold railway material collected by groups or individuals. Few are dedicated solely to railways and fall within the Museums Association's definition of a museum as an 'institution which collects, documents, preserves, exhibits, and interprets material evidence and associated information for the public benefit'.

By the 1850s, people were sufficiently aware of the importance of early locomotives to regard them as worthy of preservation. The inclusion of a core collection in what was to become the Science Museum, London, indicates that they were recognized as nationally important technological landmarks of the Industrial Revolution.

Other historical railway items, principally locomotives, were also saved for public display by several railway companies, but their permanent safe-keeping was not assured. A growing acceptance by the late 19th century of the value of preserving individual railway relics was divorced from the concept of a collection housed in a railway museum. This contrasts sharply with developments in Europe where railways featured in museums of science and industry and transport. A number of railway museums were established by the beginning of the 20th century, the earliest being at Hamar, Norway (1895) and Nuremberg, Germany (1899).

Not until 1927 was Britain's first railway museum opened, by the *London & North Eastern Railway at *York. It was a reflection of increased official interest in railway history stimulated by the *Grouping of 1923 and the popular celebration of the centenary of the opening of the *Stockton & Darlington Railway in 1925. The York museum, in the absence of any other, became the nation's railway museum, and material from other operating companies gravitated towards it. The principal companies held historical material in offices and various works, but without official museum status some collections were disposed of when financial and operational demands dictated.

This conflict between the business interest of railway management and preservation in museums is a recurrent theme. It featured in *British Railways after *nationalization. Official policy represented by the 1951 report *The Preservation of Relics and Records* set out an enlightened approach, proposing a national transport museum supplemented by regional railway museums. This centralized policy fell short of its aims and only created the Museum of British Transport at Clapham, London (1961–73), and two joint ventures with local authority museums at *Swindon and *Glasgow. In 1975 the NRM acquired the BR collection, and in 1980 London Transport opened its own museum.

As official preservation by the railway industry was highly centralized, and because of the inherent problems of preserving major railway items, Britain's provincial museums have played a lesser role. There was a short-lived railway museum at *Hull station in the late 1930s (which was destroyed during the war) and a few key locomotives and other equipment were included in technologically based museum collections at *Newcastle, *Edinburgh, and Glasgow. It was not until the 1950s that local authority museums became active collectors of railway material, and they have tended to concentrate on locomotives of local significance with an emphasis on industrial railways, as at *Birmingham, *Bristol, *Leeds, *Leicester, and *Liverpool.

The growth of open-air and site museums since the 1970s opened up new areas for the preservation of railway material. Museums like Ironbridge and Beamish include railways as part of a wider theme with growing archive collections. Historic railway stations provide the context for railway collections at Darlington, *Manchester, Monkwearmouth, and North Woolwich. Display is no longer restricted to a small number of token items. The exhibition of railway equipment in operation is a feature at a number of museums and is a valuable educational and interpretive medium as it illustrates the preservation of the working object and the dynamic process of railway transport.

The growth of amateur interest in railway preservation in the 1950s was seen as an alternative to static railway exhibits in museums. Railway preservation became no longer the monopoly of large railway companies or museums, and *enthusiasts saved increasingly large numbers of locomotives, coaches, and relics throughout the country. Sometimes this was in a museum context like the *Narrow Gauge Railway Museum at Towyn, North Wales but, more generally, redundant locomotives and rolling stock were saved to operate on a preserved railway line. Today the umbrella term of 'preserved railway' covers a diverse group of organizations from commercially operated tourist railways and hobby lines, to open-air and site museums.

As the principal museums and preserved railways have developed in the later 20th century, they have influenced one another's approach. Museums now use some of the skills of the railway *preservation movement, and an increasing number of preserved railways are adopting museum standards and practices, which will help to ensure the long-term preservation and understanding of Britain's railway history.

In Europe railway museums have also developed since the 1970s. A characteristic has been the redisplay of national collections in new museums as at Mulhouse (France), and major redevelopment at existing museums such as Utrecht (Netherlands), Nuremberg (Germany), and Odense (Denmark). The demise of the steam locomotive and modernization of railways have also stimulated the growth of railway preservation in most European countries.   DWH

R. Barker, 'Lost Preserved Railway Rolling-Stock', *Transport History*, 9 (1978), 100–9; D. W. Hopkin, 'Railway Preservation: Railway Museums and Enthusiasts', unpublished thesis, University of Leicester (1987); and 'Railway Preservation in the 1920s and 1930s', in N. Cossons (ed.), *Perspectives on Railway History and Interpretation* (1992); B. Morgan, *Railway Relics* (1969); J. Simmons, *Transport Museums in Britain and Western Europe* (1970).

music, railways and. Music has been linked with railways since the 1830s. Railway openings, even excursions, were accompanied by a band. Railway work-forces formed bands, choirs, and orchestras, including Leeds Railway Foundry and *Doncaster Plant works bands, which excelled in contests in the 1850s, and Horwich Railwaymen's Institute, open champions in 1916–17. Of major railways, the *London & North Eastern Railway had London and regional musical societies; Doncaster's embraced a male voice choir, orchestra, and an operatic section. Leslie Woodgate, Stanley Marchant, and others composed music for the LNER.

Music depicting railways is often popular and dance-like,

perhaps reflecting the rhythm of a moving train. The Viennese Strausses wrote much of it, including the gallops *Bahn Frei!* ('Line Clear!': Eduard) and *Vergnügungszug* ('Excursion Train': Johann II); they had Austrian, even Scandinavian, imitators. In Victorian England many railway songs (e.g. 'Oh Mr Porter!') and dances appeared; in France, Berlioz, Rossini, and Alkan wrote railway music. Astringent idioms encouraged 20th-century composers to explore the railways' more mechanical aspects: Honegger's *Pacific 231* (1923), Villa-Lobos's engaging *Little Train of the Caipira* (1930), and several items of band music. Modern 'minimal-ism' finds inspiration in railways: Michael Nyman, *MGV* (1993). Much railway music remains light in character: Vivian Ellis's orchestral *Coronation Scot*; and up-tempo numbers like *Chattanooga Choo-Choo*, *Tuxedo Junction*, and *Daybreak Express*. Of the countless musical sound-tracks for films featuring trains, the documentary *Night Mail* (1936: Benjamin Britten), *Brief Encounter* (1945: borrowed from Rachmaninov), and *Murder on the Orient Express* (1974: Richard Rodney Bennett) may be instanced. PLS

P. L. Scowcroft, *Lines to Doncaster* (1986), 40; and 'Railways and British Music', *JRCHS*, 30 (1992), 378–9.

naming of locomotives is a practice as old as the locomotive itself, and followed the custom of naming horses, stage-*coaches, and ships. In the earliest days, names were descriptive or allusory *nicknames, the first recorded being that of *Trevithick's locomotive *Catch-me-who-can*, in 1808. Others, such as *Hedley's *Puffing Billy* (1814) and *Stephenson's *Rocket* (1829), have passed into folklore.

The development of repair records and capital accounting required unequivocal identification of locomotives. Most companies adopted numbers, and some also retained names, while some very small railways never used numbers. The *London Chatham & Dover Railway used only names until 1874, and the *Great Western Railway named but never numbered its broad-*gauge locomotives.

Names reflected the times in which they were chosen. In the 1840s, when steam locomotives were not regarded with universal affection, names were occasionally mocking (e.g. *Ghoul*, *Bat*, *Dwarf*) but more often were evocative of speed or power (e.g. *Gazelle*, *Meteor*, *Pegasus*, *Hercules*). Mid-Victorians recognized the benefits of careful naming, and celebrated places and people. Personal names came from ancient Greece and Rome, literature, military heroes, royalty, and directors of the company; place-names came primarily from towns and cities served by the railway. The latter practice was later abandoned by some railways when passengers mistook the names for destinations.

The early 20th century saw more ordered naming, with entire locomotive classes named on single themes. Some companies abandoned naming, but it was still used extensively by many major railways as well as *narrow-gauge and *industrial lines, which between them owned several thousand named locomotives.

The 1920s and 1930s produced more prosaic names: racehorses, regiments, castles, birds, counties, rivers, warships, nations of the empire, early locomotives, duchesses, and kings of England featured prominently.

*British Railways restricted naming to express passenger locomotives, with what had become traditional themes. Under the *Modernization Plan of 1955 an effort was made to maintain public interest in diesel locomotives before BR lost interest and abandoned naming. It was reintroduced in 1975, when the *Stephenson Locomotive Society persuaded BR to name a locomotive *Stephenson*.

Naming since then has been largely haphazard, for short-term publicity. Little glamour and impact has been obtained from naming engines after newspapers, television programmes, and trade associations, except for a class of freight locomotives named after mountains and famous Britons,

while some owners of preserved locomotives have impoverished naming as a reliable identification by allowing engines to masquerade as scrapped members of the same class, again for short-term publicity.

The commonest means of applying a name is by handpainting or by affixing a plate bearing raised letters. Early examples were often wooden, but metal plates with riveted or cast letters soon replaced them. New names are often unveiled with some ceremony; removed nameplates are collectors' items.

See also NAMING OF TRAINS.   AD

naming of trains. The first name given to a British train seems to have been the 'Irish Mail', officially so named on the opening of the *Chester & Holyhead Railway in 1848.

The title 'Flying Dutchman' was applied to the chief express from *London to *Exeter in or soon after 1849, taken from a horse that won the Derby and the St Leger; but this was a *nickname, not used by the *Great Western company itself. On the same railway other trains also received unofficial names, such as the 'Zulu', of 1879, the time of the Zulu War, and the 'Jubilee' in 1887.

The *East Coast companies' principal express from London to Edinburgh was known familiarly as the 'Flying Scotsman', or 'Flying Scotchman', at least by the 1870s. But again this was a railwaymen's nickname, passing into official use only under the companies' successor the *London & North Eastern in 1923.

Official naming of British trains was of two kinds. Most of the early names represented statements of fact. The 'Irish Mail' was self-explanatory. The 'Limited Mail' was a similar train running from *Euston to Scotland, the word 'limited' making it clear that the passenger seating accommodation was fixed, and that no extra carriages would be attached. Similarly, when the first all-*Pullman-car train began to run between London and *Brighton in 1881 its title was simply the 'Pullman Limited Express'.

The other kind of naming constituted an advertisement. The Granville Hotel at Ramsgate persuaded the *South Eastern Railway in 1876 and the *London Chatham & Dover in 1878 to run special trains from London for its guests. These were officially entitled 'Granville Special Expresses'. Then in 1889 the LCDR introduced a new and luxurious train between London and Dover in connection with an International Exhibition in Paris, which excited the interest of the public, who called it the *'Club Train', a name also used by the SER for a similar train. The Chatham company adopted it officially in 1891. Here was a nickname, coined elsewhere, taken over by a railway company in order to publicize a service.

These 'Club Trains' disappeared in 1893, and did not appear again until the turn of the century. In 1904 the GWR introduced a new train from Paddington to Falmouth and Penzance, a territory to which it had already applied the name the 'Cornish Riviera'. The train became the 'Cornish Riviera Express', forming part of the development of a fast-growing tourist business. In 1905 the *London & North Western and *London Brighton & South Coast Railways officially named their through train between *Liverpool, *Manchester, and Brighton the 'Sunny South Special'.

In Scotland the practice was confined to factual statement. In 1906 the *Highland company put on a 'Further North Express' running between *Inverness and Dornoch. The *Caledonian's 'Upper Ward Express' was a businessmen's service between Moffat and *Glasgow, later renamed 'The Tinto', after the hills past which it ran.

The *Big Four companies used naming to foster their competitive services. The 'Atlantic Coast Express' appeared on the *Southern in 1926. The morning *West Coast train from Euston became the 'Royal Scot' in the following year, the afternoon one bearing the absurd and meaningless appellation the 'Mid-day Scot'. Then came the streamlined high-speed trains of the 1930s. The LNER's 'Silver Jubilee' was the first, running between London and *Newcastle, in 1935, the 25th year of George V's reign, followed by two on the main Anglo-Scottish routes in 1937, the year of his son's coronation. The LNER took the best title possible, 'Coronation'. The LMS came out with another absurdity, 'Coronation Scot'.

The afternoon train from Cheltenham was named the 'Cheltenham Spa Express', but quickly became best known by its nickname, the 'Cheltenham Flyer'. In 1931 the GWR advertised it as 'the fastest train in the world', but the diesel 'Flying Hamburger' in Germany outdid it in 1933. The Southern's 'Golden Arrow' of 1929 was equally well-known: an all-Pullman *boat train from London to Dover, connecting with a similar service from Calais to Paris named 'La Flèche d'Or'.

The nationalized railways did not at first take to naming of their trains, but gradually some of the old names crept back, and others were added, mostly with regional associations: 'Golden Hind' and 'Armada', running to and from Plymouth for example, and 'Red Dragon' in Wales. A dreary succession of 'Executives' appeared from 1967 onwards—'Bradford Executive', Hull Executive', and so on.

A number of trains still bear names, such as the 'Cornish', 'Devon', and 'Wessex Scots', and the 'Highland Chieftain', although the only indications on the trains themselves are cheap-looking paper stickers on the windows.

Nothing has been said of *freight trains. A few of them bore the stiffest titles, like 'Conditional Scotch Goods'. But some had nicknames. The chief GWR trains between London and Exeter in the Victorian age were habitually known, for some reason, as the 'Flying Pig' and the 'Tip'. A BR

*container liner train carrying domestic refuse is appropriately nicknamed the 'Bin Liner'.

There was one group of named trains of great importance in World War I, that took coal from South Wales and personnel from Euston to Scottish naval bases (see WAR). Collectively, all these services were named 'Jellicoe specials' after the First Lord of the Admiralty. But those who used the passenger train had their own private name for it: 'The Misery'.   JS

C. J. Allen, *Titled Trains of Great Britain* (1954 edn.); A. A. Jackson, *Railway Dictionary* (1992); 'Flying Pig' and 'Tip': *LTW*, iv, 46.

narrow-gauge railways: in contemporary usage, railways with track narrower than standard *gauge (4 ft 8½ in), but originally used as the opposite of broad gauge (7 ft 0¼ in) promoted by I. K. *Brunel on the *Great Western Railway. This older meaning would normally be assumed in anything written before 1860 and did not become obsolete until *c*.1870.

Standard gauge came into being through George *Stephenson, who built his first public railways to the same gauge as his earlier mineral lines, thereby enabling him to test locomotives and equipment on existing track before delivery. These railways had a gauge of approximately 4 ft 6 in to suit wagons carrying 2–2½ tons of lump coal; elsewhere in Britain railways of narrower gauges could be found, likewise determined by local circumstances such as the density of the mineral being carried, the size of underground workings, etc. The actual gauge of an isolated railway was immaterial, and only if several railways were to be joined up to form a system was it necessary to define a common gauge. Narrow-gauge railways have thus existed side by side with standard gauge right from the beginning, but were of no more than local interest until the widely publicized conversion of the *Festiniog Railway to a steam-hauled public railway in 1865.

On a misrepresentation of the Festiniog's financial performance, it was then claimed that narrow gauge was inherently more efficient than standard gauge but few practical railwaymen were taken in. Others, however, realized that the FR had completely demolished the long-running argument over centres of gravity by operating locomotives and rolling stock far larger in relation to gauge than those which had been condemned as dangerously top-heavy by the low centre of gravity school only a few years previously. This showed that equipment of standard-gauge proportions could safely be employed on track of no more than 3 ft gauge, thereby giving the capacity and economic advantages of standard gauge on a railway that was cheaper and easier to construct in difficult terrain. Thus began the widespread use of 3 ft, metre, and 3 ft 6 in gauges in developing countries. So far as the British Isles were concerned, however, the only significant use of narrow gauge in this context was on the *Isle of Man and in remote parts of *Ireland.

British narrow-gauge railways may be divided into three groups: *industrial lines, public railways, and miniature railways. Of the first-mentioned, the earliest often adopted the gauge of an existing horse-worked line or sometimes an existing, informal local standard. Thus 2 ft 8 in gauge was popular in South Wales, 2 ft 3 in gauge in mid-Wales, and 2 ft gauge in North Wales. The building of main-line railways brought into being another variation, temporary lines of varying gauges being laid down by the larger contractors to aid spoil removal. These railways were portable only in the sense of being taken up and put down as needed, but in 1838 Henry Croskill of Beverley, east Yorkshire, introduced the first commercially available, prefabricated, portable railway equipment. Of 3 ft gauge, it employed iron-faced wooden track and hand-propelled wagons of no more than one ton capacity.

After 1850 small steam locomotives began to appear for use on the more substantial industrial railways and by 1862 Fletcher Jennings & Company of Lowca, west Cumberland, were advertising a range of standard locomotives for narrow-gauge track. The next logical development, in 1877, was the introduction of Paul Décauville's prefabricated all-metal track made in a range of popular, round-figure gauges both metric and Imperial. From then on, although many earlier gauges persisted, new lines were often laid to standard sizes such as 2 ft or 2 ft 6 in. Some builders held stocks of track and equipment in the popular sizes for prompt delivery, locomotives included, and this was used both for temporary and for permanent railways. It was quickly appreciated that a small railway was much more efficient than horses and carts (by a factor of about three to one in 1890) and many industrial lines had been laid by the outbreak of World War I (see also MILITARY RAILWAYS; WAR).

The industrial narrow-gauge railway went into decline after World War II, a process accelerated by rapid industrial change in the late 1950s onward. Contractors found that modern rubber-tyred off-road vehicles were more flexible and less labour-intensive than portable railways, permanent lines succumbed to lorries, and many new factories relied wholly on road transport. By 1990 narrow-gauge industrial lines survived principally on peat mosses, where no other form could be employed, in mines, and on *tunnelling contracts.

The first British public narrow-gauge lines were built to serve a particular local need for connection to a main-line railway or harbour, being in practice mineral railways that also carried passengers. Like contemporary industrial lines they reflected earlier local practice and employed rather small equipment. Subsequent railways were built from scratch with public operation in mind and employed larger, more substantial equipment. Few such lines were built, however, because the British railway system had become so complex that few places of any importance were far enough from a station to justify one. In any case, British railway legislation treated a short narrow-gauge line no differently from a main line until, first, the *Regulation of Railways Act, 1868, and, more positively, the *Light Railways Act in 1896, under which a simple railway could be authorized by the much simpler and cheaper procedure of an Order made under that Act.

Under the term 'minimum gauge', Sir Arthur Heywood (1849–1916) tried to popularize railways of 18 in or even 15 in gauge for handling very small traffic flows, for example connecting a large estate to the nearest railway station to carry about 10,000 tons per annum. A skilled engineer, he built a 15 in gauge railway on the hillside behind his home at Duffield Bank, near Derby, in order to develop and demonstrate his ideas which included six- and eight-coupled locomotives with flexible wheelbases. Only the Duke of Westminster took up his ideas, commissioning a line to connect Balderton station with Eaton Hall (near Chester), which was completed in 1896. Heywood's work was later to influence the development of miniature railways.

The dividing line between miniature and narrow-gauge railways is confused, but in general the former is a narrow-gauge railway of 15 in gauge or less built principally for the carriage of passengers for pleasure. Originally the term 'miniature' implied the use of locomotives that were scale or close to scale reproductions of full-size originals, as for example on the 15 in gauge *Romney Hythe & Dymchurch Railway, but it was also applied to the 2 ft gauge line in Wicksteed Park, Kettering, which used standard industrial railway equipment, making only minor modification to the outline of the locomotive to achieve a quasi-steam appearance. Today, however, there are 7¼ in gauge railways using purpose-built narrow-gauge equipment as large as that built a century earlier by Sir Arthur Heywood for 15 in gauge. The 7¼ in gauge is usually regarded as the narrowest suitable for ground-level operation—the width of a pair of feet, upon which that most unstable of animals, the human being, can normally remain upright without conscious effort. Narrower gauges are generally operated on elevated tracks with vehicles on which the passengers sit astride the track to ensure stability, but 5 in gauge ground-level tracks are not uncommon.   RW

Sir A. P. Heywood, *Minimum Gauge Railways* (1898).

nationalization. At the close of the 19th century the appearance of an embryo Labour Party revived interest in railway nationalization (see NATIONALIZATION, THE CONCEPT OF), a commitment to which was made at the party conference in 1908. But it was to be nearly 40 years before a Labour government possessed a majority sufficient to redeem that commitment, though Private Members' Bills for nationalization had been introduced each year in 1906–9 and in 1911; none had obtained a second reading.

In both world wars the railways came under direct government control, though retaining their company identity. After World War I the first Minister of Transport, Sir Eric *Geddes (a former senior railway manager), proposed and even began to plan for nationalization. However, in June 1920 the Cabinet decided otherwise and Geddes had to be satisfied with *grouping the main-line railways into the *'Big Four' companies, under the Railways Act, 1921.

Between the wars the financial position of the railways deteriorated, mainly though not exclusively owing to *road competition. During World War II the railways came again under government control and their post-war organization was discussed from time to time between ministers in the wartime national government, but no conclusion was reached before Labour came to office in July 1945 with a very large majority.

The new government decided to nationalize not merely the railways but virtually all public transport under a *British Transport Commission charged with 'integrating' the various forms of transport into a single public service. The Transport Act, 1947, was passed, despite strenuous opposition, to give effect to this concept. Despite the Bill's complexity, the provisions for nationalizing the railways were comparatively simple. The four grouped railways, and virtually all the minor railways as well, together with the London Passenger Transport Board (see LONDON UNDERGROUND RAILWAYS), were vested in the BTC on the appointed day, 1 January 1948. Railway stockholders received in exchange for their securities British Transport Stock, a charge on the revenues of the Commission, but with principal and interest at 3 per cent guaranteed by the Treasury. The basis of exchange was the average market price of railway stocks over the six months prior to the general election, or the price ruling immediately prior to the publication of the Transport Bill, whichever was the higher. *Private owners' wagons were compulsorily taken over, on a simple valuation formula annexed to the Act, based upon type, capacity, and age.

The railways, although vested in the BTC, were placed under an agent of the BTC called the Railway Executive, though the title of *British Railways came into immediate use for general purposes. Relations between the RE and the BTC were difficult from the outset; moreover, the trade unions expressed disappointment that the members of the RE were predominantly former railway managers; they had expected more participation. But most rank-and-file railwaymen (rather optimistically) assumed that a brighter future lay ahead and at midnight on 31 December 1947 the drivers of night trains sounded their whistles to celebrate the act of nationalization.   MRB

Gourvish; M. R. Bonavia, *The Nationalisation of British Transport* (1987); and *The Birth of British Rail* (1979); R. Kelf-Cohen, *Twenty-Five Years of Nationalization* (1969).

nationalization: the concept of. British railways developed as joint-stock companies, authorized by *Parliament but outside *government control, in strong contrast to continental railways where governments either owned them or participated in their management. Some people in Britain, however, wished to see the railways brought directly under the state. This article outlines the development of the idea up to 1945; for the actual process, see NATIONALIZATION; BRITISH RAILWAYS; and BRITISH TRANSPORT COMMISSION.

In 1836 James Morrison tried to get Parliament to take powers to revise the railways' tolls. Two years later the Duke of Wellington urged Melbourne's government to assert itself to guard the country against their 'monopoly and mismanagement'. Both were unsuccessful.

The first widely publicized plan for state purchase of the railways came from William *Galt in 1843, in his *Railway Reform*, prompting *Gladstone to include in his *Regulation Act, 1844, a government option, exercisable from 1865 onwards, to purchase any railway company sanctioned thereafter. The issue then died down until that time approached. In 1864 Galt revised his book, and in 1865 a Royal *Commission on Railways was charged, among other duties, with re-examining the issue of nationalization. Its conclusion was that nothing should be done in that matter.

Galt was by no means alone. Walter Bagehot wrote in the *Economist*: 'It is easy to show that the transfer of the railways to the state would be very beneficial, *if only it can be effected*' (original emphasis), and demonstrated how that might be done. Sir Rowland Hill thought much the same; so did S. R. Graves, the Liverpool shipowner and director of the *London & North Western Railway, and the Board of *Trade inspector Henry *Tyler. The only strong, dispassionate argument against the policy, disregarding railway companies' and shareholders' interests, was that it would set up a new kind of patronage, in the hands of politicians, as it was said to have done in Belgium.

The first important nationalization of any British industry occurred at this time: the government's purchase of the *telegraphs from private companies in 1868. It was later cited as a precedent for the railways, when it had produced striking benefits.

The strength of the idea increased late in the century. Even *Findlay, general manager of a great railway company, though he did not support it, demonstrated in 1889 just how such a measure could be equitably framed. By this time a new political force was emerging, the *trade unions. The Amalgamated Society of Railway Servants (later the *National Union of Railwaymen) declared in favour of state ownership of the industry in 1894. Early in the new century the growing Labour Party committed itself to railway nationalization. Current unrest in the industry, displayed in *strikes, illustrated the depth of feeling against some of the companies' policies. The railways themselves enjoyed little public popularity; and their power within Parliament was diminishing. The Liberal government appointed a Royal Commission to investigate railway nationalization in 1913, but World War I terminated its work.

The war itself revealed the country's total dependence upon the railways. The state assumed temporary control (see WAR), and in 1919 the government appointed Sir Eric *Geddes to prepare a Bill concerning transport, to include nationalizing the railways; but in 1920 it abandoned nationalization in favour of *grouping the private companies into four, implemented in the Railways Act, 1921.

The Conservative party, dominating politics between the wars, ensured that the issue was not revived; the only step in this direction was the formation of the London Passenger Transport Board (see LONDON UNDERGROUND RAILWAYS) in 1933. British railways again performed well in World War II. Then, with the return of a strong Labour government in 1945, nationalization became certain.   JS

M. R. Bonavia, 'Railways and Some Politicians, 1845–1945', *JRCHS*, 29 (1987); W. Bagehot, *Collected Works* (1965–86), x, 447; Findlay, 231–7.

National Railway Museum. This was established at York in 1972 as part of the Science Museum, London, and opened in 1975. Three people have headed it, each of whom writes an account of its development in his time: John Coiley (1975–92), Andrew Dow (1993–4), and Andrew Scott (1994 onwards).

The NRM is the world's largest railway *museum with more than 100 locomotives (including *Mallard*, the world's fastest steam locomotive), 150 carriages and wagons (not all at York), and large collections of artefacts ranging from signals and track to tickets and tableware, as well as an archive of mechanical engineering drawings, prints, paintings, posters, and photographs. By 1992 the museum covered some 16 acres and had received over 16 million visitors.

The idea of a National Railway Museum first emerged shortly after the opening of the Museum of British Transport at Clapham, London, in 1961–3. The *British Transport Commission, which had been responsible for the new museum, was abolished in 1962 and the *British Railways Board, which replaced it, concentrated on the business of operating the railway. With government support, it was agreed that responsibility for all the railway historical relics (and archives relating to relics) should be passed to the Department of Education and Science. A new museum, the National Railway Museum, would be created and run as a branch of the Science Museum, London. The terms of this arrangement were confirmed within the Transport Act of 1968. After much debate it was decided that the new museum, although national, should not be in London but in York. This was a central location, with a museum and tourist tradition and possessing a suitable site. The existing BR railway museums at Queen Street, York (opened in 1927), and Clapham would be closed and their collections transferred to the new museum. The railway collections established in the early 1960s at *Swindon (*Great Western Railway Museum) and *Glasgow (Transport Museum), with their strong regional content and run by local authorities, would remain, although much of the material at Swindon was on loan from the National Collection.

The site in York chosen for the NRM was the former motive power depot alongside the *East Coast main line, just west of the station. The necessary restoration and new building work was carried out by BR to a brief drawn up by the Science Museum's team of curators and designers in close collaboration with the railway. To provide overall guidance for the museum an NRM Committee (non-executive) was appointed in 1973, comprising leading representatives from the railway, museums, universities, and industry, who continue to advise today.

An important feature of the renovation work was the retention of the rail connection and the two working turntables, around which the locomotives and carriages were to be displayed, allowing large exhibits to be changed easily. The roof and floor were renewed and a wall built to separate the adjoining operational diesel depot. New construction included a lecture theatre, library, workshops, archive storage, and a number of other modern facilities. Major

display work provided a deepened inspection pit, so that visitors could walk underneath a locomotive, and the operation (by electric motor) of two early stationary winding engines. Most of the new exhibition was a considered display of the most important objects, large and small, from the former museums at York and Clapham, using the latest exhibition ideas and equipment, together with material recently acquired. New exhibits, specially selected, were a sectioned modern express steam locomotive with wheels and valve-gear driven by electric motor, and a *signalling and pointwork display capable of demonstration.

After the museum opened, work concentrated on a number of projects. First it was necessary to establish the educational and library services. Second, a start was made on sorting, recording, and photographing all collections. A restoration programme was also drawn up for the many stored locomotives and carriages so that they could be displayed and the balance of the collection on exhibition improved by the inclusion of more modern motive power, ordinary carriages, and freight vehicles. The museum also maintained one or two steam locomotives in working order for demonstrations and the occasional main-line special train, and provided historical exhibits, some operational, including specially commissioned working replicas of historic steam locomotives, for major railway anniversaries.

Funding for such restoration work was greatly assisted by the formation, in 1977, of the Friends of the National Railway Museum. As a charitable body the FNRM could accept donations from visitors and, especially after museum admission charges were introduced in 1987, organize fund-raising for specific projects. Access, by appointment, to an enlarged library continues to be free.

An early general objective for the museum was 'to illustrate and explain the history of railways and railway engineering in Britain from the beginning of the Industrial Revolution to the present day, including the impact on the social and economic life of the community and to look at probable future developments'. The museum's collecting policy supported this objective and was mainly concerned with broadening the content of the different collections and filling significant gaps. Notable acquisitions included post-1950s diesel and electric locomotives, a British-built steam locomotive from China representing the export activities of the British railway industry, more Royal saloons, a French-built Wagons-Lits car from the London–Paris 'Night Ferry' train reflecting international services to and from Britain, and signalling equipment.

The restoration work, together with new acquisitions (many from BR without any direct charges, under the terms of the 1968 Transport Act), created storage problems in York. These were exacerbated by the loss of storage on the railway despite co-operation with other museums and the railway *preservation movement which accepted objects on loan. Fortunately it was possible to purchase buildings suitable for storage next to the museum or nearby—a large goods shed in 1976, the diesel depot and workshops in 1982, and two further railway sheds in 1989. In addition to storage, the large goods shed, with its track and loading platforms, suggested a possible future exhibition, recalling a traditional *trainshed station with appropriate locomotives and carriages displayed, coupled together, alongside the platforms.

While this and other ideas for the future development of the museum were being considered, the roof of the main exhibition hall was condemned as from April 1990, owing to deterioration of its reinforced concrete beams. Rather than close the museum completely while repairs were made, it was decided to advance the opening of the large goods shed, first with a temporary exhibition 'The Great Railway Show' with the theme 'Travel by Train', and then, after minor adjustments, permanently. Furthermore, the condemned roof was to be replaced by a completely different design, allowing better viewing. Other improvements included an interactive centre, primarily for younger visitors.

The enlarged museum opened in 1992. It comprised the original building with the new roof, housing displays all concerned with 'Railway Technology', brought up to date with a segment of the *Channel Tunnel and a 'Eurostar' train exhibit. It was linked by a tunnel under the intervening road to the 'Travel by Train' exhibition in the large goods shed, the front of which had received a new main entrance (nearer the city centre and station) with a larger shop.   JAC

The enlargement, with the re-roofed original building aptly named the 'Great Hall', allowed a far greater proportion of the collections to be placed on display. In the following year this was increased further by the reopening of the mezzanine gallery in the Great Hall with displays of railway services, technology, and pictorial art. An audio-visual facility supplemented the refurbished lecture theatre.

On the floor of the Great Hall a popular innovation was the introduction of rolling stock displays to illustrate the modern railway. Items included a Mk 3 first-class saloon from the new East Coast fleet, a Kent Link Networker electric *multiple unit, a *merry-go-round coal hopper wagon complete with displays to show the system of delivery from mine to power station, new intermodal technology, and a Central Line tube train from *London Underground.

The Friends added a fresh dimension to the services offered to the visitor by providing volunteers for information points. Railway collectors were attracted to the museum by the institution of collectors' weekends, and these provided the curatorial staff with many contacts in specialist areas which have subsequently benefited the interpretation of the museum's collection.

The foundations for interpretation of the modern East Coast main line were laid by the inclusion of a viewing gallery in the plans for a replacement workshop and storage area necessitated by the condemnation of the old diesel depot in 1993.   AD

The NRM has two main roles: managing the nation's historic railway collection and encouraging a wider understanding of railways. The museum has entered its third decade by reviewing the way in which it meets these roles.

The reorganizations which led to the museum's creation preceded a period of ever-accelerating change in Britain's railways. During this period, the museum has rightly collected widely to preserve evidence of an industry in transition. It seems likely that the pace of collecting will reduce in the future, as emphasis shifts to ensuring high-quality care for the museum's collections and access to the information they contain.

The audience has also changed. Public expectations of what museums can offer have increased, and prior knowledge of railways is likely to be less than for earlier generations. To ensure that the museum serves the needs of new audiences, its displays will increasingly explore a broader story and, in particular, the part railways have played in shaping the world in which we live.

In 1995 the NRM moved to strengthen the academic and scholarly foundations upon which its work depends by establishing the Institute of Railway Studies as a joint venture with the University of York. The post of Head of Research at the museum is now linked to a chair in Railway Studies at the University and a growing programme of postgraduate courses and research work has commenced.

The NRM has rightly acquired a reputation as the primary centre for the interpretation of Britain's railway history. These new initiatives will ensure that it develops to meet the need of a wide range of users in the years to come.   AJS

J. Simmons, *Dandy-Cart to Diesel—The National Railway Museum* (1981); D. Jenkinson (ed.), *The National Railway Collection* (1988); P. Bignell, *Taking the Train—Railway Travel in Victorian Times* (1978); D. Jenkinson and G. Townend, *Palaces on Wheels—Royal Carriages at the National Railway Museum* (1981); *Guides to the National Railway Museum* (1975–94).

National Union of Railwaymen. The NUR started life in 1872 as the Amalgamated Society of Railway Servants. As a result of a merger with two other unions it became the NUR in 1913. When a merger took place with the National Union of Seamen in 1990 it assumed the name of the National Union of Rail, Maritime and Transport Workers (RMT).

The inaugural meeting of the ASRS was held in London in 1872 in propitious circumstances. There was a trade boom and a railway labour shortage; the Trade Union Act, 1871, ruled that no union was illegal merely because it acted in restraint of trade, and the new union was set in motion by willing outside helpers. M. T. Bass, one of the country's leading brewers, and MP for Derby, deplored the way in which the *Midland Railway, which carried half a million of his barrels annually, employed its servants for excessive hours of overtime. He gave financial support to the union, subsidized its newspaper, the *Railway Service Gazette*, and spoke on its behalf in Parliament. Dr Baxter Langley, a London lawyer, gave freely of his services as organizer and conciliator.

Until the late 1880s the ASRS was a friendly society-type union. In *The Railwaymen's Catechism*, which it published in 1875, *strikes were deplored as 'an evil to masters and men'. Members were recruited from the better-paid *guards, *drivers, and *signalmen, rather than from the poorly paid *porters and *platelayers. Lest they be victimized by the companies, they gave their branch name rather than their personal names when they attended the annual general meeting. The union's main concern was a limitation of the hours of work as a means of reducing the terrible level of *accidents. In 1875 some 767 railwaymen were killed, or one in every 334 employed. In 1882, at Darlington, the union staged an exhibition of improved wagon *braking, *coupling, and labelling systems which would have both saved the lives of shunters and expedited the movement of freight; but the companies were reluctant to incur the necessary expense. Another exhibition was staged at the Nine Elms goods yard in London in 1886 with a similarly disappointing result.

The years 1887–97 marked a turning point in the history of the union which, according to its General Secretary, Edward Harford, became 'a trade union with benefit funds, instead of being a friendly society with a few mutual protection benefits'. The change was led by branches in areas where the union was stronger: in the north-east, Scotland, and South Wales. The Darlington programme of 1887 included a ten-hour day (except in busy areas where it was to be eight); overtime pay at 1¼ normal rates, and a guaranteed weekly wage. In 1890 the annual general meeting adopted these demands as the first national programme. It was encouraged to make this decision by the success of the London dock strike of August 1889, and the increase in ASRS membership from 9,000 in 1885 to 26,000 in 1890. Only minor concessions in respect of hours of work and overtime rates were gained, but on the *North Eastern Railway in 1889 the directors met union representatives and agreed to resort to arbitration.

In 1880 Fred Channing MP succeeded M. T. Bass as spokesman for railwaymen's interests in the Commons. They were both Liberals. Two legal cases early in the 20th century changed the earlier complacency. In July 1901 the *Taff Vale Railway Company was awarded £23,000 damages against the ASRS for loss of business during the previous year's strike. This decision destroyed the previous belief that the 1871 Trade Union Act had brought immunity from prosecution. The conclusion was reached that the law had to be changed through the election of more Labour Representation Committee MPs. (An ASRS member, T. Steels, had moved the resolution at the 1899 Trade Union Conference which brought the LRC into existence.) In the general election of 1906, 30 Labour MPs were elected to a Parliament which passed the Trade Disputes Act of that year, restoring the rights of trade unionists. Another ASRS member, W. V. Osborne, prompted the 'Osborne Judgment' of 1909 which declared that union financing of political action, including the sponsoring of MPs, was illegal. This decision was overturned in the Trade Union Act, 1913.

Under pressure from the railway trade unions, the leading companies agreed in 1907 to the establishment of Conciliation Boards to discuss and, it was hoped, settle issues of pay and working conditions. They did not allay discontent resulting from a rising cost of living and the absence of full union recognition. All railway unions, except the Railway Clerks' Association (see TRANSPORT SALARIED STAFFS' ASSOCIATION), joined in the first national railway strike in August 1911 and found strength in unity. On 29 March 1913 the National Union of Railwaymen was formed through a merger of the ASRS with the General Railway Workers Union, founded in 1890 principally to organize the workshop staff and the poorly paid, and the United Pointsmen's and Signalmen's Society of 1880, a craft union organization. By the end of that year there were 267,611 members in the NUR. The leaders of the new organization believed that the best interests of all railway workers would be achieved through one big industrial union.

In World War I a Railway Executive Committee ran the railways under the government as a unit. For the first time the NUR faced one body with which to negotiate wages and working conditions. A labour shortage arose as a result of wartime enlistment, and the number of *women employed on the railways rose from 4,564 in 1913 to 55,000 in 1919. A series of flat-rate war bonuses was agreed.

In 1923–39 the *'Big Four' companies established under the Railways Act, 1921, experienced unstable business conditions arising from two trade depressions, the General Strike of 1926, and the emergence of *road motor vehicle competition. Wage cuts of 2s. in the £1 were imposed in 1930 and not fully restored until 1937, though their impact was mitigated by falling prices. The NUR recruited members from the 41 *bus companies acquired by the railways under powers given them in 1928.

During World War II another Railway Executive Committee negotiated directly with the unions. The burden of work increased as traffic was shifted from eastern to western areas of the country to minimize air raid damage. In the war period *freight traffic rose by 65 per cent and passenger miles increased by 77 per cent. However, the work-force, including an all-time maximum of 114,000 women, received an average pay rise of 60 per cent, more than offsetting a 29 per cent rise in the cost of living.

In the post-war period to 1951 the NUR was at the height of its influence, with a peak membership of 462,205 in 1947, some three times the combined membership of the other two railway unions. Besides railway workers, membership included bus, *hotel, and catering employees, railway shopmen, railway-owned *canal and inland waterway employees, and those who worked in railway-owned docks.

In 1952 NUR membership was nearly 400,000; by 1994 it had fallen to 70,000. In the first years of this decline, up to 1979 the *nationalized railways were kept under unified control, but the sale of the *British Transport Commission's Road Haulage Executive assets under the Transport Act, 1953, meant that the growing deficit of the railways could not be offset by the increasing profits of the RHE. The *Modernization Plan of 1955 aimed at restoring profitability by means of increased productivity; the *Beeching Plan of 1963 by cutting 5,000 route miles of the network; but they were unsuccessful at a time when motor car registrations increased from 2½ million in 1950 to 16 million in 1980. The NUR participated in productivity agreements and played a positive role in the introduction of modern technology. In 1978 it produced the 16-page booklet *Railway *Electrification*, urging more investment in this mode of traction. In 1985 BR proposed as an economy measure the abolition of passenger train guards on the St Pancras–Bedford line. The NUR, under Sydney Greene, proposed that guards should be given new duties as travelling ticket inspectors. The arbitrator ruled a six-month trial of the proposal. Half-way through, it was announced that although passenger numbers had not grown significantly, BR's revenue on the route had increased by £7,000 a week.

The trend of events from about 1870 to 1948 was towards railway consolidation, leading to eventual nationalization; from about 1980 this process was reversed in selling off railway assets, including hotels, in the early 1980s, leading to the establishment of 25 operating companies for *privatization under the Railways Act, 1994. These changes resulted in a substantial fall in NUR membership. Even more damaging to railway workers and the union was the reduction of the government's Public Service Obligation grant for socially desirable but unremunerative services from £1,070 million in 1963 to £500 million in 1990. This placed BR in a straitjacket and toughened its resistance to wage and salary demands. Whereas in the 1950s railworkers' incomes stood favourably with those in comparable occupations, the *Financial Times* commented on 8 April 1980 that 'Britain's railwaymen are Europe's lowest paid'. The NUR had to try to maintain recruitment in an industry whose management depended increasingly on short-term contracts, and no automatic deductions of union subscriptions from pay packets were permitted.

A few months after the Railways Act, 1994 (privatization), RMT won a victory in a signalmen's strike, gaining increased earnings and shorter hours, but inevitably its future was very dependent on political circumstances.

See also ASSOCIATED SOCIETY OF LOCOMOTIVE ENGINEERS AND FIREMEN; EMPLOYMENT; TRADE UNIONISM.   PSB

P. S. Gupta, 'Railway Trade Unionism, 1887–1900', *Economic History Review*, 19 (1960); P. S. Bagwell, *The Railwaymen*, i (1963), ii (1982); P. W. Kingsford, *Victorian Railwaymen* (1970).

navvies. The construction of the British railway network created a demand for labour which reached its peak in the Railway *Mania years of 1846–7 when it is estimated that at least 200,000 men were regularly at work on a profusion of new schemes. Although this period had no equal for the sheer volume of labour involved, the navvy could find employment in railway building somewhere in Britain in all of the 80 years preceding World War I, but this increasingly took the form of improvements to existing lines.

In view of their importance in the development of the Victorian economy, it is surprising that the wealth of official sources which have enriched our knowledge of the life and work of the factory operative and collier have no parallel for the activities of the *canal, dock, or railway navvy. In 1839 and 1840 Parliament ordered railways to produce a list of the injuries sustained by men in *construction work, and the first of 14 annual returns of men engaged in railway

building compiled to the instructions of the Board of *Trade appeared in 1847. But the solitary full-scale enquiry into navvy life and labour, the Select Committee on Railway Labourers of 1846, came into existence only after the appearance of a number of lurid reports on the physical and moral dangers faced by those building the trans-Pennine Woodhead Tunnel on the Sheffield Ashton-under-Lyne & Manchester Railway (see GREAT CENTRAL). This committee obtained evidence from engineers, *policemen, *contractors, railway missionaries, etc., but, in strong contrast to other enquiries into working-class life at the time, members of the group in question had an inadequate hearing since only three of them were called and they received a total of 171 questions out of the 3,115 put to all witnesses. Parliament then failed to legislate on recommendations for the protection of workers, and the chief importance of the enquiry rests on the cornucopia of information it collected from observers of navvy life and employment.

For the origins of railway construction labour the census returns are a necessary though by no means perfect source (see POPULATION, CENSUSES OF). Some of the first railway navvies had acquired their skills in canal building, but by the mid-1830s several of the country's trunk rail routes, notably the *Great Western, *Grand Junction, and *London & Birmingham, were coming into existence and the bands of canal 'navigators' became armies of railway navvies. The incentives of higher rates of pay and non-casual work that had decades before drawn men from the Essex countryside to the scene of Hugh McIntosh's excavations for the East India Dock Company now attracted agricultural labourers and men from declining handcraft trades on to railway contracts. According to the census returns, many lines obtained a large part of their labour from the inhabitants of the villages and towns of their regions, and in intensely rural parts of the country, such as south-western England and mid-Wales, the locality accounted for the overwhelming majority of railway builders. In the words of a leading contractor, Charles R. Hemingway, navvies 'were, on the whole, the pick of the agricultural districts through which the new railways were being made, both as regards physique and intelligence'. Irishmen could be found on railway contracts throughout Britain, but they played a significant role only in northern England, the west Midlands, and, above all, in the Border and Lowland regions of Scotland. Beyond these sources of labour, one type of railway builder made a contribution out of proportion to his numbers; he was the professional, itinerant, or 'true' navvy. A census enumerator in 1841, for example, found men from the Midlands and Yorkshire at work on the *South Eastern Railway in Surrey. These people tramped the country in search of railway employment or followed a contractor from one job to another as trusted members of his work-force. Some had acquired one of the many skills that were essential for railway construction—those of the carpenter, miner, mason, blacksmith, etc.—and they were an especially large proportion of the labour force in sparsely populated districts or where the attractions of well-paid employment in industry reduced local participation. All the above groups became navvies, for a season or a lifetime, without the use of any formal and frequently used recruiting machinery on the part of prospective employers, and regular shortages of labour occurred only in the summer with the arrival of the counter-attraction of harvest work.

The extensive temporary encampments of workers, such as that in the 1870s at Ribblehead on the *Midland Railway's *Settle & Carlisle line, which have been the source of much navvy legend and innumerable anecdotes, mostly relating to squalid living conditions and civil disorder, were a comparatively rare feature of railway building. They sprang up in thinly populated parts of the country or where very heavy concentrations of labour, for example for *tunnel building, made *ad hoc* accommodation necessary. Thus a large collection of huts existed above Box Tunnel (GWR) in 1840. According to the census returns, railway workers usually lodged with the resident population and so created a new source of income to offset the upheaval which inevitably accompanied an influx of visitors; the majority of married men lived with their families and rented separate premises. Far from being social pariahs, navvies were often in some respects well integrated into the local community.

The navvy's reputation for brutality began in the age of canal building and was reinforced by the explosions of violence which occurred on some railway contracts, notably those of the *North Midland Railway in the 1830s and, later, of the *Lancaster & Carlisle and Edinburgh–Hawick lines, and involved the use of the military to restore order (see RIOTING). Lewes Gaol was full of navvy prisoners in the early 1840s during the construction of the London & Brighton Railway (see LONDON BRIGHTON & SOUTH COAST). However, the incidence of navvy crime is not the same throughout the country; the court records of the West Riding of Yorkshire and of five southern English counties during periods of intense building reveal that in these areas at least the navvy made no significant contribution to the calendar of indictable crime heard by assizes and quarter sessions. The majority of navvy prisoners appeared before petty sessions, the lowest of the criminal courts, charged with minor theft, assault without weapons, pugilism, and, above all, the offence which rose in the entire population during times of prosperity, drunkenness. Those with the responsibility for keeping the peace, chiefly the magistrates, deplored the bad example the navvies set for the indigenous population, but their apprehension was generally directed more towards the rising costs of administering the law than the possibility of serious disorder. The increase in misdemeanours which came with railway building clashed with the drive which had gathered considerable force by mid-century towards greater decorum in public behaviour and a 'respectable' Victorian society (see PRIZE-FIGHTING).

Against the picture of the turbulent and 'masterless' navvy must be set the loyalty which he showed towards enlightened and highly regarded contractors, such as Samuel Morton *Peto and Stephen Ballard, and his generous response to appeals for help from destitute fellow workers.

Violence could be his reply to those employers who failed to adopt and enforce even the most simple precautions against accidents, and so by wanton neglect added to the heavy toll of life and limb in railway building. It could be the reaction to contractors such as Edwin Warden and Robert Gale and their successors at Mickleton Tunnel on the Oxford Worcester & Wolverhampton Railway (see WEST MIDLAND RAILWAY) who, instead of paying in cash, first operated the truck system and thus depreciated wages by issuing tickets for over-valued goods in their tommy shop, and then failed to pay the men at all. Savage circumstances made savage men.

By the 1880s, the end of the heroic age of navvying, the time of the creation of the great main lines with minimal assistance from machinery had passed, and henceforth railway projects were rarely extensive and sometimes outnumbered by a wide range of reservoir, dock, and drainage schemes. Many British navvies elected to leave for work abroad, as they first did in the 1840s when Thomas *Brassey took them to France. At home, the principal organization which came into existence for their benefit, the Navvy Mission Society (founded in 1877), provided many services, including assistance for the impecunious and injured, and intelligence on the availability of work. Civil engineering contracting was now more than ever the province of major businesses which valued their best workers, provided them with decent living and leisure facilities on the contracts, and even subscribed to a pension fund for retired men.   DB

D. Brooke, *The Railway Navvy* (1983); and 'The "Lawless" Navvy. A Study of the Crime Associated with Railway Building', *JTH*, 3rd ser., 10, 2 (1989), 145–65; T. Coleman, *The Railway Navvies* (1965); G. Y. Hemingway, *The Hemingway Masons and Contractors from Dewsbury and Their Associates*, typescript (undated), 673, Huddersfield Central Library; Select Committee on Railway Labourers, PP, 1846, xiii; D. Sullivan, *Navvyman* (1983).

Neath & Brecon Railway. Having taken over the powers of two unsuccessful companies, this one opened its line throughout (72 miles long) in 1867–73. It could never look for any substantial passenger traffic, serving no towns at all between its termini. The largest parish, Devynock, had 1,800 people, spread over 29,000 acres. Coal passed over the line from Neath and the Dulais valley, but not enough to bring in any secure revenue, and the company went into receivership in 1873. In 1877 expenditure exceeded receipts by 238 per cent.

However, the big *Midland Railway was determined at this time to forge a route for itself from *Birmingham and Hereford to *Swansea by the acquisition of *running powers over other companies' lines, including the N&BR. Through passenger services between Birmingham and Swansea began in 1877, provided by the Midland. The N&BR could now concentrate its attention on the southern end of its line, where the coal traffic could be made profitable. In 1922 the N&BR became a subsidiary company of the *Great Western. Through passenger services from Hereford to Swansea continued until 1931, those to Neath until 1962. The line from Neath still remains in use for freight traffic as far as Onllwyn.

The route traversed a landscape of singular grandeur and charm, and discerning travellers admired it greatly. Adelina Patti, the celebrated Italian soprano singer, bought Craig-y-Nos castle in 1878, providing a private waiting room for herself and her numerous guests at Penwyllt station, which was renamed Craig-y-Nos.   JS

Reg. Hist., xii, 199, 204, 207–9; Murray's Handbook for South Wales (1877 edn.), 123–6.

Neele, George Potter (1825–1921), manager. Born in London, educated there and at Walsall Grammar School, Neele entered railway service with the *Eastern Counties company in 1847; he was chief clerk, *South Staffordshire Railway, in 1849–61; superintendent of the line, *London & North Western Railway, in 1862–95.

Although an efficient and conscientious officer, who managed his company's passenger business well and also contributed to the work of the *Railway Clearing House, he is remembered chiefly for his book Railway Reminiscences (1904). This summarizes his working life, year by year, sometimes critically: speaking, for example, of the LNWR's bad safety record in the early 1870s and condemning its notorious chain-brake (see BRAKES), while defending the company loyally wherever he could.

But his book has another value too. The LNWR arranged Queen Victoria's journeys (usually four a year) between England and Scotland, and Neele was in charge of the train, under the general manager, continuously from 1863 to 1895. He describes these journeys in detail (see ROYAL TRAVELLING). His record remains unique, for nobody else had the same experience. It helps to illuminate the machinery of Victorian politics.   JS

Neele's own copy of his Reminiscences is in PRO RAIL 114/62, with his unpublished additions and corrections. These are drawn upon in the 1974 edition.

network, see SYSTEM, DEVELOPMENT OF THE.

Network SouthEast, see BRITISH RAILWAYS.

Newcastle & Carlisle Railway. Various plans were considered from 1794 onwards for building a canal across England from Tyne to Solway, producing only the little Carlisle Canal at the west end, opened in 1823. A company was authorized to make a railway instead in 1829. Several engineers contributed to planning it, including William *Jessop. Its execution was entrusted to Francis *Giles.

The promoters encountered pertinacious opposition from some *landowners, and the Act forbade the use of locomotives on it. That provision being disregarded when the first section of the line was opened in 1835, one landowner secured an injunction against the company, whereupon it stopped all services for ten weeks, and his resistance collapsed. The whole line was completed in 1839.

It had some notable engineering features: very fine stone bridges at the western end, and the big, elegantly handled Cowran cutting, 2,270 ft long and up to 110 ft deep. The credit for the design of these works belongs to Giles, but he

neglected his duties in favour of other railways and was eased out in 1834 in favour of his able assistant John Blackmore.

The company soon came to encourage special kinds of traffic by offering reduced fares to *markets, and wrestling matches and *horse races. It seems indeed to have been the first British railway that made any sustained and effective attempt to address the public by means of handbills and *posters (see PUBLICITY).

In 1848 the company was leased by George *Hudson on behalf of the *York Newcastle & Berwick Railway, but that company rejected the arrangement and the NCR regained its independence in 1850. The *North Eastern Railway (the combine into which the YNBR entered in 1854) repeatedly tried to lease or purchase the NCR, but did not succeed until 1862, when Parliament authorized the merger.

The NCR built only one important branch, to Alston (1852), but it was joined near Hexham by the Border Counties line running down from Riccarton in Scotland, completed under the *North British Railway in 1862.

Conservatively managed in its later years, the NCR was by then in some respects old-fashioned. That perhaps benefited the shareholders, who in 1839–62 received an average dividend of 4.7 per cent.

Among all the important English railways built before 1850 the NCR has been the least altered. A journey along it is a rewarding and memorable experience.   JS

Tomlinson; J. S. MacLean, Newcastle & Carlisle Railway (1948); G. Whittle, Newcastle & Carlisle Railway (1979).

Newcastle and Gateshead. These two ancient towns face each other across the River Tyne from different counties (Northumberland and Durham), with separate administrations until 1974. Both were important centres of the coal trade. Horse-worked railways were spoken of at Gateshead in the 1690s; they were in use at Newcastle early in the 18th century.

The first locomotive-worked railway to serve these towns was the *Newcastle & Carlisle, opened from Carlisle to Redheugh, a suburb of Gateshead, in 1837, passengers and freight being ferried across the Tyne to a temporary station outside Newcastle. Two years later the NCR bridged the river to a station there, and extended by connecting railways into Gateshead itself. In 1844 the *Great North of England and Newcastle & Darlington Junction Railways (see YORK NEWCASTLE & BERWICK) supplied a through route from York and the south to Gateshead, prevented from reaching Newcastle by the very deep gorge of the Tyne. A long, lofty, and expensive *bridge was required to link the two towns at any sufficient height. The railway companies, prompted by their chairman George *Hudson, agreed in 1844 to finance a double-deck bridge carrying trains above and road vehicles beneath. The only old bridge across the river was at a very low level, reached on both banks by steep and crooked streets. When Robert *Stephenson's High Level Bridge was fully completed in 1850 (having cost £½million), it instantly improved the daily lives of many people in Newcastle and Gateshead. Some of them recognized that they owed this

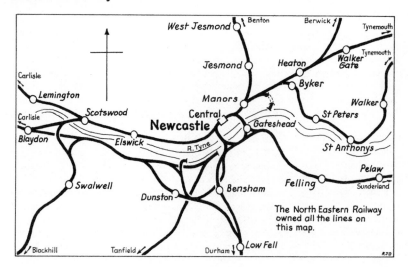

Newcastle upon Tyne, 1922

great benefit most of all to Hudson, and were grateful to him.

The opening of the bridge to rail traffic in 1849 put Newcastle on to the *East Coast main line from London to Scotland. The city got a new Central *Station (opened in 1850) which also accommodated the former Newcastle & North Shields suburban line. It was a building of great distinction, owed to Stephenson again and to the *architect John *Dobson.

All this railway development coincided with the notable reconstruction of central Newcastle under Thomas Grainger. When the station *hotel was added in 1854, railways had made a great contribution to its amenity and improvement; perhaps larger than anywhere else in Britain.

But railways brought no comparable benefit to Gateshead. A tangle of viaducts near the centre of the town was required to carry the lines through it. In 1844 the NDJR established locomotive repair *works there. Ten years later, when the *North Eastern Railway was formed in 1854 they became its principal locomotive headquarters, where about 1,000 engines were built until 1910, when the works were removed to Darlington. All this made the centre of Gateshead a pandemonium of noise, heavily polluted by smoke.

Gateshead had two stations: East, for trains to Sunderland; West, on the main line to York—but scarcely any long-distance trains called there. Passengers for stations beyond York had to drive or trudge into Newcastle to take a train that sailed through their West station without stopping. No attention whatsoever was paid by the NER board to numerous requests from the Gateshead town council for better services. The company always treated the town (in which it was the largest employer of labour) with contempt. After successfully electrifying its Newcastle suburban system in 1904, the NER never extended it to the lines south of the Tyne.

The NER's monopoly of railway services in Newcastle

was broken in 1864 when the *Blyth & Tyne Railway ran into a terminus at Picton House. But though its management was enterprising, that of the port of Blyth was not, and its business soon declined, allowing the NER to purchase it in 1874.

One operational handicap remained at Newcastle. All trains continuing northwards or southwards had to reverse in Central station. This became increasingly troublesome as the traffic mounted, and a second bridge, the King Edward VII Bridge west of the first one, was opened in 1906, allowing trains to run through the station without reversal.

Only two other important changes have been made to the system since then: the construction of the Tyne & Wear Metro from 1980 onwards (see LIGHT RAPID TRANSIT SYSTEMS), partly occupying former *BR tracks, providing Gateshead at last with a frequent electric service to Newcastle, crossing the Tyne by another new bridge; and *electrification of the East Coast main line in 1991.　　JS

Tomlinson; *Reg. Hist.*, iv; S. Middlebrook, *Newcastle* (1950); F. W. D. Manders, *History of Gateshead* (1973).

Newcomen Society for the study of the history of engineering and technology. Named after Thomas Newcomen, inventor of the first satisfactory steam, or 'atmospheric', engine, the society was founded in 1920, since when it has become a leading learned body in this field. A world-wide membership ranges from practising engineers to historians, industrial archaeologists, and academics, and interests span from the ancient civilizations to the present-day age of electronics, including water supply, construction techniques, mechanical and electrical engineering, transport, communications, and prime movers. It promotes and co-ordinates studies into the relationship between technology and society, and holds regular lecture meetings at its headquarters at the Science Museum, London, and several provincial centres. The society's most valuable contribution to historical research lies in its annual *Transactions*, containing published papers which are recognized as authoritative works in their fields, a number of which are concerned with railways. Annual residential summer meetings are held in Britain and abroad, and a monthly members' *Bulletin* contains news, short articles, and authoritative book reviews.   GJB

Newhaven, see PORTS AND DOCKS.

newspaper traffic. Newspapers were on sale at railway stations at least as early as 1839 (see STATION TRADING), but they were being conveyed to the newsagents by train earlier than that. The *Liverpool & Manchester made two agreements for this purpose in 1831.

The trunk lines offered very much faster distribution than the coaches. As soon as the *Grand Junction Railway opened in 1837 Mansell & Co. entered into arrangements with it and the *London & Birmingham (still then under construction) for the handling of newspapers to and from *Liverpool, *Manchester, *Birmingham, and *London. But a much bigger man was now entering this business. The first W. H. Smith, who had been using 'express coaches' to get London newspapers into the provinces, rapidly perceived the capabilities of the railways, and by 1850 nearly all his deliveries to the larger towns went by rail.

This was a serious threat to the provincial daily newspapers. The London papers soon came to be on sale in many of these towns in the morning, not long after those published locally, and with later news than theirs. The provincial press was rescued, however, from 1850 onwards by another new invention (closely associated with railways), the electric *telegraph, which enabled it to receive the latest news within a few minutes of its arrival in London. The competition between the London and provincial papers now became one of quality. Moreover, the provincial papers could, by using the railways, find their own London market in the morning. Before long the *Manchester Guardian* was beginning to make its mark there as an organ of liberalism.

Once established, the railways' newspaper business grew without interruption. By 1861, in the small hours of every weekday, six tons of *The Times* were being carried out of London by rail, carts clattering through the streets towards the stations up to the last minute before departure. There Smiths' men were waiting to handle the papers into the trains, where they were sorted for distribution *en route* much as the *mails were in the travelling post offices. *Acworth described the process in interesting detail in 1889.

The railways and their customers alike were concerned to foster this business. The newspaper proprietors and their distributors were now altogether dependent on the railways' services. On the other side, the traffic formed a useful component of the companies' revenue. Just how large it was can only be guessed, for the newspaper traffic was included with that of *parcels in their *returns. 'Because of the regularity, certainty, and economy of packing, newspapers represented "the commodity *par excellence*" for the railways.'

They started to run newspaper trains out of London, sometimes with just a very few passengers. In 1875 The *Times* attempted to persuade the *London & North Western Railway to provide a train solely for copies of its papers; but the *Standard* heard of the proposal and got it stopped, partly it seems through Smiths' influence. There were at least three newspaper trains, running from *Euston, *Paddington, and *King's Cross by 1876. In 1899 the new *Great Central Railway secured what the LNWR had been refused in 1875: a 2.30 a.m. train from *Marylebone to Manchester, chartered by the *Daily Mail* to bring its latest news from the Boer War.

This business remained with the railways well into the 20th century. Smiths' diverted some of theirs to motor vans during World War I, and turned to them more after the railways' brief paralysis in the General *Strike of 1926. In 1934 it formed a subsidiary company to handle its motor transport. But it was not until 1961 that the firm could be said to reckon motor transport as a 'new and dynamic factor which promised, or threatened, an impact on distribution arrangements comparable with that of the early railways'.   JS

C. Wilson, *First with the News: The History of W. H. Smith, 1792–1972* (1985: final quotation, p. 396); VR, ch. 10; Acworth, 80–3; 'commodity *par excellence*': Bagwell, 118; *The Times* and *Standard*: G. P. Neele, *Railway Reminiscences* (1974 edn.), 205; *Daily Mail*: Dow, ii, 340.

nicknames. (See also NAMING OF TRAINS.) Like many other employees of large organizations—the armed forces, for example; the police, the boatmen on canals—railwaymen used nicknames freely, attached to buildings, the appliances they handled, and the discipline imposed on them at work. The origins of most of these words and phrases are clear enough, but some remain mysterious.

Only one writer, Frank McKenna, has published any good and well-organized lists of these nicknames. His relate mainly to the third quarter of the 20th century.

They might have purely local associations. The pole supplied to men coupling and uncoupling wagons in the process of *shunting was always called a 'stick'. Many efforts were made to produce devices counteracting the dangers in its use. Among these was the 'Newcastle hook', which was fixed to the stick, allowing the attachment and detachment to be made from the side of the wagon, not by ducking underneath its buffers. Newcastle was the place where it was introduced.

Some parts of large stations acquired nicknames. A double-sided platform at *Euston was erected about 1840 to accommodate trains passing to the *Midland Railway, which carried them on to *York. Long after that traffic had ceased, and the two platform faces had been officially numbered 9 and 10, the staff continued to call it 'the York'. At *Waterloo substantial additions were made to the station in 1878 and 1885, immediately nicknamed after current political events 'Cyprus' and 'Khartoum', and they kept those names for many years.

Goods shunting-yards sometimes acquired curious nicknames. One group opened by the *London Brighton & South Coast Railway at New Cross in 1880 was at once unofficially called 'Ballarat', after the Australian gold-rush of that time. Another, at Norwood in a district isolated from all amenities, became known as 'Teetotal Sidings'.

The Stock Exchange attached its own names to the railway companies' shares. Those of the *Great North of Scotland Railway were 'Haddocks'.

Locomotives attracted many nicknames. Those built at Darlington for the *North Eastern Railway were called 'Quakers', with a reference back to the *Stockton & Darlington company and the *Pease family. The 4-4-0s of the 1265 class were always known as 'Ginx's Babies', from some connection (but what?) with a satire on sectarian education written by J. E. Jenkins and published in 1870.

Many of these nicknames were wry or derogatory. Classes of engines heavy on coal, for instance: the *Great Eastern Railway 2-4-2Ts known as 'Gobblers'; on the *London Midland & Scottish the 'Royal Scots', called 'the Miners' Friends'; and the voracious Garratts (until they were equipped with automatic firing machinery) were 'Birth Controllers' for the firemen. On the other hand, the *Lancashire & Yorkshire Railway had a set of locomotives that gained a nickname from pure affection. George *Hughes's five 0-8-2 tank engines (1908) were large machines, designed for banking trains up very steep inclines (Accrington–Baxenden, for instance) and for shunting. Grateful drivers called them 'Little Egberts', after a circus troupe of performing elephants.

Nicknames were occasionally bestowed on individual locomotives. The *North British Railway's 4-4-0 No. 224 that fell into the Tay with its train when the bridge collapsed in 1879 (see ACCIDENTS) was later rescued from the river bed, repaired, and remained in service for another 40 years. The men called it 'The Diver'. No. 16 of the *Midland & South Western Junction Railway was a 2-6-0 freight engine built in 1897, a powerful puller that sometimes showed a turn of speed. She was known as 'Galloping Alice'.

The particular appearance or characteristics of certain locomotive classes could give rise to nicknames. For instance, the prominent continuous splashers on the *London & South Western T14 class 4-6-0s produced the nickname 'Paddleboxes'; Hughes's 2-6-0s on the LMS were called 'Crabs', deriving from the crawling-like movement of their outside motion; and the name 'Black Fives' for the same company's large stud of class 5 mixed traffic 4-6-0s came from the colour they were painted.   JS

F. McKenna, *The Railway Workers* (1980), ch. 8; *VR*, 186; 'Newcastle hook': E. B. Ivatts, *Railway Management at Stations* (5th edn., 1910), 552; *Great North of Scotland Railway* (Stephenson Locomotive Society, 1954), 317.

Nine Elms, see WORKS.

Nock, Oswald Stevens (1904–94), engineer and author. Nock's working life was spent with the *Westinghouse Brake & Signal Company, latterly as CME, giving him unlimited opportunities for rail travel at home and overseas. Indeed, he proudly claimed to have ridden on nearly every railway in the world. His knowledge was prodigious, and he numbered many notable engineers among his friends.

Nock's name will always be associated with his prolific writings. He produced over 140 books—more than any other railway author—principally on engineering, operating, and rolling stock, both British and foreign, including several biographies.

Included in nearly 1,000 magazine articles was a long-running series in the *Railway Magazine* on locomotive practice and performance, in succession to Cecil J. *Allen. This, and signalling, were his specialities, permeating much of his writing, and leading to a certain imbalance when he attempted company histories, of which he wrote a number. A man of many parts and immense energy, his interests extended to archaeology, astronomy, painting, and music.

GJB

O. S. Nock, *Another Facet of an Autobiography* (1993); *The Times*, 8 Oct. 1994.

noise, see POLLUTION.

Nokes, A. G., see SEKON, G. A.

Norfolk Railway. An amalgamation, formed in 1845, of the Yarmouth & Norwich Railway, opened in 1844, with the Norwich & Brandon, which at Brandon met another line (part of the *Eastern Counties Railway) from London via Cambridge, both opened simultaneously in 1845. Robert *Stephenson and G. P. *Bidder were engineers for all these lines. On completion of the Trowse bridge at *Norwich they formed a 123-mile trunk route. The NR also built branches to Lowestoft and Fakenham, opened in 1847–9, making its own system 95 miles long.

The Yarmouth & Norwich was the first railway, other than the uniquely worked *London & Blackwall, to be equipped from the outset with the electric *telegraph, which the NR continued to Brandon. The NR's management was bold and enterprising, but accidents revealed that it was somewhat careless. The ECR leased it in 1848 (without Parliament's sanction); matters then grew much worse, until a large physical reconstruction was undertaken in 1856–7. The NR and ECR passed into the *Great Eastern Railway in 1862.   JS

C. J. Allen, *Great Eastern Railway* (1955); *Reg. Hist.*, v.

Normanton, see JUNCTIONS; MANCHESTER & LEEDS RAILWAY.

North American relationships. In the USA, primitive forerunners of the railway served as adjuncts to quarrying and mining; but the very idea of the railway, as an instrument for conveyance of public traffic over specialized tracks, was an import from Britain. Close attention was paid in the USA to developments on the *Liverpool & Manchester Railway—the *Rainhill trials were reported daily in a Boston newspaper; 'just about every major engineer associated with early US railroad construction . . . consulted with the *Stephensons in England' (J. H. White); and its *gauge was generally adopted. About 120 locomotives were imported from England in 1829–41. But conditions were so different that sharp divergencies of practice soon appeared, principally due to lightness of construction—the Americans did not invest in substantial works before traffic grew to demand them. Low axle-loads for lightly laid, unfenced tracks (running down the main streets of some cities) were beginning by 1840 to lead to differences in technical and business development that made *Acworth declare in 1891: 'In every single item, from baggage checks to bogie trucks, American railways differ from English much as cheese does from chalk.'

Britain made important contributions to the great expansion of American railroads after the Civil War, providing capital amounting to 15–20 per cent of railroad stocks in the 1890s, and rails, mostly from Wales, culminating in the years 1871–81. British capital and management controlled the Grand Trunk Railway in Canada. Dickens, Trollope, and the actress Fanny Kemble recorded their impressions as travellers; Douglas Galton reported officially to the Board of *Trade on American railways in 1857; railway directors and officers toured American railroads—G. P. *Neele, *London & North Western Railway, in 1881; Sam *Fay, *London & South Western Railway (1900); Herbert *Walker, LNWR (1902). George *Gibb, *North Eastern Railway, having studied US railroad management in 1901, introduced ton-mileage *statistics to British railways.

Some American material crossed the Atlantic. Nineteen bogie locomotives were supplied by Norris of Philadelphia to the *Birmingham & Gloucester Railway in 1840; without much success. Eighty 2-6-0s with bogie tenders were bought from Baldwin of Philadelphia by the *Midland, *Great Northern, and *Great Central Railways in 1899–1900; they had short lives. A few *narrow-gauge engines came from Baldwin, beginning with one for the Lynton & Barnstaple Railway in 1899. *Pullmans—sleeping, 'parlour', and dining cars with bogies and clerestory roofs—were imported, first for the Midland (1874), then the GNR and *London Brighton & South Coast Railway (1875), and for the *Highland Railway (1885). The *Westinghouse compressed-air brake was adopted by several important British companies. High-capacity freight *wagons and automatic *couplers were investigated but not adopted. *Track circuiting, and pneumatically operated, then electric, signals were gradually taken up in Britain, notably on the *London Underground, with its American financial backing (see YERKES, CHARLES TYSON) and technology (where the words 'car' for 'carriage' and 'truck' for 'bogie' became normal usage). Two outstanding American managers were brought over—Albert Stanley (Lord *Ashfield) to the Underground in 1907 and Henry *Thornton from the Long Island Railroad to the *Great Eastern in 1914. Locomotive *wheel notation devised by the American F. M. Whyte in 1900 was immediately adopted in Britain.

In World War I the British railways handled Canadian and US forces traffic from their own resources; but in the second it was beyond them unassisted, and by early 1944, some 400 US locomotives were taking their part in the British build-up to D-Day. US forces operated their own large depots and carried out erection and maintenance of railway equipment. American and British railwaymen were thrown together in most theatres of war and had to learn each other's terminology and outlook, which had diverged widely over the century in which they had been operating in what seemed like different worlds.

See also OVERSEAS RAILWAYS, BRITISH INFLUENCE ON; EUROPEAN RELATIONSHIPS.   RMR

C. F. Adams, *Railroads: Their Origin and Problems* (1878 edn.); W. M. Acworth, *The Railways and the Traders* (1891); C. F. Dendy Marshall, 'British Locomotives in North America', *Two Essays in Early Locomotive History* (1928), 89; D. R. Adler, *British Investment in American Railways 1834–1898* (1970); J. H. White, Jr., *A History of the American Locomotive: Its Development 1830–1880* (1979); and *The American Railroad Freight Car* (1993).

North British Railway. This company was first promoted in 1842 in the wake of the opening of the *Edinburgh & Glasgow, to build an *east-coast line south from *Edinburgh to Dunbar and Berwick. Despite the promoters offering dividends of 8 per cent, it proved difficult to raise the necessary finance in Scotland. English money came to the rescue, George *Hudson inducing the *York & North Midland Railway to invest £50,000 to create an east-coast route to *Scotland. The North British Bill was passed in 1844 and work began shortly afterwards.

The standard of construction varied: that for the Cockburnspath section was particularly ill-done, the *contractors having alienated their *navvies by the use of the truck system, which led to riotous pay days. Although the line was opened in 1846, within three months floods had washed away many of the poorly built bridges and embankments, despite which the NBR pushed on with building branch lines to Duns, North Berwick, and Hawick, the last of which pointed towards *Carlisle, forming the Waverley route, finally opened in 1862. It even invaded England, securing *running powers from Newcastle to Hexham in return for allowing the *North Eastern Railway to work its east coast expresses over the 57 miles of NBR track from Berwick to Edinburgh.

The company's inefficient operations and meagre dividends in the 1850s made it a favourite target of the press and disgruntled customers. But under a new chairman, Richard *Hodgson, things appeared to have been improved, not least with the acquisition of the Edinburgh & Glasgow against fierce opposition from the *Caledonian, thereby opening up the west to the NBR. A new company secretary, however, noticed some financial irregularities: a formal enquiry showed that the accounts had been falsified for years in order to pay the dividends Hodgson felt were necessary, and he was forced to resign. Shares plummeted, and discussions were opened in 1871 with the CR by the new chairman, John Stirling of Kippendavie, with a view to an amalgamation, but the shareholders would have none of it. What helped to revive the company's fortunes was the completion in 1876 of the *Midland Railway's *Settle & Carlisle line which allowed a through service from *St Pancras to Edinburgh. To work the greatly increased Anglo-Scottish traffic, the NBR's locomotive superintendent, Dugald *Drummond, designed a very successful class of 4-4-0 express engine.

Competition with the Caledonian, which was to recruit Drummond in 1882, remained a key feature of the NBR's existence, the two companies fighting each other over control of Fife and its coal; services from the south to *Aberdeen, culminating in the races of 1895 (see RACES TO SCOTLAND); suburban services in the *Glasgow area—the CR's home territory; and the provision of great *hotels, a contest which the NBR won hands down with its impressive building next to Waverley station, Edinburgh. It was completed in 1902, its huge clock tower quickly becoming a distinctive city landmark.

The two companies also fought on the water (see SHIPPING SERVICES). The NBR had put two passenger steamers on to the Clyde in 1866 but had been quickly forced to withdraw them; a second attempt, based on Dunoon instead of Helensburgh, resulted only in heavy losses. Agreement with the *Glasgow & South Western gave access to Greenock, which improved matters. The competition was not just coastal, but inland on Loch Lomond, where the NBR had purchased the local steamship company, only to be challenged in the 1890s by the CR which threatened to operate its own vessels. The result was a reluctant agreement between them to share the loch fleet, while fighting hard to capture the rail traffic to and from the pier at Balloch.

The NBR was also involved in a surprising range of other marine activities. Until the bridges were built, it ran the *ferries across the Forth and the Tay, and south of the border began the Silloth venture in Cumberland, a brainchild of Richard Hodgson, where the company promoted a *port and a select sea-bathing resort (see HOLIDAY-MAKING). The latter had only a little local success, despite the NBR's efforts in laying out streets, building houses, providing services, and constructing a golf course. The port was more successful in tapping traffic for *Liverpool, the *Isle of Man, and *Ireland. The NBR also operated motor services: in September 1904 two 23-seater open-sided charabancs were purchased at the combined cost of £1,120 to provide a service between the upper-class East Lothian resorts of Gullane and North Berwick. It even had a part-share in a road: the Trossachs toll road from Aberfoyle to Loch Katrine.

By the 1890s, with the opening of the *Forth Bridge and the rebuilding of the Tay Bridge, the NBR had its east coast route secure, though the NER, after beating off an NBR legal challenge in 1894, continued to work all main-line expresses north of Berwick to Edinburgh. There was, however, immense congestion at Waverley station, relieved only by quadrupling the main line through Princes Street Gardens, boring new tunnels at Haymarket and the Mound, and remodelling the station. When the new suburban platforms were opened in 1898, Waverley was said to have more platform accommodation than any other station in Britain except Waterloo. In Fife, which generated so much coal business, it had bought the Methil railway and docks in 1889. Exports of coal rose from 0.4 million tons in 1888 to 2.8 million tons in 1907. One of the last large railway schemes to be completed in Britain was the West Highland line from Craigendoran, west of Glasgow, to Fort William, opened in 1894, and the daunting Mallaig extension of 1901, a mere 40 miles which took the contractor Robert *McAl-

pine a full four years to complete after much political controversy and a Treasury *subsidy of £260,000.

The NBR's system was virtually complete; a few *light railways were to follow, and the Dunfermline to Kincardine line. During World War I the NBR, like other companies, experienced an immense increase in traffic. The new naval base at Rosyth, served by a dockyard station opened in 1915, received over 1.25 million tons of Welsh coal in 1918 as well as special trains for naval personnel. Shortages of men, many of whom had enlisted, and backlogs of maintenance created immense strain, and the war left the NBR weakened, a situation made worse by shortages of coal and engines. But the company recovered: services were reinstated and locomotive deficiencies remedied, 17 of the 'Glen' class, for example, being built in 1919–20. Despite being thought to be devitalized, the NBR fought and won a very determined battle with the government to secure adequate compensation for the wear and tear of war traffic and was awarded just under £10 million in 1921. At the *Grouping in 1923 the NBR was the largest of the Scottish railway companies with over 1,300 miles of track, 1,100 locomotives, 3,500 carriages, and 57,000 wagons. It became part of the *London & North Eastern Railway.   AJD

Reg. Hist., vi and xv; J. Thomas, The North British Railway, i (1969), ii (1975); W. Vamplew, 'The North British Railway Enquiry of 1866', in Scottish Industrial Miscellany (1978).

North Eastern Railway: an *amalgamation, authorized in 1854, of three important companies, the *York Newcastle & Berwick, *York & North Midland, and *Leeds Northern, including also the little Malton & Driffield Junction. It did not involve a total fusion: the stocks of the three companies remained separate for another 16 years. Neither did it create a complete territorial *monopoly. Two substantial railways within the territory, the *Blyth and Tyne and the West *Hartlepool, remained independent, and to the west two old-established companies, the *Stockton & Darlington and *Newcastle & Carlisle. The amalgamation produced a system 700 miles long, with administrative headquarters at *York.

In railway politics, the new company's most pressing tasks were to settle its relations with its independent neighbours. As a port, West Hartlepool threatened Middlesbrough and *Hull, and the WHR formed an alliance with the *London & North Western Railway, pertinaciously bent on thrusting into the NER's territory east and north of Leeds. In 1860 the NER offered to buy up the WHR, but failed to reach any satisfactory bargain because it was then encountering complicated legal and financial difficulties. When the proposal was renewed in 1864–5, however, it succeeded.

The Stockton & Darlington, being part of the *Pease family's empire, was much more firmly founded. But the NER was made anxious by the construction of the South Durham & Lancashire Union line in 1857–61, supported by the SDR, to link the Durham and Cumberland coal and iron fields; again with the aid of the LNWR, which actually purchased for itself a whole side of one dock at West Hartlepool. In 1862 the SDLUR was amalgamated with the SDR, which was itself merged in the NER in 1863. The NCR followed it into the combine in 1865.

These enlargements called for much laboured, and sometimes acrimonious, negotiation, but they consolidated the company's territory against invasion. The *North British Railway, it is true, formed an alliance with the still-independent Blyth & Tyne: potentially dangerous to the NER when the smaller company built lines of its own into *Newcastle and Tynemouth in 1864. But the NBR's interest in Northumberland soon cooled, and the NER was able to buy up the BTR (at a high price) in 1874.

The NER was also strengthening its partnership with the *Great Northern and the NBR in the *East Coast route from London to Scotland. In 1868–71 it shortened the route by building direct lines totalling 26 miles from Durham to Gateshead and from *Doncaster to York, where an impressive new station was built in 1872–7.

The results of this long struggle to produce a virtual monopoly of rail transport in north-eastern England were not altogether satisfactory. The NER, SDR, and NCR each had its own well-established operating practices, and integration was slow. Diversities of management were one factor in a series of four *accidents on the NER late in 1870, as revealed in the reports of the inspector, *Yolland. He pointed also to more general mismanagement and to the NER's backwardness in introducing the *block system and the interlocking of points and signals (see SIGNALLING), safety devices that nearly all the other companies were adopting. The NER board was so much disturbed by these disclosures that the general manager, William O'Brien, was sacked. Under his successor, Henry *Tennant, reforms went ahead. The expense was heavy, but the NER could well afford it. The stocks of the amalgamated companies were combined in 1870, and the new North Eastern Consols paid an annual dividend of more than 8 per cent in 1870–9.

In this strong position, the company felt able to make a good showing—at considerable expense—with celebrations of the 50th anniversary of the opening of the SDR, 'The Jubilee of the Railway System', at Darlington in 1875 (see also EXHIBITIONS).

There was, however, one town in its territory in which it was widely unpopular: Hull. This hostility originated from a series of *agreements in 1855–6 between the NER and other companies to pool the receipts from freight traffic to and from all the ports from the Tyne to the Humber, and it was strengthened when West Hartlepool came under the NER's control in 1865. Hull now showed a strong desire for a wholly new railway to bring Yorkshire coal for shipment, competing with the NER and not bound by any of the agreements.

The port of Hull was, however, suffering from grave congestion of shipping in the Humber, which the Hull Dock Company was too weak to deal with. In 1879–80, therefore, an ambitious plan was proposed, strongly backed by Hull Corporation, for building an independent railway from the south and west Yorkshire coalfields, and a new dock, much larger than those already there. The Hull Barnsley & West

Riding Junction Railway & Dock Company (see HULL & BARNSLEY RAILWAY) was authorized, after a fierce parliamentary struggle, in 1880. The 66-mile railway and the dock were opened in 1885. A war of rates with the NER followed, and the HBR (much the weaker of the two) passed into receivership in 1887–9. But the NER wisely showed a willingness to make terms, and though negotiations for union failed, largely through the corporation's implacable hostility, the two railways jointly built the big new deep-water King George V Dock, opened in 1914.

In 1870 no knowledgeable person would have pointed to the NER as a leader among British railway companies in management or methods of operation. It had created for itself an enclave within which in some ways it worked well, and in others not so well, communicating with other railways only when necessary. It was much influenced, sometimes dominated, by the interests and practices of its own region. For example, the power of the ironmasters made it the last of the great companies to abandon iron rails for steel (see TRACK), in 1877. Edward *Fletcher, the locomotive superintendent, though wise and immensely experienced, was no innovator. He retired in 1882 and was succeeded by Alexander McDonnell, who introduced new practices, some overdue. But the enginemen protested loudly and, in effect, forced his resignation. This attitude was summarized perfectly by the passenger superintendent, Alexander Christison, when the *Railway Clearing House was discussing a revision of all the companies' telegraphic codes in 1883: 'As I could not possibly agree to any alteration of our code, I think it unnecessary to have anyone at the meeting to represent the North Eastern company.'

However, these attitudes were already changing. As early as 1871–2 the NER began to foster third-class travel, deliberately and substantially as the *Midland did, though by rather different means. It came through the alarming recession in *mineral traffic (on which it largely depended) in 1875–9, adapting itself to new conditions successfully. Although Tennant was a sound railwayman, the company's management showed no brilliant flair until he was succeeded by G. S. *Gibb in 1891. Under him, the company became, in some important ways, prominent in the British railway industry.

Gibb considered that the company's senior men had too narrow an experience, and he gradually brought in outsiders. Some of them became highly respected in different fields, later: R. L. *Wedgwood, for example, Frank *Pick, and E. C. *Geddes.

He attended particularly to the reform of the traffic department. By 1899 he required more working *statistics than had hitherto been available, partly based on ton-mileage instead of train-mileage. He was helped by the economist George Paish, who publicized in London what was happening on the NER. Some of the other companies' officers, determined against changing their methods, treated this with discreditable contempt, but the NER stuck to its own path. These policies were not applicable to its region alone, and gradually, as the old guard disappeared, the NER grew respected for its forward thinking.

The company was taking its own way in other aspects of management, too. It was the first railway to negotiate directly with a *trade union on wages and hours of work, to the indignation of the rest. After Gibb left the NER to become managing director of the *London underground railways in 1906, his successor, A. Kaye Butterworth, maintained most of his policies, and before 1914 some of their merits were becoming more fully recognized.

The company's operating techniques also attracted widespread attention. Under Wilson *Worsdell and Vincent *Raven as successive CMEs, it moved steadily (though not without some qualms) into *electrification, converting its short but very awkward Quayside freight line at Newcastle in 1902, and the suburban system north of the Tyne in 1904—well ahead of all the main-line London companies. It then turned to longer-distance electrification, achieved for freight in 1915 from Shildon to Middlesbrough. Plans were already being made for electrifying the main line from York to Newcastle, for all traffic, but World War I intervened and they were not implemented until 1991.

The HBR amalgamated with the NER on 1 April 1922. The NER passed into the *London & North Eastern Railway at the 1923 *Grouping.   JS

> Tomlinson; *Reg. Hist.*, iv; R. Bell, *Twenty-five Years of the North Eastern Railway, 1898–1922* (1951); R. J. Irving, *The North Eastern Railway Company, 1870–1914* (1976); Christison's remark is recorded in G. P. Neele, *Railway Reminiscences* (1974 edn.), 290.

Northern & Eastern Railway. Authorized in 1836 to run from London to Cambridge, it was altered in 1839 to allow it to use the *Eastern Counties Railway's terminus at Shoreditch, its line branching out of the ECR's at Stratford. James *Walker was the company's first engineer, succeeded by Robert *Stephenson in 1839. After opening 37 miles to Bishop's Stortford and a branch to Hertford in 1843, the line stuck until the ECR leased it and extended its line (1845) through Cambridge to Brandon, to meet the *Norfolk Railway coming from *Norwich. The NER (like the ECR) was originally of 5 ft *gauge, but was converted to standard gauge in 1844. The lease continued until the company was purchased by the *Great Eastern Railway in 1902.

The NER was an innovator in the use of iron *fencing. In 1843 it was said to run the fastest trains in Britain, between London and Bishop's Stortford, at 36 mph (excluding stops). That ceased quickly after the ECR took control.   JS

> C. J. Allen, *Great Eastern Railway* (1955); *Reg. Hist.*, v, 102–5; on speed see Acworth, 29.

Northern Line, see LONDON UNDERGROUND RAILWAYS.

North London Railway. Only 13¼ miles long, this line had an importance disproportionate to its size. It provided the vital connecting link between the northern and western main lines and the London docks and City goods depots. Its trains worked over 54¾ miles of other companies' lines, and it was joint lessee of the North & South Western Junction Railway. In 1907 freight and miscellaneous traffic amounted to half the total receipts, suburban passenger train traffic the other half.

The NLR's origin was in the East & West India Docks &

Birmingham Junction Railway, authorized in 1846 from Camden Town on the *London & North Western Railway to the docks at Blackwall, opened in 1850–2. Happily, it was renamed North London Railway in 1853. Though primarily promoted for goods traffic, it operated passenger trains at 15-minute intervals from the start. Its first City terminus was *Fenchurch Street on the *London & Blackwall Railway. The approach was roundabout and inconvenient; but after a 2-mile line from Kingsland (Dalston) to Broad Street in the City (the 'happy afterthought') was opened in 1865, both passenger and goods traffic grew fast.

The LNWR had a two-thirds ownership of the company and dominated its relations with other lines, though the NLR had a spirited personality of its own. The North Western was able to keep *Great Northern trains out of Broad Street; instead NLR trains worked to GNR suburban stations by a curve at Canonbury from 1875. NLR trains ran over other companies' lines to Richmond on the *London & South Western, and to High Barnet, Potters Bar, and Enfield on the GNR.

To the north-west the NLR worked the services on the NSWJR Willesden–Kew link, 3¾ miles opened in 1853, jointly leased by the LNWR, *Midland, and NLR in 1871, and the Hampstead Junction Railway, 6½ miles from Camden Town to Willesden, opened in 1860, which was LNWR property with NLR participation in the stations. In the result, the NLR was the essential link in a chain of lines circling London to the north, connecting LSWR, *Great Western, LNWR, MR, GNR, *Great Eastern, and *London Tilbury & Southend Railways. Four tracks between Broad Street and Camden Town were completed in 1874, and the NLR managed by efficient working to accommodate all its own traffic and that coming off the connecting lines. It was able, with LNWR influence behind it, to defeat several rival schemes; only the Midland managed to secure an independent connection with the LTSR in 1894. The NLR came under heavy pressure in World War I, being closed to public traffic several times; and it was knocked about by enemy air raids.

The company was the last London railway to provide only first and second class for passengers; third came in 1875. In the 1880s and 1890s it was steady in traffic and dividend, declaring 7½ per cent in 1880–99 except for two years at 6¾ per cent. But electric street *tramways then began to erode its passenger receipts; *electrification was the obvious answer. In preparation, the line was worked by the LNWR from 1909 while retaining its separate company structure until 1921. Electric working, approved in 1911 as part of the LNWR's London scheme, was begun between Broad Street and Richmond in 1916, followed by Broad Street–Watford in 1922.

William *Adams began building locomotives at the railway's Bow *works in 1863, and under him and his successors J. C. Park and H. J. Pryce, the NLR possessed an efficient and largely standardized stock of engines: 4-4-0 tanks (from 1868 with outside cylinders) for passenger trains, with Adams bogies; and Park's outside-cylinder 0-6-0 tanks for goods. There were 123 locomotives in 1908.

Water-softening plant was installed at Broad Street in 1898 and at Bow. The NLR's 620 carriages were all close-coupled sets of four-wheelers, with coal-gas lighting from 1862.

A notable *signalling advance was made at Kentish Town Junction, Camden Town, in 1860 with the first installation of completely interlocked points and related signals, made at Bow. The NLR's worst *accident—in fact, a series of rear-end collisions on the GNR's connecting curve through Canonbury Tunnel, in 1881—was due to misunderstanding of NLR bell codes by a GNR signalman. The murder of Thomas Briggs in a train near Old Ford by Franz Müller in 1864 led for a time to the provision of 'Müller's lights': openings in compartment partitions.

At the last North London shareholders' meeting it was claimed that more than 33 times the population of Britain had been carried over its line in 50 years. It had strong claims to be considered the most efficient of the smaller British railways.   RMR

A. J. Chisholm, *The North London Railway* (1902); G. A. Sekon, *Locomotion in Victorian London* (1938); M. Robbins, *The North London Railway* (1983 edn.); C. P. Atkins and T. J. Edgington, *North London Railway: A Pictorial Record* (1979).

North Midland Railway. Authorized in 1836, this was a northward extension of two other railways springing from the *London & Birmingham, which was then under construction: the *Birmingham & Derby Junction and the *Midland Counties, meeting at *Derby. It was to build a 73-mile line from there to *Leeds, a large contribution to a trunk route from *London to north-east England. George *Stephenson seems chiefly to have devised it, with the banker G. C. *Glyn, chairman of the London & Birmingham, and other moneyed men in London, *Liverpool, *Manchester, and Yorkshire. He laid down the line, with his son Robert: not the most direct—that would have gone through *Sheffield and Barnsley—but an easier one, with a *ruling gradient of 1 in 250; when lines were subsequently built by the shorter route they called for long stretches at 1 in 100. There were three substantial *tunnels, one at Clay Cross a mile long. The railway was opened throughout in 1840.

The line had been expensive to build, costing nearly twice the estimated amount. Its revenue proved disappointing: enough to pay an average dividend of only 3.2 per cent in 1841–3. Glyn resigned the chair of the company in 1842, being succeeded by a Derby director, W. L. Newton. Protesting shareholders secured a committee of investigation into the company's expenditure and management, dominated by George *Hudson, already chairman of the *York & North Midland Railway: this led to drastic economies achieved by dismissing some of the company's servants, and a general reduction in the salaries and wages of those who remained. The consequences of these policies attracted the attention of the Board of *Trade in 1843, after a serious *accident had occurred; and the management was powerfully attacked in a knowledgeable book published over the pseudonym *Veritas Vincit*.

The two companies whose lines the NMR met at Derby were also in financial difficulties, much increased by quarrelling with each other. Robert Stephenson and Hudson agreed in thinking that the only satisfactory solution to the problems of all three lay in their amalgamation, and the three were combined to form a new *Midland Railway in 1844.   JS

C. E. Stretton, *History of the Midland Railway* (1901), chs 4, 6; Whishaw, 367–79; M. Robbins, 'The North Midland Railway and its Enginemen', *JTH*, 4 (1959–60), 180–6; M. C. Reed, *Investment in Railways in Britain 1820–44* (1975), 162–8.

North of England Institute of Mining & Mechanical Engineers. Formed in 1852 under the presidency of Nicholas *Wood, the institute has numbered railway engineers among its members. Robert *Stephenson bequeathed it £2,000 which formed the basis of a fund for permanent premises, and the Neville Hall and Memorial Hall in *Newcastle were opened in 1872. In 1876 the institute was granted a Royal Charter. With the University of Durham it jointly administered the College of Physical Science inaugurated in Newcastle in 1876, and forerunner of the University of Newcastle upon Tyne. Although the institute retains its autonomy, since 1889 it has also acted as the north of England branch of the national Institution of Mining Engineers. It maintains an extensive library.   GJB

North Staffordshire Railway. Known and affectionately remembered as 'The Knotty' because the Staffordshire Knot was its emblem, the NSR was a compact, highly profitable company which made a big impact on the region. Within a few years of its formation in 1845, it had opened 111 miles, almost half the total mileage with which it became the sixth largest constituent of the *London Midland & Scottish Railway at the 1923 *Grouping. Local industrialists and businessmen created the NSR to bar the surrounding big companies from the Potteries and its large coal, ironstone mining, and quarrying districts. Yet they negotiated *running powers over more than 300 miles of other companies' tracks, including access to the North Wales coast, the nearest seaside. The NSR became the largest *canal-owning railway by amalgamating with the Trent & Mersey Canal in 1846. It developed, rather than destroyed, what had long been the Potteries' main transport artery, carrying over 300,000 tons of goods and minerals annually.

*Crewe–*Derby and Colwich–Macclesfield main lines met at *Stoke, the latter providing the *London & North Western Railway with a *Euston–*Manchester route 5 miles shorter than via Crewe. The NSR projected itself as a 'purely local line' and the *Loop Line of 1875 linking the six Pottery towns helped to form what a chairman called 'a small octopus'.

That octopus embraced a north–south route, which avoided Stoke, through Leek and the pretty Churnet Valley to Uttoxeter; a branch penetrated the neighbouring heavily industrialized Biddulph Valley, and a rural branch ran to the *Great Western Railway at Market Drayton. The NSR was also joint owner with the *Great Central of the 11-mile Macclesfield Bollington & Marple Railway. *Narrow-gauge enterprise came through working the 2 ft 6 in Leek & Manifold *Light Railway of 1904.

North Sunderland Railway

In Edwardian years, the carriage of over 5 million tons of coal, coke, and patent fuel a year, almost all originating on the system, and more than 10 million passengers, helped produce 5 per cent dividends. Directors encouraged people from the industrial towns to enjoy the countryside on Sundays, their only day off, defying some shareholders' calls to reduce Sunday train services.

Many economies and changes followed the Grouping, but passenger decline was reversed by a branch opened to the war-time Swynnerton Royal Ordnance Factory, near Stone, in 1941. It carried 3 million workers a year on trains never publicly timetabled. Main line *electrification in the 1960s embraced Colwich and Stone to Macclesfield, but not the Crewe branch.   RC

CMNSR; G. Dow, North Staffordshire Album (1970); 'Manifold', The North Staffordshire Railway (1952).

North Sunderland Railway, see LIGHT RAILWAYS.

North Union Railway.
Formed by an amalgamation of the Wigan Branch and Wigan & Preston Railways in 1834, the NUR was opened throughout from Parkside, on the *Liverpool & Manchester, to *Preston in 1838, forming a through route from London—now part of the *West Coast main line. In 1843 it was joined at Euxton Junction by the Bolton & Preston Railway which, with its direct access to *Manchester, broke the NUR's monopoly. From the outset there was endless trouble over tolls charged by the NUR for the 5½ miles into Preston and the use of its station. A fares war broke out over Preston–Manchester traffic, even though the NUR's route via Parkside was longer, and the latter obstructed BPR trains at Preston. For a time the BPR conveyed passengers by road from Euxton to Preston, before suggesting amalgamation, which took place between the two companies in 1844.

The enlarged NUR was itself leased by the *Grand Junction and *Manchester & Leeds companies in January 1846, and vested in them jointly in July, shortly after the GJR had become part of the *London & North Western. In December the MLR became the *Lancashire & Yorkshire Railway. The lines from Parkside and Bolton to Preston were, therefore, now LNWR and LYR joint property, although in practice they were operated as parts of the respective companies' main lines, a situation that was officially recognized by Acts of 1888 which transferred Parkside–Euxton to the LNWR solely and Bolton–Euxton to the LYR, leaving only the northern end and Preston station in joint ownership.

Notable engineering features are the Ribble bridge at Preston and, on the BPR, a stone cutting near Chorley unusually buttressed by 16 masonry flying arches (see EARTHWORKS).   GJB

LYR, i, ch. 4; Reg. Hist., x, ch. 9 (1986 edn.).

Norwich.
Cathedral city, and county town of Norfolk, with an ancient textile manufacture, breweries, and an important market, Norwich stood in 1831 eighth town in population in England and Wales.

The *Eastern Counties Railway was authorized in 1836, from London via Ipswich, but was not completed until 1849. Another line had been opened in 1845, via Cambridge, joining one from Norwich to Yarmouth (see NORTHERN & EASTERN RAILWAY; NORFOLK RAILWAY). Unlike the London lines, the Yarmouth one attracted local finance, for it greatly improved the conveyance of coal, hitherto brought by water.

Even when the ECR was finally opened to London, intercompany squabbles at Colchester prevented the running of through trains until 1854. Quarrelling died down after 1862, when the antagonists were merged into one *Great Eastern Railway, comprehending the Cambridge line also.

Norwich now had two termini: Thorpe, accommodating the Yarmouth and Cambridge trains and reached by a specially built street (see TOWNS); and Victoria for some trains on the Ipswich line. Thorpe was rebuilt and enlarged in 1886. Victoria lingered on for passengers until 1916; for goods until 1966.

North Norfolk was late in securing railways; the GER's line to Cromer was completed only in 1877. But in 1882 the Lynn & Fakenham Railway (later part of the *Midland & Great Northern) opened a line between Norwich and Melton Constable, requiring a third station, eventually called Norwich (City).

Eight railways converged on Norwich, providing a reasonable service, although it could have been better, particularly if the council had consented to the removal of the central cattle market to the suburb of Trowse, adjoining the railway.

By 1951 Norwich was down to 30th in population, its textile trade long overtaken by Yorkshire. However, although well off the main railway system (still today over 60 miles from a motorway), it remains the regional capital of East Anglia, and a large centre of administration and distribution. It is within easy commuting distance of London; the Ipswich route was *electrified in 1991, trains taking two hours or less. Four of the eight lines that once served it still carry passengers.   JS

C. J. Allen, Great Eastern Railway (1955); Reg. Hist., v.

Nottingham,
well situated on the navigable River Trent, has an importance stretching back to the Danish Five Boroughs, but by the early 19th century it was stagnating. Although early wagonways (see WOODEN RAILWAYS) were laid down at Wollaton nearby, and mining and iron-founding followed, when the *Midland Counties Railway came, promoted by coalowners seeking wider markets, Nottingham was at the end of the line. Its subsequent industrial development was only dependent on railways in the wider sense of seeking national markets and prominence for its products: hosiery and lace, supplemented by pharmaceuticals, bicycles, and cigarettes. Nevertheless Nottingham became the focus of nine routes before finally being on an important main line.

The MCR lines to *Derby (1839) and through to *Leicester and the *London & Birmingham Railway at Rugby (1840) became part of the *Midland Railway, which opened lines from Nottingham to Lincoln (1846) and Mansfield (1848–9). An independent line opened from Grantham

Nottingham, 1922

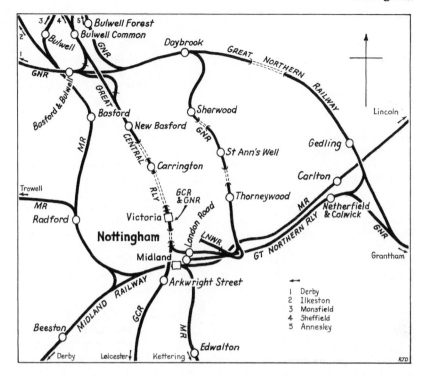

(1850); together with its attractive station at London Road, it became a vehicle for the *Great Northern Railway to break into the Derbyshire coalfield (1876) and reach Derby (1878), as well as letting in the *London & North Western Railway from Market Harborough (1879). Nottingham's dramatic mid-century expansion incorporated its industrial suburbs along the Mansfield line (1877), although in the north-east the Nottingham Suburban Railway (1889) was never as important. At Colwick the GNR built extensive yards and a locomotive depot for its coal traffic, matching the Midland's at Trent.

Nottingham was eventually put on a direct line from London when the Midland, after building the Radford–Trowell loop (1875), opened its line from Kettering (1880) and ran *Leeds and *Bradford and some Scottish expresses this way. Real competition arrived with the *Great Central Railway's London Extension (1899), with its impressive Victoria station, built jointly with the GNR (1900), causing the Midland to rebuild its own station. In its heyday Victoria provided through services to points as diverse as *Aberdeen, *Bournemouth, *Cardiff, *Hull, and *Plymouth, but it was too large and too late; *British Rail rationalization closed these routes in 1966 and Victoria itself in 1967. London Road had closed to passengers in 1944.   RVL

Reg. Hist., ix, chs 7, 8 (1984); R. Church, *Economic and Social Change in a Midland Town* (1966).

Oakley, Sir Henry (1823–1914), manager. He spent most of his working life with the *Great Northern Railway, joining in 1849.

Oakley was chief clerk in the secretary's office until appointed in 1858 as secretary to the company. He succeeded as general manager in 1870, one of a new wave of senior managers that were to govern GNR affairs for a generation. The company was concerned with fending off the territorial—and commercial—ambitions of the Manchester Sheffield & Lincolnshire (see GREAT CENTRAL) and *Midland Railways, as well as competition offered to the *east coast route by the *west coast companies, as epitomized by the *races to Scotland in 1888. There were also pressures on GNR resources and operations exacted by its London suburban traffic.

As general manager, Oakley was skilful in handling the politics of, and negotiations involved in, various issues. He was prominent during parliamentary hearings leading to the Railway & Canal Traffic Act, 1888 (see PARLIAMENT AND LEGISLATION); he also acted as secretary to the Railway Companies Association during this period. This may have influenced his receipt of a knighthood in 1891.

Oakley was elected to the board in 1897, and retired as general manager in 1898. A GNR 'Atlantic' locomotive was named *Henry Oakley* in 1900.

On retirement from the GNR, he became chairman of the *Central London Railway.   MLH

Grinling.

observation car, a carriage designed, or converted from an existing vehicle, so as to provide passengers with (relatively) unimpeded scenic views through large windows in its trailing end. Some early royal saloons were notable for having prominent end-windows, and railway officers' inspection saloons not in passenger stock were similarly endowed, to allow viewing of track and structures. The latter were usually propelled, a practice denied to passenger trains, other than with *push-pull operation, with the result that observation saloons were attached as the last vehicle of a train.

Observation saloons were built by the *London & North Western Railway in 1912–13, for use between Llandudno Junction and Blaenau Festiniog. In 1915 the *Cambrian Railways introduced on its coast lines six-wheeled saloons converted from ordinary thirds; these worked until 1936. But the most stylish was *Pullman car *Maid of Morven*, gracing the Glasgow–Oban line from 1914. Observation cars were used—and some continue to be—on *narrow-gauge

railways, notably the *Festiniog, North Wales Narrow Gauge, and Vale of Rheidol Railways.

In summer, an observation car was attached to the rear of the *London & North Eastern Railway's Coronation express, operated between London *King's Cross and *Edinburgh in 1937–9. Pullman featured an observation car on the Devon Belle which ran between London (Waterloo) and the West Country in 1947–54. During the 1960s, these cars were later deployed to routes in the Scottish Highlands such as Fort William–Mallaig and *Inverness–Kyle of Lochalsh. Other cars were used there from the 1980s and also appeared on the Royal Scotsman touring train.   MLH

officers, senior, see MANAGEMENT.

oil, carriage of. Railways began to carry oil from the 1880s, the *wagons being owned by the refiners of oil and petroleum products. They consisted of a simple riveted tank barrel resting in saddles on a standard wagon chassis. The tank was loaded and discharged through a barrel-top filler. Highly flammable oil products were classified as *dangerous goods.

Little changed in the next 50 years, most consignments of oil being moved in wagonload services. During World War II, oil traffic became a major concern, notably the movement of fuel from west coast *ports to east coast airfields—on the *London Midland & Scottish Railway alone, 200 trains were run weekly during 1943—and in preparation for the invasion of Europe, petrol to ports such as Poole.

Before World War II, most oil supplies were imported as finished products but, from 1945, the major oil companies built refineries in Britain, in particular along the Thames estuary and at Fawley, near *Southampton. By the late 1950s, up to 11 block trains of tank wagons daily were being forwarded from Thames Haven, mostly to inland distribution depots in the Midlands.

The gross load of four-wheel tank wagons was limited to 35 tons, then to 45 tons from 1960. Even so, many of the older, unfitted wagons remained in traffic.

To secure for rail the major flows of petroleum products between refineries and distribution depots, from 1963 *BR concluded long-term—usually ten-year—contracts with the oil companies, specifying that they would maintain their current tonnages plus the annual market increase, and that high-capacity brake-fitted wagons would be provided. For the railway's part, the inducements offered were low rates, and block loads conveyed at express freight speed.

To achieve further economies in operation, bogie tank wagons were built for the oil companies from 1965, leading to the construction of 100-ton (gross laden weight) cars whose strength was almost entirely in the tank barrel. Apart from Thames-side, major refineries were built in south-west Wales, which was the growth area of the 1970s. Subsequently, the movement of oil by rail began to decline, and the early 1990s saw a number of the smaller distribution depots closed to rail.   MLH

J. Johnson and R. A. Long, *British Railways Engineering 1948–80* (1981).

oil as a fuel was first used for railway traction in 1882 when Thomas Urquhart, motive power superintendent of the Grazi-Tsaritsin railway in SE Russia, successfully converted coal-burning locomotives, after eight years' work in developing a satisfactory oil burner. By 1885 some 143 oil-burning locomotives were running on this railway.

In Britain, James *Holden, locomotive superintendent of the *Great Eastern Railway, started experiments in 1886, using gas-oil residues from the production of gas for *carriage lighting. His first oil-fired locomotive, a 2-4-0 *Petrolea*, was built in 1893, and 60 engines were fitted before a new use for the waste oil put the price up. In Holden's system, used by other railways in Britain and overseas, steam was raised by a coal fire, which was then supplemented by the oil burner.

In oil-fired locomotives fuel was conveyed from a tank mounted in the tender—steam-heated if highly viscous low-grade oil was used—to a burner in the firebox, where the oil was atomized in a steam jet prior to combustion. Usually the conventional firegrate and ashpan were replaced by a flame pan and refractory brickwork.

Oil-burning had obvious advantages over coal in eliminating ash disposal and fire-cleaning work, thus increasing availability for traffic, as well as minimizing the work of the fireman. Oil-firing also gave increased boiler efficiency at high power outputs. With coal-firing this had often resulted in considerable ejection of partially burned fuel and consequent lineside *fires.

However, in Britain the substantial price differential in favour of indigenous coal over imported oil was sufficient to rule out its use except during prolonged industrial disputes restricting coal supplies, as in the *strikes of 1912, 1921, and 1926. The severe coal shortage in 1947 prompted plans for the conversion of well over 1,000 British locomotives to oil-firing, but coal production rose again in the initial stages, causing their abandonment.

In countries with abundant low-cost oil supplies, such as Mexico and the USA, oil-fired steam locomotives were widely used before the diesel era (see TRACTION, DIESEL; MULTIPLE UNITS).

Attempts were also made to burn a mixture of oil and pulverized coal in locomotive fireboxes, as on the *Great Central Railway from 1920 onwards, but with little success.

The first oil-fired internal combustion locomotive in Britain, with a Hornsby-Akroyd engine, was built in 1896, five years after the first petrol-engined locomotive (see TRACTION, PETROL) was built by Daimler in Germany. In the early 1930s considerable numbers of diesel shunting locomotives

were built in the USA, and some by the *London Midland & Scottish Railway in Britain; these showed substantial economies over steam shunters, whose efficiency was very low. In Britain the large-scale replacement of coal-fired steam *traction by oil-fired diesels began in 1957 and was completed by 1968.

In 1970 the *Festiniog Railway adopted the Laidlaw-Drew oil-burning system as an economy, where the all-round spray pattern is more suited to locomotive fire-boxes than long-flame burners. Its success has led to conversions on some other preserved railways.

Oil fuel is also normally used in gas turbine locomotives (see TRACTION, TURBINE).   GWC

W. C. Ikeson, 'Development of the Oil-Fired Locomotive', *Jnl Inst. Loco. Engineers*, 42, 229, 19.

opening ceremonies. Most early British railways celebrated their opening with some kind of ceremonial.

The *Stockton & Darlington, *Canterbury & Whitstable, and *Liverpool & Manchester Railways all did so. The third of those affairs was much the grandest, attended by the Prime Minister, Wellington, but marred by the death of Huskisson (see ACCIDENTS) and by the demonstration against Wellington on his arrival at Manchester. Remembering perhaps these dismal events, the board of the *Grand Junction Railway decided to open it in 1837 without any ceremony whatever.

In Britain the railways were free to arrange these matters as they chose, whereas in France two of the King's sons were sent to inaugurate the lines from Paris to Rouen and Orléans, on successive days in 1843.

The heart of the event in Britain was usually a massive banquet at which numerous speeches were made: ostentatious, commonplace, noisy, and jolly.

A good festivity of this kind, well organized by the railway and the towns concerned, and supported by the people, could be an agreeable, even moving, demonstration. Lady Charlotte Guest, a very cool critic, was delighted by the directors' opening journey along the *South Wales Railway in 1850, concluding in the afternoon with a municipal breakfast for 690 people in a marquee at *Swansea. On the other hand, if the directors were careless the people might take over, clambering about the trains with no regard for safety: 'very funny and very dangerous doings', a journalist called them on the *Manchester & Leeds Railway in 1840.

Every sort of misfortune might attend these functions. Exceptionally violent storms ruined those organized by the *Newcastle & Carlisle and Newcastle & North Shields Railways in 1838–40. At the opening of the Durham Junction Railway in 1838 there was a collision between trains, which determined the engineer, T. E. *Harrison, never again to permit an opening ceremony on any line for which he was responsible. Some badly organized openings served only to bring down curses on the directors, like that of the *Inverness & Perth Railway in 1863. A scandalous squabble, on a political issue unconnected with railways, ended in blows at the opening of the Exmouth Railway in 1861.

So there were risks in publicizing these events too well, and in later years they grew quieter, or were dispensed with. The opening of the *Great Central Railway's London extension in 1899 was a stately affair at Marylebone station, undertaken by the President of the Board of *Trade.

The only openings by a reigning monarch were the *Victoria Line (1969), *Piccadilly Line to Heathrow (1977), Tyne & Wear Metro (1980), and *Docklands (1987).   JS

operating costs can be defined and measured in different ways: by *accountancy, i.e. grouping together cash outlays directed to the movement function; in economics as 'avoidable costs', escaped if traffic ceases to flow; and statistically in terms of resources consumed, such as man-hours. Here changes in the nature of operating costs over the years are discussed under the simple headings of materials and labour consumed by train movement, i.e. short-term costs excluding maintenance and renewals.

At the outset, however, it is obvious that operating costs can be affected by geography. Gradients are usually a handicap, though in the South Wales valleys the heavy coal trains ran downhill and the empties uphill. A limiting factor was the level of expenditure on construction: whether or not heavy *earthworks and *tunnels could be afforded to ensure a good track alignment.

In the early days of railways, the capital outlays involved in building the infrastructure were so large, and servicing the capital so demanding, that it was often considered that a viable railway project should have an operating ratio (proportion of working expenses to receipts) not in excess of 50 per cent. As a national average this was commonly the case until the 1870s when a long slow rise started which reached almost 64 per cent just before World War I; and between the wars figures in excess of 80 per cent were usual.

While early railways could in one sense be considered capital-intensive, their operation expressed as train movements was labour-intensive owing to primitive procedures. With stopping-power limited by hand *brakes, passenger trains of any length would require two or even three *guards to act as brakesmen. The absence of proper *signalling and reliance on the time-interval system involved the employment of large numbers of *'policemen', and 'pointsmen' or 'switchmen', along the line. *Porters were needed at large stations to handle the mountains of *luggage with which Victorian families habitually travelled, and also to manhandle *carriages over *turntables to form trains. Goods *stations were very demanding in manpower, especially where transhipment was involved, as at frontier points between broad-*gauge and standard-gauge railways.

Strong efforts to contain wages costs were made, partly by imposing excessive working hours and partly by the employment of juveniles at lower wages than adults (see SALARIES AND WAGES). In fact, entry to the railway service commonly continued to be through starting grades such as 'lad porter' until World War II. But from the middle of the 19th and into the first decade of the 20th century, forces were at work in different ways to affect labour costs. The replacement of lineside 'policemen' and 'pointsmen' by signalmen in *signal boxes led to economies in manpower, as later did the replacement of hand brakes by power brakes on passenger trains—though the additional equipment needed maintenance staff. Goods stations continued to rely mainly upon barrowing, with limited *crane power, though *shunting in a few places was done expeditiously with ropes and hydraulically powered capstans, in conjunction with turntables. Sorting of wagons at *marshalling yards was also labour-intensive; even the *London & North Western Railway's renowned gravity yard at Edge Hill, *Liverpool, dating from 1873, needed an army of shunters; full mechanization with rail brakes had to wait until well into the 20th century.

All operating costs rose after the 1870s because of the increased expectations of rail users and the force of intercompany *competition, leading to heavier trains with amenities such as corridors and lavatories, *restaurant and *sleeping cars. The progressive reduction in working hours from twelve to ten, and then eight hours, grudgingly conceded by the companies (see TRADE UNIONISM), substantially increased costs.

Among the 'consumable stores' used in train operating, fuel was the largest item. Until the late 1860s locomotives (see TRACTION, STEAM) were required to burn coke to reduce smoke emission. With improvements in firebox design there was a general change to coal, which was cheaper, ten tons of coal having been needed to produce seven tons of coke. But there were wide differences in the cost of locomotive coal arising from transport costs; Jack Simmons has noted that in 1883 the Manchester Sheffield & Lincolnshire Railway (see GREAT CENTRAL), which served a coalfield, paid 6s. 6d. a ton, whereas the *London Brighton & South Coast had to pay about 17s. Locomotive engineers were concerned to design engines with efficiency in fuel consumption, and there was rivalry to produce the lowest figures of pounds of coal per unit of work. Coal purchases for locomotives were not seriously affected by *electrification until the 1920s, mainly on the *Southern Railway, which like most preferred to generate its own power.

Other major consumable stores were *lubricants and lamp oil for signals and trains. Staff *uniforms were also a substantial cost, though practice varied considerably between companies.

By the time of the *Grouping in 1923, basic railway technology had not changed in essentials. The accountancy definition of 'total operating cost' for railways in Great Britain in that year showed 'locomotive running costs' and 'traffic expenses' as representing about 58 per cent of total railway working expenditure. Effective steps to contain operating costs had begun in 1902 when (Sir) George *Gibb instituted statistical measures to assess resource costs such as engine-hours on the *North Eastern Railway. Not long afterwards, (Sir) Cecil Paget introduced a train *control system on the *Midland Railway, which was effective in reducing delays and enginemen's overtime costs.

Between the two World Wars, the most significant impact upon operating costs was made by the Southern Railway's electrification programme, each project within which was justified on cost reduction, with improved traffic estimates as a bonus, usually well exceeded in practice. Whilst still adhering to steam power, the *London Midland & Scottish Railway experienced a drive towards cost reduction inspired by Sir Josiah (Lord) *Stamp and his team of vice-presidents. All the railways imposed wholesale reductions in salaries and wages during the worst years of the depression, later to be restored in instalments. But labour costs stayed rather inflexible in sheer numbers; the all-time peak of 736,000 employees in 1921 had only fallen to 573,000 in 1938.

The most dramatic change in the composition of railway costs can be said to have begun with the *Modernization Plan of 1955, and the complete change of traction, followed by the *Beeching restructuring of the network, and the inexorable draining away of *freight traffic. Appreciable savings were obtained from the productivity agreements reached with the trade unions. From 1979, with a Conservative government seeking to reduce all types of *subsidy to *British Rail, staff savings tended to be concentrated on stations, where establishments were cut to a bare minimum, many stations becoming unstaffed halts. The disappearance of non-corridor compartment carriages facilitated a policy of 'open' stations with ticket checks carried out solely on trains. Conversely, the drive to reduce operating costs by staff savings involved substantial investment, for instance on signalling concentration schemes, and safety measures to permit driver-only operation of *multiple-unit trains.

The overall effect of these changes in 1994, including some partial *privatization, was that British Rail's total staff fell to 94,000; passenger stations fell from a peak of 7,000 to 2,500, with fewer than 60 freight depots open for traffic. The railway had become less labour-intensive. Staff costs in 1994 were 38 per cent of total operating expenditure, whereas in 1969 they had amounted to 47 per cent. Whether, in a service industry involving personal contacts, staff reductions can go much further is questionable.

See also ACCOUNTING; PROFITABILITY.   MRB

W. V. Wood and J. Stamp, *Railways* (1928); P. S. Bagwell, *The Railwaymen* (1963–82); Gourvish; Annual Reports and Statistics, British Transport Commission and British Railways Board.

opposition to railways. The opposition faced by the promoters of railways was of three main types: personal, corporate, and competitive.

The first was the most conspicuous of them in 1820–40. It was an emotional matter, the expression of an instinctive, unreasoning antipathy. King William IV was, in conversation, 'very peremptory in his dislike' of railways, and disposed to stop the progress of the *Great Western company's second Bill through Parliament in 1835, though he wisely thought better of doing that. Col. *Sibthorp's language when he spoke of them was often frantic. 'I hate your railways, I detest them altogether', said G. C. Berkeley, MP, in 1845; 'I wish the concoctions [of all railway schemes]

were at rest in Paradise.' The 6th Duke of Atholl started out from the simple position that he 'objected to all railways in the Highlands'.

Some other great *landowners thought at first in a similar way. The majority, however, came to terms with railways—as indeed this Duke did—and settled down to treat each on its merits. The Earls of Yarborough supported railway development in Lincolnshire, where their largest estates lay, in the 1840s, but in the 1860s they obstructed it in the *Isle of Wight. Attitudes might change from one generation to another. An Earl of Derby had taken a leading part in opposing the *Liverpool & Manchester Railway in the 1820s; his son actually gave railways important assistance by lending money to them on a large scale 25 years later.

Personal opposition of this kind grew negligible after 1870, except here and there in Scotland. Opposition from corporate bodies took no simple pattern. The Corporation of *Liverpool acted benevolently towards the LMR in the 1820s. But 40 years later it had grown restive under the dominance of the *London & North Western, and when that company proposed to amalgamate with the *Lancashire & Yorkshire Railway in 1871, Liverpool's opposition was uncompromising. The corporation then became the leader among English municipalities in denouncing 'railway *monopoly' on principle. The same apprehensions induced Hull Corporation to invest £100,000 in the *Hull & Barnsley Railway in 1880, to break the monopoly of the *North Eastern.

The third kind of opposition, hostility from other companies as competitors, including *canals in the earlier days, came to meet almost every important new project. A striking example was the West Highland Railway, seeking in 1889 to run from the Clyde to Fort William. This was a second attempt to get a railway into Lochaber, much desired for the assistance of an economically decaying district. The first, called the Glasgow North Western, supported by the *North British company, was defeated in 1883, chiefly through the opposition of the *Highland and *Caledonian Railways. The same opponents now fought the West Highland Bill through Parliament, backed again by the North British. But the HR and CR were dogs in the manger. For years past they had skirted the district, without making any effort to penetrate it. They now spent freely in order to stop another company from doing so. The committee examining the Bill, perceiving this essential weakness in their case, recommended that the line should be authorized, in order to provide what we should call now a necessary social service. Parliament did so and the West Highland was opened in 1894.

Railway companies wishing to extend their lines or services had to meet other types of opposition too, and whatever the outcome the motives behind them must always receive careful and fair analysis.   JS

William IV: *Holland House Diaries*, ed. A. D. Kriegel (1977), 315–16; Berkeley: *Railway Times* (1846); Duke of Atholl: J. Mitchell, *Reminiscences*, ii (1884), 190; *RTC*, 136–9 (Liverpool), 205–6 (Hull), 304 (Lord Derby's investments).

origins of railways, see WOODEN RAILWAYS; EARLY IRON RAILWAYS.

Oswestry, see WORKS.

Ottley. This is the name given gratefully to the most valuable single work of reference for the study pursued in this book: George Ottley's *Bibliography of British Railway History* (1965; 2nd edn., 1983; Supplement, 1988). The compiler was successively on the staff of the libraries at the British Museum and Leicester University. The volumes list almost 13,000 books and pamphlets (including some references to periodicals) under a well-considered and indexed scheme of classification.

No such work can ever be exhaustive. Hitherto unknown books—still more, unknown pamphlets—will always be turning up in unlikely places; so are many new publications, not supplied to the *British National Bibliography.* But the remarkable comprehensiveness achieved by Ottley's unwearied vigilance gains a decisive tribute when booksellers describe an unrecorded rarity as 'not in Ottley'; a phrase seldom required.   JS

Outram, Benjamin (1764–1805), engineer; born in Alfreton, Derbyshire, eldest son of Joseph Outram, estate agent; he joined William *Jessop as superintendent on the Cromford Canal. Discoveries of ore led to the establishment of the ironworks, B. Outram & Co., in 1792. Outram was managing partner but simultaneously constructed several *canals, including the Peak Forest Canal and Railway (i.e. *tramroad); also the Huddersfield Narrow Canal.

After 1801, Outram concentrated on management of the ironworks and on building railways, notably the Ashby (or Ticknall), and the Sirhowy and others in South Wales, with his cousin John Hodgkinson as agent. Benjamin's brother, Joseph, was involved in this contract work.

Outram developed improved specifications for railway construction, rolling stock, and operational management. After his death the ironworks became the Butterley Company. Outram's son was Sir James Outram, 'the Bayard of India'.   RBS

Overend Gurney Bank failure, see SPECULATION.

overhead railways built end-to-end as such, like New York's 'elevated', were uncommon in Britain. The *London & Greenwich Railway (1836–8), 3¾ miles on 878 brick arches, falls within this definition, together with the steel *Liverpool Overhead Railway, 6½ miles long, of 1896. In recent times the Birmingham Airport *Maglev system (1984–95) ran on an elevated concrete structure, as does the driverless overhead railway from Gatwick Airport station to the terminal building (1984), and most of the *Docklands Light Railway System in London. At various times experimental overhead *monorail systems have been tried, but none have operated commercially.

G. P. *Bidder, John Parson, and William *Baker gave evidence in favour of an elevated railway before a Lords Committee in 1863, and over some 40 years numerous schemes were promoted. The Westminster Bridge Deptford & Greenwich Railway (1839), intended to join the London &

Greenwich, was pictured as running at the Westminster end on decorative arches forming a fashionable arcade lined with shops, and the London Grand Junction Railway (1836) was to run on arches along the centre of broad streets from close to the City to join the *London & Birmingham Railway, then under construction.

In 1841 Sir Frederick Trench, MP, proposed an elevated railway on an elegant iron arcade over the Thames Embankment, then being discussed, employing *cable haulage. He was supported by Bidder and James *Walker, and in 1853 the structural engineers Fox Henderson put forward a plan for a central station for London on iron piles in the Thames, which would have required overhead approaches. A year later Sir Joseph Paxton produced a £34 million scheme for a Great Victorian Way, comprising an 11½ mile iron arcade encircling central London, and incorporating a railway. About that time an architect, James Clephan, and an engineer, William Curtis, produced a 'London Railway' plan that integrated architecture, planning, and transport. It showed an *atmospheric railway running at first-floor level on top of an iron arcade attached to elegant five-storey terraces on each side of the street, with shops underneath. Perhaps the most unlikely scheme was the London & Westminster Thames Viaduct Railway of 1864: an iron viaduct along the centre of the Thames. All these ideas were aimed at easing traffic congestion. In the event, *underground railways were built instead.   GJB

R. H. G. Thomas, *London's First Railway: The London & Greenwich* (1972); J. S. Gilks, 'Proposed Thames-Side Railway', *RM*, 107 (1961), 465; C. B. Andrews, *The Railway Age* (1937), pl. 75, 76, 80, 81; J. S. Curl, *Victorian Architecture* (1973), 60–1, pl. 31; *VR*, 166.

overseas railways, British influence on (excluding *Europe and *North America). Not only was the main-line railway a British creation, but until at least 1870 Britain was the centre of, and principal influence on, railway activity throughout the world. Thereafter, with railways opening up the largest continents, Britain's role changed character, but still remained significant.

Before 1870, Thomas *Brassey in particular contracted to build railways in India, Australia, Argentina, and Russia. British engineers established workshops and factories in a number of countries for the manufacture of locomotives, and supplies such as rails. Rolling stock—locomotives in particular—was exported from the UK to a variety of countries outside the British Empire, until such time as indigenous manufacture had been established.

Much of the investment in overseas railways was associated with mining interests. British consulting engineers were retained in a significant advisory role by many companies and were often directly involved in management. There was also the strategic dimension, by which railways were built to protect British lines of communication; before construction of the Suez Canal, to link the steamer ports in Egypt lines were built from Alexandria to Cairo, and then to Suez. Internal military requirements often dictated railway construction, such as in Sudan.

From 1870 there was major capital investment by British companies in railways outside the Empire, most notably in South America, and in particular in Argentina where the seven major British-owned railways constituted the largest UK commercial enterprise outside the Empire.

Of the total railway exports by value in the years before World War I, locomotives, rails and *track materials, and *wagons each accounted for some 25 per cent, and rolling stock materials and miscellaneous items the remainder.

Railways featured in nearly all British-controlled territories, and until the 1940s British management prevailed. Exports from the UK of motive power and rolling stock, and track and *signalling equipment, continued to be extensive. In this connection, a crucial role was played by the Crown Agents, representatives in London for the colonial railways. From the 1950s, countries that were formerly major UK markets, such as India and South Africa, began to manufacture their own locomotives and rolling stock.

The British Empire's greatest railway network was in India. Although some 50 per cent of the system was government-owned, from 1854 a guarantee system was adopted by which, in return for government supervision of routes and standards, private companies were guaranteed a set dividend, whatever the receipts in a particular year. Although the government progressively acquired company-worked lines, as late as 1930 private companies owned nearly 50 per cent of Indian railways. In 1913, India (with Burma and Ceylon) constituted the principal market for exports of British locomotives, 34 per cent by sales value of total exports. Between 1852 and 1952, Vulcan Foundry, Lancashire, alone supplied an average of one locomotive a fortnight for service in India.

The metre-gauge Federated Malay States Railways formed one of the smartest and most advanced of the British colonial railways, the network having been built up after 1885. In South Africa, railway development was initially influenced by Boer hostility towards the British, such that lines skirted their republics, but Cecil Rhodes was responsible for progress with the Cape Government Railway, connected to Pretoria in 1893. The South African War retarded progress towards a unified South African Railways system, eventually achieved in 1910. These railways were central to Rhodes' interests in gold and diamonds, and part of his dream to create a Cape to Cairo railway under British control. The Rhodesia Railways, to the same 3 ft 6 in gauge, were company-owned.

East Africa became a leading market for UK railway exports after World War II. The Kenya & Uganda Railway & Harbours undertaking was notable for integrating railway services with lake and river steamers, motor transport, and harbours, and became one of the best-run and most profitable systems in the Commonwealth. Its metre-gauge mileage totalled 1,400 compared with the 1,800-mile 3 ft 6 in gauge network of the Nigerian Government Railway, built up from 1896, and the pioneering Lagos–Jebba line. The different *track gauges of African railways militated against Rhodes' ideal of a unified system, although stock for East Africa was built with provision for conversion to the 3 ft 6 in gauge, shared by Sudan but not by Egypt which had a 4 ft 8½ in system.

Gauge problems also bedevilled Australia. Despite advice from the British government, three states refused to agree on a uniform track gauge before railway construction began, and in the event the country's network of lines featured three gauges: 5 ft 3 in, 4 ft 8½ in, and 3 ft 6 in. In Australia and New Zealand, earlier railway practice was strongly influenced by Britain, but from 1900 New Zealand followed US practice in motive power, as in time did some Australian state railways. In the period before World War I, Australasia was second only in importance to India as a market for UK railway exports.

Until *nationalization in 1948, the British-owned railways in Argentina, with their three track gauges, represented a remarkable contribution in terms of trading between the two countries. By 1914, British companies had invested £80 million in building up a 17,000 route mileage, no less than a third of this amount having been expended within the preceding decade. Some 3,000 steam locomotives were exported to Argentina in the first quarter of the 20th century, at any one time comprising over 20 per cent of UK export sales. Most railway construction had been carried out under concessions granted to the companies by the government, with a guaranteed return on investment.

Brazil was also the recipient of major British investment in railways, principally the Great Western and Leopoldina Railways. In Uruguay, British companies owned 80 per cent of the railway network. Mining interests influenced involvement in other South American railways such as the Antofagasta (Chile) and Bolivia (which survived into the 1980s under British ownership), and the London-based Peruvian Corporation which controlled that country's railway systems as subsidiaries. British interests also had an appreciable stake in Mexico's railways which were built by the contractor Weetman Pearson, featuring gradients as steep as 1 in 25 and reverse curves of 320-ft radius in linking coast and capital city.

British capital and technical assistance were significant in building up the state railway network in China after that country's defeat by the Japanese in 1895. Britain supplied the first steam locomotive to Japan in 1871, and exported locomotives and equipment for the country's electrification schemes begun in 1922.

Since 1945 there has been a growth in agencies and consultancies helping to modernize the world's railways, usually in conjunction with overseas aid funding. From 1959, this was offered through the United Kingdom Railway Advisory Service, established jointly by the Ministry of Transport and *BR. For personnel it drew on former Railway Inspecting Officers, and seconded staff from BR and the private sector. UKRAS was closely involved in the Pakistan Railways' electrification between Lahore and Khanewal.

As the scale of work increased, in 1969 BR established

Transmark as a wholly owned subsidiary to undertake consultancy services overseas, including investigating the case for new lines, and carrying out engineering, marketing, and operating studies. Transmark has been active in over 80 countries and under *privatization was sold in 1993, to join the growing number of railway consultancy organizations in the private sector. MLH

M. Robbins, *The Railway Age* (1962); Political & Economic Planning, *Locomotives* (1951); J. N. Sahni, *Indian Railways: One Hundred Years* (1953); Locomotive & Allied Manufacturers' Association, *British Locomotives* (1960); D. S. Purdom, *British Steam on the Pampas* (1977).

Oxford Worcester & Wolverhampton Railway, see WEST MIDLAND RAILWAY.

P

Paddington station, see LONDON STATIONS.

Paget, Sir Cecil, see CONTROL, SYSTEMS OF TRAIN.

parcels traffic. In addition to passengers the stage-
*coaches always carried parcels, from little consignments of
jewellery to heavy packages. The railways seized on this
business quickly. The *Grand Junction announced at its
outset in 1837 that it would convey parcels at a minimum
charge of 1s. 6d. The *Liverpool & Manchester had operated a delivery service in *Manchester since 1833. The Sheffield Ashton & Manchester Railway (see GREAT CENTRAL)
undertook in 1843 to deliver parcels within one mile of its
stations.

At that time the work of the *Post Office was confined to
letters. In 1837 Rowland Hill unsuccessfully tried to get its
powers extended to include parcels. However, he secured a
book post in 1848, and in 1863 a pattern post, but that was
abused, and discontinued in 1871. Hill and his brother continued to advocate a parcel post, carried under agreement
by the railways and delivered through the Post Office's existing services.

The railways opposed this plan strenuously, contending
that the book post had caused them substantial losses. But
they were hampered by the multiplicity of companies, each
with powers to impose what rates it might choose, subject
to any limits set by their Acts of incorporation. It took a
long time, and much argument at the *Railway Clearing
House, to get agreement on charges for carrying parcels,
but in 1865 one was at last apparently accepted by all the
companies, including some of importance that had not yet
joined the RCH.

These discussions concerned parcels carried by passenger
train. The Post Office had no ambition to handle large or
bulky articles—sacks of coal, for instance, or ironware—
which were transported on the railways as *freight.

In 1871 a serious effort was made to reach agreement
between the Clearing House and the Post Office. That failing, later in the year letter rates were considerably reduced,
making it economic to send a substantial package (i.e. a
small parcel) in that way. This ought to have been a warning
to the companies, but they continued their internecine
squabbles, and at last the government stepped in. Under the
Post Office (Parcels) Act, 1882, the Post Office was allowed
to handle them from 1883. The refusal of the railways to act
effectively together had brought about their well-deserved
defeat.

There remained the problem of fixing rates for carrying
parcels that were acceptable to the Post Office and the rail-

ways, and the battles were constant, leading the postal
authorities to experiment with other forms of transport.
They started running large horse-drawn parcels vans, by
1896 used on eight principal routes from London. From
1906 onwards motor vans were being used, running in 1913
from *London as far as *Liverpool and *Bournemouth.

After World War I railways no longer monopolized long-
distance overland transport. Road motor vehicles handled
small parcels more flexibly, though the railways developed
collection and delivery services in their own motor vans.
Their receipts from parcels traffic declined a little after 1917.
But 30 years later they rose again: to some extent naturally,
on the establishment of the *British Transport Commission
which was responsible for road as well as railway services.
But the handling of parcels in passenger trains, usually in
compartments of the guards' vans, had always been a cause
of trouble in operation. The time occupied by loading and
unloading frequently caused delays at stations.

In 1963 *BR introduced a new registered parcels service,
'Red Star', designed to provide fast and certain delivery, in
direct competition with the Post Office. The charges made
for it were high, but it proved reliable and was for a long
time widely used. But in the end this service did not prove
cost-effective. In 1991 it was brought within a new business
sector of BR, named 'Parcels Group'.   JS
  M. J. Daunton, *Royal Mail* (1986), 65–6; Bagwell, ch. 5; D. L.
  Munby and A. H. Watson, *Inland Transport Statistics* (1978), table
  A13.

Park, C. A., see LONDON & NORTH WESTERN RAILWAY.

Parker, Sir Peter, see BRITISH RAILWAYS.

parkway stations, see STATIONS, PARKWAY.

Parliament and legislation. Parliament served two main
purposes in relation to railways: as the chief—though not
the sole—agency by which the laws and regulations were
established, controlling them in the public interest; and as a
forum for the discussion of matters of any kind concerning
them.

The Process of Legislation
The two Houses of Parliament, Lords and Commons, were
more sharply different during the *Railway Age than they
are today. Excepting bishops and judges, all members of the
House of Lords sat there by some kind of hereditary right;
the creation of life peerages, in the form familiar now, dates
only from 1958. The members of the Commons (or MPs),
658 in number representing the whole of the British Isles,
were all elected.

Parliament and legislation

In the 18th century both Houses had represented predominantly the interests of landed property and agriculture. But with the growth and multiplication of manufactures in the later part of that century, demands arose more and more insistently for an alteration of the franchise for the election of MPs, in order to take account of this development. They were met in part by the Reform Act of 1832, and more fully by its two successors in 1867 and 1884–5. The franchise remained entirely with men until 1918.

Throughout the 19th century most MPs in England, Wales, and Scotland belonged to one of two parties: Tory (or Conservative), Whig (or Liberal). In many ways, however, Parliament constituted a criss-cross of interests and opinions rather than a confrontation of two united parties, each with its own programme. This was particularly true where railways were concerned. No important policy pursued by any government towards them ever became, during the 19th century, a matter of party politics.

Parliamentary legislation affecting railways took two different forms: Public General Acts (referred to here as PGAs), promoted by the government and dealing with matters of broad public policy; and either (in very early days) Private Acts, or Local and Personal Acts (LPAs). These measures came before Parliament first as Bills, those for the establishment of private companies having first been examined to see that their terms did not conflict with the standing orders of either of the Houses, and then by committees of them both. If accepted thus and passed by the two Houses they received the Royal Assent. The LPAs empowered the companies' promoters to acquire *land by compulsory purchase, to raise or borrow what *capital they needed (within stated limits), and to build and equip their lines (see PROMOTION PROCEDURE).

As soon as firm plans came forward for the construction of long-distance railways, early in the 1830s, when their lines began to take shape as a national *system, it was necessary to consider the state's attitude towards them. Should the government plan the lines of the system itself and control them, as the Belgian government set out to do in 1834? Or should the lines be laid down and built by privately financed companies, limited and to some extent guided by legislation, just as the British *canals had been? (See also GOVERNMENT, RAILWAYS AND NATIONAL.) No politician of any importance contended that the state should plan, construct, and work them. But what degree of control by the government should be established, to safeguard the interests of the public at large? The history of the *turnpike trusts and the canal companies offered little guidance here, for railways were in many respects different undertakings from them, in scale and technology and economic strength.

Although there was an outburst of wild financial speculation in 1835–7, in which railways figured prominently, Parliament paid it very little attention. But as the excitement was dying down in 1837 (and with the first trunk line, the *Grand Junction, nearing completion) the Commons appointed a 'Select Committee on Railroads'. This was the first of a long series set up by one House or the other or jointly, from their members, to investigate railways, empowered to call witnesses as they pleased (see COMMISSIONS AND PARLIAMENTARY COMMITTEES). The record of the evidence given to them and the conclusions they drew from it afford a most valuable body of evidence for the student of British railway history.

The government played no part in setting up the companies, nor did it begin to legislate on railways (save only indirectly) until 1838, when it obliged the railways to provide the *Post Office with the services it asked for at a 'reasonable remuneration', to be settled if necessary by arbitrators. The outcome was the passage of the Railways (Conveyance of Mails) Act, 1838, the first measure that shows the British government legislating to secure for the public a social benefit that the railways were equipped to supply.

This was followed by the Regulation of Railways Act (1840), the earliest in a series of nine that were passed down to 1893 (see REGULATION ACTS). These were not designed to build up a code of railway management and practice, after the fashion of the codes laid down in many European countries, where the state owned or controlled all, or most, of the railways. In Britain the government owned no railways at all, except some within military or naval bases. But it could 'regulate' anything the companies did if it chose to do so. The Act of 1840 required them to send to the Board of *Trade annual *returns of their traffic and of *accidents occurring on their lines.

The Crisis of 1844–52

When, in 1844, it appeared that a fresh outbreak of railway promotion was at hand, much larger than that of 1835–7 (see MANIAS), it became clearly desirable that new means should be found to enable Parliament to handle applications for powers to construct lines, better suited to this enormous demand. The government set up a committee of five, charged with the preliminary examination of all railway projects (see DALHOUSIE), to assist the parliamentary committees that had to consider each of them individually. It incurred the hostility of many MPs because it encroached on the old committees' powers. It was abolished in 1845, leaving the business of promotion to be handled in the following year by the traditional method alone. The quantity of that was again very large, and stretched the committees well beyond their capacity.

Reviewing the performance of Parliament in relation to railways at this critical time, many people considered it deplorable. Railway affairs were understood by only a small number of members, and those who did know something of them often had interests of their own, as investors or landowners for example, which were bound to influence the policies they supported. In 1844 a change was made in the rules governing the composition of these committees, disqualifying any MP from serving on one of them if his constituents were affected by a projected railway that it was considering; but this touched only one part of the problem.

Parliament now decided, in 1846, to establish a Railway Commission, under the chairmanship of an MP. But that experiment did not seem to turn out well, and in 1852 the Commission was abolished, its duties reverting to the Board of Trade. The Board kept Parliament continuously informed of the exercise of the powers statutorily granted to it by 'laying papers on the table' of each House, on which members were entitled to ask questions.

The Railway Interest

While the two Commons committees of 1837–9 were sitting, two informal, extra-parliamentary bodies were called together, representing the railway companies' boards, to ensure that their interests were not overlooked. Each of them concentrated its attention on one set of legislative proposals and was then dissolved. Nevertheless, it soon began to appear that a new 'interest' (or what might now be called a pressure-group) was emerging that might well become comparable with the well-recognized and powerful East and West India Interests: a 'Railway Interest'. Already 11 directors of railway companies sat in the House of Commons. Over the next 20 years that number grew strikingly, to 80 by 1847 and 96 by 1859—by which time members of the House of Lords who were railway directors numbered 44. It must not be assumed that they acted in unison, or indeed that they would act in any way whatever: as one of them put it, 'they had not been sent to Parliament as guardians of railway proprietaries'. But there were matters affecting railways on which a number of them would speak and act together, and their wishes had to be taken into consideration by governments. The Railway Interest soon began to insert itself into the machinery of Parliament.

When the excitement of the Mania had died down the Interest went further towards joint action between the companies. A committee including all railway directors sitting in either House was set up in 1855, to watch parliamentary business affecting them. In 1870 it was replaced by a *Railway Companies Association, a stronger body that lasted until 1947. (See also POLITICS, RAILWAYS IN.)

During these years individual companies obtained powers from Parliament to provide *ancillary services that had been sought but seldom granted. In 1860–4 four important companies were authorized to acquire and operate ships of their own: against the opposition of the Shipping Interest, which argued that this represented an unwarrantable extension of their powers, beyond their proper business of working railways. At the same time Parliament freely permitted them to build and run *hotels, facilitating that by passing Bills that included provisions for raising additional capital for the purpose.

Taking into account all these measures, and also two Acts passed in 1864 (Improvement of Land, and Railways Construction Facilities), together with the notable new services provided in London in the early 1860s (with the introduction of *workmen's trains, and the opening of the first *London underground line), the railways now seemed to be climbing to a new high point of achievement. But in fact this was the apex of their power, in Parliament and in the country.

The Companies' Declining Strength

The third and last speculative mania of railway promotion began in 1864, and left behind it another grim trail of disappointed hopes, bankruptcies, and lost savings. While it was in progress a Royal Commission on Railways was sitting, charged with powers to investigate the whole of their business, which it examined honestly and most laboriously, but to little effect in the end. In 1867 it advised against any extension of the government's control over the railways.

However, in 1868 Parliament passed a Regulation Act that did something to curtail the companies' freedom to run their business as they chose. It stiffened the rules regarding the preparation of their accounts and allowed the Board of Trade, in certain circumstances, to appoint inspectors to report on them: a clear commentary on the failing financial state of the *London Brighton & South Coast, *London Chatham & Dover, and *Great Eastern companies, as well as some others. It also required the companies to publish lists of *fares and *freight rates at their stations. And it attempted to require them to provide means of *communication between passengers and train crews in emergency, though perfectly aware that the techniques then employed for this purpose would prove undependable in practice.

Here were indications of some change in the attitude of Parliament towards railways. Hints of that came out into the open in 1871–2. A committee of both Houses then recommended against authorizing two powerful companies, the *London & North Western and *Lancashire & Yorkshire, to *amalgamate, thereby putting a stop also to similar proposals by others. Had these powers been granted, large tracts of England and Scotland might have passed straight away into the hands of new railway *monopolies. The stand that Parliament took here was positive and strong. More than 20 years then passed before it received any more proposals of the same kind.

Parliament now began to look further into complaints of abused monopoly that had arisen during the discussions of the amalgamation proposals, taking serious note of the rising protests made by commercial firms against the rates that the companies charged for the conveyance of their goods. Out of this deliberation there came the establishment of a new legal court in 1873, entitled (confusingly) the Railway Commission, charged with investigating any of these allegations brought before it, whether by private interests or by local government bodies, and pronouncing on their validity. The evidence given in the cases heard by the Commission showed that many of them were well founded.

The Railway Companies Association proved powerless to combat any of these measures, which in rapid succession revealed the declining strength of the Railway Interest since 1864. The number of MPs who were railway directors had not declined: indeed it reached its peak in 1873, at 132. But the railways' popularity in the country was waning for good.

Parliament also responded to public anxiety by giving increased attention to railway accidents. They were investigated by another Royal Commission, appointed in 1874, which was unable to suggest any certain remedies when it reported in 1880. That was not the Commission's fault, for while it was at work new forms of *brakes were being tried out, and it was they that in the end did most to reduce the numbers and severity of accidents. An exceptionally frightful one in 1889 prompted the passing of a new Regulation Act, two features of which were notable. First, Parliament rushed the Bill through all its stages at an exceptionally high speed. The accident itself occurred on 12 June; the Act *went into force* on 30 August. And secondly, here at last the government accepted the responsibility for dictating methods of operation to the companies, requiring all lines carrying passenger trains to be worked on the *block system and all such trains to be fitted with instantaneously working continuous brakes, the Board of Trade being authorized to fix time limits for completion of the work.

With an ill grace and some shuffling, the companies implemented the Act. As soon as they had done so, serious accidents caused by inadequate braking ceased in Britain (though it ought perhaps to be remembered that the worst railway accident that is known to have happened anywhere in Europe, at St Michel-de-Maurienne in 1917, was due to this cause, 543 French soldiers dying there). Here was the most striking example of the direct intervention of the state in the working of British railways in the 19th century, and it proved entirely beneficent.

Delegated Legislation

The Act of 1889 represented a striking exception to Parliament's usual practice. It had always been reluctant to concern itself with technological devices, not only in transport but also in manufacturing industry. Though willing to regulate hours of work in textile mills and to require the appointment of inspectors to enforce its decisions, it did not prescribe the types of machinery to be used. Where railways were concerned, it had been content to leave the execution of its broadly framed laws to be supervised by civil servants in the Board of Trade, sometimes—though not invariably—requiring the Board to report to Parliament at stated intervals on what it had done. But Parliament was always wary of adopting the expedient sometimes later called 'delegated legislation'.

Any legislative body may reasonably relieve itself of some minor responsibilities, in order to help it to pay proper attention to those of greater importance, and the authority to make *bye-laws was written into most of the LPAs establishing railway companies. The Railways Clauses Act of 1845 (sect. 109) gave this power to all railway companies alike, subject to the disallowance of any bye-law by the Board of Trade.

In 1869 Parliament took another step in the direction of delegating its legislative powers over railways. The bankrupt London Chatham & Dover Railway had fallen into a financial tangle that it was incapable of unravelling itself. Parliament then, in Clifford's words, 'confessed its helplessness, as a court of law does in hearing the main facts', and decided that it was 'not competent to deal with so complicated an issue'. Accordingly, it appointed two wise and very able men, Lord Salisbury and Lord Cairns, to formulate an arrangement straightening out the company's finances.

This they did, and their award was simply included in an LPA of 1871.

During the 1870s and 1880s English arable farming grew steadily less profitable (see AGRICULTURE), and some MPs complained that rural districts lacked the benefit of services available in and around towns. The building of branch railways had slackened off, many of them having proved commercially unprofitable, and a determined effort was made in the 1890s to find means of extending the railway system into such districts by constructing cheap *light railways, similar to those that had proved their value in France and Belgium.

Parliament now passed a Light Railways Act in 1896, to facilitate the provision of services of this sort, financed in part, if necessary, by the national Exchequer or local authorities. A Light Railways Commission was created by the Act, whose members were to be appointed by the President of the Board of Trade and empowered to give or refuse their consent to such applications, their Orders being subject to confirmation by the Board. Parliament, however, learnt of these only from a report presented to it once a year, by which time some of the work involved was already well under way.

This was delegated legislation indeed. No Acts were required for the construction of these railways. The authorizing Orders were issued by a body that Parliament *did not itself appoint*. Minor amendments were made to the Act in 1901 and 1912, but they left its principles untouched. Here Parliament surrendered some of its own powers relating to railways into hands better suited to exercising them than its own.

The public unpopularity of the railway companies increased markedly towards the end of the Victorian age, and Parliament heeded it. (In certain constituencies it was noted as an element in campaigning at the general election of 1892.) The Hood case (see STATIONMASTERS) could hardly fail to make a deplorable impression on fair-minded people, culminating in a summons to members of the *Cambrian Railways board, together with John *Conacher, who had been the company's general manager at the material time, to receive the formal admonition of the Speaker for a breach of parliamentary privilege. And an even worse showing emerged in the course of the evidence given to a Commons committee on railwaymen's hours of work, which led to the Regulation Act of 1893, designed—though not very effectively—to restrict them. It was followed in 1900 by the Railway Companies (Prevention of Accidents) Act, empowering the Board of Trade and the Railway and Canal Commission to require the companies to adopt appliances and precautions to increase the safety of their servants. They were coming now to be widely considered as bad employers, their servants needing special protection from the law while they were at work.

What had become of the Railway Interest? The RCA was active in briefing MPs and in lobbying, and the companies' defence did not go by default in Parliament. But it was in truth a losing fight, partly through the growing power of the *trade unions and the representatives of labour in the

Commons, even more because the companies' own strength was declining.

For that there were several reasons. The new technical devices they were being forced to adopt, as well as more that they chose to employ for the faster running of their intensely competitive services, cost a great deal of money, which had to be found from accumulated profits, from borrowing, and from pegging or reducing dividends; scarcely any increases in rates and fares were now permissible. In the closing years of the 19th century, moreover, they were threatened by a new kind of competition, from electric street *tramways, which made some serious inroads into their suburban traffic. The general impression they made in Britain was of an old and tired industry, battling with endless rises in costs, and their performance had come to look especially unimpressive in Parliament. *Lloyd George (not naturally at all well-disposed to the companies) remarked in the Commons in 1913: 'It is rather a difficult task in this House to recommend any measure which seems in the slightest degree to favour railway companies.'

While the country was at *war in 1914–18 and the government was responsible for running the railways, Parliament had little to say about them. But when peace returned their future came under its discussion almost immediately. The benefits that arose from central control had been widely appreciated, and there was now some determined support in Parliament for nationalizing them (see NATIONALIZATION, CONCEPT OF). But a large majority of MPs favoured leaving them in private hands, and the Railways Act of 1921 (see GROUPING) was passed without any substantial difficulty, providing for the amalgamation of 120 companies into four. It went into force on 1 January 1923.

The *Big Four

The new companies had now to accept that they no longer held a monopoly of land transport throughout the island, for mechanized haulage of traffic by road rapidly increased year by year to 1939. Parliament took note of this, and granted them some relief and assistance by the introduction of a licensing system for road vehicles, giving the authorities power to control their numbers, and it also agreed to place Treasury money at the railway companies' disposal for carrying through some large works of improvement. But the new companies, though each of them was a much larger corporation than any of its predecessors had been, and enjoyed a monopoly of rail transport over a large tract of Great Britain, were seldom able to make any powerful public impression, commensurate with their collective importance as one of the greatest industries in the country.

Moreover, in Parliament they now faced a potential danger that had never confronted them before. They had been preserved as privately owned corporations in 1921. But from 1923 onwards the Labour party constituted the main Opposition, the only one that could replace the Conservatives, then in office; and that party was committed to nationalizing the railways. The policies of the two parties on a very important railway matter now appeared as political creeds, totally opposed. Railways had become a party issue at last.

*Nationalization and *Privatization

The Conservative party dominated Parliament almost continuously from 1921 to 1940, when a coalition government was formed, which fought World War II to its end. But then the election of 1945 brought a Labour government into power, with a firm majority, and it was quick to frame and drive through the nationalization of most of the inland transport system, against fierce Conservative opposition. The Act of 1947 went into force on 1 January 1948: a thorough-going measure comprehending all but the very smallest railways, together with the inland waterways and much of the road transport industry. All these were placed under the authority of a newly created *British Transport Commission (BTC). The Commission established 'Executives' to manage different divisions of its responsibilities, a Railway Executive being one of them. The relationship between the BTC and that Executive was never easy and sometimes badly strained. The Executive was dissolved in 1953, and in the same year the road undertakings were returned to private ownership by the Conservatives. The BTC itself was abolished by them in 1962, making a *British Railways Board solely responsible to Parliament and the government for the railways.

These and similar shifts of policy, depending on the results of general elections, made it difficult to frame long-term policies. Only one serious effort was made in this direction, when in 1955 (under a Conservative government) the BTC produced a *Modernization Plan for the railways. This was a good document, but its implementation was marred by some questionable policy decisions and, in the longer term, by financial constrictions arising largely from changes of attitude taken towards the railways by successive governments.

Then came the long, unbroken series of Conservative governments, in power from 1979 onwards, moving steadily towards abolition of the nationalized railway system established in 1947, which was achieved at length in the Transport Act of 1993 (see PRIVATIZATION). This moved the railways back, in terms of their ownership, management, and operation, not merely to where they had been in 1947 but further still, to their position in 1922.

In the last period of this story one thing stands out. It was purely a battle of political parties and their programmes. Few members of either House of Parliament were ever able to speak up for the railways, explaining there why this or that proposed measure could or could not be made to work satisfactorily. Outside Parliament, *public opinion seldom showed any active interest in them, except when stirred up momentarily by some single event (usually an accident). In Parliament they were now subject solely to politicians and the party machines.   JS

J. Bigg, *Collection of the Public General Acts for the Regulation of Railways* (16 edns., 1845–1912); Local and Personal Acts: long runs of these are to be found in the BL and the copyright libraries at Oxford, Cambridge, Aberystwyth, and Edinburgh; Parliamentary Papers, or Sessional Papers: there is a separate annual series for each House—sets (none of them quite complete) are in

parliamentary plans

the BL and copyright libraries; Sir I. Jennings, *Parliament* (1919); W. Hodges, *Treatise on the Law of Railways* (7 edns., 1855–89); F. Clifford, *History of Private Bill Legislation* (1885–7); L. James, *The Law of Railways* (1980); G. Alderman, *The Railway Interest* (1973).

parliamentary plans are detailed surveys of the line of a proposed railway including all the lands which would be affected by it; from 1799 they were required by Parliament, with other documents, to be put on public deposit as part of the statutory process, and their form and content has been specified over the years by a succession of parliamentary Standing Orders.

The traditional private wayleave developed for *tramroad construction had a number of drawbacks, principally that if a particular owner refused to co-operate there was no way that the line could be built short of avoiding his land altogether; and this might be difficult or impossible to achieve. Promoters therefore petitioned Parliament for authority to build extended lines of communication, with powers of compulsory purchase cutting across the often fragmented land ownership pattern. This process necessitated accurate *surveys, and some 18th-century *canal and road Acts came to include a clause compelling the applicants, before construction commenced, to prepare and make available for public inspection a plan showing all the affected lands, refining the general route description in the text. For canal schemes this process was codified from 1792 by a parliamentary Standing Order requiring this at the time the Bill was introduced, so that owners and occupiers would have clear knowledge of the intentions and a chance to petition against anything which adversely affected their interests. The arrangements were extended to railway Bills in 1810, and by the dawn of the *railway age the requirements were for a plan at a scale of at least 4 in to the mile, details of the depth and height of cuttings and embankments, a book of reference to all the owners and occupiers likely to be affected, and (from 1846) a published index map which was to be the one-inch scale Ordnance Survey where available. By 30 November copies for the forthcoming parliamentary session had to be deposited with each county authority affected by the line, with the Private Bill Office at Westminster, and a variety of other specified bodies.

The parliamentary plan was originally a manuscript, but as the need for duplicates increased, so the use of engraved or lithographed prints spread. These were not only cheaper than laborious manual copying, but exact facsimiles were assured. From the 1840s the typical deposit would comprise a title page, a set of numbered sheets covering the whole route, a sheet of the one-inch OS map with the line picked out in colour, and a longitudinal section, either on the relevant plan sheets or separately. The whole would be bound in paper, cloth, or leather covers, and rolled. The plan showed the detailed topography of the area through which the line was proposed, with county, parish, and other boundaries; the commencement and termination of the line with some detail of other lines it was joining; the centre-line of the proposal with distances in miles and furlongs; and enlarged plans of complex areas, particularly in towns. Each

'parcel' of property affected had a unique number as a key to the separate book of reference which gave a brief description with the names of the owner, lessee, and occupier, each of whom had to be sent a formal notice advising of the intended application. Dotted lines on the plans showed the limits to which it was proposed that the railway could be deviated under the intended Act; whilst flexibility was desirable, widening the limits of deviation affected more lands and increased the potential opposition. If necessary the centre-line could lawfully be taken right out to the limit of deviation which meant that half the width of the formation might be constructed outside it. This point caused many difficulties, and later practice has been to specify that the limits shown are both of deviation and of land purchase.

Accuracy in production was essential, for one of the first tasks of a scheme's opponent was to go through it minutely to find any errors on which to mount an attack in Parliament; to prove compliance with Standing Orders was one of the promoter's earliest tasks, and surveying errors were a common cause of failure. The 1825 Bill for George *Stephenson's *Liverpool & Manchester Railway was doomed once the opposition had discovered serious discrepancies in the levels at the eastern end—his surveyors were at fault but it was Stephenson who took the blame, and lost his appointment as a result. This need for exactitude did not fit comfortably with the rapidity of completion in order to meet the November deadline, with the whole process of field surveying, checking, drawing up, and printing often squeezed between the autumn harvest and the end of November. During the *'Mania' year of 1845 when hundreds of plans for new lines were surveyed and deposited, the services of experienced surveyors were at a premium and lengthy trunk routes were drawn up by office boys and others with only a cursory knowledge of surveying techniques. That most failed to pass Standing Orders is little surprise.

The historical importance of these plans must be emphasized, particularly when read in conjunction with the other documents forming part of the statutory process. With their aid can be traced the exact route of the unfinished Manchester & Milford Railway through the mountains of central Wales, the attempts to shorten the coastal route around the Lake District by crossing the Duddon estuary, and the fierce battles to secure territory between warring companies.

Unusually for plans, the detail they record can be correctly dated to within a month or so, and is often unavailable elsewhere; as an example the *Chester & Holyhead's Chester Extension plan of November 1846 shows the layout of the first Chester stations at Brook Street before the line was diverted for the new General station. Routes proposed through colliery districts usually record shafts, pithead buildings, and the networks of tramroads serving them. The plans of 1853 for the Port Carlisle Dock & Railway give an accurate view of the canal over which it was built with all the locks, etc., and similar information can be found for the Uttoxeter Canal, Hay Railway, and other transport routes which were adapted for railway use.

Lines promoted under the *Light Railways Act of 1896

needed similar plans, although the authorization procedure was different. Useful railway information can also be gleaned from the parliamentary plans for other public schemes such as dock, *tramway, water, and gas undertakings; the plans for the Manchester Ship Canal Act include several miles of railway diversions to accommodate the waterway.

The House of Lords Record Office holds the plans for all proposals that were enacted, with supplementary deposits for amendments made in committee. County Record Offices are a better source for the full range of deposited schemes, including those that subsequently failed Standing Orders or were not progressed. In most cases each county has the complete set of plans, however small the portion of route that lay within it.

Parliamentary plans are a neglected source of information that deserve further study; few railway historians have fully exploited their potential.

See also PROMOTION PROCEDURE; MAPS AND PLANS; JUNCTION DIAGRAMS; LAND ACQUISITION.   RJD

RS; F. Clifford, *History of Private Bill Legislation* (1887); P. Hindle, *Maps for Local History* (1988); D. Smith, *Maps and Plans for the Historian and Collector* (1988); O. C. Williams, *The Historical Development of Private Bill Procedure and Standing Orders in the House of Commons* (2 vols., 1948).

parliamentary trains. The origin of these trains reaches back to Christmas Eve 1841, when a bad *accident occurred on the *Great Western Railway at Sonning, east of Reading, in which eight third-class passengers were killed, travelling by a goods train in low-sided open wagons. The *inspector's report drew attention to the dangers of carrying passengers in such accommodation, initiating within the Board of *Trade a general inquiry into the conveyance of third-class passengers throughout the country. In 1844 *Gladstone, then President of the Board, carried through an Act that compelled all future 'passenger railways' (i.e. those drawing at least one-third of their income from passenger traffic) to run at least one daily train (Sundays included), calling at every station, travelling at not less than 12 mph including stops, and carrying their passengers in enclosed vehicles provided with seats, at a *fare not exceeding 1d. per mile, including 56 lb of luggage. Having met those requirements, any railway company was exempted from the payment of passenger tax on these fares (see TAXATION, NATIONAL), then levied at 5 per cent.

This was a remarkable piece of legislation, on two counts. Here, for the first time, the British government interfered directly with the companies' operations (see GOVERNMENT, RAILWAYS AND NATIONAL). And the remission of passenger duty clearly involved a sacrifice of revenue by the Treasury, to secure what would now be called a social benefit.

The Act went into force on 1 November 1844, and Board of Trade officials set themselves to examine the vehicles that the companies were providing for these 'parliamentary trains', publishing drawings and commenting on their deficiencies. Although the Act applied only to railways not yet sanctioned, almost all companies accepted its provisions,

enticed by the tax remission. Before 1850, with unimportant exceptions, these trains were available on every line in Great Britain.

They did not supplant the old third-class trains. Any company was still free to convey passengers at whatever rates it chose, and some offered third-class and parliamentary fares side by side, the third-class being subject to passenger tax but not bound by the conditions laid down in the 1844 Act.

Bitter complaints were made by some companies that many of their passengers now travelled at 1d. a mile who could easily afford to pay more; they were particularly loud in Scotland. For this there was no remedy. A railway company could not dictate the class by which its passengers must travel.

The 12-mph minimum speed of a parliamentary train represented very fast travelling in 1844, when few of the best and most expensive horse-drawn *coaches attained a speed of 10 mph. But by the 1870s, when some railways admitted third-class passengers to *express trains, it had become very slow. Dispute grew up between the companies and the Board of Trade, leading to legal action in 1874, about the exact conditions under which exemptions from passenger duty could be granted. The courts ruled that duty was payable on 'parliamentary *tickets' used in trains that did not stop at every station, as the Act required. In 1877 a Travelling Tax Abolition Committee was established. Total abolition of all such taxation was not achieved until 1929. But under well-organized pressure from that committee, a Cheap Trains Act was passed in 1883, exempting all 1d.-a-mile fares from duty.

'Parliamentary tickets' did not then disappear. Some companies retained them, chiefly as a legal precaution. The *Cambrian Railways still informed their passengers in 1914 that 'first-class and parliamentary tickets are issued by all trains' on their system. The *Bishop's Castle Railway was still issuing tickets marked 'parliamentary' at the end of its life in 1935.

The chairman of the committee of 1877, G. J. Holyoake, paid a generous and just tribute to the parliamentary train in 1901. He described it as 'a successful invention though a tedious benefit. . . . To workmen of small means the Parliamentary train was a considerate device as it enabled thousands to travel who otherwise could not travel at all.'   JS

C. E. Lee, *Passenger Class Distinctions* (1946); Robertson, 241–3; G. J. Holyoake, *History of the Travelling Tax* (1901), 5; Cambrian Railways timetable, PRO, R927/41; E. C. Griffith, *Bishop's Castle Railway* (1969 edn.), 54.

Pasley, Sir Charles William (1780–1861). After wide military service in 1796–1809 he established the Royal Engineers Institution at Chatham, directing it in 1812–41. He then became *inspector of railways at the Board of *Trade (1841–6). His duties were at first vaguely defined, but they included the inspection of all new lines, with power to prevent their opening if he considered them unsafe, and also the investigation of serious *accidents. Though others occasionally reported on these matters, Pasley remained the sole inspector until 1844, when a second one (co-equal with himself) was appointed. He performed his very large task with great energy, as can be seen from the diary he kept daily, now in the British Library.

He had to establish a good working relationship with the railway companies; not easy when he criticized them, obliging them to spend money in rectifying errors. But his personality was genial, he appreciated the value of diplomacy, and he made himself respected.

He had also to enlarge his own knowledge of railways, and he learnt about them not only during inspections but also from visits to manufacturers—to Sharp Roberts' locomotive works at *Manchester, for example, and to the builders of the first railway swing bridge outside *Norwich (SEE BRIDGES AND VIADUCTS). Within the public service, however, his personal relationships were less fortunate, and when the Board's railway powers were transferred to the Railway *Commissioners in 1846, he was superseded, having no further connection with railways thereafter.   JS

DNB; GR; H. W. Parris, 'Pasley's Diary: A Neglected Source of Railway History', JTH, 6 (1963–4), 14–23.

passenger journeys. The numbers of 'passenger journeys' made on railways must not be confused with the 'numbers of passengers carried'. The expressions denote two different things.

The numbers of tickets booked at each station and given up at the end of journeys were recorded by the railway companies, and some of them survive (see STATISTICS). Occasionally the railways took censuses of the numbers of people travelling in selected trains, or arriving at individual stations; but they were very uncommon and usually occurred on a single occasion for some special purpose. None that is of real value covering any continuous series of years seems to exist now (though see CHESHIRE LINES). More effective attempts were made after *nationalization, some to assist a case for closing an unprofitable line, others as part of a regular routine for monitoring main-line traffic. But even such a counting of heads cannot give us exact figures of the 'numbers of passengers'. One of them arriving on his daily journey to work at 9 a.m. and returning home from the same station at 5.30 p.m. is one person, but in any census of this sort becomes two. If that passenger travels on about 230 days in the year, he or she has become 460 'passengers' by the end of it. That is how they appear in any simple total of 'numbers of passengers carried'. Observing this confusion, the Board of *Trade inspector Henry *Tyler coined the phrase 'passenger journeys', in reporting in 1877 on the *accidents of the previous year.

These figures are of more than technical importance when they are used to purport the quantity of railway travelling in Great Britain per head of population. All they are able to show is the number of journeys made, divided by the figures of population given in the preceding decennial census. For the year 1913 that figure was about 27. It is right to use these totals of *passenger journeys* as the basis of comparisons between one year and another or between railways of one country and another. But they do not tell us how many individual persons in Great Britain actually made use

of railways, or to what extent; something still unknown today, as in the past.   JS

For Tyler's phrase see PP 1871, lx. iii.

passenger mileage, see STATISTICS.

Passenger's Charter, see PUNCTUALITY.

passenger train traffic. This phrase does not, in the railways' ordinary language, refer to the carriage of passengers alone. It means 'traffic by passenger trains', including *parcels, *mails, *newspapers, *milk, and *fish, that were also conveyed in them. This usage did not establish itself at once. In the earlier annual accounts of the companies it is not always clear whether the narrower or the broader sense of the expression is being used; there is similar uncertainty in the Board of *Trade *returns. As used in this article, it means 'traffic by passenger trains'.

The early railways were built for carrying *freight, though workmen and others sometimes rode on the wagons. The first regular passenger service was provided on the *Swansea & Mumbles Railway by a *contractor, licensed by the company, in 1807. When the *Stockton & Darlington Railway was opened in 1825 it also contracted out the passenger business, as a side-line, to coach proprietors who ran their vehicles on the railway; but it took the work over itself in 1833.

The *Liverpool & Manchester Railway was also originally intended to be a carrier of freight, but at the opening in 1830 it ran only a passenger service, provided by itself. When freight traffic began, the revenue from passengers proved more valuable, to the surprise of many people within and outside the company. In 1831–45 passenger revenue furnished 56.4 per cent of its total traffic receipts. This disparity appeared also on the first trunk railway, the *Grand Junction, where in 1845, the last year of its independent operation, the share of passenger revenue was the greater by almost exactly the same amount.

These unexpected results were due primarily to one cause. After the LMR opened, the horse-drawn *coach services between *Liverpool and *Manchester were at once reduced, and within three months they had virtually ceased. Though the change came more slowly on the GJR, owing to the pertinacity of one big coach proprietor, the completion of the whole trunk route from London to Liverpool and Manchester in 1838 quickly forced him to abandon his service. The same thing happened as each new trunk line was brought into use. Travellers now had to choose between the train—quicker and cheaper—and the hiring of post-horses, more expensive than any other mode of transport. Naturally, nearly all of them preferred the train.

So, as the railways moved across the country, they acquired almost at once the whole long-distance passenger traffic between the places they served, developing it further as their systems extended. But it was not the same with freight. The *canals and coastal *shipping continued at work, some of them more vigorously in order to face this new competitor. Where heavy freight was concerned, they and the carriers could usually offer a service comparable with the railways'. Although movement was slower, speed was not usually of prime importance—in the conveyance of bulk cargoes such as *coal or *stone, for instance, or main-crop vegetables, and here the canals could often undercut the railways in price. Therefore, although most railways were willing to carry freight, some even to bid for it by lowering their charges, most of them preferred at the beginning to develop the passenger traffic they had secured so easily by the quick defeat of their competitors on the roads.

There was another consideration also. Passenger trains were usually lighter than freight trains, and moved at higher speeds. As the whole volume of traffic grew, there might be an operational problem in running services at different speeds on the same pair of rails. The faster passenger trains got priority, the freight trains having to be shunted into *sidings to let them pass.

But freight traffic increased nevertheless. By the mid-1850s the receipts from it were coming to exceed those from passengers, which thereafter yielded a lower revenue than freight every year up to 1914.

That statement refers to all the British railways taken together. It is not true of each of them individually. Most of those in south-eastern England were primarily carriers of passengers. In 1913 the *London Brighton & South Coast Railway, for instance, derived almost 75 per cent of its revenue from passenger traffic. Just as clearly, passenger traffic was of less account than freight on some railways: on those in South Wales, which were all primarily carriers of coal, and among the larger ones the *Great Central and the *North British. Some urban railways, on the other hand, carried passenger traffic alone, notably the *London underground railways.

Considerable differences appeared in the railways' handling of it. All had to keep the behaviour of passengers under close watch, to prevent them, for example, from strolling about on the tracks and from using the trains without paying their fares, imposing rules and regulations and *bye-laws upon them for these purposes. Although the controls might be necessary, they were sometimes exercised with a quite uncalled-for harshness. Moreover, it was often noticed that the manners of the railway staff varied very much in their treatment of first, second, and third-class passengers (see CLASS DISTINCTIONS).

On all the larger railways, however, the cost of providing passenger services was considerably higher than that incurred in the handling of freight. Passenger *stations had to be elaborately equipped: with *ticket offices, *waiting rooms, lavatories, at the bigger ones *refreshment rooms, even *hotels. Goods *stations, on the other hand, originally were very simple affairs, having scarcely any public facilities to provide, except weighing machines and a counter for clerical transactions, which was only carpenter's work. The station itself was hardly more than a large shed, usually wooden. Something grander did indeed appear at *King's Cross in 1852, but for a long time it remained unique in London.

Similarly with the vehicles. Those used in passenger traffic cost a great deal more than freight vans and *wagons, and as the amenities they were expected to include multiplied—gas and electric lighting, for instance, in place of oil, better upholstery, continuous *brakes, lavatories, and corridors—the cost of conveying each passenger rose (see CARRIAGES). No comparable expenditure had to be incurred on freight vehicles during the 19th century. Moreover, the railways' freedom to raise fares, to offset the cost of these improvements, was closely restricted. That was emphasized when they were statutorily obliged in 1868 to publish at every station a complete list of the fares charged for conveyance to every other station to which passengers could book direct. And then from the 1870s onwards—again under the pressure of competition—there was a marked increase in the speeds of the best trains (see EXPRESS TRAINS), which further added to the cost. By the late 1880s it was clearly recognized that these speeds were higher than any on the Continent. But it was also being pointed out that some of these trains were not well filled. There were three competing routes from London to Manchester, *Glasgow, and *Edinburgh, two to *Leeds, *Nottingham, *Birmingham, and *Exeter. J. S. Jeans, a well-informed observer, put it like this in 1887: 'If Englishmen will insist on travelling at the rate of 50 mph, and having more express trains than any other country, they must expect to have to pay somewhat more for the costly facilities thus provided.' Instead of that, the fares remained the same and—even more remarkable—they were lowered by numerous further concessions, of return, tourist, circular, and excursion *tickets, widely available in every part of the country. This may perhaps be seen as an example—one of many—of the later Victorians' propensity for living above their income.

One further feature of the working of long-distance passenger traffic became increasingly well known at this time: the provision of *cross-country services and *through carriages. This increase may be said to date from 1874, when through carriages were first run between Birmingham and *Bournemouth via the *Somerset & Dorset Railway, the modest beginning of what became a substantial service from the north to this rising new resort. It was a valuable amenity for travellers, saving them the trouble and expense of crossing London. By 1914 such services were being run to all the principal English seaside towns, as well as from Yorkshire to *Blackpool and North Wales.

This was not a mere luxury. Within a small island, much of it very densely populated, it represented a natural and proper use of the railway system. But at least a dozen separate companies were involved in making the arrangements, which required careful negotiation about *timetables and the provision of locomotives and carriages; as well as, with the aid of the invaluable *Railway Clearing House, a complicated apportionment of the expenditure and receipts between them.

Another very important branch of passenger traffic was the suburban business in and around the great towns. This did not become really dense before 1870. It then presented some quite special problems of its own. Most of the long-distance traffic was spread out over the whole day, but *commuters' services were bunched together tightly, to fit in with their hours of work, in the early morning and evening. They forced the provision of extra tracks to accommodate them, on the *Great Northern Railway for example and the *Great Eastern, which was very expensive (see MULTIPLE TRACKS). The London underground railways had a similar problem as they extended out to the west; worse indeed, because neither of the two companies involved could face quadrupling its tracks, which were almost entirely in tunnel. They dealt with it in a different way, by *electrification. Electric traction was also being introduced at the same time in Liverpool and *Newcastle, and from 1908 onwards on two of the main-line railways in London. In the inter-war years electrification extended very much further to the south. By 1939 it included main lines to *Portsmouth, *Brighton, Eastbourne, and Hastings.

All the railways' passenger services were then being threatened by the development of *road motor transport. They fought back to retain all the profitable parts, here and there with some success, and reduced unprofitable passenger services (see CLOSURE). They also collaborated with some *bus companies in the hope of developing integrated services. But the struggle was severe and its success, from the railways' point of view, very limited. In 1923–38 their revenue from passenger services was nearly 30 per cent less than that from freight.

The *nationalized railways, having always to seek economies of working, attended naturally to reducing the system, slowly at first and more quickly from 1961 onwards; and the axe fell more heavily on passenger than on freight traffic. It remained, as it had always been, more expensive to work, and at that time it was more easily turned over to road services. But when in the 1980s freight traffic declined very seriously, the importance to *British Rail of passenger business increased, and for the first time since 1855 (save in the exceptional year 1919) the revenue from passenger traffic was the higher of the two, continuing so until 1994. JS
Railway *Returns.

Passenger Transport Authorities and Executives

were foreshadowed in the 1966 White Paper by Barbara Castle, Minister of Transport, which recognized the need for comprehensive and locally accountable transport planning in the major conurbations and for new financial support mechanisms which reflected public transport's essential contribution to the functioning of these regions. In 1967 a further White Paper argued that conditions in four areas—the West Midlands, Greater Manchester, Merseyside, and Tyneside—warranted the urgent establishment of *ad hoc* passenger transport authorities, without waiting for proposed wider changes to local government. Each PTA, which was to be composed mainly of representatives from existing councils, would determine the policy and financial framework for public transport in its area, delegating planning and operational responsibilities to an appointed Passenger Transport Executive and its professional staff.

The necessary powers were included in the Transport Act, 1968, and the first four PTAs and PTEs were created by ministerial direction in 1969 and 1970, followed in 1972 by Greater Glasgow, the sole Scottish example. In 1974 the existing English bodies were assimilated into the new metropolitan county structure, with some title and boundary adjustments, and at the same time West and South Yorkshire received PTA status. With the abolition of the six metropolitan counties in 1986 their PTAs were re-established as joint boards of the constituent district authorities, and similar arrangements applied when Strathclyde Regional Council, which had assumed the former Greater Glasgow PTA functions in 1975, was abolished in 1996.

In fulfilling their wider responsibilities, the PTAs and PTEs have played a leading role in the renaissance of local railway passenger services since the 1970s, by providing substantial revenue support and by sponsoring major investment projects. They also pioneered the reintroduction of light rail technology in Britain, through *Light Rapid Transit schemes such as the Tyne & Wear Metro, the Greater Manchester Metrolink, and the South Yorkshire Supertram. MCR

Cmnd. 3057, *Transport Policy* (1966); Cmnd. 3481, *Public Transport and Traffic* (1967); Passenger Transport Executive Group, *25 Years of the Passenger Transport Authorities and Executives* (undated).

passes and privilege tickets. Directors and senior officials of railway companies have always enjoyed free travel facilities, authorization taking the form of medallions worn on the watch chain or a paper *ticket bound into a gold-blocked leather wallet. Similar free travel passes were sometimes offered to local dignitaries and landowners across whose land the line ran.

Medallions currently held by serving and retired railway officials are still honoured, although the authority to travel free is given to them and their families by plastic passes of credit card size.

Free tickets were provided to some companies' shareholders to enable them to travel by train to attend annual general meetings.

In 1852 the *Great Eastern Railway arranged an annual outing for employees at Stratford to Harwich at a fare of 4d. return for 140 miles. Twenty-six years later GER staff petitioned the company for general privilege fare facilities and by the early 1880s several companies allowed employees to travel over their own lines at reduced rates, usually the return journey for a single fare.

By 1893 staff from several companies formed the Interchange Privilege Ticket Movement to negotiate with individual railways. The *London & South Western and *Great Northern Railways immediately concluded a reciprocal agreement, and by 1896, 46 English, 14 Welsh, and 11 Irish companies were issuing interchange privilege tickets.

In 1904 the GER extended privilege fares to its ships to the Continent, and the Railway Employees Privilege Ticket Association arranged continental travel in the 1920s, resulting in today's interchange facilities with most European state railways, many private companies, and systems as far afield as Canada and India.

With the *privatization of the *BR system, staff privilege travel facilities for existing staff were safeguarded under the 1993 Act, although new entrants receive concessions only within their own operating company.　　　　MGDF

W. Sime, *REPTA Records* (1926); M. I. Bray, *Railway Tickets, Timetables and Handbills* (1986), 36, 37, 50; G. Fairchild and P. Wootton, *Railway and Tramway Tickets* (1987), 40, 41; M. Robbins, Shareholders' Passes: *RM*, 113 (1967), 470; 114 (1968), 451; 115 (1969), 43; L. Wiener, *Passenger Tickets* (1939), 27, 28, 60, 61.

patents. Engineers and others have filed a huge number of railway patents, many of which have been of great significance in operating and safety.

They can provide useful information for the railway historian, but there are pitfalls which can mislead those not familiar with the system. Patent specifications and drawings, often made before any device had been constructed, may not represent the invention as actually produced. Although a patent is intended to claim a new invention, it was not until 1905 that examination for novelty was made by the Patent Office; previously there were many examples of duplication.

From the 16th century protection of an invention was only one of a variety of privileges which could be obtained by the grant of letters patent, using archaic and expensive procedures. The increasing number of inventions led to the demand for reform of the patent laws, which came with the Patent Law Amendment Act of 1852, simplifying the application procedure and reducing the initial cost.

Throughout the 19th century there were many parliamentary committees investigating the patent laws, and their reports include the evidence of many experts including eminent railway engineers: for example, I. K. *Brunel was opposed to the whole system of patents. *Reports of Patent Cases* were published annually from 1884. Although compiled to record legal precedents, they can provide information on the history of an invention.

Until 1919 the maximum term of a patent was 14 years; it was then increased to 16 years, and in 1977 to 20 years. In exceptional cases an extension was allowed; examples were David *Joy's *valve gear patent extended in 1893, and H. W. Garratt's patent for articulated locomotives in 1923. After 1852 fees were payable in instalments so that the patent could be allowed to lapse if renewal fees were not paid. Thus a patentee would only need to pay these fees if his invention proved profitable. As a guide to the success of a patent, payment of renewal fees can be determined from records at the Science Reference and Information Service division of the British Library, where classified abridgements and name indexes can also be found.

In the 1850s the early specifications dating from 1617 to 1852 were printed for the first time and allotted numbers in a continuous series from 1 to 14,359. After 1852 all new patent specifications were printed and numbered in a sequence starting from 1 in each year, so that to identify a patent of this period it is necessary to specify the year of the application. From 1916 accepted patents were numbered in a continuous series starting from 100,001. Since 1977 a new series from 2,000,001 has been used.　　　　RTS

N. Davenport, *The United Kingdom Patent System* (1979); *Reports of Patent, Design and Trade Mark Cases*, 10 (1893), 89–92, and 40 (1923), 396–7; R. T. Smith, 'John Gray and His Expansion Valve Gear', *TNS*, 50 (1978–9), 139–54; I. Winship, 'Patents as a Historical Source', *Industrial Archaeology*, 16 (1981), 261–9.

Paterson, Murdoch (1826–98), engineer. Born near *Inverness, he worked for two years in an Inverness bank, before being apprenticed to Joseph *Mitchell in 1846 when the latter was Inspector of Highland Roads and Bridges. In 1851 he worked for the *contractor building Inverness harbour, which he completed after the bankruptcy of his employer. He rejoined Mitchell in 1854 to work on the Inverness & Nairn Railway (see HIGHLAND RAILWAY) and thereafter supervised all Mitchell's railway projects. After Mitchell's retirement in 1867, Paterson became engineer for the Dingwall & Skye and Sutherland & Caithness Railways. On completion of the latter he became resident engineer on the Highland Railway where he was responsible for building branches to Fortrose, Buckie, Strathpeffer, and Hopeman. His major work was the direct line from Inverness to Aviemore. He died just before its completion, in the station agent's house at Culloden Moor, almost within sight of his greatest work, the Culloden Moor Viaduct (see BRIDGES AND VIADUCTS). He was thus directly involved in the creation of almost the whole of the Highland Railway, an achievement perhaps overshadowed by the construction of the West Highland and *Callander & Oban lines, but no less remarkable.　　　　JRH

PICE, 135 (1898–9), 351; J. Mitchell, *Reminiscences of My Life in the Highlands*, ii (1884); H. A. Vallance, *The Highland Railway* (1985).

path: the course laid down for each train in the working *timetable, allotting to it a clear passage between those preceding and following it.　　　　JS

Pearson, Charles (1794–1862), promoter. The son of a London merchant, he became solicitor to the City Corporation in 1839–62. He was MP for Lambeth (1847–50). He interested himself very much in the physical improvement of the City, particularly in the Fleet valley, and he gave powerful support to the building of the *Metropolitan Railway. He wished to enable slum-dwellers to move out of London to live in healthier conditions, travelling in and out by train for their daily work at unusually low fares. Largely through his influence, the first such services to run in Britain were introduced on the Metropolitan and *London Chatham & Dover Railways in 1864–5 (see WORKMEN'S TRAINS). Though they did not realize all the benefits that Pearson hoped for, they were adopted widely in London and in some provincial cities.　　　　JS

Boase; *HLT*; A. A. Jackson, *London's Metropolitan Railway* (1986).

Pease, Edward (1767–1858) and his son **Joseph** (1799–1872), woollen manufacturers and railway promoters, both born in Darlington and brought up as Quakers. It is safe to assume that but for their role in founding and managing the *Stockton & Darlington Railway they would have been viewed as no more than representative of numerous nonconformist businessmen in the early phases of industrialization in Britain. Edward was a notably plain Quaker, well known for his dislike of worldly extravagances, yet in 1818 he took the lead, in collaboration with his relation and fellow Quaker, Jonathan Backhouse, in projecting the SDR as an economical means of coal shipment. It was Edward who engaged the services of George *Stephenson as engineer for the line and who also provided the bulk of the capital for the inauguration in 1824 of Robert *Stephenson and Co. of Newcastle-upon-Tyne as the world's first locomotive building establishment.

If Edward was the driving force behind the SDR as an investment project, it was Joseph who carried it forward to commercial success. A worldly Quaker, who was the first Quaker MP, Joseph was noted for his ability to capitalize on the network of credit within the Society of Friends in order to fund further railway projects. His intentions were twofold: first to secure for the collieries of south-west Durham a profitable niche in the London coal market, and secondly to open up the mineral wealth of northern England for the benefit of the iron trade. In both he was highly successful. Under his direction the newly founded settlement of *Middlesbrough became the world's greatest centre for iron production by 1870, while the SDR had in 1861–3 penetrated across the Pennines to exploit the iron ore of Furness. By then the SDR was part of the *North Eastern Railway, having been absorbed in 1863 on notably generous terms. On Joseph's death in 1872, he was a director of railway, iron, engineering, mining, and textile enterprises. He left over £400,000.   MWK

M. R. Bailey, 'Robert Stephenson and Co., 1823–1824', TNS, 50 (1980), 109–37; M. W. Kirby, Men of Business and Politics: The Rise and Fall of the Quaker Pease Dynasty of North-East England, 1700–1943 (1984); M. W. Kirby, 'The Failure of a Quaker Business Dynasty: The Peases of Darlington, 1830–1902', in D. J. Jeremy (ed.), Business and Religion in Britain (1988), 142–63; M. W. Kirby, The Origins of Railway Enterprise: A History of the Stockton & Darlington Railway, 1821–1863 (1993); Sir A. E. Pease (ed.), The Diaries of Edward Pease: The Father of English Railways (1907).

Peel, Sir Robert (1788–1850), politician. He paid no special attention to railways until 1835, when he actively supported the promotion of the *Birmingham & Derby Junction line. As Prime Minister in 1841–6 he tried to restrict government intervention in their affairs, in which he disagreed with his colleague *Gladstone, who prevailed nevertheless in 1844. Having set up a board under *Dalhousie to sift proposals for new railways before they came to Parliament, he dissolved it after only a year's work. The Railway *Mania ran its course with little attempt by the government to influence or control it. Peel's own political difficulties, culminating in the repeal of the Corn Laws in 1846 and his immediate fall from power, must be recognized in judging him here. Perhaps no leader, at that time, could have succeeded in curbing the private speculation of 1844–6 and its evil consequences (see GOVERNMENT, RAILWAYS AND NATIONAL).   JS

N. Gash, Peel (1976 edn.); GR, 83–9; Peel's non-interventionist policy: Hansard's Parliamentary Debates, 72 (1844), 251.

pensions and gratuities. In the early days of railway operation in Britain no railway company had a pension scheme for all its employees, nor was any *compensation paid in the case of injury or sickness other than occasional ex gratia payments to widows of men killed in accidents. Since there was no state provision of welfare services either, railway workers had to depend on their own meagre resources in case of emergencies. Many paid a penny a week to the *Railway Benevolent Institution and secured in return some financial help in sickness, old age, and funeral expenses, as well as minimal assistance to widows and orphans.

The *Great Western Railway's Enginemen's and Firemen's Mutual Assistance Fund, established in 1865, was confined to locomotive men, whose membership of the fund was compulsory. At age 60, men who had paid 45 years' contributions received a lump sum of £100 and a weekly pension of 12s. 6d.—some two thirds of their average wage during employment. But this was a privileged group. For the large majority of the company's workers there was an opportunity after 1838 to join the GWR Provident Society which provided small benefits in the case of sickness and, on the death of the contributor, payment to the next of kin.

The *Stockton & Darlington Railway Superannuation Society, founded in 1860 on a contributory basis, offered a weekly pension of two thirds of average working-life salary to members who had completed 45 years' service at the age of 65. As wages-grade workers were, in practice, excluded, the scheme left most of the company's employees unprotected.

Elsewhere, benefits provided by the larger railway companies before 1914 were undependable and autocratically managed. On the *North Eastern Railway intermittent payments were discretionary by directors or senior managers. The policy of the board of the *London & South Western Railway of making annual contributions to the company's Friendly Society, from the proceeds of the sale of lost property and the fines imposed on staff for various misdemeanours, was followed by other companies. The board of the *London Brighton & South Coast Railway was happy to approve the action of one of its *guards, William Climpson, who confronted passengers with his collie dog 'Help' (the name given on the collecting box it carried on its back), who raised £1,000 for the Amalgamated Society of Railway Servants' Orphans' Fund during the period of its railway 'service' from 1882 to 1887.

The *Railway Clearing House Superannuation Fund, set up in 1873, lasted longer than any railway company scheme. It provided a pension at age 60, at two thirds of average in-service salary, for those employees who had completed 45 years' service. Members' contributions were deducted from their payrolls and were matched by contributions from the RCH. Though primarily intended for clerks and supervisors, it was also open to similar classes of employees of affiliated companies. This was a great boon to clerks and supervisors in smaller companies which lacked the financial strength to establish a fund of their own. When the RCH Superannuation Fund was wound up in 1978 it had benefited a total of 48,000 members.

In 1913 railway companies in Britain employed over 615,000 persons. It is doubtful whether more than one fifth of these were covered by any pension scheme. The fortunate few were overwhelmingly in the clerical or locomotive grades.

Any hopes that the '*Big Four' main-line companies after 1923 would introduce a comprehensive pension scheme for wages grades were repeatedly dashed before World War II. Their profits were too seriously depleted by the effects of growing *road transport competition and severe trade depression in the early 1920s and 1930s for them to feel able to pay pensions.

After prolonged negotiations in 1951–3 a pension scheme for the wages grades was agreed between the railway unions and the *nationalized Railway Executive (see BRITISH TRANSPORT COMMISSION) in October 1953. It made provision for a maximum pension of 30s. a week for men who had completed 45 years' service, with lump-sum death benefit varying from £4 to £184, depending on the number of years' contributions. *London Underground, British Transport *Hotels, and Docks and Inland Waterways staff were included with those of the Railway Executive. The scheme had many shortcomings, but was accepted by a special general meeting of the *National Union of Railwaymen on 14 October as a first step which could be improved. This in fact happened. In 1966 Underground staff went into a new London Transport scheme. Under a new scheme in 1967, women employees were included for the first time and a pension was agreed which would enable a person with 40 years' service, who was also in receipt of a state old-age pension, plus a graduated state pension, to enjoy a total income of two-thirds of his or her pay when last in work. A shortage of railway labour in 1974 made it possible to negotiate further improvements. An increase in the combined railway and union contributions to the fund from 13 per cent to 23.33 per cent of pay enabled improved benefits. Finally, in 1988, employees' contributions were reduced from 10 per cent to 5 per cent of weekly pay, the lump-sum death benefit was increased from one year's to three years' pensionable pay, and retirement lump sums were increased by 25 per cent. PSB

P. W. Kingsford, *Victorian Railwaymen* (1970), ch. 9; F. McKenna, *The Railway Workers, 1840–1970* (1980); M. R. Bonavia, *The Four Great Railways* (1980); P. S. Bagwell, *The Railwaymen* (1982), ii, ch. 10.

Penson, Thomas Mainwaring (1817–64), architect. Third in four generations of Chester architects, Penson first worked for his father and then became a resident engineer under Henry *Robertson on the Shrewsbury & Chester Railway (1846–8), where he designed the stations. Most were in Tudor or Jacobean manner, with 'picturesque' half-timbering at Whittington and Baschurch, but two were quite remarkable essays in Florentine Italianate, at Ruabon and the larger Gobowen. The former was rebuilt about 1865 in a weak Tudor style, but Gobowen remains, fully restored, as one of the gems of British railway architecture. Penson's work was not restricted to stations; he designed matching crossing-houses and gate lodges as well.

His largest railway work was the handsome collegiate Tudor station at Shrewsbury (1849). Six years later he supervised an extension, and in 1893–1903 it was enlarged again in a sympathetic manner that today is indistinguishable from the original.

Penson also worked with Robertson on the *Shrewsbury & Hereford Railway (1852–5), designing the large French Gothic station at Hereford, and probably the intermediate stations too. He is recorded as the architect of Machynlleth station on the Newtown & Machynlleth Railway (1863)—later part of the *Cambrian—and as the other original stations on the line are smaller versions it seems reasonable to assume he also provided those.

He was county surveyor for Cheshire, and did much architectural work in Chester where he was responsible for reviving the traditional half-timbering for which it is noted. He designed many schools, houses, and churches in North Wales. GJB

G. Biddle, 'The Railway Stations of John Livock and T. M. Penson', *JRCHS*, 31(2), 154 (1993), 61–71; 32(2), 164 (1996), 141.

perishable traffic needed fast, reliable transits (often overnight to arrive in time for the next day's markets) and special *wagons.

From 1891 railway companies were required to provide reasonable facilities for the speedy carriage of perishable merchandise either by passenger train or other similar service. The wagons, therefore, had to be suitable for passenger train speeds and equipped with continuous *brakes; they were generally designated as 'vans', a term borrowed from road transport for a faster, lighter goods vehicle.

The vans were often fitted with ventilators in the sides, ends, roof, or all three, to allow circulation of air around the contents during the journey, and sometimes fitted with collapsible shelves for loading boxed traffic. They might also have some degree of insulation. Occasionally they were designated for particular traffics, such as butter, eggs, tea, or margarine, to avoid contamination by more pungent traffics. Insulated or refrigerator vans or containers were needed for chilled or frozen traffic (chiefly *meat and *fish), highly insulated containers for ice-cream and frozen foods, and heated vans for bananas.

See also FLOWER TRAFFIC; FOOD AND DRINK TRAFFIC; FRUIT AND VEGETABLE TRAFFIC; MILK TRAFFIC. GAB

Sir F. J. C. Pole and J. Milne, 'Parcels Traffic by Passenger-Train Services', in *Modern Railway Administration* (1925), i, 143–56.

Permanent Way Institution: promotes knowledge of railway infrastructure technology amongst some 5,700 members throughout the railway industry.

Founded in 1884, the institution has 29 local sections in the UK and Ireland, and nine in Commonwealth countries. Three home-based functions are arranged annually for all members, as well as occasional international seminars. Records of activities are published in the PWI *Journal*.

Perth

Classes for track staff, pioneered by the PWI in the 1930s, continued for about 20 years until *British Railways started its own schemes, and were complemented by publication in 1943 of *British Railway Track*, based on the instructors' notes. Publication of this textbook continued (with revision) through four further editions after the classes ceased. The completely rewritten sixth edition was published in 1993. Two supplements, *Bull-head Supplement* and *Tracks to the Cities*, are also available.   GHC

J. A. R. Turner, *The Permanent Way Institution—The First Hundred Years* (1984).

Perth. Perth General station was one of the hubs of the Scottish railway system. The first line to reach the 'Fair City' was the Dundee & Perth from the east, opened in 1847 to a temporary station at Barnhill, and into the city over a long viaduct across the Tay in 1849; quickly followed from the south by the *Scottish Central, and its northern extension, the Scottish Midland Junction Railway, providing a direct route to *Aberdeen; and the Edinburgh & Northern line through Fife from Ladybank (see EDINBURGH PERTH & DUNDEE).

Within three years Perth had become a centre for four railways, the first three becoming part of the *Caledonian and the last the *North British. Competition between the Edinburgh & Northern and Scottish Central for traffic to *Edinburgh resulted in destructive fare cutting in the early days, and in an attempt by the SCR to gain absolute control over the junction station. This went to Parliament, which decided that the station should be *jointly owned and managed by the user companies—hence the name Perth General station. It also recommended a site on a much-prized open space, which the citizens successfully resisted. The original station was designed by Sir William *Tite, and was enlarged in 1885–7 with Blyth & Blyth as consulting engineers. The long through north–south platforms accommodated the immense trains conveying families to and from the Highlands during the *shooting season; *Dundee trains used two sharply curved platforms. The Caledonian's direct line to Aberdeen was closed in 1967, and only *Inverness trains now use the north–south platforms. There was one other station in Perth—Princes Street, on the Caledonian's Dundee line.

Lines to Dunkeld (1856) and Methven (1858) were added, the former becoming part of the *Highland Railway's main line in 1865. The mergers of the 1860s had a significant effect on Perth. The integration of the Scottish North Eastern, Scottish Central, and Caledonian Railways made the city a nodal point on a major railway, and the combined company made the Perth workshops of the SCR an important locomotive maintenance point. The assimilation of the Edinburgh & Northern into the North British and the creation of the Highland Railway further increased the prestige and importance of Perth as a railway centre. There were still, however, three railway companies using the General station, each with its own offices, and locomotive and carriage servicing facilities, while the provision of through services meant that there was much remarshalling of trains.

Even after the *Grouping, when three companies became two, there was a degree of duplication, and it was only *nationalization that finally ended Perth's position as a railway frontier town. It had become even more important when the NBR built its direct route via Glenfarg (opened in 1890) linking with the new *Forth Bridge, and giving the company a shorter line to Edinburgh than the Caledonian's.   JRH

W. S. Bruce, *The Railways of Fife* (1980); O. S. Nock, *The Caledonian Railway* (1962); *Reg. Hist.*, xv.

Peterborough, situated on the Nene at the edge of the Fens, with an ancient monastery, remained overshadowed by neighbouring Stamford, well-placed on the Great North Road, until the 1840s. Lord Exeter, anxious to maintain his political control over Stamford, curbed commercial expansion and obliged the *Great Northern Railway to keep its line well to the east, through Peterborough. It expanded accordingly (from 6,959 to 30,872 in 1841–1901), gaining four companies' locomotive depots and, briefly, the GNR's locomotive repair shops, as well as other heavy engineering such as Brotherhood's and Perkins, and extensive brick works. The GNR established a substantial community at New England (see HOUSING).

The Nene pastures, valued for fattening cattle, attracted Peterborough's first railway (1845), a long branch from the *London & Birmingham Railway via Northampton. Other lines quickly followed: from Stamford and *Leicester (1846–8), Ely (1847), Lincoln (1848), Rugby via Stamford (1851), and the GNR main line from *London (1850) and on northwards through Grantham (1852). Later arrivals were lines from Wisbech (1866) and Rugby via Seaton and Wansford (1879); and a GNR service from Leicester via Seaton and the Fletton Curve (1883).

The lines to Rugby and Northampton closed in the mid-1960s, leaving the Stamford–Leicester line as a circuitous link between the Midlands and the expanding east coast ports. But Peterborough remains an important junction on the electrified *East Coast main line and in services to the north Midlands and East Anglia, aided by its burgeoning population as a new town, rising from 62,340 (1961) to 154,300 (mid-1990s).   RVL

R. A. Dane, *Railways of Peterborough* (1978); *Reg. Hist.*, v, ch. 11 (1968).

Peto, Sir Samuel Morton (1809–89), civil engineering *contractor, born near Woking, Surrey. In 1830, with his cousin, Thomas Grissell, Peto inherited the general building company of his uncle, Henry Peto, and carried out a number of prestigious projects in London. He went into railway building in the mid-1830s with contracts for the *London & Birmingham and *Great Western companies. After heavy involvement in railways, chiefly in East Anglia, in the 1840s, Peto and his second partner, Edward Ladd Betts, were joined by Thomas *Brassey in a huge programme of contracts in Britain and seven other countries. Between 1850 and 1865 they built approximately 1,400 miles of railway, including the Balaclava line during the Crimean War and the Canadian Grand Trunk Railway.

Peto's career is the foremost example in the 19th century of the extension of the role of contractor into the fields of railway finance, promotion, and management. This range of activities, and especially an imprudent association with the *London Chatham & Dover Railway, played a major part in his bankruptcy and enforced retirement following the business crisis of 1866.

Peto lived in style, became a baronet, and served successively as MP for Norwich, Finsbury, and Bristol. He was noted for his attention to the welfare of his *navvies.

DB

DBB; DNB; PICE, 99 (1889–90), 400–3; Sir H. Peto, Sir Morton Peto, A Memorial Sketch (1893).

petrol locomotives, see TRACTION, PETROL.

photography. This article is in two parts. The first surveys the emergence of photography, as a technique applicable to many departments of railway work, up to World War I. The second sets out a number of the great changes that have occurred since then in cameras, film, and reproduction, greatly enlarging the scope and power of the whole craft.

Before 1914

The earliest photographs connected with railways in Britain seem to be two dating from about 1845. One is a daguerreotype portrait (held by his family) of the young engineer Daniel *Gooch, standing beside a model of a locomotive he had designed; the other is a picture of Linlithgow, taken from a hillside and showing in the foreground the railway station with all its equipment: entrance, booking office, platforms, tracks, a crane, a passenger carriage, and a goods wagon. This was the work of David Octavius *Hill and Robert Adamson, and is in the Scottish National Portrait Gallery at Edinburgh. By 1847, I. K. *Brunel was having plans of railway structures, which he had designed in London, daguerreotyped, to be sent to his assistants working on a railway scheme in Austria, almost exactly as he might communicate instructions by fax today.

The spectacular iron bridges of the 1850s across the Menai Strait, the Wye, and the Tamar (see BRIDGES AND VIADUCTS) were all photographed while under construction. Soon after 1860 some engineers and *contractors had systematic photographic records made of the progress of their works. John *Fowler did so for the first *London underground railways, the section of what is today the Circle Line between Farringdon, *Paddington, and Gloucester Road. At the same time the Manchester firm of locomotive builders, Beyer Peacock (see WORKS), were taking photographs of the machines they built, using the pictures as a form of trade catalogue. For some of this work they commissioned the best practitioner available locally, James Mudd. The Butterley Ironworks photographed the construction of the roof of *St Pancras station in 1867–8, and the firm of Bedford Lemere took a long series of photographs, outside and inside, of the adjoining Midland Grand Hotel. Photographs now came to be taken of entire lines of railway, running over substantial distances, showing examples of the engineering works they had required: of the Mansfield–Southwell line in Nottinghamshire, for example (an album is at the *Institu-

tion of Civil Engineers), and of the *Callander & Oban line in *Scotland (prints in the Scottish Record Office, Edinburgh).

Some railway companies began to establish photographic units of their own, usually placed within their engineers' departments. Among their tasks was the recording of accidents, as soon as possible after an occurrence before the wreckage had been moved, the photographs forming part of the evidence on which an inquiry could be based. From the 1880s onwards it became a common practice to put photographs of buildings and landscape into railway carriages, as an encouragement to travel. Many of these were taken by the companies' official photographers: the Scottons, father and son, who worked for the *Midland Railway, for example, were heavily engaged in this work in 1892–3 in several districts served by the company. The *Great Eastern Railway, however, entered into an arrangement with a commercial photographer, Payne Jennings, for the same purpose. Photography had now become the basis of a great deal of the *posters and other *publicity material issued by the railways. On the *Great Western Railway some of this took the form of little books about the railway itself, and particularly its locomotives, produced for *enthusiasts and sold in substantial numbers. They included a liberal provision of photographs, playing a large part in the sale of these publications. A booklet on engine names ran through at least 15 editions between 1911 and 1946.

No satisfying photography of trains in motion was achieved until the 1880s, when new materials and faster shutter-speeds made that advance possible. One of the chief pioneers of this technique in Britain was a clergyman in Cornwall, Revd A. H. Malan, who photographed express trains running on the GWR, sometimes at 60 mph, in 1880–92. Such pictures were still all in monochrome. From 1896 onwards illustrated magazines devoted to railways were published, and they provided photographers with a new market for pictures.

This was not all to the good. The standard of reproduction in the most popular of these papers, the Railway Magazine (see PRESS), was very low, and that discouraged photographers from giving much attention to the finer points of their craft. Some did take great care, to please and satisfy themselves (P. W. Pilcher and K. A. C. R. Nunn, for example). But the magazines were content to publish an interminable series of pictures of trains, taken time after time at some well-known convenient spots, together with the dullest official photographs of locomotives.

Some admirable pictures were, however, taken in those years, to be cherished both as records and as interpretations of work connected with railways. Perhaps the most remarkable was the long series devoted to the construction of the *Great Central line from Nottinghamshire to London taken in 1893–9, and the loop line associated with it through High Wycombe in Buckinghamshire added in 1906. These photographs were the work of S. W. A. Newton, a young professional photographer in Leicester, and 1,100 glass negatives recording this operation are now in the Leicestershire Record Office. He photographed the constructional work fully and faithfully, and he also depicted the men engaged on it with all the expertise of a professional portrait photographer. JS

Since 1914

The cameras used to take official photographs for the railway companies were very cumbersome. At *Crewe and *Derby *works, for example, a handcart was needed to carry the camera and the 16 in × 12 in glass plate negatives, heavy in themselves. Although the post-1923 companies (see GROUPING) continued to use glass plates, in general the size was reduced.

Amateur railway photography at first was limited to those who could afford reflex or press cameras with glass plates, usually of quarter-plate size, the emulsion of which was quite slow. A limiting factor was still the weight of the camera and its plates. Use of a tripod was desirable. M. W. Earley, who did most to foster improved railway photographic techniques, founded the Railway Photographic Society in 1922, which survived some 50 years and outlived steam traction on *British Railways. Regular circulation of postal portfolios and criticism sheets completed by members did a great deal to improve standards. Earley's negatives survive at the *NRM, as do those of several prominent members. Sadly, many collections no longer exist, having been thoughtlessly destroyed. While many of these photographs could be described as technically perfect, most concentrated on the locomotive or train with scant regard for the railway infrastructure or environment.

In 1925 there was a significant photographic development. At this time a British-made Thornton Pickard reflex camera with f4.5 lens, using glass plates, cost £12 10s. In that year the first Leica 35 mm cameras were imported from Germany at a cost, with case, of less than £20. These lightweight cameras could fit into a reasonably capacious pocket, so avoiding the need to carry a bulky camera with a limited supply of glass plates. With 36 exposures on a film, they could be used more liberally to obtain record photographs which are now of historic interest. Furthermore, with its high-resolution lens and fine-grain film, in the hands of a competent photographer the Leica could produce results which would stand enlargement and bear comparison with those previously obtained with a large-format film camera. An early user of this medium was C. C. B. Herbert, whose negatives are also held by the NRM.

Better folding cameras, such as those by Agfa or Zeiss, were imported from Germany before World War II. These used the familiar 120 size film providing eight 6 cm × 9 cm negatives. Also available were Hasselblad, Rolleiflex, or Voigtländer single-lens reflex cameras using the same film. They mostly had compur-rapid shutters with speeds to $\frac{1}{500}$ second. The Leica had a focal-plane shutter with speeds to $\frac{1}{1,000}$ second. Railway photography to an acceptable standard was becoming within the reach of more people. Then World War II brought an end to authorized railway photography.

Colour photography became generally available in 1934 with the introduction of Dufaycolor film in large format. This had a very slow emulsion and could only be used for static subjects. Considerable research was carried out in this medium, notably in the USA, and Kodachrome film came on to the British market in the early 1950s. In December 1938 the Railway Magazine published a colour frontispiece based on a Dufaycolor transparency. In its early years the magazine had used splendid tinted lithographs by Alf Cooke of Leeds; later it had relied on tinted photographs, but not on a regular basis. Sadly it was to be many years before another colour photograph appeared.

Also in 1934 the Railway Magazine included some pages of semi-gloss paper, greatly improving reproduction quality. At this time, among many photographic contributors, the name Eric Treacy appeared. Later to become Bishop of Wakefield, he produced powerful photographic images, notably in northern England. Initially he used a heavy press camera, which he admitted having to abandon for a Zeiss roll-film camera because of its weight. His pictures were the subject of the first of many one-man photographic albums in 1950.

Despite impending paper rationing, new railway magazines emerged in World War II. Railways (later Railway World) appeared in December 1939 with a larger page size and glossy paper. It sponsored photographic competitions which encouraged railway photography. In 1946 there followed Trains Illustrated, a small-format journal initially on poor paper, and Railway Pictorial, a large-format magazine on glossy paper obtainable on subscription only. Its price and scarcity led to its demise after three volumes. After an unpromising start due to paper rationing, Trains Illustrated brought about the growth of the publisher Ian Allan Ltd, which also sponsored photographic competitions.

As soon as film became more readily available after the war, the greater circulation enjoyed by various railway publications led to an increase in railway photography. It also brought about what Earley had foreseen when he founded the Railway Photographic Society. With more photographs published there was an encouragement to achieve higher standards. At last the train ceased to be the total focus of attention; more important was the train in its setting.

Such a photographer was Ivo Peters, whose name was associated with the *Somerset & Dorset line. Peters nevertheless roamed far and wide, some of his best photographs being those taken in Treacy territory in the Lakeland fells. He also used 16 mm film, later to become available on video cassettes.

Even before publication of the 1962 *Beeching Report branch and *cross-country lines were increasingly being closed, creating an urgent need to record them. Even some main lines faced closure, and those that remained were rapidly modernized. The days of the steam engine were numbered following BR's *Modernization Plan in 1955, and although standard steam locomotives were built for a further five years their lives were short. Such changes brought about a tremendous increase in railway photography. The film manufacturers prospered, but in fairness they were constantly enhancing the quality of their films, improving definition, and marketing new high-speed films.

In the last months of steam in 1968 there were scores of photographers by the lineside, some intent on recording the rundown of steam, photographing freight trains in urban and industrial surroundings, notably in the north. The train often formed only a small part of the overall picture. Where S. W. A. Newton had recorded the construction of the Great Central Railway, its final years and those of other lines were now being recorded, and the results published.

On surviving main lines the new diesel and electric locomotives lacked the pictorial appeal of steam. Apart from BR's Southern Region, all new *electrification was carried out on the overhead system, presenting a new hazard to the photographer. Steam engines were finally withdrawn by the late summer of 1968 and breaking up was entrusted to private contractors, their yards presenting scenes to the photographer unknown since the end of the Great Western broad gauge.

Of greater importance was the growth of the railway *preservation movement, which started in the 1950s with the revival of two *narrow-gauge lines in Wales. Since 1959, preservation of standard and narrow-gauge railways has expanded dramatically, providing new scope for photographers. Further photographic opportunities arise when chartered steam excursions are run on main lines.

Colour photography is now paramount, and although Kodachrome film is still extensively used, Agfa of Germany and Fuji of Japan also command much of the market. Again, the abundance of publications affords comparison, and more adventurous photographs are reproduced. Although the quality of reproduction in British magazines is very good, the best pictorially are probably those of France, Germany, and the USA, but at a price the British enthusiast probably would not be prepared to pay.   RCR

Piccadilly Line, see LONDON UNDERGROUND RAILWAYS.

Pick, Frank (1878–1941), vice-chairman of the London Passenger Transport Board (see LONDON UNDERGROUND RAIL-WAYS). Articled to a York solicitor, he joined the *North Eastern Railway in 1902. He became personal assistant to Sir George *Gibb, general manager, in 1904 and followed him to the *Underground Electric Railways of London in 1906, taking charge of its traffic promotion in 1909. On the inclusion of the London General Omnibus Company in the Underground group in 1912, Pick became commercial manager of the combine.

After work with the Board of *Trade (1917–19) he returned to the Underground and rose to be managing director (with Albert Stanley, Lord *Ashfield) in 1928 and vice-chairman of the London Passenger Transport Board in 1933–40. In World War II he was director-general of the Ministry of Information.

Pick was a transport manager and administrator of very high quality, giving attention to the details as well as the policies of the Underground's multifarious activities. He seemed to be omnicompetent, and in Sir John *Elliot's phrase 'the power of decision came easily to him'. This made it difficult for the talents of other men close to him to grow in his shade. But with Ashfield's political skills and sense of the 'common touch', which Pick lacked, and Pick's administrative gifts and command of detail, London Transport after 1933 until the shadow of war descended forged an integrated passenger transport system that was in its day incomparable.

Underlying his management skill was a deeply felt commitment of social responsibility, implanted by his Congregational upbringing at York. He strove to make his business activity coherently directed to proper and intelligible social ends. The most obvious (but not the only) result of this cast of mind was his increasing concern with good design, from buildings and posters to teaspoons. His concern for the look of station frontages ('a station', he wrote, 'is an inviting doorway in an architectural setting that cannot be missed by the casual pedestrian') showed him to be no 'art for art's sake' aesthete but a man with a passion for fitness and seemliness in the apparatus of the workaday business of transport.   RMR

DNB; DBB; HLT: C. Barman, *The Man Who Built London Transport* (1979); papers at London Transport Museum; personal knowledge.

Piercy, Benjamin (1827–88), engineer. After training as a surveyor in his father's office, he helped to prepare Henry *Robertson's plans for the Shrewsbury & Chester Railway. He was engineer for the line from Shrewsbury to Welshpool and for nearly the whole of what became the system of the *Cambrian Railways, to Aberystwyth and Pwllheli, and southward to Three Cocks, not far from Brecon; some 200 miles in all, opened in 1863–7. He also laid out railways in north-eastern Wales at the same time, including those from Rhyl to Corwen, and in his later years he was much involved in the Wrexham Mold & Connah's Quay Railway (see GREAT CENTRAL).

From 1862 to his death he was involved as engineer in the development of railways in Sardinia: very difficult country for that work, but his Welsh experience must have assisted him in it. He bought estates there and did much to improve agriculture and cattle-breeding. He also built railways in France (Tours–Les Sables d'Olonne, 160 miles) and in Assam.

Unlike Thomas *Savin, with whom he was much associated, he had a good head for money, successfully surviving the financial débâcle of 1866. In 1881 he returned to live in Wales, acquiring Marchwiel Hall, Denbighshire. He left the very large fortune of £325,000.   JS

Dictionary of Welsh Biography; BDE; CMCR.

pier railways. Seaside piers were first built at popular resorts where there was a need for passengers and their baggage to be landed from steamboats at all states of the tide. Whenever a structure was pushed out over water, rails were laid on it for the construction; the rails could be used later to carry trolleys or other vehicles to convey baggage, and sometimes passengers too. The technical means—power and *gauge—varied from place to place; there was no reason for conformity to a standard, as the tracks would never meet. Though usually referred to as *'tramways', these lines usually had areas reserved for them. Piers suffered often from fire, collision from ships, and war. Ramsey's was blessed on opening by the Bishop of Sodor and Man; Southend's has a train-set named in memory of Sir John Betjeman.

The principal passenger-carrying installations were (in order of pier construction):

Ryde, Isle of Wight: built 1814, extended 1824, 1833; three piers side by side; standard-gauge horse-drawn tram, 1864; steam, 1881–4; electric, 1886; petrol *railcars 1927; closed 1969.

Southend-on-Sea, Essex: 1829, 1¼ miles (longest in the world); luggage tramway, c. 3 ft 6 in gauge, wooden rails; passengers in horse-cars c.1875–81; new pier and 3 ft 6 in electric railway 1890; Royal Navy use (closed to public) 1939–45; closed 1978; reopened, 3 ft gauge, 1986.

Herne Bay, Kent: 1832, with narrow-gauge tramway, horse power, sail from 1833; closed 1864; new pier with electric tramway, gauge c. 3 ft 4½ in 1899; closed 1914; re-opened, petrol electric vehicle, 1925; closed 1939.

Southport, Lancashire: 1860; tramway 3 ft 6 in gauge, hand-propelled 1863; cable haulage 1865; electric 1905; converted to 60 cm gauge, diesel locomotive 1950; closed c.1971.

Hythe, Hampshire: 1880, luggage tramway, 2 ft gauge, later used for passengers; electric 1922.

Ramsey, Isle of Man: 1886, 3 ft gauge, trucks for baggage, hand-propelled; petrol engine 1937; closed 1981.

Walton-on-the-Naze, Essex: 1898, 3 ft 6 in gauge, electric; closed 1935; 'guideway' for battery car, 1936; closed 1942; 2 ft gauge line, diesel-hauled, 1948.

Felixstowe, Suffolk: 1905, 3 ft 6 in gauge tramway operated in summer; closed 1939.

Blackpool North, Lancashire: 1991, 3 ft gauge, diesel locomotive, 3-car set of non-bogie eight-wheelers.

Baggage is reported to have been transported on rails along piers at Aberystwyth, Bangor, Beaumaris, Bognor, Hunstanton, Lowestoft, Margate, and Weston-super-Mare (Birnbeck). RMR

A. P. Herbert, *The War Story of Southend Pier* (1945); P. W. Gentry, 'Pier Railways', *RM*, 98 (1952), 413, 707; M. Robbins, 'Tramway and Railways at Ryde', *Points and Signals* (1967), 89; K. Turner, *Pier Railways* (1972); S. H. Adamson, *Seaside Piers* (1977).

pigeon traffic, see LIVESTOCK TRAFFIC.

place-names. Railways sometimes helped to fix the names of places, or their spelling where there were alternatives. They preferred 'Altrincham' to 'Altringham', for instance. The *Post Office had done much previously in this way; the Ordnance Survey too, on its maps. The spelling adopted by the railway company usually remained in all its literature thereafter, from entries in timetables to luggage labels, though in Hampshire the *London & South Western company did abandon 'Swathling' for 'Swaythling', no doubt under the Post Office's influence.

Some names the railways created. In 1899, for instance,

the *Great Central opened a station in Buckinghamshire on its new main line to London, which it called Calvert, after the landowner. No village ever appeared, but a big brick-works was opened that took the same name.

Railways had some influence on the pronunciation of place-names. Displayed in large letters on station name-boards, they came to be pronounced phonetically, as they were spelt, not as they always had been in the local dialect. So in north Norfolk, after the railway's arrival, the places that had been pronounced 'Darsingham', 'Snetsham', 'Hetcham', and 'Hunston' came to be 'Dersingham', 'Snettisham', 'Heacham', and 'Hunstanton'. The holiday-makers' bald literacy was here destroying local usage. JS

VR, 190–2.

plans, see MAPS AND PLANS.

plastics, use of. During the 1930s the *London Midland & Scottish and *London & North Eastern Railways made limited use of plastic mouldings in carriages. The latter introduced thermosetting plastics for light fittings in compartments, and clear acrylic panels for the partitions of *restaurant cars in the 1938 Flying Scotsman sets.

From the early 1950s, glass-reinforced polyester (GRP) mouldings began to be used for railway rolling stock. With the cheapness of moulds, combined with the hand-lay process, GRP was economic for applications such as the roof and body-end canopy of diesel *railcars. Increasing use was being made of melamine laminates for decorative panels in the interiors of carriages, as well as for finishes in stations and ships.

In the early 1960s a unit specializing in plastics was set up at Eastleigh *works, and developed stiffened GRP doors for suburban trains, and probably the world's first GRP-bodied carriage which entered experimental service in 1963.

GRP mouldings were used extensively in the *BR Mark 2 carriages entering service from 1965. Because of the numbers required, it was economic to use cold-press moulding for the seat shells in open second-class vehicles, while all varieties of Mark 2s featured hand-moulded vestibule-end decorative mouldings with a dark green or red finish, body-end canopies, and vestibule ceilings. These mouldings eliminated the troublesome corners and edges associated with traditional materials.

The High Speed Trains introduced from 1976 use a number of GRP items. The most notable is the hand-moulded, double-skinned driving cab module of the power car. The cavity between the skins is filled with foam, and the composite structure has successfully resisted impact in the worst head-on collisions. In the trailer cars, GRP mouldings are used for the window interior surrounds, seat shells, exterior doors, and vestibule end panels and ceilings. Hot-press moulded seat shells were used in the Class 313/315/507 series electric *multiple units.

*London Underground had to review the use of plastics following the *King's Cross station *fire of 1987. Targeted for replacement were the older types of melamine laminate and GRP widely used in its rolling stock. The former have been replaced with aluminium and enamelled steel, and the GRP by glass-reinforced phenolic mouldings, or a new, fire-resistant melamine laminate. Latest specification plastic cabling materials are used in new and refurbished Underground stock. To match the improved interiors, an attractive two-pack polyurethane exterior finish is used, this type of plastics-based paint also being employed for recent BR stock. MLH

platelayers. The term 'platelayer' appears to be derived from those who laid the plate rails of horse *tramroads in the early 19th century, but for long has been in general use to describe those who maintain the *track of ordinary railways. They were also known as 'waymen' in the 1840s, and as 'surfacemen', particularly in Scotland.

On the *London & Birmingham Railway in 1839 *Whishaw 'counted as many as eight waymen, on average, per mile'. By 1860, W. M. Mills wrote that 8,598 platelayers were maintaining the 8,863 miles of railway then open in Great Britain, or little less than one per mile; nevertheless *Acworth stated in 1889 that a thousand platelayers were employed on the line from London to Edinburgh (392¾ miles). In 1948 some 60,256 'permanent way men' were employed on the railways of Britain.

Platelayers worked in gangs under a foreman, each gang allocated to a length of line which was examined twice a day. Using hand tools—picks, shovels, hammers, wrenches, crowbars, and track gauges—they maintained its alignment, *gauge, level, and *superelevation. Loose keys had to be hammered home, fishplate bolts tightened, subsiding sleepers raised by packing ballast beneath them. Broken chairs and worn rails had to be replaced. Where the work was too extensive to be done between trains, the line was temporarily closed, traditionally at weekends. Acworth chose for his frontispiece not a romantic illustration of a great express, but 'The Railway Man's Sunday' depicting a vast crowd of platelayers, which stretches as far as the eye can see, re-laying the *Midland main line near Wickwar, Gloucestershire.

Platelayers also maintained lineside *fences, and kept culverts clear. In *fog, they served as fog signalmen.

From the 1960s onwards, changes in track materials and in maintenance techniques have much altered the task of the platelayer—who has, himself, become a 'trackman' or 'leading trackman'. Installation of continuously welded rails, and replacement of wooden sleepers by concrete, have reduced the amount of maintenance needed. Many former manual tasks, such as ballast-tamping, are now done by machine. Equipment for relaying has steadily increased in power, speed, and functions to include, notably, self-propelled hydraulic track-relaying machines, and ballast-cleaners, operated by 'on-track machine supervisors' and 'track machinemen'.

In 1995 *British Rail Infrastructure Services employed about 12,000 track staff, of whom 10,000 worked in maintenance gangs and the rest in relaying gangs or specialized activities such as track welding.

With the growth of *preserved railways since the 1950s, many of their volunteer helpers have become familiar with the platelayer's tasks and skills, both mechanized and manual.

See also BREAKDOWN TRAINS. PJGR
Acworth; Anon., *Railways and Railwaymen* (1892), ch. 11; J. Macaulay and C. Hall (eds.), *Modern Railway Working* (1912), iii, ch. 5; W. M. Mills, *The Railway Service . . .* (1867); Whishaw.

plateways, SEE EARLY IRON RAILWAYS.

Plymouth. (For map, see p. 382.) What is now called Plymouth is a merger of the 'Three Towns' of Plymouth, Stonehouse, and the naval dockyard town of Devonport. The *South Devon Railway ran in from *Exeter in 1849, its Millbay terminus being close to a new dock, owned by it and two others and served by a branch in 1850. In 1859 the *Cornwall Railway joined the SDR, with a station at Devonport, and a branch was completed to Tavistock, extended to Launceston in 1865. All were broad *gauge lines.

The standard gauge did not appear until 1876, when the Launceston branch was converted to mixed gauge south of Lydford to allow the *London & South Western Railway's trains to enter Plymouth. It had its own terminus (Friary), but could also run into the SDR's new through station at North Road (1877). The dockyard received a branch at Keyham in 1867, and a third rail was now laid on that too. The LSWR's access was greatly improved by the Plymouth Devonport & South Western Junction Railway, opened in 1890. That company's extensions had been steadily supported throughout by the municipal authorities of Plymouth and Devonport, anxious for commercial reasons to be linked with the standard-gauge system of the rest of the country. After the *Great Western Railway (which absorbed the SDR in 1876) abolished its broad gauge in 1892, and then shortened its old route between Plymouth and London by almost 20 miles in 1906, it became much the better of the two.

Devonport was one of the greatest naval bases in Britain. But the commercial business of Millbay Docks and the harbours of Plymouth and Stonehouse was also growing fast, with a considerable transatlantic traffic, and the two railways competed strenuously for it, until a pooling *agreement divided the receipts in 1910.

Plymouth was now throwing out suburbs to the north and east, served by railways (the latest of them opened in 1892-8). The Three Towns had become, collectively, the regional capital of the south-western peninsula, and were merged into one 'Plymouth' in 1914 with a population of about 200,000.

The city suffered very severely from air-raids in World War II. Millbay station closed in 1941, Friary in 1958, all passenger traffic being concentrated at the dilapidated North Road. A new station was officially opened there in 1962, although not fully completed for several more years. JS
Reg. Hist. i, ch. 6; MacDermot; Williams.

Plymouth Devonport & South Western Junction Railway

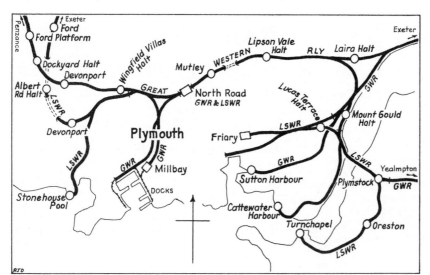

Plymouth, 1922

Plymouth Devonport & South Western Junction Railway, see PLYMOUTH.

pneumatic railways, see ATMOSPHERIC RAILWAYS.

points, see TRACK.

Pole, Sir Felix J. C. (1877–1956), manager. The son of a Wiltshire schoolmaster, he went to the *Great Western Railway as a telegraph clerk in 1891. After service under the civil engineer he entered the general manager's office in 1904. One of his tasks there was to rejuvenate the *Great Western Railway Magazine*. He became general manager (at 44) in 1921.

Under the Railways Act of that year (see GROUPING) the GWR had to absorb 21 Welsh companies, inheriting also an impressive series of docks (see PORTS AND DOCKS). *Interval services for its main-line trains out of London were introduced in 1924. Pole constantly sought to keep the GWR's public image bright. However, in 1928 he was persuaded by Sir Guy *Granet to become chairman of the very large new combine Associated Electrical Industries Ltd, and he never returned to railway service. He had been knighted in 1924.

Undaunted by blindness, he completed an interesting autobiography in 1954, three-quarters of it given to his railway service. JS

DBB; DNB; Felix Pole, His Book (1968 edn.).

police. In the early days of railways it quickly became apparent that some sort of policing was needed. For its own safety an unaccustomed public had to be restrained from venturing on to the lines. As traffic grew it also became obvious that railway property and customers' goods had to be protected.

Crowds of over 10,000 assembled to watch the *Rainhill locomotive trials on the *Liverpool & Manchester Railway in 1829, the same year as the establishment in London of the Metropolitan Police, Britain's first professional police force. Hitherto, law enforcement had been in the hands of parish constables, for long an ineffectual system in London, although it continued in the provinces until the 1850s. In times of trouble they were augmented by the military, or citizens sworn in as special constables by the magistrates. At Rainhill, for instance, the justices enrolled 300 railway labourers to keep the line clear, and at the formal opening in 1830 pickets of cavalry were posted along it at intervals.

With the rapid spread of construction, parish constables were powerless to prevent lawlessness among *navvies, leaving railways no alternative but to summon military assistance or call in the Metropolitan Police, as happened on the *Manchester & Leeds and *North Midland Railways in 1838–40 (see RIOTING). Under the 1838 Special Constables Act, railways and other undertakers of public works were liable to a charge of 5s. per day for each special constable appointed to keep the peace, while the *Regulation Act of 1840 gave railway staff powers of arrest in cases of trespassing and obstructing railwaymen in the performance of their duties.

By now the major railways had their own police. The LMR had them quite early, but the first to acquire statutory authority was the *London & Birmingham under its Act of 1833, followed by the *Great Western in 1835. Appointments could only be made by the magistrates, although directors as well as the justices had powers of dismissal. Railway police authority was restricted to railway premises, but under the LBR's 1837 Act it was extended to half a mile on either side of the line. The GWR did not gain this privilege until 1877.

One of the policeman's primary duties was to prevent theft and pilferage. But apprehending law-breakers was only one of a very wide range of the early constables' responsibilities. Each man was allocated a section of line and provided with a hut. He was expected to patrol his section, giving a hand signal to drivers to indicate whether or not the line was clear, and saluting the train as it passed. Any defects in the *track had to be reported immediately, and at stations the policemen acted as ticket collectors and booking clerks. The GWR regulations of 1841 required constables to keep order at stations and on the line, give and receive hand signals, operate fixed signals where they were provided, clear obstructions, assist at the scene of accidents, remove intruders, supervise points and crossings, announce arrivals and departures, inspect the rails, direct passengers, and guard the company's property.

They were paid 15–23s. a week, in which working days could be 12 hours or more. Inspectors on the LBR received 30s. In 1838 that company had a superintendent, ten inspectors, and 90 constables. Their *uniform, and that of the GWR, was similar to that of the Metropolitan Police: tight trousers, a tail-coat with a high collar bearing the company's initials, a top hat reinforced with leather, and a distinctive wrist-band which, as with the London police, was worn only when on duty. Constables carried a truncheon bearing the company's initials and perhaps its coat of arms, while an inspector carried a hollow baton, often with brass mountings, containing his rolled warrant.

The duty to regulate trains gradually disappeared as *signalmen were appointed, following introduction of the electric *telegraph and the concentration of signal levers at boxes, but other extraneous duties lasted for a long time. As late as 1900 *North Eastern Railway policemen rang a bell to indicate the imminent departure of a train, and they were expected to act as substitute *guards or ticket collectors if necessary.

The organization of railway police as a separate department, operating on similar lines to the civil police, was not generally adopted until after 1900. Previously, control had varied between companies. The *Edinburgh & Glasgow's Law and Land Committee in 1852–62, for instance, had a bewildering array of responsibilities, from water supplies and hotels to supervising the company's police force. The *London Brighton & South Coast Railway formed a separate department in 1900, bringing together policemen most of whom hitherto had not been sworn and were answerable to individual *stationmasters or goods agents. For special events like race meetings (see HORSE-RACING), the company had hired men from the Metropolitan Police.

By 1914 the NER had one of the most efficient forces in the country. The GWR police, though, remained under the Traffic Department until 1918, and the *South Eastern & Chatham did not have a separate force until 1920. Despite these organizational shortcomings, however, there was close liaison between railway and civil police, as is still the case. In 1880 the NER's chief superintendent became chief constable of Hull, and later the same company's own chief constable became a Commissioner of the Metropolitan Police.

Some larger companies had their own detectives. The *London & North Western started employing individual detectives in 1853, and in 1863 formed a separate detective

service in an endeavour to reduce severe losses of goods in transit. The GWR did so in 1864, and in 1918, when it amalgamated its plain-clothes and uniformed police, the detectives were dealing with 2,000 cases a year. In addition to maintaining a presence at large stations and *junctions, the police played an important part in reducing crime at *ports and docks.

All the *Big Four companies formed at the 1923 *Grouping set up police forces modelled on the civil police. In 1946 the companies combined to establish a railway police training school, with a system of cadet entry. At the same time the first policewomen were appointed, and special training began in dog handling—the NER police had been the first to use dogs, possibly in the whole country, at Hull in 1908.

After *nationalization in 1948 the four forces amalgamated as the British Transport Police under the *British Transport Commission, with responsibility for railways, docks, and canals. The force continued under the same name after the BTC was disbanded, and again under *privatization in 1994. GJB

MacDermot, i, ch. 12; J. R. Whitbread, *The Railway Policeman* (1961); D. Brooke, *The Railway Navvy* (1983), 109–18, 121–2.

politics, railways in. Railways and politics have always been inseparable. Politics was the midwife of railways. Their birth brought into being a new economic interest group which sought to defend itself through political influence and political involvement. It also produced a new source of political problems, which politicians have had, often unwillingly, to confront. The wider impact of railways upon society helped transform the conduct of politics and even the thinking behind them.

The railways were involved in politics right from their inception. Building them required parliamentary consent, in the form of legislation (see PARLIAMENT AND LEGISLATION). During the great railway boom between 1844 and 1847, 442 Acts for railway construction were passed, under private Bill legislation. It was time-consuming and expensive to pilot through both Houses of Parliament. Acceptance of new lines was not automatic. There were many to object, including rival railways (see OPPOSITION TO RAILWAYS). The routeing of railways was a frequent cause of lively political controversy, as it became again in the 1990s with the *Channel Tunnel link. Railway promoters were compelled to forge political connections and to find parliamentary allies in order to achieve their ends: the beginning of a close association between the railways and politics.

Some leading railway figures, such as *Hudson and Daniel *Gooch, often became Members of Parliament, and many MPs joined the boards of railway companies. The number of railway directors in Parliament reached a high point of 132 MPs and 54 peers in 1873.

They represented a 'railway interest'. Their ability to act jointly and effectively was often compromised by the intense inter-company rivalry which characterized 19th-century railways in Britain. But they did show themselves able to co-operate on occasion, especially when governments attempted to regulate their industry. A committee and sub-committee of the *Railway Clearing House were established in 1855–6 to monitor the effects of legislation on the railway companies' interests and to lobby in their defence. These were followed by the *Railway Companies Association (1858–61) and the United Railway Companies Committee, later known also as the Railway Companies Association, which operated from 1867 until *nationalization in 1948.

The principal task of the 'railway interest' was to oppose government control of the railways. This was something which governments, initially at least, hardly sought with relish. Governmental actions before 1840 were timid and indecisive. But the impact of the railways on the economy and society was so great that politicians were compelled to adopt a policy towards them. 'Politicians' is the appropriate word. Many early initiatives came from individual back-bench MPs rather than from governments. One such initiative resulted in the establishment of the Railway Department of the Board of *Trade in 1840. Political responsibility for the railways was thus institutionalized. The politics of railway control have rarely been off the agenda since. The *Grouping of 1923 and *nationalization were causes of major political controversy, as was the government's legislation returning ownership to private hands in 1994 (see PRIVATIZATION).

The 'railway interest' undoubtedly enjoyed some success in limiting government control before 1914. Nationalization was successfully seen off in 1844, 1867, and in the 1870s (see NATIONALIZATION, THE CONCEPT OF). But the 'railway interest' did not prevent an unusual degree of political interference in other aspects of railway operation. Only the mining industry was subject to greater state regulation by 1914.

A major incentive for political interference was *safety. Railway *accidents had consequences for politicians as well as for the railways themselves. Parliament was specially alarmed by a series of spectacular accidents which took place after 1865. The work of the Board of Trade's railway *inspectorate was increasingly supported by the power of Parliament. A Royal Commission on Railway Accidents sat in 1874–7. After the dreadful accident at Armagh in 1889, when 80 people were killed, the Board of Trade was given power to compel all railway companies to fit their passenger trains with continuous *brakes and to adopt the *block signalling system.

These considerations of safety highlight the wider political problem of railway performance. The quality of service has often been a political issue, particularly since nationalization. In the *commuter constituencies of London and the south-east the performance of the railways and the cost of tickets are 'bread-and-butter' issues which can influence elections, especially perhaps by-elections. The reductions in the rail network implemented by *Beeching in the 1960s were greatly resented in isolated rural communities which have often shown great determination to retain their railway lines. Groups of railway users have organized themselves to lobby local and central government for improved rail services, including the reopening of closed stations and abandoned lines. These now represent, perhaps, the true 'railway interest'. Investment in railways has become involved with other important political concerns, such as *pollution and the environment.

The railways also affected the conduct of politics. The revolution in the speed of communications had inevitable political consequences because it changed society. Railways greatly improved the postal system (see POST OFFICE) and the circulation of news. *Newspapers could reach almost every corner of the British Isles from London within 24 hours by the 1860s, contributing to the 'nationalization' of politics. Political parochialism began to break down. Events and issues at home and abroad were brought before a truly national audience. The railways also changed lifestyles, making possible the growth of *suburbs, improved access to leisure, and to a greater variety of cheaper raw materials and goods. The political consequences of these developments are somewhat intangible but nevertheless profound.

Railways also greatly facilitated the establishment of national political organizations. First was the radical pressure group, the Anti-Corn Law League, which used railways in the 1840s to create a sophisticated network of branches, visiting speakers, and agents administered from its headquarters in *Manchester. National political parties followed in its wake. Acceptance of political responsibility for the operation of railways induced a greater degree of government intervention in the last third of the 19th century, just as in the 1990s railways have been a subject of political attempts to reduce government spending and revitalize the market economy.   JMB

G. Alderman, *The Railway Interest* (1973); GR; REW, 214–38; N. McCord, *The Anti-Corn Law League 1838–1846* (1968 edn.), 163–87.

Pollitt, Sir William (1842–1906), railway manager. He joined the Manchester Sheffield & Lincolnshire Railway (see GREAT CENTRAL) at 15 and in 12 years rose to chief clerk to the accountant. His ability to take broad views was noticed in the 1870s and his progress was then assured. In 1885 he became assistant general manager, rising to general manager the following year.

He tackled the difficult role of GM to Edward *Watkin's chairman with aplomb, drawing to himself a first-rate team; he made overdue peace with the *Great Northern Railway, which became a staunch ally; and endured a long war with John Bell, chairman of the *Metropolitan Railway, over the shared route to *London.

Pollitt ably steered the Great Central through two changes of chairman in the crucial five years when the London extension was completed. He was knighted in 1899 and elevated to the board in 1902.   AD

Dow, ii and iii.

pollution. Railways produced pollution in several forms as soon as they began to be worked mechanically.

It arose first from the smoke from engines. Parliament tried to reduce this by requiring them to be built so as to 'consume their own smoke', which meant burning coke instead of coal. Since coke was the dearer fuel, efforts were made to reduce smoke emission, usually by new designs of coal-burning firebox, fully successful in 1859 (see TRACTION, STEAM). But the railways adopted them slowly, and local authorities made numerous attempts to enforce the smoke-restriction clauses in railway Acts. Stockport and *Liverpool councils both tried to enlist the help of others to this end in 1866–7, but without success. Only the improvement in the design of locomotives reduced it.

Many townspeople complained of another kind of pollution—noise, particularly from the engines' whistling at night; at *York, for example, in 1869 and on the *North London Railway again and again from 1871 for 30 years and more. The ears, noses, and throats of the citizens of Gateshead (see NEWCASTLE AND GATESHEAD) were continuously attacked by trains at a busy junction of main lines right at the centre of the town.

When lavatories were introduced into trains the discharge of their effluent on to the track threatened *health; it has been complained of intermittently down to the present day (see SANITATION).

In the 20th century many of these nuisances have been lessened through changes in railway operation. Shunting at night in goods yards—oppressive, for example, at *Leicester and *Carlisle—has gone. So have steam locomotives. Electric *traction involves no pollution. But the heavy oil used by diesel engines still causes it, and their fierce din on starting, set up particularly by IC 125 trains, might well have been thought intolerable by the Victorians.   JS

VR, 77, 370; York RO, York City Council minutes, 4 Feb. 1867, and Board of Health Committee, ii, 368, 373; Liverpool RO, Council Minutes, 1866–7, p. 31.

pooling, see AGREEMENTS.

population, censuses of. The census returns can be a useful aid to the study of railways. They show the growth —or decline—of communities, a process in which railways may have played an important part (see TOWNS, RAILWAYS AND THE DEVELOPMENT OF). As time went on, the scope of the census broadened from a mere figure of the number of people in each parish, district, and county to an elaborate recording of their occupations, group by group. Among the groups are the railways, and the industries associated with them.

Censuses have been taken every ten years since 1801 (except in 1941). Those of 1811–41 occurred on dates between 26 May and 7 June; all the rest in March or April except the late June one of 1921. This is important when holiday resorts are being examined. All censuses since 1931 have been taken on Sundays except those of 1961 (Saturday) and 1951 (Thursday). A special warning about the figures of railway *employment was given by the Census Commissioners themselves in 1911.

In comparing the population of a local community at one date and another, changes of boundary must be attended to, occurring in the years between. Substantial changes of this sort were made occasionally in the 19th century. They have

grown more common since; those of 1965 (in London) and 1974 have been especially important.

The published census returns deal in categories of persons, but not with individuals, as declared by themselves. For them search has to be made in the enumerators' books, which are open to public examination 100 years after the taking of each census.   JS

population, changes in. Railways took a significant part in the changing distribution of population in Great Britain up to 1914.

They contributed to it most directly by the decisions that some companies took to establish new centres of work, or to transfer those already established from one place to another. So, when the *Grand Junction Railway determined to remove its locomotive works from Edge Hill, outside *Liverpool, to an almost uninhabited site 33 miles away, which received the name of *Crewe, it added some 800 persons to the population of rural Cheshire; and the *Great Northern company's decision to concentrate its locomotive works at *Doncaster increased the population of that old town immediately by some 20 per cent.

Changes of this kind were made solely to suit the companies' own convenience. They appeared at their most arbitrary when they resulted from *amalgamation. The *Edinburgh & Glasgow Railway had its works at St Margarets, a suburb of *Edinburgh; but in 1869, after its fusion with the *North British, all its locomotive-building was removed to *Glasgow, to be undertaken in the NBR's works at Cowlairs. After the *London Chatham & Dover Railway entered into its 'working union' with the *South Eastern in 1899, its London locomotive *works at Longhedge in Battersea were gradually run down, and transferred to Ashford. That change, coupled with the *London & South Western Railway's decision to evacuate its Nine Elms works, close by, in favour of Eastleigh (Hampshire), had a considerable effect on the population—as well as on the rateable value—of the Battersea district.

All these changes can be, to some extent, quantified from the census returns (see POPULATION, CENSUSES OF). So can some other changes, temporary by their nature but conspicuous during the years of most intense railway construction in 1835–70. The census returns may record startling rises in the population of individual parishes through which railways were being built at the time at which they were taken, with corresponding falls in the next census. The causes of these changes may or may not be noted in the returns.

Other changes were longer-lasting, or even permanent.

Increases in the population of towns following the railways' arrival have often been ascribed directly to them; but that may be based on nothing but guesswork, and sometimes it is wrong, or at least incapable of proof.

The 12 largest towns in Great Britain outside *London in the Victorian age were *Birmingham, *Bradford, *Bristol, Edinburgh (with Leith), Glasgow, *Hull, *Leeds, Liverpool, *Manchester (including Salford), *Newcastle, *Nottingham, and *Sheffield. Their combined population, as shown in the first census of 1801, was 669,000. Over the next 30 years that total increased by 117 per cent. But their subsequent growth was at a much lower level: in 1831–61, by 81 per cent; in 1861–91, by 65 per cent; in 1891–1921, by 50 per cent. In other words, the greatest ferment in their expansion was already over before mechanically operated railways could have any significant effect there.

What railways did most usefully, in social terms, was to open up possibilities of new settlement, assisted and serviced by them. The speed at which these operations were realized, and their extent, depended in large measure on the attitudes of other people: on *landowners' willingness to sell for house-building; or the eagerness with which property developers came forward, having builders able and anxious to construct the streets and houses in new settlements. Railways were seldom built in Britain in advance of demand, with a vague expectation of future housing development—unlike many in America, where social, political, and economic conditions were often quite different. When British railways did that, their efforts usually failed.

In Essex the *Great Eastern Railway's Churchbury *Loop, opened in 1891, managed to bring in so little new resident population that it was closed down in 1903. Further east, the company's Fairlop Loop, opened in 1903, met with similar failure. Its large, solidly built stations stood out in an open countryside, almost unused; one of them, Hainault, was closed in 1908. In both these cases the railway's failure was caused partly by the unanticipated arrival of electric *trams, competing with it; but, allowing for this, it must be said that the GER's speculative efforts to produce new housing development had been totally unsuccessful. In the second of these cases there was indeed a large potential, but it was not fully realized until the *Central London underground line was extended, linking up with the Loop, in 1948.

By way of contrast, in north London the underground railways' system was extended from Golders Green to Edgware in 1924 only after the careful consideration of developers' plans for future building; and when the *Metropolitan Railway's Stanmore branch was opened in 1932 it served ambitious building development already completed or well under way.

These were all population changes furthered by railways in the rich south-east of England. But they had a hand in other changes also in distant parts of the island, which had the opposite effect.

After 1860 the population of some rural counties in England and Wales fell: in the mid-Welsh counties of Brecknock, Radnor, Montgomery, and Cardigan by 14.5 per cent in 1861–1911. There were even greater population falls in northern Scotland and in Wigtownshire. Most of these changes were attributable to migration, and much of that was clearly influenced by railways, as their system extended into these districts in 1862–74. Here railways, with their facilities of easy movement, were clearly important agents of change, though it is difficult to pinpoint it exactly, for families moving out in this way to another part of Great Britain seldom left much record of their journeys behind them.

But the railways also assisted longer journeys, of a kind that had been undertaken far more laboriously before they appeared: those of men who despaired of getting any satisfactory work in Britain and determined to make a new life overseas. Migration here became emigration.

The railway system in the Scottish Highlands much facilitated journeys to the western *ports, to cross the Atlantic. *Acworth's *Railways of Scotland* affords us a touching picture of some of these emigrants leaving Aberlour station on Speyside in the 1880s, to take an Anchor Line ship at Glasgow; 'going away' was the simple phrase used to describe their journey—for most of them, going away for ever. The same process appeared in England. From 1893 onwards *through carriages ran every Friday night from Whitehaven, in impoverished west Cumberland, to *Southampton, joining up with others from Bradford *en route*, to convey emigrants on their way to America and South Africa; and that service seems to have continued until 1914.   JS

Population figures from Mitchell & Deane; A. A. Jackson, *Semi-detached London* (1991); W. M. Acworth, *Railways of Scotland* (1890), 134–5; R. W. Rush, *Furness Railway* (1973), 44–5.

porters first became a familiar part of railway travel on the *Liverpool & Manchester Railway (1830): they gave directions to board trains, stowed passengers' luggage upon the roofs of carriages, unloaded it on arrival, and carried it to waiting omnibuses. Out of the public eye, the LMR employed porters to load and unload goods: by 1842, for example, there were about 110 porters working in the warehouses at *Manchester, Liverpool Road.

The LMR's example was followed by later railways such as the *Grand Junction. *Whishaw in 1842 specifically noted three porters on its staff at Warrington, and two at Whitmore. The *London & Greenwich Railway employed five porters, the Newcastle & North Shields 11; even the three-mile long Paisley & Renfrew had five. By 1860 numbers had grown to a total of 17,954 porters and messengers throughout Britain; in 1948 the totals were 18,388 goods porters and 34,469 passenger.

At large stations, porters were divided up into gangs; some had particular tasks such as washing carriages, attending to oil lamps, and sorting parcels. Platform porters attended to passengers' luggage, labelled it and loaded it into van or compartment, after finding seats for the passengers themselves. All the time there were questions to be answered, carriage doors to be shut, vans to be loaded and unloaded. Trains arrived with their brake vans full of vast amounts of luggage, and other traffic too—*milk churns, *newspapers, and boxes of *fish.

At country stations with few staff, porters' lives were much more varied still. The same individuals attended to all these tasks and many more, including selling and collecting *tickets; cleaning offices and waiting rooms; preparing goods *wagons for dispatch by putting up the doors and sheeting the wagons over; loading and unloading cattle; and cleaning out horseboxes after unloading, for return to their owning companies. At many small stations the task of porter was combined with that of *signalman, in the grade of porter-signalman, which meant that the men concerned also needed full knowledge of *signalling, block regulations, and so on.

For most of the 19th century a porter's wages were about 17s. a week. The LMR and GJR both prohibited porters from accepting gratuities; the *Midland Railway, in its 1920 rule book, forbade its servants to solicit them—a subtle distinction. In practice, tips had become a valuable means to supplement low pay; for porters with large families, probably an essential one. They were, however, generally supplied with *uniform. In the late 1830s the LMR provided a drab jacket, moleskin trousers and a cap; by 1870 a porter's uniform was typified as green velveteen jacket, vest, and trousers; in the 1890s as corduroy and brass buttons. So far as passengers were concerned, porters were noted for their variety of character, ranging from politeness and civility through indifference to downright rudeness. Some porters evidently developed a fine line in repartee, to judge from the frequency with which they featured in 19th-century cartoons in *Punch* (see HUMOUR).

Porters seem generally to have been recruited from country districts and from Ireland. For those who were ambitious, the grade of porter was the first step on a promotional ladder on which the next were goods guard or signalman and the top was senior management; but many were not, preferring instead the settled life of a country station. By the 1970s the platform porter's traditional tasks, of checking that carriage doors were shut and getting trains away on time, had passed to the new grade of 'railman'. Porters to attend on passengers have recently been reintroduced at *King's Cross and *Euston.   PJGR

Anon., *Railways and Railwaymen* (1892), ch. 7; H. Aland, *Recollections of Country Station Life* (1980); H. Chappell, *Life on the Iron Road* (1924), ch. 11; Whishaw.

Port of London Authority, see PORTS AND DOCKS.

Portpatrick & Wigtownshire Joint Railway. The Portpatrick Railway was built in 1861–2 to serve the shortest sea crossing to *Ireland: from Portpatrick to Donaghadee. Commencing from the end of the Castle Douglas & Dumfries Railway (1859), it ran through Dalbeattie, Creetown, and Newton Stewart to Stranraer and Portpatrick. It was a difficult line, crossing numerous river valleys, and climbing over steep ridges, requiring a number of large viaducts. These were cheaply built, needing extensive repair in later years. Though the line was in *Glasgow & South Western Railway territory the *Caledonian Railway exercised *running powers over it. A branch to Whithorn and Garlieston, the Wigtownshire Railway, was opened in 1876–7, but both lines got into financial difficulties. In 1885 the Caledonian, Glasgow & South Western, *London & North Western, and *Midland Railways acquired the Portpatrick Railway *jointly.

The Portpatrick crossing was abandoned in 1874, in favour of an easier route from Stranraer to Larne, requiring the construction of a pier and branch line at Stranraer Harbour. The only other branch was from Tarff to Kirkcudbright. The whole area is sparsely populated, and never

generated significant local traffic, resulting in closure in 1965, Stranraer Harbour henceforward being served by the GSWR line from Ayr: a much longer route from England although now Stranraer is principally a roll-on roll-off vehicle ferry port (see SHIPPING SERVICES). There have been proposals to rebuild the line but that is likely to be realized only if a tunnel under the Irish Sea were to be built.   JRH

D. L. Smith, *The Little Railways of South-West Scotland* (1969); J. Thomas, *Forgotten Railways: Scotland* (1976); Reg. Hist., vi.

ports and docks. Railways played a major role in the great period of Victorian port expansion. Earlier docks were difficult to adapt for railways, generally hemmed in by populous areas and only reached by laying rails through the street. Their small size meant that wagons had to be moved around them singly over *turntables.

It took some time for dock-owners to realize the changes that railways were bringing about. The new Clarence Dock, *Liverpool, for instance, opened in 1829, only a year before the *Liverpool & Manchester Railway, had no railway nearer than the LMR's Wapping goods *station 1½ miles away in the old south docks. The goods station itself at first relied on cartage to and from the quays until 1833, when rails were laid to the coal yard at King's Dock, and through the streets to timber yards at Brunswick Dock in 1835. It was 1855 before the first branch railway was opened to the expanding north docks. The *Hull & Selby Railway built a line to *Hull docks from the outset in 1840, but the new Railway Dock of 1846 was too small for the largest steamers, while the Victoria Dock of 1850–2, which could accommodate them, at first lacked good rail connections.

As dock expansion gathered pace, however, greater attention was paid to rail access. New docks were designed to take trains alongside ships instead of ships having to move one at a time to rail-served berths. Among the first, the Victoria Dock, *London, in 1855, had integrated transit sheds instead of the traditional warehouses. Fierce competition between the London dock companies at length led the East & West India Dock Company in 1886 to open a purely rail-served dock at Tilbury, 26 miles downriver, relying on the *London Tilbury & Southend Railway for land transport. It guaranteed the railway a minimum annual tonnage in return for special rates, but in two years was bankrupt. Tilbury's fortunes did not significantly improve until after the Port of London Authority was formed in 1908, in which it was included.

Three dock groups in particular developed extensive private railways: in London, on the Mersey, and on the Manchester Ship Canal.

Railway companies soon realized the advantages of control, particularly where a port was vital in maintaining a traffic or gave them competitive advantage. So they began to buy or build their own docks, gaining considerable power in fixing rates and charges. Some were within an existing port, like the *Great Western's Millbay Docks at Plymouth. Or railways might become the port authority themselves, as at Grangemouth, *Barrow—which the *Furness Railway developed from nothing—and Fishguard. At other ports the railways invested heavily in dock installations and warehousing, as the *Great Eastern did at Great Yarmouth, the GWR and the *London & North Western at Liverpool and Birkenhead, and the *Lancashire & Yorkshire at Goole. The *Midland and *North London Railways owned docks in London at Poplar. After the 1923 *Grouping the GWR found itself the largest dock-owner in the world, principally centred on South Wales, leading it to establish its docks headquarters at Cardiff.

Coal Ports

The earliest railway-owned dock was at Llanelly, which the *Carmarthenshire Railway (a *tramroad) purchased in 1802, although its line was not completed until 1806. It was also the first combined dock-and-railway company, followed by more in South Wales. All were built to export *coal, the last being the *Barry Railway in 1889. In 1897 the Bute Docks Company, which owned Cardiff docks, changed its name to the *Cardiff Railway to enable it to build short connecting lines outside.

Coal gave impetus to railway ports in the north-east, too, where early wagonways ran to riverside staiths. The *Stockton & Darlington Railway built new staiths downriver from Stockton in 1829, where there was deeper water, and in 1849 took over the dock there; Port Clarence was built by its rival the *Clarence Railway in 1834; *Hartlepool had two independent railway docks in the same port until they became part of the *North Eastern Railway. That company took over and developed the others, and also had staiths at Dunston on the Tyne, and at *Blyth. In 1859 it built the large Tyne Dock at Jarrow.

Railways also brought coal down from Fife pits to small harbours on the Firth of Forth. Burntisland was the main one, where the *North British Railway partly financed new docks in 1876 and 1901, and finally bought it in 1922. In 1887 a new dock and railway were opened at Methil, which the NBR took over in 1889, expanding it to become Fife's largest port. The company also owned Alloa docks, to which the *Caledonian Railway penetrated but never reached beyond, leaving the NBR with a monopoly of the north bank coal ports eastwards.

On the south side of the firth the NBR built a dock at Bo'ness, jointly with the harbour trustees, in 1878, taking over full control in 1895. But Bo'ness was overshadowed by Grangemouth, built by the Forth & Clyde Canal along with Bowling docks on the Clyde. The Caledonian bought the whole undertaking in 1887, immediately setting about developing Grangemouth in order to secure to itself the coal and other traffic from the Forth–Clyde valley.

On the Clyde the *Glasgow & South Western owned Troon harbour, as successors to the *Kilmarnock & Troon Railway, and leased the harbour at Ayr, purchasing it in 1920; both shipped Ayrshire coal. On the Mersey, the St Helens & Runcorn Gap Railway amalgamated with the Sankey Brook Navigation in 1845 and built a new coal dock at Garston to replace both companies' inadequate facilities at Widnes. Opened in 1853, it was developed by the LNWR into a successful general port.

The railways led in the mechanization of coal-handling equipment. In 1829 the Stockton & Darlington erected steam-operated hoists for discharging wagons bodily into ships' holds, and throughout the century there was continuous development. Hydraulic hoists at Burntisland in 1876 could handle 1,000 tons an hour, and in the late 1920s the GWR installed conveyor-loaders at Port Talbot. The decline in the South Wales coal trade was then becoming apparent, and with modest success the company tried to diversify into other cargoes by investing in appropriate handling plant.

General Ports

Dock-and-railway companies were not confined to the coal trade. In 1840 the *Preston & Wyre company opened its line to its new port at Fleetwood, but it developed slowly until the Lancashire & Yorkshire built docks in 1878 and 1909, making it Britain's third fishing port as well as taking in timber and grain, for which a huge elevator was erected. The *Eastern Counties Railway took over the Lowestoft Railway & Harbour in 1848, investing nearly £200,000 in the port over the next eight years and offering concessionary rates for cattle and coal. The ailing Carlisle & Silloth Bay Railway & Dock Company was acquired by the NBR with an eye to using the dock, opened in 1859, for traffic from southern Scotland to Ireland and Liverpool. Irish expectations were quickly reduced, but the sea route to Liverpool flourished.

The *Hull & Barnsley was the largest of these combinations. Intended to break the NER's monopoly in rail access to Hull, it opened its line and dock in 1885. Then in 1914 it combined with the NER—which meanwhile had bought out the Hull Dock Company—to open a much larger new dock. Lastly, Felixstowe: there a railway-and-dock company built a small dock in 1884 which lay moribund until the 1960s when, having escaped *nationalization, it expanded enormously and became a leading *container port.

Earlier, the Manchester Sheffield & Lincolnshire Railway (see GREAT CENTRAL) had tried to wrest port traffic from Hull by purchasing the run-down Grimsby Dock Company. In 1852 it opened the first truly modern dock in England, operated entirely by *hydraulic power from a central source. When shipowners refused to move, the company started its own services to the Continent, built a fish dock, and in ten years made Grimsby the country's fifth port in value of trade. By 1912 all the available land was used, so the Great Central opened a new dock at Immingham, six miles away, but although it was capable of taking the largest cargo vessels and was ready two years ahead of the NER and HBR's King George V Dock at Hull, its full capacity was never entirely utilized.

Inter-railway *competition left its mark on *Plymouth where, at the beginning of a long campaign to reach Devon and Cornwall, the *London & South Western in 1847 contributed to improvements to Sutton Harbour. The GWR and its local allies replied by putting money into building Millbay Docks. It was 1874 before the LSWR, through a subsidiary, obtained powers to enter Plymouth, whereupon the GWR party purchased Millbay Docks outright. Both companies competed for ocean liner passengers brought ashore by tender, for whom the LSWR built a terminal at Stonehouse Pool in 1904, only to withdraw its Plymouth *boat trains in 1910, leaving the field to the GWR. After nationalization a new ocean terminal was built at Millbay in 1952 and boat trains ran until 1963.

The LSWR owned the greatest of the railway ports, *Southampton, which it purchased in 1892. The company spent £5 million on creating a docks system capable of taking the largest liners, rivalling and eventually overtaking Liverpool in passenger and, latterly, cargo business, as well as running packet services to the Channel Islands and Le Havre. Its successor, the *Southern Railway, continued the policy, and after nationalization a new ocean terminal was opened in 1953, when 650,000 passengers a year passed through the port—half of them cross-Channel—and 12¼ million tons of cargo.

Packet Ports

Railway investment in ports for continental and Irish passengers began with the *South Eastern's purchase of Folkestone in 1844, for services to Boulogne. To improve the tidal service from Newhaven to Dieppe, the *London Brighton & South Coast Railway financed the construction of deepwater quays by the harbour company in 1878, and by 1909 annual passenger figures had risen from 75,000 to 211,000, although Newhaven's never approached Folkestone's, and neither of them Dover's where the Admiralty's harbour was heavily invested in by the South Eastern company. The Admiralty also owned the harbour at Holyhead, where the LNWR built the inner harbour in 1873 and provided all the services (see CHESTER & HOLYHEAD RAILWAY; IRELAND); and at Harwich, whence the Great Eastern operated services to the Low Countries. In 1882, when it became too small, the GER built large new berths, a station, and a *hotel two miles away, naming it Parkeston Quay, after the company's chairman.

The little *Portpatrick Railway struggled to provide an Irish short-sea crossing from Stranraer to, first, Donaghadee, and then to Larne, but it needed the joint resources of the Caledonian, GSWR, LNWR, and Midland to develop it and the railway into a popular route in 1885. The MR also competed with Fleetwood for Belfast traffic, from its new port of Heysham, opened in 1904 to replace the inadequate tidal pier at Morecambe.

At this time the GWR created a new port at Fishguard in conjunction with the Great Southern & Western Railway of Ireland, which did the same at Rosslare. The new joint service began in 1906, replacing one from Neyland to Waterford. In 1908–14 the GWR also attempted to attract transatlantic traffic to Fishguard in the same manner as at Plymouth, but with little success. In 1928–30 it tried again at Cardiff, even less successfully.

Railways also conducted numerous smaller marine operations. They included little ports like Aberdovey and Tayport (which derived from the ferry that preceded the Tay Bridge); steamer and ferry piers at Largs and Fairlie on the Clyde, New Holland on the Humber, and Gravesend; a small dock at Brentford on the Thames; and wharves at

Saltney on the Dee, Deptford in south London, and Cowes on the Isle of Wight.

After nationalization in 1948, the railways' coal and general ports were placed with the canals under the Docks & Inland Waterways Executive of the *British Transport Commission. The packet ports, however, remained under direct railway control, even though most also had cargo traffic. Shortly afterwards several small, uneconomic ports were closed, and investment was concentrated on the larger ones. When the BTC was disbanded in 1963 the docks were separated from inland waterways, and the British Transport Docks Board was formed. In 1963 the government also set up a National Ports Council on the recommendation of the Rochdale Committee, appointed to advise on the future of British ports. The committee recommended that, where practicable, ports should be amalgamated into groups on an estuarial basis, and by 1970 authorities had been set up on the Tyne, Tees, Forth, and Clyde, including former BT docks. The BT Docks Board itself became the estuarial authority on the Humber and at Southampton. In the late 1980s the government's *privatization policy led to the progressive sale of these and the other BT and railway ports.

See also SHIPPING SERVICES.   GJB

The Docks of the Great Western Railway (1924); *Ports of the London & North Eastern Railway* (various edns. 1927–38); H. N. Appleby, *Ports Owned and Served by the London Midland & Scottish Railway* (1932); G. Jackson, *The History and Archaeology of Ports* (1983); P. Bennett and D. Jenkins, *Welsh Ports of the Great Western Railway* (1994); *Reg. Hist.*, i–vi, x–xv.

Portsmouth. Railways had three duties here: to handle the general business of the town (population 52,000 in 1841; 263,000 in 1921), to meet the requirements of its naval dockyard, and to forward traffic to and from the *Isle of Wight.

The first railway in the district ran to Gosport, on the west side of Portsmouth Harbour: a branch from the London–Southampton main line (see LONDON & SOUTH WESTERN RAILWAY). It was taken through Fareham and opened in 1842, Portsmouth being served by a ferry. In 1847 the *London Brighton & South Coast Railway brought a line from *Brighton into Portsmouth itself. Next year the LSWR opened a branch from Fareham (see 'BATTLES' BETWEEN RAILWAYS). The two companies made pooling *agreements in 1848 and 1858, sharing the London–Portsmouth passenger traffic, and they agreed to use the LBSCR station jointly. The dockyard came to be served by connections from the main lines and an internal system of its own within its walls. The companies were forbidden to penetrate the landward defences to reach the harbour, so Isle of Wight traffic had to be conveyed to the steamers by road.

Both railway routes to London were about 95 miles long. The Portsmouth Direct Railway was opened by the LSWR in 1859, via Petersfield, reducing the distance to 74 miles. The LBSCR cut its distance to 87 miles in 1867, with a line through Pulborough.

In 1876, the land defences being no longer thought necessary, the railway was extended from the 1847 station to the harbour. It required a high-level platform, to allow it to bridge Commercial Road, and terminated at a new station serving the Isle of Wight steamers.

Adjoining Portsmouth lay the separate township of Southsea, steadily developing as a middle-class holiday resort. It was served from Fratton station, ¾ mile east of Portsmouth, by a privately promoted branch line 1¼ miles long, opened in 1885 and worked by the main-line companies (see JOINT RAILWAYS). It never generated much traffic, however, and the *Southern Railway was authorized to close it in 1923.

The services provided by the LBSCR and LSWR were not generous in quantity, and always slow. Both routes to London were hilly and difficult to work; the agreements between the two companies kept the speed down, and Portsmouth had a slower service to London than any other of the largest English towns. Although speeds rose after the Direct line was electrified in 1936, the statement remained true. In 1994 the fastest trains from Portsmouth to London ran at 53 mph. JS
E. Course, *Portsmouth Railways* (1969); *Reg. Hist.*, ii.

Port Talbot Railway and Docks. Port Talbot emerged only with the development of its docks from 1835 onwards. The first dock was constructed for the copper industry at Cwmavon. But in 1870 it began the shipping of *coal. The Port Talbot Railway was established in 1894, to bring down as much of it as possible through the steep hills via Maesteg, as well as coal from mines at Tonmawr, north of Cwmavon. It also acquired the docks, enlarging and modernizing them. The two lines were opened in 1897–8.

For over 20 years this 48-mile system prospered greatly. The *Great Western Railway took over the working of the lines in 1908, though not the docks, and absorbed the Port Talbot company in 1922. JS
Reg. Hist., xii, 186–91, 195–6.

postcards. A great many picture postcards were produced by or for railway companies, as advertisements.

Plain postcards had been issued by the *Post Office since 1870. In 1890–1 the number sold was 230 million. In 1894 picture postcards, commercially produced, were accepted for transmission through the British mail service. Their popularity grew, forming a short-lived national craze, and 927 million postcards (plain and pictorial together) were sent in 1913–14. Many of these cards depicted towns or landscape; railway activities appeared on a few. They were available through vending machines at some stations.

In 1899–1903 eight railways issued postcards showing holiday resorts served by their lines. Most of the other large companies were soon doing the same—and some very small ones too, including the Corris and the Vale of Rheidol. They depicted not only scenes and buildings but also the railways themselves, their locomotives and rolling stock. A number of them showed the interiors of dining cars alluringly; diners could write them at table and have them posted at the next stop.

The company that went most heavily into this business was the *London & North Western. By 1914 it had issued 11 million postcards. But there were already signs that the craze was passing. Very few more were produced by any company after the *Grouping in 1923. The pre-war cards were already being sought after by collectors, however, as they have been ever since.

Although the quality of these cards, as pictures, is seldom high, the railway scenes they present—station buildings and the passengers assembled there, for example—are often interesting now. Very few were intended to be comic, but among those that were one series stands out: the delightful cartoons of the *Southwold Railway from the drawings of Reg Carter. JS
M. J. Daunton, *Royal Mail* (1985), 80–1; *RM*, 18 (1906), 137–45; M. I. Bray, *Railway Picture Postcards* (1986).

posters are a prime medium for publicity, but this was not recognized by the Victorian railway companies. Nearly all railway posters of the 1840s and 1850s were very basic printed bills in a range of bold typefaces juxtaposed to make eye-catching announcements. Most of them were text only, occasionally relieved by a standardized woodcut illustration of a train. The design process amounted to little more than the printer assembling his blocks in a frame for letterpress relief printing carried out in no more than two colours.

Commercial lithographic production of full-colour posters became practicable towards the end of the century. By the 1880s the illustrated poster was coming into widespread use for advertising, but even at this stage the railways did not exploit it fully. Although some larger companies had *publicity departments by this time, they usually still relied on a printer for the design and layout of their posters, with predictably uninspired results. The typical railway poster of 1900 featured an assemblage of small illustrations showing beauty spots thrown together in a cluttered layout, with text in a confusing variety of typefaces. The principle that later exponents of poster art always emphasized, of keeping the impression bold, simple, and direct, was rarely demonstrated. One notable exception was the fine work by Norman Wilkinson for the *London & North Western Railway from 1905. Another was John Hassall's famous jolly fisherman poster of 1908 for the *Great Northern Railway, with its slogan 'Skegness Is SO Bracing'.

It was the *London Underground that set the pace in poster advertising when its publicity came under the inspired direction of Frank *Pick in 1908. For the first time, posters became the principal focus of a railway company's publicity and in due course created a reputation for the Underground and later *London Transport as enlightened patrons of commercial art. Pick commissioned designs from both well-established artists and students at art school. He would suggest a subject, usually an appropriate destination or leisure activity reached by the Underground, but would never impose stylistic rules. 'There is room in posters for all styles', he once wrote, 'so long as the subject remains understandable to the man in the street.'

By the 1920s the Underground was issuing up to 40 posters a year, turning its station entrances and platforms into colourful galleries of modern art with a very practical purpose. They encouraged travel, but were also a very effective means of reinforcing the Underground's image as an enlightened and progressive organization. The main-line railways found it hard to follow.

After the 1923 *Grouping the *Big Four companies began to develop a more organized approach to publicity. Posters formed an important part of the *Southern Railway's new public relations strategy led by John *Elliot, a press man brought in to manage it. Elliot liked to emphasize the SR's modernity, exemplified by its commitment to a massive *electrification programme. While some posters encouraged *commuting from Kent and Surrey, others promoted country excursions and the delights of the SR's many seaside resorts.

The *Great Western, always rather conservative, did not make very effective use of posters, preferring to concentrate on other promotional products such as *guidebooks and jigsaws. Its brief flirtation with avant-garde art, when it commissioned the Underground's star designer Edward McKnight Kauffer to design some travel posters in the 1930s, did not go down well and was not extended. With these exceptions, GWR posters were generally rather staid exercises in pictorialism advertising holiday resorts in Devon and Cornwall.

The *London Midland & Scottish Railway took a different approach in 1924 by specially commissioning posters from Royal Academicians. With a few exceptions this tended to confirm the widely expressed view that what were then termed commercial artists were better suited to poster work than fine artists. The same distinction seemed valid over 60 years later when London Underground also used Royal Academicians in its 'Art on the Underground' campaign.

The *London & North Eastern was the most adventurous of the main-line companies in its posters. The publicity manager, William Teasdale, followed Pick in commissioning widely, promoting the LNER's poster productions with annual exhibitions. Its five leading artists were given exclusive contracts in which they agreed, in return for a higher fee, not to work for the other three main-line companies. Of the five, Tom Purvis produced the most distinctive work, always recognizable by his use of strong colours in a simplified flat block style which, like all the best posters, attracts and holds the eye at a distance.

The inter-war period was a golden age of railway poster art. However, its effectiveness, either as general propaganda for the railways or in raising traffic levels, is an open question. Market research was still in its infancy and none of the companies appears to have undertaken any.

The aftermath of *nationalization coincided with an almost universal decline in the standards of poster advertising. *Photography ousted drawn artwork but was not used with much creative flair. As an advertising medium, posters were upstaged in turn by television and new colour magazines. Very few railway posters of the 1950s and 1960s demonstrate the artistic verve of the pre-war period, and the decline in quality was matched by a general reduction in the quantity produced. *British Rail's poster campaigns of the 1970s are memorable more for their slogans than for

quality of design. 'See a friend this weekend', 'InterCity makes the going easy', and 'This is the age of the train' were catchy, but were also parodied mercilessly by cartoonists and comedians.

In more recent years the railway poster has taken on a new lease of life. In the 1980s London Underground began to make direct commissions to artists again as a form of corporate art sponsorship. The subjects are loosely connected with Underground destinations, but their purpose is more to brighten up the station environment than directly encourage travel. BR, and particularly its InterCity business, increasingly took posters beyond the immediate railway environment as part of its effort to lure customers out of their cars. Railway posters on large roadside hoardings, many of them reinforcing television advertising, have brought the promotion of rail travel into the consumer marketplace. They frequently show a style and wit that matches the best in modern advertising. Far from being an outmoded publicity medium, as some have claimed, the railway poster in this new form looks set to have a creative future.

See also ART. OG

B. Cole and R. Durack, *Happy as a Sandboy: Early Railway Posters* (1990), and *Railway Posters 1923–1947* (1992); O. Green, *Underground Art: London Transport Posters from 1908 to the Present* (1990); J. T. Shackleton, *The Golden Age of the Railway Poster* (1976).

Post Office. This article deals with the Post Office itself, and its relationship with the government and the railways. For discussion of the handling of mail, see MAIL SERVICES and PARCELS TRAFFIC.

The Post Office was formed late in the 17th century, charged with the conveyance of letters only. After 1720 they were carried by 'post-boys' on horseback; but, travelling alone, they were easily delayed or robbed. It took 30–40 hours for a letter to get from London to Bristol. The improvement of the roads after 1750 somewhat accelerated the service, but no striking change occurred until 1784, when the Post Office established 'mail-*coaches' entirely under its own control, in charge of an armed guard. In ordinary weather they kept good time, providing a regular and reliable service. By the 1830s the mail-coaches' time between London and Bristol was 12¼ hours. The advent of steam-worked railways, co-operating with the Post Office from 1830 onwards, brought a great further improvement. In 1841 the London–Bristol time came down to 4 hours 10 minutes by mail train.

A most important reform was now introduced in the working of the Post Office. To understand it properly the political position of the Office itself has to be appreciated.

It was headed by a Postmaster-General, representing it in Parliament, who was never a powerful minister. No PMG sat in the Cabinet between 1830 and 1846. The Office earned a large profit, and its income and expenditure were closely scrutinized by the Treasury, as an important item in the national revenue. It had perhaps less freedom than any other government department to apportion the funds at its disposal between its various activities. By its very nature it was peculiarly exposed to popular complaints, most of them from laymen, who bore no responsibility for executing their proposals for reform.

One of these was the radical publicist Rowland Hill, whose pamphlet *Post Office Reform* (1837) included a plan for a uniform postage of one penny on every lightweight letter sent within the UK, regardless of distance. The demand for a reduction in the postal rates had been heard for a long time, and here was a way to achieve it. Hill's drastic and simple plan did not absolutely require that the distribution of the mails should be by railway, but the practice was now already coming into view and the government recognized it by passing a Railways (Conveyance of Mails) Act in 1838, obliging the companies to carry the mails for the Post Office on request, for a 'reasonable' remuneration. Hill's plan was contemptuously ridiculed in Parliament by the PMG, the Earl of Lichfield, and the Office opposed it strenuously. But the government overruled their arguments and introduced the penny post in 1840, by which time the first trunk railways had been opened, and others were under construction.

The immediate effects of the measure were startling. The number of letters posted increased by 123 per cent in the first year. It had gone up by 441 per cent in 1854, when the basic railway system was fully at work. Although the new arrangements proved far more costly to implement than Hill had forecast, the net revenue from the conveyance of letters more than doubled in these years. Results like those required exceedingly heavy work from the officials, whose job was to change the carriage of letters from the mail-coaches to the railways as they expanded, sometimes at very short notice. But as soon as the new system had settled down, it became easier to improve mail services after the chief ones had been taken off the roads, as they had been by 1860. Hill had by now joined the staff of the Post Office, serving as its Secretary in 1854–64; he was widely and understandably detested there, and thwarted in most of his later ambitions.

In the 1850s the desirability of placing the new electric *telegraph system under direct state control, exercised through the Post Office, began to be discussed, on a simple analogy between the transmission of letters and telegrams. Telegraphs in Britain were then in the hands of private joint-stock companies. The Post Office did not seek this extension of its powers, owing to the unpopularity that such an enlargement of the state's control of economic affairs would incur. The railway companies, heavily involved both as owners and as users of telegraphs themselves, feared the expansion of the power of the Post Office to interfere in their affairs. There was much troublesome argument over the compensation to be paid by the government both to them and to the telegraph companies' shareholders. Nevertheless, the government's policy prevailed, the Telegraph Act (1868) authorizing the Post Office to buy telegraph undertakings and compelling it to do so on request from any of them. Here again the government was forcing the Office to act in a way that it judged contrary to its own interest.

This exercise in *nationalization proved advantageous to

the public and profitable to the government until the telephone came to rival the telegram and finally to displace it in the 20th century—passing in turn to the Post Office in 1912.

One more large issue concerning the government, the Post Office, and the railways arose in the 1870s, over the carriage of *parcels. It was settled differently, the government legislating in favour of a policy supported by the Post Office but opposed by the railways, until they were bribed into accepting it.

The Post Office had from its earliest days been confined to conveying letters. Heavy parcels went by coach, and later by train. From the point of view of the public, this was an awkward arrangement, each railway company being entitled to charge its own rates. Patiently repeated efforts were made by the *Railway Clearing House to secure a standard charge for this service, accepted by all its member-companies, but by 1870, when there had been many absorptions of smaller companies, the number of large ones was still 25, and no unanimous agreement could be reached among them. Negotiations went on throughout the 1870s. When it looked as if an agreement had been reached in 1879, the proposals were torpedoed by the *North Eastern and *London & South Western Railways. The public was now growing restive at this shilly-shallying. In *Gladstone's second government, elected in 1880, the PMG, Henry Fawcett, became convinced that an agreement must be reached, and the government passed the Post Office (Parcels) Act in 1882, going into force the following year. The preamble stated that its new arrangements for the conveyance of parcels were proposed by the Treasury 'on the representation of the Postmaster-General'. So in this instance an agreement on policy between the Office and the government was proclaimed; achieved, however, only by awarding the railways 55 per cent of the receipts from carrying Post Office parcels, when the highest rate payable on the Continent was 40 per cent.

One effect of the high price that the Post Office had to pay the railways was that it began to look for a cheaper means of transporting parcels. In 1887 it reintroduced horse-drawn vehicles of its own, running twice daily between London and Brighton. It adopted motor-vans early in the 20th century. In 1913 they were running almost 200 miles, between London and Liverpool.

By that time the Post Office was proposing to build a tube railway of its own beneath London, to convey mails between *Liverpool Street and *Paddington stations; however, this was not completed until 1928 (see POST OFFICE RAILWAY).

The big triangular struggle between the government, the Post Office, and the railways had now ceased. The relationship between the postal authorities and the companies had become a generally co-operative one, broken occasionally by disputes on single issues which, in recent years, have been determined almost entirely by technological changes in the handling of letters and parcels, as dealt with in the articles already cited.   JS

H. Robinson, *Britain's Post Office* (1953); M. J. Daunton, *Royal*

Mail: The Post Office since 1840 (1985); Bagwell; P. Johnson, *Mail by Rail* (1996).

Post Office Railway. The first tube railway built in London for the transport of mail was the property of a private concern, the Pneumatic Despatch Company, which secured general powers in 1859 to construct under any street in the Metropolis airtight tubes in which vehicles would run by atmospheric pressure. After experiment on a 600-yd stretch at *Euston, a single-tunnel line was built from Euston via Holborn, where there was a reverse, to the General Post Office at St Martin's-le-Grand in the City, nearly 2½ miles. It was not circular in profile but rather a flattened horseshoe in shape, 4 ft 6 in wide and 4 ft 1 in high, with a rail *gauge of 3 ft 8½ in. Only a limited quantity of mail was carried in 1873–4, and the project was then abandoned.

The *Post Office's own railway, authorized in 1913, was a means to carry letters and parcels clear of the growing congestion on the London streets. It is a tube line linking *Paddington across the centre to the Eastern District Office at Whitechapel, with six intermediate stations, solely for the conveyance of mail in bags. The main tunnel was built in 1914–17 but not then used (except for the wartime storage of museum objects); it was opened for traffic in 1928. The 9 ft diameter tunnels carry two 2 ft gauge tracks, with third-rail current supply at 440 V dc. The trains are operated without drivers by automatic control through *track circuits. The original 4-wheeled cars were replaced from 1930 by bogie cars with a 4-wheeled power unit at each end; new cars were added in 1980. Though not unique (Munich and Chicago have had small-scale postal tubes), the Post Office Railway beneath London has made a useful contribution to speeding the mails and slightly reducing street congestion.

See also MAIL SERVICES. RMR
W. G. Carter, *Post Office (London) Railway* (1937); C. E. Lee, 'The Pneumatic Despatch Company's Railways', *TNS*, 45 (1972–3), 67; D. A. Baylis, *The Post Office Railway, London* (1978); D. F. Croome and A. A. Jackson, *Rails through the Clay* (1993 edn.).

Pratt, Edwin Augustus (1860–1922), writer. Pratt was a journalist on *The Times* staff from 1890 who, while producing a string of books and pamphlets on social affairs including the position of women, temperance, mission work in China, and agriculture, made a particular study of railway and *canal economics and practices. In the lively debate on the organization of the British railways after about 1900 he was a strong opponent of proposals for *nationalization. In the course of writing these contributions to current controversy, he became convinced that understanding of the issues involved would be strengthened by investigation of the history of English transport in general, and his book *A History of Transport and Communication in England* (1912) was the result. This was a pioneer in its broad scope, attention to statistical material where it was available, and assessment of the effect of railways on national life. The 7½-page list of authorities (to which detailed references were not given) showed how widely he had read. *The Rise of Rail-Power in War and Conquest 1833–1914* (1916), world-wide in scope with a 22-page bibliography, was again a pioneer work in

its field. His last book, *British Railways and the Great War* (2 vols., 1921), was a solid and careful account. All three remain valuable to students of transport history. RMR
The Times, 30 Oct. 1922; M. Robbins, 'The Progress of Transport History', *JTH*, 3rd ser., 12 (1991), 74.

preservation of railways. The railway preservation movement has ensured survival of steam trains in Britain, together with the specialized skills required to operate and maintain them. Yet in this is an essential paradox, for operating a steam train causes continuous wear and tear. Worn-out parts have to be replaced, with loss of historic authenticity. Railway preservation is ever a compromise; indeed a conflict between the needs to preserve the essential element of motion and to preserve individual items of historic significance intact for as long as possible.

This dilemma has been present at least since the late 1940s when L. T. C. *Rolt was considering what could be done to prevent closure of the dilapidated *Talyllyn Railway after the death of its octogenarian owner. His plan was to 'perpetuate' it, by re-laying it as a 10¼-in *gauge miniature railway, mixing the gauge for a short distance with the original 2 ft 3 in over which the original locomotives and rolling stock could occasionally be demonstrated. But it became clear that only an attempt to 'preserve' the railway in its original form was likely to attract adequate support. The concept of a Talyllyn Railway Preservation Society was suggested to Rolt in 1949 by O. H. Prosser, and the term 'railway preservation' has been familiar since it was formed in 1951.

Preservation of railway equipment, however, goes back much further. The first preserved locomotive appears to have been the *Canterbury & Whitstable Railway's *Invicta*, which was stored by the *South Eastern Railway in the late 1840s. The first locomotive preserved in public was the *Stockton & Darlington Railway's original locomotive *Locomotion*, placed on a pedestal at Darlington North Road station in 1857. Two important early locomotives were acquired in 1862 by the Patent Office *Museum, South Kensington (forerunner of the Science Museum): *Hedley's pioneering *Puffing Billy* of 1814, and what was left of the *Stephensons' *Rocket*. *Hackworth's *Sans Pareil* joined them in 1864.

The *London & North Eastern established a museum at *York in 1927. Railway-owned relics were joined there by the noted *London Brighton & South Coast Railway 0-4-2 *Gladstone*, purchased on withdrawal for preservation by the Stephenson Locomotive Society in 1927. This event marked the entry of voluntary societies into railway preservation.

The celebrations of the centenary of the *Liverpool & Manchester Railway in 1930 prompted restoration to full working order, by the *London Midland & Scottish Railway, of the LMR locomotive *Lion* of 1837. Then in 1938 the *London & North Eastern Railway restored to working order *Great Northern Railway 4-2-2 No. 1 of 1870. Attached to a train of coaches from the 1880s, it provided for publicity a contrast with the latest Flying Scotsman express. In that year No. 1 and train were chartered by the *Railway

Correspondence & Travel Society: the first *enthusiasts' special to use a preserved locomotive on the main line.

*Narrow-gauge railways had the appeal of the diminutive. Closure of the Lynton & Barnstaple Railway in 1935 prompted the purchase of several coaches for use as summer houses and the like, including one which has survived to reach the *National Railway Museum. The Talyllyn was too unimportant to be placed under government control during World War II, and so escaped nationalization: Lady Haydn Jones, by then widow of former owner Sir Haydn Jones, was kind enough in 1951 to give effective control to the TRPS, whose first trains ran in that year.

The *Festiniog Railway had then lain derelict since closure in 1946: but the embryonic Festiniog Railway Society (which originated in 1951) found the company heavily in debt. A benefactor appeared: Alan Pegler, who in 1954 purchased a controlling interest in the railway, and later transferred it to a charitable trust. The railway was reopened in 1955–82.

The first standard-gauge railways to be preserved, both in 1960, were the historic *Middleton Railway and the Bluebell Railway. The former was the first of many *industrial railways to be preserved; the Bluebell the first closed *British Railways branch to be reopened as a preserved railway, for which a preservation society had been formed. It in turn formed an operating company to lease, and later purchase, the line from BR which had first obtained a *light railway order for it from the Minister of *Transport, followed by a further order transferring it to the Bluebell company. The element of disinterested benevolence is seen throughout the voluntary sector of railway preservation, although the legal structures through which it has been expressed have varied, and this process or something like it was to be repeated many times over, particularly during the period of closures which followed the *Beeching Plan. From this period originate many names familiar in railway preservation, such as the Keighley & Worth Valley Railway, the Severn Valley Railway, the Dart Valley Railway, and the North Norfolk Railway. In some instances new narrow-gauge railways have been constructed on the trackbeds of closed standard-gauge lines—examples include the Brecon Mountain and South Tynedale Railways.

The 1960s also saw the virtual extinction of the steam locomotive from everyday use by BR, which itself set aside a representative selection for preservation. The principal home established for them was the Museum of British Transport at Clapham, London (1961); several *Great Western Railway locomotives went to the GWR Museum at *Swindon (c.1961), and some from Scottish railways to the Museum of Transport, *Glasgow (1964). All these were static museums. The Clapham museum's railway collection was for the most part moved to the new NRM.

During the 1960s BR restored a few historic locomotives for use on special trains, notably the record-breaking City of Truro. The general ban on steam operation which followed the 'end of steam' in 1968 put an end to this, but meanwhile individuals and groups had purchased steam locomotives for preservation. Pioneers included J. B. Latham, who purchased the 1 ft 11½ in gauge 0-6-0ST Triassic from Rugby Portland Cement Co. in 1957, and Captain W. G. Smith who bought GNR 0-6-0ST No. 1247 from BR in 1959; Alan Pegler made national news when he bought the famous locomotive Flying Scotsman from BR in 1963. In 1962 GWR 4-4-0 No. 9017 was bought from BR by a fund raised from public appeal by T. R. Gomm, and set to work on the Bluebell Railway. This was an arrangement which soon became common: on a train on a preserved railway, the likelihood is that the locomotive belongs to a separate group and the coaches to a third.

The same period saw establishment of 'steam centres' such as the Great Western Society's Didcot Railway Centre (1967) and Steamtown Carnforth. There locomotives and rolling stock could be overhauled and restored, and carry passengers over a short demonstration line. Some centres have been an initial stage in preservation of a branch line. Others became centres for the maintenance of locomotives used for main-line operation: in 1972 BR relaxed its steam ban and has subsequently allowed steam excursions over selected routes such as the *Settle & Carlisle line. Locomotives from the NRM have been regular performers on these, as well as those privately owned.

After the end of BR steam, the continuing demand for locomotives for preservation was met from three main sources: industries such as the National Coal Board; importation from the Continent and further afield; and scrapyards. Of the latter, the outstanding example was Woodham Bros of Barry, from which more than 200 steam locomotives were purchased for preservation between 1968 and 1989. A number of diesel and electric locomotives and *multiple units have also been preserved.

One hindrance which had to be overcome before the first could be released was a condition of sale for scrap by BR prohibiting resale. It was to negotiate on such matters, successfully in this instance, that the *Association of Railway Preservation Societies originated in 1959. Legislative proposals affecting railway preservation have tended to increase in recent years, from both Westminster and Brussels, and it is largely to influence the latter (such as a proposal that hot surfaces should be painted a fluorescent colour) that the association was instrumental in formation of the European Federation of Museum & Tourist Railways (FEDECRAIL) in 1994.   PJGR

L. T. C. Rolt, Railway Adventure (1953); P. J. G. Ransom, Railways Revived (1973); A. C. Butcher, Railways Restored (annually).

press, railway. Railway journalism in Britain began in 1823 with the Mechanic's Magazine, which gave much attention to railways from its outset, supporting them firmly against road interests from 1829 onwards. The founder and editor was Joseph Clifton Robertson, whose sorry conduct remained obscure until it was revealed in an article published in 1995. He was an able man, with a vision of the railways' future, but crafty and treacherous, giving a bad name to most things he touched—including, in the 1830s, the unfortunate *Eastern Counties Railway. Among his associates at this time were John *Herapath, John Braithwaite, and W. B. *Adams.

Robertson worked briefly for the *London & Greenwich Railway, under the financier John Walter, but their association ceased in 1834. Walter went on to establish a paper called the *Railway Magazine and Annals of Science*, the first in Britain that was devoted primarily to railways, selling it to Herapath in 1836. With some changes of title, the paper continued until 1903. Then in 1837 Robertson (now warring violently with Herapath) founded the *Railway Times*, in collaboration with Braithwaite. This paper continued until 1914, when it was merged with the *Railway Gazette*, which itself dated back to the *Rail Road Gazette* of 1856 and *Transport* of 1892. In 1904 they combined as *Transport and Rail Road Gazette*, becoming the *Railway Gazette* in 1905. It is still published today as *Railway Gazette International*, reflecting its world-wide reputation.

'Herapath' and the *Railway Times*, both published weekly, were concerned first of all with matters of finance and management. They included reports of company shareholders' meetings, share prices, and traffic figures. Their view of management was broad, for each would take its stand (usually opposed to the other's) on engineering questions—the types of locomotive that in its opinion should be employed, for instance—on the *gauge of railways, and the causes of *accidents. As British investment in *overseas railway companies increased, they expressed their views on them too.

Although these papers' opinions are often amusing, and sometimes shrewd, the student of railway history today will find more value in their factual information, for example on the rise and fall of traffic. But as the figures were usually supplied by the companies, their accuracy is not entirely reliable.

The *mania of 1844–7 called forth new periodicals, aimed at giving potential investors the kinds of information they wanted. At least 15 were in circulation by October 1845. Among them the *Railway Chronicle* has an interest of its own, through concerning itself with the social effects the railways were producing. It was edited by the engineer John Scott Russell, assisted by Henry Cole, who was to play an important part in the Great Exhibition of 1851. But like all the other new journals (except the *Railway Record*) it died when the speculative fever passed.

Different journals soon appeared, concerned with railway technology. The *Engineer* (first published in 1856) and *Engineering* (1866) were notable. Railways figured there a great deal, along with ships and other means of transport, mostly powered by steam. A specialist magazine, the *Railway Engineer*, was added in 1880.

Side by side with these, another group of publications recorded the proceedings of the engineers' professional bodies: the *Institutions of Civil, Electrical, Locomotive, Mechanical, and Railway Signal Engineers. They provide the texts of papers read by eminent men, accompanied by the subsequent discussions to which other prominent figures often contributed, and they repay careful study.

No single writer emerged who founded a reputation on work in any of these 19th-century journals. But from 1889 onwards a new and more widely spread interest in railways began to show itself (see LITERATURE OF RAILWAYS), which was met by a series of periodicals unlike any of their predecessors. They were headed by two that were first published in 1896–7: *Moore's Monthly Magazine*, later known as the *Locomotive* and lasting until 1962; and the *Railway Magazine*, which is still published today. In the latter Charles *Rous-Marten figured frequently, followed by others like Cecil J. *Allen, helping to make their names widely known. E. L. *Ahrons' two largest and best-known books were based on articles published in the *Engineer* and the *Railway Magazine*.

One other type of railway periodical was now proliferating: the house journal. In 1881, when working on the *London & South Western Railway, Sam *Fay started a *South-Western Gazette*, with two colleagues. The *Great Western Railway Magazine*, started in 1888 by the company's Temperance Society, became very successful under the direction of Felix *Pole and was taken over by the company in 1904. W. W. *Tomlinson worked hard and effectively on the *North Eastern Railway Magazine*, leading to his admirable history of the company. All the *'Big Four' companies produced staff magazines, perpetuated by *British Railways on a regional basis until they were eventually superseded by the national *Rail News*.

A valuable weekly, *Modern Transport*, appeared from 1919 to 1966, and in 1939 a new magazine for enthusiasts entitled *Railways* was published, the first to compete with the *Railway Magazine*. Later renamed *Railway World*, it now gives emphasis to preserved lines.

In 1920 a new society was established for the study of the history of engineering and technology: the *Newcomen Society, whose annual *Transactions* have paid careful and constant attention to railways. On the debit side, however, the *Railway Engineer* died in 1935: a significant loss, testifying to the increased public interest that was then being taken in motor vehicles and aircraft.

The *British Transport Commission produced a monthly magazine intended for its own staff, and also a very good little quarterly from 1950 onwards: the *British Transport Review*. Some of its articles are of permanent value.

Four specialist historical periodicals should be mentioned. The *Journal of Transport History* (from 1953) and the *Journal of the *Railway & Canal Historical Society* (from 1955) are available by subscription; the more recent *British Railway Journal* (quarterly) and *Back Track* (monthly) are on public sale. All contain valuable material, as do some of the *modellers' magazines from time to time. Numerous societies devoted to the study of the history of specific railway companies publish their findings in magazines for members.

Among the numbers of present-day *enthusiasts' magazines, many of which are largely devoted to nostalgia, one stands out. In 1962 the *Locomotive* combined with a monthly enthusiasts' magazine, *Trains Illustrated*, under the title *Modern Railways*. It was aimed at professionals and serious enthusiasts alike, and quickly secured a reputation for informed comment and reporting on railway affairs at home and abroad, since when its stature has continued to increase.   JS

VR, 293–5; Robertson; J. E. C. Palmer, 'Authority, Idiosyncrasy, and Corruption in the Early Railway Press, 1823–1844', JRCHS, 31, 161 (July 1995), 442–57.

pressure groups, see PUBLIC OPINION.

Preston. Local histories have generally overlooked Preston's importance on the railway, and the part it played in the town's development.

The first line was a *tramroad in 1803, crossing the valley of the Ribble to connect the southern and northern sections of the Lancaster *Canal. In 1836 the short Preston & Longridge Railway was opened from quarries. With a population of 14,000, Preston was changing from a commercial centre to a cotton and engineering town, and its position between the Pennines and the Irish Sea formed a focus for railways. In 1838 the *North Union Railway linked it to lines to *London, *Liverpool, and *Manchester, followed in 1840–9 by others: northward to *Scotland; to Fleetwood and the Fylde coast; Manchester by a shorter route through Bolton; Blackburn and East Lancashire; and a direct line to Liverpool via Ormskirk.

These railways came into *London & North Western or *Lancashire & Yorkshire ownership or, like the station and the Ribble branch to the riverside, were *joint. The final line was the West Lancashire to Southport, in 1882. The LYR soon acquired it and closed its separate station. Between 1850 and 1908 numerous connecting lines were made south of Preston to allow east–west trains to enter or avoid the station without conflicting with the *West Coast main line.

Meanwhile the town had grown, containing 115,000 people by 1900. The five original railways had separate stations, and their refusal to collaborate in through services gave Preston a notoriety which persisted long after the concentration of main-line trains at the North Union station in 1844. A busy interchange point, the station was also a refreshment stop for all Anglo-Scottish expresses until *restaurant cars appeared in the 1890s. The joint companies disagreed on sharing the cost of improvements until unbearable inadequacy and decrepitude finally forced them to rebuild and extend it in 1873–1913 (see also JOINT STATIONS). Even so, *Blackpool holiday trains continued to cause congestion, but plans for an avoiding line for them never materialized. Rationalization of track and train services for West Coast line *electrification in 1971–2 made some platforms redundant, otherwise the modernized station is substantially as it was when it was rebuilt, where once more all trains stop. Line closures have been limited to the Longridge branch (passengers in 1930, goods in 1967–80), the West Lancashire, and most of the southern connecting lines in 1969–72. Liverpool line services were terminated at Ormskirk, through trains being diverted via Wigan.

The Preston Dock railway, opened on the Ribble branch in 1892, now serves industrial premises. Preston's railway associations extended to electric tram cars made by Dick, Kerr & Co., and the prototype *Deltic diesel-electric loco-

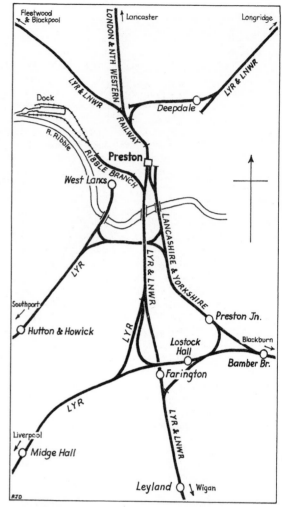

Preston, 1922

motive built by their successors, English Electric—now GEC Alsthom.   GJB

LYR, i and ii; Reg. Hist., x (1986 edn.), ch. 9; G. Biddle, The Railways around Preston: An Historical Review (1992 edn.); D. Hunt, A History of Preston (1992).

Preston & Wyre Railway. The line from *Preston to Fleetwood, opened in 1840, was promoted by Sir Peter Hesketh Fleetwood as an integral part of his scheme for a new port and town on his Rossall estate at the mouth of the River Wyre. In 1841–8 it formed part of a *London–*Glasgow route, steamers taking passengers by sea to Ardrossan, until the *Caledonian Railway was completed.

The railway was taken over by the *Lancashire & Yorkshire and *London & North Western Railways (see JOINT RAILWAYS) in 1849, which used it to encourage development of the bracing Fylde coast by opening branches to *Blackpool (North) and Lytham in 1846. An independent company built a separate Lytham–Blackpool line in 1863, but was absorbed by the joint companies in 1871, followed by an improved route to Lytham and a connection between the two railways there to form a second route to Blackpool (Central).

The LYR developed Fleetwood as a *port for Ireland and the Isle of Man, and built docks for a flourishing trade in fish, grain, and timber.

As Blackpool developed, the route from Poulton to the North station became the main line instead of the original one to Fleetwood, and after a serious derailment on Poulton curve an improved alignment was opened in 1896. Increasing Blackpool holiday traffic was further speeded up in 1903 by a direct line from Kirkham to Blackpool Central, mainly used in the summer to avoid the circuitous route through Lytham. It was closed in 1967, followed by withdrawal of Poulton–Fleetwood passenger services in 1970.   GJB

B. Curtiss, *Fleetwood: A Town Is Born* (1986); *LYR*, i, ch. 5; *Reg. Hist.*, x, ch. 9 (1986 edn.).

private-owner wagons. When the early railways changed from simply providing track for others to use, to acting as carriers using their own locomotives and vehicles, many privately owned *wagons remained, particularly for *coal. Even after *nationalization, when 540,000 passed to *British Railways, some were still operated.

Private-owner wagons produced difficulties through variations in design (many at first had dumb *buffers, for example), and maintenance, generally by independent wagon repairers, was often inferior to the railways' own. In the 1920s two Royal Commissions commented adversely on their design and condition. Failure by owners to modernize handling facilities, and to renew wagon stocks, perpetuated outdated designs with low payloads. Movement of private-owner wagons was controlled immediately by railway companies, and more generally by the *Railway Clearing House, which also attempted to set standards of design, notably the standard steel underframe of 1939 used for 4-wheel, 13-ton open and covered wagons.

As early as 1849 the *York Newcastle & Berwick Railway decided to buy up all the private-owner wagons on its system, but it is not known to what extent this was carried out. None were allowed on the *North Staffordshire and *Festiniog Railways. By the 1870s accidents were frequently attributed to faults in private-owner wagons, and in 1873 the Board of *Trade inspector, *Tyler, urged the railways to buy them up. In 1881 the *Midland Railway attempted to do so, followed by the *Caledonian, neither successfully. In 1914 private-owner wagons represented £20 million investment by 4,000 owners. A cheaper rate was conceded by the railways for coal conveyed in private-owner wagons, as opposed to company-owned vehicles—a powerful reason for their users to ensure their survival.

Apart from coal and mineral wagons, private-owner wagons (700,000 in 1925) included specialized types such as cylindrical tank wagons for petroleum products, first introduced in the late 1880s; rectangular tank wagons for tar and other viscous coal products; and tank wagons for chemicals, such as liquid chlorine. There were also hopper wagons for ore or minerals, often moved over short distances only.

In World War II, private-owner wagons were taken over by the government, and subsequently became 'common user', to be loaded with any traffic. After nationalization, a number of specialized privately owned wagons remained, principally those for petroleum products. Liaison between private owners, BR, builders, and repairers was maintained by a technical committee. This body promoted improvements, most notably in the development of 75-ton and 100-ton bogie tank wagons, and the fitting of continuous *braking and more sophisticated *suspensions.

From the 1960s, BR placed an increasing emphasis on major rail-users providing their own wagons, particularly high-capacity wagons for petroleum products, but there are privately owned double-deck car transporter wagons, pressure-discharge tank wagons for *cement, and those for substances such as caustic soda liquor and liquefied petroleum gases. In addition, wagons have been built to the order of leasing companies—sometimes associated with the wagon builders—for use by major rail freight users. Aggregates producers invested in 100-ton payload wagons in the 1980s and there have been notable purchases of trans-modal wagons for international traffic through the *Channel Tunnel.   MLH

YNBR: B. Poole, *Report to the . . . London & North Western Railway on Coal Traffic* (1849); Bagwell, ch. 9.

privatization. The first Conservative government led by Margaret Thatcher made clear its determination to privatize, or return to private ownership, a number of nationalized industries. *British Rail was instructed to divest itself of what the government considered were fringe activities such as the *hotels, *shipping, and hovercraft services, which passed to new owners by 1985. The government also directed BR to broaden the participation of the private sector in its activities. At this stage, some engineering activities were sold, along with Travellers Fare, its station catering subsidiary (SEE REFRESHMENT ROOMS).

Having instructed BR to move to an arm's-length relationship with British Rail Engineering Ltd, the government ordained its sale to the private sector, and in April 1987 BREL passed to a consortium comprising Asea Brown Boveri, Trafalgar House, and its own management team. Some workshops were previously formed into British Rail Maintenance Ltd, and these remained in the public sector until sold off with principal BR maintenance depots during 1995.

During 1988 the Downing Street Policy Unit revealed that privatization of the main railway industry was being considered, for implementation during the fourth term of the Thatcher administration. Options included selling off BR as a going concern as 'BR plc'; absorption of the railway infrastructure into a track authority, with separate train operating companies; and breaking up BR into geographically based companies. By early 1991, with John Major as Prime Minister, the government made it clear that privatization would entail open access (to all comers) to the rail network by any operator, in line with European Community policy.

Following Major's victory in the 1992 election, the Queen's Speech at the opening of Parliament confirmed that legislation would be introduced to enable the private sector to operate rail services. The outcome was the publication of a White Paper on rail privatization in July 1992.

The White Paper's proposals were that the rail freight and parcels businesses should be transferred entirely to the private sector; that private sector companies should manage and operate existing passenger services as franchisees, receiving grants in return for meeting required standards of service, with the control of franchising vested in a Franchising Director; that there should be right of access to the network for all operators of freight and passenger services, to be overseen by a Rail Regulator; that part of the existing BR would become a track authority named Railtrack with responsibility for operating all track and infrastructure, and intended for eventual privatization. As sales proceeded, the residual BR would fade away.

The appearance of the White Paper coincided with the appointment by the Department of *Transport of numerous consultants, charged with producing papers and guidelines on the process of privatization. During 1992–3, with public criticism of the privatization proposals, and a general lack of interest from potential purchasers of those rail businesses due for sale, or from possible bidders for franchises alike, the privatization strategy was modified, leading to the Railways Act, 1993, which received Royal Assent on 5 November. By this time, new aspects of the privatization process had become apparent. This included the decision that from 1 April 1994 all traction and rolling stock would be owned by three rolling stock leasing companies, known as the ROSCOs; they lease stock to the train operating units and had passed to private ownership by early 1996. Technical service units of the former rail businesses were made nominally independent companies and are progressively being sold. They have become known as the TESCOs.

The major restructuring of BR occurred on 1 April 1994. From this date, Railtrack, organized into ten (eight from 1995) regional zones, took over the track and infrastructure responsibilities of BR. Railtrack's revenue comes from charging train operators access charges. The three passenger businesses were dissolved on the same date, and their regionally based units were thereafter regarded as divisions of BR, charged with preparing for the franchising of their operations. The 25 passenger businesses thus formed became Train Operating Units and broadly followed the previous sub-divisions of the former rail businesses with the addition of two new units: Cardiff Valleys, and Merseyside. Each of the TOUs had a licence to operate only within its territory; at least temporarily, the government has had to concede the principle of open access for passenger operations.

Once vested as subsidiaries of the BRB, the TOUs became TOCs—Train Operating Companies. The TOCs were then offered as franchises, and the first privatized operations commenced early in 1996.

Separate from the TOCs was European Passenger Services Ltd, responsible for operating international services through the *Channel Tunnel, and running and maintaining the Eurostar and Euronight trains. A division of BR until 1994, EPS then became a government-owned company, the intention being that it would be absorbed by the private company successfully bidding as contractor for, and operator of, the planned high-speed rail link between *St Pancras and the tunnel. This is London & Continental Railways.

The trainload business dealing principally with Royal *Mail traffic was launched as Rail express systems (Res) in 1991, and this entity remained a separate business after 1994, with a licence to operate over the whole of the BR network. It was purchased by a US company late in 1995.

During 1994, the commodity-based freight business, and part of Railfreight Distribution, were reorganized into three regionally based organizations of roughly equal size, with the licence to operate services. They were renamed Loadhaul, Transrail, and Mainline, but were subsequently sold as one concern to the same US company in 1996. The trainload freight operation will be subject to open access from other rail freight operators, including the power generation companies. The remainder of Railfreight Distribution is principally concerned with international freight services. The freight container haulage operation, *Freightliner, remained as a separate unit, also to be sold.

Major changes occurred to the *civil engineering and non-rolling stock technical services operations of BR. The former activity, previously the civil engineers' responsibility, became a unitary authority under BR control from 1 April 1994, with the title of British Rail Infrastructure Services. This was a prelude to a complex procedure whereby adjoining, regionally based BRIS units were merged, before splitting into new track renewals and infrastructure maintenance units. All were offered for sale during 1996.

A range of nominally independent organizations has been created, and remained under BR control until passing to the private sector, including British Rail Telecommunications, Quality and Safety Services, and, from the former Production Services, six units including Sigtech and Interlogic (signalling engineering), Works Division (track and signalling services), and Railtest (the evaluation of railway vehicles and systems, and operation of the Old Dalby test track)—see TESTING OF EQUIPMENT.

Nearly 100 nominally self-standing rail businesses have derived from the breaking up of the British Railways Board.   MLH

HMSO, *New Opportunities for the Railways*, Cm 2012 (1992).

prize-fighting. Apart from *horse-racing, prize-fighting was the first spectator *sport notably aided by railways, although when they became established it was already declining, partly under moral disapproval. However, it still had aristocratic patronage, and considerable popular support.

The gathering of crowds to see these fights, and their

tumultuous behaviour, could constitute illegal assembly or riot, which local magistrates were authorized to suppress, assisted at need by soldiers. Some promoters would then adjourn a fight to another county under the jurisdiction of different magistrates, for which reason most large ones were held close to a county boundary.

In 1842 the *Northern & Eastern Railway brought large crowds to a fight at Sawbridgeworth in Hertfordshire, close to Essex. The Caunt v. Bendigo fight of 1845 took place in Buckinghamshire near Newport Pagnell, close to Bedfordshire and Northamptonshire, and many people were brought to Wolverton for it by the *London & Birmingham Railway. In 1859 a *South Eastern special train was stopped by the Kent police, near Tonbridge. It was thereupon diverted to the Hastings line, and fights took place at Etchingham in Sussex. The most celebrated of these final contests was Sayers v. Heenan, held in 1860 at Farnborough in Hampshire, which was close to Surrey and served by two railways, the SER and the *London & South Western.

At *Paddington station a savage crowd assembled in 1863 as a special train was due to leave for a fight at Wootton Bassett, and an ugly riot ensued. Parliament was now growing concerned about this and similar matters. Public executions of criminals ceased in 1867, preventing another frequent cause of disorder. By the *Regulation of Railways Act (1868) the companies were forbidden to run special trains to prize-fights or stop trains for this purpose at places lacking stations, subject to fines of £200 to £500, half of which were to go to informers. This helped to kill the sport.   JS

RTC, 89; Newport Pagnell fight: *Bell's Life*, 14 Sept. 1845; Kent episode: Kent RO, Maidstone, Q GB 41 (bundle B).

profitability of Britain's railways has been a source of continuing concern since the industry was born. Because the railway companies were financed by private capital, profits were clearly important, particularly in the development stage (c.1825–50). Actual rates of return were a function of the cost of *promotion and *construction, the degree of effective *competition, *accounting decisions, and the facility with which managers responded to the type of market chosen. The first railway companies, which catered for high-value *freight and high *fare-paying passengers when competition was limited, earned dividends considerably in excess of market rates. The *Liverpool & Manchester Railway, for example, paid its ordinary shareholders an average of 9.5 per cent a year in 1832–45. Then the government acted to inject more competition in the industry by authorizing competing companies, while at the same time producing regulations which limited charges and profits (*Gladstone's Act of 1844 introduced service and fare constraints and took powers to purchase new railways after 21 years if profits remained high). All this served to reduce the profitability of most of the established railway companies, as did the effects of the speculative investment *manias in 1836–7, 1847–9, and 1863–6. Railway managers were forced down-market in order to produce revenues sufficient to enable them to pay dividends on greatly expanded capital

accounts. For example, the *Great Western, which was promoted with an initial capital of £3 million, had raised nearly £7 million by 1845 and £14.5 million by 1851. Furthermore, the process continued after 1850; the amount invested in the UK (historic values) rose from £246 million in 1850 to £630 million by 1875 and £1,335 million by 1912.

Much has been written about the relatively high profits of the pre-1870 period and more modest earnings thereafter. In fact, profitability was always patchy and cyclical in nature, and there was a wide disparity between the earnings of individual companies, and between expected profits and actual returns: M. C. Reed has shown how wide the gap was in 1843 for six companies promoted in 1836, with an average estimated return of 10.6 per cent and an actual profit of 4.7 per cent. The manipulation of accounts to maintain dividends, especially before the *Regulation of Railways Act, 1868, also complicates the picture. The main trends may be derived from the net rate of return on paid-up capital (Mitchell & Deane), and the average return on equity capital (Mihill Slaughter). The net rate of return on UK capital rose from about 3.75 per cent in the mid-1850s to 4.5 per cent in the early 1870s. The average ordinary dividend paid by the 15 major companies followed a similar path. This exceeded 6 per cent in 1840–6, fell below 3 per cent in 1849 and 1850 in the aftermath of the mania, then rose gradually to about 5 per cent by the early 1870s.

Overall, returns were scarcely monopolistic. The average dividend paid over the period 1850–75 was a fairly modest 3.65 per cent. In the period 1875–1914 profits were more tightly squeezed as a result of greater state control, increased labour costs, competition, and the additional investment which companies were persuaded to make in less profitable lines. As a result the net rate of return on capital fell from 4.6 per cent in 1870–4 to 3.4 per cent in 1900–4, although it was not until the 1890s that returns fell below the 4 per cent level of the 1860s, and there was a modest recovery in the early 20th century to 3.6 per cent in 1912. If the return on net capital is calculated (i.e. if nominal additions to capital are excluded), the position appears healthier. On this basis the return was still 4.3 per cent in 1895–9, very similar to that in 1875–84, and although earnings dipped to 4 per cent in 1900–9, there was a recovery to 4.2 per cent in 1910–12. Of course, averages hide the disparity in corporate fortunes. Some of the companies which were in receivership in the mid-1860s, such as the *Great Eastern and the *London Chatham & Dover, struggled to pay any dividend at all; others, enjoying a secure freight market, such as the *Taff Vale, *Furness, and the *Maryport & Carlisle, paid handsome dividends for several decades. The Furness ordinary dividend averaged 7.3 per cent, 1854–82, that of the Maryport & Carlisle nearly 7 per cent, 1844–1922. Of the larger companies, the *North Eastern and the *London & North Western rewarded shareholders handsomely; the former paid 8 per cent, 1871–83 (9.1 per cent, 1871–73); the latter 6.8 per cent, 1864–90.

During World War I the railways were placed under government control. Wartime demands produced a severe drain on corporate resources, dragging the industry into an overall loss of £9 million in 1921 and casting doubt upon its future profitability. The promise to maintain net receipts at 1913 levels and leave the equity 'unimpaired' was not really kept; instead, a sum of £60 million was eventually offered to discharge all obligations. Yet although there was talk of *nationalization, the government chose a private-sector solution. It continued to view the railways much as it had done before the war, as a potentially dangerous oligopoly likely to earn excess profits unless firmly regulated. The Railways Act, 1921 (SEE GROUPING), which reorganized the companies into four regional groups, aimed at limiting shareholders to a target or 'standard' net revenue of £51.4 million a year, equivalent to that earned in 1913. In fact, the 'standard revenue' was never earned, since Britain's heavy industries were hit by recession, and the rise of mechanical *road transport eroded the railways' competitive advantage in several markets. Net revenue amounted to only £35.7 million per annum in 1923–9 and £30.1 million p.a. in 1930–8. The net rate of return on capital raised in 1934–8 was a mere 2.9 per cent, or 3.2 per cent excluding nominal additions, scarcely the profits to be expected of regional monopolies. All four companies suffered, although the experience of investors varied considerably. The Great Western was able to pay its ordinary shareholders 2.8 per cent per annum in 1935–9, while there was only 0.65 per cent for deferred ordinary shareholders in the *Southern, and nothing at all for *London & North Eastern ordinary shareholders. World War II produced a temporary but illusory improvement in profitability. In 1940–5 GWR ordinary shares paid 4.4 per cent, *London Midland & Scottish ordinaries 2.7 per cent, and Southern deferreds 1.8 per cent. In 1946/7 even the LNER was able to pay something (0.41 per cent), while the other companies paid 3.5–6.1 per cent. However, over-use and under-investment in wartime proved to be a damaging legacy for future operations, and nationalization did little to disguise the underlying financial problems.

The profitability of the nationalized railways was masked to a considerable extent by their inclusion within a multi-modal *British Transport Commission in the period 1948–62, by regular financial reconstructions and other accounting devices, notably in the charging of maintenance and the calculation of central charges, such as amortization and interest, and later on by government *subsidies paid under Acts of 1968 and 1974 for uneconomic *passenger services deemed to be socially necessary. The published data show a negative return in all years but 1952, with the annual deficit rising to £156 million in 1962, the Commission's last year. The *British Railways Board, created in 1963, fared little better. Here, *Beeching's reforms limited the published deficits to under £135 million p.a. in 1963–6, but they soon escalated again, although their true extent was disguised by government subsidies and special grants. British Rail was shown to be in surplus in 1969 and 1970 to the tune of £12 million a year, but losses reappeared thereafter, and reached a reported £52 million in 1973 and £158 million in the following year, necessitating a further financial reconstruction. Later figures are difficult to compare, given further intervention, coupled with the proceeds from property sales and the *privatization of subsidiary businesses. What the true picture really was is an issue which has attracted several commentators, notably Stewart Joy and Terry Gourvish. The latter's calculations, which cover the period 1948–73, indicate modest losses averaging £5 million a year in 1948–53 (with a surplus of £1 million in 1952), rising to £186 million in 1967–8. Substantial grants failed to halt the rising tide of passenger train losses, which reached £151 million in 1972–3 (all in contemporary prices). The introduction of a more cost-conscious Sector Management regime in British Rail in the 1980s, together with the clearer financial objectives set by a more determined government, appeared to produce some improvement. The InterCity sector, which was required to break even, recorded a modest profit of £42 million in 1988–9, but this achievement soon began to look distinctly fragile in the post-1989 recession and the run-up to privatization. However, it might be added that Britain's railways were the least subsidized and most cost-effective in Western Europe in the 1980s.

See also COSTING TECHNIQUES; FINANCING OF RAILWAYS.

TRG

M. Slaughter, *Railway Intelligence* (1849–75); M. C. Reed, *Investment in Railways in Britain 1820–1844* (1975); Mitchell & Deane; S. Joy, *The Train That Ran Away: A Business History of British Railways 1948–68* (1973); T. R. Gourvish, *Railways and the British Economy 1830–1914* (1980); Gourvish.

promotion of railways: procedure. As with other public works such as *canals, docks, and water undertakings, the promoters of a railway required a private Act of Parliament in order to obtain statutory authority to compulsorily purchase land, interfere with public rights such as stopping-up roads and footpaths, secure immunity from committing a nuisance that might be actionable at common law (other than in cases of negligence), and to gain other powers necessary for operating a railway effectively. Latterly, private Acts have also granted immunity from most of the Town & Country Planning legislation. In return for such sweeping powers, in the public interest Parliament has always insisted that the promoters of private Bills adhere strictly to a detailed and elaborate procedure, which enables it to give them the closest scrutiny.

The early railway promoters' first step was to engage an engineer or *surveyor to establish a possible route. Meanwhile, *landowners, industrialists, and other influential people were canvassed in order to obtain their names as supporters—an important factor in establishing credibility. A provisional committee was formed, public meetings were held, and a subscription list opened to defray expenses. Estimates of revenue had to be made, sometimes by taking censuses of goods and passenger traffic on roads, and estimating how much of it, and canal traffic, could be expected to transfer to rail. This information, with extracts from the survey report, was embodied in a *prospectus setting out the promoters' case. Considerable efforts were made to assess potential traffic, although later on, particularly in the *Mania period, speculative schemes often paid little attention to details of this kind, much less their accuracy.

Having gained sufficient promises of support, and with

subscriptions coming in, the committee could appoint a parliamentary agent to draw up a Bill and guide it through the intricate procedure at Westminster, beginning with a petition from a well-disposed MP asking leave to introduce it into the House of Commons. That obtained, the Bill was first considered by the Committee on Standing Orders.

To comply with standing orders, the promoters were required to publicize their intentions by notices in the *London Gazette* or *Edinburgh Gazette*, and local newspapers, at monthly intervals during the three months preceding the parliamentary session. A copy of the Bill with detailed plans and sections (see PARLIAMENTARY PLANS) had to be deposited with all counties and boroughs on the projected line, accompanied by a book of reference listing all owners, leaseholders, and occupiers of property alongside or through which it would pass; the numbers of those assenting, dissenting, or 'neuter' to the proposals; and an estimate of the construction cost. In this way, Parliament tried to ensure that everyone affected was informed of the scheme and had an opportunity to express an opinion.

If a Bill was to be accepted for the forthcoming session, all this material had to be obtained and deposited by 30 November. To avoid damaging crops, detailed surveys had to wait until after the harvest, leaving only 2½ months in which to do the work, prepare and print plans, compile books of reference, send out and receive notices of assent, try to assuage any *opposition, and put final touches to the draft Bill. It was a period of frantic activity; on the 10½ miles of the branch line proposed from Newton Abbot to Ashburton in 1846, for example, 474 notices had to be served. The Mania boom created enormous pressure on Parliament; in 1845–7 over 900 Bills were deposited. The evening of 30 November 1845—the peak year—witnessed extraordinary scenes as the offices of clerks of the peace in quiet county towns were besieged by last-minute depositors trying to meet the deadline. In the hour before midnight there was near-pandemonium in Whitehall outside the Board of *Trade, which at that time acted as the receiving office for railway Bills. Some railways promoting or supporting new lines ran special trains to get plans to London in time, but refused them to competitors.

In 1837 the Commons tried to provide more time by amending its standing orders, including an endeavour to discourage purely speculative schemes by requiring that half the capital must be subscribed at the time of deposit, but they created dissension and in 1842 Parliament reverted to its old rules. Attempts to provide some sort of order from competing schemes were made again in 1844 and 1846 (see DALHOUSIE; COMMISSIONS AND PARLIAMENTARY COMMITTEES), but essentially the procedure remained unchanged.

Examination of a Bill by the Standing Orders Committee gave opponents an opportunity to kill it at the outset if they could persuade the members that it contained inaccuracies or violations of orders, and many were rejected on pure technicalities, depending on the strength of the opposing parties.

Having successfully negotiated standing orders, the Bill underwent its first and second readings in the House, then proceeding to the Committee on Bills. To provide one more opportunity for local objections to be made, this time at parish level, at least ten days before the committee met the promoters had to deposit a further copy of the Bill with every parish clerk on the route, or in Scotland with the schoolmaster, and furnish the committee with evidence that half the capital had been subscribed. Committee hearings were conducted like a court, with counsel and witnesses. The committee could either accept or reject the Bill as it stood, or insert amendments before returning it to the floor of the House, where more amendments could be tabled. Once all objections were satisfied, the Bill had its third reading and then passed to the House of Lords, where it went through a similar process.

Safely through the Lords, the Bill became law by receiving the Royal Assent, usually in July or August, it having taken at least a year from the first survey to create a statutory company. If at any stage the Bill was rejected, the promoters had to wait for the next session before reintroducing their Bill, when the process was repeated. Some Acts took three or more applications to Parliament before they gained authorization.

Except for a few lines built under the *Light Railways Act, 1896, the entire British system was built up in this way. There was no shortage of critics, from aggrieved promoters to engineers who contended that committees were incapable of properly weighing evidence without technical advice. Another major disadvantage was that anything authorized by Act of Parliament required another Act to amend or modify it, and it became the practice of the larger railways to include minor requirements in periodic Bills for additional powers, although major schemes still required a separate Bill, a policy that was continued by *British Railways on an annual basis.

After World War II comparisons were made with the system of authorizing new trunk roads and motorways by ministerial order, under which objections were heard at a public inquiry conducted by an independent inspector appointed by the Department of *Transport. It was argued that this method enabled direct public participation, which the private Bill procedure did not. At length, in 1992 the Transport & Works Act was passed, setting up a procedure for railways, inland waterways, and works interfering with rights of navigation, that brought some consistency in authorizing transport projects. For minor, largely non-contentious railway works the new procedure is simpler, quicker, and cheaper than presenting a private Bill, but the effect on larger schemes which arouse wider opposition remains to be seen. It could take longer; a new motorway, for instance, can take seven years or more to become reality, so for major railway projects of national significance the private Bill method is still likely to be preferred, for this and other reasons, as in the case of the high-speed *Channel Tunnel link.

See also OPPOSITION; COMPETITION. GJB

H. Riddell, *Railway Parliamentary Practice* (1846); F. Clifford, *A History of Private Bill Legislation* (1885); *GR*; *RS*, ch. 2; *Transport & Works Act, 1992: A Guide to Procedures* (1992).

property, see LAND AND PROPERTY, OWNERSHIP AND DEVELOPMENT OF.

prospectuses. A railway company's prospectus was the promoters' first formal statement of its purposes, both an advertisement and an appeal for subscribers to take up its shares. A prospectus forms part of the origins of a railway company, and may reveal valuable connections between names figuring in it, as promoters for example, or engineers or solicitors.

If the promoters succeeded in getting parliamentary powers to construct the line described, the prospectus ceased to be of any practical importance. Nothing said in it was ever legally binding; construction was governed entirely by the authorizing Act and by the public Acts applicable to all railway companies (see PARLIAMENT AND LEGISLATION). It is not surprising, therefore, that many railway companies' prospectuses have disappeared, their officials considering it unnecessary to keep them. An investigation of the history of a railway should certainly include an attempt to find its prospectus, as a record of its declared purposes; but the effort may prove fruitless.

A prospectus is headed by a list of those who first came forward as the promoters of the scheme. This would ordinarily include some local magnates in the country through which the railway was to pass; large *landowners who might be willing to part with land without troublesome *opposition; industrialists whose firms could be expected to use the railway when it was built. Such people were often grouped together as a 'provisional committee', which might swell into something absurdly large: that for the Cambridge & Lincoln Extension Railway of 1845, for instance, comprised 179 members; that for the London & Edinburgh Direct 277.

Many of these lists, drawn up at great speed, contained the names of people who had not indicated their support or even of some who asserted that they had never heard of the project. Nevertheless these lists include the names of the local people who were backing the scheme seriously, and that may indicate the connections—political, financial, commercial—lying behind it, especially valuable when rival projects were before the public at the same time—e.g. to provide a railway between *London and *York.

Most prospectuses include the names of the promoters' solicitors and bankers, and of their officers. These particulars have to be looked at with critical caution. It was not an actionable offence for the name of somebody to be set down in a prospectus—e.g. an engineer—who had in fact no connection whatever with the project.

Solicitors mentioned in prospectuses were often London firms, some of which became specialists in railway business; or they were local. Firms of both kinds might appear together, a sensible arrangement if the division of work between them had been clearly defined—see LAWYERS.

The text was usually devoted mainly to making the case for building the railway as a desirable economic and social enterprise, and as a commercial undertaking that could hold out the hope of an acceptable return on the capital invested in it—perhaps the allurement of a large profit. The prospectus would generally make broad statements about the line's anticipated traffic: the minerals and other raw materials it would bring in to supply manufacturers, and the facilities it would afford for the distribution of finished products; the services to farmers in marketing their crops and cattle; the speed and simplicity of travel offered. It might claim that this notional traffic had been calculated on the basis of some kind of census. Most such statements were large and vague, deserving little respect as evidence, but some were founded on real censuses taken for the purpose. Good ones were made for the East Anglian Railway (1841), for example, and the Wear Valley Railway (1845).

Most prospectuses had also something to say about the expenditure that would be called for. Here they were apt to be misleadingly optimistic. Very few railways were built within the financial limits set out in their prospectuses. The price to be paid for land sometimes proved very much higher than could have been reasonably foreseen; the cost of equipment, e.g. of rails and locomotives, was subject to sudden and startling variations.

All the same, it must be recognized that in many of these documents the physical obstacles in the way of building and operating the line were either dismissed airily or ignored altogether. The 1844 prospectus of the *Cornwall Railway, for example, said nothing about the crossing of the formidably broad estuary of the Tamar at *Plymouth.

When all these things have been said it may appear that the value of prospectuses to the student of railways is small. However, in the busiest period of this activity, between 1825 and 1850, prospectuses were the chief instrument by which news of railway schemes reached potential investors. No one could ever assess their influence on the recipients. But it must have been considerable, in drawing attention to the project and outlining what was being done to realize it. Much investment undoubtedly arose in consequence, from people acting on their own initiative or on the advice of brokers and solicitors, who were kept informed by means of prospectuses too.

It should be added that no prospectus was required for amalgamating two existing companies into one new one. For this reason none was ever issued for the *Midland Railway, for example, or the *Glasgow & South Western. The proposals for the lines that formed them must be sought in the prospectuses of the original smaller companies.

See also PROMOTION OF RAILWAYS: PROCEDURE.   JS
Main collections: PRO, RAIL 1075, 1076; BL—Maps, 18 c. 1; 1881 b. 23; and 1890 c. 6. For a general account of the literature of the subject see *ET*, ch. 11.

public address systems, see ANNOUNCING OF TRAINS.

publicity and public relations. These are two different things, though often closely related. Publicity was at first intended primarily by the railways to attract public notice, to provide information: of the times of trains and the *fares charged, the provision of additional trains, or the opening of new branch lines. The information might be supplied by means of newspaper advertisements or by handbills. But 'public relations' denoted something much wider: the explanation and sometimes, where it seemed necessary, the defence of policies, in order to win public support, or at least to lessen antagonism.

Although the railways had many benefits to confer, their operation made them dangerous contrivances, calling for rules and regulations (see BYE-LAWS), applicable both to customers and to staff. The companies' bye-laws were displayed at their stations. They were hardly more than commands—you must do this, you must not do that; so they offered passengers a bleak welcome.

The companies might also have more cheerful communications to make, of additional services or reductions in charges. A series of handbills from the *Newcastle & Carlisle Railway at the *NRM, dating from about 1840, announces services to *markets and fairs and *excursions to *sporting events. Printed in black and white, they are enlivened by bold type and occasionally by little engravings of trains.

Larger advertisements of the railways' activities came to be plastered on hoardings in towns. This business (it was usually handled by agents, particularly W. H. Smith) increased as the railways became more competitive with one another from the 1850s onwards (see COMPETITION). An unwritten convention usually restrained one company from asserting directly that its services were better than those offered by another one, which the advertisement named, though that rule was occasionally broken. For such purposes, and for advertising excursions to the seaside, large *posters were increasingly adopted, printed in several colours and sometimes including pictures, as chromolithographic printing developed after 1870.

But there were other important means that the railways could use to speak up for themselves. Their boards of directors often included members of either or both Houses of *Parliament. In the 1840s the most conspicuous of them was George *Hudson, who organized lobbies to influence ministers, their members speaking when railway matters were under debate. The numbers of these MPs grew steadily up to 1873, when one-fifth of the House of Commons were railway directors. Collectively they came to be known as the 'Railway Interest' (see PARLIAMENT AND LEGISLATION; POLITICS, RAILWAYS IN).

No effective and continuous action by the companies collectively appeared until 1868, when the *Railway Companies Association was formed to represent them inside and outside Parliament. This was the nearest approach to an organization by which the railways could address the public as a whole.

Occasionally other opportunities arose, which could be seized for the same purpose. In 1855–77 a series of bodies was appointed by Parliament to review some large aspects of railway policy (see COMMISSIONS AND PARLIAMENTARY COMMITTEES). One, the Royal Commission on Railways of 1865, undertook a general survey. Others investigated single important issues: *accidents and *amalgamation, for example. Each one questioned numerous witnesses, among them senior officers of the companies, declaring their practices

and defending them. They were not addressing their questioners alone, but a much wider public also: for these bodies' proceedings were summarized in the press, and commented on there. By the 1860s the whole of this evidence was published for sale, verbatim.

In 1873 the railways suffered two humiliating defeats in Parliament. An application by a pair of large companies for powers to amalgamate was rejected: so overwhelmingly that no other was considered there seriously for 25 years. And a new court of law was established, one of its leading duties being to adjudicate in cases of complaint brought by the railways' customers. Neither the new Association nor the Railway Interest found any means of countering the growing unpopularity of the railway companies. But they could not yet accept the notion of addressing the public themselves.

The first effective attempts to do that were made by individuals in books published commercially, not commissioned by the companies. In 1886 the general manager of the *Great Western Railway, James *Grierson, produced his Railway Rates, English and Foreign, in an effort to provide 'an equitable and satisfactory settlement of questions now so much discussed' (see FREIGHT TRAFFIC RATES). Cogent and good-tempered, it showed that the British railways had indeed a case for charging as they did for freight.

Three years later another general manager, George *Findlay of the *London & North Western, published The Working and Management of an English Railway. This was the first attempt by any British railwayman to expound the rationale of the railways' operations in language that the public could find interesting and intelligible. At the same time a younger man, unconnected professionally with the railways, produced a short, lively, and well-informed survey: W. M. *Acworth, in his Railways of England. There was now a public willing to learn more about railways, and to understand them better (see LITERATURE OF RAILWAYS). That was proved when each of the two books ran through five editions by 1900.

Works addressed primarily to railway staff were now being put on public sale, giving anybody who chose to read them clear explanations of some practices. E. B. Ivatts' Railway Management at Stations is a good example, issued first in 1885 and reaching a fifth edition in 1910.

Stirrings of change in these matters now began to appear within the companies' management. In 1902 Sam *Fay, general manager of the new *Great Central Railway, established a Publicity Department within his own office, under a manager who handled not only advertising but also—instructed directly by himself—the company's communications with the press. Though that arrangement was not generally adopted (it did not last very long in its original form even on the GCR), similar departments to handle advertising were set up by at least three other companies before 1914.

Advertising itself was then branching out, seeking to reach a wider public. Some companies' posters now displayed a much higher quality, led by the LNWR, which commissioned paintings from Norman Wilkinson, with fine results. A number of companies produced *postcards, themselves or through commercial publishers, depicting their buildings, rolling stock, and steamships as well as some of the districts their trains served, and these could be bought from vending machines at stations. They were sold in very great numbers (some 11 million of those of the LNWR, we are told, before 1914). When the GWR went thoroughly into the production of *guidebooks to districts on its system, from 1904 onwards, they too were seized on eagerly, and over 100,000 copies of *Holiday Haunts*, its general guide to resorts and accommodation, were sold every year in 1904–14. From 1908 onwards the *London Underground Railways transformed their advertising, under Frank *Pick, into a branch of art quite new in Britain.

We know little about what all this advertising cost. The companies seldom disclosed that, since some people (shareholders no doubt among them) considered the expenditure a waste of money. But a well-qualified critic, Thomas Russell, argued persuasively in 1919 that the main-line railways would have done better to advertise their freight more extensively than their passenger business.

In 1900–14 the companies' need to appeal to the politicians and to customers grew more insistent. In the 1890s their working expenditure had averaged 56.8 per cent of total receipts: in 1900–9 that was 63.2. They were virtually prohibited from offsetting these increases by raising freight rates or passenger fares. Clashes over wage demands were serious (SEE TRADE UNIONISM). World War I cost them a very great deal (see WAR); and then the government forced a great amalgamation upon them under the Railways Act of 1921 (see GROUPING).

The new *Big Four companies attended to their public relations somewhat more thoroughly than their predecessors. The *Southern was the first to appoint an officer specifically concerned with it, in 1925: John *Elliot, who acted under the general manager, Sir Herbert *Walker. When Walker asked him to suggest a title for his new post he said, following his American experience: 'Why not call me Public Relations Assistant?' Walker agreed, remarking that 'no one will understand what it means, and none of my railway officers will be upset'.

The four companies made some energetic efforts to act together. They proclaimed the difficulties they laboured under through inability to increase rates and fares, the Railway Companies Association putting out a well-considered appeal to the general public for a 'Square Deal' in 1938–9. This campaign might well have achieved some success but for the outbreak of World War II.

After *nationalization in 1948 neither the new *British Transport Commission nor its subsidiary the Railway Executive could do much to address the public directly. The railways now depended on the *subsidies provided by the government to supplement their inadequate revenue. That was a matter for parliamentary debate, occasionally influenced by the attitude of the electorate but never determined by that alone. There were no shareholders' meetings now, at which policies could be criticized or suggestions made for their improvement. Consultative bodies were

established, including some members of the public, but like most they were seldom effective.

None of those who directed the railways now achieved any conspicuous improvement in their publicity. Their advertising was intermittent and humdrum, though the *London & North Eastern's was generally well designed. *British Rail did no better, whether on its own or through a separate company. For a time even *London Transport almost discontinued its poster work, long so widely acclaimed. The advent of television advertising brought a marked change, using well-known personalities and slogans like 'The Age of the Train', accompanied by widespread outdoor posters.

BR did, however, pay careful attention to some aspects of public relations, devoting a good deal of money and thought to one particularly important aspect of it: the training of employees in their personal attitude towards passengers, both actual and potential. Some of the results were striking. The endlessly increasing complexity of the fare systems made them very difficult to understand, and the public could no longer be expected to read a timetable. But the men and women employed in *ticket offices, in the new 'travel centres', and as *guards on trains, usually communicated very patiently with the public face-to-face, showing a marked superiority to the equivalent staff in most bus offices. Here, at the very heart of public relations, the railways showed up very well indeed.

Both the companies and the nationalized railways accepted much commercial advertising for display on their premises and inside their carriages, which brought them a substantial revenue. But stations came to be greatly disfigured by it in the Victorian age, and passengers complained that station names became difficult to distinguish among a profusion of advertisements.

No serious effort to mitigate this nuisance was made until about 1900, when the *North Eastern Railway set about controlling it. The *Caledonian company refused to display in its splendid new *Glasgow Central station any advertisements other than its own, which were carefully considered and coherent. From 1909 onwards Pick rearranged the London Underground group's advertising contracts to allow firms' posters to be brought under a well-framed plan; and the small advertisements inside the open cars of its trains were now better treated too. Gradually the main-line companies did likewise, and both London Transport and British Rail later developed a firm policy of having well-designed displays of their own advertising and others' on stations.   JS

VR, ch. 11; R. B. Wilson, *Go Great Western* (1987 edn.); Sir J. Elliot, *On and Off the Rails* (1982), 19; literature on the 'Square Deal' campaign: *Ottley, 4654, 4657, 4660, 4666, 4668–74.

public opinion. Although this is a vague phrase, something like a general voice does occasionally emerge in judgement on public actions. Where railways were concerned, governments heeded it, and the companies would sometimes try to persuade opinion by statements or to allure it by offering bribes or new facilities (see PUBLICITY AND PUBLIC RELATIONS).

Railways always had complaint to face. They might pay less for land than the owners expected (see LAND ACQUISITION). Travelling on them could be uncomfortable, sometimes dangerous. They stimulated *speculation, attracting blame for most of the bad effects to themselves, rather than to the speculators. Yet unprejudiced people acknowledged that railways enlarged the scope of business and pleasure. By 1850 the general assessment was a fairly even mixture of praise and blame.

After 1860, however, a distinct change began. In 1860–5 a fresh boom in railway building extended the system by over 25 per cent, to the accompaniment of more speculation, with a crash in 1866. The railways' growing activities and power came just when their shortcomings were being displayed by a long sequence of bad *accidents, in 1865–79.

Public opinion now saw them as greedy, cynical, and inefficient, stimulating parliamentary inquiries into plans for large-scale *amalgamation, which were turned down. But their *monopoly of all the quicker means of inland transport caused resentment that spilt over into furious agitation against their *freight rates.

When a standing Royal *Commission was set up in 1873 to investigate such complaints as these, the evidence revealed the strength of public feeling. Criticisms were often unjust, or overstated, and the Commissioners reached their judgements accordingly. But the general suspicion remained that the companies were overcharging for their services.

The shocking Armagh accident of 1889 proclaimed the dangers arising from inadequate *brakes, enabling a *Regulation Act to pass through Parliament at high speed. The long controversy about braking systems had shown, in *Acworth's words, that 'the experts were wrong and the public right'.

The railways now sank to their lowest point in public esteem. Thereafter they retrieved their reputation somewhat with improved services and some special achievements evoking widespread commendation, above all in the two world *wars. But, being monopolists, they could never become popular.

The electric *tram and the *road motor vehicle destroyed their monopoly, and after *nationalization whatever profits they made went to the public. The railways merely became less and less important to the average person in Great Britain, as was demonstrated very clearly by the country's largely unquestioning acceptance of *privatization in 1993.　　　　JS

Acworth, 194.

Pullman car: a railway *carriage with a saloon interior, arranged as either a *restaurant car or a *sleeping car, offering a high standard of comfort, usually on payment of a supplementary fare, with at-seat service of meals, light refreshments, and drinks. Pullman is a registered trade name, as applied to railway carriages, the rights being held exclusively by the Pullman Car Co., or operators inheriting those rights, such as wagon-lits.

George Mortimer Pullman (1831–97) was an American citizen. An agreement between Pullman and the *Midland Railway in 1873 brought Pullman service to Britain. The conditions of operation were that Pullman would supply the cars and their equipment at its financial risk and cover all costs of operating them, including the provision of attendants. This was in return for an exclusive contract for 15 years to provide the services and permission to charge a Pullman supplement on regular services, additional to the fare for travel.

The basis of this 1873 concession applied subsequently to all agreements reached between railways and the Pullman Palace Car Co. (Europe) and its succeeding companies, the British Pullman Palace Car Co. (1882–1915) and the Pullman Car Co. Ltd (1915–62). In 1954 the *British Transport Commission obtained control of the Pullman Car Co. Ltd, which was absorbed into the *British Railways Board under the Transport Act, 1962. Pullman entered into fixed-term agreements with British railway companies whose obligation was to clean and wash the cars and give them general service attention, including repainting, and to maintain their running gear. First-class Pullman service continues to be provided on certain InterCity trains but no supplement is charged and the carriages have standard seating, upholstery, and livery.

Pullman sleeping car services ceased to be offered in Britain after withdrawal of an Inverness–Glasgow service in 1907. Pullman catering vehicles were of specific types: parlour car, with swivel or armchairs, and sometimes end coupé compartments (usually with four seats) but without kitchen facilities or brake control; brake parlour car, with brake control; kitchen car, with swivel or armchairs and kitchen facilities able to serve main meals; bar car, including a bar with stools. Some Pullman cars, usually in Scotland, were run as restaurant cars and served main meals but no supplementary fare was charged for their use.

The traditional Pullman cars built until 1952 were generally of a distinctive design influenced by the American origins of their company, with straight body-sides as opposed to the British tumblehome (curved) profile, end vestibules with inward opening doors, large square-cornered windows to the saloons, and ornate lavatory windows. The liveries were various but, from 1906, Pullman cars were generally painted cream and umber brown, with the name or car number shown prominently on the body panels, usually accompanied by the Pullman coat of arms.

Pullman cars were operated in a variety of regular or *special trains (sometimes for royalty or heads of state) formed wholly or partly of Pullman cars, hauled by steam, diesel, or electric locomotives. There were also powered train sets entirely comprising Pullman cars, notably the Brighton Belle electric *multiple units operated between London *Victoria and *Brighton from 1933 to 1972, and the 'Blue Pullman' air-conditioned diesel units which ran from London *St Pancras to *Manchester and between *Paddington and *Bristol, *Birmingham, and *Swansea from 1960 to 1973.　　　　MLH

B. Haresnape, *Pullman—Travelling in Style* (1987).

punctuality. Assertions are frequently made by railway travellers today that the services they use are less punctual than they were in the past. The same thing was said at times during the Victorian age. These statements are worth very little unless they rest on evidence carefully marshalled and extending over adequate periods of time, not based on single days or the performance of one particular train. Otherwise they cannot be more than expressions of opinion, which seldom deserve much attention.

When the unpunctuality of trains on any railway was remarked on so frequently that its managers had to take notice, they sometimes made special inquiries into allegations and causes. The resulting reports were not published; they were considered only by senior officials or committees of directors. Some of them may have been aimed merely at covering up delinquencies, in which case the writers would have taken grave risks, for misrepresentation of that kind could be detected quite easily. Any public statement, based on such an investigation, might or might not be candid in admitting faults, stating reasons, and proffering excuses. The same may be said today.

When the *Liverpool & Manchester Railway began work in 1830 it did not publish what would now be called a *timetable, only a 'list of departures' from its two terminal stations, which did not give times of arrival. Two years later the 'first-class trains' were set to make the 30-mile journey in 1 hr 30 min, the 'second class' in 2 hrs. Travellers to and from intermediate stations had to guess approximate times. This imprecise arrangement was adopted because of the difficulties arising from unreliable locomotives, and other causes not foreseeable. It continued until 1841. The *Grand Junction Railway was the first important one in Britain to declare the exact times at which its trains were to call at every one of its 23 stations. By doing that from its opening in 1837 the company fully accepted the challenge to run a punctual service.

Well-managed railways soon came to take this challenge seriously, and their directors did not leave the examination of irregularities in the hands of their officers alone. The *Great Western board, for example, held a special meeting to consider unpunctuality in 1852, and set itself to investigate delays at *Paddington station a year later. In the 1860s the *London & South Western Railway began to acquire a long-lasting reputation for unpunctuality. The directors pressed their traffic committee to secure improvements in 1884, but met with no lasting success. In 1889 Robert Louis Stevenson wrote of a train that was running 'a little behind time, but not much for the South Western'. The LSWR's neighbours, the *London Brighton & South Coast and *South Eastern, were even worse in this respect, becoming the subject of pertinacious public attack. A leader in *The Times* (14 September 1895) debated 'which of the two has the better right to call itself absolutely the worst line in the country'. In 1890–3 Parliament required the companies to make a series of returns of the punctuality of arrivals in London. What usually emerged from this and similar inquiries was that the *Great Eastern Railway had the best record for punctuality, and the *Midland the worst. The

Midland board set up a 'commission on train delays' in 1891, which made 82 reports over the next two years, pinpointing various places on the system where it was necessary to multiply tracks or to undertake other engineering work to prevent delays. Some of it was already in progress; more was authorized accordingly. But the improvements were slow to appear and the company remained a target of derision for some expert writers on railways into the 20th century.

Many disgruntled passengers took the railway companies to court for their failure to provide advertised services, but only a few got any satisfaction there. The companies hedged round the conditions on which their *tickets were issued in such a way as to protect themselves, and it was hard for the passenger to adduce convincing proof that the loss or inconvenience resulting from unpunctuality was due to negligence or misconduct on the part of railway employees. This position remains the same today. As a 1980 treatise on railway law puts it, *BR 'do not guarantee that an advertised train shall run, or that it shall run punctually according to the timetable. . . . The contract with the Railways Board gives the passenger no enforceable right to be carried at all'.

Though most companies probably kept some record of timekeeping, little attention was paid to that matter in public statements except when services were notoriously bad. The general assumption was clearly that trains ran according to their timetables. When mechanically worked arrival indicators began to be erected at some of the larger stations, it was seldom thought necessary to show late running, such as we look for everywhere today.

There was nothing in all this peculiar to Britain. Sherrington pointed out in 1928 that scarcely any governments in the world demanded returns of punctuality from their railway administrations.

A change of attitude, on the part of both the railways and the public, emerged during World War II and its aftermath. From 1940 onwards the British railways were subjected to bombing far heavier and more extensive than anything in 1914–18. All their services were disrupted: not merely those in the districts that were hit by air-raids but everywhere else too, because of the delays to connecting trains. When the war was over repairs were very slow, and long delays to trains continued. During these years punctuality was hardly expected. If it appeared it seemed almost a bonus, and was acknowledged as such with gratitude.

This was the state of things when the railways passed into public ownership in 1948. The new management's daunting task was made much more formidable by insufficient funding (see NATIONALIZATION). Its first duty was to keep the trains moving, despite all the obstacles that destruction and neglect had caused during the war years, with an inadequate and ageing fleet of locomotives and rolling stock. Under these conditions, punctuality was impossible. The *Modernization Plan of 1955 offered some hope of improvement, but its promises were not quickly realized. The worst history of unpunctuality hitherto seen in British peace-time passenger services was in the years 1955–65, when the old steam engines, often poorly maintained, were being gradually phased out, to be replaced by new diesel and electric locomotives. A record from carefully kept notes shows that out of 40 journeys made between *Leicester and London *St Pancras in the two years following 1 October 1958, one alone reached its destination exactly on time. All the others were from 1 to 39 minutes late; and that without any special causes of delay such as an *accident, violent storms, or large engineering works on the line.

With better rolling stock, new signalling methods, and some help from the rationalization of the system (by the reduction in the number of stopping passenger and slow freight trains, many of which were discontinued altogether), punctuality slowly improved. But the service never became as regular as it had been in the years before the war. The continuity of generally correct performance was broken, and it has not been restored.

The *Passenger's Charter* (see also COMPENSATION), issued by BR in 1991, was concerned more with punctuality than with any other shortcoming in the service, and it displayed what was in some respects a new attitude towards the late running of passenger trains. It laid down minimum standards of performance that the Board hoped to achieve, and undertook, on application, to recompense passengers who had suffered substantial delays. This *ex gratia* system' offered a promise of a better compensation for inconvenience or loss due to unpunctuality than could be afforded by the courts. On that account it deserved to be welcomed.

It is, however, noteworthy that for the whole of Great Britain, with the large exception of south-east lines, the criteria were that 90 per cent of trains should arrive within ten minutes of their scheduled time; that 99 per cent of the services should actually run; and that, among London suburban services, no less than 80 per cent of trains from Southend and Reading into London should arrive within five minutes of the published times. None of this was claimed as a performance actually achieved. It was an ideal to be aimed at in the future.

One old and obvious remedy for difficulties of this kind was still open to the railways' management, and it was widely adopted now: a complete or partial slowing-down of the service offered on lines where punctuality proved impossible to achieve, by allowing *'recovery time' to be built into the schedules presented to the public. This expedient could not be welcomed by anybody, but it was often the only way in which promise could be squared with performance. And that squaring might well be accepted by passengers as the most honest and satisfactory policy that the railways could follow.   JS

GWR board meetings: PRO, RAIL 250/6, pp. 181–8, 229–30; R. L. Stevenson and L. Osbourne, *The Wrong Box* (1889), ch. 2; for the punctuality returns to Parliament see PP 1890, lxv, 802–25; MR commission on train delays: PRO, RAIL 491/740; court cases: H. W. Disney, *Law of Carriage by Railway* (6th edn., 1923), 221–9, and L. James, *Law of the Railway* (1980), 213; foreign governments' attitude towards punctuality: C. E. R. Sherrington, *Economics of Rail Transport in Britain*, i (1928), 274. Train-running between Leicester and London, 1958–60, is from notes kept by the writer.

push-and-pull train: a train comprising a locomotive coupled semi-permanently to one or more specially equipped, unpowered coaches. The locomotive either hauls or propels the coaches, and can be driven from the other end of the train so avoiding the need to 'run round' at terminal stations.

The system was developed with steam traction for lightly used services and, in addition to time-saving at terminals, push-and-pull operation usually allowed *guards to be dispensed with, the *driver controlling the train from a compartment in the leading end of the carriage when the engine was propelling. The *fireman remained on the footplate, carrying out his normal tasks of firing and maintaining the steam pressure and boiler water level, but he was additionally employed in altering the *cut-off and operating the large ejector to release the brakes. Crews working push-and-pull trains had to be specially trained.

Several systems were used for the remote control of the steam locomotive by the driver from his position in the driving coach, from where he operated the regulator and whistle, and had a vacuum (or air) brake valve to assist in braking. Control systems were mechanical, using cables and pulleys on the *Midland and *Great Central Railways, or rodding on the *Great Western. Compressed air was used on the *North Eastern and *London Brighton & South Coast Railways, and the *Southern Railway, and a vacuum system on the *London Midland & Scottish and *London & North Eastern. Earlier, communication between driver and fireman was by means of a whistle code, but electric bell signalling was later employed, with designated codes. Also, the engine whistle was supplemented by a large warning gong mounted on the leading coach, and operated by the driver's foot pedal.

Push-and-pull trains were introduced in the early years of the 20th century. To reduce train *operating costs, or to introduce services on lightly trafficked routes newly provided with unstaffed track-level halts, a number of railways experimented with steam *railcars. These did not prove very successful and railways instead turned to push-and-pull working. Unlike the railcars, such trains could be enlarged by adding extra vehicles for parcels traffic or additional passengers, and their performance was also superior.

Early applications of push-and-pull trains were on the GWR (1904), for the Southall–Brentford branch, and in the *Plymouth area; the Midland (1905), where former *Pullman cars were converted for use on services radiating from *Derby; the NER (1905), initially between *Hartlepool and West Hartlepool, then more generally; the LBSCR (1905), early services so worked being *Brighton to Kemp Town and Worthing, Horley–Three Bridges, and Epsom Downs–West Croydon; and the GCR (1906), on Aylesbury–Verney Junction, Banbury–Woodford Halse, and Lowton St Mary's–St Helens workings. Eventually, many railways operated them.

Push-and-pull trains usually comprised a pair of coaches formed into a set, but might consist of up to four; a guard was required if the number of coaches exceeded three. Only those coaches equipped with low steps were permitted for use on services featuring track-level halts. Additional vehi-cles could be attached behind a locomotive propelling a push-and-pull train. On the GWR, some services such as Plymouth–Saltash featured a locomotive sandwiched be-tween two pairs of auto-trailers (see below); the mechanical control system used by this company meant that no more than two trailers could be propelled. Push-and-pull trains were also known as steam rail motors or auto-trains on the GWR, steam autocars on the NER, or motor-trains by the southern companies.

The usual choice for push-and-pull working was the four-coupled passenger *tank engine, less commonly a small 0-6-0T such as the LBSCR 'Terriers'. The GWR also used 0-6-0 tanks, a couple of which in the early days of push-and-pull working were bizarrely disguised with dummy coach-work painted in carriage livery. Only the GWR specifically built engines for auto-train working—0-4-2Ts and 0-6-0 pan-nier tanks—in particular from the late 1920s when its stock of steam railcars was being withdrawn.

The coaches used were usually conversions of non-cor-ridor, compartment stock, although the GWR favoured saloon vehicles, referred to as auto-trailers, which were pur-pose-built or converted from steam railcars. New push-and-pull coaches were built until the early 1950s, and the last conversions took place in 1960–1. Some non-driving coaches were fitted with through controls for push-and-pull working, as were some parcels vans on the Southern Railway.

The nature of their operations, on rural or suburban branch lines, or lightly used main-line stopping services, meant that from the mid-1950s push-and-pull trains were increasingly replaced by diesel railcars or *railbuses, or the

services worked by them were withdrawn. The last ran between Seaton Junction (Leicestershire) and Stamford, and was replaced in 1965.

Opportunities for push-and-pull working increased with diesel and electric *traction. For the Bournemouth *elec-trification of 1967, BR's Southern Region evolved the high-speed propelling of trains, in which, at speeds up to 90 mph, a powered four-car electric unit, an electro-diesel locomo-tive, or a diesel-electric locomotive propelled up to eight unpowered coaches. The unmanned power unit was re-motely controlled by the driver from the cab of the leading unit.

In the 1970s and 1980s there was push-and-pull working in the Scottish Region, with multi-way cabling and control air piping for remote operation of a diesel locomotive. This was succeeded by a two-wire system employing time divi-sion multiplex control, the signals being transmitted through the lighting circuits from the cab of the driving trailer coach to the propelling locomotive. No modification of intermediate coaches is required with this system, in which there is no noticeable delay between the driver's action, and response from the locomotive. The system was initially developed for push-and-pull services in Scotland, notably between Edinburgh and Glasgow, and is currently used on the *East and *West Coast main lines, and between London and Norwich.   MLH

Railway Clearing House, *Push and Pull Trains—General Instruc-tions*, BR 30036 publication (1960); W. J. A. Sykes, 'High-speed propelling of trains on the Southern Region, BR', *Jnl Inst. Loco. Engineers*, 55, no. 304 (1965/6); K. Taylor, *Chairman's Address to I Mech E*, 1979–80, vol. 193, no. 39.

quad-arts, see ARTICULATED CARRIAGES.

quadrupling, see MULTIPLE TRACKS.

R

races, horse, see HORSE-RACING.

races to Scotland. The first railway route from London to *Edinburgh and *Glasgow was that of the *London & North Western and *Caledonian companies via *Preston and *Carlisle, completed in 1848 and known as the *West Coast route. The *East Coast route via *York and Berwick was opened throughout in 1852 by collaboration between four companies, reduced to three in 1854: the *Great Northern, *North Eastern, and *North British. Both routes competed strenuously, although total revenue was apportioned in accordance with *agreements reached in 1851–6.

They did not compete in speed, however. Although the East Coast day express from London to Edinburgh became an hour quicker than its rival in 1862, the LNWR deprecated all fast running, and the West Coast timing remained unaltered.

In 1872–6 the two partnerships were obliged to reconsider their arrangements, when the *Midland Railway admitted third-class passengers to all its trains, abolished second class, and built its own line to Scotland (longer than the others, however) via *Leeds and Carlisle (see SETTLE & CARLISLE RAILWAY).

The fastest East Coast train did not admit second-class passengers (who naturally went by the West Coast) until November 1887. In May 1888 the West Coast partners suddenly announced that from 2 June they would run from London to Edinburgh in nine hours, the time taken by their rival. On 1 August both trains were set to run in eight hours. On 13 August the East Coast schedule came down to 7¾ hours, and the train actually made the journey in 7 hr 27 min. Next day the partnerships agreed on minimum timings for their trains, and racing stopped.

It had aroused both excitement and warnings of danger. But something else was at stake besides a display of speed. The *Forth Bridge was now approaching completion, which would afford an East Coast route to *Dundee and *Aberdeen slightly shorter than its rival's. Another contest lay ahead, over a much longer distance.

That came in 1895, in races between the night trains from London to Aberdeen. Both partnerships now disregarded scheduled times, particularly on the last two nights, 21–22 August. The East Coast men then called off the racing, but their rivals made a supreme effort the following night, taking their train over the 540 miles from London to Aberdeen at 63.3 mph. No more racing took place thereafter in Anglo-Scottish traffic. It had shown what could be done by way of speed under the most favourable condi-

tions: the trains were very light (unsuited for ordinary service); on many runs two engines were used; all staff were instructed to give the racing trains utmost priority.

These races had no lasting or important effect on train operation in Britain. But they were a splendid display of the skill and endurance of the enginemen and the reliability of their locomotives. JS

O. S. Nock, *Railway Race to the North* [1958]; E. Foxwell and T. C. Farrer, *Express Trains English and Foreign* (1889), 16–26.

racing between trains. Railways in Britain may be said to have 'raced' with one another in three senses: in services running over substantial distances by different routes, competing in speed (see also COMPETITION, INTER-RAILWAY); in two famous and exceptional but short contests in 1888 and 1895 (see RACES TO SCOTLAND); and in a literal sense, here and there quite unofficially, where the trains of two different companies ran on parallel tracks, and *drivers competed as if they were jockeys riding horses.

As early as 1848 it was remarked that the English public always enjoyed a race, 'and accordingly find the different rates of the express trains a common subject of interest'. Long-distance competitive services began in 1852–7, between *London and *Birmingham, *Sheffield, and *Manchester, but at first competing in convenience rather than in speed. Although the rival *West Coast and *East Coast routes between London and *Edinburgh had already emerged, competition was for a time restricted by pooling *agreements.

The first long-distance train in Britain intended to compete with another one in speed was introduced by the *London & South Western Railway in 1862 between London and *Exeter. In response the *Great Western and *Bristol & Exeter companies accelerated their best train. Similarly, in 1868, the *Midland Railway's first express trains between London and Manchester competed with two established rivals. Again, one of the Midland's considerations in constructing its expensive Kettering–*Nottingham line (1880) was to compete more effectively with the *Great Northern in speed between London, *Leeds, and *Bradford.

The multiplication of these competing routes raised criticism on economic grounds, it being observed that many of the trains were far from full. But the companies paid no attention. By 1888 there were three expresses leaving London stations less than a mile apart at 2 p.m., reaching Manchester within five minutes of one another. The GWR and LSWR behaved similarly between London and *Plymouth until the GWR decisively shortened its route in 1906.

radio and television

After the 1923 *Grouping all such competition was much reduced, good sense prevailing, backed by the need for economy. It finished after *nationalization in 1948.

Where the trains of two companies ran on parallel tracks, racing in the fullest sense was sometimes seen. Over the seven miles southward from Gloucester to Standish Junction (GWR and MR) trains raced frequently, to the pleasure and amusement of some passengers; but an accident in 1877 helped to put an end to it. Racing appeared also on the *North Eastern Railway between *York and Church Fenton, where its trains and the *Lancashire & Yorkshire's ran side by side for 11 miles. For many years two trains southbound left York at 2.35 p.m. and raced merrily. As a rule the NER train (lighter than its rival) was victorious, until 1921, when the LYR introduced its big rebuilt *Hughes 4-6-0 engines, which won the battle for good. On the *Isle of Man, simultaneous departures for two routes from both Douglas and St John's stations prompted unofficial racing between narrow-gauge trains over short distances before the parallel tracks diverged.   JS

Journal of the Statistical Society, 2 (1848), 333; E. Foxwell and T. C. Farrer, *Express Trains English and Foreign* (1889), 15; PP 1877, lxxii, 390; E. Mason, *Lancashire & Yorkshire Railway in the Twentieth Century* (1975 edn.), 36; J. I. C. Boyd, *Isle of Man Railways* (1995 edn.).

radio and television, railways and. Radio and television have always been the mirror of life as it is lived, and hardly ever the opinion-former they have been accused of being. It is therefore fairly easy to follow the rise and fall of the popularity of railways in the public esteem by observing the placing of railway-related programmes, their content, their attitude, and their importance in the general broadcasting schedules.

The public fascination with railway subjects grew with the freeing of the microphone from the studio. Although pre-World War II programmes were mainly scripted and far removed from the immediacy of today, a microphone at a railway station, with all its sounds, was something of a catch for the average listener. When the BBC Archive Record 'Railways Remembered' was being compiled, some splendid interviews were found dating from the middle of the 1930s. The railways were at that time, in the mind of the public, a necessary and even pleasant form of transport. They were at their zenith. Although the motor car had just started to make inroads into rail traffic, nostalgia had not reared its head and even the upper middle classes still used railways for their holiday journeys. At the same time the railways had amassed a considerable and newsworthy history. Fast runs, powerful locomotives, and even *electrification, were all matters of public interest, as broadcasts following *Flying Scotsman's* 100 mph run in 1934 and an interview with the driver of *Mallard* after its record run in 1938 exemplify.

With World War II the railways assumed an important role in the day-to-day running of the nation and were given, whenever possible, pride of place in the news bulletins. They were not programme material in their own right then. Their position was of national importance, and even subject to rigorous censorship. This, in a way, removed the railways from the public eye. As delays and overcrowding worsened, the general lack of adulation of the overburdened railways turned into criticism. Not loud, but deep-felt frustration built up, and as soon as censorship was relaxed this criticism was mirrored in broadcasting. The slow and dirty trains became subject to sniping on the radio. Money was scarce and holidays had been curtailed. The glamour had gone.

This was the time when television returned after an enforced absence during the war, hungry for new and spectacular material. Railway films with visually pleasing steam engines were a cheap and ready-made programme source. The heroic performance of the war gave rise to several radio documentaries, but possibly the most dramatic was afterwards: the *Ballad of John Axon,* the story of the self-sacrifice in 1957 of a railwayman (see also HONOURS).

At this time, when the political future of the railways was in question, *nationalization brought standardization. It was realized that 'the good old days', when it was always summer on the *Great Western, were gone for ever, and nostalgia reared its head. Programmes live on sentiment, and the broadcasters began looking for long-forgotten pictorial material of the old lines. The railways themselves produced films to meet the need of the broadcasters (see CINEMA). In the 1950s railways moved from radio to television: they were, after all, a visual medium.

Television soon developed from its naïve beginnings, and presenting railways as they were did not satisfy planners, producers, or the public. With the *Beeching proposals railways were in the news again. Then the cuts began. The time had arrived for L. T. C. *Rolt to bring people together for railway *preservation. Railways once more hit the news, but their press was no longer unalloyed love. The public's fickle feelings had turned to dissatisfaction, even hate. 'Everyone' had a motor car. In the public mind those who still loved the 'old' railways had themselves become a little odd. The 'mad' cleric, the anorak-sporting youth at the end of the platform, and the grown man playing with trains in attic or garden, were mirrored in the programmes. Usually the mirror was a distorting one. By now railways had ceased to make good radio. Their rare appearances on air were after they had *accidents, failed, were late, or had to be used to portray slightly eccentric members of society.

Television, too, tended to relegate railways to the less popular afternoon time-slots, although John Betjeman's programmes on 'nostalgic railways' in the 1960s had evening slots and helped to popularize them. A brave attempt was made by BBC's Midland Region with a series of *Railway Roundabout* programmes presented by Patrick Whitehouse; they successfully lasted for over three years.

Jim Palm, a BBC employee, in 1973 made two railway programmes for Radio London, leading to a series entitled *Rail* which lasted until 1979 and then moved to Radio Medway and Radio Solent. He also made regular programmes for BBC local radio elsewhere until 1992–3. But by this time the railways had been marginalized in the public esteem, as well as on radio and television.

It then occurred to the television programme planners that travel and exploration programmes could be enhanced by combining them with celebrities and international railway travel. The *Great Railway Journeys* series on BBC 1, and then BBC 2, in 1981 reached a large audience. The follow-up series became more personality-oriented.

A commercial radio station, County Sound of Guildford, took up the rising local and national interest in railways in the 1980s with their long-running *National Railway Roundup* (monthly for four years). The railways had once more taken up attention in politics, and this programme, which was angled towards the general public, became sufficiently popular to be carried by over ten other commercial stations.

In 1989–90 the BBC produced a popular *Steam Days* series which was given a prime-time slot. In 1994 the BBC commissioned three series of *Making Tracks*, and ITV presented several railway programmes, mainly for a minority audience in a poorer time-slot.

Now the public interest in trains and railways is once more rising. It will be fascinating to see what images our media will present. RAS-S

railbuses. Early railbuses were just that—a road *bus converted to run on rails. In time, 'railbus' described a self-propelled passenger vehicle with vestigial buffing and drawgear and so unable to haul a trailing load. The mechanical parts were usually to the design standards of road buses. Railbuses were also called *railcars at times. Leyland Motors supplied three four-wheeled lightweight, 40-seater diesel railbuses to the *London Midland & Scottish Railway, which entered service during 1934. A less conventional bus derivative seen on Britain's railways was of French inspiration. This was the Micheline, a petrol-engined bus with solid rubber tyres fitted to the rims of pressed-steel flanged wheels and so riding on the rails. The power unit and cab were separate from a low-slung, lightweight passenger saloon. It ran trials during 1932. Its maker's partnership with Armstrong Siddeley brought two British-built Michelines to the LMS in 1936 but, although reasonably successful, they were out of use before 1939.

A train of three railbuses built as a private venture by Associated Commercial Vehicles in 1953 was purchased by *British Railways. Joined by eight more cars, they worked in the Watford area in 1955–9. BR also experimented with a variety of other manufacturers' railbuses which worked on various uneconomic branch lines between 1958 and 1968. From the late 1970s, a third generation of railbuses was developed by BR and the manufacturer of the Leyland National bus, which formed the basis of these vehicles. Production versions built during the 1980s were progressively changed from the original concept and are called 'Pacers'. MLH

B. Haresnape, *British Rail Fleet Survey*, parts 7 and 8 (1985, 1986).

railcars: self-propelled passenger units powered by steam, petrol, or diesel engines; or by electricity from a battery or conductor rail or an overhead wire. The term is applied to a single vehicle or several comprising a *multiple unit. Probably the earliest successful railcar was *Express*, a steam-driven vehicle, by J. Samuel and W. Bridges *Adams on the *Eastern Counties Railway, which first ran in 1847. Other steam railcars, either on a single frame, or a coupled unit including coachwork, were built before 1900, often used for official inspection purposes.

By 1900, several railways used steam railcars to combat competition from street *tramways, or to call at track-level halts built for semi-rural services. They were capable of being driven from either end, and comprised a small locomotive unit, usually four-wheeled, married to a carriage unit. Many railways termed them steam rail motors rather than railcars. Some railcars proved to be underpowered; others generated traffic beyond their capacity, so resulting in their displacement by *push-and-pull trains. A few lasted into the 1940s, the survivors including the Sentinel Cammell railcars favoured by the *London & North Eastern Railway during the 1920s.

In the attempts to apply internal combustion engines to railcars, the various early essays proved temperamental. The pioneers were two petrol-electric railcars introduced by the *North Eastern Railway in 1904 on services in the north-east. Petrol cars with mechanical transmission were built for the *London Brighton & South Coast Railway in 1905.

Straightforward conversions of road *buses for railway use were more promising, with the emergence after World War I of reliable chassis from major motor manufacturers. During the 1920s, railcars of this type offered the chance of economical passenger services for the marginal *light railways of Col. H. F. Stephens, and the narrow-gauge County Donegal Railways Joint Committee in *Ireland. The future lay with diesel-engined railcars, principally with mechanical transmission and lightweight bodywork. The best-known were those of the *Great Western Railway, 38 of which were built in 1934–42. Useful experience from their operation (and with railcars used by the Northern Counties Committee in Ireland) influenced large-scale dieselization in post-war years on Irish and British railways.

Diesel electric railcars were successfully developed by the English Electric Co. Ltd from 1933, complete sets being exported to Ceylon before World War II. EE power equipment was used from the 1950s for multiple units built by *British Railways, both for itself and for Northern Ireland Railways. A second generation of diesel railcars was produced by British Rail from the early 1980s, initially comprising bus-derived four-wheelers (see RAILBUSES), and, later, the Sprinter bogie cars. A full range of these cars is now available for cross-country express services, intensive urban workings, and in single-car form for lightly used rural routes such as the Central Wales line and Cornish branch lines. MLH

Rail, Maritime and Transport Workers, National Union of, see NATIONAL UNION OF RAILWAYMEN.

rails, see TRACK.

Railtrack, see PRIVATIZATION.

'Railway Age, The'. This phrase has often been applied in Britain to the years 1830–1914, from the opening of the *Liverpool & Manchester Railway to the outbreak of World War I. During those years the railways came to establish a monopoly in the provision of inland passenger transport. When the war was over that monopoly was at once reduced, and soon it was almost entirely destroyed.

Equivalent phrases also appeared in France and Germany, though they did not pass into such common use there. In the USA there was a 'Railroad Age' too, but it opened only with the termination of the Civil War in 1865 and the development of the transcontinental lines that quickly followed. JS

M. Robbins, *The Railway Age* (1965 edn.), ch. 1.

Railway & Canal Commission, see COMMISSIONS AND PARLIAMENTARY COMMITTEES.

Railway & Canal Historical Society. Founded in 1954, the Society is the only voluntary organization devoted to the study of transport history, including early *tramroads, *road and *air transport, docks and shipping. Its six local groups meet regularly, and a bi-monthly *Bulletin* contains news and details of events. The *Journal*, published three times a year, contains valuable articles of both academic and more general interest, correspondence, and book reviews. Books are also published. At the annual meeting, held over a weekend, visits are made to historic sites. An annual public lecture is held alternately in London and the provinces, and occasional overseas visits are arranged. GJB

Railway Benevolent Institution. This was the main charitable body supported by many of the railway companies jointly. (For their individual activities of this kind see CHARITIES, RAILWAYS AND.) It was established in 1858 to provide assistance to railwaymen in need, supplementing what their employers might afford them, making grants in cases where the companies could not or would not help. It provided small pensions to incapacitated railwaymen and to their widows and orphaned children. The Institution's funds were derived from the annual subscriptions of its members, who were railway officers and servants, and from donations made by the public.

The Institution held an annual festival in London, the accounts of which in the press kept up interest in its work and encouraged the influx of funds for promoting it. The festival of 1867 was presided over by Dickens, who made a good speech, reminding his audience of the debt they owed to the men who looked after them on their travels.

In 1881 the *Midland company's Railway Orphanage at *Derby was affiliated to the Institution. But some companies still maintained homes for the children of their own employees: notably the *London & South Western, at first in London and then in ample buildings erected at Woking.

By 1921 the grants that the Institution had made totalled £1,600,000. JS

Speeches of Charles Dickens, ed. K. J. Fielding (1860), 361–6; *RM*, 12 (1903), 297–305; *RYB* 1922, 85.

Railway Clearing House. A railway map of Britain in 1836 shows a scattering of short, unconnected lines, such as the *London & Greenwich, the *Whitby & Pickering, and the *Edinburgh & Dalkeith. By contrast, a map of December 1842 shows what looks like a system of through lines, such as those between *London and *Bristol; London, *Birmingham, and *Liverpool; Bristol and *York; *Edinburgh and *Glasgow. But although the rails were linked, the shortsightedness of many company managers stood in the way of easy through communication.

Some companies would not accept the *carriages of 'foreign' railways on their own lines; some made provision for first- and second-class travel only and would not accept third-class passengers from other lines; through booking over a number of lines was not possible; there was no common *signalling system—on the *Great Western two red discs indicated 'all clear', on the *London & Birmingham they signified 'danger'. For goods traffic, even when there was agreement on the through transit of 'foreign' *wagons, there were disputes over the division of receipts between companies as there were no generally accepted mileage tables giving distances between stations. Some companies carried *freight in their own wagons, others employed carriers on contract. There was a great variety in wagon sizes, *brakes, and axle-boxes. Even *buffers were differently positioned. There was no commonly accepted classification of goods. Not surprisingly, Chaplin & Horne, and Pickfords, the principal long-distance road haulage firms, continued to do business in 1840–50.

The chief officers of the London & Birmingham saw most clearly the need for an organization to tackle these obstacles to through traffic. They were the chairman, George Carr *Glyn (later Lord Wolverton), and the chief accountant, Kenneth Morison. Following a letter of invitation from Glyn, the representatives of nine companies attended the inaugural meeting of the Railway Clearing House held in a small house at 11 Drummond Street, near Euston, on 2 January 1842. Apart from the LBR, the original member companies were all in the central industrial heartland of England, bounded by *Manchester, *Leeds, York, *Hull, *Derby, and Rugby. Membership of the RCH was always voluntary. The Great Western, *London Chatham & Dover, and *London Brighton & South Coast Railways stayed aloof until the early 1860s. But the large majority of railway companies had joined by 1870.

The five principal objectives of the Clearing House were to organize the through booking of passengers; the through booking of personally owned carriages and horses; to divide passenger receipts on a mileage basis; to encourage through transport of goods on a rate per mile basis; and to provide that all inter-company debts should be settled at the Clearing House. Finance for running the RCH was provided by a levy of £5 per year on each station of member companies, plus additional levies proportional to receipts. From 1847 Clearing House number-takers were employed to check the numbers and contents of wagons travelling on 'foreign' lines.

Among the important decisions made in the early years of the RCH was the recommendation by the committee at its meeting in September 1847 that member companies adopt Greenwich *time at all their stations. Before the days of radio time-signals it was common practice for people to check their watches by station time. The standardization of ticket-printing and date-stamping, as devised by Thomas *Edmondson and advocated by Morison, was rapidly adopted by member companies. The first RCH book of distance tables, issued in 1853, facilitated the settlement of accounts between member companies. The Clearing House could not dictate what charges should be made for the conveyance of different types of goods. It could only make recommendations. A start was made in 1847 when the goods managers' conference published the first official classification of goods (see FREIGHT TRAFFIC RATES) into five classes on one piece of cardboard measuring 9 in × 7 in. By 1879 the RCH General Classification of Goods filled a 129-page book.

It proved easier to standardize the operating practices of member companies than the equipment they used. Most locomotives were manufactured in the larger companies' workshops, as at *Crewe, *Doncaster, and *Swindon, where in each case the chief locomotive engineer reigned supreme and expressed his own ideas in the engines he designed. In no areas were the limitations of the influence of the Clearing House more starkly evident than in the design and use of the railway wagons. It was a consequence of the easy-going, permissive policy of the goods managers' conference that there was a riot of individuality in the companies' wagons. But the railways also hauled *private owners' wagons, a still more motley assortment. In 1922 some 4,000 private owners were responsible for 650,000 wagons, including 80 different types of cattle wagons. The RCH did not even make recommendations about the minimum loading. It was not until 1902 that the RCH engineers made recommendations on the positioning of *Westinghouse or vacuum brake pipes. As a consequence of this shambles British freight trains were among the slowest-moving and costliest to operate in Europe, and as late as 1910 coastal *shipping carried about the same tonnage of freight as railways.

The standardization of operations in signalling and telegraphy was a long-drawn-out process. In the superintendents' 'Rules for working over foreign lines' of 1867, semaphore signals were recommended; but there were appended colour illustrations of other systems in use. There followed a gradual tendency to assimilation, so that by the end of the 1870s the semaphore system was almost universal. The superintendents' committee issued a code of telegraphic signals in 1884, but this was not in operation totally until 1904.

Before the age of steam-heating (see TRAIN HEATING) the attempt by the RCH to improve the comfort of travellers by issuing them with footwarmers makes pathetic reading. In 1864 the superintendents recommended their supply to first-class passengers. Lesser mortals were left to freeze in their second-class or third-class carriages. In 1872 the general managers recommended their availability to all classes. But several companies declared they would only adopt this policy if others did so first. In consequence the scheme collapsed. Winter travellers had to wrap up warm and hope to survive until the coming of steam-heated radiators.

The standardization of railway *accounts was advanced more by the companies' lobbying of Parliament and by the terms of the *Regulation of Railways Act of 1868 than by any lead given by the RCH. But once the Act was passed meetings of company accountants were held regularly in the Clearing House.

With the outbreak of World War I in 1914, the Railway Executive Committee, appointed by the government, took over the management of railways. Questions were asked as to whether the more than 3,000 staff of clerks and number-takers could still be fully employed. Over 1,000 men either volunteered or were called up into the armed forces. None of the remaining staff was dismissed as there was still useful work to be done. The Clearing House committee devised a common-user scheme for railway wagons, tarpaulins, and ropes. But although this equipment was pooled, records of movement of wagons were still kept by the number-takers and clerks. The implementation of the railway pre-paid parcel *stamp scheme employed many others.

After the passing of the Railways Act of 1921 (see GROUPING) a record number of committees met in the Clearing House and much clerical assistance was provided by RCH staff. Many clerks were employed in drafting maps of rail networks and diagrams of rail centres. A greater volume and variety of *statistics was collected. Nevertheless, employment had fallen to 1,800 by September 1939.

With *nationalization following the passing of the Transport Act of 1947, rumours of the imminent closure of the RCH were rife and a number of 'farewell' dinners were consumed. But there were still calls for their help. The Railway Clearing House was not disbanded until 31 March 1963. At least one person who had served in the 'long office', where accounts were settled, waxed nostalgic about the 'peculiar atmosphere—very Dickensian—that hung about the place'.

See also MAPS AND PLANS; JUNCTION DIAGRAMS.　　PSB
H. C. Smart, The Railway Clearing House: What It Is and What It Does (1912); GR; Bagwell; M. R. Bonavia, typescript of an interview with T. J. Lynch, last secretary of the Railway Clearing House, in author's collection (21 Jan. 1975).

Railway Club. It was founded in 1899 for those interested, professionally or otherwise, in railways. It is the oldest society of railway *enthusiasts in the world, and the only one of its kind to have a members' club room open daily. The room is situated at 25 Marylebone Road, London NW1, and it houses the reference and lending sections of the club's library. A research section is housed at the Old Station Museum, North Woolwich, and may be consulted by members. Together, the three sections contain a comprehensive collection of books, timetables, maps, periodicals, and reports.

Regular meetings are held at which members and distinguished visitors present papers covering all aspects of railways, and visits are arranged to places of railway interest.

JEN

Railway Companies Association. Its origins were at a meeting of railway chairmen in 1854, under the auspices of the *Railway Clearing House. The consequence was that to discuss issues relating to Parliament, and to legislation affecting railways, the companies formed a special committee, renamed the Railway Companies Association in 1869. With a permanent secretariat based in Westminster, this organization survived until *nationalization.

The RCA was a political organization, compared with the RCH, and although devised primarily to counter parliamentary regulation of railways, it also involved itself with resisting proposed legislation relating to *safety measures and excessive hours of work. In the 1900s the RCA reflected the railways' attempts to avoid recognition of the railway *trade unions. It lobbied successfully from 1919 against nationalization, and associated measures such as workers' representation in management; for the *grouping of the railways on its terms; and, from 1945, fruitlessly against the Labour government's proposals for nationalization. Similarly unsuccessful was the 'Square Deal' campaign, promoted from 1938 with the aim of securing freedom for the railways to fix *freight rates, and the repeal of legislation in the Railways Act, 1921 that gave powers to the Railway Rates Tribunal to review rates. MLH

P. S. Bagwell, *The Railwaymen*, i (1963); M. R. Bonavia, *The Organisation of British Railways* (1971).

Railway Correspondence and Travel Society. One of the three oldest railway societies, the RCTS was founded in 1928, and a year later began publishing its monthly magazine the *Railway Observer* which has continued uninterruptedly ever since. The society caters for all railway interests and holds regular meetings in over 20 centres. It has a large library for the use of members, which includes a comprehensive photographic collection, and has published numerous books on various aspects of railways. In particular, its long-running series of detailed locomotive histories, still continuing, makes an important contribution to literature on the subject, for example those by D. L. Bradley on locomotives of the *Southern Railway and its constituents.

GJB

Railway Development Society. With the aim of promoting the retention, modernization, and greater use of rail transport, the Railway Development Society was formed in 1978 by the amalgamation of the Railway Invigoration Society and the Railway Development Association. These organizations had originated in the early 1950s as campaigning groups opposed to the withdrawal of passenger services on *BR secondary and branch lines.

The RDS is a national, voluntary, and independent body relying on membership fees from individuals and affiliated groups. The Society's national activity is complemented by several local action groups which have been prominent in successful campaigning for the reopening of BR stations to passenger traffic. MLH

Railway Heritage Trust, see CONSERVATION.

Railway Industry Association. This manufacturers' trade association has claims to be the oldest in the world.

In the early 1870s, the *London & North Western Railway was considering a merger with the *Lancashire & Yorkshire Railway, and in the meantime supplied that company with locomotives built at *Crewe works. Amalgamation was rejected by Parliament but the LNWR supplied 100 locomotives to the LYR in the years to 1874.

This activity precipitated a meeting of private locomotive builders, with the result that it was decided that legal action should be taken against the LNWR. Subsequently, the Locomotive Manufacturers' Association was founded in London during 1875, to protect the interests of the builders and, specifically, to seek a judicial decision as to the legality of railway companies manufacturing locomotives and rolling stock for sale or hire. The association obtained a High Court injunction restraining the LNWR from manufacturing for third parties and thus established general law.

Subsequent legal applications established that any activity by a railway company such as manufacturing locomotives for sale was prohibited unless statutorily authorized. The situation was firmly defined by the 1880s and remained as such until the Transport Act, 1968, permitted the *BR workshops to manufacture equipment for sale to third parties.

With the development of diesel and electric traction, the LMA's scope was widened in 1956 to include the makers of such equipment, and so became the Locomotive and Allied Manufacturers' Association. Membership was further broadened with the formation in 1971 of the Railway Industry Association which has its headquarters in London. MLH

B. Reed, *Crewe Locomotive Works and Its Men* (1982).

railway institutes. The popularity of mechanics' institutes in early Victorian Britain was reflected by the railway companies, which quickly established their own. These were often expanded to include baths and games rooms as well as libraries and technical classes. Railway *excursions soon followed, *Swindon Mechanics' Institute (established in 1844) organizing the first works outing for 500 in 1849, the huge public excursions from *Leicester and *Nottingham in 1840 having shown the possibilities.

By the 1880s these social activities were being supplemented by the coffee taverns of the United Kingdom Railway Temperance Union, with their games rooms, sports, and societies, and by the railwaymen's unions (see TRADE UNIONISM) with fund-raising concerts and parades for Orphans Funds. As the educational and welfare aspects of the railway institutes and their kindred bodies were increasingly absorbed into the welfare state in the 20th century, these organizations metamorphosed into the British Railways

Staff Associations, concentrating on their social and recreational roles.

See also EDUCATION. RVL

railways never built, or uncompleted. It may be guessed—the statistics are too shaky for it to be proved—that the mileage of British railway schemes surveyed and presented to Parliament, but not in the event constructed, fell little if at all short of the mileage of those which were. The railways that were never built either were pure speculations, or failed to get authorized, or when authorized were not undertaken, or having been started were completed only in part.

Speculative schemes floated for financial gain, without serious intention of construction, are most characteristic of the *Mania years of 1845–6, such as the Great Eastern & Western Railway from Yarmouth to Swansea and the Southern Counties Union & Bristol Bath & Avon Direct Railway.

Projects seriously promoted might fail to secure authorization because of lack of financial support, non-compliance with parliamentary standing orders (SEE PARLIAMENT AND LEGISLATION), or, most importantly, opposition from existing companies. Schemes for a railway between London and Brighton, for which there were six competitors in 1836–7, were reduced to one; the London & York and the Direct Northern, proposing different routes, were merged into the *Great Northern in 1846. In 1836–46 and up to 1884, lines were repeatedly promoted to cross north central Wales to Porth Dinlleyn, on the Caernarvonshire coast, as a rival to Holyhead; but no railway was ever built to the place. A Glasgow & North Western Railway, 167 miles along Loch Lomond and Loch Ness, in 1883, was defeated by existing interests. The *London & North Western Railway repeatedly tried to get into north-east England but was defeated—for example, the North of England Union Railway from Settle to West Hartlepool, 1865; and beyond Carmarthen into Pembrokeshire. An ambitious scheme for a coal-carrying line from Market Rasen, Lincolnshire, to Long Stanton, Cambridgeshire, was rejected in 1871. In rural Essex and Suffolk and in the remoter parts of Scotland there were repeated schemes for *light railways, up to 1918, to Gairloch, Ullapool, and Laxford Bridge, even on Skye and Lewis; but few of them came even to promotion. From 1845 to 1914 proposals were frequently made for a peripheral line linking the railways west and north of London with the docks, with later echoes up to 1944 (see NORTH LONDON RAILWAY).

Some unexecuted schemes did, however, have the effect of stimulating existing companies, which had to defend their position by making improvements in their lines and services. The London & South Wales scheme of 1896 forced the *Great Western to undertake its cut-off line from Wootton Bassett to the *Severn Tunnel, opened in 1903. The London & Brighton Electric, defeated in 1902, prompted the *London Brighton & South Coast to widen its main line down to Balcombe Tunnel and secure powers to electrify it in 1903, but this was not achieved throughout until 1933.

Some lines on which construction had begun were abandoned: the York & North Midland's Copmanthorpe–Leeds line, after Tadcaster viaduct had been built, in 1848; the GWR–LNWR connection over Duddeston Viaduct, *Birmingham, in 1852; the Ouse Valley line, LBSCR, from Balcombe to Uckfield in 1866.

Some short lines were vestiges of grander schemes. The so-called Manchester & Milford, authorized in 1860 from Llanidloes to Pencader Junction, 52 miles, diverted its western end to run from Strata Florida to Aberystwyth, so that three miles on the abandoned section, from Penpontbren to Llangurig, completed and fully signalled in 1863, were never used. The *Bishop's Castle Railway, 10½ miles long from Craven Arms, opened in 1866 and insolvent from then until its closure in 1935, was a fragment of a larger scheme to run to Montgomery. The Potteries Shrewsbury & North Wales (later the Shropshire & Montgomeryshire—SEE LIGHT RAILWAYS), an amalgamation of 1866, operated 22 miles from Shrewsbury to Blodwell Junction but never approached the Potteries. The Lancashire Derbyshire & East Coast Railway (see GREAT CENTRAL), authorized in 1891 to run from Warrington to Sutton-on-Sea, Lincolnshire, 170 miles, with branches, was completed only from Chesterfield to Lincoln, 38 miles. See also ABANDONMENT. RMR

Railways Tribunal, see FREIGHT TRAFFIC RATES.

Railway Study Association of the London School of Economics. Formed in 1909 as the Railway Students' Association to further the study of transport, the association holds monthly lecture meetings in the winter, and in the summer organizes educational visits. Annual events include a week's convention in Britain or overseas, a seminar, and an educational weekend. Circulars and a quarterly Bulletin containing digests of papers are published. Membership generally is open to graduates, members of professional institutions, railway and London Transport managerial staff, and others approved by the association council. GJB

Rainhill trials. The construction of the *Liverpool & Manchester Railway, authorized in 1826, proceeded steadily, but the directors did not consider what form of power should be adopted for working it until the autumn of 1828: whether by horse-traction; by means of ropes, controlled by *stationary steam engines (see also CABLE HAULAGE); or by locomotives. The board engaged James *Walker and J. U. *Rastrick to investigate railways actually at work. Having visited them in January 1829, they reported separately, both somewhat in favour of stationary engines. But Walker suggested that the LMR should hold a competition, offering a substantial prize for the best locomotive entered. Presently the board agreed, fixing the prize at £500, to go to a locomotive that showed 'a decided improvement on those now in use'.

Three machines were entered that fulfilled all the conditions laid down: the *Stephensons' *Rocket*, *Hackworth's *Sans Pareil*, and *Novelty*, the work of John Braithwaite and the Swede John Ericsson. The judges were Rastrick, Nicholas *Wood, and John Kennedy, an engineer and cotton-spinner of Manchester. The trials were held on the line at

Rainhill and spread out over seven days early in October 1829.

Both *Rocket* and *Novelty* reached the unprecedented speed of 30 mph. But *Rocket* proved more consistently reliable in operation than either of its rivals, and that brought it the prize.

The trials did more than decide a contest between three machines. They persuaded the LMR directors to entrust the operation of their railway almost wholly to locomotives. The contest was followed closely outside Britain, the news of it being published day by day as far afield as Boston, Massachusetts.

See also LOCOMOTIVE TESTING.   JS

Thomas, ch. 3. Much the best account of *Rocket* is in B. Reed, *Locomotives in Profile*, i (1971), 149–72. Boston: C. F. Adams, *Railroads: Their Origin and Problems* (1886 edn.), 55.

Ramsbottom, John (1814–97), locomotive superintendent of the North Eastern Division of the *London & North Western Railway in 1846, of the combined Northern Division in 1857, and of the whole railway in 1862. A talented engineer and manager, he was responsible for several inventions, of which the most important were the modern form of piston ring (1852) and his tamper-proof safety valve (1856). He also devised the water trough for replenishing locomotive tenders on the move (see WATER SUPPLIES).

Of his locomotives, the classic DX 0-6-0 introduced in 1859 became the most numerous class ever to run in Britain, and the Problem 2-2-2 (also 1859) included the first locomotives built new with the Giffard *injector. Aided by his chief draughtsman Francis *Webb, Ramsbottom set about modernizing *Crewe works, introducing not only the use of steel but also its manufacture.

He resigned in 1871, ostensibly on health grounds, after a dispute with the chairman Richard *Moon over his salary, becoming a consulting engineer. In this capacity he was involved in modernization of the *Lancashire & Yorkshire Railway, notably in creation of their new works at Horwich, completed in 1889.   RW

BDE; F. C. Hambleton, *John Ramsbottom, The Father of the Modern Locomotive* (1937).

Ramsden, Sir James (1822–96), a key personality in the development of the *Furness Railway and of *Barrow-in-Furness. He is believed to have served an apprenticeship with Edward Bury & Co. and, possibly after service with the *London & Birmingham Railway, arrived in Barrow in 1846 as locomotive superintendent to the FR. Ramsden became secretary and general manager in 1850, and managing director from 1866 until retirement in 1895. Dominant in industry and local government, he was Barrow's first mayor in 1867 and was knighted in 1872.   PWR

J. Kellett, *James Ramsden, Barrow's Man of Vision* (1990).

Rastrick, John Urpeth (1780–1856), engineer. Articled to his Northumbrian father, a London machine-maker, he studied iron manufacturing in Shropshire and soon had charge of a foundry. He built a cast-iron bridge at Chepstow in 1815–16, and became interested in making railway track. He was engineer of the *Stratford & Moreton Railway in

1823. With George *Stephenson he reported to the *Liverpool & Manchester Railway promoters on lines in northern England in 1825, and testified in its favour to a parliamentary committee in 1826. In 1829 he built the Shutt End colliery railway in Staffordshire, with a locomotive *Agenoria* to his own design, and was a judge at the *Rainhill trials. He made a preliminary survey for what became the *Grand Junction Railway (1830), and was engineer for the London & Brighton Railway (see LONDON BRIGHTON & SOUTH COAST) in 1831–41, building it to plans originating with the *Rennies. He was entirely responsible for the *Portsmouth–*Brighton–Hastings line and most of its branches (1840–9), the Bolton & Preston Railway (1841), Gravesend & Rochester (1845), and *Nottingham–Grantham (1846). He was elected FRS in 1837, the first railway engineer to be so honoured.

Rastrick's work stood well, with no important failures. His meticulous preparation can be appreciated from his remarkable notebooks and papers at the University of London.   JS

DNB; PICE, 16 (1857), 128; TNS, 5 (1923), 48, and 26 (1947–9).

rates for freight traffic, see FREIGHT TRAFFIC RATES.

rating, local, see TAXATION, LOCAL.

Raven, Sir Vincent Litchfield (1858–1934), mechanical engineer. Apprenticed under Edward *Fletcher at Gateshead *works, he became assistant divisional locomotive superintendent, *North Eastern Railway, in 1888, chief assistant mechanical engineer in 1903, and CME 1910–22. Raven was the first to standardize the use of three-cylinder drive, with a more even torque in transmitting power to driving wheels and thus enabling heavier trains to be hauled for a given adhesive weight. He built some 200 engines of this type, with numerous 4-4-2 express, 4-6-0 mixed traffic, 0-8-0 and 4-6-2 tank freight, and 4-4-4 passenger tank locomotives. All were robustly built and capable, although the three sets of inside *valve gear were relatively inaccessible for servicing. He also experimented with Stumpf uniflow cylinders as a possible means of improving efficiency.

Raven proposed main-line *electrification between *York and *Newcastle on the 1,500 V dc overhead system, used successfully on the Newport–Shildon mineral line from 1915. The 1921 trade recession and 1923 *Grouping caused the abandonment of this project. He also introduced *automatic train control between York and Newcastle. Retiring as technical adviser to the *London & North Eastern Railway in 1924, he reported on railways in New South Wales and New Zealand, and on railway workshops in India. He was knighted for war service as superintendent of the Royal Arsenal, Woolwich.   GWC

BSRL; *The Engineer*, 57 (1934), 206.

Raymond, Sir Stanley, see BRITISH RAILWAYS.

records, see ARCHIVES AND RECORDS.

records, speed, see SPEED.

recovery time: additional time allotted for the running of a train, to allow for reductions in speed arising from operating or engineering requirements, and allowed for in the public timetable. The use of this device, frowned on at one time as a confession of weakness, came to be recognized as a necessity during and after World War II, and it is now freely used whenever it seems necessary.   JS

G. F. Allen, *British Railways Today and Tomorrow* (1959), 193–4.

Redesdale, John Thomas Freeman-Mitford, 2nd baron and 1st earl of (1805–86), politician; chairman of committees, House of Lords, 1851–86, which made him powerful in mid-Victorian legislation, especially in the consideration of private Bills. As the owner of Batsford Park, Gloucestershire, he had much trouble with the Oxford Worcester & Wolverhampton Railway (see WEST MIDLAND). He readily detected chicanery among railway managers, and favoured tighter control of railway legislation, desiring (vainly) to see a board established, much like *Dalhousie's of 1844–5, to examine proposals before they came to *Parliament. He served on the joint committee on *amalgamation, 1872. Impregnably placed, masterful in manner and thinking, quick-witted, totally honest, he did much to maintain the authority of government over the railway companies.   JS

DNB; *Complete Peerage*; E. Cleveland-Stevens, *English Railways* (1915), 210, 251–3, 264.

Red Star, see PARCELS TRAFFIC.

refreshment rooms. Where and when the first railway refreshment room was opened is uncertain, but if the Gartsherrie Inn, built by the Garnkirk & Glasgow Railway in 1832, is discounted, it was either at the *Grand Junction Railway's temporary Vauxhall terminus at *Birmingham (1837), or on the *London & Birmingham Railway at Rugby (1838) or Birmingham Curzon Street (September 1838).

Refreshment rooms were provided not only for passengers changing trains but for the meal stops made by all long-distance trains before the introduction of *restaurant cars, such as at *Swindon, *York, Normanton, *Preston, and *Carlisle. LBR trains stopped for ten minutes at Wolverton, which was half way, where the rush into the refreshment room was described by Sir Francis Head. The catering was leased to contractors, to whom the railways guaranteed a compulsory stop by all or by specified trains. At first, refreshment stops were considered necessary about every 50 miles, but as speeds increased they could be spaced further apart, making some of them unnecessary; none more so than at Swindon where the *Great Western had unwisely let the refreshment room on a 99-year lease which earned the contractor a handsome profit. The stop soon became an anachronism, but survived until 1895 when the GWR finally succeeded in buying back the unexpired lease for the enormous sum of £100,000, which remained a charge on the revenue account until 1920.

Railway refreshment rooms changed eating and drinking habits by bringing the bar, or serving counter, into widespread use in a trade where they might only be found in some of the posting inns. The bar could run the length of the room, or be circular or oval in the middle, like those at Swindon which had a central servery divided by a partition

into first and second class, and a spiral stair to the kitchens below. Third-class passengers were not usually accommodated, although *Manchester Victoria had a refreshment room for them in 1844, albeit in the basement.

Jokes about the food go back to the early days. In 1842 *Brunel complained about high prices and low quality at Swindon, Wolverton, and *Derby. Complaints became widespread, and Dickens' parody in *Mugby Junction* (1866) was based on his own experiences with tea and soup that were virtually indistinguishable, and sandwiches seemingly filled with sawdust. But standards were not always uniformly bad. At Normanton, for instance, passengers on the *Midland Railway's Scotch expresses could enjoy a six-course meal for 2*s*. 6*d*., provided they could eat it in 20 minutes, which was all the *London & North Western allowed for the same purpose at Preston.

As longer journeys became possible, the demand grew for full meals, and most large stations had a separate dining room or restaurant with table service. Some gained such high reputations that they were patronized by local businessmen, as happened after Rugby station was rebuilt in 1902, and *Aberdeen in 1915; or became popular meeting places, like the elegant Pillar Hall restaurant at *Victoria, the Surrey Room and Windsor Bar at *Waterloo, the restaurant at *Glasgow Central, and the charming *art nouveau* tea-room at York. Birmingham New Street had five refreshment rooms and three dining rooms, while *Liverpool Street even had a separate ladies' dining room.

Unlike *waiting rooms, refreshment room decor received special attention, and often complemented the station architecture. The LBR's at Birmingham Curzon Street had a large panelled ceiling supported by two rows of Corinthian columns. The handsome and well-proportioned rooms at Cambridge, Derby, and Chester were designed by the architect Francis *Thompson, who was also responsible for the Arabesques at Swindon; while *Dobson at *Newcastle and *Tite at Carlisle incorporated refreshment rooms that were respectively Classical and Gothic. The grill room at Manchester Victoria, rebuilt in 1901–4, was splendidly Edwardian with a coloured glass dome.

Contractors at first were often landlords of local *hotels. In 1850, for instance, the room at *Liverpool Lime Street was let to the proprietor of the Queen's Hotel for five years, but gradually many of the large companies set up catering organizations as part of their own hotel departments, which were also responsible for train catering. Some, however, continued to use contractors, notably the *London & South Western which in 1882 changed from piecemeal lettings to one single contractor, Simmons, and six years later to Spiers & Pond, who were the leading railway caterers. From beginnings in Australia they had gained their first British contract from the *Metropolitan Railway at Farringdon Street, going on to become caterers to the *South Eastern, *London Chatham & Dover, and *Cheshire Lines Committee, and at a number of large stations. In 1925 they ran over 200 refreshment rooms.

On *nationalization, station catering came under the Hotels Executive of the *British Transport Commission, and from 1953 British Transport Hotels & Catering Services. Self-service cafeterias were now rapidly replacing dining rooms, and as the hotels began to be sold off the brand name Travellers Fare was adopted in 1973, marking the beginning of a country-wide programme of completely redesigned refreshment facilities aimed at attracting a much wider clientele than solely railway passengers. In 1982 Travellers Fare became a division of *British Rail, but when the first moves towards railway *privatization began it was itself sold. Meanwhile, specialist buffets and bars had started appearing on large stations, and today users are offered a wide choice of both fast foods and cafeteria catering, although many mourn the loss of 'proper' dining facilities. However, local caterers can still be found at some smaller stations, from which they never completely disappeared, often offering attractive local delicacies.   GJB

C. Dickens, *Mugby Junction* (1866); GRSB; N. Wooler, *Dinner in the Diner: The History of Railway Catering* (1987); Wolverton: F. B. Head, *Stokers and Pokers* (1968 edn.).

Regional Railways, see BRITISH RAILWAYS.

Regulation Acts. Nine 'Railway Regulation Acts' were passed in 1840–93, each dealing with one large aspect, or more, of railway business. Other equally important measures were passed, for example the Railways' Clauses Act of 1845, and the Cheap Trains Act of 1883. But the word 'regulation' used in the title of each of these nine Acts gives them something of a common character, and as they are often referred to simply as 'Regulation Acts' it is worth listing them with their dates and numbers and the briefest indication of the chief matters they dealt with. The texts of them all can be found in *Bigg's General Railway Acts* (16th and best edition, 1912).   JS

1840	3 & 4 Vict., cap. 97	Powers of Board of *Trade; punishment of railway servants.
1842	5 & 6 Vict., cap. 59	Powers of Board of Trade; conveyance of troops and police.
1844	7 & 8 Vict., cap. 86	*Gladstone's Act.
1868	31 & 32 Vict., cap. 119	Accounts; companies' obligations as carriers; *smoking.
1871	34 & 35 Vict., cap. 78	*Inspectors; *accidents; *statistics.
1873(1)	36 & 37 Vict., cap. 48	Appointment of Railway *Commission.
(2)	36 & 37 Vict., cap. 76	Returns to Board of Trade.
1889	52 & 53 Vict., cap. 57	*Brakes; *signalling; *block system; railway servants' overtime; evasion of fares by passengers.
1893	56 & 57 Vict., cap. 29	Hours of work.

Reid, Sir Bob, see BRITISH RAILWAYS.

Reid, Sir Robert (1921–93), chairman. In 1947, the year of the *nationalization Act, Bob Reid, as he was known, became a traffic apprentice on the *London & North Eastern Railway. He rose to become general manager of *BR's Southern Region in 1974, and board member for marketing three years later. In 1980 he was made chief executive and became responsible for implementing changes demanded by the Conservative government whereby the railway's regional management was replaced by business sectors. By the time he was appointed chairman in 1983 these changes were well on the way to producing a stronger commercial structure, although inevitably they led to difficult relationships with the *trade unions, which had already been strained by the 1982 strike. The serious *accident at Clapham in 1988 convinced him of the correctness of his view that safety and quality of performance go hand-in-hand. An apparent diffidence and a poor public-speaking manner belied a determination to make the railways succeed, although his hopes that a clear demonstration of a new efficiency would dissuade the government from pursuing *privatization failed to be realized. He was succeeded in 1990 by a namesake, Sir Bob Reid (II) (see BRITISH RAILWAYS).   GJB

D. Kirby, 'Sir Robert Reid, 1921–93' (obituary), *Modern Railways*, 51, 545 (Feb. 1994), 75.

religion. Religious considerations entered into both the construction and the working of railways.

Much concern was expressed about offering religious teaching and assistance to the *navvies who built the lines. The contractors sometimes provided this, when they held strong beliefs themselves: *Peto, for example, David *Davies, T. A. *Walker. 'Missionaries' might be appointed to minister to the men and their families, some of them grouped together in societies. Bishop Creighton of London took special care to see that provision of this sort was made for the men building the southern tip of the *Great Central Railway's London extension in 1894–9.

The railway companies occasionally played a direct part in this matter. The *Great Western added an aisle to the parish church of Box (Wiltshire) in 1840, to accommodate the navvies working on the great tunnel there. Some companies also built, or assisted the building of, churches and chapels in the railway *towns. There, however, they might have to go cautiously, for some shareholders opposed the expenditure of company funds in this way. When the chairman of the *Great Northern Railway asked its shareholders to vote £8,000 for building a church at *Doncaster in 1854, he encountered strong opposition. 'Is it to be a railway company', said one of the objectors, 'or a Church Extension Society?' The opposition was strong enough to prevent the church from being built by this means. The money was found by private subscription among the shareholders, and the church was opened in 1858.

Proper religious observance was seen by some companies as an element in their men's duty. The *Taff Vale Railway was most explicit on this point in a rule of 1856, which 'earnestly requested' each of its servants 'on Sundays and Holy Days when he is not required on duty that he will attend a place of worship; as it will be the means of promotion when vacancies occur'.

When the interest in *education grew stronger in the country as a whole, it came to be treated by some railways in conjunction with religion. The GWR directors, for example, had a single Swindon Church and School Committee in 1845–82.

Another controversial matter concerning religion also gave the railways trouble: the provision of trains on Sundays. Some of them ran none during the hours when most people were expected to be at church or chapel. This was dubbed the 'Church Interval'. Gradually eroded or abolished, traces of it were yet to be found as late as 1921 (see SUNDAY SERVICES).

Some railway companies made other gestures in the same direction. The Frenchman Taine noted in 1862 that 'large, chained Bibles' were kept in station waiting rooms. On the remote *Settle & Carlisle line church services were held on Sundays at Ribblehead and Garsdale stations.

Looked at broadly, the provision of railways assisted the organization of national religious bodies of all denominations. As the historian of the 19th-century Anglican church put it, they slowly 'made both cathedral and bishop more effective as capitals of the diocese'. JS

Grinling, 138, 147–9; H. Taine, *Notes on England* (1957), 13; O. Chadwick, *Victorian Church* (1966), i, 524.

Rennie family, engineers. Although their most important work was concerned with *bridges, *canals, and docks, they made two substantial contributions to railways.

John Rennie (1761–1821) was the great man among them, always to be remembered for his Waterloo, London, and Southwark Bridges and for the design of *Plymouth breakwater. He undertook no railway work.

His sons **George** (1791–1866) and **John** (1794–1874) became partners in 1821 and surveyed the line of the *Liverpool & Manchester Railway, but were not invited to build it since they refused to work with George *Stephenson, whom they did not consider an engineer. Similarly in 1837, after they had laid out the route of the London & Brighton Railway (see LONDON BRIGHTON & SOUTH COAST), the directors entrusted its execution—very wisely—to *Rastrick. The Rennies' habitual superciliousness provoked immediate hostility, and they never saw any railway project through to completion.

George did better as a mechanical engineer. The partnership established works in London and built at least 16 locomotives there in 1838–42. Few of them gained a good reputation in service. George then turned successfully to marine engineering.

John was knighted in 1831 as a posthumous courtesy to his father, whose London Bridge he had completed. JS

DNB; BDE; J. W. Lowe, *British Steam Locomotive Builders* (1978), 545–6.

reopened railways. Discounting short connecting curves, and lines reopened by preservation societies (see PRESERVATION OF RAILWAYS), railways brought back into use after *closure were rare until recent years. Perhaps the most significant length to lose and then regain a passenger service before the mid-1970s was the 5-mile Churchbury Loop

opened by the *Great Eastern Railway in 1891. It failed to generate the anticipated traffic and was closed to passengers in 1909. In 1960 it was electrified and reopened to ease congestion, and renamed the Southbury Loop.

In 1977 the *Coventry–Leamington line was reopened to passenger trains, after their withdrawal in 1965, to allow re-routeing of InterCity *cross-country services between the north and the south-west, and ten years later its counterpart from Coventry to Nuneaton had regular passenger trains restored in collaboration with Warwickshire County Council. Local authorities and *Passenger Transport Authorities have played a prominent part in many reopenings, and as road congestion increases more are planned, although much depends on availability of *subsidies. In 1989 local authorities and the West Midlands PTA succeeded in having the Walsall–Hednesford line reopened, closed in 1965.

The experimental service between Kettering and Corby failed, yet the similar mainly rural Oxford–Bicester service has succeeded. Other regular services restored are those from *Cardiff to Coryton and to Maesteg, respectively withdrawn in 1962 and 1970; in the *Glasgow area on the Paisley Canal (closed in 1983) and Whifflet lines (closed 1964); and from *Edinburgh to Bathgate (closed 1956).

In Lancashire, after withdrawal of Blackburn–Hellifield passenger services in 1962, limited summer weekend trains for walkers were later introduced, followed in 1994 by a full daily service to Clitheroe. The longest reopened line is the 17 miles between Ladybank and Hilton Junction, near *Perth, restoring a shorter route from Edinburgh that had closed in 1955.

All these lines had been retained for freight trains. A parallel development has required the actual relaying of track and, at some places, the repurchase of former railway land. It began in 1974 on five miles between Carlin How and Boulby in north Yorkshire, to allow freight trains to serve a new potash mine, and then in 1978–83 the former *Cheshire Lines track between St Michaels and Garston was reopened after six years of total disuse, to extend *Liverpool's Merseyrail system.

In London the former *London Chatham & Dover Railway's line between Farringdon and Ludgate Hill, closed to passengers in 1916 and freight in 1971, was relaid and electrified in 1988 as part of BR's new *Thameslink service.

Two most ambitious examples of this kind are in the Midlands. In 1994–5 some 25 miles were reopened from *Nottingham to Mansfield Woodhouse and named the 'Robin Hood Line', involving relaying five miles of track and digging out the ½-mile Kirkby Tunnel which had been infilled with colliery waste at both ends. In *Birmingham, the short stretch of former *Great Western Railway between Moor Street and a new Snow Hill station was reopened in 1987, 19 years after it was lifted, followed in 1995 by four miles onward to Smethwick West—the 'Jewellery Line'; part of a comprehensive rail development plan. GJB

Reg. Hist., iii, vii, xv; Nottingham: J. Sully, 'Robin Hood Riding through the Glen', *Modern Railways*, 52, 565 (Oct. 1995), 607;

research and development

West Midlands: M. Causebrook, 'West Midlands Growth', *Modern Railways*, 53, 570 (March 1996), 166.

research and development. British railways quickly applied the principles of scientific method, one early application being the study of locomotive performance by means of a *dynamometer car: an activity continued into the 1960s. As manufacturers in their own right they soon became involved in the development of production processes. As considerable purchasers and users of materials they were concerned to determine the calorific value of *coal and the chemical composition of *lubricants, paints, and metals. Such analytic activities were seen as a service to various railway departments, generally at main *works, and were under the control of *mechanical and *civil engineers' departments.

The first industrial laboratory established by a British railway was that set up in 1864–5 under John *Ramsbottom of the *London & North Western Railway at *Crewe. This was initially concerned with aspects of steel production at the works. F. W. *Webb was involved there in much experimental work, in particular the thorough investigation of boiler stay design, and with the materials used. By the end of the 19th century, there were some 11 laboratories owned by British railways.

There was some collaborative work between the *'Big Four' companies, notably in the fields of wind resistance and *bridge design; the civil engineers were more amenable to research. One project of the late 1930s was the building of a *locomotive testing plant by the *London Midland & Scottish and *London & North Eastern Railways, but not opened until 1948, at Rugby.

Only in the 1930s was a concerted effort made by the LMS to co-ordinate research activities within a scientific research department. This was based at *Derby, and science graduates were employed to investigate matters such as the maintenance costs of rolling stock, and fuel economy. Yet Britain had no facility comparable to the Grünewald research station of the German railways.

The research activities inherited from the 'Big Four' companies were not amalgamated until 1951, a reflection of the tension then existing—and never entirely dispelled on *British Railways—between the mechanical engineering function and a separate research department. By the mid-1950s BR had set up development units to investigate a wide range of subjects, as a service to operators and engineers.

In the early 1960s there was governmental encouragement to set up a centralized research facility, and laboratories, test rigs, and workshops were built within the Railway Technical Centre at Derby, opened in 1964 and extended over the next decade. A move from defensive to offensive research followed the concomitant appointment of Dr Sydney Jones as BR's Director of Research. He believed that some of the fundamental principles of railway engineering were due for reassessment, and that new research priorities should be determined.

Notable among the areas of research under Jones were wheel and rail dynamics, and the riding behaviour of vehicles. This led directly to the creation of the *Advanced Passenger Train whose disappointments had an adverse effect on the prominence given to the Research Department from the late 1970s. Other more lasting areas for research have been train *control, improvements in power collection from catenary, and *track construction.

See also TESTING OF EQUIPMENT; TESTING OF MATERIALS.

MLH

J. Johnson and R. A. Long, *British Railways Engineering 1948–80* (1981); H. Williams, *APT—A Promise Unfulfilled* (1985).

restaurant car: a *carriage provided for the service of meals and refreshments, with staff working from a kitchen which is able to produce main meals. Their services are generally indicated in *timetables or *publicity.

In a restaurant-kitchen car, the kitchen normally contains a stove fired with solid fuel, or ovens with gas, electric, or microwave equipment, or a combination of these. Gas-fuelled cars have underframe storage cylinders while cars with electric cooking equipment draw on current generated by axle-driven dynamos or from a train supply. Other facilities include water tanks, sinks, and cupboards, refrigerators for the storage of foodstuffs, and a staff compartment. The seating may be fixed chairs or benches, less commonly loose chairs, with fixed tables usually laid for the service of meals with cutlery and glassware. Interior decor is generally of a higher standard than other carriages.

Some railways preferred to use open-layout carriages as restaurant cars, providing at-seat service of meals, although they were without cooking facilities. Restaurant cars once were usually designated for first- or third-class ticket-holders. Where limited dining facilities are available, accommodation now is referred to as 'either class' or 'unclassed'. Some cars include a bar counter for the service of alcoholic drinks and light refreshments and are described as a restaurant-buffet car. A vehicle with kitchen facilities only and without seating for diners is known as a kitchen car.

The first dining car to run regularly on British railways was a modified *Pullman car, operated by the *Great Northern Railway between *Leeds and *King's Cross from 26 September 1879. By 1896, the GNR, *London & North Western Railway, and *Great Western Railway were operating restaurant cars. At first, the cars were first-class only and passengers were expected to remain in them throughout their journey. British railways were initially reluctant to provide restaurant car services as they were seen as uneconomic and as adding to the weight of trains.

Concern at the incidence of train *fires led to the use of all-steel catering vehicles such as the kitchen cars used on the Flying Scotsman from 1914. Alternatively, from 1920 H. N. *Gresley on the GNR developed electric cooking equipment for restaurant cars, adopted by the *London & North Eastern Railway from 1924. As well as current generated on board the vehicle, power for cooking was obtained from supplies at termini. Composite equipment with electric and anthracite-fuelled ovens was introduced on LNER cars from the late 1930s. Restaurant cars normally used oil gas, produced at railway-owned plants. With the decline in the numbers of gas-lit vehicles, alternative fuels were sought and, from the late 1950s, most restaurant cars used propane or butane gas for cooking. More recently, cars have been all-electric.

See also BUFFET CAR.   MLH

returns, railway. In 1840, under the first *Regulation Act (see PARLIAMENT AND LEGISLATION), the Board of *Trade was authorized to call for returns from every passenger-carrying railway company established by Parliament, showing the traffic it carried, the *accidents that had occurred in working it, and the *fares and tolls it charged.

All these returns were at first included in the Board's annual reports. With the enlargement of the system they became too voluminous for this treatment, and those on accidents were split off to form a series of their own.

The phrase 'the railway returns' relates to the returns of capital, traffic, income, and expenditure. The exact forms in which they were to be made were set down in schedules attached to the Regulation Acts of 1871 and 1873. They followed that pattern until 1911, when the forms of the accounts were substantially altered and the scope of the general returns was enlarged and refined. They were now to include information, for example, about the railways' *ancillary activities, such as giving the number of *hotels owned by each company, and they did much towards unravelling the tangle into which the figures of *season and *workmen's tickets, and the numbers of journeys made by their holders, had fallen.

The first returns issued in this form were in respect of the year 1913. No figures (except a few, very much abbreviated) were published while World War I was in progress; but the series was resumed in 1919 (now produced by the new Ministry of *Transport), altered so as to omit Ireland in 1922, and carried on thereafter until 1947. Further changes, concerned primarily with the accounts, were introduced in 1928. After 1947 the annual reports and accounts of the nationalized bodies (the *British Transport Commission, 1948–62, and the *British Railways Board, 1963–94) took the place of the old returns.

The returns are by no means free from faults, some arising from defects in the information supplied by the companies, others from mistakes or misjudgements in the handling of it at the Board of Trade. But all students of British railways, of their *management, finance, and operation, need to use them. Above all they offer, together with the railway companies' reports to their shareholders, a continuous view of the fortunes of each railway, its achievement and failings, from 1840 to 1947, that is to be had in no other way.

Sets of the returns (incomplete here and there) are to be found in the British Library, the Bodleian Library (Oxford), and the University Library at Cambridge; also in the National Libraries of Wales (Aberystwyth), Scotland (Edinburgh), and Ireland (Dublin). A long run of them, from 1858 to 1923, is also available in the library of the *NRM.   JS

Rhondda & Swansea Bay Railway: incorporated in 1882, to provide an alternative route for bringing coal from the Rhondda valley to the sea through a port other than *Cardiff, which was choked with traffic. It was to run from Treherbert to Briton Ferry, and included the 2-mile Rhondda Tunnel. Until this was completed (1890) the railway's main business could not begin. The system came to be 29 miles long.

In 1906 the *Great Western Railway made an offer to acquire control of the RSBR, which was accepted. The smaller company was merged with the larger one outright in 1922.   JS

Reg. Hist., xii, 192–5, 203–4.

Rhymney Railway. The 'Old Rumney' Railway, an antiquated *tramroad, connected the Rhymney Ironworks with Newport. In 1851 the Bute Trustees, about to build a new dock at *Cardiff, encouraged its replacement by a modern railway to the port. The Rhymney Railway was established accordingly in 1854–5, reaching Cardiff by *running powers over six miles of the *Taff Vale Railway, and opened in 1858.

The running powers gave trouble immediately. Although the courts soon reduced one of the TVR's charges by 80 per cent, the RR's financial difficulties compelled it to lease itself to the Bute Trustees, which Parliament refused to sanction.

With coal traffic mounting, it turned the corner nevertheless by 1862, and in 1864 secured powers to build its own line into Cardiff, opened in 1871. Two other important extensions were also completed then. One, made jointly with the *London & North Western Railway, went from Rhymney to Nantybwch. The other, with running powers over the *Great Western, penetrated the Aberdare valley. The steep Taff Bargoed line, built jointly with the GWR, brought the RR to Dowlais in 1876, extended to Merthyr Tydfil ten years later.

Most of the RR's lines, originally single, had to be doubled in the 1870s. In 1875 the company paid no dividend, but over the next 22 years the rate rose to 10½ per cent, under the tight control of Cornelius *Lundie. The RR suffered in 1889 by the opening of the *Barry Railway which, with the *Brecon & Merthyr, parallel with the RR, took away some of the RR's traffic for shipment at Barry.

Caerphilly was now the most important place on the RR system after Cardiff. Locomotive repair shops were opened there in 1902; passenger traffic grew so large that the station had to be reconstructed in 1913.

In 1909–10 the TVR tried to absorb the RR and the *Cardiff Railway, but Parliament refused to agree. In 1917, however, the TVR and Cardiff companies accepted E. A. Prosser, the RR's manager, as their manager too, and the three were worked as one. They became constituents of the GWR in 1922.   JS

D. S. Barrie, *Rhymney Railway* (1952); *Reg. Hist.*, xii, chs 5 and 6.

Riddles, Robert Arthur (1893–1983), mechanical engineer. Following apprenticeship at *Crewe under C. J. Bowen *Cooke, 1909–14, in 1920 he became assistant to the works manager and in 1925–7 was responsible for its major reorganization under the *London Midland & Scottish Railway, including a new erecting shop and introduction of a line-production belt system, reducing time in locomotive repairs by two thirds. In 1928–31 he did the same at *Derby, returning to Crewe as assistant works manager. In 1933–7 he was principal assistant to the CME, William *Stanier, and in 1937 became mechanical and electrical engineer (Scotland). In World War II he controlled the supply of locomotives and rolling stock for military use overseas. Stanier 2-8-0s were first built in railway workshops, but Riddles developed a simpler and cheaper alternative for war-time mass production. Of 1,100 2-8-0 and 2-10-0 engines to his design, most returned to work on *BR.

In 1946–7 he was LMS vice-president, engineering, and after *nationalization, member of the Railway Executive for mechanical and electrical engineering, 1948–53. There, Riddles realized that there would be no funding for main-line *electrification, which he had long felt to be desirable, so he built a series of simple, robust standard steam locomotives, with maximum *route availability. Nearly 1,000 were built, including 250 freight 2-10-0s which provided a step-change in performance.   GWC

E. S. Cox, *Locomotive Panorama*, i and ii (1965–8); H. C. B. Rogers, *The Last Steam Locomotive Engineer—R. A. Riddles* (1970).

rioting. Amid a commotion audible in neighbouring villages, Lord Harborough's stalwarts battled against the Syston & Peterborough Railway's prize fighters while its *surveyors hurriedly took their measurements in his park. This 'Battle of Saxby' (1844) was no isolated incident in the early years of railway promotion as antagonistic landowners sought to defend their property. Subterfuge was often necessary, including working by night when the surveyors might be taken for poachers. Confrontation with agents and keepers was common; the Riot Act was read near Bicester, the yeomanry threatened in Hampshire, and clan rivalries surfaced in Glen Falloch.

Railway companies themselves, anxious to protect their territory from interlopers, on occasion resorted to blockades of rolling stock, supported by employees (see 'BATTLES' BETWEEN RAILWAYS).

Disorder among construction *navvies was endemic, especially during the 'randies' (drunken brawls) after payday, as they worked prodigiously hard and relaxed accordingly, but racial violence was common too, especially against the Irish. Incidents during the building of the *North Midland Railway (1838–40) culminated in an attack on them and their families which was finally quelled by armed Metropolitan *Police, while in 1846 they were attacked by the Welsh at Penmaenmawr, the English at Penrith, and the Scots near Edinburgh. Despite the frequency of confrontations, however, railway navvies generally quickly gave way before small numbers of professional police or military, pending their return to sobriety.

Equally reprehensible was the two-day confrontation between engineer and *contractor—the so-called 'Battle of Mickleton' (1851)—when *Brunel (no less), despite the presence of armed police, troops, and magistrates reading the Riot Act, twice attempted to use force to remove the contractors responsible for building Campden Tunnel before wiser counsels prevailed.

Popular discontent in the early 19th century, increased by unemployment, mechanization, and poor harvests, was met by magistrates reading the Riot Act, reinforced as required by the local militia. The coming of the railways and the electric *telegraph assisted the maintenance of order as they enabled troops to be moved quickly; during the Chartist outbreaks of 1842, some 700 troops were sent to *Manchester via *Birmingham, while in 1848 three companies were kept at Weedon barracks, Northamptonshire, ready for immediate despatch to *Liverpool or Manchester. The early prominence of former military men in railway administration, like Captain Mark *Huish on the *Grand Junction Railway, was undoubtedly helpful. As late as 1883 rail-borne troops assisted police in controlling militant Sabbatarians at Strome Ferry in the western Highlands.

Paradoxically, this ready availability of rail-borne troops aided Liberal politicians in encouraging the establishment of local police forces, and the railways concurred, feeling vulnerable to rioters; in 1848, some 478 railway employees at Wolverton (see WORKS) were sworn in as special constables before the great Chartist demonstration. Labour unrest after 1900 revived these fears: in the great railway *strike of 1911 bearskinned guardsmen assisted police in protecting critical points of the system, while in the General Strike (1926) troops with machine guns again appeared. Nor were these fears groundless: in 1926 striking miners overturned an express at Cramlington in Northumberland and jeered at rescuers, crew, and passengers.   RVL

D. Brooke, *The Railway Navvy* (1983), ch. 5; D. Brooke, 'The "Great Commotion" at Mickleton Tunnel, July 1851', *JRCHS*, 30, 145 (1990); G. Body, *Great Railway Battles* (1994).

road-rail vehicles. From the earliest days of railways, there has been the ideal of a trans-modal vehicle, moving easily from road to rail. Road carriages were conveyed by rail (see HORSE-DRAWN CARRIAGES, CONVEYANCE OF) but, with *freight, transhipment proved unavoidable. Railways sidestepped the difficulty by building up extensive road cartage facilities for freight and parcels, as well as becoming energetic *bus operators. But interest in road-rail vehicles remained. Few proved successful because of the problems of converting from road to rail, and the weight of the equipment. One well-publicized example, if probably only experimental, was the Ro-Railer: a heavy road coach produced by Karrier during 1931 in association with the *London Midland & Scottish Railway. In appearance a conventional single-deck bus with doors on both sides, the road and rail wheels were co-centric. Transfer from road to rail running was done quickly by locking the steering and raising the road wheels to clear the rails, and the vehicle was intended to serve the LMS's recently opened *hotel at Stratford-upon-Avon which was some distance from the railway. It worked for only a few months.

Road-rail freight vehicles featured at various times, usually demountable tankers with fixed road wheels and loaded on to flat wagons. A truly trans-modal vehicle was developed during the 1950s in the USA and the licence to manufacture was obtained by the Pressed Steel Company. Known in Britain as the Roadrailer, it comprised a semi-trailer capable of running on road and rail, with independent braking in either mode. On rail, the front of one Roadrailer was coupled to the rear of the preceding vehicle, all running behind an adaptor wagon attached to the locomotive. On road, the semi-trailer formed an articulated vehicle with a tractor unit. Trials were run on *British Railways during 1963 but the train of Roadrailers never entered revenue service. Bi-modal piggyback vehicles were operated by Charterail during 1991–2, others are being developed, and doubtless more will be seen with international freight traffic through the *Channel Tunnel.   MLH

road transport. Railways both competed against and were complementary to road transport. They were preceded by a long-established network of reliable and regular road services conveying goods and passengers over both short and long distances. Carriers catered for the higher-value or more urgent consignments, for which water transport was too slow or which could bear road transport's higher price. This wagon and stage-*coach traffic was seen as an important potential source of revenue by railway promoters.

Road transport's major weakness was its dependence on the slow and costly horse. Railways could provide cheaper and, above all, faster carriage. However, even the long-distance services did not disappear immediately, since it took time to create a widespread railway network. A few coachmasters sought to compete head-on with the railways, but most recognized the inevitable, sometimes turning their services into railway feeders. Goods carriers were in a stronger position in the short term: they had 'connections' of regular customers, who very often required door-to-door conveyance, which it was difficult for the railway companies to provide. The long-distance carriers mostly began to use the railways (usually at special rates)—not running their own trains, but doing the loading and unloading, and bookkeeping, themselves and providing horse-powered transport at each end of the line. However, as the railway companies became better established and their networks developed, they began to see advantage in conducting their own carrying, and had little difficulty in supplanting the carriers. Most of the major carrying firms disappeared in the 1850s, though a few survived as railway agents—notably Pickfords (for the *London & North Western Railway from 1847) and, in Scotland, Wordie & Co.—together with the former coachmasters, Chaplin and Horne.

The railways' effect on short-distance road transport was very different. *Freight and *passenger traffic to and from the railway *stations was greatly stimulated, both in the growing towns and in the country, where even at their fullest extent the railways directly served at most about one in six villages. Many country carriers became railway agents. The number of commercial road vehicles increased from about 161,000 to 702,000 between 1851 and 1901, and the number of commercial horses (post-horses, hackneys, and

those hauling public passenger vehicles or goods vehicles) rose from about 251,000 in 1811 to 264,000 in 1851 and 1,166,000 in 1901 (a quarter of them in London). Country carriers, omnibuses, hackney cabs, and privately owned carriages all multiplied. Far from railways eclipsing road transport, the golden age of railways was also the peak period for horse-drawn road transport. But the trend in urban areas was for the railways to become carriers, and their road collection and delivery fleets grew until at *nationalization in 1948 they comprised nearly 12,000 motors, over 26,000 horse-drawn vehicles, and 8,500 horses.

Road vehicles could be improved, as in the case of the omnibus and the horse-drawn tram, but road transport would only become a threat to railways once it escaped from its dependence on the horse. This began with steam lorries (numerous by the 1890s), the electric *tramway (from the mid-1890s), and reasonably reliable petrol-driven motor vehicles (from the mid-1900s). Passenger transport was mechanized sooner than goods transport, owing to its greater requirement for speed and less demanding technical requirements: the process was virtually complete by World War I in London and other large cities. Between the wars the number of private cars gradually increased, reaching 2 million by 1939, but was overshadowed by the huge increase in *bus services, especially in rural areas in the 1920s. The railways lost much of their short-distance passenger traffic.

Before World War I, the economic range of motor lorries was about 40 miles, though some travelled further. Road and rail remained largely complementary, though traffic figures suggest that the railways were already losing traffic they would otherwise have carried. The number of lorries increased substantially after the war; their operating costs fell and economic range increased. They could be much more flexible than the railways in terms of both operation and pricing. By the 1930s there was increasing road competition over distances of 75 to 100 miles. After obtaining road powers in 1928, the railways purchased Pickfords, the parcels carrier Carter Paterson, and others, together with some trunk hauliers such as Joseph Nall. This alarmed the Road Haulage Association, which was appeased by a promise to avoid cut-throat competition.

The full impact of motorized road competition was felt after World War II, with improved vehicles and better roads. Car registrations increased dramatically, from 2 million in 1950 to nearly 20 million in 1990, though partly at the expense of public road transport. Passenger mileage by rail held up well, being little changed since the immediate post-war period, but the share of railways (including *underground railways) in total passenger mileage declined from 20 per cent in 1952 to 6 per cent in 1990. While the share of buses and coaches fell from 41 to 6 per cent in that period, the share of cars, taxis, and motorcycles rose from 27 to 86 per cent.

Although the Transport Act, 1947 imposed a duty to integrate nationalized road and rail services, the Road Haulage Executive (see BRITISH TRANSPORT COMMISSION), which inherited the railways' road freight investments (though not the collection and delivery fleets), concentrated on building up British Road Services independently of railway associations.

The Transport Act, 1953 replaced 'integration' by the even vaguer 'co-ordination'. Soon the 1960s concept of liner trains for fast *container services using road and rail developed into the *Freightliner. But the Transport Act, 1968 transferred not only *BR's road collection and delivery fleet, along with the terminals for sundries traffic, to the road-based National Freight Corporation but also gave the NFC a 51 per cent shareholding of Freightliners. This was, however, later returned to BR pending privatization. Containers remain the only real example of road–rail co-ordination today, apart from some ventures with 'swap-body' vehicles (see ROAD-RAIL VEHICLES).

Railway freight traffic has declined sharply, from 22,600 million ton-miles in 1952 to 9,700 million in 1990. Long-distance road haulage grew impressively, as did the number of very large lorries. Ton-miles of freight by road first exceeded that by rail in the mid-1950s, and the roads in 1990 accounted for 62 per cent of total ton-miles, compared with rail's 8 per cent, the remainder being by water or pipeline.   DJG

T. Barker and D. Gerhold, *The Rise and Rise of Road Transport, 1700–1990* (1993); P. S. Bagwell, *The Transport Revolution* (1988); G. L. Turnbull, *Traffic and Transport: An Economic History of Pickfords* (1979); E. Paget-Tomlinson, *The Railway Carriers: The History of Wordie & Co.* (1990); Dept of Transport, *Transport Statistics: Great Britain* (1991); Gourvish.

Robertson (Baron), General Sir Brian (1896–1974),
soldier and chairman. The longest-serving chief executive of *British Railways, Robertson was a very distinguished military administrator chosen to become chairman of the reconstituted *British Transport Commission in September 1953. His chief remit was to provide leadership in what was seen as an undisciplined organization and to decentralize the railways, in addition to selling back to the private sector the recently nationalized road haulage firms.

He designed for the newly enlarged BTC a detailed organization reflecting Army 'line and staff' principles; it proved cumbersome in practice. The deteriorating financial position led him to support the 1955 railway *Modernization Plan which scored an initial success with the government but it was hampered in its execution partly by the headquarters organization, partly by interference from the railways' Area Boards, and partly by some technological and commercial misjudgements.

Robertson took all the key decisions but was at a disadvantage through his lack of 'inside' railway experience; he depended upon what in Army terms he would have designated 'good staff work', and this he had missed in the BTC. He tried to rectify it by creating his own 'General Staff' of advisers, who were soon very unpopular with engineers and managers.

His tall, imposing presence, and the stiff shyness which precluded small talk made him seem intimidating, though they masked a real humanity and he could unbend well with railwaymen at grass-roots level. He saw the railway as essentially a public service, which he was charged to deliver to a high standard. He expected to be given the resources in money and manpower to deliver this. He instigated the Railway Research Centre at Derby and the British Transport Staff College.

His later years brought some disillusionment through the increasing deficits and the attitude of the *trade unions. Robertson was subject to much unfair criticism; those who knew him best resented this. He retired on 31 May 1961 and was created Baron Robertson of Oakridge.   MRB

Gourvish; M. R. Bonavia, *The Organisation of British Railways* (1971); M. R. Bonavia, *British Rail: The First 25 Years* (1981).

Robertson, Charles James Alan (1939–92), historian.
Having taken his degree at St Andrew's, he went to the University of Pennsylvania to pursue post-graduate work, returning to his old university to teach economic and social history for the rest of his life. In 1983 he published *The Origins of the Scottish Railway System, 1728–1844*, a very highly finished work; the best account yet produced of the history of railways in any part of Great Britain. He continued the study in the face of gruelling ill-health, but was obliged to leave it uncompleted at his death.   JS

Economic and Social History Society of Scotland Newsletter (1993).

Robertson, Henry (1816–88), civil engineer, ironmaster,
railway promoter, politician; born at Banff, Scotland, the youngest son of an excise officer; educated at King's College, Aberdeen. He embarked on a mining career but became a pupil of Robert *Stephenson and *Locke. Under Locke, he was credited with levelling and setting out the *Lancaster & Carlisle Railway over Shap Fell. Invited in c.1841 to report on the mineral potential of north-east Wales, he collaborated in the development of Brymbo Iron Works, and built the North Wales Mineral Railway to the River Dee and to join the *Chester & Holyhead Railway. The NWMR later formed part of his Shrewsbury & Chester Railway (1846), featuring majestic viaducts (see BRIDGES AND VIADUCTS) at Cefn and Chirk. Robertson was closely associated with other lines, including Chester–Birkenhead; Ruabon–Blaenau Festiniog; *Shrewsbury–*Birmingham; Shrewsbury–Hereford; and Central Wales. He represented Shrewsbury in Parliament in 1862–8 and 1874–85, and Merioneth in 1886.

Always a proud Scot, Robertson was enchanted by the beauty of the upper Dee and rebuilt Palé Hall, Llandderfel, where he died, highly regarded for his expertise, industry, and integrity.   GB-J

P. J. Anderson, *Officers and Graduates of King's College, Aberdeen* (1893); G. C. Lerry, *Henry Robertson: Pioneer of Railways in Wales* (1949); Robertson Papers, National Library of Wales, and Clwyd RO.

Robinson, John George (1856–1943), locomotive engineer. The son of a divisional locomotive superintendent on the *Great Western Railway, he was apprenticed at *Swindon; in 1884 he became assistant locomotive superintendent

on the Waterford Limerick & Western Railway in Ireland. Becoming superintendent in 1888, he reorganized the workshops and renewed most of the locomotives and rolling stock.

In 1900 he joined the *Great Central Railway as locomotive and marine engineer, taking responsibility for *carriages and *wagons in 1902, as CME.

Robinson produced modern, efficient equipment, using extensive standardization. His coaches were comfortable, his wagons capacious. His locomotives included 4-4-2s, widely regarded as the most beautiful of locomotives, for fast passenger services; mixed-traffic locomotives for fast *fish trains; handsome heavy freight locomotives in large numbers both for the GCR's growing *coal traffic and as the Ministry of Munitions' standard locomotive for overseas service in World War I; and powerful tank locomotives for suburban traffic on the London Extension.

He was an inventor, notably of a superheater (see TRACTION, STEAM) and a system of oil-burning for locomotives, and *buffers and fenders for carriages to prevent telescoping in accidents.

Robinson was a firm disciplinarian but popular with his men, including the *drivers and *firemen who daily proved the excellence of his designs.   AD

Dow, iii; *RM*, 7 (1900), 82.

Robinson, W. Heath, see ART.

rolling stock, see CARRIAGES; WAGONS.

Rolt, Lionel Thomas Carswell (1910–74), writer. In his early years he endured much adversity. Apprenticed to Kerr Stuart, the locomotive manufacturing firm of *Stoke-on-Trent, he was turned adrift when it collapsed in 1930. In 1934 he and two friends opened a garage near Basingstoke, specializing in the rehabilitation of old motor cars. He bought a canal boat in 1939, living on it until 1951. His first book, *Narrow Boat* (1944), an evocation of canal life, was the result, followed by his *Inland Waterways of England* (1950).

Among those who have written extensively about railways, Rolt stands out as the engineer of most diverse practical experience. He became directly involved with them only in 1950, when he took a leading part in saving the *Talyllyn Railway from total closure, helping to float a preservation society for the purpose and taking part in the management of the reopened line. All this he recorded very well in his book *Railway Adventure* (1953).

In 1957–60 he published good biographies of I. K. *Brunel, *Telford, and the two *Stephensons. He did much for the railway *preservation movement, giving experienced advice to a number of the societies formed for this purpose. He also afforded valuable assistance to the Science Museum in connection with the establishment of the *National Railway Museum at *York.   JS

DNB: Missing Persons; personal knowledge. Rolt's own two volumes, *Landscape with Machines* (1971) and *Landscape with Canals* (1977), form a vivid autobiography.

Romney Hythe & Dymchurch Railway. The world's largest and best-known 15-in *gauge railway was built as a public railway by Captain Jack Howey to serve the coast of Kent between Hythe and Dungeness. It was authorized in 1925 and built under the supervision of the eminent miniature railway engineer Henry Greenly, who designed the ⅓ full size 4-6-2 and 4-8-2 locomotives that still handle most of the traffic. The double-track line from Hythe to New Romney opened in 1927 and the line was extended to Dungeness two years later.

Though some freight traffic was carried, the line was from the start principally a tourist attraction and its buildings, locomotives, and rolling stock were intended to create the effect of a main-line railway in miniature. Taken over by the Army during World War II, the railway operated a miniature armoured train and later helped to build PLUTO (Pipe Line Under The Ocean—supplying fuel to allied forces). Post-war reconstruction singled the line between New Romney and Dungeness. Following Howey's death, there was a period of uncertainty until the present administration took over to perpetuate and develop the railway without losing its essential character.   RW

J. B. Snell, *One Man's Railway* (1983).

Rous-Marten, Charles (1844–1908), writer. Born in New Zealand, he made his name in South Island politics. He came to Britain in 1887 to study its railways. On his return the New Zealand government asked him to report on railways there, in some Australian colonies, and other countries.

He settled in England in 1893. In 1897 he studied locomotive practice in France, reporting enthusiastically on French compound express passenger engines (see TRACTION, STEAM). He wrote for the *Engineer* from 1894 onwards. In 1895–1907 he contributed annual reports on British locomotives to the *Bulletin of the International Railway Congress*. He began a series of articles in the *Railway Magazine* on 'British Locomotive Practice and Performance' in 1901, continued ever since.

Rous-Marten was a pioneer in recording speed from the footplate and the carriage. 'Long experience and special aptitude enabled him to do the work of at least two ordinary men', said the *Engineer*. Though his accuracy has sometimes been questioned, and subsequent practitioners have refined on his methods, he founded the study in Britain. He was held in affectionate esteem by many railwaymen, not least because of his strict impartiality. He declined the Legion of Honour lest it should be supposed that it influenced his commendation of French locomotive work.   JS

Engineer, 105 (1908) 431, 477; *RM*, 22 (1908), 455–7.

route availability. In considering which vehicles may be allowed to run over a particular route, account must be taken of their weights in relation to the carrying capacity of *bridges on the route, *clearances, and occasionally of very sharp curves. Any new bridge will be designed for a combination of four concentrated loads representing four adjacent axles, with a uniformly distributed load of indefinite length, defined in British Standard 5400: Part 2 as 'RU' loading. This incorporates the recommendations of the International

Union of Railways (UIC), and allows for all combinations of vehicles currently running or projected to run on main-line railways in Great Britain or Europe. Many older bridges may have been designed to lower standards than this, or their condition may have deteriorated. Hence the railway continuously assesses and updates the capacity of individual bridges, the results being codified as route availability numbers (e.g. RA8). The RA number of a route will usually be the lowest RA number of any track-carrying structure on it. New types of vehicle are similarly assessed and are only permitted to travel (without special dispensation) over a route having the same RA number as the vehicle, or a greater one.

Historically, maximum concentrated loads were produced by the driving wheels of steam locomotives and the impact factors were determined by their hammer-blow. These were reflected in the design loadings of the time, and on the *Great Western Railway engines carried an appropriate colour code. Today, however, the RU design loads and impact factors represent the heaviest axles of freight wagons. GHC

British Standard Specification 5400: Steel, concrete, and composite bridges; Part 2.

route selection. A number of factors affected engineers' choice of route for a railway, not least *landowners' attitudes (see LAND ACQUISITION), but the overriding influence was geography. Early lines followed *canal practice in devising long level lengths interspersed with short steep sections: locks on canals, *cable-worked inclines on railways. Ideas about cable haulage on the *Liverpool & Manchester Railway were dispelled when locomotives easily surmounted short 1 in 96 gradients, although the *Stephensons believed that an appreciable distance steeper than 1 in 330 would overtax locomotives, hence Robert's insistence on the enormously expensive Kilsby Tunnel on the *London & Birmingham Railway. I. K. *Brunel designed the original *Great Western main line with gradients no steeper than 1 in 660, except for two short inclines at 1 in 100–200 where he intended to use additional engines. But engineers quickly modified their opinions when they saw how rapidly locomotive power was increasing.

The first main lines generally took natural routes used by predecessors. South of Kilsby the LBR broadly follows the Roman Watling Street, *Telford's Holyhead Road, and the Grand Junction Canal, while the *Great Northern Railway's main line is only once more than five miles from the original Great North Road. The *Edinburgh & Glasgow Railway is never far from the Forth & Clyde and Union Canals. Later, the *Highland Railway followed Telford's road for 92 miles across the Grampians.

Hilly areas in particular made the natural route the first choice. The *Manchester & Leeds and Huddersfield & Manchester Railways crossed the Pennines by hugging rivers, roads, and canals through narrow valleys, and tunnelling through the watershed. Likewise in South Wales, lines taking out coal clung to narrow, parallel valleys, often

alongside competing railways. Only three crossed them laterally, needing heavy engineering works to do so.

Where directness was the prime consideration, arduous engineering could not be avoided in hill country. The Sheffield Ashton & Manchester Railway (see GREAT CENTRAL) was particularly difficult, and had to tunnel for three miles under the high Pennine watershed at Woodhead, while even in Sussex the London & Brighton Railway (see LONDON BRIGHTON & SOUTH COAST), in rejecting five easy but circuitous routes in favour of a direct one, had to accept three major tunnels and a long viaduct.

In keeping to natural routes early lines might miss important traffic centres. The London & Birmingham ran four miles west of Northampton, and the *Grand Junction Railway passed through nowhere of importance between Stafford and Warrington, completely ignoring the Potteries. Consequently some major towns like *Sheffield, Halifax, *Bradford, Worcester, and St Helens for some years had to be content with a branch or loop line. This factor had now to be considered when planning routes: important intermediate places could no longer be disregarded, particularly as advances in civil engineering were making tunnels and viaducts less expensive. The Scottish Midland Junction Railway, for instance, left the easy route down Strathmore in order to serve Forfar and Montrose, adding eight miles to the line from *Perth to *Aberdeen. Later still, competing lines found the best route already occupied, leaving no alternative to expensive engineering works, as happened on the GNR's extensions in West Yorkshire and Derbyshire.

Contours were followed wherever possible, producing serpentine courses on some secondary and branch lines where speed mattered less than cost. *Settle & Carlisle Railway surveyors skilfully used contours to the opposite effect and produced a direct route, but at the expense of numerous tunnels and viaducts between heads of valleys. Coastal routes, too, could require tunnels through headlands and viaducts across estuaries; or the coast might form a barrier like the Ord of Caithness which forced the Highland Railway into a long detour inland rather than face the cost of getting past it, although there was pressure to open up the interior as well.

Always, route selection was a continuous balancing act between terrain, cost, and the wishes of promoters. GJB

J. H. Appleton, *The Geography of Communications in Great Britain* (1962); A. C. O'Dell and P. S. Richards, *Railways and Geography* (1971 edn.); D. Turnock, *Railways in Britain: Landscape, Land Use and Society* (1982); RS, 110–15.

Royal Engineers; Royal Corps of Transport, see MILITARY RAILWAYS.

Royal Institution of Chartered Surveyors. Railways played a leading part in the formation of the RICS. They brought *surveyors together in field work, at arbitration and valuation hearings, and in parliamentary committees. The Surveyors' Club was founded in 1834, and in 1868 it became the Institute of Surveyors. The royal charter was granted in 1881.

Fifteen of the 20 founder members were prominent in railway work, and some present-day firms began by surveying and valuing for railway companies, including Cluttons, who worked for the *Midland Railway, and Drivers Jonas. John Clutton, the first president, was land agent for the *South Eastern Railway, and Edward Driver bought land for the *Great Western and *London Brighton & South Coast companies. Clutton and Edward Ryde, who was surveyor for the SER in 1855–92, were regarded as co-fathers of the Institution. Ryde became an authority on railway rating and valuation (see TAXATION, LOCAL). The Institution is the professional body for railway estate surveyors.

See also LAND AND PROPERTY, OWNERSHIP AND DEVELOPMENT OF; LAND ACQUISITION; LAND, SURPLUS.   GJB

F. M. L. Thompson, *Chartered Surveyors: The Growth of a Profession* (1960); RS.

royal travelling. Most of what has been written on this subject has been devoted mainly to royal trains. But there is more to be said about it than that, for the railway travelling of royalty became an ingredient in the political life of the United Kingdom.

The journeys made by reigning monarchs had been elaborately organized in the past, when they went 'on progress', surveying their realm and showing themselves to their people. Such tours ceased almost entirely in Britain after 1640, and over the next 200 years the sovereigns' ordinary travelling within the island became much more limited. George III went to Weymouth in pursuit of health, politely acknowledging when he could salutations of those who watched as he passed. George IV travelled a great deal (constantly to and from *Brighton), but he swept along at high speed, paying little attention to anyone. When Queen Victoria made the first journey by train, from Windsor to London on 13 June 1842, she opened a new chapter in the history of the British monarchy.

The train permitted her, when it seemed appropriate, to show herself, Prince Albert, and presently her family, to her subjects through the broad glass windows of her carriage. The monarchy now began to become a physical reality to many ordinary people, not merely an institution.

Railway travelling added to the Queen's comfort. In a horse-drawn carriage she had always moved fast (in popular places in order to prevent mobbing by an enthusiastic, or possibly a dangerous crowd), rocking violently from side to side. The train was somewhat steadier, and the crowds could generally be controlled at stations. Moreover, she was now able to read, write, and transact state business *en route*.

She was never in a railway *accident of any consequence herself, though she had a narrow escape from one at Forfar in 1863, and her eldest son had another at Drumlithie in 1869. She disliked travelling at more than 40 mph. Her trains' timetables were always carefully discussed in advance between her private secretary and the railway officials, and when she was conveyed faster than she liked, in order to make up time for instance, she protested vehemently. There was trouble at *Carlisle in 1886 when she had

come too rapidly over the *North British Railway from *Edinburgh, and the *London & North Western, which took her on from there, was specially instructed to keep speed down.

The first vehicle designed for royalty was provided by the *Great Western Railway in 1840, its body supplied by a London coachbuilder and its iron frame constructed by the railway itself. The *London & Birmingham company commissioned two in 1842–3, one for the Dowager Queen Adelaide, the other for Victoria and Albert. These carriages all ran on four wheels, but the GWR's was replaced by an eight-wheeler in 1849. That vehicle and one built by the *South Eastern company at the same time had a form of lavatory (see SANITATION).

None of these carriages proved wholly smooth to ride in, even at the moderate speed insisted on by the Queen. Better accommodation came to be provided by the LNWR and GWR in 1869–74. The LNWR's two saloons were enlarged to make one 12-wheeled vehicle in 1895.

The pattern of the Queen's journeys soon changed greatly. In the 1840s she and her husband had travelled much throughout the UK, showing themselves freely to many of her people. But though she performed her duties conscientiously, she also felt herself entitled to a private life. Accordingly, she acquired two country estates, Osborne in the *Isle of Wight in 1843, and Balmoral, west of *Aberdeen, five years later: the first of them 85 miles from London, the second 600. Osborne was reached easily by train, a short sea-crossing, and a coach drive. The railway reached Aberdeen in 1850, but a much longer coach drive ensued to Balmoral until a branch line was opened to Ballater, nine miles from the castle, in 1867.

After Albert's death in 1861 the Queen's life became much more secluded. Most of her long-distance journeys were made between Osborne or Windsor and Balmoral, on a regularly fixed system. She travelled twice a year, in spring and autumn, usually overnight, though sometimes she performed a public duty on her way: for instance, visits to *Glasgow in 1888, and to *Manchester in 1894.

The organization involved was very complicated, the royal train running over four companies' lines successively. It was preceded by a pilot engine, travelling 15 minutes in advance, to test the track and provide warning of danger. The passage of the Queen's train caused a large disruption of normal traffic. The pilot and the train itself had each to be allotted a *path of its own in the regular timetable. No trains were allowed to pass the royal train in the opposite direction, except mail trains; no freight trains might move at all after the pilot's passage. These arrangements became much harder to apply whenever, for some reason, the royal train was running late. At various times extra precautions had to be taken to meet threats from Irish terrorists.

In Scotland the arrangements for spectators of the Queen's arrival and departure were more relaxed than in England, especially at Ferryhill, south of Aberdeen, where her train stopped to reverse. Even more elaborate precautions were called for to protect some of the foreign visitors to Balmoral, notably the Emperor and Empress of Russia, who arrived at Leith in 1896 and travelled on by train.

The Queen recognized that by removing herself so far from London she made the conduct of government more difficult. Her part in that was by no means wholly formal; she kept up continuous discussions with her ministers on matters of high policy. Here she was aided by the *telegraph, which allowed messages to be despatched and received not only at Osborne and Balmoral but also at stations on the way. She worked hard to maintain the flow of political communication. In 1894—she was then 75—her train had to be held at Carlisle until 12.30 a.m. to allow her to complete her day's work.

King Edward VII made changes in his travelling arrangements, from 1901 onwards. He liked higher speeds than his mother, going from London to Devon and back at an average of 52 mph in 1902; next year his son (later George V) went from London to Plymouth at 63 mph. He dispensed with a pilot on many of his journeys, and he frequently used motor cars over short distances. To meet his tastes and requirements the LNWR and *London Brighton & South Coast Railway built impressive new royal trains.

This expensive travelling was not made free of charge. The bills that the companies presented to the royal household have yet to be investigated. The normal basis became the charge made to anyone hiring a *special train, with additions in respect of the pilot engine and some exclusive services. Detailed figures survive of the LNWR's charges made to Edward VII in 1904–9, giving the numbers of passengers to be paid for, including each dog.

During the two world wars these trains came to serve another purpose. As George V and George VI moved about the country they afforded reasonable security from air attack, and on long journeys were frequently placed in quiet sidings, for stops overnight.

Although today most of royalty's travelling is made by road or air, a royal train is still sometimes called for, and in 1985 BR provided a handsomely refurbished one for Queen Elizabeth II. JS

C. H. Ellis, *The Royal Trains* (1975); P. Kingston, *Royal Trains* (1985); G. P. Neele, *Railway Reminiscences* (1904), chs 16–18; LNWR charges, 1904–9: PRO RAIL 410/1302. A number of the royal saloons are at the NRM.

rule-book; rules and regulations, see BYE-LAWS, ORDERS, RULES, AND REGULATIONS.

rule of the road: 'the fixed custom which regulates the side to be taken by vehicles . . . in progressing or passing each other' (*Oxford English Dictionary*, first citation, 1871). Practice on roads was variable until codified by the Highways Act, 1835, which provided for drivers to keep to the left, in general. The *Liverpool & Manchester Railway, opened as a double line throughout in 1830, adopted left-hand running (an Ackermann aquatint showing right-hand running on Chat Moss is due to a reversed impression or artist's licence), and this became the rule on railways in Britain and those countries where British engineers inaugurated the systems. It was laid down in the bye-laws govern-

ing a number of companies. A few with right-hand running were the *Newcastle & Carlisle Railway until 1863–4; the *Clarence and West Hartlepool Railways, Co. Durham, until after 1863; the Manchester & Bolton until 1846; and the *Taff Vale for a short time after 1845. The *London & Greenwich was an exceptional case, running right-handed from 1850 until 1901, to minimize 'fouling' movements at North Kent Junction with the *South Eastern Railway. The *London Underground tube railways crossed over to right-hand running at some places so as to reduce the sharpness of curves (White City–Shepherd's Bush and Bank–London Bridge) or to give cross-platform interchange (Euston and King's Cross, *Victoria Line). On long sections of single line, non-stopping trains sometimes used the straight track at passing stations or loops where a stopping train had 'gone inside', either to the left or the right. RMR

'The Rule of the Road', *RM*, 80 (1937), 85; J. S. Maclean, *The Newcastle & Carlisle Railway* (1948); R. H. G. Thomas, *London's First Railway* (1972).

ruling gradient: the steepest gradient on any section of line, which determines the minimum power required for handling a train over it. Thus the ruling gradient between *Crewe and *Carlisle is the 1 in 75 of the last four miles of the northward climb to Shap. JS

running powers. These were powers given to one railway company to run its trains, hauled by its own locomotives, over the lines of another. They might be established by agreement between the companies concerned or imposed compulsorily, by special provisions in an Act of Parliament.

The power to make such arrangements was put beyond doubt by the Railways Clauses Act (1845), sect. 87, conditional on the payment of 'such tolls and under such conditions and restrictions as may be mutually agreed upon' by the companies concerned.

The device was obviously cumbersome, demanding much paperwork, that would have been unnecessary if the line in question had been controlled by one company alone. It might, however, avoid the need to construct a second one, superfluous otherwise, and it was particularly welcome to companies seeking to enter large towns, where the price of land was high. The arrangement by which the *Manchester & Leeds Railway reached *Leeds by running powers over the *North Midland in 1840 is an example, and it never caused any serious trouble. On the other hand, when in 1837–9 the *South Eastern Railway decided to abandon its first route from London to Dover, with much tunnelling, by accepting another, lengthier one, which involved running powers over the London & Brighton's line (SEE LONDON BRIGHTON & SOUTH COAST RAILWAY) as far as Redhill, it laid the foundation of innumerable angry disputes between the companies, only partly relieved by the building of the SER's very expensive direct line to Tonbridge in 1868.

The smooth working of these arrangements might depend on the urgency of the companies' need for them in each particular instance, and on the good sense and temper of the railway officers responsible. Necessity enforced collaboration between companies that were bitter enemies elsewhere. The *North British Railway had to enter *Aberdeen and *Carlisle by means of running powers over the hated *Caledonian. The *Midland Railway entered *Birmingham in a similar way, though peacefully, over the lines of the *London & North Western. The Isle of Wight Central Railway (see ISLE OF WIGHT RAILWAYS) could not have offered a service between Newport and Ryde except by running powers for 2 miles over other companies' lines. The *London & South Western gained its own terminus at *Plymouth in 1890 over the *Great Western from Devonport Junction to Friary Junction (2½ miles)—an arrangement written into the Plymouth Devonport & South Western Junction Railway's Act of 1882.

An agreement might be made by two or more companies to provide or work a line jointly (see JOINT RAILWAYS). In some cases, when it could be made acceptable, a simpler device was adopted: an *agreement for the leasing of the smaller company by the larger one, a procedure also sanctioned by the Clauses Act of 1845, sects. 112–13. Or they could be joined together by a complete *amalgamation. For most of the foregoing purposes, however, the concession of running powers continued to be preferred.

The general public was seldom aware of this contrivance of the railways: perhaps only once, indeed, in 1895, when it became momentarily conspicuous in the second series of *races to Scotland. The competing *East and *West Coast companies ran trains from London to Aberdeen over widely separate routes as far as Kinnaber Junction, just north of Montrose, where the East Coast (NBR) route continued to Aberdeen by means of running powers over the West Coast (CR) line. Both trains had left London at 8 p.m., and whichever train reached Kinnaber first had won the race. At the climax on 21 August the West Coast train reached Kinnaber at 4.16 a.m., the East Coast train at 4.17 a.m.

The quantity and extent of running powers were extraordinary. There were some 800 in force in 1914, covering all traffic or, in some instances, certain kinds only; and over 300 more were in existence, but not then exercised. This very complex organization was essential to the working of the multi-company railway system in Britain.

Running powers were maintained by the *Big Four companies after they were established in 1923: at Aberdeen and Carlisle, for example, and on the approaches to *Manchester and *Peterborough. But not many of them were now left, and those were worked without any overt disagreement. All of them ended with *nationalization.   JS

Railway Clearing House Junction Diagrams (1915 edn., reprinted 1969); O. S. Nock, *Railway Race to the North* [1958].

Russell, Samuel, artist. He depicted scenes on the *North Midland and *Chester & Holyhead Railways, which were lithographed.

The first series were probably issued as a set; but if they were no copy of it survives in Britain, though there is one (apparently complete) in Harvard University Library. Most of his prints showed stations, and they are important as almost the only known pictures of these greatly admired buildings, designed by Francis *Thompson. Others show railway scenes of a different kind: the splendid masonry of the long cutting at Belper, and the elaborate one of Bull's Bridge, where the railway is crossed by the Cromford Canal, along which a sailing boat is moving.

Russell also portrayed (at the same time as George *Hawkins) the construction of the *Britannia Bridge in 1848–9. His pictures include a carefully observed view of the building of one of the tubes on the shore of the Menai Strait.   JS

Ryde, Edward, see SURVEYORS.

S

Sacré, Charles Reboul (1831–89), engineer. Of Huguenot origin, he was articled to Archibald Sturrock of the *Great Northern Railway, and put in charge of its *Peterborough works at the age of 28. The following year he was appointed engineer and superintendent of the locomotive and stores departments of the Manchester Sheffield & Lincolnshire Railway (see GREAT CENTRAL).

His responsibilities were extraordinarily wide, embracing *civil engineering, *canals, *shipping, *carriages and *wagons, *works, and docks (see PORTS) as well as locomotive design and manufacture.

Sacré built strong, long-lived locomotives, but was conservative in his approach, declaring his opposition to bogie carriages and clinging to the single-driver locomotive when four-coupled designs had proved their worth. Yet he was forward-looking, using steel for switches and crossings (see TRACK) in 1863 and equipping Gorton Works to manufacture steel rails in 1886. He experimented with locomotive feed-water heaters in 1871, and with Sturrock's steam *tenders on locomotives for heavy coal trains.

Sacré was popular with his men and proved an effective negotiator with staff. He retired in 1886.   AD
Dow, ii.

safety. From an early stage in the development of Britain's railways it has been recognized that safety is a fundamental issue in their design, construction, and operation. The safety of the public, on and off the railway, and of employees soon became paramount in new works, developments, day-to-day operations, and emergencies. As far as possible two simple principles have prevailed: if something cannot be done safely it should not be done; and equipment and systems should be designed to fail safe.

The public in Britain, perhaps more so than elsewhere in the world, have demanded very high standards in railway safety, expecting effectively an accident-free system, yet have apparently accepted a certain number of *accidents as almost a fact of life in other areas, as, for example, on today's roads. Railways have therefore been subject to much legislation (see PARLIAMENT AND LEGISLATION) regulating their activities and setting safety standards. While the pursuit of safety cannot be criticized, it has to be balanced with the risk of pricing rail transport out of the market, causing users to transfer to less safe modes. Levels of concern could be understood in the early days, when trains were so much larger and faster than anything else and the means of stopping them were poor, but it has continued to the present day. For example, Britain is one of the few countries in the world where its railways are compelled to be completely *fenced.

The single greatest force in railway safety has been the Railway Inspectorate (see INSPECTORS, GOVERNMENT). Set up under an Act of 1840, the Inspecting Officers were successively part of the Board of *Trade, the Ministry of *Transport (1919), and the Health and Safety Executive (1989). Curiously, the inspectorate was never given comprehensive powers and the legislative framework was patchy. Much of what was gained was accomplished by a combination of tact, diplomacy, and persistence. The inspectorate's single greatest achievement was the *Regulation of Railways Act, 1889, a slim document that made compulsory the adoption of interlocking (see SIGNALLING) and the *block system on passenger lines, and continuous *brakes on passenger trains. These three things are still the corner-stones of railway safety today.

The railways are obliged to report to the railway inspectorate all accidents involving injury to the public or railway staff. There were Royal *Commissions into railway accidents in 1875 and 1877. Rules and regulations (see BYE-LAWS) govern railway employees' conduct and safe procedures for undertaking their duties. They are also specifically covered by legislation, for example the Railway Employment (Prevention of Accidents) Act, 1900, which resulted from the Royal Commission on Accidents to Railway Servants of 1899. Orders under this Act included rules for the protection of permanent way staff working on the line and for the lighting of sidings and stations. Brakes on both sides of new wagons were required by an order of 1907. Other orders of 1907 were made under the Factory & Workshop Act, 1901, to cover the safety of men working in connection with *shunting yards and train operation. Later, the Offices, Shops & Railway Premises Act, 1963, covered working conditions.   RDF
GR; H. R. Wilson, *The Safety of British Railways* (1909); L. T. C. Rolt, *Red for Danger* (1966).

St Pancras station, see LONDON STATIONS.

St Rollox, see GLASGOW; WORKS.

salaries and wages. The railways of Britain were a rapidly expanding industry in the middle years of the 19th century. Route miles increased from 1,500 in 1840 to 14,500 in 1875 while the number of employees (exclusive of clerks) rose from 2,000 in the census of 1841 to 157,000 in that of 1881. To attract workers it was generally necessary to offer somewhat higher rates of pay than were available in comparable occupations. This was particularly the case in the skilled grades such as engine *drivers, switchmen, pointsmen, and goods *guards. The classification of employment changed over the years. The *police who kept order among the *navvies who built the lines provided recruits for pointsmen and switchmen who, in turn, were the source of supply of *signalmen. Until World War I wages in urban areas were above those of the country districts.

Throughout the decades of the period before 1914—and even after—there was a traditional hierarchy of wages by different grades. Drivers headed the list with pay ranging from 4s. 8d. to 7s. 2d. per day in the 1840s, and from 5s. 0d. to 7s. 6d. per day in the 1870s. *Firemen were usually paid at about three fifths of the drivers' rate. Those who dealt with goods generally earned more pay than those who were concerned with looking after passengers. Thus, passenger *porters' average weekly earnings were fixed a shilling or so above agricultural labourers' wages, and varied from 15s. to 20s. in the 1840s but fell to 12s.–20s. in the 1870s; goods porters' rates were from 20s. to 21s. in the 1840s and 17s.–21s. in the 1870s. With pay ranging from 21s. to 30s. in the 1840s and from 21s. to 36s. in the 1870s, goods guards were among the better-paid railway workers. Passenger guards could not often match goods guards in pay, but because of their contact with passengers they wore a better-looking free *uniform and could receive tips. Shunters rose from the ranks of porters and were not recognized as a distinct grade of the service by the Board of *Trade until 1875. They had the most dangerous occupation on the railways (see SHUNTING) and deserved, by their hard work and the many risks they were called upon to take, every penny of their rise from an average weekly wage of between 18s. and 21s. in 1840, to between 20s. and 25s. in the 1870s. *Level crossing gate-keepers were among the lowest paid employees of the railway. Besides opening and closing the crossing gates they had sometimes to work the points and signals as well. They did, however, enjoy the benefit of the rent-free cottage by the gates; but the meaner companies gave them no other compensation.

Railway clerks were a very disparate group. Their pay and conditions of service varied between the companies, their location within the company network, and the tasks they performed. At an office on the *Great Western Railway in 1879 H. A. Simmons (*Earnest Struggles*, 1879) found the clerks 'out at elbows, looking miserably thin' and 'all standing to write' with 'bundles of papers before each enough to turn each poor fellow's heart sick'. These were certainly general clerks on the lower grade of pay of no more than £50 a year. Clerks-in-charge (of a station) sometimes occupied a company house for which they paid a less than economic rent. In the 1840s their pay varied between £50 and £150; this had changed to between £65 and £120 some 30 years later. Head office clerks' pay rose as companies grew bigger. A range of pay of £60–£150 in the 1840s had become £65–£300 in the later 1850s. *Stationmasters' pay varied enormously, depending on the importance of the rail centre where they were employed. The range of pay rates rose from £40–£100 in the 1840s, to £65–£200 in the 1870s.

A feature of the period 1880–1910 was the *amalgama-tion and consolidation of smaller companies. By 1911 fifteen large companies, many of them regional *monopolies, controlled 84 per cent of the total mileage. Accompanying this merger movement was a reduction in the number of distinct grades of employees. This is revealed in the results of a remarkable census of wages paid and hours and overtime worked in 1907 by men in the traffic grades, filling 136 printed pages and published by the Amalgamated Society of Railway Servants (see NATIONAL UNION OF RAILWAYMEN). It shows, however, that the old difference in rates of pay still survived, through the Victorian and Edwardian eras.

What also survived were the benefits of railway employment. Stationmasters, head clerks, and some signalmen and *platelayers, among others, lived in company houses for which they paid rent. But generally *housing was not a significant addition to the real wages of railway workers. Free uniforms did make a significant addition to real wages: for example, a goods guard employed by the *Great Northern Railway in the 1850s, who was issued free jacket and trousers, boots, cap, and greatcoat which would have cost him £4 1s. 2d. to buy, when he was earning 26s. a week. One other worthwhile benefit was the free travel-pass or *passes for the railway worker and his wife. It offered some relief from what in many cases would be the complete drudgery of railway work.

In World War I some 184,000 railwaymen, over 29 per cent of the work-force, joined the armed forces; 19,000 of them were killed. Some of their places in the railway industry were taken by *women. In 1914 there were 4,562 railway women and by 1919 these numbers had grown to 55,000. The unions' fear was that their presence would depress the rate of wages. In the course of the war the Railway Executive Committee conceded seven separate war bonus awards; when men were awarded a bonus of 5s. a week in September 1916 the REC allowed women only 3s. When its decision was challenged by the NUR the REC gave the explanation that women's labour was only three-fifths as productive as men's. When the NUR asked 'did this apply to women ticket collectors?' the REC gave no answer, but in the last war-time bonus, awarded in September 1918, both women and men received 5s. Prices rose more rapidly in World War I than they did in World War II and bonus awards were made retrospectively, so that the real value of wages in November 1918 was slightly below what it had been in August 1914.

Following the strikes of August–October 1919 new rates of wages were agreed between the government and the unions. Drivers were to be paid 72s. in the first year of their employment, rising after six years to 90s. Firemen's rates were 57s.–66s. in the tenth year. Both passenger guards and goods guards rose from 58s. to 68s. Parcel porters' wages were 53s.–63s., slightly less than the ticket collectors' and checkers' 54s.–64s., and much the same as the shunters' 53s.–64s. With a wage of 54s.–57s., platelayers had the lowest prospect of improvement, though porters started at the lower rate of 49s. with prospects of rising to 55s.

Under the Railways Act of 1921 (see GROUPING), charges fixed by the Railway Rates Tribunal (see FREIGHT TRAFFIC

RATES) were designed to secure for the four main-line companies their 'standard' revenue, based on the exceptionally good year 1913. Unfortunately they were unable to achieve this objective and this caused them to demand reductions of wages. A 2½ per cent reduction on all wages and salaries was agreed for 1928–9 since the cost of living fell sharply in the later 1920s. However, the companies' problems deepened in the depression of the early 1930s and there were further wage cuts in 1932–7.

During World War II the trade unions negotiated seven instalments of a war bonus, increasing rates of pay by over 60 per cent in 1939–45. This compared favourably with a rise of 46 per cent in other service industries. Thus, although it was the case that just before the war railway pay was less than that in comparable occupations outside the industry, in 1945 it compared favourably. Improved rates of pay and working conditions agreed with management in July 1945 raised Sunday duty rates of pay from 1½ to 1¾ the weekday rates; night duty was redefined as from 10 p.m. to 6 a.m. instead of 10 p.m. to 4 a.m.; holiday entitlement for traffic grades was raised from six to 12 days per year and for salaried staff from 12 to 15 days. But labour was then in short supply, with only 1½ million private cars and less than ½ million lorries on the roads. Railways were exceptionally busy.

Under the Transport Act, 1947, the railways were controlled by the *British Transport Commission, which had the duty to pay its way 'taking one year with another'. From 1948 to 1955 gross receipts exceeded working expenses, but from that time working deficits increased and there was a large deficit on capital account due to interest on monies borrowed for the Railway *Modernization Plan. The growth of working deficits was due in part to the easing of petrol rationing in 1950 to motorists, especially to lorry-owners, not paying the costs incurred by the road system, and to denationalization of British Road Services, the most profitable part of the BTC's assets, under the Transport Act of 1953. These background conditions made it extremely hard for the BTC, and its successors, to pay their way 'taking one year with another', and to pay wages similar to those in comparable occupations, for the greater part of the second half of the 20th century.

After prolonged negotiations through the established machinery in 1954–5 the NUR gave notice that its members would take strike action, whereupon the Minister of Labour and National Service appointed Sir John Cameron, QC, to enquire into the crisis of railway wages. The Cameron Committee report concluded that the argument of the BTC that its offer was fair and reasonable, but that it was not able to offer such wages as were desired because of the financial limits imposed under the Transport Act, 1947, was contradictory. The committee went on to add that: 'The nation has provided by statute that there shall be a nationalized system of railway transport. Having willed this end the nation must will the means.' Within a fortnight of the publication of the report the railways' chairman, Sir Brian *Robertson, with the authority of the Cabinet, negotiated wage increases to all grades from porters to engine drivers.

In the late 1950s and early 1960s the attention of the Ministry of Transport turned to the question of comparability. The unions were claiming that railway wages were below the levels paid in comparable industries. But what were the comparable industries and by how much had railway wages fallen behind? A committee of inquiry under Professor G. W. Guillebaud was appointed 'to conduct an investigation into the relativity of pay of salaried and conciliation [i.e. wages] staff in British Railways, with the pay of staff on other nationalised industries, public services and appropriate private undertakings'. The committee's report, published on 2 March 1960, pointed out that railway rates of pay were about 10 per cent behind those of comparable industries. Shortly afterwards pay increases were awarded, ranging from 8 to 10 per cent, and backdated to 4 January 1960.

Throughout these years there had been steady reductions in the numbers of staff. There were 339,000 persons employed by *British Rail in 1966 and only 182,188 in 1978, yet the number of passenger miles travelled over the same period of time rose from 18.6 million to 19.1 million.

These trends to increased productivity were given extra emphasis in the talks between unions and management at Penzance and Windsor in 1967–9. Under the Penzance Agreement of July 1968 a new grade of 'railman', incorporating the duties of 41 previous grades, was introduced. As old occupational barriers were swept away, the keynote word was 'flexibility'. Simultaneously it reduced BR's costs and offered the employees who remained—many redundancies were declared—slightly higher wages for greater responsibilities.

A decisive turning-point came with the thoroughly commercially minded Serpell Report of 1983 which in many ways ceased to regard the railways as an essential public utility. It provided a backdrop to the *privatization plans of the early 1990s. PSB

Amalgamated Society of Railway Servants, *Census of Wages, Hours of Labour, etc. Report* (1908); P. W. Kingsford, *Victorian Railwaymen, 1830–1870* (1970); P. S. Bagwell, *The Railwaymen* (1963–82); Gourvish, ch. 7.

Salisbury, Lord, see GREAT EASTERN RAILWAY.

salt traffic. From the late 1860s the railways became the principal carrier of crystalline salt for human consumption and, in larger quantities, for industry, sometimes in the form of brine. Previously, the output from the Cheshire salt mines had been principally transported by *canal. Rock salt was moved in open *wagons but, for domestic salt, distinctive covered wagons with pitched roofs were used.

One company, Salt Union Ltd, had 20 or so private *sidings in 1904, primarily located in the Northwich area of Cheshire. Salt deposits were worked by this and other companies at Haverton Hill and Port Clarence in Co. Durham, and at Stoke Prior, near Droitwich. Another location was Middlewich, associated with Murgatroyd Salt Co.

Opened in 1867 by the *Cheshire Lines Committee, two branch lines totalling four miles were dedicated to serving the works and mines in the Northwich area, and were known as the Salt Branches. Another branch was constructed by the CLC in 1870, linking Greenbank and Winnington, and later fed salt products to the major chemical works operated by Brunner Mond, later ICI Ltd. By the 1970s the remaining rail movements were in trainloads only, such as between Cheshire and the Baglan Bay chemical works in South Wales. MLH

Cheshire Libraries and Museums, *Transport in the Salt Industry* (n.d.); R. P. Griffiths, *The Cheshire Lines Railway* (1947).

sanitation. After the Romans left Britain, it was not until the 1870s that public conveniences again began to become common. Before then, railway stations were virtually the only public places providing them. From the early 1840s most stations had separate ladies' and gentlemen's lavatories, although as late as 1894 lady passengers at Weston, Lincolnshire, had to be shown into a station house bedroom. Large stations had generous provision, often incorporating bathrooms and hairdressing saloons. Nowadays, as all trains have lavatories, only the larger stations generally still have public toilets.

Railway outdoor employees were less well served; in yards and out on the line earth closets or buckets were often the only provisions while some permanent way cabins had nothing. Signal boxes had an outside lavatory, or one in the interlocking room.

Queen Victoria's saloon on the *Great Western Railway, and a vehicle on the *South Eastern, had the first train lavatory in 1848–50: a washbasin, with a chamber pot in a cupboard underneath. In the 1860s lavatories were provided in family saloons, and in sleeping cars from the 1870s, but it was only when corridor coaches appeared in the late 1880s that lavatories started to become general. Elaborate instructions were issued for the provision of paper, soap, and towels; the *North Eastern Railway's ran to 32 pages.

Water closets were flushed directly on to the track from large tanks in the roof, relying on the speed of the train to atomize solid waste. In 1984 the Department of *Transport stipulated that in future controlled-emission toilets must be fitted, requiring retention tanks. After rejecting aircraft-type chemical toilets, the pressure-sluice system was adopted, which uses less water and allows flexible layout design. The latest innovation is the vacuum toilet, which requires even less water. GJB

C. Hamilton Ellis, *Railway Carriages in the British Isles, 1830–1914* (1965); 'Train Toilets', *Modern Railways*, 51, 554 (Nov. 1994), 682; Weston: PRO RAIL 487/97; NER: *Equipment of Train Lavatories* (1912).

Saunders, Charles Alexander (1795–1864), manager. Educated at Winchester, he became a government clerk but left that service for commercial business. He was appointed secretary to the London committee of the *Great Western Railway in 1833 and took a large share in its promotion, canvassing throughout the territory it was designed to serve. In 1840 he became the chief administrator of the whole company, as 'secretary and general superintendent'. A quiet, immensely hard-working man, he was always directly—not just formally—the executive officer of the board, which kept a very firm hold on the management of the company. Having no taste for self-advertisement, he was little known to the general public, but he shone out as a witness before parliamentary committees. On his death Sir Daniel *Gooch, then chairman, observed that he 'undoubtedly knew more of the temper of Parliament . . . than any railwayman in the country'.

In defending the company's actions he necessarily made enemies. Some Bristol proprietors never forgave what they believed to be his responsibility for the GWR's northern thrust to *Birmingham and Birkenhead. In truth he was himself uneasy about that policy, but was obliged to implement the board's decisions.

When on his retirement, through ill health, in 1863 the directors proposed to reward his services with a *pension (very unusual then), his critics tried to stop them from doing so at a shareholders' meeting, but they were defeated by a large majority. No railwayman ever earned a specially voted pension more fully. JS

MacDermot, esp. i, 4, 77, 236–71; ii, 14.

Savin, Thomas (1826–84), promoter. He was a partner in a drapery business at Oswestry, and mayor of the town in 1863.

He and David *Davies entered into a partnership to build the Llanidloes & Newtown Railway in 1855, Davies already being an established *contractor and Savin knowing nothing of that work, though he soon began purchasing stone quarries. Benjamin *Piercy was its engineer.

The principal undertaking that these men engaged in together was the mountainous Newtown & Machynlleth Railway, begun in 1858. But in 1860, while it was under construction, Savin and Davies quarrelled. Savin was launching a grandiose scheme for an Aberystwyth & Welsh Coast Railway, to continue the NMR to Aberystwyth and build a long northward branch skirting Cardigan Bay to Pwllheli, together with *hotels to assist the establishment of a new holiday district (see CAMBRIAN RAILWAYS). The plan showed Savin's imaginative grasp of potentials in railway development, but also his disregard of financial realities, of which Davies had a very firm grasp indeed; and the break between the two men was final. The line was authorized in 1863. At the beginning of 1866 Savin went bankrupt, and he played no further important part in railway work thereafter. JS

CMCR, i.

Saxby and Farmer, see SIGNALLING EQUIPMENT MANUFACTURE.

Scholes, John H. (1914–77), museum curator. Born in Lancashire, he first became a museum curator at Southport in 1936, then curator, Castle Museum, *York, where he was mainly responsible for establishing its reputation and its famous 18th-century street.

His appointment by the *British Transport Commission in 1951 as Curator of Historical Relics was notable, reflecting the enlightened attitude of the Commission towards preservation of relics and records. It also endorsed the view that there was a need for a London collection of relics, as distinct from those in the Railway *Museum, York (opened in 1927). The choice of Scholes, with a proven museum record, from outside the railway industry, was imaginative and contrasted with the usual practice in Europe. He achieved much by constructive communication within the railway, and by pioneering liaison with the then embryonic private railway *preservation movement from which he received much support.

His endeavours culminated in the opening of the British Museum of Transport, Clapham, London, in 1961–3. He was involved in preliminary planning for the new *National Railway Museum, York (opened in 1975) but was unable to take up a senior position there due to ill health, retiring in 1974.   JAC

Railway Gazette (29 June and 14 Sept. 1951), 732 and 300–1; W. O. Skeat, 'John Scholes: An Appreciation', RM, 123 (1977), 452.

Scotland. The railways of Scotland grew out of the network of wagonways established to move coal in the 18th century. It was across one of these that the Highland army advanced in 1745 during the rout of General Cope at the battle of Prestonpans. Steam, as opposed to horse haulage, was first introduced in Scotland on the *Kilmarnock & Troon Railway in 1817 and soon a number of mineral lines were following suit. The Garnkirk & Glasgow, which was built to the so-called 'Scotch *Gauge' of 4 ft 6 in, has some claim to the title of the first proper railway in Scotland: from 1831 it offered a range of passenger and freight services worked by steam power, albeit over a relatively short distance. Other lines quickly followed, particularly in Lanarkshire, then a rapidly expanding centre of coal and iron production. The horse-drawn *Edinburgh & Dalkeith had started passenger services in 1832 and in the first year of operation carried no fewer than 150,000 people. Advocates of railways such as Charles Maclaren, editor of the *Scotsman*, sensed the possibilities of passenger traffic between centres of population: the Forth & Clyde *Canal in 1836 was already carrying an appreciable traffic of some 200,000 passengers a year between *Edinburgh and *Glasgow.

Another centre of railway experiment, even though isolated from developments elsewhere, was *Dundee, which had its own network of local lines. But generally speaking, Scotland lagged behind England in the 1830s: not until 1838 was the much-needed *Edinburgh & Glasgow Railway authorized, and some quite feasible projects put before Parliament, such as the Glasgow & Hamilton in 1842, came to nothing. But when the EGR did finally open in 1842, the returns were well up to expectation: 200,000 passengers in the first year of operation and over a million by 1846. The rail network was pushed north to *Aberdeen by 1850, from *Perth to *Inverness in 1863, and south across the border by three routes: via Dumfries, Carstairs, and Berwick in 1846–50. A fourth, the Waverley route via Hawick, re-

mained halted there as its southern terminus until 1862 when the final stretch to *Carlisle was opened; whether it took the best route through the southern Borders is open to question, going via Liddesdale rather than Langholm which would have generated much more traffic.

The second half of the 19th century saw the Scottish railway network continue to expand, with significant routes being added much later than was the case south of the border. The *Highland Railway pushed north from Inverness to Wick and Thurso (1874), an undertaking backed financially by the Duke of *Sutherland. Nor was the north-west neglected: the Skye line reached Strome Ferry in 1880, the same year that saw the completion of the *Callander & Oban Railway, the latter place a rising tourist resort, dubbed the Charing Cross of the Highlands. The last of the great schemes was the West Highland Railway (see NORTH BRITISH RAILWAY) with an extension to Mallaig opened in 1901, thanks in part to a Treasury *subsidy.

By 1900 no centre of any significance in mainland Scotland was without its railway service. Some indeed, thanks to *competition between companies, had an over-provision: Peebles and Banff, for example, were provided with competing stations. There were also the suburban services of Glasgow, Edinburgh, and Aberdeen, and the *Light Railways Act of 1896 induced the construction of a number of lines such as that from Fountainhall Junction to Lauder, The Mound to Dornoch, Fraserburgh to St Combs, and, perhaps the least commercially viable of them all, the Invergarry & Fort Augustus, which was opened in 1903 and on which regular passenger services were suspended for two years. There was also a myriad of *industrial and construction lines. One of these was the Edinburgh Waterworks Railway from Broughton, built to facilitate the construction of the new reservoir and waterworks at Talla, and dismantled in the 1920s. Curiously, it used granite from Italy in its bridge across the Tweed.

*Construction costs generally were higher in Scotland than elsewhere: the terrain required more viaducts, inclines, and *bridges, to say nothing of *landowners who insisted upon sunken routes as at Kippenross on the *Scottish Central south of Dunblane. An early example of a formidable engineering undertaking was the 36-arch viaduct over the River Almond on the EGR. The challenges called forth some remarkable engineering responses; the contractor Robert *McAlpine ('Concrete Bob') pioneered the extensive use of mass *concrete for the Glenfinnan Viaduct and bridges on the Mallaig extension. The successful second bridging of the Tay (1887) and the *Forth (1890) were major achievements; against them, of course, must be set the disaster of the first Tay Bridge (see BRIDGES AND VIADUCTS).

At times, nature imposed severe restrictions on the operation of railways in Scotland; some winters brought heavy *snow which paralysed operations, as in 1894–5 when every Highland Railway line except one was closed. Another hazard was periodic *flooding which damaged bridges and embankments; the August 1948 floods swept away every main-line bridge in the Ayton and Grantshouse area on the *East Coast main line. By contrast, blown sand caused endless trouble on the Burghead branch of the Morayshire company. Falling boulders were a serious hazard on the Callander & Oban, something which prompted Anderson's 'piano-wires': a screen of wires connected to semaphore *signals to warn drivers of rock falls. And if nature did not pose enough difficulties, another problem, not unique to Scotland but at its worst there, was the vexed question of *Sunday services, a debate which rumbled on for many decades of the 19th century.

The railways as carriers were of immense significance to the Scottish economy prior to 1914 in many ways: in the movement of *perishable goods, such as *fish and *meat from Aberdeen and the north-east to the south, and *milk from country areas to the cities. Grain was moved to distilleries and whisky taken from them. The movement of *coal from pithead to market was always a major consideration to the railways. The Midlothian coalfield alone sent by the *North British Railway 1.3 million tons in 1902, and 3.2 million tons in 1909. Much of the Scottish coal industry's output went for export via the *ports of Ardrossan, Ayr, Burntisland, Methil, Bo'ness, and Grangemouth. The manufacture of engines and rolling stock provided employment for both private builders (Neilson, and Dübs of Glasgow, for example) and for company *works such as those at Glasgow and Inverurie. The numbers were substantial: the NBR alone, according to a company investigation in 1905, had some 900 engines and 3,700 carriages.

While business travellers and goods traffic were the staple of the Lowland lines, the role of tourist traffic was particularly important for Highland and coastal lines (see TOURISM). Additional staff had to be taken on each summer. North Berwick, a popular resort for professional Edinburgh, was allowed in the 1890s three additional summer appointments: a *guard, a *porter, and a parcel-deliverer. The decline after 1900 in the receipts from first-class summer traffic caused great anxiety. A correspondent to the *Railway Magazine* in 1904 observed that the more 'intensive use of motor cars by visitors from the south' was making serious inroads into the receipts of the Highland Railway from first-class fares. Significantly, the *Caledonian and the NBR found themselves prompted in 1909 by the newly formed Scottish Shareholders Association into a pooling *agreement, designed not just to share receipts but to end competitive capital expenditure and achieve the most economical way of working traffic. Scottish railway companies did their best to keep a grip on the tourist business; operating steamers on the Clyde under a pooling agreement reached in 1909 after years of bitter competition, running motor-*buses, and even providing special carriages to carry *bicycles, an innovation of the *Great North of Scotland Railway in 1902.

In 1914 the Scottish railway system was under the control of five companies. The demands of World War I tested them all, but none more so than the Highland. Short of staff, and with much of its mileage single-track, it had to cope with a vastly increased traffic, naval and military—3,500 special trains in 1918 alone (see WAR). Other companies also had their problems: the Quintinshill disaster

at Gretna in 1915 left 227 dead, some of whom were never identified (see ACCIDENTS). The war left the NBR, in John Thomas's word, 'devitalised': short of engines and coal, and with terrible arrears of maintenance. After fierce argument to secure better terms it obtained belated compensation from the government, and undertook a programme of locomotive building that gradually surmounted the difficulties. Prestige trains which had been suspended during the war reappeared; *excursions were arranged.

The 1923 *Grouping saw the end of the separate identity of the Scottish companies, though not of their traditions. The inter-war years were difficult times, particularly during the worst years of depression when freight traffic slumped, and expensively created port facilities lay idle. The level of coal exports from Methil, in Fife, which the NBR had purchased in 1889, fell by over 40 per cent between 1907 and 1936. Passenger and freight services were suspended or cut back in many localities, some never to be resumed, as, for example, at Gullane, which lost its passenger service in 1932. Suburban services were also under increasing pressure from road competition: Aberdeen was to lose its 'subbies' in 1937. But the post-Grouping railways in Scotland did not merely submit to what some saw as inevitable, the supremacy of *road transport. They provided what have been described as some of the finest and cheapest long-distance excursions available in Britain. On a Sunday trips were run from Glasgow and Edinburgh to places quite far afield, and arrangements were made for weekend excursions from London to Staffa and Iona, both destinations long familiar to southern visitors.

After World War II, the Scottish railways enjoyed a resurgence in both freight and passenger traffic. But the improvement of roads, and the increased efficiency of road transport, ate into their business. In August 1959, four special trains were required to forward 30,000 sheep and lambs from Thurso market to Inverness and onward destinations, and as late as 1960 weekly workings of cattle trains to Gorgie market in Edinburgh were still in operation. But the withering of freight business when it came was sudden and awful, catching *British Railways on the hop. It had invested heavily in new freight *marshalling yards, as at Millerhill near Edinburgh, which was no sooner opened than redundant. Progressively the roads took over most of what traffic there was, and the railways were left with some movement of bulk commodities such as *cement, *oil, and *timber; they lost almost everything else during the 1970s and 1980s, including such long-time staples as the distillery traffic in whisky, malt, and grain, the movement of *parcels, and the Royal Ordnance Factory business which used to be significant for centres such as Stirling. Passenger traffic, too, was contracting; the longer-distance business traveller went by air to London. Closures were inevitable, yet the cuts when they came were deep. Some were of minor lines that had seen but a weekly coal train. Others were not: the closure of the Waverley route in 1969, despite furious opposition, was perhaps the most substantial casualty. The timing was unfortunate in many instances; the Aberdeen–Peterhead line closed finally to freight in 1970 just when it seemed

North Sea oil would justify its continuing operation. But it always proved easier to shut a line than to reopen it, though the West Highland and the Far North lines somehow survived in the teeth of economic reality. The formation of ScotRail in 1984 did signal a surge of enterprise in marketing and operations and there has been, of late, some *reopening of several lines and stations; Macmerry on the East Coast main line and Camelon at Falkirk, to name but two. Serious talks have even taken place about the reopening of some lines such as Stirling to Alloa.   AJD

Robertson; W. M. Acworth, *The Railways of Scotland* (1890); O. S. Nock, *Scottish Railways* (1960); *Reg. Hist.*, vi and xv.

ScotRail, see BRITISH RAILWAYS; SCOTLAND.

Scott, Sir George Gilbert, see LONDON STATIONS (ST PANCRAS).

Scotter, Sir Charles (1835–1910), manager and chairman; appointed goods clerk, Manchester Sheffield & Lincolnshire Railway (see GREAT CENTRAL) in 1853; passenger superintendent, 1860; goods manager, 1873; general manager, *London & South Western Railway, 1885.

That company was now concentrating its attention mainly on Hampshire, seeking to aid *Bournemouth to rival Torquay as a seaside resort. In 1883–8 it built a new direct line approaching Bournemouth from the east, which led to a great improvement in the London–Bournemouth service.

The LSWR faced great difficulties at *Southampton, and Scotter, coming to them afresh, set himself to solve them. The company had long been a greedy monopolist there, rendering poor service. The Southampton Docks Company was inadequate to its task. Scotter seized the opportunity at once. Having made himself personally acceptable in the town (as no previous LSWR general manager had been), he persuaded his directors to offer to purchase the docks, and to invest substantially in their development. This proposal was authorized in 1892, and acted on promptly. The port now grew to become the successful rival of *Liverpool and *Glasgow in the transatlantic passenger trade.

Scotter had a natural gift of communication, and he used it with the LSWR's men no less than with its customers. He handled negotiations with most uncommon skill. He was knighted in 1895. On his retirement then he became a director of the LSWR, and its chairman 1904–10.   JS

Williams.

Scottish Central Railway. Running from Larbert and Stirling to *Perth, the SCR was a key railway in the developing Scottish network, offering the first through link between central Scotland and the north. It was authorized in 1845, with *Locke and Errington as engineers, and a construction contract was signed with Thomas *Brassey: amongst its principal subscribers in 1844 was the railway protagonist John Campbell, second Marquess of Breadalbane, and owner of the most extensive estates in Scotland after the Duke of *Sutherland. The route presented challenges: there were several bridges to construct, including one across the *Forth; a tunnel at Kippenross insisted upon by the local laird so as not to spoil the view from his house; a stiff climb

out of Bridge of Allan; and a 1,200-yd long tunnel on the southern entrance to Perth at Moncrieff. Over 1,800 men were employed at one time on the line's construction.

But once the line was opened in 1848, it proved an immediate success. Not just the commercial and passenger traffic from *Glasgow and the west to the north was attracted. Many passengers from *Edinburgh took the 69-mile journey to Perth via the SCR rather than the shorter Edinburgh & Northern route (see EDINBURGH PERTH & DUNDEE RAILWAY), which required a *ferry crossing to Burntisland. Not surprisingly, the SCR was highly profitable, paying the second highest dividends in Scotland, of 5½–7 per cent. Its summer traffic was particularly heavy as tourists passed north; traffic returns for the early 1860s show a doubling of passengers during July and August. Goods traffic was also buoyant, the chairman reporting a 16 per cent increase in 1863. *Excursion trains were significant, too: one for *Aberdeen in June 1850 left Larbert at 5.30 a.m. and Stirling 24 minutes later requiring 49 coaches, so that the train had to be divided into two. By 1863 the company's works at Perth were maintaining 78 engines, 288 passenger coaches, and over 1,300 goods vehicles.

Shortly before its amalgamation with the *Caledonian Railway in 1865, the SCR had taken over the Crieff Junction Railway, which joined the main SCR line between Blackford and Auchterarder at what came to be named Gleneagles station. The SCR had a number of branches: to Perth Harbour, Denny, and in 1865 to Plean where new coal pits were being sunk. The amalgamation of the CR and the SCR, and the merger with the Scottish North-Eastern, allowed a complete Caledonian route through Strathmore to Aberdeen.   AJD

Reg. Hist., xv, ch. 2.

Sealink. With *nationalization, the fleets of ships of the *Big Four companies, and the *ports associated with them, passed to the *British Railways' Regions although limited functions were centralized. Little changed until 1968 when all the Regional activities were transferred to the BR Shipping and International Services Division.

With the launching of the BR corporate identity, a new style was evolved for the painting and design of the shipping fleet. With its continental partners, the Shipping and International Services Division owned the largest fleet of its kind in European waters and, to emphasize its identity, the brand name Sealink was used from 1970, being applied to the ships, and in marketing the services. By now, Sealink had moved from a shipping activity which was an adjunct to railways, to a major ferry-operator with multi-purpose ships primarily catering for accompanied car and roll on-roll off lorry traffic.

Under the *privatization policies of the Conservative governments from 1979, Sealink at first was organized as a quasi-independent division of BR then, as a subsidiary company, it was prepared for sale as Sealink UK Ltd. Sold in 1984 to British Ferries Ltd, a subsidiary of Sea Containers Ltd, its principal operations were later resold to Stena Line, and in 1996 trades as Stena Sealink.   MLH

season tickets. Season or contract tickets offer regular travellers between two stations unlimited travel in either direction for a fixed period, usually a week or any consecutive seven days, a month, quarter (3 months), or year.

The *Stockton & Darlington Railway encouraged regular travellers by offering season tickets in the 1830s, sometimes describing them as 'free tickets', indicating freedom of use and not the price.

For many years season tickets were offered only to first- and second-class passengers. Third-class passengers had to purchase their tickets daily. Figures published by *London Transport in 1928 showed that annual sales of monthly and quarterly tickets were 865,066, issued at a total cost of £652,117. Weekly tickets were introduced at this time and quickly proved popular with the travelling public, who were saved the trouble of queueing to buy a ticket each day, without the capital outlay of a monthly season.

From the 1840s some railways had encouraged building development by offering season tickets to house-buyers, and between the world wars railways serving the London hinterland encouraged city workers to live further out from the central area. The *Metropolitan Railway's subsidiary estates company, for instance, advertised houses for sale with the incentive of season tickets (see METRO-LAND).

Firms spending large sums on freight traffic could apply for special traders' season tickets, presented by the railway in leather or cloth-bound wallets and taken up as first class for management or second or third class for staff. Before the bulk transport of cars, delivery drivers were given season tickets covering a wide area to enable them to return to their base. An all-country first-class annual ticket cost £600 in 1971 (£400 for second class); in 1995, £360 would only buy a first-class weekly All-Line Rover (£220 standard).

Season or contract Runabout and Rover tickets have given leisure travellers unlimited travel within specific holiday areas. A week's travel by train in the Isle of Wight cost 7s. 6d. before World War II; in 1995 a Cornish Rover ticket cost £31 for a similar period.

Season ticket prices have in recent years tended to rise more steeply than individual fares. Whilst any railway is grateful for a regular income from a daily flow of passengers, *commuters are not operationally cost-effective, as it is necessary to maintain sufficient coaching stock and track facilities to handle the peak-hour load which are not required for the greater part of the day.

See also FARES; TICKETS; PASSES AND PRIVILEGE TICKETS; COMMUTING. MGDF
G. Fairchild and P. Wootton, *Railway and Tramway Tickets* (1987), 37–42; M. I. Bray, *Railway Tickets, Timetables and Handbills* (1986), 175–9; D. G. Geldard, 'Tickets and Fares on the Stockton & Darlington Railway', *Jnl. Transport Ticket Society*, 144 (1975), 443–4; J. P. Thomas, *Handling London's Underground Traffic* (1928), 12.

Sekon, George Augustus (1867–1948), writer. His real name was Nokes. A land agent and surveyor (and later a partner in his firm), he wrote in his spare time for the *Railway Herald*. He published short histories of the *South Eastern, and *London & South Western Railways in 1895–6 and

a more substantial one of the *Great Western in 1898. When the *Railway Magazine* was launched in 1897 he became its editor. He drew in some good contributors, notable among them the New Zealander Charles *Rous-Marten. His own writing was brisk, forceful, and always opinionated (from the railways' point of view alone). He egged every company on, for example, to appeal against increased rating assessments (see GOVERNMENT, RAILWAYS AND LOCAL), irrespective of the reasons for raising them. He left the *Magazine* in 1910, having quarrelled with its proprietors, and immediately started up another (much inferior to it), the *Railway and Travel Monthly*, which lasted until 1922.

He also edited the *Railway Year Book*, first published in 1898, an annual that remains a useful work of reference. His last book is also his best: *Locomotion in Victorian London* (1938), an admirable survey of its very broad subject. JS
RM, 94 (1948), 145; *Engineer*, 185 (1948), 199.

Selbie, Robert Hope (1868–1930), general manager, born at Salford, Lancashire. He joined the *Lancashire & Yorkshire Railway in 1883 and worked in various head office posts, from 1899 as assistant to the chief traffic manager.

In 1903 he was appointed secretary of the *Metropolitan Railway (which ever since the days of Edward *Watkin had personal links with *Manchester), and general manager in 1908. His energy, good sense, and commercial acumen pulled the company round. Heavy investment in *electrification had not yet yielded adequate new receipts, and it was in a depressed state. He expanded the outer suburban services to Harrow and beyond, with quadrupling of the line and new rolling stock. He initiated station improvements and skilful publicity, including the *Metro-land campaign in 1915. From 1919 Metropolitan Railway Country Estates Ltd undertook building development close to stations. Ordinary dividends rose from ½ per cent in 1907 to 3½ per cent in the late 1920s. In 1922 Selbie became a director as well as general manager, at a salary of £7,000 a year. He was a founder member of the *Chartered Institute of Transport (1920) and a forceful and straightforward speaker. He held that to stop capital spending was never the right response to hard times.

Selbie made several attempts to secure an agreed scheme for co-ordination of London's passenger transport while maintaining the Metropolitan's independence; but he did not live through the proceedings leading to the London Passenger Transport Act of 1933 (see LONDON UNDERGROUND RAILWAYS). RMR
DBB; HLT; A. A. Jackson, *London's Metropolitan Railway* (1986).

Settle & Carlisle Railway. Determined to provide a third route from London to Scotland, but denied *running powers from Ingleton to the *London & North Western Railway's Lancaster–Carlisle line, the *Midland Railway in 1866 obtained an Act to build a 72-mile line from Settle to Carlisle across some of the wildest and remotest terrain in England, supported by the *Lancashire & Yorkshire, *Glasgow & South Western, and *North British companies.

Severn Tunnel

Alarmed by the prospect of competition it would be unable to control, the LNWR hastily concluded an *agreement with the MR, whereat the latter sought to abandon the now unnecessary project. However, the LYR and NBR forced it to carry on, so with characteristic energy the Midland threw itself into construction under its engineer, J. S. *Crossley.

The line is the most spectacular in England, and was the most difficult ever built over such a distance, starting with a climb of 15 miles mostly at 1 in 100 to reach the 1,000-ft contour, above which it continued for another 15 miles before descending 48 miles to almost sea level at Carlisle; all achieved at the cost of 13 tunnels and 21 viaducts, four over 100 ft high. The estimated four years' construction extended to 6½, expenditure rose from £2.2 million to £3.8 million, and the severe working conditions caused a labour turnover of 73 per cent. The railway opened in 1875–6, the last of the 'heroic' lines in its concept and in its construction.

Unable to compete with the *West Coast and *East Coast routes from London in distance, the Midland vigorously promoted it by concentrating on superior standards of comfort in through trains to *Edinburgh and *Glasgow from London, *Liverpool, and *Manchester, these two over the LYR via Hellifield. Originating traffic was sparse. Connections with the *North Eastern Railway were made at Appleby, and by a branch from Garsdale to Hawes.

The long gradients made the line difficult to work, and in winter it was regularly blocked by snow. In the 1960s *BR began to run it down, and in 1970 closed all the stations except Settle and Appleby. The last remaining long-distance train ran in 1982, after which there were only two passenger trains a day, virtually no freight, and periodic diversions from the West Coast main line.

Meanwhile, BR's financial figures were being challenged, and an increasing body of the public opposed closure, supported by local authorities who subsidized excursions for walkers for which some stations were reopened at weekends. When, in 1981, BR's announcement that the largest viaduct, Ribblehead, was becoming dangerous seemed to signify the end, the newly formed Friends of the Settle & Carlisle Line mounted a country-wide campaign to keep the railway and promote its potential. In 1989 the government finally decreed that the line should be retained and developed. Services were improved, eight stations were reopened, revenue rose, and with national and local assistance Ribblehead viaduct was repaired. After an abortive attempt by BR to sell the line as a going concern an investment programme began, and the Settle & Carlisle Railway Trust was formed by local authorities to raise money for restoration of historic structures, while the Rural Development Commission and the English Tourist Board set up the Settle & Carlisle Development Company to encourage small business investment along the route. Economic recession and *privatization uncertainties caused a setback, but initiatives were later resumed.   GJB

F. W. Houghton and H. Foster, *The Story of the Settle–Carlisle Line* (1948); P. E. Baughan, *The Midland Railway North of Leeds* (1987 edn.); D. Jenkinson, *Rails in the Fells* (1980 edn.); S. Abbott and A. Whitehouse, *The Line that Refused to Die* (1990).

Severn Tunnel. The wide estuary of the River Severn has always been an obstacle to traffic between South Wales and the *Bristol area. From the earliest times there were ferry crossings, the last of which was the New Passage, with rail connections to jetties at each side. On the Gloucestershire side there was a line from Pilning while on the Monmouthshire side a short branch joined the South Wales main line. In charge of the construction of the rail jetties for the New Passage was Charles Richardson. He realized the feasibility of a *tunnel under the Severn and in 1863 he unsuccessfully put a Bill before Parliament.

Increasing traffic and transhipment problems of the New Passage caused the *Great Western Railway to seek parliamentary powers to build a tunnel, and in 1872 the Act was passed. Richardson, the originator of the scheme, was appointed engineer in charge, with Sir John *Hawkshaw as consulting engineer. Work started early in 1873.

The scheme was for seven miles of railway from Pilning to a junction at Rogiet, later called Severn Tunnel Junction. The tunnel was to be nearly 4½ miles long with 2¼ miles under water. The gradients from each end, falling towards the centre, would be 1 in 100 with 12 chains level under the deepest part of the river, known as the Shoots, where the cover over the tunnel would be 30 ft, later modified to 45 ft. This modification necessitated a steepening of the gradient to 1 in 90 on the Rogiet side. The engineering opinion was that once the problematical section under the Shoots was completed no untoward difficulties should arise from the remainder of the project.

In the event, however, the greatest hazard was a large spring, later named the Great Spring, which broke into the tunnel in October 1879. A huge inrush of water totally flooded the workings. Large steam pumps were installed but it took until late 1880 for the water to be cleared.

Following this serious mishap Hawkshaw was appointed engineer-in-chief with Richardson joint engineer, and Thomas *Walker, a contractor with tunnelling experience, was entrusted with completion of the works. Nine years after work started the two pilot headings met on 26 September 1881. Work progressed well until October 1883 when further setbacks occurred. First, the Great Spring again broke through, flooding all the works at Sudbrook and under the river. Then one of the largest pumps broke down, and finally, on 17 October, a high tidal wave inundated all the surface works, imprisoning 83 men working below who were rescued next day by boat.

After several weeks of pumping, the installation of an extra shaft, and additional pumps, work resumed at full pace. A side heading was built into which the Great Spring was diverted, and ever since its waters have been extracted at Sudbrook by large pumps, originally steam but now electric. The completed tunnel, 4 miles 629 yds in length and, excepting the *London Underground tunnels, the longest railway tunnel in Britain, was opened in 1886. It was then the longest underwater tunnel in the world.   AB

Sheffield and Rotherham, 1922

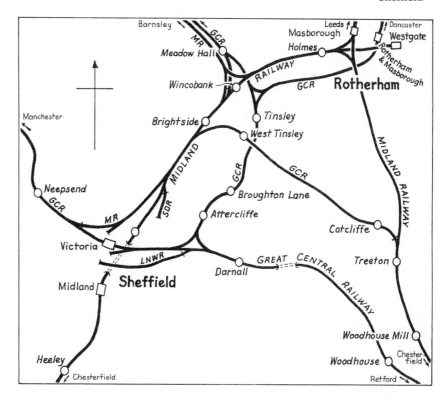

T. A. Walker, *The Severn Tunnel, Its Construction and Difficulties, 1872–1887* (1891 edn.).

shares and shareholding, see FINANCING OF RAILWAYS; COMPANIES; SPECULATION.

Sheffield was known to Chaucer, who made his well-known reference to 'a Sheffield thwitel' (table knife), but it was not until the *Railway Age that a relatively small cutlery centre was transformed into one of the world's major producers of steel.

The town's population tripled between 1843 and 1893, and at the same time two railway companies incessantly rivalled one another to provide competitive facilities. Wherever the *Midland Railway went, the Manchester Sheffield & Lincolnshire (see GREAT CENTRAL) was also sure to go, the ultimate result being that virtually everything from main lines to the tiniest siding was provided in duplicate.

In railway terms Sheffield suffered from having its sole natural routeway facing in the wrong direction, the only level exit being along the Don valley to the north. George *Stephenson insisted on minimal gradients on his *North Midland Railway connecting *Derby with *Leeds, and routed it directly through the Rother valley to the east, thus completely bypassing Sheffield. On the NMR's opening in 1840, the town found itself at the end of a branch line, a spur at Masborough giving a connection on to the locally promoted Sheffield & Rotherham Railway. Completed two years earlier in 1838, this line's terminus at Sheffield Wicker

was later described by the *Railway News* as 'a miserable station, small in size, hideous in aspect, dirty, dilapidated and situated in one of the least inviting districts of the town'.

Frustration in Sheffield was heightened by delays in building a direct rail link to *Manchester, only 35 miles away yet separated by the formidable barrier of the Pennines. The Sheffield Ashton-under-Lyne & Manchester Railway was incorporated in 1837, but financial difficulties and problems with the infamous 3-mile-long *tunnel under the watershed at Woodhead delayed completion until 1845. Even then Sheffield had to make do with a temporary terminus at Bridgehouses.

Two years later the company became part of the MSLR, and an eastwards extension to Gainsborough and Grimsby was completed in 1849. This and the Manchester line met at the new Victoria station, completed in 1851, with a 'light glass roof like that of the Crystal Palace'.

As the local railway network developed so did the steelworks, and by now the town was producing 86 per cent of Britain's cast steel. Yet it still had no direct rail outlet to the south. Both stations were distant from the centre, and in 1864 a local effort was made to build a direct north–south line, largely underground in the town area, with seven urban stations. It failed, but authorization was given for a Midland line from Chesterfield down the Sheaf Valley to a new station at Pond Street. Opened in 1870, it ended the bypassing of Sheffield, where the population was now 200,000. It was an expensive piece of construction, involving the compulsory purchase of over 1,000 houses, many of them newly built.

The new line became the jumping-off point for a competitive Midland route to Manchester via the Hope Valley. One of the last major pieces of railway construction in the area, it was opened in 1894 and included Totley Tunnel, at 3 miles 950 yds the longest in Britain after the *Severn. The MR station at Pond Street was rebuilt for much larger traffic in 1906.

Work on *electrifying the rival Woodhead route at 1,500 V dc was started by the *London & North Eastern Railway in 1936 but not finally completed until 1954. Its future thus seemed secure, but only 16 years later passenger traffic was withdrawn as part of a rationalization scheme which saw closure of Victoria and concentration of all services at the former Midland station. Amid massive controversy, the tunnel was closed completely in 1981, the bulk of trans-Pennine *freight movements being transferred to the inadequate roads between Sheffield and Manchester, two cities which still do not have a direct motorway link.   DJ
Reg. Hist., viii, ch. 6; S. R. Batty, *Rail Centres: Sheffield* (1984).

Shildon, see WORKS.

shipping, coastal. The application of steam power to commercial shipping predated that on land. Henry Bell's *Comet* of 1812 plied the Clyde and nearby coastal waters 13 years before the *Stockton & Darlington Railway opened. Throughout the 19th century innovations were often pioneered in coastal shipping, reducing costs and improving reliability and speed.

The coastal ship was the most tenacious and effective competitor to the railway system in the 19th and early 20th centuries. In contrast to road and *canal transport, the coaster continued to carry large quantities of cargo and improved its technology and organization to compete more effectively. It had a particular advantage in carrying low-value bulky goods, such as *coal, china *clay, grain, and *salt, and it was also most effective on long hauls of over 100 miles, such as from *Aberdeen to *London, Cornwall to Runcorn, and South Wales to the Thames. It also carried high-value manufactured goods such as soap, meat extract, and even pianos and cigars, and this ability to offer a range of services was another of its strengths.

The evidence comes in many indirect forms. A number of writers have shown that the railways perceived the coaster as a real threat, and adjusted their pricing, speeds, and frequencies to allow for this. More directly, the registered tonnage of coastal shipping entering British ports grew steadily from the 1830s to 1914 at around 2 per cent per annum, demonstrating that the trade co-existed with the growth of the railway system. An extensive network of coastal liner companies, linking virtually all major ports with a regular, reliable, and frequent service, could not have survived and flourished without ample patronage. Evidence of the coaster taking traffic from the railways comes in the London coal trade where, from 1867, the train was bringing the lion's share of coal to the capital. However, by 1898 the coaster had competed so effectively as to recapture the

greater part of the trade which it retained until World War I. This abrupt turnaround was aided by the abolition of London port dues in 1890, the rise in railway rates, and the establishment of riverside gas works and power stations.

The seriousness with which the railways viewed coastal competition is demonstrated by the collaboration which took place between them. On a number of long-distance routes, particularly from London to Scotland, the railway companies consulted the coastal shipping firms, agreed prices and timetables, and in some cases had joint-purse agreements. In a few examples the coastal companies were full members of *Railway Clearing House pools or conferences. An attempt has been made to calculate the work, in ton-miles, performed in 1910 by railways, coasters, and canals, which concluded that railways and coastal vessels performed about equal amounts of work while canals performed a fraction of either. However, the manner in which the two dominant forms of transport achieved roughly equal outputs was quite different. The railways' average haul was 50 miles, whereas the coaster carried a much lower tonnage over a much longer average distance: 250 miles. So, just before World War I, when the railway network was at its peak, the coaster competed very effectively.

The economic advantage of the coaster lay especially in large quantities and long distances. Throughout the 19th century the average railway *wagon capacity was about ten tons and in 1871 the average train load was about 57 tons, whereas the average coaster carried about 200 tons. The difference was even greater for bulk cargoes like coal. In 1890 the average cargo of sea-borne coal entering the port of London was over 800 tons, and by 1900 over 1,000. The coaster had advantages in the long haul. Many of its costs were incurred at the point of departure or arrival; for example loading and unloading, wharf and harbour dues, pilotage, ballast charges, etc. The impact of these fixed costs per mile fell as the journey distance increased. By comparison, the railway's costs were much more proportional to the journey's length. The railway owned land, track, and equipment, and employed a large staff to operate this vast empire of fixed capital. By contrast the coastal ship, once it was at sea, incurred no equivalent costs, and so charged freight rates for long hauls well below the equivalent on the railway.

The coaster competed with the railway by segmenting the market and offering a different service to each. Four can be broadly identified. The premier service was the coastal liner. By the mid-19th century an extensive network of coastal lines linked all the major British ports. The service was scheduled, frequent, and reliable, and performed by the newest, largest, and fastest ships. Often both goods and passengers were carried; there was no minimum quantity and the only goods excluded were those that were obnoxious, such as fresh hides, or dangerous, such as dynamite. The service was the most expensive, as liners sailed whether full or not and incurred the greatest costs. They were able to compete with the railways by virtue of speed and reliability at a time when goods trains were slow and uncertain, with much marshalling and shunting, inadequate *braking, and priority assigned to passenger trains. Although bad weather had a greater impact in delaying shipping than it did railways, this only impinged significantly on sailing ships.

The second market segment might be termed that of the regular traders. These had ships dedicated to one route or commodity which shuttled back and forth, though not to a fixed schedule. Prime examples are the screw colliers of the east coast, which carried only coal and sought no return cargo. Their characteristics lay between the liner and the tramp steamer, suiting the customer who needed large regular deliveries, like power stations, gas works, or potteries.

The third identifiable segment was served by the coastal steam tramp. It ran to no timetable, picking up a cargo as and when available; preferred to sail with full holds and thus was more suitable for bulky goods; and, being steam-powered, was predictable, even if only travelling at nine knots (10 mph), thereby competing with the slow goods train on price and reliability.

The final segment was that served by the sailing coaster. Its major drawback was unpredictability, being subject to wind and tides, but it was cheap and, for durable bulk goods of low value, was an ideal form of transport. Even in 1900 over 12 per cent of the coastal tonnage entering British ports with cargo was sail-powered. For bulky low-value cargoes like *stone, sand, and gravel, and for routes entirely on navigable water, the sailing coaster remained until well into the 20th century a cheap carrier.

In more recent times, aided by North Sea gas and oil exploration and extraction, the volume of coastal shipping has continued to be important, though the coastal liners have all gone and the coal trade, once the mainstay of coastal shipping, has faded away.

See also SHIPPING SERVICES. JA

P. S. Bagwell, *The Transport Revolution* (2nd edn., 1988), 49–75, 265–70, 348–53; G. Channon, 'The Aberdeenshire Beef Trade with London', *Transport History*, 2 (1969), 1–24; D. H. Aldcroft, 'The Eclipse of British Coastal Shipping, 1915–21', *Studies in British Transport History* (1974), 144–68; J. Armstrong, 'The Role of Coastal Shipping in UK Transport: An Estimate of Comparative Traffic Movements in 1910', *JTH*, 8 (1987), 164–78; and 'Railways and Coastal Shipping in Britain in the Later Nineteenth Century', in C. Wrigley and J. Shepherd (eds.), *On the Move—Essays in Labour and Transport History presented to Philip Bagwell* (1991), 76–103.

shipping services. Britain's railway companies owned and operated a wide range of ships from 1846 to 1984. During that time, a total of about 60 operating companies owned some 1,250 ships of different types, including tugs, dredgers, estuary and cross-channel ferries, and pleasure steamers, according to their needs. This was investment on a massive scale, and at least as far as many of the larger companies were concerned, emphasized the utmost importance they placed on extending their services across the water by providing ships capable of making comfortable and reliable short-sea crossings.

To provide for this business, it was sometimes necessary to construct special harbours (see PORTS AND DOCKS) with connecting railways. They often gave rise to the need to own tugs, dredgers, and other harbour craft. Pleasure steamers, as such, assumed a position of strategic importance in only a few railway-owned fleets, notably on the Clyde. There was also some railway ownership of *canal craft.

A significant feature of most railway-owned cross-channel services was, therefore, that they tended to take the shortest practicable sea route. Short-sea services offered by other shipowners, whose origins very often predated competing railway services, tended to serve existing city centres in tidal waters, requiring longer passage times. Examples were Swedish-Lloyd (London–Gothenburg), W. Müller's Batavier Line (London–Rotterdam), and the Coast Lines group which operated many routes, including those between *Glasgow and Dublin, and between *Liverpool and Cork. While very few of the latter have survived, the railway companies' main routes remain largely intact, although the emphasis has switched from rail-borne cargo and foot passengers to road haulage vehicles and passengers with cars.

The inauguration of cross-channel services led to the introduction of special *boat trains connecting with steamers. By the late 1950s vehicular traffic had become of increasing importance, although the first drive-on car ferry, *Princess Victoria*, had appeared on the Stranraer–Larne route as early as 1939. The first English Channel drive-on ferry, the *Lord Warden*, appeared on the Dover–Boulogne service in 1952, although cranes had to be used at Dover until a linkspan was opened in 1953, from which date the railway's first true drive on-drive off cross-Channel ferry service began. As similar services developed from other ports, so the importance of boat trains diminished and most were withdrawn, although there are still some connecting trains.

In the early days of railway operation, the companies were not authorized to own or operate steamers because the government did not want existing enterprises to be placed at a disadvantage. So the railways sought devious ways of outflanking the legislation by setting up associated or suitably disguised subsidiary companies. Thus, the *London & South Western Railway had interests in the South Western Steam Navigation Co., founded in 1842, and the *London Brighton & South Coast Railway in the Brighton & Continental Steam Packet Co. (1847). In fact, the LBSCR had taken one risk too many when it was found that the Steam Packet Co. was a wholly-owned subsidiary. Within two years it had been forced to cease trading, legal action having been taken by opposing factions.

From the mid-1840s, railway companies could seek parliamentary powers to run steamers, but had to stipulate specific routes. The LSWR gained powers for services to the Channel Islands and Le Havre in 1848. From 1863 the power to run passenger steamers was freely granted to railway companies collectively, but individual routes still had to be authorized. Pure cargo operations were subject to separate arrangements. These provisions were not altered until the *British Railways Act, 1967, which at one stroke swept away the conditions imposed by all previous Acts by enabling the Railways Board to operate services on any routes it wished. A new route between Harwich and Dunkirk was opened almost immediately, followed shortly afterwards by another between Holyhead and Belfast, although both were basically for freight and neither lasted very long.

The first railway shipping service was authorized in 1846 when the Great Grimsby & Sheffield Junction Railway (see GREAT CENTRAL) obtained powers to operate a ferry service across the Humber between New Holland and *Hull, although there was in fact no railway link to New Holland until the following year. This service was operated by successive railways until the opening of the Humber road bridge in 1981. In 1848 the *Chester & Holyhead Railway obtained powers to run Irish packet services from Holyhead to Kingstown (now Dun Laoghaire), or Howth. The former route still operates (see IRELAND, RELATIONSHIPS WITH).

The first railway-owned English Channel packets were operated by the *South Eastern Railway, which obtained powers in 1853 for a Folkestone–Boulogne service. This route survived until *privatization in 1984. From the 1850s enabling powers were obtained for an increasing number of shipping services to Ireland and the Continent from many ports, although some railways continued to rely on contract services until much later.

As railway *amalgamations took effect, ships and routes passed from owner to owner without the need for further applications for shipowning powers. There were changes in funnel colours and liveries, the companies being very jealous of their identities. After the *Grouping of 1923 the *Big Four companies began to effect a high degree of ship standardization, which was accentuated after *nationalization in 1948.

Prior to 1923, *competition between railway companies was rife as, for example, that for Irish traffic between the *Midland *Railway from Heysham, and the *Lancashire & Yorkshire and *London & North Western Railway joint operation from Fleetwood. The English Channel companies were, of course, also in competition. After 1923 little inter-railway rivalry remained, though Channel Islands traffic was still fought over by the *Southern Railway from Southampton and the *Great Western from Weymouth.

Joint operations with overseas railway companies were not uncommon, as for example between the LBSCR and the then Chemin de Fer de l'Ouest on the Newhaven–Dieppe service in 1863. This Anglo-French co-operation continued in slightly different forms under successive railway owners until privatization. Similarly, the service from Fishguard to Rosslare was inaugurated in 1906 by the Fishguard & Rosslare Railways & Harbours Company, which was jointly owned by the GWR and the Great Southern & Western Railway in *Ireland. This arrangement also survived to 1984, latterly under the control of BR and Coras Iompair Eireann (Irish Transport Board).

On the Clyde, three railway companies became responsible for most services to islands and further reaches of the mainland, and for building up an extensive excursion trade. At first they extended their lines to the coast. The *North

British Railway, on the north bank, reached Helensburgh in 1865, extending to Craigendoran in 1883. On the south shore the *Caledonian Railway reached Greenock (but not the pier) in 1851, Wemyss Bay in 1865, and Gourock in 1889. The *Glasgow & South Western reached Ardrossan in 1854 and Greenock Pier in 1869. The CR also reached Ardrossan in 1890.

But for a number of years these railways were unable to obtain powers to operate their own ships, so until nearly the end of the century, Clyde sailings were undertaken by nominees or contracted operators. The CR applied for powers in 1889 but Parliament refused, so immediately the Caledonian Steam Packet Co. was formed to own and operate a fleet for the CR, ships' departure times being tied to the arrival times of trains. The GSWR managed to obtain powers in 1891, the NBR in 1902. These years were characterized by highly intensive competition, leading on occasions to racing between rival ships, and causing many small private operators to go out of business. From 1893 various working *agreements were entered into by the Caledonian Steam Packet Co. and the GSWR, followed by a pooling agreement in 1910. After, first, the Grouping, then nationalization, only the Caledonian Steam Packet Co. survived alone, with a very much reduced network. It finally passed out of railway control when, under the Transport Act, 1968, it was transferred to the Scottish Transport Group on 1 January 1969. Railways also had interests in running steamers on several Scottish lochs, including Loch Lomond and Loch Awe.

Over the years, railways have also taken interests in other shipping companies, either wholly or in part. These have included Soc. Anon. Angleterre-Lorraine-Alsace (latterly the Dover–Dunkirk train ferry), Associated Humber Lines (services from Humber ports), British Rail Hovercraft ('Seaspeed', an early entrant to hovercraft operations in 1966, sold off in 1984), and David MacBrayne Ltd. (Western Isles).

From early days, railway companies were associated with the operation of steamers from the Humber ports of Goole, Grimsby, and Hull. The emphasis was on cargo rather than passengers, so that there was rarely accommodation for more than 12 on routes to, for example, Amsterdam, Antwerp, Bremen, and Ghent. The exceptions were those linking Grimsby with Hamburg and Rotterdam, and Hull with Rotterdam, on which up to 450 passengers could be accommodated. From 1935 all Humber services were operated under the management of Associated Humber Lines. The longest route regularly operated by any railway-associated service anywhere was that between Goole and Copenhagen (12 passengers), lasting 2½ days each way. AHL operations finally came to an end in 1971 when the remaining service, between Hull and Rotterdam, was closed down. By now, too much business had been lost to North Sea Ferries, which had been offering roll on-roll off and improved passenger facilities on the same route since 1965.

The design of cross-channel ships became very specialized, according to requirements. On short routes such as Dover–Calais, *Portsmouth–*Isle of Wight, and on the

Clyde, sleeping accommodation was not required so a 'day-boat' design emerged with deck space, lounges, and eating facilities but with few or no cabins. Longer journeys usually undertaken overnight, like Grimsby–Hamburg and Heysham–Belfast, required considerable sleeping accommodation, at the expense of other public rooms. In profile, a day-boat usually looked much like a night-boat, and a 'typical' packet emerged, like the Southern Railway's *Invicta*. When she entered service in 1946 between Dover and Calais she was the largest ferry on the Channel with a gross tonnage (a measurement of size, not weight) of 4,191. The largest ferry now operating across the English Channel has a gross tonnage of over 33,300.

The first train *ferry was operated across the Firth of Forth in 1850, followed by the Tay in 1851. Wagons were carried on rails laid on the decks, gained by movable ramps from the shore. After they ceased on the opening of the bridges, train ferries were not used again until World War I when they were required for transporting railway rolling stock to France. The first public continental train ferry began operations in 1924 between Harwich and Zeebrugge, for freight only, followed by a Dover–Dunkirk service in 1936 which also carried through sleeping cars from *Victoria to Paris and Brussels: the well-known 'Night Ferry' train.

During both world wars, railway steamers were in great demand by government for use as hospital and troop ships, for which work their speed, relatively shallow draught, and berth accommodation made them eminently suitable. Other ships found work as convoy rescue vessels and in coastal cargo convoys, and went as far afield as mid-Atlantic and the Mediterranean. During World War I most routes remained operational, with some changes, as long as there were ships available. During World War II, only routes from Holyhead, Heysham, and Stranraer were kept open, but were often interrupted.

Railway-owned shipping operations contributed a great deal to the maritime industry as a whole, in terms of technical innovation, design, speed, and reliability. Railway management was often in the forefront in testing new ideas. It was, for example, to a railway ship, the Southern Railway's *Isle of Sark*, that the prototype of what became famous as the Denny-Brown stabilizer (then known as a gyro-stabilizer) was fitted in 1936. Speeds of 18 to 21 knots were usual, although on certain routes, notably Newhaven–Dieppe and, to a lesser extent, Holyhead–Dun Laoghaire, 25 knots was not uncommon.

In 1970, BR's shipping services were renamed *'Sealink' for marketing purposes—including, oddly, the Windermere steamer services acquired by the *Furness Railway in 1875—and were sold in 1984.

Most of the key passenger routes had survived, notably Harwich–Hook of Holland, Dover–Calais and Dunkirk, Folkestone–Boulogne, Newhaven–Dieppe, Portsmouth and Weymouth–Channel Islands, Fishguard–Rosslare, Holyhead–Dun Laoghaire, and Stranraer–Larne. Those which had been closed since nationalization included Hull–Rotterdam, Harwich–Antwerp, the Harwich–Zeebrugge train

ferry, Folkestone–Calais, all services from Southampton (formerly to the Channel Islands, Le Havre, and St Malo), Fishguard–Waterford, Heysham–Belfast, several Clyde services, and all cargo-ship operations.   WPC

W. P. Clegg and J. S. Styring, *British Nationalised Shipping* (1969); M. Cowsill and J. F. Hendy, a range of books covering various aspects of railway shipping (from 1988); C. L. D. Duckworth and G. E. Langmuir, *Railway and Other Steamers* (1948); D. Haws, *Britain's Railway Steamers* (1993–4).

shooting. Few sports benefited more from the coming of the railways than shooting. The railways allowed access to regions previously out of reach, and made the letting of estates, moors, and deer forests a commercial proposition in northern England, central Wales, and the Highlands of Scotland. They also permitted the movement of fresh game and venison to markets in the south.

In Victorian times, a most sought-after and fashionable pastime was grouse-shooting, favoured both by the established upper classes and by those with new money. Bankers, brewers, and stockbrokers alike vied for ground in the north, using publications such J. Watson Lyall's *Sportsman's Guide* which first appeared in 1873. Their guests came by rail with enthusiasm; it was estimated in 1895 that 5,000 out of the 6,000 who travelled north incurred no more outlay than their rail fare. Such sportsmen packed the railways in August on the eve of 'the Glorious Twelfth' when the season began, with their guns, dogs, equipment, and servants. By 1887, for example, there were three overnight expresses from *Euston, all discontinued after 10–11 August. The practice of engaging private saloon *carriages for their families led to some very long and complicated trains, and considerable confusion at *Perth.

Proximity to stations and the anticipated 'bag' were key factors in the price a moor could command. In came the guests, their servants, and supplies for the lodge: out went their mail and hampers of game. In good years, the capacity of lines such as the *Highland Railway north of Perth was stretched almost beyond limit. But there was another side. A poor year for the grouse could mean sharply diminished receipts: fewer shooters came, and they stayed for a much shorter time. In 1873 the *Railway News* noted that the 'shooting traffic in the Highlands had suffered a heavy diminution from the failure of the grouse this season'.

There were no comparable services in England and Wales, although shooting parties were, of course, carried by ordinary trains.   AJD

R. Eden, *Going to the Moors* (1979); E. G. Mackenzie, *Grouse Shooting and Deer Stalking* (1907).

shops, see STATION TRADING.

Shrewsbury was an important transport centre long before railways arrived, standing on the London–Holyhead mail-coach road and with two bridges across the navigable Severn. The first railway to reach the town was the Shrewsbury & Chester in 1848, followed by the Shrewsbury & Birmingham with a connecting line to Stafford built by the *Shropshire Union company, completed in 1849. Then came the *Shrewsbury & Hereford, in 1853. Shrewsbury was linked with Welshpool and Aberystwyth in 1862. The *London & North Western and *Great Western Railways fought for control of the Shrewsbury companies. The Shrewsbury & Hereford and most of the line between Shrewsbury and Welshpool eventually came under their *joint ownership.

In Shrewsbury itself a single *joint station for all these lines was built on the narrow neck of the Severn's horseshoe loop, impinging on the medieval castle. Externally it was the work of T. M. *Penson.

The engineer responsible for the railways into Shrewsbury from Chester and Hereford was Henry *Robertson, Liberal MP for the town in 1862–8 and 1874–85.

Among the industries fostered by the railways was *wagon building, from which emerged the important Sentinel Wagon Works. In 1923 this firm joined with the Metropolitan-Cammell Carriage & Wagon Company to construct *shunting locomotives and *railcars, creating a substantial export market for the cars. The works closed in 1957.

Shrewsbury was much the largest railway centre between Chester and *Bristol. The LNWR and GWR ran competing services from London, some going on to Aberystwyth and Pwllheli over the *Cambrian Railways. The LNWR provided trains through Llandrindod Wells to *Swansea. In collaboration the two companies ran *cross-country services from *Liverpool and *Manchester via Shrewsbury to Bristol and the West Country by the *Severn Tunnel.

After the railways were *nationalized, and competitive services abolished, Shrewsbury's importance on the railway system declined, and cross-country trains were now rerouted through *Birmingham. Through services to London were withdrawn in 1992. Today the big station accommodates only small units of 1–3 cars.   JS
  MacDermot, i, ch. 8 and pp. 227–8; *Reg. Hist.*, vii and xi; J. W. Lowe, *British Steam Locomotive Builders* (1975), 569–73.

Shrewsbury & Hereford Railway: a line 51 miles long, authorized in 1846 and engineered by Henry *Robertson. In 1850 *Brassey contracted to build it, and he agreed to work it on lease for eight years from 1854. Opened in 1852–3, it ran into a *joint station at *Shrewsbury, to which it subscribed with the Shrewsbury & Chester and Shrewsbury & Birmingham Railways. At Hereford it joined the Newport Abergavenny & Hereford (see WEST MIDLAND RAILWAY).

Brassey appointed George *Findlay (then aged 22) to manage the line. The shareholders did well out of the lease, but the railway was run on the cheap (see CONTRACT, WORKING OF RAILWAYS BY). It threw off no branches, though subscribing to an eight-mile one to Tenbury, opened in 1861, and working it.

The *London & North Western and *Great Western companies were now developing their interests in the South Wales coalfield, and when Brassey's contract ended in 1862 they agreed to lease the Shrewsbury & Hereford company jointly, paying the ordinary shareholders a guaranteed dividend of 6 per cent.

It now formed part of a north-west to south-west main

line, which grew more important with the opening of the *Severn Tunnel in 1886. Though the principal north to west expresses now run via *Birmingham, it still carries about 17 passenger trains on weekdays in each direction, mostly running between *Manchester and *Cardiff.   JS
  MacDermot, i, 227–8.

Shropshire & Montgomeryshire Light Railway, see LIGHT RAILWAYS.

Shropshire Union Railways & Canal Company. This represented the fullest attempt made in Victorian Britain to create an organization for running *canals and railways together, forming an integrated transport system, though canal and railway companies were frequently merged.

In 1845 the Ellesmere & Chester and Birmingham & Liverpool Junction Canals amalgamated. The directors of the enlarged company then began to consider converting part of their system into railways. The Shropshire Union Railways & Canal Company was statutorily authorized in 1846, based on the Ellesmere & Chester Canal, with the Shrewsbury and the Shropshire Canals brought into the union, together with the Montgomeryshire, purchased in 1847–50: a system of waterways 190 miles long. The new company also built a 19-mile railway from Stafford to Wellington, opened in 1849.

The *London & North Western Railway leased the Shropshire Union in 1847. The railway's interests were always paramount thereafter, but the Shropshire Union board sometimes stood up for its canals with a stubborn determination that might prove effective. The company remained in being until it was absorbed into the LNWR in 1922, and so into the *London Midland & Scottish at the *Grouping of the following year.

The Union company embodied an intelligent idea, which suffered from misfortune. Had it been set up two years earlier it might have established itself more firmly and perhaps have set useful examples elsewhere.   JS
  C. Hadfield, *Canals of the West Midlands* (1966), ch. 13.

shunters, see SHUNTING.

shunting might be defined as slow-speed, short movements of *carriages or *wagons, generally for the purpose of making up a train before its journey, changing its formation *en route*, splitting it up at the end of the journey, or positioning vehicles for a static operation such as unloading or maintenance. It might take place on running lines; this was more so in the past, when it was common for *through carriages to be detached from one train and attached to another at *junction stations, when passenger trains conveyed horseboxes or other non-passenger stock, and when every line had its daily local goods train. But shunting is an activity more associated with *sidings.

Shunting is normally carried out by a locomotive—either the train's own engine or a small engine provided for the purpose—pulling the vehicles in one direction and propelling them in the other. Where wagons are allowed to run under their own momentum after an initial push, this is known as 'loose shunting'. A resident shunting engine at a passenger station was often called the 'station pilot'. The coupling and uncoupling of the vehicles and overall direction of the operation are performed by a shunter or, where none is provided, the train *guard, using hand signals, or at night a hand-lamp, to pass instructions to the driver.

However, shunting by locomotive was not always the only, or indeed the most efficient, option. The early four-wheel carriages and wagons were light enough to be pushed manually. When they became heavier, horse-towing was often adopted, even in large flat *marshalling yards; e.g. Toton yard, near *Nottingham, employed 50 *horses in 1889. *British Railways inherited 238 shunting horses and the last, at Newmarket, was not withdrawn until 1967. Another method of moving wagons in docks and large *goods depots was by rope and capstan; steam-, hydraulically-, or electrically-powered.

A disadvantage of shunting with a locomotive is that it can be trapped at the end of a siding unless there is a cross-over or run-round loop for its release. There were various practices to overcome this, but all involved risks:

1. At some branch line termini where no loop was provided to release the arriving engine, *'gravity shunting' provided the answer. The train was propelled up an incline; then after the engine had run forward into a siding, the carriages were allowed to roll into the platform under the control of the guard's handbrake. The engine could then be attached at the other end ready for the return working.

2. In 'fly shunting', wagons were uncoupled while the train was being drawn forward. The engine and front portion accelerated ahead on to one line and the detached wagons, following a little behind, were diverted on to another line.

3. 'Tow-roping', or 'towing', describes wagons being towed by a rope attached to an engine on an adjacent track.

4. 'Propping' was the practice of pushing wagons by an engine on an adjacent track by means of a timber prop between the engine and the last wagon.

Gravity shunting was also used in gravity and hump marshalling yards; in the latter case it was called 'hump shunting'. Except where retarders were installed, the speed of the wagons, as in loose shunting, was controlled by a shunter running alongside while applying pressure on the hand-brake lever with a wooden brake stick. Damage to goods caused by a 'rough shunt', or heavy impact between moving and stationary wagons, and *accidents to shunters were common.

The shunting pole was introduced in the late 1870s, to avoid the need for shunters to go between wagons to couple or uncouple them, and was in general use from 1886. In spite of this improvement, the Royal Commission on Accidents to Railway Servants in 1900 found that the accident rate for shunters (5.08 fatalities per year per thousand employed) was even worse than for miners and second only to merchant seamen. It recommended abolition of tow-roping and propping as far as possible, provision of brake levers and destination labels on both sides of wagons to avoid shunters continually having to cross the track, and

lighting where there was frequent shunting at night, but it felt unable to make a recommendation for automatic *couplers. The Railway Employment (Prevention of Accidents) Act, 1900, empowered the Board of *Trade to make and enforce rules on these matters, following which conditions slowly improved.

The continuous *brake was adopted only slowly for goods trains partly because it needed shunters once more to go between wagons to uncouple and recouple the vacuum pipes, slowing down shunting and reintroducing a hazard. BR commissioned development of an automatic wagon coupler incorporating vacuum pipe connections. It received trials in 1958–9 but would have been an expensive solution. In the event the amount of shunting was considerably reduced by the adoption of trainload working (see FREIGHT TRAFFIC). GAB

P. S. Bagwell, *The Railwaymen* (1963), 101–8.

Sibthorp, Charles de Laet Waldo (1783–1855), politician; he came of a Lincolnshire landed family and served in the dragoon guards in the Peninsular War. He was MP for Lincoln almost continuously from 1832 to 1855, and became conspicuous for his eccentricities, constantly denouncing in the wildest language Catholic emancipation, parliamentary reform, and free trade.

His opposition to railways, which became notorious, did not spring from any dislike of steam-worked machinery: he chaired a Commons committee on steamships quite sensibly in 1831. He opposed railways for their invasion of the rights of private property, through their powers of compulsory land purchase.

In 1844 he claimed that he had fought 'every proposition of every railroad whatever' (forgetting that he had presented a petition from his constituents in favour of one in 1830). *Punch* (see HUMOUR) delighted in his gross absurdities, likening him to a pantomime clown. His political importance in railway matters proved quite negligible. JS

DNB; Boase; Hansard, 72 (1855), 255; *Punch*, 6 (1844), 83; Sir F. Hill, *Victorian Lincoln* (1974), 115.

siding. The word 'siding' was used by Nicholas *Wood in 1825 to indicate a short track at the side of the railway. Although there are exceptions, sidings are generally distinguishable from running lines in that they are operated at slow speeds and not controlled by a *signalling system; they were often laid with reused materials removed from main lines. The term 'road' is often used to refer to a siding, particularly in conversation. A group of sidings may be called a 'yard', and those associated with a station the 'station yard'.

In the early years, much use was made of *turntables, rather than points, to connect sidings. They suited the practice of manually *shunting individual *carriages and *wagons, which was possible with the light rolling stock of the period, and were more economical of space in the confined layouts of large passenger *stations, city goods stations, and dock warehouses (see GOODS SHEDS AND WAREHOUSES). They were a feature at many small *London & North Western

Railway stations where, by means of a siding at right angles across the running lines, they were used to transfer wagons from one side to the other, allowing traffic in both directions to share common loading and unloading facilities. They were also necessary for turning the LNWR's many vans that had doors in one side only. Turntables disappeared from passenger stations when coaches became too long for them, but wagon turntables continued in use in large goods depots and warehouses until the 1960s or 1970s.

Groups of sidings serve different purposes, the most common being: sidings in goods depots, where wagons are loaded or unloaded; 'sorting sidings', where wagons are marshalled into freight trains (large groups of sorting sidings were called *'marshalling yards'); 'carriage sidings', where coaches are cleaned, maintained, stabled, and formed into trains for their next working; and sidings at maintenance depots and repair *works. 'Mileage sidings' catered for goods traffic subject only to mileage charges, i.e. where handling and cartage were performed by the consignor or consignee.

Each siding within a group needs to be identifiable by its own name. Generally this describes its specific function, e.g. the 'cripple siding', where defective vehicles are placed for repair, or the 'van kip', where brake vans slumbered until next required in a marshalling yard, if necessary supplemented by a number, e.g. *Up Reception Siding No. 2; or it might refer to its location, e.g. the Back Road. But some had names that reflected their history, such as the Volunteer Siding at Wimbledon, which until 1889 handled the traffic for the annual volunteer riflemen's camp on Wimbledon Common, or the period in which they were built: many places had their Klondike, Crimea, or Jubilee Siding.

'Private sidings' are owned by, or leased to, a freight customer for his exclusive use. Except where they are shunted entirely by the railway company, the handover of wagons between the company and the customer takes place in 'transfer sidings'. 'Private siding agreements' define the ownership and lease boundaries, the track maintenance responsibilities and charges, and the arrangements for safe working.

See also TRACK; LOOP.   GAB

N. Wood, *Practical Treatise on Railways* (1825); R. Foster, 'Wagon Turntables', *British Railway Journal*, 2 (1986–7), 58–70.

signal boxes. The traditional British railway signal box as we know it—a two-storey structure with a glazed operating floor upstairs and a locking room below—evolved in the 1860s, following the introduction of interlocked lever frames which required some 6 ft headroom beneath operating floor level. Prior to that, *signalmen at stations had small huts. At many *junctions elevated signal platforms had been provided in the 1840s and 1850s, but these, whilst they were a predecessor of the fully developed signal box, usually had the levers in the open, with a small hut for the signalman. There were also some junction 'towers' whose great height enabled signalmen to see trains approaching from afar in the days before *block working.

The classic signal box of the 1860s–1920s was variously built of brick, brick-and-timber, or wholly timber, largely according to companies' preferences, although some did use all-timber on unstable sites. Stone was occasionally instead of brick. Roofs were variously hipped or gabled, the latter often with decorative bargeboards and finials. A few boxes, where space was constricted, had to be cantilevered out or built on gantries over the tracks. As layouts expanded, the average size of boxes increased, some being built over 80 ft long. Lever frames were at first always placed in the front of the box so that the signalman faced the line, but increasing equipment on the 'block shelf' above the frame began to obstruct the signalman's view, and from the 1900s some companies placed the frame at the back instead. Almost all boxes had a hearth or stove, and many latterly had lavatories.

Many companies employed *signalling contractors who had their own signal box designs, which appeared in identical form on different railways, particularly in 1860–80. Latterly, however, most large companies designed and built their own identifiably standard structures, sometimes of attractively elaborate appearance. Signal boxes could take curious forms, such as the rooms in the island platform buildings at *Perth and the *Midland Railway stations at *Leicester and *Nottingham, with bay windows overlooking the platforms; the wooden box at Broughty Ferry, Angus, which was integral with the station footbridge; and several specially designed to match a station, like the 'Arts and Crafts' styled example at Nutfield, Surrey.

From the 1930s many signal boxes reflected contemporary designs, with flat reinforced-concrete roofs, steel-framed plate-glass windows, and concrete sills and lintels. Architects were now more often used. In the late 1930s and during World War II many boxes were built with thicker roofs, to withstand air-raids. Small mechanical boxes continued to be built in significant numbers until the 1970s, but line closures and the evolution of 'power boxes' and electronic signalling centres controlling many miles of line have brought the number down from some 13,000 at *c.*1900 to 1,000 in 1994.   PK

Signalling Study Group, *The Signal Box; A Pictorial History and Guide to Designs* (1986).

signalling: the equipment provided and the processes required to ensure the safe operation of trains. The system can be separated into four basic elements. Signals indicate to drivers the state of the line ahead: whether they are required to stop or regulate their speed, and the route to be taken at *junctions and stations. They are generally 'fixed' (i.e. permanent), but hand signals can be used for certain purposes such as local movements and emergencies. 'Interlocking' is provided to ensure as far as possible that the signalman cannot move points to set up conflicting routes, or give 'proceed' signals to trains which could lead to collisions. It can be achieved mechanically or electrically. The *'block system' keeps trains apart by maintaining an appropriate space between them. These physical elements are drawn together in a series of rules and regulations (chiefly the rule book, Block Regulations, and Signalmen's General

Instructions) which must be followed by *signalmen, *drivers, *guards, and others who operate trains (see BYE-LAWS). Many safety devices back up these basic elements to produce a safe railway where high speeds and frequent services can be provided with confidence.

Early Signalling

As soon as the first railways opened it was realized that there must be some means of giving information to drivers. The starting-point was hand signals by flags or lamps. However, permanent signals were soon found necessary at stations and junctions. Various devices were tried, usually based on the principle of raising on a post something easily visible, such as flags, balls, discs, lamps, etc., when the train was required to stop or take a particular route. They evolved into two basic types: discs and semaphore arms. Disc signals usually comprised a circular board on a post which could be rotated to show the disc face-on for 'stop' and edge-on for 'proceed'.

The first semaphores were installed by (Sir) Charles Hutton *Gregory at New Cross Gate on the *London & Croydon Railway in 1841. The arms were mounted on a pivot in a slot in the post and showed three positions: horizontal indicating 'stop'; lowered to 45 degrees for 'caution'; and vertically downwards (and therefore hidden inside the slot in the post) for 'proceed'. Lamps on the posts originally rotated to show different coloured lights: red for 'stop', green for 'caution', and white for 'proceed'. Soon they were fixed in position and coloured glasses, mounted in 'spectacle plates', were attached to the rod working the arm so that they moved across the lamp's lens and showed the appropriate colour.

A characteristic of most early signals was the effective absence of a signal that denoted proceed. This was unsatisfactory as it was not fail-safe—later a fundamental principle of signalling—in that the signal could simply have fallen down. *Brunel on the *Great Western Railway addressed this weakness in 1840 by attaching below the disc signals a crossbar mounted at right angles, so that either disc or crossbar always showed a positive indication. Most other discs and the semaphore continued to rely on drivers looking only for the post for a 'clear' indication.

These first signals were hand-operated and usually only located at junctions and stations. They were placed at a point convenient to the operator, such as the centre of a station or at junction points, rather than the position where the train should stop, frequently requiring them to halt at a considerable distance short of the signal. Often it was difficult for drivers to stop in time. Additional signals were gradually introduced, known as 'auxiliary' or 'distance' signals, to give some advance warning. They were worked by wire from a hand lever at the station or junction, but their use was somewhat muddled. Some companies required trains to stop at them, some to stop and proceed after a set time, and some just to proceed cautiously. Eventually their use was consolidated as the 'distant' signal, which at danger signified 'proceed at caution and expect the next stop signal to be at danger'. They were, however, fitted with red lamps

Semaphore signals

Lower quadrant

Distant signal at 'caution'   Stop signal at 'clear'

Upper quadrant

Stop signal at 'clear'

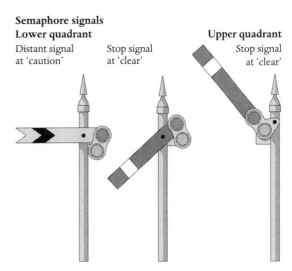

and arms, making them indistinguishable from 'stop' signals. The distinguishing 'fishtail' notch in the arm was introduced on the *London Brighton & South Coast Railway in 1872 and became universal after 1877.

Interlocking

Initially there were no links between signals and points, other than by the men working them, and there was nothing to prevent the signals showing indications that conflicted with the direction in which the points were set, or even with each other. Point and signal levers were generally adjacent to or on the signal post. As several might be in the charge of one man this did not encourage careful working, especially in bad weather. Gradually point and signal levers began to be concentrated at one place where more could safely be under the control of one man, although there was no connection or interlocking between them. This practice was actively encouraged by the government *inspectors and it became one of their standard requirements when these were first published in 1858.

Concentration aided working, but did not prevent conflicting signals being given. A means of 'interlocking' between the signals and points was needed. The first step came in 1843–4 when Gregory erected some signals operated by foot stirrups at Bricklayers Arms Junction, interconnected so that conflicting signals could not be given. The idea was developed by Stevens & Sons, who patented an improved stirrup frame in 1847. The first interlocking between points and signals was at East Retford Junction, Manchester Sheffield & Lincolnshire Railway (see GREAT CENTRAL) in 1852, when Atkinson arranged a rod from the points to lock the operating rod to the relevant signal. In 1856 John Saxby made a significant step by patenting junction interlocking. The signal rods were attached to the point levers so that the signals automatically repeated the position of the points. Auxiliary levers allowed arms to be put to danger. The 'simultaneous motion' of this device limited its application.

signalling

Arrangement of signals at a small station

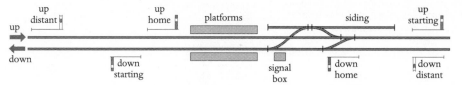

The big breakthrough came in 1859 when Col. *Yolland of the Board of *Trade refused to sanction the opening of Kentish Town Junction on the *North London Railway. He considered that the stirrup frame provided by Stevens, which did not interlock points with signals, was insufficiently safe for the heavy traffic. Austin Chambers, a NLR engineer, devised a frame where the signal stirrups and point levers interlocked with each other so that one could be moved only when all the others were in the correct position. This 'successive motion' was the basis of all subsequent interlocking frames. Chambers patented his frame early in 1860. Both Saxby and Stevens recognized the importance of the idea and within weeks had produced their own interlocking frames based on Chambers' principle. The industry never looked back. Demand for signalling equipment and interlocking apparatus increased rapidly from 1860, creating a thriving industry (see SIGNALLING EQUIPMENT MANUFACTURE).

Much development and improvement took place over the next two decades. McKenzie & Holland developed the cam-and-soldier frame in 1866, the first really durable design. It was improved in 1873, and developed in 1886 into the 'T bar'. Catch-handle actuation of the locking, which prevented the full force of a lever movement being put on to it, was developed by Saxby and Easterbrook in 1867. Saxby produced his 'rocker' frame in 1871 and improved it in 1874, while Stevens patented the tappet locking frame in 1870. Tappet locking proved to be the simplest and most versatile form of interlocking, and from about 1880 was gradually adopted. Special forms of locking, such as sequential and conditional, were generally much easier to achieve with tappet locking, and the system suited the miniaturization needed for the early power frames which had mechanical locking.

Large sums were soon being spent on signalling and several of the largest companies manufactured most of their own equipment. The *Midland Railway always did, the GWR started in about 1863, the *London & North Western in 1874, and the *Lancashire & Yorkshire in 1889.

Block *Telegraph

Increasing traffic soon required means of preventing collisions between trains following each other along the same track, or joining, leaving, or crossing it. Theoretically the *timetable should prevent conflicts, but in practice the protection was lost by delays, breakdowns, or running extra trains. The problem was that only very limited communication was available to ascertain the whereabouts of trains.

Early attempts to regulate their passage were therefore based on imposing a 'time interval' between them. A train was not allowed to leave a station, or other point, before a specified period of time (typically five minutes) after the preceding one had departed.

As a further precaution, drivers of trains passing within a further five minutes or so were usually warned that there was a train not far ahead. The idea was that drivers would then take extra care. It was a cheap and simple system, needing no special equipment, and the existing staff such as *stationmasters and *policemen could normally do the work. No communication was needed between stations; the telegraph was in the early stages of development and was expensive, although of course it helped.

None the less there was a fundamental flaw: allowances for trains travelling at different speeds were rather hit-and-miss. Although a fast train might leave a station after the correct time interval, it could quickly catch up with a slower one, while some were often delayed at stations and *sidings. Thus a train might still come unexpectedly on the one ahead, sometimes resulting in a collision. In addition, uncertainty over the whereabouts of trains made it difficult to deal with those joining and leaving the line, while a train could arrive just when the track was blocked by vehicles or shunting movements. The weaknesses of the system were sometimes compounded by rather lax attention to the rules by the men themselves or with the tacit approval of management, both in the supposed interest of expediting operations.

The development of the electric telegraph by Cooke and Wheatstone between 1836 and 1845 provided a solution enabling information on the locations of trains to be passed on. In some cases the time interval was supplemented by the telegraph, to give improvement in working.

The telegraph allowed the system of keeping trains apart to be rethought. Cooke issued a pamphlet, *Telegraphic Railways*, in 1842. He suggested that lines should be split into 'sections', each governed by a separate telegraph. A second train would not be allowed to enter a section until the first had left it. Although he was principally addressing the even more pressing problem of safe working of *single lines, it also had clear application to double lines. The system relied on an interval of space, rather than time, being maintained between trains, and this has remained the fundamental principle of the block system ever since. Cooke's system was first tried on the single-line *Norfolk Railway between Norwich and Yarmouth in 1844. A five-needle instrument at each of the six stations showed the state of the line in all five sections. It was consequently cumbersome and costly.

The idea was developed by Edwin Clark of the Electric Telegraph Company. He simplified it so that there was a separate circuit for each section, and information on the state of the line was not transmitted further afield. This substantially reduced both cost and complexity, making it a practical proposition for widespread application on double lines. In 1852 C. V. Walker combined the single-stroke electric bell with the block telegraph, using it to attract the signalman's attention and to send descriptions of trains, etc., by means of coded sequences of rings.

Initially there was much opposition to the block telegraph on the grounds of cost, and a belief that it would reduce line capacity. Eventually it was found to be the only suitable means of control on most lines, and was widely adopted, fears about capacity proving groundless. After a very serious *accident at Armagh, Ireland, in 1889, block working and interlocking were made compulsory under the *Regulation of Railways Act of that year.

Signal Aspects

The concentration of levers in interlocking frames, and the block system, were brought together in *signal boxes under the control of a signalman. The block system rendered the three positions of the semaphore unnecessary and too complex, so signals were altered to show only two aspects. At junctions and stations where caution was required, the horizontal (stop) and 45 degrees (caution, with green light) positions were adopted but in some cases the horizontal and vertical (clear) positions were retained.

The invisible position of the vertical signal arm led to an accident at Abbots Ripton, *Great Northern Railway, in 1876 when a signal arm froze inside the slot in the post, leading to a false 'clear' indication; it was consequently abandoned. This and other factors also led to a change from signals normally showing clear (unless the line was occupied or blocked) to normally standing at danger. The accident discredited the slotted post form of signal and there was a general change to mounting signal arms on the outside of the posts, although slotted-post signals continued in use for many years. In September 1877, Edward French of the GNR devised a novel form of centre-balanced arm, normally referred to as the 'somersault', which solved the problems of the slotted post and allowed the arm to take a visible vertical position for clear. This was used extensively on the GNR, the *Barry, and the *Rhymney Railways.

A white light for 'clear' was eventually recognized as unsatisfactory. There was an increasing number of other white lights, at stations and alongside the railway, which could lead to confusion, and if the red spectacle glass on the signal broke, a white, apparently clear, light would be shown while the signal was at danger. This broke the fail-safe rule and from 1893 green was adopted for the 'proceed' aspect. Conversion took a long time and it was the beginning of the 20th century before the process was completed. White was then regarded as a danger signal.

Eventually the unsatisfactory nature of the red distant signal was addressed. Yellow lights for distants first appeared on tunnel sections of *London Electric Railway, followed in 1917 by an open-air installation between *Marylebone and Neasden on the *Great Central. This retained red semaphore arms but it soon became the practice to paint them yellow. They were made a requirement for new work by the inspectors in 1925, and conversion of existing signals was largely completed around 1930.

Standardization and Colour Lights

In 1919 the war-time Railway Executive (REC) set up a sub-committee to devise a range of signalling equipment which could be universally adopted to give economies and the benefits of standardization. The chairman was A. T. Blackall, the GWR signal engineer, although much of the design and development work of the mechanical equipment was done at *Derby by the Midland and later the *London Midland & Scottish under W. C. Acfield. A whole range of new equipment and parts was devised, of which the most publicly obvious was the upper-quadrant signal arm. Light pressed-steel construction could be used, as the weight of the arm ensured that the signal returned to danger if the wire broke, whereas a lower-quadrant required a heavy spectacle for the same purpose.

In the late 1920s the upper quadrant was adopted as standard by the LMS, *London & North Eastern, and *Southern Railways, while the LMS made most of the REC designs its standard. The GWR decided to go its own way and retained the lower quadrant, a policy continued by the Western Region of *BR.

The period from about 1910 to the 1930s was filled with discussion and controversy over how, and in what form, signals should be developed. It was recognized that the existing semaphores were inadequate, at least for main lines, where an additional aspect was needed to give drivers a better idea of the state of the line ahead and the speed he should proceed at. The first idea to be tried was the three-position semaphore. The upper-quadrant arm was horizontal for stop, 45 degrees (yellow light) for 'proceed with caution', and vertical (green) for 'proceed at speed, next signal at caution or clear'. The first full-scale installation, of four signals each way, was installed at Keadby, GCR, in 1916, a large installation at London *Victoria following in 1920.

*Underground railways needed only lights for signals in tunnels and hence the colour-light signal was born. Light signals without semaphore arms appeared on the *Waterloo & City Railway in 1898. The breakthrough was lamps and lenses which produced a light powerful enough to be seen over distances in daytime. The first daylight colour-light signals in Britain appeared on the *Liverpool Overhead Railway in 1920. Change became rapid. In 1922 the *Institution of Railway Signal Engineers set up a committee to consider three-position signalling. By the time they reported in December 1924, the three-position semaphore was out of date, and the report principally concerned colour lights and recommended a fourth aspect. The first four-aspect signalling was installed between Holborn Viaduct and Elephant and Castle in 1926. There was much discussion over whether signals should indicate route, the normal British practice, or speed. The only installation of 'speed' signalling in Britain was at Mirfield, Yorkshire, in 1932.

Two types of colour-light signal were developed. The 'searchlight' had one lamp and lens, coloured glasses moving over the lens giving the different aspects. The other featured separate lamps and coloured lenses for each aspect. Both types were installed up to the 1960s, after which the multiple lamp type became standard.

Power Signalling

By the late 1890s it was recognized that power working was to be the way forward in the operation of points and signals, although change-over proved to be very slow. The first significant installations were brought into use within days of each other in 1899: an all-electric system at Gresty Lane, *Crewe, LNWR, and an electro-pneumatic one, employing compressed air-operated points and signals, at Bishopsgate, *Great Eastern Railway. Generally, miniature lever or slide frames were used, with mechanical interlocking. Electrical circuits gave savings in the number of levers; one could operate the signals for several routes, for instance. This and the small lever size made it possible to control large layouts with fewer and smaller signal boxes, which also saved manpower. The British Pneumatic Railway Signal Co.'s system featured slides, rather than levers, with pneumatic operation of points and signals. One of the largest installations was 14 signal boxes between Ardwick and Hyde Junction, GCR, in 1905–6.

The next breakthrough was the introduction of electrical interlocking which reduced space requirements and made larger frames easier to build and modify. The first installation was a *Westinghouse style 'L' frame at North Kent East Junction, Southern Railway, in 1929. The style 'L' frame proved popular, the largest installations being *Cardiff West, 339 levers (1932) and *Waterloo, 309 levers (1935).

Power working and electrical interlocking meant that the movement of a lever was not necessary, allowing the introduction of the signalling 'panel' in which points and signals are operated by switches and buttons. Since the switches were not themselves interlocked, many extra relays were required to set, prove, and interlock the routes. However, they allowed much larger areas of control and further reductions in manpower. First installed in the 1930s, panels became the predominant form of control for power signalling installations from the 1950s to the beginning of the 1990s.

Different forms of control systems were developed for the panels. The 'one function switch' system was derived from the style 'L' frame, the switches effectively replacing the levers, the first installation being at Goole Bridge in 1933. One switch set an entire route, via route relay interlocking, in the 'one control switch' system which was first used at Thirsk in 1934. Large relay interlockings were installed at *Leeds in 1937 (individual switches) and *Hull in 1938 (one control switch).

The entrance-exit ('NX') system of control of relay interlocking, where buttons are provided at the beginning and end of each route section, was first used in a small panel at Brunswick, *Cheshire Lines Committee, in 1937. On pressing the buttons the interlocking checks that the line is clear and that no conflicting routes are set, selects and operates the points, and, when proved correct, clears the signals. A further important step forward occurred in 1939 at Northallerton where the full extent of a route set-up was indicated on the diagram by a chain of white lights. World War II delayed progress, and the first large NX panel, *York, was not commissioned until 1951.

Panel boxes are generally associated with continuous *track circuiting and track-circuit block, which was formalized in the Block Regulations in 1964. Train describers provide details of each train's identity, type, and route. The descriptions could step forward on the panel, or describer, in unison with the occupation of the track circuits. From 1961, standard four-character train numbers were introduced (see HEADCODES).

The 1955 *Modernization Plan marked the beginning of a process of resignalling which has continued at varying speeds ever since. Much of the work has centred on the installation of multiple-aspect colour-light signalling (MAS) and power signal boxes controlling progressively larger areas, much of it based on the principles of relay interlocking and the 'NX' panel. A development of the late 1950s was 'geographical circuitry' where the interlocking was broken down into a series of basic units (such as a point or a signal), the relay sets for which are standardized, and factory preassembled and wired. This saved design and installation time and simplified fault rectification. Early examples included part of Tilbury Riverside (1961), Paddock Wood (1962), and Rugby (1964).

Recent developments have been solid-state interlocking, developed jointly by BR, GEC-General Signal, and Westinghouse Signals, and first used at Leamington in 1986; and Integrated Electronic Control Centres (see SIGNALLING, AUTOMATIC).

See also CONTROL, SYSTEMS OF TRAIN; FOG; SAFETY. RDF
M. G. Tweedie and T. S. Lascelles, *Modern Railway Signalling* (1925); R. Blythe, *Danger Ahead: The Dramatic Story of Railway Signalling* (1951); O. S. Nock (ed.), *Railway Signalling* (1980); M. A. Vanns, *Signalling in the Age of Steam* (1995).

signalling, automatic: a system whereby the signal movements are controlled by the passage of trains alone, no other agency being required; not to be confused with power *signalling, panels, etc., where some manual control is still needed. Control of the signals is usually achieved by *track circuits, which change the signals to danger behind the trains as they proceed and return them to 'clear' when the appropriate *block sections ahead are unoccupied again. Most systems operate on the principle of the signals normally displaying the 'clear' aspect, contrary to the practice in manually operated systems where the signals are normally at danger.

Automatic signalling is most commonly applied to plain sections of line where trains simply follow each other, and is particularly suited to urban passenger lines where services are frequent and repetitive. Its advantages are that line capacity can be substantially increased by placing signals at optimum spacing, manpower is reduced, operation is quick and reliable, and there is a high degree of safety due to the elimination of the human factor.

In most cases installations are supplemented by some means of automatic train control such as 'train stops' (notably on *London Transport lines—see TRIP COCK) or an *automatic warning system on *BR lines.

The track circuits ensure that there is a space interval between trains, and conventional block working is not required. Train describers (see BLOCK WORKING) are normally provided to indicate trains' identities to signalmen.

The first installation, employing electrically operated semaphores actuated by contacts, was on the *Liverpool Overhead Railway in 1893. A low-pressure pneumatic system, actuated by track circuits, was installed on the *London & South Western Railway between Andover and Grateley (the first main-line use) in 1902, followed by a 24-mile section between Woking and Basingstoke, with controlled signals at stations. The *Underground Electric Railways of London began installing automatic signalling in 1903, utilizing electro-pneumatic operation, while an ac variant appeared on the *Central London Railway. The *North Eastern Railway installed an electro-gas system over 11 miles between Alne and Thirsk in 1905. An all-electric upper quadrant two-position semaphore system was installed between Baker Street and Harrow, *Metropolitan Railway, in 1908, while a three-position semaphore system was used on the *Great Western's Shepherd's Bush and Ealing extension line when it opened in 1920.

Daylight colour-light signals were first employed on the Liverpool Overhead Railway in 1920; the first main-line installation with multiple-aspect colour-lights was between Neasden and Marylebone in 1923. Most power signalling installations feature lengths of automatic signalling between areas of controlled signals. Some normally automatic signals can be switched to controlled working and are usually known as 'semi-automatic'.

Repetitive operation of points at stations and junctions suited automation, and automatic operation of the low-level terminal station at *Liverpool Central, *Mersey Railway, commenced in 1923. Train descriptions or the timetable provide a means of extending automatic working to more complex junctions and stations. London Transport devised 'programme machines' that use a punched roll representing the timetable, extensively installed in the 1960s. It advances with the passage of trains, automatically setting route and signals for the next train after cross-checking with the train number.

Automation culminated in the automatic *Victoria Line of 1968. *Computers have allowed the principle to be extended to much larger and more complex areas. The first, trial, installation of Automatic Route Setting (ARS) was at Three Bridges in 1983. BR's Integrated Electronic Control Centres (IECC) allow most or all of the day's operations to be automatically computer-controlled in association with timetable, track circuits, and train descriptions. The signalmen need only intervene for special movements such as *shunting and engine-changing, and in cases of incidents, failures, and out-of-course running. The first installation was *Liverpool Street in 1989, closely followed by Yoker on Tyneside, and *York.   RDF

W. F. Raynar, *Railway Signalling: Automatic* (1922).

signalling equipment manufacture. Most railway *signalling equipment is of a specialist nature and from the 1850s a number of specialist suppliers have existed. Initially, although most of them supplied everything, manufacturers could be divided into two groups: those supplying mechanical and power signalling equipment (signals, interlocking frames, *signal boxes, etc.); and those supplying electrical instruments and systems such as *block instruments, *single-line apparatus, electrical indicators, and train describers. Some early mechanical suppliers began as general iron manufacturers, such as Stevens & Sons of Southwark, founded by John Stevens in the 1820s, who commenced signalling work in 1841.

Another ironworks that became a major signalling supplier was McKenzie & Holland of Worcester. Originally formed in 1861 as a partnership between John McKenzie, Thomas Clunes, and Walter Holland, it became McKenzie & Holland in 1873. Lesser-known examples included E. S. Yardley & Co. of *Manchester (often referred to as Smith & Yardley) and Ransomes & Rapier of Ipswich, better known for agricultural machinery. Some companies were established specifically for signalling work.

Perhaps the best-known name was John Saxby (1821–1913). Originally an employee of the *London Brighton & South Coast Railway, he began manufacturing signalling equipment at Haywards Heath in 1857, and formed a partnership with John Stinson Farmer (1827–92) when he needed finance for a new works at Kilburn in 1863. Saxby & Farmer was the dominant force in signalling from the 1860s to the 1880s.

The market for mechanical signalling grew rapidly in that period, when a second wave of manufacturers, mostly formed by former employees of the earlier companies, became established. They included Easterbrook & Co., formed in 1867 by Walter Easterbrook (1842–1914) from Saxby's. Diversification into signalling by the Gloucester Wagon Co. in 1876 was supervised by George Edwards, originally from Saxby's and signal superintendent of the *London & North Western Railway, 1873–6. Edwards went on to set up the Railway Signal Co. in 1881, probably the most successful contractor in the 1890s. Samuel Telford Dutton, from McKenzie's, set up Dutton & Co. in 1888. The last significant new mechanical contractor was Evans, O'Donnell & Co. of 1894–5, with a works at Chippenham. Other firms which achieved smaller but significant volumes of sales included I'Anson & Sons of Darlington and J. Tweedy & Co. of *Carlisle.

The market for mechanical equipment began to decline in the late 1890s while power signalling demanded more resources. This led to a restructuring of the industry. Agreements between Saxby & Farmer, McKenzie & Holland, Evans O'Donnell, and J. F. Pease & Co. (successors to Dutton) led to the formation of the Pneumatic Electric & General Engineering Co. as a holding company in 1901, renamed Consolidated Signal Co. in 1903. Saxby and McKenzie continued to trade as separate companies but competition was kept to a minimum.

At the same period it became clear that the future lay with power signalling. Saxby marketed a hydraulic system, which did not find favour in Britain; the Railway Signal Co. had a licence for the 'Crewe' all-electric system, while McKenzie obtained a licence to sell the American Union Switch & Signal Co.'s pneumatic system. The last was the most successful, leading to the formation of the McKenzie, Holland & Westinghouse Power Signal Co. in 1907 (McKH&WPSCo) (see WESTINGHOUSE). J. P. O'Donnell formed the British Pneumatic Railway Signal Co. in 1900 (British Power Railway Signal Co. from 1918) with a licence for another American system. Siemens Bros & Co. (Siemens & General Electric Railway Signal Co. (SGE) from 1926) sold the German parent company's system.

Further restructuring in 1915–17 brought the Consolidated Signal Co., McKenzie, Saxby, and McKH&WPSCo under one managing director and in 1920 the signalling interests were transferred to the Westinghouse Brake & Saxby Signal Co.

Electrical instruments and systems were supplied by various companies whose principal work was in *telegraphs and *telephones, and by two specialist railway equipment companies. Edward Tyer (1830–1912) established Tyer & Co. (initially Tyer & Norman) in 1851, with premises at Dalston in London. Tyer specialized in the supply of block telegraph instruments and other electrical aids for *signalmen and was the largest commercial supplier of block instruments. The firm is best known for the electric train tablet system for single-line railways. After acquiring J. Tweedy & Co., mechanical signalling equipment was also supplied and around 1934 it became B. P. & Tyers Signals, combining the Tyer and British Pneumatic businesses. William Robert Sykes of the *London Chatham & Dover Railway set up the W. R. Sykes Interlocking Signal Co. primarily to supply electrical signalling equipment, and best known for the Sykes interlocking block. The firm was continued by his sons and was eventually absorbed by Westinghouse.

The process of change in the signalling business through closures, amalgamation, change of name, and new entrants has continued to the present day. The Consolidated Signal Co. became a shareholder in the Railway Signal Co. from 1903, but it continued to trade independently, specializing in mechanical equipment. It went into liquidation in 1974. Another American company, General Railway Signal Co., joined forces with Metropolitan Vickers Electric Co. to trade as Metropolitan Vickers GRS Ltd, and subsequently with SGE to form GEC-General Signal Ltd, now GEC Alsthom Signalling. The Swiss Integra system has been marketed for many years by Henry Williams Ltd, itself a long-standing supplier of signalling components.

Today the major suppliers are Westinghouse, GEC Alsthom, and EB Signal (UK), formerly M. L. Engineering (Plymouth) Ltd. RDF

Signalling Study Group, *The Signal Box* (1986).

signalmen: the persons responsible for ensuring the safe and expeditious passage of trains by the operation of the *signalling system in accordance with the rules and regulations (see BYE-LAWS).

In the early days of railways, the *stationmasters normally authorized the movements of trains and departures from stations. Most railways employed *policemen to patrol the line to prevent trespass, help ensure safety, and assist in emergencies. Most were required to indicate to passing trains that all was well or stop them in emergencies. As more fixed signals were installed and lines got busier it became the practice for policemen to attend to the signals and help regulate the passage of the trains. At large and busy stations pointsmen were employed to operate the points.

With the introduction of interlocking (see SIGNALLING) and the *block system, control of points and signals was brought together in *signal boxes. Full-time attendance was required and the pointsmen, and those policemen who were spending most of their time on signalling duties, became 'signalmen'. A reminder of the origins of the signalman has lingered on in the railwaymen's slang term 'bobby'.

In mechanical signalling the signalman was the link between the block system, the lever frame and its interlocking, the signals and points, the rules and regulations, and the passage of the trains. Originally he was the only link between the block and interlocking, although electrical controls were gradually introduced and were a feature of power signalling. He was required to enter in a 'train register' details and times of all signals received and sent on the block instruments and bells. This was a valuable discipline to ensure correct working, as well as a memory-aid and a source of evidence in inquiries into *accidents. At busy boxes, 'booking boys' were employed to keep the register.

Signalmen were graded in responsibility and pay according to the importance of the boxes they worked. At the bottom of the scale were 'porter-signalmen' who were only required to undertake signalling duties for part of their day's work. 'Relief signalmen' covered for holidays, rest days, and sickness.

In addition to the rule book there were 'Regulations for Train Signalling' and 'Signalmen's General Instructions' which were written to suit the block (or token: see SINGLE LINES) system in use. Further information to aid the work, such as distances between signal boxes, numbers of running lines, gradients, maximum loads, and special instructions, appeared in the 'Appendix to the Working *Timetable' and related publications, while all signal boxes had their own special instructions or 'footnotes'.

The signalmen had to be familiar with all the documents relevant to the box(es) they worked, and were examined and 'passed out' before taking responsibility for a box. The men were re-examined at regular intervals, usually by their district inspector. Many railways provided signalling schools where the men received formal training through full- or part-time courses. Prizes were often given for outstanding performance in examinations.

Signalmen were responsible for regulating the passage of trains, that is, allowing fast trains to overtake slower ones, deciding the order of trains at junctions, and the line over which they travelled. Timetables, and tables of running times were provided to assist them. The advent of the train *control system spread responsibility and improved decision-making. Power signalling made it possible for one man to control a much larger area, giving economies in manpower and improved operation. As a result of this and line closures the number of signalmen has declined from about 28,000 in 1938 to fewer than 10,000 today.   RDF

J. Aitken, *The Railway Signalman* (c.1944).

signals, see SIGNALLING.

Sinclair, Robert (1817–98), engineer. Educated at Charterhouse School, he was apprenticed to a family firm of engineers at Greenock and then under *Buddicom on the *Grand Junction Railway. He followed Buddicom to France and then found his way into the service of the *Caledonian Railway, becoming its locomotive superintendent in 1847. In 1856 he moved to the same post with the *Eastern Counties Railway, serving for ten years with it and its successor the *Great Eastern.

He was a much better manager than J. V. Gooch, from whom he took over, and he equipped the two companies with locomotives well up to their work, experimenting early with *injectors and the use of steel instead of *iron. He was the first engineer of a southern English main-line company to provide substantial cabs to protect the engine crews.

He avoided the storms that had beset the GER and its predecessors. Nevertheless in 1866 he retired (before he was 50) and lived in Italy for the rest of his life.   JS

Boase; *BDE*.

single lines, working of. The objective in single-line working (nor to be confused with *wrong-line working) is to prevent collisions between following trains or trains travelling in opposite directions on the single line. The earliest and simplest system required that each train be accompanied by a 'pilotman'—only one man, which ensured only one train on the single line. This remains the basic method of temporary single-line working. Pilotman working was soon replaced by use of a staff made of wood or metal (the train staff), marked to show the section of single line to which it referred. The advent of the electric *telegraph and *block working permitted a system (train staff and ticket) under which trains could follow each other on a single line, block working maintaining the space interval between them. The driver of the first train of a series travelling in the same direction was shown the train staff and given a paper ticket authorizing him to proceed on to the single line, and the driver of the last carried the staff through the section.

In 1880 Tyer & Co., with the *Caledonian Railway, produced a system in which a number of metal discs (train tablets) were held in two instruments, one located at each end of the section, electrically interlocked so that only one tablet could be released at any time. Tablets were made in different shapes so that a tablet for one section could not be put into an instrument for an adjacent section. In 1888 *London & North Western Railway officers devised instruments, licensed to the Railway Signal Co., which—though similar in principle in using the polarity of current transmitted from one end of the section to the other to control the electric interlocking—used metal staffs (electric train staffs) not tablets. In 1912 *Great Western Railway signalling engineers developed a system, licensed to Tyer & Co., which used a smaller token, operated in the instrument in the same manner as a key in a lock.

Little-used points on single lines were generally controlled by ground frames, released by the tablet, staff, or key token for the section concerned. Where a train needed to be 'shut inside' a *siding so that other trains could pass, an intermediate instrument was provided.

Train crews exchanged tablets, staffs, or tokens with *signalmen using one of a variety of designs of carrying hoop. This was dangerous even at the maximum authorized speed, usually 15 mph. Methods of automatic exchange were developed, notably by J. Manson, A. Whitaker, and W. Bryson.

The problems of exchanging tokens led to experiments with tokenless block systems. The 1960s saw significant developments of tokenless block, with systems devised in Scotland, on the Western Region of *BR (later adapted to become standard), and on the *Isle of Wight. Where the expense of *track circuiting through the section can be justified, a different form of tokenless working without block instruments can be used, with acceptance levers or switches. In either version of tokenless working, clearance of the section starting-signal (rather than possession of a staff or token) is the driver's authority to enter on to the single line.

Radio Electronic Token Block has been developed as a strategy for cost reduction. Signal boxes at passing loops can be abolished, the token taking the form of a cab display of authority to proceed issued by radio from a central computer, which operates the interlocking.

See also ANNETT'S KEY; SAFETY; SIGNALLING.   MC

G. M. Kichenside and A. Williams, *British Railway Signalling* (1963); Signalling Record Society Papers: 10: F. Alexander, *The Scottish Region Tokenless Block*; 11: D. S. Stirling, *Electric Token Block Instruments*.

slate traffic. Slate quarrying has long been centred on *Wales, and especially on the mountains of Snowdonia. Output peaked in 1898, when Wales produced 507,000 tons, England 91,000, and Scotland 43,000, providing roof coverings for most of Victorian Britain. Without reliable transport through the difficult terrain no slate quarry could succeed, and *narrow-gauge railways—the Penrhyn (1801), Dinorwic (1824), Nantlle (1828), and *Festiniog (1836)—to the nearest ports gave an incalculable stimulus to the four major centres of the Welsh industry. The Penrhyn's greatest annual output was 130,000 tons, the Dinorwic's 98,000, and the Festiniog's 150,000. Other lesser lines followed.

Standard-gauge railways reached the slate regions late: *London & North Western branches to Port Penrhyn and Port Dinorwic (1852), Nantlle, by conversion of the tramway (1866–72), and Blaenau Ffestiniog (1879); the *Cambrian to Portmadoc (1867) and the Festiniog interchange (1872); the *Great Western to Blaenau Ffestiniog (1883). The tradition of shipping by sea took long to break; only after 1900 did more Ffestiniog slate depart by standard-gauge railway than by ship. With the decline of the industry, all the main purpose-built railways closed between 1946 and 1963.

The two largest slate quarries in England were likewise much boosted by rail links—Burlington in the Lake District (*Furness Railway, 1846) together with others in the area, and Delabole in Cornwall (*London & South Western Railway, 1893).

All the narrow-gauge lines had special slate *wagons, as did some of the main-line companies, notably the Furness. MJTL

J. Lindsay, *A History of the North Wales Slate Industry* (1974); *Reg. Hist.*, i, 73; xi; xiv, 99–102.

sleepers, see TRACK.

sleeping car: a *carriage with accommodation for overnight travel, either in berths or compartments, usually with some form of bedding. For use of the facilities a charge is made, in addition to the travel fare. Most sleeping cars have lavatories and an attendant working from a staff *compartment, usually serving refreshments to passengers.

The earliest carriages with seating that was adaptable for sleeping were called 'bed carriages'. The first genuine sleeping car was introduced by the *North British Railway in 1873 between *Glasgow and London *King's Cross. This and other pioneering vehicles, including the early *Pullman sleeping cars imported from the USA, had communal sleeping, with longitudinal berths convertible from seats. The *Great Western Railway was responsible for the genesis in 1890 of the familiar sleeping car layout with an internal side corridor and compartments containing berths—in this case, double berths. This became the conventional British sleeping car, introduced by a variety of railways principally on Anglo-Scottish services, but also between London and the West Country, and London and northern cities.

Third-class facilities were restricted to seated compartments until the GWR, *London Midland & Scottish, and *London & North Eastern Railways simultaneously introduced third-class 'lying-down' accommodation during 1928. A supplement was payable for the hire of a pillow and rug in a four-berth (two upper, two lower) compartment. Washing facilities were available at each end of the carriage only. Third-class sleeping cars were improved after 1948 when two-berth compartments with full bedding and wash-basins were gradually introduced. MLH

slip carriages: *carriages that are designed to be detached from the rear of a train in motion so as to serve intermediate stations. Before the train passed through the station to be served, the coupling of the carriage being detached was 'slipped' by a *guard travelling in this vehicle. He then brought it to a stand, in earlier days using a hand *brake, later using vacuum or air brakes, discharging into and charged by brake reservoirs on the carriage.

The practice was inaugurated in 1858 by the *Great Western, *London Brighton & South Coast, and *South Eastern Railways. The early system of slipping employed rope actuation to slip the coupling and, at later date, to seal the brake pipes of the slip carriage and the main train. A safer arrangement was used by the GWR in which the brake pipe of the slip carriage was not self-sealing, such that the brakes were automatically applied once the vehicle had parted; the guard then released the brake sufficiently to control its deceleration. The GWR slip coupling had a hinged end, and was dropped forward through the coupling link to disengage it by release of a lever in the guard's compartment of the slip carriage. The train heating pipes were designed to part under tension.

Most slip carriages did not have gangway connections. They might be slipped in company with one or more carriages coupled behind. Special tail lamps were carried on the slip carriage and on the last vehicle of the main train. Slipping was discontinued in *fog or falling *snow. The last slip carriage was operated in 1960, at Bicester on the former GWR Paddington–Birmingham line. MLH

Smiles, Samuel (1813–1904), writer. A Scotsman, born at Haddington, he practised as a doctor there in 1832–8. He was then editor of the left-wing *Leeds Times*, 1838–43. In 1845 he became assistant secretary of the Leeds & Thirsk (later *Leeds Northern) Railway, publishing his able analysis *Railway Property: Its Condition and Prospects* in 1849. When his company was merged into the new *North Eastern Railway he became secretary of the *South Eastern Railway, taking a substantial share in planning the company's extension from *London Bridge to *Charing Cross and *Cannon Street.

He helped the establishment of municipal public libraries and advocated state education. But he also championed self-education, and wrote a life of George *Stephenson to show what a man could achieve by his own efforts: an honest and careful book, it deserved the enthusiastic reception given to it when published in 1857. His *Self-Help* (1859) had much greater commercial success: 55,000 copies were sold in 1859–64.

Smiles extended his biographical work with his *Lives of the Engineers* and *Industrial Biography*, besides other popular books treating the theme of self-help more directly. After leaving the SER, he devoted himself mainly to writing and travelling. His *Autobiography* was published in 1905. JS

DNB; *Ottley, 189, 2471–2, 5272, 7118, 7203, 7285.

smoking of tobacco was generally, though not quite universally, prohibited on railway premises and trains from the 1830s until 1868. From then on legislation required the railways to provide accommodation for smokers, until in the 1980s changing social attitudes and perception of *fire risk reversed the process and complete bans on the practice were introduced in many areas.

The *Liverpool & Manchester Railway in 1831 prohibited smoking in first-class carriages, even with the consent of the passengers present. It was the dislike of smoke pollution on upholstery and fittings that weighed; as there were none in second- and third-class accommodation, smoking was at first tolerated there. But the LMR prohibited any smoking on its trains and premises from 1838, mainly it seems for fear of fires in its warehouses.

The *London & Birmingham, *Great Western, and *South Eastern Railways put a total ban on smoking from the start, and the Railways Clauses Act, 1845, authorized the companies to pass *bye-laws forbidding smoking 'and the commission of any other nuisance' in trains and premises. The SER in 1845 stopped smoking on *London & Greenwich trains (permitted until then) and the sale of cigars or tobacco at refreshment rooms. On the other hand, the *Eastern Counties Railway in 1846 provided some special saloon carriages—travelling 'cigar-divans', with apparently some sort of air extractor in the roof. A first-class carriage for smokers was run on the *North Eastern Railway's Tynemouth branch in 1856, and there was one on the *Stockton & Darlington in or shortly before 1863.

But such provision was exceptional; people smoked in defiance of the bye-laws and penalties. The GWR was specially active in trying to stamp out smoking by special order in 1865; but the *Great Northern reported that it was 'universal' in trains, and in that year it agreed to mark smoking compartments on its local trains between London and Hitchin; in 1867 it provided smoking accommodation on its expresses to Yorkshire, but not to *Manchester.

In 1868, however, all this was changed by a clause (the 'Sheridan' clause) in the *Regulation of Railways Act, warmly supported by the social reformer John Stuart Mill. This provided that a smoking carriage must be attached to every train containing more than one carriage of each class, unless the Board of *Trade gave a special exemption. This it did for the underground railways in London; but when the *Metropolitan District, on its extension to Hammersmith in 1874, provided smoking compartments, the *Metropolitan reluctantly followed suit. The *Highland Railway never provided more than one smoking compartment in each class.

Smoking accommodation was normally specially marked—the GWR at first used a large 'S' painted on the door exterior. Later 'no smoking' signs were shown. Baedeker's London guide for 1923 noted that the *South Eastern & Chatham Railway alone labelled 'non-smoking' carriages. The *London Underground began to do so in 1926, and this soon became general practice.

After 1960, in response to changed demand, the proportion of areas in which smoking was permitted was progressively reduced. It was banned in *London Transport trains and underground areas from 1985 and throughout the whole system from 1987, after fires at Goodge Street (1981), Oxford Circus (1984), and *King's Cross (1987), where lighted cigarettes or matches were suspected of being the cause. At the same period, smoking accommodation was withdrawn from a number of *British Rail services, including the whole London suburban system and from the first class on certain long-distance trains; also in underground areas at stations.

See also CARRIAGES.   RMR

C. E. Lee, *Passenger Class Distinctions* (1946), 35; C. Hamilton Ellis, *Railway Carriages in the British Isles from 1830 to 1914* (1965), 37, 117.

Snaefell Electric Railway, see ISLE OF MAN RAILWAYS; MOUNTAIN RAILWAYS.

snow. Of all the hazards which afflict railways, snow is arguably the worst: unpredictable in arrival, in both date and location, and variable in quantity and, particularly, form. One cu ft of snow may weigh between 7 and 60 lb.

Trains have become embedded in dramatic drifts. Even a light coating of snow underfoot restricts movements of staff and hinders their arrival at work, leading to labour shortages and long working hours. Snow has blocked points, formed insulating ice on conductor rails, and brought down overhead cables and telegraph wires. It has caused derailments and collisions, and makes it difficult for enginemen to see signals, or indeed anything much at all.

Snow caused delays on the *Liverpool & Manchester Railway as early as 1830. It blocked the *Great Northern Railway in 1854, and was the root cause of the disastrous multiple collision at Abbots Ripton in 1876 (see ACCIDENTS): snow had frozen the arms of slotted post signals (see SIGNALLING) into the 'clear' position. In 1906, at Elliott Junction near Arbroath, a blinding snowstorm caused a collision which killed 22 people.

In 1880–1 heavy snowfalls obstructed the *London & South Western and *Great Western Railways, and blocked the *Settle & Carlisle line: and in 1941 snow fell continuously in north-east England between 19 and 21 February. The main line and all alternative routes between Darlington and *Newcastle upon Tyne were blocked, and the lines into Newcastle from west, north, and east also. In March 1947 blizzards seriously dislocated railways in the home counties, South Wales, and south-west Scotland; the Settle & Carlisle line was blocked for a month.

The *Highland Railway's main line to *Inverness was blocked by snow for the first time in 1865, and subsequently snow blockages became almost an annual occurrence. Particular danger points were Drumochter Summit, and near Altnabreac on the line to Wick. Trains became first stuck, then buried in snow drifts. During the severe winter of 1894–5 the Dingwall & Skye line was blocked for a week, when snow also badly affected the West Highland Railway in its first year of operation, becoming a recurrent problem.

The winter of 1962–3 was the worst of the 20th century, with much of Britain under snow for several weeks, disrupting rail services. On 31 December a blizzard blew up in south Devon. It was the last day of passenger trains on the

Plymouth–Launceston branch, but the final scheduled trains never ran as earlier trains were already stranded. Recent winters have been less severe, although in 1982 the Inverness–Wick line was blocked for a week. Nationwide snow in February 1991 saw much dislocation of routes operated by electric *multiple units, which succumbed to powdered snow penetrating the traction motors. The railways received much opprobrium when they described it as 'the wrong kind of snow'.

The basic cure for snow blockages throughout most of the railway era has been gangs of railwaymen with shovels, aided in wartime by servicemen. The snows of 1854 prompted Archibald Sturrock to design snowploughs for the GNR, and William *Stroudley, locomotive superintendent of the HR in 1865–9, designed snowploughs for that line in three sizes: nose-ploughs attached to locomotive buffer-beams for drifts up to 2 ft deep; a larger type for drifts up to 5 ft; and the largest of all, one which reached to the top of the smokebox and could deal with 12-ft drifts. A similar range of snowploughs was still being used by *British Railways, Scottish Region, in the 1960s. The *North Eastern Railway, in the 1880s, built snowploughs upon the frames of scrapped locomotives. In 1995 several classes of diesel locomotives and multiple units are fitted permanently with small snowploughs, while Railtrack has 20 large snowploughs—some of them built on old steam locomotive tenders—and two powerful snowblowers with rotating blades.

Prevention is better than cure. On the HR, point rods were boxed in and signal wires elevated at crucial locations. Snow fences made from old sleepers were set up alongside the line at exposed places, and on the West Highland line after its first winter; the worst affected cutting was roofed over to become the only snow-shed in Britain. In 1978 it was arranged for trains on the Highland and West Highland lines to carry survival hampers containing emergency supplies.

To prevent points freezing, *London Transport was using point heaters on surface lines by the early 1960s, and BR was starting to install them. Subsequently they came into general use on main lines. De-icing trains, to scrape electric conductor rails and spray them with anti-freeze, came into use on London Transport and the Southern Region of BR at the same period.

Sometimes snow brings benefits: early in 1963 BR found valuable business carrying to London motor cars which had been left behind by their owners in the snowbound West Country.   PJGR

G. R. Parkes, *Railway Snowfighting Equipment and Methods* (1961); H. A. Vallance, *The Highland Railway* (1985 edn.); L. T. C. Rolt, *Red for Danger* (1955), ch. 4; RM, 109 (1963), 159–70; 137 (1991), 268–71.

Snowdon Mountain Railway, see MOUNTAIN RAILWAYS.

social effects of railways. 'We see, in this magnificent creation, the well-spring of intellectual, moral and political benefits beyond all measurement and all price.' So the Tory *Quarterly Review* saluted the opening of the *Liverpool &

Manchester Railway in 1830. This article indicates a few of the effects that the 'magnificent creation' produced on the development of British society.

The most conspicuously impressive of all the benefits that the early railways brought was the quite new speed of communication they offered. 'Everything is near', wrote Sydney Smith, referring to them, in 1842; 'everything is immediate—time, distance, and delay are abolished.' And by 1845 a different sort of speed, equally astonishing, had appeared, in close association with railways. The electric *telegraph was then providing almost instantaneous communication from Yarmouth to Norwich (20 miles apart) and from *London to Gosport (88 miles), the railways allowing the telegraph lines to be laid beside their tracks and the public being able to send and receive messages by this means.

Over the next 20 years these developments extended. Railway travel then became possible from *Aberdeen to Penzance, and from Holyhead to Dover, and these places were all linked by the telegraph as well. By 1862 the journey from *London to *Edinburgh could be made in 10½ hours; in 1836 it had taken 43.

The railways and the telegraphs, in conjunction, soon displayed their power in other ways too. They wrought great changes in the provincial daily press (see NEWSPAPER TRAFFIC); and they caused the adoption of one standard *time throughout the country, taken from Greenwich. A new concept of the meaning of 'time' itself now began to appear, as something to be watched constantly, hoarded so that none of it should be lost. All life, public and private, came to be regulated with a new awareness of time, precisely expressed. These changed habits of thinking gradually came to pervade the whole of Victorian society.

Here was a new rigidity, a tightening of the rules governing social and commercial behaviour. But the railways also did much to loosen those rules. They opened the way to a quite new personal mobility. And—what makes this social liberation most remarkable—it was not conferred, as had invariably happened in the past, only on those who could buy it at a high price. It quickly came to be offered to all but the very poor.

The principle of imposing a standard low minimum *fare to be charged by all railway companies was established by *Gladstone's Act in 1844. In accordance with it, every line came to provide *parliamentary trains at penny-a-mile fares; and though that was not as cheap as might be supposed (a penny could buy half a pound of bread in London in 1844), it was much lower, given the quality of the service offered, than what had been charged for any kind of public transport in the past. The welcome it received speaks for itself. By 1850 more than 50 per cent of British *passenger journeys were being made at the parliamentary rate or less; by 1875 journeys at the lowest fares were 80 per cent; by 1913, 96 per cent; in 1994, 99 per cent.

The same tendency appeared in most European countries. But the British railways' practices differed from those of nearly all of them in two important respects. First, by

1890 they admitted third-class passengers to nearly every train they ran (a policy that had then been adopted on the European mainland only by Denmark), and they charged scarcely any supplements for travelling even by the fastest *express trains. So, except in matters connected with seating, the British third-class passenger travelled almost on an equality with the first (see CLASS DISTINCTIONS). Secondly (doubtless, in part, as a consequence), the total number of passenger journeys made every year in Great Britain was very much larger than in any other European country. In 1880–1 it was twice as many as in France and Belgium combined; 30 years later it was still one third higher, and 43 per cent higher than in Germany. British people evidently used their railways much more than any of their neighbours.

That may be attributed in part to higher wages in Britain, to a generally higher standard of living, to a shorter working week, and an increasing acceptance by employers (the railway companies included) of the principle of granting holidays with pay. It also sprang from the *competitive system established on British railways, impelling them to run faster and more numerous trains than any of the governments that controlled the railways elsewhere in Europe.

The higher numbers of people travelling on British railways can be accounted for in another way too: by the extraordinary density of movement into, round, and beneath London and many of the other large cities in the country. That was greater in the 19th century than any found elsewhere in Europe, though the multiplication of *underground railways there (on British models) has changed that preponderance in the 20th.

When the volume of third-class travel in Britain is looked at and analysed with care, it leads to the conclusion that the railways assisted the development of social democracy there—using that phrase in a broad sense, not a narrowly political one. The density of the system, pervading all the most heavily populated areas; the railways' favourable treatment of third-class passengers; the lavish competitive services they offered, impeded very little by the restrictions that were imposed by most other European railways on the use of the fastest trains; the provision of *workmen's trains on a large scale, and of extra-cheap *excursion trains, to an extent quite unknown elsewhere: all these policies, taken together, constituted a great levelling-up of opportunity, in close accordance with the enlargement of voting powers and the lowering of the barriers between men and women. No railway company adopted them from any specifically political motive—that could scarcely be looked for in joint-stock companies' directors, managers, or shareholders. But they all came to face and accept them: freely and deliberately, like the *Midland Railway and the *Great Eastern; slowly, yet in the end whole-heartedly, as on the *London & North Western and *Great Western.

One of the prospective effects of the extension of railways that was welcomed by the reviewer of 1830 was 'a better distribution of our population—a check to the alarming growth of cities, especially of manufacturing towns, and of this Babylon in which we write': i.e. London, whose growth

many people had already been deploring for over 200 years. His wishes here were not fulfilled. The population of Greater London steadily increased, by a factor of 2.5 in 1831–1911; that of the 12 largest provincial cities, added together, by almost 4. The railways assisted that expansion by the services they afforded out into *suburbs, none of which prospered in the 19th century if it remained without a railway for long.

Another great change they assisted was to encourage migration, most of which went from thinly populated rural districts into the towns or overseas. The part that railways took in this process can be observed with particular clarity in mid-Wales and the Scottish Highlands. But they did more than that. The cheap travel they offered served to aid movement from one town or manufacturing district to another: first, in the search for new employment; then, when it had been found, in the quick removal of whole families to new homes. This increased the mobility of labour, sometimes following the lines of the railways themselves, so that colonies of people from South Wales came to be found at Swindon, and of Scots in and around Kettering.

Had that reviewer foreseen what the real redistribution of the British people would turn out to be, aided by railways, he might have denounced it with the vigour of Jeremiah. But we, looking back now, can see that it brought benefits with it as well as evils, particularly in the growth of suburbs, affording many bread-winners and their families a healthier, more pleasurable life than they had led near the increasingly polluted town centres; though that might be offset by miserable conditions on the railway travelling to and from work.

The last large-scale effect of the railways' development to be discussed here is one that was frequently mentioned, with dislike or approval: their tendency to impose standardization, even complete uniformity, on the country as a whole. Regional differences within the island, in food or clothing, prices or social customs, were lessened or destroyed by them. From 1851 onwards each census of England showed a greater preponderance of dwellers in towns over those who lived outside them, and the towns' standards and practices inevitably grew more powerful. Here the railways were clearly in part responsible (see TOWNS, RAILWAYS AND THE DEVELOPMENT OF). Their system itself had been based on towns from the start, such as Stockton & Darlington, Liverpool & Manchester, London & Birmingham. Those connections grew steadily stronger. In the railways' hands small towns became, more and more, the satellites of large ones.

The development of chains of shops, particularly in the grocery business from the 1880s onwards, increased the power of the towns in the economy of country districts; and they all purveyed standard articles—brands of tea, sugar, to an increasing extent tinned foods—identical in Lancaster, Leicester, and Launceston. Their prices were usually lower than those charged in the village shops, largely owing to bulk conveyance by railway. Here was a great strengthening of the forces making for uniformity in daily life.

But uniformity was strengthened by the railways in another way: in the power of the government over the whole country. Its business could be much more efficiently conducted, from its awkward centre in the south-eastern corner of the island, now that it could impose orders instantly by means of the telegraph, backing them up in an emergency by the rapid conveyance of police or troops by rail to a centre of disorder. Some of its own services were now also enlarged and improved in collaboration with the railways, having profoundly beneficial effects on the whole community of Britain: notably the *Post Office, with the telegraphs, nationalized in 1868 and attached to it.

In the greatest emergencies, those arising from the two world wars, the railways formed a loyal and effective instrument in governments' hands in the defence of the country, in the dispersal of much of its urban population from bombing, and in mounting the great counter-attacks of 1918 and 1944–5 that brought the wars to a victorious conclusion (see WAR; GOVERNMENT, RAILWAYS AND NATIONAL).

It cannot be said that the politicians showed any serious appreciation of the debt that Britain owed to its railways, whether in the Railways Act of 1921 (see GROUPING) or in the *privatization Act of 1993. A perceptive and just-minded historian may some day expose the ingratitude, and judge it with severity.   JS
    Quarterly Review (1830); S. Smith, *Works* (1869 edn.), 793; *VR*, chs 14–16.

Somerset & Dorset Joint Railway. In 1862 two companies amalgamated as the Somerset & Dorset Railway. The Somerset Central had opened from the *Bristol & Exeter Railway at Highbridge to Glastonbury, Wells, and Burnham-on-Sea in 1854–9. Steamers plied to Cardiff from Burnham from 1860 to 1888. In 1860–2 the Dorset Central had opened from the *London & South Western Railway at Wimborne, through Templecombe—where later there was another junction with the LSWR—to meet an extension of the SCR. After the new company underwent four years in receivership, it nearly bankrupted itself again by opening in 1874 a northward extension from Evercreech across the Mendips to Bath, which became the main line.

Realizing the line's strategic potential as a route from the Midlands and the north to the growing resort of *Bournemouth, the LSW and *Midland companies leased it jointly in 1875. Shortly afterwards 13 people died in a head-on collision near Radstock (see ACCIDENTS). The Bridgwater Railway from Edington Junction, leased to the LSWR and opened in 1890, was worked as part of the SDJR.

The total route mileage was 102. Parts of the 64-mile main line were doubled, leaving 26 miles single which, with the hilly northern section, made it difficult to work. Heavy expresses frequently required two engines. The line had its own management, and a works at Highbridge. Locomotives, which were built by the Midland, and *carriages bore a striking blue livery.

After the 1923 *Grouping the line started losing money, and despite economies in 1930 when the *Southern Railway assumed responsibility for infrastructure and signalling, and

the *London Midland & Scottish for locomotives and operating, it remained unprofitable. *BR progressively closed it in 1951–66.   GJB
    R. Atthill, *The Somerset & Dorset Railway* (1970 edn.); *Reg. Hist.*, i (1988 edn.), ch. 10.

sources of railway history. This note is a brief guide to some of the chief sources of British railway history as used in this book.

What are often called 'primary sources'—meaning the most important, original sources—may be either in manuscript or printed. It is a mistake to suggest that manuscript documents are the more valuable, merely because they have not been printed. Parliamentary Papers, Railway *Returns, and *Accident Reports are collections of printed documents that are of primary importance. The printed Acts of Parliament (see PARLIAMENT AND LEGISLATION) constitute the foundation of all public railways.

The article ARCHIVES AND RECORDS surveys the main categories of manuscript documents, official and unofficial. The articles LITERATURE OF RAILWAYS, GUIDEBOOKS, and PRESS, RAILWAY, offer a broad general view of printed works, in addition to those referred to above. *Maps and plans and *timetables are also particularly important, and local newspapers provide valuable contemporary material. Other sources of knowledge are treated under PHOTOGRAPHY, ART, MUSEUMS, and NATIONAL RAILWAY MUSEUM.

The railways themselves, their earthworks, bridges, tunnels, track, and stations, are (so far as they survive or can be traced) part of the evidence for their own history (see ARCHAEOLOGY OF RAILWAYS).   JS

Southampton. In 1815 Southampton was a quiet seaside resort, with few remains of its ancient commercial prosperity. Its maritime business revived, however, in the 1820s with the introduction of steamships running to the Channel Islands and France.

When the London & Southampton Railway was projected in 1831–3 it was well backed locally, and also in *Manchester, which took up 40 per cent of the original shares. It was authorized in 1834 and opened in 1838–40; a westward extension to Dorchester followed in 1847. The Royal Pier was built in 1833, and a dock followed ten years later, used by ships engaged in the south Atlantic and Indian trades. For passengers to and from London, Southampton had a great advantage. The long, dangerous sea passage round Kent into the Thames could now be replaced by a railway journey made in three hours.

The relationship between the railway and the town, however, became unhappy. The company changed its name to *London & South Western in 1839, declaring its intention to become more than a railway between London and Southampton. But it held a *monopoly, and many townspeople complained that it charged high rates for poor service. Their antagonism to the company came even to affect parliamentary elections.

In the scale of Victorian towns, Southampton remained small. Its population reached 50,000 only in 1871, and 100,000 in 1901. It had no substantial manufactures, nor any industrial hinterland, lying as it did far from large coalfields. Its development depended entirely on the docks, which were under-capitalized and soon grew inadequate. Attempts to bring in another railway to compete with the LSWR (supported by the rival *Great Western Railway) met with small success. But with the development of *Bournemouth the town got a better service. The LSWR now came to appreciate the potential value of its Southampton traffic, and bought the docks in 1892. The port soon shot ahead, rivalling *Liverpool in the transatlantic trade. It handled the conveyance of soldiers to the South African war of 1899–1902 with admirable efficiency, and did equally well in meeting the same demands in both world wars.

Southampton remained predominantly a passenger port. Two disasters struck it: from air-raids in World War II, and then from the growth of transatlantic air travel. The *Southern Railway projected the construction of a very large Ocean Terminal, but the impressive building was not completed until 1953. Already by that time 500,000 passengers were flying the Atlantic annually. Within ten years that number had multiplied by five, and the fares were coming down.

Southampton now became a big oil port (with Fawley refinery close by) and a principal centre of Britain's maritime *container traffic, handled at first chiefly by rail, but now increasingly by road. (See also SCOTTER, SIR C.)   JS
A. T. Patterson, *History of Southampton* (1966–75), and *Southampton: A Biography* (1970); Manchester investment: M. C. Reed, *Investment in Railways in Britain, 1801–44* (1975), 147–51.

South Devon Railway.
Following the authorization of the *Bristol & Exeter Railway in 1836, plans were prepared for a broad-gauge line on to *Plymouth, surveyed by *Brunel, but not authorized until 1844.

The line had to cross the foothills of Dartmoor, demanding steep gradients and extensive *tunnelling. The route was 53 miles long, against 45 by the hillier coach road. Brunel now determined to work the line with stationary engines and pneumatic power (see ATMOSPHERIC RAILWAYS). The level 20 miles from Exeter to Newton Abbot were opened in 1846, but the impracticalities of the system prevented its extension, and it was abandoned, at a heavy cost, in favour of locomotives. The line reached Plymouth in 1849. A branch to Torquay had been opened in 1848.

The *Great Western Railway at first supplied locomotives, but in 1851–66 *contractors undertook to work the line, at high cost, giving them large profits. One of them, Daniel *Gooch, designed the highly successful 4-4-0 saddle-tank engines that did most of the work.

In 1859–68 the Torquay branch was extended to Paignton, Kingswear, and Brixham by a nominally independent company, as were the branches to Tavistock (1859), which was extended to Launceston in 1865; Moretonhampstead (1866); and Ashburton (1872). The SDR system then totalled 126 miles.

The Tavistock and Launceston line occasioned protracted disputes with the *London & South Western Railway which, determined to get to Plymouth via Okehampton, secured *running powers from Lydford to Plymouth, requiring a third rail to accommodate its standard-gauge traffic, and LSWR trains reached Plymouth in 1876, three months after the SDR had agreed to amalgamate with the GWR. The arrangement was validated by Parliament in 1878.

The SDR owed a substantial debt to Thomas Woollcombe, a Devonport solicitor and its patient and tenacious chairman in 1849–74. F. P. Cockshott, its traffic superintendent in 1851–65, became the *Great Northern Railway's superintendent of the line, 1865–95.   JS
MacDermot, ii, ch. 6; C. H. Gregory, *The South Devon Railway* (1982).

South Eastern Railway.
This was not the first railway in Kent, but earlier ones were quite small: the short *Canterbury & Whitstable (1830), the *London & Greenwich, opened in 1836, and a short mineral railway at Swanscombe laid in 1825 by a cement maker. There had been no lack of plans for railways, including one by Thomas *Telford in 1829 from London to Dover, and by Henry Palmer to Ramsgate in 1830. Out of a jumble of projects, the South Eastern Railway Bill came to Parliament, and the Act was gained in 1836, for a line to Folkestone and Dover.

No sooner had work started than the London & Brighton Act of 1837 (see LONDON BRIGHTON & SOUTH COAST RAILWAY) required both lines to enter London on the same metals, from a junction at Redhill, then called Reigate Junction. The SER abandoned its route via Oxted, and the shared route was built, the Brighton Railway being required to sell the portion from Reigate Junction to Stoats Nest (Coulsdon) to the SER. The joint line met the *London & Croydon Railway at the latter point, and all three met the Greenwich Railway in Bermondsey, over which they ran to stations at *London Bridge. Thus the SER began life working over three other railways, to two of which it paid tolls.

Once the SER climbed out of Redhill and entered its own county, it ran direct to Ashford, which it made a railway *town, reaching Folkestone in 1843 and then traversing the foot of the cliffs to Dover in 1844. Its first train had run as far as Tonbridge in 1842. At London Bridge every train on the SER had to cross the LGR track, so an exchange of stations took place.

It took the SER less than 20 years to cover the county with its main network: Ramsgate and Margate, 1846; Deal, 1847; Tunbridge Wells, 1845; Hastings, 1851; Gravesend, 1849; Maidstone via Strood, 1856. The Reading branch (1858) was a financial disaster. The North Kent line involved taking over the 1844 Gravesend & Rochester Railway, which was built on a *canal towpath and had a *tunnel 4,012 yds long with a small open gap near the middle. The North Kent was regarded for many years as separate, with its own station at London Bridge after an abortive attempt to persuade its passengers to use a terminus at Bricklayers Arms.

The company started a cross-channel service, at first through a wholly owned subsidiary, in 1845; the first paddle steamers of 300 tons gave passengers a rough 2½ hours of crossing in bad weather, but the ships' tonnage had risen to 1,000 by the end of the century (see SHIPPING SERVICES). The Folkestone service was tidal until 1880 (see BOAT TRAINS); a misunderstanding about tidal timings led to the severe *accident at Staplehurst in which Charles Dickens was involved.

Sir Edward *Watkin became chairman in 1866 and controlled the company until his retirement in 1894; his vaulting ambition was for a 'Watkin' route from *Manchester to Paris, by way of the Manchester Sheffield & Lincolnshire (see GREAT CENTRAL), *Metropolitan, SER, and a *Channel Tunnel. In 1868 the direct SER line to Tonbridge was opened; this saved 13 miles, and ended disputes with the LBSCR, but called for a long and punishing climb, the so-called Halstead Bank, ten miles at up to 1 in 120 for southbound trains. Fortunately by 1878 James Stirling was CME, and producing excellent engines; his predecessors had provided very few of adequate power and almost no tank engines for suburban work. His carriages were less praiseworthy. However, some luxurious American 'cars' were put on the Hastings service, followed in 1897 by another 'American Car Train' (but built in Britain) on the Folkestone line.

In 1864 the imposing *Charing Cross terminus was opened, with a large *hotel. The equally impressive *Cannon Street followed in 1866.

For most of its life the company was in bitter dispute with the *London Chatham & Dover Railway, resolved by forming a joint *South Eastern & Chatham Railways Managing Committee, which started work in 1899.   RWK

G. Measom, *Official Guide to the South Eastern Railway* (1858); G. A. Sekon, *History of the South Eastern Railway* (1895); A. Gray, *South Eastern Railway* (1990); Acworth, 357–81.

South Eastern & Chatham Railway.
A Joint Committee was set up in August 1898, under the chairmanship of Cosmo *Bonsor, to run the *South Eastern and London Chatham & Dover Railways as one. The original companies would remain in being; the agreement was sealed to start on 1 January 1899. Rationalization was not thorough; the competing branches to Margate and Ramsgate remained until after the *Grouping. The SER took 59 per cent of receipts. Its rolling stock was in better shape, so more of its old rival's engines and carriages were scrapped.

Both companies had poor reputations and the public needed to see the new SECR as more than the sum of its parts. *Wainwright's graceful D class 4-4-0 locomotives and red painted carriages set the pace. An important step was the joining of the two main lines where they crossed near Bickley by four long spurs; continental trains could now be handled with greater flexibility. These high-quality trains, with *Pullmans from 1910, deflected attention from the sordid suburban stock. A grand new dockside station called Dover Marine was opened in 1919.

World War I fully strained the SECR, which equipped a number of hospital trains, and loaned engines for shunting in France. Afterwards the Committee put in hand as much

modernization of engine and carriage stock as was possible, bearing in mind many restricted-weight bridges and some narrow tunnels; there were also plans for the *electrification of the suburban lines, later carried through under *Southern Railway auspices.   RWK

C. F. Dendy Marshall, *History of the Southern Railway* (rev. R. W. Kidner, 1963), pts I and IV; R. H. Clark, *Southern Region Chronology and Record* (1964); N. Wakeman, *SE&CR Locomotive List* (1953).

Southend-on-Sea, see LONDON TILBURY & SOUTHEND RAILWAY.

Southern Railway.
Smallest of the four *'Groups' created by the Railways Act, 1921, the SR was compact, with a virtual rail monopoly over the south of England and a straggling main line to the West Country meeting *Great Western competition, e.g. at *Exeter and *Plymouth. Its constituent companies were the *London & South Western, the *London Brighton & South Coast, and the *South Eastern & Chatham Railways.

At its birth in 1923 the SR inherited a network of overlapping suburban routes in South London and no fewer than seven London terminal stations, the product of wasteful 19th-century competition. A few suburban lines had been *electrified (on two different systems) by the LSWR and the LBSCR, but the steam services, particularly of the SECR, attracted widespread criticism for slowness, unpunctuality, and obsolete carriages.

There were, however, main-line services to coastal resorts such as *Brighton and *Bournemouth, and continental boat trains, some with *Pullman cars or *restaurant cars operated by contractors, that were well regarded. The SR was unique in relying on passenger traffic for three-quarters of its total receipts. In the absence of much profitable freight, it was creditable that its net revenue of £6.5 million in 1923 survived road competition and was £6.2 million in 1937. This was chiefly due to the energetic policy of electrification pursued by the SR general manager, Sir Herbert *Walker.

Walker supported the third-rail dc system against the overhead ac system adopted by the LBSCR; but gaps in the conductor rail were considered to preclude using locomotives, so all freight on electrified lines continued to be steam-hauled.

The SR directors supported Walker's 'rolling programme' of electrification under which teams were continuously employed under Alfred Raworth. By 1931 293 route miles had been electrified, covering virtually the whole suburban network; the former LBSCR overhead system had also been converted to third rail to promote standardization and through running.

In 1933 a start was made with main-line electrification. Brighton and Worthing were reached first, followed by Eastbourne and Hastings in 1935, *Portsmouth by the ex-LSWR route in 1937, and by the ex-LBSCR route (together with Bognor and Littlehampton) in 1938.

These schemes displaced many steam locomotives; however, the SR's successive CMEs, R. E. L. *Maunsell and

O. V. S. *Bulleid, designed and built some impressive express passenger locomotives as well as some for freight work.

While the suburban services were being improved by the provision of clean, frequent, and regular-interval train services, new corridor coaches as well as restaurant cars were being built for long-distance expresses. Most expresses on electrified routes included a Pullman or *buffet car. Steam-hauled all-Pullman trains included the Golden Arrow continental boat train, with a special fast steamer connection, and the Bournemouth Belle. The Brighton Belle was unique as an all-Pullman electric train.

The SR developed the continental and Channel Islands *shipping services which had been operated by its constituent railways. After replacing vessels lost on war service, by 1931 the SR fleet comprised 44 ships on cross-channel services and 12 Isle of Wight ferries. In 1930 Parliament rejected the proposal for a *Channel Tunnel, and the SR embarked, in association with the Nord Railway of France, upon building train ferry ships to carry both wagons and the Night Ferry sleeping car service operated by the International Sleeping Car Company. The Night Ferry and the Golden Arrow partially succeeded in meeting the new airline competition.

The SR invested substantially in the development of *Southampton as a major liner port by building the West Docks and a graving dock; it started to build an impressive Ocean Terminal after World War II, completed after *nationalization.

The SR was heavily engaged during World War II with armed services traffic (especially during the Dunkirk evacuation and the D-day landings) and suffered severely from bombing, though the third-rail electrification system proved capable of rapid restoration to service after damage.

Electrification was not resumed between the end of the war and nationalization in 1948, when the SR became the Southern Region of *British Railways. Sir Herbert Walker had retired in 1937. He was succeeded by G. S. *Szlumper, and then by E. J. (Sir Eustace) *Missenden.   MRB

C. F. Dendy Marshall, *History of the Southern Railway* (1963 edn.); E. Course, *The Railways of Southern England* (1976); C. F. Klapper, *Sir Herbert Walker's Southern Railway* (1973); *Reg. Hist.*, ii (1992); M. R. Bonavia, *History of the Southern Railway* (1987).

South Shields Marsden & Whitburn Colliery Railway, see INDUSTRIAL RAILWAYS.

South Staffordshire Railway: an amalgamation, effected in 1846, of two newly authorized companies, the South Staffordshire Junction and the Trent Valley Midlands & Grand Junction. It ran from Dudley across the great coal and iron-working district of the Black Country, via Wednesbury and Walsall, to Wichnor on the *Midland Railway's Birmingham–Derby line, with *running powers beyond to Burton-on-Trent. It was opened in 1847–50. The engineer J. R. McClean took a lease of the company, confirmed by Act of Parliament in 1850, the first that sanctioned such a lease to an individual person (see CONTRACT, WORKING OF RAILWAYS BY).

G. P. *Neele, chief clerk to the company in 1849–61, recorded interesting details of the operation of the line under this lease, especially of *signalling arrangements. Among its locomotives were two of the earliest *tank engines in their fully developed form. McClean's interests extended into waterworks and coal-mining. He developed the Marquess of Anglesey's Cannock Chase coalfield, into which a branch ran from the SSR in 1859.

The *London & North Western Railway was anxious lest the Midland should take over the SSR and thereby gain an assured entrance into the Black Country. It accordingly negotiated with McClean to take over his lease. This was settled in 1861, and the LNWR absorbed the SSR outright in 1867.   JS

Reg. Hist., vii, ch. 7; G. P. Neele, *Railway Reminiscences* (1904), chs 2–4; *BSRL*, 103–5.

South Wales Railway. Incorporated in 1845, this was an offshoot of the *Great Western, designed to run from a point near Gloucester to Fishguard, where it was to connect with steamships for *Ireland. It was opened to Carmarthen in 1852 but never reached Fishguard, being diverted instead to Milford Haven, whence a steamer service ran to Waterford. *Brunel was the engineer. The work included big viaducts at Chepstow, Newport, and Landore, and a lifting bridge at Carmarthen.

It was laid down to the 7-ft broad *gauge, necessary for the running of through trains from the GWR. But nearly all the lines coming down from the Monmouth and Glamorgan coalfields and ironworks to the sea were built to the standard gauge. Any freight from them consigned over the SWR had therefore to be transhipped where the lines crossed, adding substantially to its market price.

The company did not prosper and, with some reason, its shareholders blamed the GWR. C. R. M. Talbot, who became chairman in 1852, managed by patience and diplomacy to prevent a rupture between the companies, but there was never real peace until they amalgamated in 1863.

All the company's locomotives and rolling stock were supplied by the GWR. The line was operated, however, by its own staff. Its passenger service was exceedingly slow. Few trunk railways in Britain can have been as unpopular in their localities as this one. In 1866 South Wales industrialists and freighters presented a memorial to the GWR board, signed by 269 firms, asking for the provision of the standard gauge. Their request was met at last in 1872, when (during a single weekend) the broad gauge was replaced by the standard throughout the SWR system—263 route miles in all.

Only six weeks later an Act went into force sanctioning the construction of the *Severn Tunnel. When that great work was completed in 1886, the new line reduced the distance between Newport and London by 25 miles.

At the same time various efforts were made by independent companies to extend the line to Fishguard. They succeeded only in 1899, under the GWR, which proceeded to construct a deep-water port there, in alliance with Irish interests (see PORTS AND DOCKS). It was brought into use in

1906 for services to and from Ireland, and three years later for a time it accommodated the fastest ships crossing the Atlantic from America.   JS

MacDermot, i, 293–308; ii, 218–19, 227–8, 234–5; *Reg. Hist.*, xii, ch. 2.

Southwold Railway: a 3-ft *gauge line, 8¾ miles long, from Halesworth on the *Great Eastern Railway's Ipswich–Lowestoft line to Southwold (population 2,100), opened in 1879. It gave valuable assistance to the town's fishing industry, which had languished, and conveyed summer holiday-makers in substantial numbers. The company unwisely declined an offer to purchase from the GER in 1893. It just made ends meet, until in 1911–13 it paid a 2 per cent dividend. The railway was ruined by *bus competition from 1926 onwards and closed in 1929. Reg Carter's delightful caricatures of it are mentioned under HUMOUR.
                                                                   JS

Reg. Hist., v, 95–6; A. R. Taylor and E. S. Tonks, *The Southwold Railway* (1979).

special trains were passenger trains provided by the railways for some particular purpose, usually in addition to the regular services set out in the public *timetables. The phrase has borne several different meanings in Britain.

Some of the pre-*Grouping companies applied the word 'special' to certain trains running in normal service. The *South Eastern ran 'Special Cheap Fast Trains' from London to Hastings, Margate, and Dover, which appeared in the public timetables, the passengers paying less than standard fares. The *London & North Western used the word 'special' from 1893 onwards for the *boat trains it ran from London to *Liverpool to connect with transatlantic liners, describing them as such in handbills.

But the phrase 'special train' was then generally understood to mean something else: a train hired by a private person for his or her exclusive use, sometimes with family and servants. In the Victorian age, when railways had a monopoly of fast inland travel, these trains were often requested at very short notice, the prospective hirer arriving at a station and asking for a train as quickly as possible. To meet this demand, the railway had to produce a spare engine, at least one carriage, and a crew, and then to fit the journey into the pattern of normal services. Before the development of the *telegraph it was difficult to give advance warning of such a train to the lineside staff on its route, and even after it had been installed it could not prevent *accidents being caused by misunderstanding or inadequate instructions, as happened to a special train of this kind at Ponders End on the *Eastern Counties Railway in 1851, which was due largely to a misuse of the apparatus.

This practice sometimes gave rise to other troubles. Having paid their fare, some passengers stood on what they considered their rights when the service they received let them down. In 1876 a traveller from Liverpool to Scarborough missed his connection at Leeds through the LNWR's unpunctuality, so he hired a special train to take him on and sued the company for the cost of it. But the Court of Appeal dismissed his action on the ground that the inconvenience he had suffered did not justify his claim.

For the hiring of these trains the companies charged what seems to have become a standard rate of 5*s.* a mile for a single journey, 7*s.* 6*d.* for a return one, in addition to the fares payable by the occupants, with a minimum charge of £3. Some published their rates in their timetables.

Early in the 20th century wealthy people could afford large, luxurious, fast motor cars which, by taking them from door to door, were more convenient than the train. Thereafter the single private carriage—the 'family saloon' —became very uncommon, although a splendid vehicle was built for the Duke of *Sutherland by the LNWR in 1899.

The *Big Four and *British Railways provided special trains in quite substantial numbers, chartered by clubs, businesses, and other organizations for private parties, or for the general public, as for race meetings (SEE HORSE-RACING), football matches, and other spectator *sports, being akin to *excursions.

Following an American idea, special trains called 'land cruises', often lasting several days, were introduced into Britain. The passengers occupied sleeping berths or stayed at hotels overnight *en route*. The *London & North Eastern Railway's 'Northern Belle' of 1933 was an example, running from London to the western Highlands.

In the 1980s BR energetically upgraded its charter business by creating a Special Trains Unit which also operated the *Royal Train. In addition, steam specials were organized, either by outside organizations or by BR itself, using privately preserved steam locomotives, and sometimes privately owned rolling stock which was certified for running on BR's tracks.   JS

Ponders End accident: PP 1852, lxviii, 144; LNWR case: H. W. Disney, *Law of Carriage by Railway* (1923 edn.), 229; M. Vincent and C. Green, *The InterCity Story* (1991).

speculation, in its financial meaning of taking risks in the hope of gain, has frequently been associated with the development of the railway system in 19th-century Britain, primarily because of the notoriety of the Railway *Mania. Such speculative excesses were not, however, intrinsic to railways as such. Many other forms of enterprise have attracted the attention of speculators, as was demonstrated by some of the British privatizations during the 1980s–1990s.

The scale of the capital requirements of railway companies quickly dwarfed all previous joint-stock ventures. At the start of the *Railway Age, the *canal companies, the closest parallel, had a total share capital of less than £20 million. Between 1820 and 1844 alone railway companies in England raised more than double that amount from shares, and by the end of 1850 the paid-up share capital of UK railways amounted to £187 million. Though company shares had been traded in London since the 18th century, the sheer volume of railway share issues transformed the capital market, revolutionizing the London Stock Exchange and leading to the establishment of organized stock exchanges in the main provincial cities. The development of the railway system was therefore accompanied by the creation of a greatly extended market in company securities.

Like any other market, that in railway shares was subject to fluctuations. Some of these were due to external factors, such as changes in interest rates, or problems overseas. For example, railway share prices fell sharply after the outbreak of the Franco-Prussian war in 1870. They also, of course, reflected factors which affected individual companies, such as the authorization of a particular scheme, or the publication of a critical report: *North British Railway shares plummeted in 1866 after serious defects were found in the company's accounts. Variations in prices offered obvious opportunities for speculators, but in this respect railway issues were no different from other securities.

The stage when railways were particularly exposed to speculation, however, was during the early years of a new undertaking's life. There were a number of specific reasons why this was the case, but in general they all related to the risks involved in promoting and constructing a railway, and the manner in which funds were gathered for that purpose. Although even a relatively small railway would have a substantial capital after its completion—for example, by 1848 the 30-mile *Taff Vale Railway had a share capital of over £600,000—shares were called up in gradual instalments as constructional expenditure was incurred. At the outset, when a scheme was in the initial stages of promotion, little or no financial commitment was necessary, and even as a Bill progressed through Parliament no more than 10 or 15 per cent of the nominal value of a subscription might be required. At the beginning of a company's life, therefore, investors could obtain an interest in it for only a fractional outlay.

At all stages prior to the completion of a railway, however, a subscriber faced considerable risk. At the outset there was the possibility that the undertaking might fail to gain parliamentary authorization, and that preliminary expenditure, while small in relation to the total projected costs, might prove entirely abortive. If the project was successful at that stage, there were then all the risks inherent in the building process; the ultimate *construction costs of many early railways proved to be more than double the original estimate, and the time required was frequently longer than expected. Only when those uncertainties were over, and the line was brought into productive use, could the final element be brought into the financial calculation: the actual traffic revenue and *operating costs, rather than estimates prepared perhaps five years earlier.

Accordingly, investors whose object was to obtain a secure return would have been ill-advised to commit their funds early in a new railway's life, since not only would there be a delay of several years before a dividend could be earned, but it would also be impossible to assess with any degree of accuracy what the ultimate return would be. But if those who subscribed to a company at the outset could not do so on the basis of a reliable projection of future revenue, the only other means of earning a return (unless they were motivated by a philanthropic or wider personal financial interest in the development benefits a railway might bring) was from capital gains during the scheme's progress. As contemporary commentators recognized, the market played a beneficial role in this process by allowing those who were prepared to accept the high risks of subscribing at the start of a project to dispose of their holdings at a later stage to those who wanted a more secure investment. The capital gains created in this process represented the reward for bearing the risk, and of course, because the price of failing to make an accurate assessment of the balance between risk and reward could be a loss, it was reasonable to expect a high price for accepting a high degree of exposure. Since, however, the speculative excesses which characterized the mania periods were driven primarily by expectations of capital gains, the distinction between speculation and the legitimate operations of a market in which risk interacted with price is one which it is hard to draw with any accuracy, especially in a historical context. Nevertheless, contemporary sources provide considerable evidence of the questionable devices that were used at the height of the mania periods by those who sought to make quick profits from the sale of railway securities. They also suggest that some promoters consciously exploited this aspect of the market.

However, its overall significance needs to be assessed with some caution. Most of the pathological gambling in railway securities took place in 'light' paper: the documents issued by companies before incorporation. While the losses to individuals who misjudged the timing of their transactions may have been significant, the sums were small in relation to the overall capital requirements of the railways. In addition, the nature of the *promotional and parliamentary processes—factors which themselves contributed to the riskiness of railway investment—meant that many of the schemes which were caught up in the speculative manias made little progress, and so incurred only preliminary expenditure.

Such speculation did, however, have consequences beyond its effects on immediate participants. By contributing to an overall market climate, it perhaps accelerated the progress of schemes which, if not unsound, were possibly premature. Since the financing of railway constructional expenditure during the late 1840s almost certainly had a distorting effect on the economy, the role of speculation in generating this peak in expenditure needs to be taken into account. Conversely, the speculative extremes seen at the height of the manias were, at least in part, a reflection of the processes involved in promoting and financing risky capital projects with a long gestation period. The reduction or elimination of such speculation would almost certainly have entailed restrictions on the transfer of railway securities, at least before incorporation. But such a measure (which was in fact implicit in the parliamentary requirements until 1858, though virtually unenforceable) would also have limited the markets' capacity to reflect gradations of risk. Thus the extent of participation in railway share transactions would have been reduced, and with it the overall availability of investment funds for railway development.

Speculation in railway securities was in any event not repeated on a comparable scale after the 1840s, primarily because of the changing nature of the system. In the initial phases of railway development, most mileage was built by separate companies, but as the network matured and consolidated many extensions were undertaken by established railways, which were able to finance the necessary investment by adding to existing capital. Where there were gaps in the network which existing companies were not prepared to fill, new undertakings continued to be floated, though their financial requirements were small in relation to the total existing capitalization of the railways. The experience of some of these companies, particularly in the 1860s, provided evidence that financing a new railway remained a risky and speculative business. In contrast with earlier periods, however, much of this speculative activity was channelled through *contractors, who accepted securities in place of cash and then placed these through City finance houses.

The vulnerability of this method of financing was spectacularly demonstrated in 1866, when tightening credit produced a series of bankruptcies. Among the first casualties were two contractors who were active participants in the promotion of new lines in Wales: Thomas *Savin and the firm of Watson & Overend. Both defaulted at the beginning of 1866, causing immediate difficulties for the railways with which they were financially associated. These included the Mid Wales Railway (see CAMBRIAN RAILWAYS), which Watson & Overend had built and was currently operating. Despite the similarity of name, there was no connection between Watson & Overend and Overend, Gurney & Co., a prominent London finance house; however, by unhappy coincidence the latter's holdings included Mid Wales Railway bonds. Though railways formed just one element in its portfolio, the firm was already over-extended, and a court ruling that the Mid Wales securities had been issued illegally, and were therefore unenforceable, led to Overend, Gurney & Co.'s failure on 10 May, with gross liabilities of over £18 million.

The bankruptcy of a firm of such standing caused immediate panic in the money markets, necessitating an increase in Bank Rate to 10 per cent. While the general collapse in confidence curtailed new promotion and created short-term difficulties for some existing railways, the financial links between City discount houses and the leading contractors meant that there were even more direct consequences for the railway industry. *Peto & Betts, one of the foremost British contracting firms, was forced to cease trading because of its liabilities to Overend, Gurney & Co. These had been secured against debentures issued by the *London Chatham & Dover Railway, which in turn went into receivership because of its reliance on Peto & Betts to finance its extensions.

However, the interaction with railway development in Britain was just one aspect of the crisis: the international role of contractors such as Peto & Betts meant that overseas undertakings were also involved, while railway transactions were only one factor contributing to the collapse of Over-

end, Gurney and the other finance houses which failed in the same year. The events of 1866 were the outcome of a broad range of speculative commercial activity, of which railway promotion was a component rather than the prime cause.

See also FINANCING OF RAILWAYS; LLOYD'S BONDS. MCR
P. L. Cottrell, 'Railway Finance and the Crisis of 1866: Contractors' Bills of Exchange and the Finance Companies', *JTH*, N.S. 3 (1976), 20–41; D. M. Evans, *The Commercial Crisis, 1847–1848* (1969 edn.), 1–52; W. T. C. King, *History of the London Discount Market* (1936), 229–56; H. Pollins, *Britain's Railways: An Industrial History* (1971), 35–54; M. C. Reed, *Investment in Railways in Britain* (1975), 83–98.

speed. The coming of railways revolutionized the speed at which people could travel over land, and rapidly displaced horse-drawn *coaches. Despite 20th-century developments in other transport modes, high-speed railways can still offer shorter travelling times for journeys of up to 300 miles.

Initially the significance of steam railways was their ability to move greater quantities of minerals than could be handled on the roads. At the opening of the *Stockton & Darlington Railway in 1825 the *Newcastle Courant* referred to the vast difference between the loads hauled by *Locomotion* and the four horses of the stage-coach it passed. Improvements in *track, motive power, and rolling stock soon enabled trains to outstrip a galloping horse.

High-speed travel, by whatever mode, is only obtained at a price, so economics, as well as engineering developments, have always exerted a significant effect on the speeds offered to the travelling public. The aerodynamic drag of a vehicle increases with the square of its speed, and the energy cost, as well as the ability to deploy the power required, has always been important. Train speeds have never increased steadily, but have made a series of quantum steps upwards.

Fast railway journeys have always made news, instantaneous maxima, as well as start-to-stop averages, being quoted. The latter more closely correspond with what will be offered to the travelling public, who, although primarily interested in journey times, respond more to speeds. There is also interest in the scheduled averages inclusive of stops, as well as between calling points.

During the first century of rail travel there were difficulties in recording speeds accurately. Locomotives were not regularly provided with speedometers until well into the 20th century, although special vehicles were used from the 1840s onwards. Railways were required to install markers every ¼-mile along their tracks (see MILE AND GRADIENT POSTS), but few passengers had the means to determine speeds. Many railway speeds that were claimed were never accurately measured, although from the beginning of the 20th century there were sufficient amateur train-timers to justify a monthly article in the *Railway Magazine* (see ALLEN, CECIL J.).

Speeds during the *Rainhill trials of 1829 were very carefully noted, but these were low compared with the 36 mph at which George *Stephenson drove the mortally injured George Huskisson to Eccles aboard *Rocket* on the *Liverpool & Manchester Railway's opening day. Few railway speed records were established in more tragic circumstances.

*Whishaw's 1842 book provides the next insight into speeds, but, although comprehensive, his accuracy is suspect. Nevertheless, he probably recorded just over 50 mph down Madeley incline on the *Grand Junction Railway. During the Gauge *Commission's work in the 1840s more accurate recordings were made, and the *Great Western Railway's 2-2-2 *Ixion* averaged 54.6 mph between *Paddington and Didcot.

In 1848 Daniel *Gooch mentioned that one express 'was in constant practice' of averaging 63–6 mph over this stretch, and once achieved 67 mph. Using a *dynamometer car, maxima of 78 mph were recorded with his eight-footers descending Dauntsey bank. Unfortunately this was the highlight of the broad *gauge, and half a century was to elapse before economic circumstances again enabled the Great Western to come to the forefront.

Railways enabled newspapers to be distributed quickly (see NEWSPAPER TRAFFIC), on occasions using special trains. When George *Hudson became MP for Sunderland in 1845, a special took the poll results to London, and was back in his constituency with copies of *The Times* by 11 a.m. the following day. Another notable run took place in 1862, when the Queen's Messenger, carrying papers from America after the boarding of the British vessel *Trent*, was whisked from Holyhead to London (264 miles) in exactly five hours. This was possible because of the new watertroughs at Mochdre, in North Wales, a feature which was important in the subsequent development of high-speed schedules during the steam era (see WATER SUPPLIES).

It was direct railway rivalry which prompted the *'races to Scotland' of 1888 and 1895. During the former, the *East and *West Coast routes were each trying to get their day trains to *Edinburgh first, and the original 9-hour East Coast schedule was eventually cut to 7 hr 27 min. This included the 20-minute *York lunch-stop, as well as a delay caused by the swing-bridge at Selby. The railways realized how much the high-speed running was costing them, and agreed not to cut their London–Edinburgh times below 8¼ hr.

In 1888 the overnight races to Scotland began, repeated in 1895. Eventually the companies realized the financial cost of these high speeds, but on each occasion, ordinary schedules improved. By the end of the 19th century there were over a dozen well-authenticated British speeds of over 80 mph.

In the 20th century competition developed between the GWR and the *London & South Western Railway with transatlantic mails for London from *Plymouth. In 1904 the former's *City of Truro* was timed at 100 mph descending Wellington bank, but the details did not appear until 1922. Although the recorder claimed a maximum of 102.3, such accuracy is not possible from the stop-watch measurements made, but detailed analyses indicate that *City of Truro* was the first steam locomotive to reach 100 mph. Equally outstanding was the Dean 'single' *Duke of Connaught*, which

took the train on from *Bristol to London at an average of 71.4 mph. The GWR also worked a *royal train from London to Plymouth in 1903 at an average of 63.4 mph, and the introduction of the 7-hour Penzance express in 1904 was a commercial success.

World War I set back train speeds for a decade, but in 1923 the GWR's afternoon Cheltenham–Paddington express was accelerated to become the fastest train in Britain. Later known as the 'Cheltenham Flyer', subsequent accelerations produced the first 70-mph schedule in the world (*Swindon–London), with a record run averaging 81.6.

The 1930s were the 'streamline' era, and the *London & North Eastern and *London Midland & Scottish Railways also exploited it as a means of publicity. The former, after trials with successive maxima of 100 and 108 mph, introduced the 'Silver Jubilee' train in 1935. Booked to average 70.4 mph between Darlington and London, on its press run it ran at over 100 mph for 25 miles continuously, twice reaching 112. The 71.9 mph schedule of their 1937 'Coronation' from London to York was the fastest ever to appear in Britain with steam. On the LMS, anxious to keep up the competition, a Stanier 4-6-2 worked a special from London to *Glasgow in 1935 at a non-stop average of 68.2 mph, and increased this to 70.0 when it returned next day. In June 1937 a press trip with the first 'Princess Coronation' locomotive achieved a new British record of 113 mph, but the following year this was trumped by the LNER when Gresley's *Mallard* reached 126 descending Stoke bank, still a world record for steam.

Elsewhere, the fastest trains in the world were now being hauled by electric or diesel power (see TRACTION), but it was not until well after World War II that Britain began to exploit these forms of traction. Service maxima of 100 mph first appeared with the East Coast *'Deltics' in 1964, but in 1962 three pairs of trains between London and Edinburgh had matched the 'Coronation's' 6-hour timing. Infrastructure improvements reduced the best timings to 5 hr 27 min in 1977, inclusive of a *Newcastle stop. Many averages of over 80 mph appeared in the timetables, the fastest being 91.4 between London and Newark in 1979.

On the electrified West Coast route there were also numerous averages of over 80 mph, and a maximum of 129 mph was reached during a 1971 trial. The tilting *Advanced Passenger Train (APT), which never entered full commercial service, achieved the current British rail speed record of 162.2 mph in 1979, and five years later worked a special from London to Glasgow at an average of 103.4 mph.

The prototype InterCity 125 train, with its 125-mph service maximum, set a number of world records for diesel traction between York and Darlington in 1973, culminating in a speed of 143.2 mph. The commercial introduction of these trains on the Western Region of *British Railways in 1976 immediately produced a record scheduled average of 95.7 mph, but a special from London to Bristol achieved 104.4 in 1977. As these sets spread throughout the country, more world diesel records were achieved, culminating in 115.4 from Newcastle to London six years later. On the last a new world record maximum of 144 mph was attained, but this was later pushed up twice, to reach 148.5 during bogie trials for the forthcoming electric InterCity 225s. These latest East Coast trains are designed for 140 mph, and have reached a maximum of 161.7 on test, but are limited nominally to 125 mph in service. On the press run in September 1991, Edinburgh was reached in 3 hr 29 min from London at 112.5 mph.

These high-speed trains materially improved BR's economics, and the InterCity sector operated without *subsidy for six years. As well as providing competitive journey times, faster speeds also increase the trains' productivity, for they regularly travel over 1,000 miles per day. This benefit of high speed is demonstrated when adverse weather limits East Coast speeds to 80 mph, which necessitates the frequency of the London–Newcastle services dropping from half-hourly to hourly.

Although British railways cannot match the maxima achieved on purpose-built high-speed lines in other countries, in 1991 InterCity operated more trains travelling at over 100 mph than any other railway in Europe. In 1992 there were 119 daily start-to-stop runs averaging over 100 mph on the East Coast route alone. From January 1996, Eurostar trains (see CHANNEL TUNNEL) between Ashford and Paris have been scheduled to average more than 125 mph start-to-stop, but most of the distance covered is in France.

Since 1825 the speeds of freight trains have also increased from the 15 mph reached by *Locomotion*. Fast vacuum-*braked freights were introduced between the world wars, and 3,000-ton mineral trains now also run at 60 mph. The resulting shorter journey times reduce the cost of goods in transit, as well as enabling orders to be fulfilled more promptly. PWBS

Whishaw; O. S. Nock, *Speed Records on Britain's Railways—A Chronicle of the Steam Era* (1971); P. W. B. Semmens, *Speed on the East Coast Main Line* (1990); and 'May 9 1904: A Legend is Created', in N. Harris (ed.), *City of Truro—A Locomotive Legend* (1992 edn.).

Speedlink, see FREIGHT TRAFFIC.

Spooner family. It was prominent in the development of *narrow-gauge railways at home and abroad. James (1790–1856) moved to North Wales with the Ordnance Survey, settled there, surveyed the *Festiniog Railway, oversaw its construction during 1832–6, and served it as engineer and manager until his death. His son Charles Easton (1818–89) then oversaw the line's development into a steam-hauled public railway in 1863–5; another son, James Swinton, engineered the *Talyllyn Railway. Charles Spooner vigorously promoted the cause of narrow gauge, but ambition sometimes outran his actual abilities. Of his sons, George Percy (1850–1916) designed the FR's later double *Fairlie locomotives and the integrally framed bogie coaches introduced in 1871, while Charles Edwin (1853–1909) became first engineer and manager of the Federated Malay States Railways. RW

D. H. Wilson, 'The Spooners Up to Date', *Festiniog Railway Magazine*, 77 (1977).

sports, field, see ANGLING; SHOOTING; LIVESTOCK TRAFFIC; FOX HUNTING; WINTER SPORTS.

sports, spectator. The development of mass spectator sports was one of Victorian Britain's most enduring legacies. The railways made an important contribution to it.

Between c.1860 and c.1880 many of the world's leading spectator sports were invented or codified in Britain. Association Football, Rugby Union, tennis, and athletics joined well-established sports such as cricket and *horse-racing as major leisure activities. Golf developed rapidly in the 1890s and during the Edwardian period took a firm grip on the male middle class.

Railways made possible sporting fixtures between teams miles apart, for which rapid travel was essential, especially when the majority of players were amateur or part-time and could afford only a limited amount of time away from their jobs. In 1879 Queen's Park, the famous Scottish amateur soccer team, was able to leave *Glasgow late on Friday night, arrive in *Manchester at 4 a.m., play a game on Saturday afternoon, and return to Glasgow overnight.

Railways also enabled large numbers of spectators to follow their teams or view the spectacle. This constituted a logistical problem to the railways. It also presented a financial opportunity.

In the 1880s it was not uncommon for 10,000 people to arrive at White Hart Lane station in London to watch Tottenham Hotspur, in trains arriving at five-minute intervals. The station was fitted with specially wide doors to ease the crush. An idea of the problem can also be glimpsed in the calculations of the manager of the *Cheshire Lines Committee, concerning a proposed station at the Manchester United football ground at Trafford Park in 1908. He estimated that there were 10,000 spectators to be brought to the ground per match, for 20 Saturdays in the year, together with athletics and cycling meetings at other times: a total of 220,000 passengers a year and bringing in £2,950 from local patronage alone.

Traffic flows of this kind presented a considerable challenge, but they were small beer compared with the problems posed by the success of the Football Association's Challenge Cup, inaugurated in 1872. Its early years were dominated by public-school and amateur teams from the south of England. But this era came to an end in 1883 when Blackburn Olympic defeated the Old Etonians. The foundation of the professional Football League in 1888, without a single team from further south than Birmingham, continued the era of northern dominance. Only two southern teams, Southampton and Tottenham Hotspur, reached the F.A. Cup Final between 1883 and 1914. Even between the two world wars London teams reached the final on only five occasions. There was no all-London Cup Final until 1967.

The railways were thus faced with the prospect of moving very large numbers of people from distant places, such as *Newcastle, Sunderland, and *Cardiff, to the capital, where the Final was always played. A crowd of 110,000 was recorded at Crystal Palace in 1901 for the drawn Final between Tottenham Hotspur and Sheffield United. This was almost certainly the biggest football crowd yet gathered in British history. The *London Brighton & South Coast and *South Eastern & Chatham Railways conveyed 50,000 people from their London termini to their two Crystal Palace stations. Some 60,000 people were reckoned to have been carried in 1907.

Playing the Finals in London, particularly with so many of the participating teams coming from the north and Midlands, was not ideal from a railway point of view. The decision to move the Final to Wembley Stadium, built for the British Empire Exhibition of 1923, was partly influenced by its excellent rail links, not only with the capital, but also from the north. In 1924 the existing stations at Wembley Park and Wembley Central were joined by a third, Wembley Stadium, built by the *London & North Eastern. It was situated on a single-track loop from the Northolt line. Until 1968 this enabled a circular shuttle service to run every five minutes from *Marylebone for Cup Finals and other big sporting occasions, such as the Olympic Games of 1948.

Wembley's accessibility was confirmed by the first Cup Final, between Bolton Wanderers and West Ham United, in 1923: 126,047 people passed through the turnstiles, but an estimated 100,000 more entered the ground by other means. The game only went ahead owing to the valiant crowd-control efforts of Police Constable George Scorey on his white horse 'Billie'. The size of the crowd is a testimony to the railways' logistical achievements. Unfortunately, large numbers who failed to get into the ground poured back on to the rail network, surface and underground, before the scheduled end of the game, and rapid adjustments to time-tabling had to be made.

Wembley catered not only for football but also for grey-hound racing and speedway and, from 1929, the annual Rugby League Cup Final, an occasion of another great northern working-class excursion to the capital.

Railway access was a consideration in the siting of other football grounds besides Wembley. Chelsea moved to Stamford Bridge in 1905, close to Walham Green (now Fulham Broadway) station. When the station was reconstructed in 1910 special facilities for the crowds were provided. Charlton Athletic had its enormous ground, The Valley, close to a station on the *South Eastern Railway. The *Great Western even leased Queen's Park Rangers a new stadium on surplus land at Park Royal in 1907. Woolwich Arsenal moved to their present home at Highbury in 1913 in part, at least, to be alongside the *London Underground station at Gillespie Road. The mutual significance of this link was confirmed in 1932, when Arsenal's formidable manager, Herbert Chapman, persuaded the Underground authorities to change the name of Gillespie Road station to 'Arsenal'.

This relationship continues. West Bromwich Albion football ground at The Hawthorns was from 1931 to 1968 served by The Hawthorns halt, one of the very few stations ever to open on Christmas Day. It was rebuilt and reopened in 1995 on the new Centro line (see BIRMINGHAM).

The opportunity presented by spectator sports was also apparent to railway managers. As commercial enterprises,

they could not afford to forgo potential revenue, and far from simply responding to the demand, the railways encouraged it. Sporting events, football in particular, usually took place on Saturday afternoons, when the rail system had spare capacity, also bringing in income from leisure travel during the winter as well as in the summer.

No one did more to encourage rail travel to sporting events than the innovative vice-chairman of the London Passenger Transport Board Frank *Pick (1933–40). During the 1930s, perhaps the golden age of spectator sport, a series of striking *posters advertised the accessibility of the capital's sporting arenas by Underground: not only football, but also cricket, rugby, greyhound racing, speedway, athletics, tennis, and the annual University Boat Race.

Railway promotion of travel to sporting events came not only through advertising but also through the provision of cheap *excursion trains. The majority of spectators, certainly at football matches, were working-class men with limited means. They had to buy a ticket for the match and feed themselves, sometimes during journeys lasting many hours, as well as finding the fare: if they were to be attracted to the railways, this had to be kept low. The result was the football excursion (or 'footex') which became an enduring element in railway operations and part of the fabric of British social life for 80 years until the growth of private car ownership and the construction of the motorway network in the 1960s changed the pattern of travel.

The *Hull & Barnsley Railway, as early as the 1880s, was assiduous in developing excursion services to the numerous West Yorkshire towns that had football and Rugby League teams. Although the company's passenger traffic was never profitable, its excursion business, especially to football matches, was.

The final years of the railway football excursion were not happy ones, with considerable *vandalism being inflicted on trains and their passengers by drunken and unruly supporters. Now its decline is almost total. On 31 May 1993, 40,000 West Bromwich Albion supporters travelled to Wembley to watch their team play Port Vale in the Second Division Play-off Final. *British Rail provided one excursion train for the occasion. It arrived late and those who travelled on it missed the start of the match. The vast majority of the spectators, including 12,000 Port Vale supporters, made their way to the ground by private car and motor coach.

Football was a game particularly well suited to the railway age. Many grounds were town-centre affairs, to which 'home' supporters could easily walk, while 'away' supporters could walk to and from stations at both ends of their journey.

Bolton, *Nottingham, *Stoke, and Wolverhampton (all with teams in the original Football League) were towns in this category. Aston Villa, the dominant team of the early years of professional football, was able to draw large numbers of people by rail from the Black Country, and was well served by the suburban station at Witton on the Birmingham–Walsall line. Where close proximity between station and football ground did not occur, as in *Sheffield, the railways were quick to emphasize the availability of connecting tram services, which grew rapidly from the 1890s. It is difficult to see how the Football League, with its fixed programme of home and away matches, could even have been envisaged, much less have succeeded, without railways.

This mutually beneficial relationship is less apparent in other spectator sports. There was at least one 'cricket ground station', at Old Trafford, on the *Manchester South Junction & Altrincham line in 1857–87, which in later years also served Manchester United football ground. But it took the first Australian tour, in 1878, for the game to capture the national imagination. The railways quickly realized this and provided special excursion trains, in both London and the provinces. Their contribution helped to make the tour a major success and so confirm cricket as a national sport.

The great London cricket grounds, at Lord's and the Oval, were both established before the high point of railway involvement in spectator sports. Lord's (1814), situated at St John's Wood, was something of an obstacle to the development of underground and surface railways. In the late 1890s the Marylebone Cricket Club vehemently opposed the extension of the *Great Central line into London for fear of desecrating the Mecca of cricket, and a special tunnel was made. Lord's, however, was well served by the Metropolitan station at St John's Wood. In 1890 the *City & South London Railway—an underground line—provided the Oval (built in 1845) at Kennington with its own station of the same name. This may be the first example of a sporting arena giving its name to a railway station.

Rugby Union, tennis, and golf, unlike football and Rugby League, were predominantly middle-class sports. Rugby grounds tended to be located in suburbs of the great metropolitan centres: Blackheath, Richmond, Twickenham (London); Moseley (Birmingham); and Sale (Manchester). Rugby Union did not develop a league system until the 1980s. Matches tended to be lacking in the competitive edge associated with an urban tribal sport like football. Crowds were not large for club matches and many grounds were little better than playing fields, such as the Old Deer Park at Richmond and the Rectory Field at Blackheath. Rugby Union has been, for much of its history, essentially a game for players rather than spectators. The great exception to this is the Five Nations' Championship between England, France, Ireland, Scotland, and Wales. Both the headquarters of English rugby at Twickenham and of Welsh rugby at the Cardiff Arms Park were well served by railways. The Arms Park is as close to a major railway station as any large sporting venue in Britain.

The All England Club held its first tennis championships in south London at Wimbledon in 1877. Mass spectator interest did not really develop until the 1920s and 1930s when charismatic and athletic male and female players from France, Germany, and the USA as well as Britain began to capture the public imagination. Tennis presented the railways with a more subtle problem than football. It was considered enough to disgorge football spectators into the heart of a town to make their way on foot to the ground. The residents of Wimbledon, however, looked without favour on having thousands of spectators making their way

from South Wimbledon or Southfields stations through quiet residential streets to the stadium. The *Underground Group and London General Omnibuses therefore provided buses to take them from the stations to the courts. The wonderfully striking posters which the Board used to advertise the All-England Championships and the Davis Cup, dominated by Britain in the 1930s, and the provision of travel to such a peripheral location, played a significant part in bringing tennis to a wider audience and turning it into a genuine spectator sport, for two weeks in the year at least.

Golf was probably the spectator sport which has been least influenced by railways. It was slow to develop in England. The first club, at Blackheath, did not open until 1864. But its growth was rapid in the 1890s; 29 golf courses opened between 1890 and 1895 in the West Riding of Yorkshire alone. By 1914 golf had established a firm hold on the sporting affections of the professional and commercial middle classes.

As a game golf was ill-suited to railways. Although a national game in Scotland, in England it was much more exclusive and was played on extensive and expensively constructed courses, with lavish club houses, designed for the socially and financially acceptable, and it did not attract spectators. Some courses had good railway access. Denham Golf Club Halt opened in 1912, and Carpenders Park for a golf course in 1914. Rickmansworth club was also well served. But golf did not seek ease of rail access. Railways were too public, and made access too easy. Many golf courses seemed to go out of their way to be inaccessible, particularly the most famous. By the time golf became a major spectator sport, in the aftermath of the British and Irish Ryder Cup victory over the United States in 1953 and the advent of television coverage, the motor car had become the dominant means of access for player and spectator alike. But most of the great golfing *hotels and their courses built by pre-*Grouping Scottish railway companies still thrive.

See also WINTER SPORTS. JMB

VR, 302–3; RTC, 88–9; T. Mason, *Association Football and English Society 1863–1915* (1981), 146–7; *Reg. Hist.*, iii, 143, 145; PRO RAIL 110/352/1.

staff, see EMPLOYMENT.

staff-and-ticket working, see SINGLE LINES, WORKING OF.

Stalbridge, Richard de Aquila Grosvenor, 1st Baron (1837–1912), chairman. The fourth son of the 2nd Marquis of Westminster, Stalbridge was MP for Flintshire in 1861–86, a privy councillor in 1872, and Vice-Chamberlain, 1872–4. Created baron in 1886, he was *Gladstone's chief whip in 1880–5.

For over 40 years he was a director of the *London & North Western Railway (1870–1911), and chairman for 20, following *Moon in 1891 and ending a long period of over-strict economy. Under his guidance the company embarked on major capital projects which rapidly improved its services, to become the 'Premier Line'. Stalbridge made himself conversant with all aspects of operation, particularly locomotive construction. He was said to have ridden more miles on the footplate than any other railway director. A strong advocate of provision for employees' welfare, he instituted a superannuation fund, a savings bank, and a widows' and orphans' fund. He was president of the LNWR Ambulance Association.

A firm believer in the benefits of a physical rail link with the Continent, he was prominent in the first Anglo-French *Channel Tunnel project in the 1870s. But he was utterly opposed to the abolition of second-class travel, which was why the LNWR did not abolish it until 1912 (see CLASS DISTINCTIONS). Most of his estate being entailed, he left negotiable assets worth only £2,849.　　　　　　　　GJB

W. L. Steel, *History of the London & North Western Railway* (1914); *DNB*; *The Complete Peerage* (1987 edn.), vol. 5.

Stamp, Sir Josiah Charles, Baron Stamp of Shortlands (1880–1941); he entered the Inland Revenue at 16 and rose rapidly, acquiring many academic distinctions and writing textbooks on taxation and finance. In 1919 he became secretary and a director of Mond Nickel Co., later part of ICI.

In 1926 Stamp joined the *London Midland & Scottish Railway as president of the executive and then chairman. He headed an executive committee of vice-presidents on the American model, mostly professional railwaymen, including his eventual successor, W. V. *Wood, who provided the statistical analyses Stamp demanded. On paper Stamp's policies were highly successful, as operating performance and workshop productivity rose markedly. But away from major centres strict financial controls produced dilapidation, while centralized and authoritarian management lowered morale.

Stamp ended sterile in-fighting in traction and rolling stock departments in 1932 by importing W. A. *Stanier from the *Great Western Railway as CME; his new standard designs greatly improved performance. Stamp also introduced an innovative Research Department. A School of Transport was another important innovation.

Stamp was remote from most of the staff, partly because he preferred to work through his vice-presidents and partly because of his governmental and academic work; he was also a lay preacher. But he was a very effective spokesman for the railways with the government, and spearheaded the 'Square Deal' campaign of 1938–9.

In 1940 he declined the Chancellorship of the Exchequer. He was killed, together with his wife and eldest son, in an air-raid in 1941.　　　　　　　　MRB

J. H. Jones, *Josiah Stamp, Public Servant* (1964); C. H. Ellis, *London Midland & Scottish* (1970).

stamps, letter and parcel. Three categories of prepayment stamps have been issued by British railway companies: *newspaper, *parcel, and letter. *Amalgamations, *joint lines, joint committees, and company name changes have all been reflected by the inscriptions on these stamps.

Between 1712 and 1855, a tax was levied on newspapers which allowed them to be sent by post without further charge, and when the tax was repealed a minimum postal rate of one penny per newspaper was established. The conveyance of newspapers was not a part of the *Post Office's monopoly and railway companies were therefore able to offer cheaper rates for their carriage.

Each company produced stamps of its own design which were issued in a variety of colours and values, some for single and others for parcels of newspapers. Stamps for general parcels were introduced in the 1870s, replacing a system of cash payments and waybills, and by the end of the century most companies had produced a series of values between ½d. and one shilling. In later years, values up to £1 were issued by the larger companies and post-*Grouping values up to £100 are known.

Parcel stamps were generally less ornate in design than the newspaper issues and many consisted of simply the name of the company, a large value figure, and sometimes the issuing station. A few companies also issued stamps for the specific conveyance of small quantities or samples of sugar, corn, grain, coal, milk, and agricultural produce.

The Post Office monopoly made it illegal for railway companies to carry letters except in the mails, and although a few had issued special stamps for news intelligence, reporters and others needing a faster service than the postal service provided were having to tie string around letters to allow their carriage as parcels.

Eventually, in 1891 the Postmaster-General came to an agreement with the railway companies permitting them to carry letters provided that normal postage stamps were affixed in addition to any railway stamp. Railway letter-stamps were to be printed in green and to a standard design specified by the Post Office. In 1920 this rule was relaxed, and thereafter any railway stamp of the appropriate value could be used.

A new Post Office agreement in 1974 enabled members of the Association of Minor Railway Companies to operate a letter-post, and although *British Rail ended its letter service in 1984, stamps are still issued for collectors by these independent lines.　　　　　　　　CPT

H. L'Estrange Ewen, *Railway Newspaper and Parcel Stamps of the United Kingdom 1855–1906* (1906); H. T. Jackson, *The Railway Letter Posts of Great Britain* (1970); N. Oakley, *Great Britain & Ireland Railway Letter Stamps 1957–1988* (1989).

standardization of design and practice. The principal agency for standardizing railway practice was the *Railway Clearing House. In simplifying and co-ordinating the through booking and movement of passengers and goods over the various railway companies' lines, the RCH helped to standardize operating and commercial activities. Its influence was limited, because it could reach agreement only by levelling the regulations of the better lines with those having lower standards.

Other important influences were regulatory legislation, such as the *Regulation of Railways Acts of 1844, 1871, and 1889, by which the Board of *Trade represented governmental and public interests, principally in the matter of *safety, and in making some aspects of safe working compulsory.

Even within individual railways, there was little measure of standardization of locomotive classes, or rolling stock types, except on the *Great Western Railway. From 1839, Daniel *Gooch introduced standard locomotives with interchangeable parts. *Ramsbottom on the *London & North Western Railway was notable for the introduction both of standard locomotive types, and of parts standardization from 1858. The process on the GWR was intensified from the time of G. J. *Churchward when major locomotive components such as boilers, cylinders, bogies, axle-boxes, and coupled-wheel diameters were standardized.

The RCH promoted standardization by specifications such as those for *wagon axle-guards and axle-boxes. Another influence was pragmatic: the design of locomotives and rolling stock to a common loading gauge (see CLEARANCES) to permit through working. When *Grouping took place, many locomotives were modified to comply with a standard loading gauge so that they could work freely over the lines of the constituent companies of the *Big Four. But most GWR locomotives and carriages were barred from much of the national network.

Grouping increased the opportunities for the RCH and the *Railway Companies Association to effect standardization. During 1923, the RCH Superintendents' Conference reached agreement on displaying the dimensions of stock on the ends of coaching vehicles, and on the number of annual *timetable issues. On the GWR and *London Midland & Scottish there was standardization of locomotive design, in the latter case only after Sir W. *Stanier became CME.

The first, abortive, attempt to evolve a standard range of locomotive designs came in 1917. The government asked the Association of Railway Locomotive Engineers, a body composed of the CMEs and locomotive superintendents of British and Irish railways, to design a range of standard locomotives.

In 1939 the Ministry of Supply selected the LMS Stanier 2-8-0 locomotive for war service overseas, and in 1942 decided that this type should be constructed by the four companies for domestic working. Simplified versions of the 2-8-0, a comparable 2-10-0 engine, and an 0-6-0ST were designed under R. A. *Riddles' control for the MoS, with the intention of domestic use after the war.

With *nationalization, all the barriers to standardization were withdrawn, and early in 1948 locomotive standards, carriage standards, and 'ideal stocks' committees were set up. The first-named established a range of standard steam locomotives; the next, the *BR standard designs of vestibuled and non-vestibuled *carriages, these owing something to principles for standard stock laid down by the RCA during World War II. The last-named made recommendations for reducing the number of types of new wagons to 71.

After World War II, standardization was increasingly influenced by the International Union of Railways (UIC), set up in 1922. Until the 1960s BR's involvement in UIC was limited, but BR designs of rolling stock components and freight *container types, rails, and some signalling practice have been influenced by participation in UIC.   MLH

J. Johnson and R. A. Long, *British Railways Engineering 1948–80*

(1981); E. S. Cox, *British Railways Standard Steam Locomotives* (1966); H. W. Holcroft, *Locomotive Adventure*, i (1962); MacDermot, i; B. Reed, *Crewe Locomotive Works and Its Men* (1982).

Stanier, Sir William Arthur (1876–1965), CME, *London Midland & Scottish Railway, 1932–44; knighted in 1943.

Apprenticed on the *Great Western Railway at *Swindon under William *Dean in 1892, Stanier became locomotive works manager in 1920. In 1922 he was appointed principal assistant to the CME, *Collett. When he succeeded Sir Henry *Fowler on the LMS there was an acute need for heavy express passenger and freight locomotives, which he met by introducing a fleet of capable, reliable, and efficient engines. Over 2,000 were built in 1932–47, combining many features of GWR practice, such as tapered boilers, with LMS features such as outside Walschaerts *valve gear which improved accessibility. His early boilers with low-degree superheat and other Swindon characteristics were unsatisfactory, which he quickly overcame by revising the design, with larger superheaters. Among his highly successful designs a total of some 1,500 Class 5 4-6-0 mixed traffic and Class 8 2-8-0 freight locomotives were built, considerable numbers of the latter also being built by other companies for World War II service. His 'Princess Royal' class of 1933 finally introduced the 4-6-2 express type to the LMS, almost ten years after *Hughes and Fowler had first proposed it, and his enlarged 'Coronation' class of 1937 was probably the most powerful British express type. He also introduced 90 diesel-electric heavy *shunting locomotives, including the type later standardized by *British Railways and, in 1938, a prototype three-coach articulated diesel-hydraulic train. In 1942 he became scientific adviser to the Ministry of Production and later a director of Power Jets Ltd.   GWC

Chartered Mechanical Engineer, 8 (1961), 497–505; O. S. Nock, *William Stanier, An Engineering Assessment* (1964); E. S. Cox, *Locomotive Panorama*, i (1965); J. Bellwood and D. Jenkinson, *Gresley & Stanier: A Centenary Tribute* (1976).

stationary engines were used for several purposes prior to the advent of electricity and portable power plants with petrol and, more recently, diesel engines. Certain applications were common to other industries, such as driving workshop machinery or pumping water, for which engines were usually similar in design to those used for the same purpose elsewhere, and they developed in the same way. The earliest were small beam engines of one form or another, later ones the simpler vertical or horizontal form that gradually displaced other types from the 1840s onwards. Where they were used to drive machinery, purely mechanical transmission was employed, there being one or more line shafts driven from the engine and mounted along the roof beams of the workshop(s), with pulleys from which leather belts drove individual machines.

Some railways built their own engines, both for these tasks and occasionally as winding engines, often using standard locomotive parts. Another variation was to adapt a redundant locomotive for stationary duties, sometimes using just the chassis but occasionally retaining the original boiler. An example was one of McConnell's unsatisfactory

'Patent' engines which was adapted to drive a rolling mill at *Crewe and survived in that form for about 50 years.

Two types of stationary engine were specific to railways. Winding engines used to work steep inclines were basically large low-speed engines driving one or two large drums that hauled in and paid out the haulage rope(s), but sometimes the engine powered a continuous rope that was taken round a pair of large pulleys in the engine house (see CABLE HAULAGE). They often resembled contemporary colliery winding engines, e.g. George *Stephenson used the local crank-overhead form on the Hetton Colliery and *Stockton & Darlington Railways.

The pumping engines used on the short-lived *atmospheric railways were a mixed bunch, the best being the horizontal engines of Boulton & Watt design for the *London & Croydon and *South Devon Railways. Earlier Boulton & Watt engines for the South Devon were, however, of inverted form with the larger air cylinders above the steam cylinders, while Maudslay, Son & Field used conventional rotative beam engines. Many atmospheric engines were subsequently sold for use elsewhere, possibly as foundry blowing engines, which they so closely resembled.

There were few oil or gas stationary engines on railway premises because the majority of railways moved straight from steam to electricity in their workshops.   RW

stationmasters. This title was one of several given by the railway companies to the men placed in charge of their stations. 'Agent' was another, favoured for a long time in Scotland. On some lines (e.g. the *London Brighton & South Coast) the larger stations were presided over by 'superintendents'. Small stations were frequently managed by 'clerks', or 'station clerks'. These officials appear side by side with stationmasters in the *London & North Western Railway's first book of rules and regulations (see BYE-LAWS), issued in 1849.

There the basic duties of a stationmaster are set out plainly. First, he is to be 'answerable for the office and buildings', inspecting them daily. He must ensure that the most economical use is made of stores and stationery, of coal, gas, and oil. He must take note of the appearance of the station staff and their behaviour to passengers. When a dispute arises about the order in which trains are to be dispatched —if, for instance, one of them is running late—the responsibility for settling it rests with him, after proper consultation with the men concerned.

It came to be usually accepted on British railways that at larger stations the stationmaster was responsible for passenger traffic, but goods were under the control of a 'goods agent', each of them falling into a different division of the company's administration.

The stationmaster became, above all, the senior railway official who was in the public eye. H. A. Simmons, himself a stationmaster, self-important indeed and perpetually at war with his superior officers, is yet, in matters of this kind, an acceptable witness. He was stationmaster at Aynho (south of Banbury) on the *Great Western Railway in 1863–4, with a staff of four under him, and then at Thame

(1864–5), at the higher salary of £80 a year. In 1867 he attained the important post of stationmaster at Windsor. He often refers, not untruthfully, to the prominent position he enjoyed, by virtue of his office, in the communities the railway served; to the numerous minor emoluments that came his way also, from the brace of pheasants from My Lord to the pair of sole from the fishmonger. As a modern writer puts it, speaking of the LNWR station at Sandy (Bedfordshire) as it was at that time, the stationmaster 'wore a frock coat and a top hat, and was well known in the town, for he made it his business to call on everyone who could provide custom for the railway. He was a person who would be asked for references.'

It is difficult to make any useful statements about stationmasters' earnings. They varied considerably from one station to another and, in real terms, depended on bonuses and gratuities, together with other concealed additions. The top salaries paid at the great terminal stations appear to have been £200–£250 a year in the 1860s, the average for the whole grade a little over £100. But the stationmaster usually had a house, rent-free, on or near the station, which it was his duty to occupy. These salaries seem to have remained more or less stationary thereafter, or perhaps to have fallen a little. A return made to the government of the average remuneration of 'stationmasters and clerks' in 1914 puts it at about £85. But 'clerks' is a vague term in this connection, probably including a fair number of men with much smaller responsibilities than stationmasters, earning considerably less. It is worth noting that the same return shows the average pay of guards as £82, of signalmen as £71: but they were seldom provided with free houses.

Though some stationmasters were local celebrities, few of them became more widely famous. Two may, however, be mentioned.

Roger Langdon, stationmaster at Silverton, east of Exeter, on the GWR achieved some celebrity in 1867–94 as an amateur astronomer. He wrote an interesting autobiography (published, with additions by his daughter, in 1908), which illuminates some of the by-ways in the duties falling on a country stationmaster. John Hood was stationmaster at Ellesmere on the *Cambrian Railways. In 1891 the House of Commons set up a committee to inquire into excessive hours of labour by railwaymen. Hood wrote to his general manager, John *Conacher, seeking permission to give evidence before it. Conacher returned no reply, and he ignored a second request; whereupon Hood got into touch with two MPs, and he was asked for evidence by the committee itself. He gave it. He was no agitator, only a man who had seen a good deal of the practices into which the committee was inquiring and felt he should testify to them. For this he was dismissed by the company, though it was alleged—subsequently—that he had falsified a pay-sheet. Two of the Cambrian directors and Conacher were called to the bar of the House for breach of privilege and admonished by the Speaker. Hood lived on in retirement, widely respected, until 1920.

In the 20th century the importance of the stationmaster's office was gradually reduced. The big companies of 1923 (see GROUPING) evolved practices that concentrated authority as far as possible into regional and central offices, and they came to group the responsibility for several small stations together under one stationmaster. In the *nationalized railways the same tendency went much further. Stationmasters, as such, disappeared. By a subtle verbal change they came now to be 'station managers' or 'area managers', and these officers were to be found only at the bigger and more important stations.

See also UNIFORMS.   JS
LNWR rules: Sir F. B. Head, *Stokers and Pokers* (1849), 186–90; [H. A. Simmons], *Ernest Struggles* (1879–80); salaries: P. W. Kingsford, *Victorian Railwaymen* (1970), 96, and PP 1914, lxxvii, 614; Langdon: *Notes and Queries*, 177 (1939), 428; Hood case: *CMCR*, ii, 12–15.

stations, goods. The term 'goods stations', or 'depots', usually referred to establishments in towns which were controlled by a goods agent or superintendent, as opposed to those that were part of a small passenger *station supervised by the *stationmaster.

The *Liverpool & Manchester Railway's goods stations (1830) at its termini were alongside the passenger stations, although at *Liverpool there was from the outset a second one at Wapping serving the docks (see PORTS AND DOCKS). Curzon Street and Lawley Street goods stations at *Birmingham, on the *London & Birmingham and *Grand Junction Railways respectively (1837), were similarly located. At *Bristol the *Great Western's goods station was 12 ft lower than the passenger station (1840), alongside the Floating Harbour. Wagons were transferred by *turntables and *hydraulic *lifts.

Goods stations had to be at street level, so where the railway was on a viaduct, wagon lifts were installed, as at Salford and *Leeds Central; later, steep inclines might be built to supplement or replace them. The *Manchester & Leeds Railway's elevated passenger station at *Manchester Oldham Road (1841) had the goods station underneath, an arrangement copied at Manchester London Road (1842), Liverpool Great Howard Street (1848)—although the passenger station was regarded as temporary—and *Broad Street, London (1865). All required wagon lifts.

Soon passenger and goods stations were separated, generally when the former was moved to a more central location, or a terminal line became part of a through route. The London & Birmingham's Camden goods station was a mile out from Euston, although more by accident than design, but others took over redundant passenger terminals, as happened at Manchester Oldham Road when Victoria was opened; Hunslet Lane, Leeds; and *Bradford Adolphus Street. In London, Nine Elms gave way to *Waterloo, becoming a carriage workshop before it was part of the goods station, and Bishopsgate to *Liverpool Street; the same thing happened at smaller places like Godalming and Lancaster.

A goods station served one or more of three main purposes: to receive and despatch goods; to transfer goods from one train to another *en route* between other places; and to provide warehousing (see GOODS SHEDS). As well as dealing with general merchandise, it could provide facilities for *coal, cattle, grain, and potato storage. Alternatively, some functions might be on other sites, particularly cattle pens which were often alongside a market (see LIVESTOCK TRAFFIC). *King's Cross, for instance, had them all except cattle, which were accommodated next to the Metropolitan Cattle Market. Like a number of other goods stations close to *canals, it had wharves for the exchange of traffic, and the main buildings catered for all transport modes under one roof.

Railways were markedly reluctant to rebuild goods stations, preferring piecemeal extensions and adaptations, resulting, as was the case at King's Cross, in complicated, confusing, and inconvenient layouts, sometimes intersected by streets requiring level crossings, like Salford and Liverpool Great Howard Street, and abounding in sharp curves. But after the 1870s numbers were completely reconstructed or new ones built, embodying the latest equipment, among them Ancoats (*Midland) and Deansgate (*Great Northern) goods stations in Manchester, Birmingham Central (MR), Forth goods station at *Newcastle (*North Eastern); and, in *Glasgow, Buchanan Street for the *Caledonian, College for the *Glasgow & South Western, and the *North British's huge High Street goods station.

A typical example of a multi-storey warehouse was opened at Huddersfield by the *London & North Western and *Lancashire & Yorkshire Railways in 1883. The ground floor was devoted to loading and unloading merchandise, and the first and third were warehouses for baled cotton, wool, wool waste, and rags. On the second, more loading platforms for potatoes and general goods were served by an external hydraulic wagon hoist and, later, an internal electric *traverser for manoeuvring wagons sideways, which took current by trolley poles from overhead wires, rather like a tramcar. The fourth floor was a granary. In the yard a hydraulic pump house provided the power.

Certain goods stations were specialized. Round Oak, in the Black Country, was provided by the GWR solely for Round Oak steelworks; in 1948 it was handling 300,000 tons of raw materials and finished steel annually.

Competition ensured a multiplicity of depots. Liverpool had 13 along the docks alone, six more elsewhere in the city, and a cattle station. Only Glasgow had any form of 'union' goods station, the General Terminus. Opened in 1848 to serve five companies, it eventually became part of the Caledonian. Some large depots had smaller satellite goods stations which fed in wagons for assembly into trains. The goods superintendent at Hockley, the GWR's main goods station at Birmingham, controlled five subsidiary depots.

Big city goods stations gave next-day delivery at other large centres for merchandise accepted by late afternoon, over a distance of about 200 miles, by overnight express goods trains. Camden, which covered 14 acres, in 1883 employed 1,500 men who each night despatched 670 wagons in 27 trains, followed by the reception of similar numbers for deliveries in London the next morning.

Goods were shifted manually between dray and railway wagon using pillar *cranes and barrows. At Broad Street the outward section was beneath the passenger station and the inward on the ground floor of the warehouse alongside. A system of designated 'stalls' corresponded with destinations on consignment notes, sorted by clerks and transcribed on to invoices which accompanied the shipments on the train. Wagons were shunted by *horses until the introduction of, first, steam and then hydraulic capstans. Hydraulic power started to become general after the 1850s, usually from a central pump house that also supplied cranes, lifts, and hoists. In 1889 Manchester London Road could handle 90 wagons an hour with hydraulic machinery, although horses were still needed for cartage. In that year Broad Street stabled over 300, and at small depots they continued to be used for *shunting.

The cramped, awkward layouts at so many of the older goods stations, and lack of finance, hampered modernization to counter *road competition after the 1923 *Grouping. The advent of electric battery trucks was the biggest innovation, which with electric and travelling cranes helped to reduce labour costs. In the early 1920s the GWR rebuilt its Bristol Temple Meads goods station, increasing wagon throughput from 432 to 748 a day, using electric lift-trucks and pallets, mobile petrol-electric cranes, an external 10-ton gantry crane, and 26 electric capstans.

But that was one of few. Most goods stations continued to be hydraulically operated and gas-lit, while motor collection and delivery services were very slow to oust the horse. At *nationalization in 1948, *British Railways took over 7,600 road-vehicle and shunting horses. In the 1950s and early 1960s some further modernization was carried out, such as new or improved depots like *Peterborough and Birmingham Curzon Street, but it was too late to affect the reductions being made in wagonload traffic by road transport and the '*container revolution'. Goods stations were steadily closed, replaced by concentration depots, privately operated distribution depots at railheads, and *Freightliner yards which only required open space for stacking containers, perhaps no more than six *sidings, and straddle cranes to lift containers between wagons and lorries. A few large city warehouses remain, used for other purposes or empty, but most have been demolished and their sites redeveloped.

See also FREIGHT TRAFFIC.   GJB
F. S. Williams, *Our Iron Roads* (1883), 418–20; Acworth, ch. 3; Findlay, ch. 12; F. W. West, *The Railway Goods Station: A Guide to Its Control & Operation* (1912); C. E. R. Sherrington, *Economics of Rail Transport in Great Britain* (1928), ii, ch. 9.

stations, parkway. These are situated on main lines close to large cities or other catchment areas of passenger traffic, affording ample parking space for private cars.

The first was opened north of Bristol in 1977: new and purpose-built, and succeeding well. Six others followed, adapted from earlier stations: Alfreton & Mansfield (no longer a 'parkway', simply 'Alfreton'), Bodmin, Didcot, Haddenham & Thame, Southampton (now 'Southampton Airport & Parkway'), and Tiverton.   JS

stations, passenger. The first railways were built for freight, and when passenger traffic began they turned to stage-coach practice for selling *tickets, which were issued at inns near designated stopping-places where passengers clambered into trains from the lineside. The *Leicester & Swannington Railway of 1832 hired a room in the Ashby Road Hotel as a booking office, and later bought the whole building which continued in use as part of Bardon Hill station until its closure in 1952. The *Stockton & Darlington Railway used a converted warehouse at Darlington, and the termini of the *Leeds & Selby (1834) accommodated goods on one side and passengers on the other, devoid of platforms. Tickets were purchased at the superintendent's house.

The *Liverpool & Manchester pioneered purpose-built termini with full facilities for passengers, and at *Liverpool there was a roof over the tracks (see TRAINSHEDS). These termini were 'side stations', having a single platform alongside the station buildings, a layout that persisted for some years at important through stations like *Derby, Chester, and Huddersfield. But it soon became obvious that termini and through stations alike needed separate platforms for trains travelling in opposite directions. Arrival and departure platforms began to be provided at termini, generally with carriage sidings in between—a practice that became widespread. Soon the platforms were connected by a cross-platform at the head of the station, which developed into the circulating area, or concourse, which is familiar today. In turn, the station offices and entrance were erected in front of it, forming 'head stations'.

Continued growth of traffic required more platforms, first displacing the carriage sidings—although they did not finally die out until close to the end of the century—and then added piecemeal outside the original station, often producing a complicated hotch-potch. *King's Cross, *Euston, *Waterloo, and *Manchester Victoria were among notoriously confusing stations.

*Brunel devised an idiosyncratic layout on the *Great Western, where his larger through stations had two platforms from the outset, but both on the same side of the line, like side-stations facing the town; in effect, a separate station for each direction, with cross-over tracks between them. They required two sets of accommodation and staff, and the unavoidable conflicting movements of trains made them awkward to operate, yet despite these disadvantages they went on being built until 1854 (at Wolverhampton Low Level), and lasted until the reconstruction of Reading in 1899. Cambridge still retains a long single platform.

Extra platforms for starting and terminating trains at through stations could be provided by dead-end *'bays', or 'docks' as they are called in Scotland, let into the ends of the main platforms. Some large stations were combinations, having through and terminal platforms in two distinct parts, as at *London Bridge, Blackfriars, Manchester Victoria, and *Bristol Temple Meads. Until 1868 the two sections at *Edinburgh Waverley were at right angles, with a street dividing them, emanating from what had been separate stations.

Waverley typified the reluctance of railway companies to embark on large-scale reconstruction until it was forced on them by sheer congestion. From about 1870, however, managements began to realize that there was no alternative, although the cost and the need to maintain train services meant that progress was slow. The rebuilding of Waterloo, for instance, even allowing for the intervention of World War I, took 20 years. Some were completely rebuilt more than once—*Birmingham Snow Hill, for example, in 1871 and 1912—while at others it took place in stages: *Crewe in 1867 and 1896–1906; *Preston in 1879–80, 1903, and 1913. *Glasgow Central was a completely new station built in two stages in 1879 and 1901–6, to form one of the finest and most convenient terminals in the country. Usually it was possible to extend sideways, as happened at *Liverpool Street and Birmingham New Street, but London's *Victoria terminus could only be extended lengthways. This was done ingeniously in 1906–8 by doubling the lengths of the platforms and inserting a third track at the outer ends which, by means of suitable cross-overs half-way, allowed two trains to arrive or depart simultaneously—although some passengers had a long walk.

During this period the concept of the island platform gained popularity. With tracks on both sides it represented considerable economy in buildings and staff, and if it was made sufficiently wide it could accommodate bay platforms. Among large stations Crewe, Preston, *Leicester London Road, and Birmingham Snow Hill had two or more, while some like Darlington Bank Top, Edinburgh Waverley, and Rugby each comprised one very broad island platform, long enough to have series of bays at the ends, and take two full-length trains at the sides. Central cross-overs connected to through lines on the outside allowed trains to arrive, depart, or overtake without conflicting. Entry was either from a road overbridge and stairs, as at Crewe, or through a side entrance and a subway, as at Darlington and Rugby. Some stations, like Preston, had both a subway and a footbridge.

Island platforms later became common at small suburban stations, while all but two stations were built to this plan on the *Great Central Railway's London Extension of 1899 between Annesley, Nottinghamshire, and Quainton Road, Buckinghamshire. They avoided the need for the two platforms hitherto required as a minimum at stations on double lines. Country junctions and more important stations might combine single-sided platforms and islands. Some two-platform stations had them staggered on either side of a level-crossing. A stopping train could then draw up clear of the gates which could be opened to road traffic behind it. But by no means all of them were like this, and there are a number where the reason for staggered platforms is not at all clear.

Junction station layouts varied immensely. A not uncommon type was V-shaped, with platforms in the angle of the junction, while several triangular junctions had sharply curved platforms on all three sides. At Ambergate in Derbyshire, Queensbury near *Bradford, and Forres on the *Highland Railway, they joined at the ends. At a few junctions the branch line platform was separate from the main station, reached by a footpath, as at Ashby-de-la-Zouch,

Leicestershire, and Sowerby Bridge, Yorkshire. At Watford Junction the St Albans branch platform was actually relocated in this manner when the main line was electrified in 1966.

Because early carriages had step-boards, platforms could be low, but as rolling stock improved they were increased in height to compartment level, unlike those in most other countries. The Board of *Trade required them to have ramps to ground level at each end. Nowadays, health and safety regulations stipulate platforms of standard height, long enough to accommodate the full length of trains normally using them. A footbridge or subway was often a later refinement, although at many smaller places a foot-crossing had to suffice. For instance, none of the 19 stations opened on the *Midland Railway's *Settle–Carlisle main line in 1876 had a footbridge. Appleby received one in 1901, and Settle in 1993.

The basic accommodation at the first proper stations comprised a *ticket office, a *waiting room or shelter, a lavatory for each sex (see SANITATION), and a lamp-room for attending to the station's oil lamps. As traffic grew, facilities were steadily increased. Separate ladies' rooms and *stationmaster's offices became fairly standard, to which were added, according to size, parcels and left-luggage offices, *refreshment rooms, separate classes of waiting rooms (see CLASS DISTINCTIONS), bookstalls, and administration offices. At large city stations they were usually ranged around the concourse. Later, shops and sales kiosks were added (see STATION TRADING).

A particular feature characterized the British railway station above all others: the platform canopy, or awning. It varied in form immensely: for instance, the flat timber decks, favoured by the *London & North Western and *Great Northern; light, elegant, glass-and-iron ridge-and-furrow canopies such as were popular on the Midland; lengthwise pitched awnings that were widely used in later years by the GWR and the *London & South Western; curved-topped on the *South Eastern. They were supported on brackets fixed to the wall of the building or by rows of columns, sometimes extending the full length of the platform. The most distinctive feature was the wooden—or occasionally iron—valance fitted to the front to deflect wind, smoke, and steam. It might be relatively plain, but generally it had a serrated lower edge cut and pierced in an infinite variety of decorative designs.

The unstaffed 'halt', a short, low platform with perhaps a simple shelter, was the railways' attempt to provide more stopping places without the expense of a proper station, and thus stimulate local traffic, particularly after tram and *bus competition began. The GWR had an intermediate category, the 'platform' (as in Wood End Platform, south of Birmingham), which was slightly less basic and had a small staff. Today, with more facilities provided on trains, many wayside stations have become unstaffed halts with nothing more than a glass-sided shelter.

See also ARCHITECTURE; STATIONS, PRIVATE. GJB
VS; GRSB; G. Biddle and J. Spence, *The British Railway Station* (1977); J. Richards and J. M. MacKenzie, *The Railway Station: A*

Social History (1986); H. Paar, 'Staggered Platforms', *JRCHS*, 26, 1 (March 1980), 16, and 26, 3 (Nov. 1980), 101; S. Bragg, 'Bizarre Station Layouts', *JRCHS*, 30, 8 (July 1992), 151, 396.

stations, private: defined here as stations not advertised for public use. Altogether there have been some 1,600, including those on *military, hospital (see HEALTH), and *industrial railways. Many became public; conversely, some closed public stations were retained for a time for use by the military, schools, etc.

Four private stations were provided solely for royalty: Nine Elms, London; at Gosport dockyard, where Queen Victoria embarked for Osborne on the *Isle of Wight; Whippingham, the station for Osborne itself; and St Margarets, Edinburgh. Others were built under a bargain with a *landowner, or for railway directors. The small *Maryport & Carlisle Railway had two: Crofton for a landowner, and Dovenby for a former chairman. Among others, Avon Lodge, Hampshire, and Watchingwell, Isle of Wight, were for landowners; Hall Dene was retained by Lord Londonderry for his personal use when he sold his colliery railway to the *North Eastern. Best known was the Duke of *Sutherland's station at Dunrobin (see HIGHLAND RAILWAY).

Stations for miners were quite numerous, such as Groesfaen Colliers Halt in South Wales, Apedale Colliery in North Staffordshire, and Arley Colliery in Warwickshire. Industrial firms' names were given to stations: Daimler Halt (Coventry); Singer Works Platform on Clydeside, now simply 'Singer'; Acrow Halt, Saffron Walden, for Acrow Engineering; and Slough Trading Estate, for instance. Briery Bobbin Mill was a halt near Keswick, Irlam Halt served the Co-operative soap works, and the curious Salvation Army Halt served the salvationists' printing works at St Albans. Three modern works stations feature in the Great Britain *timetable, with a footnote that they are only accessible from or to be used for nearby factories: Sinfin North, at Derby; 'British Steel Redcar'; and the ill-named 'IBM' near Greenock.

Military stations, other than on military railways, were fewer, like Kidwelly Flats Halt in South Wales and Barry Links Halt (also known as Barry Review Platform) in Angus. The Royal Naval College at Dartmouth had its Britannia Halt, reached by ferry. Lympstone Commando station near Exmouth is now public. Sport had special stations, for cricket and football grounds (see SPORTS, SPECTATOR), race-courses (see HORSE-RACING), and, in Scotland, curling (see WINTER SPORTS). Hedon Halt near *Hull briefly served a speedway in 1948.

Atlantic Park Hostel Halt served a reception centre for American emigrants near *Southampton (now Southampton Airport station), while the little Isle of Man Railway had as many as three private stations, all unique: Braddan Halt for open-air church services; Quarter Bridge for motorcycle races; and Bishop's Court Halt for the Bishop of Sodor & Man.

Certain railway locations had special employees' platforms, like Caerphilly Works, Barassie Workshops, and Cadder Yard. Durnsford Road, Wimbledon, is still used, and

a small platform for crew-changing was built at Queens Road depot on the *Manchester Metrolink system (see LIGHT RAPID TRANSIT). Platforms for railway families were provided at a number of remote places, such as Sugar Loaf Summit on the Central Wales line, Hoo Junction in Kent, and several in Scotland.

See also STATIONS, PASSENGER.   GJB

G. Croughton, R. W. Kidner, and A. Young, *Private and Untimetabled Railway Stations* (1982).

station trading. Apart from *refreshment rooms, retailing on Victorian stations comprised little more than bookstalls and, later, automatic vending machines. The *Liverpool & Manchester Railway allowed vendors to sell newspapers on the platform at *Liverpool Lime Street, and the first bookstall is thought to have been let to Horace Marshall & Son by the *London & Blackwall Railway at *Fenchurch Street station in 1841. The business became competitive, but because contracts were let piecemeal, often to former railway employees, bookstalls were shabby, with newspapers, unwholesome literature, cakes, and soft drinks all mixed up.

In 1848 the *London & North Western Railway accepted from W. H. Smith & Son an exclusive offer to sell papers at all its stations, starting Smiths' rise to become the largest newspaper and book retailer in Britain. The LNWR also led in negotiating rentals as percentages of receipts, subject to a minimum figure, in contracts that allowed the railway to prohibit anything of which it disapproved, including indecent publications, dubious patent medicines, and advertising trade union activities. Smiths started taking over advertising, too (see PUBLICITY; POSTERS). In 1851–2 they paid £8,790 for contracts with 11 railways.

In 1905 Smiths lost their important LNWR and *Great Western contracts, probably through clashes of personalities. Foreseeing the possibility, the firm had started to diversify into town shops and other activities, and quickly recovered, but the two railways placed their contracts with Wymans, who were printers, had no experience, and had to be subsidized.

The first Scottish bookstall was probably at Dunkeld in 1856, and John Menzies opened his first at *Perth and Stirling in 1857, quickly followed by leases on all the bookstalls between *Edinburgh and *Aberdeen. Smiths' sole Scottish venture, at Edinburgh in 1851, lasted only five years; thereafter Menzies steadily acquired a monopoly. Today, Menzies and Smiths share the bulk of the business throughout Britain.

Fruit and flower stalls, hairdressing salons, and bootblacks were allowed at larger stations; then specialist sweets and tobacco kiosks and, after about 1900, a few chemists and post offices, although the latter were found earlier on a few of the remoter country stations. The first station news cinema was opened at *Victoria in 1933, followed by *Waterloo and *Leeds City. But, unlike in Europe and America, it was the 1970s before the real potential of station trading was realized in Britain. In 1985 *British Rail successfully promoted the idea of a station concourse as a shopping area for other than passengers. Platform barriers were replaced by shops, and rooms around the concourse were converted.

Today there is a wide variety of trading on stations, large and small, which in 1988–9 earned BR over £26 million in rentals. GJB

C. Wilson, *First with the News: The History of W. H. Smith* (1985); *RS*, 188–91, 230–2; D. M. Scott, 'Something for the Train' (John Menzies), *The Scots Magazine* (Feb. 1994); W. Vincent, *Seen from the Railway Platform* (1919).

statistics. The management of the complexities of traffic movements, the variety and scale of daily cash transactions, and a financial structure which contained high fixed costs required an unprecedented flow of statistical information, for which the managers of large railway companies from the 1830s had to devise methods of handling. They turned first to financial *accounting, which involved the collecting, collating, and auditing of hundreds of daily transactions to provide information for compiling annual balance sheets and accounts.

Under the first two Railway *Regulation Acts, of 1840 and 1842, the Board of *Trade was authorized to require annual *returns of traffic, tolls, and accidents. Though these provided some of the information necessary for assessing the companies' performance, they did not range widely over railway business, and their insufficiency was sharply complained of in 1850 by *Lardner in his *Railway Economy*, compared with those available for the railways of Belgium and France. In later years the British government called for much additional statistical information (particularly under the Regulation Acts of 1871–3 and 1911), increasingly detailed and carefully defined.

Innovations in cost accounting came more slowly than in financial and capital accounting. The most commonly used method to describe and compare the performances of companies was the 'operating ratio': the relationship between working expenditure and gross revenue at a particular time, with the first expressed as a percentage of the second. It was used as a measure of changes in expenditure in relation to particular traffics and companies, or in relation to the railway industry as a whole. However, variations might be the result of factors outside the control of the company, rendering the ratio an imperfect guide to changes in the efficiency and the relative positions of companies. Despite these weaknesses it was the most commonly used statistical measure in 1870–1914.

Statistical departments came to be established by most of the great railway companies. Some of their reports, now preserved in the PRO, took special care to set their own figures against those available from other railways.

All these series related to the companies' business as a whole, or to large divisions of it; they reveal nothing of what was transacted at individual stations for passenger or goods traffic, into which the government scarcely ever thought it necessary to inquire. But the Royal Commission on London Traffic of 1903 did publish some important series, relating particularly to the traffic at the great terminal stations. In this department of the railways we are dependent therefore on the station traffic statistics that have survived at the PRO and SRO.

The most extensive are those of the *North Eastern Railway, which include some from the companies it took over. The oldest are the *Stockton & Darlington Railway's traffic records for 1833–5. The *Midland Railway's 'station books' are complete from 1872 to 1922. There are similar series at the SRO, coming from all the three largest companies in Scotland. Many of these records deal also with freight, and with the annual cost of working stations, from those serving hamlets in sparsely peopled districts (some of them at a loss) to the great termini of *London, *Edinburgh, and *Glasgow.

Apart from the NER, under its general manager, George S. *Gibb (1891–1906), British railway companies before World War I were well behind their American counterparts in the collection and analysis of data. Statistics on train- and engine-mileage and receipts per train mile were collected and used as measures of performance. However, what was required, so it seemed, was a measure that could be used to assess changes in working methods, in particular train loadings. More widespread use of the ton-mile, as had been used in the USA and India for many years, would have enabled companies to secure better efficiency in train working, and to identify marginal traffic.

The harsher competitive conditions of the inter-war period exposed the statistical immaturity of the majority of companies, including the setting of rates and *fares. Charges were set according to 'what the traffic will bear' rather than a close analysis of costs. However, more sophisticated approaches were introduced in the final years before *nationalization.

See also COSTING TECHNIQUES; FINANCING OF RAILWAYS.

GCh

G. Paish, *The British Railway Position* (1902); H. Pollins, 'Aspects of Railway Accounting before 1868', in M. C. Reed (ed.), *Railways and the Victorian Economy: Studies in Finance and Economic Growth* (1969), 138–61; T. R. Gourvish, *Mark Huish and the London & North Western Railway: A Study of Management* (1972); R. J. Irving, *The North Eastern Railway Company: An Economic History* (1976), 219–22; station statistics: *RTC*, 336–8.

steam locomotives, see TRACTION, STEAM.

steamships, see SHIPPING SERVICES; SHIPPING, COASTAL; FERRIES.

steel, see IRON AND STEEL INDUSTRY; IRON AND STEEL, USE OF.

Stephens, Col. H. F., see LIGHT RAILWAYS.

Stephenson, George (1781–1848), engineer, possibly the most famous ever, thanks to Samuel *Smiles, who immortalized the rise of the some-time pit boy to the presidency of the *Institution of Mechanical Engineers.

Born at Wylam, Northumberland, and trained as a colliery enginewright, he invented a miner's safety lamp independently of Sir Humphrey Davy and went on to become engineer of the *Stockton & Darlington Railway (1825).

Stephenson is credited with many achievements, including discovering that iron wheels adhered to iron rails, developing the steam blast-pipe, and the tubular boiler, and triumphantly combining these first in *Rocket*, then in the first modern railway, the *Liverpool & Manchester, where his civil and mechanical engineering talents converged to form a technological archetype. Later he was engineer of the *Birmingham & Derby Junction (1839), *Manchester & Leeds (1840), *North Midland (1840), *York & North Midland (1839), and other railways, but was forced to relinquish the *Grand Junction to Joseph *Locke. The dream of a nationwide railway system, however, already belonged to Thomas Gray and William *James, with whom it had remained so. The peculiar genius of George Stephenson was that he made it happen.

He was actually a very conservative engineer and sometimes when, as at Chat Moss on the LMR, he took charge, he made serious errors. The technology lay with the younger men, chiefly his son Robert and Locke. But their talents were as yet unproven to investors. George formed them into a team and carefully built a cumulative record of achievement, giving them a 'brand name' through the sister companies of Robert Stephenson & Co. and George Stephenson & Son. He obtained the support of wealthy and influential backers by not hesitating to claim credit for the work of others or to blame errors on underlings.

Recent research suggests that no significant technical development entirely belonged to George, and much of his substantial wealth came from colliery ownership and share-dealing. The somewhat unreliable stories about him were increasingly exaggerated as time passed, but his commercial skills and relationships, and impressive public image, were central to the establishment of early railways. 'Inventor of Railways' he was not, but the claim that he was 'Father of Railways' remains true. AJ

W. O. Skeat, *George Stephenson: The Engineer and His Letters* (1973). For further references, see STEPHENSON, ROBERT.

Stephenson, Robert (1803–59), engineer. He gained early experience when helping his father, George, then enginewright at Killingworth Colliery, Northumberland, who ensured that, unlike himself, Robert had a good engineering training. By 1823 he was placed in charge of Robert Stephenson & Co., *Newcastle, the first purpose-built locomotive works in the world. There he designed and mostly constructed the *Active*—later to become famous as *Locomotion No. 1*—followed by a string of innovative designs: *Rocket, Planet, Patentee*, which established the basic form of the steam locomotive for the rest of its history (see TRACTION, STEAM).

He assisted in surveying the *Stockton & Darlington and *Liverpool & Manchester Railways and was appointed engineer for the *Canterbury & Whitstable and *Leicester & Swannington, but it was his appointment as engineer-in-chief for the *London & Birmingham Railway (1838) which really completed his emergence from his father's shadow. He subsequently became engineer for the *Chester & Holyhead Railway (1850) and the Royal Border Bridge, Berwick (1850). He also showed considerable expertise in

structural ironwork, and despite the collapse of his Dee Bridge at Chester, he successfully completed the *Britannia Bridge over the Menai Strait, Newcastle High Level Bridge, and numerous others, including the Victoria Bridge, Montreal, then the world's longest (see BRIDGES AND VIADUCTS). Later his reputation was such that he was called to adjudicate in widely disparate fields, even in cases where he had a personal interest. Alongside *Brunel and *Locke, he was among the most notable and prolific of early railway engineers and was unusually accorded the presidency of both the *Institution of Civil Engineers and the *Institution of Mechanical Engineers.

Yet he remains something of an enigma. In 1824 he left the locomotive works to become a mine engineer in Bolivia, causing the works virtually to collapse in his absence, and he quietly manœuvred his father out of some major contracts, notably the LBR and the Chester & Holyhead. Even so, the source of Samuel *Smiles' assertion that Robert was always proud to help his father was almost certainly Robert himself, and he positively encouraged Smiles to attribute some of his own achievements to his father. He was MP for Whitby 1847–59 and is buried in Westminster Abbey. AJ

S. Smiles, *Lives of the Engineers*, v (1874); L. T. C. Rolt, *George and Robert Stephenson* (1960); D. Smith (ed.), *Perceptions of Great Engineers* (1994)—see particularly papers by Haworth and Jarvis.

Stephenson Locomotive Society. Founded in 1909, the SLS is the second oldest railway society catering for amateurs, as well as professionals, and has numbered among its members such well-known locomotive engineers as Sir William *Stanier, O. V. S. *Bulleid, and André Chapelon. Its title belies the society's widespread interests, and publications have included some carefully compiled company histories. Regular meetings and visits are held in various parts of the country, and the SLS *Journal* holds a respected position in railway periodical *literature. Long predating the present-day *preservation movement, in 1927 the society secured the preservation of *London Brighton & South Coast Railway 0-4-2 locomotive *Gladstone*, now at the *National Railway Museum. GJB

Stevens & Son, see SIGNALLING EQUIPMENT MANUFACTURE.

Stirling, Patrick (1820–95), engineer. He was apprenticed at a foundry; then worked with marine engines and locomotive builders, and went to the *Glasgow & South Western Railway in 1853 as locomotive superintendent. In 1866 he was appointed assistant locomotive superintendent, *Great Northern Railway, and chief locomotive superintendent soon after.

On the GSWR, Stirling was required to select a site for a new locomotive works at *Kilmarnock, and in 1857 the first locomotive type to be built there was his '2' class 2-2-2. From 1860 he adopted the domeless boiler, also used by his brother James, and son Matthew, on the GSWR and *South Eastern Railway, and *Hull & Barnsley Railways respectively.

Stirling's first locomotives on the GNR were 2-4-0s, then came 2-2-2s in 1868, 0-6-0s, 0-4-2s, and 0-4-4T engines. His masterpiece was the 8-ft driving wheel 4-2-2, built in 1870–95. These excellent performers, elegant in design, ran some of the fastest passenger trains in the world during the 1870s.

Stirling was becoming out of touch with modern practice by the end of his time in office, and was hostile to the idea of coupled express engines and bogie passenger stock. Yet the design for the trains of new East Coast Joint Stock (see also CARRIAGES) introduced in 1896 was produced under the aegis of Stirling, and to time.   MLH

Railway Correspondence & Travel Society, *Great Northern Locomotives*, ii (1989); F. A. S. Brown, *From Stirling to Gresley* (1974).

Stockton & Darlington Railway. The first public railway to be empowered by Parliament to convey goods and passengers by steam traction has been dismissed by some historians as fulfilling little more than a precursory role in the inauguration of the *'Railway Age'. This view has several foundations. The company's original route ran only from the collieries of south-west Durham, via Darlington, to Stockton—a distance of less than 30 miles. Traffic was dominated from the outset by the carriage of heavy minerals and this factor, combined with the company's long-lasting commitment to subcontracting significant aspects of its operations, differentiated it from the later trunk-line companies with their more varied traffic and centralized managerial procedures. Finally, the company's commitment to steam haulage was initially uncertain, at least until 1828 when the first locomotive superintendent, Timothy *Hackworth, succeeded in developing more reliable engines at the company's Shildon *Works. On these grounds, the SDR, authorized in 1821 and opened in 1825, has been subject to invidious comparison with the succeeding *Liverpool & Manchester Railway. While the innovatory significance of the latter is recognized widely, new perspectives in economic and business history have refocused critical attention on the achievements of the earlier company.

In the first instance, the SDR provided an invaluable testing ground both for the technical development of locomotives and for improvements in *track. In these respects, the company's first engineer, George *Stephenson, was able to gain experience which redounded to his advantage in future railway projects. Secondly, the SDR offers significant insights into capital formation in the early 19th-century economy. As a public company its sources of finance were unusual in that they were drawn principally from the Society of Friends in general, and the Quaker *Pease family of Darlington, in particular. It is now accepted that personal networks of this kind played a critical role in financing Britain's early industrialization. Thirdly, although the railway began operations with a limited route, by the early 1860s it occupied a vitally strategic position in the evolving network in northern England. By that time the company had a number of subsidiary enterprises exploiting heavy mineral resources in the region. In this context, the South Durham & Lancashire Union Railway, completed in 1861, was outstanding in so far as it permitted access across the Pennines to the iron ore of Furness. Ownership of the SDLUR, more-

over, enabled the SDR to block the entry of the predatory *London & North Western Railway into north-east England.

In 1828 the SDR had extended the original line from Stockton to *Middlesbrough in order to enter the coastal trade in coal. By 1870, however, Teesside had diversified to become the most important iron-producing district in the world, the product, in large measure, of the SDR's cheap transport. It is a testimony to the company's regional importance that it was absorbed by the *North Eastern Railway in 1863 on generous terms. Finally, the railway provides ample evidence of dynamic entrepreneurship in a crucial phase of Britain's industrial growth. The Pease family directed it with a combination of efficient management and an ability to engage in well-founded railway promotions. In terms of its dividend record, the company was the most profitable British railway before 1860, enjoying a mean annual dividend of 9.5 per cent in the latter half of the 1850s.   MWK

J. S. Jeans, *Jubilee Memorial of the Railway System: A History of the Stockton & Darlington Railway and a Record of Its Results* (1875; reprinted 1975); M. W. Kirby, *Men of Business and Politics: The Rise and Fall of the Quaker Pease Dynasty of North-East England, 1700–1943* (1984); M. W. Kirby, *The Origins of Railway Enterprise: The Stockton & Darlington Railway, 1821–1863* (1993); M. C. Reed, *Investment in Railways in Britain, 1820–1844: A Study in the Development of the Capital Market* (1975); Tomlinson.

Stoke-on-Trent. Even though the *North Staffordshire Railway's presence at Stoke included ownership of the Trent & Mersey Canal, it was not quite strong enough to make it a railway town. The pottery and other industries were far bigger locally. All lines were built by the NSR, the first, from Stoke to the *London & North Western at Norton Bridge (10½ miles), being opened in 1848. A temporary terminal at Whieldon's Grove was quickly replaced by a magnificent station which became the company headquarters. It has a Jacobean-style frontage to a small square completed by a company hotel, almost equally imposing, and small houses for its workers. The centrepiece is a statue to Josiah Wedgwood, founder of the pottery industry in the 18th century. With Stoke and smaller attractively designed stations, the NSR gave the Potteries some of its most distinctive *architecture.

Stoke was also linked to *Crewe, Uttoxeter, and Burton-on-Trent in 1848 and a route to *Manchester followed in 1849 after Macclesfield was reached. Most famous of subsequent lines was the 8-mile Stoke–Kidsgrove Potteries *Loop line constructed in 1861–75. As work began, Measom's LNWR *Guide* (see GUIDEBOOKS) noted that the NSR 'binds together the range of Pottery towns like a thread stringing beads'. The Loop was a sharply curved, steeply graded new circle linking the six pottery towns which formed the conurbation of Stoke-on-Trent in 1910, when its population was approaching 250,000.

The NSR was admired for running smartly timed trains between Stoke and towns and villages nearby. W. D. Phillipps, general manager 1882–1919, once stated: 'most of our runs are so short that drivers are afraid to put on much speed for fear of running 20 or 30 miles on to somebody else's line before they stop'. Frequent 6 a.m.–11 p.m. Loop Line trains helped to keep tram competition down.

In Edwardian years, over 200 daily trains arrived at and departed from Stoke, short trains using the two long platforms two at a time. Most prestigious were LNWR Euston–Manchester (London Road) expresses, for which the NSR was 'fined' £1 for every minute lost while on the system. Like the Loop, the 'Eustons' were immortalized by Arnold Bennett, whose writings captured the air of expectancy which surrounded their arrival at Stoke.

Up expresses were often worked from Manchester by sturdy NSR *tank locomotives. They were built at the NSR Stoke *works where 500 men built and repaired locomotives and 400 worked on carriages and wagons. The Stoke locomotive building industry collapsed between 1926, when the *London Midland & Scottish Railway closed the NSR works and transferred most men to Crewe, and 1930 when Kerr Stuart ceased locomotive building at Stoke after nearly four decades. The NSR works were near a roundhouse at Stoke locomotive shed, biggest on the system.   RC

CMNSR; A. C. Baker, The Potteries Loop Line (1986); G. Body, Railway Stations of Britain (1990); RTC.

stone, use of. Railways had to traverse an undulating and sometimes rugged topography, bringing about the need for *bridges and viaducts, *tunnels, retaining walls, culverts, roadways, and embankments. It was fortunate that these same locations by their very nature often contained rock from which stone could be quarried for use in the construction work. The transport cost of building materials was also a major practical and economic factor, so a source of supply close to the works was an added bonus. The resulting structures of various types and forms correspondingly fitted well into the same local environment, borne out in the way that many of them have to a great extent developed considerable character and integrity over the years.

One of the most notable features of railways built up to the 1860s, and a number that followed, is the use of local stone where it was available. Where cheapness and speed in construction of bridges and viaducts was paramount, imported *timber was used, but later replacement by more permanent structures was usually wholly or partly in stone. Typical examples can be found on the *Settle & Carlisle line, in the Derbyshire Peak District, in the West Country, and on nearly all the Scottish railways. The first-mentioned, mostly now in a National Park, was constructed in 1870–6, and comprises many fine stone structures, notably the viaducts at Arten Gill, Dent Head, and Ribblehead. Everywhere stone underbridges and road overbridges, together with retaining and boundary walls, fit well into the landscape, from pale limestone at the southern end to gritstone further north and dark red sandstone in the Eden Valley.

The Derbyshire Peak District is also a National Park, and another area of natural beauty in which the prospect of a railway originally caused hostility. Several lines were built through it, although some have now closed. The extensive use of local limestone and gritstone in construction has pro-

duced a compatibility with the *landscape and its vernacular architecture that is in many ways similar to that on the Settle & Carlisle route. Some of the *disused lines in the Peak District can be used for walking and cycling, which permits continuing usefulness and a means of observing the works.

Influences can be observed elsewhere in the railway system where different stones such as granite, slate, and sandstone exist, not only in civil engineering structures but also in stations, warehouses, and railway houses. Flint was used in areas where it was the indigenous building material, such as parts of East Anglia, Hertfordshire, and Wiltshire. Local stone might not always be suitable, of course, in which case it had to be brought from further afield when it was considered essential, by canal or river or, as the system spread, by the railways themselves. Thus we have a splendid heritage of railway buildings and structures in stone, many of which are excellently preserved and documented. Nearer the end of the 19th century, however, *brick, carried by the railways themselves, began to supplant stone where it was cheaper to use it, thereby ending the harmonious relationship with the landscape that marked the earlier years.

Depending on the type and quality of the rock, stone was quarried, crushed, and processed to fulfil a variety of needs. The use of stone in embankments enabled a structure of considerable strength to be formed. The larger stones were tipped at the bottom, reducing in size towards the top, with their angular shapes locking together, forming a strong mechanical bond. Stone embankments could have steeper sides than earth structures, thus requiring less land at the base. The surface of the embankments was in some locations 'fair faced' with hand-placed random stone, forming features sometimes referred to as 'breast walls'. There are examples on the Cromford & High Peak Railway (1831) in Derbyshire.

A great deal of foresight is evident in the way in which stone was used for protection of the railway against river and coastal erosion, such as embankment faces, river beds under bridges, areas around bridge abutments and piers prone to scouring, sea walls, groynes, and breakwaters. Long lengths of sea wall were required in order to build the *Chester & Holyhead Railway along the North Wales coast, for instance, on the *South Devon Railway between Dawlish Warren and Teignmouth, and in west Cumbria. Not only the obvious places need scour protection, but also the potentially abnormal situation. For instance, many lines are built in river valleys in which flood waters gently rise. When they fall the railway embankment acts as a dam, and the receding flood waters rush back to the river through any convenient bridge opening or culvert, causing scour unless suitably protected.

The railways also needed stone for building many roadways, some of which are still owned by them and require stone for maintenance. Several early lines used stone for *track, such as the Haytor and West India Docks granite tramways.

The largest continuing demand for stone is for track ballast, and although ash was used in goods yards and other similar locations, and on some main lines, stone has been the main material now for many years. Originally it was specified as bottom ballast, consisting of hard stone up to 9 in long, and top ballast of maximum 2 in. However, it is the practice nowadays not to use bottom ballast, but to provide top ballast to an increased depth.

Ballast is obtained from crushed granite or limestone, the former being favoured for main and heavily used routes as limestone tends to powder and become less efficient. In addition to the main track ballast, stone dust is sometimes used for formation blanketing (or sealing), and chippings for sleeper packing and maintenance of track levels. Crushed stone is also used for many other construction works, such as drainage systems, and at one time a number of railways owned their own quarries, like the *North Staffordshire's at Caldon Low and the Manchester Sheffield & Lincolnshire's (see GREAT CENTRAL) at Doveholes in Derbyshire. Best-known, probably, was the extensive Meldon quarry on Dartmoor, bought by the *London & South Western Railway in 1897 and only sold by *British Rail in 1994. The *South Eastern used shingle from Dungeness for ballast, whilst the *Great Northern dredged gravel from the River Trent at Newark.

Apart from the need for coursed and shaped stones in the construction of masonry, other demands existed for stone products, such as sett paving, flagstones, road kerbs, machine bases, copings, slabs, etc., all of which needed some degree of prior preparation and shaping. Early *tramroads and the first longer-distance railways such as the *Stockton & Darlington, *Liverpool & Manchester, and *London & Birmingham used roughly shaped stone blocks for sleepers, with holes drilled in them for the iron spikes or bolts that secured the rails. After they were superseded by wooden sleepers, many of the blocks were used for walling and other purposes. Some had to be transported considerable distances where local stone was either unsuitable or not available. On the *Glasgow Paisley Kilmarnock & Ayr Railway, for example, stone for blocks and other purposes was shipped across from the Isle of Arran. Sett paving in particular was used in many railway locations, being very common in goods and coal yards, station approaches, and roadways to provide what might be considered the ultimate wear-resistant surface. It was highly suitable for horse-drawn traffic, but became unpopular as motor vehicles came into use. In the 1950s and 1960s considerable areas of setts were replaced by macadam and asphalt surfaces. Sometimes they were taken up, and at other places were covered over, the latter method frequently proving unsuccessful as eventually the hard granite pierced the overlying surface. The setts comprised granite blocks approximately 5-in cube, and sometimes bigger.

Masonry may be described as 'the art of building in stone'. Railway masonry structures are numerous and wide-ranging in type and application, displaying to the full the ingenuity and skill that is the mason's art. As a structural material, stone is strong in compression, but its tensile abilities are poor, so in arch construction it is used in compression, enabling it to withstand the heaviest loads. In addition

to bridges and viaducts the railways used masonry for many other purposes, such as *stations, offices and workshops, *engine sheds, river weirs, water towers, reservoirs, docks and wharves, tunnels and tunnel shafts, retaining walls and buttresses, culverts and subways, and even on occasions monuments and *memorials. This wide variety of buildings and structures involved the use of many different types of stone, from marble and granite to slate, limestone, gritstone, and softer sandstone. Construction varied from random and rough block stonework to fine ashlar. Frequently, specially cut and shaped features were needed for such work as columns, cills, mullions, lintels, balustrades, parapets, copings, drip courses, plinths, keystones, voussoirs, and quoins. Stone sculpture and ornamentation is not uncommon, including armorial devices. It can be found on station buildings, tunnel portals, and monuments.

Although much experience and knowledge existed in building stone arch bridges, the effects of long-term railway loading and vibration on them were unknown. The engineers' original assumptions, calculations, and configurations appear in the majority of cases, however, to have been more than adequate as proved by the test of time, despite increased speeds and weights of trains. As a result, thousands of masonry structures remain in service after well over 100 years' life, and form the core of the present-day railway infrastructure. On viaducts and tunnels the builders' skills and workmanship, often applied in hostile conditions, are displayed with particular eloquence. Examples of notably fine masonry work can be seen, for instance, in the curved retaining walls interspersed by bridges at Belper, Derbyshire; throughout the *Edinburgh and Glasgow Railway; in the ashlar retaining walls, bridges, and viaducts on the *Great Western through Bath; and in the flying arches buttressing the walls of a cutting between Chorley and Preston. Fine flying-arch bridges in ashlar were built on the London & Birmingham near Coventry, and in rockfaced stone in the West Country and South Wales.

Even the finest and most robust masonry, of course, requires maintenance. Mortar joints have deteriorated, requiring re-pointing, and some stones have perished, needing replacement. Water seepage, particularly in tunnels, has occurred in places, while wind and frost action have damaged both mortar and stone. Stone-faced piers, abutments, and arches were in some cases originally backed-up or infilled with rubble and mortar, which has decayed—possibly as a result of water seepage—requiring cement grouting and, in some cases, the addition of steel reinforcement and stitching bars. Generally speaking, vibration has caused more damage to arches than direct loading, particularly where the mortar points have become weak; strengthening has therefore been necessary and remedial measures have included the removal of the old backfill in the arch spandrels and replacement with concrete and steel reinforcement. Steel tie-bars and pattresses (washer plates) on the face of the arch have also been used sometimes, unfortunately to the detriment of a structure's appearance.

See also ARCHITECTURE; CONSERVATION; BRICKS, USE OF; TIMBER, USE OF; IRON AND STEEL, USE OF; STONE TRAFFIC.　　KUR

G. Biddle and O. S. Nock, *The Railway Heritage of Britain* (1983); P. J. G. Ransom, *The Archaeology of Railways* (1981); A. M. Sowden, *The Maintenance of Brick, Stone and Masonry Structures* (1990); F. S. Williams, *The Midland Railway: Its Rise and Progress* (1968 edn.).

stone traffic. In the wide range of freight designated by the railway as *mineral traffic, excluding *coal, stone predominated. *Slate, *cement, china *clay, and *iron ore have separate articles; here we are concerned with cut and crushed stone.

Many early *tramroads carried stone. Ralph Allen's wooden tramroad (1731–64), for example, carried stone from his quarries into Bath, and in Fife the Halbeath line built in 1783 to take coal to Inverkeithing carried freestone as well. After the railways were built, quarries on or near the coast continued to ship stone by sea, and still do so, although they frequently had short railways or inclines to the pier. The Penlee Railway at Newlyn, Cornwall, was like that, and only operated when a ship came in. A longer line, the Liskeard & Caradon (1844), at first carried Cheesewring granite to the Liskeard & Looe Canal, and later continued to Looe harbour. The Plymouth & Dartmoor Railway (1823–1900) carried stone for 23 miles for shipment at Sutton Pool. In Lancashire, the Preston & Longridge Railway (1840) carried Longridge Fell stone for *Preston's public buildings, *Liverpool docks, and coastal works.

These were all local lines. After the *Great Western Railway was built it was realized that the Bath stone in the Box area of Wiltshire could provide a lucrative traffic in taking it further afield, and other railways did the same. The well-known Idle Moor quarries near *Bradford, for instance, sent out most of their products over the *Great Northern Railway's Shipley branch. Stone for buildings and streets in the towns of northern England and Scotland usually came from nearby quarries until they began to run out. When Liverpool's were exhausted in the 1850s stone was carried from North Wales, mainly but not entirely by sea. *Glasgow's supplies lasted until the 1890s, when Arran and Dumfries-shire sandstone was substituted, in both cases carried by sea, although large quantities from the Dumfries area also travelled by rail. Corncockle quarry, which was connected to the *Caledonian Railway near Lockerbie, provided stone for many Glasgow buildings, while the opening of the Dumfries & Castle Douglas Railway in 1859 revived large-scale quarrying at Dalbeattie, noted for its polished granite. Although most of this went by sea, by 1907 some 70,000 tons of crushed stone a year were despatched by rail, and 400 men were employed. In north-east Scotland the Alford Valley Railway (1859) in Aberdeenshire deliberately took a different route in order to serve granite quarries near the hamlet of Kemnay, which grew to house 1,000 people. Near Arbroath the Earl of Dalhousie built the Carmyllie Railway in 1864 to connect his 'pavement' quarries to the main line.

Harbour works might have their own separate railways, like the breakwater railways at Weymouth, Holyhead, and Peterhead.

Road improvements begun in the latter part of the 19th century required increasing quantities of crushed stone, usually granite or limestone, and many county councils had their own roadstone sidings. Limestone was even more important for lime works, and for the iron and steel industry. George *Stephenson owned quarries at Crich, Derbyshire, and lime kilns at Ambergate, 2½ miles away, which in 1837 he connected by a 3-ft gauge tramway. The Cromford & High Peak Railway (1831) was built primarily to carry limestone, and in 1860 some 6,000 tons a month were passing off the northern end at Whaley Bridge. Elsewhere in Derbyshire the *London & North Western Railway built the Ashbourne–Buxton line principally to take out limestone, and today large quantities are carried by rail from quarries and lime works in the Buxton area. In Durham, too, in 1850 the *Stockton & Darlington Railway was moving 66,700 tons a year along its Weardale branch, first opened in 1847, rising to 500,000 tons in 1868. Other limestone-bearing areas owed their development to railways: north-west Yorkshire, where today the truncated Grassington branch remains open for block limestone trains; south Derbyshire; and the Mendips in Somerset, where in 1986 Foster Yeoman, owners of the large Merehead quarries, began haulage over *BR tracks with their own American-built locomotives, the first to do so since the National Coal Board ceased running over BR in Durham in the 1960s. In 1988 some 20 trains a day were leaving Merehead, and another large quarry-owner in the same area, ARC, has formed a joint operation with Foster Yeoman called Mendip Rail. In 1900, 1 million tons of crushed granite was taken by rail from quarries in the Charnwood Forest area of Leicestershire: traffic that is still substantial today. See also STONE, USE OF. GJB

Reg. Hist. (all vols.); Glasgow: M. Lindsay, *Portrait of Glasgow* (1972); Dumfries-shire: I. Donnachie, *Industrial Archaeology of Galloway* (1971); Dalbeattie: D. Frew, *The Parish of Urr* (1909); Liverpool: T. A. Roberts, 'The Welsh Influence on the Building Industry in Victorian Liverpool', in M. Doughty (ed.), *Building the Industrial City* (1986).

Stratford (London), see WORKS.

Stratford & Moreton Railway. This owed its origin to William *James, who surveyed a 'Central Junction Railway' in 1819–20, from Stratford-upon-Avon to London through Moreton-in-Marsh and Oxford. That failed, but the idea of bringing coal from the navigable Avon to Moreton attracted local support, and the Stratford & Moreton Railway, authorized in 1821 (17 miles long), was the result.

James urged that it should use locomotives. But in 1823 J. U. *Rastrick was appointed the company's engineer, and under him the line was laid down to be horse-worked.

The undertaking never prospered. Opened in 1826, the line was reported to be in poor condition two years later. A branch was taken to Shipston-on-Stour in 1836, which did quite well. But when the Oxford Worcester & Wolverhampton Railway (see WEST MIDLAND RAILWAY) was authorized in 1845, passing through Moreton, it leased the small company, controlling its management in 1852. The Stratford–Moreton passenger service terminated in 1859. The OWWR eventually passed to the *Great Western in 1863,

Stratford-upon-Avon & Midland Junction Railway

and the Stratford & Moreton company was liquidated in 1868. In 1889 the GWR opened a new line between Moreton and Shipston, partly on the old railway's track-bed; closed to passengers in 1929, and to freight in 1960.   JS

C. Hadfield and J. Norris, *Waterways to Stratford* (1968 edn.), 127–55; *ET*, 11–17.

Stratford-upon-Avon & Midland Junction Railway. Based on Stratford, the 'SMJ' was an impecunious minor railway that managed to survive to the *Grouping and be absorbed into the *London Midland & Scottish. An amalgam of four smaller companies—the earliest opened in 1866—its single line straggled through 69 miles of middle England between the *Midland Railway's Bedford–Northampton branch at Ravenstone Wood Junction and its Barnt Green–Ashchurch line at Broom Junction, including branches from Towcester to the *London & North Western's main line at Blisworth and the Banbury branch at Cockley Brake Junction—all names indicative of the SMJ's deeply rural character. There were also connections into the *Great Central and *Great Western Railways.

In receivership, with no other railway prepared to buy it, some order was restored by reorganization in 1908. Originating traffic was sparse and efforts to bring traffic to 'The Shakespeare Route' included through services to Stratford from *Euston and *Marylebone. The MR and LMS used it for Avonmouth–London freight traffic, but it was only in the two world wars and the early 1950s that the line came into its own as an east–west freight route.

The company's collection of engines once included a 'double *Fairlie', the first locomotive in Britain to have Walschaerts *valve gear. In 1932 the LMS experimented with a 'Ro-Railer' *road-rail coach. By 1965 the line had closed except for 3¼ miles from Fenny Compton to a military depot.   GJB

J. M. Dunn, *The Stratford-upon-Avon & Midland Junction Railway* (1952); A. Jordan, *The Stratford-upon-Avon & Midland Junction Railway* (1982).

Stretton, Clement Edwin (1850–1915), writer. Educated at Rugby, he lived in Leicester for the remainder of his life. After training as an engineer, he became a consultant and advised the *Midland and other railway companies, particularly on matters concerning *safety. He assisted railwaymen also, and they showed much appreciation of his help. His book *Safe Railway Working: A Treatise on Railway Accidents* went through three editions in 1887–93.

He also investigated the history of individual railway undertakings in Leicestershire and elsewhere, publishing over 100 pamphlets about them, together with a substantial *History of the Midland Railway* (1901), a well-organized and comprehensive account, including valuable chapters on the administrative structure of the company.

Stretton has often been criticized for his inaccuracy, and the charge is true, yet one has to admire his output. His pamphlets were based mainly on newspapers—often inaccurate themselves; he seems to have had no access to the MR records. But he was a pioneer in this study, opening up a wide view of the subject (eight of his pamphlets were devoted to the shipping services across the Irish Sea), and his work is always worth referring to, provided one can check his statements.   JS

Leicester Daily Post, 22 Feb. 1915; *Ottley; collections of his pamphlets at BL and Leicestershire RO.

strikes. The incidence and character of railway strikes may be grouped into six main periods: (a) from 1830 to 1873 they were all of a purely local character and affected mainly single grades of railway employees; (b) from 1873 to 1900 strikes were less risky to undertake because of the protection given to *trade unions in 1871; (c) in the turbulent years from 1900 to 1919 inclusive, there were national all-grade disputes which shook the governments of the day; (d) between the two world wars there were both comprehensive strikes involving all grades, and sectional strikes involving the footplate men; (e) in 1945–65, largely due to a much-improved negotiating machinery, there were only two official national strikes though there were unofficial stoppages; (f) after 1965 such few strikes as there were generally took the form of 'working to rule', or a succession of one-day stoppages.

The large majority of the first generation of railway employees had no experience of strikes. Research has revealed only 11 of them between 1836 and 1870 inclusive; most lasted only a few days, concerned one grade of employee—generally enginemen and porters—were confined to one district, and came in the aftermath of the Railway *Mania of 1845–55, or the financial crisis of 1866–7. The infrequency and small scale of the strikes before 1870 may be partly attributed to the much-prized relative security of railway employment; the alternative, of petitioning the general managers, and the fear of the consequences of taking industrial action in the light of the existence of the old combination laws, deterred them.

Two developments in the boom of the early 1870s made strike action more feasible. The Trade Union Act, 1871, gave trade unions legal status and the protection of their funds; and the Amalgamated Society of Railway Servants (see NATIONAL UNION OF RAILWAYMEN) was established in 1872. In the slump of the later 1870s which followed the boom, many railway companies tried to cut their wages costs. On the *Midland Railway in January 1879 there was a reduction of wages successively in the different grades which led to a walkout of goods *guards at Toton sidings, followed by strikes of other grades in the company's employment. The strike was beaten by the importation of 'scab labour' from the *North Eastern, the *Great Eastern, and other railways. In 1887 the *Associated Society of Locomotive Engineers & Firemen, founded in 1880, backed a strike of Midland Railway enginemen.

In the period after 1900 strikes took on a more aggressive and widespread character, particularly in 1911–13. Both sides in the railway industry strengthened their bargaining power through consensus and amalgamation. In 1893 the principal railway companies agreed that they should help each other to 'sit out' strikes, i.e. that they should hold on until union forces were exhausted in a gradual war of attrition. At the same time the ASRS sponsored 'all grades' campaigns in 1897, 1907, and 1911. This was followed by three unions combining to form the NUR in 1913.

Although the main tendency in this period was towards national movements, the Taff Vale strike of August 1900 was an exception. In its earlier years the *Taff Vale Railway enjoyed great prosperity through the expansion of the coal trade, but competition from the *Barry and *Rhymney Railways forced it to reduce its tonnage charges and the dividend paid to its shareholders. A 'hard-line' general manager, Ammon Beasley, was brought in to cut labour costs. Impetuously, many ASRS members came out on strike without handing in their stipulated notices. When the strike was ended after 11 days, Mr Justice Farwell's judgement was highly critical of union power. It changed the balance of industrial forces by making unions liable for damages after strikes. The law this represented was overturned in the Trade Disputes Act, 1906.

The first national railway strike in August 1911, sponsored by all four of the railway unions except the Railway Clerks' Association (see TRANSPORT SALARIED STAFFS' ASSOCIATION), was basically one of union recognition. The railway directors at first invoked the assistance of the prime minister, H. H. Asquith, who declared that the government would 'use all the civil and military forces at its disposal' to ensure that trains would continue to run. But, despite the deployment of 58,000 troops at key *junctions, *stations, and *signal boxes, the strike was effective. When the railway directors still refused to meet the union leaders, a House of Commons resolution, moved by J. Ramsay Mac-Donald, urging a meeting of the two sides to the dispute, was carried without a division. Discussions between the representatives of the men and the companies followed.

In 1919, at discussions at the Board of *Trade, the coalition government, the leading railway companies' directors, and union representatives agreed a policy of 'standardization upwards' for railway wages, i.e. adding the total of war bonuses to the highest pre-war rates paid to each grade. This policy was applied by the Railway Executive Committee first to the locomotive grades in August 1919 in the hope that they would be less likely to support other categories of railwaymen should a dispute arise about their pay. When the wages proposed for the rest of the railway workers were announced it was seen that several grades were to have their wages cut. Before the national railway strike in September, J. H. *Thomas, general secretary of the NUR, was so convinced that the dispute would be settled by negotiation that he made no provision for a strike emergency and the need to give strike benefit of 12s. a week to 481,000 members. The NUR had but £3,000 readily available, though its total funds amounted to £1,218,327. The help given by the Co-operative Wholesale Society in this emergency was crucial. Its printing department issued cheques encashable at CWS banks and stores, and the CWS bank gave cash for vouchers issued by local strike committees. The strike was also notable in that, for the first time, use was made by both sides of advertisements in *The Times* and other newspapers. The charge made by the government

that Thomas was leading an 'anarchist conspiracy' lacked credibility. Following all-day discussions on 5 October, the government yielded and abandoned its plan to reduce railway wages. The strike, the most important in railway history, marked a decisive turning-point in railway industrial relations. The unions had demonstrated their considerable power, and henceforward government and railway management realized that co-operation with labour, rather than confrontation, was the wisest policy.

A strike of members of ASLEF took place in January 1924. It followed a ballot of the union's members who voted 6–1 for industrial action in opposition to worsened mileage allowances and special duty rates. NUR members were instructed to remain at work because all the unions, including ASLEF, had agreed to a National Wages Board decision of the preceding November accepting some wage reductions. The result of the strike was that the changes in enginemen's working conditions were postponed to a later date.

The greatest expenditure of the railway unions' funds took place as a result of their participation in the General Strike of 1926. No direct railway issue was at stake since it was a sympathetic strike in support of the miners, who were threatened with large wage cuts and loss of jobs which were seen by most railway workers as a precursor of general attacks on wage-earners' living standards.

Following the conclusion of World War II and *nationalization of transport in 1948, though there were a number of unofficial strikes which helped to give the public the impression of a strike-ridden industry, there were very few official stoppages. In May and June 1955 ASLEF members struck work to restore their differentials, and secured a part of their objectives. There was a national one-day railway strike in 1962 against *Beeching's proposal to reduce the number of railway workshops. The case for these reductions was that diesel locomotives required less detailed maintenance than did the steam locomotives they were in the process of replacing, and that the more streamlined railway after 1948 required fewer workshops. After intensive discussions Beeching agreed to reduce the pace of workshop closures and to improve the compensation paid to those men and women made redundant.

Early in 1973 ASLEF organized a ban on rest-day working, unrostered overtime, and Sunday working on different regions at different times, which led to some modifications of the terms of employment in the union's favour. In the summer of 1994, in a series of 24-hour strikes called on different days in successive weeks, the *signalmen members of the NUR withdrew their labour. In the previous ten years the number of signalmen employed had been reduced from 6,695 to 4,600, though the train mileage controlled by the staff was not significantly different. In 1970 there were 180 *signal boxes controlling the *East Coast main line between King's Cross and the Scottish border. In 1994 there were five. The signalmen considered that they had not been adequately rewarded for the very substantial increases in their productivity. After a ballot which was 4–1 in favour of strike action, the dispute lasted from 15 June to 27 September. The complicated settlement brought concessions in the form of lump sum payments and 3.4 per cent average increases in pay, concessions to Railtrack (see PRIVATIZATION) on rostering, and simplification of salary payment arrangements. PSB

P. W. Kingsford, *Victorian Railwaymen* (1970); M. R. Bonavia, *British Railway Policy between the Wars* (1981); C. D. Foster, *The Transport Problem* (1975 edn.); Gourvish.

Stroudley, William (1833–89), locomotive engineer. The self-educated son of a paper-mill machinist, he worked for a Birmingham millwright, and then served in the *Great Western Railway workshops at *Swindon and the *Great Northern's at *Peterborough. He became works manager at Cowlairs, *Edinburgh & Glasgow Railway, 1861–5; locomotive superintendent, *Highland Railway, 1865–70, and *London Brighton & South Coast Railway, 1870–89.

The HR and the LBSCR were both impoverished, and there was a miscellaneous assortment of locomotives at *Brighton. To contain costs, Stroudley introduced standardization, based on five locomotive types of his own devising, from the nimble little 'Terrier' tank engines for suburban and branch-line traffic to the 'Gladstones', with their remarkable front-coupled (0-4-2) wheel arrangement, for express service. They were finished to a very high standard and were therefore not cheap, but they were economical and very long-lived. Stroudley never convinced his board that he was economizing enough, and they might have quarrelled if he had not died suddenly in 1889. JS

DBB; H. J. C. Cornwell, *Stroudley: Craftsman of Steam* (1968); *PICE*, 81 (1884–5).

subscription contracts. Lists of subscribers to large public undertakings were required by Parliament before it considered their Bills, showing names, addresses, and professions, together with the amount that each contracted to subscribe (see PROMOTION OF RAILWAYS: PROCEDURE). In 1836 there was widespread complaint that many names had been obtained improperly, and in the following year a Commons committee investigated six projects. It was said that 'needy and indigent persons' appeared in the lists, obviously unable to find the capital they subscribed for, and that they included numerous 'false and fraudulent signatures'. The committee examined many witnesses (among them the journalist John *Herapath, who was clearly involved in much malpractice of this sort) and concluded that the complaints were well founded. Some tightening-up of the procedure for introducing railway Bills followed. But it could not be fully effective. Given Parliament's confined and rigid timetable, it was impossible to check the lists of signatures adequately. They continued to include many that had been wrongfully obtained and were, as guarantees for the investment of capital, worthless. The number of these contracts multiplied enormously in the *Mania of 1845–6. The Railway *Commissioners derided them in 1847, and though they continued to be required until 1858, they received little attention.

Historians disregarded them too until the 1970s, when it was realized that, with all their faults, the lists deserved serious analysis. They reveal something of the geographical distribution of the subscribers; and where registers of shareholders still exist, with which they can be compared, they also show how many subscribers were seriously committed, and how many failed to take up their shares or sold them off. Subscription contracts also show something of the relative strength of the great centres of capital—*London, *Liverpool, and *Manchester—in the total investment in individual companies.

Careful discrimination still needs to be applied to the signatures; but these documents may be valuable indicators of the financial support the early railways enjoyed. JS

Committee of 1837: PP 1837, xviii; lists and particulars of subscribers: PP 1845, xl; 1846, xxxviii. Many original contracts are in HLRO. S. A. Broadbridge, *Studies in Railway Expansion* (1970); M. C. Reed, *Investment in Railways in Britain, 1820–1844* (1975); Robertson, 150–62.

subsidies. The Exchequer Loan Commission was set up in 1817 to lend money for public works. The *Liverpool & Manchester Railway benefited, but only four other English and four Irish railways received advances in 1830–44. More applied, but were rejected. Under the 1896 *Light Railways Act £1 million was set aside for loans and grants, but little more than 20 per cent was spent. In the 1890s, the Mallaig line (*North British) was guaranteed interest and alleviation of local rates, while the Kyle extension (*Highland) received an outright subsidy. Between the wars the Guarantees and Loans Act, 1934, authorized government assistance for public works in an endeavour to alleviate unemployment, and a number of railway modernization schemes received loan interest guarantees and grants.

These were the only instances of state aid for railways until Barbara Castle's 1968 Transport Act, and they can hardly be considered to have been true subsidies. The new Act, however, was different. Under Section 20, *Passenger Transport Authorities were set up in large conurbations, with power to contribute to unremunerative passenger services and to sponsor new railway investment. Section 56 authorized direct government subsidy of other loss-making services which it considered desirable to retain on social grounds, in the form of Public Service Obligation grants.

Section 8 of the 1974 Transport Act took subsidy into the freight sector. Grants could be made to *BR and private firms for new or improved rail facilities, such as private *sidings, with the object of encouraging traffic to move from road to rail. PTAs and PSO grants have been very successful in retaining and enlarging the passenger network, but the impact of Section 8 grants on freight traffic has at best been marginal, due in part to Treasury insistence on a rate of return which many consider to be unrealistically high.

A form of government subsidy was also made in meeting deficits incurred by BR in a number of years.

The *privatization Act of 1993 contained revisions. PSO grants—now made under European Commission regulations—may be part of franchise agreements under which payments are made to private operators or PTAs. Passenger services not forming part of a franchise can be subsidized by the government through the Franchising Director.

Freight operators may be subsidized to offset track access

charges in respect of traffic from which it is agreed that social or environmental benefits will accrue, and finance is available for infrastructure work that ensures the retention of traffic on the railway, replacing Section 8 grants.

Financial assistance is also available for formulating 'management buyouts' by railway employees.

See also FINANCING OF RAILWAYS; IRELAND; PARLIAMENT AND LEGISLATION.   GJB

M. C. Reed, *Investment in Railways in Britain, 1820–1844* (1975), 249–52; Gourvish; Transport Act, 1993.

suburbs and railways. Although sometimes a powerful agent in suburban growth, a railway was rarely the primary factor. Even during the building booms of the early 20th century when the network was highly developed, elements such as the availability of cheap building land usually played the major role; indeed in *London, large developments, such as North Ilford and North Romford, would occasionally be located without regard to public transport. And, as at Hayes, Kent, Victorian railway promoters hoping for profits from residential growth could be frustrated when landowners refused to break up their estates. Established railway companies, when projecting lines into districts seemingly ripe for development, could overlook the predominance of local employment or fail to foresee the emergence of the cheaper and more convenient street *tramway, as demonstrated by the *Great Eastern Railway's Churchbury Loop of 1891, in 1909 one of the first passenger closures.

Suburban rail travel associated with separation of middle-class home and work-place, notably in London, emerged in the 1860s. From around 1875 it grew strongly, remaining important today (0.74 million in 1994), despite dilution caused by dispersal of city offices and the onset of automation. Railways have always been the most efficient means of handling this traffic and, although the main-line companies north of the Thames regarded it as something of an unavoidable nuisance, for those companies with little income from freight or no long-distance passenger services, it was a staple item, particularly that from the outer areas, with its high proportion of first-class *season ticket-holders. After the mechanization of *road transport, such longer-distance traffic, less vulnerable to road competition, was carefully cultivated. For local companies, like the *Metropolitan, suburban traffic formed a substantial portion of income. Until the 1960s brought expansion in car ownership, all suburban railways reaped lucrative off-peak revenues from travel to schools and shopping centres, and for leisure activities. Except on the *London Underground, they also carried *milk, *newspapers, *parcels and *mail, retailers' supplies, solid fuels, and building materials—all these lost to road or through changes in domestic heating after the 1950s.

Until around 1900, the *Great Western, *Midland, and *London & North Western Railways paid scant regard to London suburban traffic. From the 1860s, reacting to demand from the favoured 'Northern Heights' and elsewhere, the *Great Northern opened new suburban facilities. Find-

ing its terminal capacity swamped, in 1875 it invited the *North London Railway to divert some of the flow. Seeking to confine its heavy but unremunerative *workmen's-fare traffic to its north-east London lines and other inner area stations, the GER unintentionally became social engineer, so strongly did its policy dictate the type of housing development in north-east London in 1875–1900.

An early demonstration of the ability of electric railways to generate suburban traffic came with the emergence from green fields of an entirely new community, Golders Green, within seven years of the tube railway's 1907 arrival from *Charing Cross. Vigilant speculators made large profits. Extension to Edgware in 1923–4 saw the process repeated, albeit at first a little sluggishly. So intense was the development at Golders Green that the extension had difficulty in breaking through it, demolishing quite new houses.

Between 1925 and 1932, following the example set in the 1910s by two of its constituents, the *Southern Railway electrified virtually all its London suburban services, 293 route miles, also constructing two new electric railways: Wimbledon–Sutton (1929–30) and Motspur Park–Chessington South (1938–9). The latter, through an area already partly built over, was intended as the first section of a loop (not completed) to relieve an existing line overloaded by new housing. With electrification, services were substantially improved.

In the 1920s and 1930s infrastructure improvements and extensions were also undertaken by the Metropolitan and the Underground, and by their successor, *London Transport, in 1933–41 and 1946–57. Station *architecture often made a notable contribution to new suburban areas. During the inter-war housing boom, railway improvements generated very large traffic increases. Between 1920 and 1940, some 70 new stations were opened in London's suburbs, many eagerly subsidized by developers anxious to advertise 'station on the estate'.

With distances between home and work-place usually shorter, the association between railways and provincial suburban development was generally less marked; for many years trams and buses carried much of what traffic existed. Although no consistent pattern appeared (a few flows were from city centre homes to suburban work-places) most conurbations developed middle-class railway suburbs, as around *Birmingham, where the London pattern was repeated on a small scale along the GWR line to Solihull and beyond. An exclusively suburban branch, to Harborne (1874), was hampered by its circuitous route; the arrival of motor bus competition brought closure to passenger traffic in 1934. The Birmingham West Suburban Railway (1876) fulfilled a very different purpose when it became part of the Midland's Birmingham–Bristol main line in 1885, after which suburban traffic was secondary. Then in 1993 its suburban characteristics were revitalized when it became part of the electrified 'Cross-City Line' from Lichfield to Redditch.

The Nottingham Suburban Railway (1889), also suffering from an indirect route, was a victim of tramway competition before 1914; subsequently passenger services dwindled to a token level, ceasing in 1931. In contrast, the 'Robin Hood Line', linking Nottingham, Mansfield, and Worksop over an old railway *reopened in stages from 1993, has proved a success. The *Manchester South Junction & Altrincham Railway (1849) and the Manchester South District Railway (1880) were both built to serve anticipated suburban expansion, the former so successfully that it was electrified in 1930. The latter quickly became part of a main line, local traffic succumbing to train and bus competition. *Glasgow's considerable network of suburban railways, electrified from 1960, continues to be expanded and improved. *Liverpool's lines, reaching the Wirral, Southport, and Ormskirk, were electrified in 1903, 1913, and 1938, and in 1978 were linked under the central area and extended to Garston. More recently, Tyneside, Greater *Manchester, and *Sheffield have turned to *light rapid transit, often using former railway alignments, while in the conurbations served by *Passenger Transport Authorities a policy of opening new suburban stations has been pursued.

See also COMMUTING; METRO-LAND. AAJ

J. R. Kellett, *The Impact of Railways on Victorian Cities* (1969); *RTC*, 59–75, 81–5, 91–4, 112–23, 162–4; A. A. Jackson, *Semi-Detached London: Suburban Development, Life and Transport, 1900–39* (1991); *LLR*; A. A. Jackson, *London's Metropolitan Railway* (1986).

Sunday services. These are of two kinds: the regular services provided (or not provided) on Sunday in the railways' *timetables; and the temporary services required by necessary engineering works on that day, when the regular timetables are suspended.

On the opening of the *Liverpool & Manchester Railway in 1830 no train left either terminus between 10 a.m. and 4 p.m. on Sundays, in order to facilitate religious observance. Many other companies adopted a similar practice; it came to be called the 'church interval'. In *Scotland the religious opposition to running Sunday trains was exceedingly strong. In 1847, while all but four companies in England and Wales ran some Sunday trains, in Scotland every railway but two was closed. Sabbatarian thinking was widely accepted throughout Great Britain long before 1830 and it asserted itself here stoutly (see also EXCURSION TRAINS).

But it was not a matter of religion alone. The *Post Office had power to require mail trains on Sundays, and exercised it. The employment of railwaymen seven days a week might threaten railway *safety.

When the railways had been at work long enough to analyse their profitability it became obvious that some lines carried a very light Sunday traffic, and in the 1860s many companies determined to reduce expenditure by closing them on that day. So whereas in 1861 only 5.7 per cent of the system in England and Wales had no Sunday passenger services, by 1871 it was 18.9 per cent, rising thereafter to 22.3 per cent in 1914. In Scotland however, it then reached nearly 60 per cent.

Economic considerations accounted for almost all these closures. Sabbatarianism had little to do with them; its power was then declining, though it revived momentarily around 1900. The railways were out to reduce losses, and here they wielded the axe. This policy affected *freight traf-

fic very little, for the amount carried on Sundays was always small.

Nothing similar occurred in Europe where, with insignificant exceptions, the Sunday timetable was the same as on weekdays. It appears that in 1914 only one line there (16 miles long, in Switzerland) closed on Sundays.

The British Sunday service was apt to differ in another important respect. To minimize disruption, the railways tried to restrict heavy engineering work to Sundays. Advance warning was given at stations, and usually accepted by the public as a troublesome necessity. Nowadays, however, arrears of maintenance caused by under-funding bring more frequent closures, some involving lengthy diversions, e.g. of *East Coast trains via Lincoln, or substitute bus services, while some work that used to be executed at night or weekends is done on weekdays to avoid overtime payments, with consequent delays. Sunday passengers are officially exhorted to enquire by telephone before travelling; the wise ones do not travel on Sunday unless they must.   JS

VR, 252–9.

superelevation. When a train travels round a curve it creates sideways thrust, or centrifugal force. If speed is constant but radius reduces, this force will increase; if radius is fixed then force increases with speed. On a flat curve the train may mount and increase wear on the outer rail, or even overturn if the force is sufficiently great. To counteract this action, the outer rail is elevated over the inner by a difference in level known as superelevation, or cant. This was negligible on the earliest railways where speeds were relatively low and curves of 1–3 miles radius were adopted.

A theoretically correct equation for cant was published by C. B. *Vignoles in 1835; railways were increasingly designed with cant over the next 25 years as economies of construction sometimes necessitated radii of 10 to 20 chains.

In moving from a straight to a curved track, the full effect of centrifugal force is applied at the tangent point, to reduce which a 'transition curve' is introduced at both ends of the curve, the radius of which increases gradually from infinity to that of the curve. Cant is gradually increased, or reduced, along the transitions respectively at entry and exit. In practice, cant is less than theory dictates because tension along a train tends to counteract centrifugal force.

Transitions were not widely adopted by 1845. Accordingly, cant was applied gradually on the straights leading to, and from, circular curves, attaining design values at the tangent points. William Gravatt recognized the need to combine cant with transition design and formulated his cumbersome 'harmonic curve transition', probably by 1828. William Froude, his one-time assistant, devised the simpler 'curve of adjustment', or cubic parabola, in 1837, first used on railways in south-west England.

See also TRACK. RBS

W. J. M. Rankine, *Manual of Civil Engineering* (1900), 648–56.

superheating, see TRACTION, STEAM.

surfaceman, see PLATELAYERS.

Superelevation

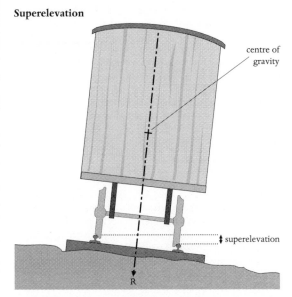

centre of gravity

‡ superelevation

R

Superelevation is calculated so that R, the resultant of all forces acting on the vehicle, is at right angles to the track. This prevents overturning.

Surrey Iron Railway. This, the world's first public railway, was sanctioned by Parliament in 1801 to run from the Thames at Wandsworth to Croydon, a distance of 8¼ miles. It followed closely the River Wandle along whose banks many mills and factories had been built and whose proprietors supported the enterprise.

The line, planned by William *Jessop, was double track and the rails were cast-iron tram plates of L-section in 3-ft lengths with a tread of 3½ in, secured to stone blocks at 4 ft 2 in *gauge. It was practically level and a horse could pull five or six loaded wagons, each of 3½ tons, at about 2½ mph. The users of the railway supplied their own trucks and horses; the maximum tolls were listed in the authorizing Act (see EARLY IRON RAILWAYS).

During the summer of 1802 the SIR promoters determined to extend the railway to Portsmouth, and as a first step obtained an Act in 1803 for the Croydon Merstham & Godstone Iron Railway. By 1805 the first 8½ miles had been opened to Merstham and traffic began from the quarries in the neighbourhood; the railway was never taken any further.

The advent of steam railways in Surrey saw the end of both plateways. The London & Brighton Railway (see LONDON BRIGHTON & SOUTH COAST) required part of the CMGR and was obliged to purchase the whole line, and the SIR terminus was sold to the *London & Croydon Railway for its Epsom extension in 1845. The CMGR was finally dissolved by Act in 1839, the SIR in 1846.   RHGT

D. A. Bayliss, *Retracing the First Public Railway* (1985).

surveying methods. Before the 1860s, when the Ordnance Survey commenced issuing six-inch *maps, railway

*route selection relied on reconnaissance surveys, using such instruments as box sextants and hand levels.

Accurate surveys were then made with Gunter chains, theodolites, and dumpy levels for the preparation of *parliamentary plans. Land corridors, known as limits of deviation, were laid down in railway Acts, 100 yds each side of the provisional centre-line in open country, less in urban areas, within which the line would be confined.

Although triangulation survey methods had been practised since the 18th century, the less rigorous technique of traversing was generally preferred. Interconnected lines marked along the corridor (the base-line) were measured, as were their included angles. Lateral stations on distant objects were selected and their angles recorded from base-line stations; secondary lines were also marked to facilitate surveys of buildings and other features. The accuracy of the linear and angular measurements was then checked by trigonometrical calculation, after which a framework of triangles was drawn on paper with beam compasses, and the detail plotted.

Levels were taken along and across the provisional centre-line at intervals and plotted, with possible rail levels indicated between vertical limits.

On approval of the plans, the centre-line was staked, with formation levels noted on each peg. The extremities of the *earthworks were marked and the slopes set by clinometer. Long straights were aligned and curves ranged, generally by theodolite.

Electro-magnetic distance-measuring equipment would be preferred nowadays for such surveys.

See also CIVIL ENGINEERING; SURVEYORS; TUNNELS AND TUNNELLING.   RBS

P. Bruff, *Practical Land Surveying for Railways etc.* (1838); J. Quested, *Railway Surveying and Levelling* (1846); J. Whitelaw, *Surveying* (1924).

surveyors, *civil engineers, and *architects in the early days of railways often combined all three disciplines. Although by 1834 each had its own professional body, considerable overlapping continued for many years, quite unlike the distinctions of today.

Preliminary surveys for the main trunk lines were frequently made by well-known engineers. Some had started their careers as land surveyors: Sir James *Brunlees, Thomas *Grainger, and Benjamin *Piercy, for instance; while that visionary but unfortunate surveyor William *James carried out the first surveys for the *Liverpool & Manchester Railway. Country surveyors and land agents were often responsible for the preliminary surveys of other lines, their routes frequently being adopted later by established engineers.

When a line had to be set out in detail, and *parliamentary plans prepared, the engineer employed surveyors for the task; often local men whose knowledge was valuable. Several developed substantial businesses in railway surveying, like the Fairbanks of Sheffield who worked for engineers in many different parts of the country. During the *Mania period of the mid-1840s the demand for surveyors was so intense that unqualified men with no experience were engaged as 'pseudo surveyors ... utterly incompetent and yet paid immense salaries ... hardly able to tell the right end of a theodolite'. For those who were competent it was hard, though lucrative, work in all weathers, to meet the parliamentary deadline (see PROMOTION OF RAILWAYS: PROCEDURE).

So far as railways were concerned, land surveying eventually became the province of the civil engineer, aided by the slow northward advance of the Ordnance Survey, founded in 1791 but not completed until 1853. It materially reduced the amount of preliminary work required. Surveyors increasingly concentrated on valuations and general land and property management, coming to play an important role in the legal and financial affairs of a railway.

Valuations, negotiations, purchases, sales, and rating work (see TAXATION, LOCAL) were usually carried out on a fee or contract basis by outside professionals such as Edward Driver, who was extensively employed by the *London Brighton & South Coast Railway. Many firms of surveyors and land agents which are well known today began with railway work, and most of the leading figures who established the Surveyors' Institution (now the *Royal Institution of Chartered Surveyors) were heavily engaged in it.

The day-to-day work of letting property, collecting rents, and general property supervision, on the other hand, was usually done by a salaried officer of the company, but as time went on the two arms of property management slowly began to merge. As an example, Frederick Wood, a former canal engineer, undertook the valuation, buying, and selling of land for the *London & North Western Railway, and was appointed land agent, on a retainer basis, in 1855. But the general administration of the company's estate south of *Preston was the responsibility of a salaried surveyor; northward it remained with the divisional engineer until 1880, when a combined land and estate agent was appointed for the whole of the railway. The *South Eastern's surveyor, Edward Ryde, was an authority on valuation and a leader of the surveying profession. He was in private practice, and even after he became a salaried officer he carried on with extensive private work.

The railway companies' practices varied widely. The *Great Western's estate management, for instance, was very fragmented until 1919, coming partly under the legal, finance, stores, civil engineer's, and locomotive departments. Conversely, the *North Eastern and *Midland Railways had more centralized estate departments. Rating remained separate on many railways, continuing so after the 1923 *Grouping. It was 1946 before the *London & North Eastern's rating functions were transferred from the finance department to the estate surveyor.

After *nationalization the Railway Executive of the *British Transport Commission appointed a chief estate and rating surveyor, but he was only responsible for co-ordinating policy. In 1953 a property committee was formed, but the regional estate surveyors' primary responsibility continued to be to their regional managements. In 1970 the first real change occurred with the formation of the *British Rail Property Board, which took the estate department into a new corporate structure responsible for all BR's property (see LAND AND PROPERTY). Under it, the work of land and building surveyors, rating, the upkeep of land plans, parliamentary work, commercial development, and all the other diverse functions of a large corporate estate department finally came together.

See also CIVIL ENGINEERING; SURVEYING METHODS.   GJB

F. C. Hockridge, 'The Work of the Surveyor's & Estate Department', *GWR (London) Lecture & Debating Society*, 282 (8 March 1934); F. M. L. Thompson, *Chartered Surveyors: The Growth of a Profession* (1968); RS; Ryde: diaries, Surrey RO (Guildford Muniment Room); unqualified surveyors in the Mania: *The Builder*, iii (5 May 1845).

suspension systems. Vehicle suspension is provided to absorb shocks due to track irregularities and tyre wear, to ensure safety against derailment, and to provide a stable ride for the vehicle. Yet, above a critical speed, the track itself is less influential in creating the standard of ride than the forces acting between wheel and rail, and the restraints imposed by the vehicle's suspension.

Early suspension systems for rail vehicles followed contemporary road practice. Laminated, cart-type springs were used over the axle-boxes of two- or three-axle vehicles, and indeed these remained the principal form of *wagon suspension for 150 years. The springs constituted what is termed primary suspension, that is between the axle-box and vehicle frame. The aim was to achieve resilience between the vehicle body, wheels and axle-boxes, and the rails. Limited damping of the suspension was achieved by the friction between the leaves of the laminated springs.

With the use of bogie vehicles from the 1870s, suspension became more sophisticated, and increasingly incorporated a secondary suspension, that is between the vehicle body and the bogie. Until the 1960s, most coaching stock bogies featured a suspension system with laminated springs above the axle-boxes, and auxiliary springs fitted at the ends of the spring hangers. The auxiliary springs were either of helical, volute, or coil types, or of rubber. The bogie bolster springs were of the elliptical, laminated type, or were coil springs. Later designs of bogie featured coil springs above the axle-boxes with laminated or coil bolster springs, or had side beams which rested on the axle-boxes, carrying coil springs with laminated or coil bolster springs.

For maximum comfort in passenger vehicles, the ideal is to obtain as soft a suspension as possible, but it must be restrained so as to avoid deflection which might cause the vehicle to become out-of-*gauge, or to lock *buffers with an adjacent vehicle, and oscillations that would be uncomfortable for the passenger. Accordingly, suspension systems incorporate some form of damping, using friction dampers or, more recently, hydraulic shock absorbers.

From the 1960s, passenger vehicle suspensions have become more complex to accommodate the lightweight vehicle bodies increasingly used in pursuit of higher train speeds, and to eliminate friction from components; also as a consequence of a better understanding of the interaction between wheel and rail which was derived from research associated with the *Advanced Passenger Train. It was recognized that wheel tyre profiles had to be regarded as part of the overall suspension, and suspension components are nowadays designed to accommodate worn rather than new profiles.

Particularly for suburban and *light rapid transit stock, rubber springs became a popular choice for primary suspension, often with a chevron rubber unit positioned over the axle-box bearing. But the 1970s saw the increasing adoption of air springs for secondary suspension, in view of their superior performance over the range of loading conditions, and without altering a vehicle's height. A convoluted design of air spring was used in conjunction with a bolster for the Mark 3 stock of IC 125 units and locomotive-hauled trains, and a diaphragm design for suburban stock. Air springs have replaced mechanical dampers.

In place of the multi-plate leaf spring of traditional wagon suspensions, in the 1970s *BR produced the 'Taperleaf' design comprising a simplified steel spring, with swing links and rubber shear springing. Freight bogie design concentrated on providing one-piece bogie frames flexible enough to run on poor track in *sidings, and with load-proportional suspension damping. The cross-braced bogie has since been developed by BR, in which the wheelsets are connected diagonally, and while they have limited lateral movement in relation to each other, they can move freely to 'steer' round curves. Among other benefits, the combination of cross-bracing and reduced secondary suspension constraints has contributed to a smoother ride.

The traditional British steam locomotive (see TRACTION, STEAM) had plate frames to which were bolted steel castings or forgings known as horn plates in which the axle-boxes for the driving or coupled axles moved up and down, usually some 2 in; a laminated leaf spring either rested directly on each axle-box, or on struts above it, or was placed under the axle-box and secured to it by links.

The ends of these leaf springs might be coupled to each other by balance beams or compensating levers, to ease stresses and so improve riding. The bogie and pony truck (a radiating two-wheeled truck based on the designs used for horse-drawn vehicles) of steam locomotives featured a number of suspension types, dependent on the bogie centre pin and traversing gear, and usually comprised leaf or coil springs to steady riding and control side play, and swing links uniting the bogie with the locomotive front end.

MLH

L. Lynes, Railway Carriages and Wagons: Theories and Practices (1959); Railway Industry Association, Sixth Motive Power Course 1977: Digest of Lectures and Support Papers; K. Taylor, Chairman's Address to I Mech E Railway Division, 1979–80 session, 193, 39; J. Johnson and R. A. Long, British Railways Engineering 1948–80 (1981).

Sutherland, George Sutherland-Leveson-Gower, 3rd Duke of (1828–92), landowner.

He succeeded to the dukedom in 1861 but took little part in politics, devoting himself almost wholly to his vast estates, which in 1883 were second in size only to those of the crown. The most valuable were in Staffordshire and Shropshire; by far the most extensive lay north of *Inverness, an area without any railways until 1862, when the Duke became the chief driving force behind the expansion of the line to Wick and Thurso, completed in 1874 (see HIGHLAND RAILWAY).

More was involved here than investment for the benefit of his estates. He had a strong personal interest in railways and a thorough knowledge of them, recognized respectfully even by officers of the *London & North Western Railway (of which he was a director) in the 1850s. He had his own locomotive, kept at his private *station at Dunrobin, which he drove himself over local companies' lines.

When, in 1889, he opposed the West Highland Railway (see NORTH BRITISH RAILWAY), on the grounds that Fort William was served adequately by steamers, his proof of evidence to the parliamentary committee put his total investment in railways at £355,000.

JS

DNB; Complete Peerage; J. Bateman, Great Landowners of Great Britain and Ireland (1971 edn.); G. P. Neele, Railway Reminiscences (1974 edn.), 67; proof of evidence: Staffordshire RO, D543 P/33/12.

Swansea: an old town at the narrow mouth of the River Tawe, which acquired new importance in the 18th century through smelting copper brought by sea from Cornwall, the ships returning with Swansea Vale coal. The harbour was improved in the 1790s, and a canal was built to it from Ystradgynlais.

The first railway opened into the town was the *Swansea & Mumbles in 1806, a horse-worked line along Swansea Bay, serving quarries and small coal mines. The first steam railway to reach Swansea was the *South Wales in 1850–2, forming part of a route from London via Gloucester and *Cardiff. It was continued westwards in 1852–6 to a port on Milford Haven, whence steamers ran to southern Ireland. Swansea now stood on a one-mile branch from Landore.

Meanwhile the Swansea Vale Railway was under slow construction, reaching Pontardawe in 1860 and absorbed in 1876 by the *Midland Railway, which gained access to it via Hereford and Brecon. Falling profits prompted the Swansea Canal to lease itself in 1872 to the *Great Western Railway, which had by then taken over the South Wales company. The *London & North Western Railway arrived in 1867, with Swansea as the terminus of its Central Wales line from Craven Arms in Shropshire.

The mineral business of the district was now growing more complex. The Vale contained the largest deposit of anthracite in Europe, a fuel that had begun to be used successfully for smelting in 1837. By 1906 more than half the total production was going overseas (the French valued it particularly for domestic stoves), and 90 per cent of that export passed through Swansea. The Vale's tinplate industry had almost a world monopoly until the USA entered the business in 1890, and its products were shipped through Swansea, Llanelly, and Neath.

Swansea's population rose uninterruptedly from 10,000 in 1801 to 165,000 in 1931; the fastest increase, by 68 per cent, was in 1851–71, during the opening of steam railways. In 1991 it was 189,000.

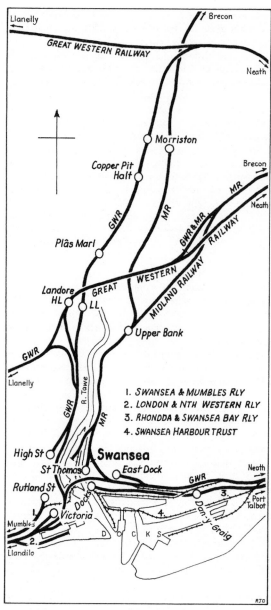

Swansea, 1922

Company	Name of station	Date opened	Date closed
GWR	High Street	1850	Still open
LNWR	Victoria	1867	1964
MR	St Thomas	1860	1950
RSBR	Riverside	1895	1933
SMR	Rutland Street	1860	1960
Vale of Neath Ry	East Dock	1863	1936

GWR	Great Western Ry	RSBR	Rhondda & Swansea Bay Ry
LNWR	London & North Western Ry	SMR	Swansea & Mumbles Ry
MR	Midland Ry		

Merthyr Tydfil, was extended to Swansea by a subsidiary in 1863. Much later, the *Rhondda & Swansea Bay Railway was promoted by Swansea interests, headed by the wealthy and masterful H. H. Vivian, and opened in 1895, passing under GWR control in 1906.

The highly inconvenient multiplicity of stations exemplified the wasteful consequences of *competition, although at Swansea it had two special causes. For the competing companies, access to the docks was paramount, and their routes were determined accordingly. For passenger traffic it would undoubtedly have been better to provide a single large station, like an American Union Terminal, but Swansea's topography made that almost impossible. The GWR's High Street station, much the biggest, scarcely found room for itself on a ledge cut into the cliff on the west bank of the Tawe, and was always inadequate. The town could never have had a station like *Newcastle Central or *Hull Paragon. Closure of local lines has now left it as Swansea's only station.   JS

H. Pollins, 'The Swansea Canal', *JTH*, 1 (1953–4), 135–54; *Reg. Hist.*, xii, esp. chs 8 and 9; for anthracite: H. S. Jevons, *The British Coal Trade* (1915), ch. 23.

Swansea & Mumbles Railway. This originated as the Oystermouth Railway, authorized in 1804 to build a 5-mile line along Swansea Bay. Opened for freight traffic (horse-drawn) in 1806, in 1807 it contracted out the right to run 'a waggon or waggons . . . for the conveyance of passengers', which was exercised for over 20 years: the earliest known record of the regular carriage of passengers by railway in the world.

The line was not profitable, and by 1855 it had become derelict. However, it was then repaired, carrying freight again, and the passenger service was resumed in 1860. In 1874 a Swansea Improvements & Tramways Company purchased the right to work the railway, introducing steam locomotives in 1877. Some trains were hauled by horses, others by locomotives. Horse-traction was discontinued in 1896. The line was extended by 1¼ miles to Mumbles in 1900. Strange processions of enormous double-decked tramcars with open tops passed along slowly by the sea, teeming with passengers at holiday times, hauled by diminutive *tank engines.

In 1925 *electrification was authorized, and an entirely new service was introduced in 1929, using double-deck enclosed tramcars, each seating 106 passengers. A large in-

Because of its preoccupation with Irish traffic and its broad *gauge, the South Wales Railway brought no great benefit to Swansea. Other short lines were soon opened, however, more immediately useful. Swansea eventually had six passenger termini, each built by a separate company and all in use simultaneously: more than any other British town outside London (see table). Two of these smaller lines brought coal for shipment from the huge field further east. The Vale of Neath Railway, running from Aberdare and

crease in passenger traffic resulted, especially during World War II, when petrol rationing limited bus services and private motoring. In 1925 some 700,000 passengers were conveyed; in 1945, 5 million. After that, however, their numbers dropped, and the railway closed in 1960. JS

C. E. Lee, *The Swansea & Mumbles Railway* (1970 edn.).

Swindon. With the coming of the *Great Western Railway, the fortunes of the small Wiltshire town of Swindon were irrevocably changed. Few residents could have been prepared for the enormous changes that were to occur in the next century; the extensive workshops established by the GWR were to dominate the economic, social, and political life of the town until after 1945, and the green fields near the town on the hill were transformed into a new community which grew up around the works, known as New Swindon.

The decision to site the company's *works at Swindon was made in 1841 when the board of directors authorized construction on the recommendation of I. K. *Brunel and Daniel *Gooch. The site chosen was at the junction of the London–*Bristol main line and the branch to Gloucester and Cheltenham. Eighty miles from Paddington, Swindon was also a suitable place for changing locomotives, in readiness for the steeply graded section of line westwards.

The works opened fully in 1843, but were originally intended only as a repair facility. By 1846 new construction had begun, with the works turning out its first Gooch locomotive, the *Great Western*. By 1855 the company was building standard- as well as broad-*gauge engines, since the GWR had begun to acquire some standard-gauge lines, particularly in the west Midlands.

Further expansion of the works occurred in 1868 when the GWR established its carriage works. After 1869 the GWR began the long task of converting both locomotives and rolling stock from broad to standard gauge, although it was not until 1892 that the process was complete. Gooch's successor, William Armstrong, began this process, but it was William *Dean, locomotive superintendent from 1877 to 1902, who guided the works through this difficult period as well as producing numerous new locomotives, including the Dean Goods and 'Achilles' designs.

From 1902 onwards a new locomotive superintendent, George Jackson *Churchward, transformed the old broad-gauge works into a modern factory. Both new buildings and equipment were provided to build locomotives such as the 'Saint' and 'Star' classes. One innovation was the *locomotive test plant, which allowed locomotives to be run at speed for experimental or running-in purposes. Little used between the wars, it was used extensively in the 1950s to test new *BR standard designs.

The high standards set before 1914 were continued after the war, the works by this time covering an area of over 323 acres, and employing over 12,000 people. Churchward's successor, C. B. *Collett, refined his predecessor's work to produce the 'Castle' and 'King' classes which were to become the mainstay of GWR express services until well after World War II.

Collett retired in 1941, leaving his successor, F. W. Hawksworth, little opportunity to make drastic changes during the difficult war years. As in World War I, Swindon played a key role in the production of armaments and other war materials. The years following 1945 saw a gradual decline; under British Railways, steam locomotives continued to be built, and although it produced a number of new diesel designs, the naming of the last steam locomotive to be built for British Railways in 1960, 2-10-0 *Evening Star*, was the end of an era.

The closure of the carriage works and concentration of activity in the area west of the Gloucester line was part of this decline which, despite a resurgence in the 1970s, saw the closure of the works in 1986. Sold for redevelopment, the old workshops will eventually house shops, industrial units, and leisure facilities.

With the establishment of the workshops, the GWR constructed an estate of houses later known as the Railway Village, to provide accommodation for the work-force, many of whom had been brought from other parts of England (see HOUSING). Old Swindon was too small to cope with this influx and a whole range of facilities evolved to cater for the needs of the growing community. These included the Mechanics' Institute, set up in 1843, which came to be the social, cultural, and educational centre; the GWR Medical Fund—a cradle-to-grave medical service paid for by contributions from the work-force; a church, a school, and a public park. The Railway Village is now a conservation area, having been purchased by the local authority from British Rail in 1966.

From the Railway Village, development spread out in all directions and it was inevitable that the community on the hill should eventually be absorbed by its newer neighbour. This was formally recognized by the creation of the Borough of Swindon in 1900. The town has now undergone a second transformation, much enlarged and a centre for light engineering, electronics, and financial services industries.

Swindon station opened in 1842, some months before the workshops; its construction led the GWR to enter into what became an unsatisfactory arrangement with the contractors, Rigby's, who agreed to build the station in return for a lease of the *refreshment rooms. The agreement required that all trains should stop at Swindon for 10 minutes. Not only did the GWR have to bear the brunt of the many complaints which ensued regarding the standard of fare served; they also found the 10-minute stop increasingly inconvenient as train speeds increased and services improved, despite legal attempts to have it removed. In 1895 the GWR eventually managed to buy out the lease, but only at the enormous cost of £100,000, which remained a charge against revenue until 1920.

Trains from the Highworth branch ran into the station. The *Midland & South Western Junction Railway had its own station, Swindon Town, closed in 1961. The main line station was severely rationalized in the 1960s, and only one island platform now survives. TB

A. S. Peck, *The Great Western at Swindon Works* (1994); R. Tompkins, R. Sheldon, and P. Sheldon, *Swindon and the GWR* (1990); A. Williams, *Life in a Railway Factory* (1915); J. Cattell and K. Falconer, *Swindon, the Legacy of a Railway Town* (1995).

Sykes, William Robert, see SIGNALLING; SIGNALLING EQUIPMENT MANUFACTURE.

system, development of the. The railways of Britain were not planned to form a coherent set of main lines, with branches springing from them. Ideas of that sort were put forward by William *James; then, more convincingly, by Thomas *Gray, who published sensible proposals in 1820 for steam-worked lines of railway stretching out across England. But they were not adopted. Instead, in 1825–30 there emerged a series of short lines far apart from one another. They had all been authorized by the government (see PARLIAMENT AND LEGISLATION), but they were promoted, financed, and managed independently of it. Having observed this policy in action, the countries on the European mainland adopted others of an entirely different kind. The Belgian government planned a railway system in 1834 based on four lines, from Antwerp, Ostend, Brussels, and Liège, meeting at Malines. In 1842 the French chose a system of five separate companies established by the state, each of them starting from Paris and occupying a whole sector of the country that was assigned to it as a *monopoly, with a view to preventing *competition.

The *Oxford English Dictionary* defined the word 'system' in 1919 as 'a whole composed of parts in orderly arrangement according to some scheme or plan'. By those standards, Britain has never had a railway system at all. There was nothing orderly about it; no general 'scheme or plan' entered into it. What the country got was a network of lines, knitted together haphazardly, and that is what it retains today.

Yet, in another and looser sense, it is reasonable to talk about a British railway system: as the aggregate of the lines serving the country, from the long fingers reaching out through sparsely populated districts into western Wales and the far north of Scotland to the dense labyrinth of railways in, beneath, and round London. We need a name for all these lines collectively. 'Network' is too tidy, for the net has always been full of holes and tangles. So it seems best in the end to speak here of a 'system', though with the strong qualifications just made.

A student of British railways must want an outline guide to the growth of this collection of lines. Table 1 summarizes the totals of route *mileage over a period of about 150 years: first in a figure for the year 1844, calculated with care by scholarly methods; then from 1850 onwards at ten-yearly intervals, based primarily on the official *returns made to the government. Let us now look at the changes in the system that occurred during four stages of its history: 1825–69; 1870–1922; 1923–47; 1948–94.

The system is treated in this article almost wholly in terms of growth, though in the 20th century it has also to refer to reduction, through the closure of lines that had proved unprofitable. That process is dealt with more ex-

tensively in another article (CLOSURE OF RAILWAYS), which should be read in conjunction with this one.

1825–1869

The railways opened before 1825 made no direct contribution to the development of a national system. Those of 1825–30 were instruments devised to serve local needs—the West Durham and the Monklands coalfields, for example. But the 'local' business of *Liverpool and *Manchester was so large that the railway linking them was recognized from the outset as an enterprise of national importance. It was itself, however, only 30 miles long.

Ideas of building trunk railways over much greater distances began to be realized in 1833–5, when Parliament sanctioned the formation of the *London & Birmingham, *Grand Junction, London & Southampton (later *London & South Western), and *Great Western companies. In 1836 a total of 28 new companies was authorized to build railways in Britain. Thirteen of these, taken in conjunction with the four previously established trunk lines, offered something that made up a coherent plan of railway communication across England south of *York. These 17 companies undertook between them to supply rather more than 1,100 miles of railway. All but 62 of those miles were opened for traffic in 1837–45.

The lines authorized in 1836 included a series of four that, taken together, made up a continuous chain of communication stretching over 175 miles from Gloucester to York. At *Birmingham this chain met the London & Birmingham and Grand Junction lines, then already under construction. Putting all these lines together, they formed a great St Andrew's cross, its arms reaching out from Bir-

Table 1. **Route miles of line open in Great Britain 1844–1993**

Year ending 31 December	Route miles	% increase or decrease
1844	2,236	
1850	6,084	+172.0
1860	9,069	+ 49.0
1870	13,562*	+ 49.5
1880	15,563	+ 14.8
1890	17,281	+ 11.0
1900	18,506	+ 7.1
1910	19,772	+ 6.8
1920	20,147	+ 1.9
1930	20,243	+ 0.5
1940	19,931	− 1.5
1950	19,471	− 2.3
1960	18,369	− 5.7
1970	11,799	− 35.8
1980†	10,964	− 7.1
1990†	10,305	− 6.0
1993†	10,270	− 0.3

* This figure is of miles constructed, not of miles open.   † Years ending 31 March.

Sources

1844, calculation by H. G. Lewin in his *Early British Railways* (1925), 186; 1850–90, Mitchell and Deane, 225–6; 1900–70, D. L. Munby and A. H. Watson, *Inland Transport Statistics: Great Britain 1900–70* (1978), 117, 209–10; 1980–93, *Annual Reports* of British Railways.

mingham. No one planned this intersection as such, after the fashion of the Belgian government; and the centre of the British railway system soon turned out to be not Birmingham but *London. Though there were some connections between the people who had launched these four companies—promoters who supported more than one of them, for instance, and investors from Lancashire, especially from Liverpool—none of them resulted from any deliberate planning as part of a larger enterprise. Each was carried through as a separate unit.

A few efforts were made on the part of the government to lay down some sort of plan for the growth of trunk railways. In 1839 it appointed commissioners to investigate possible routes for lines linking London with *Ireland and *Scotland. They reported in favour of one from Chester to Holyhead (for steamships to Dublin), and of another running from *Carlisle up Annandale, forking into two branches to *Edinburgh and *Glasgow. These formed the basis of plans that were gradually realized. In 1846, again by means of a special inquiry, the government made a serious though ineffective attempt to solve the problems presented by the threatened admission of railways into the heart of London. But each of these investigations was directed to one route, or one group of routes. None of them was charged with the planning of a national system.

Some of the drawbacks of the piecemeal building and management of the companies appeared very soon. Travellers from Manchester to *Hull, for instance, making a journey less than 100 miles long, had to use the lines of four companies, which might or might not co-operate. The three railways of 1836 converging on *Derby came to be on most uncomfortable terms until they were persuaded to amalgamate to form one *Midland Railway in 1844.

A new expedient was devised at this time, adapted to the special needs of the British railways. In 1842 nine companies came together to establish a 'Railway Clearing House for 'facilitating the process of booking through connected lines of railway'. This grew into a central organization to regulate the debits and credits that necessarily arose from the flow of traffic between one company and another. Although the British railways had been established in accordance with no 'orderly arrangement', in their Clearing House they created a smooth-working device for enabling traffic to move across the country with the least possible hindrance.

The rate of promotion of new companies was low in 1838–42, largely from the weak state of the economy and the tightness of money. By 1843, however, capital was seeking higher returns, and railway investment seemed promising. Eighteen new companies were set up in 1844, and much more promotion was evidently on the way.

In August 1844 a new board was established for the examination of plans for the building of railways before they came to Parliament. It comprised five members under the chairmanship of Lord *Dalhousie. It was given very onerous duties and no powers. The Board's business was to consider the bearing of each proposal on the railways already opened or authorized and on other new plans relating to the same district. But it could make nothing more than

recommendations; the decision lay with Parliament. The board did as much as any men could have done in these conditions, but it was abolished in July 1845. Its work represented the sole effort ever made by any British government to control the growth of the railway system.

In many of the discussions concerning lines proposed for the Midlands and southern England one question now appeared prominently: were they to be built to the standard *gauge or to the 7-ft broad gauge of the GWR and its associated companies? The confusion that arose when lines of different gauges met had now become notorious, and the device of laying down a third rail, to produce a 'mixed gauge', accommodating both standard- and broad-gauge trains, never proved satisfactory. A British system built to one gauge was plainly desirable. By 1845 seven-eighths of the lines open in England were laid to the standard gauge, one-eighth to the broad. Commissioners appointed to investigate this problem came up with a carefully considered report in 1846, recommending that in future all new railways should be built to the standard gauge. An Act was passed, laying down exactly this requirement, but at the same time making it into nonsense by exempting from it any line governed by 'a special enactment defining the gauge of such railway, or any part thereof'. So new broad-gauge lines went on being built, under special enactment, for another 30 years. The 7-ft gauge did not pass entirely out of use until 1892. As long as it lasted, the broad gauge stood as the negation of the idea of a national railway system in Britain.

By 1852 there were 6,628 miles of railway in Great Britain, extending from London west and north as far as *Plymouth, *Swansea, Holyhead, Glasgow, and *Aberdeen. Ten years later this mileage had increased by over 40 per cent, and a number of new main lines were appearing that had been built largely for competitive purposes. That example had been set in 1852 by the GWR and *Great Northern companies, with their competitive routes, rivalling established ones, from London to Birmingham and to Yorkshire. In 1860–1 new lines, manifestly competitive in purpose, were opened from London to *Exeter and Dover; the Midland completed two very costly lines of the same sort to bring it into Manchester and London in 1867–8; and the *Caledonian equipped itself fully to compete for the traffic between Edinburgh and Glasgow when its Midcalder–Holytown line came into use in 1869. Competition provided a powerful new impulse behind railway building, constantly apparent in the extensions of the system down to 1910, when the last substantial line of this sort was opened.

1870–1922

One more great rush of railway promotion came and went in the 1860s. The building of the lines authorized then went ahead very slowly after the financial crisis of 1866 (see SPECULATION). The most impressive of these, the MR's line from *Settle to Carlisle, undertaken in order to provide a third route between London, *Leeds, and Scotland, took ten years from authorization to completion (1866–76). The other lines comparable in length opened after 1870 lay,

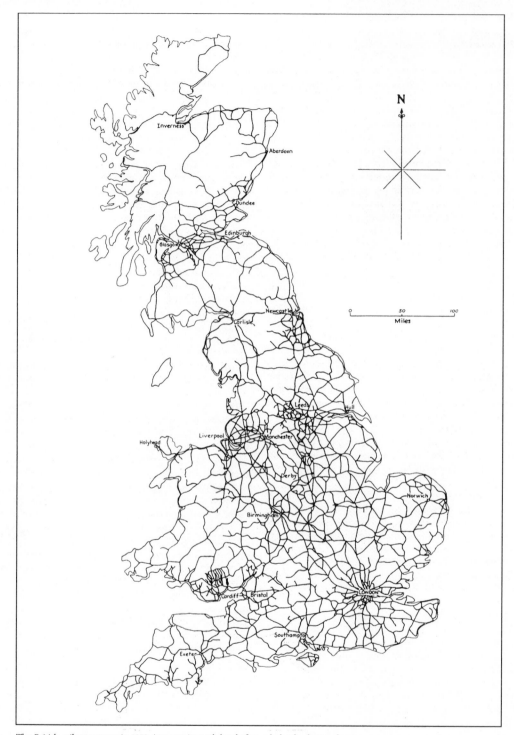

The British railway system in 1952, just past its peak but before wholesale closures began

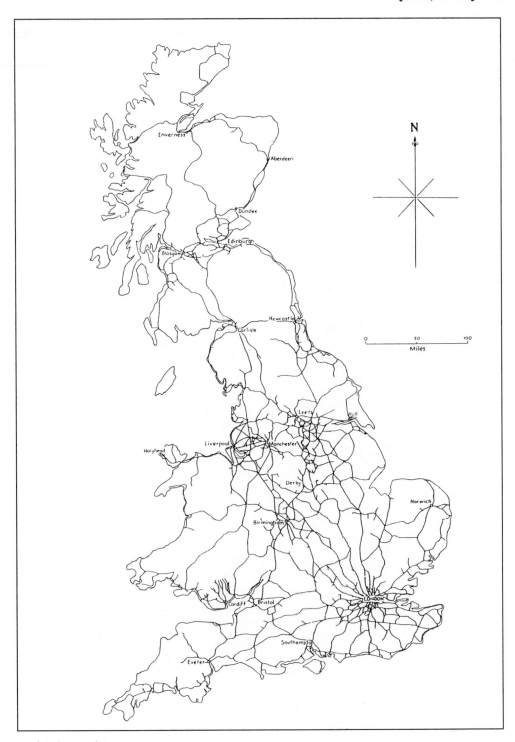

British Rail's network in 1985

with one exception, in the Scottish Highlands, reaching out northwards to Wick and Thurso and westwards to Oban, Mallaig, and Kyle of Lochalsh; over 350 miles in all.

One more long line was built in the 1890s, the last in England. This was the London extension of the Manchester Sheffield & Lincolnshire Railway, running from Annesley in Nottinghamshire to Quainton Road, Bucks.; thence over the *Metropolitan Railway to a new London terminus at *Marylebone. Its purpose was entirely competitive. The Sheffield company was determined to secure part of the constantly increasing traffic from Lancashire and Yorkshire southwards, then in the hands of the *London & North Western, MR, and GNR. It required the construction of 102 miles of new railway and was opened (the company having changed its name to *Great Central) in 1899. The undertaking proved, even on the most lenient view, no more than a very partial success.

Not so imposing as this venture, though more important, was the first group of electrically operated underground railways in London (see LONDON UNDERGROUND RAILWAYS), opened in 1890–1907. They were undertaken by seven separate companies, with capital raised outside Britain as well as inside it, and only one of them (the shortest, the *Waterloo & City) proved to be, in financial terms, profitable. But they rendered great services to London, their deep-level lines being permitted (as hardly any railways had been in the past) to criss-cross its centre.

In 1870–1914 many smaller lines were built, often as branches from the main system. Their number increased after 1896 when *light railways were laid down, generally at a lower cost than had formerly been incurred in building branches. Some of these lines served small towns hitherto left off the system: Callington and Lyme Regis, for example; Aberayron and Holywell; Mildenhall and Easingwold; Lauder and Dornoch. Others were built to assist agriculture, such as the Wrington Vale Railway in Somerset and the Goole & Marshland in south Yorkshire and Lincolnshire.

In this period most of Britain's offshore island railways were built. Although the Alderney Railway had been opened as early as 1847 for building a breakwater, and the first on the *Isle of Wight dated from 1862, others came later. The Isle of Wight lines and one on Jersey were standard gauge; the other Jersey line and those on the *Isle of Man were narrow. Guernsey had only a short electrified tramway, but during World War II a military system was operated there and on Jersey by the German occupation forces.

The railway companies, which had substantial *shipping services of their own, were promoters or partners in the development of many *ports; and they became part of the system too. The *Barry Dock & Railways Company is an outstanding example. Fishguard, Heysham, and Immingham were all offshoots of large railway companies. And though Tilbury Docks (opened in 1886) were financed by the East & West India Docks Company, they were built beside an existing railway, which was linked up to the 50 miles of line laid down within the docks themselves.

One other group of new railway lines comprised those built to improve the system by doing away with detours, through the construction of 'cut-off' lines (see LOOP). The *North Eastern Railway shortened its route between York and *Newcastle (and so the whole *East Coast main line) in this way in 1868–71. The MR opened a new line from Kettering to *Nottingham in 1880, furnishing a second pair of tracks, in addition to those on its existing line via *Leicester, available for all the company's traffic between London and Yorkshire.

The two greatest engineering works on British railways in the late Victorian age both stood on lines of the same sort. The *Severn Tunnel, completed in 1886, shortened all the distances between the South Wales coalfield and southern England. The *Forth Bridge, opened in 1890, was the chief component in the *North British company's new route from Edinburgh to Aberdeen, which was 34 miles shorter than that of its rival the Caledonian. Further north the *Highland company completed its Carr Bridge line in 1898, providing a direct route from Aviemore to *Inverness without the previous detour via Forres; a reduction of 18 per cent in the distance.

The chief improvements of this kind are shown in Table 2 on p. 497. The total mileage of new construction recorded there amounts to less than 9 per cent of all the additions made to the British railway system during these years. Nearly two thirds of the total mileage of these lines formed part of competitive routes.

The GWR's work of this sort in 1900–10 stands out. Although its original main line from London to Bristol was splendidly direct, the westward extensions built in conjunction with it produced some very circuitous routes. The LSWR's line from London to Exeter, completed in 1860, was 13 per cent shorter than the GWR's before the GWR direct route was completed in 1900–6; the LNWR's to Birmingham shorter by 14.4 per cent until 1910. Then, in both cases, the distances became almost identical.

Only one further piece of construction of this kind was undertaken by any of the old companies. The GNR was much handicapped in the operation of its line out of King's Cross by eight tunnels in the course of its first 25 miles. A rapidly growing suburban traffic clogged the working here, and though additions were made to the two southernmost tunnels, taking four and then six tracks, the company shrank from the expenditure required for enlarging the remainder. Instead, in 1898 it secured powers to build a wholly new line further east, running from Enfield to Stevenage and familiarly known as the Hertford Loop; designed to provide, in conjunction with the old line, a four-track route. But the first five-mile section of the Loop was not opened until 1910; eight years later, under war-time pressure, the rest of it was brought into use for freight trains; the whole was not opened fully until 1924. The Loop, 19 miles long, had taken 26 years to complete.

1923–1947

No substantial additions were made to the mileage of lines open for passenger traffic under the four large companies

Table 2. Major improvements to the main line system 1868–1924

Date of completion	Company	Route	Mileage
1868	SER	Lewisham–Chislehurst–Tonbridge	24
1869	NER	Durham–Birtley–Gateshead	14
1869	CR	Holytown Jcn–Midcalder Jcn	20
1869	LNWR	Ditton Jcn–Runcorn–Weaver Jcn	20
1871	NER	York–Selby–Doncaster	32
1871	MR	Chesterfield–Sheffield	12
1876	MR	Settle–Carlisle	78
1880	MR	Kettering–Melton Mowbray–Nottingham	36(a)
1883	LNWR	Roade–Northampton–Rugby	24
1886	GWR	Pilning–Severn Tunnel Jcn	7
1888	LSWR	Brockenhurst–Sway–Christchurch	12
1889	LYR	Pendleton–Hindley–Pemberton	19
1890	NBR	Saughton Jcn–Forth Bridge–Burntisland	17
1896	LBSCR	Coulsdon–Earlswood (Quarry Line)	7
1898	HR	Aviemore–Carr Bridge–Inverness	34
1899	GCR	Annesley Jcn–Aylesbury–London (Marylebone)	95(b)
1900	GWR	Patney–Westbury	14
1903	GWR	Wooton Bassett–Badminton–Pilning	30(c)
1906	GWR	Castle Cary–Somerton–Curry Rivel Jcn.	19
1906	GWR/GCR	S. Ruislip Jcn–High Wycombe–Ashendon Jcn	34(d)
1908	GWR	Birmingham–Stratford-upon-Avon–Cheltenham	39(e)
1910	GWR	Ashendon Jcn–Bicester–Aynho Jcn	18
1924	GNR(LNER)	Enfield–Langley Jcn	19(f)
TOTAL			624

Notes
(a) Excluding 16 miles Manton–Melton Mowbray, already built.
(b) Excluding 42 miles Quainton Road–Canfield Place (London), already built by the Metropolitan Railway.
(c) Excluding 4 miles Patchway–Pilning, already built.
(d) Excluding 8 miles High Wycombe–Princes Risborough, already built by the GWR.
(e) Excluding 13 miles Birmingham–Tyseley, and Stratford-upon-Avon–Honeybourne, already built.
(f) Opened for freight traffic 1918.

Key

CR	Caledonian Ry	LNWR	London & North Western Ry
GCR	Great Central Ry	LSWR	London & South Western Ry
GNR	Great Northern Ry	LYR	Lancashire & Yorkshire Ry
GWR	Great Western Ry	MR	Midland Ry
HR	Highland Ry	NBR	North British Ry
LBSCR	London Brighton & South Coast Ry	NER	North Eastern Ry
		SER	South Eastern Ry
LNER	London & North Eastern Ry		

that came into being in 1923. The *Southern Railway added 41 miles to its system in 1925–39, half of them by the opening of the line from Halwill to Torrington in North Devon. The diminutive Hatherleigh, which stood on it, was the last town in Britain to receive railway communication. Otherwise the only new lines opened in these years were bypassing *loops: the last and shortest of the GWR 'cut-offs', enabling express passenger and freight trains to avoid bottlenecks at Westbury and Frome stations; on the SR in east Thanet and at Lewisham. The London underground railways extended their system by new lines to Edgware, Cockfosters, Morden, and Stanmore in 1924–33.

None of the new companies spent much on the replacement or reconstruction of important *stations that demanded it imperatively. Two of the very worst were tinkered about with—Glasgow Buchanan Street by the *London Midland & Scottish Railway, Doncaster by the *London & North Eastern. Some other discreditable stations—at *Peterborough, Banbury, and Plymouth, for example—remained unaltered. The GWR did perhaps the best it could with its most uncomfortably sited terminus at Swansea. The Southern made some determined efforts at improvement, quite successfully at Surbiton, Margate, and Ramsgate. The only really large-scale expenditure, imaginative and determined, that was undertaken by the four companies for the purpose of improving the system in these years was that of the Southern by means of the *electrification of its London suburban lines. Otherwise the overriding instruction everywhere, to all the staff, was 'make do and mend'.

The system reached its greatest extent, with 20,267 miles of standard-gauge route, in 1926, though its track *mileage continued to grow until 1932. The lines that have been spoken of here added in all less than 70 miles to the system. Against those 70 must be set some 1,650 miles that were closed to passenger traffic in these years (see CLOSURE OF RAILWAYS). The managers of these great companies were confronted now with the full effects of the development of the internal combustion engine; but most of them were still railwaymen, brought up in the tradition that it was their duty to maintain a public service, and some statutory restrictions fettered the companies' freedom to relinquish that duty, even when its continuance had become hopelessly unprofitable. The 1,650 miles were made up of very small lines; the longest single unit among them (Alnwick–Coldstream, closed by the LNER in 1930) comprised less than 36. The closures did not follow a considered investigation of the problem, conducted by any of the companies, with a view to formulating a policy. Each case was examined on its own.

This treatment did not lead to wholly negative results, confined to the closure of unprofitable lines. Ever since 1903 some railway companies had been running road motor-*bus services of their own, to get to places that their system had not touched, or to supplement the facilities their trains provided. They now decided to invest substantially in bus undertakings, and they secured full power to do that in 1928. Bus services run in this way could connect with their trains at stations. Here was a method of reaching places that lay off the system without increasing the mileage of railway lines; and also a means of reducing that mileage by the provision of bus services in place of trains. But it was—yet again—quite unsystematic, making few efforts to secure a bus service integrated with the railways', at the stations where they met. The British railways might have learnt useful lessons in this matter from France; but they did not. From this time onwards the mileage of lines that were open for freight traffic alone steadily increased.

Szlumper

1948–1994

The *nationalized railways added very little to this system. Nearly all the lines they built were short stretches, most of them being designed to improve operation rather than to provide facilities not available before.

To that statement there is, however, one important exception. As airports grew bigger and their number multiplied, they called for links with railways. Where the airport was situated close to a line, interchange of traffic could be provided by stations specially equipped for the purpose. An example of this had already been set by the Southern Railway at Gatwick in 1935. That station was rebuilt and extended in 1958 by *BR, which provided others like it, as at *Southampton, Birmingham, and Dyce, close to Aberdeen. The extension of the *Piccadilly underground line to Heathrow (1977) was the first in Europe to link air services with a great city's urban railway system. Other links of the same kind were provided by short new branches from old-established lines at Stansted and Manchester.

In the earlier years of the nationalized administration, the railways' freight traffic still called for enlargement. Under the *Modernization Plan of 1955 some new, or greatly extended, *marshalling yards were constructed: at Ripple Lane on the Tilbury line, for instance, and at Kingmoor, north of Carlisle—a very big operation, adding 56 track miles to the system and costing £4.5 million. Completed in 1963, it was useful for a time. But the time was short. By 1972 BR's freight-train mileage was less than it had been in 1948; and the Kingmoor yard was phased out almost completely in 1972–82.

The only new line of any considerable length built by BR was the 'Selby diversion', 14 miles long, completed in 1983. This was not an improvement, undertaken by BR as such, however. It was necessitated by coal-working under the East Coast main line near Selby, and the cost was met by the National Coal Board. But it produced a great uncovenanted benefit to the working of high-speed trains by cutting out the awkward passage through Selby, where for many years the speed limit over the swing-bridge crossing the River Ouse was 40 mph.

Everywhere else the history of the system in these years was almost wholly one of reduction. Nearly 10 per cent of it was closed to passenger traffic in 1948–62. That was a substantial amount, but small by comparison with what followed. By 1973 about one third of the system, as it was in 1962, had been closed to passenger traffic (see CLOSURE OF RAILWAYS). During the whole period since nationalization, the route mileage open for passenger and freight traffic had sunk by 1973 from 19,639 to 11,537, or by 41 per cent.

At this point, however, the process of reduction slowed down very markedly. At the end of BR in 1994 that total mileage was around 10,300, by when some modest *re-openings had begun.   JS

Szlumper, Alfred W. (1858–1934), engineer. He entered the civil engineering department of the *London & South Western Railway as a young man, and was for many years occupied with the long-drawn-out reconstruction of *Waterloo station and the widening of the approaches, in later years as London divisional engineer. In 1914, following the untimely death in a riding accident of J. W. Jacomb-Hood, Szlumper succeeded him as chief engineer, a post in which he saw the final touches put to the new Waterloo in 1922.

At the *Grouping he was appointed chief engineer of the *Southern Railway, where he saw through many important new works including the reconstruction of the lines in the Ramsgate and Margate area and the remodelling of *Cannon Street station. His character was once described as 'bluff, chunky and capable'. He retired in 1927 and was appointed consulting engineer. He was the father of G. S. *Szlumper.   MRB

C. F. Dendy Marshall, *History of the Southern Railway* (1963 edn.); J. N. Faulkner and R. A. Williams, *The London & South Western Railway in the Twentieth Century* (1988); M. R. Bonavia, *History of the Southern Railway* (1987).

Szlumper, Gilbert Savill (1884–1969), manager. Son of A. W. *Szlumper, chief engineer, *London & South Western Railway, he was a pupil in his father's department, 1902–5, and then engineering assistant until 1913 when he became assistant to the general manager, (Sir) Herbert *Walker. After serving as secretary to the Railway Executive Committee in World War I, he returned to the LSWR to become docks and marine manager in 1920, where he planned and initiated huge extensions to *Southampton docks. In 1925 he became assistant general manager to Walker on the newly formed *Southern Railway, when he received the CBE, succeeding him in 1937.

Tireless, and a clear thinker, Szlumper's prime task was to complete the Southern's large-scale *electrification programme, with which he had been closely associated under Walker. In 1939–40 he again assumed duties at the War Office as Director-General, Transportation, and after his formal retirement from the SR in 1942 he became Director-General at the Ministry of Supply until 1945.   GJB

Who Was Who; C. F. Klapper, *Sir Herbert Walker's Southern Railway* (1973); J. N. Faulkner and R. A. Williams, *The London & South Western Railway in the Twentieth Century* (1988).

T

Taff Vale Railway, the oldest and largest of the South Wales coal railways.

The Glamorganshire Canal was opened throughout in 1798 to link Merthyr Tydfil and the adjoining ironworks with the sea at *Cardiff. As ironworking and coalmining grew, the canal became inadequate. The TVR was authorized to build a Merthyr–Cardiff railway, 24 miles long, in 1836. I. K. *Brunel was the engineer, adopting the 4 ft 8½ in *gauge rather than the 7 ft he was using on the *Great Western Railway. Construction was not very difficult. The railway was completed in 1841, when two branches were added: one, to Dinas, the first mechanically worked railway in the Rhondda valleys. Meanwhile, in 1839 what became known as the Bute West Dock was opened at Cardiff, to which the TVR had access.

In 1845 a branch was opened from Navigation House (Abercynon) to Aberdare, which the TVR worked, leasing it permanently in 1847. The Aberdare valley had been the chief source of South Wales steam coal, but in 1855 that business began in the Rhondda, which became by 1880 the chief supplier in Europe.

The TVR soon prospered, paying an average dividend of 5 per cent in 1850–9, rising steadily to 14.9 per cent in 1880–8: the highest maintained by any British railway over so long a period (see PROFITABILITY). Revenue was hard-earned, for the TVR was beset by enemies: the *Rhymney Railway the most important of them, from 1858 to 1888. The Taff Vale's strength had at first been largely due to its position at Bute West Dock. But the Bute Trustees soon allied with the RR, and in 1856 the TVR developed a new port at Penarth, lower down the Taff, through a company leased by it in 1862. Despite its success, congestion at Cardiff continued to worsen. Some of the chief coalowners then promoted the *Barry Railway, with its own docks on the open sea: a grave threat to the TVR from 1889.

The TVR fought back on several fronts. It opened a 7-mile line in 1892 to Aberthaw, a small port west of Barry—to which, however, it presented no real threat. It courted passenger traffic, increasing the service by nearly 40 per cent in the 1890s. Later challenges were contained: notably when, in 1916, after long litigation, it prevented the *Cardiff Railway (into which the Bute Docks Company had turned itself) from opening a finished, competitive line near Taff's Well. In 1900–1, in the celebrated 'Taff Vale Case', the TVR established that a *trade union could be sued in a representation action (see STRIKES). That was largely due to the pugnacious tenacity of the general manager, Ammon Beasley. When he retired in 1917 to become a director and deputy-chairman, he was succeeded by E. A. Prosser, who was already managing the Rhymney and Cardiff Railways, and the three were then worked in unison. The TVR became a constituent of the GWR in 1922.　　　JS

D. S. Barrie, *Taff Vale Railway* (2nd edn., 1950); *Reg. Hist.*, xii, chs 6, 7.

Tait, Arthur Fitzwilliam (1819–1905), artist. The son of a Manchester businessman, he became a lithographer. But he could get little work except by drawing churches, which as a convinced atheist he greatly disliked. He published a series of 19 lithographs of the *Manchester & Leeds Railway in 1845, accompanied by a text written by Edwin Butterworth. Their detail is sharp, and Tait showed careful observation of some of the railway's civil engineering works, for example the Gauxholme viaduct, as well as what was most congenial to him, the railway's passage through the open landscape. He then began work on another set devoted to the northern division of the *London & North Western Railway, but it was not finished and remained unpublished. In 1850 he emigrated to the USA, where he became a well-known and successful painter of wild animals. He never returned to England.　　　JS

G. W. Cadbury, *Arthur Fitzwilliam Tait* (1986); copies of the LNWR lithographs are at the NRM.

Talyllyn Railway. Proprietors of the Bryn Eglwys quarries, dissatisfied with the transport of their slate down to the sea, secured powers in 1865 to build a 2 ft 3 in *gauge railway, seven miles long, to the new port of Towyn. They bought two locomotives from Fletcher Jennings, Whitehaven. The line carried passengers from 1866.

The quarries were sold in 1911 to Sir Haydn Jones, MP for Merioneth. The railway's passenger business kept up, attracting some tourists, until it lost out to motor-*buses. O. H. Prosser suggested to L. T. C. *Rolt the formation of a society of volunteers to operate the railway. After Sir Haydn's death in 1950, the Talyllyn Railway Preservation Society was established, and with the generous support of Lady Jones it set about raising funds. With Rolt as general manager for the first season, members of the society (including some ex-railwaymen) got it reopened in 1951, and a summer service has been maintained ever since, in the hands of the two original engines (now 130 years old) and others acquired from elsewhere. It was the first railway preserved in this fashion anywhere (see PRESERVATION OF RAILWAYS).

A small museum has been created at Towyn Wharf station devoted to the *narrow-gauge railway as such, not to the Talyllyn alone. The cost was met partly by the Pilgrim Trust.   JS

L. T. C. Rolt, *Railway Adventure* (1971 edn.).

Tanat Valley Light Railway, see CAMBRIAN RAILWAYS.

tank engine, a steam locomotive fitted with one or more tanks to contain water and also to carry some coal in a bunker, thus dispensing with the need for a separate *tender. The French term for such a machine is *locomotive tender*, which is logical, for a tank engine combines both functions.

The first to run in Great Britain were two built for the *London & Greenwich Railway in 1836. Each had a tank beneath its boiler—what was later called a well tank. When the tank was placed on top of the boiler it was known as a saddle tank. But the most widespread practice was to have two tanks, one on each side of the boiler, making a side-tank engine. A variant, much favoured by the *Great Western, was the pannier tank, where the tanks were placed well above the frames and were much wider. Dispensing with the tender enabled the engine to run forwards or backwards without needing to be turned, and it occupied less than half as much space on the line as a tender engine, although limited water and coal capacities restricted it to relatively short journeys. For the development of the type, see TRACTION, STEAM.

See also WHEEL NOTATION.   JS

R. H. G. Thomas, *London & Greenwich Railway* (1986 edn.), 176–7; pannier tanks: H. Holcroft, *Outline of Great Western Locomotive Practice* (1971 edn.), 82–3.

taxation, local. Until the beginning of reform in 1888, local government comprised a plethora of overlapping authorities for separate functions such as poor law, highways, sewerage, etc., based primarily on the parish, except in those towns and cities which had corporations set up by royal charter or established under the Municipal Corporations Act, 1835. Before county councils were formed in 1888, wider powers in rural areas were exercised by magistrates at quarter sessions, or sheriff courts in Scotland. Revenue was mainly raised by a property tax applied to a net annual value based on a notional rent, called 'rating'. The sums collected were called 'rates'.

The system was extraordinarily difficult to apply to a railway. The companies always considered that they carried an unfair share of the rates burden, while the authorities maintained that railways tried to ride roughshod over them by employing superior skills and unfairly invoking their statutory powers. The method of calculation was heavily weighted against the railways, imposing rateable values quite disproportionate to the land they occupied. For example, in 1849 the *London & North Western Railway contributed over 35 per cent of the total rates income in Huyton parish, Liverpool, in respect of under 1 per cent of the parish land. The railways were particularly aggrieved at effectively being penalized for building lines which benefited localities and thereby increased overall rateable values —one reason why in some areas they were reluctant to pro-

vide stations in new suburbs. Worse, they gained no greater representation in parish affairs in return for their major financial contribution.

Case law in 1841–4 resulted in a uniform method of calculation, but it was extremely cumbersome and did not reduce the burden. The estimated rental of a railway was based on the amount its owners could expect to receive from a lessee. Although this could be applied to buildings, the actual track could not be said to have a rental value, so instead the company's net receipts were used for that part of the assessment. It was the only form of rating that took account of profits, and in consequence railways paid as much as 20 times more per employee than industry and agriculture.

Rates, therefore, received the railways' considerable attention, and appeals were commonplace. For example, in 1850 the *Great Western's chairman attended an Aylesbury parish vestry meeting to appeal against the rating of the station. Demand grew for specialist *surveyors, and a number of firms very successfully branched out into this business. In time the larger companies employed their own rating surveyors, usually distinct from estate departments.

Although the Local Government Act, 1858, limited railways' assessments to a quarter of the net annual value, their share of local rates continued to be disproportionate, and their surveyors became increasingly skilled at contesting assessments. In 1904, for instance, the local valuer contended that the new Woodford Halse–Banbury line warranted higher assessment than the *Great Central Railway's revenue in neighbouring parishes because it made a greater contribution by enabling the company to gain West of England traffic. At arbitration he was out-argued by the company's surveyor, and a reduction was agreed.

A body of rating legislation and accumulating case law tended to make the railways' position worse, culminating in an attempt to codify accepted practice in valuing net receipts in the Railways (Valuation for Rating) Act, 1930. The Bill was strongly opposed by the *Big Four companies, and its enactment set off a round of appeals through the Railway & Canal *Commission and the courts. By this time much rating work had been assimilated into the companies' estate departments, which undertook valuations, and negotiations with local authorities. A separate assessment was necessary in every parish through which a railway passed, requiring the company to keep special plans and records to ensure that it paid no more than it could argue for. Even so, rates continued to be a heavy expense. In 1913, for instance, the GWR paid around £1 million, rising to £2¼ million in 1921.

Eventually, simplification was achieved by the 1948 Local Government Act. It introduced standard overall values for operational property, subject to periodic revision, although non-operational property continued to be valued in the accustomed manner. The 1988 Finance Act replaced domestic rates by the community charge (the infamous 'poll tax'), but continued to recognize the special position of operational railways by valuing them on a percentage of turnover, to which the standard business rate was applied, with an adjustment factor.

Nineteenth-century railways also faced other forms of local taxation, such as tithe payments and periodic dues to *turnpike trusts, obligations which usually derived from the acquisition of land. In 1851 the LNWR paid £93 13s. 6d. as a release from further payments to the Lichfield trust. The cities of *Carlisle and *Newcastle were entitled to levy tolls on goods entering and leaving. The difficulty in collecting them from railways was overcome by an annual commutation, which was agreed fairly cordially in Carlisle—where in 1880 it amounted to £615, or 42 per cent of the total revenue—but not in Newcastle where they created acrimony. In Scotland, the small burgh of Sanquhar in Dumfriesshire had a similar right, which was commuted to £40 a year for the *Glasgow & South Western Railway until the levies were abolished in 1889.

School Boards were introduced in 1870, with powers to levy rates to build new schools in places where church schools were absent or inadequate. As large ratepayers, railways would be liable for major contributions, and with this knowledge church schools began to seek donations for improvements from the companies and other large property owners, correctly judging that they would rather make a grant or a small annual subscription than see a School Board set up. In 1883 the *Cheshire Lines Committee volunteered to pay a rate of £1 4s. 8d. to prevent the establishment of a School Board at Mouldsworth, Cheshire, and in 1891 it donated £15 to Christ Church school, Chester, for the same purpose. In 1906 the GCR preferred to subscribe £20 15s. 11d. towards a new school in Haydock, Lancashire, rather than pay an estimated rate of 2¾d. in the pound for the next 30 years.   GJB

T. F. Hedley, 'The Rating of Railways', *Trans. Inst. of Surveyors*, 11 (9 Dec. 1878); *GWR (London) Lecture & Debating Society*: F. W. Showers, 'Local Government and Taxation', 86 (11 Jan. 1912), and F. C. Hockridge, 'The Work of the Surveyor's & Estate Department', 282 (8 Mar. 1934); F. M. L. Thompson, *Chartered Surveyors: The Growth of a Profession* (1968), 107–8; J. R. Kellett, *The Impact of Railways on Victorian Cities* (1969), 388–91; Lichfield turnpike: PRO RAIL 220/10; Carlisle and Newcastle: *RTC*, 188; CLC: Estate Committee Minutes; GCR: PRO RAIL 226/133.

taxation, national. The British government's taxation of the means of transport has a curious history.

Taxation as a means of paying for the maintenance of roads was introduced in 1555. Persons owning carriages were taxed from 1747 onwards, according to the number that they owned: carriage horses too, from 1785. Stage-coaches began to be taxed in 1775, as well as coach-makers for every coach or carriage they produced. But mail-coaches, since they ran primarily on government service (see POST OFFICE), were exempted from taxation when they went into service in 1784.

*Canals were never subjected to any such taxation at all. The younger Pitt intended to tax their carriage of freight in 1797, but withdrew the proposal in face of the opposition it aroused, and no other attempt of this kind was made.

This article deals only with the direct taxation of rail-

ways. They also paid numerous indirect taxes, some of which were particularly onerous in the earliest days of their construction: the tax on bricks, for example (removed in 1850); that on timber, which ended ten years later. Like all other business corporations (and private persons) they also contributed substantially to the national revenue through the stamp duty charged for validating documents. If that were ever reckoned up separately, the amount of it would probably be found surprising.

Railways were first taxed in 1832, when a duty of a half-penny a mile became payable by each company on every four passengers it carried. The yield was at first trifling: £13,000 a year in 1835–7, compared with £750,000 from the stage-coach taxes. This 'passenger duty', as it came to be called, was applied to all travellers alike, without distinction of class: so when reflected in *fares the charge fell much more heavily on poor passengers than on the rich. This was pointed out plainly by a parliamentary committee in 1842, and after two years of dispute between the railways and the government a *Regulation of Railways Act was passed, which altered the basis of this taxation of fares by exempting from duty all that were paid (at a penny a mile or less) by passengers travelling in specially cheap trains which must conform to rules laid down in the Act (see GLADSTONE'S ACT; PARLIAMENTARY TRAINS). In form, this new provision applied only to railways authorized from 1844 onwards, but very soon almost every company was providing trains that qualified to claim the exemption. The passenger duty continued to be applicable in respect of travellers paying higher fares.

It continued to be criticized, often on the ground that it was based upon a wrong principle. The amount of travelling by train increased enormously. In 1844 the number of *passenger journeys made in Great Britain was 1.3 per year per head of the population. By 1869 the corresponding figure was 7.8, and the second of these figures was seriously understated because it did not include the holders of *season tickets, whose daily journeys to and from work were now becoming very numerous. The true figure must have been close to ten. Railway travel was now recognizably a matter of national concern. Ought it to be taxed so heavily, or taxed at all?

In 1869 the Chancellor of the Exchequer, Robert Lowe, proposed in his budget to abolish the railway passenger duty, on a principle stated trenchantly: 'A tax on the means of locomotion is as bad a tax as any that can be devised.' He found himself obliged to retain it, however, because the railway companies refused to accept the terms he intended to impose in the revisions. He did not revive this plan, nor was it taken up again by any of his successors for over ten years. The duty, yielding more from year to year, made a contribution to the national revenue that was not insignificant: £315,000 in 1855, £810,000 in 1883. Still, Lowe was the first Chancellor to make any serious effort to get rid of the passenger duty. Faithful to his doctrine, he discontinued the taxation of stage-coaches in 1870—but by then most of them had gone; the *turnpike trusts, with their tolls, were then beginning to be wound up. Of all the 'means of locomotion', only the railways were still being taxed, the brunt of the imposition still falling most heavily on their poorer passengers.

The duty came under constant fire in the 1870s. But the argument was complicated by divided attitudes among the railway managements; the *Railway Companies Association found it hard to keep them in step during negotiations with government. As in 1844, the formula that was sought was one based not on abolition of the duty itself but on the granting of exemptions to companies willing to provide *workmen's trains which were now multiplying. Special attention was due to them now, as well as to parliamentary trains.

Social reformers of many kinds took part in assaulting the duty. In 1874 a Travelling Tax Abolition Committee was formed under the left-wing direction of G. J. Holyoake and C. D. Collet, which helped to publicize the issue. In the end an agreement was hammered out with the government and the Railway Companies Association, which was embodied in the Cheap Trains Act of 1883. This did not remove the passenger duty altogether, but it laid down new conditions on which the companies could obtain exemptions from it, designed to ensure that they provided adequate services of workmen's trains in every large urban district (as defined in the Act), the fares paid for travelling on them being freed from duty.

The duty continued to be levied on fares above one penny a mile, until it was finally abolished in 1929, on condition that the revenue should be capitalized by the government to form a fund for the improvement of rail transport. Here at last the direct taxation of railways by the government ceased. JS

S. Dowell, *History of Taxation and Taxes in England* (1887–8); C. E. Lee, *Passenger Class Distinctions* (1946), ch. 5; G. Alderman, *The Railway Interest* (1973), ch. 5; yield of railway and coach taxation, 1835–7: PP 1837, xx, 219.

Tay Bridge, see BRIDGES AND VIADUCTS; NORTH BRITISH RAILWAY.

telegraph, electric: a form of communication utilizing electric impulses in a wire to transmit information over distances. The impulses conveyed the messages by coded needle indications, or morse code. It was the precursor of all forms of communication by wire, notably the *telephone.

A number of experimenters realized in the 1820s and 1830s that electricity and magnetism could be harnessed to transmit simple messages. (Sir) William Fothergill Cooke began developing ideas in 1836 when he published a pamphlet which led to a trial in the *Liverpool tunnel on the *Liverpool & Manchester Railway. As a result he became acquainted with (Sir) Charles Wheatstone and the two improved the electric telegraph, taking out a joint patent in 1837. The *London & Birmingham Railway was persuaded to have an experimental installation between Euston and Camden. Despite its success the company declined to ex-

tend it (the system was crude and expensive), but the *Great Western was more impressed and had it installed between Paddington and Hanwell in 1839. After a slightly uncertain start it was repaired and extended to Slough in 1843. The telegraph's reputation was sealed in December 1845 when a murderer made his escape by train from Slough to Paddington; it was used to send details to London where the man was apprehended.

Originally the telegraphs featured multiple dials, with the Cooke–Wheatstone system using five needles. A two-needle system was devised in 1837, and this was followed by a letter-showing dial in 1840 and a printing telegraph in 1841. Wheatstone patented a single-needle apparatus in 1845, which was the basis of almost all future instruments and became the core of the *block telegraph system of train signalling, propounded by Edwin Clark in 1854.

Two types of instrument developed, one giving primary indication by sound and the other visually. In both the transmission of messages was based on the morse code (invented by S. F. B. Morse). The former used different sounds, or intervals between sounds, to indicate the 'dots' and 'dashes', while the latter used combinations of left and right deflections of a normally vertical single needle. The system naturally became commonly known as the 'speaking telegraph'. The railways standardized on needle instruments. As words had to be spelt out, a complex series of code words was devised for whole messages or phrases, thus reducing transmission time.

The success of the telegraph led to the establishment of a number of telegraph companies which quickly set up a national network largely along the routes of *canals and railways. The railways used a mixture of their own circuits and those of the telegraph companies. The telegraph companies and their circuits were nationalized by an Act of 1869 and placed under the *Post Office. Special arrangements were made for the railway companies to continue to use their own systems. The process of disentangling the systems and agreeing ownership and compensation took some years to complete.

On the railways the telegraph comprised three parts: the public system of the PO; the railways' commercial and message circuits; and the block telegraph system. Early references to the introduction of the telegraph need careful interpretation about which was the primary use. As the railways became more complex and the number of trains increased, there was a growing need for message circuits to reinforce the block telegraph with additional information to ensure efficient regulation and control of trains.

Telegraph circuits were much cheaper than telephones, allowing earth returns and much lower-quality insulation. Therefore the railway companies were very slow to convert telegraph circuits to telephones. Even at nationalization a significant proportion of BR's internal message system was still by telegraph—particularly in *signalling and train *control. The speaking telegraph was in use for train operation and regulation at the southern end of the *East Coast main line as recently as 1972. Teleprinters were an adaptation of the system. RDF

J. Kieve, *The Electric Telegraph* (1973); F. B. Head, *Stokers and Pokers* (1968 edn.); W. E. Langdon, *The Application of Electricity to Railway Working* (1877).

telephones were rapidly recognized as being a valuable aid to railway operations, and extensive internal systems were established.

Within five years of the invention of the telephone by Alexander Graham Bell in 1875, wires connected *Cannon Street and *Charing Cross stations, and also *signal boxes on the *Lancashire & Yorkshire Railway. By the close of the century considerable numbers of telephones were in use, including 'omnibus' circuits of the local battery and magneto ringing types. These had several telephones on the same line, coded rings being used to attract the appropriate person. The railway companies were early users of *Post Office lines in stations and depots for commercial purposes.

By 1914 private exchanges were in use at large centres, connected by trunk lines and Post Office junctions. The railways were quick to exploit the carrier telephony technology of the 1920s, which enabled many conversations to be transmitted between exchanges over a single pair of wires, and by the mid-1930s complex trunk systems had been established. For the most part, lines were carried on open poles.

Traffic *control systems, established on several railways between 1909 and 1914, relied on telephony for reporting train movements. Dedicated 'control' circuits were often used in parallel with the ordinary local omnibus circuits. Teleprinters were later used in control offices and elsewhere.

Railway exchanges tended to be complex, with common battery, magneto, and omnibus lines. Facilities for connecting omnibus circuits were also installed in signal boxes and elsewhere, some of which were equipped with 'concentrators'. These brought a number of separate lines together in an apparatus from which the user could have access to any line via a single handset. Modernization of exchanges brought auto-dialling facilities, leading to Extension Trunk Dialling (ETD) in the 1960s and 1970s, while open wires have been replaced by underground cables. Eventually most outlying locations were equipped with ETD extensions.

In the 1990s, digital technology is being introduced and the system has been extended to encompass radio links to telephones in the driving cabs of trains. 'Cab Secure Radio' gives exclusive communication between driver and signalman, while 'Driver to Shore Radio' is in effect an extension of the ETD system. Railway modernization has led to considerable expenditure on signal post telephones (SPT) and dedicated lines to electric traction control rooms, provided more recently with touch-screen terminals. There is still a requirement, however, for independent circuits such as direct lines between signal boxes and to *level crossings.

See also SIGNALLING; TELEGRAPH, ELECTRIC.   MRLI
A. E. Tattersall, *Railway Signalling and Communications* (1940); (Anon), *The Railway Signal and Permanent Way Engineer's Pocket Book* (Loco Publishing Co.) (1915).

television, see RADIO AND TELEVISION, RAILWAYS AND.

Telford, Thomas (1757–1834), engineer. His chief work was with roads and canals. But his involvement with railways calls for brief notice here.

He laid out one railway himself, in 1809. This was 125 miles long, linking Berwick with *Glasgow, to be worked by *horses and *cable haulage; but it remained unbuilt.

As President of the *Institution of Civil Engineers (1820–34) he was frequently consulted on railway matters. He advised the *Stratford & Moreton and *Newcastle & Carlisle Railways to adopt horse traction. He was engineer to the Exchequer Loan Commissioners, with whom the *Liverpool & Manchester Railway had dealings, and inspected its works on the Commissioners' behalf in 1829. His report criticized some of the methods employed in construction and management, while commending the 'very perfect' masonry on the Sankey viaduct. It had nothing to say about locomotives. Telford was not opposed to them as such. In his last years he had careful tests made to compare their efficiency with that of other means of traction and accepted the value of their total superiority in speed. But he never came fully to terms with them.   JS
Robertson, 32–4; L. T. C. Rolt, *Thomas Telford* (1958), esp. 154–61.

temperance movement. Among all the offences against discipline that the servants of a railway company might be punished for under its rules and regulations (see BYE-LAWS), none was more serious than drunkenness when on duty. If that severity appears excessive, two things should be considered. First, a drunken driver or signalman might endanger the lives of all those travelling in the trains he controlled; a drunken porter too, if he had charge of points (see TRACK) at a station. And, secondly, it so happened that the greatest extension of the railway system, in 1850–76, coincided precisely with the rise in the consumption of alcoholic drinks to the highest figure it has ever reached in Britain.

Some of those who observed that rise had set themselves to combat it by the formation of voluntary societies which, though they differed at some points from one another, may be called collectively 'the temperance movement'. All their members undertook to abstain from alcoholic refreshment or to limit their consumption of it. Those societies included directors and senior officers of railway companies, many of whom used their influence to extend that work among railwaymen.

Quakers, who exercised much power in some railway companies, supported any policy designed to further temperance. Nathaniel Worsdell was president of the Crewe Temperance Society from 1843 to 1871. At the Railway Jubilee celebrations in 1875 Edward *Pease claimed that the *Stockton & Darlington Railway's extraordinary freedom from *accidents (it never killed a passenger) was partly due to its refusal to sell 'spirituous liquors' at its stations. Where, as in some railway *towns, the companies could control the numbers of pubs, they kept a careful watch over them. Yet such policies could not go so far as some of their directors wished, because the boards might also include brewers, and those who disliked the temperance movement for its interference with personal liberty.

*Excursion trains presented the companies with another aspect of the same problem. The jollity they promoted among their passengers often over-spilled into drunkenness, and they would seek to persuade train crews and other railway staff to drink with them too. The inspector's report on the bad accident on the *London Tilbury & Southend Railway at Barking in 1875 applies a microscope to this process. But the biggest excursion agent was a very prominent temperance man, Thomas *Cook, and his influence, as well as that of some rival firms, was constantly exercised in trying to curb these propensities among the travellers under his care.

By command and punishment and persuasion, variously exercised, the railway companies managed to keep the drinking habits of their staff and passengers fairly well under control. Yet Brian Harrison was probably right in his contention that 'sobriety in the 19th century probably owed more to faster trains than temperance agitation'. The new freedom, the flexibility of life, that the railways introduced opened up new—and often cheaper—forms of enjoyment than the excessive consumption of beer and spirits.   JS

B. Harrison, *Drink and the Victorians* (1994 edn.); W. L. Burn, *The Age of Equipoise* (1964), 280–4; W. H. Chaloner, *Social and Economic Development of Crewe* (1950), xviii, 151; J. S. Jeans (ed.), *Railway Jubilee at Darlington* (1875), 35; Barking accident: PP 1875, lxvi.

tender. The purpose of the locomotive tender is to carry coal and water. Some very early locomotives appear to have had no tender. Coal was carried on the footplate, and their low-pressure boilers could work for several hours without replenishment, which was probably done from lineside hot water boilers. *Hackworth's early *Stockton & Darlington engines had return-flue boilers fired from the smokebox end, requiring the tender to be at the front, while his preserved *Derwent* (1845) had a coal tender at the front and a water tender behind. Robert *Stephenson's *Rocket*, and others of the time, merely had a small wagon carrying coke and a water barrel.

*Gooch on the *Great Western Railway probably designed the first six-wheel tenders (1840–2), with iron-and-wood 'sandwich' frames. The *London & North Western used 2,500-gallon wooden-framed tenders until as late as 1903; they were cheap, and their relatively low water capacity was no disadvantage on a line well-provided with water-troughs (see WATER SUPPLIES).

The more general British pattern of outside iron-framed tenders with springs above the platform evolved in 1842–51; thereafter springs were increasingly placed below the platform, allowing wider water tanks, which for many years were U-shaped around three sides of the tender. From 1870 rectangular tanks of up to 3,500 gallons capacity began to appear, with sloping tops which helped coal to be shovelled forward. Coal capacity was increased by fitting rails above the sides.

The first eight-wheel tenders were built for James Manson's *Great North of Scotland Railway 4-4-0s in 1890, followed by the *Caledonian and *Midland Railways' twin bogie tenders in 1897 and 1900, carrying 4,500 gallons of water and nine tons of coal; the *London & South Western's of 1901 were larger. *Gresley's eight-wheeler for his *Great Northern 4-6-2 (1922) could hold 7,000 gallons. After the 1923 *Grouping the *London & North Eastern and *Southern Railways built eight-wheel 5,000-gallon tenders—the former with rigid axles—for their large express passenger engines, but the GWR and *London Midland & Scottish standardized on six-wheel types, the latter introducing steam-operated coal pushers on their 'Princess Coronation' class 4-6-2s. The rear tenders of the LMS Beyer-Garratt locomotives had rotary mechanical coal bunkers.

GJB

BSRL, 1–32, 366–71; (Railway Gazette) *British Locomotive Types* (1946); P. Ransom-Wallis, *Last Steam Locomotives of British Railways* (1966).

Tennant, Henry (1823?–1910), manager. After education at the Quakers' Ackworth School, he entered railway service with the Brandling Junction company in 1844 and held the combined posts of traffic superintendent and accountant on the Leeds & Thirsk and *Leeds Northern Railways. He was involved in the formation of the amalgamated *North Eastern Railway in 1854, serving as its accountant in 1854–71 and general manager in 1871–91. He then retired, with a seat on the board. He was also chairman of the Central London Railway (see LONDON UNDERGROUND RAILWAYS) in 1895–8.

Tennant was a highly capable manager, benefiting from his early experience both of operation and of finances. He initiated or supported some progressive policies, doing much, for example, to foster travel at the cheapest rates in the early 1870s, in improved third-class *carriages. But he knew little of the world outside north-eastern England, and his successor *Gibb became increasingly irked by his narrow-minded obstruction. He kept a tenacious hold on the NER board, which elected him deputy-chairman at the age of 81 and kept him there till his death at 86.   JS

Tomlinson; R. Bell, *Twenty-five Years of the North Eastern Railway* (1951); C. H. Ellis, 'Lewin Papers Concerning Sir George Gibb', *JTH*, 1st ser., 5 (1961–2), 226–32.

terminal charges (or 'terminals') were sums added to the mileage charge made by British railways for carrying merchandise, to cover handling costs at each end of its journey. They had already been charged in the past by the road carriers to the customers whose loads they put on to the railways, but the railway companies assumed that task themselves quickly and added these charges to the customer's total bill.

In 1847 the goods managers of the companies that were then members of the *Railway Clearing House agreed certain rates for 'terminals'. Other companies, on joining afterwards, accepted them too. As general goods traffic increased with the growth of industry, the railways' handling methods, particularly in the large industrial towns, expanded and became much more complicated. It demanded greatly enlarged goods *stations and warehouses (see GOODS SHEDS), for reception, sorting, and despatch. In 1876–85 the

*London & North Western Railway spent over £3¼ million on goods stations in *Liverpool, *Manchester, and *Birmingham, the greatest part of it on large buildings and their equipment. One contribution towards meeting this great expenditure came from the quiet, steady increase of charges, in which the railways were not obliged to disclose the proportion for handling.

'Terminals' played a large part in the bitter arguments that developed from the 1870s onwards between the railways and traders (see FREIGHT TRAFFIC RATES). The legality of levying them was challenged repeatedly in the courts, but without success. In the leading case of *Hall v. *London Brighton & South Coast Railway* (1886) it was sustained on appeal to the House of Lords.

When the Railway Rates Tribunal was set up under the Railways Act of 1921, the sender of goods was for the first time given a right to see a breakdown of the total charge proposed, and if there were any charges for services that he did not wish to use, he was entitled to a rebate. 'Terminals' disappeared altogether when rates themselves were abolished under the Railways Act of 1962.   JS

J. S. Jeans, *Railway Problems* (1887), 435, 509–16; E. A. Pratt, *Railways and Their Rates* (1905), 16–20, 195–7; H. W. Disney, *Law of Carriage by Railway* (1923 edn.), 260–4; Bagwell, 85–9.

testing of equipment. During the 19th century there was no shortage of technical innovations on British railways, many of them being *patented in the name of engineers such as *Webb. But most work was purely empirical, and formal testing of equipment was limited until the 20th century. Most of what had been undertaken related to locomotive engineering (see LOCOMOTIVE TESTING; DYNAMOMETER CAR).

Among the earliest railway testing procedures were bridge deflection tests in which a locomotive was run across a bridge to check the deflection induced by static loading of the structure, as compared with the predicted deflection for the designed load. It took until the 1920s for locomotive and civil engineers to understand the dynamic loading characteristics of locomotives, the balancing of the reciprocating parts, and the effects of hammer-blow on track and bridges.

It is difficult to reproduce the service conditions of railway equipment in a laboratory. To simulate the effect of braking a complete train, and to assess the speed and performance of *brake applications, static test-rigs of vacuum and air brake equipments were established in factories by manufacturers such as *Westinghouse and Davies & Metcalfe. GEC built a 'combined test' installation at its Preston works in 1984 so that testing could be undertaken of the complete electrical propulsion system of a train, including its auxiliaries.

Preliminary testing of designs under service loading, or to destruction, dates from the early 1950s, notably with the structural testing of Mark 1 carriage underframes (see CARRIAGES). A full-scale stress analysis was undertaken of the structure of a Swindon-built InterCity diesel unit car when under load.

Study of the interaction between wheel and rail led to

*BR conducting an extensive testing programme from the early 1960s which was accompanied by experimental work. This aimed at an understanding of vehicle dynamics (see ADVANCED PASSENGER TRAIN). The work was assisted by the availability from 1969 of the Old Dalby test track for rolling stock where high-speed testing could be conducted away from public services.

Various research and testing programmes on BR aimed to achieve full train *control with two-way communication between track and train, and systems were tested in service conditions. Of these, the APT Control System (CAPT) included track-mounted transponders and train-borne microprocessors, while another development in this field—the signal-repeating automatic warning system (SR AWS) —combined the *automatic warning system with a visual indication in the driver's cab of the next signal ahead (see also SIGNALLING).

Other notable subjects for full-scale testing on BR included the development from the mid-1950s of disc brakes for passenger stock.

Spectrographic analysis of samples of *lubricating oil from a diesel engine was developed into a routine test procedure involving BR's regional laboratories. Examination of the oil for trace metals provided early warning of some types of engine defect, and allowed engines to continue in service without the need to open them up solely for inspection.

There was an exceptional test in 1984 when, in conjunction with BR, the Central Electricity Generating Board staged a crash on the Old Dalby test track between a remote-controlled train and a flask used for the transport of spent nuclear fuel rods. This £1.6 million demonstration attempted to allay public fears about the safe movement of nuclear materials on rail.

See also TESTING OF MATERIALS; RESEARCH AND DEVELOPMENT.   MLH

J. Johnson and R. A. Long, *British Railways Engineering 1948–80* (1981); R. Ford, 'Traction and Rolling Stock Testing', *Modern Railways* (Jan. 1985), 40; Old Dalby nuclear flask demonstration: 'Smash!', *Modern Railways* (Sept. 1984), 460; spectrographic analysis of lubricating oils: Railway Industry Association, *Sixth Motive Power Course 1977: Digest of Lectures and Support Papers*; stress analysis of InterCity diesel unit: R. A. Smeddle, *Presidential Address to the Institution of Locomotive Engineers, 1959/60*.

testing of materials began with William *Fairbairn's pioneering investigation of the factors affecting the strength of iron. By 1850 it was realized that by controlling chemical composition and the method of forging wrought iron one could predict its mechanical properties, and from that point iron founders were able increasingly to produce special materials for specific purposes, which created the need for determining and guaranteeing their properties without destroying whole components or structures as Fairbairn had done.

Typical of early proof-testing was dropping a rail across a metal trestle from a given height: if it bent or otherwise deformed it was rejected. More scientific tests were soon developed such as tensile-testing, impact-testing, hardness-testing, and fatigue-testing, the last of these being developed specifically for railway axles. With chemical analysis and structural assessment, by examining under a microscope the polished and etched surface of a section though an actual component or test piece, these were the principal techniques available to the early metallurgist, and in modern form they are still used today.

Railways began to install their own laboratories, usually to overcheck the results claimed by their suppliers, but one of the first was associated with the steelworks set up at *Crewe by the *London & North Western Railway in the late 1860s. Up to that point, testing was largely confined to new materials and parts, but the railways introduced an important principle by developing non-destructive testing (NDT) for checking used parts in service or during overhaul. The *wheel-tapper's hammer was the earliest example of NDT: if a tyre rang when struck it was sound, if it gave out a dull thud it was cracked. The modern counterpart is ultrasonic testing, used to check wheels and axles and capable of pin-pointing flaws hidden deep in outwardly solid metal. Another technique, developed by the LNWR, is to pass a heavy electric current along the suspect part, when any high localized voltage drop indicates a serious, hidden flaw.

Penetrant crack-detection began with the oil-and-chalk system applied to crank axles, connecting rods, and other moving parts of LNWR engines by F. W. *Webb in 1887–8. This technique is now widely used, the most sensitive form using fluorescent penetrant which is viewed under ultraviolet light. Magnetic inks are also used to show up cracks in highly magnetic steels, the sides of the crack acting as the poles of a magnet when a current is passed.

Other industries have now taken the lead with the development of advanced inspection and testing techniques, but the modern railway is not far behind. Techniques apart, materials-testing has been revolutionized by the advent of computers. It is now possible, for example, to build up a three-dimensional picture of an internal defect, while of equal importance is the ability to carry out detailed statistical analysis of accumulated test results. Statistical process-control can lead to refinement and optimization of testing requirements and is required by today's ISO 9000 quality systems.

See also LOCOMOTIVE TESTING; TESTING OF EQUIPMENT; RESEARCH AND DEVELOPMENT. RW

Thameslink: the name applied to cross-*London electrified passenger services, linking Bedford and Luton with Wimbledon, Sutton, and *Brighton via Farringdon, *Blackfriars, and *London Bridge.

The *London Chatham & Dover Railway (Metropolitan Extensions) Act, 1860, gave powers for a line into London from the south, and a branch to Farringdon Street station on the *Metropolitan Railway. The lines were fully open to traffic in 1866 and provided a link from south London across the Thames, through the Snow Hill Tunnel, to join the Widened Lines of the Metropolitan and linking with the northern main lines. Through services were operated via

Snow Hill until 1916 when regular passenger traffic ceased. Until 1969 the route was used by freight trains to and from South London, but it was then disused and the track partly lifted.

In 1983 the Greater London Council commissioned a study into reopening the line, to link the passenger services of the London Midland and Southern Regions of *BR. The study's positive findings were endorsed by BR, and a modernization scheme was approved by the government in 1985. Included were restoration of the track between Farringdon and Ludgate Hill, *electrification, and the provision of dual-voltage electric *multiple-unit trains able to use the electrified third rail of the Southern Region, and the 25 kV overhead system north of Farringdon. The service was launched as Thameslink in 1988.

The services have proved very successful, and a new station has been provided, called City Thameslink, replacing Holborn Viaduct terminus (see LONDON STATIONS: BLACKFRIARS). But investment in infrastructure north and south of the central core, including resignalling, upgraded power supplies, an improved station at *King's Cross–*St Pancras, and additional track capacity between Blackfriars and New Cross, would allow increased service frequencies. The project to realize this is known as Thameslink 2000, and has been given government approval. MLH

theatre. Railways made three quite different contributions to the theatre: (1) they provided a source of new themes, allusions, and settings for stage entertainments; (2) they opened theatre-going to a wider public by providing improved transport; (3) they greatly facilitated the movement of travelling theatrical companies.

(1) *Speculation in railway shares (see MANIAS) provided the theme for Edward Stirling's play The Lucky Hit, or Railroads for Ever (1836). The railway itself began to appear on the stage in 1840 with T. E. Wilks' farce The Railroad Station, set at *Birmingham, a train passing by a window behind the stage. The speculation of 1845 helped to evoke several pantomimes, wildly predicting the railways' potentiality to provide journeys to the moon in ten hours, or to China in one. The underground *Metropolitan Railway in London was treated in Du Terreaux's Waiting for the Underground (1866), set entirely at its *King's Cross station, and by Dion Boucicault in After Dark (1868), which required a train to be brought on stage.

But the railways never achieved a permanent place in the Victorian theatre, beyond casual allusions: to a comic director in W. S. Gilbert's Thespis; to tipping the guard, in a delightful exchange in Sydney Grundy's comedy A Pair of Spectacles (1890). Bad services, or over-exacting employers, might figure at music halls, as the *Brecon & Merthyr Railway did, for example, at Newport in the rousing chorus of a song:

Six and five trains up to Dowlais
Six and five trains back same way
Wherever I wass finish, I wass get no extra pay!

A sudden revival of interest in railways appeared after 1900. At least 15 plays alluding to them were licensed in

1908–14. The advent of the *cinema—a dangerous rival to the stage, offering stronger realism—had something to do with it. A response to rising speed did more. One of these plays was entitled *A Mile a Minute*, another *Sixty Miles an Hour*.

Only one railway play ever enjoyed any striking theatrical success in Britain: Arnold Ridley's thriller *The Ghost Train* (1925), which also appeared in three film versions (1927–41).

(2) Railways came to offer additional late services after performances, from London to Aylesbury and *Brighton, for example, at least once a week; some *London Underground railways ran trains up to 1 a.m., allowing a post-theatre supper. This may not have been good for the plays themselves, however. 'What would you think', wrote Henry James in 1890, 'of any other artist—the painter or novelist—whose governing forces should be the dinner and the suburban trains?'

(3) The transport of unwieldy theatrical equipment presented problems to the railways, until low-loading *wagons were used for big stage flats. Provincial theatres depended more and more on travelling companies. Some continued to move about by road, like *circuses and travelling zoos. But theatre managers could not ignore the economies arising from the railways' much greater speed. When the company packed up on Saturday night it could be taken on Sunday to open in another distant town on Monday, either in a special train or in carriages and vans attached to ordinary trains. In 1898 one theatrical company travelled on four successive Sundays, starting from *Southampton, for a tour of Southport, *Plymouth, *Sheffield, and *Cardiff—over 1,100 miles altogether. This benefited managements, and it must have paid the railways too, for they all discounted the fares by 25 per cent.

See also RADIO AND TELEVISION. JS

VR, 207–9; D. S. Barrie, *Brecon & Merthyr Railway* (1957), 144; Henry James, *The Tragic Muse* (Penguin edn.), 50; RM, 3 (1898), 555–61.

Thomas, James Henry (1876–1949), *trade union official and politician. J. H. ('Jimmy') Thomas was brought up in poverty by a devoted and hard-working grandmother. Between the ages of five and 12 he attended Newport national schools. He worked for the *Great Western Railway, first as call-boy, then as engine-cleaner. In 1894 he was *fireman and by 1900 *driver. He rose to prominence in the affairs of the Amalgamated Society of Railway Servants (see NATIONAL UNION OF RAILWAYMEN) in 1900–19, a time of rapid growth in membership and national influence. In 1905 he was elected its youngest-ever president, and in 1906 organizer for the *Manchester district. His impressive organizing ability and his forthright eloquence led to his election as assistant general secretary in 1910, and general secretary in 1917. He played a large part in settling the first national railway strike in 1911, and the more decisive strike of 1919 which brought union recognition.

Thomas' political career began as a *Swindon councillor in 1901. In 1910 he was elected MP for *Derby where he

retained his seat until 1935. He held Cabinet office in the Labour governments of 1924 and 1929–31 and in the National Government of 1931–5. In 1936 he was found guilty of leaking budget secrets and resigned from Parliament. PSB

DNB; J. H. Thomas, *Red Light on the Railways* (1921); H. R. Phillpott, *The Rt. Hon. J. H. Thomas* (1922); J. H. Thomas, *My Story* (1937).

Thomas, Ronald Henry George (1914–96), writer. After working in the City, followed by war service, Thomas entered the teaching profession. A contributor to transport journals, he was an early member and a London Group secretary of the *Railway & Canal Historical Society, and lectured on railway history for London University extra-mural department.

He will be long remembered for two fine books: *London's First Railway: The *London & Greenwich* (1972) and *The *Liverpool & Manchester Railway* (1980). The articles in this *Companion* on those two lines are by him, as well as those on the *London & Croydon and *London & Blackwall Railways.

In both of his books he had to dispel misunderstandings, fill in large omissions, and correct previous writers' mistakes, which he did firmly but without needless asperity. He enjoyed the great advantage of having access to contemporary records, to which he paid meticulous attention.

Both companies, although important, had short independent lives. Thomas' sure command of the copious evidence enabled him to observe and record their operations almost as if they were unfolding before our eyes. His *Liverpool & Manchester Railway* stands among the best histories of an important British railway company. JS

Thompson, Edward (1881–1954), mechanical engineer. He held various appointments in industry, and on railways, before becoming carriage and wagon superintendent of the *Great Northern Railway, 1912; area workshops manager, *London & North Eastern Railway; mechanical engineer, Stratford *works, 1930; and CME of the LNER on the death of *Gresley, 1941; he retired in 1946.

Thompson's work at Stratford included the successful re-building of many of the *Great Eastern 'B12' 4-6-0s, and 'D16' 4-4-0s, in 1932–3. As CME, he had to confront the problems in wartime with the conjugated *valve gear of Gresley engines. Some of the solutions involved the drastic and expensive rebuilding of these and other engines, often proving to be 'new wine in old bottles'. Classes appearing in his time as CME included the serviceable 'B1' 4-6-0s, from 1942, and the less satisfactory 'L1' 2-6-4Ts. Steel-panelled corridor carriages with transverse gangways were built from 1945, following extensive surveys of public opinion.

Personal animosity between Thompson and Gresley has been the subject of conjecture in railway circles. MLH

G. Hughes, *LNER* (1986); P. Townend, *East Coast Pacifics at Work* (1982).

Thompson, Francis (1808–95), architect. Son of a Suffolk county surveyor, Thompson first practised in Quebec in

1830–7. On his return to England he began a long association with Robert *Stephenson, working first on the *North Midland Railway (1840) where he designed 26 stations, including *Derby and *Leeds, the *hotel at Derby, *engine sheds, and tunnel portals. The stations, of which only Wingfield survives, were all different, and were among the most delicate designs ever to grace a railway, attracting wide attention.

On the *Eastern Counties Railway from Bishop's Stortford northwards (1845), Thompson worked with the architects Sancton *Wood and Henry Hunt (the exact division of responsibility is not clear), including Cambridge station. The intermediate stations were to a basic plan that differed only in size and detailing. Association with Wood continued on the *Midland Railway's *Leicester–*Peterborough line, where the division of responsibility is also unclear. Oakham and Luffenham certainly bore his characteristics, which were later adopted by others on various lines in eastern England.

Thompson took the same style to the *Chester & Holyhead Railway (1848), where he also designed the fine masonry work for Stephenson's Conway and *Britannia tubular bridges. Chester station, like Derby, had an immensely long frontage, in a strikingly Italianate style. The intermediate stations, some of which remain, again varied only in size and detail; particularly so at Holywell and at Bangor.

In 1853–9 Thompson was back in Canada, designing stations for the Grand Trunk Railway, the masonry for Stephenson's Victoria Bridge over the St Lawrence, and similar work.

Other achievements by this talented architect remain obscure, probably because so many of them were in North America.   GJB

O. Carter, 'Francis Thompson, 1808–95: An Architectural Mystery Solved', *Backtrack*, 9, 4 (April 1995), 213–18.

Thompson, Stephen Harry (?–1874), chairman. Of a Yorkshire landowning family, he became a director of the *York & North Midland Railway and then of the *North Eastern, of which he was chairman from 1855 to 1874.

In that office he was strong, quiet, and calm. When the company was assailed as a *monopolist in 1866, he said that 'they held their district for so long, and so long only, as the majority of thinking men in the district believed that they were as well served by the North Eastern as they could be served by other companies'.

He rode out two storms well. When in 1867 a shareholder accused the company of misappropriating funds, he and the officers rebutted the charge completely. A crisis arose in 1870 from the lax administration of the general manager, William O'Brien, but Thompson achieved his dismissal without exciting the least public comment. He also showed, however, that the affair had taught him and the company necessary lessons.   JS

Tomlinson, 621, 630–2, 770–1; J. Simmons, 'The Removal of a North Eastern General Manager', *ET*, ch. 9.

Thornton, Sir Henry Worth (1871–1933), manager. Born at Logansport, Indiana, USA, he joined the Pennsylvania Railroad in 1894 and became general superintendent of the Long Island Railroad (part of the PRR) from 1911 to 1914, when he was appointed general manager of the *Great Eastern Railway. He was the only American who ever managed a large British railway company, and he did that with distinction.

His first big task was to produce a new suburban *timetable, issued in October 1914. He was then drawn into the national administration of the railways, under government control (see WAR). There he rose to become inspector-general of transportation and was made KBE in 1919. Back with the Great Eastern, he set himself to improve the handling of suburban traffic still further. The new timetable of 1920 was justifiably proclaimed as 'The Last Word in Steam-operated Suburban Services'. All such work was performed by interdepartmental teams. Thornton chose men well: F. V. Russell as his superintendent of operations, for example, and John *Miller as chief civil engineer.

He was president of the Canadian National Railways in 1922–32.   JS

DBB; C. J. Allen, *Great Eastern Railway* (1955); E. A. Pratt, *British Railways and the Great War* (1921).

through carriages were taken off trains at junctions, and attached to others.

Their provision first came under public discussion in 1839, when the arrangements for handling them at Parkside (Lancashire) were complained of before a parliamentary committee. The through carriage supposed to run from *Preston to *London sometimes did not in fact do so, and even when it did there were difficulties in transferring passengers' luggage from one train to another; moreover, travellers also had to rebook at Parkside and *Birmingham.

Facilities of this kind were welcomed by the public, nevertheless, and they were soon multiplied. By 1844 a through carriage was provided each way between London and *Hull, travelling over the lines of six companies. The apportionment of the fares paid by passengers making the whole journey was a task for the newly created *Railway Clearing House. In 1860 a single *Great Northern Railway express was conveying through carriages from London to *Manchester, *Liverpool, Huddersfield, Halifax, *Bradford, *Leeds, and *Newcastle.

The provision of through carriages called for additional station work, besides complicating operation and increasing its cost. But their popularity was evident. *Hawkshaw, for instance, having in the 1860s to make much use of the Belgian railways, remarked that Englishmen would find the constant changes of carriage there intolerable.

Some British railways provided through services by means of *slip carriages, fitted with special apparatus allowing a guard to detach them from moving trains which did not then have to stop at the station. The first of these appeared in 1858. Such services could, however, only form a substitute for outward-bound stops, for no means were found of attaching carriages to trains passing through in the opposite direction without stopping. Slip carriages were provided by some companies, but rejected by others, like the *North Eastern Railway. They were to be found hardly anywhere else in Europe.

Through carriages were usually worked singly or in pairs. When the traffic justified more expansive accommodation, it might be provided in complete through trains, running over main or secondary lines from London or (increasingly from 1875 onwards) between provincial cities (see CROSS-COUNTRY SERVICES).

It would be impossible to list the numbers of through carriages that were provided. They are shown irregularly in *Bradshaw's Guide*, which was compiled on the basis of information provided by the companies. Some of them offered lists of through carriages available, set out in their own public *timetables, but not all. For the rest, our knowledge of them may arise partly by chance. A report on an accident on the *Midland Railway at Hereford in 1889 reveals that the company was then providing a through carriage between London (St Pancras) and Brecon.

The services continued to be valued, and we must presume they were well used. In that year *Acworth remarked that 'if there is one thing the British public appreciates more than another, it is through carriages'.

One notable new through carriage working was introduced in the 20th century, which stood quite alone in the distance it travelled: the 785 miles between *Aberdeen and Penzance, taking about 21 hours and involving the collaboration of four companies: the *North British, North Eastern, *Great Central, and *Great Western. It never constituted a train of its own, being a single vehicle attached to other trains that included *restaurant cars, together with *sleeping cars southwards from *Swindon and northwards from *York. It ran from 1921 to 1939.

The number of through carriages was then being gradually thinned down, partly for a technical reason. The old small carriages, running on four or six wheels, had given way to bogie vehicles, each offering perhaps 50–60 seats —often more than were required. By the 1930s private motor cars now offered door-to-door conveyance, more convenient for many of their owners than the trains. So—by way of example—through carriages were still provided in 1930 from London to towns as small as Buckingham and Horncastle, but by 1939 they had gone.

The massive *closure of lines and stations under *British Rail removed railway facilities from many towns and districts that had enjoyed through services in the past. And in the 1970s another technical change put an end to the possibility of providing them. The fixed *multiple units now running in shuttle services could not haul additional vehicles.

JS

PP 1839, x, 311, 336, 362; Hawkshaw: PP 1867, xxxviii (1), 808; Acworth, 184; Aberdeen–Penzance services: C. J. Allen, *London & North Eastern Railway* (1971 edn.), 196.

ticket office. Until recent times this was known as the 'booking office', deriving from the stage-coach practice of issuing handwritten *tickets torn from a book, which early railways adopted before *Edmondson card tickets became general. At first, tickets were issued at a local inn or hotel, but with the establishment of permanent stations the railways provided their own booking offices. The *Liverpool & Manchester Railway for a time used both systems at its termini. Tickets could be bought at a city-centre hotel or office, the fare including an omnibus to the station.

Large stations would have a number of booking offices, segregated according to *class, destination, railway company (if more than one used the station), or all three, often resulting in a formidable array. The LMR's *Manchester terminus at Liverpool Road (1836), for instance, had separate first- and second-class offices. Later, segregation at the second Lime Street station at *Liverpool (1849) was geographical, for Manchester, Bolton, and *Preston, and for London and *Birmingham, respectively. When Birmingham New Street was extended in 1886 separate offices were provided for the *London & North Western and *Midland Railways at each of three locations; six in all. Multi-user stations such as *York, *Carlisle, and *Perth had offices for each company, and it was to the passenger's advantage to have some knowledge of railway geography. Large stations, such as those with heavy commuter traffic, could have one big office with windows for ranges of alphabetical destinations, *season tickets, *excursions, etc.

The booking office itself might be in a separate room with a partition separating the clerks from the passengers, in which small ticket-issuing windows were fitted with thick glass or a wire grille containing a pigeon-hole, covered by a sliding hatch when the office was closed. Or it might form a separate structure on the concourse, as at *Edinburgh Princes Street, or within a booking hall like that at *St Pancras. Some had a waist-high barrier in front of each window. Smaller stations would have the booking office adjoining the entrance-hall, passageway, or *waiting room.

Behind the window was a counter containing a ticket-dating press, alongside racks of pre-printed tickets in vertical slots labelled according to destination and type. Williams in 1883 described the counter as having five bowls set in it containing the clerk's change, covered by a sliding lid. Above each row of tickets in the rack was chalked the serial number of the first one issued. By comparing it with the number of the lowest one, which was the next awaiting issue, the clerk knew how many had been sold. At the end of his shift he entered in a book the numbers of tickets issued to each destination and the total fares, which had to balance with the cash taken. With the advent of paper money the cash bowls were fitted into drawers containing slots for notes.

Mechanical ticket machines for heavily used suburban routes appeared in the early 1900s, but otherwise the system remained unchanged until the 1960s when *BR started equipping its larger offices with machines that printed paper tickets on the spot, simplifying accounting. Later, electronic APTIS machines (see TICKETS) became standard, linked to a central computer. Ticket offices, as they had become, are now frequently part of a travel centre at large stations, where enquiries and reservations can be made and tickets purchased in one place. The traditional window remains, however; much enlarged and fitted with a voice-amplifier to assist conversation between customer and clerk.   GJB

Thomas, 189; R. Foster, *Birmingham New Street*, ii (1990); F. S. Williams, *Our Iron Roads* (1883), 309–10.

tickets. Many early railway companies used stage-coach practice as a precedent for fare collection. Thus passengers reserved their places in advance and their names were recorded on waybills, or on paper tickets torn from books containing counterfoils, hence the origin in coaching days of the term 'booking'. The ticket acted as a receipt for the fare.

The *London & Greenwich and *Leicester & Swannington Railways sold passengers reusable metal tokens or checks as permits-to-travel, whilst other lines provided a skeleton printed ticket for the clerk to complete by hand with individual journey details.

There was then little check on the honesty of passengers or railway servants, and to regulate fare collection Thomas *Edmondson pioneered a system of prepared card tickets whilst working at the *Newcastle & Carlisle Railway's Milton (now Brampton) station.

His tickets met the three basic needs for revenue control:

1. To provide a receipt for the passenger's money.
2. To authorize the passenger to travel a certain distance by a specified route and in a particular class.
3. To ensure that the company received its dues in full. Each ticket was serially numbered, so that the clerk had to account for either the cash or the unused tickets.

Edmondson moved to the *Manchester & Leeds Railway, where he introduced his ticket system over the entire line. To enable sometimes illiterate railway staff to check tickets he printed different patterns on the reverse side. *Manchester, for example, had wavy lines.

The *Railway Clearing House adopted this system, so that it became a virtual condition of membership that Edmondson tickets were employed. Participating railways paid him a royalty of 10*s*. per route mile for using his pasteboard tickets, size 2¼ in × 1³⁄₁₆ in, and most standardized the colours of card for different classes, finally using white for first-class ordinary tickets and green for third.

Tickets issued under *Gladstone's Act of 1844 usually carried the term *'parliamentary'. The same legislation provided for cheaper travel for children: free for those under three years old and half fare between three and 12.

Where traffic densities allowed, separate tickets were printed for children; otherwise an adult ticket was adapted, either by cutting it in half or by removing a portion with hand clippers or scissors. Enough information was printed on the portion removed to identify the journey and fare, so that the clerk could be credited with the value of the unpaid half fare. Until the 1960s most stations issued 1*d*. (later 2*d*.) platform tickets granting admission only.

The main drawback of the Edmondson system was that each station had to hold stocks of pre-printed tickets to

Two Edmondson card tickets: Great Central & Midland Joint Committee third-class single; Bishop's Castle Railway third-class parliamentary return.

every destination regularly used, multiplied by each of the many types of fare—single, day return, period return, excursion, dog, cycle, and so on. The serial numbers had to be recorded meticulously and each clerk's sales accounted for accurately. Tickets presented a security risk as they might be stolen *en route* from the printer to the station.

To cater for bookings for infrequently used journeys or routes, every station was provided with blank card or paper tickets, completed in manuscript by the clerk. Guards of trains calling at unstaffed halts often carried racks of tram-type paper tickets, marked on issue with a punch.

The *London Underground and other suburban railways mechanized ticket issue to speed the flow of passengers. Coin-operated machines were first installed on station forecourts in 1904, and in 1921 ticket offices began to be equipped with hand- and electrically-operated machines to date and record ticket issues automatically.

Main-line railways, too, experimented with new ticket systems, including the *Great Western at Birmingham in 1912. However, it took another 40 years for *British Railways to introduce at its major stations equipment that printed tickets at the point of sale, simplifying accounting and eliminating the need for producing, transporting, and storing stocks of pre-printed tickets. At smaller offices, agencies, and the majority of BR stations, Edmondson's ticket system, with his heavy metal dating-press, continued in use for up to 40 years after *nationalization.

The 1960s brought the use of commercial cash registers to date and price tickets upon issue, meeting the legal need for ordinary tickets to carry the correct fare, and speeding up accounting.

To take advantage of computer-age technology, after various trials British Rail chose APTIS (All Purpose Ticket Issuing System), whose *ticket office consoles are linked through the BR telephone network to a central computer at

Nottingham, which gathers information each night from station machines and transmits fare revisions.

Conductor-guards handle on-train ticket issues with SPORTIS machines, the portable equivalent of APTIS, which are regularly linked at their home stations to the same computer network.

'Tribute', the latest British Rail development, provides a comprehensive rail travel information and booking system. The airline-style tickets can be issued for domestic journeys and for travel on Eurostar services through the *Channel Tunnel.

See also FARES; SEASON TICKETS; PASSES AND PRIVILEGE TICK-
ETS.   MGDF

G. Fairchild and P. Wootton, *Railway and Tramway Tickets* (1987); M. I. Bray, *Railway Tickets, Timetables and Handbills* (1986); M. Farr, *Thomas Edmondson and His Tickets* (1991); D. G. Geldard, *The First Fifty Years (The Early Development of the Railway Ticket)* (1984); J. P. Thomas, *Handling London's Underground Traffic* (1928), 154–8.

Tilbury, see PORTS AND DOCKS.

timber, use of. A large proportion of the huge quantities of timber used by the Victorians was consumed by the railways, most of it imported. Railway workshops manufactured all manner of wooden products, from *carriages and *wagons to small items like curtain rings and pick handles. A *Crewe joiners' shop even turned out artificial limbs for injured employees.

Until well past the turn of the century carriages and wagons were almost entirely wooden, apart from wheels and axles. Oak was used for wagon under-frames, with bodies of oak, teak, or red pine. In 1889 the *London & North Western Railway's Earlestown wagon works employed 1,600 men, most of them in woodworking trades, who could turn out 18 wagons a day, together with horse-drawn delivery vans and drays, barrows, and other items, quite apart from large numbers of repaired vehicles.

Carriage-building needed greater skills and a wider variety of timber. In 1849 Crewe used oak for floors and under-frames, ash for body frames, mahogany for panelling, and willow for brake-blocks. Forty years later, Wolverton carriage works was using mahogany, baywood, pine, teak, Quebec and English oak, and ash, with fine veneers for internal finishes. Some 2,000 men were employed, again predominantly in woodworking, including carpenters, joiners, coach-builders, and cabinet-makers. Furniture and ticket racks were among the miscellaneous wooden products. The LNWR kept two years' supply of timber at Wolverton, and other large railway workshops did the same. At *Derby carriage works, for instance, it was estimated in 1883 that the *Midland Railway had 10,000 tons of unsawn timber seasoning in its yards, and the independent carriage and wagon builders would keep proportionate quantities.

Sleepers took larger amounts of timber. In 1845–50 some 12 million were required for new lines alone, and nearly a century later, in 1938, some 4.4 million were used. They were mostly sawn from Baltic redwood or Douglas fir, although in earlier days some lines used French or home-

grown larch, or Scots fir. They might be half-round, or sawn into a rectangular section, which was more expensive. Some companies creosoted them. In 1871 the general manager of the Manchester Sheffield & Lincolnshire Railway (see GREAT CENTRAL) investigated the practice on other lines, finding that prices could vary between 2s. 1½d. per half-round creosoted sleeper on the *South Eastern Railway, and 4s. 0½d. for a *Kyanized sleeper on the *Great Western. The cheapest were the Midland's at 1s. 7d., but no details were given. Sleepers were purchased from specialist importers who bought from the shippers; in the early 1950s, for instance, there were 14 supplying *BR and *London Transport, and the Timber Trade Federation had a sleeper and pole importers' section.

When some lines were built, timber was used for *bridges and viaducts, mainly pine. Although they had to be replaced with more durable structures later, their cheapness helped to keep down the initial costs while speed of construction meant that a line could be opened as quickly as possible and start earning revenue. I. K. *Brunel specified yellow pine for his numerous viaducts in Devon, Cornwall, and South Wales. Other lines which had series of wooden bridges included the SER between Redhill and Ashford, the *Great Northern Railway through Lincolnshire, and the *Caledonian between Carlisle and Carstairs.

Baltic pine was also used for signal posts, the very tall ones being shaped from a whole tree (see SIGNALLING). Wooden signal arms were usually of mahogany, cedar, teak, or baywood, and it was not until the latter part of the century that steel came into use: in 1883 on the LNWR, but not until the 1930s on the Great Western. Derby works was using 15,000 cu ft of timber a year for signals in 1883. *Level crossings, of which there were 25,500 in 1956, required at least two wooden gates, and in the same year the railways had some 550,000 wooden *telegraph poles.

Timber was widely used in buildings. *Signal boxes usually had wooden superstructures in standardized patterns, and some were entirely wooden. Most lines had some wooden *stations. The SER, GWR, and LNWR in particular had significant numbers, frequently to a standard design which enabled quick and cheap construction. Many other buildings were in timber: small goods sheds and yard cabins, for instance. Most of this construction, of course, was done by *contractors working to railway companies' specifications. *Fencing, whether post-and-rail or post-and-wire, also used up large quantities of timber, often from old sleepers.

The railways themselves, the carriage and wagon builders, signalling manufacturers, and building and civil engineering contractors collectively formed a large body of customers for timber merchants and importers, particularly those engaged in the Baltic trade. Price Walker & Co. of Gloucester, for instance, were large suppliers, particularly to the Midland, of which W. P. Price was chairman in 1870–3. The firm had timber yards and sidings at Gloucester docks, and at the MSLR's Grimsby docks from where that company was supplied. In 1860, as Price & Co., they joined with the Gloucester Wagon Co. to enter into a hire-purchase agreement to supply the MSLR with 200 wooden timber wagons, followed in 1863 by 600 more. A year later the Manchester Railway Steel & Plant Co. supplied another 800 under similar arrangements. These figures also give some indication of the amount of *timber traffic on one major railway. In 1864 the same railway also bought 200 wooden coal wagons on hire purchase from the Gloucester company.

Another timber firm, James Kennedy of Glasgow, imported American oak scantlings sawn to size for wagon frames before shipment, hardwood for carriage panels and furniture, and fir sleepers. They had a sawmill and sidings at Bo'ness dock on the Forth, and at Kinning Park, Glasgow.

After World War II timber was in short supply for some years, but by 1953 the railways were buying more than before the war and, with London Transport, were the country's second largest consumers. Thereafter the use of timber began to decline as reinforced *concrete was increasingly used for sleepers and some structural work. Now, steel frames and *asbestos or steel cladding have supplanted wooden buildings, just as they have replaced a good deal of *brick construction. Rolling stock is almost entirely steel, with extensive use of *plastics for carriage interiors. New small stations, however, often still have wooden platforms. GJB

F. S. Williams, *Our Iron Roads* (1883 edn.); Acworth; F. B. Head, *Stokers and Pokers* (1968 edn.); *Facts and Figures about British Railways* (1956 edn.); Findlay; Dow; R. Fitzgerald and J. Grenier, *Timber: A Centenary History of the Timber Trade Federation, 1892–1992* (1992), 85, 92, 93.

timber traffic. Since the 18th century a very high proportion of Britain's timber requirements have been imported, chiefly from Scandinavia, the Baltic, and North America. Most of the railways' timber traffic was therefore forwarded from the principal ports involved in this trade: West *Hartlepool, *Middlesbrough, *Hull, Grimsby (and later Immingham), *London (Surrey Commercial Docks), *Bristol, *Cardiff (Bute Dock), Birkenhead, *Liverpool (Canada Dock), and *Glasgow. All of them handled softwood, but hardwood was concentrated on London and Liverpool. Pit wood (with bark) and pit props (stripped of bark) generally came in through the coal-exporting ports, providing for the coal wagons a return load back to the collieries.

Timber merchants had private *sidings, although for many years there was dissatisfaction with the railways' classified rates and charges, leading directly to the formation of the Timber Trade Federation in 1892, through which Parliament was lobbied on railway rates legislation. In 1893 the companies agreed to negotiate with individual traders, although relationships continued to be strained.

In 1920 some 8 million tons of timber were consigned by rail, 43 per cent of it pit wood and pit props, excluding the considerable quantities of sleepers and other material for the railways' own use. The biggest carrier was the *North Eastern Railway. By 1938 the tonnage carried had halved.

The pattern of movements changed radically during both world wars, when imported supplies were severely curtailed and the gap had to be filled by a massive increase in felling of British woodlands, particularly in northern *Scotland. The former *Highland and *Great North of Scotland Railway lines both carried large quantities of timber in World War II. Temporary sidings and *narrow-gauge railways were installed to handle this traffic.

Detailed guidance on the loading and securing of timber, both sawn and 'round' (unsawn), was given in the railways' loading instructions. Lengths up to about 20 ft might be loaded within an open *wagon, or overhanging one end of it. Longer lengths, such as telegraph poles, were loaded on two or more four-wheel bolster wagons or, later, on a bogie bolster wagon. These were flat-decked wagons fitted with transverse wooden baulks, or 'bolsters', on which the timber rested; it was held in position by vertical stanchions at each end of the bolsters, as well as by securing chains. Overhanging loads also required a 'runner' wagon under the overhang. Pit wood and pit props were tightly packed and roped in open wagons, in a variety of horizontal and vertical configurations, depending on their length. From the 1950s it became the practice to strap sawn timber together into packages suitable for handling by fork-lift truck.

Since the late 1970s most of the timber traffic carried by rail has been home-grown logs, notably from Scottish Highland plantations to the paper mills, and continental sawn timber and chipboard imported via train ferry.

See also TIMBER, USE OF. GAB

E. A. Pratt, *British Railways and the Great War* (1921); D. Cox and C. Krupa, *The Kerry Tramway and Other Timber Light Railways* (1992); R. Fitzgerald and J. Grenier, *Timber: A Centenary History of the Timber Trade Federation, 1892–1992* (1992), ch. 2.

time. The development of railways produced considerable changes in people's appreciation of time.

Hitherto their awareness of it had seldom been acute, or seemed at all important. The longest east–west journey between large English towns was from *London to *Plymouth: 220 miles, performed by the mail coaches in 22 hours. At Plymouth the traveller found that the local time was 20 minutes later than it was in London; but that was a trifling difference, easily adjusted.

As the national railway *system developed, however, time differentials soon became an impediment. The two trunk lines that ran almost directly from east to west, the *Great Western and *London & South Western, adopted Greenwich time for all purposes from their opening in 1838–41. It was also used by the companies that in 1841 formed the line from *Leeds to Rugby, where it joined the *London & Birmingham Railway, which observed local time. How were the movements of their respective trains to be synchronized precisely, as all railway working demanded?

Henry *Booth, secretary of the *Liverpool & Manchester Railway, advocated the adoption of Greenwich time by all railway companies. His own petitioned Parliament to impose it in 1845. That effort failed, but his arguments soon came to be accepted as unanswerable. They were indisputable when the electric *telegraph enabled time signals to be transmitted instantaneously. By 1852 Greenwich time was established everywhere along the railways from London to Plymouth, Holyhead, and *Glasgow.

The change made itself felt elsewhere too. In 1847 *Manchester Corporation ordered all clocks in the town to be set to Greenwich time, at the request of the *Lancashire & Yorkshire Railway. The number of public clocks now began to multiply. The railways themselves provided many of them, placed conspicuously above their *stations at *Norwich, Malvern, *Shrewsbury, and Scarborough, for instance; very notably in London, at *King's Cross and *St Pancras. Clock towers now came to be widely adopted as public monuments, standing in the streets of towns as dissimilar as *Leicester and Machynlleth.

This all served to express the importance of time as an element in ordinary life, inculcating *punctuality as a duty and a virtue. Businessmen were quickly referring to it in ordinary conversation, solely in figures, just as they were presented in the railways' timetables. 'There is a late train, 3.15; you will be there by 4.30': that is a Stalybridge mill-owner, speaking in Disraeli's novel *Coningsby* (1844).

Time thus came to be quietly forced into the minds of people living in Britain—a majority of them in towns by 1851. It should be noted too that 'Greenwich Time', correctly so called, came to be referred to in ordinary speech more loosely as 'Railway Time' or, when the railways' victory here was complete, 'London Time': a silent reminder of the increasing power of London.

British railways never adopted the 'continental' 24-hour system in their timetables ('1 p.m.' becoming '1300', and so on) until 1965, after *nationalization.   JS

D. Howse, *Greenwich Time* (1980); VR, 345–7; *Coningsby*, Book IV, ch. 2.

timetables. This word was invented by the railways, derived from 'tide tables', which had been compiled for use at ports since the 16th century. The mail-coaches' 'time bills' were something different: not a schedule but a device perfected by the *Post Office for checking the punctuality maintained by its coaches in running over each stage of their journeys. The *Liverpool & Manchester Railway advertised its trains in newspapers by means of a 'scheme of departures'. It was the *London & Birmingham that first produced something called a 'time table', in 1838.

Public Timetables

Every important railway company came to publish its own timetables, sold to the public for a penny or two before 1914. These usually contained more than the times of trains: lists of typical fares, and arrangements for conveying luggage; notices, setting out some of the conditions on which tickets were issued; and a wide range of miscellaneous advertisements.

Each of these related primarily to the services provided by one company. But by 1838 over 700 miles of railway were open to passengers in Great Britain, owned by some 40 companies, and one-third more miles again were under construction. An observant printer in Manchester, George *Bradshaw, then set himself to publish booklets containing timetables for all the railways in the country whose services

he was able to ascertain. In 1841 the information he had collected was brought together to form *Bradshaw's Monthly Railway Guide*, which soon became the national timetable for the British Isles, remaining so for 120 years.

The *Guide*'s success was immediate. Although rivals sprang up, only one maintained itself, and it had a more limited purpose: the *ABC Railway Guide*, first produced in 1853 and still appearing monthly today. It set out the services and fares between London and each station in the country, with departure and arrival times for the more important and, for the minor ones, the stations at which passengers had to change into connecting trains. *Bradshaw's Guide* had attempted to supply fares too, but never wholly successfully, and as pressure on its space increased, with the continuing growth of the system, it gradually gave up stating any fares at all.

However, the *ABC Guide* (well produced today, and easy to use) gives its best service only to those travelling to and from London. It offers much more limited help to anybody who wants to go, say, from Bristol to Edinburgh.

The companies still went on issuing their own timetables, side by side with *Bradshaw's Guide* and the *ABC*. They varied in quality and character, as a critical survey of a number of them in 1902 showed. In addition, local railway timetables soon came to be produced, giving the services into and out of one town or all those in a substantial district. At the head of them stands the publication familiarly known in *Glasgow as *Murray's Time Tables*, which continued under various titles from 1843 to 1966. These comprehended the railway services throughout Scotland. Elegantly produced (to a much higher standard than Bradshaw's), there is a long run of them in the Mitchell Library, Glasgow.

The *Grouping of the railways in 1923, to form (with minor exceptions) four large companies, necessarily called for the production of new public timetables. The *London Midland & Scottish and *London & North Eastern Railways did the job thoroughly, the LNER's being much the better designed. For the *Great Western it was an easier matter, since its long-distance services ran almost unchanged; all that now had to be done was to add those of the smaller companies it had absorbed. The *Southern Railway never designed a timetable of its own. It arranged with *Bradshaw's Guide* to print its services in the three sections into which the company divided itself, Western, Central, and Eastern. It then bound up sheets of them together to form its all-line timetable.

For more than half their history the *nationalized railways produced timetables that were a discreditable make-shift. Each region issued one; they were not even uniform in size. Further arrangements with Bradshaw changed the size of the old *Guide* and some of its typography, to meet the wishes of the new corporation. Then in 1961, the *Guide* itself ceased to be published, so that there was no single national railway timetable at all. The country's services had to be sought for in five or six separate volumes, imperfectly correlated. Perhaps no aspect of British Railways' *public relations was worse than this one, until at last that department under an able controller, Eric Merrill, took the task in hand, to produce a single-volume timetable, properly designed, for the whole system in 1974. That lasted, with only minor changes, until after *privatization.

Working Timetables

All the timetables mentioned so far showed passenger services only. The companies must have run their freight trains to some kind of schedule, but no timetable of them is known to survive that is older than a London & Birmingham one of 1846, at the *NRM. The earliest we have that show passenger and goods trains in one book date from 1852–4. These are what came to be known as 'working timetables' (on some railways 'service timetables'). They were not published, but printed for the companies' servants alone; and it was ordered, or at any rate generally understood, that each copy was to be destroyed as soon as it had been replaced by a later one. Not many of them are now in existence. However, sets were kept for reference at some companies' headquarters, and a number of these have passed into the national archives. Among the companies for which long runs of working timetables have survived in this way are the Great Western, *London & South Western, *Midland, and *North Eastern at the PRO, together with the *Great North of Scotland, the *Highland, and the *North British at the SRO (Edinburgh).

These timetables grew into substantial books. On the biggest railways they came to be issued in several volumes, one for each division of the system. Most of them came out two or three times a year.

At first they usually included permanent (or at least long-term) instructions for the working of trains: of speed restrictions, for example, at individual points or over some stretches of line continuously; of types of locomotive that might be prohibited from travelling over lines not strong enough to carry them; of arrangements made for the working of *single lines and for the running of *mixed trains. As their systems grew larger and more complicated, some companies took to removing their standard instructions from the timetables, to form pamphlets, or eventually stout volumes, on their own. These were known as the Appendixes to the Working Timetables. They should be consulted, if possible, by anybody who is trying to discover the amount of traffic any line carried and the special ways in which it was worked—which might, of course, affect the speed at which trains were permitted to run over it.

The earliest of these appendixes now in the national collections are of 1877 and 1879, for the NER, at the NRM and PRO respectively. The number surviving from the turn of the century onwards is larger, though nearly always in single copies, not in long continuous runs. The only complete set of them from any one company in Great Britain seems to be that of the Highland Railway at the SRO, from their first issue in 1897 to the end of the company's life in 1922.

But the schedules contained in the working timetables might have to be temporarily altered for unforeseen reasons: for example owing to a landslide or a flood; or to a serious accident on the line, which might close some or all of its tracks; or on account of heavy engineering works, like the reconstruction of a bridge. Warnings of these occurrences had to be given to the whole staff responsible for the operation of trains on the part of the line affected, and they would be set out in special notices. Since some of these comprised no more than one sheet and most related to individual arrangements lasting only a short time, not many sets of them are now to be found. The largest for any British company is that for the MR (1886–1922, NRM), but they relate solely to engineering works, not to more general arrangements or to the provision of extra trains. The full range of these is best gleaned from the series for the GNSR and NBR (1888–1922 and 1889–1922 respectively) at the SRO.

The notices have one special importance of their own. They reveal the greatest degree of flexibility in working that could be achieved by alteration of the timetables, communicated on paper in advance to every member of the staff directly concerned. The news of a sudden calamity, imperilling the safety of all trains (some of them actually on their way), would have to be transmitted from one *signal box to the next by *telegraph or *telephone, or a member of the staff would have to be sent out on foot to meet an oncoming train, bearing a flag.

So the working notices show us, more clearly than any other documents, the effects of special occurrences on regular practice. It is only by the use of all these timetables and appendixes and notices—what may perhaps be called for convenience 'the working literature'—that any general view can be formed of the actual operation of a railway. Here we see the whole traffic the railway carried: passengers, merchandise, minerals, mails, newspapers, together with all the movements of empty rolling stock that were required and of the locomotives that had to travel 'light', on their own, to the trains they were assigned to haul. A railway was a device for moving vehicles and their loads, of all kinds. In the working literature, and nowhere else, the full extent and complexity of those movements are revealed.

Two examples may be given of important matters that can be understood only by reference to the working timetables, both concerning freight operations.

From 1867 onwards the MR had difficulty in working its enormous coal traffic to London. It was all carried in slow, heavy trains on the same tracks as the expresses. From Nottinghamshire to Kettering an alternative line via Melton Mowbray was completed in 1880, relieving the pressure on the original main line; and a beginning had been made in 1874 with the provision of additional tracks between Kettering and London, primarily for freight trains. This work was extended, piecemeal and very slowly, completed throughout only in 1905.

What improvement in the handling of the traffic resulted from this protracted and expensive work? The working timetables help us to answer that question. In 1888, 28 mineral trains were scheduled to run on weekdays from Wellingborough (the central point on the route) to London. By 1912 that number had increased by nearly half, to 40, now being worked on segregated tracks clear of fast passenger trains, and thereby opening up the possibility of improving their time-keeping, too, which for long had been notoriously bad (see PUNCTUALITY).

The working timetables offer us a microscope to be applied to the running of every kind of freight train. The humblest of all, for example, the 'pick-up goods', stopped at each station on its way, to deliver and collect consignments. At what speed did it move? Samples taken from three companies, the LSWR, MR, and NER, show that up to 1922 such trains usually ran at between 3½ and 8 mph, including stops: taking a whole long day, for instance, to cover the 50 miles from Leicester to Bedford. Even at that leisurely pace, they were going twice as fast as any corresponding service had ever done, hauled by horses. But when motor goods vehicles grew numerous after 1922, nimbler and more flexible, it was another matter, and the traffic steadily passed away to them.

To set out and explain the successive changes that have been introduced into the working timetables from the 1970s with the progress of *computerization, and to explain how to use them, would require space disproportionately large within the scope of this book. Sets of these timetables in their new form can be found at the PRO and SRO.

A final word about the use of timetables for the study of railway history. It must be re-emphasized that none of them is, or could ever be, more than a set of directions issued to the staff for the working of the traffic, and to passengers for enabling them to know what facilities the railways offered them. They are a record of intention, not performance, and they must always be treated as such.

See also TIME.   JS

R. E. Charlewood, 'The Public Timetable Books of Our Chief Railways', RM, 17 (1902), 335–42; J. House, The Romance of Murray (1952); ET, 194–212; J. V. Gough, The Midland Railway: A Chronology (1989).

Tite, Sir William (1798–1873), architect. A pupil of David Laing, before he was 30 Tite established himself by winning two competitions in one year: for Regent Square Presbyterian church, London, and Mill Hill school, after which he developed one of the first of the very large Victorian architectural practices. Inheriting and marrying into money, he invested profitably, e.g. in the *Great Western Railway, for which he bought its first office in London. He was chairman of the *Eastern Counties Railway's provisional committee and purchased land for it and for the *London & Blackwall, whose terminus he designed. Until 1871 Tite was architect and surveyor for the *London & South Western Railway, designing most of its stations including Nine Elms, Southampton, and Windsor. There he began an association with the engineer *Locke and the contractor *Brassey, with whom he worked on the *Lancaster & Carlisle, *Caledonian, and *Scottish Central Railways, and the lines between Paris and Le Havre, designing all the stations. Many of his stations were built in collaboration with Edward N. Clifton. He built the new entrance block for the 1846 enlargement of *Liverpool Lime Street.

Forceful in manner, Tite had many commercial interests. He was director of two banks, and as MP for Bath in 1855–73 was a hard-working member of Commons committees. Not above taking improper advantage, he survived questions about his commission for rebuilding London's Royal Exchange (1844)—his best-known work—and suggestions concerning the *London Tilbury & Southend Railway in 1863, to be knighted in 1869. Twice president of the RIBA, he was respected as an archaeologist and antiquarian. He died childless, leaving a large fine art collection, a valuable library of rare books and manuscripts, and the considerable sum of £400,000.   GJB

'Memoir', Proc. RIBA (1873–4), 209–12; M. S. Briggs, 'Sir William Tite, M.P.: His Life and Work', The Builder (13 & 20 Jan. 1950), 39–42, 95–8; H. M. Colvin, Biographical Dictionary of British Architects, 1600–1840 (1978).

token working, see SINGLE LINES, WORKING OF.

Tomlinson, William Weaver (1858–1916), writer. Son of a secretary of the Hull & Selby Railway (see LEEDS & SELBY RAILWAY), Tomlinson joined the accountant's office of the *North Eastern Railway at *Newcastle in 1873, in which he served for the rest of his life.

Northumberland was then new to him, and he entered with zest into studying its history and topography. His admirable Comprehensive Guide to Northumberland (1888) was the result. He began work on a history of the NER about 1900, the first experienced local historian ever to write such a book in Britain. It was published in 1914. He died less than two years later.

The North Eastern Railway: Its Rise and Development offers a detailed account of all the lines forming the company down to 1879, followed by a brief sketch of its history in 1880–1904: a shortening that appears to have been due partly to Tomlinson's declining health. But this imbalance is the book's only fault. It is accurate, well written and documented (references for its statements are meticulously supplied), proper attention being paid to both passenger and freight business, to the company's financial performance, and its management. The book is illustrated liberally and thoughtfully, and it carries a good index. It retains a high place in the historiography of British railways.   JS

North Eastern Railway Magazine (Jan. 1917), 19; Archaeologia Eliana, 3rd ser., 14 (1917), 133–43.

ton-miles, see STATISTICS; COSTING TECHNIQUES.

TOPS: an acronym derived from Total Operations Processing System, a *computerized freight information system implemented by *BR between 1971 and 1975.

TOPS was introduced to improve the efficiency of the wagonload *freight business, in particular by increasing utilization of rolling stock and terminals to match traffic demand, and to provide reliable information on transits to customers. Previously, details of train loads, and rolling stock requirements for traffic flows, were sent by railway *telegraph, usually in code, later supplemented by *telephone advice via the *control offices. In the late 1950s, BR Eastern Region uniquely made use of teleprinters, telex, and radio for advance traffic information between *marshalling yards.

The computerized database for TOPS was originally developed for the Southern Pacific Railroad in the USA, and was maintained by continuous updating, from principal locations on the railway network, of information relating to the status of individual wagons in the fleet. A modern internal telecommunications network was an essential provision of the scheme as implemented by BR, and this links the terminals around the system with the main computer at the BR headquarters in London. In time, TOPS has been extended to cover the control and movements of locomotive and coaching stock, and maintenance planning, and remains in use.   MLH

R. T. Munns, *Milk Churns to Merry-Go-Round* (1986).

tourism. The railways of Britain played a central role in converting tourism from an élite experience which had been enjoyed only by the monied few, into a mass phenomenon in which all classes and sections of society participated. And their coming opened up localities formerly out of reach except to the very intrepid; the Scottish Highlands, the resorts of Devon and Cornwall, the Yorkshire Dales, and the Lake District. By the end of the 19th century, travel for pleasure and for leisure, by either regular or special services, was an integral part of railway business, especially during the summer months which saw sportsmen travelling north, families heading for the seaside, works *excursions, innumerable Sunday school outings, and other specials (see HOLIDAY-MAKING).

The roots of tourism lie partly in the search for health at spas, or through sea-bathing, but also in the growing fashion of the later 18th century for the picturesque, which led increasing numbers of travellers to undertake coach tours to look at scenery, ruins, and remote places. The closure of the Continent by revolution and war further encouraged an interest in Britain as a tourist destination. The coming of the steamship was very significant for some areas; by the 1830s there was a substantial sea-borne traffic from the Clyde to Staffa and Iona, from *Bristol to North Devon, and from *London to Kentish and East Anglian resorts. But important though the improvement of river and coastal transport had been (see SHIPPING, COASTAL), the railways were totally to change the scale and scope of tourism in Britain, in terms of both where people came from and where they went.

Right from the earliest days, the railway companies were able to tap into the growing thirst for travel amongst an ever-widening market. The *Liverpool & Manchester, for example, was alert to the possibilities that cheap *fares might allow: its first excursion train in May 1831 was a Sunday school trip, which was charged at one-third the normal fare. The Garnkirk & Glasgow Railway organized 'Railway Pleasure Trips' during the summer months: their handbills assured customers that 'Genteel Parties will find the trip an agreeable and healthful mode of spending part of the day'. The emphasis is an interesting one, and not untypical; the pleasure of the excursion lay as much in the trip itself and the sights along the line, as in destination. In the next decade came the concept of the 'monster' excursion: the *Man-

chester & Leeds Railway ran an 82-carriage (four-wheelers) excursion from Hebden Bridge in 1844, and it was by no means the largest. Demand appeared insatiable; it was reported of one *temperance excursion from *Glasgow to Ayr that even despite the hasty provision of extra coaches, on some carriages passengers 'were clustering outside like bees'.

From these early ventures was to spring what has been argued to be one of the distinctive features of the British railway experience: the strength of the excursion system for which there was no continental parallel. There is, unfortunately, no way of establishing how much this traffic grew, though there are occasional statistics: the *Midland Railway carried nearly 400,000 excursionists in 1865, an average of 700 passengers per train. But not all tourists were excursionists: many (and their families, servants, and luggage) travelled by the standard services during the summer when many lines found their traffic considerably augmented. Indeed, the possibilities of the pleasure traffic were much stressed by railway promoters.

The promotion of travel for pleasure became an important element in railway practice. The railway companies themselves did much to publicize resorts through advertising campaigns, *posters (Merrie Morecambe, Health-making Herne Bay, and the like), and *guidebooks. Many had their own *hotels, made complete in Scotland by an attached golf course. The best of these made money, as did Gleneagles and Turnberry; others did not. The 1891 edition of Baddeley's *Thorough Guide to the English Lake District* gives a representative sample of railway advertising. All the principal companies are present: the Midland stressing itself as 'The Tourist Route to Scotland' and also offering to convey picnic, pleasure, and school parties at reduced rates. It announced that there would be a full programme of excursion trains from all the principal towns within its system, the details of which would be announced 14 days prior to the trains being run. That two weeks' notice was deemed sufficient is an interesting comment. The *Cambrian Railways were promoting tours in Wales, for bathing, boating, fishing, coaching, and mountaineering. The *Great Western offered tourist tickets to *Exeter, Penzance, and other resorts, tickets which were valid for two months—the length of stay at the seaside that a better-off family might expect. The *Caledonian advertised over 100 tours in Scotland, and stressed the plethora of steamer connections for Arran, Bute, and the other islands of the Clyde.

Some tours involved a combination of rail, coach, and steamer services: the *North British Railway's popular tour from *Edinburgh to the Trossachs went by rail to Aberfoyle, coach to Loch Katrine, boat to Stronachlachar, coach to Inversnaid, boat again on Loch Lomond to Balloch, and then finally back by rail via Dumbarton. But the advent of the touring motor car was to leach much of the first-class tourist traffic away from the railways, even before World War I: by then no superior hotel's facilities were complete without a garage and inspection pit.

Railways did much to promote their services, but there were also *travel agents in whose hands much of the excursion business was. Though other factors were at work, such as the rise in incomes and growing opportunities for time off in the artisan and working classes, the railways had much to do with the growth of tourism in Victorian Britain. Though they were seldom actively involved in the actual development of resorts, with the exception of Saltburn, Skegness, and a few others, their speed of service and cost of travel opened up localities previously too remote for tourists to reach in any number. The coming of the railway in 1845 to south Devon reduced the time of travel from London to Exeter from 16½ hours by the fastest coach to 4½, and the cost by more than half, to the great benefit of resorts such as Dawlish and Teignmouth. But the railway was not always welcomed when it started to bring in working-class day-trippers and excursionists, who were not all as well-behaved as Thomas *Cook's clientele seem to have been. In 1846 Wordsworth expressed his concern about the projected Kendal & Windermere Railway, which certainly did increase the numbers of visitors tenfold. What did not improve his temper is that he himself was gaped at as a tourist attraction.

> Hear YE that whistle? As her long-linked Train
> Swept onwards, did the vision cross your view?
> Yes, ye were startled;—and, in balance true
> Weighing the mischief with the promised gain
> Mountains, and Vales and Floods, I call on you
> To share the passion of a just disdain.

From the railways' viewpoint, the most serious problem of the tourist trade was always its seasonality, with too much of the business concentrated in the summer months. At peak periods every piece of rolling stock that could run had to be pressed into action. But for much of the rest of the year, the holiday lines were light in traffic, the extra sidings for excursion traffic unused.

In the inter-war years the railways did try to encourage an 'early holidays movement', but to little result. Nevertheless, traffic held up and even grew. Between the late 1920s and 1930s the volume of holiday traffic on the railways trebled, and the companies were forced to make additional provision at the more popular resorts. But there was the increasing competition of the coach and the rise in private car ownership. The railways did respond in a variety of ways: new 'Tourist Trains' and camping coaches. The *London Midland & Scottish Railway, in partnership with Thomas Cook, opened a holiday camp at Prestatyn in 1939.

After the 1950s the picture was one of steady decline as patterns of tourism changed; more and more Britons were taking at least one annual holiday away from home, but their attention was increasingly focused, thanks to the charter flight and the package holiday, on destinations such as Spain, where the sun was guaranteed. Some resorts suffered more than others, but the railways were squeezed on both sides: less tourism within Britain, and fewer by rail. The outcome was inevitable. When the *Beeching axe came, some very well-known tourist lines closed. Who would have conceived of a resort like St Andrews losing its service in 1965? By the mid-1960s through tourist services were virtually extinct: the once-popular Lakes Express from London

*Euston was just one of the many casualties of the decade. Very little now remains of the tourist traffic, as the rusting or lifted sidings at Scarborough attest. There is some increase of traffic in the summer, a few steam-hauled specials, and a luxury train or two, like The Royal Highlander, but little otherwise to remind us of what a large part tourism once played in the life of many British railways.   AJD

VR; D. N. Smith, *The Railway and Its Passengers: A Social History* (1988); J. Walton, *The English Seaside Resort: A Social History 1750–1914* (1983); J. Walvin, *Beside the Seaside* (1978).

Towle, Sir William (1849–1929), and **Arthur** (1878–1949), hotels and catering managers. The Towle family became one of the best-known names in the British *hotel industry. At the age of 15 William joined the staff of the Midland Hotel, *Derby (near his birthplace) and in 1871, aged 22, became its manager, including the station *refreshment rooms. His introduction of refreshment baskets for travellers in 1875 was copied by other railways. In 1884 he became manager of the Midland Grand Hotel at *St Pancras, and a year later was given control of all the *Midland Railway's hotels. His energetic, innovative approach earned him and his company a high reputation. He had virtually a free hand in planning the new Midland Hotel, *Manchester (1903), and the Adelphi, *Liverpool (1914), after visiting America to gain ideas. Towle strongly advocated central control as the only way to ensure consistently high standards.

After retirement in 1914, he was succeeded by his sons Francis and Arthur jointly, and in 1920 he was knighted. Francis moved to Frederick Hotels in 1921, and Arthur became sole manager. In 1925 he was appointed hotel and catering controller of the *London Midland & Scottish Railway, the largest hotel group in Europe, and supervised the planning of the new Midland Hotel, Morecambe, and the Queens, *Leeds. He retired in 1945.   GJB

N. Wooler, *Dinner in the Diner: The History of Railway Catering* (1987); O. Carter, *British Railway Hotels, 1838–1983* (1990).

towns, railways and the development of. Some of the services rendered by railways to 40 individual towns are the subject of separate articles. Here they are considered collectively.

Apart from *Crewe, railways did not actually *found* any town of importance entirely by their own efforts, though they were closely involved from the outset in the establishment of *Middlesbrough, Fleetwood, and *Barrow-in-Furness; and Redhill (Surrey) would never have existed had it not been a railway junction (see TOWNS AND VILLAGES, RAILWAY-CREATED). But they added large quarters of their own to existing settlements, containing *engine sheds and *works. Within great cities, or on their edges, there grew distinctive railway districts: in *London, for instance, at Nine Elms, Willesden, and Stratford; in *Liverpool, Edge Hill; in *Manchester, Gorton; in *Glasgow, Cowlairs. None of these developments added directly to urban amenities. Far from it: the smoke and dirt generated by them befouled the atmosphere (see POLLUTION), and only the very poor, who could not afford to move, would live in these districts. There the railways were helping to create slums, or at least to extend them: as, very plainly, in the Ancoats district of Manchester and in Saltley, east of the centre of *Birmingham.

It has often been supposed that railways were the cause of large increases in the population of towns. That statement needs to be reconsidered, critically. Indeed, judged by one fair test, it turns out to be the opposite of the truth (see POPULATION, CHANGES IN). Nevertheless, railways were clearly responsible for substantial growth in some places, where they established works in them.

They helped to increase the population of many other industrial towns too, by facilitating the migration into them of very poor agricultural workers, anxious to secure better-paid employment in factories, or with the railway companies themselves. In the past this movement had been undertaken on foot or in carts or carriages; almost never by *canals, even though they had played a vital part in the towns' industrial development. But railwaymen and their families formed a clearly recognizable element in the expanding population of large towns.

In smaller towns, without any large industries, the story might be different. In 1801 Bath, with 33,000 people, stood about 14th in population among all the towns of Great Britain, and it still grew for a time, though much more slowly than the industrial towns of the Midlands and the north. When the railway arrived there in 1841 the figure was 53,000, and growth then entirely stopped; in 1911 the population was 2,000 less. A stranger case was that of Macclesfield, a town given up largely to silk-making, which attained its highest population (39,000) in 1851, just after the railway reached it, and was down to 34,000 in 1911. Both these towns stood on main lines, not on branches. But Bath had strong rivals to contend with in its old-established business as a spa, like Cheltenham, Buxton, and Harrogate; and Macclesfield lost out through the emigration of many of its silk-workers to the USA.

There were some little towns that railways never reached. The largest in England that were more than three miles from a station were Painswick (Gloucestershire), Kingsclere (Hampshire), and Ambleside (Cumbria), all with populations of about 2,500 in 1911. Seven attempts to secure a railway to Painswick were made in 1866–1901, but none succeeded. The business these places had to offer never appeared to justify the necessary expenditure. But they all went on, not unprosperously, until in the 20th century they began to be served by motor *buses.

Railways made very little contribution to the adornment or improvement of towns in any physical sense. Nowhere in Britain were large, handsome squares laid out in front of stations, as in many continental towns (though of course nearly all have now been turned into car parks). Only a few of the greatest British *stations presented a really striking front to the world, to become one of the town's chief monuments, like many of those in the USA. Liverpool (Lime Street) strove to do that, *Newcastle Central, Huddersfield, and *Stoke-on-Trent; in London, *Euston (until it began to be seriously marred in the 1870s), *King's Cross and *St Pancras, *Charing Cross and *Cannon Street (see ARCHI-

TECTURE). Some of these very important stations had no frontage whatever. In London for a third of a century the two at Victoria remained entirely hidden behind hoardings of advertisements. Manchester (Central) never received a façade of any kind.

But if railways added little to the beauty of the towns they served, they did a great deal to increase the comfort of living and working in them. They could almost guarantee regular and unfailing supplies of the commodities most needed in daily life (coal above all), and their passenger services were as a rule dependable (see PUNCTUALITY). In the big cities they provided many lines of communication crossing or skirting their central districts: outstandingly in London, Liverpool, and Glasgow. As London and Glasgow streets grew more crowded, the steady pace of the *underground railways rendered them much preferable; and when they were electrified, from 1890 onwards, their merits shone out more brightly still.

The facilities offered by the railways helped to change the character of towns as places of work. Great numbers of people had walked in and out daily, and some continued to do so well beyond the end of the 19th century. But by that time most workers used some kind of public transport.

The practice of *commuting—making regular journeys from *suburbs into the city centres several days in the week—was common even before railways arrived. By 1850 middle-class workers were travelling into London by train from Blackheath, Croydon, Watford, Hertford, and Brentwood; they were even making the 50-mile journey from *Brighton. New suburbs were then appearing also in *Bristol, Liverpool, Manchester, and *Leeds, with similarly easy access. The range of this kind of travel steadily extended. By 1914 such journeys were being made to London from *Bournemouth, Bristol, *Nottingham, and *Norwich; from Windermere to Manchester; from Morecambe to Leeds and *Bradford. The high-speed trains of the 1970s–1990s greatly extended these distances.

These were facilities for wealthy businessmen. But *workmen's trains, at specially low fares, were provided into London from the 1860s onwards, traversing distances of 15 miles and more, and into Liverpool and Manchester. So the work-force within the great towns, whether of company chairmen or labourers, reached them from many districts beyond their boundaries.

To put all this discussion into its right perspective, one comparative statement of fact must be borne in mind. In the second half of the 19th century the percentage of people in Great Britain living in towns with a population of 20,000 and more was substantially higher than in any other country in the world (Australia and the USA included). There was no dissent from the judgement made in 1899 by the American economist A. F. Weber that this concentration was due chiefly to railways. In the 20th century the same process has continued everywhere, but the strongest influence behind it has been mechanized *road transport.   JS

J. R. Kellett, *Impact of Railways on Victorian Cities* (1969); *LLR*; *RTC*; A. F. Weber, *Growth of Cities in the 19th Century* (1963 edn.), 142–54; *RTC*.

towns and villages, railway-created. Of the towns built by railways to accommodate employees at their *works, only two were on virgin sites: *Crewe, which before 1843 had only a few scattered dwellings; and Melton Constable, Norfolk, where there was even less before the Lynn & Fakenham Railway built workshops in 1882, and it subsequently developed as the *Midland & Great Northern Railway's headquarters. Although it called itself a town Melton was really no more than a works village.

The first 'railway town' in the broader sense was Shildon, where in the early 1830s the *Stockton & Darlington Railway established its works next to a small village. The *London & Birmingham did likewise at Wolverton, where it laid out a town which by 1906 housed 7,000 people. So did the *Great Western in 1841, close to the market town of *Swindon, and later in that decade the *Furness Railway developed a small hamlet into *Barrow-in-Furness. The *South Eastern Railway transferred its works to Ashford in 1847, built a 'New Town' next to the old one, and began the growth of today's town. In 1884–6 the *Lancashire & Yorkshire transformed the small textile town of Horwich when it moved its works there, tripling the population within five years. The same happened at the village of Bishopstoke, to which the *London & South Western moved its works in 1891. Renamed Eastleigh, it was a town of 15,200 by 1904.

Some established regional centres were chosen for railway works. Before railways began to transform them, *Derby was a county town, and Darlington had markets and industries. Gateshead (SEE NEWCASTLE), too, was an ancient place, on to which a railway works was grafted and then greatly enlarged by the *North Eastern company in 1852–4.

At other historic towns distinct railway communities sprang up, among them *Peterborough, *Carlisle, Boston, *Doncaster, and, above all, *York, which like Derby, housed a major company's headquarters, creating a wide social structure.

Many large cities had substantial railway enclaves: Willesden, Cricklewood, Nine Elms, and Stratford in *London; Springburn in *Glasgow; and Gorton in *Manchester. The last two grew around both company and private locomotive builders' works. Smaller ones were established for works at quiet towns like Oswestry and Inverurie, while the *London & North Western built a colony of 340 houses for its wagon works by the ancient borough of Newton-le-Willows, Lancashire, and named it Earlestown, after a director.

Villages where junctions were located might evolve into small towns, like Bletchley, Didcot, Redhill, Normanton, and Carnforth, sometimes attracting other industries in turn. Others remained villages with distinctive urban-like appendages. When the *Great Central Railway constructed a major junction at Woodford Halse, the stone Northamptonshire village was transformed by 170 red brick houses, shops, and a gas works.

At other locations, new 'railway villages' were built close to an existing settlement, as happened at Tebay and Hellifield, or perhaps some distance away but taking its name.

Carstairs Junction is a mile from the old village, and Halwill Junction the same distance from Beaworthy, whose name the station originally bore. Other junctions produced villages where none previously existed, taking the station name, like Builth Road, Llandudno Junction, Seaton Junction, and Craven Arms (itself named after an inn which was the sole establishment before the railway). Horbury Junction also became known for Charles Roberts' wagon *works. Often the name 'Junction' remained long after the station closed, as at Horbury and Seaton, while at Halwill Junction the entire railway has gone.

Railway villages solely comprising a company's own *houses for employees were fewer, usually at remote locations such as Battersby, Garsdale, and Riccarton Junction. The last had no road, requiring everything and everybody to be taken by rail, including the doctor. The *North British Railway provided gas, a school, and a recreation room, and there was a shop and post office on the station. After the line closed in 1969, the place was razed.

See also TOWNS, RAILWAYS AND THE DEVELOPMENT OF.   GJB
RTC, ch. 6; RS, ch. 6; P. S. Richards, 'The Influence of Railways in the Growth of Wolverton', Record of Bucks, 17 (1976); B. J. Turton, 'The Railway Towns of Southern England', Transport History, 2, 2 (July 1969); G. Turner, Ashford, the Coming of the Railway (1984); B. Lingham, The Railway Comes to Didcot (1992); J. Cattell & K. Falconer, Swindon: The Legacy of a Railway Town (1995); W. H. Chaloner, The Social and Economic Development of Crewe (1950).

track: an assembly of rails and sleepers, generally resting on and contained by ballast.

Rails

By 1826 plate rails (SEE EARLY IRON RAILWAYS), often supported continuously on longitudinal timber 'waybeams', typical of early *tramroads, had largely given way to 'edge rails', mostly of cast iron, typically fish-bellied, of inverted-tee-shaped design and about 5 ft long. Between 1826 and about 1860 as the main-line railway system developed, rails in Britain evolved into, firstly wrought iron, and then steel rails, of two main types: bull-head and bridge rails.

The change from cast to wrought iron made possible the manufacture of rail in much longer pieces (albeit initially only about 15 ft). With increased length the rails could no longer be supported at their ends only, and this led to the abandonment of the fish-bellied profile, in favour of the constant cross-section now taken for granted. At the supports the rails were wedged by wooden (latterly steel) 'keys' into 'chairs' carried on sleepers, which were initially stone blocks, and later wooden beams laid transversely.

The actual cross-section used for the rail gradually became more I-shaped than tee-shaped. By about 1830 it was realized that by making its foot very broad, and with a flat underside, the rail could be sufficiently stable to sit on a sleeper without being wedged upright. This flat-bottomed (FB) rail section came into widespread use except in Britain and in areas influenced by British engineers. The names of R. L. Simpson in the USA and C. B. *Vignoles in Europe are associated with the development of FB rail.

Whilst eliminating the chair cheapened and simplified track construction, the contact area on the sleeper was reduced, so that FB rails tended to cut into the tops of the sleepers. Spikes were used to hold the rail in position, and these did not restrain the rail against longitudinal movement (creep) as well as the keys used in the chairs. For these reasons British engineers preferred rails with chairs, and about 1835, *Locke developed a rail for use in chairs in which the head and foot were the same size. The idea was that when the head wore down, the rail could be inverted, so doubling rail life. This concept was a failure, and by the late 1840s was replaced by a rail in which the head and foot were the same width, but the head was much deeper. This was called bull-headed (BH) rail.

Other alternatives were tried. *Brunel, on the *Great Western Railway, developed the 18th-century principle of the plate rail into 'bridge rail', screwed down to longitudinal sleepers and held to correct *gauge by transoms. W. H. *Barlow designed a very short-lived modification of this with its bottom flange converted into prongs to hold the rail in place in ballast without needing timbers. A somewhat similar rail, bolted to a triangular piece of timber, formed the 'Seaton' rail. MacDonnell plates were a longitudinal rolled iron plate supporting a bridge rail and, like the Barlow rail, intended to eliminate the longitudinal sleeper.

None of these ideas found favour on standard-gauge railways, and BH became nearly universal throughout Britain until after World War II, although there are records that FB rail was occasionally used experimentally, e.g. on the GWR in place of bridge rail. Bridge rails continued in use on that line until after the gauge conversion in 1892.

Wrought-iron rails weighed 35 to 50 lb per yd, and being relatively soft had a very short life. Mass production of cheap steel (see IRON AND STEEL, USE OF), with its superior hardness and strength, extended rail life from a few months to around 16 years. The first recorded use of steel rails was in 1857 on the *Midland Railway at *Derby, and their use rapidly became universal, increasing in weight from 60 to 103 lb per yd by around 1910, and in length to 60 ft.

Apart from the impracticality of making long rails, it was long considered essential to provide joints to permit expansion. Rail joints consist of two bars (fishplates) placed in the webs to link the two rails together, with up to three bolts passing through both fishplates and rails on either side of the joint. As traffic and speed increased, damaged and even broken rail-ends and fishplates became a problem and much effort went into improving joint design. Finally, the possibility of welding was examined. It became clear by the 1920s that even the heaviest BH rails were no longer adequate, and British engineers re-examined American and European experience, where FB rail had been standard for a century. These developments were halted by World War II, although *London Underground standardized on welded BH rail in 1939.

After the war, rail welding development was resumed. It was found that buckling under thermal compression in hot weather could be prevented by pretensioning the rails, with fastenings capable of both longitudinal and torsional restraint, heavier and more closely spaced sleepers, and more

Types of rail section

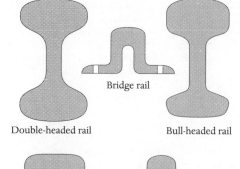

Bridge rail

Double-headed rail   Bull-headed rail

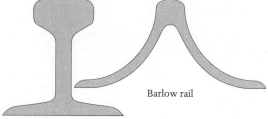

Barlow rail

Flat-bottomed (Vignoles) rail

Components of modern flat-bottom continuously-welded track

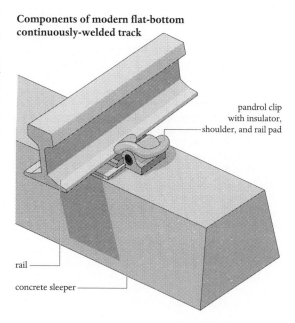

pandrol clip
with insulator,
shoulder, and rail pad

rail

concrete sleeper

and better ballast. New FB rail sections were designed to meet these conditions, weighing up to 113 lb per yd. Simultaneous development of sleepers and fastenings allowed continuous welded rail (CWR) track to become standard for all new main-line relaying in 1965.

Rail development culminated around 1970 in the British Standard 113A (113 lb per yd) rail section, replacing BS 110, from which it differs in its thicker web, which reduces fatigue at joints. Consideration has since been given to using even heavier rail, following European practice, but the change has not yet been found economically justifiable. Modernization of the manufacturing processes since 1950 has much improved the strength, wear resistance, and freedom from internal defects of rails. Rail is now supplied in 120-ft lengths, and wear-resistant steels can be made by altering the proportions of *alloying elements, and by various types of heat treatment.

One of the features leading to the success of CWR track was the development of efficient fastenings for FB rails. By the 1930s, when British engineers were looking anew at FB rail, the unsatisfactory traditional fastening was already superseded elsewhere by spring steel spikes and baseplates. Many millions of these were installed up to about 1965. It was realized, however, that if the securing of the FB rail to the baseplate, and of the baseplate to the sleeper, were separated, as with BH rail, performance would be improved.

A fully creep- and torsion-resistant fastening which would secure the rail directly to a *concrete sleeper was also needed. All these requirements were met by the Pandrol clip and its accessories, which became standard on *BR in the mid-1960s.

Sleeper

This is any beam-like member acting as intermediary between rail and ballast. The earliest sleepers developed from the timber rails laid longitudinally to form early wagonways (see WOODEN RAILWAYS). When iron rails were introduced, stone blocks could be used to support the chairs which held the rail-ends. In both these cases transoms or tie-bars were required to ensure correct track gauge. Stone blocks were normal until the 1830s, when they began to be replaced by transverse timbers (cross-sleepers) which hold the rails together as well as distributing the loads from the rails over the ballast surface. Cross-sleepers are the commonest form of rail support, and are currently manufactured from timber, steel, concrete, and even (but not in Britain) plastics.

Most sleeper timber is imported: softwoods such as Scots pine from Scandinavia, or Douglas fir from Canada, and latterly hardwoods, such as jarrah from Australia (see also TIMBER, USE OF). Softwood sleepers are mostly impregnated under pressure with creosote, and some railway companies had their own impregnation plants (see also KYANIZING). The best preserved softwood sleepers last about 20 years, depending upon the amount of traffic and the environment. Whilst jarrah is certainly durable, it is expensive and reserves are limited. Thus there has always been an incentive to find alternatives to timber.

Iron sleepers are recorded very early in railway history (the use of Barlow rail and MacDonnell plates has already been noted), and steel sleeper manufacture started around 1860. As steel is a good electrical conductor, the rails must be well insulated for *track circuiting. For this and other reasons, steel sleepers have been little used on BR.

During World War II, shortage of imported timber impelled experiments with prestressed, pretensioned concrete 'monobloc' sleepers, but their weight, and the tendency of early designs to crack under rail-joints, made them unpopular until most of the rail-joints were eliminated by welding, when weight became an advantage. Production rose to over 1 million per year by 1965, and continued at about that rate for over 25 years, whilst the use of softwood sleepers fell almost to nothing. Concrete monobloc sleepers continue to be standard, although production has substantially declined because of economic restrictions on relaying, the effect of rationalization, and because they last longer than softwood.

After many years of virtual oblivion, the ancient principle of individual blocks under each rail, tied together with a steel transom, in the form of twin-block concrete sleepers, re-emerged in France in the early years of the 20th century. These have been popular and successful there ever since, and were specified for the Cheriton terminal of the *Channel Tunnel. Consequently, manufacturing facilities are now available in Britain, where they are slowly coming into use.

Longitudinal sleepers, termed 'wheel timbers', 'waybeams', or 'rail bearers', are still occasionally used on bridges, either to save weight or to minimize constructional depth.

Ballast

This supports and restrains the sleepers, assists drainage, and distributes traffic loads over the underlying ground. Lack of proper appreciation of these functions led to inadequate quantities of cheap and readily available but sometimes unsuitable material such as ash or gravel being used, subsequently creating problems and expense in maintaining acceptable standards of track geometry.

Present-day track ballast is high-strength crushed igneous or at least metamorphic rock with good abrasion resistance in wet conditions. Since its useful life is limited, there is a continuing need to obtain around 3 million tons of fresh ballast per year, and to dispose of a similar quantity of spent material, tasks which present environmental challenges. Some ballast stone is nowadays even being imported from overseas (see STONE, USE OF).

Non-ballasted track

Occasionally the sleepers are replaced or surrounded by a continuous slab of concrete, either because of subgrade problems, shallow construction depth, or because of very small *clearances. The *London Underground tube railways used concreted-in timber cross-sleepers for this last reason. The need for a maintenance-free trackform in tunnels and on Metro and *Light Rapid Transit-type railways has led since the 1960s to the development of various other types of concrete slab track. BR developed paved concrete track (PACT), where the rails are fastened directly to the slab, and on the *Docklands Light Railway the rails are carried on baseplates bolted to the trackform slab.

Train speed on curves

The speed at which a train can be allowed to traverse a curve depends on the radius of the curve and the applied *superelevation ('cant'). A sinuous track layout which was acceptable for the low speeds of, say, 1840 has become less so over the years, even though allowable cants and unbalanced centrifugal force have increased as *suspension design has improved. In many cases speed increases have been achieved by re-aligning track, thus increasing radius, and extending transition curves within the confines of the original earthworks, but sometimes widenings have been necessary. There are examples of this on the *East Coast main line, such as a slew of 34 ft at Offord. In really difficult terrain, however, such as the *West Coast main line through the Lake District, the inherited alignment now restricts further improvement.

Points and crossings

In *junctions trains are diverted from one track to another by a 'turnout', comprising a pair or set of points (or 'switches') which perform the diverting function, and a crossing to enable one line of rails to cross another. A 'diamond', where two tracks cross, contains four 'crossings' of two different types. The term 'points' is often extended to mean the whole turnout, whilst the term 'crossing' is often used to denote a diamond. In Britain, points and crossings were traditionally made from currently used plain-line rail, suitably machined. In the 1970s the special 'shallow-depth' rail used throughout Europe to make the tapered movable 'switch rails' was tried out, and is now coming increasingly into use. Metallurgical research has enabled various types of steel casting to replace machined rails in crossings.

The turnout radius, and hence its allowable speed, is limited by the length of the rail available to make the switch. In 1840 manufacture of switch rails with a taper longer than about 10 ft was impracticable. By contrast, 32-ft long switches were available to the GWR by 1939, the length of the tapered tongue being 17 ft 3 in. These were coupled

Points open to main line

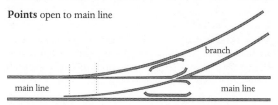

main line / branch / main line

A diamond crossing

C=check rail

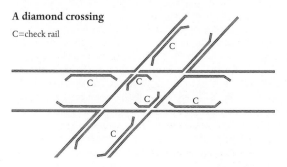

with a 1-in-20 crossing to give a turnout speed of about 50 mph. The most modern switches are up to 91 ft long with a 57 ft 5 in taper suitable for speeds up to 125 mph.

Track maintenance and renewal

For many years, all work was done manually. About the turn of the century, jacks replaced levers for lifting, and simple methods of calculating the amounts by which the track needed to be lifted or slewed were introduced, but significant mechanization only began with the introduction of twin-jib track-relaying cranes in the 1940s. These were followed by automatic on-track ballast cleaners, single-line track-relaying gantries, rail changers for CWR re-railing, ballast regulators, etc., many of which had to be imported from Switzerland and Austria. More recently, relaying geometry has been improved by laser control of ballast-handling plant.

Automatic track lifting and re-aligning machines (also mostly Austrian), introduced in the 1960s, brought unprecedented changes in track maintenance. Small local gangs maintaining a few miles of track have been replaced by larger gangs transported, with their equipment, by road over distances of 25 miles or more. This concentration of resources, together with the Offices, Shops and Railway Premises Act, 1963, required depot and booking-on points to be provided. For the first time in railway history, trackmen had proper washing and toilet facilities, whilst mess facilities in the road vehicles replaced the old lineside cabins.

Simultaneously, management became more sophisticated, and is now assisted by surveillance equipment such as track geometry recording and ultrasonic rail-testing cars, while record-keeping, forward planning, and trend-detection are computerized.

Overall, therefore, track is now constructed, maintained, and renewed to a higher technical standard, and more cost-effectively, than ever before.

See also TRACK GAUGE; IRON AND STEEL INDUSTRY; NARROW-GAUGE RAILWAYS; PLATELAYERS. GHC

H. J. P. Taylor, 'The Railway Sleeper—Fifty Years of Pretensioned Prestressed Concrete Sleepers', *Permanent Way Institution Journal*, 111 (1989); J. K. Yates, *Rail Manufacture and the Available Range*, Railway Industry Association, Track Sector Course (1986); M. G. Reynolds, 'Development in Civil Engineering Management and Practice on British Rail', *PICE: Transportation*, 95 (1992); G. H. Cope (ed.), *British Railway Track* (1993 edn.).

track circuit: a safety device provided by an electric current passing through the rails, which allows the presence of a train or vehicle to be detected when the wheels and axles complete a circuit. At its simplest the circuit tells the signalman of the location of the train. However, it is capable of doing much more: it can lock block instruments, lock and release signals and points, and convey train descriptions (see SIGNALLING).

In most power-signalling systems the running lines are continuously track-circuited, forming, with the signals, what is known as 'Track Circuit Block' (see BLOCK WORKING). The space between the signals (with appropriate safety margins) effectively forms block sections. The track circuits control the signal aspects and, in automatically signalled areas, will return the signals progressively to 'clear' after a train has left the section.

The principle of the track circuit was propounded as long ago as the 1860s, W. R. Sykes conducting experiments in Britain and William Robinson in the USA, but within the limitations of the power supplies and other equipment then available it was difficult to achieve reliability. Electrical leakage through poor or wet ballast could prevent a train being detected, while many passenger vehicles had wooden *wheel centres which would not conduct the current. It was not until nearly 1900 that improvements in track and electrical equipment made possible track circuits with all-weather reliability. Initial use was limited to special locations: St Paul's station, London (by Sykes) in 1886; Gas Works Tunnel at *King's Cross in 1894; and Grateley in 1901; also some *London Underground lines from 1905 (see SIGNALLING, AUTOMATIC). It was about 1910 before the main-line companies began to install them on a large scale. Several of the smaller companies, such as the *Cambrian and *Highland, still had none at the *Grouping in 1923.

Improving technology has brought recent problems. Modern vehicles are so light and ride so smoothly that they sometimes do not cut through the resistive films of grease, rust, or leaves on wheels and rail, hence failing to operate the track circuits reliably. Both circuits and vehicles have had to be modified to overcome the difficulty.   RDF

D. C. Gall, *Railway Track Circuits* (1933); O. S. Nock, *Railway Signalling* (1980).

tracked hovercraft. This research and development project was undertaken, between 1969 and 1973, by Tracked Hovercraft Ltd, a subsidiary of the government agency, the National Research Development Corporation.

Air-cushion suspension and guidance, and linear induction motor (LIM) propulsion, offered potential for a high-speed ground transport (HSGT) system. Commercial speeds of 250 mph, rising to 350 mph, would reduce city-centre travel times compared with rail and air services. Several inter-city routes in Britain were investigated and were seen as part of a European-wide HSGT network.

A test centre and full-scale test track was established at Earith in Cambridgeshire. 75.5-ft long hollow, rectangular-section, concrete beams, weighing 49.2 tons, sat on columns, whose height varied according to gradient and topography.

The RTV31 test vehicle had two suspension and six guidance peripheral-jet 'hoverpads', with air supplied by 12 mixed-flow fans, which accommodated pitching, rolling, and jolting forces. The vehicle's single-sided LIM reacted with a steel-backed aluminium plate set into the top of the track, with a clearance of 0.98 in. Trackside power supply at 50 Hz was transformer-controlled, with a maximum output of 6.6 kV.

Advances in LIM technology, with vertical magnetic forces being redirected upward, led to trials of magnetic suspension, which was favoured over hover suspension by the end of the programme.

The project ended in 1973, when government funding was terminated. The test facilities were demolished. German and Japanese magnetic-suspension HSGT programmes have continued, and inter-city routes in those countries remain under active consideration at the time of writing.

See also MAGLEV.   MB

M. R. Bailey, 'The Tracked Hovercraft Project', *TNS*, 65 (1993–4), 129–45.

track gauge is the distance between the vertical inner faces of the rail heads of a railway *track, or alternatively the tool used for measuring it. On almost all railways in Great Britain and very many in other parts of the world, the track gauge is 4 ft 8½ in (1,435 mm, but on *BR modified to 1,432 mm). This became known as standard gauge after the Gauge Act, 1846, forbade, with certain exceptions, construction of passenger railways to any other dimension. Gauges are often categorized as broad or *narrow, depending upon whether they are greater or less than standard.

The 4 ft 8½ in dimension originates in horse-and-cart technology. Horse-drawn vehicles have throughout history commonly been built with their wheels about 5 feet apart because this suits the proportions of the horse. There is some evidence that grooved stones were used for guidance on trackways built for bulk horse-drawn transport, from which early railways and *tramroads developed. Thus, when rails replaced the grooved stones, it was natural that the distance between them should be about 4 ft 8 in. The first steam locomotives merely took over from horses on some of the existing tramroads, and by the time of the first main-line passenger railways, e.g. the *Liverpool and Manchester (1830), the 4 ft 8½ in gauge was well established.

The broad gauge of 7 ft 0¼ in was conceived by I. K. *Brunel. In a letter to the *Great Western Railway directors in 1835 he pointed out that with a gauge of 4 ft 8½ in, the body of the carriage must extend over the tops of the wheels, and a space must be left for the action of the springs. This entailed raising the vehicle body and limited the wheel diameter. By broadening the track gauge he reasoned that the body of the vehicle could be kept between the wheels, so that the centre of gravity could be lowered, thereby providing a steadier motion and reducing wear and tear. At the same time larger-diameter wheels could be used.

In the event, very few vehicles were ever constructed on this principle. Even these had their axle bearings outside the wheels, like all standard-gauge carriages and wagons, rather than between the wheels as was the case with road vehicles, which appear to be the model upon which Brunel based his reasoning. However, the load gauge (see CLEARANCES) adopted on the GWR was up to 11 ft wide, allowing even their conventionally designed vehicles to be significantly wider than those on other railways.

The locomotives designed by Daniel *Gooch for the GWR took full advantage of the broad gauge and were more powerful and faster than standard-gauge engines. Experience also confirmed Brunel's prediction of a smoother ride, the wider gauge apparently helping to reduce the twisting effect of longitudinal track imperfections, even though the centre of gravity was not, in the event, lowered. Because of wider carriages, faster average speeds, and smoother ride, broad-gauge passenger trains were relatively popular with passengers.

The Achilles' heel of the broad gauge was the inconvenience of transhipment of freight, passengers, and luggage, where it met the standard gauge, first experienced at Gloucester in 1844. This brought about violent controversy between the proponents of the two gauges. The report of the Royal *Commission appointed to study the problem admitted the technical superiority of the broad gauge but nevertheless recommended its abolition, because the difficulty of either widening the standard-gauge railways which formed the majority, or allowing the status quo to remain, was too great. This decision was extremely unpopular with the broad-gauge faction and, faced with protests and demands for compensation, Parliament lacked the resolve to adopt the Commission's recommendation. Hence the Gauge Act neither enforced conversion to standard gauge, nor even ruled out the possibility of authorizing further railways of non-standard gauge, thus incidentally leaving the way open for *narrow-gauge railways. It also allowed a number of broad-gauge schemes then under way to continue.

The immediate result of this weak stance was that the broad gauge, which at the end of 1845 amounted to only about 250 miles of route, continued to extend, to some 544 miles by about 1860, from London to Penzance, Neyland (Pembrokeshire), and Wolverhampton. In addition there were about 78 miles of mixed-gauge track, where a third rail at standard gauge was placed between the broad-gauge pair, allowing vehicles of either gauge to run on the same line.

The broad gauge was, however, always in a very small minority, leading the GWR directors to recognize the commercial imperative of standardization. No further broad-gauge track was laid after about 1860, and existing track was progressively converted, achieving the recommendation of the Gauge Commissioners without compensation. The *South Wales Railway was converted in 1872, and the final act was the dramatic re-gauging of the main line from Paddington to Penzance, when 213 track miles were converted over the weekend of 20–23 May 1892, since when all British main-line railways have been standard gauge.   GHC

Brunel and broad gauge: MacDermot.

track-laying, see TRACK.

track mileage, see MILEAGE.

traction, diesel. Rudolf Diesel's engine was the first in which the heat of compression alone was sufficient to ignite the fuel, and when put into production in 1897 it made possible, in theory, locomotives with a thermal efficiency three or four times greater than that of contemporary steam engines. But it was a heavy, low-speed engine employing air-blast fuel injection, and the only way to build

locomotives of reasonable power within a European loading gauge (see CLEARANCES) was to employ direct-drive and start the locomotive by using compressed air. In Britain this concept developed into the ingenious Kitson-Still locomotive built in 1927. It had an oil-fired boiler supplying steam to undersides of the pistons in an eight-cylinder direct-drive engine, being used to start the locomotive or when extra power was required; normally the locomotive was driven by the upper, diesel cylinders alone. The exhaust gases from these were passed through flues in the boiler before discharge, to augment steam production. It was tested on the *London & North Eastern Railway with encouraging results, but the business failure of Kitson & Co. halted development.

The advent in the 1920s of the airless-injection diesel engine greatly reduced its size and complexity relative to power, and with improvements in transmission technology the diesel locomotive as we know it today could be developed. Three basic forms of infinitely variable drive to couple the engine to the wheels came to the fore.

Electric transmission, in which the engine drives a generator supplying current to one or more traction motors, most closely approaches the ideal of stepless infinite variability and was used in both Europe and America in the 1920s. Two British firms, Beardmore and Armstrong Whitworth, made major contributions to its development, the former supplying engines for the first main-line locomotives in *North America and the latter building some pioneer trainsets for Argentina and Brazil. Armstrong Whitworth later formed a separate diesel division and produced some excellent low-power *shunting locomotives and *railcars. One built in 1934 was still at work in 1994. They built in 1933 an 880 hp 1-C-1 mixed traffic locomotive which was tested extensively on the LNER. Further developments were cut short when the builder decided to concentrate on its core business of armament production.

In 1932 the *London Midland & Scottish Railway obtained from Armstong Whitworth a 250 hp diesel-electric shunting engine with single traction motor and jackshaft drive, followed by a 300 hp type from English Electric with two axle-hung motors. Both demonstrated large economies in operating costs compared with steam shunters, and were the forerunners of a large fleet that eventually totalled some 1,400 under *British Railways.

The great upsurge in main-line diesel-electric traction was in the USA, in the mid-1930s. It was closely studied in Britain, when in the immediate post-war period a shortage of high-grade coal, combined with accumulated arrears of maintenance and staffing problems, made it difficult to regain pre-war standards of steam locomotive reliability. In 1945 *Fairburn, CME of the LMS, made proposals for 1,500 hp diesel-electrics and in 1947 introduced the first main-line diesel-electric to run in Britain—a 1,600 hp Co-Co. *Bulleid of the *Southern Railway instigated the design of two 1,750 hp 1-Co-Co-1 locomotives, with a lower axle-loading than the LMS machines but using the same type of English Electric 16-cylinder four-stroke engine and traction equipment, built in 1950 under BR. These prototypes demonstrated their ability to equal or improve on the average performance of steam locomotives of considerably higher maximum-rated power. The constant horsepower characteristic of diesel-electrics showed improved acceleration in the lower and medium speed ranges when compared with steam. However, the much higher capital costs and continued financial stringency on BR delayed further development until 1955, when the *Modernization Plan included provision for 2,500 diesel main-line locomotives in replacement of steam. Prototypes of between 800 and 2,300 hp, to 14 different designs, mostly diesel-electric, were ordered with the intention of evaluating fully the merits of the various types of diesel engines and traction equipment. Before this could be done, fears of coal strikes paralysing the railways created government pressure to order a further 500 locomotives, resulting in the teething troubles in some of the prototypes being continued in production runs, and subsequent large-scale modifications.

The new BR main-line diesel-electric fleet was powered almost entirely by medium-speed four-stroke English Electric, Sulzer, and Mirrlees engines, all pressure-charged to increase power. However, the most powerful, with a 2,500 hp Sulzer engine, barely equalled the maximum short-term output of the most powerful express steam types, and in 1961 BR's Eastern Region ordered twenty-two 3,300 hp Co-Co locomotives with twin Napier *Deltic two-stroke engines, each driving a generator, enabling *East Coast main-line trains to be drastically accelerated. For general main-line service, 507 Class 47 Co-Cos with 2,750 hp Sulzer engines were built by Brush from 1962, together with 309 Class 37 1,750 hp Co-Cos by English Electric.

In 1976 BR introduced into regular service the first 4,500 hp High *Speed Trains (HSTs), capable of a sustained 125 mph. They comprised a 2,250 hp diesel-electric power car, with a Paxman Valenta 1,500 rpm four-stroke engine, at each end of six to eight passenger cars in fixed sets. Recent higher-powered diesel-electric Co-Co locomotives of Classes 58, 59, and 60, primarily intended for heavy freight service, have 3,200–3,500 hp Ruston Paxman (English Electric) or Mirrlees four-stroke medium-speed engines. Combustion air delivered by turbocharger blower is intercooled, enabling power to be further increased.

Hydraulic transmission takes a number of forms. The earliest was the Hele Shaw-Compayne system in which a variable-output, reversible pump coupled to the engine supplied oil under pressure to one or more constant-displacement motors driving the wheels, this being the archetypal 'hydrostatic' transmission. It was first applied to rail traction in an 85 hp petrol railcar built by Baguley Cars Ltd in 1913, but was ahead of its time; hydraulic oils and seals suitable for high-power hydrostatic transmissions only became available some 50 years later, and although many low-power diesel-hydrostatic locomotives and railcars have been built the system has yet to become established at main-line level.

The next development was the fluid coupling (fluid flywheel) which could be used in conjunction with a manual or automatic gearbox, thus eliminating the clutch. This form of 'hydro-mechanical' transmission became popular for small shunting engines and railcars between 1930 and 1965, notably using a Wilson epicyclic gearbox (the Wilson-Drewry transmission). For more powerful applications, hydro-mechanical transmissions were developed which combined a torque converter with an automatic gearbox, as for example the Mekhydro transmission applied to some of the BR Western Region 'Warship' class.

The torque converter, which unlike a fluid coupling acts as a torque multiplier as the speed of the output side falls below that of the input, was developed in Germany in 1926 and can be used on its own as a transmission. 'Hydro-kinetic' transmission was first used in Britain in 1931 on two 21-in gauge steam-outline Pacifics for the North Bay Railway at Scarborough, using Vickers-Coates torque converters. In 1935 the Voith-Sinclair turbo-transmission using three converters, engaged (filled with oil) sequentially to match converter efficiency to locomotive speed, was applied to a 330 hp diesel locomotive built for the Northern Counties Committee (see IRELAND) lines of the LMS. In the 1950s the Western Region of BR purchased over 300 B-B and C-C type diesel-hydraulic locomotives of 1,700, 2,200, and 2,700 hp deriving from German designs. However, their maintenance costs, using faster-running 1,500 rpm engines, were higher than on diesel-electrics of equivalent power with medium-speed engines, and they were phased out by the mid-1970s. Recently Voith turbo-transmission has been reintroduced on BR Class 158 and 159 diesel power cars.

In 1950 British Railways tried an experimental 2-D-2 2,000 hp locomotive designed by L. F. R. Fell of Rolls-Royce, in which power from four Paxman engines was transmitted mechanically through an ingenious system of primary and secondary differential gears and fluid couplings, without orthodox change-speed gearing.

See also MULTIPLE UNITS. GWC and RW
J. M. Doherty, 'Evolution of the Internal Combustion Locomotive', Jnl Inst. Loco. Engineers, 46, 251 (1956); J. M. Doherty, 'Diesel Railway Traction', in P. Ransome-Wallis (ed.), Concise Encyclopaedia of World Railway Locomotives (1959), 25–106; B. Webb, The British Internal Combustion Locomotive, 1894–1940 (1973); R. M. Tufnell, The Diesel Impact on British Rail (1979).

traction, electric. Electric locomotives and *multiple units differ fundamentally from self-propelled types in drawing power from an external source. The major advantage is the removal from the traction vehicle of the prime mover, with its associated maintenance costs, as confirmed by recent experience on British, French, and Japanese railways where they are about one third of those for diesel traction. A proportion of the cost of maintaining power distribution and catenary systems must be added to that of the locomotive, but these are relatively low per unit on routes carrying heavy traffic. Furthermore, much higher outputs can be achieved in an electric locomotive or unit of given weight than in self-propelled vehicles.

Electric locomotives and units require traction motors, control equipment, and auxiliaries, such as blowers supplying motor-cooling air. Alternating current needs transformers; also rectifiers if direct current is used.

The first electric locomotive that picked up current was a small 2.5 kW, 150 V dc machine built by Siemens in 1879 for hauling passengers at a Berlin exhibition. Its single motor was mounted longitudinally and drove the two axles through spur-and-bevel gears. Most early electric locomotives were of rigid frame, two axle, type, such as the 500 V dc machines for the *City & South London Railway. These were 'gearless' with traction motor armatures on the axles.

In 1899 Charles Brown, of Brown Boveri in Switzerland, built the first ac locomotive, taking a three-phase supply at the low voltage of 750 (due to local safety restrictions) to asynchronous induction motors. In 1903 great interest was aroused by high-speed trials on the Marienfeld–Zossen military railway, near Berlin, where a 1,440 kW motor-coach, working on 10 kV, 45 Hz, three-phase ac supply, attained 130 mph. The potential of electric traction had earlier been foreseen by the British locomotive engineer F. W. *Webb, who envisaged 100-mph running on the *West Coast main line.

However, the contact wire system for three-phase ac traction was rather complicated and in 1905 single-phase ac working at 15 kV, 15 Hz—which required only a single contact wire—was introduced in Switzerland using B-B locomotives having monomotor bogies with rod drive. Low frequency ac can satisfactorily be switched by a commutator and hence used in series motors as fitted to dc locomotives, and this type of motor became standard in Germany and Switzerland where 15 Hz or 16⅔ Hz current was adopted. Series motors have a smooth torque/speed characteristic and were until recently preferable to the outwardly simpler, commutator-less induction type which produces useful power only over a very narrow speed range. The induction motor is now making a comeback because modern electronics make it possible to convert incoming current into variable-frequency ac, enabling the near-constant speed characteristic of a simple induction motor to be exploited by the speed and acceleration control systems now employed in modern trains.

Single-phase ac commutator motors were also used on motor-coaches for two early British ac *electrifications—the *Midland Railway's Lancaster–Morecambe–Heysham conversion of 1908, and the *London Brighton & South Coast's London suburban of 1909.

The *North Eastern Railway introduced Bo-Bo 600 V dc freight locomotives on its *Newcastle Quayside line in 1904, and in 1915 ten Bo-Bo machines, with interconnected bogies also carrying the traction drawgear, were built to haul mineral trains on the Newport (*Middlesbrough)–Shildon line. This was the first British line to be electrified at 1.5 kV dc with overhead catenary.

From 1910 onwards many powerful electric locomotives were built in Europe with body-mounted traction motors driving axles mounted in the rigid frame, either individually through resilient final drive or from one or two large motors with rod drive to coupled wheels, following steam locomotive practice. British examples included the *Lancashire & Yorkshire Railway's 1-B-1 rod-drive machine for its experimental 3.6 kV dc Bury–Holcombe Brook line, and Sir Vincent *Raven's prototype 2-Co-2, 1.5 kV dc express locomotive, with individual axle drive, built in 1922 for the intended NER *York–Newcastle electrification. This was stopped by the 1923 *Grouping, as were proposals for electrification of the *London & North Western *Crewe–*Carlisle line using 2-Do-2 express locomotives, also deriving from Swiss practice.

Locomotives with chassis-mounted motors caused less wear on the *track than early double-bogie types with heavy axle-hung, nose-suspended motors, adding considerably to unsprung weight. Motor-coaches, of course, shared the latter objection and the need to reduce or eliminate unnecessary unsprung weight was first demonstrated by *Aspinall in 1920 on the LYR *Liverpool–Southport line, where quite high speeds were achieved by the 600 V dc multiple-unit trains. Rigid-framed locomotives with chassis-mounted motors and resilient drive were not suitable for fast traffic unless fitted with carrying axles fore and aft, which reduced the available adhesive weight, and continuing improvements in electric motor technology led by the late 1930s to traction motors sufficiently compact to be mounted resiliently in a four- or six-wheeled bogie, since when the double-bogie locomotive has become universal. Motor-coaches have undergone a similar development, but despite Aspinall's pioneering work Britain did not begin to desert the axle-hung motor until the early 1960s.

The first large British electric locomotive order was for 58 Bo-Bo mixed traffic locomotives for the 1.5 kV dc *Manchester–*Sheffield electrification of the *London & North Eastern Railway, authorized in 1936 but not completed until after World War II. Seven Co-Co express locomotives were built for this route in 1954.

The *Southern Railway's extensive 600 V dc electrified network used only multiple-unit trains—freight and through passenger trains from elsewhere were steam-hauled—until 1942 when the first Co-Co type mixed traffic locomotive was built. The major problem of current collection at gaps in the conductor rail at points and crossings —which did not arise in trains with a power bus-line connecting the collector shoes at each end—was overcome ingeniously by the SR's electrical engineer, Alfred Raworth, in conjunction with the English Electric company. Current drawn from the conductor rail drove a motor-generator which fed the traction motors. A heavy flywheel interposed between motor and generator provided sufficient kinetic energy for continued power generation when the locomotive was passing over a conductor-rail gap. Twenty-four 1,800 kW Bo-Bo type locomotives working on the same principle were built from 1959 onwards for freight and passenger working.

Although the 1951 Cock Report had confirmed the recommendation of the 1931 Weir Report for 1.5 kV dc electrification in Britain, the highly successful electrification of French main lines at 25 kV ac single-phase, using industrial frequency at 50 Hz which greatly reduced fixed installation costs, induced a change to this system in *British Railways' 1955 *Modernization Plan.

A hundred 25 kV Bo-Bo locomotives of about 2,000 kW were built from 1960 for the *London–Manchester–Liverpool electrification. French experience had shown that it was preferable to supply rectified current to dc traction motors, and this was adopted by BR. Sixty had mercury-arc rectifiers and the remainder used solid-state silicon or germanium types, which proved more satisfactory in service. All these locomotives had axle-hung nose-suspended traction motors, but the high track stresses at 100 mph resulted in 135 subsequent locomotives, whose rated power was finally increased to 3,730 kW, being provided with 'flexicoil' suspension and resilient drive to the wheels.

Developments in electronics enabled thyristor circuits to be applied to 50 further Bo-Bo type Class 90 locomotives built in 1987–90, compared with tap-changer control of transformer motor output in earlier locomotives. Microprocessors provide automatic control of acceleration up to the maximum speed pre-set by the driver.

From 1960 onwards BR introduced a large fleet of some 1,300 25 kV power cars—the largest in Europe—in its intermediate and suburban multiple units, and in 1973 produced an experimental *Advanced Passenger Train (APT) with vehicle-tilting mechanism to enable it to run at up to 156 mph over the West Coast main line. The 14-coach production train had two power cars in the middle, but after protracted troubles the project was abandoned.

BR's most recent electric locomotive to date is the 4,540 kW Class 91 Bo-Bo, built in 1988–91 for the 25 kV *East Coast main line. Designed for 140 mph running, the suspended traction motors minimize unsprung weight and drive the axles through cardan shafts, universal couplings, and final drive gears. On test a maximum speed of 162 mph was attained, the highest yet in Britain.

For freight and sleeping-car trains through the *Channel Tunnel, 46 Co-Co locomotives have been built to work on both 25 kV ac and 750 V dc systems. Maximum power is 5,000 kW.

The 20-vehicle Eurostar high-speed passenger trains operating between London, Paris, and Brussels (see CHANNEL TUNNEL) comprise a Bo-Bo power car at each end of 18 coaches, the first and last of which have motored bogies adjacent to the power cars. Derived from the French TGV trains, they run at 186 mph on 25 kV ac in France, and at 100 mph on the British side of the tunnel on 750 V dc where maximum power is limited to 35 per cent of that for 25 kV working.

See also ELECTRIFICATION. GWC

A. T. Dover, Electric 'Traction' (1963); F. J. G. Haut, 'Electric Motive Power', in P. Ransome-Wallis (ed.), Concise Encyclopaedia of World Railway Locomotives (1959), 143–233; Y. Machefert-Tassin, F. F. Nouvion, and J. Woimant, Histoire de la Traction Electrique, i and ii (1980, 1986).

traction, horse, see HORSES, USE OF.

traction, petrol. This appeared at the end of the 19th century and marked the first serious challenge to steam power for other than main-line and suburban passenger services. It was based largely on contemporary automotive practice and shared a common difficulty—early gearboxes were difficult to operate and needed to be made much more massive for a locomotive than was the case in a motor car of the same power. Except in the smallest sizes this held back development of locomotives with mechanical transmission and encouraged the more progressive builders to experiment with electric or hydrostatic transmission.

Small war-surplus petrol locomotives flooded on to the market at the end of World War I, together with men who knew how to drive them, while steady development work enabled reliable, easily used locomotives of greater power to be produced at highly competitive prices. No petrol locomotives of more than 100 hp were, however, used in Britain before the advent of airless-injection diesel engines, which were not only more suitable for the purpose but also more economical. A diesel engine uses fuel roughly in proportion to its power output; a petrol engine uses proportionately more as power is reduced. New production apart, many existing petrol locomotives were subsequently fitted with diesel engines, but although the first British diesel locomotives (see TRACTION, DIESEL) appeared in 1927 it was more than 30 years before air-cooled diesel engines finally displaced petrol engines from the smallest and lightest locomotives.

See also RAILCARS; LIGHT RAILWAYS. RW

B. Webb, The British Internal Combustion Locomotive, 1894–1940 (1973).

traction, steam. Pioneered in Britain, the steam locomotive was the predominant form of railway motive power for more than a century. It was, perhaps, unique in the extraordinary continuity of its basic form and principles of functioning. Although a number of primitive locomotives were built from 1804 onwards (see below), the first definitively established form was Robert *Stephenson's *Rocket* of 1829. It combined a multi-tubular boiler—using induced draught to regulate the rate of combustion and steam production—with direct rod drive from cylinders to rail wheels. The extent of its subsequent development is illustrated by comparing the 25 hp, 7½-ton *Rocket* with recent 2,500 hp, 150-ton machines—a fivefold increase in power-to-weight ratio.

A fundamental feature of the Stephensonian locomotive concept was the linkage achieved between steam production in the boiler and steam usage in the cylinders, using the energy in exhaust steam discharged through the blast-pipe nozzle in the smokebox to create a proportional induced draught on the fire through the boiler tubes.

Origins and early history

The first practical steam engine was built by Thomas Newcomen in 1712 for pumping water at collieries. The first steam-driven vehicle was Cugnot's steam carriage which ran on the roads of Paris in 1769. The first successful steam railway locomotive was built by Richard *Trevithick in 1804 for the Penydarren ironworks railway in South Wales.

Initially it was questioned whether the adhesion, or frictional grip, between wheels and rails was sufficient to enable locomotives to haul trains of mineral wagons up appreciable gradients. Locomotives built in 1812 for the *Middleton Colliery, Leeds, used rack-and-pinion final drive patented by John Blenkinsop, but tests made by William *Hedley at Wylam Colliery, Northumberland, demonstrated that simple wheel-to-rail adhesion was adequate for all normal conditions of loading and gradient, and that rack-and-pinion drive was an unnecessary complication.

Hedley's Wylam locomotives of 1813 and George *Stephenson's at nearby Killingworth had vertically mounted cylinders and connecting rods. Axles were coupled by gear trains or chains, but in Stephenson's Locomotion of 1825 coupling rods were used. Robert Stephenson's Rocket cylinders were inclined at 40° from the horizontal, but the piston thrusts still exerted considerable forces on the track and the cylinders of subsequent machines were mounted almost horizontally to minimize this effect.

The blast-pipe draughting system was first applied in Trevithick's locomotive of 1804, then in Hedley's Puffing Billy at Wylam in 1813 and, later, in improved form with contracted nozzle, in Timothy *Hackworth's Royal George of 1827 for the *Stockton & Darlington Railway.

The earliest steam locomotives worked on mineral railways. However, the *Rainhill locomotive trials of 1829, in which the Rocket 0-2-2 ran at up to 30 mph, confirmed the ability of steam locomotives to handle passenger as well as freight trains on the newly built *Liverpool & Manchester Railway.

Developments in Design and Construction

The multi-tubular boilers of locomotives built from the 1830s generally had short barrels and fireboxes of small volume, and were unsuitable for coal-burning, coke being the normal fuel. In the 1850s rapidly increasing demand outstripped coke supplies and prices rose steeply. After attempts to improve combustion of coal and to reduce smoke emission by using special types of firebox, a simple and effective solution was found in tests made by Charles Markham on the *Midland Railway in 1856–60. In this, an inclined arch of firebricks was provided at the front of a conventional firebox to lengthen the flow path of combustion gases before they passed through the boiler tubes, and an inclined deflector plate inside the firehole directed secondary air downwards to the fire.

Until 1860, feedwater was delivered to the boiler by axle- or crosshead-driven pumps. These could only operate when the locomotive was in motion. In 1859 the French engineer Henri Giffard invented the *injector, which used live steam to force feedwater into the boiler and could be used when in motion or standing. It rapidly replaced the feed pump.

The earliest locomotive *valve gear, controlling steam admission to the cylinders, did not permit expansive working with steam *cut off at a selected point in the piston stroke, after which it would do additional work by expan-

sion for the remainder of the stroke. In 1841 Robert Stephenson invented his link motion valve gear which permitted expansive working in the cylinders, increasing the power developed from a given volume of steam. Combined with Howe's expansion link, Stephenson's motion was used on many thousands of locomotives. In 1844 the Belgian engineer Egide Walschaert, dissatisfied with the need to use two eccentrics to drive a single valve, invented his single eccentric-drive radial valve gear. Widely used in France and Germany as well as Belgium, its application became almost universal.

From the 1870s steel (see IRON AND STEEL, USE OF) was used instead of wrought iron for locomotive wheel tyres; also for boilers and frames. This harder material greatly reduced the rate of tyre wear, especially on locomotives with coupled wheels. It had previously been so great as to discourage their more widespread use on fast passenger engines, where increased loading underlined the frequently inadequate adhesive weight of single driving-axle locomotives.

To secure improved locomotive stability, needed with the higher speeds of passenger trains from the 1880s, two-axle leading bogies, with springs to control lateral displacement, were widely used in place of single radial axles. These were first applied by William *Adams in 1868 on the *North London Railway.

In earlier days, crank-axle failures in locomotives with inside-cylinder drive were fairly frequent, which some railways used outside cylinders to avoid. Improved metallurgy enabled stronger and more reliable crank-axles to be produced, and from the 1850s to around 1900 most British passenger and freight locomotives had inside cylinders, which gave greater stability in riding. Inside cylinders were also better-protected from cold air, thus reducing condensation, while there was a preference in the Victorian era for clean, uncluttered appearance, although accessibility for maintenance was considerably reduced.

Towards the end of the 19th century two major developments in locomotive practice—compounding and superheating—were first applied, coinciding with demands for more powerful locomotives.

Compound drive

This involves the expansion of steam through two stages, in high- and low-pressure cylinder groups. Well-designed compounds can give a 10–15 per cent increase in power output and efficiency over simple expansion machines of similar overall dimensions, as well as a more even torque, or turning moment, in applying cylinder power to the driving wheels.

Two-cylinder compound 0-4-2T locomotives designed by Anatole Mallet and built in 1876 for the Bayonne–Biarritz Railway showed substantial fuel economies over simples. From 1880 August von Borries introduced the type on the Prussian State Railways, where some 6,500 were built over the next 30 years. He collaborated with T. W. *Worsdell, locomotive superintendent of the *North Eastern Railway, where some 270 were built in 1886–92 for both passenger and freight service. Unlike von Borries' machines, Worsdell's had inside cylinders, as British structure gauge restrictions (see CLEARANCES) prevented the large low-pressure cylinder being mounted outside the frames. This resulted in some mechanical and structural problems, although appreciable fuel economies were achieved.

The first three-cylinder compound was F. W. *Webb's 2-2-2-0 built for the *London & North Western Railway in 1882. It had two outside high-pressure cylinders and one large inside low-pressure, restricted platform clearances preventing the use of two outside low-pressure cylinders of adequate diameter. The driving wheels of this and 100 further passenger locomotives were uncoupled to reduce frictional resistance, and avoid the need for long coupling rods for which current steel technology was inadequate (see IRON AND STEEL, USE OF). This cylinder layout was also applied to 113 0-8-0 freight engines. The alternative three-cylinder compound layout was used by W. M. Smith of the North Eastern in 1898 in rebuilding a two-cylinder 4-4-0. The locomotive was the inspiration for S. W. *Johnson's first Midland compound 4-4-0s of 1902, the forerunners of a class totalling 240 machines built up to 1932. Tests made by the *London Midland & Scottish Railway in 1924–5 showed that the Midland compounds gave greater fuel economy than larger simple-expansion 4-6-0s, and an enlarged 4-6-0 version was designed but not built.

Webb's four-cylinder compounds, with two inside low-pressure cylinders, of which 270 0-8-0s, 4-4-0s, and 4-6-0s were built from 1897, had only two inside sets of Joy's valve gear, the outside valve spindles being driven through rocking shafts.

In 1903–5 G. J. *Churchward, CME of the *Great Western Railway, introduced three du Bousquet–de Glehn four-cylinder 4-4-2 compounds from France, for comparative trials against his own latest two-cylinder simple machines. These had four sets of valve gear with independent control of high- and low-pressure valves and compound-to-simple changeover arrangements, as used on some 4,000 French and other European locomotives. Churchward adopted the four-cylinder divided-drive layout for his own 4-6-0 machines, but retained simple expansion, to avoid the complicated control arrangements of the French engines.

In the mid-1920s the remarkable performance of the four-cylinder compound 4-6-2s of the French Nord Railway inspired Sir Henry *Fowler, CME of the LMS, to have designs prepared for large 4-6-2 compound passenger and 2-8-2 freight locomotives. These were ultimately frustrated by the operating department, partly owing to the cost of providing larger turntables. In 1929 H. N. *Gresley, CME of the *London & North Eastern, built a notable four-cylinder compound 4-6-4 with a 450 psi water-tube boiler. Its full development was delayed by the economic recession, but by 1935, after modifications suggested by the French locomotive engineer André Chapelon, it gave good results. However, its higher initial cost and special boiler maintenance procedures, as well as improvements to Gresley's standard three-cylinder simple 4-6-2s, militated against its reproduction.

Superheating

Steam vapour generated in a boiler is known as saturated steam and, being in contact with water, contains moisture. In saturated steam locomotives, contact with the metal surfaces of the steam pipes and cylinders cools the steam and results in the formation of water droplets, which create resistance to movement of the pistons and thus reduce power and efficiency.

When sufficient additional heat is applied to saturated steam to convert it to a gas, it is said to be superheated, and its moisture content is turned into additional steam. If its temperature is raised sufficiently, it will be kept at above saturation temperature throughout its passage through steam pipes and cylinders, until it is exhausted through the blast-pipe, thereby eliminating power losses due to condensation.

The other great advantage of superheating is that steam expands progressively in volume as more heat is absorbed, enabling more power to be developed from a given weight of steam produced by the boiler. Depending on the degree of superheat used, locomotive power could thus be increased by up to about 25 per cent, compared with saturated machines of similar boiler dimensions.

Steam-drying, by passing saturated steam through a chamber in the boiler before delivery to the cylinders, was applied to a locomotive built by Hawthorn in 1842. Patents for a superheater with element tubes housed inside the boiler flues were taken out in 1850 by Quillac and Montcheuil in France. However, nearly 50 years elapsed before developments in metallurgy and lubricants capable of withstanding the severe cutting action of superheated steam made superheating a practical proposition.

In 1898 Wilhelm Schmidt's superheater, with several steam element tubes housed in one large flue, was applied to two Prussian 4-4-0s, and an alternative design, with element tubes in the smokebox, on other locomotives. However, the latter system had poor accessibility for cleaning and maintenance, and the Belgian engineer Jean-Baptiste Flamme applied a third Schmidt design from 1903, using multiple rows of boiler flue tubes, each housing four steam element tubes. Its use rapidly became universal.

In Britain, George *Hughes of the *Lancashire & Yorkshire Railway and Churchward of the GWR introduced this form of superheater in 1906, the latter railway having 750 superheated locomotives by 1913, giving a fuel saving of about 15 per cent, or 60,000 tons of coal per annum. Churchward's early experiments showed that carbonization of cylinder lubricants took place at steam temperatures around 600 °F, and he used only moderate superheat. Later, improved lubricants were developed enabling the maximum steam temperatures to be raised to 750–800 °F, making possible further increases in power and efficiency.

The use of superheated steam at higher temperatures resulted in lubrication and wear problems with slide valves, and circular piston valves, first introduced by Robert Stephenson in 1832 and later in improved form by W. M. Smith in 1887, rapidly replaced them.

Many British locomotive engineers accepted the theories of Robert Garbe of the Prussian Railways that superheating made compounding unnecessary. However, tests made by Fowler with the Midland compound 4-4-0s in 1914 showed that equally important savings in fuel and water consumption were achieved in superheated compounds as in superheated simples, when compared with saturated steam machines, and that a combination of superheating and compounding gave the largest economies.

Evolution, 1900–39

The continued increase in passenger train loadings and speeds, and the demand for more powerful locomotives than the prevalent 4-4-0 types, resulted in substantial numbers of 4-4-2 and 4-6-0 machines being introduced, whose power was further increased by superheating. Outstanding examples were H. *Ivatt's large 4-4-2s on the *Great Northern Railway and Churchward's 'Saint' and 'Star' class 4-6-0s on the GWR.

The introduction of express freight trains running at 50–60 mph required more powerful and stable locomotives than the standard 0-6-0 freight types. Larger 2-6-0 designs were produced by Churchward and Gresley in 1911–12 to meet this need.

The transmission of higher power output in larger inside-cylinder locomotives resulted in highly stressed crank-axles and increased maintenance, which induced many British railways to revert to the use of outside cylinders. Other railways introduced three- or four-cylinder locomotives to reduce crank-axle stresses. The first modern three-cylinder simple expansion locomotive was J. *Holden and F. Russell's *Great Eastern Railway 0-10-0T of 1902, which demonstrated acceleration performance equalling that with electric traction. Sir Vincent *Raven of the NER built 200 three-cylinder passenger, freight, and mixed traffic locomotives from 1909, and Gresley was responsible for over 800 for the GNR and LNER.

Four-cylinder simple 4-4-0s were built in 1897, followed from 1906 by Churchward's 'Star' class 4-6-0s, the forerunners of over 550 British four-cylinder locomotives, culminating in Sir William *Stanier's LMS 'Duchess' class 4-6-2 type of 1938.

Although some 1,900 multi-cylinder locomotives ran in Britain, they represented only about 10 per cent of total locomotive stock. Except on the LNER, two-cylinder locomotives were preferred for all but the heaviest passenger duties, whilst nearly all heavy freight and mineral trains were hauled by two-cylinder 0-6-0, 0-8-0, and 2-8-0 machines. Only on the LMS were articulated Garratt-type 2-6-0 + 0-6-2 freight locomotives introduced for mineral train haulage, replacing pairs of 0-6-0s, although the LNER in 1925 introduced an even larger six-cylinder 2-8-0 + 0-8-2 for banking mineral trains up a short, severe gradient.

The search for higher efficiency

From the mid-1920s, increasing fuel costs highlighted the need for improved fuel efficiency in steam locomotives: i.e. the percentage of heat in the fuel burnt actually turned into useful work. This did not exceed about 6–7 per cent, or about one third of that for electric traction, which was then ruled out on account of its high fixed installation costs. This low efficiency was due primarily to the relatively small proportion of heat energy in steam which could be turned into useful work before being exhausted to atmosphere.

In theory, an increase of about one-third in thermal efficiency could be achieved by expanding steam to a pressure lower than atmospheric, and exhausting it to a condenser. However, despite several experiments with vacuum-condensing locomotives, dating back to the Reid–Ramsay machine of 1910 with turbine drive and electrical transmission, the difficulties in accommodating suitable condensing units within the restricted space of a locomotive have prevented any worthwhile improvement in efficiency.

Experiments with condensing and other non-conventional types of steam locomotive confirmed that, in British conditions where coal was relatively cheap, increased construction and maintenance costs could more than offset improved fuel efficiency.

The work of the French engineer André Chapelon from 1929, in which the power and efficiency of existing locomotives was increased by 40 per cent or more, showed the substantial scope for improvement by eliminating pressure losses through tortuous and constricted steam-pipes, and steam chests of inadequate volume, where no useful work was done. Chapelon's principles were first applied in Britain in Gresley's 2-8-2 and 4-6-2 types of 1934–5, then by Stanier on the LMS and *Bulleid on the *Southern Railway. Chapelon's Kylchap exhaust system, which greatly reduced the power absorbed in exhaust pressure required to draught the boiler, was applied to over 200 LNER and *BR locomotives, including Gresley's 4-6-2 *Mallard* in which it contributed to the attainment of the world speed record for steam of 126 mph in 1938.

Post-1939 Developments

Shortages of labour, especially skilled artisan staff, during and after World War II, combined with lower grades of coal, resulted in major difficulties in resuming pre-war standards of performance and reliability. The use of rocking grates and hopper ashpans, which radically simplified fire-cleaning and ash-disposal, was greatly extended. G. Ivatt's new LMS locomotives also incorporated self-cleaning smokeboxes, in which the smaller particles of ash and partly burned fuel were passed through mesh screens and exhausted through the chimney. His locomotives also had running plates raised well clear of the coupled wheels, providing improved access to the driving rods and valve mechanism.

After *nationalization in 1948, it was decided to produce a series of nine standard steam locomotive types, all two-cylinder simples, embodying the best features of previous company locomotive practice, and having wider *route availability than some former types of equivalent power. About 900 of these locomotives were built from 1951 until the cessation of steam building in 1960, some of the later machines being fitted with improved poppet valve gear which greatly reduced the frequency and cost of valve gear maintenance. Of these BR standard types the Class 9 2-10-0 freight locomotives, of which 250 were built under R. A. *Riddles, demonstrated a considerable increase in perform-ance capacity over previous 2-8-0s.

In 1968 steam locomotives were finally withdrawn from British Railways, 138 years after the opening of the Liver-pool & Manchester Railway, but a number of preserved machines still operate on special enthusiasts' and tourist trains.

See also TRACTIVE EFFORT. GWC

BSRL; O. S. Nock, *The British Steam Railway Locomotive*, ii: *1925–1965* (1966); J. T. Van Riemsdijk and K. Brown, *The Pictorial History of Steam Power* (1980); A. Briggs, *The Power of Steam* (1982); J. T. Van Riemsdijk, *Compound Locomotives* (1994).

traction, turbine: an attempt to achieve the same advan-tages of compactness, reliability, and economy in a steam locomotive that were obtained in stationary and marine in-stallations of considerably greater power. The Reid-Ramsay condensing steam turbine-electric locomotives of 1910 and 1922 were indeed miniature power stations on wheels, but proved far too heavy for their disappointingly small power outputs. Simpler locomotives with mechanical transmission tested in 1924 and 1926 were no more successful. In 1935 there appeared *London Midland & Scottish Railway No. 6202 (nicknamed *Turbomotive*), an otherwise standard 'Princess Royal' class Pacific in which the four conventional cylinders were replaced by forward and reverse turbines. It performed well and, turbines apart, required less main-tenance than a standard locomotive; the most successful British turbine locomotive yet, it lasted until 1952.

Attention then turned to gas turbines, which appeared the way to construct locomotives of high power-to-weight ratio burning relatively cheap fuel. Shortly before *nationalization the *Great Western Railway ordered two turbine-electric locomotives, one from the Swiss gas turbine pioneers Brown Boveri, the other from Metropolitan Vickers. They arrived in 1950 and 1952 respectively, but such was the accumulated experience with jet aircraft that their turbines were already obsolete. Despite satisfactory performance, they had been withdrawn by 1960. Subsequently English Electric built and tested GT3, a direct-drive gas turbine locomotive based on a steam locomotive chassis, and small turbines were used to power a prototype *Advanced Passenger Train. RW

P. Ransome-Wallis (ed.), *Concise Encyclopaedia of World Railway Locomotives* (1959), 465–71, 478, 487–9.

traction, unusual forms of. Thomas Shaw Brandreth's *Cycloped*, entered in the *Rainhill trials, was powered by a horse walking on a series of rollers, as was a similar ma-chine tried on shunting duties by the *London & South Western Railway in 1850. Neither was successful because the horse is an expensive and inefficient way of developing comparatively little power, even without the losses inherent in a geared transmission.

Wind power was used in 1698 on a railway at Neath. Later, trolleys fitted with sails were used on a few exposed coastal railways where the direction and regularity of the prevailing wind made this practicable, for example that from Patrington to Spurn Head, and on the Thames Haven branch in 1905, but were no more than the easy way of making a journey that would otherwise involve pushing the trolley or waiting for the next proper train.

The Adkins-Lewis 'Never-Stop Railway' employed an articulated screw laid in the centre of the track, engaging rollers beneath each vehicle; varying screw pitch speeded up or slowed down the cars which were kept a constant time apart. Demonstration lines were laid at Southend Kur-saal (1923) and the Wembley Exhibition (1924–5).

A modern super-flywheel can store appreciable amounts of energy and, unlike a storage battery, can be 'recharged' quickly; an Oerlikon-Sentinel flywheel-electric shunting lo-comotive was tested by the National Coal Board in 1957.

Manpower was employed for light inspection trolleys before the advent of small, cheap, and reliable air-cooled petrol engines. Discounting trolleys that were simply pushed, there were bicycle-like vehicles with pedals, and pump-trolleys whose riders worked a rocking beam con-nected to a crankshaft which was geared to one axle.

See also GRAVITY WORKING; CABLE HAULAGE. RW

B. G. Wilson and J. R. Day, *Unusual Railways* (1957), 194–8.

tractive effort is the force exerted by a locomotive for its own propulsion and for train haulage. Effective or drawbar tractive effort is the force exerted for useful work at the coupling between locomotive and train. When the drawbar tractive effort exceeds the total train resistance that is due to mechanical friction in bearings and suspension, wind resis-tance, and gravity, the train will accelerate; when tractive effort is less it will decelerate.

In steam locomotive practice reference is also made to indicated cylinder tractive effort—the force exerted on the pistons—and to wheel-rim tractive effort at the driving wheels, as frequently recorded at the rollers of *locomotive testing plants. Indicated and wheel-rim tractive efforts are appreciably higher than the drawbar effort at a given rate of steam supply and road speed, the difference in the former being the force absorbed in frictional resistance of the driv-ing mechanism and axle bearings, together with wind re-sistance; in the latter, driving mechanism and coupled axle bearing resistances only are involved.

The maximum tractive effort exerted in the cylinders of a simple-expansion steam locomotive, in lb force, is expressed in the following formula:

$$TE = \frac{N}{2} \times \frac{D^2 \times S \times 0.85P}{W}$$

where N is the number of cylinders; D, S, and W the cylin-der diameter, piston stroke, and driving wheel diameter in inches; and P the boiler working-pressure in lb force. In compound locomotives separate calculations are made for high- and low-pressure cylinders, requiring knowledge or assumption of the intermediate receiver pressure.

Tractive effort differs fundamentally from horsepower, which is time-related to work performed. Where a locomotive is exerting a given horsepower its tractive effort varies inversely with speed, horsepower being defined as

$$\frac{TE \times Speed}{375}.$$

GWC

Trade, Board of. Before 1840 the Board had been concerned primarily with overseas trade and shipping, never directly with transport inland. But as the outlines of a railway system emerged in 1833–5, some people felt that the *government should make a strong effort to regulate them. Two Commons committees were appointed to investigate this matter, the second of which recommended in 1838 that an additional board should be set up, annexed to the Board of Trade, to be concerned wholly with railways. It was established, as the Railway Department of the Board of Trade, in 1840, charged with responsibilities defined in two *Regulation Acts, passed in 1840 and 1842.

The Board was ill-equipped to meet these new obligations. None of its staff had any personal knowledge of railways or their working, though its Statistical Department, set up under G. R. Porter in 1832, was already assembling information. Porter was quick to foresee some of the consequences of the development of this new mode of transport, and he was placed in charge of the Railway Department. Samuel *Laing became its law clerk. In addition, the Acts empowered the Board to appoint *inspectors to examine new lines, certifying that they were fit for opening, and to investigate *accidents; and each company was obliged to send the Board statistical *returns of its traffic.

The inspectors were officers of the Royal Engineers, and therefore aware of some of the technical problems in building and operating railways, though they knew nothing about their mechanical equipment, about which they had to learn from literature, observation, and experience. Naturally, mistakes were made. Porter, for example, was convinced in 1845 that no railway could meet the competition of steamboats on the Thames. When the boilers of locomotives exploded, the true explanations, if they arose from faulty design or materials, were sometimes missed.

With a staff of no more than five (the whole Board's then was only 30) much of the Railway Department's work was performed by discussions between its members and the political heads, the President and Vice-President of the Board of Trade. This was just adequate in 1840–3, when railways were not growing fast, but that ceased to be true in 1844. A Commons committee on railways of that year, chaired by *Gladstone, then President of the Board, included among its recommendations the provision of cheap travel at specially low fares, in vehicles constructed to minimum standards (see PARLIAMENTARY TRAINS). This involved large-scale inquiry into the accommodation currently being provided and that which was proposed, and the whole work fell on the Railway Department, which did it with a care and attention that reflected a lively understanding of its social importance.

Before it was completed a new and far more onerous task had to be faced. In the summer of 1844 a great mass of new railway proposals came before *Parliament (see MANIAS).

The task of classifying them, and appraising their merits and defects, was evidently beyond the resources of the Railway Department, and in August a new board was established, still a part of the Board of Trade, whose President, Lord *Dalhousie, became its chairman. It fulfilled its duties with an efficiency remarkable in the circumstances, but it was abolished in 1845. New railway proposals were then handled by parliamentary committees, much less well. On a change of government in 1846 railway matters were removed from the Board of Trade and handed to a new body of Railway Commissioners, who achieved nothing notable. They were dissolved in 1851 by the government that had appointed them and the Railway Department of the Board of Trade was re-established, and was to last until 1919.

In 1853 a fresh attempt was made by a Commons committee, chaired by Edward *Cardwell (then President of the Board), to secure a standing committee on general matters of railway policy and legislation, to be advised by the Railway Department. That failing, the authority of the Board necessarily grew stronger. The Royal Commission on Railways of 1865–7, which surveyed the British railways very broadly, recommended no change in the Board's powers or functions.

The care and skill of its inspectors earned it a high reputation in the investigation of the growing number of serious railway accidents. The annual reports by its chief inspector Henry *Tyler, from 1870 onwards, afforded a carefully framed running commentary on safety precautions, considered very broadly. The reports on individual accidents became steadily bolder in pointing to the failure to adopt proved new equipment, primarily on account of cost.

The Regulation Act of 1871 reflected this changing attitude in its redefinition and extension of the inspectors' duties, which were now concerned with all accidents, including those to railwaymen as well as to passengers. The 1873 Regulation Act transferred certain powers concerning the approval of working *agreements between railway companies, and their running of steamships, from the Board of Trade to a new court, the Railway Commission.

In 1878 each railway company was required to furnish the Board, twice yearly, with returns of the extent of the fitting of continuous *brakes, a matter that had now become prominent through improved braking systems. Despite repeated assertions by some of the companies that no system had proved wholly satisfactory, the inspectors' accident reports became steadily more insistent that they should be fitted. Then in 1889 the government's hand was forced by the Armagh accident, and under a new Regulation Act the Board of Trade was authorized to compel railway companies to adopt the *block system and the interlocking of points and signals on lines carrying passenger traffic (see SIGNALLING), and to fit continuous brakes on all passenger trains.

This represented an important change in the government's attitude to the Board. It was being directed to act on its own responsibility, without reference to the government or Parliament, exercising powers that were compulsory and unqualified. If the order was disobeyed, the Board could refer the matter to the Railway Commission for legal enforcement.

Most European governments included a Ministry of Communications. The British government was not prepared to do that yet, but went on to give the Board an important part in enforcing legislation to restrict the working hours of railway employees in 1893. The whole development of *light railways was placed under its ultimate control in 1896. In 1900 the Railway Employment (Prevention of Accidents) Act extended the Board's powers in a new way, allowing it to require the use of any appliances that in its opinion might reduce the danger of accidents to staff (automatic *shunting devices were then much under discussion) and authorizing it to test them free of charge to the companies. Provision was made for discussions with the companies, and for arbitration when they and the Board disagreed. But the Board itself was specifically allowed to take the initiative.

It now undertook a number of inquiries of its own, which would formerly have required a committee of one or both Houses of Parliament. The Departmental Committee on Railway Agreements and *Amalgamation of 1911 is an important example. The annual reports of the London Traffic Branch of the Board from 1908 onwards provided a valuable commentary on quickly changing traffic patterns in the capital.

In World War I the government assumed direct control of the railways, placing them under a Railway Executive Committee: a group of railway managers with the President of the Board of Trade as its titular chairman. In 1919, when reorganization of the railways in peace-time was being worked out, a Ministry of *Transport was established, to which the whole of the Board's railway responsibilities was transferred.

A survey of the Board's entire work for and with the railways must surely accord it high respect. It started out with no strong support from the government, faced with powerful enemies resenting its interference. In 1844–5 its associated railway board was given the impossible task of forging a coherent system from a welter of rival proposals. Railways were then removed from the Board's scope for over four years. Yet after this most unpromising start the Board went on to discharge its duties as effectively as its powers and facilities allowed.

It had only six or eight clerks in the 1860s; the number of its inspectors grew slowly in 1840–67 from one to four. The Board took a minor place among the government departments, and it was seldom headed by outstandingly able men. After Cardwell, no front-rank politician was its President under Queen Victoria for any substantial period, except Joseph Chamberlain. Only one of its Permanent Secretaries stayed a long time, T. H. Farrer (1865–86). But the corporate effort of this small group, working quietly behind the scenes, gave the Board real power in the surveillance, and eventually in the working, of the British railway system, which it maintained firmly until World War I.   JS

Sir H. Ll. Smith, *The Board of Trade* (1928); *GR*; Porter and steamboat competition: SRO, GD45/7/36, 13 Jan. 1845.

trade unionism. Collective bargaining did not exist on British railways for the greater part of the 19th century. A typical view of the directors and general managers of the railway companies was that expressed by Cosmo *Bonsor, chairman of the *South Eastern & Chatham Railway, when he declared, even as late as 1907, that 'the company had refused and would continue to refuse, to permit a third party to come to their Board Room to discuss with them as to how they were to carry on their business'. The reason given for this attitude of intransigence was that reliable time-keeping and safe railway operation required strict discipline and unquestioning obedience to the companies' rules and regulations. George *Findlay, general manager of the *London & North Western Railway, asserted in 1892: 'if the railway company were to deal with the Amalgamated Society on questions affecting matters of discipline, I say no discipline or good order would be maintained'. To enforce these rigorous standards, ex-army or navy officers were often recruited to the boards of directors or appointed as general managers. Among these were Captain Laws of the *Lancashire & Yorkshire, Captain William O'Brien of the *North Eastern, and Captain Mark *Huish, from 1846 general manager of the London & North Western.

The methods used to maintain full control of the staff were a combination of reprimands, cautions, fines, suspensions, and dismissals, all of which were carefully noted in the staff registers. On the *London Brighton & South Coast Railway between August 1862 and December 1863 inclusive, 432 fines were imposed on a total staff of 1,800. The obverse of the coin of strict discipline was paternalism. The widows of long-serving and loyal railwaymen were often given small grants of £8 or £10 to help them through the early stages of bereavement (see COMPENSATION). The directors of each company did everything possible to encourage the belief that, because of the regularity of employment offered in an expanding railway industry, it was a privilege to be 'in the service', and in the service of a particular company whose name was shown on the uniform. The staff was split not only into different grades, e.g. *porters, *guards, and *drivers, but within each grade between those classed as 'loyal' and those regarded as 'troublemakers'. That is why the directors' claim, made in response to demands for collective discussions, that the board room was always open to deal with the problems of any individual railwayman, was regarded as a hollow one. Staff were astute enough to realize that a worker voicing a general complaint was liable to be considered untrustworthy when it came to a question of promotion. Loyalty was instilled through the teaching given in schools and churches controlled by the larger companies, as in the cases of *Crewe, Wolverton, and *Doncaster. While it is true that I. K. *Brunel considered it an advantage if engine drivers were illiterate, since being able to read might distract them from their practical tasks, on the Brighton line managers insisted that their employees should be literate (see LITERACY).

It was easier to secure unquestioning obedience from staff who were recruited in the country areas, where deference was expected to the squire and the parson, than it was from those enrolled in the towns and in urban areas where such influences were weaker.

In view of the many discouragements to independent thought and insubordination it is not surprising that no lasting trade union for railway workers existed before 1872.

The first steps towards collective bargaining were taken in the last quarter of the 19th century in the industrial areas of the north-east and South Wales. It is true that a number of railway unions were formed on the North Eastern and Brighton lines in the wake of the Overend, Gurney financial crisis of May 1866 (see SPECULATION); but none survived to December 1867. The most substantial and promising of them, the Engine Drivers' and Firemen's United Society, survived for just over a year from April 1866, but in April 1867 its members who struck on the North Eastern had to surrender in consequence of management's employment of blackleg labour from other companies. The union disappeared in the following month.

Following the establishment of the Amalgamated Society of Railway Servants (see NATIONAL UNION OF RAILWAYMEN) at the beginning of 1872, union recruitment was brisk in Durham. In the business boom of the early 1870s market forces brought about some improvement in railway workers' pay; but when depression followed in the later years of the decade the NER imposed wage cuts. These stimulated a further rise in union membership, so that by the late 1880s it totalled over 2,000 in Durham alone, or 13.2 per cent of the union's national total. The Darlington Programme, as it became known, included the demand for a maximum ten-hour day, the payment for overtime at 1¼ times the daily rate, and a guaranteed day's employment. The NER board met a deputation of the company's employees on 7 October 1889. This meeting was notable in that the directors did not insist on seeing the men in their separate grades, but as a single body. Another milestone was reached on 16 November 1889 when a committee of the directors met representatives of the employees accompanied by union officials. The directors insisted that the officials were present as 'advisers' and not as negotiators; but an important further step towards collective bargaining had been taken. When further negotiations were deadlocked in December 1889 the union suggested arbitration, the company agreed, and both sides accepted Dr Spence Watson as arbitrator. An important reason why these advances towards collective bargaining had been achieved was that the NER directors were industrialists who had grown accustomed to it in the main industries of the area, coal and iron.

Somewhat similar background economic conditions were present in South Wales. In August 1890 a *strike on the *Taff Vale, *Rhymney, and *Barry Railways was settled when Edward Harford, general secretary of the ASRS, negotiated directly with James Inskip, the chairman of the TVR. But this agreement was a recognition of necessity rather than something arising from a principled belief in the advantages of a continuing close understanding with trade unions. Harford also took up the case of James Hood on the *Cambrian Railways, but was eclipsed by action in Parliament (see STATIONMASTERS).

Following separate grade conferences of its members the ASRS launched its first national All Grades Programme in October 1896 with comprehensive demands for shorter hours and improvements in pay. The railway companies' chairmen and general managers, at a conference at *Euston on 4 November 1897, decided to close ranks in outright opposition to the union's demands, and refused to negotiate. The NER was the one exception. Its board agreed to accept Richard *Bell, general secretary of the ASRS, as negotiator and submitted the entire All Grades Programme to the arbitration of Lord James of Hereford. His award included shortened hours and improved overtime and Sunday duty rates.

On 18 January 1907 all railway company general managers received a copy of a new All Grades Programme including an eight-hour maximum working day for traffic grades. By this time the ASRS was in a considerably stronger bargaining position with over 90,000 members. Nevertheless all the large companies, except the NER, came to the unanimous decision 'not to yield in the slightest degree' to the union's demands. It took all the energy, charm, and negotiating skill of *Lloyd George, President of the Board of *Trade, to establish a compromise. The unions dropped their claim for full recognition in exchange for the companies' agreement to the setting up of Sectional (i.e. grade) and Central Conciliation Boards, and the reference to arbitration of any disputes which could not be settled in them. The companies claimed a victory in so far as union officers were excluded from membership of the boards; the union leaders argued that this railway conciliation scheme was a step forward to eventual union recognition.

However, the subsequent awards of the arbitrators reflected the companies' loss of revenue in a slump in trade, and the railway workers' average weekly wage in 1910 of 25s. 9d. was a penny less than it had been in 1905. The result was that railwaymen were caught up in the widespread industrial unrest of the hot summer of 1911. What began as an unofficial strike on the Lancashire & Yorkshire Railway soon became a national strike backed by all the railway unions except the Railway Clerks' Association (RCA)—see TRANSPORT SALARIED STAFFS' ASSOCIATION. On 15 August the union leaders offered the companies 24 hours in which to open negotiations. At first the directors resisted any idea of discussions, but with the threat of war over Morocco in the background, Lloyd George succeeded in bringing together the two parties in one room. There were some further delaying tactics by the companies, but a revised conciliation scheme was eventually hammered out by 11 December. It was notable for the fact that, for the first time, trade union officers were allowed to represent their members.

When war broke out in August 1914 an Order in Council, made under the Regulation of Forces Act, 1871, established a Railway Executive Committee comprising ten leading general managers. It was given full powers to use the railways of the country, as a unit, for the successful prosecution of the war. The government, for its part, guaranteed the companies a revenue not less than that they had achieved in 1913—a prosperous year. J. H. *Thomas, assistant general secretary of the NUR, then maintained that the railway workers should also be guaranteed real wages at least comparable to those of 1913. The reason why from January 1915 there were direct negotiations between the REC and the railway unions, rather than a resort to the conciliation machinery set up in 1911, was that food prices rose very rapidly in the early months of the war and negotiations on a company-by-company basis as provided for in 1911 would have been too time-consuming. Thus it came about that at the Midland Grand Hotel, *St Pancras, on 12 February 1915 there was signed the first-ever agreement between representatives of the railway companies (through the REC) and union officers for *national* rates of railway wages. The fact that six other 'war bonus' agreements proved necessary to offset the rising cost of living meant that by the war's end both parties became familiar with procedures for nation-wide settlements. The extremists on both sides of the negotiating table began to admit that their opposite numbers were not the ogres they had previously come to believe.

Until the coming into operation of the Railways Act, 1921 (see GROUPING) in January 1923 disputes between the two sides of the industry continued to be negotiated directly between the REC and the unions. In Part IV, paragraph 61 of the Act, the arrangements for negotiations with the four main-line companies were clearly stated: 'all questions relating to rates of pay or conditions of service . . . shall, in default of an agreement between the railway companies and the trade unions concerned, be referred to and settled by the Central Wages Board, or, on appeal, the National Wages Board as reconstituted under this Act'. The Central Wages Board comprised eight representatives of the companies and eight of the trade unions, including four from the NUR and two each from the *Associated Society of Locomotive Engineers & Firemen and the RCA. The National Wages Board comprised six representatives of the railway companies and six from the unions (two from each).

This new machinery of negotiation proved effective in settling disputes without resort to lock-outs or strikes. Following its participation in the General Strike of 1926, the NUR called its members out on a national strike only once before 1972. In 1922 the railway workshops' men were brought into the negotiating machinery when an Industrial Court Award No. 728 ruled 'that the principle of regarding the railway service as an industry was a sound one and the principle should be applied to the manufacturing side of the railway companies' activities'.

In March 1933 the companies gave notice to end their participation in the arrangements established under the Railways Act, 1921. This notice came into effect in March 1934. In the light of government financial restraints, they wanted to reduce costs and found the delays experienced in the National Wages Board an obstacle to achieving this objective. At the same time they declared that 'they had no desire to depart from the established policy of discussing labour problems with the unions', and they worked out a new scheme in co-operation with the union leaders. The Memorandum of Agreement for a Machinery of Negotia-

tion for the Railway Staff came into operation from 1 March 1935. Five stages of negotiation were recognized, including (a) local representatives and Local Departmental Committees (LDCs) which had responsibilities for such matters as shift turns and holiday arrangements; (b) Sectional Councils on each railway to consider the application of national agreements; (c) direct discussions between the companies and the unions on national agreements; (d) the Railway Staff National Council which should, if necessary, forward matters to (e) the Railway Staff National Tribunal, which would be the final body of appeal.

At one time in the emergency of World War II it looked as if these arrangements would be thrown aside. In February 1941 the chairman of the REC, Sir Ralph *Wedgwood, prompted by the government, proposed submitting a wage claim to an independent tribunal. The unions were unanimous in rejecting this proposal and the government and the REC chairman then conceded that there should be no change in the negotiating machinery. Thus, in 1995 this apparently cumbersome and roundabout negotiating machinery had continued in use for 60 years—far longer than any of its predecessors and, despite its time-consuming characteristics, it had contributed more successfully to the achievement of industrial peace.   PSB

F. McKenna, *The Railway Workers, 1840–1970* (1980); G. Alderman, *The Railway Interest* (1978); P. S. Bagwell, *The Railwaymen*, i (1963), ii (1982).

trading on stations, see STATION TRADING.

train ferries, see FERRIES; SHIPPING SERVICES.

train heating. Until the 1890s few passenger *carriages had a heating system. Passengers relied on footwarmers —flat, metal containers filled with hot water and available from platform staff for a small charge. They were introduced in the 1850s and, at first, were supplied to first-class passengers only. During the 1880s, F. W. *Webb patented the idea of sealed footwarmers, filled with a solution of soda acetate. These were preheated at stations and gave out heat as the solution recrystallized. As an indication of the number of footwarmers in use on a major railway, in 1905 the *Midland Railway reported that it owned 27,000.

An alternative arrangement for train heating dated back to 1843 when a saloon used by Queen Victoria on the *London & Birmingham Railway featured a boiler with oil-burners, supplying hot water to a radiator inside a double floor. In the USA there was the Baker heater, a small coil-tube boiler with closed-circuit hot water pipes heating the coach interior; this system was included in the *Pullman cars put into service on the Midland Railway from 1874. The West Lancashire Railway was an early user of train heating, with a boiler in the guard's van supplying water to adjoining carriages.

By the last decade of the 19th century, there were three train heating systems available: hot water supplied from the engine and circulated through the carriages; the steam storage system with radiators in the carriages filled with a soda acetate solution, and at intervals heated by high-pressure steam supplied from the engine; and the low-pressure system by which steam from the engine first passed through a pressure-reducing valve (to obviate the danger of steam at boiler pressure bursting pipes within the carriages) and then by way of a flexible hose from the tender and between carriages to piping inside the vehicles to supply radiators, usually placed under seats. This system predominated by the start of the 20th century, and later thermostats were used to control radiator temperature.

The *East Coast companies adopted the low-pressure system in 1895, while the Midland conducted comparative trials with the circulating hot water and the low-pressure steam systems as late as 1902. The following year, the MR adopted the low-pressure steam system devised by its engineers, with heat regulated in the *compartments by passengers; two years later this company had 1,350 vehicles with steam or hot-water heating.

At first, steam heating was used for radiators only, but an arrangement was devised for the steam heating of water to wash-basins in lavatories. Because *sleeping cars required hot water for wash-basins when steam heating was not available in summer months, they had auxiliary electric or gas heating.

Electric railways used electrically heated elements under seats, and there were experiments with pressure ventilation and heating on steam-hauled stock from 1908 (see AIR-CONDITIONING). Pressure loss, and leaks, made the effective steam heating of lengthy trains problematic and caused H. N. *Gresley to look first at the electric heating of compartments, but this was difficult other than by using current from quickly exhausted batteries. A solution lay in the pressure ventilation systems adopted by the *London & North Eastern and *London Midland & Scottish Railways from 1930, in which warmed (or cooled) air circulated through ducts in the compartments. Fully automatic pressure ventilation was employed by Gresley from 1934, with pre-heating of carriages before departure, and steam heating supplied from the engine once the train was under way. Later, steam heating was dispensed with entirely in prestige LNER stock.

The majority of diesel locomotives supplied under *BR's 1955 *Modernization Plan were equipped with steam generating boilers, as the coaching stock in use was fitted with steam heating only. From 1960, new carriages, and many older vehicles, too, on the London Midland and Southern Regions were fitted with electric train heating, working from an 800 V dc supply, but steam-heated stock continued to be built for other regions until 1964. Current was available from an electric, or electro-diesel locomotive, from an auxiliary generator driven by the power-unit of a diesel-electric locomotive, or a generator van. From 1971, fully air-conditioned Mark 2 carriages were put into service on InterCity trains, and with the withdrawal of older vehicles steam heating was eliminated on BR by 1986–7.   MLH

trainsheds, or overall roofs, were traditional not only at large stations but, in earlier days, at many smaller ones. The first were wooden, as at *Liverpool Crown Street on the

*Liverpool & Manchester Railway (1830). *Brunel's belief in timber for viaducts extended to his larger stations, which have been called 'Brunel's barns', although that sobriquet does not apply to *Bristol, where Tudor detailing was applied to the imitation hammer-beams that disguised ingenious cantilever construction.

Low, but not inelegant, light wrought-iron pitched roofs, clad with slates and glass, were designed for *Euston (1837) by Charles Fox under Robert *Stephenson. Easy and cheap to erect, his roof was developed with glazed gable screens by many railways, particularly the *London & North Western where it survives in its final form at Preston (1879–80). G. T. *Andrews designed a light iron roof with hipped ends for a number of stations in the north-east like Beverley, which had a new roof in 1908 still in Andrews' style.

The widest of these roofs were only half the width of some of the wooden or iron single spans in naval dockyards. They were not exceeded until the arched roof was developed to satisfy demands for platform space unobstructed by columns, and greater height to dissipate smoke and steam. The twin arcades of 105-ft-wide laminated timber ribs designed by Lewis *Cubitt for *King's Cross formed the last of the large wooden roofs—later replaced by iron.

Among the early iron-arched roofs, *Newcastle Central (1850), built on a sharp curve by John *Dobson and Robert Stephenson, produced dramatic geometrical perspectives surpassed only at *York (1877).

The completion of *Birmingham New Street on an irregular site in 1854 marked a big advance. The single-span arched roof was 212 ft at its widest point. A variety of others followed, some with multiple spans: in London at *Paddington (with intricately designed transepts), *Charing Cross, *Cannon Street, *London Bridge, particularly gracefully at *Victoria, and elsewhere, such as *Glasgow Queen Street, *Manchester London Road and Exchange, Darlington, and *Aberdeen, to name a few. But New Street was equalled only by the enlarged Liverpool Lime Street in 1867, and exceeded by the finest of them all, William *Barlow's great arched trainshed at *St Pancras (1868), 243 ft wide and 110 ft high, springing directly from the ground. The platforms and track rested on an elevated iron deck which reduced the downhill gradient into the station, acted as a tie for the ribs, and provided a street-level warehouse below. The smaller roofs at Glasgow St Enoch (1876) and Manchester Central (1880) were somewhat similar.

Nearly 90 years after the last major arched roof was built, at *Hull (1904), a spectacularly novel design by Nicholas Grimshaw & Partners was executed in 1993 at *Waterloo International, fully upholding the tradition of dramatic station engineering, and the antithesis of the only other modern trainsheds: the portal-framed roofs at *Leeds (1967), and King's Cross Thameslink (1984).

From the 1850s many flat ridge-and-furrow roofs were built, both transverse and longitudinal, based on Paxton's principles for the Crystal Palace. Usually they were low with a narrow profile, like *Stoke-on-Trent (1893), although some had a broad, lofty cross-section, making them more airy, like *Carlisle (1880), *Perth (1887), and—particularly impressive—the later part of Glasgow Central (1906).

GJB

A. T. Walmisley, *Iron Roofs, Examples of Design* (1888); *VS*, ch. 5; *GRSB*, ch. 8; R. J. M. Sutherland, 'Shipbuilding and the Long Span Roof', *TNS*, 60 (1988–9), 107.

train spotting, see ENTHUSIASTS.

train staff, see SINGLE LINES, WORKING OF.

tramroads; tramways. These terms are used in a somewhat bewildering fashion to describe various kinds of railway, regardless of *gauge. They should not be confused with street *tramways.

The word 'tram' itself is of ancient mining derivation, originally meaning a sledge or wheelbarrow, later fitted with wheels and running on rails. From about 1800 the term gave way to the more generally used 'wagon', only to be revived with the construction of street tramways when 'tramcar' came to mean the passenger-carrying vehicle, or 'tram' for short. Where operation was by steam, the specially enclosed locomotives were called 'tram engines'.

'Tramroad' generally refers to early horse-operated lines that pre-date railways (see EARLY IRON RAILWAYS). It can include those with wooden rails, more usually known as 'wagonways' (see WOODEN RAILWAYS). But there are pitfalls. For instance the *Stratford & Moreton Railway (1826) and, initially, the Cromford & High Peak Railway (1830–1) were, in fact, tramroads while, conversely, as late as 1888 a company that leased the Brill Tramway, an agricultural railway in Buckinghamshire, called itself the Oxford & Aylesbury Tramroad. As a further anomaly, the Blackpool & Fleetwood Tramroad (1898) is an extension of the *Blackpool street tramway system.

Then there were officially titled tramways which in effect were *light railways running alongside roads or across country with minimal earthworks, although not all were built under the Light Railways Act. Examples were the Wantage, Wisbech & Upwell, Rye & Camber, and the picturesquely named Hundred of Manhood & Selsey Tramways. *Pier railways and *cliff railways are also sometimes called tramways, as were many short *industrial lines, either officially, like the Croesor Tramway in North Wales, or by local custom.

Again, some lines with the title 'railway' were, in fact, essentially electric street tramways, perhaps including substantial lengths of fenced track in open country, like the Llandudno & Colwyn Bay Electric Railway and the Kinver Light Railway. On the other hand, the Burton & Ashby, Camborne & Redruth, and Dearne District Light Railways were laid entirely or for the greater part on public roads. This category also included what were essentially railways but used tramcar-type vehicles and overhead equipment, such as the Manx Electric (see ISLE OF MAN RAILWAYS AND TRAMWAYS), Grimsby & Immingham Light, and *Swansea & Mumbles Railways.

GJB

tramways, street. The definition of a street tramway has been a subject for debate. Here we are concerned with a system of rail vehicles running mainly on public roads and carrying passengers to various parts of a town, especially from suburbs to the centre. While in other countries they frequently extended to link outlying places, in Great Britain this was exceptional.

Street tramways first appeared in the USA in the 1830s, and by the middle of the century extensive systems existed in several towns. The first European line was laid in Paris in 1853. The proprietors also tried unsuccessfully to obtain powers to construct a tramway in *London. It was therefore in *Liverpool that British tramways had their beginnings when in March 1859 William Curtis started a service of 'railway omnibuses' along existing railway tracks on the waterfront. Because of delays caused to freight traffic this lasted only nine months. However, its popularity caught the attention of George Francis Train, an eccentric young American working there. Unable to run trams in Liverpool, he obtained approval in Birkenhead and on 30 August 1860 opened the Birkenhead Street Railway. In most respects it was an outstanding success and Train swiftly followed with lines in London, Darlington, and Hanley in the Potteries. Unfortunately, although an astute publicist, he persisted in using the step-rail, which projected above the road surface, rather than grooved rail, so his lines were short-lived with the exceptions of those in Birkenhead and Hanley.

Apart from a curious guide-rail system in Salford (see MANCHESTER) it was not until the end of the decade that enthusiasm for tramways really began. Sensing the need for uniformity, Parliament passed the Tramways Act in 1870, which formed the basis of most subsequent street tramway Acts. It contained various standard clauses of which two gave considerable trouble later. One authorized a local authority to purchase an undertaking compulsorily after 21 years (and every subsequent seven years), and the other required a tramway company to maintain the road surface between, and 18 in on either side of, the rails. Local authorities were enabled to reject tramway proposals and, although several owned tramways, they could only run them by employing contractors. Not until 1882 was municipal operation authorized, commencing in Huddersfield. One other factor that came to have an adverse effect was the liability of tramway undertakings to pay rates (see TAXATION, LOCAL) on the full value of their track, confirmed by the courts in 1873. Because of the restrictions imposed by the Act a number of later lines were constructed under the *Light Railways Act, 1896.

Only animal power was permitted by the 1870 Act, and the vast numbers of horses required at the usual ratio of 10 or 11 horses per tramcar was a major expense. Steam was the only practicable alternative and several inventors produced locomotives or self-propelled cars. To use these required special dispensation from the Board of *Trade, but in 1879 the Tramways Orders Confirmation Act permitted mechanical power. About six firms produced locomotives but the market was dominated by the patented designs of Kitson and of Wilkinson. The definitive type of steam tram consisted of a locomotive, totally enclosed and consuming its own smoke as required by the Act, pulling a large bogie passenger trailer, often a double-deck car with a roof to protect passengers from the engine's exhaust.

There were about 530 steam trams in Britain, operating on about 50 systems. Other mechanical systems had little success, although almost everything from gas to clockwork was tried. A few lines were operated by cables from a winding engine in a central power station, running in a sunken conduit between the rails, attached to the cars by detachable grippers, but only *Edinburgh had a widespread cable system.

Electricity was the answer for tramway propulsion. The principles had been understood from the 1830s but it was not until 1879 that the first successful electric railway was demonstrated, in Germany, by Werner von Siemens. In 1883 Magnus Volk opened a curious line on the shore at *Brighton (still running today) and in the same year the first conventional electric tramway was opened for tourist traffic to the Giant's Causeway, at Portrush in Northern Ireland. In Britain the *Blackpool tramway began running to the designs of Holroyd Smith in 1884, with power collection from conductors in a conduit below the road. Meanwhile, in America basic problems of current-control through resistances, axle-mounted motors, and current collection by overhead trolley and wire had been resolved, mainly by Frank Sprague. The first British line using trolley poles opened at Roundhay, *Leeds, in 1891.

Throughout the 1890s several new electric tramways were built, and although many experiments were made, most followed the proved method of overhead trolley current-collection on doubled-ended, four-wheel or bogie cars. Usually these had an enclosed lower saloon and an uncovered upper deck, with end-staircases. In central London and several other towns environmental concerns forced the use of conduit current-collection, while a few systems, principally Wolverhampton and Lincoln, supplied current through a series of studs in the road which, if working properly, were only 'live' as the car passed over them. Apart from the London conduit, these variations were relatively short-lived.

Throughout the 1900s tramways proliferated throughout Great Britain, and by World War I all major cities and many smaller towns were equipped. The typical system was usually municipally owned and operated, taking current from a municipal power station and using simple but sturdy four-wheel double-deck cars (or larger bogie cars in big cities) on frequent and cheap services from around 6 a.m. to midnight. In most cases the tracks, usually of standard *gauge but sometimes narrower, ran in the centre of the main roads into the town. Where they penetrated country areas, building development might soon follow. The majority of British tramcars were built by the *Preston firm of Dick Kerr & Co. or the Brush Electrical Engineering Co. of Loughborough, although there were a few smaller manufacturers. Many municipal and some company systems built some of their own cars.

Some tramways carried freight. Huddersfield had two

special cars to take coal from railway sidings to mills, while railway wagons were hauled by electric locomotives through *Glasgow streets to shipyards in Govan, and also over part of Blackpool's reserved track. Many systems carried *parcels, for which *Manchester had a fleet of special cars.

Following World War I some of the smaller systems were losing money, partly because reliable *buses, often based on war-time lorry chassis, were available to rival private operators who could offer a more flexible service. Sheerness was the first electric system to close, in 1917, and over the next 20 years most of the smaller concerns followed as their original track and equipment wore out. Conversely, most major towns saw the tram as the only means of handling dense traffic and steadily developed their systems. Many bought new totally enclosed cars and modernized older cars. Often larger motors and air *brakes were fitted for higher service speeds. Large cities often took over smaller neighbouring systems as they expanded, resulting in extensive and heavily used layouts. Glasgow, for instance, had over 1,200 tramcars operating on 133 miles of route in the city and surrounding burghs.

British tramways reached their maximum extent in 1927 when 14,481 cars operated on 2,554 route-miles. 184 local authorities owned tramways at various times, though only 112 actually operated trams. The remainder were worked either by neighbouring municipalities or by one of over 70 private companies. However, most of the private operators owned all or part of their tracks, with an estimated 2,850 cars working a maximum of 800 route-miles in 1920.

In spite of the industry's size it began to decline in the face of bus competition. Several larger towns, such as *Newcastle and *Portsmouth, started scrapping trams in the 1930s, often turning to the trolleybus to maintain the use of municipal electricity. All the London tramways became part of the London Passenger Transport Board (see LONDON UNDERGROUND RAILWAYS) in 1933, which did not favour trams. A shortage of new buses during World War II ensured the survival of most remaining tramways, although *Coventry and *Bristol were casualties of enemy action, but afterwards most systems had closed by the mid-1950s. The last was Glasgow in September 1962, except for the seafront tramway at Blackpool which still remains, an extension of the pioneer electric line.

Various efforts were made to preserve cars and other relics, resulting in the setting up of the National Tramway Museum at Crich, Derbyshire, in 1959. A representative selection of trams is on display, with several operating a demonstration service in the summer months. The museum also houses the official national collection of tramway archives and an extensive film library. There are several other tramcars, some in running order, preserved at various industrial and transport *museums.

European experience has shown the value of railed electric traction in reducing congestion and pollution in cities, resulting in the opening of the tramway's successor, the *Light Rapid Transit System, first in Newcastle (1980) and then in Manchester and *Sheffield. Plans for others are well advanced.

See also ISLE OF MAN RAILWAYS AND TRAMWAYS; SWANSEA & MUMBLES RAILWAY; SUBURBS, RAILWAYS AND.   CRI

(Sir) Philip Dawson, *Electric Railways and Tramways, Their Construction and Operation* (1897); C. Klapper, *The Golden Age of Tramways* (1961); W. H. Bett and J. C. Gillham, *Great British Tramway Networks* (1962); J. S. Webb, *The British Steam Tram* (1981).

Transport, Ministry and Department of. Since the coming of the railways, the nation has had an equivocal attitude to them, in which governments—of all political persuasions—have been tempted to interfere but for which they have been unwilling to be held responsible. The history of the Board of *Trade clearly indicates the inability of politicians to decide what quality, quantity, and type of transport the country wants and can afford, and it was not until 1919 that a separate transport ministry was set up. The first minister, Sir Eric *Geddes, announced that 'upon efficient transportation depends the comfort, if not the very existence, of each and every one of us'.

The main reason for the creation of the new ministry in 1919 was the parlous state of Britain's railways after four years of war, during which the then existing 120 independent railway companies had been under government control. *Nationalization was considered, but in the event the numerous companies were amalgamated into four by the Railways Act, 1921 (see GROUPING). In so doing, *Lloyd George's coalition government had sought a compromise between state and private ownership. The merger proposals were formulated by Geddes—a former deputy general manager of the *North Eastern Railway—without consultation with the companies that were covered by the Act.

The Railways Act had been drafted with a view to controlling a railway monopoly, but the Ministry of Transport had not anticipated the extent of the threat to the railways created by the growth of *road traffic, both personal and commercial. The Road Traffic Act, 1930, helped the railways in part by introducing regulations relating to the construction and operation of vehicles and requiring road passenger operators to obtain public service licences, but the abolition of the 20-mph speed limit for cars increased the attractiveness of private motor vehicles. Three years later, goods vehicle operators were also required to obtain carriers' licences.

On the outbreak of World War II in 1939, government control over the railways was exercised much as during the earlier conflict, but this time through the ministry which, in 1941, became part of the Ministry of War Transport whose responsibilities also included *shipping and road transport. Ministerial control of the railways was exercised by the Railway Executive Committee (REC), appointed under the Emergency (Railway Control) Order of 1940 to co-ordinate the running of all railways, but not their financial control. The headquarters of the REC was ingeniously and speedily constructed in the disused subways and on the platforms of the closed Down Street station on the *Piccadilly Underground line, where its location remained a secret throughout the war.

In general, the quality of the equipment and infrastructure, and the profusion of alternative routes inherited by the REC, could hardly have been better preparation for the conflict for which the railways were to be so poorly remunerated. Negotiation as to the revenue that should be allocated to the shareholders of railway companies was both prolonged and difficult, and the government drove a hard bargain by calculating compensation by reference to the (bad) financial years of 1935, 1936, and 1937.

After the war, responsibility for shipping remained with the Ministry of Transport, to which name it had reverted, until transferred to the Board of Trade in 1965. In the air, the Ministries of Transport and Civil Aviation combined in 1953: aviation also moved to the Board of Trade in 1965 but returned again in 1983. In 1971, the Ministry of Transport merged with the Ministry of Housing and Local Government and the Ministry of Works to form the Department of the Environment, and in 1976 the Department of Transport was created to which shipping was returned in 1983.

The ministry—under whatever name—has often been accused of being a 'Ministry for Roads'. Support for this view can be gauged by the fact that in 1985, for example, no fewer than seven under-secretaries were responsible for roads compared with two dealing with railways: the figures for assistant secretaries were 13 and four respectively. Similarly, statements by ministers and department officials about 'investment' in roads are to be compared with complaints about railway *subsidies and deficits. New roads and road improvements are proposed within the ministry and justified on a social cost-benefit basis, including in the calculations such matters as reduced journey times and safety-enhancement, whereas every request for railway investment is scrutinized by ministry officials and has to demonstrate at least an 8 per cent return on capital. Under this regime, a vast motorway network has been constructed throughout the country since 1960, during which period main-line *electrification has been extended only to the *East and *West Coast main lines, and more lines in the south-east.

Between the date of its creation in 1919 and the beginning of 1995, there have been no fewer than 37 transport ministers or secretaries of state compared with 41 presidents of the Board of Trade in 1840–1919. The numerous changes of name borne by the ministry, and the frequent reallocations of its duties, testify to the low estimate of the importance of transport in the minds of British politicians. Ministers have seen the post either as a stepping-stone to higher office, to which they wish to aspire at the earliest opportunity, or as an indication that their ministerial career has peaked. In either case, enthusiasm for the post is likely to be in short supply. The most famous transport ministers are probably Herbert *Morrison, Leslie Hore-Belisha, Lord Reith, Ernest Marples, and Barbara Castle. One Labour minister, Richard Marsh, was subsequently appointed chairman of the *British Railways Board by a Conservative government.   CSH

Gourvish; M. R. Bonavia, *Twilight of British Rail?* (1985), and *British Rail: The First 25 Years* (1981); O. S. Nock, *Britain's Railways at War, 1939–1945* (1971).

Transport 2000. This international transport campaigning group had its origins in Britain. It is an umbrella group, launched in February 1973 by the railway trades unions, environmental groups, amenity societies, and the *Railway Industry Association.

The organization represents the interests of its constituent groups by seeking to maximize the role of public transport, notably rail, and by recommending the reduction of car traffic and road freight transport.

Transport 2000 has received funding from the railway trades unions, the railway industry, and *British Rail. From the late 1970s it has maintained a full-time staff, and commissioned transport studies and publications, as well as achieving good access to the media.　　　　　MLH

P. S. Bagwell, *The Railwaymen*, ii (1982).

Transport & Works Act, see PROMOTION OF RAILWAYS: PROCEDURE.

transporter wagon: a wagon for transporting another rail vehicle, usually of a different *track gauge, to avoid transhipment. The usual application was on *narrow-gauge railways.

The 4-ft gauge Padarn Railway in North Wales, of 1843, used special wagons to carry four 2-ft gauge *slate wagons, two abreast, from Dinorwic quarries, near Llanberis, to Port Dinorwic, where they were off-loaded and lowered down inclines to the quay. It closed in 1961.

E. R. Calthrop, engineer of the 2 ft 6 in gauge Leek & Manifold Light Railway, opened in 1904, designed a flat transporter wagon to convey a standard-gauge wagon whose wheel-flanges rested in grooves. Probably the first of its type on a public narrow-gauge railway, the idea was also used in India, and Germany. There were four wagons on the Leek & Manifold, which closed in 1934.

These should not be confused with the use of flat wagons to carry *containers, well wagons, or Roadrailers (see ROAD-RAIL VEHICLES). Wagons to carry road tankers containing milk or edible oil saw limited use in the 1930s, and more recently intermodal wagons have appeared on *BR, such as were operated by Charterail, and through the *Channel Tunnel.　　　　　MLH

D. C. Carrington and T. F. Rushworth, *Slates to Velinheli* (1973).

Transport Salaried Staffs' Association. The TSSA started life in Sheffield in 1897 as the National Association of General Railway Clerks, which changed its name a year later to the Railway Clerks' Association (RCA). It was known as that until 1950 when it was decided that, as membership was opened up to all transport clerical workers, a more appropriate name would be the Transport Salaried Staffs' Association.

At the close of the 19th century railway clerical staff conditions were often unhygienic and the hours excessive. Railway clerks did not have the protection of the Factories Acts or of the Employers' Liability Act. It was claimed that a separate organization of railway clerks, supervisors, and *stationmasters was needed to protect their interests.

In its early months the future of the RCA looked bleak.

Recruitment was sluggish. At an executive meeting on 13 November 1898 a resolution to wind up the organization was defeated by five votes to four. Some of the minority considered they would be better off inside the Amalgamated Society of Railway Servants (see NATIONAL UNION OF RAILWAYMEN), which already had clerical staff members. Others thought that railway victimization of trade union activists, by blocking their promotion, or by their transference to remote country stations, would beat all attempts to establish a strong union. But the efforts of the pioneers continued and membership crept up to 4,666, organized in 59 branches, in 1904.

Two events stimulated growth. The Trade Disputes Act, 1906, removed the obstacles to trade union membership and activity, and the election of A. G. Walkden, a very able founder-member, as general secretary of the RCA in the same year was later described in the union's journal (May 1987) as 'a stroke of genius'. Walkden remained in office until retirement in 1936. He had the wisdom to see that the RCA, acting alone, lacked the power to obtain full recognition by the companies. The union had affiliated to the TUC in 1903 and it sought its help, and that of the Labour Party after 1906, in a policy of blocking railway Bills until it gained concession from the companies, or union recognition. Thus a Bill to amalgamate the *Great Northern, *Great Eastern, and *Great Central companies was held up until an agreement was reached that railway clerks should be free to join the RCA. The Bill subsequently failed in Parliament.

It was the union's policy under Walkden to secure full unionization of all railway clerical and supervisory staff by negotiation and the strength of its case, rather than by industrial action. One of the persistent arguments of the companies that had to be countered was that clerks handling confidential information should be banned from union membership since, otherwise, there would be a conflict of loyalties.

The RCA did not join the other unions in a strike over union recognition in August 1911, but in the general upsurge of workers' organization its membership shot up from 9,476 in 1910 to 25,791 at the end of 1913.

The closing years of World War I and its immediate aftermath saw an enormous increase in industrial militancy, with six million working days lost in strikes in 1918 and no fewer than 35 million in 1919. During these months, for the first time, the majority of railway clerks were in the RCA. Full union recognition was obtained under the Railways Act of 1921 (see GROUPING).

After the war the union avoided involvement in other railway strikes; but in 1921 its executive voted £1,000 to the miners on strike against heavy wage cuts. It supported the TUC's call in the 1926 General Strike, though slightly under half of its members stopped work.

In 1952, under its new name of TSSA, the union achieved a peak membership of 91,514, partly caused by recruiting from linked concerns, such as Thomas *Cook and Sons. In the 1980s and 1990s TSSA did not experience membership decline on the scale in the other two railway unions, because *BR and its successors shed jobs more drastically in the operating grades. It had a total of 38,000 men and women members in 1994.

See also TRADE UNIONISM. PSG

A. G. Walkden, *The Life of a Railway Clerk* (1911); A. G. Walkden, *The RCA and Its Path of Progress* (1928); A. Tranter, 'Walkden, Alexander George, 1st Baron Walkden of Great Bookham, 1873–1951', in J. M. Bellamy and I. Saville, *Dictionary of Labour Biography*, v (1979); 'The History of the TSSA', *TSS Journal*, April, May, July, and Sept. 1987.

Transport Tribunal, see FREIGHT TRAFFIC RATES.

Transport Users' Consultative Committees. When the railways were *nationalized by the Transport Act, 1947, the government recognized that users of the new monopoly might need some protection. In section 6 of the Act, the government established a Central Transport Consultative Committee (CTCC) and regional committees 'to consider . . . and make recommendations in regard to any matter (including charges) affecting services and facilities provided by the *British Transport Commission which has been the subject of representations . . . by users . . . or which appears to be a matter to which consideration ought to be given, or which the Minister or Commission may refer to them for consideration'.

Regional committees were initially established for Scotland, Wales, London, and eight other areas in England. The Minister stressed that they were 'free and independent bodies' which had not been set up to act as 'rubber stamps', but generally in the 1950s there was little conflict between recommendations of the committees—such as *electrification of the Hastings line—and the desire of the BTC and government to improve services and reduce costs. Even *closure proposals considered by the regional committees were so evidently desirable that subsequent recommendations in favour of closure to the CTCC and thence to the minister created no problems.

However, a recommendation to retain the Westerham (Kent) branch in 1961 was overturned by the minister and, perhaps in anticipation of the more robust attitude likely to be adopted to the numerous and more difficult closure proposals that would follow the publication of the *Beeching Report, the powers of the TUCCs were reduced by the Transport Act, 1962. Henceforth, the committees would only be required to advise the minister on the hardship that might result from a closure, not on the closure proposal itself. The limited powers and duties of the committees in closure cases have rarely been understood by the public, which also does not appreciate the less dramatic aspects of committee business such as commenting upon quality of service and timetable proposals.

Members of the CTCC and the regional committees were appointed originally by the Minister of Transport, and later by a minister from the Department of Trade and Industry. Under the Railways Act, 1994 (see PRIVATIZATION), the CTCC was abolished and replaced by a Central Rail Users' Consultative Committee (CRUCC). The regional committees (other than the London Regional Passengers' Committee) were also replaced by new regional Rail Users' Consultative Committees. All members of CRUCC and the regional committees are now appointed by the Rail Regulator, save for the chairmen who are still appointed by the Secretary of State after consultation with the Regulator.

CSH

Annual Reports of CTCC, 1939–1994; Annual Reports of London Regional Passengers' Committee, 1984–1994; Gourvish.

travel agents. No such people were ever heard of before the development of railways. At the larger coaching inns there were booking offices, where places could be reserved in the coaches based on them; but none of these offered a choice of places in several coaches, starting from different inns.

A new kind of agency originated with the *excursion train. Thomas *Cook soon began arranging long-distance trips that involved the guaranteed co-operation of more than one provider of travel facilities: in 1845–6 from *Leicester to *Liverpool and North Wales, for example, and to the Scottish Highlands, a single booking with him covering all the travel involved, by land and water. At the same time Joseph Crisp was advertising excursions from Liverpool to Paris, with all the arrangements for rail and sea journeys made by him in advance.

Crisp seems to fade out in the 1850s, but another man appeared in Liverpool, Henry Marcus, working with the *London & North Western Railway as its excursion agent until 1866, when he was replaced by Henry Gaze of *Southampton, who moved to London shortly afterwards, building up a very large business with branches or agencies of his own across the world, until it went down in the less competent hands of his sons to insolvency in 1903. Dean & Dawson, founded as a travel agency at *Sheffield in 1878 and subsequently based chiefly in Stockport, was taken over by the *Great Central Railway in 1904. The business of John Frame of Northampton, conducted strictly on *temperance principles, grew extensive enough to allow him to become agent for one Scottish railway company, the *Caledonian. Agents also appeared offering specialized types of excursions and tours: Quintin Hogg's Polytechnic Training Association (1886), appealing largely to students at the London Polytechnic, and Sir Henry Lunn (1893), whose business was specifically addressed to the promotion of travel to winter sports in the Alps. John Restall chartered trains for day and weekend excursions, working with the *London Brighton & South Coast Railway and some others, selling tickets for them at his London office.

In the 20th century travel agency became big international business. Cook's was very active in the USA, American Express in Britain. Yet no large firm of travel agents like these ever appeared in any continental country, except Wagons-Lits, based in Belgium, whose attention was given chiefly to the provision of *sleeping and *restaurant cars.

The scale of this industry—it was now hardly less than that—continued to grow and, generally speaking, it flourished in the 1920s and 1930s. After World War II it took on quite new dimensions with the huge expansion of air travel, and its cheapening in the 1950s, and at the same time the great increase in holiday cruises, on all the oceans, employing to a large extent the large liners as they yielded up their original business to aircraft.

This new world-wide travelling intensified the demand for agencies. Few holiday-makers could master the complications involved in it. Fewer still could accurately compute the price of one projected journey against another. Firms of travel agents now multiplied everywhere: some quite large, others very small, Cook's and American Express still outdistancing the rest.

One change affecting all of them took place in these years. Their concern with railway travel grew less and less important. Where, in earlier days, people commonly turned to a travel agent to arrange their summer holidays for them in *Bournemouth or Scarborough, they now wanted to go to Majorca or Rimini or Florida. The railways' holiday business contracted. But the travel agents' grew.   JS

W. F. Rae, *The Business of Travel* (1893); P. Brendon, *Thomas Cook* (1991); Dean & Dawson: Dow, iii, ch. 3; several sets of figures for Restall's business with the LBSCR are in PRO, RAIL 414/537.

Travellers Fare, see REFRESHMENT ROOMS.

Travelling Post Office, see MAIL SERVICES.

traversers, or transfer tables as they are appropriately described in North America, are travelling rail-bridges moving transversely to link groups of tracks on either side, usually serving workshops and stores, and taking much less space than points and crossings. They are used primarily in locomotive and carriage-building and repair *works, and enable rolling stock to be transferred between shops on opposite sides of the traverser pit, or between those on the same side, during the various stages of construction and overhaul. Their disadvantage was that as vehicle lengths increased, they could be found to be too short. *London & North Western Railway *carriages were restricted to 42 ft for many years, due to the length of just one or two traversers. They were sometimes used in goods depots for wagon transfer, and in several early passenger stations. Two remained in use at *Birmingham Moor Street station until 1967.

Located at right angles to the tracks to which they provide access, traversers consist of two main girders carrying the rail track, braced by cross members. Their length now of up to about 100 ft is sufficient for the longest locomotive or coach. They run on flanged wheels at each end, travelling on rails at the longitudinal sides of the pit. At one time operated by steam, normally they are now powered electrically.

In workshops run on a production-line system, locomotives or coaches are moved by overhead travelling *cranes, so that traversers tend to be used less.   GWC

trees, planting of. Many railway embankments and cuttings were planted with trees when the lines were built, with the intention that their roots should help to bind them together: particularly on loose, sandy soils and on chalk. The most extensive example in Britain is on the 42 miles of main line between Woking and Winchester, completed under *Locke in 1838–40. The long, deep cutting east of Farnborough is planted with noble trees, including Spanish chestnuts. On the chalk at Micheldever there is much more of this rich planting, with a preponderance of beech. The *Great Western and *Great Central companies came to use conifers, particularly firs, for this purpose, cheap and quick-growing; their gloomy presence still characterizes the GWR 'cut-off' lines of 1900–10 (see LOOP).

But such planting could serve another purpose too. Some *landowners insisted, as a condition of their assent to the building of railway embankments across their property, that trees and shrubs should conceal them, and also perhaps, when full-grown, damp down the railways' noise. One at Bradford-on-Avon got the Wilts Somerset & Weymouth Railway to agree that embankments crossing his land 'should be planted by the company at the proper season next after their construction with ornamental shrubs or evergreens, and protected and from time to time renewed'.

Public bodies might be equally demanding. *Preston Corporation required the *East Lancashire Railway to plant its embankment approaching the town in 1847; 'plane and other suitable trees' had to be planted, on the insistence of the Enfield Urban District Council, on the embankment carrying the *Great Northern Railway's extension to Gordon Hill in 1898.   JS

Bradford-on-Avon: Bodleian Library Oxford, MS Top. Wilts. b.3, fol. 22v; Preston: *LYR*, i, 121–2; Enfield: *LLR*, 240.

Trevithick, Richard (1771–1833), engineer. Born at Camborne in the tin-mining area of Cornwall, the son of a mine manager, he eagerly participated in local efforts both to evade James Watt's stationary steam engine monopoly and to harness high-pressure steam which would increase engine output while saving on coal; in 1800 he built a double-acting high-pressure engine with crank which was soon widely in demand in Cornwall and South Wales, the forerunner of his world-famous 'Cornish Engines'.

After experimenting with models, in 1801–3 he built and patented three high-pressure steam road carriages which ran in Camborne, London, and Coalbrookdale, but poor roads aborted this line of progress. As the result of a wager, in 1804 he built a steam locomotive for the Penydarren Ironworks near Merthyr Tydfil, which successfully hauled 10 tons over the 9½-mile-long *tramroad, although difficulties were encountered with the iron plate-rails breaking. It was then put to work driving a hammer, as intended. A second locomotive was built for Christopher Blackett at Wylam (see HEDLEY, WILLIAM) but not used.

Although his third locomotive, *Catch-me-who-can*, was built in 1808 as a publicity venture (it gave rides on a circular track near Euston), it was an advance on the Penydarren one in having a vertical cylinder driving directly to the wheels on one side without the clumsy flywheel or hazardous trombone-like slide arrangement.

On home ground in Cornwall, Trevithick had a deserved reputation for hard work and innovation, but elsewhere he flitted from one project to another (e.g. a steam dredger for the Thames, a brick tunnel under the Thames) without having the tenacity to overcome the inevitable problems, whether technical or financial. Many of his ideas—the return-flue boiler, the blast-pipe, coupled wheels, even his demonstration that smooth wheels had sufficient adhesion on smooth rails to pull a load—were adopted by others while he ultimately frittered away his talents and fortune in ill-considered mining ventures in South America, dying penniless. It was symptomatic that when Trevithick, in desperate circumstances, met the young Robert *Stephenson in Colombia in 1827, after the initial joy of recognition they had little to say to each other. His son Francis, however, went on to become the first locomotive superintendent of the *London & North Western Railway.   RVL

J. Hodge, *Richard Trevithick* (1973); J. B. Snell, *Railways: Mechanical Engineering* (1971).

tripcock: a device to prevent trains from passing stop signals, adopted as standard practice on *London Transport lines and some other urban lines. A short arm mounted close to the rail at each stop signal lies flat when the signal shows 'clear', and rises to a vertical position when it is at 'danger'. If a train passes a signal at danger the trip arm comes into contact with a trip lever or cock on the train, which operates a valve in the braking system and stops it. The driver has to reset the tripcock before he can proceed.

See also SIGNALLING; SAFETY; UNDERGROUND RAILWAYS.
     RDF

G. M. Kichenside and A. Williams, *British Railway Signalling* (1968).

Trubshaw, Charles (1841–1917), architect. After training under his father, who was architect and surveyor for Staffordshire, Trubshaw joined the *London & North Western Railway in 1864. In 1874 he was appointed architect for the northern division of the *Midland Railway, and from 1884 until his retirement in 1905 for the whole system. One of his early works was a new station at Skipton, in which he modified the company's characteristic ridge-and-furrow glass-and-iron platform awning in a manner subsequently used extensively elsewhere. Among his major stations *Leicester London Road, *Bradford Forster Square (including the *hotel), and *Sheffield Midland stand out, and he was a prolific user of terracotta as a facing and decorative material. He used it in several standardized styles developed for smaller stations, and particularly in his most notable work, the Midland Hotel in *Manchester, designed in collaboration with the Midland's hotels manager, Arthur *Towle.   GJB

D. E. Ware, *A Short Dictionary of British Architects* (1967); S. J. Dixey, 'Charles Trubshaw: A Victorian Railway Architect', *Backtrack* (1994), 65–8.

tube, see LONDON UNDERGROUND RAILWAYS.

tunnels and tunnelling. From the beginnings of railway construction and throughout the years of expansion up to the early years of the 20th century, the construction of tunnels was an essential feature in affording reasonably direct routeing with acceptable gradients, as opposed to the alternative of a circuitous route around high ground, in order that gradients should not be steeper than the *ruling gradient for the line.

The total number of tunnels on main-line railways in Britain is officially stated to be 1,049. Included in this figure are structures built by cut-and-cover method as well as tunnels driven through the ground as a bore or heading. In the former case the ground is opened out and abutments constructed which are surmounted by an arch or some other form of superstructure. A tunnel in this category is in reality an elongated bridge. Examples are the tunnels on the sub-surface railways beneath the centre of *Glasgow and the Circle Line on the *London Underground.

British Tunnels over 2 miles long

Tunnel	Location between	and	Length (miles)	(yds)	Opened
Channel	Folkestone	Coquelles, France			
Running Tunnel North			31	636	1994
Service Tunnel			31	606	1994
Running Tunnel South			31	611	1994
Severn	Pilning	Severn Tunnel Jcn	4	629	1886
Totley	Dore	Grindleford	3	950	1893
Standedge	Marsden	Diggle	3	62	1849[a]
Woodhead	Dunford Bridge	Woodhead	3	22	1845[b]
Sodbury	Badminton	Chipping Sodbury	2	924	1903
Disley	Chinley	Cheadle Heath	2	346	1902
Bramhope	Horsforth	Arthington	2	241	1849
Festiniog	Roman Bridge	Blaenau Festiniog	2	338	1879[c]
Cowburn	Edale	Chinley	2	182	1893

Note: The longest continuous tube tunnel is on London Transport's Northern Line, East Finchley to Morden via Bank, 17 m 528 yds.

[a] Single line. Second single-line tunnel opened 1871; third (double-line) tunnel opened 1894 (3 m 64 yds); single-line tunnels closed 1966.

[b] Single line. Second single-line tunnel opened 1852; new (double-line) tunnel opened 1954 (3 m 66 yds) and single-line tunnels closed; new tunnel closed 1981.

[c] Single line.

Since the vast majority of British tunnels were built by traditional tunnelling methods it is pertinent, therefore, to deal with tunnels in this category alone.

The progenitors of railway tunnelling in Britain were the coal-mining tunnels carrying rails, and the *canal tunnels built during the 18th century and the very early years of the 19th. Those early constructions include a 1¾-mile tunnel at Norwood on the Chesterfield Canal, built by Brindley and Henshall, Brindley's mile-long tunnel at Harecastle on the Trent & Mersey Canal, the 2½-mile Sapperton Tunnel through the Cotswolds near Kemble, and the 3-mile Stand-edge Tunnel on the Huddersfield Narrow Canal.

The development of tunnelling on a really large scale, in terms of both length and sectional dimensions, was unreservedly attributable to the demands of railway construction under the great railway engineers: the two *Stephensons, *Locke, *Brunel, and others. Their works in the field of tunnelling surpassed by far anything previously undertaken in earlier canal construction. Considering the very simplicity and inadequacy of the available tools and equipment, which were mainly picks, shovels, and bars, and the fact that the only source of power was men and horses, their early tunnel engineering accomplishments were monumental by any standards.

Between 1826 and 1830 the Stephensons had already built two double-line tunnels under *Liverpool for the *Liverpool & Manchester Railway: the Victoria Tunnel, 1 m 946 yds in length, and the Wapping Tunnel, 1 m 351 yds. Robert Stephenson's 1 m 36 yds tunnel at Glenfield on the *Leicester and Swannington Railway was opened in 1832 and later in that decade work started on the first trans-Pennine bore, Summit Tunnel, 1 m 1,125 yds, at Littleborough on the *Manchester & Leeds Railway with T. L. *Gooch in charge of the site works under the direction of George Stephenson. When it opened in 1840 it was the longest tunnel in Britain. Meanwhile, construction of Brunel's tunnel under Box Hill between Chippenham and Bath on the Bristol main line of the *Great Western Railway had been started in 1836. Construction took 4½ years and, after encountering particularly difficult geological conditions, the tunnel, 1 m 1,452 yds in length, was opened to traffic in 1841.

From those early years of the railway building era the basic method of tunnel construction has remained much the same. Now, just as in those days, the main stages are, firstly, the sinking of exploratory borings and trial shafts along the line of the tunnel to ascertain the nature of the strata. Next follows the construction of working shafts to a depth from which the pilot headings are driven in opposing directions. At the same time, the approach cuttings at each end of the tunnel are excavated and, from these, pilot headings are also driven. This system enables excavation of the headings to be effected from twice as many working faces as there are headings, plus the two faces being driven from the portals. In the early years of tunnelling, before accurate *surveying instruments were available, it was necessary for the several pairs of driven headings to link up before the longitudinal line of the tunnel could be set out with due precision. The link-up of the headings also facilitated ven-

tilation and drainage. Following the driving of the headings comes the opening-out to the full sectional dimensions of the tunnel, allowing, of course, for the thickness of the tunnel lining. Finally the tunnel lining and portals are built and permanent drainage installed.

The decision as to whether a tunnel or a cutting was appropriate depended on several factors, such as the nature of strata and whether or not the excavated spoil was required for nearby embankments, but a rough rule was that where a cutting would be more than 60 ft in depth it was more economical to bore a tunnel.

The extent of resources engaged in tunnel construction has always been, and continues to be, massive because of the very nature and scale of the activity. On earlier projects every operation was very labour-intensive, slow, sometimes cumbersome, and often not without danger. This may be judged from the fact that at the peak of activity during the construction of Box Tunnel no fewer than 4,000 men and 300 horses were employed. A ton of candles and a ton of gunpowder were used every week and the many accidents during the course of the job took a toll of nearly 100 men's lives.

Access to the working level was by means of winding devices called gins, which were worked by horses. The same means were used for bringing excavated spoil up to the surface. If blasting of the rock was necessary, drilling for the shots was done by hand. The only explosive was gunpowder. Even the process of setting out the line of the tunnel was quite primitive. It necessitated the building of a substantial tower around 30 ft high over the centre-line of the tunnel at a high point, to afford sighting of the whole length. Surmounting the tower was a telescope, called the transit instrument, which could rotate in the vertical circle only, thus limiting its use to the setting out of points on a straight line.

By around the 1850s and 1860s a gradual and continuing improvement in tunnelling equipment was taking place. Steam engines replaced the horse-gins and steam power was being applied to other surface activities. There were improvements to pumping machinery, air compressors, rock-drilling equipment, and the disposal of excavated spoil. Following Nobel's invention of dynamite in 1865 more effective explosives became available, hydraulic equipment such as jacks were in use, and, later in the century, portable steam engines and boilers were available to drive generators that provided electric lighting underground, thus giving considerable improvement in working conditions.

The tunnelling 'shield', a device which minimises collapse when excavating soft groud, was devised by Sir Marc Brunel for the Thames Tunnel (1825–43, see LONDON UNDERGROUND RAILWAYS: EAST LONDON RAILWAY). It was developed by P. W. *Barlow and J. H. *Greathead, and first used on the Tower Subway (1870).

Throughout a century and more of railway tunnelling in Britain, despite the most thorough investigation of geological conditions, it has not been unusual for problems to be encountered which have called for changes in methods, or design changes in the form of lining.

At Box Tunnel the original intention was that half a mile at the eastern end, where it was driven through Bath stone, would not need to be lined. However, the friable nature of the rock meant that a brick lining had to be provided over much of that length. At Primrose Hill Tunnel (1837), north of *Euston, where London clay was encountered, it was found that the ground pressures were so great that measures to strengthen the entire structure were necessary. This was achieved by the provision of an extra ring of brickwork to the lining, the provision of an invert, and the substitution of 'Roman Cement', a mixture of cement and sharp furnace ashes, for the normal jointing mortar. Further north on the *London & Birmingham line at Kilsby, the usual trial borings had been put down to prove the strata and nothing to cause concern was indicated. However, when work on the 1 m 666 yds tunnel was under way in 1835, quicksand which had not been shown up by the trial borings was encountered. Water flooded the workings, and before construction could continue additional shafts had to be sunk and powerful pumps installed. A century later, when the double-line Woodhead New Tunnel was being driven, the *London & North Eastern Railway had the advantage of a detailed longitudinal section made by the resident engineer when the first Woodhead Tunnel (see GREAT CENTRAL RAILWAY) was built between 1838 and 1845, yet even with such information it became necessary to change the way of drilling and revise the working methods.

The 45 years from 1825 to 1870 formed the most active period of railway construction in Britain. During those years the essential system encompassing all the main lines was virtually completed. The railway network of 1870 included numerous tunnels, 28 of which exceeded a mile in length. These were at that time the major tunnels of the system. Two of them exceeded 3 miles and one was more than 2 miles long. The remaining 25 were of lengths ranging from 1 m 6 yds to 1 m 1,693 yds. These 28 tunnels aggregated in length to a total of 47½ miles.

The succeeding 35 years saw the completion of another 23 tunnels more than a mile long. The most notable of these was the 4 m 629 yds *Severn Tunnel, built between 1873 and 1886.

The 20th century has seen the construction of only three major tunnels. Noteworthy among these is the Woodhead New double-line tunnel, 3 m 66 yds long, which was built between 1949 and 1953 to replace two single-line bores.

The outcome of development of 19th-century main-line tunnelling are the deep tubes of the London Underground. Their construction has been favoured by a deep stratum of clay enabling boring with a shield and the use of cast-iron or precast concrete segments for the lining. There are 175 miles of deep tubes plus 45 miles of sub-surface railways. The longest tube, 17 m 528 yds, opened in 1939, is on the Northern Line between East Finchley and Morden via Bank. Until completion of the 33 m 809 yds single-line Seikan Tunnel, Japan, in 1988, this was the world's longest railway tunnel.

Judged by any standards, whether boldness of concept, magnitude of construction, or quality of workmanship, tunnels rank among the greatest civil engineering achievements of railway construction in Britain. There is one, however, which eclipses all others in terms of its complexity and magnitude, and which can fairly be said to be the greatest civil engineering accomplishment of all time: the *Channel Tunnel, comprising three bores, each over 31 miles long.

See also UNDERGROUND RAILWAYS; CIVIL ENGINEERING.   AB

F. W. Simms, *Practical Tunnelling* (1896 edn.); A. Blower, *British Railway Tunnels* (1964). Tunnelling shields: C. E. Lee, *The Tower Subway*, TNS, 43 (1970–1) 41–51.

turbine locomotives, see TRACTION, TURBINE.

turnpike trusts were legal instruments that did much to improve the British road system in the 18th century. From 1700 onwards Acts were passed, empowering named trustees to levy tolls for the maintenance of specified sections of road. The system grew rapidly from 1750 onwards and lasted for nearly two centuries.

The word 'turnpike' was an old one, meaning simply a barrier, applied to the gates where the tolls were collected at the beginning of each trust's road. The tolls were farmed out by auction annually, providing the trustees with funds for the repairs and improvements, supplemented by mortgages where necessary.

When passenger-carrying railways were projected the trustees usually opposed them, as rivals likely to diminish or destroy their revenue. A standard printed form for the use of trustees petitioning Parliament against a railway Bill was drawn up about 1834. These fears were often justified. The receipts from the auction of the Tewkesbury tolls fell by 36 per cent in 1839–40, with the opening of the *Bristol & Gloucester Railway; those of the trusts where roads paralleled the *Lancaster & Carlisle Railway by 40 per cent in 1846–8. On the other hand, trusts that had no railway competition continued to be able to maintain their roads adequately. The Ambleside trust, for instance, remained profitable until its abolition in 1885.

The growth of the railway system reduced the need for well-repaired roads. Maintenance ceased to be a national problem, though it remained one for some localities. The trusts now seemed effete survivals from the past. In 1871 all turnpike tolls in London were abolished; by 1883 all had gone in Scotland. The very last disappeared in Anglesey in 1895.   JS

W. Albert, *The Turnpike Road System in England, 1663–1840* (1972); draft printed form: Kent RO (Maidstone), AG 54; *Tewkesbury Register*, ii (1850), 11; L. Williams, *Road Transport in Cumbria in the 19th century* (1975), 147, 185; S. and B. Webb, *Story of the King's Highway* (1913), 222.

turntables. From the earliest days of railways simple turnplates were used extensively, for example on the *Liverpool & Manchester Railway (1830) and at early termini, where they were situated on arrival tracks adjacent to buffer stops to enable the small locomotives and four-wheel carriages of the day to be released, or moved about the station. Another example was *Derby, where the line from the *engine shed crossed eight running lines at right-angles, each equipped with turnplates at intersections. Additional turnplates were spaced along the tracks which were all parallel to the single platform. G. P. *Neele recalled trains jarring across turn-plates in stations in 1857–60, although by then they were starting to disappear with the advent of larger vehicles, to be superseded by locomotive turntables of more sophisticated design outside. However, they continued in use in goods yards for four-wheel wagons until recent times.

Locomotive turntables were originally of 20–30 ft diameter, with carrying beams of cast or wrought iron mounted on a central pivot in a circular pit, deep enough to accommodate the beams, to the ends of which were attached pairs of wheels which ran on a circumferential race-rail around the base of the pit. Running rails were mounted on the top of the beams which also carried wooden platforms for access. This turntable was the balanced type, as the locomotive had to be carefully positioned, balanced about the centre pivot which then carried the total load, the outer race wheels merely performing a steadying function. Around the edge of the turntable pit a slatted path was usually laid to enable locomotive crews, after withdrawing the locking catches, to push the table round manually, finally bringing it to rest gradually to enable the locking catches to be replaced.

As locomotive sizes increased, larger turntables were required. At first, geared windlass-type winding handles were used, followed by geared motor drives using either vacuum from the locomotive braking system or independent electric power. The advent of still larger locomotives in the 1920s, and later some exceeding 60-ft wheelbase, created balancing difficulties. New designs of turntables of up to 70-ft diameter were introduced using steel articulated girders with three-point suspension, so avoiding the necessity to balance. The outer race-rails, accurately levelled, then carried part of the load on ball-bearing wheels, while the centre portion mounted on the pivot carried its load on the pivot ball-race.

In addition to turning at stations and junctions, turntables were also necessary at *engine sheds. As part of a locomotive's servicing, it had to be turned in readiness for its next working, and a turntable would be situated strategically in the shed yard or, in the case of a roundhouse, in the centre of the building with stabling roads arranged radially around it.   FGC

For early station layouts, see *GRSB*, ch. 6.

Tyer, Edward, see SIGNALLING EQUIPMENT MANUFACTURE.

Tyler, Sir Henry (1827–1908), inspector. Educated at the Royal Military Academy, Woolwich, he was commissioned into the Royal Engineers, but moved in 1853 to the Board of *Trade as an *inspector of railways. He made his mark quickly with a report on an accident on the *Lancashire & Yorkshire Railway in which he commended Fay's continuous *brake. He strongly advocated the extension of interlocking (see SIGNALLING), which brought him into conflict with the *Midland Railway, whose general manager, *Allport, resisted all the Board's recommendations. In 1864 he produced an excellent report for *Parliament on *communication between passengers and train crews. But it was ignored, resulting in long and discreditable confusion.

As Chief Inspector of Railways (1870–7) Tyler wrote annual reports, providing a good commentary on railway technology, backed by informative *statistics. He was respected by many railway officers, as *Neele put it, for 'his unfailing courtesy and fairness'.

He was a director of the Grand Trunk Railway of Canada, and in 1877 (just before his retirement from the Board) its chairman. He also became chairman of the British *Westinghouse Brake Company, to the strong disapproval of his colleague *Yolland, who disliked that company's marketing methods. He was a Conservative MP in 1880–92 and knighted in 1877.   JS

DBB; *GR*.

U

underground railways. The very origin of the railway lies under ground, in the 'adits' or near-horizontal 'drifts' tunnelled into hillsides for mining, along which vehicles —wheelbarrows, sledges, or trucks—were drawn or propelled on prepared tracks giving some form of guidance from the 15th century (see WOODEN RAILWAYS; EARLY IRON RAILWAYS).

These were all private railways for minerals. 'Underground railways', in the sense of sub-surface or deep-mined systems for the conveyance of passengers (rarely freight also) between underground stations having access from and to the surface, were first operated by the *Metropolitan Railway in London in 1863, worked by steam locomotives. This line was excavated from street level ('cut-and-cover') apart from one bored tunnel. The *East London Railway used the *Brunels' Thames Tunnel of 1843. The *Mersey Railway from Liverpool to Birkenhead, 1886, was at first steam-worked.

Construction of tunnels under cities by traditional methods was difficult and eventually prohibitively expensive. P. W. *Barlow's method of driving a 7-ft circular iron tube was used for the Tower Subway, London, in which a rail vehicle was run briefly in 1870; with J. H. *Greathead's improvements, it was developed for the *City & South London Railway (1890) and later lines. There were two major technical problems to be solved: the means of traction (steam being inadmissible) and the vertical movement of passengers at stations. *Cable haulage was used on the circular *Glasgow Subway (1896), but the City & South London had already opted for electric traction from a current rail. Lifts were provided at most stations: at first hydraulic on the Mersey Railway in 1886 and the CSLR in 1890; then electric, on the Central London Railway in 1900; finally largely displaced by escalators (see LIFTS AND ESCALATORS). Safe working was particularly important, and many advances in *signalling and *track-circuiting techniques were first introduced on underground lines.

Special characteristics of underground railways are the need to keep tunnels watertight or effectively drained; adequate ventilation without excessive draughts; stations designed to cope with surges or peaks of passenger movement, with the shortest possible train stopping times; good lighting and stringent *fire precautions; connection with surface train depots; and adequate periods with power cut off to permit maintenance of structures and equipment. Their potential advantage, compared with general-purpose railways, is that their traffic is homogeneous and is best dealt with in standardized train units, being particularly suitable for automatic control. RMR

A. J. F. Wrottesley, *Famous Underground Railways of the World* (1956); *HLT*; J. R. Day, *Railways under the Ground* (1964); O. S. Nock, *Underground Railways of the World* (1973).

Underground railways of London, see LONDON UNDERGROUND RAILWAYS.

undue preference. The Railways Clauses Act, 1845 (sect. 90), and the Railway and Canal Traffic Act, 1854 (sect. 2), forbade the companies to charge differential rates, giving one customer any 'undue or unreasonable preference' against another. That principle remained in force, with some amendments, until 1954. Over those 100 years the courts debated the meaning of 'undue' and 'unreasonable'.

It was held unreasonable for a railway to carry one trader's goods between his premises and the railhead free, and to charge another for the same service. But in 1895, when *Southampton complained that the *London & South Western Railway was carrying agricultural produce from overseas to London for less than it charged local producers, the company showed that its own costs were less—the foreign goods being conveyed in larger loads and better packed—and the Court of Appeal accepted that the lower rate was 'reasonable'.

See also FREIGHT TRAFFIC RATES; COMPETITION. JS
O. Kahn-Freund, *Law of Inland Transport* (2nd edn., 1956), 107–14.

uniforms. Because many navy and army officers became railway managers in the 1840s, it is not surprising that railway companies decided to provide staff with uniforms. These consisted of trousers with frock coats or jackets and waistcoats, according to grade, and a cap or top-hat. Garments were either of corduroy or woollen cloth, with distinctive designs of buttons and badges for the different companies.

Uniforms were issued to virtually everybody who came into contact with the public—except for clerical grades —and to footplate crews, *signalmen, messengers, and carters. They remained the property of the company and had to be returned for periodic replacement, or on leaving the railway. Second-hand uniforms were sometimes sold to *overseas railways, especially those owned by British companies, presumably after removal of buttons and badges. Frequency of issue varied. For instance, the *North Eastern Railway issued suits on 20 March each year, with overcoats in alternate years. Winter trousers were provided on 1 November. Measurements were taken at stations and depots, and inevitably the quality of the fitting varied. The larger companies maintained central stores, and some had their own clothing workshops. Certain manufacturers specialized in railway uniforms, including John Hammond of *Crewe and Redman Brothers of Hebden Bridge, Yorkshire. Practice varied; the *London Tilbury & Southend Railway, for instance, contracted for the supply of uniforms annually.

When uniforms were introduced in the 1840s, among the first to receive them were passenger train *guards, following mail-coach practice. Some were red and others green, although by 1900 navy blue was standard. The *London & North Western Railway retained green double-breasted frock coats and caps for their passenger guards for many years, with buttons bearing the company's crest. The *London & South Western Railway issued a similar uniform but with cap badges that included the word 'Guard', with a number identifying the wearer. From 1893 the LSWR issued all grades with red neckties which could be used in an emergency as danger signals, a practice followed by some other companies. A ticket collector's uniform was similar to a guard's, and both might wear a button-hole flower, an engaging practice which lingered among *Great Western Railway *stationmasters. Outside *porters, normally retired railway servants who were permitted to operate from station premises, were issued with numbered armbands.

After the 1923 *Grouping, changes were gradual, and in 1930 the stationmaster at Tilbury still appeared in his *Midland Railway frock coat. On the *Southern Railway, many former *London Brighton & South Coast locomotive men continued to wear cap badges which incorporated an LBSCR locomotive. With the spread of electrification on the SR there came a new grade of driver who had 'Motorman' on his cap badge. In World War I *women joined the railway service, requiring special uniforms. In World War II caps and trousers found more favour than skirts and hats. After *nationalization in 1948, change was slow. A 1950 photograph shows an engine crew, platform *inspector, and passenger guard all wearing SR uniforms. In 1955 the stationmaster at Ealing Broadway was wearing his full GWR uniform when he received a visiting party.

There were variations, both official and unofficial. Stationmasters at some major stations, particularly those used by royalty or important people, were issued with frock coats and top-hats, including most London terminals and stations such as *Edinburgh Waverley. Bowler hats were much more general. Supervisors and inspectors had bowlers, navy blue suits and raincoats. Unofficial variations were more restricted. However, in the 1950s and 1960s, while drivers continued to wear their shiny-topped caps, locomotive firemen frequently covered their heads with knotted handkerchiefs, and secured the bottoms of their overall trousers with cycle clips.

Changes in grades and duties in the 1960s brought new styles of uniform. Lighter material was used, navy blue gave place to grey, and professional designers were employed. Striped shirts were introduced, and when porters were abolished, their traditional sleeved waistcoats went with them. Further changes were made in the 1980s, when ticket and enquiries staff also received uniforms. Modern fabrics and styling have been conducive to much smarter appearance, and in 1994 the instruction issued by the NER in 1905, on balance, was being fully honoured: 'All grades in receipt of uniform must keep same in good order and appear neat and clean on all occasions'. EC

D. J. Froggatt, *Railway Buttons, Badges and Uniforms* (1986); J. Mackay, *Railway Antiques* (1978).

unusual railways, see TRACTION, UNUSUAL FORMS OF.

'up' and 'down'. On all railways leading into *London, trains were said to travel 'up' in that direction and 'down' in the opposite one, following accepted road practice. Some provincially based railways ran 'up' to their headquarters location, hence the *Lancashire & Yorkshire company's trains travelled 'up' to *Manchester, the *North Eastern's 'up' to *York, and the Midland's to *Derby until it extended to London in 1868. The five large Scottish companies all adopted a geographical plan, their trains going 'up' when they ran southwards. On the *Edinburgh & Glasgow Railway, where they travelled east and west, trains ran 'up' to Edinburgh and 'down' to *Glasgow. Since the *Grouping, on all lines the London-bound direction has been 'up', although on those with no connection towards London a more arbitrary designation has been necessary. JS

Vale of Rheidol Railway, see CAMBRIAN RAILWAYS.

valve gear (see diagrams on p. 550) operates the valves admitting steam to and releasing it from the cylinders of a steam locomotive, being the means both of reversing and of adjusting the *cut-off. Most British locomotives employed reciprocating valves operated by valve gears that derived their motion from eccentrics mounted on the crank-axle, from the connecting rod or from the crosshead. Though mechanically different, all achieve the same basic effect. The motion of a reciprocating valve (i.e. slide or piston valve) can be split into two components: a primary component that is 90° out of phase with the crank, and a secondary component that is in phase with, or 180° out of phase with (opposite) the crank. The primary component determines how far the valve opens and at what point in the stroke it closes (cut-off); the secondary component—also known as 'lap plus lead'—determines the exact point at which the valve opens to steam at the beginning of the stroke.

Early locomotives usually had fixed eccentrics for each direction of travel, one or other of which was connected to the valve as required; they had no provision for varying cut-off. There were a few attempts to produce mechanisms giving variable cut-off but none succeeded until the Williams-Howe link motion of 1843, long known as *Stephenson valve gear, in which valve travel is adjusted by combining that of both eccentrics in different proportions using a slotted link. Stephenson was the commonest British valve gear, two other important gears being *Joy, which took its motion from the middle of the connecting rod, and Walschaert's, which was preferred for many 20th-century locomotives. In Walschaert's gear the primary component of motion is taken from an eccentric on the driving axle, the secondary from the crosshead; unlike Stephenson or Joy, it is usually mounted externally.

Reciprocating valves are either flat (slide valves) or cylindrical (piston valves) and are located in the steam chest. As they move they cover and/or uncover ports connecting the cylinder with the steam chest or with exhaust.

Poppet valves similar in action to those of a motor car engine have been tried several times, sometimes driven by a conventional valve gear with an oscillating camshaft but usually by rotating cams. They were never popular in Britain, where Caprotti gear was the system most frequently used. RW

P. Ransome-Wallis (ed.), *Concise Encyclopaedia of World Railway Locomotives* (1959), 294–304.

vandalism by railways. This term here means environmental violation caused by railways during construction.

For vandalism suffered by the railways themselves, see MALICIOUS DAMAGE.

Although there had been complaints about cutting canals through open parkland (see LANDOWNERS), most of them were concerned more with anticipated practical consequences—e.g. changes in the water-table or flooding—than with the defacement of the landscape. In towns the widening of streets and bridges for stage-coaches caused the removal of some historic structures, e.g. at *Leicester and Bedford, also a consequence of the erection of the new London Bridge in 1824–31.

The building of railways presented new and more serious threats, for they cut paths much more directly than roads. Some people indeed thought that nothing should be allowed to stand in a railway's projected line. One even considered that Blenheim Palace should not be sacrosanct, if need be, though he allowed that if the obstacle were Westminster Abbey the railway might have to avoid it.

However, in 1833 the *London & Birmingham Railway had to accept statutory restrictions to safeguard the ruins of Berkhamsted castle. Other castles were less fortunate; railways were permitted to impinge on or remove parts of those at Berwick and Huntingdon. Special conditions were imposed in 1844 on the *Chester & Holyhead Railway at Chester and alongside Conway castle.

A public outcry arose at Dorchester in 1846, which forced the Wilts Somerset & Weymouth Railway to accept statutory safeguards for a notable prehistoric monument, Maumbury Rings. Protesters also triumphed in *Scotland in 1844, in saving not a structure but a public amenity. When it was proposed (with Board of *Trade approval) to site *Perth station on the South Inch, an open space the citizens rightly prized, they opposed the plan in Parliament and had it rejected. So the railway had to skirt the Inch and build its station elsewhere. These are the first important battles won by local people in defence of monuments and amenities threatened by railways.

London was not at first affected, chiefly because in 1846 Parliament discouraged construction in the central area. But in 1859 the *London Chatham & Dover Railway challenged that decision by seeking to build a line across the forbidden zone, bridging the Thames at *Blackfriars and traversing the City on a viaduct. Because the scheme made sense as a railway it succeeded, even though its bridge over Ludgate Hill marred the view of St Paul's, one of the grandest street scenes in London. That outrage continued until the hideous bridge was replaced by a tunnel in 1991.

In the 1860s Parliament considered plans for nearly 900

valve gear

Stephenson valve-gear for inside cylinders
and slide or outside admission piston valves

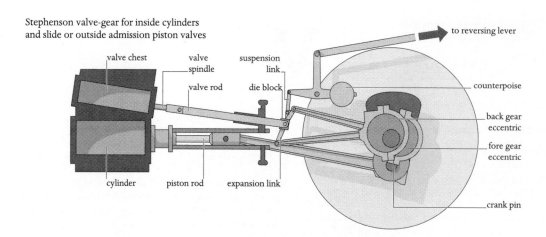

to reversing lever

valve chest valve spindle suspension link die block

counterpoise

back gear eccentric

fore gear eccentric

cylinder piston rod expansion link

crank pin

Joy valve-gear for inside cylinders
and slide or outside admission piston valves

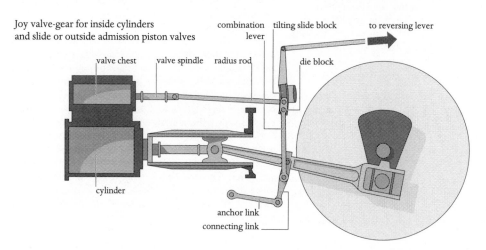

combination lever tilting slide block to reversing lever

valve chest valve spindle radius rod die block

cylinder

anchor link
connecting link

Walschaert's valve-gear for outside cylinders
and inside admission piston valves

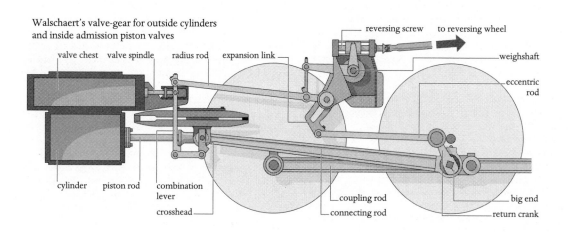

reversing screw to reversing wheel

valve chest valve spindle radius rod expansion link

weighshaft

eccentric rod

cylinder piston rod combination lever

crosshead

coupling rod
connecting rod

big end
return crank

miles of railway in Greater London—many vehemently opposed. Some were indeed astounding. One, for a Thames Railway (1864), shows the line striding down the middle of the river on iron stilts. Others were hardly less offensive.

Railway vandalism appeared at its worst in 1882–4. One line was to run across the Lower Close at *Norwich; another, to intersect the Avenue at Stonehenge. One of the many schemes for taking railways right into the Lake District was launched in 1882; so was one that included an 80-ft-high bridge over Aysgarth Force in Wensleydale. None succeeded.

In 1890 the Manchester Sheffield & Lincolnshire Railway (see GREAT CENTRAL) proposed to cross the western edge of Leicester, through an important Roman site and immediately below the medieval castle, evoking opposition from cultural societies and the borough council. The whole scheme proved unacceptable, the Bill failed, and for its reintroduction in 1891 the plans were modified, to satisfy its critics. The railways now saw the need to come to terms with their opponents.

In the 20th century the railway was victorious in the notable case of the great Doric portico at *Euston station. Its demolition in 1961 was widely condemned as a supreme example of corporate vandalism. But when in 1966 *BR proposed to close, and perhaps demolish, *St Pancras station, the campaign against it owed much to the strength of feeling demonstrated at Euston. The issues here concerned the operation of a big station as well as the preservation of a notable monument. This time the preservationists succeeded, not only in saving the building but in improving plans for its rearrangement. The result showed what could be achieved by long and patient discussion of difficulties that, although real, were capable of solution.

See also CONSERVATION.   JS
For the theme of vandalism and preservation in its historical context see D. Lowenthal, *The Past Is a Foreign Country* (1985), 389–412; *VR*, ch. 6.

vandalism on railways, see MALICIOUS DAMAGE.

vegetables traffic, see FRUIT AND VEGETABLES TRAFFIC.

ventilation, see AIR-CONDITIONING; TUNNELS AND TUNNELLING.

viaducts, see BRIDGES AND VIADUCTS.

Victoria Line, see LONDON UNDERGROUND RAILWAYS.

Victoria station, see LONDON STATIONS.

Vignoles, Charles Blacker (1793–1875), engineer. A soldier, who became a surveyor in the USA, he returned to England in 1823, where he was employed in docks and drainage works, and on the *Liverpool & Manchester Railway, 1826–7. He became engineer of the Wigan Branch and St Helens & Runcorn Gap Railways, 1830–3.

His most important lines in the British Isles were the Dublin & Kingstown, *North Union, and *Midland Counties, all opened in 1832–40, together with the Sheffield Ashton & Manchester (see GREAT CENTRAL RAILWAY), which he did not complete, resigning through a dispute with the directors in 1841. His chief contribution to railway engineering was the Vignoles rail, laid directly on to the sleepers without resting on a chair (see TRACK), employed extensively in France but much less in Britain.

His greatest single works were on the mainland of Europe: the road bridge over the Dnieper at Kiev in Russia (1847–53), and the Tudela & Bilbao Railway in Spain (1857–64). He was president, ICE, 1870–1.   JS
K. H. Vignoles, *Charles Blacker Vignoles* (1982). Vignoles' remarkable diaries (BL, Add. MSS 34528–36, 35071), used in that work, would still repay much further study.

wagon building. The presence until 1948 on British railways of so many *private-owner wagons meant that by the 1850s a flourishing wagon-building and repair industry had become established. It was a low-technology industry for the most part and relied on little more than the skills required for building horse-carts—woodworking and smithy work. Components were drop-stamped or forged and riveted together. By the 1950s, almost the only development had been the adoption of welding for steel underframes and bodies.

The railway companies established extensive workshops for the production and repair of wagons. At the *Great Western Railway's *Swindon *works, no fewer than 10,000 wagons were built between 1869 and 1877. Some railways moved their wagon-building and repair shops to new premises, e.g. the *London & North Western Railway which transferred its wagon department from *Crewe to Earlestown as early as 1855. Major wagon works also became established at Ashford, Kent; *Doncaster Carr; Faverdale and Shildon, Co. Durham; and Temple Mills, east London.

The private industry exported large numbers of wagons, but indigenous manufacture was gradually established in major markets such as India. Leading British wagon builders included Cambrian Wagon, *Cardiff; Central Wagon, Wigan; Derbyshire Carriage & Wagon, Chesterfield; Gloucester Carriage & Wagon; Metropolitan-Cammell, *Birmingham; Charles Roberts, Wakefield; and Standard Railway Wagon, Reddish and Heywood, Lancs. These were active into the 1960s. Subsequently, the number of builders and repairers has declined significantly, despite a minor boom in the demand for high-capacity, bogie private-owner wagons during the 1970s.   MLH

wagon-lits, see PULLMAN CARS.

wagons. From 1603, wagons with flanged wooden wheels were running on a wooden track (see WOODEN RAILWAYS). The earliest surviving wagon in Britain dates from 1797: a quarry truck with metal wheels designed to be hauled behind a horse along metal rails. Chaldron-type wagons were used in the north-east from the 1800s for the conveyance of *coal on colliery railways and their descendants remained at work into the 1960s. Because coal was the staple of the British railways, the chaldron wagon, with bottom-discharge from its hopper-shaped body, became the basis of the railway freight wagon. By 1856, there are said to have been some 15,000 chaldron wagons in use, usually with a capacity of at least three tons. They lacked springs, had dumb *buffers, and were often devoid of *brakes.

From 1830, general freight wagons had a two-axle chassis carrying an open body. Their design was to alter little in 120 years. The underframe was usually of oak, the axle-guards being attached by rivets and positioned outside the wheels which had laminated, cart-type springs. Wood gave way to steel underframes over the years. The axles ran in bearings within boxes with detachable fronts, *lubricated by grease; later by oil-saturated fabric pads. The wheels were originally cast iron, on an iron axle. Wrought-iron axles and open-spoked wheels were the next step but, after invention of the Bessemer process, steel tyres were adopted. Buffers progressed to self-contained, sprung designs, and *couplings were of simple three-link type attached to drawhooks. Braking was no more than a hand-lever connected to rigging which applied brake blocks to the wheel tyres. The brake lever could be pinned in various positions to retard progress. Bodies were built from planks of largely imported softwood, with iron or steel fittings. Many loads were conveyed in open wagons of two to seven planks' depth, with tarpaulin sheets, because these were easier to load and unload. Covered wagons had cambered roofs covered with canvas.

The survival of simple, small capacity, four-wheel wagons into the 1980s reflected the inertia of users as much as the provider. Collieries, coal yards, private *sidings, and *freight depots were designed for Victorian, short-wheelbase wagons able to negotiate sharp curves and poor track. At collieries in particular, handling was primitive and only the loose-coupled, non-continuously braked wagon was acceptable. Failure to invest in modern handling facilities was widespread and, as coal constituted the major rail traffic, wagon design generally was anachronistic well into the motor age. Most coal was carried in 13-ton wagons owned by collieries or merchants, their specification being regulated by the *Railway Clearing House.

Individual railways noted overseas developments, particularly in the USA, attempting without much avail during the 1900s to impose high-capacity bogie wagons. From about this time, vacuum or air brakes began to be fitted to wagons used for merchandise and *perishable traffics. The *Great Northern Railway pioneered fast braked freight trains between West Yorkshire and *London, and another advance was the introduction of all-metal wagons for locomotive coal and for specific flows of coke. Design improvements were effectively limited to oil-lubricated or roller bearing axle-boxes and the greater use of steel. Corrugated steel ends began to be used from the 1930s, helping to reduce damage to wagons and their loads, a significant hazard as *shunting caused appalling impacts. Another palliative was wagons with shock-absorbing underframes.

The sheer scale of the problem militated against modernization. Low payloads were endemic, with the average wagon load just under 8 tons. On *nationalization, *British Railways inherited 1.25 million wagons of 480 types. Seventy-one new types were chosen to replace this fleet, including the most numerous single type of railway vehicle to be built in Britain, the all-metal 16-ton mineral wagon —over 200,000 of them, mostly hand-braked. Apart from standard open and covered wagons, there was a myriad special types: vans for *livestock, *fruit, *fish, and refrigerated traffic, including those for international consignments travelling by train *ferries; four-wheeled and bogie wagons, with bolsters and securing chains for *timber and steel (see IRON AND STEEL); well wagons with low-level centre sections for conveying boilers and machinery; hopper wagons for *iron ore, some capable of being unloaded by tippler. Tank wagons existed in a variety of forms, nearly all owned by producers of petroleum products, tar, and hazardous substances (see DANGEROUS GOODS). Coal and mineral wagons with vacuum brakes began to appear in the 1950s, while carrying capacities were increased to up to 24 tons, particularly for slack for the large, new power stations. The major advance came in 1965 with the introduction of *merry-go-round coal trains in circuit between colliery and power station.

The revolution in rail freight finally eliminated the problems of numerous types and low technology. From the early 1960s the emphasis was on block train movements, mainly employing privately owned specialized wagons, or *containers. BR's wagon fleet declined dramatically, particularly with the elimination by 1984 of conventional wagonload traffic. Remaining traffic to and from private sidings was accommodated on the Speedlink network of air-braked services for which BR built wagons during the 1970s and 1980s. In turn, Speedlink was discontinued from 1991 and the BR wagon fleet (other than for engineering purposes) now numbers less than 20,000.   MLH

R. T. Munns, *Milk Churns to Merry-Go-Round* (1986).

wagonways, see TRAMROADS; WOODEN RAILWAYS; EARLY IRON RAILWAYS.

Wainwright, Harry Smith (1864–1925), engineer. He held varied posts in locomotive and *carriage departments, latterly on the *South Eastern Railway, until appointed locomotive carriage and wagon superintendent of the *South Eastern & Chatham Railway, 1899.

He effected the move of the carriage and wagon shops to Ashford in 1899, and the locomotive *works from 1911; introduced a range of capable locomotive classes—'D' and 'E' class 4-4-0s, 'C' class 0-6-0s, and 'H' class 0-4-4Ts—and rebuilt earlier designs inherited from the *London Chatham & Dover Railway and SER; standardized train *braking on automatic vacuum (the LCDR was air-braked); and introduced 900 or so coaching stock vehicles, most with electric

lighting and steam heating (see TRAIN HEATING). His 'D' and 'E' class 4-4-0s were finished in an elaborate and attractive paint scheme. Probably the chief draughtsman, Robert Surtees, was responsible for the design of those locomotives attributed to Wainwright.

In 1913 the SECR experienced a motive power shortage, because of a backlog in locomotive repairs, not helped by the closure of Longhedge works before sufficient capacity had been created at Ashford. For this, and other alleged shortcomings, Wainwright was asked to resign 'on grounds of ill-health'.   MLH

K. Marx, *Wainwright and His Locomotives* (1985); D. L. Bradley, *The Locomotive History of the South Eastern & Chatham Railway* (1980); D. Gould, *Carriage Stock of the SE&CR* (1976).

waiting rooms. For long, station waiting rooms were depicted as cheerless places, just as they had been at the coach offices. Trollope said of Taunton: 'Everything is hideous, dirty and disagreeable . . .'; and Samuel Sidney in 1851 described the first-class room at *Euston as 'dull to a fearful degree and finished in the dowdiest style of economy'. The second-class was 'a dark cavern'.

The *Liverpool & Manchester Railway (1830) provided waiting rooms only at its termini. The intermediate stations were merely lineside stopping places, and 15 years passed before a full complement of permanent stations appeared, with proper facilities. Early railways considered waiting rooms of little importance. Francis *Whishaw, an acute observer, in 1842 made no comment on their appointments. He approved a combined booking office and waiting room at Aylesbury, and thought that the ladies' room at Arbroath ought to have a separate entrance, but the rooms under arches at Lea Bridge received scant notice.

Larger stations were soon given more generous provision, with separate first-, second-, and, later on, sometimes third-class rooms for both sexes. *Liverpool Lime Street in 1836 had five waiting rooms: first- and second-class ladies' and gentlemen's, and one simply designated 'ladies' waiting room'. In 1894 *Edinburgh Princes Street also had five, one of them a 'general waiting room'. Smaller stations generally had first-class, ladies', and 'general' rooms, and the smallest a 'general' and a 'ladies'.

Apart from the Great Hall at Euston, the large, lofty combined waiting and concourse hall found in Europe and America was not favoured in Britain. The smaller waiting rooms that led off the concourse, plain though they were, had fewer draughts, and nearly always possessed a fireplace. Seating, too, generally was better, with upholstered benches instead of wood. At a few of the more important stations waiting rooms received special attention, like those at *King's Cross which were 'elegantly fitted up and furnished', but in the main little expense was lavished on them.

Passengers at smaller stations were often looked after better, particularly in country districts. There would be a fire in winter, and later on posters and sepia prints of places served by the railway began to adorn the walls. But these comforts would probably be confined to the main building.

As often as not the other platform had only an open-fronted shelter containing a wooden bench.

Private waiting rooms for the privileged were provided at certain stations. Queen Victoria had sumptuously furnished suites at Euston, *Paddington, and the two Windsor stations, while Wolferton, the station for Sandringham, had three waiting rooms for the royal family. The Duke of Rutland's waiting room at Redmile was fitted out with a vast carved-oak chimneypiece depicting Belvoir Castle and the chase. The Duke of Westminster had his own room at Waverton, and Earl Brownlow a suite at Berkhamsted. The first-class room at Rowsley was given superior furniture for the benefit of visitors to Chatsworth House.

But it was left to *British Rail to do the obvious thing and combine waiting rooms with buffets, to the advantage of passengers and staff alike, and at some stations to call them passenger lounges.   GJB

A. Trollope, *The Belton Estate* (1865); S. Sidney, *Rides on Railways* (1851, reprinted 1973), 13; Whishaw, 4, 12, 364; Thomas, 123, 128–30; VR, 259.

Wales. The railway system of Wales was quite different from those in England and *Scotland. The forces behind its construction were different, and it took a physical shape peculiar to itself.

The trunk lines roughly formed a reversed capital E (∃), with the vertical stem close to the English border and comprising four lines built by separate companies to make a continuous route from Chester to Newport, completed in 1853. The top and bottom horizontal arms represent the only two first-class trunk lines the country ever had: the *Chester & Holyhead Railway, along the north coast (completed in 1851); the *South Wales Railway to Milford Haven (1856). Both linked up with trunk lines coming from London, at Chester and Gloucester. The middle arm formed the east–west main line of the *Cambrian Railways, running from junctions with the *Great Western and *London & North Western systems through mid-Wales to Aberystwyth and opened in 1864.

The prime purpose of the two trunk lines was to carry traffic from London to Dublin and to southern Ireland; the stem, a *cross-country line, became a trunk route only with the opening of the *Severn Tunnel in 1886; the last was built largely to carry agricultural traffic, but also to open up Cardigan Bay to *holiday-making. None of these lines generated much industrial traffic.

English interests did much to promote the two coastal lines. The *London & Birmingham Railway (later part of the LNWR) was authorized in 1844 to subscribe £1 million to the CHR; the GWR likewise invested £½ million in the SWR. Both were absorbed by their English partners, in 1859 and 1863 respectively.

Great *landowners played a very small part in development. Wales had no estates comparable in extent with the greatest in Scotland. By far the largest one in Wales was the Williams Wynn estate (reckoned in 1883 at 146,000 acres, one ninth of the Scottish acreage of the Duke of *Sutherland). But no member of the Wynn family contributed not-

ably to railway development. The next largest estate was Cawdor (52,000 acres in Wales), and it provided the GWR with a very able chairman in 1895–1905. In rural Wales, however, the determined efforts of small landowners helped to secure the building of railways where no large profits could be looked for, as a service to their own districts. In mid-Wales their success owed much to the contractor David *Davies, the developer Thomas *Savin, and the engineer Benjamin *Piercy (see also CONTRACTORS' LINES).

The most powerful driving-force behind Welsh railway development came from the industrialists in the south, particularly the ironmasters of Merthyr Tydfil and Dowlais, who had been chiefly responsible for constructing canals running down to the sea at *Cardiff, *Swansea, and Newport, completed in 1794–9. But they all proved inadequate for rapidly growing traffic, and the industrialists turned towards supplementing them by steam-powered railways. The first to be completed was the *Taff Vale Railway (1841), followed by the Monmouthshire at Newport (1850 onwards, springing from a canal company), the Vale of Neath (1853), the Swansea Vale (1852–64), and the *Rhymney (1857–8). Further west the Llanelly Railway served a similar purpose in Carmarthenshire (1839–57).

On these foundations the railways in Glamorgan and Monmouthshire became the densest in Great Britain outside London. In 1915 H. S. Jevons considered that this tract of the country included 'a greater total length of railways than any area of the same size chosen in any part of the world, excepting possibly London, with its tubes'.

It was an extraordinary tangle. By 1900 seven companies ran trains into Merthyr Tydfil. Swansea came to have six passenger termini. A most intense rivalry subsisted between the companies. Three big English ones (the GWR, LNWR, and *Midland) fought to carry South Wales coal away over great distances inland. Eight separate local companies conveyed it down to the sea.

This intensity of competition between railway companies over a comparable period was never matched anywhere else. It grew much stronger with the opening up of coal working in the Rhondda valleys from the 1850s onwards. The quality of the steam coal they produced was never excelled and the demand grew insatiable: e.g. as fuel for steamships elsewhere, including for the world's expanding navies. It also found a ready market with some railways abroad. The Italian State Railways had permanent offices in Cardiff, charged primarily with purchasing coal.

Despite this virulent competition, the Glamorgan railway companies became very profitable. In 1880–8 the Taff Vale company paid an annual dividend of 13 per cent.

There was also competition between ports and docks. The facilities at Cardiff, provided almost entirely by the Bute estate, were by the 1850s growing incapable of accommodating all the traffic, so the TVR supported the construction of a new port at Penarth. That became busy at once, and within 20 years had itself grown inadequate. Some of the coalowners in the Dare and Rhondda valleys were now looking westwards, to take their traffic, through great physical barriers, to *Port Talbot, Neath, and Swansea. Others, led by Davies, banded together to construct a railway running to a new port at *Barry, close to Cardiff, opened in 1889. This hit the TVR very badly: yet it recovered, to be able to pay 8 per cent in 1913. There was enough business to keep all these railways and ports profitable.

The other, much smaller, industrial district, in north-eastern Wales, also produced coal, iron, and later steel. It had one railway of its own: the Wrexham Mold & Connah's Quay, opened in 1866 to carry traffic down to a tide-water port. Always under-financed, it gave a poor service, passing into the hands of the *Great Central Railway in 1905.

North Wales relied chiefly on two English railway companies: the GWR, with a main line from *Shrewsbury and a long branch from Ruabon to Dolgelley; and the LNWR, eventually controlling the entire standard-gauge system of Anglesey, Caernarvonshire, and Denbighshire. On the whole, the LNWR monopoly benefited this large tract of country. It generated a very profitable traffic in holiday-making, which brought a constantly increasing revenue into the district during one third of the year, causing Llandudno, Rhyl, and the other coastal resorts to grow, with increasing hotels and boarding-houses for visitors who stayed, and many *excursion trains for those who came for the day. The railway company made special *publicity efforts to promote this business. It even went into the *cinema as early as 1907, collaborating with an American company in the production of an 800-ft film depicting North Wales as 'the Land of Castles and Waterfalls'.

But very different railways were also at work: the *narrow-gauge lines in and around Snowdonia, built primarily for handling its enormous *slate traffic. The largest of these, the *Festiniog, was opened in 1836, worked by *horses, man-power, and *gravity on a 2-ft gauge track to suit narrow spaces and sharp curves. In 1863 it began experimenting successfully with double-boilered steam locomotives (see FAIRLIE, R. F.). This railway and the *Talyllyn, also a slate-carrier, became profitable tourist attractions. Preserved and worked affectionately, they remain that still.

The north-coast holiday business had a counterpart on Cardigan Bay, where the Cambrian Railways threw off, from their main line to Aberystwyth, a 53-mile branch that hugged the sea all the way to Pwllheli. The resorts that developed were small, but their quietness recommended them to the numerous visitors who returned to them every year.

The interior of Wales, north of Merthyr Tydfil and Carmarthen, was the quietest area of the country; the only part where the population declined in the 19th century. (The railways helped removal from it.) But pastoral agriculture, above all sheep-farming, prospered—its traffic passing, however, after World War I, largely into the hands of road operators. When the closing of unprofitable lines was debated in the 1960s, the arguments in this district were considered with some care. The Mid-Wales line, running southwards through Rhayader to provide a service to Merthyr, was closed in 1962, but the Central Wales (now called the 'Heart of Wales') line, also threatened, was reprieved—like the line

skirting Cardigan Bay—largely to meet social needs, in districts where roads were awkward and few.

The reduction of the railway system in South Wales under *BR has been much more drastic. Only five lines now have passenger trains running up the valleys, from Cardiff to Coryton, Rhymney, Merthyr, Aberdare, and Treherbert. There had been 14 in 1921.

A number of valuable experiments were made for the first time on Welsh lines. C. E. *Lee rightly suggested that 'the earliest example of "power" traction on rail' was provided by the use of sails on wagons conveying coal at Neath in 1698. The *Carmarthenshire Railway, authorized in 1802, was the first railway and dock worked under one ownership. The first locomotive capable of hauling a heavy load was *Trevithick's, at Penydarren in 1804. The earliest regular railway passenger services were introduced on the *Swansea & Mumbles line in 1807. The wrought-iron *Britannia Bridge over the Menai Strait was a great landmark in the history of civil engineering: the first long-span flat-beam bridge ever built. The Festiniog Railway's locomotives were studied, and purchased for service in different versions in many countries abroad.   JS

Reg. Hist., xi, xii; S. Owen-Jones, Railways of Wales (1981); K. O. Morgan, Wales: Rebirth of a Nation, 1880–1980 (1981); J. Bateman, Great Landowners of Great Britain and Ireland (1971 edn.); H. S. Jevons, The British Coal Trade (1969 edn.), 59.

Walker, Sir Herbert Ashcombe (1868–1949), manager. He joined the *London & North Western Railway at 17, and became outdoor goods manager, Southern Division; then general manager, *London & South Western Railway, in 1912, aged 43. He was soon involved in rebuilding *Waterloo station, already under way, and *electrification of the suburban network by third-rail dc system. He insisted upon fixed-*interval or 'clock-face' timetabling. In World War I he was acting chairman of the government's Railway Executive Committee despite his comparative youth, commanding universal respect. He was knighted in 1917.

When the *Southern Railway was formed Walker became general manager and soon started to weld the three main constituents into a single undertaking, embracing continued electrification, development of *Southampton as an ocean port, improvement of continental services (introducing the all-*Pullman 'Golden Arrow'), and, after rejection of the *Channel Tunnel, train ferry services (see SHIPPING SERVICES). He developed on-train catering, especially by Pullman.

Walker had a remarkable financial grasp, and ensured that major schemes were carried through with economy, such as rebuilding steam-hauled *carriages for electric trains. The results of suburban electrification were so favourable that Walker obtained authority for main-line schemes to *Brighton, *Portsmouth, Hastings, Bognor, and Littlehampton. He retired in 1937 and was appointed a director of the Southern. He died in 1949.

He was described as deeply impressive, with a remarkable grasp of all aspects of railway work; quiet, yet authoritative, stimulating his subordinates to give their very best.   MRB

C. F. Klapper, *Sir Herbert Walker's Southern Railway* (1973); Sir J. Elliot, *On and Off the Rails* (1982); M. R. Bonavia, *History of the Southern Railway* (1987).

Walker, James (1781–1862), engineer. He was a general engineer, involved much in works concerned with water: the first Vauxhall bridge in London, for example (1816), and a 30-mile cut through the Fens. He was one of the founders of the *Institution of Civil Engineers, and its president in 1834–45.

Walker was frequently called into consultation on matters concerning railways. He reported on railways in the north of England to the board of the *Liverpool & Manchester company in 1827 and proposed the competition that became known as the *Rainhill trials. He surveyed two of the early lines projected to run from London to *York, forerunners of the *Great Northern Railway. But he was responsible for the construction of only two lines of importance: the *Leeds & Selby and the Hull & Selby. Some of the elliptical over-bridges he designed for the LSR are still intact, and he had the foresight to recommend the company to provide space for four tracks if required.   JS

Boase; *BDE*.

Walker, Thomas Andrew (1828–89), *contractor. He began railway work at 17, serving under the contractor Thomas *Brassey on the *North Staffordshire Railway and the Grand Trunk Railway of Canada, where he continued in railway work; then in Russia and Egypt. Resident manager for a contractor building *London Underground lines (1865–7), he went on to construct part of the *East London Railway, completed in 1876. The engineer was *Hawkshaw, who was also consultant for the *Severn Tunnel and, after he became sole engineer for it (1879), he secured Walker as contractor. It was finished in 1886. Walker was a good employer, housing his men well, keeping them under firm discipline, and allowing no work on Sundays.

He also constructed the final stage of London's Inner Circle line (see LONDON UNDERGROUND RAILWAYS—METROPOLITAN DISTRICT RAILWAY) in 1883–4, turning to work on docks at Buenos Aires and *Barry, and on the Manchester Ship Canal. He died in 1889, leaving £597,000.

He produced an admirable account of the Severn Tunnel: the only important book devoted to a great British railway structure that was written by the contractor responsible for it.   JS

T. A. Walker, *The Severn Tunnel: Its Construction and Difficulties* (1889); MacDermot, ii, 186–91.

Walschaert, see VALVE GEAR.

Wantage Tramway. Opened in 1875, this 2½-mile line was one of the few in Britain running alongside a public highway (see TRAMWAYS, STREET). It linked the town of Wantage (population 3,300 in 1871) with Wantage Road station on the *Great Western's London–Bristol main line, where passengers had to change, although freight vehicles were taken through. Steam traction was employed from 1876 onwards.

The company prospered, paying its shareholders an annual average dividend of 4.6 per cent in 1876–1914.

Motor-*bus competition killed passenger traffic in 1925, but freight continued for another 20 years. The company was wound up in 1947. Its locomotive, *Shannon*, has been preserved.   JS

S. H. P. Higgins, *The Wantage Tramway* (1958).

War. From the earliest days of main-line railway promotion, the Admiralty and the War Office were concerned that their interests were not overlooked, especially in regard to continuous communication, without break of *gauge, to bases and embarkation ports. The London & Southampton Railway (1834)—see LONDON & SOUTH WESTERN RAILWAY—was seen in that light. The government in 1842 imposed on the railways a requirement to convey troops as needed, more for the preservation of internal order than for overseas expeditions. This was enlarged in 1844 and 1867 until full state control in war-time was provided for by the Regulation of the Forces Act, 1871. From then on, planning was based on the premise that the government would take control on the outbreak of war, giving overall directions to the companies which would continue to manage the operation of their lines.

The use of railways was then considered principally for the movement of troops and supplies to embarkation ports. The government sometimes intervened to press for alignments that paid regard to defence on lines along the coast (e.g. Ashford–Rye–Hastings, *South Eastern Railway, 1850); and it opposed lines that would penetrate land defences (see PORTSMOUTH). There was, however, no general railway strategic policy. The War Office opposed extension of the *London Tilbury & Southend Railway to Shoeburyness (the gunnery school) in 1877 but approved it in 1882.

Under the influence of invasion scares from 1859 onwards, measures for the active use of railways in defence began to be considered. Proposals for a circular line round London on which armoured trains with artillery should be stationed came to nothing. No railway, except within bases and depots (see MILITARY RAILWAYS), was built solely for defence purposes. An Engineer & Railway Staff Volunteer Corps was formed in 1865, including railway and docks officers and civil engineers, to prepare railway plans for the event of war. An Army (later War) Railway Council was set up in 1896, and plans were constantly reviewed and revised.

For the South African War in 1899–1902, the railways were not taken over under the Act but handled the military traffic in liaison with the War Office and the Admiralty. Most of the burden fell on the LSWR and *Southampton docks, where 528,000 troops, with their horses and equipment, were embarked from trains.

Between then and 1914 organization was strengthened, and railway access to concentration areas near Salisbury Plain was improved. In World War I the government took control through the Railway Executive Committee, consisting of 11 general managers under the nominal chairmanship of the President of the Board of *Trade, in practice under (Sir) Herbert *Walker, general manager of the LSWR. Heavy movements of troops and supplies were carried out efficiently; Southampton was again much pressed;

the contribution of coastal *shipping to *coal movement was limited, and the Grand Fleet based on Scapa Flow had to be supplied by 'Jellicoe specials', mostly from Pontypool Road, *Great Western Railway, to Grangemouth, on the *Caledonian Railway, 375 miles. From August 1914 to March 1919, 13,630 coal specials were run from South Wales to Scotland using *West Coast, *East Coast, and *Midland routes. In Scotland the *Highland Railway came under severe strain. The passenger counterpart, the 'naval specials', ran nightly from February 1917 between Euston and Thurso, 717 miles in 21½ hours.

Civilian passenger services were curtailed, and a few were withdrawn, but still traffic increased. Train ferry services (see SHIPPING SERVICES) to France were provided from Southampton and a new port was built at Richborough, Kent. The government looked to railways, already operating more than their peace-time loadings of traffic, also to furnish men and equipment, especially locomotives, for overseas operations. In 1914–18, 184,475 or 49 per cent of the railway staff of military age joined the colours and over 600 locomotives were taken; large quantities of equipment, including shells and fuses, were manufactured in railway *works. Most difficult to handle were large volumes of passenger and freight traffic arising at ordnance factories set up at places with few existing railway facilities, as in the Gretna area. Coaches were converted to form ambulance trains.

In 1921 control was returned to the *grouped railways; liaison and planning for war-time were continued, with new dimensions in air-raid precaution and anti-gas measures. In World War II government control was again effected through a Railway Executive Committee, now consisting of four general managers and Frank *Pick, succeeded by Lord *Ashfield, from *London Transport. In the regular absence of the Minister of Transport, Sir Ralph *Wedgwood, former chief general manager of the *London & North Eastern Railway, took the chair until August 1941, followed by Sir Alan Garrett Anderson.

In addition to the tasks of moving and supplying the armed forces, the railways had immediately to provide for evacuation of civil population from cities; to operate with much reduced lighting (the 'black-out'); and to take precautions against chemical warfare. After June 1940 possible invasion had to be very much in mind. Twelve armoured trains carrying anti-aircraft guns were deployed on the east and south-east coasts and in Scotland (three were manned by the Polish army); even the 15-in gauge *Romney Hythe & Dymchurch Railway was pressed into military service. At Martin Mill on the Kent coast several spur lines were built for the use of heavy rail-mounted guns, and the Elham Valley line was taken over for this use. Canadian troops began to arrive in December 1939, USA forces in large numbers from May 1942. Their movements, including leave traffic, were normally handled by rail. On top of the crushingly heavy 'Overlord' programme for the D-Day landings in Normandy and supplies for the ensuing battles, came the need to redeploy anti-aircraft and balloon units to counter flying bombs.

As in World War I, the railways were required to give up men and equipment. With closer attention given to the retention of men in 'essential occupations', the four main lines released nearly 110,000 staff for national service, over 100,000 of them in the armed forces. They provided 298 steam and 45 diesel locomotives for overseas service, together with much other equipment, including tanks (642 manufactured complete at Horwich and Crewe *works); guns and gun mountings from *Swindon and *Doncaster; shells, ball-bearings, bridges, and landing craft from Swindon and Eastleigh. The Transportation Corps, US Army, had the use of railway workshops at Ebbw Junction, Eastleigh, and Hainault, for assembling and reconditioning its equipment.

During the war the British railways discharged heavy burdens with a remarkable degree of success, taking enemy bombing and emergency operations like the transport of troops from the Dunkirk evacuation (over 300,000 between 27 May and 4 June 1940), if not exactly in their stride, still with high professional competence. Their safety record was good; the worst accident attributable to war-time loads was a fire on ammunition wagons culminating in explosion at Soham, Cambridgeshire (LNER), on 1 June 1944. They emerged to face the post-war world with what a Labour minister called 'a poor bag of assets'. They had demonstrated again what Ludendorff had concluded in 1918: 'There comes a time when locomotives are more important than guns.' RMR

E. A. Pratt, *The Rise of Rail-Power in War and Conquest 1833–1914* (1916), and *British Railways and the Great War* (2 vols., 1921); R. Bell, *History of British Railways during the War, 1939–45* (1946); C. I. Savage, *Inland Transport* (History of the Second World War) (1957); M. Robbins, *The Railway Age* (1962), ch. 14.

warehouses, see GOODS SHEDS AND WAREHOUSES.

water columns, see WATER SUPPLIES.

Waterloo & City Railway, see LONDON UNDERGROUND RAILWAYS.

Waterloo station, see LONDON STATIONS.

water supplies. The advent of railways to small communities in the earliest days brought considerable changes, and the creation of new industry such as large locomotive *works required living accommodation for its staff. New *towns grew up and in addition to providing *housing, services such as water and gas were provided by the works of the railway company. Locomotive water was obtained from bore holes, small reservoirs, or, in some cases, rivers and canals. The *Great Northern Railway, for instance, pumped water from the River Trent for its troughs at Muskham, near Newark, while the *Great Western took water direct from its Stratford-on-Avon Canal where the Alcester branch passed beneath Bearley Aqueduct.

*Engine sheds required large elevated water storage tanks, often located above coaling stages, to provide constant supplies to the many water columns and supply points situated around the depot, neighbouring yards, and stations. At some locations a small 'parachute' type of elevated water tank was provided, supported on a cast-iron column, delivery to the locomotive being by a horizontal swan-neck pipe attached to which was a leather trunk. A chain-operated lever at ground level lifted a valve, allowing water to flow down into the locomotive tank. Some of the out-based water columns in stations and freight yards had quite elegant designs with a cast-iron column supporting an ornate swan-neck of cast iron or copper, with a wheel-operated control valve at ground level.

Water Troughs

With increasing traffic and longer distances of operation, water supplies became the limiting factor for long-distance non-stop trains. In 1860 John *Ramsbottom, the locomotive superintendent of the *London & North Western Railway, solved the problem by introducing the first means of taking up water whilst on the move, from troughs situated between the rails, at Mochdre in North Wales. A scoop beneath the locomotive's *tender was lowered into the water, which the forward speed of the locomotive forced up a vertical pipe into the tank. Lineside boards were placed to indicate to the *fireman where to lower and raise his scoop. The system was highly successful and subsequently troughs were situated at about 30-mile intervals on many main lines. All the large English railway companies adopted them except the *London & South Western, but only two in Scotland. Some remained in use after dieselization so that heating-boiler tanks could be topped up on the move, enabling the *Deltic locomotives to run non-stop between *King's Cross and *Edinburgh.

Water Treatment

As locomotives increased in power, so did demands on boilers, and pressures increased steadily from the 50–60 psi of the early days to 250 psi for the larger express locomotives (see TRACTION, STEAM). Such developments brought with them problems of corrosion of copper fireboxes. It was realized that there was considerable variation in water quality, depending on locality, and water-softening using lime-soda was introduced to remedy it. The larger engine sheds were equipped with their own water-softening plants.

They had electric automatic pumps, float-switch controlled, the lime-soda ash being loaded manually. A pressure sand filter was provided to collect the sludge, which was then disposed of by pressing it into solid cakes or by carrying it away in semi-liquid state using specially adapted old tenders. Softened water, however, sometimes brought priming troubles on locomotives, and on the *London Midland & Scottish Railway a continuous blow-down valve was fitted to alleviate this problem. It opened when the locomotive regulator was opened, and actually discharged a small amount of boiler water through a cooling coil in the tender tank, before allowing it to run out on to the track. This, coupled with the more frequent washing out of boilers, appeared to control the problem. However, in the 1930s copper corrosion was evident on high-pressure boilers where high alkaline water was used even though it was being softened. The LMS then decided that further treatment was necessary, and small chemical treatment plants were intro-

duced at certain depots, automatically controlled, in which all locomotive water was treated with sodium agents and tannin. These so-called Wayside Treatment Plants were very successful and at smaller depots similar treatment was applied manually by placing compressed briquettes in the storage tanks. This careful control of water-softening and treatment, together with more frequent washing out of boilers, did much to reduce considerably the rate of boiler corrosion, leading to improved efficiency of locomotive operation.   FGC

A. J. Parsons, *Some Aspects of Locomotive Boiler Feed Water Treatment*, Institution of Locomotive Engineers, Paper No. 572 (1957); J. S. A. Hancock, *Brief History of Locomotive Feed Water Treatment on the London Midland Region of BR*, Institution of Locomotive Engineers, Paper No. 573 (1957).

water troughs, see WATER SUPPLIES.

Watkin, Sir Edward (1819–1901), railway manager and chairman—perhaps in 1870–95 the most well known in Britain. Born in *Manchester, he entered his father's cotton merchant's business, but in his twenties made a reputation running anti-Corn Law and other campaigns. In 1845 he became secretary of the Trent Valley Railway, and then assistant to *Huish, the *London & North Western Railway's general manager, where he gained a wide experience of railway management and negotiations with other companies. In 1854 he was appointed general manager of the Manchester Sheffield & Lincolnshire Railway (see GREAT CENTRAL), a smaller company which soon played off larger companies and gave the *Great Northern Railway access to Lancashire at the LNWR's expense.

He resigned in 1862 after disagreement on policy adopted while he was in Canada attempting to revive the Grand Trunk Railway, but returned as chairman in 1864–94.

Involved in many railway and other companies at home and abroad, he was also chairman of the *South Eastern (1866–94) and *Metropolitan Railways (1872–94), which with his unsuccessful *Channel Tunnel project and the MSLR's London extension, he saw as part of a continuous Manchester to Paris route. Renamed the Great Central Railway, the last opened in 1899 after his retirement.

Quick-witted, adept at controlling meetings, ambitious, domineering, and restless, he pursued large ideas on many fronts. His combative and expansionist attitude led to unprofitable competition, particularly with J. S. *Forbes of the *London Chatham & Dover and *Metropolitan District Railways, but the MSLR, Metropolitan, and SER under Watkin were only as successful as the average British railway judged by their return on capital and measures of managerial efficiency, though quality of service probably suffered.

Knighted in 1868 for his work in assisting Canadian federation, and made baronet in 1880, he was MP for Great Yarmouth (1857), Stockport (1864–8), and Hythe (1874–95).   DJH

DNB; *DBB*; Dow; A. A. Jackson, *London's Metropolitan Railway* (1986); T. R. Gourvish, 'The Performance of British Railway Management After 1860: The Railways of Watkin and Forbes', *Business History*, 20 (1978), 186–200; P. S. Bagwell, 'The Rivalry and Working Union of the South Eastern and London, Chatham & Dover Railways', *JTH*, 2 (1955), 65–79.

Waverley route, see NORTH BRITISH RAILWAY.

Webb, Francis William. (1836–1906), engineer. He displayed in childhood a remarkable engineering talent, served an apprenticeship on the *London & North Western Railway at *Crewe under Francis Trevithick, and on completion was retained at an enhanced salary. Two years later he became chief draughtsman under Trevithick's successor John *Ramsbottom. In 1866 he went (or was sent) to manage a steelworks in Bolton; he returned in 1870 to manage Crewe steelworks, but within months succeeded Ramsbottom.

As engineering supremo of the largest joint-stock company in the world, his job was to provide the best possible equipment and services at minimum cost, and he did so with conspicuous success, especially when train weights and speeds began to increase rapidly towards the end of the century. His compound locomotives (see TRACTION, STEAM) received a worse press than they deserved but were a small percentage of his overall contribution to the LNWR. His value to that cost-conscious railway was reflected in a salary that reached £7,000 a year (including £2,000 for use of his many patents)—roughly £400,000 at 1994 value.

Webb was a pioneer in the use of steel, of compound locomotives, of *electricity, and of the *telephone. An early motorist, he recognized the threat of *road transport and before 1900 was advocating *electrification of the London–Glasgow main line to permit 100 mph running. He took a close interest in the town of Crewe, serving as mayor in 1886–7, and left much of his considerable fortune to deserving causes in the district.   RW

W. H. Chaloner, *Social and Economic Development of Crewe* (1850); J. R. Spink, unpublished thesis in Crewe library (1965); R. Weaver, 'Francis William Webb', *Railway World*, 47 (1986), 538–43, 606–11.

Wedgwood, Sir Ralph Lewis (1875–1956), manager. From Cambridge he joined the *North Eastern Railway's traffic apprenticeship scheme. He rose rapidly: company secretary at age 30; chief goods manager at 36. After distinguished war-time service as director of ports, he became deputy general manager and, in 1922, general manager. He was knighted in 1923.

Outstanding ability and his comparative youthfulness (48) gained him the position of chief general manager of the new *London & North Eastern Railway after the *Grouping. A decentralized area management system left Wedgwood and his team free to concentrate upon finance and policy, though he did occasionally give directives to the divisional general managers and was a final court of appeal in disagreements. Wedgwood established a good relationship with his chairman, William *Whitelaw.

He was an impressive advocate and witness. He was a member of the 1931 government Committee on Main Line *Electrification (the Weir Committee); in 1936 he led an enquiry team to India; and played a leading part in the *'Big Four's' 'Square Deal' campaign (see FREIGHT TRAFFIC RATES). He retired in 1939, but was asked to continue as chairman

of the government's Railway Executive Committee, exercising war-time government control over the railways. He retired in 1941.   MRB

C. J. Allen, *The London & North Eastern Railway* (1966); M. R. Bonavia, *History of the London & North Eastern Railway*, i and ii (1981–2); G. Hughes, *LNER* (1986).

weekend. The weekend holiday predated the railways. In *London some professional men had suburban villas, at Hampstead or Norwood for instance, or on the river, driving out to them on Friday evenings and returning on Mondays.

The railways began to cater for it in 1842 when the *London & South Western offered cheap tickets from London to *Southampton or Gosport and back on Saturdays–Mondays. It soon made headway in Lancashire, stimulated by a growing *Manchester practice of closing banks, public offices, and warehouses on Saturday afternoons. In 1850 the *Lancashire & Yorkshire Railway was including in its timetable the rates for weekend tickets from Manchester to *Blackpool and Fleetwood. By 1863 an additional express left Manchester for Blackpool at 1.15 p.m. on Saturdays, with a corresponding return train on Monday mornings.

The companies had various reasons for liking this practice. The *London & North Western favoured it because it reduced the demand for *Sunday trains. On the coasts of Lancashire and North Wales it brought additional business to seaside resorts that the railways wished to develop, like Southport and Llandudno. Similarly in London: extra trains were then running up early on Mondays from Eastbourne, Ramsgate, and Yarmouth.

In the 1870s the expression 'the weekend' had entered the English language. At least by 1906 the French had taken *le week-end* into theirs. By 1914 some French railways were beginning to offer the same facilities as the British.

Since then this type of *holiday-making has come to be widely accepted throughout Europe. But it appeared first as a social institution in Britain, and the railways were chiefly responsible for developing it.   JS

REW, 133–4; *VR*, 292–4.

Welsh Highland Railway, see FESTINIOG RAILWAY.

Welshpool & Llanfair Light Railway, see CAMBRIAN RAILWAYS.

West Coast Main Line (WCML) is the current name for the route between London *Euston and Scotland. It comprises the major part of the former *London & North Western and *Caledonian Railways' main line from Euston to *Glasgow, *Edinburgh, and *Aberdeen, and was directly competitive with the *East Coast route from *King's Cross (see RACES TO SCOTLAND).

The line was built by a number of smaller companies in 1837–50, originally via *Birmingham, to avoid which the LNWR in 1847 opened the more direct Trent Valley Railway between Rugby and Stafford, followed by a short cut-off (see LOOP) north of Warrington in 1864. The Edinburgh route diverged at Carstairs, and the lines to Glasgow and Aberdeen at Motherwell. When Glasgow Central station was opened in 1879 the distance from London was 401 miles, and to Aberdeen 540.

Progressive widenings and the use of loop lines eventually made four tracks available for the greater part of the line as far north as *Preston, although compared with the East Coast route it has always had the disadvantage of severe gradients over Shap and Beattock summits, and to Aberdeen was some 16 miles longer. In 1967 Aberdeen services were concentrated on the East Coast line, after which the Perth–Kinnaber Junction section was closed. Since then the WCML has been regarded as comprising the Euston–Glasgow line, the Birmingham and *Stoke-on-Trent loops, and the lines from *Crewe to *Liverpool and *Manchester, all of which were electrified in 1959–74. The Carstairs–Edinburgh section was electrified in 1991. Political prevarication over renewal of ageing electrical and signalling equipment continued in 1995 to lead to extended journey times on this prime route. GJB

West Cornwall Railway. This standard-*gauge line originated as the Hayle Railway, running from Hayle to Redruth, authorized in 1834 and opened for freight in 1837–8. Its total mileage, including branches, was 17. Two miles of inclined planes were worked wholly or partly by *stationary engines. Locomotives were used elsewhere on the railway from the outset.

Hayle was the chief port of north Cornwall. Much of the tin and copper mined around Redruth passed through it. No regular service for passengers seems to have been provided until 1843.

In 1846 a new company was authorized, the West Cornwall, empowered to purchase the Hayle Railway and extend it to Truro and Penzance, as well as to make deviations to eliminate the inclines. W. S. Moorsom was the original engineer, but was superseded by *Brunel in 1845, becoming chairman of the board in 1847–50. The railway was single-line throughout and had nine timber viaducts (see BRIDGES AND VIADUCTS).

The opening of the broad-gauge *Cornwall Railway from Plymouth to Truro in 1859 produced an inconvenient break of gauge. The Cornwall company had been authorized in 1850 to require the West Cornwall to lay down a third rail, to accommodate broad-gauge rolling stock. When it made this demand in 1864 the West Cornwall could not find money to comply with it, and was forced to transfer its property to the 'Associated Companies' (see CORNWALL RAILWAY) already responsible for the Cornwall Railway. By some curious oversight, however, the company continued its nominal existence until *nationalization in 1948. JS
MacDermot, ii, ch. 8.

West Highland Railway, see NORTH BRITISH RAILWAY.

Westinghouse: one of the best-known names in the fields of railway *brakes and *signalling, and one with which associations in the USA date back to the 1850s. George Westinghouse was an American, born in 1846, who patented the straight air brake in 1869. The same year he set up the Westinghouse Air Brake Company in Pittsburgh and began

supplying his system to the American railways. A visit to Britain in 1871 resulted in a redesign so that a train which became divided would automatically stop, still a fundamental feature today. The braking trials of 1875 established the advantages of the air brake and led to Westinghouse forming the Westinghouse Continuous Brake Company in Britain in 1876, which became the Westinghouse Brake Company in 1881. Subsidiaries of the British company were eventually set up in a number of European countries and in Australia.

Westinghouse realized from his visits to Britain that signalling there was more advanced than in the USA. He took back ideas and rights to products, and set up the Union Switch & Signal Company (USSCo) in 1880. This company eventually developed a system of power operation of points and signals, and miniature frames for working them. In order to develop the system for the British and European markets arrangements were made for the Westinghouse Brake Company of Britain to undertake manufacturing and sales. This led in 1895 to a licence arrangement with McKenzie & Holland, which was consolidated in 1907 by the formation of a jointly owned company, the McKenzie Holland & Westinghouse Power Signal Company. Subsequently the USSCo became an equal partner. Manufacturing was largely undertaken at the Brake Company's works at York Road, *King's Cross.

Changes in the railway signalling industry led to the formation of the Pneumatic Electric & General Engineering Company in 1901, renamed Consolidated Signal Company in 1903, which became the owner of several signalling contractors, including Saxby & Farmer, McKenzie & Holland, and Evans O'Donnell. The Saxby works at Kilburn was closed and manufacture transferred to the Evans O'Donnell works at Chippenham.

The Brake Company eventually decided that a combined brake and signal business would help to even out fluctuations in the two markets. In 1920 it took over Consolidated's interests in the signal companies and changed its name to the Westinghouse Brake & Saxby Signal Company. This was shortened to the Westinghouse Brake & Signal Company (WBSCo) in 1935. At first there was American money in the British company but by the 1940s this was no longer the case. The company's head office was at King's Cross, the old Brake Company's premises, and McKenzies' works at Worcester closed in 1921, the work being transferred to Chippenham.

Major resignalling schemes in which WBSCo has been significantly involved include *Charing Cross, *Cannon Street, and *London Bridge (1925–9 and 1975–6), Brighton line (1932 and 1982–4), *Euston (1952 and 1965), *Manchester Victoria and Exchange (1929), Manchester Piccadilly (1959 and 1988), *Glasgow Central (1907 and 1956), and *York (1951 and 1983).

See also SIGNALLING EQUIPMENT MANUFACTURE. RDF
WBSCo, A Centenary of Signalling (1956); The Signalling Study Group, The Signal Box (1986); J. D. Francis, Westinghouse, The Style 'L' Power Frame (1989).

West London and West London Extension Railways.
These two lines, together some seven miles long, came to
link the trunk lines approaching *London from the north
and west with those from the south and south-east.

The Birmingham Bristol & Thames Junction Railway
was authorized in 1836 to connect the *London & Birmingham Railway with the Kensington Canal. In 1839 it purchased the canal and became the West London Railway, its
line crossing the *Great Western Railway on the level. It
was opened in 1844. Though handling some freight traffic it
conveyed scarcely any passengers (attracting the ridicule of
Punch in consequence: see HUMOUR). It was closed after six
months, and was reopened only in 1862. It then formed part
of a West London Extension Railway, joining the *London
& South Western, *London Chatham & Dover, and *London Brighton & South Coast Railways at Clapham Junction.

Its Kensington station lay close to the site of the second
Great *Exhibition, and later of Olympia. Freight and suburban passenger services now passed along it in both directions. Later it came to be used for a number of
long-distance passenger trains from the Midlands and the
north to the south coast (see CROSS-COUNTRY SERVICES).

See also JOINT RAILWAYS.   JS
H. V. Borley and R. W. Kidner, *West London Railway* (1968).

West Midland Railway. This company was constituted in
1860 by an amalgamation of the Oxford Worcester & Wolverhampton, Newport Abergavenny & Hereford, and
Worcester & Hereford Railways.

The OWWR (authorized in 1845) was intended to be a
broad-*gauge line running from a junction with the *Great
Western Railway at Oxford to the Black Country, where
almost all the railways were standard-gauge. *Brunel was its
engineer. The cost much exceeding the estimate, the GWR
consented to guarantee additional capital up to £2.5 million
(a limitation not, however, disclosed to the OWWR shareholders). The *contractors, *Peto & Betts, and Treadwell,
gave further financial assistance, putting in John Parson as
the company's solicitor. Clever, crooked, and greedy, he
dominated its affairs from 1850 to 1856.

The line (92 miles long) was completed in 1854, now
with mixed gauge and in alliance with the *London &
North Western Railway, determined to exclude the broad
gauge from its territory. The mixed gauge was a sham, for
no regular broad-gauge trains ran over it.

One of Parson's most effective devices was to ignore
court and Board of *Trade orders. When in 1854 the *Railway Times* exposed his appropriation of the company's
money through stock-jobbing and other malpractices, he
remained silent, thereby confirming its allegations.

Operating results were unsatisfactory, and the board was
changed in 1856, Peto becoming deputy-chairman. The
GWR agreed in 1859 to accept abandonment of the broad
gauge over all but two miles of the line; a defeat for it, yet
in the long run a gain when the gauge was mixed from
London to Oxford in 1861, allowing through running of
OWWR standard-gauge trains.

The Newport Abergavenny & Hereford Railway was incorporated in 1846 and constructed in 1852–4 as a standard-
gauge line with the help of the LNWR, giving that
company access to South Wales. The engineer was Charles
*Liddell. A branch westwards to Quaker's Yard, built in
1855–7, included the spectacular Crumlin Viaduct (see
BRIDGES AND VIADUCTS).

The Worcester & Hereford Railway, incorporated in
1858, was the result of a long parliamentary tussle. The
OWWR, NAHR, and *Midland Railway undertook to work
it jointly. Seven miles were opened in 1859–60, but Malvern
and Ledbury tunnels gave the engineer (Liddell, again)
much trouble, and the line was not completed until 1861,
after merging into the WMR.

The LNWR had made several attempts to secure a direct
line from London into this territory, and in 1860–1 it backed
a project for one from London to the former OWWR near
Oxford. But a GWR and WMR working *agreement in
April 1861 stopped it. The two companies were fully amal-
gamated two years later.   JS
MacDermot, i, ch. 10; S. C. Jenkins and H. I. Quayle, *The Oxford
Worcester & Wolverhampton Railway* (1977).

Whale, George (1842–1910), CME of the *London &
North Western Railway, 1903–9; he presided over a complete transformation of the locomotive fleet. Formerly running superintendent, responsible for the operational side of
the locomotive department, he had little 'works' experience
and his appointment almost four months after F. W. *Webb
had officially retired suggests a 'safe' choice in the absence
of an obvious successor.

Making up ground lost during Sir Richard *Moon's austere rule took time, and Webb's locomotives had successfully handled heavier and faster trains while the principal
routes were upgraded to take heavier locomotives. Whale's
job was to build them. He could rely upon the experience
of Thomas Sackfield and John Jackson (chief designer and
chief draughtsman), who supervised and no doubt influenced the design of such excellent locomotives as the Precursor, Experiment, and G (0-8-0) classes. His engines were
therefore of unmistakable Webb ancestry: bigger, rather
lightly built, excellent value for money, and capable of
remarkable performance in the right hands. Whale's crucial
contribution was to ensure continued support from a board
which had been rather reluctant to spend money on locomotives.   RW

**Wharncliffe, James Archibald Stuart-Wortley-Mac-
kenzie,** 1st Lord (1776–1845), politician. He gave valuable
help to the *Great Western Railway's second Bill in 1835, as
chairman of the committee of the House of Lords that
examined the proposals. During the discussion he pounced
on some false statements circulated by the Bill's opponents.
*Brunel's noble viaduct at Hanwell, completed in 1837, was
named after him and bears his arms.

'Wharncliffe meetings' were named after him. Under his
influence the Lords made an order requiring the directors of
any company wishing to extend its powers to secure the
agreement of at least three-fifths of the shareholders at a

special meeting before taking the proposal into Parliament. The order went into force in 1846 shortly after his death, and Wharncliffe meetings were often required by railway companies.　　　　　　　　　　　　　　　　　　JS

　　Complete Peerage; OED.

wheel notation. Two systems came to be generally used in Britain, one for steam, the other for electric and diesel locomotives.

The Whyte notation for steam locomotives was that proposed in 1900 by the engineer F. M. Whyte of the New York Central Railroad. It was based on the enumeration of the leading, coupled driving, and trailing wheels under the engine, from front to rear, as shown in the diagram. Where the driving wheels were uncoupled, each pair had to be shown separately: hence the 'Teutonic' class of the *London & North Western Railway were correctly described as '2-2-2-0'.

*Tank engines were indicated by the suffix 'T'—e.g. 0-6-2T—with the sub-divisions (in Britain) of 'PT' for pannier tank, 'ST' for saddle tank, and 'WT' for well tank.

Steam locomotives with certain types of wheel arrangement came to be known by special names. They all originated in the USA, many of them referring to the titles of the companies that pioneered them. Four passed into common use in Britain: Atlantic (4-4-2), Baltic (4-6-4), Mogul (2-6-0), and Pacific (4-6-2).

For electric and diesel locomotives the accepted notation gives letters to the motored axles, and numerals to the carrying ones; where the motored axles are driven separately, the letter is followed by the suffix 'o'. Thus, the 'Peak' diesel locomotives of 1959 (Class 44–45) were 1 Co-Co 1, having two sets of separately motored axles, flanked by single leading and trailing axles; the main-line electric locomotives built from 1962 onwards are all classified Bo-Bo. The Whyte notation has been retained for coupled diesel shunting engines (0-4-0, 0-6-0).　　　　　　　　　　　　　JS

wheels. The first to be fitted to railway vehicles were of wood or cast iron, the latter often used as cast, and discarded when worn out. Steam railways required something

Whyte's steam locomotive notation

0 – 6 – 0　　　　2 – 4 – 2　　　　4 – 4 – 0

4 – 6 – 0　　　　4 – 6 – 2　　　　2 – 8 – 0

Diesel and electric locomotive notation

Bo – Bo　　　　　　　Co – Co

1 Co – Co 1

Examples of wheel notation

better and soon adopted cast- or wrought-iron wheel centres on to which were shrunk wrought-iron tyres, a system which, with improvements in design and materials, remained almost universal throughout the steam age.

Railway wheels are rigidly attached to their axles and have profiled treads to render them self-steering, so that as the wheelset moves outwards the rolling radius of the outer wheel increases slightly, causing it to overtake the inner wheel and steer the wheelset back to a central position. So effective are modern computer-generated tyre profiles that the flanges of today's high-speed trains seldom if ever touch the rails. The anonymous experimenter who discovered the effect of profiled wheel treads made the single most important contribution to railway technology since the invention of the wheel itself.

Steam locomotive wheels usually had spoked centres to save weight. Wrought iron was used at first, but after 1870 cast steel wheels (see IRON AND STEEL, USE OF) were introduced, often centrifugally cast in rotating moulds to ensure soundness; these became invariable on passenger locomotives but cast-iron wheels continued in use in less demanding applications. Carriage and wagon wheels initially had spoked forged centres, too, but to give quieter running many carriages later had *Mansell resilient wheels in which a segmental wooden disc was pressed into place between boss and tyre. As speeds and wheel loads increased, iron and later steel disc wheel centres became normal.

Wheels are held on to their axles by friction, the bore of the boss being made slightly smaller than the seat on the axle; the wheel is then forced into place by hydraulic pressure. Once in place, a force in excess of 50 tons is required to shift it. Keys are used to maintain the correct angular relationship of steam locomotive driving wheels coupled by rods, as they are pressed on.

Tyres were retained by friction, but because of their size they were shrunk rather than forced on to the centre. The tyre was heated using gas burners, which caused it to expand slightly, and the wheel centre was lowered into the tyre until it came up against a lip on the outside face. On cooling, the tyre gripped the centre firmly. It was always made much thicker than necessary so that it could safely be re-turned several times to restore its profile.

Since the early 1970s, tyred wheels have given way to monobloc wheels which are simpler and cheaper to produce and better able to withstand the stresses of modern railway operation. When worn out, they are pressed off the axle and new ones fitted.

Pneumatic tyres were tried in the 1930s but, while giving better grip, were unsuitable for any but the lightest vehicles and absorbed considerably more power than steel wheels doing the same job.　　　　　　　　　　　　　　　　　RW

　　P. Ransome-Wallis (ed.), *Concise Encyclopaedia of World Railway Locomotives* (1959), 292, 309.

wheel tapping. The sight and distinctive sound of the wheel-tapper was, until recent times, a familiar part of the scene at major stations. A long-handled hammer was struck against the tyres of *carriage wheels. From the ringing note produced, the experienced man could detect any flaws such as loose tyres or cracks in the wheels or axles, and the regular clang of his hammer marked his progress along the train. His job, however, involved more than this. The carriage undergear, *couplings, and other connections between vehicles were inspected, brake blocks and wheels were checked for evidence of brake-drag and overheating, while the back of the hand placed near each axle-box detected a hot bearing. The object was to discover defects before they could cause a breakdown or *accident, and enable remedial action to be taken. The work was not confined to stations or to passenger trains. It went on in *marshalling yards, *goods depots, and carriage *sidings. While trains still have to be examined, the man with the hammer has disappeared. Better materials and such things as ultrasonic testing and automatic lineside hot axle-box detectors have rendered his manner of examination unnecessary.   RDF

Whishaw, Francis (1804–56). Articled to James *Walker, he worked on an abortive scheme for a railway serving the London docks, and on the *Manchester & Leeds Railway from 1830.

In 1837 he produced an *Analysis of Railways*, examining current railway projects and including a glossary of railway terms, probably the first ever compiled. A much larger work followed in 1840, his *Railways of Great Britain and Ireland* (2nd and best edition, 1842), a most valuable account of 58 companies with lines open or under construction, together with records of experiments made on them.

He was secretary of the Society (now Royal Society) of Arts in 1843–5, instilling new life into what seemed an expiring body. He then returned to railways, lured by the opportunities that the *Mania offered. His name figures in some *prospectuses, but he was not responsible for any line actually built. He was interested in *telegraphs too; in 1847 he published a paper on telegraphic communication between Britain and India. But he is not heard of again until his death from apoplexy in the Marylebone workhouse in 1856.   JS
  Boase; *Journal of the Society of Arts*, 4 (1855–6).

Whitby & Pickering Railway. This line, 24 miles long and engineered under George *Stephenson, was authorized in 1833, providing primarily for the conveyance of lime and stone from the Vale of Pickering for shipment at the port of Whitby. Though one section of its Act permitted the use of locomotives, another forbade it. When the line was opened in 1835–6, traction was wholly by horses except on the Goathland incline (nearly a mile long), which was worked by *cable haulage. Passengers were carried from the outset. The WPR was purchased by the *York & North Midland company in 1845, which immediately strengthened it to carry locomotives (1847). It was taken into the *North Eastern Railway in 1854. After closure in 1965 the 18-mile section of the line from Grosmont to Pickering was reopened as the North Yorkshire Moors Railway in 1973 (see PRESERVATION OF RAILWAYS).   JS
  H. G. Lewin, *Early British Railways* (1925); Tomlinson.

Whitechapel & Bow Joint Railway: a line promoted in 1897 jointly by the *Metropolitan District and *London Tilbury & Southend companies; only two miles long, but an important link in the London railway system. It provided those living in the south Essex suburbs (East Ham, Barking, later Dagenham and Upminster) with easy access by the MDR to central London and provided the LTSR with additional means of getting passengers into the City, bypassing the overworked terminus at Fenchurch Street. The line was opened in 1902, having cost £1.2 million. It became part of *London Underground.   JS
  H. D. Welch, *London Tilbury & Southend Railway* (1951), 19; *HLT*, ii, 76.

Whitelaw, William (1868–1948), Scottish landowner and bank director, taking an active part in the affairs of the Church of Scotland. He was a director of the *Highland Railway, 1899, and chairman 1902–12; also a director of the *North British Railway, and chairman 1912–23.

His selection in 1923 as chairman of the newly formed *London & North Eastern Railway surprised many; but he lasted 15 years and was generally considered successful. The sprawling LNER was very different from the Scottish companies where staff knew him personally; he liked making footplate trips. Once respective responsibilities were defined, Whitelaw's relations with top management were cordial.

Whitelaw's Scottish caution and financial rectitude were reinforced by the LNER's difficulties from over-capitalization. In 1932 he insisted upon dividend restraint which made the LNER's prior charges ineligible for investment by trustees. The following year he disquieted fellow chairmen by publicly stating that *nationalization of the railways might be acceptable.

Whitelaw was universally respected for his courteous manner. Despite exerting financial stringency he took great pride in the LNER's achievements, such as its high-speed trains, *Gresley's splendid locomotives, and the mechanized *marshalling yard at Wath. He retired in 1938.   MRB
  C. J. Allen, *The London & North Eastern Railway* (1966); M. R. Bonavia, *The History of the London & North Eastern Railway* (1981); G. Hughes, *LNER* (1986).

'Widened Lines', see LONDON UNDERGROUND RAILWAYS (METROPOLITAN RAILWAY).

Wilkinson, Norman, see ART.

Williams, Frederick Smeeton (1829–86), writer; a Congregational minister; English tutor and financial secretary, Congregational Institute, Nottingham, 1863–86. He published *Our Iron Roads: Their History, Construction, and Social Influences* (1852; 7th edn., 1888) and *The Midland Railway . . . A Narrative of Modern Enterprise* (1876; 5th edn., 1888).

Our Iron Roads lived up to the claim made in its sub-title: the 12th chapter of the 1852 edition did indeed try to assign railways their place in society. It was the first truly comprehensive account of the railways of England. The book was conscientiously revised and brought up to date in subsequent editions. *The Midland Railway* was the first extended work devoted to any one of the largest British railway companies. It is good as both history and description. JS

Boase; *Nottingham Guardian*, 28 Oct. 1886.

winter sports. Curling and skating, both traditional Scottish sports, were changed from local to national sports by the railways. Until the development of artificial indoor rinks, these activities depended on a hard winter to freeze lochs and ponds. When the ice was judged sound enough—in the case of curling, to bear the weight of the 'rinks' (teams of four players) and their stones—competitions had to be quickly organized. The value of the railways was their ability at short notice to provide special trains to take the curlers and ice-skaters to their destination as did, for example, the *Great North of Scotland Railway in the 1890s from *Aberdeen to the Loch of Aboyne. The national bonspeils (or 'big matches'), which drew curlers from all over Scotland, relied on rail services. These inter-regional competitions between the north and the south of Scotland were held when the ice was hard-frozen at Loch Leven, Fife, or the Lake of Menteith, Perthshire, or Carsebreck Pond near *Perth, to which over 340 rinks and supporting spectators from all round Scotland came in January 1903. The *Stirling Observer* commented how convenient the venue was, with its small *Caledonian Railway siding, 'specially constructed where curlers and their luggage can easily detrain in the morning or entrain at night'. Mountaineering and later ski-ing also benefited from the access to the winter hills afforded by the railways, mainly centred on Aviemore.

See also SPORTS, SPECTATOR. AJD

A. J. Durie, *Sport and Leisure in Victorian Scotland* (1988); D. B. Smith, *The Roaring Game: Memories of Scottish Curling* (1985).

Wirral Railway. This line successfully encouraged people from *Liverpool and Birkenhead to live along the breezy north Wirral coast or to enjoy day trips.

It was formed in 1891 from short lines dating back to the Hoylake Railway, which opened in 1866 between that fishing village and Birkenhead docks. It grew to 13½ miles with extensions to West Kirby (junction with the *Great Western and *London & North Western *Joint line), Birkenhead Park, Birkenhead Docks, New Brighton, and Seacombe (for the Liverpool ferry). Its passenger receipts totalled several times those for freight traffic. Sometimes it paid small dividends.

Frequent West Kirby and New Brighton services connected at Birkenhead Park with those of the underground *Mersey Railway from Liverpool Central (Low Level). There were also through tickets from Liverpool to New Brighton and West Kirby via Seacombe ferry.

*Accidents were few, although in a head-on collision at Hoylake in 1888 five passengers and six railway workers were injured, one dying later. The Hoylake *stationmaster was held responsible and gaoled for manslaughter.

The WR and Mersey Railway both got *electrification powers in 1900, but whereas the MR opened its electrified line in 1903, it was 1938 before third rails were laid to West

Kirby and New Brighton by the *London Midland & Scottish Railway, allowing through running to Liverpool.

See also PASSENGER TRANSPORT AUTHORITIES. RC

C. Highet, *The Wirral Railway* (1961); J. W. Gahan, *Steel Wheels to Deeside* (1983).

Wisbech & Upwell Tramway, see LIGHT RAILWAYS.

Wolverhampton, see WORKS.

Wolverton, see WORKS.

Wolverton, Lord, see GLYN, G. C.

women, employment of. Women have been employed since railways began, but their contribution has barely been acknowledged by most railway historians. This disregard of women's work on railways is puzzling, as their labour, even in their traditional domestic tasks, was without question essential to the industry, and in war-time the railways would have foundered without them.

The history of women's railway work is distinct from that of men. It is one in which all decisions about the work they were to perform were made by men: local managers, head offices, unions, and Parliament. It is a history of exploitation as cheap labour, and of segregation in 'women's work'; followed by two episodes of war service in 'men's work', each one succeeded by expulsion. Segregation was resumed until, finally, legislation made it illegal.

Contrary to the common belief that few women were employed by railways until recently, just before World *War I there were over 13,000, or about 2 per cent of the workforce, compared with about 9,000 in 1984. Women were automatically assigned to traditional women's work and assumed to be unsuitable for other tasks. Nevertheless, the work allocated to female employees was integral to the railway service and their labour was vital to passengers and staff. They were employed as ladies' *waiting room attendants and *refreshment room staff, and as inspectors and manageresses in those areas. In workshops they were machinists, french-polishers, painters, blind-dyers, and needlewomen, and labourers. They provided a large part of the staff of companies' *hotels, their laundries, and printing works; cleaned offices, workshops, and messrooms; managed railwaymen's lodging-houses and staffed their canteens. A few worked on board trains as ladies' attendants. The only operating post they filled was that of crossing-keeper. Out of the public eye, women began to replace men as clerks, tracers, and copyists. That which was labelled men's work was closed to women, although there were some exceptions to this rule. Rural station mistresses (see STATIONMASTERS) were employed as early as 1832, thinly distributed across Britain, and a few women labourers appear alongside *navvies in the 1851 census. In 1858 two female booking clerks were noted at *Edinburgh, and there were solitary instances of a bridgekeeper (*North Eastern Railway) and a signalwoman (*Great Western Railway). From the late 19th century increasing numbers of women clerks were recruited, and paid about half the male rate—which provoked protest from men fearing for their jobs. The men were placated when women were given the monopoly of the new technologies of *telephones, *telegraphs, and typing, for all of which they showed special aptitudes, but women were barred from the usual promotional steps, and dismissed on marriage, thus removing them from competition with men. Although these constraints were artificial they were cited as reasons not to train women or accord them equal pay.

By July 1914 approximately 5,500 worked in hotels and catering, 1,300 in workshops, and 2,500 in offices. The remaining c.3,700 were in miscellaneous manual grades.

In World War I thousands of railwaymen enlisted in the forces and by April 1915 the barrier against women performing men's work was of necessity removed. Women demonstrated immense eagerness to undertake men's jobs and inundated the railways with requests for work. In 18 months 34,000 were engaged, as clerks, carriage cleaners, *porters, goods porters, ticket collectors, engine *cleaners, electric truck drivers, horse-van drivers, number-takers, messengers, operators of lifts, cranes, and points, and in many other grades. They attracted considerable press attention, and the influx generated extensive debate among railwaymen. The *National Union of Railwaymen negotiated the terms and conditions of women's employment before lifting its ban on their membership in July 1915. To safeguard men's jobs and rates, enlisted railwaymen were guaranteed reinstatement, and women paid no less than the male minimum rate. As the manpower shortage grew in 1917, women trained as signalwomen, shunters, and *guards—despite considerable opposition from railwaymen. By September 1918, some 52,000 women were replacing men. The war-time cost-of-living bonus that was paid only to men created inequality of pay between the sexes and women protested about it throughout the war. There were two episodes of industrial action: a small walk-out in 1916 on the GWR, and a larger one in London in 1918 when women on the underground railways joined those employed on buses and trams in their equal pay *strike. Improvements were obtained, but not equality. Despite this, war-workers in male grades earned nearly double the wage of their sisters in women's work.

Women substituting for men were dismissed when railwaymen returned from the forces. Heavy losses left 20,000 vacancies but women were not permitted to remain, although many had performed the work satisfactorily for up to five years. However, the number of women employed did not revert to pre-war levels because the companies retained many as carriage cleaners and clerks.

Women clerks campaigned fruitlessly throughout this period for equal pay and opportunities and abolition of the marriage bar, as in many other occupations. It is ironic that many completed 30 or 40 years' service (and more) while a timeworn stereotype of women as unambitious, temporary workers who left on marriage was cited as reason to deny them equality. Manual staff were not dismissed on marriage but were rigidly excluded (with very few exceptions) from all male grades. Increasingly through the 1920s and 1930s women replaced men as crossing-keepers and carriage cleaners, on lower pay. By 1939 there were 26,000 women employed by the railways, of whom 11,500 were clerks.

In World War II, once again, the staff shortage caused by enlistment and conscription meant that women were considered suitable for male work. They filled the same grades as in World War I, but this time many more worked as guards, as signalwomen, and on the permanent way. In the workshops women became welders, blacksmiths, sleeper-makers, lathe operators, hammer-drivers, signal repairers, drillers, planers, *fitters, and electricians.

There was again opposition from railwaymen. In some locations men were antagonized when companies suspended the minimum height requirement and circumvented the usual seniority-based promotional structure in order to utilize women as passenger guards. Senior men resented being relegated to old-fashioned, grimy steam trains so that women could take the more prestigious work on electric trains. Generally, men's attitudes ranged from grudging resentment to fatherly protectiveness. By June 1944, over 114,000 women were employed. Of these, 74,500 were in male grades from which women were barred in peace-time.

The jobs women performed were infinitely more hazardous and stressful during war-time, when the railways were enemy bombing targets (see WAR). Nearly 400 staff were killed and 2,500 were injured. In June 1941 the Great Western steamer St Patrick was bombed and sunk. Stewardess Elizabeth Owen repeatedly dived into submerged cabins to rescue passengers. She was awarded the George Medal, and the Lloyd's War Medal for bravery, the first woman railway employee ever given such accolades. Porter Violet Wisdom, of Bramley, *Southern Railway, witnessed a terrifying air attack on a nearby train. It was bombed and machine-gunned, killing the driver and guard and injuring passengers. Without hesitation, she ran to the wreckage and helped the dazed fireman to deal with the catastrophe. Isabella Gilder, a guard at Lennoxtown, near Glasgow, recalled: 'The black-out was so horrible—not knowing where one was. Going out into strange yards, and listening to trains moving and not seeing them, not knowing where the points were, and nobody to ask, is very alarming. My first run was to Clydebank. The station had been bombed and we went into another. We then had to shunt up the line. I had to get out of the van to change the rear lamp. There was hardly anything there but rubble. I did not know where I was. I had the greatest desire to run, but it seemed there was no place to run.'

In spite of the dangers and difficulties, women asserted that they enjoyed railway work immensely and were sad to leave.

After the war women were again dispensed with when no longer needed, and were supposed to have reverted to being unsuitable for men's work. A few signalwomen and portresses were retained, however, and women clerks and carriage cleaners continued to increase in number. From 1958 women on *British Railways were entitled to equal pay for equal work, predating the enforcement of the Equal

Pay Act by 17 years. However, this applied solely to those performing the same work as men, and in most cases the sexes were segregated, with women banned from the majority of promotional moves. In the late 1950s an acute shortage of men resulted in the limited recruitment of women in *signal boxes and in *track maintenance, but when the same problem led *Beeching to contemplate employing women guards in 1960 his proposal was blocked by protesting railwaymen. A few individuals pioneered their way into technical and engineering positions during the 1960s and 1970s. The clerks' marriage bar was lifted, but they were still artificially held back from reaching higher grades, especially that of stationmaster.

The Sex Discrimination Act, 1975, in theory threw open all so-called men's work to women, on the same terms, conditions, and rates of pay as those enjoyed by men. Within five years women had penetrated the last few male bastions, including the British Railways Board and the NUR National Executive. However, the pioneer women drivers, guards, shunters, technicians, and station managers suffered from varying amounts of prejudice and discrimination, as revealed in a government report, *Wanted: Railman*. Twenty years on, railwaymen have become accustomed to women colleagues and the former hostility has almost entirely evaporated.   HW

Equal Opportunities Commission, *Wanted: Railman* (1986); E. A. Pratt, *British Railways and the Great War* (1921); H. Wojtczak, *Women Workers on the Railways* (1996).

women's emancipation. Railways opened up opportunities to women that they had never known before. Previously, few of them had ever travelled alone. A wealthy widow might go in her own carriage, attended by servants. Others—certainly of the upper and middle classes—when they travelled accepted the need for a male escort.

Railways brought about a change. The numbers of people travelling were far larger than they had been by coach and, particularly if a woman could be seen off and met at each end of her journey, she was much safer. A ladies' *waiting room was provided by the *Liverpool & Manchester Railway at Liverpool in 1831, and as time went on all but the smallest *stations had one, often with a woman attendant. As early as 1844 the *Quarterly Review* could write that women were now released 'from the prohibition from travelling in public carriages, which with the majority was a prohibition from travelling at all'.

By that time some companies were beginning to label *compartments in their trains 'Ladies Only', and a demand arose that they should be obliged to do that on every train by law. But the companies pointed, fairly enough, to the difficulties that would thereby arise in the making up of some of their trains, and this compulsion was not placed upon them.

As the number of travellers grew, cases of sexual assault on railway trains became common in the courts, and the objection of allowing women to travel alone began to be voiced loudly again. In Trollope's novel *He Knew He Was Right* (1868) Miss Stanbury laid it down that 'there's no

place a young woman is insulted in so bad as those railway carriages, and I won't have her come by herself'. Men too had a complaint of their own here. Any of them who found himself travelling alone with a woman in a railway compartment might be vulnerable to blackmail.

The provision of 'Ladies Only' compartments was investigated by the Board of *Trade in 1887, when it appeared that most railways would reserve one on request, but that those permanently reserved for ladies were noticeably under-used.

In all other respects the gains made by women from their opportunities to travel easily by train were clear. On the railway they were equal with men and enjoyed without question any new services the railways afforded. When early-morning *'workmen's trains', for example, began to run in 1863 at very cheap fares, they were open to travellers of both sexes. The *Great Eastern Railway provided special waiting rooms for them at *Liverpool Street station. The employment of women, apart from factory working and the numerous branches of domestic service, was still small, but it grew steadily. The census of 1881 recorded 7,000 women clerks in Great Britain: 30 years later the number had become 146,000. By that time railway companies themselves were employing them in many capacities (see WOMEN, EMPLOYMENT OF). The war of 1914–18 opened up a great deal of railway work that had hitherto been performed wholly by men, and though this contracted again from 1919 onwards it remained much larger than it had been earlier. The range of opportunities and employment open to women grew steadily greater, and wherever they needed the assistance of the railways in taking up new work they called on it, as they did in their leisure activities too (see HOLIDAY-MAKING). They could still complain, however, that they were paid less than men for the same work.

Railways gave women new energies and incentives to pursue demands for political and economic equality with men, which began to succeed in 1918 when they got the parliamentary vote, and in 1975 when they became entitled to equal pay.   JS

VR, 332–6; *Quarterly Review*, 74 (1844), 250; A. Trollope, *He Knew He Was Right* (old World's Classics edn.), 73.

Wood, Nicholas (1795–1865), engineer, closely associated with the Stephensons.

Wood's demonstration of ability induced Sir Thomas Liddell, his father's landlord, to send him for training as a colliery manager at Killingworth, where he met George *Stephenson and became closely associated with early steam locomotive developments. There Robert *Stephenson was apprenticed to Wood. In 1820 he proposed the use of steam as a compressible medium for locomotive springing: the same principle as that used over a century later in air springs. In 1825 he produced the first edition of his classic and influential work *A Practical Treatise on Railroads*. That year there was great controversy over the merits of steam locomotives, *horses, or *stationary engines and *cables; Wood made a convincing case for locomotives (see TRACTION). He gave parliamentary evidence in favour of the

*Liverpool & Manchester Railway Bill, and in 1829 was one of three assessors for the *Rainhill trials to select the most suitable locomotive for the line. In 1838 he correctly identified fallacies in *Brunel's case for the broad *gauge, but did not convince the *Great Western board. He also held railway directorships.

In 1844 he became manager of the Hetton Coal Company's collieries, in which he was a partner. He played a prominent part in mining safety investigations leading to the Mines Inspections Act, 1851. GWC

PICE, 31 (1866), 236–8; *Trans. North of England Institute of Mining Engineers*, xv (1866), 49–59; *DNB: Missing Persons* (1993), 729.

Wood, Sancton (1816–86), architect; articled to Sir Robert Smirke. In the early 1840s Wood was engaged to design stations on the *Eastern Counties Railway, where he built the Italianate Bishopsgate terminus in London (1849) and probably others, although there is uncertainty about his relationship with Francis *Thompson and Henry Hunt who also worked for the ECR. All three made contributions to Cambridge station (1845). In 1846 Wood designed the Italianate first station in Blackburn, and the extraordinary but very imposing station at Bury St Edmunds, finished in 1847. Thompson and Wood were also active on the *Midland Railway's *Leicester–Stamford–*Peterborough line (1848), where there were stations with the characteristics of each of them, and shortly afterwards Wood was working on the Rugby–Stamford line of the *London & North Western, where the stations were undistinguished. The fine Gothic stations at Ketton and Stamford, however, have strong affinities with Wood's stations from Monasterevan to Limerick Junction (1847–8) on the Great Southern & Western Railway of *Ireland, for which he was architect in 1845–50. His best work there, or indeed anywhere else, is the imposing classical terminus at Dublin Kingsbridge (now Heuston), which equals Huddersfield and *Newcastle as one of the finest station frontages in the British Isles. Wood went on to build many private houses and offices in London, where he was also a District Surveyor. As well as his fellowship of the RIBA he was an Associate of the *Institution of Civil Engineers. GJB

D. Ware, *A Short Dictionary of British Architects* (1967); *VS*, 34, 53, 82; *The Builder* (22 May 1886), 761; J. Sheehy, 'Railway Architecture, its Heyday', *Jnl. Irish Railway Record Society*, 12, 68 (Oct. 1975), 125–38; Bury St Edmunds: N. Pevsner, *The Buildings of England: Suffolk* (1975 edn.), 147; H. Moffat, *East Anglia's First Railways* (1987), 133–6.

Wood, Sir William Valentine (1883–1959); born in Belfast, he began his railway career as a junior accountant with a local company. During World War I he worked for the Irish Railway Executive Committee, and subsequently for the Ministry of *Transport. In 1924 Wood became assistant to the accountant-general of the *London Midland & Scottish Railway, and soon encountered Josiah *Stamp, chairman from 1926. His next post was controller of costs and statistics in 1927, and three years later came a massive promotion to a vice-president of the executive committee. During the 1930s he cemented his high reputation as a master

of railway *statistics, an expert on the complex pricing system, and a competent spokesman for the company and the industry before official bodies. Wood worked effectively with the more eloquent Stamp, supplying him with a flow of relevant facts and figures. He was the principal author of the book *Railways* which they published jointly in 1927. Wood succeeded to the presidency of the LMS in 1941. He also served during World War II as a member of the Railway Executive. After *nationalization he was recruited by *Hurcomb to spend five years as a member of the *British Transport Commission. He was knighted in 1937. GC

P. B. Whitehouse and D. St J. Thomas, *LMS 150* (1987); *Railway Gazette*, 7 Aug. 1953.

wooden railways played a crucial role in establishing the fundamentals of the railway. The first in Britain comprised small hand-pushed trucks guided by a pin running in a slot between plank-like rails, a type long established underground in continental metal mines. Imported by Austrian copper miners to Cumberland in the 1560s, they barely influenced future development. This was, rather, stimulated by the burgeoning *coal industry, which demanded an all-weather means of transport, more efficient than unmetalled roads, from pit-head to (normally) navigable water.

The resulting British railway differed from its continental predecessors in scale, in carrying coal above ground with horse traction, and in its method of guidance. Every respectable colliery acquired one. Purely private, with essentially one-way traffic, it appeared almost simultaneously in the east and west Midlands and followed two distinct lines of evolution. The earliest on record was built at Wollaton just west of *Nottingham in 1603–4 by Huntingdon Beaumont, who about 1605 took the idea north. By 1660 perhaps nine wagonways, as they were locally known, had appeared in Tyneside, which became the real nursery of the railway and from the 1720s exported it to other coalfields—Yorkshire, Cumberland, and *Scotland—under its technical influence.

The building of wagonways was intimately tied up with the internecine warfare between coalowners, who could block a rival's passage by refusing wayleaves. The profession of 'waggonway-wright' arose, to lay out routes up to 12 miles in length, taming the rough terrain with cuttings and embankments, though gradients could be precipitous by later standards. While most bridges were spindly wooden structures, the stone Causey Arch of 1726 had the largest span (105 ft) in Britain at that time (SEE BRIDGES AND VIADUCTS). Traffic could be high: in 1727 the Tanfield Way carried 450,000 tons; equivalent, on working days, to one wagon every 45 seconds.

Single *track gave way to double. The rails, typically of oak some 4½ in square, were pinned to close-set sleepers laid in deep ballast on a well-drained formation; splendid examples have been unearthed at Bersham near Wrexham and, very recently, at Lambton, Co. Durham. Under heavy traffic, rails needed replacing every year, and from the 1750s an upper layer of rail was often added to protect the lower, and sometimes plated with thin wrought-iron straps. Check rails, and rodded and self-acting points were all employed. Wagonways being physically unconnected, Tyneside *gauges varied, between 3 ft 10 in and 5 ft; the standard gauge originated with the 4 ft 8 in of the Killingworth Way of 1764–5, on which George *Stephenson later worked. From 1660 to 1800 wagon capacity grew from 33 cwt to 53 cwt. *Wheels were flanged—evidently a British invention of about 1600—and were wooden until, from 1732, cast iron was gradually adopted. The normal motive power downhill was gravity (controlled by brake), and one horse per wagon up.

Simultaneously there evolved the Shropshire railway, first heard of near Broseley on the Severn in 1605; within 20 years another eight are attested nearby. Whether they imitated Wollaton, or Wollaton imitated some earlier line at Broseley not recorded in the skimpy sources, is not certain. Railways rapidly proliferated, with a particularly complex system serving Coalbrookdale and its satellite ironworks from 1748, and carrying not only coal but lime, ore, and pig iron; and from 1665 Shropshire-style railways were introduced to other west Midlands coalfields, South and North Wales, Scotland, and Lancashire.

Many details differed from Tyneside. The local nomenclature was 'railway' (by 1681) or 'railroad' (1702). The early Shropshire railway was short, running uninterruptedly from the coalface, out of the adit (horizontal shaft) and down the river bank by rope-worked incline. The result was a narrow gauge (2 ft to 3 ft 9 in) and a small wagon-capacity (normally up to 30 cwt). Only the 50- or 60-cwt wagons of Coalbrookdale seem to owe something to Tyneside. Cast-iron wheels were usual from at least 1729. Engineering was light and gradients steep, with sometimes three horses needed to haul one wagon. Most importantly, from 1767 Coalbrookdale protected its wooden rails with cast bars, the precursor of the all-iron rail.

Underground, wooden railways were adopted in the 18th century in collieries, notably the horse-operated 'rolley-ways' of Tyneside, and in larger metal mines. Also on Tyneside, around the 1750s, the hand-pushed tram was put on flanged wooden rails. This was the *tramroad or tramway, a name and a rail type soon to become prominent on surface lines.

From 1757, many railways were built to feed *canals. A largely Midland phenomenon, these lines borrowed more from Shropshire than from Tyneside, which is why 'railway' became the standard name. Some, built as extensions to canals in terrain where waterways were impracticable, were the first public railways, like the canals themselves open on payment of toll to all comers; perhaps the earliest (1778) was at Caldon in Staffordshire. From the 1790s, iron rails spelt the end for wooden railways, although a few survivors lasted until the 1840s.

See also EARLY IRON RAILWAYS.   MJTL

M. J. T. Lewis, *Early Wooden Railways* (1970); G. Bennett, E. Clavering, and A. Rounding, *A Fighting Trade: Rail Transport in Tyne Coal 1600–1800* (1990); S. Grenter, 'A Wooden Waggonway Complex at Bersham Ironworks, Wrexham', *Industrial Archaeology Review*, 15 (1993), 195–207.

workmen's trains. These were run, at specially low fares, for those going to work in the early morning and returning at night.

The first railway to provide them seems to have been the *Eastern Counties, in 1847: from Canning Town to North Woolwich, for the Woolwich ferry, taking workers across the Thames to the dockyard. The *Stockton & Darlington provided similar trains from *Middlesbrough to the iron-working village of Eston from about 1852.

As early as 1846 Charles *Pearson advocated moving by railway 'a large portion of the mechanic population' to and from London for work. In 1860, when the *London Chatham & Dover Railway sought to enter the City at Blackfriars, he proposed, in giving evidence on its Bill, that it should be compelled to provide a stated minimum service of 'workmen's trains'. This obligation was accepted by the company (though not, as usually stated, written into its Act), which introduced services in 1865. Nine months earlier the *Metropolitan Railway had, voluntarily, inaugurated similar trains, crossing London from west to east. In 1864 the House of Lords required that all railway Bills for new lines into London should include the provision of workmen's trains.

Demolition for new railways in London and other large towns created widespread homelessness. Efforts were made to oblige the companies to provide other accommodation for the people displaced, but few succeeded. When the *Great Eastern Railway secured power to extend its line to *Liverpool Street in 1861–4, it was on condition that it should run workmen's trains from Edmonton and Walthamstow to London at a return fare of 2d. a day, enabling workers to live 6–8 miles out. These trains multiplied and extended. By 1899 there were 104 in London, conveying 23,000 passengers each weekday.

The London County Council, formed in 1889, constantly tried to secure more trains, partly on the ground that as the companies were running more than they were obliged to, they must be profitable. But this was false logic. C. H. Parkes, chairman of the GER, told its shareholders in 1891 that these trains paid *only when they were full*, which the earlier trains never were. By 1904, however, the company admitted that the twopenny fare from Enfield (the greatest distance) was remunerative. That railway enjoyed the great advantage of scale; on others, workmen's trains formed a relatively small part of their operations.

To what extent did these trains solve the problem of overcrowding? H. J. *Dyos concluded that although, south of the Thames, they 'broke down at least some of the economic obstacles to suburban migration', they also accelerated the decay of the central districts that were vacated.

Workmen's trains were not provided in London alone. Some *Birmingham and *Glasgow services differed from those in London in running outbound: to Bournville (for Cadbury's), for example; to the great Singer sewing-machine factory down the Clyde. Workmen's *tickets sometimes formed a substantial proportion of total passenger revenue: for instance, on the *Liverpool Overhead Railway in 1913, it was 23.8 per cent.

From 1900 onwards, in some districts, electric trams (see TRAMWAYS, STREET) captured an increasing quantity of this traffic, though their impact was uneven. They did not reach Enfield, for example, until 1913. In that year there were 1,000 workmen's trains in London, and the annual number of journeys in Great Britain was 255 million. In 1938 it was 328 million.

After World War II workmen's fares, under that name, were phased out, though opposition to their proposed abolition on *London Transport was successful in 1952. Thereafter they gradually became assimilated with 'early morning fares', a more general and vague concession.

JS

C. E. Lee, *Passenger Class Distinctions* (1946), ch. 7; H. J. Dyos, 'Workmen's Fares in South London', *JTH*, 1 (1953–4); *HLT*; *RTC*.

works, railway manufacture and repair. The first works to be established primarily for manufacture of railway equipment was that of Robert Stephenson & Co., in 1823. The partners included George and Robert *Stephenson: they had foreseen a rapid increase in demand for *locomotives, *stationary engines, *wagons, and *track, and established their works at Forth Street, *Newcastle. In 1825 it completed its first locomotive: *Locomotion*, for the *Stockton & Darlington Railway.

In the earliest days of locomotives, however, and for a long time afterwards, it was usually the established engineering firms which built them. The Coalbrookdale Co. in 1802 and Penydarren Ironworks in 1804 both built *Trevithick locomotives for their own use; the first locomotive for a customer seems to have been the Trevithick locomotive built in 1805 by John Whinfield of Gateshead for Christopher Blackett.

Hazeldine & Rastrick, who had built many Trevithick stationary engines, built Trevithick's noted demonstration locomotive *Catch-me-who-can* of 1808. The first locomotives to run successfully in commercial service—Blenkinsop and *Murray's *Middleton Railway locomotives of 1812—were also built by a firm with much experience of stationary engines: Fenton Murray & Wood of Leeds.

George Stephenson's early locomotives were built using the engineering facilities of his coalowning employers, but the first which he designed for an outside customer, the *Kilmarnock & Troon Railway, was built in 1817 by, probably, the Walker Ironworks at Newcastle. In 1829 Foster & Rastrick built four primitive locomotives, one of which, *Agenoria*, has survived to become the *National Railway Museum's oldest locomotive.

The *Rainhill trials in the same year greatly encouraged not only improvements in design, but also development of the manufacturing industry. Construction of *Rocket*, not without difficulty where the multi-tubular boiler was concerned, was a triumph for Robert Stephenson's works. John Braithwaite of London had been building successful steam fire engines, designed by John Ericsson, and together they adapted the design to produce the Rainhill runner-up *Novelty*. Timothy *Hackworth, who built *Sans Pareil* for Rainhill

while locomotive superintendent of the SDR, set up his own works at Shildon in 1833. At Robert Stephenson's suggestion in 1831, a works was set up in Lancashire to obviate difficulties of transport from Tyneside: at first called Charles Tayleur, it later became well known as the Vulcan Foundry Co. Its first locomotives were completed in 1833.

Some of the firms which turned to locomotive building at this period became famous. Edward *Bury completed his first locomotive in 1830. Others include R. & W. Hawthorn (later Hawthorn Leslie), who were building locomotives from 1831; Sharp Roberts, later Sharp Stewart (1833); Nasmyth Gaskell, later Nasmyth Wilson (1839); Tulk & Ley, later Fletcher Jennings (1840); Stothert & Slaughter, later Avonside (1841); and Neilson & Mitchell (1843).

Tracing the development of the industry is much hampered by the frequent changes of name which resulted from the ease and frequency with which partnerships were formed and dissolved. An extreme example is Todd, Kitson & Laird, well known as builders of that famous surviving locomotive *Lion*—and probably better-known now than to contemporaries, for the firm bore that name only during 1838, the year of *Lion's* construction. The Kitson element, however, remained constant through many changes; Todd left in 1838 to form Shepherd & Todd and establish the Railway Foundry at *Leeds, which later became well known as E. B. Wilson. When it failed in 1858 there arose in its place and location, Manning Wardle, Hudswell Clarke (1860), and the Hunslet Engine Co. (1864). Other noted locomotive builders established at this period included Beyer Peacock (1854), Andrew Barclay (1859), Fox Walker, later Peckett (1864), Dübs (1865), and W. G. Bagnall (1876). Kerr Stuart, originally a dealer, was building locomotives from 1893.

There was, however, another trend. The plant and skills required for heavy repairs to steam locomotives are scarcely less than those required for building. So again and again one finds railway companies equipping themselves for repairs, and subsequently taking up new construction. Frequently parts from earlier locomotives were reused. The first instance seems to have been at Shildon, SDR, in 1827 when Timothy Hackworth designed and constructed *Royal George*, and incorporated parts from the unsuccessful *Chittaprat*. The Monkland & Kirkintilloch Railway was building its own locomotives from 1834, and the *Liverpool & Manchester from 1841. All the important railway companies, and many of the lesser ones, eventually built their own locomotives (see table). They could build, however, only for their own use: when the *London & North Western Railway built locomotives for sale, the independent builders in 1875 formed the Locomotive Manufacturers' Association (see RAILWAY INDUSTRY ASSOCIATION) and successfully contested the LNWR's right to do so.

Yet although new construction was the glamorous aspect of railway workshops' work, maintenance and overhauls always formed the greater part of it. The *Cambrian Railways established Oswestry works in 1865, but built only two locomotives there. Even the *Festiniog Railway was able to build two new locomotives, double *Fairlies, at its

Boston Lodge works, in 1879 and 1885. The *Furness Railway had its works at *Barrow, but built no locomotives of its own.

The origin of the rolling stock industry may be taken as the manufacture, by Robert Stephenson for the SDR in 1828, of the first wagon to be fitted with springs and outside bearings in axle-boxes: the first piece of rolling stock specifically suited to steam trains. For the bodies of passenger *carriages, however, there was a precedent in road *coaches, and it was their makers who built the first railway carriages. Coachbuilders *Worsdell & Son—members of the family would later have distinguished railway careers —built carriages for the LMR. Stage-coach builder and operator Joseph Wright of London set up in 1845 at Saltley, *Birmingham, the rolling stock building firm which eventually became the Metropolitan Railway Carriage & Wagon Co. Coachbuilders Brown & Marshall started to build railway rolling stock at the same period. Other manufacturers who also built road vehicles, at least initially, included Ashbury (established 1837), Gloucester Wagon Co. (1860), and Bristol Wagon Co. (1866)—names metamorphosed down the years, often to include the words 'Railway Carriage & Wagon'. Manufacturing and leasing wagons to *private owners was big business: the Midland RCW Co. started to build only in 1864 after over 20 years of hiring out stock built by others. At least five other important builders of rolling stock were established in the mid-19th century.

The railway company works also maintained and, in many cases, built rolling stock. Locomotive, carriage, and wagon maintenance was often undertaken in the same works: specific rolling stock works included Bromsgrove (established 1840), Cowlairs, *Glasgow (1842), Stratford, London (1847), Ashford (1850), Earlestown (1852), *Doncaster carriage (1853), *York (1865), *Derby (1873), Newton Heath, *Manchester (1877), Gorton, Manchester (1881), Lancing (1888), and Doncaster wagon (1889). Some of these represent the dispersal of rolling stock work from locomotives: Wolverton, by contrast, after locomotive repairs were moved away in 1877, became exclusively a rolling stock works.

Some of the independent builders compensated for the lack of orders from main-line companies by concentrating on building for *industrial railways and *contractors. Virtually all of them found an important export market (see OVERSEAS RAILWAYS). This was almost as old as the industry itself: by 1831 six of the first 90 locomotives built in Britain had been exported to America, and by 1857 British-built locomotives had been sent to Belgium, Germany, Canada, Russia, India, and Argentina, among other countries. Subsequently they were distributed almost world-wide. Export markets became vital.

J. W. Lowe, in *British Steam Locomotive Builders*, estimates that by the turn of the century the private builders and the railway works between them were producing about 2,000 locomotives a year. But competition from builders on the Continent and in the USA was becoming increasingly intense. Seeking economies from large-scale construction, three Glasgow firms—Neilson Reid, Dübs, and Sharp Stewart—merged in 1903 to form the North British Locomotive Company, one of the largest locomotive builders outside North America. Other firms concentrated on particular types of locomotive: Kitson on the Meyer type from 1903, Beyer Peacock (with great success) on the Beyer-Garratt from 1908.

The rolling stock industry saw rationalization also, with the formation in 1902 of the Metropolitan Amalgamated Railway Carriage & Wagon Co. Ltd in which Metropolitan RCW was joined by Ashbury, Brown Marshalls and others. Railway companies set up new C&W works at Eastleigh (1891), Temple Mills, London (1896), Barassie, Ayrshire (1901), and Faverdale, Darlington (1923).

Works conditions had improved since the early days when the SDR's repair shops comprised a building similar to a barn, divided into a joiners' shop and a smithy with two hearths. Tools then were all hand-tools, except for hand-lathes, and boilers and engines could be lifted only by jacks. Tallow candles provided illumination.

Machine tools gradually made their appearance—wheel-lathes, for instance, from about 1840, steam-hammers from 1847—and more and more specialized and advanced equipment was introduced. Eventually G. J. *Churchward constructed a stationary test plant for completed locomotives at *Swindon in 1903 (see LOCOMOTIVE TESTING). At Horwich, *Lancashire & Yorkshire Railway—a large modern works —in 1912 the erecting shop had space for 100 locomotives and 30 tenders and was served by two overhead travelling cranes of 40 tons capacity. To feed it were the boiler shop and the machine shop, both vast and the latter in turn fed by steel, iron, and brass foundries, and the smithy, where much of the work was mechanized. Much use was made of *hydraulic power, for instance for flanging firebox plates; compressed air was used for riveting and caulking machines and other tasks; and the works generated its own electric power for cranes, motors, and lighting.

Among the many products of Horwich were the bogies and traction motors for the LYR Liverpool–Southport electric trains. But *electrification and construction of electric traction equipment were more commonly the preserve of specialist companies. Siemens Bros and Dick Kerr had been active since the 1880s, and eventually merged with others to form English Electric in 1919. Brush Electrical Engineering was formed in 1889 to take over Falcon, builder of steam locomotives and tramcars, and gradually phased out steam in favour of electricity. The British Westinghouse Electric & Manufacturing Co. was formed in 1899 and completed electrification of the *Mersey Railway in 1903. In 1919 it was renamed Metropolitan-Vickers Electrical, having been acquired, along with Metropolitan, by Vickers to form a group for steel-making, rolling stock construction, and electrical engineering. Only nine years later, however, it was sold to the American company General Electric, which formed Associated Electrical Industries as a holding company for it and other British subsidiaries, although trading as Metrovick continued until 1959.

In the meantime there had been further amalgamations on the rolling stock side. In 1919, in the aftermath of World

War I, Cammell Laird adapted their munitions factory at *Nottingham for manufacture of rolling stock, and took over Midland RCW. Four years later they also acquired Leeds Forge which had pioneered pressed steel construction of rolling stock in 1887. In 1927 Vickers and Cammell Laird merged their rolling stock interests to form Metropolitan-Cammell Carriage, Wagon & Finance Co.: Metro-Cammell. Production was concentrated at the west Midlands plants and the outlying ones closed. Exports continued to be of paramount importance. A notable success was construction in quantity of those most quintessentially foreign vehicles, the *sleeping and *restaurant cars of the Compagnie Internationale des Wagons-Lits: travel from Paris to the Riviera in the late 1920s was in *wagons-lits* built by Leeds Forge.

The slump between the wars hit the locomotive industry very hard indeed: at its deepest in 1933 North British Locomotive Co., with the capacity to build 600 locomotives a year, built no more than 16. The company survived, but others did not. Manning Wardle, Kerr Stuart, Avonside, Kit-son, and Nasmyth Wilson all closed in 1927–39. The locomotive building activities of Hawthorn Leslie were taken over by Robert Stephenson in 1937. Also in the 1920s and 1930s, however, were the first attempts to build diesel locomotives in quantity—by, for instance, Vulcan Foundry, Hunslet, Andrew Barclay, and English Electric. The latter found in the *London Midland & Scottish Railway a ready market for diesel-electric shunting locomotives. In general, however, until as late as the 1950s overseas railways tended to be a more favourable market for diesel traction than those at home.

One of the consequences of the 1923 *Grouping was that the *Big Four railway companies tended to concentrate construction and maintenance of locomotives and rolling stock at their principal works. Small works inherited from constituents were either closed, or used only for maintenance. The companies could have stopped buying from the independent manufacturers, but in fact they continued to give them some support. The *Great Western Railway

Principal railway company works at which steam locomotives were built.
Locations are mentioned in text, except where stated below

Works	Railway	Date opened	Date first loco built	Post-1922 owners	Date last steam loco built
Shildon	SDR, NER	1826	1827	LNER, BR	1867[a]
Edge Hill, Liverpool	LMR, GJR	c.1830	1841	—	1848
Nine Elms, London	LSWR	1839	1844	—	1909[b]
Cowlairs, Glasgow	EGR, NBR	1841	1844	LNER, BR	1924
Wolverton	LBR, LNWR	1838	c.1845	LMS, BR	1862[c]
Crewe	GJR, LNWR	1843	1845	LMS, BR, ABB	1958
Miles Platting, Manchester	MLR, LYR	1846	1846	—	1881
Swindon	GWR	1843	1846	GWR, BR	1960
Stratford	ECR, GER	1847	1851	LNER	1924
Derby	NMR, MR	1840	1851	LMS, BR, ABB	1957
Brighton	LBSCR	1852	1854	SR, BR	1957
Ashford	SER, SECR	c.1850	1853	SR, BR	1944
St Rollox, Glasgow	CR	1854	1854	LMS, BR	1928
Cardiff	TVR	c.1845	1856	GWR	1903
Kilmarnock	GSWR	1856	1857	LMS, BR	1921
Gorton	MSLR, GCR	1848	1858	LNER, BR	1950
Wolverhampton	SBR, GWR	1849	1859	GWR, BR	1908
Gateshead	YNBR, NER	1854	1859	LNER, BR	1910[d]
Bow, London	NLR	1853	1863	LMS	1906
Darlington	SDR, NER	1863	1864	LNER, BR	1957
Doncaster	GNR	1853	1867	LNER, BR	1957
Stoke-on-Trent	NSR	pre-1868	1868	LMS	1923
Longhedge, London	LCDR, SECR	1862	1869	—	1904
Inverness	HR	c.1865	1869	LMS, BR	1906
Melton Constable, Norfolk	EMR, MGNJR	1883	1897	LMS/LNER	1910
Horwich	LYR	1887	1888	LMS, BR	1957
Caerphilly	RR	1901	—[e]	GWR, BR	1963
Inverurie, Aberdeenshire	GNSR	1902	1909	LNER, BR	1921
Eastleigh	LSWR	1909	1910	SR, BR	1950[f]

Notes

[a] Subsequently C&W works.
[b] Work transferred to Eastleigh.
[c] Locomotive construction transferred to Crewe; locomotive repairs until 1877, subsequently C&W works.
[d] Construction transferred to Darlington.
[e] Rebuilding of locomotives; but the most important railway works in Wales from 1901.
[f] 1955–61, Bulleid Pacifics rebuilt at this works.

Company abbreviations:

ABB	Asea Brown Boveri
BR	British Railways
CR	Caledonian Ry
ECR	Eastern Counties Ry
EGR	Edinburgh & Glasgow Ry
EMR	Eastern & Midlands Ry
GCR	Great Central Ry
GER	Great Eastern Ry
GJR	Grand Junction Ry
GNR	Great Northern Ry
GNSR	Great North of Scotland Ry
GSWR	Glasgow & South Western Ry
GWR	Great Western Ry
HR	Highland Ry
LBR	London & Birmingham Ry
LBSCR	London Brighton & South Coast Ry
LCDR	London Chatham & Dover Ry
LMR	Liverpool & Manchester Ry
LMS	London Midland & Scottish Ry
LNER	London & North Eastern Ry
LNWR	London & North Western Ry
LSWR	London & South Western Ry
LYR	Lancashire & Yorkshire Ry
MGNJR	Midland & Great Northern Joint Ry
MLR	Manchester & Leeds Ry
MSLR	Manchester Sheffield & Lincolnshire Ry
MR	Midland Ry
NBR	North British Ry
NER	North Eastern Ry
NLR	North London Ry
NMR	North Midland Ry
NSR	North Staffordshire Ry
RR	Rhymney Ry
SBR	Shrewsbury & Birmingham Ry
SDR	Stockton & Darlington Ry
SECR	South Eastern & Chatham Ry
SER	South Eastern Ry
SR	Southern Ry
TVR	Taff Vale Ry
YNBR	York Newcastle & Berwick Ry

placed orders with Kerr Stuart and Yorkshire Engine Co., the LMS with Vulcan Foundry, the *London & North Eastern with Kitson. Most notably, when the LMS needed improved express locomotives in a hurry, it had the Royal Scots built by North British.

By the late 1940s ten surviving steam locomotive manufacturers employed about 13,000 people; in 1914 there had been 16 firms employing 21,000. The railway companies' own locomotive works in 1947 employed approaching 43,000 people, the great majority of whom were concerned with repairs rather than new construction.

The independent steam locomotive manufacturers were coping with a post-war boom. 'Never has the industry been more virile', stated the Locomotive Manufacturers' Association Handbook in 1949. Most of them could also build diesels, which were 'more attractive in countries where oil is cheaply available or water scarce'. By then, General Motors in the USA was presenting dieselization as a virtual *fait accompli*. Late in 1947, a few weeks before it was *nationalized, the LMS produced its first main-line diesel-electric locomotive at Derby: engine and electrical equipment were by English Electric.

In 1949 a main-line steam locomotive cost one-third, or less, of the cost of a diesel-electric. Although the newly nationalized *British Railways adopted diesel locomotives for shunting, for other work a range of standard steam locomotive classes was designed. The companies' works became the responsibility of BR's regions, but production of each class was in principle allocated to a single works: *Brighton, *Crewe, Darlington, Derby, Doncaster, Horwich, and Swindon.

In 1954, however, there emerged from Derby C&W works the first BR diesel *multiple-unit train—a harbinger of the *Modernization Plan which would end construction of steam locomotives by BR. The last, *Evening Star*, was completed at Swindon in 1960. Comparable dates for last steam locomotives completed by the private builders were: Vulcan Foundry, 1956; Peckett, North British, and Beyer Peacock, 1958; Hudswell Clarke, 1961; Andrew Barclay, 1962; and Hunslet, as late as 1971. The Hudswell Clarke order was for the National Coal Board; the remainder were all for export. Small steam locomotives continue to be built by and for preserved and tourist railways and as replicas of early locomotives, and there are hopes of constructing anew full-size examples of main-line locomotives from classes which were entirely scrapped.

BR works which built diesel and/or electric main-line locomotives under the modernization plans included Crewe, Derby, Swindon, and Doncaster. Engines and electrical equipment were bought in. Unlike the standard steam locomotive range, the modernization plans brought business to private locomotive builders and rolling stock manufacturers. The distinction between the two became ever more blurred, with rolling stock manufacturers constructing multiple-unit trains and even locomotives, and locomotive builders eventually turning to diesel trains and rolling stock. Among the principal initial beneficiaries of the modernization plans were English Electric (which had ab-

sorbed Vulcan Foundry, Robert Stephenson & Hawthorns, and Bagnall), Brush, North British, Beyer Peacock, Metrovick, and Metropolitan-Cammell. Not all were able satisfactorily to make the transition from steam: notable casualties were North British Locomotive, liquidated in 1962, and Beyer Peacock, which ceased building locomotives in 1966.

In 1962 British Railways transferred control of main works from the regions to its newly established Workshops Division. Their main function was to be repairs, with some new construction. Some works were developed, but during the years 1962 to 1968 three locomotive works and at least 12 carriage and wagon works were closed, some of the latter being merged with adjoining locomotive works. The same period brought contraction in private rolling stock building too, with several old-established firms either going out of business or ceasing to manufacture rolling stock.

In early 1970 BR's Workshops Division was transformed into British Rail Engineering Ltd, a wholly owned subsidiary of BR—with freedom to undertake work for outside customers. Before long BR workshops were producing not only high-speed trains for Britain, but shunting locomotives for Kenya and wagons for Malaysia. Nevertheless there were still further closures, notably Shildon in 1984, and Swindon in 1986.

In 1987 BREL was split up. Four works—Eastleigh, Wolverton, Doncaster, and Glasgow (formerly St Rollox)—were formed into BR Maintenance Ltd, a new BR subsidiary intended to concentrate on maintenance and repairs. During 1988 Doncaster Wagon Works and Horwich Foundry were sold. The other four remaining works—Crewe, Derby Loco., Derby Litchurch Lane, and York (the last two formerly being C&W works) were formed into BREL (1988) Ltd to concentrate on new construction and heavy overhauls. This was a preliminary to offering the company for sale: it was bought in 1989 by a consortium of BREL management and employees, Trafalgar House, and Asea Brown Boveri. ABB subsequently bought out Trafalgar House, and in 1992 the company was renamed ABB Transportation. As such it forms part of a world-wide multinational group with other distinguished constituents, and is now called Adtranz.

The constant changes of name, product, ownership, and alliances make tracing the recent history of the industry as confusing as that of its early years. Hunslet took over Andrew Barclay in 1972, and was taken over by Telfos in 1987. This acquired a 51 per cent holding in Ganz of Budapest in 1989, but was itself taken over in 1992 by the Austrian Jenbacher Transport Group. Brush Traction functions under the umbrella of the BTR Group conglomerate. AEI was acquired by the British concern General Electric Co. in 1968, and in 1969 GEC took over English Electric too. In 1989 the Power Systems Division of GEC was merged with Alsthom (France) to form GEC Alsthom Transport Division; this acquired Metro-Cammell Ltd later the same year. GEC Alsthom therefore is the true descendant of many of the early builders of locomotives and rolling stock; particularly the earliest of all, Robert Stephenson & Co.   PJGR

J. W. Lowe, *British Steam Locomotive Builders* (1975); E. J. Larkin and J. G. Larkin, *The Railway Workshops of Britain 1823–1986* (1988); J. H. Price, *Tramcar, Carriage & Wagon Builders of Birmingham* (1982); J. G. H. Warren, *A Century of Locomotive Building by Robert Stephenson & Co. 1823–1923* (1923, reprinted 1970); R. P. Bradley, *Power for the World's Railways: GEC Traction and Its Predecessors—1823 to the present day* (1993).

Principal locations of records of locomotive and rolling stock builders: Robert Stephenson: Science Museum; North British Locomotive: Mitchell Library, Glasgow; Beyer Peacock: Museum of Science & Industry, Manchester; Hunslet: Leeds Industrial Museum; Vulcan: National Museums & Galleries on Merseyside, Liverpool; Metro-Cammell: Birmingham Central Library, Archives Dept; Birmingham RCW: Staffordshire Record Office.

Worsdell, Thomas William (1838–1916), mechanical engineer, son of Nathaniel Worsdell, carriage superintendent of the *London & North Western Railway.

He was apprenticed at his uncle's engineering works in Birmingham, then worked in the LNWR *Crewe drawing office, 1858–60, leaving to become manager of an engineering works. In 1865 he joined the Pennsylvania Railroad, USA, becoming master mechanic at its Altoona works. In 1871 Worsdell became works manager at Crewe under F. W. *Webb, and locomotive superintendent, *Great Eastern Railway, 1881.

There, Worsdell's excellent 0-6-0s of 1883 numbered 289 engines by 1913, and his 2-4-2 suburban tanks were the forerunners of a large fleet. His express 2-4-0s were followed by two-cylinder compound 4-4-0s, which gave a fuel economy of 14 per cent over the previous type.

Appointed to the *North Eastern in 1888, Worsdell introduced two-cylinder compounding on a large scale, inspired by the success of von Borries' locomotives in Germany, but, because of the smaller British structure gauge (see CLEARANCES), with inside cylinders, making maintenance more difficult.

He built 270 two-cylinder compounds, including 4-4-0 and 4-2-2 express and 171 0-6-0 freight engines, as well as 0-6-2 tanks. Worthwhile fuel economies were achieved, but the large inside low-pressure cylinders caused some structural failures. Many were rebuilt as simples by his brother Wilson, who succeeded him in 1890 when he retired prematurely due to ill health. GWC

BSRL; *Locomotive, Railway Carriage & Wagon Review* (1939), 115–18.

Worsdell, Wilson (1850–1920), mechanical engineer, brother of T. W. *Worsdell. He was a pupil at the Pennsylvania Railroad's works, Altoona, USA, where his brother was master mechanic, 1867–71. He joined the *London & North Western Railway in 1871, working at *Crewe works erecting shops and several locomotive depots. Joining the *North Eastern as assistant mechanical engineer, Gateshead, in 1883, he worked under his brother until succeeding him, 1890–1918.

With increasing passenger and freight traffic, more powerful locomotives were needed, which Worsdell met with new designs of greatly increased boiler capacity. In 1899 he introduced the first 4-6-0 passenger type in Britain, followed

in 1901 by a powerful 0-8-0 heavy freight and mineral engine, and in 1903 by a large 4-4-2 passenger type—all with outside cylinders, following American practice. Equally successful were his inside-cylinder 4-4-0 express and large 0-6-0 freight classes. His chief draughtsman, Walter Mackersie Smith, played a prominent part in this design work and was responsible in 1898 for the first British three-cylinder compound 4-4-0, which inspired the 240 similar locomotives built by S. W. *Johnson, Deeley, and H. *Fowler for the *Midland and *London Midland & Scottish Railways. Smith's four-cylinder compound 4-4-2s, built in 1906 under Worsdell, were more powerful and efficient than the latter's large simples, but problems over royalties after Smith's premature death in 1906 prevented further application of either system and Worsdell reverted to his simple-expansion type. GWC

BSRL; O. S. Nock, *Locomotives of the North Eastern Railway* (1954); G. Hill, *The Worsdells: A Quaker Engineering Dynasty* (1991).

Wrexham Mold & Connah's Quay Railway, see WALES.

wrong-line working. Movement of trains in the *up direction on a down line, or vice versa, is only permitted in a limited, and in many cases specified, number of situations, each of which is strictly regulated by rules and regulations. The most important of these is 'wrong-line working', also called 'single-line working', although that should not be confused with working a railway that has only a *single line. When one of the tracks on a double line is blocked, perhaps for engineering work or through an accident, trains have to be worked in both directions over the other line, requiring special safety procedures to prevent collisions.

Wrong-line working normally takes place between the nearest crossover points on either side of the obstruction and used to be controlled by a designated official (traditionally the *stationmaster or district *inspector) who prepared a series of wrong-line working forms for issue to all staff concerned. A 'pilotman' is appointed to have sole charge of train movements, and he now prepares and issues the forms after ensuring that the line is safe. Wrong-line working can then start. He has to accompany each train personally through the single-line section, but if several trains are to follow each other he will authorize each one to proceed, travelling on the last himself. When double-line working can be resumed the pilotman withdraws all the forms and authorizes the reintroduction of normal operations.

Other situations where trains may be permitted to run in the wrong direction are between signal boxes in station and yard areas; within station limits; in connection with emergencies such as train failures and runaways; and on lines which are signalled for both directions. RDF

J. Aitken, *Single Line Working During Repairs or Obstruction, by Means of Pilotman* (c.1944); G. M. Kichenside and A. Williams, *British Railway Signalling* (1968).

Wythes, George (1811–83), *contractor. The son of a Worcestershire farmer, he secured three contracts for the

Wythes

London & Brighton Railway in 1838–9 with a partner, John Hale. Others followed, making up between them the whole *London Brighton & South Coast Railway line from *Portsmouth to Hastings, together with that from Wivelsfield to Lewes and the Newhaven and Eastbourne branches. These 100 miles were opened in 1840–9, all under J. U. *Rastrick as engineer. His partnership with Hale was dissolved by 1848.

He shared in building the Harwich branch in 1854, but otherwise all his British contracts lay south of the Thames, predominantly in Kent and Sussex. His largest works were the *Charing Cross and *Cannon Street lines for the *South Eastern Railway. Wythes also undertook some overseas contracts with *Brassey, in India and elsewhere. He invested in landed property, and especially in building development in west Kent. He left £1,525,000: after Brassey's, the largest fortune ever based mainly on railway contracting within the British Isles.   JS

Boase; *PICE*, 74 (1883), 294–7; L. Popplewell, *Gazetteer of Railway Contractors and Engineers* (1983–9).

Y

Yerkes (pron. Yer-kes), **Charles Tyson** (1837–1905), financier and chairman of London's *Underground group. Born in Philadelphia, Yerkes was active in street railway promotion in Chicago, and then turned to London (see LONDON UNDERGROUND RAILWAYS). In 1900 he acquired the powers for the Hampstead tube, and in alliance with the solicitor Robert William Perks he established the *Metropolitan District Electric Traction Co. Ltd in 1901, expanded in 1902 to become the Underground Electric Railways Co. of London Ltd, to electrify the District and to build and equip three tube lines. He was a deft financier, using devices then unknown to (and suspected by) orthodox British railway directors; but he succeeded where they failed in raising £16 million capital, largely from the USA and other foreign banking sources. Yerkes, who had a somewhat disreputable private life (fictionalized by Theodore Dreiser), spent lavishly and acquired a notable art collection, all of which had to be auctioned after his death to pay his debts. It was very largely due to him and the American men and technology that he introduced that London's internal local railway system was transformed in the Edwardian decade.   RMR

Dictionary of American Biography; C. E. Lee, 100 Years of the District (1986); HLT; D. F. Croome and A. A. Jackson, Rails through the Clay (1993 edn.).

Yolland, William (1810–85), government *inspector. The son of a land agent, he entered the Royal Engineers in 1828; was an officer of the Ordnance Survey, 1841–53; *inspector of railways, 1854–77, and chief inspector, 1877–85; CB, 1881.

The longest-serving of all the Board of *Trade railway inspectors, he was very strict in his investigations, but was not harsh, and he came to command general respect in the world of railways. He was quick to discover the improper intrusion of commercial interests into their working (see BRAKES) and he advocated quietly but firmly the extension of government power over the companies, achieved, not long after his death, in the *Regulation Act of 1889 (see PARLIAMENT AND LEGISLATION).   JS

Boase; GR; ET, 126–9.

York. At the first census in 1801, the population of this ancient cathedral city was 16,000. It was an important market and commercial centre, with busy wharves on the River Ouse that connected it to *Hull. After a period of low growth in the 1830s the openings of, first, the *York & North Midland and then the *Great North of England Railway put York on the line from *London, *Leeds, and Hull to the north, which for a decade speeded up expansion. In 1931 the population was nearly 85,000, and in 1981 was 101,000.

These two railways were followed by lines to Scarborough, Market Weighton (later to Beverley), and Harrogate in 1845–8, and two years later the line northward had reached *Edinburgh. York was firmly established as the most important junction on the *East Coast route to Scotland south of *Newcastle.

The lines were all promoted by George *Hudson, then York's most influential citizen. The city Council gave ready support, even to the extent of agreeing to siting the station in Tanner Row, inside the city, which required the walls to be breached by arches. A terminus, the station included a *hotel, and a new street called Hudson Street was built to improve access. After Hudson's disgrace in 1849 it was renamed Railway Street, but it was again renamed George Hudson Street in 1971.

The city's cordial relationship with its railways continued after they became part of the *North Eastern Railway in 1854, when York, with the rest of north-east England, was served by a monopoly, although the trains of seven other companies reached it by means of *running powers. In 1871 a direct line from Selby and the south was opened, to be replaced in turn by a second new one in 1983. The station had for long been totally inadequate, causing frequent accidents, and at length the NER built a large through station with a dramatic arched roof (see TRAINSHEDS) on a sharp curve outside the walls. It was opened in 1877, with 13 platforms (later increased to 16), and trains no longer had to reverse. A year later a large new hotel was opened alongside it. The old station and hotel which, with a number of other railway buildings in the city, had been designed by the York architect G. T. *Andrews, became offices and sidings.

In 1842 locomotive and rolling stock workshops were built west of the station, and after numerous extensions they became one of the NER's main *works. Locomotive work mainly comprised repairs, and in 1905 it was moved to Darlington. York continued to build *carriages and *wagons, however, and in 1884 became the company's sole carriage works. Under *British Railways the wagon works closed, but carriage-building continued and eventually was *privatized.

Buildings near the station were acquired over the years for more headquarters accommodation to accompany the NER's expansion. Then in 1906 an entirely new building was opened; large and handsome, it was designed by the company's architect William *Bell, and Horace Field. But by now the railway's position as the city's largest single employer, which it had enjoyed virtually from the outset, was beginning to be challenged. Rowntrees' and Terrys' chocolate factories were expanding. After the 1923 *Grouping York ceased to be a railway headquarters, although it was not until after World War II that railway employment began to decline seriously. Indeed, in 1968 it received a boost when BR's Eastern and North Eastern Regions were combined, with a headquarters once more at York, the only one of the railway's English regions to be based outside London. To supplement the 1906 building a large concrete office block named Hudson House was erected in the old station yard, an ugly, confusing building sitting inside the city wall alongside Andrews' original station.

In 1928 the NER's successor, the *London & North Eastern Railway, had opened a museum in two separate parts, to be greatly enlarged when the former steam and diesel depot in Leeman Road was acquired for the *National Railway Museum which opened in 1975. Today the museum is one of York's major tourist attractions. *Tourism itself, of course, owes much of its enormous growth to the railway.

York also had another railway, the tiny Derwent Valley *Light Railway, an agricultural line running from Layerthorpe, in the eastern part of the town, to Cliff Common on the NER's Selby–Market Weighton line. Opened in 1913, passenger trains ceased in 1926, but the company escaped *nationalization and survived for goods traffic until it closed in stages in 1965–81.   GJB

Tomlinson; K. Hoole, *Rail Centres: York* (1983); *GRSB*; *RTC*, 185–7; *VCH: City of York*.

York & North Midland Railway. The making of a railway between *York and *Leeds began to be discussed at York in 1833. The *North Midland Railway, running from Leeds to *Derby, was authorized in 1836, and at the same time a separate York & North Midland Railway, 32 miles long, joining it west of Castleford. The driving-force behind both these railways came to be George *Hudson. George *Stephenson was their engineer.

Its line presented no difficulties of construction, being virtually level over the first 15 miles southwards from York. It was opened in 1839, the much longer North Midland following in 1840. The YNMR now became part of the great trunk route from London to York via Rugby and Derby. At Milford two spurs were built, linking the YNMR to the *Leeds & Selby, and so to its eastward continuation, the Hull & Selby. In 1840 the Hull & Selby company was leased to the YNMR and NMR jointly.

Hudson was chairman of the company from 1836 to 1849. Its system expanded further, to reach Scarborough and Pickering in 1845; 49 miles of line altogether, built within a year at a cost of less than £6,000 a mile—a most creditable achievement. Robert *Stephenson was the engineer. In 1845 the YNMR purchased the Leeds & Selby and *Whitby & Pickering Railways.

Early in 1849 a majority of the company's shareholders, having grown suspicious of the financial activities of Hud-

son, forced him into resigning the chairmanship. One of his last important acts was to make an amicable agreement with the *Great Northern Railway (hitherto his bitterest enemy), facilitating its access to York. In 1854 the company joined in the *amalgamation to form the *North Eastern Railway. The total length of the YNMR system, including the East & West Yorkshire Junction Railway from Knaresborough to York, which it had taken over in 1851, was 113 miles.   JS

Tomlinson.

York Newcastle & Berwick Railway: a combination of the York & Newcastle and Newcastle & Berwick Railways, effected in 1847 by George *Hudson, following his successful creation of the *Midland Railway (1844). He was already chairman of the *York & North Midland Railway, approaching York from the south. He carried the fusion through with great skill and force, having already gained the support of *Newcastle by promising the corporation that his railway should cross the Tyne there by a high-level bridge, carrying road as well as railway traffic. Hudson made a bid to include the *North British Railway in the new combine, but that company's board rejected the surprisingly liberal terms he offered it.

In 1848 the YNBR was 149 miles long. It took a lease of the *Newcastle & Carlisle and Maryport & Carlisle Railways and also gained control of some other small companies, including the Hartlepool and West Durham Railways. But as Hudson tottered to his fall in 1849 these arrangements began to collapse. The Newcastle & Carlisle and Maryport companies regained their independence in January 1850.

Meanwhile the strength of the YNBR's only important competitor, the *Leeds Northern Railway (which had never come into Hudson's hands), was growing, and by 1852 it had become clear, both to the YNBR and to the YNMR, that the wisest and most economical policy must be to *amalgamate the three companies into one. The negotiations were complicated and troublesome but, led by the three companies' managers, T. E. *Harrison, A. C. Sheriff, and Henry *Tennant, they were successfully concluded with the combination of the three to form a new *North Eastern Railway, sanctioned by Parliament in 1854.

The YNBR was a progressive concern. It made some enterprising experiments with locomotives, including one of the first to be fitted with three cylinders. It was the first large railway company to face the difficulties presented by *private-owners' *wagons and to begin buying them up. Its central station at Newcastle remains today one of the finest anywhere in England; the bridges built for it at Newcastle and Berwick (see BRIDGES AND VIADUCTS) are among the outstanding achievements of British railway engineering.   JS

Tomlinson; purchase of private-owners' wagons: B. Poole, *Report to the . . . Directors of the London & North Western Railway Company on Coal Traffic* (1849), 6.

APPENDIX 1

1923 Grouping

Constituent and Subsidiary Companies: First Schedule, Railways Act, 1921, 11 & 12 Geo V, c55.

Southern Group (Southern Railway)

Constituent Companies

London & South Western; London Brighton & South Coast; South Eastern; London Chatham & Dover; South Eastern & Chatham Railway Companies Managing Committee.

Subsidiary Companies

Bridgwater; Brighton & Dyke; Freshwater Yarmouth & Newport (Isle of Wight); Hayling; Isle of Wight; Isle of Wight Central; Lee-on-the-Solent; London & Greenwich; Mid Kent; North Cornwall; Plymouth & Dartmoor; Plymouth Devonport & South Western Junction; Sidmouth; Victoria Station & Pimlico.

Western Group (Great Western Railway)

Constituent Companies

Great Western; Barry; Cambrian; Cardiff; Rhymney; Taff Vale; Alexandra (Newport and South Wales) Docks & Railway.

Subsidiary Companies

Brecon & Merthyr Tydfil Junction; Burry Port & Gwendraeth Valley; Cleobury Mortimer & Ditton Priors Light; Didcot Newbury & Southampton; Exeter; Forest of Dean Central; Gwendraeth Valleys; Lampeter Aberayron & New Quay Light; Liskeard & Looe; Llanelly & Mynydd Mawr; Mawddwy; Midland & South Western Junction; Neath & Brecon; Penarth Extension; Penarth Harbour Dock & Railway; Port Talbot Railway & Docks; Princetown; Rhondda & Swansea Bay; Ross & Monmouth; South Wales Mineral; Teign Valley; Vale of Glamorgan; Van; Welshpool & Llanfair Light; West Somerset; Wrexham & Ellesmere.

North Western, Midland, and West Scottish Group (London Midland & Scottish Railway)

Constituent Companies

London & North Western; Midland; Lancashire & Yorkshire; North Staffordshire; Furness; Caledonian; Glasgow & South Western; Highland.

Subsidiary Companies

Arbroath & Forfar; Brechin & Edzell District; Callander & Oban; Cathcart District; Charnwood Forest; Cleator & Workington Junction; Cockermouth Keswick & Penrith; Dearne Valley; Dornoch Light; Dundee & Newtyle; Harborne; Killin; Lanarkshire & Ayrshire; Knott End; Leek & Manifold Valley Light; Maryport & Carlisle; Mold & Denbigh Junction; North & South Western Junction; North London; Portpatrick & Wigtownshire Joint Committee; Shropshire Union Railways & Canal; Solway Junction; Stratford-upon-Avon & Midland Junction; Tottenham & Forest Gate; Wick & Lybster Light; Wirral; Yorkshire Dales.

North Eastern, Eastern, and East Scottish Group (London & North Eastern Railway)

Constituent Companies

North Eastern; Great Central; Great Eastern; Great Northern; Hull & Barnsley; North British; Great North of Scotland.

Subsidiary Companies

Brackenhill Light; Colne Valley & Halstead; East & West Yorkshire Union; East Lincolnshire; Edinburgh & Bathgate; Forcett; Forth & Clyde Junction; Gifford & Garvald; Great North of England Clarence & Hartlepool Junction; Horncastle; Humber Commercial Railway & Dock; Kilsyth & Bonnybridge; Lauder Light; London & Blackwall; Mansfield; Mid-Suffolk Light; Newburgh & North Fife; North Lindsey Light; Nottingham & Grantham; Nottingham Joint Station Committee; Nottingham Suburban; Seaforth & Sefton Junction; Sheffield District; South Yorkshire Junction; Stamford & Essendine; West Riding Railway Committee.

Imperial and Metric Measures

Length

	1 inch	=	2.54 cm
12 inches	=	1 foot	=	30.48 cm
3 feet	=	1 yard	=	0.9144 m
22 yards	=	1 chain	=	20.1168 m
10 chains	=	1 furlong	=	201.1680 m
8 furlongs	=	1 mile	=	1.6093 km

Area

144 sq in	=	1 sq ft	=	0.0929 sq m
9 sq ft	=	1 sq yd	=	0.8361 sq m
4,840 sq yds	=	1 acre	=	0.4057 hectares

Weight

1 oz	=	28.35 g
1 lb	=	0.4536 kg
1 stone	=	6.3503 kg
1 cwt	=	50.802 kg
1 ton	=	1.016 tonnes

Capacity

1 gallon	=	4.546 litres

Volume

1 cu inch	=	16.3871 cu cm
1 cu foot	=	0.0283 cu m
1 cu yard	=	0.7646 cu m

Velocity

1 mph	=	1.6093 km ph

Money

s.	d.	p	s.	d.	p
	1d.	$\frac{1}{2}$p	6s.		30p
	2d.	1p	7s.		35p
	3d.	1p	8s.		40p
	4d.	$1\frac{1}{2}$p	9s.		45p
	5d.	2p	10s.		50p
	6d.	$2\frac{1}{2}$p	11s.		55p
	7d.	3p	12s.		60p
	8d.	3p	13s.		65p
	9d.	4p	14s.		70p
	10d.	4p	15s.		75p
	11d.	$4\frac{1}{2}$p	16s.		80p
	12d. (1s.)	5p	17s.		85p
2s.		10p	18s.		90p
3s.		15p	19s.		95p
4s.		20p	20s. (£1)		100p (£1)
5s.		25p			

APPENDIX 3
Historical Money Values

Year	Contemporary value (£)	1995 value (£)
1825	1,000	45,737
1830	1,000	55,807
1845	1,000	55,300
1851	1,000	66,846
1866	1,000	50,692
1872	1,000	47,523
1875	1,000	51,991
1895	1,000	84,486
1900	1,000	66,846
1913	1,000	57,387
1920	1,000	19,435
1933	1,000	61,444
1938	1,000	53,832
1945	1,000	29,673
1948	1,000	18,775
1951	1,000	16,441
1960	1,000	11,951
1963	1,000	10,882
1965	1,000	10,038
1970	1,000	8,046
1975	1,000	4,370
1980	1,000	2,231
1985	1,000	1,577
1995	1,000	1,000

Based on: Rousseaux wholesale price index all items; Sauerbeck-Statist wholesale price index all items; CSO Producer Price Index.

TRG

Sectional maps of the Railways of Great Britain showing ownership in 1922

Approximate scale: 1 inch = 20 miles

Boxed areas on the sectional maps appear as larger scale maps with the appropriate text entry, except South and West Yorkshire on map 5, which is enlarged on map 10.

Railway company abbreviations used in these maps

Ba	Barry Railway
BC	Bishop's Castle Railway
BM	Brecon & Merthyr Railway
BPGV	Burry Port & Gwendraeth Valley Railway
BWHA	Bideford Westward Ho! & Appledore Railway
C	Cardiff Railway
Ca	Cambrian Railways
Cal	Caledonian Railway
CKP	Cockermouth Keswick & Penrith Railway
CLC	Cheshire Lines Committee
CMDP Lt	Cleobury Mortimer & Ditton Priors Light Railway
CM Lt	Campbeltown & Machrihanish Light Railway
Co	Corris Railway
CVH	Colne Valley & Halstead Railway
CWJ	Cleator & Workington Junction Railway
DV	Dearne Valley Railway
DV Lt	Derwent Valley Light Railway
E	Easingwold Railway
EK Lt	East Kent Light Railway
EWY	East & West Yorkshire Union Railway
F	Furness Railway
Fe	Festiniog Railway
FYN	Freshwater Yarmouth & Newport Railway
GC	Great Central Railway
GE	Great Eastern Railway
GN	Great Northern Railway
GNS	Great North of Scotland Railway
GSW	Glasgow & South Western Railway
GVT	Glyn Valley Tramway
GW	Great Western Railway
H	Highland Railway
HB	Hull & Barnsley Railway
IM	Isle of Man Railway
IW	Isle of Wight Railway
IWC	Isle of Wight Central Railway
KE	Knott End Railway
KES Lt	Kent & East Sussex Light Railway
LB	Lynton & Barnstaple Railway

LBSC	London Brighton & South Coast Railway
LMM	Llanelly & Mynydd Mawr Railway
LNW	London & North Western Railway
LSW	London & South Western Railway
LTS	London Tilbury & Southend Railway (Midland Railway)
LY	Lancashire & Yorkshire Railway
M	Midland Railway
MC	Maryport & Carlisle Railway
ME	Manx Electric Railway
Met	Metropolitan Railway
MSJA	Manchester South Junction & Altrincham Railway
MS Lt	Mid-Suffolk Light Railway
MSW	Midland & South Western Junction Railway
NB	North British Railway
NBn	Neath & Brecon Railway
NE	North Eastern Railway
NS	North Staffordshire Railway
NS Lt	North Sunderland Light Railway
NV Lt	Nidd Valley Light Railway
NWNG	North Wales Narrow Gauge Railway
PDSW	Plymouth Devonport & South Western Junction Railway
PT	Port Talbot Railway
RE	Ravenglass & Eskdale Railway
Rhy	Rhymney Railway
RSB	Rhondda & Swansea Bay Railway
SDJ	Somerset & Dorset Joint Railway
SEC	South Eastern & Chatham Railway
S Lt	Selsey Light Railway
SM	Snowdon Mountain Railway
SMJ	Stratford-on-Avon & Midland Junction Railway
SM Lt	Shropshire & Montgomeryshire Light Railway
So	Southwold Railway
SSMWC	South Shields Marsden & Whitburn Colliery Railway
Tal	Talyllyn Railway
TV	Taff Vale Railway
W	Wirral Railway
WCP	Weston Clevedon & Portishead Light Railway
WT	Wantage Tramway

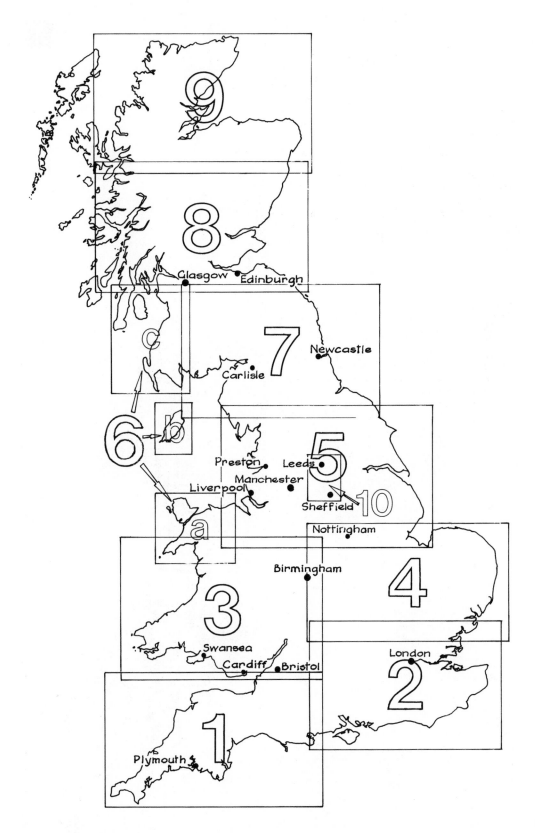

1
2
3
Penarth
Abertham
Barry Island
Weston-super-Mare
Clevedon
Yatton
Bath
Devizes
Blagdon
Trowbridge
Hallatrow
Radstock
Westbury
Wells
Shepton Mallett
Frome
Warminster
Bulford
Burnham
Highbridge
Glastonbury
Bridgwater
Castle Cary
Salisbury
Lynton
Ilfracombe
Minehead
Barnstaple
Appledore
BWHA
Bideford
Torrington
Taunton
Bampton
Templecombe
Yeovil
Yeovil Junction
Hemyock
Tiverton
Tiverton Junction
Chard
Chard Junction
Wimborne
Christ-church
Bude
Holsworthy
Halwill Junction
Crediton
Sidmouth Jnctn
Honiton
Axminster
Lyme Regis
Maiden Newton
Seaton Jnctn
Bridport
Poole
Wareham
Exeter
Okehampton
Moretonhampstead
Seaton
Sidmouth
Abbotsbury
Budleigh Salterton
Launceston
Exmouth
Weymouth
GW/LSW
Easton
Swanage
Bournemouth
Dawlish
Teignmouth
Tavistock
Princetown
Ashburton
Newton Abbot
Padstow
Wadebridge
Callington
PDSW
Bodmin
Liskeard
Totnes
Torquay
Newquay
PLYMOUTH
Brixham
Kingswear
Dartmouth
St Austell
Yealmpton
Perranporth
Looe
Fowey
Kingsbridge
Truro
St Ives
Redruth
Camborne
Falmouth
Penzance
Helston
GW
LSW
SDJ
LB

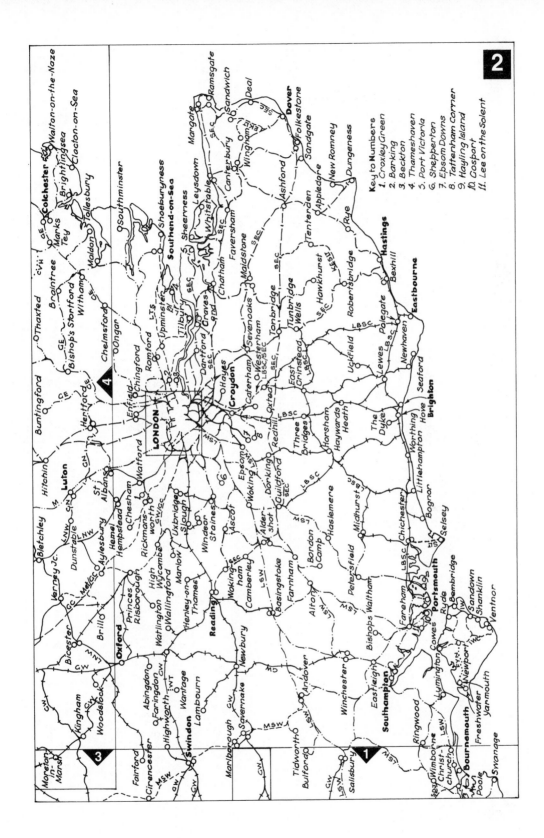

Key to Numbers
1. Croxley Green
2. Barking
3. Beckton
4. Thameshaven
5. Port Victoria
6. Shepperton
7. Epsom Downs
8. Tattenham Corner
9. Hayling Island
10. Gosport
11. Lee on the Solent

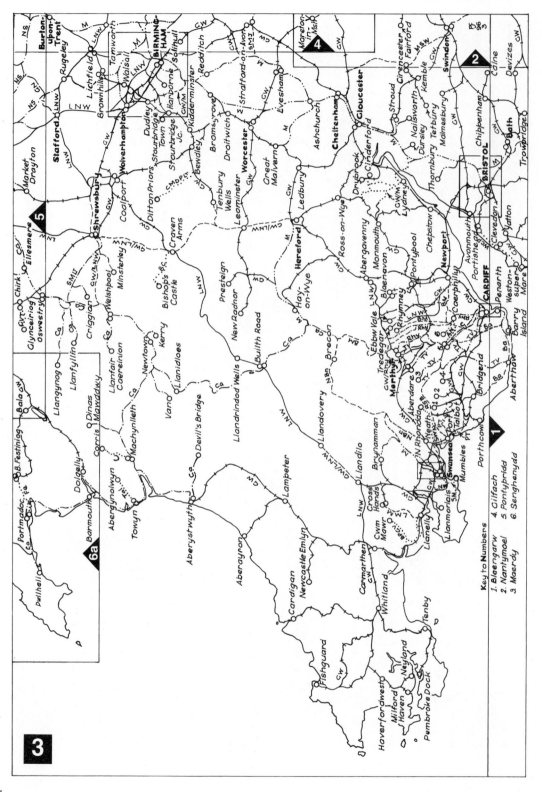

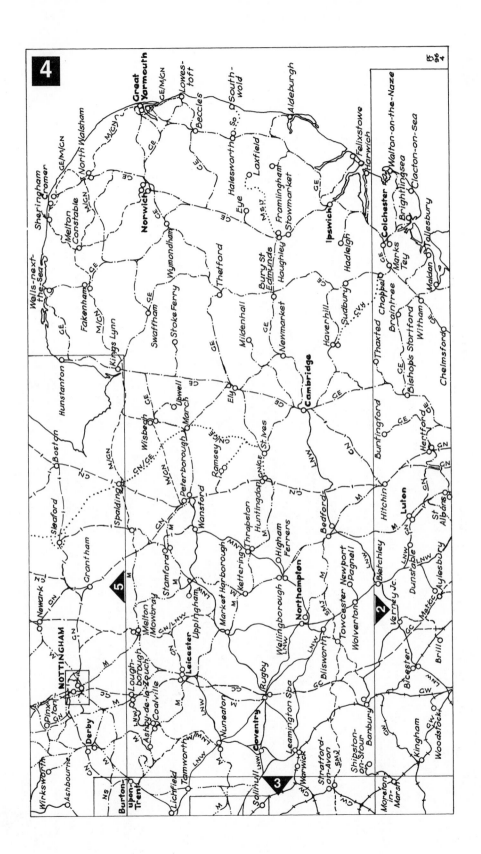

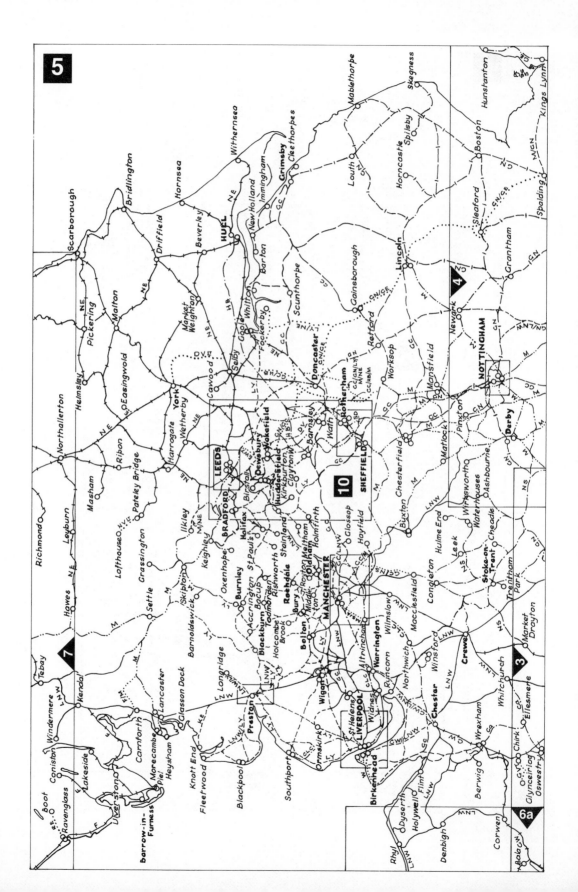

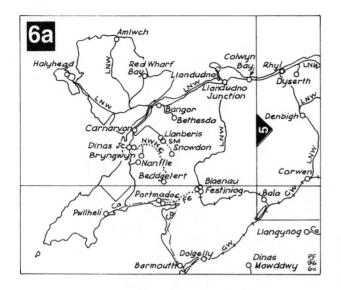

6a

Amlwch

Holyhead
LNW
Red Wharf
Bay
Colwyn
Bay
Rhyl
Dyserth
LNW
Llandudno
Llandudno
Junction
LNW
Bangor
Bethesda
LNW
Denbigh
Carnarvon
Llanberis
SM
NW&C
Snowdon
Dinas Jc.
Bryngwyn
Nantlle
Corwen
Beddgelert
Blaenau
Festiniog
Bala
C.W.
Portmadoc
Fe.
Ca.
Pwllheli
Llangynog
Ca.
Dolgelly
C.W.
Barmouth
Dinas
Mawddwy

5

PF
96
6c

6b

IM
Ramsey
Snaefell
Peel
IM
ME.
Foxdale
Douglas
Port
Erin
IM
Castletown

PF
96
6b

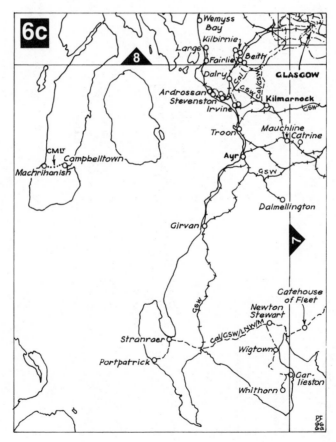

6c

Wemyss
Bay
Kilbirnie
Largs
Fairlie
Beith
Dalry
GLASGOW
Cal
Ardrossan
Cal/GSW
Kilmarnock
Stevenston
Irvine
GSW
Troon
Mauchline
Catrine
Ayr
CMLt
Campbeltown
GSW
Machrihanish
Dalmellington

8

Girvan

7

Gatehouse
of Fleet
Newton
Stewart
Cal/GSW/LNW/M
Stranraer
GSW
Wigtown
Portpatrick
Gar-
lieston
Whithorn

PF
96
6a

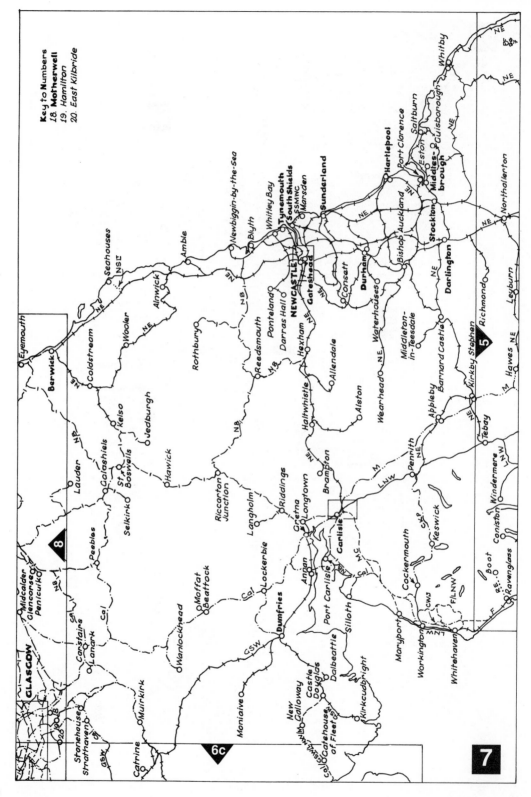

Key to Numbers
18. **Motherwell**
19. *Hamilton*
20. *East Kilbride*

GLASGOW

Midcalder
Glencorse
Penicuik

Stonehouse
Strathaven

Carstairs
Lanark

Catrine
Muirkirk

Wanlockhead

Moffat
Beattock

Moniaive

New
Galloway

Castle
Douglas

Dalbeattie

Gatehouse
of Fleet

Kirkcudbright

Dumfries

Lockerbie

Annan

Port Carlisle

Silloth

Maryport

Workington

Whitehaven

Cockermouth

Keswick

Coniston

Windermere

Boot

Ravenglass

Gretna

Longtown

Brampton

Carlisle

Penrith

Appleby

Tebay

Kirkby Stephen

Hawes

Leyburn

Richmond

Northallerton

Langholm

Riddings

Riccarton
Junction

Hawick

Selkirk

St.
Boswells

Galashiels

Peebles

Lauder

Jedburgh

Kelso

Coldstream

Wooler

Alnwick

Seahouses

Eyemouth

Berwick

Rothbury

Reedsmouth

Ponteland

Darras Hall

Hexham

Haltwhistle

Alston

Allendale

Wearhead

Middleton-
in-Teesdale

Barnard Castle

Newbiggin-by-the-Sea

Blyth

Whitley Bay

Tynemouth

South Shields

Marsden

SMWC

NEWCASTLE

Gateshead

Consett

Waterhouses

Durham

Bishop Auckland

Sunderland

Hartlepool

Port Clarence

Eston

Saltburn

Guisborough

Whitby

Stockton

Middles-
brough

Darlington

Amble

8

6c

5

7

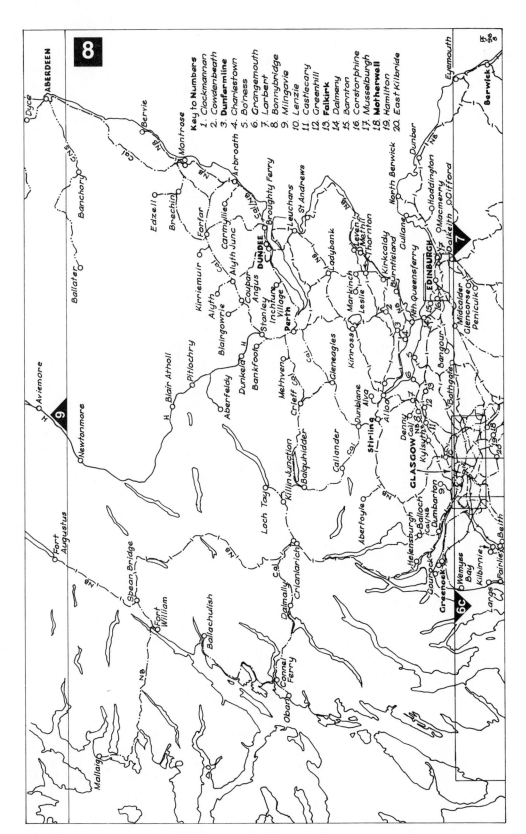

8

Key to Numbers

1. Clackmannan
2. Cowdenbeath
3. **Dunfermline**
4. Charlestown
5. Bo'ness
6. Grangemouth
7. Larbert
8. Bonnybridge
9. Milngavie
10. Lenzie
11. Castlecary
12. Greenhill
13. **Falkirk**
14. Dalmeny
15. Barnton
16. Corstorphine
17. Musselburgh
18. **Motherwell**
19. Hamilton
20. East Kilbride

ABERDEEN

Dyce

Bervie

Montrose

Banchory

GNS

Cal

NB

Ballater

Edzell

Brechin

Forfar

Arbroath

Kirriemuir

Carmyllie

Aluth Junc

Broughty Ferry

DUNDEE

Cal

NB

Aviemore

Newtonmore

9

H Blair Atholl

Pitlochry

Aberfeldy

Dunkeld

Bankfoot

Blairgowrie

Alyth

Coupar Angus

Stanley

Inchure

Village

Perth

Leuchars

St Andrews

Ladybank

Cal

NB

NB

Markinch

Leven

Methil

Thornton

Leslie

Kirkcaldy

St Andrews

Fort Augustus

Spean Bridge

Fort William

Ballachulish

Connal Ferry

Oban

Dalmally

Crianlarich

Cal

Killin Junction

Balquhidder

Loch Tay

Callander

Methven

Crieff

Cal

Gleneagles

Kinross

Dunblane

Alva

Alloa

Stirling

Cal

NB

Aberfoyle

Denny

Cal

Kilsyth

NB

Helensburgh

Balloch

Ca/NB

Dumbarton

GLASGOW

Greenock

Gourock

Wemyss Bay

Largs

Fairlie

Kilbirnie

Beith

Mallaig

NB

Gullane

North Berwick

Bunntisland

Wth Queensferry

EDINBURGH

NB

Dunbar

Haddington

Macmerry

Gifford

Dalkeith

Midcalder

Glencorse

Penicuik

Bangour

Bathgate

Bo'ness

Berwick

Eyemouth

NB

NB

BR 96 8

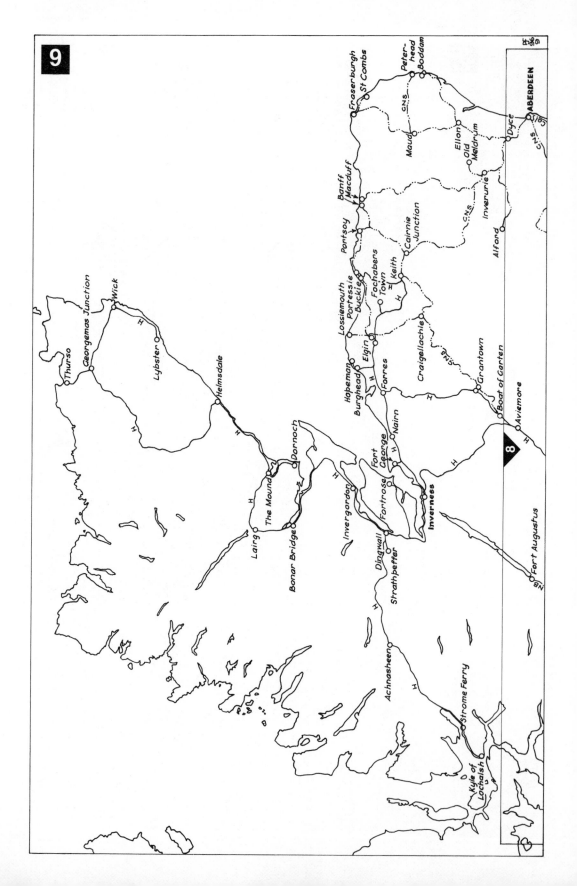

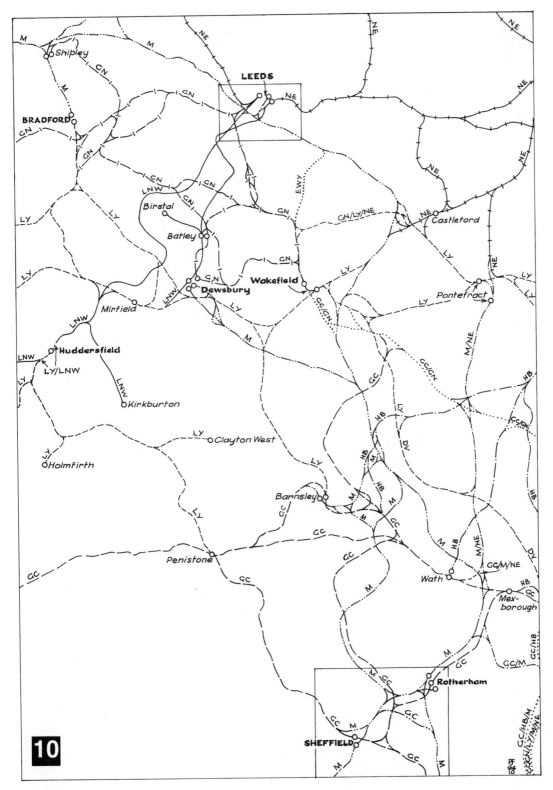

10